Tools to Enhance the Learning Experience

CHAPTER OPENING CASES

Each chapter begins with a case scenario about an actual company, product, or situation that illustrates key concepts discussed in the chapter.

- Ch. 1 Who Wants to Dive with Dolphins?
- Ch. 2 Marketing Research Drives Marketing Decisions
- Ch. 3 Targeting Women for Financial Services
- Ch. 4 Putting Products in the Spotlight
- Ch. 5 An Old Brand Targets New Customers
- Ch. 6 Changing Attitudes Toward the Military
- Ch. 7 Squawking about a Brand Raises Awareness
- Ch. 8 Nostalgia Marketing Jogs the Memory
- Ch. 9 Finding Wheels on the Web
- Ch. 10 Wheels and Deals in Thailand
- Ch. 11 Are Foreign Brands Better than Local Brands?
- Ch. 12 After Consumers Click and Buy
- Ch. 13 Broadcasting Product Placement
- Ch. 14 Class Clash in China
- Ch. 15 Generation and Gender Gaps in China
- Ch. 16 Pepsi and Ford Pass the Word on the Web
- Ch. 17 Something for Everyone
- Ch. 18 The Symbolism of Harley-Davidson
- Ch. 19 Driving into the Future
- Ch. 20 Battling Over Better Pizza
- Ch. 21 Who Is Collecting Your Personal Data—and Why?

MARKETING IMPLICATION SECTIONS

For every major concept discussed, marketing implication sections show how consumer behavior applies to the practice of marketing, including such basic marketing functions as market segmentation, target market selection, positioning, market research, promotion, price, product, and place decisions.

EMPHASIS ON GLOBALIZATION AND E-COMMERCE

Interwoven throughout the text are many cross-cultural examples and information on how the Internet has impacted consumer behavior. The wealth of these examples emphasizes the text's practical and contemporary orientation.

CURRENT AND CUTTING-EDGE COVERAGE

In addition to providing a balanced perspective, including both psychological (micro) and sociological (macro) topics in the field of consumer behavior, the text provides the most up-to-date research possible. This includes several *novel chapters* that often do not appear in other textbooks: "Symbolic Consumer Behavior," "Knowledge and Understanding," and "The Dark Side of Consumer Behavior and Marketing."

3RD EDITION

Consumer Behavior

Wayne D. Hoyer
University of Texas at Austin

Deborah J. MacInnis
University of Southern California

Houghton Mifflin Company Boston New York

DEDICATION

To my wonderful family, Shirley, David, Stephanie, and Lindsey, and to my parents, Louis and Doris, for their tremendous support and love. To all of you I dedicate this book.

Wayne D. Hoyer
Austin, Texas
May 2003

To my loving family—my life-spring of energy and my center of gravity.

Debbie MacInnis
Los Angeles, California
May 2003

V.P., Editor-in-Chief: George T. Hoffman
Associate Sponsoring Editor: Joanne Dauksewicz
Senior Project Editor: Tracy Patruno
Manufacturing Manager: Florence Cadran
Marketing Manager: Steven W. Mikels

Cover illustration: © James Steinberg/the *i* spot showcase

Printed in the U.S.A.

Library of Congress Control Number: 2002109477

ISBN: 0-618-26482-5

456789-DOW-07 06 05

ABOUT THE AUTHORS

Wayne D. Hoyer

Wayne D. Hoyer is the James L. Bayless/William S. Farrish Fund Chair for Free Enterprise, Chairman of the Department of Marketing, and Director of the Center for Customer Insight in the McCombs School of Business at the University of Texas at Austin. He received his Ph.D. in Consumer Psychology from Purdue University in 1980. Wayne has published over 60 articles in various publications including the *Journal of Consumer Research, Journal of Marketing, Journal of Marketing Research, Journal of Advertising Research,* and *Journal of Retailing.* A 1998 article in the *Journal of Marketing Research* (with Susan Broniarczyk and Leigh McAlister) won the O'Dell Award in 2003 for the article that has had the most impact in the marketing field over the five year period. In addition to *Consumer Behavior,* he has co-authored two books on the topic of advertising miscomprehension. Dr. Hoyer's research interests include consumer information processing and decision making (especially low-involvement decision making), customer relationship management, and advertising effects (particularly miscomprehension and the impact of humor). He is a former associate editor for the *Journal of Consumer Research* and serves on the editorial review boards of the *Journal of Marketing, Journal of Consumer Research, International Journal of Research in Marketing,* and the *Journal of Public Policy and Marketing.* Dr. Hoyer is a member of the American Psychological Association, the Association for Consumer Research, and the American Marketing Association. His major areas of teaching include consumer behavior, customer strategy, and marketing communications.

Deborah J. MacInnis

Debbie MacInnis is Professor of Marketing at the University of Southern California in Los Angeles, CA. She received her Ph.D. in marketing from the University of Pittsburgh in 1986. She also holds a B.S. degree in psychology from Smith College. Debbie has published papers in the *Journal of Consumer Research, Journal of Marketing Research, Journal of Marketing, Journal of Advertising, Journal of Advertising Research,* and *Journal of Personality and Social Psychology* in the areas of marketing communications, information processing, imagery, emotions, and brand images. She has served as a member of the editorial review boards of the *Journal of Consumer Research, Journal of Marketing Research, Journal of Marketing, Journal of the Academy of Marketing Sciences, International Journal of Internet Marketing and Advertising, Journal of Market Focused Management,* and *Journal of Consumer Behaviour,* and served as a reviewer for the *Journal of Advertising* and *Journal of Consumer Psychology.* She is currently President of the Association for Consumer Research, and has served that organization as Treasurer and conference co-chair. She has served as Vice President of Conferences and Research for the Academic Council of the American Marketing Association. Debbie is recipient of the Alpha Kappa Psi award, an honor awarded to the best paper published in the *Journal of Marketing.* She has received the Teaching Innovation Award from the Marshall School of Business and has been named as a Faculty Fellow at USC's Center for Excellence in Teaching. Debbie's major areas of teaching include consumer behavior, integrated marketing communications, and marketing management.

BRIEF CONTENTS

CONTENTS

PART TWO
The Psychological Core

MOTIVATION, ABILITY, AND OPPORTUNITY

EXPOSURE, ATTENTION, AND PERCEPTION

KNOWLEDGE AND UNDERSTANDING

CHAPTER 19

ADOPTION OF, RESISTANCE TO, AND DIFFUSION OF INNOVATIONS

PART SIX
Consumer Welfare

CHAPTER 20

CONSUMERISM AND PUBLIC POLICY ISSUES

CHAPTER 21 THE DARK SIDE OF CONSUMER BEHAVIOR AND MARKETING

PREFACE

At just about every moment of our lives, we engage in some form of consumer behavior. When we watch an ad on TV, talk to friends about a movie we just saw, brush our teeth, go to a ball game, buy a new CD, or even throw away an old pair of shoes, we are behaving as consumers. In fact, being consumers reaches into every part of our lives.

Given its omnipresence, the study of consumer behavior has critical implications for areas such as marketing, public policy, and ethics. It also helps us learn about ourselves—why we buy certain things, why we use them in a certain way, and how we get rid of them.

In this book we explore the fascinating world of consumer behavior, looking at a number of interesting and exciting topics. Some of these are quickly identified with our typical image of consumer behavior. Others may be surprising. We hope you will see why we became stimulated by and drawn to this topic from the very moment we had our first consumer behavior course as students. We hope you will also appreciate why we choose to make this field our life's work, and why we developed and continue to remain committed to the writing of this textbook.

WHY THE NEW EDITION OF THIS BOOK?

There are a number of consumer behavior books on the market. An important question concerns what this book has to offer and what distinguishes it from other texts. As active researchers in the field of consumer behavior, our overriding goal was to provide a treatment of the field that is up-to-date and cutting-edge. There has been an explosion of research on a variety of consumer behavior topics over the last twenty years. Our primary aim was to provide a useful summary of this material for students of marketing. In drawing on cutting-edge research, however, we wanted to be careful to not become too "academic." Instead, our objective is to present cutting-edge topics in a manner that is accessible and easy for students to understand.

Specific changes and improvements to the third edition of this book include:

- Marketing Implications sections have been expanded and updated to show students how chapter concepts apply to the strategy and practice of marketing.
- Coverage of Internet-related consumer behavior issues has been expanded.
- New coverage of contemporary techniques such as ethnographic research, conjoint analysis, data mining, and viral marketing has been added.
- New coverage of research and behavioral concepts related to post-decision regret, sexual orientation, teenagers around the world, brand communities, frugality, and special possessions has been included.
- New chapter-closing Questions for Review and Discussion help students remember, analyze, and understand every chapter's content.
- Supplemental chapter-closing exercises challenge students to sharpen their skills and apply chapter concepts.
- Extensively revised, student-friendly writing style and headings make the text even more accessible.
- Numerous new advertisements offer concrete illustrations of consumer behavior concepts in action.

- Numerous new global, small-business, and high-tech examples highlight how all kinds of organizations use consumer behavior in their marketing efforts.

TEXTBOOK FEATURES

As award-winning teachers, we have tried to translate our instructional abilities and experience into the writing of this text. The following features have been a natural outgrowth of these experiences.

Conceptual Model. First, we believe that students can learn best when they see the big picture—when they understand what concepts mean, how they are used in business practice, and how they relate to one another. In our opinion consumer behavior is too often presented as a set of discrete topics with little or no relationship to one another. We have therefore developed an overall conceptual model that helps students grasp the big picture and see how the chapters and topics are interrelated. Each chapter is linked to other chapters by a specific model that fits within the larger model. Further, the overall model guides the organization of the book. This organizing scheme makes the chapters far more *integrative* than most other books.

Practical Orientation, with an Emphasis on Globalization and E-Commerce. Another common complaint of some treatments of consumer behavior is that they reflect general psychological or sociological principles and theories, but provide very little indication of how these principles and theories relate to business practice. Given our notion that students enjoy seeing how the concepts in consumer behavior can apply to business practice, a second objective of the book was to provide a very practical orientation. We include a wealth of contemporary real-world examples to illustrate key topics. We also try to broaden students' horizons by providing a number of international examples (often more than twenty per chapter). Given the importance of consumer behavior to electronic commerce, we also provide a number of examples of consumer behavior in an e-commerce context. The abundance of global and e-commerce examples makes our book *more global and e-commerce based* than other texts on the market.

Current and Cutting-Edge Coverage. Third, we provide coverage of the field of consumer behavior that is as current and up-to-date as possible (including many of the recent research advances). This includes several *novel chapters* that often do not appear in other textbooks: "Symbolic Consumer Behavior," "Knowledge and Understanding," and "The Dark Side of Consumer Behavior and Marketing." These topics are at the cutting edge of consumer behavior research and are likely to be of considerable interest to students.

Balanced Treatment of Micro and Macro Topics. Fourth, our book tries to provide a balanced perspective on the field of consumer behavior. Specifically, we give treatment to both psychological ("micro") consumer behavior topics (e.g., attitudes, decision making) and sociological ("macro") consumer behavior topics (e.g., subculture, gender, social class influences). Also, although we typically teach consumer behavior by starting with the more micro topics and then moving up to the more macro topics, we realize that some instructors prefer the reverse sequence. The *Instructor's Resource Manual* therefore provides a revised table of contents and model that show how the book can be taught for those who prefer a macro first, micro second approach.

Broad Conceptualization of the Subject. Fifth, we present a broad conceptualization of the topic of consumer behavior. While many books focus on what products or services consumers *buy,* consumer behavior scholars have recognized that the topic of consumer behavior is actually much broader. Specifically, rather than studying buying per se, we recognize that consumer behavior includes a *set* of decisions (what, whether, when, where, why, how, how often, how much, how long) about *acquisition* (including but not limited to buying), *usage,* and *disposition* decisions. Focusing on more than what products or services consumers buy provides a rich set of theoretical and practical implications for both our understanding of consumer behavior and the practice of marketing.

Finally, we consider the relevance of consumer behavior to *many constituents*, not just marketers. Chapter 1 indicates that consumer behavior is important to marketers, public policy makers, ethicists and consumer advocacy groups, and consumers themselves (including students' own lives). Some chapters focus exclusively on the implications of consumer behavior for public policy makers, ethicists, and consumer advocacy groups. Other chapters consider these issues as well, though in less detail.

CONTENT AND ORGANIZATION OF THE BOOK

One can currently identify two main approaches to the study of consumer behavior: a micro orientation, which focuses on the individual psychological processes that consumers use to make acquisition, consumption, and disposition decisions, and a macro orientation, which focuses on group behaviors and the symbolic nature of consumer behavior. This latter orientation draws heavily from such fields as sociology and anthropology. The current book and overall model have been structured around a "micro to macro" organization based on the way we teach this course and the feedback that we have received from reviewers. (As mentioned previously, for those who prefer a "macro to micro" structure, we provide in the *Instructor's Resource Manual* an alternative Table of Contents and model that reflect how the book could be easily adapted to this perspective.)

Part One presents an introduction to consumer behavior. Chapter 1 provides students with an understanding of the breadth of the field as well as its importance to marketers, advocacy groups, public policy makers, and consumers themselves. It also presents the overall model that guides the organization of the text. Chapter 2 focuses on the groups who conduct research on consumers and how that research is both collected and used by different constituents.

Part Two, "The Psychological Core," focuses on the inner psychological processes that affect consumer behavior. We see that consumers' acquisition, usage, and disposition behaviors and decisions are greatly affected by the amount of effort they put into engaging in behaviors and making decisions. Chapter 3 describes three critical factors that affect effort: the (1) *motivation* or desire, (2) *ability* (knowledge and information), and (3) *opportunity* to engage in behaviors and make decisions. In Chapter 4, we then examine how information in consumers' environment (i.e., ads, prices, product features, word of mouth communications, and so on) is internally processed by consumers—how they come in contact with these stimuli *(exposure)*, notice them *(attention)*, and *perceive* them. Chapter 5 continues by discussing how we compare new stimuli to our knowledge of existing stimuli, a process called *categorization,* and how we attempt to understand or *comprehend* them on a deeper level. In Chapters 6 and 7, we see how attitudes are formed and changed depending on whether the amount of effort consumers devote to forming an attitude is high or low. Finally, because consumers often must recall the information they have previously stored in order to make decisions, Chapter 8 looks at the important topic of consumer *memory.*

Whereas Part Two examines some of the internal factors that influence consumers' decisions, a critical domain of consumer behavior involves understanding how consumers make acquisition, consumption, and disposition decisions. Thus, in Part Three we examine the sequential steps of the consumer decision-making process. In Chapter 9, we examine the initial steps of this process—*problem recognition* and *information search*. Similar to the attitude change processes described earlier, we next examine the consumer decision-making process, both when *effort is high* (Chapter 10) and when *effort is low* (Chapter 11). Finally, the process does not end after a decision has been made. In Chapter 12 we see how consumers determine whether they are *satisfied* or *dissatisfied* with their decisions and how they *learn* from choosing and consuming products/services.

Part Four reflects a macro view of consumer behavior that examines how various aspects of *culture* affect consumer behavior. First, we see how *regional, ethnic,* and *religious* factors (Chapter 13) can affect consumer behavior. Chapter 14 then examines how *social class* is determined in various cultures, and how it affects acquisition, usage, and disposition behaviors—such as how we strive to improve our standing, impress others, and distribute wealth to our progeny. Chapter 15 examines how *age, gender,* and *household* influences affect consumer behavior. Chapter 16 considers how, when, and why the specific *reference groups* (friends, work groups, clubs) to which we belong can influence acquisition, usage, and disposition decisions and behaviors. Combined, these external influences can influence our *personality, lifestyles,* and *values,* the topics covered in Chapter 17.

Part Five, "Consumer Behavior Outcomes," examines the effects of the numerous influences and decision processes discussed in the previous four sections. Because products and services often reflect deep-felt and significant meanings (e.g., our favorite song or restaurant), Chapter 18 focuses on the interesting topic of *symbolic consumer behavior.* Chapter 19 builds on the topics of internal decision-making and group behavior by examining how consumers adopt new offerings, and how their *adoption* decisions affect the spread or *diffusion* of an offering through a market.

Part Six, "Consumer Welfare," covers two topics that have been of great interest to consumer researchers in recent years. Chapter 20 directs our attention to *consumerism and public policy* issues. Chapter 21 examines the *dark side of consumer behavior* and focuses on some negative outcomes of consumer-related behaviors (compulsive buying and gambling, prostitution) as well as marketing practices that have been the focus of social commentary in recent years.

PEDAGOGICAL ADVANTAGES

Based on our extensive teaching experience, we have incorporated a number of features that should help students learn about consumer behavior.

Chapter Opening Cases. Each chapter begins with a case scenario about an actual company or situation that illustrates key concepts discussed in the chapter and their importance to marketers. This will help students grasp the big picture and understand the relevance of the topics from the start of the chapter.

Chapter Opening Model. Each chapter also begins with a conceptual model that shows the organization of the chapter, the topics discussed, and how they relate to both one another and to other chapters. Each model reflects an expanded picture of one or more of the elements presented in the overall conceptual model for the book (described in Chapter 1).

Marketing Implication Sections. Numerous *Marketing Implications* sections are interspersed throughout each chapter. These sections illustrate how various consumer behavior concepts can be applied to the practice of marketing, including such basic marketing functions as market segmentation, target market selection, positioning, market research, promotion, price, product, and place decisions. An abundance of marketing examples (from both the U.S. and abroad) provides concrete applications and implementations of the concepts to marketing practice.

Marginal Glossary. Every chapter contains a set of key terms that are both highlighted in the text and defined in margin notes. These terms and their definitions should help students identify and remember the central concepts described in the chapter.

Abundant Full-Color Exhibits. Each chapter contains a number of illustrated examples, including photos, advertisements, charts, and graphs. These illustrations make important topics personally relevant and engaging, helping students to remember the material and making the book more accessible and aesthetically pleasing, thereby increasing students' motivation to learn. All diagrams and charts employ full color, which serves to both highlight key points and add to the aesthetic appeal of the text. Each model, graph, ad, and photo also has an accompanying caption that provides a simple description and explanation of how the exhibit relates to the topic it is designed to illustrate.

End of Chapter Summaries. The end of each chapter provides students with a simple and concise summary of topics. These summaries are a good review tool to use with the conceptual model to help students perceive the big picture.

End of Chapter Questions and Exercises. Each chapter includes a set of discussion and review questions and application exercises designed to involve students on a more experiential and interactive level. Exercises include experiential exercises (e.g., watching and analyzing consumers and ads), mini-research projects, or thought-provoking questions.

COMPLETE TEACHING PACKAGE

A variety of ancillary materials have been designed to help the instructor in the classroom. All of these supplements have been carefully coordinated to support the text and provide an integrated set of materials for the instructor.

Instructor's Resource Manual. The *Instructor's Resource Manual,* prepared by Professor John P. Eaton, has been completely revised and updated to provide a thorough review of material in the text, as well as supplementary materials that can be used to expand upon the text and enhance classroom presentations. An alternate table of contents and consumer behavior model for presenting the text in a "macro to micro" approach has been provided, as well as different sample syllabi. Included for each chapter are a chapter summary; learning objectives; a comprehensive chapter outline; a list of useful Web sites, with descriptions of how they might assist the instructor in preparing for or teaching a class session; and several suggested classroom activities. Classroom activities include questions for each chapter that stimulate group discussion, suggestions for bringing additional examples (videos, readings) into the classroom, and special experiential activities created by Professor Sheri Bridges, with detailed guidelines for facilitation.

Expanded Set of Color Transparencies. A set of 50 color transparencies includes illustrations not found in the text. The transparencies consist of print ads that may be used to illustrate various concepts discussed in the chapters. Teaching notes are provided to facilitate integrating the transparencies with lectures.

Test Bank/Computerized Test Bank. An extensive test bank prepared by Professor David Ackerman is available to assist the instructor in assessing student performance. The test bank contains approximately 2,100 questions, including a mix of both conceptual and applied questions for each chapter. All test bank questions note the page in the book from which the relevant item came. An electronic version of the printed test bank is available for Windows. This computerized test bank allows instructors to edit and easily generate multiple forms of tests.

PowerPoint Presentation Package. A package of professionally developed PowerPoint slides is available for use by adopters of this textbook. Slides include some text illustrations as well as additional presentations that highlight chapter concepts. Instructors who have access to PowerPoint can edit slides to customize them for their classrooms. A view is also provided for instructors who do not have the program. Slides can also be printed for lecture notes and class distribution.

Videos. A completely new video package has been provided to supplement and enliven class lectures and discussion. Videos include many real-world scenarios that illustrate certain concepts in a given chapter. The clips are intended to be interesting, ground the concepts in real life for students, and provide an impetus for stimulating student input and involvement.

STUDENT AND INSTRUCTOR WEB SITES

Specially designed Web pages enhance the book's content and provide additional information, guidance, and activities.

The **student site** includes chapter previews, chapter outlines, learning objectives, Internet exercises with hyperlinks, interactive quizzes that help students assess their progress, chapter links to key companies mentioned in the opening cases and chapter examples, a resource center providing links to consumer behavior research sites, and term paper help.

The **instructor site** provides lecture notes, PowerPoint slides, suggested answers to the Internet exercises, additional teaching tips, sample syllabi, and various classroom enhancement materials, such as additional experiential exercises and project ideas.

ACKNOWLEDGMENTS

Special recognition is extended to Marian Wood, whose assistance was instrumental to the completion of this project. Her tireless work on this project is greatly appreciated. We have also been extremely fortunate to work with a wonderful team of dedicated professionals from Houghton Mifflin. We are very grateful to Joanne Dauksewicz, Tracy Patruno, and Naomi Kornhauser, whose enormous energy and enthusiasm spurred our progress on this third edition. We also appreciate the efforts of Sheri Bridges at Wake Forest University for her work on the experiential exercises, John Eaton at the University of Arizona for his work on the *Instructor's Resource Manual,* and David Ackerman from Cal State Northridge for his work on the test bank.

The quality of this book and its ancillary package has been helped immensely by the insightful and rich comments of a set of researchers and instructors who served as reviewers. Their thoughtful and helpful comments had real impact in shaping the final product. In particular, we wish to thank:

Larry Anderson
Long Island University

Sharon Beatty
University of Alabama

Russell Belk
University of Utah

Joseph Bonnice
Manhattan College

Margaret L. Burk
Muskingum College

Carol Calder
Loyola Marymount University

Paul Chao
University of Northern Iowa

Dennis Clayson
University of Northern Iowa

Joel Cohen
University of Florida

Sally Dibb
University of Warwick

Richard W. Easley
Baylor University

Richard Elliott
Lancaster University

Abdi Eshghi
Bentley College

Frank W. Fisher
Stonehill College

Ronald Fullerton
Providence College

Philip Garton
Leicester Business School

Peter L. Gillett
University of Central Florida

Debbora Heflin
Cal Poly–Pomona

Elizabeth Hirschman
Rutgers University

Raj G. Javalgi
Cleveland State University

Harold Kassarjian
U.C.L.A.

Patricia Kennedy
University of Nebraska–Lincoln

Robert E. Kleine
Arizona State University

Scott Koslow
University of Waikato

Phillip Lewis
Rowan College of New Jersey

Kenneth R. Lord
S.U.N.Y.–Buffalo

Bart Macchiette
Plymouth State College

Lawrence Marks
Kent State University

David Marshall
University of Edinburgh

Anil Mathur
Hofstra University

Martin Meyers
University of Wisconsin–Stevens Point

Vince Mitchell
University of Manchester Institute of Science and Technology

Lois Mohr
Georgia State University

James R. Ogden
Kutztown University

Thomas O'Guinn
University of Illinois

Marco Protano
New York University

Michael Reilly
Montana State University

Gregory M. Rose
The University of Mississippi

Mary Mercurio Scheip
Eckerd College

Marilyn Scrizzi
New Hampshire Technical College

John Shaw
Providence College

C. David Shepherd
University of Tennessee–Chattanooga

Robert E. Smith
Indiana University

Eric R. Spangenberg
Washington State University

Bruce Stern
Portland State University

Jane Boyd Thomas
Winthrop University

Phil Titus
Bowling Green State University

Stuart Van Auken
Cal State University–Chico

Janet Wagner
University of Maryland

Tommy E. Whittler
University of Kentucky

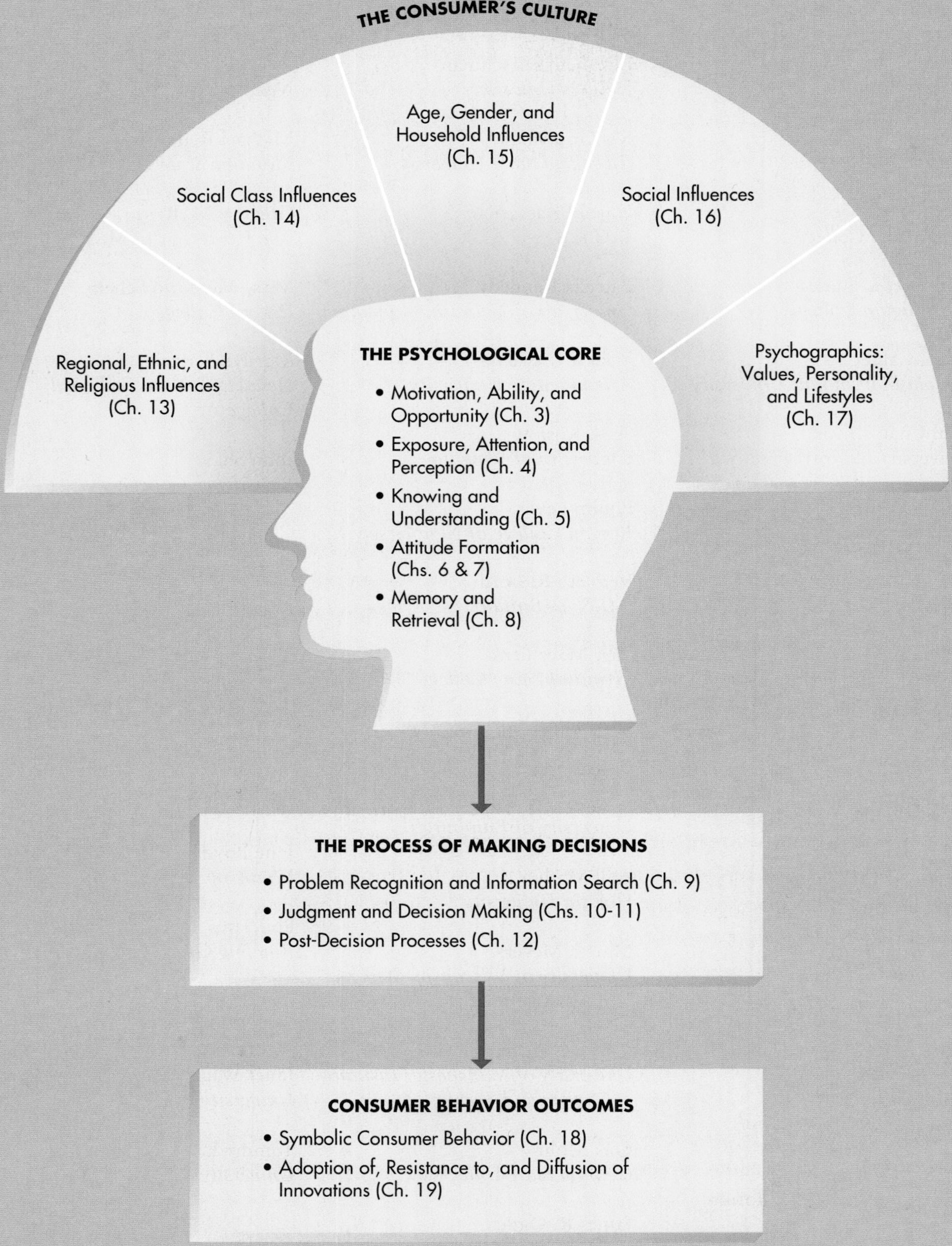

THE CONSUMER'S CULTURE

Regional, Ethnic, and Religious Influences (Ch. 13)

Social Class Influences (Ch. 14)

Age, Gender, and Household Influences (Ch. 15)

Social Influences (Ch. 16)

Psychographics: Values, Personality, and Lifestyles (Ch. 17)

THE PSYCHOLOGICAL CORE

- Motivation, Ability, and Opportunity (Ch. 3)
- Exposure, Attention, and Perception (Ch. 4)
- Knowing and Understanding (Ch. 5)
- Attitude Formation (Chs. 6 & 7)
- Memory and Retrieval (Ch. 8)

THE PROCESS OF MAKING DECISIONS

- Problem Recognition and Information Search (Ch. 9)
- Judgment and Decision Making (Chs. 10-11)
- Post-Decision Processes (Ch. 12)

CONSUMER BEHAVIOR OUTCOMES

- Symbolic Consumer Behavior (Ch. 18)
- Adoption of, Resistance to, and Diffusion of Innovations (Ch. 19)

PART ONE

An Introduction to Consumer Behavior

Part One introduces the subject of consumer behavior and provides an overview of the various topics it encompasses. You will learn that consumer behavior involves much more than the purchasing of products—it also involves consumers' use of services, activities, and ideas. In addition, you will find out that marketers are always studying consumer behavior for clues to who buys, uses, and disposes of what products, as well as when, where, and why.

Chapter 1 defines consumer behavior and examines its importance to marketers, advocacy groups, public policy makers, and consumers themselves. It also presents and explains the overall model that guides the organization of this text. As this model indicates, consumer behavior covers four basic domains: (1) the psychological core (the internal processes that consumers use to make decisions), (2) the consumer's culture (the external factors that influence consumers' decisions), (3) the process of making decisions, and (4) the outcomes of consumer behavior.

Chapter 2 focuses on the critical importance of consumer behavior research and its special implications for marketers. You will learn about various research methods, types of data, and ethical issues related to consumer research. With this background, you will be able to understand how consumer research helps marketers develop more effective strategies and tactics for reaching and satisfying customers.

chapter 1

Understanding Consumer Behavior

Introduction: Who Wants to Dive with Dolphins?

Paradise at a price—that's the premise of Discovery Cove, an interactive tropical adventure park in Orlando, Florida. Owned by Anheuser-Busch's Busch Entertainment Corporation, Discovery Cove is designed to give visitors a special experience they'll never forget (see Exhibit 1.1). Visitors spend the day swimming with dolphins, feeding tropical birds, wading with stingrays, and snorkeling in a cove filled with colorful fish.

Victor G. Abbey, Chairman of the Board and Presdent of Busch Entertainment Corporation, explains that the company conducted research to determine consumer interest in this new type of entertainment park. Despite the unusually high price for a one-day pass—set at $179 for the first year and later raised to $199—Abbey notes that Discovery Cove is not just for wealthy vacationers: "There's a segment of the market that sees this experience and says, 'I have to do this.'" The opportunity to get close to nature by riding a dolphin or patting a stingray has proven to be a strong draw for consumers well acquainted with Disney World, Universal Studios, and other Orlando attractions.

Busch Entertainment's marketers also realized that Discovery Cove visitors wanted to get away from the lengthy lines, crowded exhibits, and frenetic atmosphere of the typical theme park. In response, they decided to limit Discovery Cove's attendance to 1,000 visitors per day. Then they built a scale model and positioned 1,000 tiny figurines throughout the different attractions to check that the park would not seem crowded at full capacity.

The ticket price covers everything for a daylong tropical adventure. Every visitor gets snorkel gear, a locker and beach towel, wildlife-friendly sunscreen, an outdoor lunch, food for feeding birds in the aviary, and training for a half-hour swim with the dolphins. The ticket price also includes a one-week pass to Busch Entertainment's Seaworld Orlando. Although some industry analysts initially thought the high price would deter visitors, Discovery Cove is often fully booked months in advance and has even added new attractions—while maintaining its 1,000-visitor cap.[1]

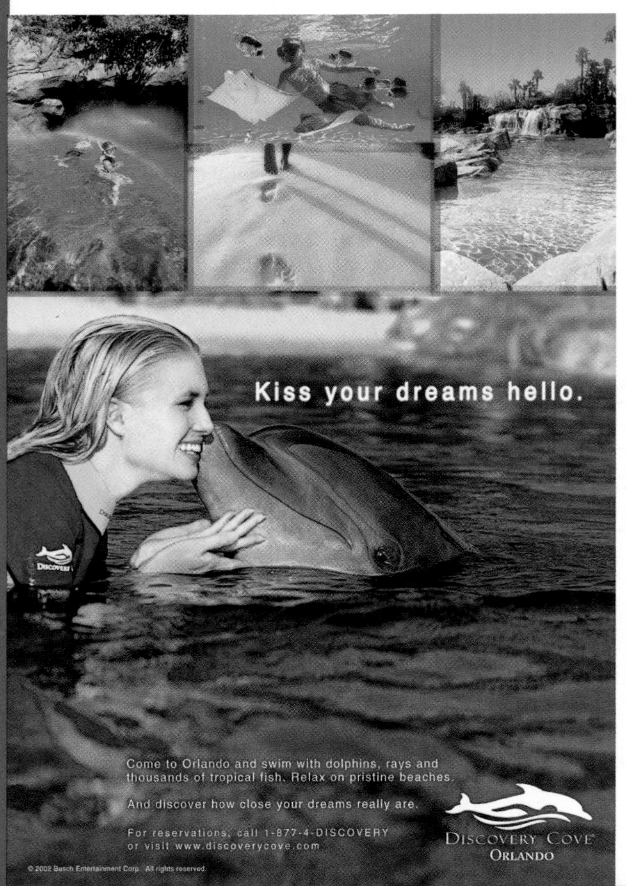

Kiss your dreams hello.
Come to Orlando and swim with dolphins, rays and thousands of tropical fish. Relax on pristine beaches.
And discover how close your dreams really are.
For reservations, call 1-877-4-DISCOVERY or visit www.discoverycove.com
Discovery Cove
Orlando
© 2002 Busch Entertainment Corp. All rights reserved.

EXHIBIT 1.1 Discovery Cove

Source: Copyright Busch Entertainment Corp.

The success of Busch Entertainment's Discovery Cove is largely due to its astute understanding of consumer behavior. First, Busch Entertainment developed a park that meets visitors' desire for an exciting, yet carefully controlled, experience with nature. Second, it created a sense of exclusivity and eliminated the frustration of waiting in line by limiting the number of visitors allowed into the park daily. Third, it trained its animal tenders and psychologists to help visitors get the most from their encounters with nature while ensuring that the animals are protected. Finally, it set a single, all-inclusive price, encouraging visitors to take advantage of every feature and to get more value by visiting SeaWorld next door.

Although Discovery Cove's total yearly attendance is not even 5 percent of Disney World's 15 million annual visitors, consumer response has been so strong that management had to expand the park less than two years after its opening. No doubt the tens of thousands of satisfied visitors have told friends and family about their positive experience and urged them to visit. Understanding consumer behavior can therefore be critical to the success of a new product or service—using this type of knowledge is the way that businesses such as Discovery Cove can truly thrive.

This chapter provides a general overview of (1) what consumer behavior is, (2) what factors affect it, and (3) why you should study it. Because you are a consumer yourself, you probably have some thoughts about these three issues. However, you may be surprised at how broad the domain of consumer behavior is, how many factors help explain consumer behavior, and how important the field of consumer behavior is to marketers, ethicists and consumer advocates, public policy makers and regulators, and consumers like yourself. ●

DEFINING CONSUMER BEHAVIOR

If you were asked to define **consumer behavior**, you might say it refers to the study of how a person buys products. However, this is only part of the definition. Consumer behavior really involves quite a bit more, as this more complete definition indicates:

consumer behavior The totality of consumers' decisions with respect to the acquisition, consumption, and disposition of goods, services, time, and ideas by people over time.

> Consumer behavior reflects the totality of consumers' decisions with respect to the acquisition, consumption, and disposition of goods, services, time, and ideas by (human) decision-making units [over time].[2]

This definition has some very important elements, summarized in Exhibit 1.2. Let us look at each element more closely.

Consumer Behavior Involves Products, Services, Activities, and Ideas

Consumer behavior means more than just how a person buys products such as laundry detergent, breakfast cereal, personal computers, and automobiles. It also includes consumers' use of services, activities, and ideas. Visiting a theme park, going to the dentist, signing up for aerobics classes, taking a trip, celebrating Thanksgiving, getting children immunized, saying no to drugs, and donating to the Boys and Girls Clubs of America are all examples of consumer behavior.

offering A product, service, activity, or idea offered by a marketing organization to consumers.

Marketing efforts therefore also focus on our consumption of services, activities, and ideas, such as the consumption activities shown in Exhibit 1.3. Because consumer behavior can reflect such diverse entities as products, services, activities, or ideas, the term **offering** is often used to refer to the entity around which marketing efforts revolve.

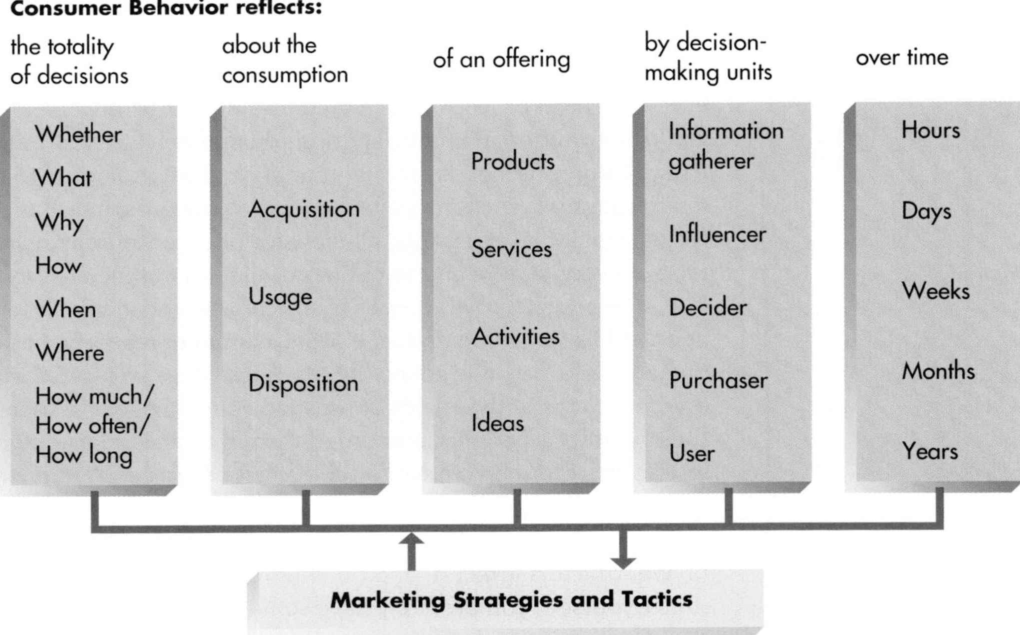

EXHIBIT 1.2
What Is Consumer Behavior?

This exhibit shows that consumer behavior reflects more than simply how a product is acquired by a single person at any one point in time. Think of some marketing strategies and tactics that try to influence one or more of the dimensions of consumer behavior shown in the exhibit.

Consumer Behavior Involves More Than Buying

The manner in which consumers buy is extremely important to marketers. However, marketers are also intensely interested in consumer behavior related to using and disposing of an offering.

acquisition The process by which a consumer comes to obtain an offering.

Acquiring Buying represents one type of **acquisition** behavior. (See Exhibit 1.4 for some interesting information on how consumers spend money.) As you will see in greater detail later in the chapter, acquisition includes other ways of obtaining products and services, such as leasing, trading, or borrowing.

usage The process by which a consumer uses an offering.

Using After consumers acquire a product or service, they typically use it in some manner. Although researchers have studied consumer acquisition in great depth, **usage** is at the very core of consumer behavior.[3] First, usage has important symbolic implications for the consumer. The products we use at Thanksgiving (pumpkin pie, whether made from scratch or store bought) may symbolize the importance of the event, how much we have worked to make a nice dinner, and how important our guests are to us. The music to which we listen (Dave Matthews Band or Tony Bennett) and the jewelry we wear (diamond rings or belly button rings) can also symbolize who we are and how we feel. As you will see in later chapters, an understanding of consumers' usage of products and services can guide marketing strategy and tactics.

Second, usage can also influence other behaviors. Dissatisfied and angry consumers may communicate negative experiences to others, sometimes with devastating results.[4] For example, negative word-of-mouth can quickly kill a

Hollywood film. Dissatisfied consumers may also complain—sometimes to the offending company and sometimes to agencies like the Federal Trade Commission (FTC) or the Federal Bureau of Investigation (FBI). For instance, after the FBI established an Internet Fraud Complaint Center, nearly half of the consumer complaints it received were about online auction fraud.[5]

disposition The process by which a consumer gets rid of an offering.

Disposing Finally, consumer behavior examines **disposition**—how consumers get rid of an offering they previously acquired. Disposition behavior can have extremely important implications for marketers.[6] For example, many consumers are concerned about the environment and will pay extra for products that are biodegradable, are made from recycled materials, or do not pollute when disposed of.[7] Some companies make considerable money from disposition behavior by buying trash and recycling it.[8]

Consumer Behavior Is a Dynamic Process

Consumer behavior suggests that the sequence of acquisition, consumption, and disposition can occur over time in a dynamic sequence. As shown in Exhibit 1.2, this sequence can occur over a matter of hours, days, weeks, months, or even years.

To illustrate the sequence, assume that a family has acquired and is using a new car. Usage provides the family with information—whether the car drives well, is reliable, impresses others, and does minimal harm to the environment—that affects when, whether, how, and why the family will dispose of the car by selling, trading, or junking it. Because the family always needs transportation, disposition of the car is likely to affect when, whether, how, and why its members acquire another car in the future.

Entire markets are designed around linking one consumer's disposition decision to other consumers' acquisition decisions. For example, when consumers buy used cars, they are buying cars that others have disposed of. Organizations like Goodwill Industries, antique stores, electronic auctions, and used clothing and used CD stores are all examples of businesses that link one consumer's disposition behavior with another's acquisition behavior. Markets have also developed in response to the decisions consumers make about time consumption. Travelers who want to make the most use of layovers between flights can work out at airport fitness centers, shop in airport malls, or rent DVD players to watch movies and play games.[9]

EXHIBIT 1.3
Affecting Consumers' Decisions about Activities
Consumer behavior includes consumers' decisions about how they spend their time. Sports teams, travel agencies, software companies, and television entertainment networks are only some of the organizations that develop marketing efforts designed to influence consumers' decisions about what activities they will pursue.

Source: Courtesy of National Geographic Channels International © 2002.

Les morts parlent, écoutons-les.
Les momies ne révèlent pas facilement leurs secrets. C'est pourquoi nos archéologues ne se contentent pas de creuser – ils mènent l'enquête.
Le Mystère des Momies Incas
DIMANCHE 19 MAI à 21H
Disponible sur CANALSATELLITE et sur certains réseaux câblés.
NATIONAL GEOGRAPHIC CHANNEL

Consumer Behavior Can Involve Many People

Consumer behavior does not necessarily reflect the action of a single individual. A group of friends, a few coworkers, or an entire family may plan a birthday party, decide where to have dinner, or visit Discovery Cove. Moreover, the individuals engaging in consumer behavior can take on one or more consumer roles. In the case of an automobile purchase, for example, one or more family members might take on the role of information gatherer by collecting information about potential

EXHIBIT 1.4
It All Adds Up: What do we buy?
We buy lots of different things from a host of product categories. A few of the more common categories of consumption are shown here.

Source: U.S. Bureau of Labor Statistics. Used with permission.

AVERAGE ANNUAL CONSUMER-UNIT EXPENDITURES BY CATEGORY, 2000		
INCOME BEFORE TAXES[1]		$44,649
AVERAGE EXPENDITURES		$38,045
FOOD		$5,158
FOOD AT HOME	$3,021	
CEREALS AND BAKERY GOODS	$ 453	
MEATS, POULTRY, FISH AND EGGS	$ 795	
DAIRY PRODUCTS	$ 325	
FRUITS AND VEGETABLES	$ 521	
OTHER FOOD AT HOME	$ 927	
FOOD AWAY FROM HOME	$2,137	
HOUSING		$12,319
SHELTER	$7,114	
UTILITIES, FUELS AND PUBLIC SERVICES	$2,489	
HOUSEHOLD OPERATIONS	$ 684	
HOUSEKEEPING SUPPLIES	$ 482	
HOUSEHOLD FURNISHINGS AND EQUIPMENT	$1,549	
APPAREL AND SERVICES		$1,856
TRANSPORTATION		$7,417
VEHICLE PURCHASES (NET OUTLAY)	$3,418	
GASOLINE AND MOTOR OIL	$1,291	
OTHER VECHICLE EXPENSES	$2,281	
PUBLIC TRANSPORTATION	$ 427	
HEALTH CARE		$2,066
ENTERTAINMENT		$1,863
PERSONAL CARE PRODUCTS AND SERVICES		$ 564
READING		$ 146
EDUCATION		$ 632
TOBACCO PRODUCTS AND SUPPLIES		$ 319
MISCELLANEOUS		$ 776
CASH CONTRIBUTIONS		$1,192
PERSONAL INSURANCE AND PENSIONS		$3,365
LIFE AND OTHER PERSONAL INSURANCE	$ 399	
PENSIONS AND SOCIAL SECURITY	$2,966	

[1]Income values are derived from "complete income reporters only"

models. Others might assume the role of influencer and try to affect the outcome of a decision. One or more members may take on the role of purchaser by actually paying for the car, and some or all may be users. Finally, several family members may be involved in the disposal of the car.

Consumer Behavior Involves Many Decisions

Consumer behavior involves understanding whether, why, when, where, how, how much, how often, and how long consumers will buy, use, or dispose of an offering (look back at Exhibit 1.2).

Whether to Acquire/Use/Dispose of an Offering Consumers must decide whether to acquire, use, or dispose of an offering. They may need to decide whether to spend or save their money when they get a raise. They may need to decide whether to eat dessert, whether to clean out their bulging closets, or whether to go to a movie. In some cases decisions about whether to acquire, use, or dispose of an offering are related to safety concerns. For example, some consumers are concerned about whether to buy and use cellular phones because the phones may adversely affect pacemakers and are suspected of contributing to brain cancer. While the World Health Organization and others investigate possible health problems, Great Britain has already ordered cell phone makers to include a health warning on handsets.[10] Concerns about economic risk, social risk, and psychological risk may also motivate consumer decisions.

What to Acquire/Use/Dispose of Consumers in each household in the United States spend an average of $90 per day on goods and services. Clearly, we make decisions every day about what to buy.[11] In some cases we make choices among product or service *categories*. Exhibit 1.4 summarizes the major categories of offerings that U.S. consumers buy. In other cases we choose between *brands,* such as the decision between acquiring a Sony PlayStation 2 or a Nintendo GameCube. Our choices multiply daily, as marketers introduce new products, new sizes, and new packages. Marketers are even creating distinctive Web-only offerings, such as online comics, to spur acquisition and use of movies, T-shirts, and other traditional products.[12]

Why Acquire/Use/Dispose of an Offering Consumption can occur for a number of reasons. Among the most important, as you will see later, are the ways in which an offering meets someone's needs, values, or goals. For example, some consumers have various body parts pierced as a form of self-expression. Others do it to fit into a group. Still others believe body piercing is a form of beauty, whereas for some piercing is done to enhance sexual pleasure.[13] Some consumers buy and use products because they want a fantasy experience. In Phnom Penh, Cambodia, tourists can fantasize that they are in a war, firing grenades or using Uzis or AK-47s from a specially designed shooting range.[14]

Sometimes our reasons for using a product or service are filled with conflict. Teenagers may smoke, even though they know it is harmful, because they think smoking will help them gain acceptance. Low-fat margarine is probably healthier than regular margarine, but many consumers avoid it because its taste has been described as similar to "melted plastic."[15] These conflicts can lead to some difficult consumption decisions.

Some consumers may be unable to stop acquiring, using, or disposing of products. People may be physically addicted to products such as cigarettes, drugs, or alcoholic beverages; or they may have a compulsion to eat, purge, gamble, or buy. Finally, consumers who want to consume may not be able to do so. In Hungary, for example, many consumers are desperate for new housing. However, so few new apartments and houses are available that people must either stay in dingy and deteriorating places or invest in extensive repairs and redecorating.[16]

Why Not to Acquire/Use/Dispose of an Offering Marketers also want to know why consumers do *not* acquire, use, or dispose of an offering. For example, consumers may put off buying a DVD player because they do not think they can handle the technology or they do not believe it offers anything special. They may believe that technology is changing so fast that their purchase will soon be outdated. They may even believe that some DVD suppliers will go out of business, leaving them without after-sale support or service.

How to Acquire/Use/Dispose of an Offering Marketers gain a lot of insight from understanding the ways in which consumers acquire, consume, and dispose of an offering.

Ways of Acquiring an Offering How do consumers decide whether to pay for an item with cash, a check, a debit card, a credit card, or an electronic payment system? In China, where bank notes are in short supply and the use of counterfeit money is widespread, the government is encouraging consumers' use of debit cards.[17] On the Internet, more than 13 million consumers use the PayPal service to pay for their purchases rather than typing in credit card numbers or mailing checks.[18] Yet buying is only one way of acquiring an offering:

- *Buying.* Although we typically recognize buying as a common form of acquisition behavior, consumers can acquire products and services in other ways.
- *Trading.* Consumers could receive a product or service as part of a trade. For example, some music stores allow consumers to trade in old CDs, albums, or tapes for new CDs, new tapes, or cash.
- *Renting or Leasing.* Goods like tuxedos, carpet cleaners, furniture, vacation homes, and computers can be rented or leased. Leasing is now a very popular way of acquiring automobiles.
- *Bartering.* Thousands of businesses and consumers worldwide engage in the practice of bartering. More than half of the largest U.S. companies, including PepsiCo and Hilton Hotels, exchange their offerings for goods and services they want to acquire, such as advertising space. In Argentina, a lengthy recession and high unemployment have driven many consumers and businesses to join barter clubs and barter $400 million worth of products per year.[19]
- *Gift Giving.* Consumers can also acquire products as gifts. Gift giving is common throughout the world, and most societies have many gift-giving occasions. Each society also has formal and informal rules that dictate how gifts should be given, what is appropriate as a gift, and what is an appropriate response to gift giving. Marketing efforts are sometimes designed to induce gift giving on traditional and nontraditional occasions ranging from Mother's Day to Boss's Day.
- *Finding.* In some instances consumers simply find goods that someone else has lost (books left on the bus, shampoo left at the gym, umbrellas left in class) or thrown away.
- *Theft.* Goods can also be acquired through theft. Some marketers have developed products to deter this mode of acquisition. For example, antitheft devices like The Club, LoJack, and car alarms attempt to reduce the likelihood of car theft.
- *Borrowing.* Another way to acquire products is by borrowing. Although we typically think of borrowing as a willing and conscious exchange between borrower and lender, some types of "borrowing" are illegal and border on

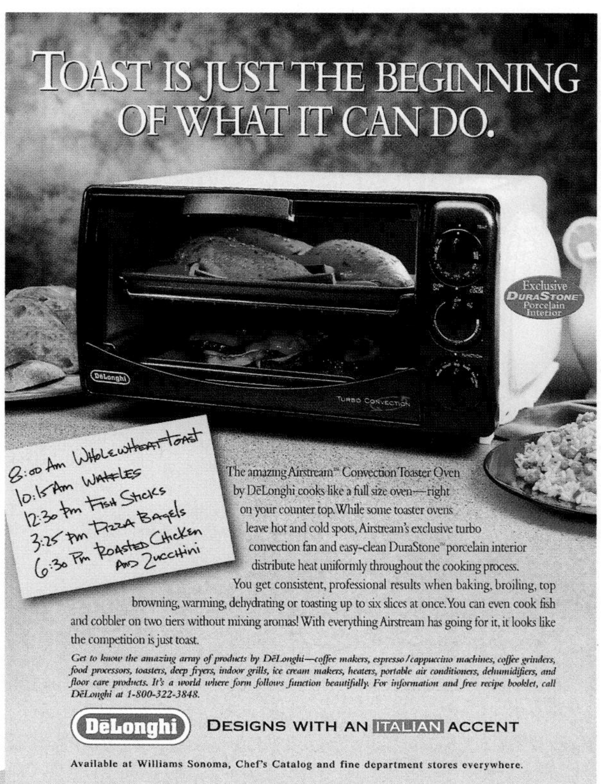

EXHIBIT 1.5
Affecting How a Product Is Used
Consumers' decisions about how an offering is used can affect how satisfied they are with it. Companies sometimes use marketing communications such as this ad to communicate appropriate or innovative uses of their products.

Source: Used by permission of DeLonghi America, Inc.

theft. It is not uncommon, for example, for some consumers to pay for new clothes, wear them, and then return them for a full refund. This happens frequently with formal wear, especially during hard economic times.[20] Illegal borrowing is also hurting publishing companies, movie studios, software producers, and musical artists who produce copyrighted material. Products in digital format, such as music and video files, are particularly vulnerable to this form of "bootlegging," since they can easily be copied and exchanged via computer.[21]

Ways of Using an Offering In addition to understanding how consumers acquire products and services, marketers are also interested in how consumers use an offering.[22] For example, marketers have found that consumers are using their cars and vans as mini-homes, complete with phones, faxes, radios, stereos, TVs, VCRs, refrigerators, and automatic alarms, and that this usage is reducing demand for traditional automotive features such as stick shifts.[23] An ad designed to influence consumer usage is shown in Exhibit 1.5.

For obvious reasons, marketers want to ensure that their offering is used correctly. For example, marketers of the female condom have found that their biggest challenge is not in getting consumers to buy the condom but rather in educating them about how to use it correctly.[24] Improper usage of some products or services, such as oven cleaner or cough medicine, can create health and safety problems for a consumer.[25] Because of these hazards, potentially dangerous products must have warning labels; unfortunately, many consumers ignore label warnings and directions. Therefore, to make these warnings more effective, marketers must understand how consumers process label information.

Ways of Disposing of an Offering Finally, consumers can decide how to dispose of products. In making this decision, they generally have several options:[26]

- *Finding a New Use for It.* Using an old toothbrush to clean rust from tools or making shorts out of an old pair of jeans are some of the ways in which consumers deal with an original item without actually disposing of it.
- *Getting Rid of It Temporarily.* Renting or lending an item is one way of getting rid of it temporarily.
- *Getting Rid of It Permanently.* Throwing an item away probably represents the most common option for permanently getting rid of it; but there are also the options of trading it, giving it away, or selling it.

Some consumers refuse to throw away things they regard as special, even if the items no longer serve a functional purpose. Other consumers are interested in collecting, not disposing of items.[27] Consumers collect many things, from stamps, CDs, dolls, and teddy bears to string, coffee beans, and flip-top lids. Preferred Plush, for example, markets its collectible stuffed animals to

EXHIBIT 1.6
Problems in Disposition
Some consumers create public health problems by failing to throw anything away, even things that have lost their functional value.

Source: © Mug Shots/CORBIS.

preteens. "We have found that if [preteens] like one of our collection products, they will keep coming back for more," says company founder Jennifer Lee.[28] Taking collecting to an extreme, some consumers are "pack rats" who can alienate neighbors and create health risks by failing to throw out anything (see Exhibit 1.6).

When to Acquire/Use/Dispose of an Offering Our tendency to rent videos, hire plumbers, call a tow truck company, or shop for clothes is greatly enhanced in cold weather. These same weather conditions reduce our tendency to eat ice cream, shop for a car, or look for a new home.[29] Dentists have found that the demand for teeth bleaching increases dramatically among politicians and lobbyists in the pre-election season.[30] Time of day also influences consumption decisions. Few of us want wine and lobster for breakfast, although we may happily anticipate the same items in the evening.

Our need for variety can affect when we acquire, use, or dispose of an offering. We may decide not to eat yogurt for lunch today if we have had it every day this week. Transitions such as graduation, birth, retirement, and death also affect when we acquire, use, and dispose of offerings. For instance, we buy products like wedding rings, wedding dresses, and wedding cakes only when we get married.

Moreover, when we consume can be affected by traditions imposed by our families, our culture, and the area in which we live. Every spring, St. George, South Carolina, hosts the World Grits Festival. In addition to serving up considerable quantities of grits, the festival features a contest in which participants roll in a huge vat filled with cooled grits, vying for prizes based on who gets covered with the most grits.[31]

Our decisions about when to use an offering are also affected by knowing when others might or might not be using it. Thus we might be motivated to travel by air, eat dinner, go on vacation, work out, or get a haircut when we know that others will *not* be doing so. In addition, we may wait to purchase goods and services until we know they will be on sale—or we may try to be among the first to purchase an offering expected to be in short supply, as when shoppers lined up to buy the Sony PlayStation 2 when it became available.[32]

Another decision we commonly face is when to acquire a new, improved version of a product we already own. This can be a difficult decision when the current model still works well or has sentimental value. However, marketers may be able to affect whether and when consumers buy upgrades by providing economic incentives for trading up from older products.[33]

Where to Acquire/Use/Dispose Of an Offering Consumers have more choices of where to acquire, use, and dispose of an offering than ever before. They can shop for groceries at discount stores such as Wal-Mart and buy low-priced clothing at supermarkets like Britain's Asda chain.[34] Beyond traditional stores and outlets, advances in information technology now allow us to buy goods and services through the mail, over the telephone, from TV, over the Internet, and using wireless handheld devices.

Consider that consumers who have traditionally traveled to places like Las Vegas and Reno to gamble now can do so in Internet-based casinos.[35] Online shopping has dramatically changed where we acquire, use, and dispose of goods. Internet purchases already top $100 billion annually and continue to grow. Many consumers buy online because they like the convenience or the price.[36] At the Williams-Sonoma Web site, for example, brides-to-be can log on to the gift registry and see who has bought them what. Online customers of Sears, Roebuck and Co. can apply for store credit cards and buy thousands of items. Circuit City and Penney's even let customers return merchandise purchased online at local stores.[37] The Internet has also changed where we acquire services. In one recent year, consumers bought more than $12 billion worth of travel services through Internet sites.[38] As another example, some banks allow consumers to get a loan through automated loan machines set up at supermarkets.[39]

Consumers sometimes choose to buy products that have been used. Indeed, buying secondhand goods has become almost chic. Some consumers even believe that certain secondhand items make wonderful gifts.[40] And 34 million people have registered to buy or sell millions of used items in eBay's online auctions, from cars to antique clocks.[41]

In addition to acquisition decisions, consumers also make decisions about where they wish to consume various products. For example, the need for privacy motivates consumers to seek the privacy of their own homes to get drunk or to use products that determine whether they are ovulating, pregnant, or diabetic. Consumers use laptops and Web-enabled cell phones to check e-mail on the road, handle banking transactions, and follow news headlines. Workers face daily decisions about what and where to eat lunch; 40 percent of American working women eat a brown-bag lunch on the job at least once a week.[42]

Finally, consumers make decisions regarding where to dispose of goods. Should they toss an old magazine in the trash or the recycling bin? Should they store an old photo album in the attic or give it to a family member? Older consumers, in particular, may worry about what will happen to their special possessions after their death and about how to divide heirlooms without creating family conflict. These consumers hope that as a result of their decisions, heirs will have mementos that serve as a legacy.[43]

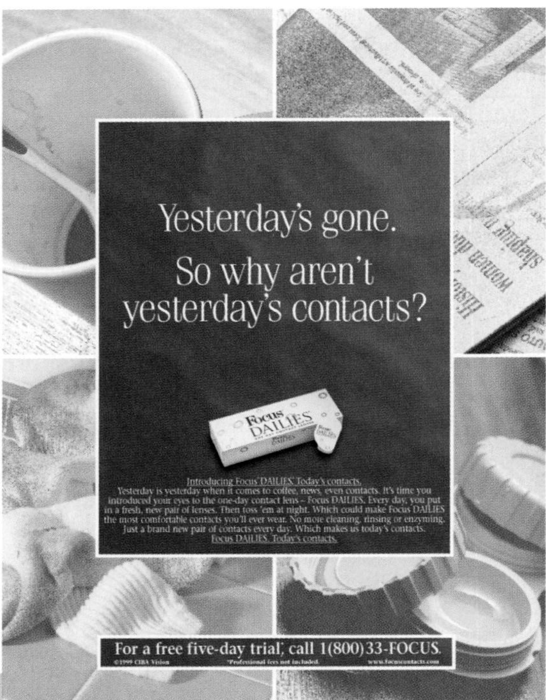

EXHIBIT 1.7
Affecting How Often a Product Is Used
Marketers can often stimulate sales not by getting more consumers to buy the offering but by making existing consumers acquire, consume, or dispose of it more often.

Source: Courtesy of CIBA Vision.

Clearly, marketers and retailers try to influence consumers' decisions about where to acquire and dispose of products. Web sites like Quotesmith.com and Insweb.com encourage consumers to buy life insurance, car insurance, and other insurance policies over the Internet.[44] Many restaurants give consumers the option of consuming meals in or taking them out. Some marketers seek to influence where consumers dispose of goods. Consumers can pay IBM a flat fee of $29.99, including shipping, to responsibly dispose of old personal computers and parts. Only 11 percent of obsolete computers are being recycled, creating a major waste disposal problem. IBM's program encourages consumers to recycle their old computers when they buy new ones.[45]

How Much, How Often, and How Long to Acquire/Use/Dispose of an Offering Consumers must make decisions about how much of a good or service they need; how often they need it; and how long they will spend in acquisition, usage, and disposition.[46] Usage decisions can vary widely from person to person and from culture to culture. For example, consumers in India drink an average of only 5 nine-ounce bottles of soft drinks per year, while consumers in China drink 17 and consumers in America drink 280.[47]

Sales of a product can be increased when the consumer (1) uses larger amounts of the product, (2) uses the product more frequently, or (3) uses it for longer periods of time. The ad in Exhibit 1.7, for example, is designed to influence how often a product is used. Estée Lauder's cosmetics salespeople are trained in techniques that will increase sales, such as recommending complementary products.[48] Bonus packs help motivate consumers to buy more of a product, just as frequent-flyer programs encourage them to fly more often.[49] Usage may also increase when consumers sign up for flat-fee pricing covering unlimited consumption of telephone services or other offerings. However, because many consumers who choose flat-fee programs overestimate their likely consumption, they often pay more than they would with per-usage pricing.[50]

Some consumers experience problems due to excessive consumption or a compulsion to engage in more acquisition, usage, or disposition than they would like. Such compulsions can occur in spending, gambling, smoking, exercising, drug abuse (including legal drugs), and eating. In the United States, for example, roughly 55 percent of all adults are overweight (see Exhibit 1.8).[51] Excessive consumption can cause many kinds of problems. For instance, doctors are blaming a rise in drug-resistant strains of bacteria on consumers' excessive use of antibiotics.[52]

In summary, consumer behavior reflects the multitude of factors revealed in Exhibit 1.2. You now can see that consumer behavior involves much more than understanding which products a consumer buys.

WHAT AFFECTS CONSUMER BEHAVIOR?

What affects consumers as they make their acquisition, usage, and disposition decisions? The many factors are organized into four broad domains, as shown in the model in Exhibit 1.9, which also serves as an organizing framework for this book.

EXHIBIT 1.8
Growing Larger
Are we getting fat? Do we consume too much? From the data, it appears that the number of people who are overweight has been increasing over time.

Source: Reprinted from *American Demographics* magazine, June 1997. Copyright 1997. Courtesy of Intertec Publishing Corp., Stamford, Connecticut. All rights reserved.

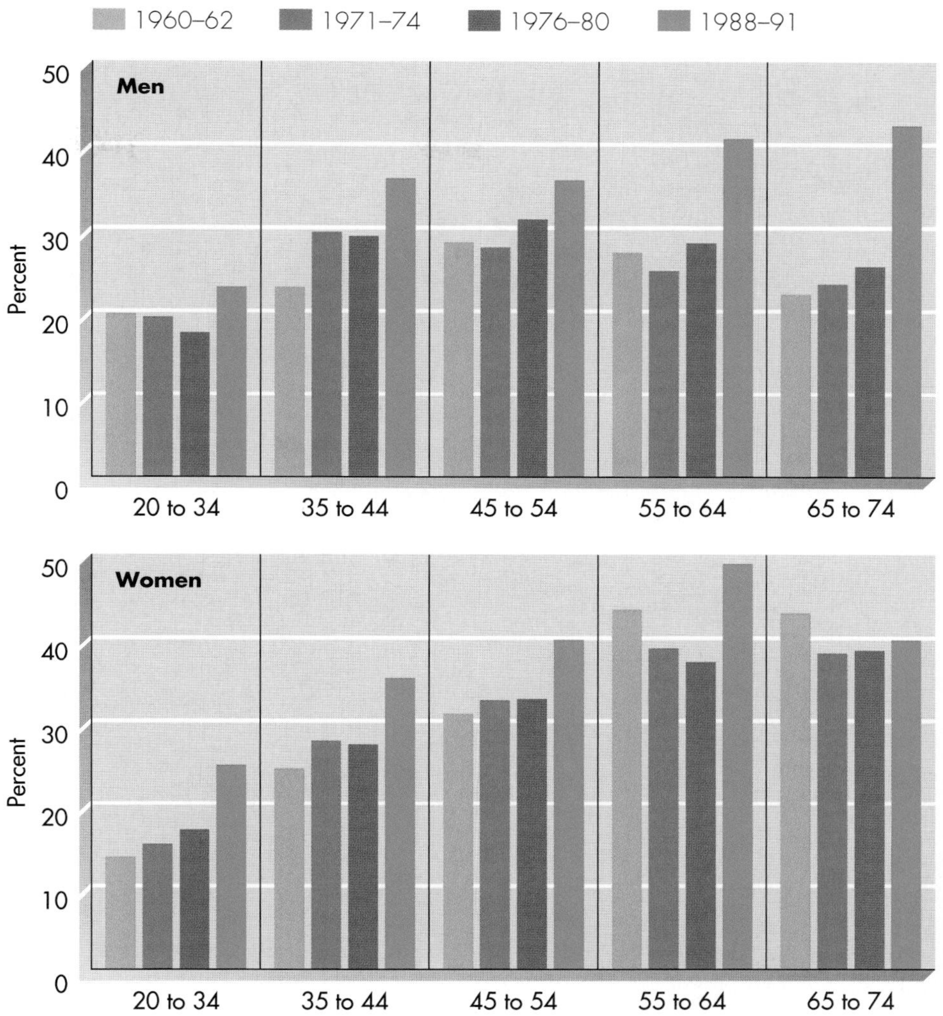

Note: Percent of U.S. adults aged 20 to 74 who are overweight, by sex and age, 1960–62, 1971–74, 1976–80, 1988–91.

The four domains of consumer behavior are: (1) the psychological core, (2) the process of making decisions, (3) the consumer's culture, and (4) consumer behavior outcomes. Although the four domains are presented in separate sections of this book, each domain is related to all the others. For example, to make decisions that affect outcomes like buying new products or using products for symbolic reasons, consumers must first engage in processes described in the psychological core. They need to be motivated, able, and have the opportunity to be exposed to, perceive, and attend to information. They need to think about this information, form attitudes about it, and form memories.

The cultural environment also affects what motivates consumers, how they process information, and the kinds of decisions they make. Age, gender, social class, ethnicity, families, friends, and other factors affect consumer values and lifestyles and, in turn, influence the decisions that consumers make and how and

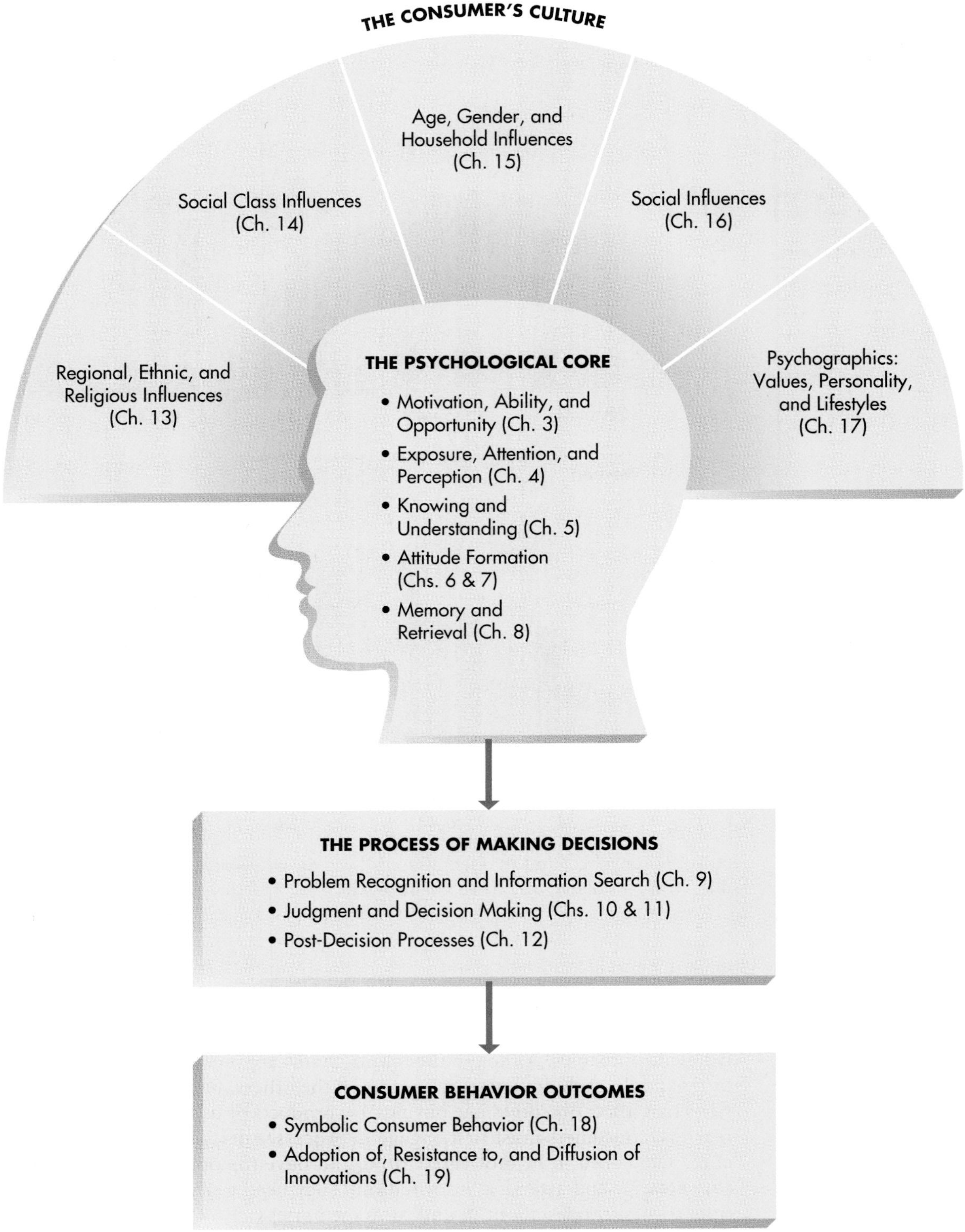

THE CONSUMER'S CULTURE

Regional, Ethnic, and Religious Influences (Ch. 13)

Social Class Influences (Ch. 14)

Age, Gender, and Household Influences (Ch. 15)

Social Influences (Ch. 16)

Psychographics: Values, Personality, and Lifestyles (Ch. 17)

THE PSYCHOLOGICAL CORE

- Motivation, Ability, and Opportunity (Ch. 3)
- Exposure, Attention, and Perception (Ch. 4)
- Knowing and Understanding (Ch. 5)
- Attitude Formation (Chs. 6 & 7)
- Memory and Retrieval (Ch. 8)

↓

THE PROCESS OF MAKING DECISIONS

- Problem Recognition and Information Search (Ch. 9)
- Judgment and Decision Making (Chs. 10 & 11)
- Post-Decision Processes (Ch. 12)

↓

CONSUMER BEHAVIOR OUTCOMES

- Symbolic Consumer Behavior (Ch. 18)
- Adoption of, Resistance to, and Diffusion of Innovations (Ch. 19)

EXHIBIT 1.9
A Model of Consumer Behavior

Consumer behavior encompasses four domains: (1) the psychological core, (2) the process of making decisions, (3) the consumer's culture, and (4) consumer behavior outcomes. As the exhibit shows, Chapters 3–19 of this book relate to the four parts of this overall model.

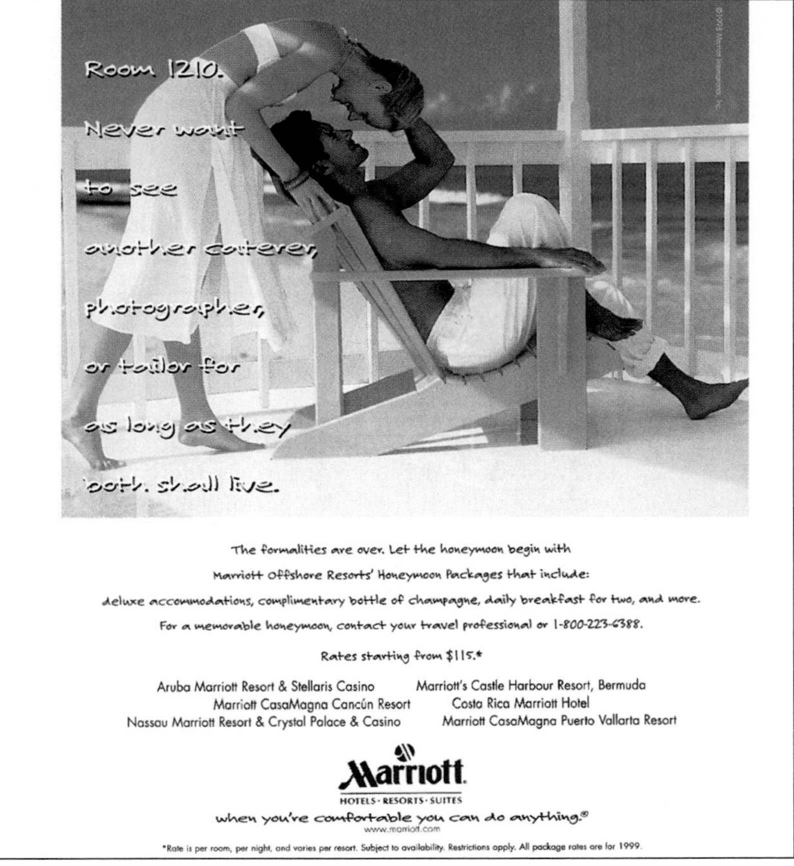

EXHIBIT 1.10
Categorizing a Vacation
Whether we decide to search for more information about an offering (e.g., a vacation destination) depends on how we categorize it (e.g., as a honeymoon vacation). If we categorize it as something different from what we want, we will not consider it further.

Source: Marriott International, Inc.

why they make them. Let us consider each domain separately and illustrate the interrelationships among the domains with an example of a vacation decision.

The Psychological Core: Internal Consumer Processes

Before consumers can make decisions, they must have some source of knowledge or information upon which to base their decisions. This source—the psychological core—covers motivation, ability, and opportunity; exposure, attention, and perception; categorization and comprehension of information; and formation and change in attitude.

Having Motivation, Ability, and Opportunity Consider the case of a hypothetical consumer named Jessica who is deciding on a ski vacation. In Jessica's mind, a vacation decision is very risky—her vacation consumes lots of money and time, and she does not want to make a bad choice. In light of this risk, Jessica is very motivated to learn as much as she can about various vacation options, think about them, and fantasize about what they will be like. She has put other activities aside to give herself the opportunity to learn and think about this vacation. Because Jessica already knows how to ski, she has the ability to determine what types of ski vacations she would find enjoyable.

Exposure, Attention, and Perception Because Jessica is greatly motivated to decide where to go on vacation and she has the ability and opportunity to do so, she will make sure she is exposed to, perceives, and attends to any information she thinks is relevant to her decision. She might look at travel ads, read travel-related newspaper and magazine articles, and engage in discussions with friends and travel agents. Note, though, that Jessica's attention is selective. She will probably not attend to *all* vacation information; she is likely to be exposed to information she will never perceive or pay attention to.

Categorizing and Comprehending Information Jessica will use the information that she does perceive and attempt to categorize and comprehend it. For example, she might categorize the vacation in Exhibit 1.10 as a honeymoon vacation. Because she does not want this type of vacation, she will not consider it further. She might infer that Kitzbühel, Austria, is a reasonably priced vacation destination because the brochures show images consistent with this interpretation.

Forming and Changing Attitudes Jessica is likely to form attitudes toward the vacations she has categorized and comprehended. She may have a favorable attitude toward Kitzbühel because a brochure describes it as affordable, educational, and fun. However, her attitudes might undergo considerable change as she encounters new information.

Attitudes do not always predict our behavior. For example, many of us probably have a positive attitude toward working out. Nevertheless, our positive attitude and our good intentions do not always culminate in a trip to the gym. For this reason, attitudes and choices are considered as separate topics.

Forming and Retrieving Memories One reason that our attitudes may not predict our behavior is that we may or may not remember the information we used to form our attitudes when we later make a decision. Thus Jessica may have formed memories based on certain information, but her choices will be based only on the information she retrieves from memory.

The Process of Making Decisions

The processes that are part of the psychological core are intimately tied to the process of making decisions. Four stages characterize the process of making consumer decisions: problem recognition, information search, decision making, and post-purchase evaluation.

Problem Recognition and the Search for Information Problem recognition occurs when we realize we have an unfulfilled need. Jessica realized she needed a vacation, for example. Her subsequent search for information gave her insight into where she might go, how much it might cost, and when she might travel. She also examined her financial situation. Elements of the psychological core are invoked in problem recognition and search because once Jessica realizes that she needs a vacation and begins her information search, she exposes herself to information, attends to and perceives it, categorizes and comprehends it, and forms attitudes and memories.

Making Judgments and Decisions Jessica's decision is characterized as a *high-effort decision,* meaning that she is willing to exert a lot of time and mental and emotional energy in making it. She identifies several decision criteria that she thinks will be important in making her choices. First, she wants the trip to be educational. She also wants it to be fun and exciting. Third, she does not want to spend a lot of money. Finally, she wants to make sure the place she selects is safe.

Not all decisions involve a lot of effort. Jessica also faces low-effort decisions such as deciding what brand of toothpaste to take on the trip, whether to use traveler's checks, and whether to bring a camera. Again, the psychological core is invoked in making judgments and decisions. With a high-effort decision, Jessica will be motivated to expose herself to lots of information; she will think about it deeply, analyze it critically, and form attitudes about it. She may have lasting memories about the information she sees because she has thought about it so much. In making a low-effort decision, such as a decision about what brand of toothpaste to buy, she would probably conduct a less extensive information search, do less information processing, and form less enduring attitudes and memories.

Making Post-Decision Evaluations Evaluating the decision is the final step of the decision-making process. This step allows the consumer to judge whether the decision was the correct one and whether the product or service is one that will be purchased again. When she returns from her vacation, Jessica will probably evaluate the outcome of her decisions. If her expectations were met and the vacation is everything she thought it would be, she will feel satisfied. If the vacation exceeds her expectations, she will be delighted. If it falls short, she is likely to be dissatisfied. Once again, aspects of the psychological core are invoked in making post-decision evaluations. Jessica may expose herself to information that validates her experiences, she may update her attitudes, and she may selectively remember aspects of her trip that were extremely positive or negative.

The Consumer's Culture: External Processes

culture The typical or expected behaviors, norms, and ideas that characterize a group of people.

Why did Jessica decide to go on a skiing trip in the first place? In large part, our consumption decisions are affected by our culture. **Culture** refers to the typical or expected behaviors, norms, and ideas that characterize a group of people. It can be a powerful influence on all aspects of human behavior. Jessica had certain feelings, perceptions, and attitudes because of the unique combination of groups to which she belongs. Culture can clearly affect the decisions we make as well as how we process and communicate information.

Regional and Ethnic Influences Jessica is a member of many groups that directly or indirectly affect the decisions she makes. For example, her decision to ski at a place far from home is fairly typical for a working woman from North America; it is doubtful that a consumer from the Third World or a single woman from a Hindu culture would have made the same vacation choice.

Age, Gender, and Household Influences Jessica's social class, as well as her age, gender, and household circumstances, might have affected her impressions of what constitutes a good vacation. The fact that she is a woman in her 20s and a college graduate who has moved in with her parents might have affected her decision to go skiing abroad, as opposed to staying at home, for instance.

reference groups A group of people we compare ourselves with for information regarding behavior, attitudes, or values.

Reference Groups When Jessica sees groups of others she perceives as similar to herself, she regards them as **reference groups**, people whose values she shares and whose opinion she values. She might also see people whom she admires, even though she does not know them, as people whose behavior she would like to emulate. Thus well-known athletes, musicians, artists, politicians, or movie stars may serve as reference groups for some consumers.

Reference groups can exert influence by conveying information. They can therefore influence the psychological core and the process of making decisions by affecting whom we get information from and how we evaluate it. Reference groups can also make us feel as if we should behave in a certain way. In this example, Jessica may feel some pressure to go to Kitzbühel because her friends think that doing so is cool. Jessica's personality is also likely to affect her decisions. Because she is an extrovert and a moderate risk taker, she wants a vacation that is exciting and affords opportunities to meet people.

symbols External signs we use, consciously or unconsciously, to express our identity.

Consumer Behavior Outcomes

As the conceptual model in Exhibit 1.9 indicates, the psychological core, decision-making processes, and the consumer's culture affect consumer behavior outcomes such as the symbolic use of products and the diffusion of ideas, products, or services through a market.

Consumer Behaviors Can Symbolize Who We Are The groups we belong to and our own sense of self can affect the **symbols** or external signs we use, consciously or unconsciously, to express our identity. For example, while she is on vacation, Jessica may use clothing and brand-name merchandise such as her Nike sneakers to communicate her status as a young female from the United States. She might also take home objects that symbolize her vacation, such as postcards and T-shirts.

In our culture, jewelry such as engagement rings and wedding bands have obvious symbolic meaning. The ad in Exhibit 1.11 illustrates the cultural meaning of the engagement ring and attempts to convey the notion that the symbol is definitely worth the price.

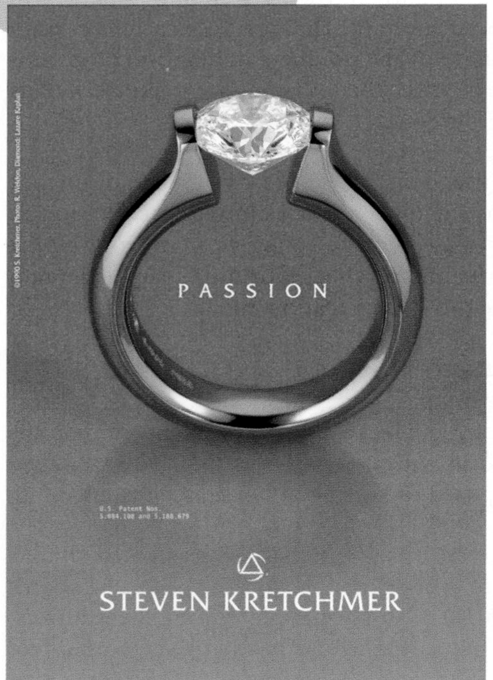

EXHIBIT 1.11
Consumption Symbols
Products like diamond engagement rings and wedding bands can symbolize meaning. Some brands and companies also have symbolic meaning. Think about the symbolic meaning of different products, brands, and companies. Is the meaning specific to a certain culture or group?

Source: © 1990 S. Kretchmer. Photo: R. Weldon. U.S. Patent Nos. 5,084,108 and 5,188,679.

Consumer Behaviors Can Diffuse Through a Market After she makes her vacation decision, Jessica may tell others about her prospective trip. Her choice of Kitzbühel as a vacation destination therefore becomes known to other consumers and may influence their vacation decisions as well. In this way, the idea of going to Kitzbühel on vacation may diffuse, or spread, to others. Had Jessica resisted going to Kitzbühel (perhaps because she thought it was too expensive or unsafe), she might have communicated information that made others less likely to vacation there. Thus the diffusion of information can have both negative and positive effects for marketers.

In the following chapters we expand on the concepts outlined in Exhibit 1.9. We first consider the psychological core (Part One) and then delve into decision-making processes (Part Two). We next consider how the consumer's culture affects consumer behavior (Part Three) and how individual and cultural factors affect consumer behavior outcomes (Part Four). In the final two chapters, we conclude by examining consumer welfare issues (Part Five).

Clearly, every consumer is unique and is affected by a unique set of background factors. Consider the vacation choices shown in Exhibit 1.12 and try to imagine the background factors that predispose consumers to choose these as vacation options.

EXHIBIT 1.12
Vacation

The word *vacation* means different things to different people. Your idea of a "relaxing getaway" may be quite different from someone else's idea. Can you see how factors like social class, ethnic status, economic conditions, group affiliations, and gender affect the kinds of vacations we are likely to find attractive? These examples show us that some marketers are successful precisely because they understand their customers and what they value.

Sources: Kevin Helliker, "Guests Pay Better Than Cattle for Many Ranchers," *Wall Street Journal,* August 1, 1997, pp. B1, B7; Linda K. Nathan, "Spas Ask: May I Check Your Heart Rate?" *Wall Street Journal,* January 19, 1996, p. B7; Timothy Aeppel, "For Great Adventure, What Could Match a Prairie-Dog Safari?" *Wall Street Journal,* August 1, 1995, pp. A1, A5; Jim Carlton, "Japanese Skip Waikiki, Head for Kmart," *Wall Street Journal,* June 29, 1995, p. B1; Timothy Aeppel, "At One with Indians, Tribes of Foreigners Visit Reservations," *Wall Street Journal,* August 6, 1996, pp. A1, A6; Josh Greenberg, "Some Lawnmowers Stay Home: Others Like Life in the Fast Lane," *Wall Street Journal,* March 27, 1997, p. B1.

ON VACATION, WOULD YOU LIKE TO...?

BE A RANCHER? You can visit one of the more than 100 ranches in Wyoming and Montana, and at some pay upwards of $150.00 per day. At all, you can help herd cattle and ride horses on beautiful terrain. Some have you stay in luxurious accommodations. At others, you can sleep in a cabin and use the local outhouse.

VISIT YOUR DOCTOR? At some vacation spas you can have your blood tested, have your metabolism checked, have a cardiogram, and get a mammogram. Of course, the spas also have the standard fare as well: mineral soaks, facials, massages, exercise and diet classes, outdoor activities, and a tranquil environment.

SHOOT PRAIRIE DOGS? At various places in the Great Plains (from Texas to Montana), vacationers can buy or rent hunting clothes and high-powered rifles with scopes, buy maps indicating prairie dog sites, and go with a trail guide on a prairie dog safari. Hunters argue that shooting prairie dogs is good for the environment as the animals carry disease and eat grass intended for sheep and cattle. Others, however, have a different point of view.

FLY TO KMART? In the mid 1990s, the Waikiki Hawaii Waikele Factory Mall, which includes such discount warehouse shops as Kmart, Home Depot, and Eagle Hardware, became one of the hottest Japanese tourist destinations, attracting roughly half a million Japanese consumers per year. Coming with empty suitcases and bags, these tourists would hunt up bargains in categories that included bulk spaghetti and crates of dog food.

BECOME A NATIVE AMERICAN? You can sleep on a grass floor of a teepee, ladle water onto heated rocks in a sweat lodge, visit a medicine man, pick organic vegetables, make jewelry decorated with porcupine quills, clear grass from the powwow ring, and observe sacred ceremonies on Native American reservations. These vacations are particularly popular among European travelers. Approximately 60,000 Germans belong to clubs that focus on Native American culture.

RACE IN A RIDING LAWNMOWER COMPETITION? On or around Labor Day, finalists—members of the U.S. Lawnmower Racing Association—will compete for the national championship of the national riding lawnmower competition. Races, held on specially prepared tracks, last for about 20 minutes at speeds of up to 55 miles per hour. In addition to paying for travel to the competition site in Rockford, IL, contestants spend upwards of $3,000 souping up their machines for the race.

WHO BENEFITS FROM THE STUDY OF CONSUMER BEHAVIOR?

The final question we address in this chapter is why people study consumer behavior. The reasons are as varied as the four different groups who use consumer research: marketing managers, ethicists and advocates, public policy makers and regulators, and consumers.

Marketing Managers

marketing A social and managerial process by which individuals and groups obtain what they need and want through creating and exchanging products and value with others.

The study of consumer behavior provides critical information to marketing managers for developing marketing strategies and tactics. We can emphasize this point by examining a classic definition of **marketing**:

> Marketing is a social and managerial process whereby individuals and groups obtain what they need and want through creating and exchanging products and value with others.[53]

According to this definition, marketing managers must clearly understand consumers' needs and wants in order to effectively market a product or service. The study of consumer behavior provides this information and suggests how marketers can design programs to bring about the exchange process. In Chapter 2 we expand on the role of marketing research and the strategic and tactical decisions it supports.

Ethicists and Advocacy Groups

Marketers' actions sometimes raise important ethical questions. For example, R.J. Reynolds Tobacco International provided the city of Bucharest, Romania, with a year's supply of yellow traffic light bulbs bearing the Camel cigarette logo.[54] A case can be made that such a "gift" might influence Romanians' decisions to smoke. Indeed, even as the World Health Organization pushes for a global ban on all cigarette promotion, major tobacco marketers are voluntarily decreasing media advertising and product placement to show they are not trying to encourage underage smoking.[55]

Consumers concerned about ethical marketing practices sometimes form advocacy groups to create public awareness of inappropriate practices. They also influence other consumers as well as the targeted companies through strategies such as media statements and boycotts. For example, advocacy groups have publicly criticized some music publishers and artists for promoting song lyrics that are sexually explicit and portray violence against women and gay people. In response, some artists and publishers have withdrawn or changed selected songs, and retailers have started using warning stickers to alert parents to albums with explicit content.[56]

Consumer groups have also denounced interactive video games featuring murder, physical violence, and rape. Many object to games that show women being beaten and brutalized or scantily clad and depicted in stereotypical ways.[57] We explore ethical issues throughout this book, particularly in Chapter 21, "The Dark Side of Consumer Behavior and Marketing."

Consumers sometimes band together to form cooperatives—institutions in which consumers minimize costs and control marketing practices by acting as both owners and consumers. Food co-ops are common in the United States. In Canada and Europe, an increasing number of funeral co-ops have been formed to help consumers avoid skyrocketing funeral costs.[58]

Public Policy Makers and Regulators

Lawmakers and public policy groups strive to protect consumers from unfair, unsafe, or inappropriate marketing practices. In the 1960s, President Kennedy declared that consumers have four basic rights: the rights to safety, to information, to choice, and to be heard. The right to a clean environment and protection for minorities and the poor were added later. Many governmental groups develop detailed regulations and enforce laws related to these basic consumer rights.

For example, the U.S. Food and Drug Administration (FDA) ensures that the labeling of medical products such as contraceptives adequately explains usage instructions, risks, and side effects. The agency approved the Today contraceptive sponge for reintroduction to the U.S. market only after insisting on a more explicit label warning women of the possibility of contracting toxic shock syndrome.[59]

In protecting the right to be informed, consumer researchers have investigated deceptive and misleading advertising. Therefore, understanding how consumers comprehend and categorize information is important to recognizing and guarding against misleading advertising. Researchers want to know what impressions an ad creates and whether these impressions are true.

For example, the FDA recently expressed concern about ads for anti-AIDS drugs that show people with AIDS and those who are HIV-positive climbing mountains and engaging in other vigorous activities. Through research, the San Francisco health department had discovered that gay men exposed to such ads were willing to participate in unsafe sex. After the FDA asked the drug manufacturers to more clearly explain the limitations of their products, Pfizer added a notice stating that its Viracept drug does not cure AIDS or prevent HIV.[60]

Consumer researchers also investigate advertising to children. Research has shown that children under the age of 6 do not have the cognitive abilities to understand that advertisements are trying to persuade them. Consequently, many people believe that young consumers need to be protected against messages that may depict products in overly glamorous or attractive ways. Policy makers have also moved to protect youngsters who use the Internet by passing the Children's Online Privacy Protection Act. This law forbids online marketers to collect personal data from children under 13 without parental notification and consent.[61]

Public policy decisions about consumer behavior can clearly affect marketers. Food marketers, for example, must be sure their products conform to government-established definitions before they can be labeled "low fat" or "lite." Moreover, companies need to define these terms on the product's packaging.[62] You will learn about these issues in Chapter 20, titled "Consumerism and Public Policy Issues." For now, the important point is that consumer behavior can be quite useful to regulators and government agencies in developing laws and policies to protect consumers.

EXHIBIT 1.13
Advertisement for Recycling
Understanding consumer behavior can help make a better environment for us all, as the trend toward recycling shows.

Source: Courtesy of the Environmental Defense Fund and the Ad Council.

Consumers

An understanding of consumer behavior can help make a better environment for consumers. For example, research indicates that we better understand the differences between brands when we can view a chart, matrix, or grid comparing brands and their attributes.[63] Thus, matrices such as those presented in *Consumer Reports* are likely to help many consumers make more effective decisions.

Product and service developments designed to protect certain consumer segments have also grown out of understanding how consumers behave. As discussed in other parts of this chapter, many people want to protect children against explicit song lyrics, invasion of privacy online, inducements to start smoking, and other stimuli they consider inappropriate. Some companies have changed their marketing voluntarily, while others have waited until legislators and regulators forced changes in their marketing.

Finally, consumer research on disposition behavior has the potential to affect programs that conserve natural resources. Exhibit 1.13 shows an ad that aims to educate consumers about the benefits of recycling.

SUMMARY

The term *consumer behavior* actually goes beyond the subject of consumer purchasing. It involves understanding the set of decisions (what, whether, why, when, how, where, how much, how often) that consumers make over time about the acquisition, use, or disposition of products, services, ideas, or activities.

The psychological core exerts considerable influence on consumer behavior. A consumer's motivation, ability, and opportunity affect his or her decisions and influence what a consumer is exposed to, what he or she pays attention to, and what he or she perceives. These factors also affect how a consumer categorizes or interprets information, how he or she forms and changes attitudes, and how he or she forms and retrieves memories. Each of these aspects of the psychological core has a bearing on consumer decision making. The consumer decision-making process entails four steps: (1) problem recognition, (2) information search, (3) judgment and decision making, and (4) evaluation of satisfaction with the decision.

Behavior is also affected by the consumer's culture. Culture refers to the typical or expected behaviors, norms, and ideas of a particular group. Consumers belong to a number of groups, share their cultural values and beliefs, and use their symbols to communicate group membership. Consumer behavior can be symbolic and express an individual's identity. In addition, consumer behavior is indicative of how forcefully or quickly an offering can spread throughout a market.

Marketers study consumer behavior to gain insights that will lead to more effective marketing strategies such as market segmentation, target market selection, and positioning. This type of knowledge can also guide decisions about marketing tactics like product, pricing, distribution, and promotion decisions. In addition, ethicists and advocacy groups are keenly interested in consumer behavior. Public policy makers and regulators also consider consumer behavior when designing protective laws and regulations. Finally, the study of consumer behavior can improve consumers' own lives as marketers learn to make products more user-friendly and to show concern for the environment.

QUESTIONS FOR REVIEW AND DISCUSSION

1. How is consumer behavior defined?
2. What three broad categories of consumer activity do marketers and researchers study in consumer behavior?
3. What are some of the factors in the psychological core that affect consumer decisions and behavior?
4. What are some of the external processes that influence consumer decisions and behavior?
5. How is marketing defined?
6. How do public policy decision makers and marketers use consumer research?

EXERCISES

1. Answer the following questions about a product or service category in which you are interested:
   a. How can this product or service be acquired? (Try to think of more than one way.) What are the implications for marketing strategy?
   b. How is the product or service consumed? How can marketers use this information when developing marketing strategy?
   c. How can the product or service be disposed of? How might this factor influence the next acquisition?
2. Based on the definition of consumer behavior presented in the first part of the chapter, identify the consumer behavior activities you have engaged in today.
3. How might a study of the way children process advertisements be useful to public policy makers? What kinds of industries might be affected by findings from such research? Explain your answer.
4. Consider the time period in which acquisition, consumption, and disposition take place when answering these questions:
   a. What products, services, or categories are typically acquired over the course of days? Over the course of weeks or months? How does the timing affect marketing decisions about these offerings?
   b. What products, services, or categories are typically used over the course of months? Over the course of years? How does the timing affect marketing decisions about these offerings?

c. What products or categories are typically disposed of over the course of days or weeks? How does the timing affect marketing decisions about these offerings?

5. Locate an ad that aims to influence the disposition of an offering and answer the following questions about it:

a. Referring to Exhibit 1.2, identify the specific consumer decisions and the decision-making units that might be affected by this ad.

b. Which aspects of the consumer's culture are mentioned or implied in this ad? How do you think these aspects are likely to affect the consumer's response to the ad?

chapter 2

Developing and Using Information about Consumer Behavior

The automotive industry is a pioneer in the use of consumer research to support marketing decisions about strengthening customer ties and to help customers make better decisions. Consider how Mazda is using research to support customer-focused marketing of its Protegé line (see Exhibit 2.1).

INTRODUCTION: Marketing Research Drives Marketing Decisions

Working with a marketing research firm and undertaking research on its own, Mazda conducted surveys and observational studies to find out who its customers are, where they shop, how they spend their time, and how they drive their cars. The car maker learned that its customers were typically men and women in their 20s who like to use the Internet. This information was instrumental in helping Mazda develop promotions for the Protegé, including a Web site featuring an online launch party where visitors could take a virtual road trip and learn more about the car. By tracking hit rates—the number of times Internet users visited the site—Mazda confirmed this promotion's popularity among its target customers. When introducing its Protegé 5 hatchback, aimed at college-educated consumers under 34 years old with annual household incomes of about $70,000, the company again used online promotion, sponsoring a Web-based racing game and inviting players to sign up for more information.

An additional survey revealed that 84 percent of consumers in the Protegé's target market described themselves as "risk takers," and 61 percent described themselves as "out of the box" (people who think independently and creatively). Based on this information, Mazda chose a celebrity endorser whose image was consistent with the image of target customers: Jane Krakowski, who starred as an independent-minded secretary on the TV show *Ally McBeal*.

Research also helps Mazda develop its products. For example, by watching consumers in the target

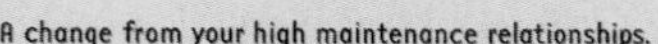

EXHIBIT 2.1
The Mazda Protegé
Mazda's consumer research led to a number of decisions about Protegé's features, promotion, and price.
Source: Copyright (1999) Mazda North American Operations. Used by permission.

market use their cars, Mazda found that most listen to CDs while driving and many are interested in MP3 music players. In response, Mazda offered a CD player as standard equipment in the Protegé and teamed up with a car audio firm to provide a CD/MP3 receiver as standard equipment on the Protegé MPS sedan. Finally, Mazda managers use research data to support price decisions. Knowing the income and spending habits of its target customers, Mazda is pricing its Protegé models under $20,000.[1]

As Mazda's experience shows, marketers often need to collect information about current and prospective customers. Consumer research is, in fact, a fundamental tool that marketers use to gain insights such as identifying specific segments within markets, determining the demographic and psychographic characteristics that describe consumers within a segment, and learning whether customers are satisfied with existing offerings. Companies also use research to guide decisions about the four elements that constitute the marketing mix: product, promotion (marketing communications), price, and place (distribution).

Furthermore, consumer research can help marketers uncover information about the consumer behavior issues described in Chapter 1. Understanding these issues is essential to developing effective marketing strategies such as target market selection, positioning, and marketing-mix plans. Marketers sometimes use consumer research to explore consumers' motivation, ability, and opportunity to process information from marketing communications and the media. At other times, they use research to uncover whether customers are exposed to, perceive, and pay attention to stimuli in their environment, including ads, TV programs, and products on store shelves.

In addition, marketers use consumer research to learn what image consumers have of the company and whether they understand the company's marketing communications. Marketers also spend considerable time determining whether consumers' attitudes toward a particular offering are positive or negative and how well consumers like and remember a company's brand name and product features based on its advertising. Another common use of research is to assess how and where consumers search for information about products and how they make their decisions. Finally, marketers often conduct research to learn whether consumers feel satisfied after they have purchased and used an offering.

Companies frequently undertake marketing research to learn about the external influences that affect consumers' behavior. As you will see, marketers conduct research on consumer demographics (age, gender, ethnic background, and so on), lifestyles, reference groups, and the types of symbols consumers use to communicate who they are to others. This information can be critical to making effective product, marketing communications, pricing, and distribution decisions. Marketers also collect information about consumers' reactions to new products; this information helps companies improve the ways in which they introduce future offerings and increases their chances of success.

This chapter describes the tools marketers use to collect information about consumers. Next is a general overview of the players in the marketing research industry, followed by a discussion of the broad purposes of consumer research (application, protection, and general knowledge). This chapter emphasizes application, showing how research helps marketers segment their markets, select a target market, develop a positioning strategy, and develop their marketing mix. Finally, the chapter explores some ethical issues related to consumer research. ●

CONSUMER BEHAVIOR RESEARCH METHODS

A number of tools are available in the consumer researcher's "tool kit." Some are based on what consumers say, others on what they do. Some researchers collect data from relatively few people; others compile data from huge samples of consumers. These tools are valuable precisely because they are so different. Each can provide unique insights that, when combined, reveal very different perspectives on the complex world of consumer behavior.

Surveys

survey A written instrument that asks consumers to respond to research questions.

One research tool with which we are all familiar is the **survey**, a written instrument that asks consumers to respond to a predetermined set of research questions. Some responses may be open-ended, with the consumer filling in the blanks; others may ask consumers to use a rating scale. Surveys can be conducted in person, through the mail, or over the phone. Researchers are increasingly using the Web to collect survey data very quickly and with minimal expense.[2] Procter & Gamble, for example, conducts about 1,500 online consumer surveys every year and obtains results 75 percent faster than with traditional survey methods—at half the cost.[3]

While companies often undertake specialized surveys to better understand a specific customer segment, some research organizations carry out broad-based surveys that are made available to marketers. The U.S. Bureau of the Census is a widely used source of demographic information. Its Census of Population and Housing, conducted every ten years, asks U.S. consumers a range of questions regarding their age, marital status, gender, household size, education, income, child care arrangements, and home ownership. Marketers often find this database valuable for learning about population shifts that might affect their offerings or the industry in which they operate. The survey itself and the data collected from it are available online (www.census.gov), in libraries, or on CD-ROM.

Survey data can also tell marketers something about media usage and product purchase. Mediamark Research Incorporated conducts yearly surveys from over 26,000 consumers about their media habits, demographics, and product purchases products. These surveys are useful because they tell marketers which media consumers use. Exhibit 2.2 shows some of the data found in one of Mediamark's summary volumes.[4] This page characterizes the media habits of consumers who are "mall shoppers," defined as consumers who have shopped at one of 7 department stores in the last 3 months and who say they like to shop. The column labeled "% Coverage" shows which media these consumers use. For example, the value in the % Coverage column for the magazine *Good Housekeeping* is 8.5 percent. This means that among people who very often visit shopping malls, 8.5 percent read *Good Housekeeping*. This data is useful to marketers trying to target mall shoppers, as it tells them that they will reach a comparatively large sample of mall shoppers by advertising in this magazine compared with many others. This particular set of data from Mediamark shows retail store patronage. However, Mediamark data includes media habits of people who purchase a variety of products and services, such as computers, frozen pizza, and checking accounts, as well as the habits of those who use specific brands, such as Tony's Pizza.

Focus Groups

focus group A form of in-depth interview involving 6 to 12 consumers led by a moderator who asks participants to discuss a product, concept, or other marketing stimulus.

Unlike a survey, which may collect input from hundreds of people responding individually to the same questionnaire, a **focus group** brings together groups of 6 to 12 consumers to discuss an issue or an offering. Led by a trained moderator, the people in the focus group express their opinions about a given product or topic. Often the researcher does not have prior insights about how the group might feel. Instead, a group's views become known only as the discussion un-

EXHIBIT 2.2

Mediamark Research: Media Usage of Consumers Who Are "Mall Shoppers"[1]

Every year, Mediamark surveys thousands of people, obtaining information on purchase and media habits.

Source: Media Usage of Consumers Who Are "Mall Shoppers," from Mediamark Research, Inc. 2001. Reprinted with permission.

	Shopped at a department store in the last 3 months (any 1 of 17)			
	Audience	%Comp[2]	%Coverage	Index
Magazines				
Gentlemen's Qtrly	3450	57.1	3.6	117.9
Good Housekeeping	8267	56.9	8.5	117.6
Midwest Living	985	56.8	1.0	117.4
Victoria Magazine	1355	56.8	1.4	117.4
Woman's Day	7422	56.8	7.6	117.4
Entrepreneur	1615	56.8	1.7	117.3
Family Circle	7932	56.7	8.2	117.2
Travel Holiday	1228	56.6	1.3	117.0
TV Programs				
NBC Sportsworld Sunday	1955	57.7	2.0	119.2
Friday: ABC in Concert	491	57.6	0.5	118.9
Extra: Weekend	1409	57.3	1.5	118.4
NBC Sports Showcase	1018	57.3	1.0	118.3
The Practice	10043	57.2	10.3	118.3
Extra	2471	57.2	2.5	118.2
Martha Stewart Living Weekend	4262	57.1	4.4	117.9
CBS NCAA Women's College Basketball	1670	57.0	1.7	117.8

1. A "mall shopper" is someone who has shopped at one of 7 department stores in the last 3 months and who says s/he likes to shop.
2. Represents the percentage of consumers who are mall shoppers who are reached using this particular medium.

folds. Focus groups provide qualitative insights into consumer attitudes, as opposed to the quantitative (numerical) data resulting from surveys. Focus groups are particularly useful for testing new product ideas.

Although most focus groups are conducted in person, marketers are finding that for some groups of consumers, such as teens, telephone focus groups can yield useful data, particularly when the topic is sensitive or embarrassing. For example, boys who participate in telephone focus groups sometimes admit that they watch educational TV and avoid violent video games. Telephone focus groups also give teens more opportunity to disagree with the group—something that is less likely to happen in a traditional focus group.[5]

Some companies prefer computer-based focus groups. With this method, consumers go to a computer lab where their individual comments are displayed anonymously on a large screen for viewing by the group. Like telephone focus groups, this method can help researchers gather information on sensitive topics. However, the anonymity prevents researchers from collecting other relevant data, such as nonverbal reactions conveyed by facial expressions and body language that would be available in a traditional focus group.

New market research companies have recently sprung up to conduct focus groups on the Web. In one project for PBS, focus group participants were asked to watch PBS documentaries and then discuss them online. Although these types of focus groups are very economical and relatively easy to conduct, researchers worry that they may not have much control over the size of the group as Web users can join or leave the discussion at will. Also, researchers may have difficulty stimulating online interaction among group members (called "group dynamics"), which is so central to traditional focus groups.[6]

Interviews

Like focus groups, interviews involve direct contact with consumers. Interviews are often more appropriate than focus groups when the topic is sensitive, embarrassing, confidential, or emotionally charged. They are more appropriate than surveys when the researcher wants to "pick consumers' brains." A researcher who wants to really understand the symbolic significance of a brand to consumers, for example, may ask respondents open-ended questions about their usage of the product; its meaning; their purchase and usage history; and the people, activities, and events they associate with it.

In some interviews, researchers ask customers about the process they use to make a purchase decision. One marketing research company assigns professional interviewers to tape record consumers' thoughts while they shop for groceries. This research helps marketers understand how factors in the shopping environment motivate or hinder a purchase. For example, a company might learn that a consumer didn't buy a particular cereal because it was placed too close to the laundry detergent.[7] Seeking to spur meat sales, the National Cattlemen's Beef Association recently hired researchers to interview grocery shoppers browsing the refrigerated meat case. Finding that consumers didn't know how to cook unfamiliar cuts, the group began printing basic cooking instructions on meat packages and helped stores display meat products by cooking method.[8]

Traditional interviews require a trained interviewer who attempts to establish rapport with consumers. Interviewers also note nonverbal behaviors like twitches, fidgeting, eye shifting, voice pitch changes, and folded arms and legs as clues to whether the respondent is open to the discussion or whether certain questions are particularly sensitive. Researchers often record interviews for later transcription so they can examine the results using qualitative or quantitative analysis. Sometimes researchers use videotapes to record nonverbal responses that cannot be captured in the transcription process. Later, trained researchers cull through the interviews to identify patterns or themes. As a result, interviews can be an expensive data collection method.

Storytelling

storytelling A research method that asks consumers to tell stories about product acquisition, usage, or disposition experiences.

A new and fairly provocative tool for conducting consumer research is **storytelling**, in which consumers tell researchers stories about their experiences with a product. At Patagonia, researchers collect consumer stories about backpacking, river rafting, and other outdoor experiences for use in developing the company's catalogs. In some cases the catalog shows real consumers in the clothing they wore on their adventures. Storytelling not only provides information relevant to the marketing of the product but also shows that Patagonia is in touch with its customers and values what they say.[9]

Although storytelling involves the real stories of real consumers, sometimes marketers ask consumers to tell or write stories about hypothetical situations that the marketer has depicted in a picture or scenario.[10] The idea is that a consumer's needs, feelings, and perceptions will be revealed by the way he or she interprets what is depicted in the picture or scenario. For example, researchers may show a picture of a woman standing in line at a Costco store with a thought bubble above her head and ask consumers to write inside the bubble what they imagine the woman is thinking. These kinds of stories can provide valuable information about what consumers think of a particular store, purchase situation, and so on.

Use of Photography and Pictures

Some researchers use a technique in which they show pictures of experiences that consumers have had. This helps the consumers remember their experiences and report them more completely to the researcher.[11] Researchers may also ask consumers to draw or collect pictures, either their own photographs or clippings from magazines, to represent their thoughts and feelings about the topic at hand (e.g., What does Ivory soap mean to me?). Still another practice is to ask consumers to put pictures together in a collage that reflects their lifestyles. Researchers then ask questions about the pictures and the meaning behind them. Having the consumer write an essay can help pull together the images and thoughts suggested by the pictures.[12]

For example, Wrigley's marketers asked teenagers to select pictures and write a story about Juicy Fruit Gum. The company learned that teens chewed the gum when they craved sweets. With this insight, Wrigley's ad agency launched the "Gotta Have Sweet" campaign—and Juicy Fruit sales climbed.[13]

In addition, researchers sometimes use pictures to learn how consumers perceive other consumers and the products they use. A car company might ask consumers to sort pictures into categories that reflect different types of product users, such as a Mercedes user, a Volvo user, and so on. One stocking manufacturer used picture research to better understand women's experiences with nylon stockings. Results from traditional research methods indicated that women hated wearing stockings. However, consumers' pictures, coupled with interview results, revealed that stockings made them feel sexy, sensual, and attractive. With this knowledge, the company developed new ads depicting a less "executive" and a more "sexy" view of women in stockings[14] (see Exhibit 2.3).

EXHIBIT 2.3

Pictures as a Research Tool

Pictures were used to uncover women's attitudes toward stockings. The stories and pictures revealed that women associated stockings with feeling sexy. Other associations are also revealed by these pictures.

Sources: Picture from Seeing the Voice of the Customer Lab, Gerald Zaltman, Olson Zaltman Associates. Article by Ronald B. Lieber and Joyce E. Davis, "Storytelling: A New Way to Get Close to Your Customers," *Fortune*, February 3, 1997, pp. 102–108.

Seeing Inside The Mind Of Your Customer

To measure customers' true feelings about pantyhose, Du Pont asked women to assemble magazine clips that evoked their emotions about the product. The composite of clips at right, produced at the Harvard business school, was used to improve marketing tactics.

Shopping for stockings can be confusing. This photo suggests the experience should be as easy as picking out fruit from an outdoor stand.

The spilled ice cream symbolizes the disappointment involved in buying an expensive pair of hose, only to have them run again after only two or three wearings.

These secretaries, hunched over their spartan desks, evoke the discomfort and frustration of having to wear stockings at work.

Joan Crawford represents glamour and sensuality. Her choice suggests that women really do like hose because they feel sexy.

Diaries

Asking consumers to keep diaries can provide important insights into their behavior, including product purchasing and media usage. Marketers have, for example, asked preteens and teenagers to keep diaries of their everyday lives. These documents often reveal how friends and family affect decisions about clothes, music, fast foods, videos, concerts, and so on.[15] When Unilever was planning a new deodorant, it asked a group of women to keep an "armpit diary" noting how often they shaved, what their underarms looked like, and how frequently they used deodorant. Finding that the women were concerned about the condition of their underarm skin, Unilever created a moisturizing deodorant product and promoted its skin-care benefits.[16]

The research firm NPD Group asks approximately 925,000 consumers worldwide to maintain online diaries tracking their purchases in dozens of product categories. Companies buy NPD's diary data to learn whether consumers are brand loyal or brand switching and whether they are heavy or light users of the product category. By linking the data with demographic data, marketers can also learn more about these consumers. Burger King, for example, can use the NPD system to look at burger consumption according age group, geographic location, and even time of day. This information helps the chain better target or change promotions, plan new products, and make other marketing decisions.[17]

Experiments

Consumer researchers can conduct experiments to determine whether certain marketing phenomena affect consumer behavior. For example, they might design an experiment to learn whether consumers' attitudes toward a brand are affected by the brand name, as opposed to factors such as product features, package, color, logo, room temperature, or the consumer's mood.

During experiments, researchers randomly assign consumers to receive different "treatments" and then observe the effect of these treatments. For example, consumers might be assigned to groups that are shown different brand names. The researchers collect data about participants' attitudes toward the name and compare attitudes across groups. In a taste-test experiment, they might randomly assign consumers to groups and then ask each group to taste a different product.

independent variable The "treatment" or the entity that researchers vary in a research project.

An important aspect of such experiments is that the groups are designed to be identical in all respects except the treatment, called the **independent variable**. Thus, in a taste-test experiment, only the taste of the food or beverage is varied. Everything else is the same across groups—consumers eat or drink the same amount of the product, at the same temperature, from the same kind of container, in the same room, in the presence of the same experimenter, and so on. After consumers taste and rate the product, researchers can compare the groups' responses to see which taste is preferred.

Researchers also use experiments to determine what attracts consumers' attention and affects their purchase decisions. One researcher has designed a virtual shopping environment in which consumers use a computer to "walk down" store aisles, "pick up" products, and "put" them in their shopping baskets (or not). By varying package colors, space arrangements, layouts, and product features, and then comparing how consumers' attention and behavior differ across different store situations, researchers can determine what makes a retail environment most effective.[18]

Companies sometimes use experiments to determine whether certain ads are effective. For example, they might expose consumers to different test ads. By measuring emotional arousal, salivation levels, and eye movements of participants, marketers may determine which ads are most arousing and attention getting.

Field Experiments

market test A study in which researchers study one or more elements of the marketing mix by evaluating product sales in an actual market.

Although experiments are often conducted in controlled laboratory situations, sometimes marketers are interested in conducting experiments in the real world, known as "field experiments." One common type of field experiment, a **market test**, reveals whether a product is likely to sell in a given market and which marketing-mix elements most effectively enhance sales. As an example, marketers can use a market test to determine how much advertising support to give to a new product. First they would select two test markets with similar size and demographic composition. They would then spend a different amount on advertising in each market. By observing product sales in the two markets over a set period, the marketers would be able to tell which level of advertising expenditure resulted in higher sales.

Conjoint Analysis

conjoint analysis A research technique to determine the relative importance and appeal of different levels of an offering's attributes.

Many marketers use the sophisticated research technique of **conjoint analysis** to determine the relative importance and appeal of different levels of an offering's attributes. To start, researchers identify the specific attributes of the offering, such as package size, specific product features, and price points. Next, they determine the levels to be tested for each attribute (such as small-, medium-, and large-sized packages). Then they ask consumers to react to a series of product concepts combining these attributes in different ways. For example, researchers might ask how likely consumers are to buy a large package of Tide laundry detergent that has added stain removal power and costs $4.75; they might also ask how likely consumers are to buy a small package of Tide laundry detergent that does not have added stain removal power and costs $2.50. By analyzing the responses to different combinations, the researchers can see how important each characteristic (e.g., size, price) and each level of that characteristic (e.g., $2.50 vs. $4.75) is to consumers' purchase decisions. Fuji Film has used conjoint analysis to learn how brand, price, and packaging influence film buyers; similarly, Sterling Jewelers in Akron, Ohio, used this method to find the most effective marketing message for each targeted segment.[19]

Observations

At times, researchers observe consumers to gain insight into potentially effective product, promotion, price, and distribution decisions. At the Fisher-Price Playlab (see Exhibit 2.4), researchers observe children's reactions to toys. At the Gerber lab, scientists observe babies' reactions to Gerber food and use the information to modify products, such as removing oregano from the firm's Italian Spaghetti baby food and changing the texture of its beef stew. Gerber also conducts research in other countries, observing how mothers feed their babies to uncover clues to local behavior and preferences. After watching parents feed babies in Japan, for example, Gerber developed freeze-dried Sardines and Rice baby food for that market.[20]

Some companies conduct **ethnographic research**, in which researchers

EXHIBIT 2.4
Hello, Kids
At the Fisher-Price Playlab, researchers observe children's reactions to determine whether they like Fisher-Price toys.

Source: © Mike Greenlar/The Image Works.

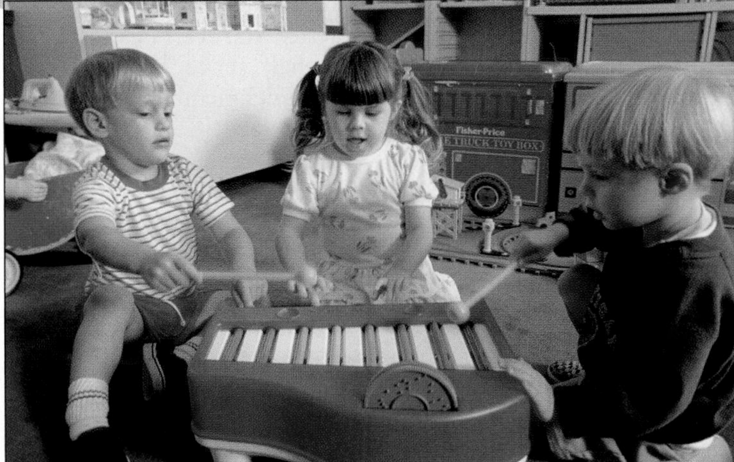

ethnographic research A technique in which researchers observe how consumers behave in real-world surroundings.

observe (and perhaps videotape) how consumers behave in real-world surroundings. In contrast to interviews and focus groups, ethnographic research does not involve interaction between researchers and consumers, simply observation. This method allows marketers to see what consumers actually *do*, not what they *say* they do. Procter & Gamble, for example, is using ethnographic research to study everyday household routines around the world. By getting permission to videotape 80 families at home in the United Kingdom, Germany, and Italy, the company is aiming to identify unspoken needs and then create new products and packages to satisfy these needs.[21]

Intuit, the maker of the financial software Quicken, watches consumers use its program at home. By observing the problems these users experience, the company learns how it can improve its product. Intuit also studies non-Quicken users in their homes, noting how they track and manage their finances. These observations help Intuit develop new product features that might convert nonusers to users.[22]

In another twist on observational research, marketers can now use Web tracking software to observe where consumers go and what they do on the Internet. This technology shows researchers which Web sites consumers visit, which pages they look at, how long they visit each site, and related data. By analyzing consumer browsing patterns, marketers can determine how to make Web sites more user friendly and better target online advertising, as well as make other decisions about Web-based marketing activities.[23] However, privacy advocates are concerned that Web tracking—especially when conducted without the consumer's knowledge or consent—is intrusive. While U.S. officials consider legal and regulatory action, companies are taking the initiative by posting privacy policies and, in some cases, allowing consumers to view and edit collected data or even "opt out" of tracking systems.[24]

Purchase Panels

Although the research described so far studies individual consumers, sometimes marketers electronically research the behaviors of large numbers of respondents. This kind of research, conducted by BehaviorScan, IRI, and other firms, simply records whether a behavior occurred; for instance, did a consumer buy Heinz or not? Such behavioral data may be collected from special panel members, from consumers chosen to be representative of the general population, or from the marketer's target market. Every time panel members go shopping, the cash register records their purchases. By merging purchase data with demographic data about panel members, marketers can tell who is purchasing a product, whether those consumers are also buying competitors' products, and whether the purchase was motivated by a coupon or other sales promotion tactic. Marketers can also use this data to determine whether, for example, the shelf space allocated to a product, or added advertising in the test area, affected panel members' purchases.

Database Marketing

Recently, marketers have attempted to combine different forms of consumer research into a common database. A common database might contain information about targeted consumers' demographics and lifestyles combined with data about their purchases in various product categories over time, their media habits, and their usage of coupons and other promotional devices. Using **data mining**, the company searches for patterns in the database that offer clues to customer needs, preferences, and behaviors.[25]

data mining Searching for patterns in the company database that offer clues to customer needs, preferences, and behaviors.

Harrah's Entertainment has been developing one of the gambling industry's more comprehensive consumer databases. Its database includes banking, credit card, and casino usage data, along with information about which meals consumers ordered at Harrah's restaurants, what products consumers purchased at Harrah's gift stores, how much consumers spent on gambling, whether they gambled at competing casinos, the size of their mortgages, and how much they are likely to spend on gambling when they next visit a Harrah's casino. Then the company analyzes this information using data mining to more effectively target customers with communications and vacation offers specifically geared to their lifestyles and spending patterns.[26] Although some might question whether the collection of such data invades consumers' privacy and perpetuates a behavior with potentially dysfunctional consequences (issues discussed in Chapter 21, "The Dark Side of Consumer Behavior and Marketing"), Harrah's is clearly adept at database marketing.

A recent move is the development of marketing databases geared to electronic retailing, allowing marketers to send consumers e-mail messages and electronic pictures of products they might find appealing.[27] Virgin Entertainment, for example, gave a free Internet appliance to 10,000 U.S. consumers who were willing to provide personal data and receive targeted advertising messages from Virgin and other firms.[28] Although companies like e-mail because it is fast and inexpensive compared with other marketing communication methods, consumers are being inundated with more and more electronic marketing messages. Therefore, to trigger a response, an e-mail campaign must be based on customer needs—for instance, be in response to requests for information—and should tailor the content and timing to each individual.[29]

TYPES OF CONSUMER RESEARCHERS

Many types of entities use market research to study consumer behavior for different reasons, as shown in Exhibit 2.5. On the one hand, organizations such as

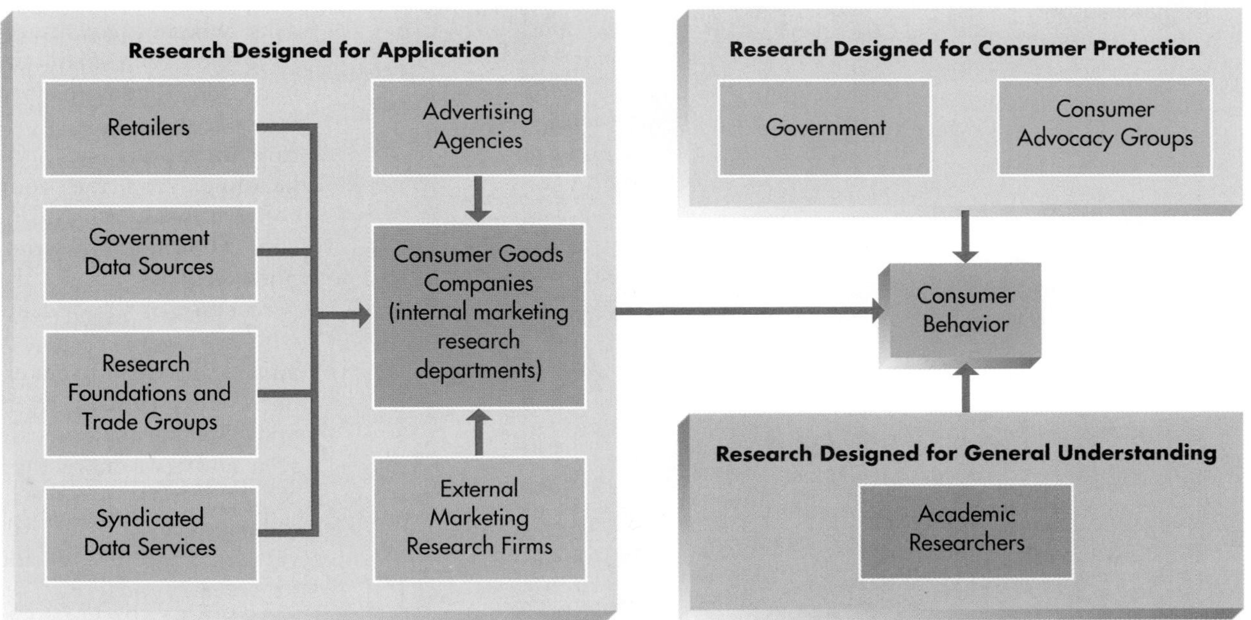

EXHIBIT 2.5
Who Conducts Consumer Research?

A number of different organizations conduct research on consumers, though they differ in their objectives. Some do research for application, some for consumer protection, others to obtain general knowledge about consumers.

consumer goods and service companies, ad agencies, and marketing research firms conduct research to make decisions about the marketing of a specific product or service. On the other hand, government organizations and academics conduct research to protect consumers or simply to understand why and how consumers behave as they do.

In-house Marketing Research Departments

The benefits of conducting "in-house" research are that the information collected can be kept within the company and that opportunities for information to leak to competitors are minimized. However, internal departments are sometimes viewed as less objective than outside research firms since they may have a vested interest in the research results. For example, employees may be motivated to show that the company is making good decisions, which may unwittingly bias the nature of their research or the outcomes they report. Consequently, some companies use outside research companies to gather their consumer research.

External Marketing Research Firms

External research firms often help design a specific research project before it begins. They develop measuring instruments to measure consumer responses, collect data from consumers, analyze the data, and develop reports for their clients.

Some marketing research firms are "full service" organizations that perform a variety of marketing research services. Others specialize in one or more types of research. For example, one company named Roper Starch Worldwide has (among other products) a product called STARCH scores. Panels of approximately 200 readers of a specific magazine go through a recent issue with a trained interviewer. The interviewer asks whether consumers have seen each ad in the issue and, digging deeper, whether they saw the picture in the ad, read the headline, read the body copy, and saw the ad slogan. The company compiles reports about the percentage of respondents who saw each part of each ad and sells them to advertisers who want to determine whether their ads are seen and read more than other ads in the issue or in the product category. Advertisers may also decide to redesign ads that receive low STARCH scores. Exhibit 2.6 shows an ad for which STARCH scores have been tabulated.

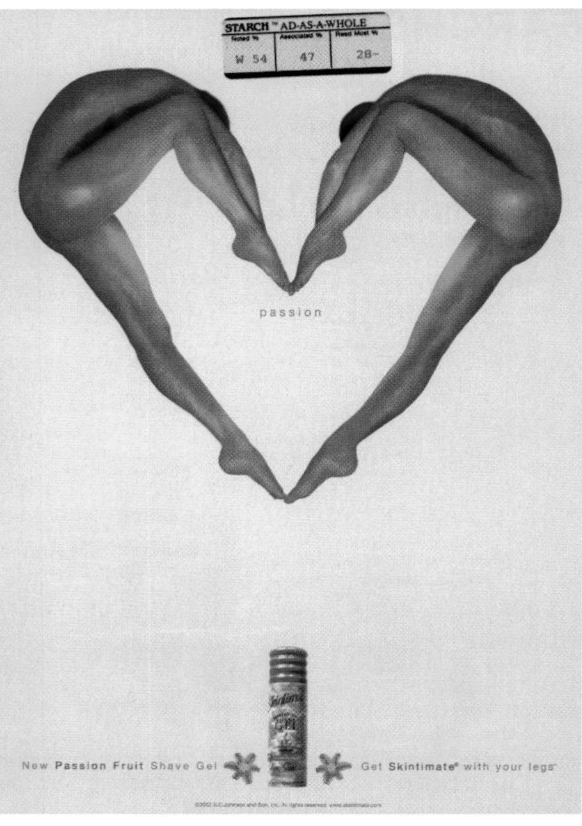

EXHIBIT 2.6
A "Starched" Ad
Companies like Starch collect data on what, if anything, consumers remembered from an ad. The numbers noted on the stickers placed at the top of the ad indicate the percentage of respondents sampled who remembered having seen or read various parts of the ad.

Source: Courtesy of S.C. Johnson.

Advertising Agencies

Some advertising agencies have their own in-house research departments to test advertising concepts as part of the service they provide to clients. They may also conduct advertising pretesting, using drawings of ads or finished ads, to make sure that an ad is fulfilling its objectives *before* it is placed in the media. In addition, ad agencies conduct tracking studies to monitor the effectiveness of advertising over time. For example, tracking studies can determine whether the percentage of target market consumers who are aware of a brand has changed as a function of the amount, duration, and timing of its advertising.

Syndicated Data Services

Syndicated data services are companies that collect and then sell the information they collect, usually to firms that market products and services to consumers. For example, the research firm Yankelovich Partners collects data on consumer lifestyles and social trends in two and one half hour interviews at the homes of approximately 2,500 adults. Its reports describe current and projected lifestyle trends. Advertising agencies may buy these reports and use them to develop creative content for advertising.

Nielsen is a syndicated data service that tracks TV viewing. Approximately 5,100 households are equipped with an electronic device called a people meter that sits on their TV. When a member of the family turns on the TV, they use a special remote control to record their presence. The people meter then records who is watching what shows and for how long the consumer is watching. Nielsen provides a rating that indicates the number and percentage of all households watching a particular TV program, and a specific commercial along with demographic analyses of the audience.[30]

By combining demographic and TV viewing behavior, Nielsen can also examine who is watching which shows. Networks, cable stations, and independent channels use this information to determine whether TV shows should be renewed and how much the stations can charge for advertising time on a particular show. The more popular the show (the higher its rating), the more it costs companies to advertise on that show. Advertisers who buy Nielsen data can assess which TV shows they should advertise in, based on the match between the demographic characteristics of viewers and the demographic characteristics of the sponsor's target market.

Retailers

Large retail chains often conduct consumer research. By using electronic scanners to track sales of a brand or product category, they can determine which are their best- and worst-selling items. They also use scanner data to examine the relationship between sales of an item and the item's location in the store and to see how consumers respond to coupons, discounts, and other promotions. Because salespeople often interact directly with customers, retailers sometimes use research to measure customer satisfaction and determine how they can improve service quality.

research foundation
A nonprofit organization that sponsors research on topics relevant to the foundation's goals.

Research Foundations/Trade Groups

Many research foundations and trade groups collect consumer research. A **research foundation** is a nonprofit organization that sponsors research on topics relevant to the foundation's goals. As an example, the Advertising Research Foundation is a nonprofit association seeking to improve the practice of advertising, marketing, and media research. The organization sponsors conferences related to the conduct of research in these areas and publishes reports on research issues and trends. It also publishes the *Journal of Advertising Research,* which reports advertising research findings from academics and practitioners.[31] The Marketing Science Institute is another nonprofit organization that sponsors academic research studies to uncover information useful to companies.

trade group
A professional organization made up of marketers in the same industry.

Specialized trade groups may also collect consumer research to better understand the needs of consumers in their own industries. A **trade group** is an organization formed by people who work in the same industry, such as the Recording Industry Association of America, a group whose members are involved in the recorded music industry through recording, distribution, or retailing activities. This organization has sponsored a host of research projects, including studies to understand how American music tastes have changed over the years.

Government

Unlike the organizations mentioned in previous sections, government agencies do not use research to help market an offering. However, marketers frequently use government research for marketing purposes; for instance, they can examine census data to estimate the size of various demographic markets (see Exhibit 2.7). Many government studies are designed for consumer protection. Agencies such as the Consumer Products Safety Commission, the Department of Transportation, and the Food and Drug Administration research product features and set safety standards or recall unsafe products.

The Federal Trade Commission (FTC) conducts research on the potentially deceptive, misleading, or fraudulent nature of certain brands' advertising. When the FTC filed a case against Kraft, it argued that consumers might have been misled by ads claiming that one slice of its cheese was made from 5 ounces of milk. The FTC worried that consumers might infer that the cheese had as much calcium as 5 ounces of milk (which it did not) or that Kraft cheese was superior to its competitors in terms of calcium content (which it was not). The FTC conducted consumer research to assess the existence and severity of these inferences.[32]

Consumer Organizations

Independent consumer organizations also conduct research, generally for the purpose of protecting or informing consumers. Consumers Union is an independent, nonprofit testing and information organization designed to serve consumers. The organization publishes the well-known *Consumer Reports* magazine. Many of the products described in *Consumer Reports* are tested in Consumers Union's independent product-testing lab, and the results are posted on the organization's Web site (www.consumersunion.org).

Academics and Academic Research Centers

Finally, academics often conduct consumer research. Although academic research involving consumers can be used for application purposes and may have implications for public policy, it is often designed simply to enhance our general understanding of why consumers behave as they do. Indeed, much of the research we report in this book describes state-of-the-art consumer behavior studies conducted by academics.

	TOTAL POPULATION	TOTAL	WHITE	BLACK OR AFRICAN AMERICAN	AMERICAN INDIAN AND ALASKA NATIVE	ASIAN	NATIVE HAWAIIAN AND OTHER PACIFIC ISLANDER	SOME OTHER RACE
Median age (years)	**35.3%**	**35.6%**	**37.7%**	**30.2%**	**28.0%**	**32.7%**	**27.5%**	**24.6%**
% DISTRIBUTION								
Total population	**100.0**	**100.0**	**100.0**	**100.0**	**100.0**	**100.0**	**100.0**	**100.0**
Under 18 years	**25.7**	**25.3**	**23.5**	**31.4**	**33.9**	**24.1**	**31.9**	**35.9**
Under 1 year	1.4	1.3	1.2	1.6	1.7	1.3	1.6	2.2
1 to 4 years	5.5	5.3	4.9	6.5	6.9	5.3	6.8	8.5
5 to 13 years	13.2	13.0	12.0	16.5	17.6	12.0	16.3	17.9
14 to 17 years	5.7	5.7	5.4	6.8	7.7	5.5	7.2	7.3
18 to 64 years	**61.9**	**62.1**	**62.2**	**60.4**	**60.5**	**68.1**	**62.9**	**61.1**
18 to 24 years	9.6	9.6	8.9	11.0	11.6	11.1	13.7	15.0
25 to 44 years	30.2	30.3	29.6	30.9	30.9	36.0	32.6	34.2
45 to 64 years	22.0	22.2	23.7	18.6	18.0	21.0	16.6	11.9
65 years and over	**12.4**	**12.6**	**14.4**	**8.1**	**5.6**	**7.8**	**5.2**	**3.0**

EXHIBIT 2.7
U.S. Census Data

The U.S. government collects primary data on the size of the population every 10 years. Many marketers analyze this data to learn more about the demographics of certain target markets.

Source: U.S. Census Data from the U.S. Census Bureau, Census, 2000.

Academics sometimes develop research centers focusing on a specific area of consumer behavior. Georgia State University, for example, has a center for the study of mature consumers. SUNY Albany has a center for the study of social and demographic analysis; the University of Michigan has a center for the study of consumer satisfaction; and the University of Texas at Austin has a center called the Center for Consumer Insight.

PRIMARY VERSUS SECONDARY DATA

Researchers collect two types of data: primary and secondary. Data that a research entity collects for its own purpose is called **primary data**. When marketers gather data using surveys, focus groups, experiments, and the like to support their own marketing decisions, they are collecting primary data. When the FTC conducts research to determine whether consumers are forming mistaken impressions from advertisements, it is engaging in primary research.

primary data Data a research entity collects for its own purpose.

secondary data Data collected for one purpose and subsequently used by another entity for a different purpose.

Data collected by an entity for one purpose and subsequently used by another entity for a different purpose is called **secondary data**. For example, after the government collects census data for tax purposes, marketers can use the results as secondary data to estimate the size of markets in their own industry. Many marketers use secondary data drawn from government studies. Likewise, when companies use research reports of syndicated data services or reports developed by trade associations or research centers in developing marketing ideas, they are using secondary data.

MARKETING IMPLICATIONS OF CONSUMER BEHAVIOR

As you learn about consumer behavior in this course, you may wonder how and why marketers use different concepts and techniques. This section is the first of many highlighting the marketing implications of consumer behavior. Starting with Chapter 3, you will find numerous sections titled "Marketing Implications" that illustrate how various consumer behavior concepts are applied to the practice of marketing.

In general, consumer research helps marketers develop product-specific plans as well as broader marketing strategies. These broader strategies determine, for instance, how the firm might approach its market segmentation, targeting, and positioning decision, as well as how it can make decisions about product, promotion (marketing communications), price, and place (distribution)—traditionally known as the four Ps.

Developing a Customer-Oriented Strategy

One hundred years ago, companies held a production-oriented view of marketing, focusing their activities on efficiently producing products. Later they shifted to a sales emphasis, developing tactics designed to move the most units of the product. In contrast to these earlier views, the prevailing view today is that marketing activities are designed *to fulfill consumer needs.* This consumer-oriented, market-driven approach automatically makes consumer research pivotal within the company. In other words, marketers must conduct considerable research to understand and describe the various segments or groups of targeted consumers—all of whom may have different needs—as part of the process of developing offerings that actually meet customers' needs. This consumer orientation guides research practices in each of the strategic and tactical marketing decisions described below.

How Is the Market Segmented? All consumers in a market are unlikely to have the same needs and wants. For example, Mobil Oil found that patrons of gas stations belong to one of the five segments noted in Exhibit 2.8. By understanding what these segments are and how well existing companies tapped the needs of each, Mobil identified the segments it would find most profitable. One Mobil study designed to identify consumer segments around the world found four distinct segments: deal makers, price seekers, brand loyalists, and luxury innovators.[33] These studies have helped Mobil formulate offerings targeted to particular segments.

How Profitable Is Each Segment? Knowing the size of a market segment can be important, because marketers can profit substantially by concentrating on large segments that competitors are not targeting. For example, marketers have found that the biggest users of the prepaid calling card are immigrants and consumers who do not have residential phone service.[34]

Consumer research can also help marketers identify underserved segments—consumers who have clearly identifiable needs that are not being met. For example, demographic research has shown that more than 80 percent of consumers who buy classical music are over age 45. To appeal to younger and underserved segments, marketers of classical music are adding popular performers to its lineup, while others are offering free concert tickets to college students.[35] In addition, marketers have used research to identify consumers' need for hybrid vehicles and have combined sport-utility pickups and light-duty pickups with four carlike doors.[36] As another example, gay men and

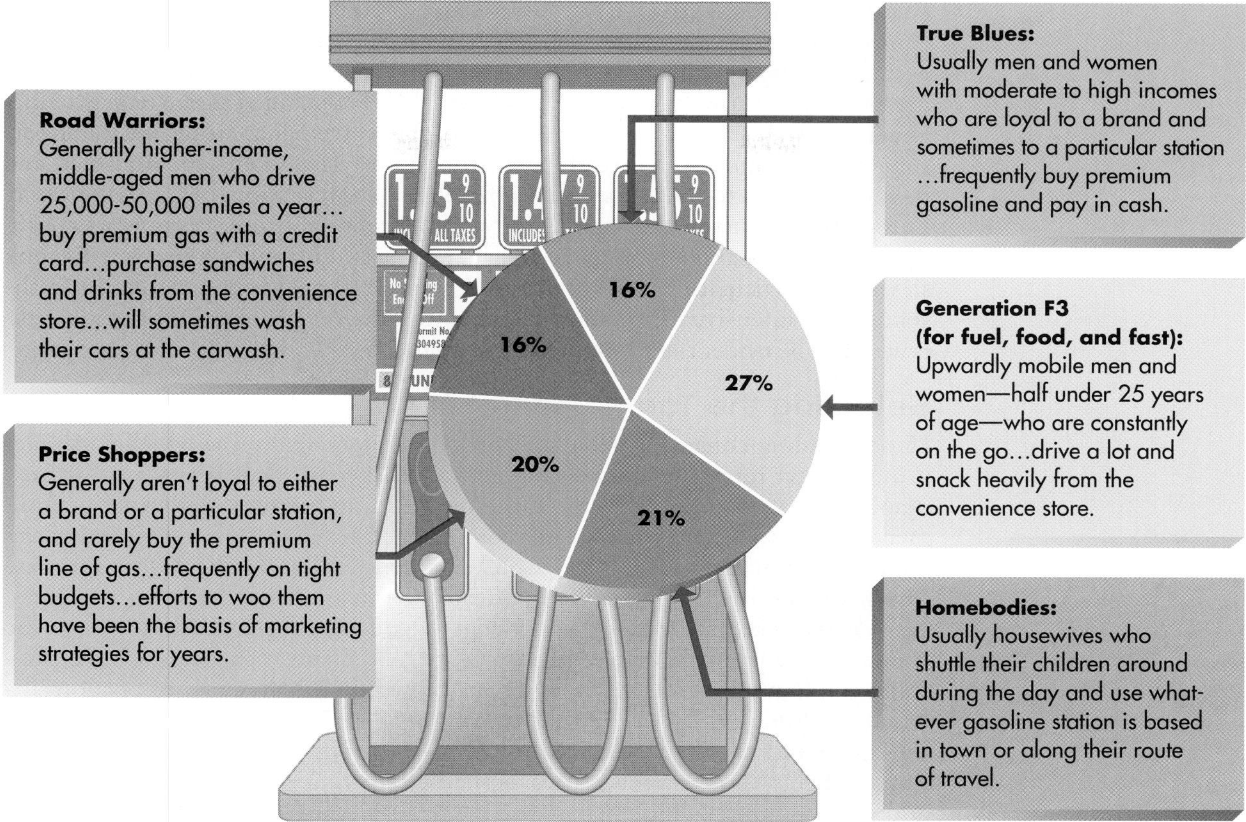

Road Warriors:
Generally higher-income, middle-aged men who drive 25,000-50,000 miles a year...buy premium gas with a credit card...purchase sandwiches and drinks from the convenience store...will sometimes wash their cars at the carwash.
Price Shoppers:
Generally aren't loyal to either a brand or a particular station, and rarely buy the premium line of gas...frequently on tight budgets...efforts to woo them have been the basis of marketing strategies for years.
True Blues:
Usually men and women with moderate to high incomes who are loyal to a brand and sometimes to a particular station ...frequently buy premium gasoline and pay in cash.
Generation F3 (for fuel, food, and fast):
Upwardly mobile men and women—half under 25 years of age—who are constantly on the go...drive a lot and snack heavily from the convenience store.
Homebodies:
Usually housewives who shuttle their children around during the day and use whatever gasoline station is based in town or along their route of travel.
16%
16%
27%
20%
21%

EXHIBIT 2.8
Mobil's Segmentation Study

By understanding consumer behavior, marketers may discover different segments with different needs. Mobil found that the needs of the Road Warrior, True Blue, and Generation F3 segments were not being met. Their marketing activities therefore focused on capturing those segments.

Source: Data from Allanna Sullivan, "Mobil Bets Drivers Pick Cappuccino over Low Prices," *Wall Street Journal*, January 30, 1995, pp. B1, B4.

women are being targeted by more and more marketers who have traditionally ignored them.[37]

What Are the Characteristics of Consumers in Each Segment? After determining how the market is segmented and whether it is potentially profitable, marketers need to learn about the characteristics of consumers in each segment. This helps marketers project whether the segment is likely to grow or to shrink over time, which affects future marketing decisions. For example, condominium marketers project sales increases as baby boomers enter retirement in the coming years.

Understanding each segment's demographics, values, and lifestyles, how they are influenced, and how they make their decisions also provides valuable information about how consumers in each segment can be reached and persuaded. The Mobil Oil study revealed that consumers in the Homebody segment were women with small children. Their lifestyle is characterized by considerable shuttling of kids to school and afterschool events. Their decisions about where to buy gas are largely driven by what station is along their route and whether it offers full service. These insights help Mobil reach, attract, and retain customers in the Homebody segment.

Are Customers Satisfied with Existing Offerings? Marketers often do considerable research to determine whether consumers are currently satisfied with the company's offerings. Based on its market segmentation study and its understanding of customers in each segment, Mobil concluded that Road Warriors and True Blues wanted better snacks from the convenience stores, fast and personal service, and special treatment. Generation F3s wanted *f*ood and *f*uel, and they wanted it *f*ast (hence the term *F3*).[38] Reebok International has a unique way of researching customers' satisfaction with its running shoes: It sponsors a 100-mile running race in Colorado to test its products. Entrants receive free Reebok shoes and participate in a 30-hour run designed to uncover design glitches in the shoes. This intensive usage allows Reebok to uncover problems that would otherwise not be evident until months after a purchase.[39]

Selecting the Target Market

Understanding consumer behavior helps marketers determine which consumer groups might represent the best targets for marketing tactics. In China, for example, numerous marketers are targeting children because, under the government's "one child per family" regulation, parents, grandparents, aunts, and uncles have fewer children to indulge. Consequently, family members dote on these "Little Emperors" and buy a wide variety of baby products.[40]

Marketers also use their knowledge of consumer behavior to identify who is likely to be involved in acquisition, usage, and disposition decisions. To illustrate, condom marketers see tremendous growth in the purchase of condoms by women. Although women do not actually wear traditional condoms, they often buy them and are very influential in men's use of condoms. Recognizing these gender effects, more marketers are explicitly targeting women.[41] In recent years, automobile manufacturers and dealers have learned, through research, that women (and children) play key roles in searching for information, influencing the decision, financing the car, using it, servicing it, and disposing of it. Using observation, one Volvo dealer in Virginia found that more than two-thirds of the customers bringing in cars for servicing were women with children. To more effectively serve these customers, the dealer added toys in the waiting area, put in a TV set to show cartoons, and brightened up its customer rest rooms.[42]

Positioning

Another strategic choice is how an offering should be positioned in consumers' minds. The desired image should reflect what the product is and how it is different from the competition. Slogans like BMW's "The Ultimate Driving Machine," Ford's "Ford Tough," and Maxwell House's "Good to the Last Drop" reflect the image these companies would like consumers to have of their offerings.

How Are Competitive Offerings Positioned? Consumer research can show marketers how consumers perceive and categorize different brands in the marketplace. In turn, this information gives marketers some interesting perspectives on how their offering should be positioned. Indeed marketers sometimes conduct research to see how consumers view other brands in comparison with their own and plot the results on a graph called a "perceptual map." The map in Exhibit 2.9 shows how consumers perceive various music retailers. Those in the same quadrant of the map are perceived to offer similar benefits to consumers. Hence the closer various companies are to one another, the more likely they are to be competitors.

EXHIBIT 2.9

Consumer Perceptions of Brands in a Market

A perceptual map, like the one shown here for music stores, plots consumers' perceptions of how various brands compare with one another along two dimensions. The top map compares the stores on variety and service. The bottom compares them on family friendliness and environment.

Source: Class project for Professor Debbie MacInnis, University of Southern California, by Alexander Moreno, Robert Frahm, Daniel McGill, and Jillian Weinstein, April 1998. Reprinted with permission.

(a) Perceptual Map Comparing Variety and Service

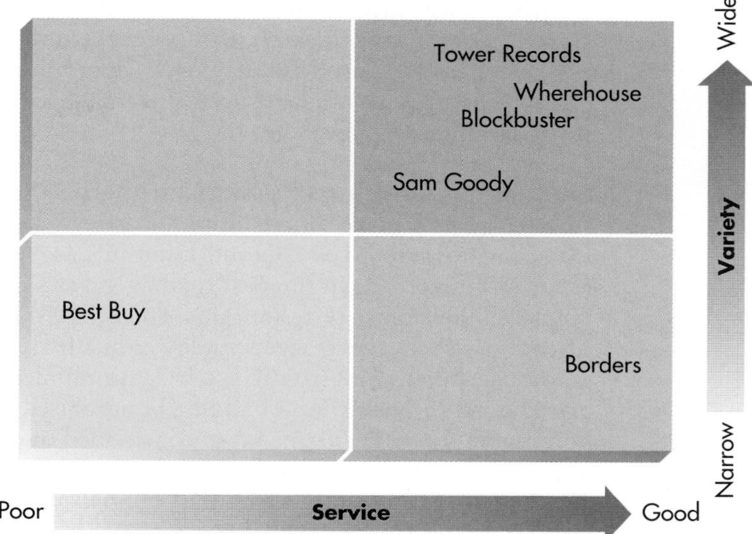

(b) Perceptual Map Comparing Environment and Family Friendliness

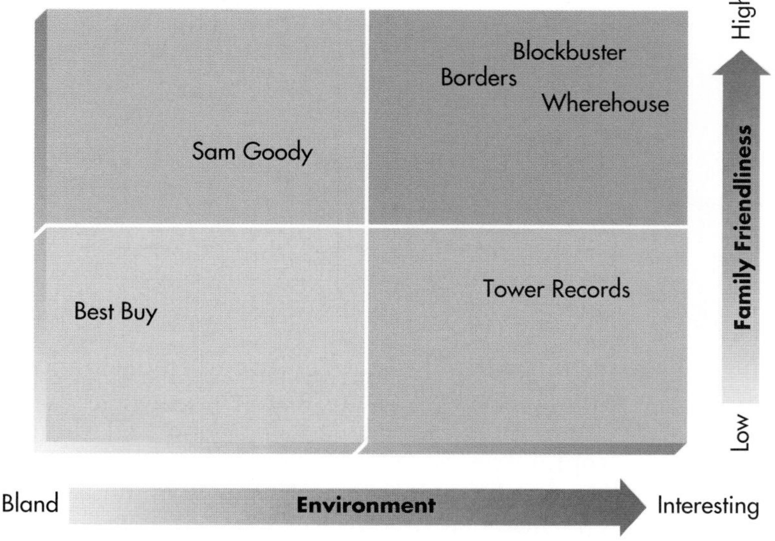

How Should Our Offerings Be Positioned? Companies use consumer research to understand what image a new offering should have in the eyes of consumers. For example, when Bissell acquired the rights to a European steam-cleaning device, the research director set out to determine how women who clean their own homes would respond to it. The company recruited 20 women from a local Parent Teacher Association, gave each the device, and asked them to keep diaries of their cleaning experiences. The company also observed women using the product at home. The research found that the device was especially appealing to women who were serious about house cleaning. They also discovered that the women were accustomed to using chemicals rather than cleaning with steam alone. Based on this research, Bissell renamed the product Steam N' Clean and positioned it as a product that uses super-hot steam to clean hard-to-reach places. The product was so successful that Bissell introduced an entire line of steam-cleaning appliances.[43]

Should Our Offerings Be Repositioned? Yet another use of consumer research is to help marketers reposition existing products (i.e., change their image). Consider how the MGM Grand hotel in Las Vegas used research in a recent repositioning effort. In the past, management shied away from trumpeting the hotel's 5,000 rooms, 16 restaurants, and 3,700 slot machines because consumers tended to associate large size with lower-quality service. Instead, the hotel sought a "value" positioning to attract bargain-minded gamblers interested in low-priced hotel rooms. After a building boom raised the total number of Las Vegas hotel rooms to 121,000, management decided to differentiate the hotel by focusing on the overall guest experience. Using ads in *People* and other magazines, plus billboards in West Coast cities, officials created a new image of the MGM Grand as a self-contained "City of Entertainment," complete with a casino, pool, and other resort touches.[44]

Developing Products or Services

Developing products and services that satisfy consumers' wants and needs is a critical marketing activity. Marketers apply consumer research when making a number of decisions about products.

What Ideas Do Consumers Have for New Products? First, marketers need to design an offering that has the benefits desired by target consumers. For example, focus groups helped one company uncover a new product idea. Mothers participating in the groups complained that their children didn't want to use soap. In response, the firm created a bar of soap with a plastic toy inside. The more children wash, the more they can see the toy.[45]

What Attributes Can Be Added to or Changed in an Existing Offering? Marketers often use research to determine when and how to modify or tailor a product to meet the needs of new or existing groups of consumers. For example, consumer research revealed that Japanese consumers prefer less lather in skin-care products, prompting Amway to produce a low-lather product. A major bicycle manufacturer developed new color combinations, redesigned its frames, and created new accessories after asking kids for new bike ideas.[46] In response to its segmentation research, Mobil made its facilities cleaner and encouraged its attendants to be more helpful in meeting the needs of the Road Warriors, True Blues, and Generation F3 consumers.[47] And Burger King has changed its french fry recipe several times to do a better job of giving fast-food customers what research says they want: a crispy fry.[48]

What Should Our Offering Be Called? Consumer research plays a vital role in decisions about product and brand names. Goodyear conducted considerable consumer research when naming its tires. It chose the name Eagle Aquatech EMT (for extended mobility technology) for a tire that, when flat, can go for 50 miles at 55 mph on wet surfaces.[49] Other companies create brand names like Obsession (for perfume) and Country Hearth (for bread) because consumer research suggested that these names would be understood, easy to remember, and suggestive of the brand's benefits.

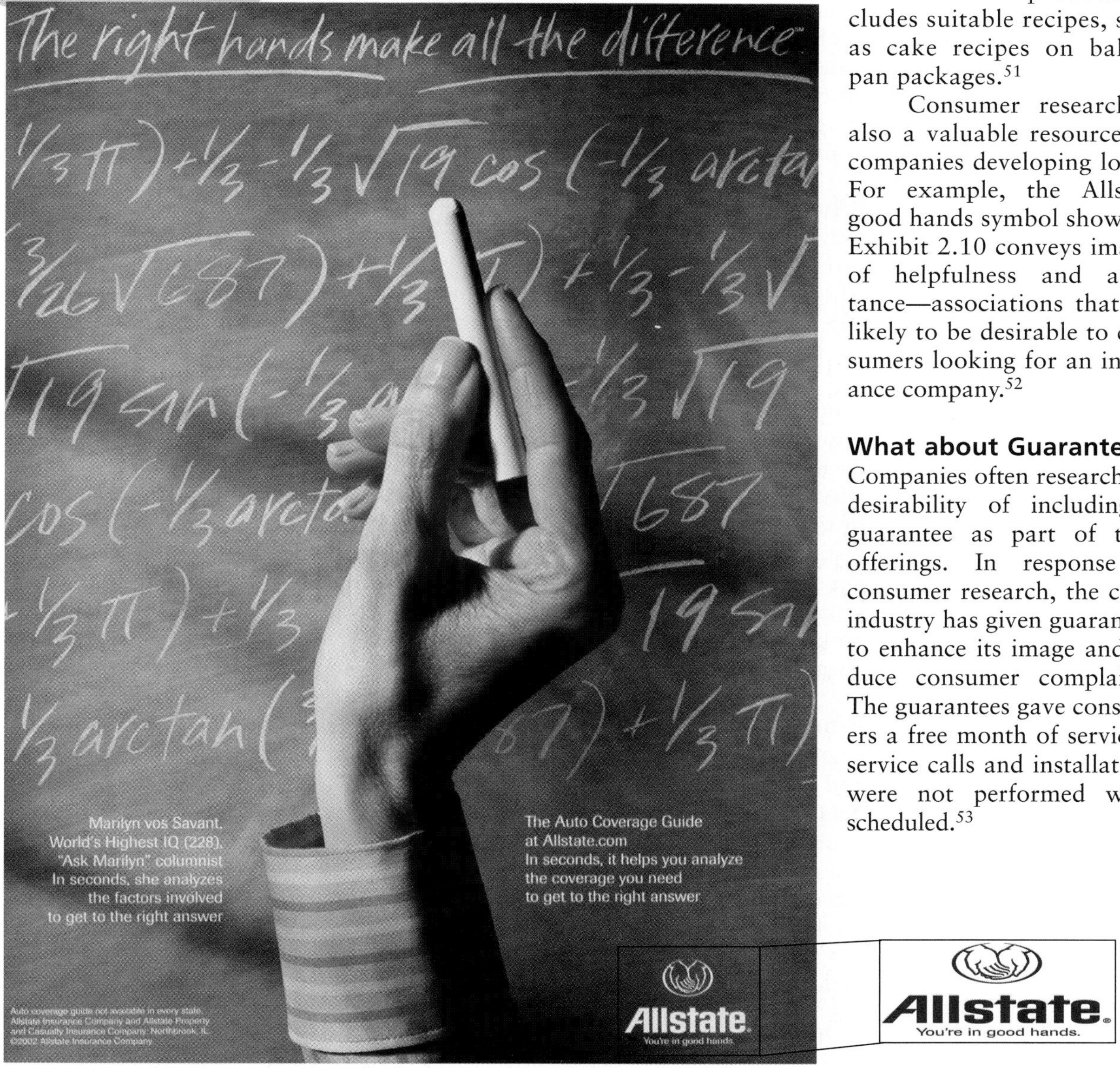

What Should Our Package and Logo Look Like? Many marketers use consumer research to test alternative packaging and logos. Research shows, for instance, that consumers are likely to think that food (including cookies) is good for them if it comes in green packaging.[50] This information is valuable in the design of packages for products with a "healthy" positioning. Research has also been instrumental in planning the packaging for Kmart's Martha Stewart Everyday household products. Knowing that consumers expect information as well as inspiration from Martha Stewart, the packaging for her kitchen products includes suitable recipes, such as cake recipes on baking pan packages.[51]

Consumer research is also a valuable resource for companies developing logos. For example, the Allstate good hands symbol shown in Exhibit 2.10 conveys images of helpfulness and assistance—associations that are likely to be desirable to consumers looking for an insurance company.[52]

What about Guarantees? Companies often research the desirability of including a guarantee as part of their offerings. In response to consumer research, the cable industry has given guarantees to enhance its image and reduce consumer complaints. The guarantees gave consumers a free month of service if service calls and installations were not performed when scheduled.[53]

EXHIBIT 2.10
Helping Hands
Research sometimes helps a company develop brand symbols. The Allstate symbol conveys the idea that the company will be there to offer help in a time of need.

Source: Reprinted by permission of Allstate Insurance Company.

Making Promotion (Marketing Communications) Decisions

Consumer research can help companies make decisions about a wide range of promotional/marketing communications tools. These include advertising, sales promotions (premiums, contests, sweepstakes, free samples, coupons, and rebates), personal selling, and public relations.

What Are Our Advertising Objectives? Consumer research can be very useful in determining what objectives should guide the development of advertising. It may reveal, for example, that very few people have heard of a new brand, suggesting that the primary advertising objective should be to enhance brand-name awareness. Other research may suggest that consumers have heard of the brand but don't know anything about it. In this case the advertising objective should be to enhance brand knowledge. If research reveals that consumers know the brand name but don't really know the characteristics of the brand that make it desirable, the advertising should aim to enhance brand knowledge and brand attitudes. Bank of America, for example, launched a $100 million multimedia image-building campaign after learning, through consumer research, that its brand was not as strong as expected across all targeted segments.[54]

What Should Our Advertising Look Like? If a marketer wants to establish brand-name awareness, research about making ads more memorable might prove relevant and useful. For example, a brand name is better remembered when the ad in which it is placed contains interesting and unusual visuals that relate to it. If the visuals are interesting but unrelated, consumers may remember the visuals but forget the name.

Consumer research can also help marketers understand which visuals should accompany ad copy. Recent research indicates not only that a car with "power" is desirable to both men and women but also that the word *power* means different things to different people. Men associate power with excitement, whereas women associate it with being able to maneuver quickly and safely out of tight or dangerous situations.[55] This information suggests the use of clearly distinct visuals and associated copy depending on whether the ad is designed to appeal to men or women. Marketers can also learn, through research, how different groups respond to different wording. For example, saying a product is a good "value for the money" does not work in Spain. Instead, marketers use the phrase "price for product."[56]

Where Should Advertising Be Placed? When marketers start to select specific media vehicles in which to advertise, they find demographic and lifestyle data and data from companies like Nielsen and Mediamark very useful. Mediamark data, for example, shows the percentage of a target market that is reached by a particular medium (refer to Exhibit 2.2). In addition, companies are finding, through research, that more people split their time among many different media—and often use recording technology to avoid television commercials. With this knowledge, marketers are increasingly seeking more targeted ways of reaching consumers.

Procter & Gamble, for instance, says television's audience is "too broad." Instead, the company is using data mining to identify promising groups for direct mail offers of new products. To launch its Physique hair-care products, P&G mailed 500,000 samples to women who, according to research, spend considerable time on their hair. The company also set up a Web site offering a free bottle of shampoo to customers who sent the Web address to ten others. Later, P&G

Rocher is perfect for Easter:
It's a good indication of how much the Easter Bunny loves you.
FERRERO ROCHER
Luscious chocolate, crunchy hazelnut, crispy wafer and always in good taste.
www.RocherUSA.com

EXHIBIT 2.11
Ferrero Rocher and the Easter Bunny
Because candy consumption increases significantly during Easter, Ferrero Rocher makes a point of advertising its chocolates in advance of the holiday. During what other periods should Ferrero Rocher advertise?

Source: Image Courtesy of Ferrero U.S.A., Inc. Photography by Victor Schrager.

followed up with television and print ads to reinforce key product points. This mix of traditional and untraditional media helped make the product introduction successful.[57]

When Should We Advertise? Research may reveal seasonal variations in purchases due to weather-related needs, variations in the amount of discretionary money consumers have (which changes, for instance, before and after Christmas), holiday buying patterns, and the like. Candy manufacturers know, for example, that consumption spikes during holidays such as Easter and Valentine's Day (see Exhibit 2.11). Researching such variations can help marketers decide on the most effective timing of advertising.

Has Our Advertising Been Effective? Finally, advertisers can undertake studies to determine whether advertising has been effective. This research can be gathered at various points in the advertising development process. Some times marketers or ad agencies conduct research called advertising *copy testing* or *pretesting*, which tests ads for their effectiveness before they are placed in the media. If the advertising objective is brand-name awareness and the tested ad does not enhance awareness, the company may replace it with a new ad.

Effectiveness research can also take place after the ads have been placed in the media. The STARCH scores described earlier in the chapter are one way of assessing how effective ads are in building brand-name awareness. In addition, advertisers sometimes conduct tracking studies to see how effective their advertising is in achieving particular objectives over time.

What about Sales Promotion Objectives and Tactics? When developing sales promotions, marketers can use research about advertising objectives to suggest sales promotion objectives and identify appropriate tactics to achieve them. A racetrack outside Los Angeles is using a database to develop its sales promotion objectives and tactics. By tracking attendance through database analysis, the company found it needed to focus on getting customers to come to the racetrack more often. To achieve this objective, the track created a Thoroughbred Club and issued members a card that entitled them to reduced admission. Furthermore, every time these customers came to the track, their admission price became lower, encouraging more frequent attendance.[58]

Sometimes the chosen tactics are so effective that a promotion exceeds its objectives, as S.C. Johnson & Son's experience shows. To promote its Raid bug killer in Thailand, Johnson offered to pay one baht (about 2 cents) for every dead bug and allow participants to bid for prizes using the bounty they earned. The promotion captured the public's imagination as people turned in thousands of bugs.[59]

When Should Sales Promotions Happen? Companies can also use consumer research to time their sales promotions. The racetrack managers, for example, can use their marketing database to determine when sales have been slowest and hence when sales promotions might be most needed to attract customers.

Have Our Sales Promotions Been Effective? Consumer research can answer this question. By counting how many consumers use the Thoroughbred Club card and evaluating how much they receive in discounts, the racetrack can determine whether the card is effective in enhancing attendance.

How Many Salespeople Are Needed to Serve Customers? By tracking store patronage at different times of the day or on different days of the week, retailers can determine the appropriate number of store personnel needed to best serve customers.

How Can Salespeople Best Serve Customers? Finally, research can be helpful when managers are selecting salespeople and evaluating how well they serve customers. For example, although there is some debate about it, one general finding suggests that the more similar the salesperson is to the customer, the more effective he or she will be.[60] Research has shown that salespeople can better serve customers when the salespeople are in a good mood.[61] This information implies that managers should devise tactics to enhance the moods of their sales personnel.

Making Pricing Decisions

The price of a product or service can have a critical influence on consumers' acquisition decisions. It is therefore very important for marketers to understand how consumers react to price and to use this information in their pricing decisions.

What Price Should Be Charged? Why do prices often end in 99? Consumer research has shown that people perceive $.99, $9.99, or $99.99 to be cheaper than $1.00, $10.00, or $100.00. Perhaps this is one reason that so many prices end in the number 9.[62]

Although economic theory suggests that a decrease in price will increase the likelihood of purchase, consumer research shows this isn't always so. A low price may make consumers suspect the product's quality, since higher price generally means higher quality.[63] Research shows that consumers have complicated reactions to price. For example, if catalog customers can save $8 on shipping charges, they will spend an average of $15 more on catalog purchases. This finding has caused some catalog marketers to absorb shipping fees.[64] Also, when making a purchase, consumers consider how much they must pay in relation to the price of other relevant brands or the price previously paid for that product, which means marketers must be aware of these reference prices.[65] Finally, when consumers buy multiple units of a service for one bundled price (such as a multiday ski pass), they may not feel a great loss if they use only some of the units, because they have difficulty assigning value to each unit. In contrast, when consumers buy multiple products for one bundled price (such as a case of wine), they are likely to increase their consumption because unit costs seem low.[66]

How Sensitive Are Consumers to Price and Price Changes? According to consumer research, consumers have varying views of the importance of price. Some consumers are very price sensitive, meaning that a small change in price will have a large effect on consumers' willingness to purchase the product. Cruise lines, for example, have found that lower prices help fill their ships.[67] Other consumers are price insensitive, meaning they are likely to buy and use the offering regardless of price. When U.S. gasoline prices skyrocketed, consumers did not stop driving or stop buying gas-guzzling sport-utility vehicles.[68] Marketers can use research to determine which consumers are likely to be price sensitive and when. For fashion or prestige goods in particular, a high price symbolizes status. Thus some consumers, particularly those seeking status, may be less sensitive to the price of a product and pay more than $50 for a simple T-shirt with a prestigious label.

When Should Certain Price Tactics Be Used? Research on consumer behavior also helps us understand when consumers are likely to be most responsive to various pricing tactics. Historical data, for example, shows that consumers are very responsive to price cuts on linens and sheets during January. These "white sales" are effective because consumers have come to anticipate them and are unlikely to buy these products after Christmas without a financial incentive to do so.

Making Distribution Decisions

Another important marketing decision involves the manner in which products or services are distributed. Here, too, marketers use consumer research when considering how to get their products to customers.

Where Are Target Consumers Likely to Shop? Marketers who understand the value consumers place on time and convenience have developed distribution channels that allow consumers to acquire or use goods and services whenever and wherever it is most convenient for them. For example, 24-hour grocery stores, health clubs, and catalog ordering and online ordering systems give consumers flexibility in the timing of their acquisition, usage, and disposition decisions. As another example, consumers can now shop for cars through the Internet, auto brokers, warehouse clubs, giant auto malls, and used-car superstores, as well as traditional auto dealers.

How Should Stores Be Designed? Supermarkets are generally designed with similar or complementary items stocked near one another because consumer research shows that customers think about items in terms of categories based on similar characteristics or use. Thus stores stock diapers near toilet paper because both have similar uses, and they stock peanut butter near jelly because those are often used together.

Consumer research can also help marketers develop other aspects of their retail environments. Research has shown that bright colors and loud, up-tempo music make consumers move quickly through the store. Softer, subdued colors and gentler music have the opposite effect.[69] According to research, consumers feel less satisfied shopping in stores with narrow aisles and closely spaced fixtures and merchandise.[70] Stores and Web sites can also be designed to convey the image marketers wish them to have. Frederick's of Hollywood recently redesigned its 200 stores and Web site to look classier and deemphasize risqué imagery.[71] As Exhibit 2.12 indicates, Restoration Hardware's store design and atmospherics go a long way toward conveying its upscale image.

EXHIBIT 2.12
Atmosphere Creates a Mood
Colors, textures, and lighting all have an important psychological impact on consumer behavior. What mood and image do you associate with the restaurant depicted here?

Source: ©Alan Klehr.

ETHICAL ISSUES IN CONSUMER RESEARCH

Although marketers rely heavily on consumer research in the development of successful goods and services, the conduct of this research raises important ethical issues. As the following sections show, consumer research has both positive and negative aspects.

The Positive Aspects of Consumer Research

Both consumers and marketers benefit from consumer research. Consumers generally have better consumption experiences, and marketers can learn to build stronger customer relationships by paying attention to consumer research.

Better Consumption Experiences Because consumer research helps marketers become more customer focused, consumers get better designed products, better customer service, clearer usage instructions, more information that helps them make good decisions, and more satisfying postpurchase experiences. Consumer research (by government and consumer organizations) also plays a role in protecting consumers from unscrupulous marketers.

Potential for Building Customer Relationships From the marketer's perspective, consumer research is helpful for identifying ways of establishing and enhancing relationships with customers. Consumers will be motivated to develop and continue a relationship with companies that seem to understand them and want to serve their needs. Consumer research can also show marketers how to build and retain a loyal customer base.

The Negative Aspects of Consumer Research

Consumer research is a very complex process, with a number of potentially negative aspects. These include the difficulty of conducting research in foreign countries, the high costs of conducting research, concerns about invasion of privacy, and the use of deceptive practices.

Tracking Consumer Behavior in Different Countries Marketers who want to research consumer behavior in other countries face special challenges. For instance, focus groups are not appropriate in all countries or situations. U.S. marketers often put husbands and wives together in a focus group to explore attitudes toward products like furniture. However, this approach won't work in countries like Saudi Arabia where women are unlikely to speak freely and are highly unlikely to disagree with their husbands. Focus groups must also be conducted differently in Japan, where cultural pressures dictate against disagreeing with the views of a group.

Although telephone interviewing is common in the United States, it is far less prevalent in Third World countries. Marketers must also think about a country's literacy rate when planning survey research. At a minimum, researchers should word questions carefully and check that the meaning is being accurately conveyed by first translating questions into the other language and then back into English.

Companies may not be able to directly compare secondary data gathered in another country with data gathered in the United States, in part because of different collection procedures or timing. Countries may also use different categorization schemes for describing demographics like social class and education level. Moreover, different or fewer syndicated data sources may be available in other countries, which limits the research available to marketers.

Potentially Higher Marketing Costs Some consumers worry that the process of researching behavior leads to higher marketing costs, which in turn translates into higher product prices. Some marketers, however, argue that they can market to their customers more efficiently if they know more about them. For example, product development, advertising, sales promotion costs, and distribution costs will be lower if marketers know exactly what consumers want and how to reach them.

Invasion of Consumer Privacy A potentially more serious and widespread concern is that marketers' conduct and use of research—especially database marketing—may invade consumers' privacy. Consumers worry that marketers know too much about them and that personal data, financial data, and behavioral data may be sold to other companies or used inappropriately without their knowledge or consent. This issue is discussed in more detail later in the text, in the context of public policy decisions (see Chapter 20) and the dark side of marketing (see Chapter 21).

Deceptive Research Practices Finally, unscrupulous researchers may engage in deceptive practices. One such practice is lying about the sponsor of the research (e.g., saying it is being conducted by a nonprofit organization when it is really being conducted by a for-profit company). Another deceptive practice is promising that respondents' answers will remain anonymous, when in fact the company is adding identifying information to individual answers so the company can use the data to market to these consumers later on. Unscrupulous researchers may also promise to compensate respondents but fail to deliver on this promise.[72]

SUMMARY

Consumer research is a valuable tool that helps marketers design better marketing programs, aids in the development of laws and public policy decisions regarding product safety, and promotes our general understanding of how consumers behave and why. Researchers for-profit and nonprofit organizations utilize a variety of research tools, including techniques that collect data on what consumers say (surveys, interviews, storytelling, focus groups, use of photography, diaries, conjoint analysis) and techniques that collect data on what consumers do (observations, purchase panels, experiments, database marketing). These tools may involve data collection from relatively few individuals or from many individuals and may study consumers at a single point in time or track their behavior across time.

Many types of organizations collect consumer research. Some firms have internal marketing research departments; others use external research firms to conduct research activities. Advertising agencies and syndicated data services, for example, are two types of outside agencies that collect consumer research information. Large retail chains often conduct consumer research through the use of electronic scanners to track sales of a brand or product category. Research foundations and trade groups, as well as the government and consumer organizations, also collect consumer information. Many academics and academic research centers conduct consumer research simply to enhance our general understanding of consumer behavior, although this research may have application purposes as well.

Marketers utilize consumer research information to understand how markets are segmented and to determine the characteristics of consumers in each segment. Consumer research information is also helpful in selecting a target market and deciding how an offering should be positioned. Research is essential to product, promotion, price, and distribution marketing-mix decisions.

Consumer research raises some ethical issues. The positive aspect of consumer research is that it supports a consumer-oriented view of marketing and can help companies provide better consumption experiences and strengthen customer relationships. However, some critics point out that research may invade consumers' privacy and lead to higher marketing costs. In addition, unscrupulous marketers can misuse consumer information.

QUESTIONS FOR REVIEW AND DISCUSSION

1. How do researchers use surveys, focus groups, interviews, and storytelling to learn about consumer behavior?
2. How do experiments differ from field experiments?
3. Why do researchers use observation and purchase panels to study consumer behavior?
4. How is primary data different from secondary data?
5. What is a perceptual map and why do researchers use it?
6. What are some of the positive and negative aspects of consumer research?

EXERCISES

1. Look up any three of the following sites on the Web and determine (a) whether they provide primary or secondary data, (b) which research tools they use, and (c) whether they design research for a specific industry or for many industries.

   www.claritas.com
   www.ars1.com
   www.secondarydata.com
   www.acnielsen.com
   www.npd.com
   www.qualtalk.com
   www.maritzresearch.com
   https://fyi.co.la.ca.us/city/demo/index.html

2. Ask a friend to identify a favorite possession. Interview your friend to find out as much as you can about it. Ask your friend to find photographs from magazines that best symbolize why that item is meaningful. Then ask him or her to keep a diary for a few days that indicates whether and how he or she used the possession. Finally, conduct a focus group with a few of your friends about their special possessions. What do these combined tools reveal to you about these possessions?
3. Imagine you're a marketing manager for Burger King. You need consumer research to support future decisions about menu items and promotions. Which research tool(s) would you use to uncover the answers to the following questions—and why?

a. Do Burger King customers prefer the chain's french fries over those of McDonald's?

b. Which Burger King sandwich is the most popular in California, Texas, and Florida?

c. Do coupons increase sales of the discounted menu items?

d. Would Burger King sell more burger sandwiches if it added bacon and cheese without raising the price?

e. Which media vehicles do Burger King customers prefer?

f. What condiments, if any, do take-out customers add to Burger King burgers eaten at home?

g. What new side dishes should Burger King introduce?

4. Choose two of the following Web sites and follow the indicated links to the page where each company invites consumer comment about products, problems, and ideas. What type of consumer data are these two companies collecting along with comments? How can the companies use the information gathered from these consumer comments in their marketing activities? What other data would you recommend that the companies request from consumers who initiate contact with them—and why?

www.gatorade.com (feedback link)

www.ford.com (contact link)

www.apple.com (contact link)

www.tylenol.com (customer service link)

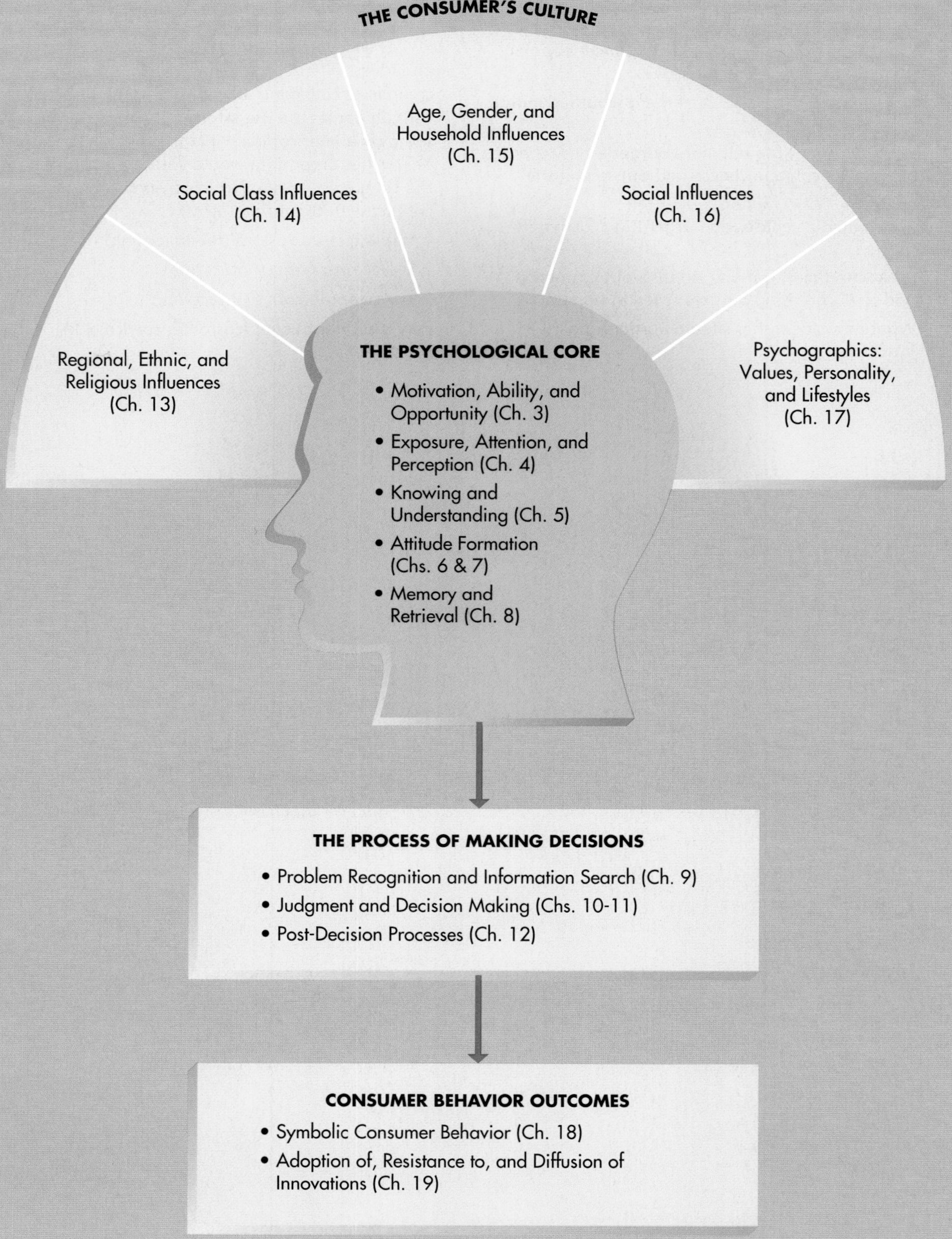

THE CONSUMER'S CULTURE

Age, Gender, and Household Influences (Ch. 15)

Social Class Influences (Ch. 14)

Social Influences (Ch. 16)

Regional, Ethnic, and Religious Influences (Ch. 13)

Psychographics: Values, Personality, and Lifestyles (Ch. 17)

THE PSYCHOLOGICAL CORE

- Motivation, Ability, and Opportunity (Ch. 3)
- Exposure, Attention, and Perception (Ch. 4)
- Knowing and Understanding (Ch. 5)
- Attitude Formation (Chs. 6 & 7)
- Memory and Retrieval (Ch. 8)

THE PROCESS OF MAKING DECISIONS

- Problem Recognition and Information Search (Ch. 9)
- Judgment and Decision Making (Chs. 10-11)
- Post-Decision Processes (Ch. 12)

CONSUMER BEHAVIOR OUTCOMES

- Symbolic Consumer Behavior (Ch. 18)
- Adoption of, Resistance to, and Diffusion of Innovations (Ch. 19)

PART TWO

The Psychological Core

Consumer behavior is greatly affected by the amount of effort consumers put into their consumption behaviors and decisions. Chapter 3 describes three critical factors that affect effort: the (1) motivation, (2) ability, and (3) opportunity that consumers have to engage in behaviors and make decisions.

Chapter 4 discusses how consumers come into contact with marketing stimuli (exposure), notice them (attention), and perceive them. Chapter 5 continues the topic by discussing how consumers compare new stimuli with their existing knowledge (a process called categorization) as well as attempt to understand or comprehend the data on a deeper level.

Chapter 6 describes what happens when consumers exert a great deal of effort forming and changing attitudes. Chapter 7 discusses how attitudes can be influenced when consumer effort is low.

Finally, because consumers are not always exposed to marketing information when they actually need it, Chapter 8 focuses on the important topic of consumer memory.

chapter 3

Motivation, Ability, and Opportunity

INTRODUCTION: Targeting Women for Financial Services

Women are a growing market for companies that offer financial management and planning services. Indeed, many financial services firms gear TV and magazine ads exclusively toward women (see Exhibit 3.1). And it is no wonder. More women have more money to invest—on their own or with their husbands—so they are actively searching for financial services information, advice, and products. Research shows that women are equal partners in making decisions about investments, financial planning, and other important financial matters in 75 percent of all U.S. households. Yet nearly half of the women in a recent poll agreed that investing was "scary," and even more said that investing was like gambling. Another survey revealed that 14 percent of women feel uninformed about money and investments, which may explain why thousands are turning out for financial management seminars conducted by Charles Schwab, Morgan Stanley, American Express, and other companies.

This increased interest in financial services is driven, in part, by the fact that women today have greater motivation, ability, and opportunity to engage in investment decisions. They may be more motivated to learn about personal finance and plan for financial security because they fear Social Security benefits will not be available when they retire and because they want to avoid the risks of an uncertain financial future. Women are also participating in the workforce in greater numbers, which means they have more income and therefore more opportunity to invest. In addition, as more financial services firms target this market, women gain more opportunity to acquire and process relevant information from diverse sources.

Knowledge, education, and age play a role, as well. When women go to financial management seminars, search the Internet for financial data, or consult with financial planners, they enhance their ability to process information about investment opportunities and to make sound investment decisions. Although

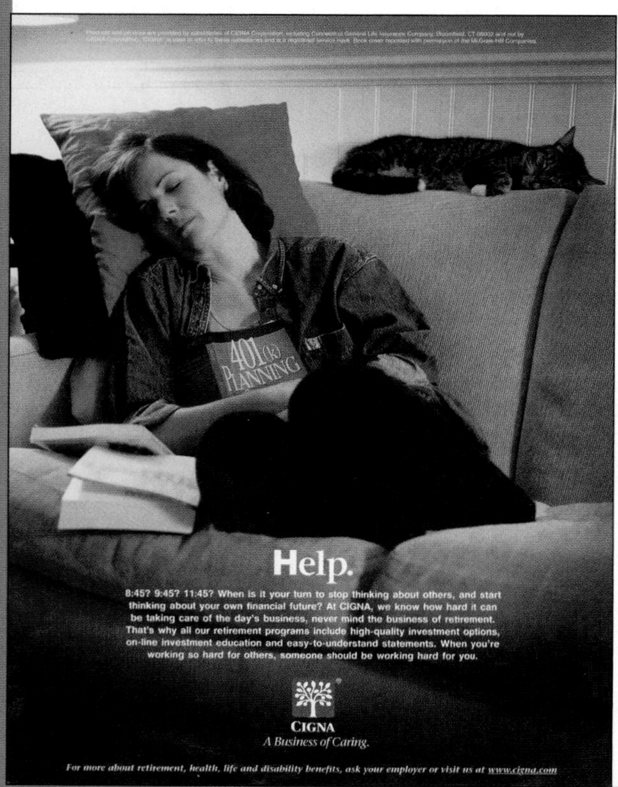

401(k) PLANNING
Help.
8:45? 9:45? 11:45? When is it your turn to stop thinking about others, and start thinking about your own financial future? At CIGNA, we know how hard it can be taking care of the day's business, never mind the business of retirement. That's why all our retirement programs include high-quality investment options, on-line investment education and easy-to-understand statements. When you're working so hard for others, someone should be working hard for you.
CIGNA
A Business of Caring.
For more about retirement, health, life and disability benefits, ask your employer or visit us at www.cigna.com

EXHIBIT 3.1

Targeting Women

Financial services marketers are increasingly targeting women given women's motivation, opportunity, and ability to use financial management services.

Source: Courtesy of Cigna Corporation.

women are 16 percent less likely than men to maintain an IRA retirement account, women with graduate degrees are 86 percent more likely than the general population to maintain an IRA. Moreover, women aged 55 to 64 are 50 percent more likely to maintain an IRA.

Financial services firms are noticing these differences. The Charles Schwab brokerage firm, for example, recognizes that "women feel differently and learn differently about investing," says Carrie Schwab Pomerantz. In response, Pomerantz developed the company's strategy for serving this market through women-only investment seminars, Web-based research resources, targeted ads, and other communications. "We're trying to speak to women in terms relevant to their lives and in language that's appealing to them," Pomerantz notes, by avoiding jargon and instead discussing the financial implications of real-life decisions such as considering a divorce or starting a family.[1]

Charles Schwab and other financial services firms understand that motivation, ability, and opportunity exert a powerful influence on a consumer's acquisition, usage, and disposition decisions. These three factors affect whether consumers will pay attention to and perceive information, what information they notice, how they form attitudes, and what they remember. These factors also influence how much effort consumers put into searching for information, how they make choices, and how they judge whether their experience has been satisfactory.

This chapter examines motivation, ability, and opportunity in detail. Exhibit 3.2, which offers an overview of the chapter, shows that motivated individuals may invest a great deal of thought and activity in reaching their goals. As shown, motivation is enhanced when consumers regard something as (1) personally relevant; (2) consistent with their values, goals, and needs; (3) risky; and/or (4) moderately inconsistent with their prior attitudes. Whether motivated consumers actually achieve a goal depends on whether they have the ability to achieve it, based on (1) knowledge and experience; (2) cognitive style; (3) intelligence, education, and age; and, in the case of purchase goals, (4) money. Achievement of goals, like processing information about financial management, also depends on whether consumers have the *opportunity* to achieve the goal. If the goal is processing information, opportunity is determined by (1) time, (2) distractions, (3) the amount of information to which consumers are exposed, (4) the complexity of that information, and (5) the extent to which it is repeated. ●

CONSUMER MOTIVATION AND ITS EFFECTS

Motivation is defined as "an inner state of arousal," with aroused energy directed to achieving a goal.[2] The motivated consumer is energized, ready, and willing to engage in a goal-relevant activity. For example, if you learn that your favorite music group is playing at a nearby concert venue, you may be motivated to buy tickets. Consumers can be motivated to engage in behaviors, make decisions, or process information, and this motivation can be seen in the context of acquiring, using, or disposing of an offering. Let's look first at the effects of motivation, as shown in the middle of Exhibit 3.2.

motivation An inner state of arousal that denotes energy to achieve a goal.

Goal-Relevant Behavior

One outcome of motivation is goal-relevant behavior. When motivation is high, people are willing to do things that make it more likely they will achieve their goals. For example, if you are motivated to buy a good car, you will visit dealerships, take test drives, ask friends for advice, and so on. Likewise, if you are motivated to lose

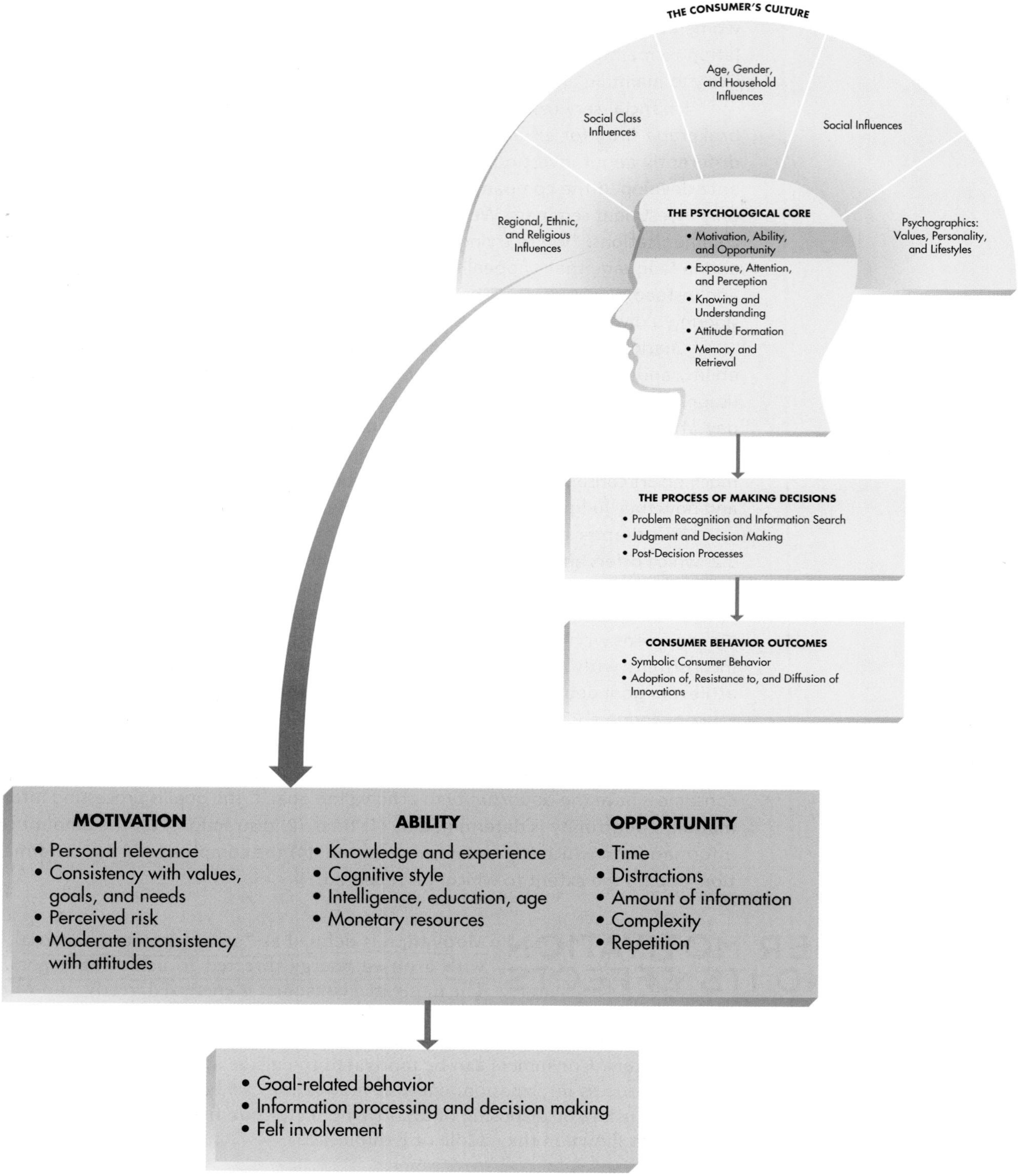

THE CONSUMER'S CULTURE

Regional, Ethnic, and Religious Influences

Social Class Influences

Age, Gender, and Household Influences

Social Influences

Psychographics: Values, Personality, and Lifestyles

THE PSYCHOLOGICAL CORE

- Motivation, Ability, and Opportunity
- Exposure, Attention, and Perception
- Knowing and Understanding
- Attitude Formation
- Memory and Retrieval

THE PROCESS OF MAKING DECISIONS

- Problem Recognition and Information Search
- Judgment and Decision Making
- Post-Decision Processes

CONSUMER BEHAVIOR OUTCOMES

- Symbolic Consumer Behavior
- Adoption of, Resistance to, and Diffusion of Innovations

MOTIVATION

- Personal relevance
- Consistency with values, goals, and needs
- Perceived risk
- Moderate inconsistency with attitudes

ABILITY

- Knowledge and experience
- Cognitive style
- Intelligence, education, age
- Monetary resources

OPPORTUNITY

- Time
- Distractions
- Amount of information
- Complexity
- Repetition

- Goal-related behavior
- Information processing and decision making
- Felt involvement

EXHIBIT 3.2
Chapter Overview: Motivation, Ability, and Opportunity

Motivation, ability, and opportunity (MAO) to engage in various consumer behaviors is affected by many factors. Outcomes of high MAO include (1) goal-relevant behavior, (2) high-effort information processing and decision making, and (3) felt involvement.

weight, you will buy low-calorie foods, measure food portions, and exercise. Motivation not only drives behaviors consistent with a goal but also creates a willingness to expend time and energy engaging in these behaviors. Thus someone motivated to attend a concert may earn extra money for tickets, wait in line for hours to buy them, and drive through adverse weather conditions to get there.

High-Effort Information Processing and Decision Making

Motivation also affects how we process information and make decisions.[3] When consumers are highly motivated to achieve a goal, they are more likely to pay careful attention to it, think about it, attempt to understand or comprehend information presented about it, evaluate that information critically, and try to remember it for later use. Doing all this takes a lot of effort. For example, if you are motivated to go to a sold-out Linkin Park concert, you might scour the classifieds hoping to find someone who is selling extra tickets. If someone mentions the name of a person who is selling tickets, you might actively try to remember this person's name and phone number.

When consumers have low motivation, however, they devote little effort to processing information and making decisions. For example, your motivation to purchase the best pad of paper on the market is likely to be low. You wouldn't devote much attention to learning about the characteristics of paper pads or examining paper ads. Nor would you think about what it would be like to own and use various types of pads. Once in the store, you are unlikely to spend much time comparing brands. You may use decision-making shortcuts, such as deciding to buy the cheapest brand or the same brand you bought last time.[4] The purchase of most common grocery products falls into the same category.

Felt Involvement

A final outcome of motivation is that it evokes a psychological state in consumers called *involvement*. Researchers use the term **felt involvement** to refer to the psychological experience of the motivated consumer.[5] There are four kinds of felt involvement: (1) enduring, (2) situational, (3) cognitive, and (4) affective.[6]

felt involvement The psychological experience of the motivated consumer. Includes psychological states such as interest, excitement, anxiety, passion, and engagement.

enduring involvement Interest in an offering or activity over an extended period of time.

Enduring Involvement

Enduring involvement exists when we show interest in an offering or activity over a long period of time.[7] Car enthusiasts are intrinsically interested in cars and exhibit enduring involvement in them. Enthusiasts engage in activities that reveal this interest (e.g., going to car shows, reading car magazines, visiting dealerships). A consumer might express enduring involvement in any object or activity—adding CDs to a personal collection or working out, for instance. However, most consumers exhibit enduring involvement for relatively few offerings or activities.

situational involvement Temporary interest in an offering or activity, often caused by situational circumstances.

Situational Involvement

In most instances, consumers experience **situational (temporary) involvement** with an offering or activity. For example, consumers who exhibit no enduring involvement with cars may be involved in the car-buying process when they are in the market for a new car. After they buy the car, their involvement with new cars declines dramatically. Involvement with gift giving is often situational. Involvement is usually high only when the consumer is trying to achieve the goal of deciding on a gift.

cognitive involvement Interest in thinking about and processing information related to one's goal.

Cognitive Involvement

Researchers distinguish between cognitive and affective involvement.[8] **Cognitive involvement** means that the consumer is interested in thinking about and processing information related to his or her goal. The goal therefore includes learning about the offering. A sports enthusiast who is interested in learning all he can about basketball player Dennis Rodman or a car enthusiast interested in learning all she can about a new-model sports car would be exhibiting cognitive involvement.

affective involvement Interest in expending emotional energy and heightened feelings regarding an offering or activity.

Affective Involvement **Affective involvement** means that the consumer is willing to expend emotional energy in or has heightened feelings about an offering or activity. The consumer who listens to music to experience intense emotions is exhibiting affective involvement. As another example, if we watch a tender scene in a movie and begin to cry, we are displaying high affective involvement.

Objects of Involvement

In analyzing consumer involvement and its influence on behavior, we can also identify the various objects with which consumers may be involved. These include involvement with product categories, brands, ads, media, and decisions.

Involvement with Product Categories As many of this chapter's examples indicate, consumers may exhibit cognitive and/or affective involvement in a certain product category, such as cars, computers, or clothes.[9] Involvement may also involve a pastime or activity. For example, a growing number of U.S. consumers are showing high involvement in soccer, an international sport that was once barely noticed in this country.[10]

Involvement with Brands Consumers can also exhibit cognitive and/or affective involvement with a brand, a phenomenon called *brand loyalty*. As you will see in later chapters, brand-loyal consumers consistently purchase the brand, hold strong beliefs about its quality, are devoted to it, and often resist competitors' efforts to attract them. Some product collections represent brands toward which people are loyal. Until recently, kids in the United States and Japan were crazy about buying, collecting, and trading Pokemon cards.

EXHIBIT 3.3
Creating Involvement in the Ad
Marketers might use a variety of tactics—like the sex appeal used in this ad—to stimulate consumers' involvement in an ad.

Source: Courtesy of Unilever Bestfoods North America.

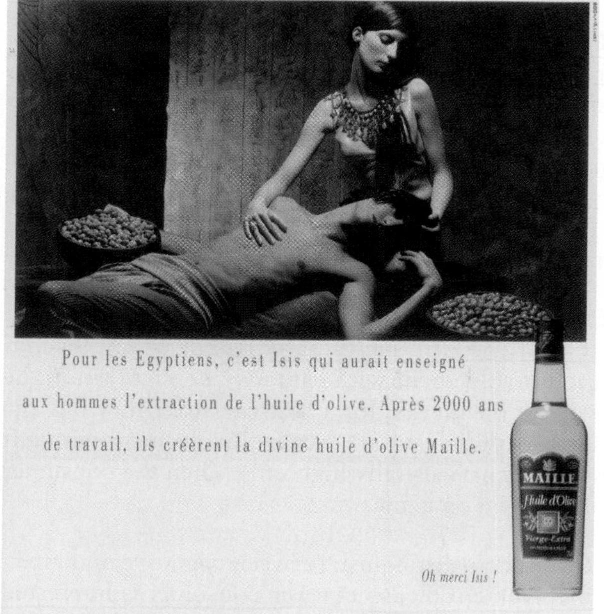

Pour les Egyptiens, c'est Isis qui aurait enseigné
aux hommes l'extraction de l'huile d'olive. Après 2000 ans
de travail, ils créèrent la divine huile d'olive Maille.
Oh merci Isis !
MAILLE

Involvement with Ads Involvement with ads may be revealed by consumers' motivation to attend to and process information contained in the ad. Typically, involvement in an ad is high if consumers view the advertised message as relevant to them.[11] Consumers can become involved in an ad simply because they find it interesting. Ads for shaving cream that present sports questions and ask readers to "make the call" usually elicit involvement among sports fans. In Japan, ads that emphasize interpersonal relationships, social circumstances, and nonverbal expressions generate more involvement than ads with clearly articulated and spoken messages.[12] Advertisers use many techniques to increase consumers' involvement in an ad and hence increase their motivation to process the ad's contents. To illustrate, the ad in Exhibit 3.3 may be involving for many consumers because of its focus on sexuality. We consider other methods for stimulating involvement in ads and motivation to process them later in the chapter.

Involvement with a Medium At times, consumers get involved with the medium in which an ad is placed. Television, for example, is a relatively low-involvement medium because viewers are typically passive and do not have to think much to process what they see. Print media such as magazines and newspapers, on the other hand, usually generate higher levels of involvement because the reader must interact with these media.

Consumers can also be involved in a specific television or radio program or a particular magazine or newspaper.[13] When companies advertise their brands on television shows in which consumers become involved, the ads tend to be more effective.[14] On the other hand, research has found that higher levels of involvement with a TV show can sometimes lower consumers' ad involvement, because an interesting program can be distracting and suspend processing of an ad.

response involvement Interest in certain decisions and behaviors.

Involvement with Decisions and Behaviors Finally, consumers experience **response involvement** when they are involved in certain decisions and behaviors.[15] For example, consumers may be highly involved in the process of deciding between brands. Someone who loves shopping may do a lot of browsing and not buy anything. Consumers can also find the act of using certain products or services involving. Many people enjoy reading books, watching movies, playing video games, or attending sporting events because these activities are highly involving.

Specifying the Object of Involvement Consumers can be involved with many different entities, so it is important to specify the *object of involvement* when using the term "involvement." For instance, brand-loyal consumers are highly involved in the brand, but because they believe their brand is the best, they are unlikely to be involved in making a decision about which brand to buy. Likewise, consumers can be very involved in an ad because it is funny, interesting, or novel—yet they may show little involvement in the advertised brand because they are loyal to other brands.

WHAT AFFECTS MOTIVATION?

Motivation is influenced by the extent to which the ad, brand, product category, or other characteristic is personally relevant to consumers. Consumers see something as personally relevant and important when it is (1) consistent with their values, goals, and needs; (2) risky; and/or (3) moderately inconsistent with their prior attitudes.

Personal Relevance

personal relevance Something that has a direct bearing on the self and has potentially significant consequences or implications for our lives.

A key factor affecting motivation is the extent to which something is **personally relevant**—that is, the extent to which it has a direct bearing on and significant consequences or implications for your life.[16] For example, if you learn that your car model is being recalled because its gas tank explodes on impact, chances are you will find this issue to be personally relevant. It has a direct bearing on you, and its consequences are very important. Careers, college activities, romantic relationships, a car, apartment or house, clothes, and hobbies are likely to be personally relevant because their consequences are significant for you.

self-concept Our view of who we are and the way we think others view us.

In addition, something may be personally relevant to the extent that it bears on our **self-concept**, or our view of ourselves, and the way we think others view us. Our self-concept helps us define who we are, and it frequently guides our behavior. When we buy clothing, we are often making a statement about who we are—a professional, a student, or a member of a sports team. Some consumers find brands like the Volkswagen Beetle and Harley-Davidson to be

#1
BECAUSE
IT WORKS.
#1
Dermatologist
recommended.*
#1
Wrinkle-fighter
Retinol.
Neutrogena
HEALTHY
SKIN
ANTI-WRINKLE
CREAM
SPF 15
A Retinol
Facial Treatment with
Multi-Vitamins
#1
Selling
anti-wrinkle
cream.*
EDITORS' & READERS' CHOICE
allure
AWARDS
www.neutrogena.com
Neutrogena
DERMATOLOGIST RECOMMENDED

EXHIBIT 3.4

Appealing to Personal Relevance

Marketers can enhance consumers' motivation to process their message by making sure it is personally relevant to them. Older women may be motivated to process this message because it focuses on the types of skin problems that increase with aging.

Source: Neutrogena Corporation.

relevant to their self-concept. Thus owning these branded products is important to their self-definition and, of course, is personally relevant.

We will be motivated to behave, process informa tion, or engage in effortful *decision making* about things that we feel are personally relevant. And we will experience considerable involvement when buying, using, or disposing of them. Think about all the behaviors you engaged in when deciding where to go to college—obtaining applications and information packets, searching the Internet, talking with friends, calling alumni, and so on. You probably devoted considerable time and effort to processing the information about each school and deciding where to go. Chances are, you found the task of making this decision personally involving. You may even have found that it preoccupied you and that reading material about various schools generated interest, enthusiasm, and perhaps a bit of anxiety.

MARKETING IMPLICATIONS Marketers can enhance consumers' motivation to process promotional materials by trying to make the information as personally relevant as possible. Salespeople can explore consumers' underlying reasons for a purchase and tailor sales pitches to those reasons.

Similarly, ads can be geared toward consumers' special concerns. Consumers seeking positive outcomes such as advancement or achievement will find an ad more personally relevant if it appeals to those outcomes. In contrast, consumers seeking to avoid negative outcomes such as gaining weight, developing cavities, and getting AIDS will find an ad more personally relevant when it tells them how the good or service can avoid those negative outcomes.[17] Volvo once ran a campaign designed to make Volvo seem more personally relevant to consumers by appealing to the avoidance of a very negative outcome. The campaign, called This Car Saved My Life, showed real-life accident victims who had been saved from serious injury by riding in a Volvo.

Exhibit 3.4 is a good example of an issue that some women might find personally relevant and that might generate motivation and its effects. Older women are likely to be motivated to attend to and process the information in this ad because they are concerned about preventing wrinkles. ●

Values, Goals, and Needs

People perceive something as personally relevant when it is consistent with their values, goals, and needs. In turn, this relevance fuels their motivation to process information, make decisions, and take actions.

values Enduring beliefs that a given behavior or outcome is desirable or good.

Values Consumers are more motivated to attend to and process information when they find it relevant to their **values**, beliefs that guide what people regard as important or good. Thus, if you see education as extremely important, you are likely to be motivated to engage in behaviors that are consistent with this value, such as pursuing a degree. We will discuss values in greater depth in Chapter 17.

goals Objectives that we would like to achieve.

Goals A second factor affecting personal relevance and motivation is goals.[18] A **goal** is a particular end state or outcome that a person would like to achieve. You might have goals about saving money, getting a good job after graduation, and meeting an attractive member of the opposite sex at Friday's party. Some goals are specific to a given behavior or action and determined by the situation at hand. If you are tired, one of your goals for the evening might be to go to bed early. If you have repeatedly been late for class, one of your goals might be to arrive at class on time. Other goals may be much more abstract and endure over a long period, such as being a good student, being cool, or looking beautiful.[19]

Whether they are situational and concrete or enduring and abstract, we are likely to be very motivated to engage in behaviors that are relevant to achieving our personal goals. As shown in Exhibit 3.5, goal-attainment activities follow a certain pattern. After we set a goal (such as to lose five pounds this month), we are motivated to form a goal intention, plan to take action (identify low-calorie foods and exercises to burn fat), implement and control the action (through diet and exercise), and evaluate success or failure in attaining the goal (by weighing ourselves at the end of the month). Finally, we use what we learned by achieving or not achieving the goal as feedback for future goal setting.[20] Thus, setting and pursuing goals becomes a highly motivating, relevant factor driving behavior.

need An internal state of tension caused by disequilibrium from an ideal/desired physical or psychological state.

Needs A third and very powerful factor affecting personal relevance and motivation is needs. A **need** is an internal state of tension caused by disequilibrium

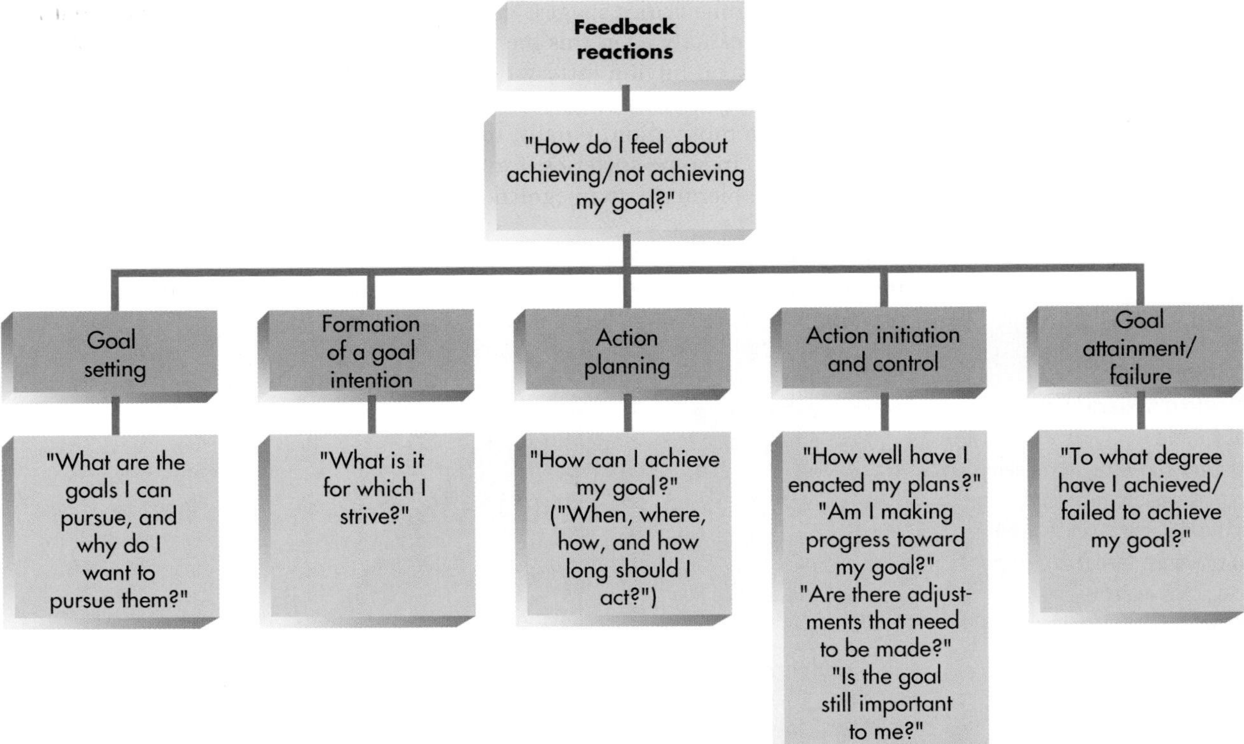

EXHIBIT 3.5 Goal Setting and Pursuit in Consumer Behavior

The process of setting and pursuing goals is circular: how a person feels about achieving or not achieving a goal affects what new goals that person sets and why. This process affects the individual's motivation to initiate or continue behaviors relevant to the goal that has been set.

Source: Richard P. Bagozzi and Utpal Dholakia, "Goal Setting and Goal Striving in Consumer Behavior," *Journal of Marketing*, vol. 63, 1999, p. 20. Used with the permission of the American Marketing Association.

from an ideal or desired state. As this definition indicates, each need has an equilibrium level at which it is in a state of satisfaction. The individual feels tension when there is any departure from this equilibrium and is motivated to find some way of fulfilling the need. For example, at certain times of the day, your stomach begins to feel uncomfortable and you realize it is time to get something to eat. You are motivated to direct your behavior toward certain outcomes (e.g., going to the refrigerator, going to a certain restaurant, ordering take-out food). Eating satisfies your need and removes the tension—in this case, hunger.

Just as needs can lead us toward a product or service, they can also keep us away. For example, have you ever put off going to the dentist? If so, you were probably motivated by a need to avoid pain.

A variety of needs can operate in a given situation. But what needs do consumers experience? One well-known theory of needs is based on the research of psychologist Abraham Maslow.[21] Maslow grouped needs into the five categories shown in Exhibit 3.6: (1) physiological (the need for food, water, and sleep), (2) safety (the need for shelter, protection, and security), (3) social (the need for affection, friendship, and acceptance), (4) egoistic (the need for prestige, success, accomplishment, and self-esteem), and (5) self-actualization (the need for self-fulfillment and enriching experiences). These categorized needs are arranged in a hierarchy in which lower-level needs must be satisfied before higher-level needs become activated. Thus before we can worry about prestige and success, we must meet our lower-level needs for food, water, and shelter.

Although Maslow's hierarchy brings useful organization to the complex issue of needs, some critics suggest it is too simplistic. Specifically, needs are not always ordered exactly as in this hierarchy. For example, some consumers place a higher priority on buying lottery tickets than on acquiring necessities such as food and clothing. The hierarchy also ignores the intensity of needs and the resulting effect on motivation. Finally, the ordering of needs may not be consistent across cultures. In some societies, for example, social needs and belonging may be higher in the hierarchy than egoistic needs.

Types of Needs Another way to categorize needs is as (1) social and nonsocial needs or (2) functional, symbolic, and hedonic needs[22] (see Exhibit 3.7).

EXHIBIT 3.6
Maslow's Hierarchy of Needs
Maslow suggested that needs can be categorized into a basic hierarchy. People fulfill lower-order needs (e.g., physiological needs for food, water, sleep) before they fulfill higher-order needs.

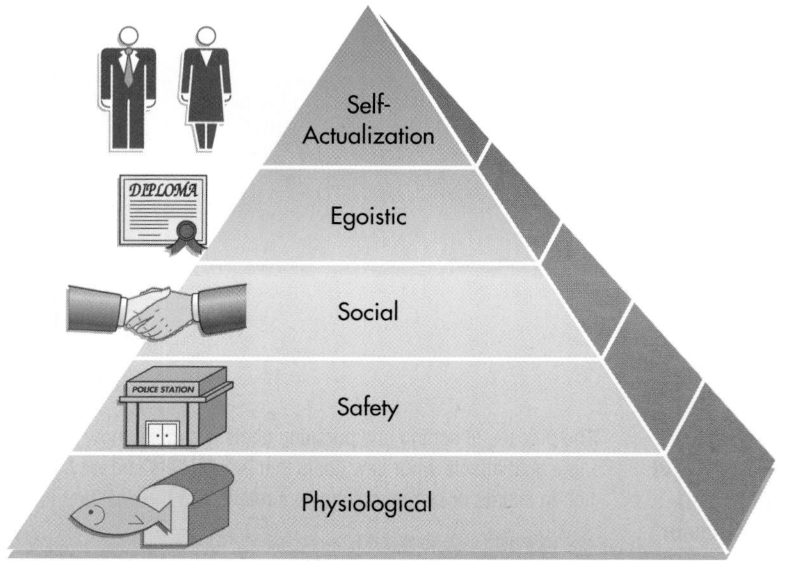

EXHIBIT 3.7
Types of Needs
Needs can be categorized according to whether they are (1) social or nonsocial and (2) functional, symbolic, or hedonic in nature. This categorization method helps marketers think about consumers' needs.

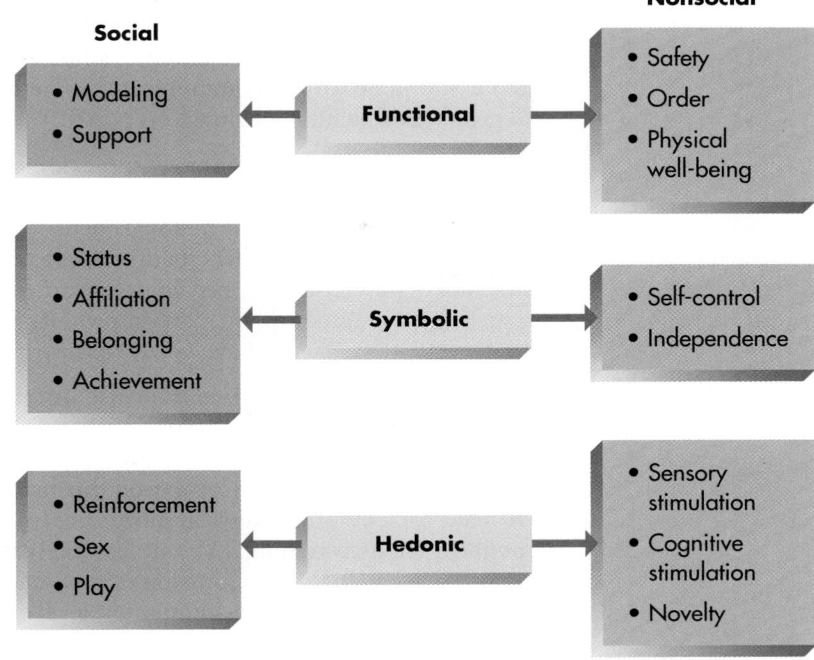

- *Social needs* are externally directed and relate to other individuals. Fulfilling these needs thus requires the presence or actions of other people. For example, the need for status drives our desire to have others hold us in high regard. In our need for support, we want others to relieve us of our burdens; and the need for modeling reflects a wish to have others show us how to behave. We may be motivated to buy products and use services like Hallmark cards and AT&T long-distance dialing because they help us achieve our need for affiliation. Other products may be valued because they are consistent with our need for status or to be unique.[23] We also have antisocial needs—needs for space and psychological distance from other people. Plane seats that are too close together violate our need for space and motivate us to escape the confining environment.
- *Nonsocial needs* are those for which achievement is not based on other people. Our needs for sleep, novelty, control, uniqueness, and understanding, which involve only ourselves, can affect the usage of certain products and services. We might purchase the same brand repeatedly to maintain consistency in our world—or we might buy something totally different to fulfill a need for variety.

functional needs Needs that motivate the search for products to solve consumption-related problems.

symbolic needs Needs that relate to how we perceive ourselves, how we are perceived by others, how we relate to others, and the esteem in which we are held by others.

- *Functional needs* may be social or nonsocial. **Functional needs** motivate the search for products that solve consumption-related problems. For example, you might consider buying a product like a Volvo wagon with side airbags because it appeals to your safety needs (a functional, nonsocial need). Hiring a nanny would solve the need for support (a functional, social need).
- *Symbolic needs* affect how we perceive ourselves and how we are perceived by others. Achievement, independence, and self-control are **symbolic needs** because they are connected with our sense of self. Similarly, our need for uniqueness is symbolic because it drives consumption decisions about how we

express our identity.[24] The need to avoid rejection and the need for achievement, status, affiliation, and belonging are symbolic because they reflect our social position or role. For example, some consumers wear Abercrombie & Fitch clothing because it communicates something about their age and the social group to which they belong.

- *Hedonic needs* include needs for sensory stimulation, cognitive stimulation, and novelty (nonsocial hedonic needs) and needs for reinforcement, sex, and play (social hedonic needs). These **hedonic needs** reflect our inherent desires for sensory pleasure. Some consumers fly first class to enjoy gourmet meals and plusher seats; others purchase CDs, perfume, and art for the sensory pleasures they can bring.[25] For the same reason, certain products (e.g., food products made with fake fat or without sugar) have failed because they have not met hedonic needs.

hedonic needs Needs that relate to sensory pleasure.

- *Needs for cognition and stimulation* also affect motivation and behavior. Consumers with a high need for cognition[26] (a need for mental stimulation) tend to be highly involved in mentally taxing activities like reading and are more likely to actively process information during decision making. People with a low need for cognition may be more involved in activities that require less thought, such as watching TV, and less likely to actively process information during decision making. Consumers also need other kinds of stimulation. Those with a high optimum stimulation level enjoy high levels of sensory stimulation and tend to be involved in shopping and seeking brand information.[27] They also show heightened involvement in ads. Consumers with thrill-seeking tendencies enjoy activities like skydiving, bungee jumping, mountaineering, and whitewater rafting. In contrast, consumers who feel overstimulated want to get away from people, noise, and demands—a desire revealed in the increasing popularity of vacations at monasteries or other such sanctuaries.[28]

Characteristics of Needs Each of the needs described above has several characteristics:

- *Needs are dynamic.* Needs are never fully satisfied; satisfaction is only temporary. Clearly, eating once will not satisfy our hunger forever. Also, as soon as one need is satisfied, new needs emerge. After we have eaten a meal, we might next have the need to be with others (the need for affiliation) or the need to study (a need for achievement). Thus, needs are dynamic, because daily life is a constant process of need fulfillment.
- *Needs exist in a hierarchy.* Although several needs may be activated at any one time, some assume more importance. You may experience a need to eat during an exam, but your need for achievement may assume a higher priority—so you stay to finish the test. Despite this hierarchy, many needs may be activated simultaneously and influence your acquisition, usage, and disposition behaviors. Thus your decision to go out for dinner with friends may be driven by a combination of needs for stimulation, food, and companionship.
- *Needs can be internally or externally aroused.* Although many needs are internally activated, some needs can be externally cued. Smelling pizza cooking in the apartment next door may, for example, affect your perceived need for food.
- *Needs can conflict.* A given behavior or outcome can be seen as both desirable and undesirable if it satisfies some needs but fails to satisfy others. The result is called an **approach-avoidance conflict** because we both want to engage in the behavior and want to avoid it. Teenagers may experience an approach-avoidance conflict in deciding whether to smoke cigarettes. They may believe that

approach-avoidance conflict A conflict that occurs when a given behavior or outcome is seen as both desirable and undesirable because it satisfies some needs but fails to satisfy others.

others will think they are cool for smoking (consistent with need for belonging). However, they may also know that smoking is bad for them (incompatible with need for safety).

approach-approach conflict A conflict that occurs when a consumer must choose between two or more equally desirable options that fulfill different needs.

An **approach-approach conflict** occurs when someone must choose between two or more equally desirable options that fulfill different needs. A consumer who is invited to a career-night function (consistent with achievement needs) might experience an approach-approach conflict if he is also invited to attend a basketball game with friends (consistent with affiliation needs) on the same evening. This consumer will experience conflict if he views both options as equally desirable.

avoidance-avoidance conflict A conflict that occurs when the consumer must choose between two equally undesirable options.

An **avoidance-avoidance conflict** occurs when the consumer must choose between two equally undesirable options, such as going home alone after a late meeting (need for safety) or waiting another hour until a friend can drive her home (need for affiliation). Conflict arises because neither option is desirable.

Identifying Needs Because needs influence motivation and its effects, marketers are keenly interested in identifying and measuring them. Yet consumers are often unaware of their needs and have trouble explaining them to researchers. Inferring consumers' needs based only on behaviors is also difficult because a given need might not be linked to a specific behavior. In other words, the same need (affiliation) can be exhibited in various and diverse behaviors (visiting friends, going to the gym), and the same behavior (going to the gym) can reflect various needs (affiliation, achievement). Consider the activity of shopping. One study found that when women shop in drug stores, they are seeking information about items that provide peace of mind (satisfying needs for safety and well-being). When they shop in club stores, they are seeking adventure and entertainment (satisfying the need for stimulation).[29]

Inferring needs in a cross-cultural context is particularly difficult. For example, some research indicates that U.S. consumers use toothpaste primarily for its cavity-reducing capabilities (a functional need). In contrast, consumers in England and some French-speaking areas of Canada use toothpaste primarily to freshen breath (a hedonic need). French women drink mineral water so they will look better (a symbolic need), whereas German consumers drink it for its health powers (a functional need).[30]

Given these difficulties, marketers sometimes use indirect techniques to uncover consumers' needs.[31] Essentially, these techniques ask consumers to interpret a set of relatively ambiguous stimuli such as cartoons, word associations, incomplete sentences, and incomplete stories. For example, using Exhibit 3.8, one consumer might reveal needs for esteem by interpreting the man in the cartoon as thinking, "My friends will think I'm really cool for riding in this car!" Another might reveal needs for affiliation by filling in the cartoon with, "I could take all my friends for rides with me." Still another might reveal needs for novelty by saying, "This car will be so different and so much more exciting than the one I have now."

When one study asked cigarette smokers why they smoked, most said they enjoyed it and believed that smoking in moderation was fine. However, when they were given incomplete sentences like "People who never smoke are _______," respondents filled in the blanks with words like *happier* and *wiser*. And when given sentences like "Teenagers who smoke are _______," respondents answered with words like *crazy* and *foolish*. These smokers were clearly more concerned about smoking than their explicit answers indicated.[32]

Researchers can also use projective techniques to identify consumers' images of brands and their users. In one study, consumers were given two nearly identical shopping lists; the only difference was that one list contained the name

EXHIBIT 3.8
Projective Techniques
Marketers sometimes uncover needs using ambiguous stimuli like cartoon drawings, sentence completion tasks, and tell-a-story tasks. The idea is that consumers will project their needs, wishes, and fantasies onto these ambiguous stimuli.

Source: B and C adapted from Mary Ann McGrath, John F. Sherry Jr., and Sidney J. Levy, "Giving Voice to the Gift: The Use of Projective Techniques to Recover Lost Meanings," *Journal of Consumer Psychology*, vol. 2, 1993, pp. 171–191.

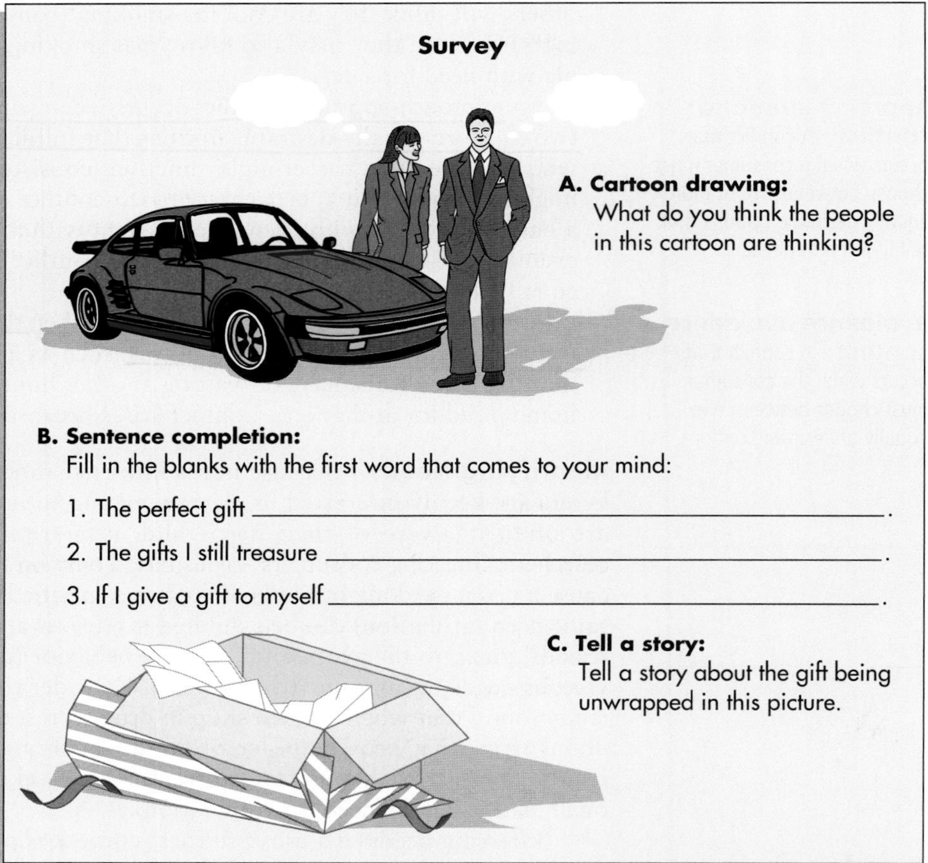
Survey
A. Cartoon drawing:
What do you think the people in this cartoon are thinking?
B. Sentence completion:
Fill in the blanks with the first word that comes to your mind:
1. The perfect gift ______.
2. The gifts I still treasure ______.
3. If I give a gift to myself ______.
C. Tell a story:
Tell a story about the gift being unwrapped in this picture.

of deodorant brand A and the other contained the name of deodorant brand B. Respondents described the shopper whose list contained brand A as less clean, less intelligent, and less popular than the shopper whose list contained brand B.[33]

MARKETING IMPLICATIONS

Consumers' needs, values, and goals have some important implications for marketers.

Segmenting markets based on needs. First, marketers can use needs to segment markets. Diet and caffeine-free soft drinks were developed by marketers who recognized the needs of different consumer segments. Financial services companies often segment markets based on consumers' needs and then develop specific products relevant to each segment (e.g., consumers interested in buying securities over the Internet versus those preferring more traditional methods).[34]

Creating new needs. Sometimes marketers attempt to create new needs. For example, eyeing the popularity of sports trading cards, companies introduced other types of trading cards (featuring soap opera stars, Pokemon characters, and others) to create a need for a new type of entertainment. As another example, many marketers are creating a need for online privacy. American Express, for example, offers its customers the option of paying for purchases on the Web without revealing their card numbers to merchants. Earthlink, an Internet service provider, is differentiating itself from America Online and other competitors by promoting itself as a privacy protector.[35]

Developing need-satisfying offerings. Marketers can also identify currently unfulfilled needs or develop better need-satisfying alternatives. Indeed, this type of research is often essential to the development of new products, as discussed in Chapter 19. Consider the following examples:

- Sales of alternative newspapers have been on the rise, particularly among twentysomethings, fulfilling needs for information delivered in a hip and irreverent format.
- Research indicating that kids are often bored (and hence need stimulation) has prompted publishers such as Houghton Mifflin Co. to use more photo essays, full-color covers, how-to projects, and fun facts in their school and college textbooks.[36]
- Sales of products like gates, fences, walls, security systems, video-surveillance cameras, guard dogs, and car alarms have all benefited from consumers' needs for safety coupled with their perception that the outside environment is unsafe.

The importance of developing need-satisfying offerings clearly operates cross-culturally as well. Over the years McDonald's has successfully satisfied international consumers' desires for fast food by altering its offering according to cultural differences. In Germany, the McRib sandwich is one of the top sellers because Germans eat a lot of pork. McDonald's also offers beer in Germany and wine in France.[37] In Japan, Tokyo Disneyland has so successfully fulfilled a strong desire for American-style entertainment that Disney recently opened a second theme park, DisneySea, right next door.[38]

Managing conflict. Companies can develop new products or use communications to resolve need conflicts. For instance, the marketers of Propecia, a prescription tablet for treating male baldness, must promote the drug's benefits while countering the perception that it will reduce sexual desire (which it can).[39]

Appealing to multiple goals and needs. Marketers may want to create bundled offerings that allow consumers to achieve more than one goal or satisfy more than one need during a single consumption episode.[40] For instance, a pizza restaurant might offer healthy fruit juices or smoothies (so consumers can achieve their goals of losing weight or eating better) as well as a wide variety of specialty pizzas (so consumers can satisfy hedonic needs or cravings for variety).

Enhancing communication effectiveness. By suggesting that the product or service fulfills a need, value, or goal, marketers can increase the likelihood that consumers will process the message (ad, sales message, etc.) and engage in desired behaviors. The makers of Head and Shoulders shampoo, for example, recognize that consumers have a strong need to be accepted by others. The manufacturer effectively appeals to this need by suggesting that having dandruff will lead to social rejection. Thus needs are an effective way of positioning a product or service.[41]

Companies should also develop marketing communications that portray the offerings as relevant to consumers' needs, values, and goals. The ad in Exhibit 3.9 is designed to appeal to both functional and hedonic needs. ●

EXHIBIT 3.9

Appealing to Functional and Hedonic Needs

Consumers are more motivated to engage in a behavior (e.g., process information in an ad) when the stimulus (e.g., the ad) is relevant to their needs, values, and goals. This ad for Carb Solutions is designed to appeal to consumers' functional and hedonic needs.

Source: Courtesy of Carb Solutions™.

Perceived Risk

perceived risk The extent to which the consumer is uncertain about the consequences of an action (e.g., buying, using, and disposing of an offering).

Perceived risk is another factor affecting personal relevance and motivation.[42] **Perceived risk** reflects the extent to which the consumer is uncertain about the consequences of buying, using, or disposing of an offering. If negative outcomes are likely or positive outcomes are unlikely, perceived risk is high. Consumers are more likely to pay attention to and carefully process marketing communications when perceived risk is high. In addition, as perceived risk increases, consumers tend to collect more information and evaluate it carefully.

Perceived risk can be associated with any product or service, but it tends to be higher when:

- little information is available about the offering.
- the offering is new.
- the offering has a high price.
- the offering is technologically complex.
- there are fairly substantial quality differences between brands, so the consumer might make an inferior choice.
- the consumer has little confidence or experience in evaluating the offering.
- the opinions of others are important, and the consumer is likely to be judged by the acquisition, usage, or disposition decision.[43]

Perceptions of risk vary across cultural groups. In particular, high levels of risk tend to be associated with many more products in less-developed countries, perhaps because the products in these countries are generally of poorer quality.[44] Also, perceived risk is typically higher when travelers purchase goods in a foreign country.[45] In addition, risk perceptions vary within a culture.[46] For example, Western men take more risks in stock market investments than women take, and younger consumers take more risks than older ones take.

Types of Perceived Risk Researchers have identified six types of risk:[47]

performance risk Uncertainty about whether an offering will perform as expected.

financial risk Risk associated with monetary investment in an offering.

physical (or safety) risk The potential harm that an offering might pose to one's safety.

- **Performance risk** reflects uncertainty about whether the product or service will perform as expected. If a car buyer is uncertain whether a new or used vehicle will be reliable, perceived performance risk is high. General Motors reassures buyers who are concerned about this risk by advertising that its certification program screens out severely damaged or heavily repaired cars.[48]
- **Financial risk** is higher if a product or service is expensive. For instance, a home is an expensive purchase, and the level of risk associated with this kind of monetary investment is high.
- **Physical (or safety) risk** refers to the potential harm a product or service might pose to one's safety. Many consumer decisions are driven by a motivation to avoid physical risk. For example, some consumers in markets underserved by a traditional police force have taken to hiring private security guards to ward off break-ins, shootings, and drug dealing.[49] Parents who worry that their Web-surfing children may inadvertently put themselves at risk by giving out personal information can control online activities using special software. Research shows that the way consumers behave toward health and safety risks varies from area to area; for example, consumers in Hawaii take considerable health and safety precautions. Exhibit 3.10 summarizes how various states stand on these risk-avoiding tendencies.[50]

	HAVE FAIR/POOR HEALTH	CURRENT SMOKER	DONT ALWAYS USE SEATBELT	BINGE DRINKING PAST MONTH	EVER DRINK AND DRIVE	OVERWEIGHT MEASURED BY BMI*	NO PHYSICAL LEISURE ACTIVITY PAST MONTH	DON'T GET 5 FRUITS/ VEGGIES DAILY
Alabama	18.3%	24.5%	16.3%	13.6%	2.6%	31.8%	45.8%	75.0%
Alaska	8.2	25.0	17.9	19.2	1.3	31.4	22.8	81.2
Arizona	13.4	22.9	12.7	13.5	2.7	24.5	33.5	75.7
Arkansas	18.6	25.2	17.5	8.8	1.5	30.1	35.1	74.7
California	14.3	15.5	5.5	15.3	1.9	26.4	22.7	71.0
Colorado	10.7	21.8	17.5	16.3	3.1	21.9	17.2	78.4
Connecticut	10.9	20.8	17.9	14.4	2.5	24.7	21.9	66.5
Delaware	13.4	25.5	17.7	8.6	1.4	29.5	36.4	83.3
Florida	14.3	23.1	12.1	13.1	2.6	29.8	27.9	74.6
Georgia	12.3	20.5	17.2	12.0	2.2	28.2	32.9	73.6
Hawaii	11.6	17.8	4.5	12.4	2.1	21.8	20.7	80.3
Idaho	11.2	19.8	19.6	12.9	2.0	27.2	21.8	78.3
Illinois	14.0	23.1	18.8	13.6	1.8	30.1	32.4	77.8
Indiana	14.7	27.2	24.2	12.8	2.6	34.7	29.6	80.3
Iowa	11.3	23.2	16.2	18.0	3.3	31.6	33.3	82.1
Kansas	12.2	22.0	24.5	13.9	3.2	27.8	28.2	79.1
Kentucky	21.1	27.8	17.6	9.7	0.6	28.8	45.9	82.7
Louisiana	17.2	25.2	18.9	14.0	2.8	30.7	33.4	80.7
Maine	12.9	25.0	37.8	11.5	0.9	26.9	40.7	79.0
Maryland	10.4	21.2	11.4	8.2	1.1	29.1	30.2	79.6
Massachusetts	12.3	21.7	25.8	17.8	3.5	21.9	24.0	69.7
Michigan	14.7	25.7	13.5	18.3	3.3	31.6	23.0	69.4
Minnesota	9.7	20.5	19.4	18.0	4.9	28.4	21.7	80.5
Mississippi	21.4	24.0	25.4	8.7	1.1	31.6	38.4	86.1
Missouri	12.7	24.3	18.9	14.1	2.1	32.9	31.8	79.0
Montana	11.3	21.1	22.6	14.3	3.4	24.9	21.0	78.8
Nebraska	10.6	21.9	24.6	15.8	2.8	29.2	24.2	80.2
Nevada	14.1	26.3	14.7	19.0	3.7	26.9	21.6	79.1
New Hampshire	10.2	21.5	32.5	16.6	1.6	25.9	25.6	73.1
New Jersey	10.9	19.2	20.3	14.0	2.0	24.4	30.2	70.3
New Mexico	17.2	21.2	6.7	14.1	3.3	23.8	19.4	76.7
New York	11.6	21.5	15.1	12.4	0.9	27.8	37.1	80.1
North Carolina	18.6	25.8	5.7	5.8	1.1	28.9	42.8	81.1
North Dakota	13.5	22.7	33.0	17.0	4.2	30.7	32.0	82.3
Ohio	14.2	26.0	18.4	9.9	1.6	31.5	38.0	78.4
Oklahoma	13.1	21.7	22.6	6.7	1.2	24.1	40.6	81.6
Oregon	11.3	21.8	5.6	13.9	1.8	28.8	20.8	78.8
Pennsylvania	13.2	24.2	21.1	19.4	3.6	30.1	26.3	75.3
Rhode Island	14.2	24.7	33.6	18.7	3.7	24.9	–	–
South Carolina	15.5	23.7	11.7	9.2	1.4	28.7	36.1	75.9
South Dakota	12.7	21.8	29.3	14.4	5.2	28.7	38.2	79.1
Tennessee	17.7	26.5	21.4	5.2	1.0	31.0	39.7	74.3

(continued)

*BMI means Body Mass Index.

EXHIBIT 3.10 How Risky Are People in Your State?

In some states, more consumers engage in risky behaviors like not using a seat belt or drinking and driving. What accounts for these differences between states?

Source: Reprinted from *American Demographics,* August 1997, Copyright 1997. Courtesy of Intertec Publishing Corp., Stamford, Connecticut.

	HAVE FAIR/POOR HEALTH	CURRENT SMOKER	DONT ALWAYS USE SEATBELT	BINGE DRINKING PAST MONTH	EVER DRINK AND DRIVE	OVERWEIGHT MEASURED BY BMI*	NO PHYSICAL LEISURE ACTIVITY PAST MONTH	DON'T GET 5 FRUITS/ VEGGIES DAILY
Texas	17.2%	23.7%	10.4%	15.3%	3.7%	28.6%	27.8%	76.9%
Utah	11.8	13.2	17.7	9.9	1.2	25.0	20.9	77.9
Vermont	11.5	22.1	13.3	16.0	2.4	25.4	23.2	71.7
Virginia	11.5	22.0	13.2	14.5	2.5	29.2	27.0	70.2
Washington	10.8	20.2	9.1	13.4	2.1	25.4	18.2	78.6
West Virginia	22.6	25.7	14.8	5.9	0.9	31.9	45.3	77.3
Wisconsin	10.1	21.8	21.2	22.9	4.5	30.2	25.9	78.8
Wyoming	11.0	22.0	23.7	15.6	3.2	27.3	23.6	76.5
U.S. average	13.9%	22.2%	15.3%	13.7%	2.3%	28.5%	29.8%	76.1%

social risk Potential harm to one's social standing that may arise from buying, using, or disposing of an offering.

psychological risk Risk associated with the extent to which an offering fits with the way consumers perceive themselves.

time risk Uncertainties over the length of time consumers must invest in buying, using, or disposing of an offering.

- **Social risk** is the potential harm to one's social standing that may arise from buying, using, or disposing of an offering. For example, although you may secretly adore the Backstreet Boys, you may know that others in your group do not. Therefore, going to a Backstreet Boys concert entails social risk, because your friends might tease you if they learn that you went to one.
- **Psychological risk** reflects consumers' concern about the extent to which a product or service fits with the way they perceive themselves. For example, if you see yourself as an environmentalist, buying disposable diapers may be psychologically risky.
- **Time risk** reflects uncer-tainties over the length of time that must be invested in buying, using, or disposing of the product or service. Time risk may be high if the offering involves considerable time commitment, if learning to use it is a lengthy process, or if it entails a long commitment period (such as a health club that requires a 3-year contract).

Risk and Involvement As noted earlier, products can be described as either high- or low-involvement products. Some researchers have classified high- versus low-involvement products in terms of the amount of risk they pose to consumers. Consumers are likely to be more involved in purchasing products such as homes and computers than in purchasing picture frames or coffee because the former generate higher levels of performance, financial, safety, social, psychological, or time risk and can therefore have more extreme personal consequences.

In general, consumers find high risk uncomfortable. As a result, they are usually motivated to engage in any number of behaviors and information-processing activities to reduce or resolve risk. To reduce the uncertainty component of risk, consumers can collect additional information by conducting online research, reading news articles, engaging in comparative shopping, talking to friends or sales specialists, or consulting an expert. Consumers also reduce uncertainty by being brand loyal (buying the same brand as last time), ensuring that the product should be at least as satisfactory as the last purchase.

In addition, consumers attempt to reduce the consequence component of perceived risk through various strategies. Some consumers may employ a simple decision rule that results in a safer choice. For example, someone might buy the most expensive offering or choose a heavily advertised brand in the belief that this brand is of higher quality than other brands.

If You Can't See Why 100% Acrylic Paint Is Important, Maybe in A Few Years You Will.
BEHR
Premium Plus
EXTERIOR
Unlike most paints, Behr Premium Plus Exterior Paint is made with 100% acrylic. Which is why it carries an impressive lifetime warranty against peeling, blistering and fading. Plus, Behr guarantees their paint will hold up even after continued washing and scrubbing. Behr Premium Plus, available at The Home Depot. The premium paint with a Home Depot price.

EXHIBIT 3.11
Enhancing Perceived Risk of Not Using Products
Sometimes marketers develop communications to make consumers see that not using their offerings could be very risky. If consumers see that not using an offering (e.g., a certain brand of paint) is very risky, they may be motivated to use it.

Source: Agency: The Richards Group. Creative Director: Gary Gibson.

MARKETING IMPLICATIONS Perceived risk has a number of marketing implications.

Reducing risk perceptions. When perceived risk is high, marketers can either reduce uncertainty or reduce the perceived consequences of failure. Pharmacia, for instance, markets Rogaine to men and women who want to avoid going bald. By stressing prevention—urging these consumers to start using Rogaine before they see significant hair loss—Pharmacia reduces the perceived risk of going bald in the future.[51]

Enhancing risk perceptions. When risk is low, however, consumers are less motivated to think about the brand and its potential consequences. Marketers sometimes need to enhance risk perceptions to make their promotional appeals more compelling. For example, the ad in Exhibit 3.11 is clearly enhancing the perception of risk for paint buyers who do not buy the Behr brand. As another example, Merck advertises its Varivax chicken pox vaccine by warning that children could require hospitalization or even die due to complications from the disease.[52]

Interestingly, consumers do not always see a particular action as risky, even when it is. As one example, consumers do not think they will have negative outcomes from unprotected sex, which explains why condom sales are not higher and why safe-sex ads are not more effective.[53] To counter this view, condom ads attempt to enhance risk perceptions and position the product as a tool to prevent potentially negative outcomes.[54] Marketers can also enhance consumers' understanding of how their own behavior can create risky negative outcomes. Research shows that when consumers think about the role their own behavior plays in acquiring AIDS, they are more likely to follow the advice in ads designed to reduce that risk.[55] ●

Inconsistency with Attitudes

A final factor affecting motivation is the extent to which new information is consistent with the consumer's previously acquired knowledge or attitudes. We tend to be motivated to process messages that are moderately inconsistent with our existing knowledge or attitudes because they are perceived as moderately threatening or uncomfortable. Therefore, we try to eliminate or at least understand this inconsistency.[56] For example, if a consumer sees a car ad that mentions slightly negative information about the brand she currently owns—such as the brand getting lower gas mileage than a competitor—she will want to process the information so she can understand and perhaps resolve the uncomfortable feeling.

On the other hand, consumers are less motivated to process information that is highly inconsistent with their prior attitudes. Thus someone who is brand loyal to Heinz ketchup would not be motivated to process information from a comparative ad suggesting that Heinz is bad or that other brands are better. The consumer would simply reject the other brands as not being viable options.

CONSUMER ABILITY: RESOURCES TO ACT

Motivation may not result in action unless a consumer has the ability to process information, make decisions, or engage in behaviors. **Ability** is defined as the extent to which consumers have the necessary resources to make the outcome happen.[57] If our ability to process information is high, we may engage in active decision making. As shown in Exhibit 3.2, knowledge, experience, cognitive style,

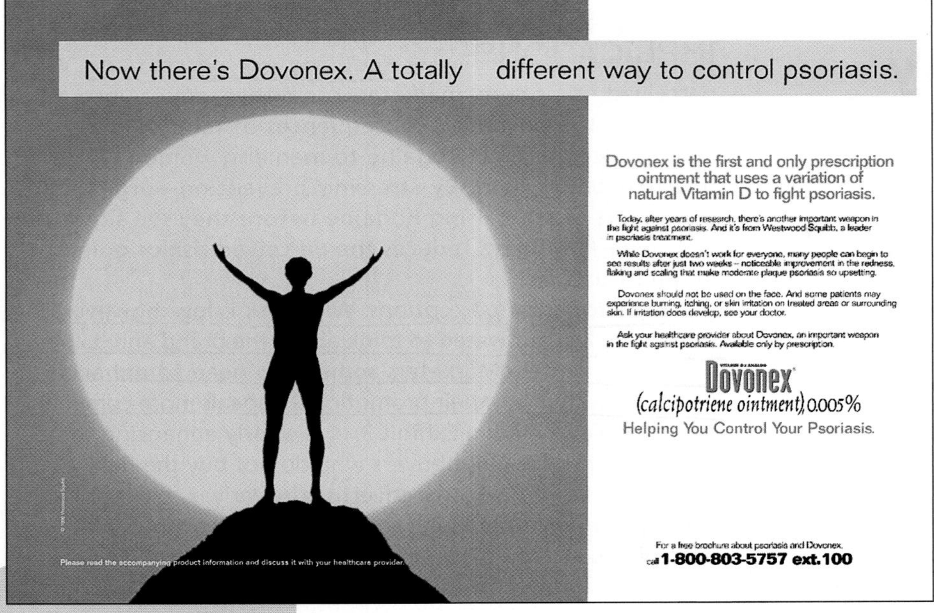

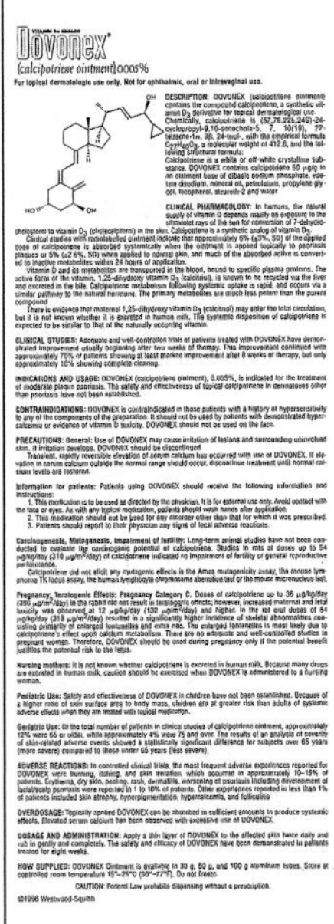
Dovonex
(calcipotriene ointment) 0.005%

EXHIBIT 3.12

Ability to Process Information from Marketing Communications

Consumers may lack sufficient background knowledge or expertise to understand the technical information that the federal government requires drug companies to provide. The technical information to the right of this ad appeared on the reverse side of the original ad.

Source: Copyright Westwood-Squibb Pharmaceuticals. Illustration used with their permission.

intelligence, education, age, and money are factors that affect consumers' abilities to process information about brands and make decisions about buying, usage, and disposition.

Product Knowledge and Experience

Consumers vary greatly in their knowledge about an offering.[58] They can gain knowledge from product or service experiences such as ad exposures, interactions with salespeople, information from friends or the media, previous decision making or product usage, or memory.

A number of studies have compared the information-processing activities of consumers who have a lot of product knowledge or expertise with consumers who do not.[59] One key finding is that knowledgeable consumers, or "experts," are better able to think deeply about information than equally motivated but less knowledgeable consumers, or "novices." These differences in prior knowledge clearly affect how consumers make decisions. For example, consumers trying to lease a car rarely understand the concept of capitalized costs (the figure used to determine lease payments), how these costs are determined, or the need to negotiate lower costs to lower their payments. The inability to understand these costs may result in a less than optimal decision.[60] Consider also cases in which less-knowledgeable consumers try to process the information in a prescription drug ad. The federal government strictly regulates these ads, and the company marketing them must provide detailed information about the product (as shown in Exhibit 3.12.) Although these ads used to contain highly technical information that was difficult for consumers to understand, many companies are trying to make this information more "user friendly" so that consumers can understand it. In this way, the ad content is consistent with consumers' abilities to process it.

ability The extent to which consumers have the resources (knowledge, intelligence, and money) necessary to make an outcome happen.

One study found that novices and experts process similar amounts of information but in different ways.[61] Experts were able to process information when it was stated in terms of its attributes (what the product has—such as a Pentium chip), whereas novices could do so only when the information was stated in terms of its benefits (what the product can do for the consumer—such as enhance

EXHIBIT 3.13
Learning by Analogy
Sometimes when we are unfamiliar with something, we can understand it only in terms of its similarity to something else. In this ad, advertisers are trying to show how a new digital camera is similar to an expert skier.

Source: JVC Company of America.

efficiency). Still, novices may be able to process information when marketers provide a helpful analogy. For example, the product shown in Exhibit 3.13 may be unfamiliar to consumers, who may not be able to relate it to their prior knowledge. However, an analogy between the new product and the expert skier makes the attributes of the product more understandable.[62]

Cognitive Style

Consumers can differ in **cognitive style**, or their preferences for ways information should be presented. Some consumers are adept at processing information visually, whereas others prefer to process information verbally. For example, some consumers prefer to check a map and others prefer to read directions when planning to reach a destination.

One important aspect of cognitive style is **cognitive complexity**.[63] A cognitively complex individual is more likely to engage in complicated processing of information from marketing communications, accepting new and/or contradictory information, making finer distinctions when processing information, and considering a greater diversity of information when making a decision.

cognitive style
Preferences regarding how information is received (e.g., visually or verbally).

cognitive complexity
The extent to which consumers prefer information to be presented in a simple or complex manner.

Intelligence, Education, and Age

Intelligence, education, and age have also been related to the ability to process information. Specifically, consumers who are more intelligent and more educated can better process more complex information and make decisions. Age also accounts for differences in processing ability. Older children seem to be more sensitive to the fact that the benefits of searching for information sometimes outweigh the costs, while younger children don't seem to have this same ability.[64] Old age has been associated with a decline in certain cognitive skills and thus reduced ability to process information. In one study, older consumers took more time to process nutrition information and made decisions that were less accurate compared with younger consumers.[65]

Money

Obviously, the lack of money also constrains consumers who might otherwise have the motivation to engage in a behavior that involves acquisition. Although motivated consumers who lack money can still process information and make buying decisions, they are definitely constrained in their immediate ability to buy from marketers.

MARKETING IMPLICATIONS

Factors affecting ability suggest several implications for marketers.

Understand consumers' knowledge and processing styles. First, marketers should be sure that target consumers have sufficient prior knowledge to process marketing communications. If not, the company may need to develop educational messages as a first step.

Match communications with knowledge and processing styles. Marketers also need to be sensitive to the potentially different processing styles, education levels, and ages of target consumers. For example, highly motivated but visually oriented parents may not be able to assemble toys for their children if the written instructions are too complex and, thus, incompatible with their processing style. Putting instructions in both words and pictures covers both processing styles.

Facilitate ability. Finally, because a lack of money constrains purchase behaviors, marketers can facilitate first-time and repeat buying by providing monetary aid. Car manufacturers have enhanced consumers' purchasing ability—and boosted sales—by offering low- or no-down-payment programs, offering low financing rates, deferring payment for several months, and offering installment payment programs. Marketers can also provide education and information that help consumers better process information, make more informed decisions, and engage in consumption behaviors. For example, many companies set up Web sites to provide product information, explain product features, and show how these features differ from those of competing products.[66] ●

CONSUMER OPPORTUNITY

The final factor affecting whether motivation results in action is consumers' opportunity to engage in a behavior. For example, a consumer may be highly motivated to work out and have sufficient money to join a health club (ability); however, she may be so busy that she has little opportunity to actually go. Thus even when motivation and ability are high, we may not take action because of lack of time, distractions, and other factors that impede our ability to act.

Time

Time can affect the consumer's opportunity to process information, make decisions, and perform certain behaviors. Some studies show that consumers are more likely to buy things for themselves during the Christmas season. The reason is that holiday shopping provides one of the few opportunities time-pressed consumers have to actually go shopping.[67] Time affects leisure-time consumption behavior, as well. Knowing that would-be gardeners have little time (or patience) to plant, weed, and water, companies are successfully marketing seed-embedded mats, low-maintenance plants, and fast-maturing trees.[68]

Consumers under time pressure to make a decision will engage in limited information processing. For example, a consumer who has to buy 30 items in a 15-minute grocery shopping trip will not have time to process a lot of information about each item. According to research, time-pressured consumers not only process less information but also put more weight on negative information; they are quicker to reject brands because of negative features.[69] In an advertising context, consumers have limited opportunity to process information when a message is presented in a short period; when they cannot control the pace of message presentation, as is the case with television and radio ads; or when they zip (fast-forward) through the ads.[70]

Distraction

Distraction refers to any aspect of a situation that diverts consumers' attention. For example, an important exam can divert a consumer's attention from a yoga class she really wants to take. If someone talks while a consumer is viewing an ad or making a decision, that distraction can inhibit the consumer's ability to process the information. Certain background factors in an ad, such as music or attractive models, can also distract consumers from an advertised message.[71] Consumers may be distracted from TV commercials if the program during which the commercials appear is very involving.[72]

EXHIBIT 3.14
Amount of Information and Opportunity
This ad contains so little information, consumers may not have much opportunity to process it.

Source: © David Young-Wolff/ PhotoEdit.

Amount of Information

The amount of information present can also affect consumers' opportunity to process a message. PepsiCo learned the hard way that its targeted consumers for PepsiOne, a low-calorie soft drink, needed real information from the introductory advertising messages—not just edgy imagery—to make a purchase decision. Facing lower-than-expected sales, the company revamped its ads to provide details about PepsiOne's taste and diet benefits.[73] Similarly, processing information related to the ad in Exhibit 3.14 would be very hard even if you had the ability and the desire to do so because there is so little information presented.

Complexity of Information

As information becomes more complex, our opportunity to process it decreases. What makes information complex? Studies indicate that consumers find technical or quantitative information more difficult to handle than nontechnical and qualitative data,[74] which inhibits processing. Many technological and pharmaceutical products entail complex information (as shown in Exhibit 3.12). In addition, research shows that messages containing only pictures, without words, tend to be ambiguous and therefore hard to process.[75] Information may also be complex if the individual needs to sort through a huge volume of it. This is why more consumers are using the Internet to locate complex information about specific health conditions or medicines when needed as Web sites often provide search functions that help them search for information efficiently. Aware of this tendency, medical products' Web sites are competing for the attention of online searchers.[76]

Repetition of Information

Whereas consumers' ability to process information is limited by time, distraction, and the quality and complexity of the information, one factor—repetition—actually enhances it.[77] If consumers are repeatedly exposed to information, they can more easily process it because they have more chances to think about, scrutinize, and remember the information. Advertisers who use television and radio, in particular, must therefore plan to get their messages to the target audience more than once, to enhance the opportunity for processing.

Control of Information

Research shows that consumers remember and learn more when they can control the flow of information by determining what information is presented, for how long, and in what order. With print ads, for example, consumers have a lot of control over which messages they pay attention to, how long they spend processing each message, and the order in which they process the messages. They therefore have more opportunity to select what is appropriate for their own needs and goals, process the information, and apply it to consumption decisions. In contrast, consumers who hear radio commercials or watch television commercials have no such control, so they have less opportunity to process and apply the information.[78] As consumers become proficient in controlling the information flow, they have the opportunity to put more effort toward processing the information content rather than focusing on the control task.[79]

MARKETING IMPLICATIONS Often marketers can do little to enhance consumers' opportunities to process information, make careful decisions, or engage in purchase, usage, or disposition behaviors. For example, advertisers cannot make living rooms less distracting during TV commercials or give consumers more time for shopping. However, companies can play some role in enhancing opportunity.

Repeat marketing communications and make them easy to process. Repeating marketing communications (up to a point) increases the likelihood that consumers will attend to and eventually process them. Marketers can also increase the likelihood of processing by presenting messages at a time of day when consumers are least likely to be distracted and pressed for time. Communications should be stated slowly and in simple terms so consumers understand them. One caution: although repetition increases the opportunity to process information, it can also reduce consumers' motivation to process it!

Reduce distraction and time-pressured decision making. Marketers can make decisions less time pressured. For example, retailers may extend their hours so consumers can take advantage of the store, product, or service at times that are least distracting and least time pressured. Many catalog companies and all online shopping sites allow consumers to place orders 24 hours a day. Marketers can also offer ancillary services that remove time constraints. For example, some health clubs offer extended hours and baby-sitting services for consumers who would otherwise be unable to attend.

Reduce purchasing/using/learning time. In addition, marketers can reduce the amount of time needed to buy or use a product and the time needed to learn how to access information about the product or service. Charles Schwab, for example, reduces learning time on its Web site by allowing consumers to enter questions in plain English.[80] The result: consumers spend less time figuring out how to do a search and more time analyzing information for investment decisions. In stores, clear signs and directories can help consumers locate goods more quickly and increase the likelihood that they will actually buy the goods.

Provide information. Sometimes the simple availability of information enhances consumers' abilities to process it, make decisions, and engage in consumer behaviors. In Zimbabwe, consumers are increasingly becoming overweight, given the influx of fast food and processed food. Some of these consumers are joining Weight Watchers and benefiting from the availability of information about the fat and calorie content of different foods, which gives them the opportunity to make healthier choices.[81] ●

SUMMARY

Motivation reflects an inner state of arousal that directs the consumer to engage in goal-relevant behaviors, effortful information processing, and detailed decision making. We are motivated to attend to, approach, and think about things that are important and personally relevant.

Motivated consumers often experience affective or cognitive involvement. In some cases, this involvement may be enduring; in other cases, it may be situational, lasting only until the goal has been achieved. Consumers can also be involved with product categories, brands, ads, the media, and consumption behaviors. Consumers experience greater motivation when they see a goal or object as personally relevant—meaning that it relates to their needs, values, and goals; when it entails considerable risk; or when it is moderately inconsistent with their prior attitude.

Even when motivation is high, consumers may not achieve their goals if their ability and/or opportunity to do so are low. If consumers lack the knowledge, experience, intelligence, education, or money to engage in a behavior, process information, or make a decision, they cannot achieve a goal. In addition, they may not achieve the goal if they are attending to information that is incompatible with their processing styles or if the information is presented in too complex a fashion. Highly motivated consumers may also fail to achieve goals if lack of time, distractions, insufficient or overly complex information, or lack of control over information flow limit the opportunity to do so.

QUESTIONS FOR REVIEW AND DISCUSSION

1. How is motivation defined, and how does it affect felt involvement?
2. What are some objects of involvement for consumers?
3. What determines the ranking of needs in Maslow's hierarchy?
4. How does perceived risk affect personal relevance, and what are six types of perceived risk?
5. In what ways can ability affect consumer behavior?
6. Identify some of the elements that contribute to consumer opportunity for processing information and making decisions.

EXERCISES

1. Randomly select ten advertisements from a magazine. Develop questions designed to assess a consumer's involvement in an ad (both cognitive and affective) and motivation to process information from the ad. Select a sample of 20–30 consumers to look at the ads and answer the questions. Which types of ads tend to be higher in involvement? Which types of ads tend to be lower in involvement? How do these ads tend to differ in terms of (a) recognition of consumers' needs, (b) structure and content, and (c) assumption of consumer knowledge or expertise?
2. Develop your own projective test, depicting some purchase or usage situation for a product or service of your choice. What kinds of needs are revealed by your test? What are the implications for the marketer of that product or service?
3. Watch TV and the associated ads for half an hour. At the end of your viewing, write down the ads you remember. Use the concepts of motivation, ability, and opportunity to describe why you processed and remembered these commercials. What was it about the ad, your prior knowledge or use of these products, or the environment in which you viewed the ads that made them memorable?
4. Visit a Web retail site (such as BestBuy.com, JCPenney.com, or Barnesandnoble.com) and carefully examine the description and information provided about one of the featured products. Also read the site's descriptions of shipping and payment options. What perceived risks are being addressed by the information on this site? How does the retailer either reduce risk perceptions or enhance risk perceptions with respect to the featured product or the shipping and payment options?
5. Select a high-involvement product you are interested in buying, such as a new car or a new computer system. Identify the factors that make this product personally relevant to you, such as how it relates to specific goals or needs. Next, consider how product knowledge/experience, age, and money affect your ability to process marketing information about this product and make a purchase. Finally, analyze how the opportunity factors related to time, distraction, and information affect your behavior toward making this purchase. What can marketers of this type of product do to enhance your motivation, ability, and opportunity to buy from them?

chapter 4

Exposure, Attention, and Perception

Introduction: Putting Products in the Spotlight

Sales of Reese's Pieces jumped after the candies were featured as a favorite treat of the character E.T. in Steven Spielberg's 1982 movie. Since then, hundreds of brand-name consumer products have been prominently featured in films and on TV (see Exhibit 4.1). Some advertisers report incredible success with product placement. Ramada, for instance, built a hotel on the CBS studio lot for use in various television shows, from *The Drew Carey Show* to *ER.* Two days after the hotel appeared in a *Drew Carey* episode, Ramada reservations shot up to levels that the company usually experiences during a major ad blitz. Miller Brewing also looks for opportunities to place its products in movies. Of the top 100 box-office hits in one recent year, 45 included beer-drinking scenes—and 24 of those showcased Miller beers.

Products are routinely shown as props in TV shows, movies, and computer and virtual-reality games, and are woven into other media. Not long ago, the upscale jewelry firm Bulgari commissioned author Fay Weldon to write a novel incorporating the company's products. Companies can even pay for a prominent position in search results presented by GoTo.com and other Internet search sites.

However, TV shows and movies do not always show products in the best light. For example, in the British comedy *Absolutely Fabulous,* actress Joanna Lumley's character carried Stolichnaya vodka in her purse and drank it right from the bottle. In some cases, the presence of products on TV shows causes a public outcry. For example, Philip Morris was asked to remove or relocate billboards in sports arenas so consumers would not be exposed to its cigarette ads when watching sports on TV.[1]

Product placement raises some interesting questions. First, are these product appearances dangerous because they blur the lines between programming and advertising? Second, are people less resistant to messages about products that appear in programs? Third, do the products force exposure to advertising messages? (Although consumers can avoid advertising messages in regular commercials by changing channels, they are less likely to do so

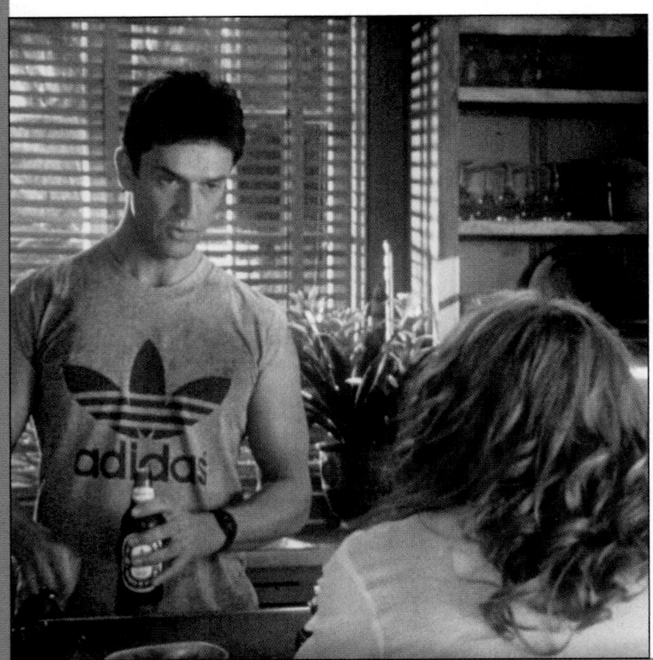

EXHIBIT 4.1
Brand Exposure through Product Placement
Source: Photofest

when the same products appear in TV shows or on film.) The complex answers to these questions are examined in this chapter.

If consumers are to be affected by a communication, they must first be exposed to it. Marketers recognize the importance of exposure, and they have been relying on product placement and other nontraditional forms of advertising to increase consumers' exposure to their brands. As noted above, however, marketers cannot completely control the exposure of their product on TV programs or in films. Generally, advertisers do not make direct payments to have products placed in films and on TV. Instead, they pay product placement firms who work with set decorators. In turn, the set decorators use various products to enhance the realism of the film or TV show. Yet advertisers sometimes arrange special sponsorships, as Campbell's did when it paid ABC to feature its soups on *The View* talk show and run related ads during the commercial breaks.[2]

After exposure, if consumers are to register any message about the brand, they must pay attention to the product. Whether they do so depends on a host of factors, such as whether the product is relevant to them, prominent, or surprising in its context. Whether consumers are affected by exposure to the products in these media also depends on whether the consumers can perceive the product in the show or film. For example, the brand name might be out of focus, too much of the package might be obscured, or the product might appear too fleetingly.

This chapter examines exposure, attention, and perception in detail, along with the resulting marketing implications. As Exhibit 4.2 indicates, exposure, attention, and perception are important because they affect what consumers comprehend, the attitudes they have, and what they remember. All this information affects the decisions and actions that consumers make. ●

EXPOSURE

exposure The process by which the consumer comes in physical contact with a stimulus.

marketing stimuli Information about products or brands communicated by either the marketer (via ads, salespeople, brand symbols, packages, signs, prices, and so on) or in nonmarketing sources (e.g., the media, word of mouth).

Before any type of marketing stimulus can affect consumers, they must be exposed to it. **Exposure** reflects the process by which the consumer comes into physical contact with a stimulus. **Marketing stimuli** are messages and information about products or brands communicated by either the marketer (via ads, salespeople, brand symbols, packages, signs, prices, and so on) or by nonmarketing sources (e.g., the media, word of mouth). Consumers can be exposed to marketing stimuli at the buying, using, or disposing stages of consumption. Because exposure is critical to consumers' subsequent processing of any stimulus, marketers need to make sure that consumers are exposed to marketing stimuli.

MARKETING IMPLICATIONS Marketers start the process of gaining exposure by selecting media, such as radio, product placements, and the Internet, and by developing promotions for the targeted consumers. For example, many car buyers enjoy watching car racing events. Therefore, Mercedes-Benz, BMW, Honda, and other car manufacturers sponsor racing teams, create racing-related commercials, and use racing elements in car designs to increase exposure to products and brands. Mercedes-Benz has used racing sponsorship to update its image and gain wider exposure through association with cutting-edge Formula One racers. "It would have cost us two, three, or four times as much in advertising to get the same exposure," says one board member. And this exposure translates into sales: in 1999, 36 percent of all Mercedes-Benz cars sold were in the company's silver racing colors, compared with just 20 percent five years earlier.[3] ●

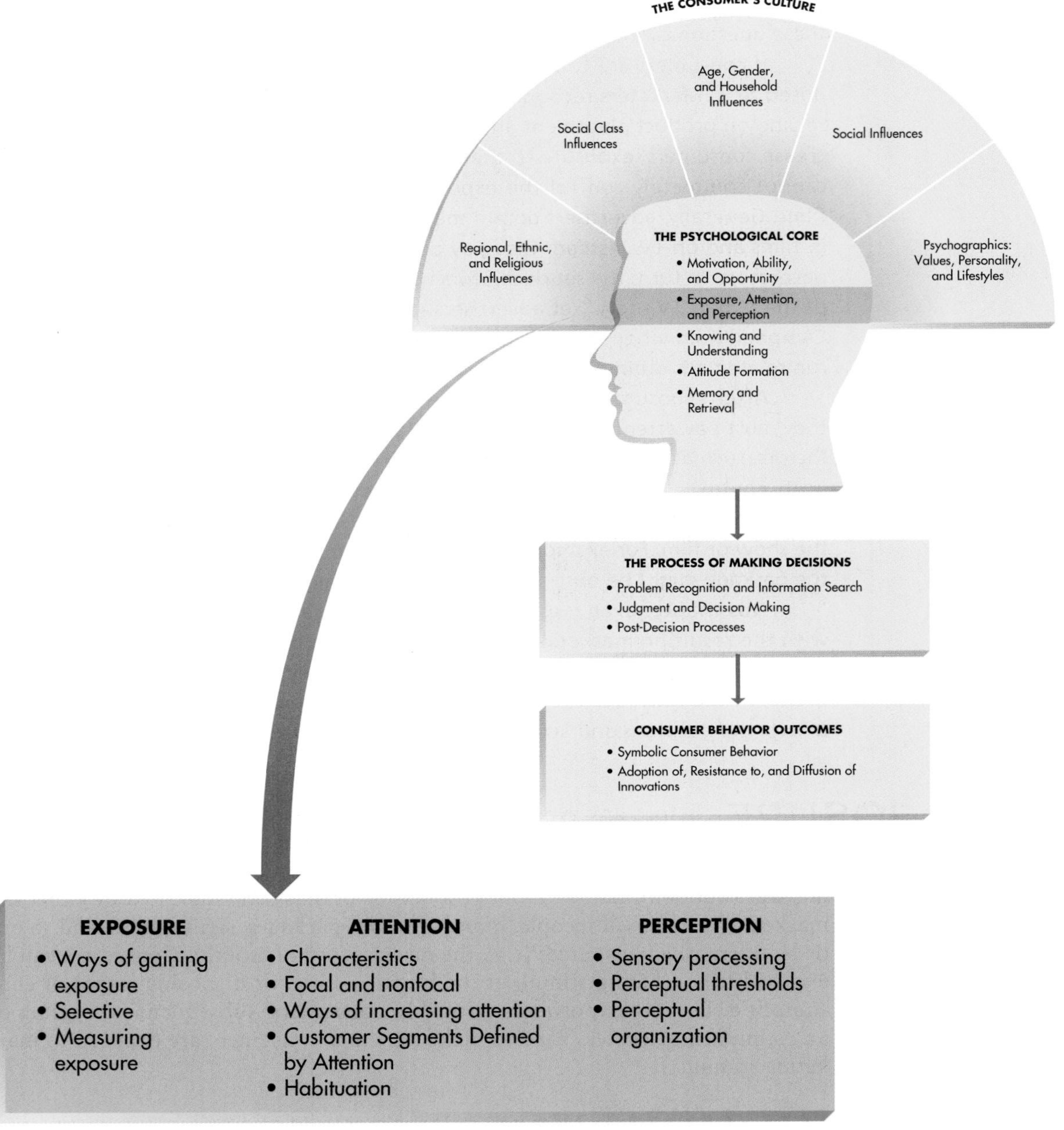

EXHIBIT 4.2
Chapter Overview: Exposure, Attention, and Perception

Consumers do some processing of a stimulus (e.g., an ad, brand) once they have been exposed to it, pay attention to it, and perceive its characteristics. Once it is perceived, consumers may attend to it some more.

Factors Influencing Exposure

The *position of an ad within a medium* can affect exposure. Exposure to commercials is greatest when they are placed at the beginning or end of a commercial break within a program because consumers are still involved in the program or are waiting for the program to come back on. Exposure to magazine ads is greatest when they appear on the back cover because the ad is in view whenever the magazine is placed face-down. Also, consumers are most likely to be exposed to ads placed next to articles or within TV programs that interest them.[4]

Finally, *product distribution and shelf placement* affect exposure. The more widespread the brand's distribution (the more stores in which it is available), the greater the likelihood that consumers will encounter it. Likewise, the location or the amount of shelf space allocated to the product can increase consumers' exposure to a product. Consumers are most likely to be exposed to products that are featured in an end-of-aisle display or that take up a lot of shelf space. Products placed from waist to eye level get more exposure than those placed higher or lower. Exposure also increases for products placed at points in the store where all consumers must go and spend time. For example, sales of some products increase because of higher exposure in point-of-purchase displays at the checkout counter of supermarkets, automotive stores, and restaurants.[5]

MARKETING IMPLICATIONS In addition to the traditional ways of reaching consumers, such as strategic placement of television commercials or effective product displays and shelf placement, marketers have been experimenting with other communications that gain exposure for marketing stimuli. Shell has installed TV sets at some of its pumps to advertise products sold at its gas station convenience stores, and BP Amoco is testing Web-based coupon distribution at selected stations.[6] Advertising in media such as airlines' in-flight entertainment programs, luggage carousels, home video rentals, shopping carts, school news programs, hot air balloons, and turnstiles at sports arenas are other ways of increasing exposure.

Cash-strapped governments in some cities are allowing companies to place ads on public buses, garbage trucks, police cars, even subway tunnels (see Exhibit 4.3). Subway riders in downtown Atlanta have been exposed to ads for Coca-Cola's Dasani bottled water. Even Beijing bus shelters and subway stations are plastered with ads for Internet sites and other products.[7] In Egypt, some advertisers use feluccas (boats that sail along the Nile River) to advertise brands.[8] Using "human directionals"—people in crazy outfits who stand on street corners waving their hands

EXHIBIT 4.3
Creating Exposure Through Transit Advertising
This bus in Shanghai, China increases consumers' exposure to messages and packages of Asahi beer.

Source: Getty Images.

and shouting information—is one way that retailers and home developers affect consumers' exposure to the store or development.

Consumers seem more receptive to ad messages when they can control exposure. Through the Polk Company's ChoiceMail program, consumers can sign up to receive direct mail advertising in specific product categories. More than six million consumers have requested advertising about women's clothing, gardening products, kitchen products, and other items.[9] Similarly, Internet users resent uninvited instant messages from companies, but many will agree to receive messages if they can control their timing. The alternative rock band Radiohead invites Internet users to sign up for messages from GooglyMinotaur, a software-driven instant message "buddy" that delivers information about the band's concerts and CDs on request. This software buddy sent out more than one million requested messages during its first week of operation.[10] ●

Selective Exposure

While marketers can work very hard to affect consumers' exposure to certain products and brands, ultimately consumers control whether exposure occurs or not. In other words, consumers can actively seek certain stimuli and avoid others. Readers of *Vogue* magazine selectively expose themselves to its fashion-oriented ads, whereas readers of *Car and Driver* choose to look at different kinds of ads. Some readers may ignore the ads altogether.

Consumers' avoidance of marketing stimuli is a big problem for marketers.[11] One survey reveals that the 54 percent of U.S. consumers and 68 percent of German consumers avoid ads.[12] Consumers can simply leave the room or do something else when TV commercials air. Zipping and zapping are two common avoidance practices. **Zipping** occurs when consumers videotape television shows and fast-forward through the commercials when viewing the shows. Consumers zip through up to 60 percent of the ads in recorded programs. Although some digital video recorders allow consumers to skip commercials at the touch of a button, users don't zip through all ads; instead, they choose to watch specific ads that seem relevant and interesting.[13] **Zapping** occurs when consumers avoid ad exposure by using remote controls to switch to other channels during commercial breaks. Approximately 20 percent of consumers zap at any one time; more than two-thirds of households with cable TV zap on a regular basis. Men zap significantly more than women do. People are more likely to zap commercials at the half-hour or hour mark than during the program itself.[14]

zipping Fast-forwarding through the commercials recorded on a VCR or Personal Video Recorder.

zapping Use of a remote control to switch channels when a commercial comes on.

Why do consumers want to avoid ads? In part, it is because people are exposed to so many that no one can possibly process them all. *Bride's* magazine now has more than 1,000 pages, approximately 800 of which are ads. Readers of *Harper's Bazaar, Mademoiselle,* and *Elle* must sometimes flip through more than 125 pages of ads before they find the first feature article.[15] Consumers avoid ads for product categories that they don't use and are therefore irrelevant to them. Consumers also tend to avoid ads they have seen before because they know what these ads will say.

Finally, many adult consumers want to limit their children's exposure to ads, because youngsters have difficulty distinguishing between ad messages and media content. This is an especially contentious issue online. For instance, FoxKids.com labels its game-and-ad entertainment as "sponsored content," but some advertisers use anonymous messages and Web sites to promote products without clearly labeling the content as advertising.[16] Yet parents can't always limit children's exposure to ads for inappropriate products—such as R-rated movies—because of massive multimedia campaigns that combine television, billboards, and many other media. Recognizing this, Warner Brothers attempts to shield children by not advertising its R-rated films on television programs where 35 percent or more of the audience is younger than 17.[17]

Now the rising tide of unsolicited ad exposure has created a backlash among consumers. After an online marketing firm distributed thousands of unsolicited e-mail messages (known as *spam*) to promote the book *Plan B,* some recipients posted negative comments on Amazon.com's review pages; the flap even received coverage in the *Wall Street Journal*.[18] Spam is particularly annoying to people outside the target market, which is why Doubleclick and other Internet advertising agencies are using technology to track Web browsing and gear ads to each consumer's online behavior.[19]

Measuring Exposure

In February 2003, advertisers paid over $2 million for a single 30-second spot during the Super Bowl. Why spend so much? In part, because of projections of exposure rates indicating that hundreds of millions of consumers around the world watched the preceding year's game. Super Bowl advertising is so coveted that advertisers even pay to put messages in a pocket on the official seat cushion.[20] Marketers are very interested in determining which media will generate exposure to their marketing stimuli and whether the desired exposure rates have actually been reached.

As discussed in Chapter 2, many marketers use data from specialized research firms to track advertising exposure. The Simmons Market Research Bureau and MediaMark Research collect data about the audiences for different media vehicles. Neilsen researches exposure to TV programs and commercials by installing people meters on the TV sets of 5,100 U.S. households. Arbitron uses diaries to collect information about which radio stations consumers listen to. Traffic counters are sometimes used to count the number of cars that drive by billboards every day. Unfortunately, counters tabulate only car traffic (not pedestrians) and cannot tell how many consumers are in each car or whether they actually see the particular billboard. Similarly, marketers are looking for ways to measure the effect of ads on free postcards distributed in trendy bars, restaurants, and other retail outlets.[21]

Advertisers are increasingly concerned about measuring exposure to online advertising. At present, advertisers have no way of knowing exactly how many consumers see their Internet ads, though they can track the number who click through to them. Also, different methods of counting ad exposures often yield very different numbers. For example, NetRatings projects exposure levels by tracking the surfing behavior of a panel of 37,000 U.S. consumers. However, its exposure figures—and those of its rivals—often differ from those of Web sites that keep traffic logs of site visits. The advertising industry is therefore working on a standard system for measuring Internet exposure levels.[22]

ATTENTION

Attention is the process by which we devote mental activity to a stimulus. A certain amount of attention is necessary for information to be perceived—for it to activate our senses. Furthermore, after consumers perceive information, they may pay more attention to it and continue with the higher-order processing activities discussed in the next few chapters. This relationship between attention and perception explains why marketers need to understand the characteristics of attention and find ways of enhancing attention to marketing stimuli.

attention The process by which an individual allocates part of his or her mental activity to a stimulus.

Characteristics of Attention

Attention has three key characteristics: (1) it is selective, (2) it is capable of being divided, and (3) it is limited.

Attention Is Selective One important aspect of attention is that it is selective. *Selectivity* means that we decide which items—out of possibly hundreds—we want to focus on at any one time. The number of stimuli to which we are exposed at any given time is potentially overwhelming. For example, although you are currently paying attention to the information in this book, you are simultaneously being exposed to other stimuli. You may hear traffic through an open window, see a stack of unanswered mail, or smell a meal simmering on the stove. In daily life, we are also exposed to hundreds of marketing stimuli. Shoppers in a supermarket are exposed to numerous products, brands, ads, displays, signs, prices, logos, and packages all at the same time. We are generally unable to examine all these marketing stimuli simultaneously. Instead, we must somehow determine which are worthy of processing. For instance, research shows that people pay less attention to things they have seen many times before.[23] Because attention is selective, we can control what we focus on.

Attention Can Be Divided A second important aspect of attention is that it is capable of being divided. Thus we can parcel our mental resources into units and allocate some to one task and some to another. For example, we can drive a car and talk at the same time. We can allocate attention flexibly to meet the demands of things in our environment, but we also have the potential to become distracted when one stimulus pulls our attention away from another. If we are distracted from a product or ad, the amount of attention we devote to it will be greatly reduced.[24] Knowing that viewers can divide their attention, TV networks reinforce their brands and flash reminders of upcoming shows at the bottom of the screen during programs. "Viewers are more confused than ever about what is on TV and when it is on," says a CBS executive. "It is incumbent on us to help them navigate our programming."[25]

Attention Is Limited A third, and critical, aspect of attention is that it is limited. Although we may be able to divide our attention, we can attend to multiple things only if processing them is relatively automatic, well practiced, and effortless.[26] For example, you can sometimes watch a TV ad and listen to your friends talk, but if the conversation turns serious, you will need to turn down the TV so you can devote your attention to your friends. The fact that attention is limited explains why consumers browsing in an unfamiliar store are less likely to notice new products than when those same consumers browse in a familiar store. Consumers will inevitably miss some products when they try to attend to many unfamiliar products.

Focal and Nonfocal Attention

These three characteristics of attention raise questions about whether we can attend to something in our peripheral vision even if we are already focusing on something else. For example, when we read a magazine article, can we process the information in an adjacent ad—even if our eyes are concentrating on the article and we are not aware of the ad? When we drive down the highway, can we process any information from a roadside billboard even if we are focusing only on the road?

Preattentive Processing To the extent that we can process information from our peripheral vision even if we are not aware that we are attending to it, we are

preattentive processing The nonconscious processing of stimuli in peripheral vision.

engaged in **preattentive processing.** With preattentive processing, most of our attentional resources are devoted to one thing, leaving very limited resources for attending to something else. We devote just enough attention to an object in peripheral vision to process *something* about the object. But because the amount of attention is so limited, we are not aware that we are attending to and processing information about that object.

Hemispheric Lateralization Our ability to process information preattentively depends on (1) whether the stimulus in peripheral vision is a picture or a word and (2) whether it is placed in the right or left visual field (to the right side or the left side of the object on which we are focused). These factors are influential because of how the two halves of the brain—the two hemispheres—process information (see Exhibit 4.4). The right hemisphere is best at processing music, grasping visual and spatial information, forming inferences, and drawing conclusions. The left hemisphere, in contrast, is best at processing units that can be

EXHIBIT 4.4
Hemispheric Lateralization
The two hemispheres of our brain specialize in processing different types of information. When a stimulus is in *focal* vision, it is processed by *both* hemispheres. When it is in *peripheral* vision (i.e., it is not being focused on), it is processed by the *opposite* hemisphere. Information presented in the left visual field is therefore processed by the right hemisphere.

Source: Adapted from Chris Janiszewski, "The Influence of Nonattended Material on the Processing of Advertising Claims," *Journal of Marketing Research,* August 1990, p. 265. Reprinted with permission of the American Marketing Association.

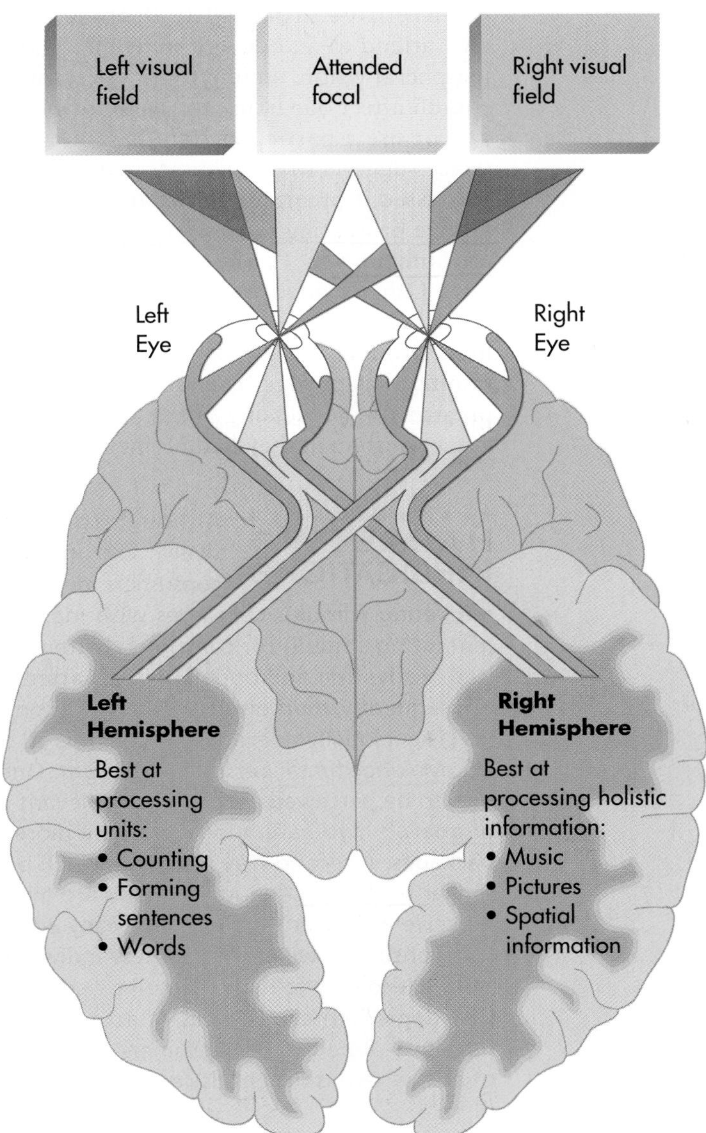

combined. This hemisphere performs tasks such as counting, processing unfamiliar words, and forming sentences.[27]

Interestingly, stimuli placed in the right visual field (ads on the right side of the focal article or billboards on the right side of the road) tend to be processed by the left hemisphere; those in the left visual field tend to be processed by the right hemisphere. Stimuli on which we focus directly are processed by both hemispheres. These findings suggest that people will most likely preattentively process stimuli such as pictures in ads if the pictures are placed to the left of a magazine article, because the processing takes place in the right hemisphere—the hemisphere that is best at processing visual stimuli. Likewise, stimuli such as brand names or ad claims are most likely to be preattentively processed if they are placed in the right visual field because they will be processed by the left hemisphere. Several studies have indeed found that consumers' ability to preattentively process pictures, brand names, or claims in ads depends on whether the ad is placed in the right or left visual field.[28]

Preattentive Processing, Brand-Name Liking, and Choice Although we may attend to and devote some minimal level of processing to stimuli placed in peripheral vision, an important question is whether such preattentively processed stimuli affect our liking for an ad or brand or, more important, our decisions to buy or use a particular brand. Some research suggests that they do: some evidence suggests that consumers will like the same brand name more if they have processed it preattentively than if they have not been exposed to it all.[29] Preattentive processing makes a brand name familiar, and we tend to like things that are familiar.[30]

Other evidence suggests that stimuli processed preattentively can affect consumer choices. In one study, consumers were more likely to consider choosing a product if they had previously been preattentively exposed to an ad containing that product than if they had not been exposed to the ad. In this case, preattentive processing of the ad affected consumers' consideration of the product, even though they had no memory of having seen the ad.[31]

MARKETING IMPLICATIONS Although consumers can process information preattentively, the information will have more impact when consumers devote full attention to it. Unfortunately, a marketing stimulus competes with many other types of stimuli (including other marketing stimuli) for consumers' attention. Moreover, consumers may have limited motivation and opportunity to attend to marketing stimuli in the first place. Consequently, marketers try to attract consumers' attention by making the stimulus (1) personally relevant, (2) pleasant, (3) surprising, and (4) easy to process.

Making stimuli personally relevant. One of the most powerful ways for a stimulus to be perceived as personally relevant is for it to appeal to your needs, values, or goals.[32] If you are hungry, you are more likely to pay attention to food ads and packages. A second way to make stimuli personally relevant is by showing sources similar to the target audience. You are more likely to notice individuals whom you perceive as similar to yourself.[33] Many advertisers use "typical consumers," hoping that consumers will relate to these individuals and thereby attend to the ad.

A third way to make stimuli personally relevant is using dramas—mini-stories that depict the experiences of actors or relate someone's experiences through a narrative—to enhance consumers' attention. Some dramas unfold through a series of ads, whereas other ads convey an entire story in 30 seconds. Dramas draw the

EXHIBIT 4.5
Rhetorical Questions Capture Attention
Rhetorical questions can be relevant to the self and can attract attention.

Source: Photo courtesy Campbell Soup Company.

consumer into the action and make the action in the ad relevant to the consumer. And a fourth way to capture attention and draw a consumer into the ad is to ask rhetorical questions—those asked merely for effect.[34] No one really expects an answer to a rhetorical question like "How would you like to win a million dollars?" because the answer is so obvious. These questions appeal to the consumer by implicitly including the word *you* and by asking the consumer (if only for effect) to consider answering the question. The ad in Exhibit 4.5 attracts the consumer's attention by asking, "Got that daily vegetable thing down yet?"

Making stimuli pleasant. People tend to approach things that are inherently pleasant. Marketers can use this principle to increase consumers' attention to marketing stimuli.

- *Using attractive models.* Advertisements containing attractive models have a higher probability of being noticed because the models arouse positive feelings or a basic sexual attraction.[35] Lingerie retailer Victoria's Secret has used attractive models such as Tyra Banks and Heidi Klum to draw viewers to its fashion shows. One million people logged on to its online fashion show in 1999, and more than 12 million tuned into the network television broadcast in 2001.[36] Clearly, individual differences influence people's opinions on what is attractive. For example, although some people enjoy seeing naked bodies in advertisements, other viewers find these images offensive. Cross-cultural differences also account for what is considered attractive. Ultrathin models represent a Western standard of beauty; elsewhere in the world, such models would be perceived as poor, undernourished, and unattractive.
- *Using music.* Familiar songs and popular entertainers have considerable ability to attract us in pleasant ways.[37] For example, snack food advertisers pay Reba McEntire to appear in commercials because she attracts attention. Music that recalls a pleasant and nostalgic past also attracts attention. This is why Budweiser commercials include the song "Ants," and commercials for Burger King play the song "That's the Way I Like It." Music can draw attention to an ad and enhance the attention consumers pay to the ad's message—provided that the music fits with the ad's theme.
- *Using humor.* Humor can be an effective attention-getting device.[38] Pepsi used humor in a recent ad showing a sweet little girl dining with her grandfather.

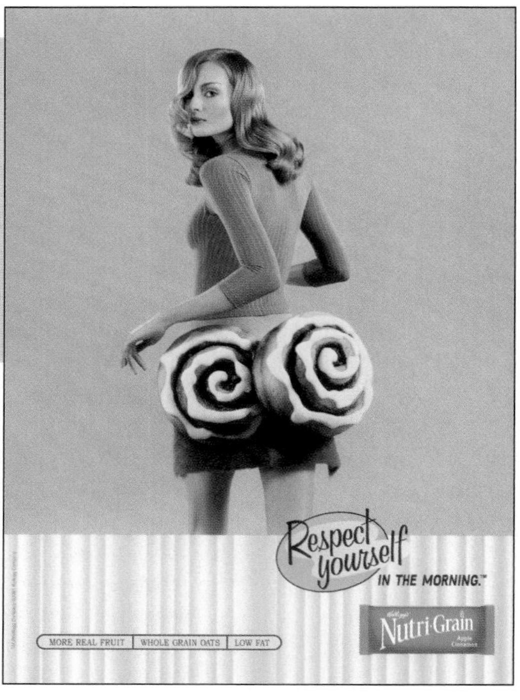

EXHIBIT 4.6
Humor in Ads
This ad uses both an unexpected image and humor to attract attention to the ad and convey the point.

Source: KELLOGG'S and NUTRI-GRAIN are registered trademarks of Kellogg Company. © 2002 Kellogg Company.

When the girl is told that the restaurant serves only Coke, her voice changes into something straight out of *The Exorcist.* The frightened waiter runs away, only to return moments later with a Pepsi.[39] The girl returns to her sweet normal self after the Pepsi is delivered. The ad in Exhibit 4.6 also illustrates the use of humor.

Making stimuli surprising. Consumers are also likely to process a stimulus when it is surprising. Three characteristics make a stimulus surprising: novelty, unexpectedness, and a puzzle.

- *Using novelty.* We are more likely to notice any marketing stimulus (a product, package, or brand name) that is new or unique—because it stands out relative to other stimuli around us. The fragrance Catalyst for Men is packaged in test tubes and laboratory flasks. Because the packaging looks like a chemistry set, the product stands out from other brands on the shelf. A perfume company is attracting attention with novel perfume fragrances such as Dirt (potting soil aroma), Carrot, and Snow.[40] As shown in Exhibit 4.7, the makers of King Tut's Party Mix developed a novel package so the brand would stand out.

Companies can attract attention using novel advertising formats: magazine ads with graphics that appear to move; color newspaper ads that stand out against the black-and-white background of the surrounding news; black-and-white magazine or TV ads that stand out against more colorful ads; stamps or dollar bills inserted into direct mail messages; and online ads that invite participation. A Gatorade marketing executive confirms that her product's black-and-white ads featuring well-known sports figures dotted with colorful beads of sweat are "a way to stand out and get attention."[41] Novel ads also command attention. To communicate that British Airways flies more people each year than the population of Manhattan, the carrier ran a now-famous campaign showing Manhattan Island flying overhead.

EXHIBIT 4.7
Novel Packaging
Consumers pay more attention to things that are novel or different. This package for King Tut's Party Mix is very different from most party mix packages. Can you think of some brand names, packages, ads, promotions, or stores that attract attention by being novel or different?

Source: Designed by Debora Michel.

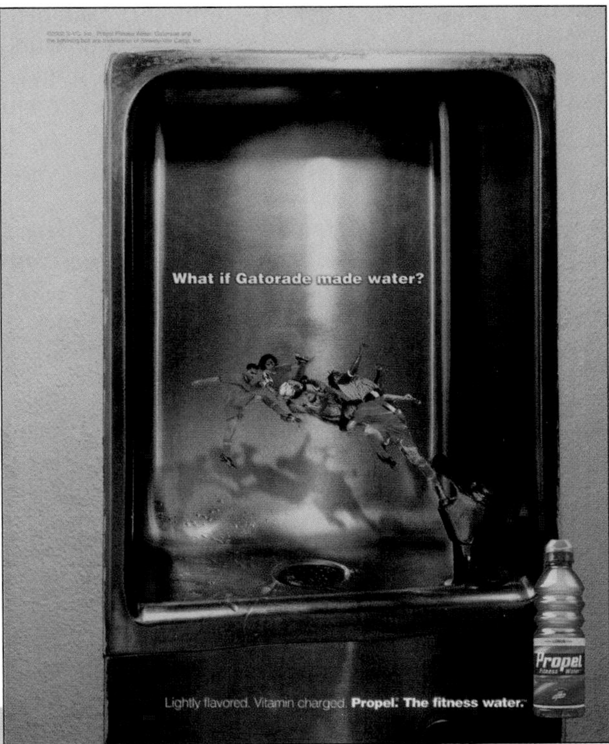

What if Gatorade made water?
Lightly flavored. Vitamin charged. Propel: The fitness water.
Propel

EXHIBIT 4.8
Using Unexpectedness to Attract Attention
Few people expect to see athletes coming out of a drinking fountain. The image therefore attracts consumers' attention to the ad.

Source: Courtesy of Stokely-Van Camp, Inc.

Although novel stimuli attract attention, we do not always like them better. For example, we often dislike food that tastes different from what we usually eat, new clothing styles that deviate from the current trend, or new and unusual music. Thus the factors that make a stimulus novel may not be the same factors that make it likable.

- *Using unexpectedness.* Unexpected stimuli are not necessarily new, but their placement differs from what we are used to. Because these stimuli are different, they arouse our curiosity and cause us to analyze them further to make sense of them.[42] Jergens attracted attention for its Naturally Smooth leg moisturizer using a TV commercial that mimicked a public service announcement about addiction. The commercial seemed to be a typical drug addiction message—until the product suddenly appeared and the woman said she was addicted to shaving her legs, an unexpected development.[43] Unexpectedness can affect the extent to which consumers perceive an ad as humorous.[44] The ad for Propel in Exhibit 4.8 uses an unexpected picture of athletes coming out of a water fountain to capture attention.
- *Using a puzzle.* Visual rhymes, antitheses, metaphors, and puns are puzzles that attract attention because they require resolution. Consumers tend to think more about information in ads that contain these elements. However, consumers from other cultural backgrounds may find it difficult to understand some puns and metaphors in U.S. ads that American consumers can easily comprehend.[45]

Making stimuli easy to process. Although personal relevance, pleasantness, and surprise attract consumers' attention by enhancing their motivation to attend to stimuli, marketers can also enhance attention by boosting our *ability* to process stimuli. Four characteristics make a stimulus easy to process: (1) its prominence, (2) its concreteness, (3) the extent to which it contrasts with the things that surround it, and (4) the extent to which it competes with other information.

prominence The intensity of stimuli that causes them to stand out relative to the environment.

- *Prominent stimuli.* Prominent stimuli stand out relative to the environment because of their intensity. The size or length of the stimulus can affect its **prominence**. For example, consumers are more likely to notice larger or longer ads than to notice smaller or shorter ones.[46] Yellow Pages advertisers have reported that doubling an ad's size increases sales fivefold, whereas quadrupling the size increases sales by a factor of 15.[47] Help-wanted ads have traditionally been small and wordy. These days, more companies are placing full-page ads with large headlines and graphics to attract the attention of job seekers.[48] Making words prominent by the use of boldfaced text also enhances consumers' attention.[49] The principle of prominence explains manufacturers' use of huge end caps and store displays. Sales of Barnum's animal crackers rose more than 15 percent in one year, in part because of very prominent 76-inch-high, gorilla-shaped cardboard store displays filled with cookie boxes.[50]

Movement makes an ad more prominent. Attention to commercials tends to be enhanced when the ad uses dynamic, fast-paced action.[51] Moving billboards and

EXHIBIT 4.9
Concreteness and Abstractness
We may pay more attention to things that are concrete and capable of generating images than to things that are abstract and difficult to represent visually.

Source: Allan Paivio, John C. Yuille, and Stephen A. Madigan, "Concreteness, Imagery, and Meaningfulness Values for 925 Nouns," *Journal of Experimental Psychology, Monograph Supplement,* January 1968, pp. 1–25. © 1968 by the American Psychological Association. Adapted with permission.

CONCRETE WORDS	ABSTRACT WORDS
Apple	Aptitude
Bowl	Betrayal
Cat	Chance
Cottage	Criterion
Diamond	Democracy
Engine	Essence
Flower	Fantasy
Garden	Glory
Hammer	Hatred
Infant	Ignorance
Lemon	Loyalty
Meadow	Mercy
Mountain	Necessity
Ocean	Obedience

concreteness The extent to which a stimulus is capable of being imagined.

moving store displays are other examples. A billboard in Orlando, Florida, promoting Disney's Animal Kingdom attracts attention by using rotating panels to display three different images and messages. Nike uses video technology to display a series of sharp, colorful images on its billboards.[52]

Loud sounds can also enhance prominence. Television and radio stations sometimes turn up the volume for commercials so they will stand out relative to the program. Loud rock or dramatic classical music can serve the same purpose.

- *Concrete stimuli.* Stimuli are easier to process if they are concrete rather than abstract.[53] **Concreteness** is defined as the extent to which we can imagine a stimulus. Notice how easily you can develop images of the concrete words in Exhibit 4.9 compared with the abstract words. Concreteness applies to brand names, as well. Consider the brands of well-known dish-washing liquids. The name Sunlight is much more concrete than the names Dawn, Joy, or Palmolive and may therefore have an advantage over the others in attention-getting ability.
- *Contrasting stimuli.* A third factor that makes stimuli easier to process is contrast. Notice in Exhibit 4.10 that the Palmolive bottle stands out much better in the left photo than in the photo on the right, thanks to color contrast. Similarly, a color advertisement in a newspaper is more likely to capture attention because everything around it is black and white, just as a black-and-white ad on color TV is likely to stand out. Wine makers have found that packaging their wine in blue bottles instead of the traditional green or amber profoundly affects sales because the blue bottles stand out on the shelf.[54] Although research indicates that consumers are more likely to consider Yellow Pages ads in which color is used only for the sake of attracting attention, they are more likely to actually call the companies when the color enhances the product's appeal in an appropriate manner.[55]
- *The amount of competing information.* Finally, stimuli are easier to process when few things surround them to compete for your attention.[56] You are

EXHIBIT 4.10
Contrast and Attention
The Palmolive bottle stands out and attracts attention only when its color contrasts with (is different from) the bottles that surround it. What implications does contrast have for merchandising products?

Source: Lawrence L. Garber Jr., Appalachian State University. "The Role of Package Appearance in Consumer Choice," dissertation, University of North Carolina at Chapel Hill.

more likely to notice a billboard when travelling down a deserted rural highway than in the middle of a congested, sign-filled city. You are also more likely to notice a brand name in a visually simple ad than in one that is visually cluttered. ●

Customer Segments Defined by Attention

One set of researchers asked the following question: If we do pay attention to things that are relevant, pleasant, surprising, and easy to process, can we identify groups or segments of consumers who are more affected by relevance, pleasantness, surprise, and ease of processing? To answer this question, the researchers hooked up consumers to eye-tracking devices that monitored the focus of their visual attention on a print ad. The ad was divided into basic parts like picture, package shot, and headline and categorized as big or small, in color or black and white. The researchers identified three groups of consumers by how they attended to the ad.

One group paid minimal attention to the ad because the elements in the ad were not relevant to them. A second group spent a longer time looking at the ad and seemed to focus on things that were visually pleasant, such as the picture. The last group spent the longest time looking at the ad. These consumers were affected by the size of the ad, but they devoted equal amounts of time to the picture, package, headline, and body text. The researchers concluded that this group may have attended to each element because the product was personally relevant and its purchase potentially risky. Hence consumers need a period of sustained attention to properly evaluate the ad's information.[57]

Habituation

habituation The process in which a stimulus loses its attention-getting abilities by virtue of its familiarity.

When a stimulus becomes familiar, it can lose its attention-getting ability, a result called **habituation.** Think about the last time you purchased something new for your apartment or room (such as a plant or picture). For the first few days, you probably noticed the object every time you entered the room. As time passed, however, you probably noticed the item less and less to the point where you probably do not notice it at all now. You have become habituated to it.

MARKETING IMPLICATIONS Habituation poses a problem for marketers because consumers readily become habituated to ads, packages, and other marketing stimuli. The most straightforward solution is to alter the stimulus every so often. Advertisers sometimes develop multiple ads that all communicate the same basic message but in different ways. Habituation is also the reason that marketers sometimes change product packaging. A fresh package or label often attracts consumers' attention anew. ●

PERCEPTION

After we have been exposed to a stimulus and have devoted at least some attention to it, we are in a position to perceive it. **Perception** occurs when stimuli are registered by one of our five senses: vision, hearing, taste, smell, and touch.

perception The process by which incoming stimuli activate our sensory receptors (eyes, ears, taste buds, skin, and so on).

Perceiving through Vision

What arouses our visual perception?

- *Size.* Size attracts attention. When choosing among competing products, consumers tend to buy products in packages that appear taller.[58]
- *Color.* Color is an extremely important factor in visual perception. Research suggests, in fact, that color determines whether we see stimuli.[59]

- *Color dimensions*. A given color can be described according to three dimensions: hue, saturation, and lightness. *Hue* refers to the pigment contained in the color. Researchers have classified colors into two broad categories or color hues: warm colors such as red, orange, and yellow, and cool colors such as green, blue, and violet. *Saturation* (also called "chroma") refers to the richness of the color, leading to distinctions such as pale pink or deep, rich pink. *Lightness* refers to the depth of tone in the color. A saturated pink could have a lot of lightness (a fluorescent pink) or a lot of darkness (a mauve).
- *Effects of color on physiological responses and moods*. Color can also influence our physiological responses and moods. Color psychologists have discovered that warm colors generally encourage activity and excitement, whereas cool colors are more soothing and relaxing. Thus cool colors are more appropriate in places such as spas or doctors' offices, where it is desirable for consumers to feel calm or spend time making decisions.[60] In contrast, warm colors are more appropriate in environments such as health clubs and fast-food restaurants, where high levels of activity are desirable.[61] One study found that deeper and richer colors (greater saturation) and darker colors evoked more excitement than did less deep and lighter colors.[62]
- *Color and liking*. Colors can have a great effect on consumers' liking for a product. For example, one reason consumers were initially attracted to Apple's iMac computers was their eye-catching colors.[63] H.J. Heinz's Blastin' Green EZ Squirt ketchup has been extremely successful because children like its color.[64]

MARKETING IMPLICATIONS Because colors can have a great effect on consumers' liking for a product, marketers often rely on the advice of "color forecasters" when deciding which colors to use in products and on packages. For example, the Color Association of the United States and the Color Marketing Group provide information to manufacturers and designers about the colors consumers are likely to prefer 2 to 3 years into the future. These forecasts are very important—the right color can make consumers believe they are buying products that are very current. Researchers have also found dif-

EXHIBIT 4.11
Color Segments
One set of researchers found that consumers could be classified as falling into one of three color segments. Where do you fall? Can you think of people who fall into the other two segments?

Source: Reprinted with permission from *Marketing News*, published by the American Marketing Association, Tim Triplett, August 28, 1995. Vol. 30, pp. 1, 39.

SEGMENT NAME	COLOR PREFERENCES	CHARACTERISTICS
The Color Forward Segment	First to try a new color Willing to spend more for a product in a fashionable color	Women under 30 or over 50 Men under 30 City dwellers Impulse buyers People who make < $35,000/year
The Color Prudent Segment	Buy a new color only after seeing friends buy it Put quality ahead of color in purchase decisions	Men and women aged 30–50 Suburban People who make > $50,000/year
The Color Loyal Segment	Replace a product with another of the same color Prefer safe colors such as blue and gray as opposed to fashionable colors	Men over 60 Suburban or rural People who dislike shopping

ferences among social classes in color preferences. Hot, bright colors have historically appealed to lower-end markets, whereas deep, rich colors have historically appealed to higher-end markets.[65] Some research has identified other color segments described in Exhibit 4.11.[66] ●

Perceiving through Hearing

Sound represents another form of sensory input. A major principle determining whether a sound will be perceived is its auditory intensity.[67] Consumers are more likely to notice loud music or voices and stark noises. In magazines, advertisers have used a technique in which ads "sing out" with a phrase or jingle. To illustrate, during one holiday season, the producers of Absolut vodka created a talking magazine ad by embedding a computer chip into the magazine page. When a company uses one person to speak the voice-over lines during many ads, consumers come to associate that person's voice with the product over time. Thus, when consumers hear Billy Crudup's voice in an ad, they will probably think of MasterCard; when they hear James Earl Jones's voice in an ad, they may think of Verizon.[68]

MARKETING IMPLICATIONS Fast music, like that played at aerobics classes, tends to energize; in contrast, slow music can be soothing. The type of music being played in a retail outlet can have an interesting effect on shopping behavior.[69] Specifically, a fast tempo creates a more rapid traffic flow, whereas a slower tempo has the opposite effect. A slow tempo can increase sales as much as 38 percent because it encourages leisurely shopping. Consumers tend to be completely unaware of this influence on their behavior.[70] Alternatively, a fast tempo is more desirable in restaurants because consumers will eat faster, thereby allowing greater turnover and higher sales.[71]

Music can also affect moods.[72] Likable and familiar music can induce good moods, whereas discordant sounds and music in a disliked style can induce bad moods. This effect is important because, as you will see in later chapters, bad moods may affect how people feel about products and consumption experiences.[73] ●

Perceiving through Taste

Food and beverage marketers must stress taste perceptions in their marketing stimuli. For example, the major challenge for marketers of light or low-calorie products is to provide healthier foods that still taste good. Yet what tastes good to one person may not taste good to another. Knowing this, White Wave has persuaded consumers to buy soymilk partly on the basis of what they *won't* taste: no beany flavor, just a slightly creamy milk-like taste.[74] Moreover, clear cross-cultural differences in taste preferences have important marketing implications.

MARKETING IMPLICATIONS Marketers often try to monitor consumers' tastes through taste tests. Many food and beverage products are thoroughly taste tested before they are placed on the market. Sometimes, however, these taste tests can backfire, as happened when Coca-Cola introduced new Coke. Because Coca-Cola's market share among younger consumers had been shrinking relative to Pepsi's, Coca-Cola designed a cola that tasted more like Pepsi. This decision was bolstered by blind taste tests in which consumers preferred the newer formula to the old one. But Coca-Cola executives failed to realize the power of the brand name. Longtime Coca-Cola drinkers were firm in their preference for the original formula. Thus when the old and new formulas were identified by name, consumers strongly preferred the original formula. New Coke provoked such a public outcry that Coca-Cola was forced to reintroduce the old formula as "Coca-Cola Classic." ●

Perceiving through Smell

If you were blindfolded and asked to smell an item, you would probably have a hard time identifying it; most consumers do.[75] However, consumers also differ in their ability to label odors. Compared with younger consumers, the elderly have a harder time identifying smells,[76] and men in general are worse at the task than are women.[77] Marketers are concerned with the effects of smell on consumer responses, product trial, liking, and buying.

Effects of Smells on Physiological Responses and Moods Like the other senses, smell produces physiological and emotional outcomes. For example, the smell of peppermint is arousing, and the smell of lily of the valley is relaxing.[78] In fact, some studies report that people can feel tense or relaxed depending on whether a scent is present and what it is.[79] This theory has been key to the development of aromatherapy. Some of our most basic emotions are also linked to smell. For example, children hate having their security blankets washed, in part because washing removes the smells that comfort the child. In addition, the smell of the ocean or of freshly baked cookies can revive very emotional and basic childhood memories.[80]

Smells and Product Trial Companies can expose consumers to marketing stimuli through their sense of smell. Smell (often in combination with other sensory perceptions) can entice consumers to try and buy a food product. Krispy Kreme designs its outlets so customers can smell—and see—the doughnuts fresh out of the oven.[81] Scratch-and-sniff advertisements expose consumers to fragrances and other types of products that involve the use of smell. Also, some perfume and cologne ads are doused with the product to increase sensory processing. However, this technique can backfire, because some consumers are offended by scented ads and some even have allergic reactions to the smells.

Smell and Liking Retailers also realize that smells can attract consumers. When Kmart Corp. reconfigured its Super Kmart stores, it positioned the bakery kiosk (with its smell of freshly baked breads, pretzels, cinnamon rolls, and muffins) as the first food area customers encounter in the store. The smell also draws consumers to other food attractions.[82]

Smell and Buying Research has found that providing a pleasant-smelling environment can have a positive effect on shopping behavior. In one study shoppers in a room smelling of flowers evaluated Nike shoes more positively than did consumers in an odor-free room.[83] Tesco, a U.K. grocery chain, seeks to stimulate coffee purchases by fitting its store-brand coffee packages with special aroma-releasing valves that let the scent waft out.[84]

MARKETING IMPLICATIONS Obviously, we like some products, for example, perfumes and scented candles, for the smell they produce. However, we may like other products, such as mouthwashes and deodorants, because they mask aromas. One company has introduced a spritzer that hides cigarette smells on hair and clothing.[85] Several other companies have introduced perfumes for dogs. Les Pooches, for example, is a dog perfume sold in chic department stores. The perfume is packaged in a bottle with gold tassels.[86]

Smell can also work to marketers' disadvantage. For example, many consumers dislike the smell of plastic containers that are used to pack prepared deli salads.[87] The smell of gasoline, paint, fertilizer, greasy food, or bleach is offensive to many and even harmful to some. One problem with using scent in the ambient retail environment is that consumers might dislike the scents or find them irritating. On the other hand, consumers value some products because they are devoid of smell, such as unscented deodorants, fabric softeners, carpet cleaners, and laundry detergents.

Finally, consumers' preferences for smells differ across cultures. Spices that are commonly used in one culture can literally make consumers ill in another. Only one smell (cola) is universally regarded as pleasant, which is good news for companies such as Coke and Pepsi that are expanding globally.[88] ●

Perceiving through Touch

Although we know far less about the sense of touch than of smell, we do know that touch (both what we touch with our fingers and how things feel as they come in contact with our skin) is a very important element for many products and services.

Effects of Touch on Physiological Responses and Moods Like the other senses, touch has important physiological and emotional effects. Depending on how we are touched, we can feel stimulated or relaxed. And research has shown that consumers who are touched by a salesperson are more likely to have positive feelings and are more likely to evaluate both the store and salesperson positively. In addition, customers who are touched by the salesperson are more likely to comply with the salesperson's requests.[89] Yet the effectiveness of being touched in sales situations differs from culture to culture. Compared with U.S. consumers, those in Latin America are more comfortable with touching and embracing. In Asia, however, touching between relative strangers is seen as an inappropriate gesture.[90]

Touch and Liking Clearly, consumers like some products because of their feel. Consumers buy skin creams and baby products for their soothing effect on the skin, and go to massage therapists to experience tactile sensations and feel relaxed. When making a purchase, consumers often want to touch before they buy. The way shoes and clothing feel when worn is a critical factor in purchasing decisions for those products. Knowing that consumers prefer to touch and try many products before they buy, the REI chain of sporting goods stores invites shoppers to test any product on display, from boots to bicycles. REI stores also maintain climbing walls and other simulated outdoor environs so shoppers can get a better sense of how products feel in use before they make a purchase decision.[91]

When Do We Perceive Stimuli?

Our senses are exposed to numerous inputs at any given time. To perceive each one would be overwhelming and extremely difficult. Fortunately, our sensory processing is simplified by the fact that many stimuli do not enter conscious awareness. For us to perceive something, it must be sufficiently intense.

Stimulus intensity is measured in units. The intensity of a smell can be measured by the concentration of the stimulus in a substance or in the air. Stimulus intensity of sounds can be measured in decibels and frequencies, and stimulus intensity of colors can be measured by properties like lightness, saturation, and hue. In the area of touch, stimulus intensity can be measured in terms of pounds or ounces of pressure.

absolute threshold
The minimum level of stimulus intensity needed to detect a stimulus.

Absolute Thresholds The **absolute threshold** is the minimum level of stimulus intensity needed for a stimulus to be perceived. In other words, the absolute threshold is the amount of intensity needed to detect a difference between something and nothing. As a marketing example, suppose you are driving on the highway and a billboard is in the distance. The absolute threshold is that point at which you can first see the billboard. Before that point, the billboard is below the absolute threshold and not sufficiently intense to be seen.

MARKETING IMPLICATIONS The obvious implication is that consumers will only consciously perceive a marketing stimulus when it is sufficiently high in intensity to be above the absolute threshold. Thus if images or words in a commercial are too small or the sound level is too low, consumers' sensory receptors will not be activated and the stimulus will not be consciously perceived. ●

differential threshold/ just noticeable difference (j.n.d.) The intensity difference needed between two stimuli before they are perceived to be different.

Weber's Law The stronger the initial stimulus, the greater the additional intensity needed for the second stimulus to be perceived as different.

Differential Thresholds Whereas the absolute threshold deals with whether a stimulus can be perceived, the **differential threshold** refers to the intensity difference needed between two stimuli before people can perceive that the stimuli are different. Thus the differential threshold is a relative concept; it is often called the **just noticeable difference (or j.n.d.)**. For example, when you get your eyes checked, the eye doctor often shows you a row of letters through different sets of lenses. If you can detect a difference between the two lenses, the new lens is sufficiently different to have crossed the differential threshold.

The psychophysiologist Ernst Weber first outlined the basic properties of the differential threshold in the 19th century. **Weber's Law** states that the stronger the initial stimulus, the greater the additional intensity needed for the second stimulus to be perceived as different. This relationship is outlined in the following formula:

$$\frac{\Delta s}{S = K}$$

where S is the initial stimulus value, Δs is the smallest change (Δ) in a stimulus capable of being detected, and K is a constant of proportionality.

Here is an example. Imagine that consumer testing found that 1 ounce would need to be added to a 10-ounce package before consumers could notice that the two packages weighed different amounts. Suppose we now have a 50-ounce box and want to know how much we must add before consumers could detect a difference. According to Weber's Law, K would be = 1/10 or 0.1. To determine how much would need to be added, we would solve for Δs as follows:

$$\frac{\Delta s}{50} = .10$$

The answer is .10 of the package weight, or 5 ounces.

MARKETING IMPLICATIONS The differential threshold has several important marketing implications.

When marketers do not want a differential threshold to be crossed. Sometimes marketers *do not* want consumers to notice a difference between two stimuli. For example, marketers might not want consumers to notice that they have decreased the size of the product or increased the price. Consumers got angry when they noticed that Long John Silver's was serving smaller food portions at the original price. In the airline industry, a j.n.d. was reached when consumers noticed that the seats in airplanes were being pushed closer together (leaving less and less leg room).

Although these practices raise some interesting ethical issues, marketers also use the differential threshold concept in more positive ways. Marketers of nonalcoholic beers, for example, have hoped that consumers would not be able to tell the difference between the taste of real and nonalcoholic beers.[92]

When marketers do want a differential threshold to be crossed. In other instances marketers do want consumers to perceive a difference between two stimuli. For example, McDonald's once increased the size of its regular hamburger patty by 25 percent but left the price the same, hoping that consumers would notice the change.[93] Likewise, if marketers decided to lower the price of a brand or service to stimulate sales, the sale price would need to be perceived as different from the regular price. If a product is improved in some way, the changes must be above the differential threshold for the consumer to notice. To illustrate, one brand of sunscreens differentiates itself on the basis of length of wear. Whereas other sunscreens last only 80 minutes, this brand lasts 6 hours—a difference that consumers will surely notice. As another example, the success of movies on DVD depends at least in part on their ability to look and sound perceptibly better than movies on videotape.

Many marketers hope that consumers can tell the difference between an old and an improved product. However, sometimes consumers cannot make the distinction because differential thresholds vary from sense to sense. For example, since our sense of smell is not well developed, we often fail to differentiate the smell of two versions of the same object. •

Subliminal Perception The concept of the perceptual threshold is important for another phenomenon—subliminal perception. Suppose you are sitting at a movie and are exposed to messages like "Eat Popcorn" and "Drink Coke." However, each message is shown on the screen for only a fraction of a second, so short a time that you are not consciously aware of them. Stimuli like these, presented below the threshold level of awareness, are called subliminal messages, and our perception of them is called **subliminal perception**.

subliminal perception The activation of sensory receptors by stimuli presented below the perceptual threshold.

Subliminal perception is different from preattentive processing. With preattentive processing our attention is directed at something other than the stimulus, for instance, at a magazine article instead of an ad in our peripheral vision. With subliminal perception our attention is directed squarely at the stimulus. Also, with preattentive processing the stimulus is fully present—if you shift your attention and look directly at the ad or billboard, you can easily see it. In contrast, subliminal stimuli are presented so quickly or are so degraded that the very act of perceiving them is difficult.

MARKETING IMPLICATIONS The question of whether stimuli presented subliminally affect consumers' responses has generated considerable controversy in the marketing field. A widely known but fraudulent study in the advertising industry claimed that consumers at a movie theater were subliminally exposed to messages on the movie screen that read "Eat Popcorn" and "Drink Coke." Reportedly, subliminal exposure to these messages influenced viewers' purchase of Coke and popcorn.[94] Although advertising agencies deny using such stimuli, some people have claimed that marketers are brainwashing consumers and attempting to manipulate them. These people also believe that ads containing these stimuli are effective.[95] This perception is perhaps fostered by the availability of self-help tapes with subliminal messages that claim to help consumers stop smoking, lose weight, and feel more relaxed. •

Does Subliminal Perception Affect Consumer Behavior? Despite public concern, research suggests that subliminal perception has limited effects on consumers.[96] Such stimuli have not been found to arouse motives like hunger. Nor do subliminally presented sexual stimuli affect consumers' attitudes or preferences. Research has also failed to show that subliminal stimuli affect consumers' explicit memory for ads or brands. As a result, the advertising community tends to dismiss subliminal perception research.

Interestingly, however, there is some evidence that stimuli presented below the threshold of conscious perception can reach our sensory registers. Researchers have found that if consumers are subliminally exposed to a word (e.g., razor), that word is recognized faster than words to which they have not been exposed subliminally.[97] Moreover, some preliminary evidence suggests that stimuli perceived subliminally can affect consumers' feelings. Consumers in one study were found to have stronger responses to ads with sexual subliminal implants than to those without.[98] Thus stimuli perceived subliminally are somehow analyzed for their meaning, and they can elicit primitive feeling responses. However, these effects do not appear to be sufficiently strong to alter consumers' preferences or to make an ad or brand more memorable. Exposing consumers to the message at or above the threshold level of awareness should have just as much or more impact, making the use of subliminal stimuli unnecessary.[99]

How Do Consumers Perceive a Stimulus?

Some research has focused on how individuals organize or combine the visual information they perceive. Consumers tend not to perceive a single stimulus in isolation; rather, they organize and integrate it in the context of the other things around it. Also, many stimuli are really a complex combination of numerous simple stimuli that consumers must organize into a unified whole using **perceptual organization**. This process represents a somewhat higher, more meaningful level of processing than simply having stimuli register on our sensory receptors. Marketers have borrowed some basic principles from Gestalt psychology to understand this phenomenon. These include the principles of figure and ground, closure, and grouping.

perceptual organization The process by which stimuli are organized into meaningful units.

Figure and Ground The principle of **figure and ground** suggests that people interpret incoming stimuli in contrast to a background. The figure is well defined and in the forefront, whereas the ground is indefinite, hazy, and in the background. In other words, the figure is the focal point of attention and perception, and the ground is everything else around it. The key point is that individuals tend to organize their perceptions into figure-and-ground relationships, and the manner in which this process occurs will determine how the stimulus is interpreted.

figure and ground The principle by which people interpret stimuli in the context of a background.

This principle suggests that advertisers plan for important brand information to be the figure, not the background. Moreover, the background should not detract from the figure. Advertisers often violate this principle when using sexy or attractive models in ad messages, with the result that the model becomes the figure and focal point, leaving the product or brand name unnoticed.

Closure **Closure** refers to the fact that individuals have a need to organize perceptions so that they form a meaningful whole. Even if a stimulus is incomplete, our need for closure will lead us to see it as complete. We therefore try to complete the stimulus. The key to using the need for closure, then, is to provide consumers with an incomplete stimulus.

closure The principle by which individuals have a need to organize perceptions so that they form a meaningful whole.

For example, putting a well-known television ad on the radio is effective in getting consumers to think about a message. The radio version of the ad is an in-

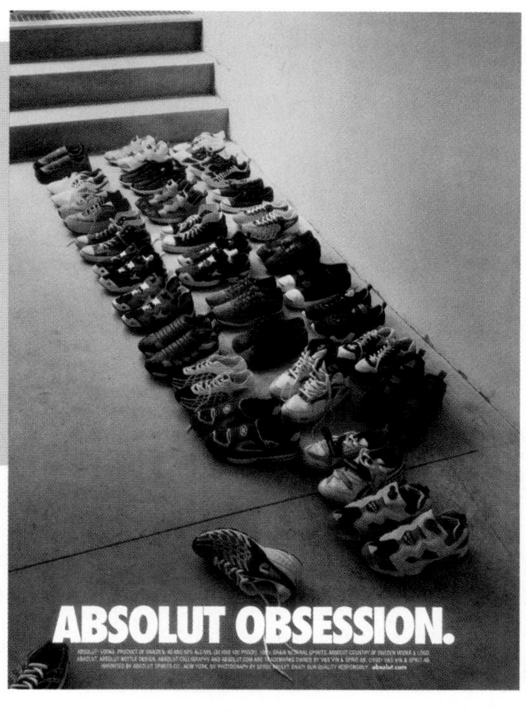

EXHIBIT 4.12
Closure
Because of our need for closure (to organize perceptions so they form a meaningful whole), we try to complete incomplete stimuli. Here we obtain closure by filling in the gaps between the shoes to see that they form a bottle of Absolut Vodka.

Source: Courtesy of TBWA/Chiat/Day.

grouping A tendency to group stimuli to form a unified picture or impression.

complete stimulus, and our need for closure leads us to picture the visual parts of the ad. Likewise, severely cropping objects in ads so that they appear ambiguous may be one way of getting consumers to think about what the object is and to gain closure.[100] The ad in Exhibit 4.12 cleverly uses the closure principle to get consumers to fill in the spaces between the shoes to form a bottle of Absolut vodka.

Grouping **Grouping** refers to the fact that we often group stimuli to form a unified picture or impression, making it easier to process them. We view similar or nearby objects as belonging together. Marketers can often influence the image or perception of a product or service by grouping it with other stimuli. For example, in the right photo of Exhibit 4.10, the green bottles are grouped together, and they are seen as different from the bluish green bottle.

In advertising, companies sometimes include more than one brand or product in an ad message to generate exposure through grouping. Target, for example, ran a series of ads featuring a famous brand or product alongside a Target item. The connection between the two was a play on words: Ruffles potato chips were shown next to a ruffled blouse; the Tide detergent logo was shown next to a jeans-clad model wading in the tide.[101] In merchandising, marketers often create a unified impression by displaying related items as a group. Consumers may perceive a table setting as elegant when the napkins, napkin holders, wine goblets, silverware, dishes, and serving bowls are cleverly grouped.

SUMMARY

For a marketing stimulus to have an impact, consumers must be exposed to it, allocate some attention to it, and perceive it. Attention and perception are mutually reinforcing processes. Consumers need a basic level of attention to perceive a stimulus; only then can they use additional mental resources to process the stimulus at higher levels. Exposure occurs when the consumer is presented with a marketing stimulus. Marketers are using a variety of traditional and nontraditional tactics (such as product placement) to increase stimulus exposure, particularly because consumers' exposure to marketing stimuli is selective.

Attention occurs when the consumer allocates processing capacity to the stimulus. Attention is selective, divided, and limited. Hence even tactics such as product placement do not guarantee that consumers will directly attend to marketing stimuli—though consumers may attend to the stimuli preattentively. Marketers believe that because the marketing environment is so cluttered they must attract consumers' attention to their own offerings. Making a stimulus personally relevant, pleasant, surprising, or easy to process enhances its attention-getting properties, and a number of marketing tactics influence these outcomes.

Consumers perceive a stimulus through one of their five senses. The processing of visual stimuli is influenced by size and color. Intensity and music are important aspects of aural stimuli. Taste perceptions are critical for some products, although taste perceptions can vary across cultures. Finally, the use of both smell and touch can be an effective marketing strategy for some products.

Perceptual thresholds determine the point at which stimuli are perceived. The absolute threshold is the lowest point at which an individual can experience a sensation. For a marketing stimulus to be perceived, it must be above the absolute threshold. The differential threshold is the minimal difference in stimulus intensity needed to detect that two stimuli are different. The differential threshold is important both when marketers do not want consumers to notice a difference between two stimuli (like a price increase) and when they do (such as in the case of product improvements).

Consumers can sometimes perceive things that are outside their conscious level of awareness, a phenomenon called subliminal perception. However, the perception of these stimuli seems to have limited impact on consumers' motives or behaviors. Finally, perceptual organization occurs when consumers organize a set of stimuli into a coherent whole. The Gestalt principles of figure and ground, closure, and grouping affect this process. These principles raise some interesting implications for how consumers perceive items in ads and in merchandise displays.

QUESTIONS FOR REVIEW AND DISCUSSION

1. How do zipping and zapping affect consumers' exposure to stimuli such as products and ads?
2. What is attention, and what are three key characteristics?
3. In what ways do prominence and habituation affect consumer attention?
4. What is perception, and what methods do we use to perceive stimuli?
5. Differentiate between the absolute threshold and the differential threshold, and explain how these concepts relate to Weber's Law.
6. What are the three main principles in perceptual organization?

EXERCISES

1. Select a good or service that would typically be considered high in involvement and one that would be considered low in involvement. Design an advertisement to encourage attention to and perception of each chosen good or service. How are these two situations similar? How are they different? Exchange your work with a classmate, and explain your rationale for each advertisement. Critique your classmate's work as he or she critiques yours on the basis of how effectively each ad attracts attention and perception.
2. Browse through a copy of one of your favorite magazines looking for three ads that you think are most effective for generating exposure, attention, and perception. Also find three ads that are ineffective for each process. What makes the good ones effective? What do you think is wrong with the others, and how could they be improved?
3. Watch TV for one hour (recorded on a VCR if possible). During this period, describe the ads that got your attention. Why were they successful in attracting you? For which ads did you want to engage in zipping or zapping and why?
4. Identify as many examples as you can in which marketers want consumers to perceive a just noticeable difference between their product and a competitor's, or between an old product and a new one. Also find examples in which marketers do not want consumers to perceive such a difference. Consider not only visual aspects of the product or service, such as how big or small it is, but other perceptual differences as well (how it tastes, feels, smells, sounds).
5. Visit a local shopping mall and examine the interiors of three or four stores. Describe the physiological and psychological responses that different stores try to create. How do they do so through the use of color, brightness, and contrast? What other sensory stimuli do these stores use to encourage consumer response?
6. Read about color trends and future color predictions in the press releases and reports of the Color Marketing Group (www.colormarketing.org). What colors are expected to be popular in the next few years—and why? Choose a particular product, such as a specific car model, and explain how the color forecasts you reviewed might affect the marketing of that product.
7. Examine the home pages of two competing online retailers, such as Amazon.com and Barnesandnoble.com. How does each site use the principles of perceptual organization to focus consumer attention on specific offerings? How does each make its stimuli pleasant, surprising, or easy to process? Which home page appears to be most effective in attracting your attention and perception—and why?

chapter 5

Knowledge and Understanding

Introduction: An Old Brand Targets New Customers

Can an old brand become a hit with a new generation? That's the challenge facing Redox Brands of West Chester, Ohio, which recently bought the 70-year-old Oxydol laundry detergent brand from Procter & Gamble. Lacking marketing support from P&G, Oxydol's annual sales had fallen below $6 million—less than one-tenth of its sales level in 1950. Then two former P&G executives, Richard Owen and Todd Wichmann, teamed up to form Redox and buy Oxydol. They believed that baby boomers would buy the product because it was so familiar—consumers would remember seeing it in the family laundry room when they were children. To reinforce this familiarity, the company repackaged Oxydol in its original bull's eye box and arranged for national exposure through product placement in the 106 stores of the Restoration Hardware chain.

However, when Redox officials conducted research to better understand how consumers view Oxydol, they learned that their assumptions were inaccurate. In focus groups, baby boomers and older consumers proclaimed their loyalty to Tide and other popular brands of today. They also said they would not change to a detergent that cost about the same as their current brand. In contrast, the twentysomethings in these focus groups expressed no loyalty to currently popular brands, said they didn't want to buy the same detergent as their parents, and weren't concerned with price. They also said they preferred to use liquid rather than powdered detergents.

Based on this research, Redox decided to target Oxydol to twentysomethings. It quickly created a new green package with a label stating: "Don't freak. Help conquer your most extreme dirt, not to mention laundrophobia." The X in Oxydol was made

EXHIBIT 5.1
Targeting Oxydol to Twentysomethings
Redox has revamped the marketing of Oxydol laundry detergent to appeal to consumers in their twenties, who say they don't want to use the same detergent as their parents.

Source: Courtesy of Redox Brands, Inc.

especially prominent on the label to suggest a link with Generation X. To launch the product, Redox created ads featuring a mud-caked dirt biker. The company also put up a campy Web site (www.the-extreme-clean.com) with cleaning hints, games, and more. Just a few months later, it introduced Liquid Oxydol Extreme Clean, again with green packaging and an outsized X in the brand (see Exhibit 5.1). Only time will tell whether twentysomethings become loyal to a brand that was a category leader decades before their birth.[1]

Oxydol's situation illustrates many concepts relevant to this chapter. First, some consumers have a number of favorable associations linked with various laundry detergent brands. Different detergent brands have different images and personalities, which means consumers view them as different from one another. Consumers also see liquid and powdered detergents as part of the broader category of laundry detergents, in which Tide is the prototypical brand. In addition, consumers have prior knowledge that allows them to categorize brands and products as specific detergent varieties. Finally, consumers' knowledge serves as a basis for interpreting information from Oxydol advertising and other sources.

In the preceding chapter, you learned how consumers attend to and perceive things. This chapter goes a step further, asking how consumers understand the world around them. To answer this question we need to know how consumers relate what they perceive and attend to with what they already know—their prior knowledge. As Exhibit 5.2 shows, this chapter describes two broad domains of knowledge—knowledge content (stored information) and knowledge structure. The chapter also describes how prior knowledge is used for understanding, including categorization and comprehension. •

OVERVIEW OF KNOWLEDGE AND UNDERSTANDING

knowledge content
Information we already have in memory.

knowledge structure
The way in which knowledge is organized.

categorization
The process of labeling or identifying an object. Involves relating what we perceive in our external environment to what we already know.

comprehension
The process of deepening understanding. Involves using prior knowledge to understand more about what we have categorized.

Knowledge content reflects the information we have already learned about brands, companies, product categories, stores, ads, people, how to shop, how to use products, and so on. Companies sometimes use marketing to develop, add to, or change consumers' knowledge content. **Knowledge structure** refers to the way we organize knowledge. Consumers often organize knowledge into categories, with similar things stored in the same category. For example, certain brands of toothpaste, such as Gleem and Pearl Drops, may be stored in a category called whitening toothpastes. These brands, along with others, for example, Crest and Close-Up, may be stored in a more general category called toothpaste. All these brands plus dental floss and other related products might be stored in a category called dental hygiene products.

Prior knowledge is essential for two levels of consumer understanding—categorization and comprehension. **Categorization** is the process of labeling or identifying an object that we perceive in our external environment based on its similarity to what we already know. Thus you might label Trident dental gum as a dental hygiene product as opposed to a candy product and relate it to your knowledge of other dental hygiene products. **Comprehension** is the process of using prior knowledge to understand more about what has been categorized. For example, you might relate the picture, headline, and ad copy in a Trident ad and understand that "Trident dental gum is good for teeth and can achieve some of the same benefits as brushing."

We say that we "know" something when we have encountered it before and have somehow come to understand what it means and what it is like. Knowing therefore has to do with our prior knowledge—both what we have encountered (knowledge content) and how it relates to other knowledge (knowledge structure).

KNOWLEDGE CONTENT

schema The set of associations linked to a concept.

The content of our knowledge reflects the set of things we have learned in the past and may consist of many facts. For example, you may know that a banana has 100 calories, that Utah is the Beehive State, and that you need to change your car's oil every 5,000 miles. These facts are not stored as random facts; rather, they are generally linked to or associated with a concept. The set of associations linked to a concept is called a **schema**.[2]

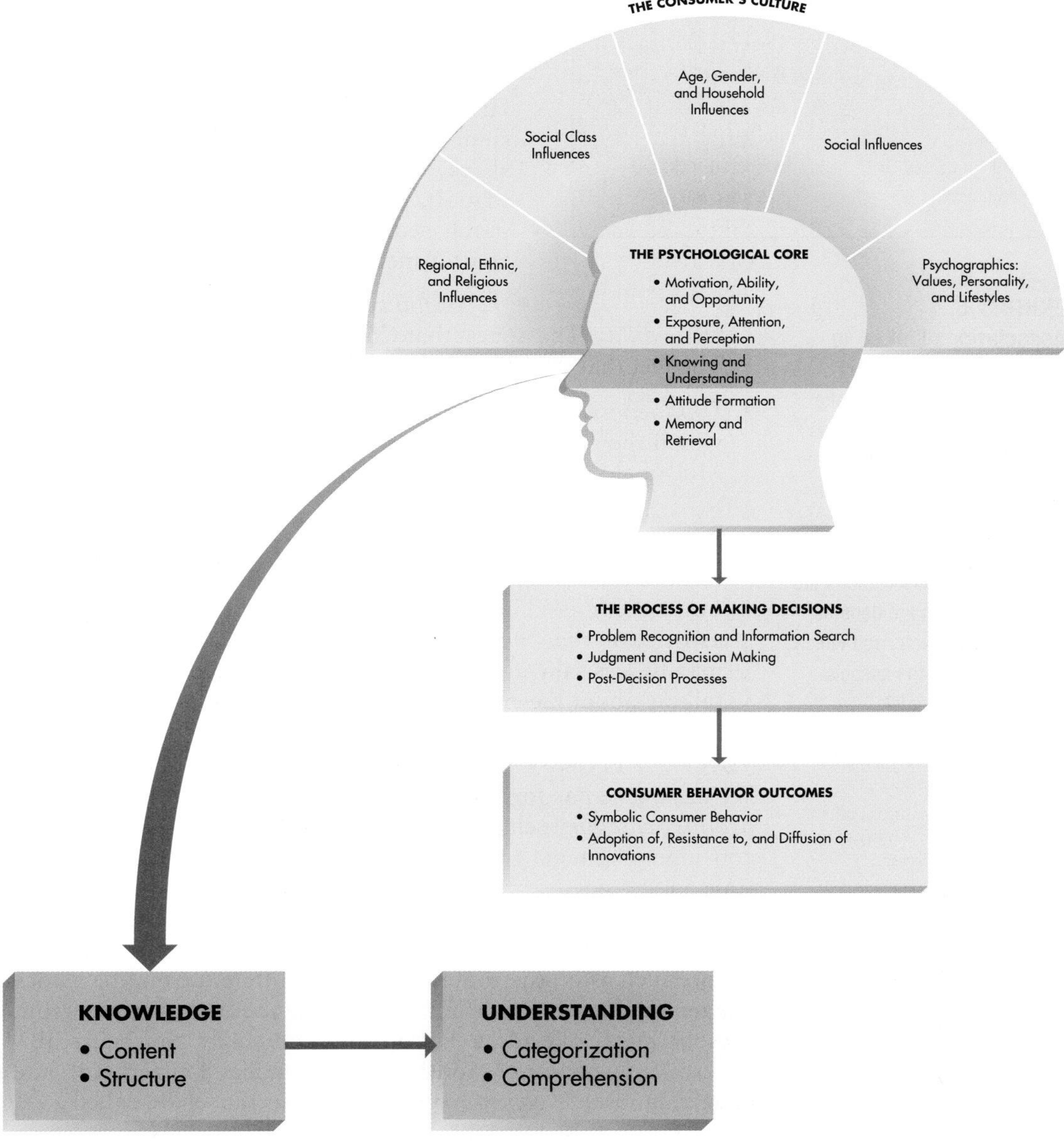

EXHIBIT 5.2
Chapter Overview: Knowledge and Understanding

We categorize information that we perceive by comparing it with what we already know. Prior knowledge includes two basic domains: content and structure. Once something is categorized, we use prior knowledge to comprehend more about it.

GUCCI	PRADA
Los Angeles	New York
Goldie Hawn	Uma Thurman
Brad Pitt	Willem Dafoe
Bamboo/calf bag	Black nylon backpack
Swingers	Intellectuals
Hip-huggers	Flat-front pants
Skin-tight	Boxy
Frivolous	Utilitarian
High tart	High concept
Boisterous	Ethereal
Stiletto	Clunky square toe
Strapless	Patchwork
Edgy	Minimal
Caviar	Truffles
Single-malt scotch	Vodka on rocks
Bikini wax	Eyebrow wax

EXHIBIT 5.3
Associations Linked to Gucci and Prada
Different brand names evoke different associations. Here is a set of associations that some consumers link to the names Gucci and Prada. What associations do you link with these names? Which associations are attributes, which are benefits, which are favorable, and which are unique? Are the associations equally salient?

Source: From "Houses of Style" from "How to Tell Two Hot Fashion Names Apart," from *The Wall Street Journal*, January 27, 1999, B1, B4. Used by permission of *The Wall Street Journal* via The Copyright Clearance Center.

A schema for the concept banana has many associations—for example, it has 100 calories, is yellow, bruises easily, and can be very slippery if stepped on. The associations that some consumers link to the brand concepts Gucci and Prada are noted in Exhibit 5.3. A schema is elaborated when we have many associations linked to the concept.

Schemas and Associations

The associations in schemas can be described along several dimensions.[3]

- *Types of associations.* Consumers have many types of associations. One schema for banana might include associations that reflect (1) the attributes of a banana (yellow, long, soft, has a lot of potassium), (2) its benefits (nutritious, low in fat), (3) people who use it (athletes who lose a lot of potassium through sweating), (4) times when it is used (as a snack, for breakfast), (5) places it is used (at home, at school), (6) ways it is used (peeled, sliced), (7) places it is purchased (at a grocery store), (8) places it is grown (in South America), and so on.
- *Favorability.* Associations can be described in terms of their *favorability.* The notion that Coke tastes great might be evaluated as favorable. The fact that Afghanistan has been associated with terrorism might not.
- *Uniqueness.* Associations vary in their *uniqueness*—that is, the extent to which they are also related to other concepts. "Greasiness" is not unique to McDonald's, but the Golden Arches and Ronald McDonald are.
- *Salience.* Associations vary in their *salience,* or the ease with which they come to mind when the concept is activated. For example, a consumer might always retrieve the association of Golden Arches upon hearing the McDonald's name. Less salient associations may be retrieved only in certain contexts. Thus the association that McDonald's is making its packaging environmentally friendly may be less salient, and a consumer may think about it only if someone starts talking about the environment.

Types of Schemas

We have schemas for many entities. The banana example is an illustration of a *product category* schema; however, we also have schemas for *brands.* Russian consumers' schema for Aeroflot, the state airline, includes associations such as stale air, cramped seats, and dilapidated interiors. We also have schemas for *people* like our mothers, Tiger Woods, teenagers, working-class people, and so on. We have schemas for *services* and for *stores,* although the associations linked to a store such as Nordstrom may be quite different from the associations linked to Kmart. We have schemas for *salespeople* (cosmetics salesperson, used car salesperson), *ads* (Coke ads, Benetton ads), *companies* (Starbucks, IBM), *places* (Lake Tahoe, Vail), *countries* (South Africa, Somalia, Switzerland), and *animals* (lynx, cougar, moose). We even have a schema for ourselves, called a *self-schema.*

brand image A subset of salient and feeling-related associations stored in a brand schema.

Images

An image is a subset of associations that reflect what a brand stands for and how favorably it is viewed.[4] For instance, our **brand image** of McDonald's may be favorable, and it may include such associations as a family-friendly place and fast food. An image does not represent *all* the associations linked to a schema—only those that are most salient and make the brand different from other brands in the category. Thus although we may know that McDonald's serves some low-fat foods, this knowledge need not be used to form our brand image. We also have images for other marketing entities like stores, companies, places, and countries. The Gap and Victoria's Secret have very strong images in the United States.[5] In Japan, images of companies such as Sony, Takashimaya, and Matsushita Electric are very strong.[6]

brand personality The set of associations that reflect the personification of the brand.

In addition, schemas can include associations that reflect the **brand's personality**—that is, how the consumer would describe the brand as if it were a person.[7] Consumers from one study described the Whirlpool brand as gentle, sensitive, quiet, good-natured, flexible, modern, cheerful, and creative. Researchers found that these associations suggested a modern and family-oriented suburban woman who is neighborly, successful, attractive, and action-oriented. Whirlpool's personality was quite different from KitchenAid's, whose name personified a smart, aggressive, glamorous, wealthy, elegant, and fashionable career woman.[8] When Whirlpool began expanding in Europe, it used an advertising campaign to create a brand personality linked to powerful goddesses. The success of this campaign led Whirlpool to adapt the campaign for U.S. markets, where it is targeting working mothers.[9]

Stores, places, and salespeople may also have personalities. Sometimes brand personalities are embodied in brand characters like Spuds MacKenzie, Charlie the Tuna, Tony the Tiger, and the Maytag repairman. Think about the personality exemplified by each of these characters and how the character's personality says something about the personality of the brand. One study found that many brands could be described according to their position on the five brand personality dimensions shown in Exhibit 5.4.

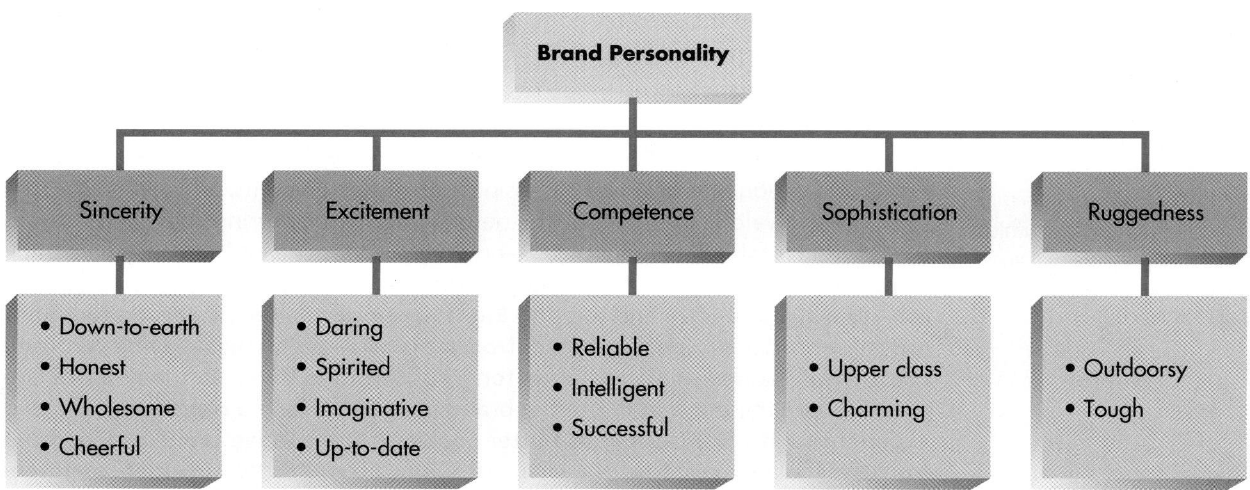

EXHIBIT 5.4
A Brand Personality Framework

One researcher found that many brands can be described according to one or more of the five personality types depicted here. Which dimensions best characterize Pepsi's brand personality? Which describe the personalities of Starbucks? Dell? Vespa? AT&T?

Source: Reprinted with permission from *Journal of Marketing Research*, published by the American Marketing Association, Jennifer L. Aaker, August 1997, vol. 34, pp. 347–356.

MARKETING IMPLICATIONS Because schemas, images, and personalities are important to consumer knowledge, marketers must work on creating these elements, developing them, changing them, and protecting them.

Creating new schemas, images, and personalities. When an offering is new, the marketer has to create a schema, image, and/or personality to help consumers understand what it is, what it can do for them, and how it differs from competitive offerings. Creating schemas is especially important for new products because consumers may not yet understand what these new products are or what they offer. Clear Channel Communications, for example, created a schema to help consumers understand its online radio music subscription service. The idea is to position the service as a kind of music club where members can download songs and replay them as often as desired—as long as members continue subscribing.[10] Because this service differs from other radio and music services, Clear Channel must use marketing to effectively communicate the features and benefits of the offering.

Creating schemas and images for a company is also important so that consumers understand the general types of products produced by the firm. Georgia-based AFLAC, for instance, offers supplemental health and accident insurance. Consumers didn't know much about the company until it adopted a friendly white duck as its mascot in print and television advertising, giving AFLAC a concrete personality. Within a year, AFLAC had increased its brand recognition among Americans to 90 percent—and sent annual U.S. sales growth up 30 percent.[11]

Schemas, images, and personalities can sometimes be created by means of brand extensions, licensing agreements, and brand alliances.

brand extension A marketing strategy in which a firm that markets a product with a well-developed image uses the same brand name but in a different product category.

licensing A marketing strategy in which a firm sells the rights to the brand name to another company that will use the name on its product.

brand alliance A marketing strategy in which two companies' brand names are presented together on a single product.

- A **brand extension** occurs when a firm uses the brand name from a product with a well-developed image, like Jell-O gelatin, on a product in a different category, such as Jell-O pudding pops. Other examples of brand extensions include Victoria's Secret cosmetics and Skippy peanut butter cookies.
- **Licensing** occurs when a firm sells the rights to the brand name to another company that will use the name on its product. For example, DaimlerChrysler has licensed the Jeep brand to be used on baby strollers, clothing, eyeglasses, luggage, toys, and bicycles.[12]
- A **brand alliance** occurs when two companies' brand names appear together on a single product. Examples include Intel chips in Compaq computers, Breyer's ice cream with Reese's Pieces in it, and the Northwest Airlines Visa card.

One consequence of brand extensions, license agreements, and alliances is that consumers develop an image for the new brand by transferring to it their associations and favorable feelings from the original brand's schema.[13] If consumers think Skippy peanut butter is rich and smooth, they may infer that Skippy peanut butter cookies will also be rich and smooth. But if the Skippy name appears on too many different products—cookies, bread, frozen dinners—consumers may be confused about what Skippy actually stands for. Thus, a brand extension may make the schema less coherent and dilute the brand image.[14] Also, if a consumer has a bad experience with Skippy peanut butter cookies, the negative feelings generated from the cookies may affect the image of Skippy peanut butter. Given these potential problems, marketers need to be concerned about the long-term effects of these strategies.[15]

At a more fundamental level, creating a set of associations linked to an offering helps to position the offering so that consumers understand what it is and what it competes against. For example, the Body Shop's association with social responsibility differentiates it from Avon (associated with personal selling) and other cosmetics competitors.[16]

Developing existing schemas, images, and personalities. Although marketers must sometimes create new schemas, in other cases they must develop or elaborate a schema—that is, add information to an existing schema so that consumers understand more about it.[17] One way to develop schemas is with multiple brand extensions. Although the name Arm & Hammer was once associated only with baking soda, the extension of the name to such categories as kitty litter, carpet deodorizer, and refrigerator deodorizer has reinforced its deodorizing image. Another way is to link the product to sponsorship in an appropriate sporting event, as a way of strengthening and developing the existing schema and personality.[18] A third way is to highlight different features and benefits, as Avis Rent A Car has done with ads focusing on quality customer service as well as other aspects of its offering.[19]

Changing schemas, images, and personalities. Sometimes consumers' schemas, images, and brand personalities contain associations that require change. When a brand image becomes stale or outdated or when negative associations develop, marketers need to find ways to add new and positive associations. White Rain recently overhauled the image of its 35-year-old Dippity-Do women's hair styling gel by changing the product name, targeting, packaging, and advertising. Dippity-Do Sport Gel for teenage boys now comes in a cobalt blue squeeze bottle and is advertised using professional athletes such as Brian Griese of the Denver Broncos.[20] As another example, Lipton has retired its traditional brand symbol, Sir Thomas J. Lipton, in favor of a trendier tea-drinking character, as shown in Exhibit 5.5.[21]

The images of stores, tourist destinations, services, and entire product categories may also require change. Selfridges, a venerable British department store, is transforming its image by stocking hipper, more upscale brands and hosting appearances by Iman and other popular celebrities, in a bid to attract younger customers.[22] Similarly, gun makers and retailers are working to portray guns as sporting equipment, not as deadly weapons used in crime.[23] And Sony and other electronics manufacturers are changing their brand images in line with younger consumers' associations with cutting-edge technology and styling. After research showed that teenagers viewed the Walkman brand as outdated because of associations with older cassette technology, Sony changed the brand image by introducing sleek new digital music devices for MP3 files.[24]

Protecting brand images. Brand images may be threatened during crises that involve potential harm, such as reports of contaminated products or health problems linked to specific products. St. Joseph Aspirin, which originally made low-dose aspirin for children, faced this challenge after doctors discovered that children who took aspirin for viral infections might develop deadly Reye's syndrome. The company kept the St. Joseph brand but changed its marketing, targeting adults who want to take low-dose aspirin to reduce the risk of strokes and heart problems. To build on positive associations formed decades earlier—when today's adults were given St. Joseph's aspirin as children—the company switched back to an older packaging design.[25]

How a company responds to a crisis affects its brand image, but research indicates that consumers' prior expectations also play a critical role. Companies whose customers held a strong positive image of the

EXHIBIT 5.5
Lipton Makes a Change
Lipton has replaced the brand symbol of founder Thomas J. Lipton, which appeared on packaging and marketing materials for more than 100 years, with a trendier tea-drinking fellow. This move is part of Lipton's strategy to attract younger consumers and compete more effectively with other beverages.

Source: © 2001 Lipton. Courtesy of Unilever Bestfoods North America.

EXHIBIT 5.6

A Script for Product Usage

A script is a set of associations linked with how we do something. Radio Shack's Gift express service may be relevant to consumers because it performs all the activities that are part of a consumer's script for "giving a gift to someone who is far away."

Source: Ad reprinted with permission.

brand prior to the crisis suffered less image damage than companies whose customers had lower expectations. Thus, firms with weaker brand images should be prepared to act aggressively in supporting their brands after a crisis.[26] ●

Scripts

Schemas represent our knowledge about objects or things.[27] A **script** is a special type of schema that represents knowledge of a sequence of events. For example, you may have a script for how to arrange roses bought from the store: you open the cellophane wrapping, get scissors, fill a vase with water, run the roses under water, cut them, and then arrange them in the vase. This knowledge helps you accomplish tasks quickly and easily. In contrast, when you do something for the first time, such as assembling a piece of Ikea furniture, having no prior script may prolong the task.

script A special type of schema that represents knowledge of a sequence of events.

MARKETING IMPLICATIONS Scripts help marketers understand how consumers buy and use an offering. In turn, marketers use this knowledge to make marketing decisions that improve products or services. Marketers may also perform tasks that are part of consumers' scripts. As the ad in Exhibit 5.6 indicates, Radio Shack facilitates gift buying by performing the packaging and shipping tasks that are normally part of consumers' gift-buying scripts. In other cases, marketers may want consumers to consider using a particular brand or product as part of a scripted activity—incorporating hands-free devices as part of their cell phone usage script, for example. Interactive shopping and advertising are changing the way consumers perform scripted activities such as buying products and processing ads. Amazon.com, for instance, offers wish lists as a way for consumers to quickly identify, buy, and ship gifts they know are wanted by family and friends. ●

KNOWLEDGE STRUCTURE

Although schemas and scripts reflect the content of what we know, our lives would be utter chaos if we did not have some way of organizing or structuring our knowledge. Fortunately, as shown in the next sections, we are adept at organizing our knowledge and categorizing information.

Categories and Their Structure

taxonomic category An orderly classification of objects, with similar objects in the same category.

Objects can be organized into **taxonomic categories.**[28] A taxonomic category is an orderly classification of objects with similar objects in the same category. For

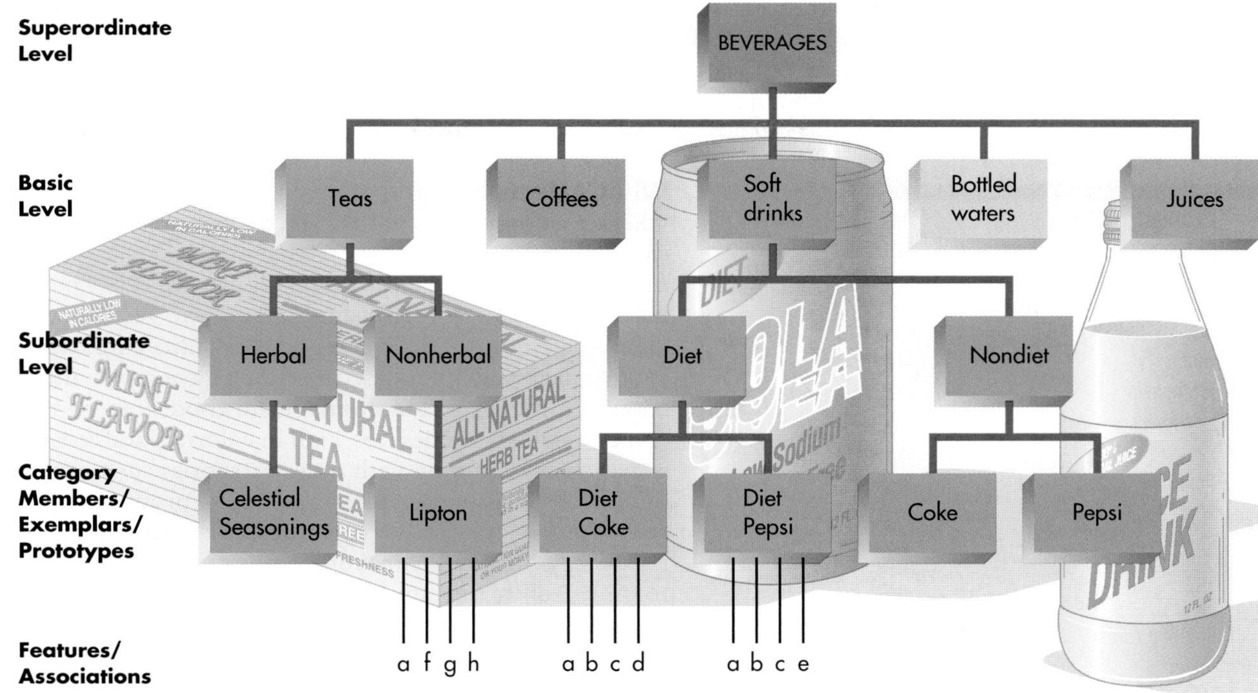

EXHIBIT 5.7
Taxonomic Category Structure

Objects can be organized in ordered, hierarchically structured categories, with similar objects in the same category. For example, herbal and nonherbal teas are subordinate to the basic-level category of teas. Teas, coffees, and soft drinks are members of the superordinate category, beverages. The letters under each brand signify attributes linked with each brand. Brands with the same letters have the same attributes. For example, the three brands share a common attribute "a" (e.g., caffeine) while only Diet Coke and Lipton share attribute "b" (e.g., artificial sweetner).

example, although we have schemas for Coke, Pepsi, Diet Coke, and so on, these schemas might be clustered in a category called soft drinks. Moreover, we may use subcategories to cluster specific brands and separate them from others. Thus we might have one subcategory for diet soft drinks and a different subcategory for nondiet soft drinks. In turn, soft drinks may be part of a larger beverage category that also includes coffees, teas, juices, and bottled water, as shown in Exhibit 5.7.

Graded Structure and Prototypicality Things that are in the same taxonomic category share similar features, and the features they share are different from the features that characterize objects in other categories. So a category member such as Diet Coke shares many associations with members of its own category of diet colas but shares few associations with members of other categories. Note that in Exhibit 5.7, Diet Coke has associations a–d, and Diet Pepsi has many but not all of the same associations (a–c and e). Lipton tea has associations a and f–h, which means it has few associations in common with Diet Coke.

Even though a category includes members that share similar features, not every member is perceived to be an equally good category member. For example, you might perceive a robin to be a better example of the category bird than a flamingo is. Likewise, you might view Coke as a better example of a soft drink than Shasta is. The fact that category members vary in how well they are perceived to represent a category illustrates the principle of **graded structure.**[29]

graded structure
The fact that category members vary in how well they represent a category.

prototype The best example of a category.

Within a category, you as a consumer can rank specific category members according to how well you believe they represent the category. The category **prototype** is that category member perceived to be the best example of the category. Thus a robin is a prototypical bird, and Coke is a prototypical soft drink. Exhibit 5.8 identifies brands generally regarded as prototypes in their product categories.

PRODUCT CATEGORY	PROTOTYPICAL BRANDS
Children's entertainment	Disney
Laundry detergent	Tide
Film	Kodak
Toothpaste	Crest
Electronics	Sony
Peanut butter	Skippy
Tuna fish	Starkist
Soup	Campbell's
Bologna	Oscar Mayer
Ketchup	Heinz
Bleach	Clorox
Greeting cards	Hallmark
Jeans	Levi's
Tires	Goodyear
Grape jelly	Welch's
Copiers	Xerox
Mustard	French's
Gelatin	Jell-O
Hamburgers	McDonald's
Baby lotion	Johnson & Johnson
Tools	Black & Decker
Cereal	Kellogg's
Tissue	Kleenex
Acetaminophen	Tylenol

EXHIBIT 5.8
Prototypical Brands
Brands viewed as the best examples of a product category are called prototypical brands. Prototypical brands tend to have many features in common with other brands in the category, are encountered frequently, and may have been the first entrant in the product category.

What Affects Prototypicality? Several factors affect whether a consumer regards something as a prototypical category member.[30] The first is shared associations: a prototype shares the most associations with other members of its own category and shares the fewest with members from different categories. Potato chips are a prototypical snack food because they have associations common to many snack foods (taste good, finger food, come in many varieties, are high in calories) and few associations in common with other categories such as dinner foods. A second feature that affects prototypicality is the frequency with which an object is encountered as a category member. Amazon.com is regarded as a prototypical place to buy books on the Internet because consumers are likely to have frequently encountered its name when online or when searching for online sources of books. The first or "pioneer" brand in a category may also be a prototype because it sets a standard against which brands introduced subsequently are compared. Amazon.com is a prototypical brand in this regard as well.

MARKETING IMPLICATIONS Prototypes represent the main point of comparison that consumers use to categorize a new brand. Therefore, a brand can develop its identity by being positioned as either close to or different from the prototype.

Positioning close to the prototype. Positioning a brand as close to the category prototype is appropriate when the goal is to appeal to a broad segment of consumers. Because the prototype best defines the category and is well liked, a new brand positioned as similar to it may appeal to a large segment of consumers. Comparative advertising may be a useful tool for making a brand seem similar to a prototype. If a challenger brand such as Barnesandnoble.com comes into the market and directly compares itself to Amazon.com, the challenger may be seen as similar to the prototype.[31] After Red Bull, based in Austria, pioneered the U.S. market for energy soft drinks, competitors Anheuser-Busch, Coca-Cola, and Snapple brought out their own energy beverages positioned close to the Red Bull prototype.[32]

Positioning away from the prototype. An alternative strategy is to position the new brand away from the prototype. Häagen-Dazs successfully promoted its ultrarich ice cream when consumers were fixated on bran and low cholesterol.[33] Red Hat, which offers Linux computer operating systems, positions itself as an alternative to the dominant Windows operating systems offered by Microsoft.[34] This is a good strategy when the brand is different from others (particularly from the prototype) and the point of difference represents a credible reason for buying. It is also appropriate when the goal is to appeal to consumers with specific needs. For example, whereas most rental car companies offer basically the same service, Enterprise differentiated itself by providing vehicle delivery and customer pickup service.[35] ●

Correlated Associations While graded structure reflects one way knowledge is structured, another way depends on whether the associations linked to category members are correlated, or go together. For example, in the category of automobiles, car size is positively correlated with safety (larger cars are generally safer), and engine size is negatively correlated with miles per gallon (the bigger the engine, the fewer miles per gallon). If consumers believe that car size, miles per gallon, and safety are generally correlated, they may infer that a new car with a large engine is safe but not very fuel efficient—inferences that may or may not be true of the brand. Thus **correlated associations** can have important effects on the inferences consumers make about a new brand that is seen as a member of a particular category and the types of communications marketers need to make to overcome potentially false inferences.

correlated associations Associations linked to a schema that go together.

Hierarchical Structure A final way in which taxonomic categories are structured is hierarchically. As Exhibit 5.7 indicates, taxonomic categories can be hierarchically organized into basic, subordinate, and superordinate levels. The broadest level of categorization is the **superordinate level**. The superordinate level groups objects that share a few associations but also have many different ones. Diet Coke and Arrowhead bottled water are both members of the beverages category. Although they have some common associations, they also have many that are different.

Finer discriminations among these objects are made at the **basic level**. Beverages might be more finely represented by categories such as teas, coffees, and soft drinks. The objects in the teas category have more in common with each other than they do with objects in the coffee category. The finest level of differentiation exists at the **subordinate level**. For example, soft drinks might be subdivided into categories of diet and nondiet soft drinks. Again, members of the diet soft drink category have more associations in common with each other than they do with members of the nondiet category. Consumers often have many levels of subcategorization; for beverages, they may consider whether soft drinks are diet or nondiet, colas or not colas, caffeinated or decaffeinated.

superordinate level The broadest level of category organization, containing different objects that share few associations but are still members of the category.

basic level A level of categorization below the superordinate category that contains objects in more refined categories.

subordinate level A level of categorization below the basic level that contains objects in very finely differentiated categories.

Consumers use more associations to describe objects in progression from the superordinate to the basic to the subordinate levels. They may apply associations "drinkable" and "used throughout the day" to all members of the beverages category. However, they may add other associations—carbonated, served cold, and sold in six-packs—to describe members of the soft drink category, then add the associations of no calories and artificial sweeteners to describe members at the subordinate diet drink level.

MARKETING IMPLICATIONS Understanding consumers' hierarchical category structure helps marketers identify their competitors. Although consumers often make choices among brands at the basic or subordinate level, in some cases they choose from brands that belong to a common superordinate category. For example, if you are deciding whether to buy an MP3 player for your home or a new car stereo, you are making a decision among products that belong to different basic categories within a common superordinate-level category (music entertainment products). The brands in both categories might be compared based on higher-order attributes that link the brands to the same superordinate-level category (how much entertainment they provide, how much they cost). And although marketers of MP3 players might not normally think about competing with car stereo brands, they are rivals in this situation. In line with this thinking, Nestlé is trying to get consumers to think about its Nescafé coffee as being a beverage, not just a coffee product. Positioning it more widely may make consumers think about Nescafé coffee whenever they want any kind of beverage.[36]

Establishing a competitive position. By understanding consumers' superordinate-category structure, marketers can glean a broad view of their competition and use this understanding to establish an appropriate competitive position. Understanding subordinate categories also helps marketers determine which attributes to emphasize so consumers will properly categorize their offering. For example, nonalcoholic beer is positioned as a subordinate category of beer, which suggests that its advertising should not only stress features central to beer (great beer taste) but also clarify its subordinate-category membership by promoting associations (without the alcohol).

Designing retail channels and Web sites. Basic, subordinate, and superordinate category levels also have implications for consumer search and the design of retail environments and Web sites. Generally, grocery stores are designed so that objects in taxonomically similar categories are shelved together, as are items in the same basic- and subordinate-level categories. For example, most grocery stores have a dairy (superordinate level) section with shelves for milk, yogurt, cheese, eggs, and so on (basic level). Within each of these sections are subordinate categories of items such as low-fat, nonfat, and whole milk. Placing items in ways that are consistent with the structure of consumers' knowledge helps consumers find products efficiently. This is why White Wave markets its soymilk by packaging it in milk cartons and placing it in the refrigerated milk section of the store as a subcategory of milk.[37]

Similarly, Web sites are likely to be easier to use if they take consumers first to superordinate categories (such as toys) then to more basic-level categories (such as toys for boys) and finally to subordinate categories (such as toys for boys aged 7 to 8). Sites such as KBToys.com do a good job of matching a typical consumer's hierarchical structure for the product category. ●

Goal-Derived Categories

goal-derived category Category of things that are viewed as belonging together because they serve the same goals.

In addition to taxonomic categories, we may also organize our prior knowledge according to **goal-derived categories**. A goal-derived category contains things that consumers view as relevant to the goal. Sometimes we assign things to the same category because they serve the same goals—even though they belong to different taxonomic categories.[38] For example, when traveling on an airplane, you might see novels, blankets, and peanuts in the same category because all are part of the goal-derived category "things that make air travel more pleasant." Because we have many goals, we can have many goal-derived categories. For example, if you are on a diet, you might form a category for "foods to eat on a diet." Likewise, you might have goal-derived categories like "things to do on Friday nights" or "interesting sites on the Web."

Consumers frequently encounter certain goals and therefore have firmly established categories of prior knowledge for those goals. For example, if you give a lot of parties, the goal-derived category of "things to buy for a party" probably comprises a fairly stable and constant set of products. In contrast, you may create relevant categories on a situation-by-situation basis for less frequently encountered goals.

Category structure is flexible: the same object can be part of a goal-derived and a taxonomic category. Thus, Diet Coke might be part of the taxonomic categories diet colas, soft drinks, and beverages. It might also be a member of the following goal-derived categories: things to eat on a diet, things to take on a picnic, and things to drink at a ball game.

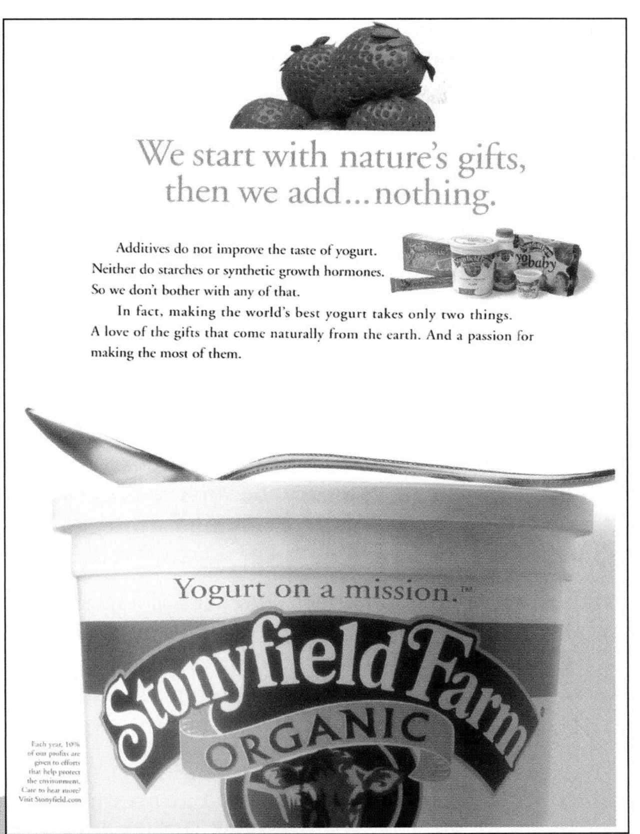

We start with nature's gifts,
then we add... nothing.
Additives do not improve the taste of yogurt.
Neither do starches or synthetic growth hormones.
So we don't bother with any of that.
In fact, making the world's best yogurt takes only two things.
A love of the gifts that come naturally from the earth. And a passion for making the most of them.
Yogurt on a mission.™
Stonyfield Farm
ORGANIC
Each year, 10% of our profits are given to efforts that help protect the environment. Care to hear more? Visit Stonyfield.com

EXHIBIT 5.9
Natural Things
Companies use pictures, ad copy, and packages to help consumers think of products as part of a goal-derived category. Here Stonyfield Farm Organic yogurt uses pictures of fresh strawberries, copy indicating lack of additives and hormones, and packaging tactics such as the words "organic" and "yogurt on a mission" to help consumers categorize the yogurt as part of the goal-derived category "things that are natural.".

Source: Courtesy of Stonyfield Farm.

Like taxonomic categories, goal-derived categories also exhibit graded structure. Consumers regard some members as better examples of a particular category when they best achieve the goals of the category. As an example, lettuce is lower in fat and calories, so it is a better example of foods to eat on a diet than baked crackers. Because goal-derived categories exhibit graded structure, consumers can also identify prototypes of goal-derived categories. As with taxonomic categories, the frequency with which an item is encountered as a category member affects its prototypicality. We tend to classify lettuce as a prototype for things to eat on diet and would probably rate it as more prototypical than a food that is equally appropriate but encountered less frequently, like kohlrabi.

MARKETING IMPLICATIONS Positioning a product or service as relevant to a goal can be an important marketing objective. To illustrate, Special K is positioned as consistent with the goal-derived category of "things to keep you thin." Wal-Mart discounts all manner of goods and services—including gasoline—to maintain is prototypical position in the goal-derived category of "saving money."[39] The ad in Exhibit 5.9 uses pure and simple images like fresh strawberries and copy indicating naturalness to convey the notion that Stoneyfield Farm Organic yogurt is part of the goal derived category of "things that are natural."

Supermarkets also apply goal-derived category structures when planning store design. Many stores display baby bottles, diapers, baby food, and juice in the same aisle despite their taxonomic differences (diapers are usually seen as similar to tissue, baby juice as similar to juice for older kids, and baby food as similar to other foods). However, because these products are part of a goal-derived category—things you need to take care of a baby—they are shelved together so parents can easily find the items and decide which brands to buy. Similarly, Web sites can be designed with consumers' goal-derived categories in mind. Travelzoo.com, for instance, is designed so segments of consumers with different travel goals can search efficiently for options such as adventure vacations, ski vacations, luxury vacations, and romantic vacations. ●

Why Consumers Differ in Their Knowledge

Several background factors affect our knowledge structure and content. These include the cultural system in which consumers exist and the consumer's level of expertise based on prior knowledge.

The Cultural System The cultural system in which consumers exist affects their knowledge base in many ways:

- *Different associations linked to a concept.* The nature and strength of associations linked to a concept may vary considerably across cultural systems.[40] In the United States, for example, American Express is associated with Tiger

Woods and golf. These associations are unlikely to be as meaningful in countries where Tiger Woods is less well known and golf is less popular. This information would clearly have implications for American Express's ability to use Tiger Woods as a global endorser.

- *Different category members.* Although consumers may have similar goal-derived categories such as "things to have for breakfast," cultural groups vary considerably in what they regard as relevant category members. In the United States, category members might include cereal, donuts, fruit, and eggs; in Japan, category members include fish, rice, and pickled vegetables.
- *Different category prototypes.* Category prototypes and members may vary across cultures, requiring companies to position brands differently for different cultures. In the Netherlands, Heineken beer is like Budweiser in the United States—frequently encountered and prototypical. In the United States, however, Heineken's associations are linked with an imported, expensive, status beer, which puts Heineken in a subordinate category. Because the beers have different competitors in the two markets, the same positioning strategy is unlikely to work equally well in both countries.
- *Different correlated associations.* Culture may affect whether associations are correlated and the direction of their correlation. For example, in the United States megastores like Price Club and Wal-Mart tend to price products lower than small stores because the large stores are often discounters. In India and Sri Lanka, however, large stores tend to price products higher to cover their higher overhead costs.
- *Different goal-derived categories.* Consumers in different cultures may not only have different members in goal-derived categories but, in fact, have different goal-derived categories. For example, the goal to have clothing that looks sexy is not likely to apply in cultures with strict religious values.

Level of Expertise Consumers vary in their ability to process information based on the extent of their prior knowledge. *Experts* are people whose prior knowledge is well developed, in part because they have had a lot of experience and familiarity with an object or a task. The content and structure of experts' prior knowledge differs from that of novices in several ways.[41] For one thing, experts' overall category structure is more developed than the category structure of nonexperts. They have more categories, more associations with concepts in a category, and a better understanding of whether associations in a category are correlated. Experts also have more subordinate-level categories and can therefore make finer distinctions among brands. For example, car experts would have many subordinate categories of cars such as vintage cars and roadsters. It is important to note that people are sometimes overconfident in their knowledge and think they know more than they actually do.[42] Still, people who consider themselves experts tend to search for information and make decisions differently from those who do not consider themselves experts, which in turn, affects how companies market to these groups.

USING KNOWLEDGE TO UNDERSTAND

Consumers' decisions are not influenced by simply attending to and perceiving stimuli. Individuals must also interpret or give meaning to the objects they perceive in light of their prior knowledge.

Categorization

A first step in this process occurs when consumers categorize an object. Categorization occurs when consumers use their prior knowledge to label, identify, and classify something new. Consumers might categorize iMac as a type of computer, eBay as a new place to buy secondhand merchandise, and *Behind the Music* as a place to get the scoop on the past lives of music stars. Once we have categorized an object, we know what it is, what it is like, and what it is similar to. How we categorize an offering has many implications for marketers, since categorization affects how favorably we evaluate an offering, the expectations we have for it, whether we will choose it, and how satisfied we may be with it. Research shows, for instance, that consumers who are exposed to brand extensions can more quickly categorize the parent brand correctly. Given the speed at which consumers are exposed to marketing stimuli when shopping, this faster categorization can be an advantage for the parent brand.[43]

Yet consumers do not always categorize things correctly. For example, Japanese women initially and incorrectly categorized *Good Housekeeping* magazine as a magazine for housemaids.[44] Lever Brothers once distributed samples of Sunlight dish-washing liquid to U.S. households. Based on the product's yellow package and the lemon on the label, some consumers categorized the product as lemon juice—and added it to their iced tea![45]

Once consumers have categorized an offering, they may not be able to categorize it differently. This is why the California Dried Plum Board is changing the name of prunes to dried plums. "Unfortunately, the stereotype among the women that we're targeting is of a medicinal food for their parents rather than a healthful, nutritious food for women who are leading an active lifestyle," explains the executive director. The industry's research shows that women aged 35 to 50 much prefer the dried plum name; the industry's challenge now is to encourage consumers to recategorize this offering.[46]

MARKETING IMPLICATIONS Categorization is a basic psychological process that has far-reaching implications for marketers, including the following:

- *Inferences.* If we categorize a product as a member of a category, we may infer that the product has features or attributes typical of that category. For example, we may infer that because a particular brand is a computer, it comes with a color monitor and a disk drive. These inferences may be correct in many but not all cases.
- *Elaboration.* Categorization influences how much we think about something. We tend to be more motivated to think about or process information that we have trouble categorizing. We are more motivated to watch ads that are different from the typical ad, and we are more motivated to think about products that look different from others in the category.[47] Seeing a Honda Accord with a spoiler and racing stripes might prompt elaboration because these features suggest a mixture of the sports car and compact car categories.
- *Evaluation.* Categorization also influences how we feel about an object, also known as our "affect" toward it. Once we categorize something as a member of a category, we may simply retrieve their evaluation stored about the category and use it to assess the object.[48] For example, if we hate lawyers and see an ad for a lawyer, we may use the category-based affect and decide that we hate this one, too. Likewise, if our category for chocolate bars contains positive affect, we may retrieve and use this affect to evaluate a new brand in the category.

- *Consideration and choice.* Whether and how we label a product or service affects whether we will consider buying it. For example, if a new phone/fax/printer is categorized as a phone, we will consider it if we are in the market for phones. If it is categorized as a printer, we won't consider it if we are in the market for phones.
- *Satisfaction.* Finally, categorization has important implications for consumer expectations and satisfaction.[49] If we categorize something as a skin moisturizer, we will expect it to meet all the performance characteristics of products in that category; if it does not, we are likely to be dissatisfied. ●

Comprehension

objective comprehension The extent to which a receiver accurately understands the message a sender intended to communicate.

subjective comprehension Reflects what we think we know, whether or not it is accurate.

While categorization reflects the process of identifying an entity, comprehension is the process of extracting higher-order meaning from it. Marketers are concerned with the two aspects of comprehension. The first is **objective comprehension**—whether the meaning that consumers extract from a message is consistent with what the message actually stated. The second is **subjective comprehension**—the different or additional meaning consumers attach to the message, whether or not these meanings were intended.[50]

Objective and Subjective Comprehension Objective comprehension reflects whether we accurately understand the message a sender intended to communicate. Interestingly, many people miscomprehend marketing messages due to the way the information is presented (its language) or differences between the sender's and the receiver's prior knowledge—or both. Subjective comprehension reflects what we think we know, whether or not it is accurate. Marketing mix elements such as price and advertising can play a powerful role in influencing what we think we know. To illustrate, you may infer that a specific brand of dental gum is as powerful as whitening toothpastes are in getting teeth white because the package uses white sparkles, the model in the ad has very white teeth, and the package uses terms like *whitening agent*. Yet the product may not actually be such a powerful whitening agent. The inferences that consumers make and why certain marketing communications prompt these inferences raise some important public policy implications.

miscomprehension Inaccurate understanding of a message.

Miscomprehension Although marketing communications such as ads and packaging are often fairly simple, consumer research reveals that achieving objective comprehension is quite a challenge for marketers. **Miscomprehension** occurs when consumers inaccurately receive the meaning contained in a message. Several studies have found a surprisingly high level of miscomprehension of TV and magazine ads, across all demographic segments. The estimated rate of comprehension was only about 70 percent for TV ads and 65 percent for print ads. Furthermore, the rates of miscomprehension for directly asserted information and implied information were fairly equal. Miscomprehension rates for programming, editorial material, and advertising were also roughly equal.[51]

In addition, consumers sometimes fail to understand how to use a product. This tendency has led to some rather bizarre warning signs on products, as Exhibit 5.10 illustrates. Consumers can also miscomprehend nonverbal actions, because the same gesture may have different meanings in different cultures. Forming a circle with the thumb and forefinger means "okay" in the United States, means "money" in Japan, and is a rude comment in Brazil.[52]

On a hair dryer:	Do not use while sleeping
On a bag of corn chips:	You could be a winner! No purchase necessary! Details inside.
On a bar of soap:	Directions: use like regular soap
On frozen dinners:	Serving suggestion: defrost
On a hotel provided shower cap:	Fits one head
Printed on *the bottom* of a Tiramisu dessert:	Do not turn upside down
On bread pudding product:	Product will be hot after heating
On packaging for an iron:	Do not iron clothes on body
On sleep aid:	Warning: may cause drowsiness
On jar of peanuts:	Warning: contains nuts
On packet of nuts:	Instructions: open packet, eat nuts
On a child Superman costume:	Wearing of this garment does not enable you to fly

In some cases, manufacturers' labels for products used in other countries do not always convey the intended meaning.

On a string of Christmas lights:	For indoor or outdoor use only
On a Korean kitchen knife:	Warning: keep out of children
On a Japanese food processor:	Not to be used for the other use.

EXHIBIT 5.10
Comprehension and Product Warnings

Consumers don't always understand how to use products, and may use them in inappropriate ways. Unfortunately, sometimes it is difficult for manufacturers' in other countries to convey the exact usage description they mean.

Effect of MAO Miscomprehension is clearly affected by consumers' motivation, ability, and opportunity (MAO) to process messages. Consumers seem most likely to miscomprehend something when their motivation to process it is low.[53] Even when consumers have high motivation, however, their comprehension may not be accurate. One study found that although consumers want to see nutritional information on packaging (implying high motivation to process it), most do not comprehend it once they read it.[54] Still, comprehension may improve with expertise and ability, which is why adults often better comprehend the finer points of a message than young children.[55] Furthermore, consumers are more likely to miscomprehend messages when they have limited opportunity to process the information. Miscomprehension is generally greater when messages are complex, shown for only a few seconds, and viewed only once or twice. Finally, experts are better able to comprehend information about a highly innovative product when prompted by marketing stimuli to make the connections and tap existing knowledge in more than one category.[56]

Effect of the Cultural System The cultural system can also affect comprehension and miscomprehension. Low-context cultures such as those in North America and northern Europe generally separate the words and meanings of a communication from the context in which it appears. Consumers in these cultures place greater emphasis on what is said than on the surrounding visuals or the environmental context of the message. But in high-context cultures (such as many in Asia), much of a message's meaning is implied indirectly and communicated visually rather than stated explicitly through words. The message sender's characteristics, such as social class, values, and age, also play an important role in the interpretation of a message.[57]

Because cultures differ in the level of attention they pay to the content and context of the message, we might expect differences in consumers' comprehension of the same message across cultures. For example, when the Michigan-based Big Boy fast-food chain opened its first restaurant on a busy street in Thailand, some local customers mistook its giant Big Boy statue for a religious icon, not a marketing feature.[58] Miscomprehension can also occur because of the way consumers interpret the meaning of a marketing message translated from another language (see the bottom half of Exhibit 5.10 for a few examples). Language differences further raise the possibility of miscomprehension. For example, Volkswagen tried to use the German concept of *fahrvergnugen,* or driving pleasure, in the U.S. market.[59] Unfortunately, U.S. consumers did not understand what this term meant, and most could not pronounce it.

Culture also affects the meaning consumers attach to words.[60] For example, in the United Kingdom, a *billion* is "a million million," whereas in the United States a billion means "a thousand million." Likewise, in the United Kingdom a movie that is a *bomb* is a "success;" in the United States, a *bomb* means a "failure." One U.S. airline promoted its "rendezvous lounges" in Brazil—however, among the Brazilians the phrase implied "a room for lovemaking."

Improving Objective Comprehension Fortunately, consumer researchers have provided some guidelines for improving objective comprehension.[61] One obvious method is to keep the message simple. Another is to repeat the message—stating it multiple times within the same communication and repeating it on multiple occasions. Finally, comprehension can be improved by presenting the message in different forms, such as visually and verbally in a television commercial.

Subjective Comprehension

Subjective comprehension describes the meanings consumers generate from a communication, whether or not these meanings were intended by the sender.[62] Public policy makers are often concerned that what consumers take away from an ad may be different from what the ad objectively states. Not long ago, the Federal Trade Commission took issue with ads from R.J. Reynolds over concerns that consumers would infer that a new brand of cigarettes advertised as having no additives would be safer than other cigarettes. In this case, the claim refers to the brand's flavor, not its safety.[63]

Levels of Subjective Comprehension Some researchers use a series of levels to describe the interpretations consumers make when they process a message. In this scheme each level indicates more thinking or elaboration.[64] For example, suppose a consumer sees an ad for a car CD player that says, "If you have an FM radio in your car, you can play CDs." The ad also states that the advertised CD player comes with a six-disc magazine. The consumer exposed to this ad might think, "I guess if you only have an AM radio, you can't install a CD player in your car." At a higher level of elaboration, the consumer might make logical inferences derived directly from what the ad says. In this example, she might logically infer that CD players and FM radios involve similar electronic interconnections because the radio is necessary for this CD player to work. At even higher levels of elaboration, the consumer might make inferences based on her general knowledge; thus, she may infer that because the CD player has a six-disc magazine, it might also have programmable functions. At the highest level, the consumer might think about or imagine future interactions with the stereo. Here, she may think that such a system would be attractive to thieves and therefore might wonder whether getting one also requires getting a car security system.

ALL IN ONE.
SAME HERE.
Total Digital Connections Plan
TOTAL DIGITAL CONNECTIONS PLAN.
Includes Sprint PCS Wireless Web℠ / Nationwide Long Distance / Voice Command / Crystal-Clear Calls
Now you can get all the best features Sprint PCS has to offer in one simple plan, using any Sprint PCS Phone.℠ To find out more, visit www.sprintpcs.com or call 1-800-480-4PCS.
Sprint.
The clear alternative to cellular.℠
Sprint PCS®
Leatherman® and the appearance of the Leatherman tool are trademarks of the Leatherman Tool Group, Inc. Service requires a phone compatible with the Sprint PCS Nationwide Network. Included minutes are not good for calls made while roaming off the Sprint PCS Nationwide Network, whether local or long-distance. Sprint PCS Voice Command℠ and Sprint PCS Wireless Web℠ are available on the Sprint PCS Nationwide Network and are not available while roaming off the Sprint PCS Nationwide Network. Copyright ©2001 Sprint Spectrum L.P. All rights reserved. Sprint, Sprint PCS, Sprint PCS Phone, Sprint PCS Wireless Web, Sprint PCS Voice Command, Sprint PCS Total Digital Connections, Sprint PCS Advantage Agreement and the diamond logo are trademarks of Sprint Communications Company L.P.

EXHIBIT 5.11
Analogies
Sometimes marketers can communicate information about their brands by drawing analogies to other things.

Source: Photography: David Campbell.

MARKETING IMPLICATIONS Like categorization, subjective comprehension involves some interaction between what is in a message and what consumers know. As a result, a marketer can strongly influence what consumers subjectively perceive from a message by designing or structuring it in a way that is consistent with prior knowledge. Sometimes, when consumers know little about a new product, marketers may be able to convey information effectively by drawing an analogy between the product and something with similar benefits. For example, a marketer may try to communicate the idea that a particular brand of boots is waterproof, soft, and lightweight by using the analogy of a duck.[65] The Sprint PCS ad in Exhibit 5.11 draws an analogy between a multi-use tool and a Sprint PCS phone plan—emphasizing the phone plan's many features in one simple device.

Marketers are often successful in designing an ad so that consumers form the "correct" inferences about the offering. At times, however, marketers may (knowingly or unknowingly) create inferences that do not accurately characterize a product or service and result in miscomprehension.[66] Situations in which marketers deliberately create false inferences about an offering raise some important ethical and legal implications, as discussed further in Chapter 21. ●

Consumer Inferences

Specific elements of the marketing mix can work with consumers' prior knowledge to affect the correct or incorrect inferences they make about an offering. The following sections describe how brand names and symbols, product features and packaging, price, distribution, and promotion can affect the inferences consumers make about products.

Brand Names and Brand Symbols Subjective comprehension of a marketing communication can be based on the inferences consumers make from a brand symbol. The Pillsbury Dough Boy has slimmed down over the years because the company's marketers are afraid that consumers will infer that he is fat from eating Pillsbury products.

Brand names can also create subjective comprehension and inferences. For example, alphanumeric brand names like BMW's 740 iL tend to be associated with technological sophistication and complexity. In addition, consumers tend to carry over certain inferences from existing products within a brand when evaluating a new product that is a brand extension.[67] Moreover, foreign brand names may create inferences based on cultural categories and stereotypes. Thus Häagen-Dazs, a German-sounding name, may evoke favorable associations when applied to ice cream even though it is manufactured in the Bronx. French and Italian names like Armani, Vuarnet, Paco Rabanne, and Pierre Cardin imply high fashion.

Descriptive names can also create inferences. Brand names such as Obsession for perfume, Speedo for bathing suits, Gleem for toothpaste, Ray Ban for sunglasses, and Sure View for contact lenses may create inferences about the particular brand's benefits.[68] On the other hand, Procter & Gamble changed the brand name of its Oil of Olay skincare products to simply *Olay* because, says an executive, "Many consumers thought oil meant a greasy product."[69] Finally, companies marketing products whose quality cannot be observed can communicate quality to consumers by offering a warranty, selling through a credible retailer, or forging an alliance with another reputable brand. Under these circumstances, consumers are likely to infer that the allied product would lose its reputation or its future profits if the quality claims were untrue.[70]

Inferences Based on Misleading Names and Labels Although some brand names may accurately characterize a product's attributes and benefits, others

EXHIBIT 5.12
Confusing Brand Names
Brand names may create inferences about attributes or benefits of the product. People may not agree on what these attributes or benefits are, and these inferences may not be correct.

Source: Adapted by permission from Bonnie B. Reece and Robert H. Ducoffe, "Deception in Brand Names," *Journal of Public Policy and Marketing*, vol. 6, 1987, pp. 93–103.

EXAMPLE NAMES*
"Salad's" Lo-Cal Italian Dressing
"Oatman's" Natural Cereal
"Lean" meals
"Lisson" Trim Beef Cup-a-Soup
"Fruitobia" Low-Sugar Grape Spread
"Just Desserts" Plus Chocolate Cake Mix

	INFERENCES	PERCENTAGE WHO AGREE THAT THIS IS WHAT THE NAME IMPLIES
LO-CAL	⅓ fewer calories than regular dressing	49†
	⅓ fewer calories than regular Salad's	59†
	Not fattening	30
	Made with no oil	11
NATURAL	Nothing artificial added	81†
	No preservatives	75†
	Fewer calories than most cereals	8
	No sugar added	20
LEAN	⅓ fewer calories than regular	56
	½ less fat than regular	34
	Smaller portions than regular	45
	Healthier than regular	30
TRIM	⅓ fewer calories than regular	52†
	10 calories per serving	35†
	All fat removed	21†
	Less flavor	21
LO-SUGAR	½ sugar of regular	62†
	Artificial sweetener	54
	10 calories per serving	19
	⅓ fewer calories than regular	47†
PLUS	Richer taste than regular	64
	Nuts or chocolate bits added	36
	More calories than regular	28
	Pudding added for moistness	61†

* Consumers in this study were presented with the names of actual brands. These brand names have been replaced with hypothetical brand names.
† Indicates what the name actually means.

have been called misleading because they suggest false inferences about the product's benefits. For example, consumers may infer that "lite" olive oil has fewer calories when it is really only "lite" in terms of its color.[71] Exhibit 5.12 reveals the confusion consumers feel over the meaning of terms used in brand names. This confusion has prompted the development of labeling laws designed to ensure that product names and ingredients accurately describe the offering. The U.S. Department of Agriculture has enacted regulations standardizing the use of the term *organic*. The term is restricted to crops untouched by herbicides, pesticides, or fertilizers for at least three years or to livestock raised without antibiotics or hormones.[72]

Inferences Based on Inappropriate or Similar Names Some brand names lead to inappropriate inferences about the product. One gas company came up with the new name Enteron, but later learned that *enteron* is a real word that means "the alimentary canal" (i.e., intestines).[73] Other names fail because they do not create unique associations or inferences that help their brand stand out from others. Pets.com is only one of many failed Internet-based companies whose names lacked differentiation and strong associations. "A fanciful name that is well branded—and examples of this are plentiful: Intel, Yahoo!—will resonate in the consumer's mind and conjure the supplier of specific products and services," says one Web marketing expert. "A generic domain name lacks that distinctive association."[74] Thus, Web marketers must find a name that suggests what they do but also helps them stand out from other companies.

Sometimes brand or company names are too similar. Consumers may inadvertently infer that the brands are similar or that they are made by the same company. Typically these situations create legal battles, with companies fighting over who can use the original brand name. This is what happened when *Polo* magazine repositioned itself from a magazine devoted to the sport of polo to an upscale magazine—a magazine with an image similar to that of Polo Ralph Lauren.[75]

Product Features and Packaging Consumers can also subjectively comprehend aspects of an offering based on inferences they make from the product and the way it is packaged.

Inferences Based on Product Attributes Knowledge that two attributes tend to be correlated in a product category may lead consumers to infer that the presence of one attribute in a brand implies the other. Thus consumers may infer that a product with a low repair record also has a long warranty.[76] Consumers may make inferences about products based on package size. A consumer who encounters a large, multipack item may use prior knowledge about the correlation between price and package size to infer that the large-sized brand is also a good buy.[77] Also, when two companies form a brand alliance for marketing purposes, consumers tend to infer that their brand attributes are similar even when one is incompletely described in marketing communications.[78]

Inferences Based on Country of Origin Knowledge about a product's country of origin can affect how consumers think about it.[79] Just as we stereotype people based on where they were born, we also stereotype products based on where they are made. Products labeled "Made in France" are likely to create inferences about elegance and style.[80] Research shows that consumers in developing countries infer higher quality from brands that are perceived as foreign.[81] Many Latin American consumers, for instance, infer that foreign telephone companies offer better service

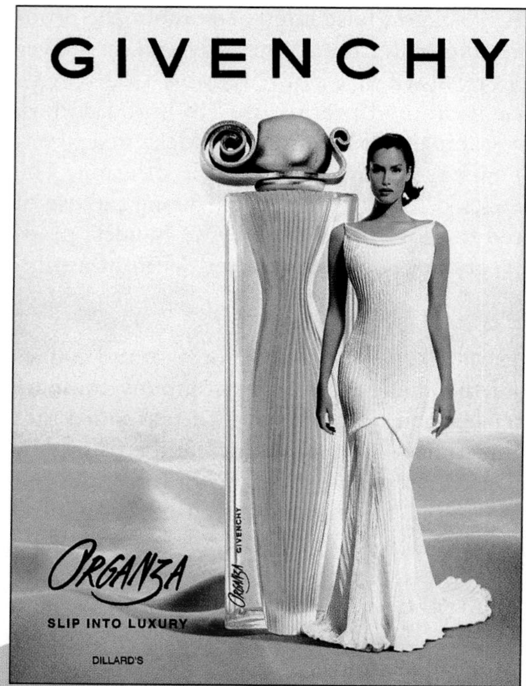

EXHIBIT 5.13
Inferences Based on Packaging
Organza perfume uses packaging shaped like a long organza gown, conveying the notion that the brand is elegant and sexy.

Source: Courtesy of Givenchy.

and quality than local companies.[82] Consumers are less likely to make inferences about a brand based on its country of origin when they are highly motivated to process information about that brand or when their processing goal guides attention away from origin information.[83]

Furthermore, country of origin inferences can also work to a product's disadvantage. In one study, Japanese consumers inferred that the quality of Japanese-made products was higher than the quality of American-made products—even when the Japanese products were not superior. This preference for own-country origin underlies the marketing strategy used by Kao Corporation to maintain its dominance of the Japanese diaper market by stressing its Japanese roots, despite intense competition from U.S. brands.[84]

Inferences Based on Package Design Package characteristics can also create inferences. Consumers in one study inferred that potato chips packaged in polyvinyl bags were crisper and better tasting than chips packaged in wax-coated bags, even though the bags contained the exact same chips.[85] Moreover, consumers may make inferences about a brand if its package, name, or design looks like that of other brands in the category. For example, the packaging for Organza shown in Exhibit 5.13 is shaped like the organza dress worn by the model. The silhouette of the female form creates inferences about the elegance and sexiness of the product. At the same time, packaging can suggest a brand's uniqueness. After the maker of Southern Comfort liquor learned, through research, that twentysomething consumers perceived its brand as not very unique or contemporary, the company updated its bottle and label to suggest more modern inferences and stand out among competing brands.[86]

Sometimes packages are designed to look like the packages of well-known brands. Walgreen's Impressions fragrances are designed to look like major designer brands, such as Drakkar Noir and Polo. At times, packaging similarity spurs legal battles, as when Kendall-Jackson sued Gallo, alleging that Gallo's Turning Leaf Chardonnay copied Kendall-Jackson's colored leaf logo, its tapered neck, the design of its label, and its leaf-stamped cork. Kendall-Jackson complained that the packaging similarity would make consumers believe that the Gallo wine was a Kendall-Jackson brand when it was not.[87]

Inferences Based on Color Finally, consumers can make inferences about an offering based on its color or the color of its package. We have color categories stored in prior knowledge. The category of things that are green includes grass, trees, leaves, and mint as members and has associations like refreshing, new, organic, peaceful, and springlike. Because of this category-based knowledge, consumers can make inferences about a stimulus based on its color. They may infer that a brand of green toothpaste that comes in a green package is refreshing, minty, and healthy.

Knowing that colors can affect consumers' inferences, some companies have taken legal steps to protect the color of their brand. Owens-Corning gained trademark protection for its pink home-insulation products, and Keds gained trademark protection for the blue rectangular label on the heels of Keds shoes. Such protection prohibits other firms from using these colors on their products—

and thus reduces the possibility that consumers will either categorize the product incorrectly or draw false inferences about it.[88]

Because category content varies with culture, the meaning associated with colors and consumers' inferences based on color will also vary.[89] For example, Western consumers usually associate white with purity and cleanliness, while in Asian countries white signifies death. Green is a popular color in Muslim countries but is negatively perceived in Southwest Asia. Black has negative overtones in Japan, India, and Europe but is perceived positively in the Middle East. Marketers must therefore consider these cultural differences when marketing in other cultures.

Price At times, consumers make inferences about a product or service based on its price. For example, category-based knowledge suggests that price and quality are correlated, so a consumer may infer that a high-priced product is also high in quality.[90] Consumers often make this inference when they believe brands differ in quality, when they perceive high risk in choosing the low-quality product, and when they have no information—such as a known brand name—to assess quality before buying.[91] In such instances, consumers may simply use price as a shortcut to infer quality.

Retail Atmospherics and Display Category-based knowledge about aspects of the distribution mix, such as retail design, displays, layout, merchandising, and service, can also affect consumers' inferences. For example, the inferences you might make walking into a warehouse-type store like Price Club are likely to be different from the inferences you might make entering a more upscale, service-oriented store like Nordstrom's. Research indicates that an aesthetically pleasing retail atmosphere causes consumers to infer positive quality perceptions of socially communicative products such as gifts (but not of utilitarian products such as household appliances) and affects consumers' intentions to shop at the store.[92] Consumers also infer differentiation among brands from the way in which products are displayed in stores. Furthermore, the display context can lead consumers to rely less on prior knowledge and more on external cues—so a brand's positioning may be undermined by inappropriate retail display decisions.[93] Atmospherics are a major tool used by retailers to develop, elaborate, and change their store images. Radio Shack is using atmospherics to change its image from a male-oriented do-it-yourself electronics retailer to a service-oriented home electronics store for the entire family.[94]

Advertising and Selling Advertising and selling efforts clearly affect the inferences consumers make about an offering. In personal selling and advertising, inferences can be based on body language. An advertisement that shows a woman touching a man's hand for longer than a second could lead us to believe that they are romantically involved. Consumers might infer that a salesperson whose handshake is weak is not interested in their business. The nonverbal aspects of communication are particularly important in Asian cultures.[95] In Japan, for example, a verbal yes often means "no"; the speaker's body language communicates the true intent.[96] In addition, consumers who infer that a salesperson is deliberately trying to persuade them, not just inform them—especially by the use of hard-sell or pressure-selling tactics—may be less likely to buy the product being sold.[97]

Physical space, or the distance between people, may also be interpreted differently in different cultures. Compared with Westerners, Asians tend to leave

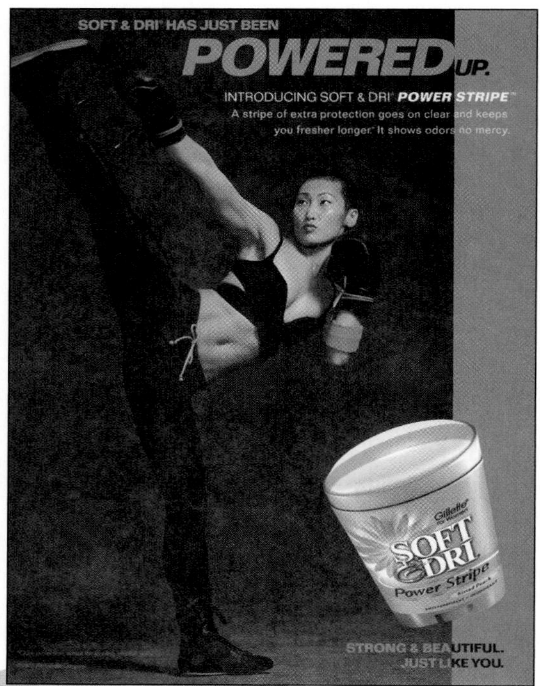

EXHIBIT 5.14
Stimulating Inferences with Pictures
The fact that Soft and Dri antiperspirant and deodorant is powerful is likely to be inferred by consumers, not only on the basis of the product shot and headline, but also the picture of the kick boxer—who herself is depicted as strong and powerful.

Source: The Gillette Company.

much more distance between people and prefer limited physical contact. A U.S. salesperson who is accustomed to less space and more contact may give Asian consumers the impression of being pushy and unacceptably physical. However, compared with U.S. consumers, Latin American consumers are comfortable with a much smaller distance between people and may therefore infer that a U.S. salesperson who maintains more distance is standoffish.[98]

Pictures Advertisers frequently use pictures to stimulate inferences. To illustrate, the ad shown in Exhibit 5.14 uses a picture of a strong kickboxer to reinforce the idea that Soft and Dri antiperspirant and deodorant is strong and powerful.

Language Just as specific words like brand names or adjectives can affect inferences, the way in which words are structured into sentences can also affect subjective comprehension.[99] The word structure of the hypothetical ad in Exhibit 5.15 can lead to the following (potentially incorrect) inferences:

- *Juxtaposed imperatives.* The headline contains two sentences placed next to one another (juxtaposed). Consumers might interpret the headline as saying, "The Starfire AD7 gives you luxury and sportiness at its finest," even though the ad does not actually make this statement.
- *Implied superiority.* Another inference commonly made from advertising is implied superiority. The statement "nobody gives you more," as in the exhibit, could be technically true if all brands offered equal performance benefits. However, consumers may interpret such statements as implying superiority—that is, "This brand is the best." Likewise, the statement provides an incomplete comparison. Nobody gives you more of what? Consumers are likely to fill in a comparison object, right or wrong.
- *Incomplete comparisons.* Ads sometimes provide a comparison but leave the object or basis of comparison either incomplete or ambiguous, which can lead to incorrect inferences.[100] The statement "it's less expensive" in Exhibit 5.15, for example, does not indicate what the Starfire AD7 is less expensive than. Is it less expensive than the other brands listed in the ad, last year's model, or the most expensive car on the market?
- *Multiple comparisons.* Some ads make comparisons with multiple brands. For example, the ad in Exhibit 5.15 states that the Starfire AD7 performs better than a Porsche in interior comfort, better than an RX7 in braking ability, and better than a Corvette in smoothness of ride. However, consumers may infer that the AD7 is better than all these brands on all these attributes. Readers may also infer that the Porsche offers the best interior comfort because it is the standard for comparison. Note that the ad could still technically be true if the Porsche were less comfortable than an RX7 and a Corvette but marginally less comfortable than the AD7.

In addition, language can lead to misleading inferences drawn from comparative ads, as Exhibit 5.16 shows. This exhibit shows three versions of the same ad

EXHIBIT 5.15
A Hypothetical Car Ad
The way a message is worded can affect our inferences. What do you think this ad is saying? Is it really saying what you think? How does the wording affect what you comprehend?

Headline: **Experience luxury and sportiness at its finest. It's the AD7 from Starfire.**

Body copy: Automotive Worlds toughest tests found that no other brand gives you more than Starfires AD7. It performs better than the Porsche in interior comfort, has better braking ability than the RX7, has a smoother ride than the Corvette, and its less expensive.

Tag: **Starfire's AD7. Nobody gives you more.**

NEW DAZZLE TOOTHPASTE IS
THE BRAND FOR YOU.
HERE ARE 4 REASONS WHY.

REASON #1: EFFECTIVE CLEANING ABILITY
Independent clinical tests conducted at Stanford, Harvard, and Northwestern dental schools have documented Dazzle's cleaning ability — Dazzle removes plaque!

REASON #2: POWERFUL WHITENERS
Other clinical tests have shown that Dazzle is effective in removing stains from your teeth.

REASON #3: A REFRESHING TASTE
Recent tests conducted by Consumer Reports have shown that 9 out of 10 consumers tested liked the refreshing taste of Dazzle.

REASON #4: AN ALL-NATURAL FORMULA
Dazzle is all natural — it contains no artificial colors or preservatives.

NEW
DAZZLE
FLUORIDE TOOTHPASTE

Try New Dazzle Toothpaste!
A Complete Toothpaste for Today's Consumer!

NEW DAZZLE TOOTHPASTE IS
THE BRAND FOR YOU.
HERE ARE 4 REASONS WHY.

REASON #1: MORE EFFECTIVE CLEANING ABILITY
Independent clinical tests conducted at Stanford, Harvard, and Northwestern dental schools have documented Dazzle's cleaning ability — Dazzle removes twice the amount of plaque than Crest!

REASON #2: POWERFUL WHITENERS
Other clinical tests have shown that Dazzle is effective in removing stains from your teeth.

REASON #3: A REFRESHING TASTE
Recent tests conducted by Consumer Reports have shown that 9 out of 10 consumers tested liked the refreshing taste of Dazzle.

REASON #4: AN ALL-NATURAL FORMULA
Dazzle is all natural — it contains no artificial colors or preservatives.

NEW
DAZZLE
FLUORIDE TOOTHPASTE

Try New Dazzle Toothpaste!
A Complete Toothpaste for Today's Consumer!

NEW DAZZLE TOOTHPASTE IS
THE BRAND FOR YOU.
HERE ARE 4 REASONS WHY.

REASON #1: MORE EFFECTIVE CLEANING ABILITY
Independent clinical tests conducted at Stanford, Harvard, and Northwestern dental schools have documented Dazzle's cleaning ability — Dazzle removes twice the amount of plaque than Crest!

REASON #2: MORE POWERFUL WHITENERS
Other clinical tests have shown that Dazzle is effective in removing stains from your teeth. In fact, Dazzle has been proven to get teeth over 60% whiter than Crest.

REASON #3: A MORE REFRESHING TASTE
Recent tests conducted by Consumer Reports have shown that 9 out of 10 consumers tested preferred the refreshing taste of Dazzle over the taste of Crest.

REASON #4: AN ALL-NATURAL FORMULA
Unlike Crest, Dazzle is all natural — it contains no artificial colors or preservatives.

NEW
DAZZLE
FLUORIDE TOOTHPASTE

Try New Dazzle Toothpaste!
A Complete Toothpaste for Today's Consumer!

EXHIBIT 5.16
Ad Stimuli Used in One Study

Consumers may inappropriately conclude that the second version of this ad (the partial comparative ad) says that the brand is superior to the compared brand on all attributes. Really, the ad says that the brand is superior on the first attribute only.

Source: Reprinted with permission from *Journal of Marketing Research*, published by the American Marketing Association, Michael Barone and Paul W. Miniard, February 1999, vol. 36, p. 63.

for a hypothetical brand of toothpaste called Dazzle. The first ad is a noncomparative ad—it simply describes the brand's benefits, but makes no competitive comparisons. The second is a partial comparative ad. It compares Dazzle to Crest, but only on the benefit of cleaning ability. The third is a direct comparative ad that compares the product to Crest on all benefits. Partial comparative ads can be misleading because consumers are likely to infer that the advertised brand is better than the compared brand on all benefits, not just the stated one.[101]

Ethical Issues

These inferences raise a number of interesting ethical and public policy questions. On the one hand, marketers are apparently able to use marketing mix elements (such as brand name, visuals, price, store atmosphere, and ad copy) to not only make their brand look better but also to mislead consumers. On the other hand, some may argue that consumers allow themselves to be misled by marketers and that marketers cannot be held accountable for inaccurate inferences and miscomprehension of ads. What do you think? See Chapter 21 for further discussion of the potential negative effects of marketing.

SUMMARY

We understand something in our environment by relating it to what we already know—our prior knowledge. Knowledge content is represented by a set of associations about an object or an activity linked in schemas and scripts. Understanding the content of consumers' knowledge is important because marketers are often in the position of creating new knowledge—that is, developing brand images or personalities, creating brand extensions, positioning a brand—as well as developing existing knowledge or changing knowledge through repositioning.

Our knowledge is also organized or structured into categories. Objects within a category are similar to objects in the same category and different from objects in other categories. Objects within a category exhibit graded structure, meaning that some are better examples of the category than are others. The best example of the category is the prototype. Knowledge may be hierarchically organized, with similar objects organized in basic, subordinate, or superordinate levels of categorization. Furthermore, within a category, objects may have associations that are correlated. Categories may also be organized around things that serve similar goals. How consumers organize knowledge has important marketing implications for product positioning, product development, and retail design. Consumers obviously differ in their knowledge. One reason is that consumers live within different cultural systems. Another reason is that their levels of expertise differ, with some consumers having more knowledge than others.

Prior knowledge combined with information from the external environment affects how we categorize something and what we comprehend. In turn, categorization has far-reaching implications for what we think about a product, how we feel about it, what we expect from it, and whether we choose and will be satisfied with it. One way of thinking about comprehension is to ask whether consumers accurately understand what was stated in a message, a concept called objective comprehension. Consumers often fail to accurately acquire the meaning of marketing communications. Limited motivation, ability, and/or opportunity to attend to and process a message often affect miscomprehension. A second aspect of comprehension is subjective comprehension, or what consumers think they know or have understood from a message, which may not always match what a message states. Consumers may fail to accurately understand what is explicitly stated in a communication because they form inferences based on elements of the marketing mix. Unscrupulous marketers can take advantage of consumers' tendencies to make inferences and deliberately mislead consumers, raising ethical and public policy issues.

QUESTIONS FOR REVIEW AND DISCUSSION

1. What is a schema and how can the associations in a schema be described?
2. How do brand extensions, licensing, and brand alliances relate to schemas, brand images, and brand personalities?
3. What is a category prototype, and what affects prototypicality?
4. What does it mean when consumers organize knowledge according to goal-derived categories?
5. How do culture and level of expertise affect a consumer's knowledge base?
6. In what way is objective comprehension different from subjective comprehension and miscomprehension?
7. What are some examples of ways in which a company can use the marketing mix, in combination with consumers' prior knowledge, to affect the inferences consumers make about a product?

EXERCISES

1. Identify a brand whose image you believe is negative.
   a. Indicate your schema for that brand.
   b. How is that brand currently being positioned? How might it be better positioned?
   c. Should the brand be positioned close to or away from the category prototype?
   d. Describe some brand symbols, visuals, packaging decisions, and advertising strategies that might be used to develop a new image for the brand.
2. Take a well-known brand and describe its associations. Based on these associations, state what its brand personality might be. Then indicate how this knowledge would facilitate your brand name, packaging, pricing, advertising, and product decisions.
3. Go to the supermarket and to a large department store and find as many examples of brand extensions as you can. For each, indicate the following:
   a. Whether you think they are good brand extensions or not, and why.
   b. Whether any negative effects might be associated with these brand extensions.

   Then take a new product for which no brand extensions exist. Indicate new product categories this brand might successfully extend to.
4. Go to a Web site where you can buy products (such as Amazon.com, eBay.com, or Travelocity.com). Think about how the Web experience alters the basic "shopping-for-products" script that consumers would enact in a typical store. Does this site enable you to perform activities that you would normally perform if you were actually shopping for products in a store? How could the site be improved to enable you to perform scripted activities more easily?
5. Find a brand that is positioned close to the category prototype and another that is positioned away from the category prototype. Why do you think marketers chose to position these brands in this way?
6. Illustrate the principles of basic-, subordinate-, and superordinate-level categories for a product category of your choosing. In one case, assume that consumers' subordinate-category structure is complex; in another case, assume it is simple. Now assume that one of the manufacturers is planning to introduce a new brand. Indicate in which case the new brand will compete with the brands the firm already makes.
7. Find an advertisement that contains juxtaposed imperatives, implied superiority, multiple comparison inferences, or incomplete comparisons.
   a. Let half the class work for the Division of Advertising Practices at the Federal Trade Commission. The commission is charging the company with creating misleading advertising. Argue that the ad is misleading and explain why the advertiser is at fault. Indicate how the ad should be rewritten, or use added or different visuals to create inferences that are more likely to be correct about the product.
   b. The other half of the class works for the legal division of the company. Argue that the ad is not misleading and that advertisers should not be held accountable for the incorrect inferences consumers may make about the brand.
8. Think about a personal goal you want to achieve, such as losing weight or learning to speak Japanese. Identify at least ten goods or services that you would include as members of this goal-derived category, then rank these members from most to least prototypical. Which is the prototypical member of this category, and why? Now consider how the marketing of this prototype might affect your decision to buy or use it in achieving your goal. How is the company using its marketing mix to position its product or service as relevant to your goal? What other steps might this company take to strengthen this position?

9. Visit a local retailer and examine two competing products from a single category, such as two shampoo brands or two cell phone brands. What inferences do you draw from the brand names and symbols? Do the brand names accurately characterize each product's features and benefits? How does the packaging affect the inferences you make about each product? If either product mentions country of origin, how does this influence your thinking about it? What inferences do you make about these products based on color? Contrast and compare your responses for each competing product. Overall, which product carries the most favorable associations and inferences, and why?

chapter 6

Attitudes Based on High Consumer Effort

INTRODUCTION: Changing Attitudes toward the Military

Remember *Full Metal Jacket?* More than a decade after the movie's release, its vivid images continue to influence teenagers' attitudes toward the U.S. military. The armed services have been struggling to recruit and retain men and women, in part because of strong, persistent, and unfavorable attitudes toward the military. When advertising experts researched the problem by conducting focus groups with teenagers, they learned that *Full Metal Jacket*—with its darker view of military training and service—was mentioned more often and had far more influence over attitudes than newer military movies such as *Saving Private Ryan.* Research by the Army's advertising agency revealed that people in the 14-to-24 target age group had no realistic sense of military life and saw the service as a threat to their individuality. Small wonder that the Army, Navy, and Air Force were struggling to meet recruiting goals. Yet the Marine Corps was meeting its goals, thanks to an ad campaign stressing the service's selectivity and life-transforming potential with the slogan "The few. The proud. The Marines."

In response to the research, the armed forces changed their advertising approaches. The Army replaced its long-standing slogan "Be all that you can be" and downplayed college funding offers in favor of the slogan "An Army of one," backed up by a multimedia campaign stressing individual achievement and previewing the rigors of training. It also set up a special Web site (www.goarmy.com) where potential recruits could follow six actual recruits through the various stages of basic training. The U.S. Navy switched its slogan to "Accelerate Your Life" to showcase self-actualization opportunities. Building on renewed patriotic fervor following terrorist attacks on New York and Washington, the Air Force aired "Freedom Forever" ads reinforcing its vital role in protecting civilians. These changes helped all three services meet their recruitment goals within a year of starting the new campaigns.[1]

These military recruitment campaigns (see Exhibit 6.1) illustrate a number of important points that stem directly from the concepts covered in the preceding chapter. First, consumers probably had certain beliefs

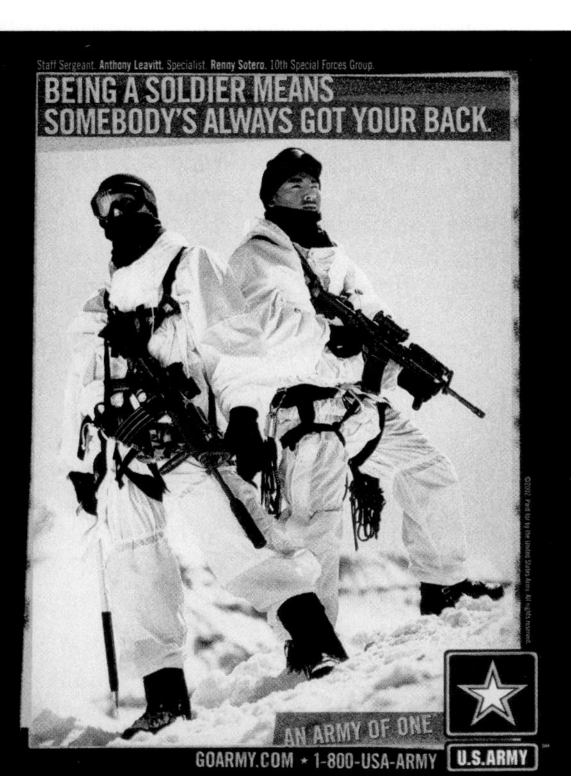

EXHIBIT 6.1
Enlisting Advertising to Boost Enlistments

Source: Army materials courtesy of the U.S. Government.

about the armed services based on the mental associations they had linked to each (unpleasant conditions, for example). Second, these beliefs likely affected consumers' attitudes toward the military (whether or not they liked a particular service) and their behavior (they might enlist if they understood what they were getting into and believed they would gain significant personal benefits). Finally, attitudes can be based on either the functional features of the offering (such as the length of service or the technical skills to be learned) or the emotional aspects (such as the satisfaction to be gained from personal achievement). Therefore, in trying to change consumers' attitudes, the armed services began portraying military life and achievement in their ad campaigns, thereby creating new beliefs and associations—central issues addressed in this chapter. •

WHAT ARE ATTITUDES?

attitude A relatively global and enduring evaluation of an object, issue, person, or action.

An **attitude** is an overall evaluation that expresses how much we like or dislike an object, issue, person, or action.[2] Attitudes are learned, and they tend to persist over time. Our attitudes also reflect our overall evaluation of something based on the set of associations linked to it. This is why we have attitudes toward brands, product categories, ads, people, types of stores, activities, and so forth.

The Importance of Attitudes

cognitive function How attitudes influence our thoughts.

affective function How attitudes influence our feelings.

connative function How attitudes influence our behavior.

Attitudes are important because they (1) guide our thoughts (the **cognitive function**), (2) influence our feelings (the **affective function**), and (3) affect our behavior (the **connative function**). We decide which ads to read, whom to talk to, where to shop, and where to eat, based on our attitudes. Likewise, attitudes influence the acquisition, consumption, and disposition of an offering—our buying behavior. Thus, marketers need to change attitudes in order to influence consumer decision making and change consumer behavior.

The Characteristics of Attitudes

favorability The degree to which we like or dislike something.

attitude accessibility How easily an attitude can be remembered.

Attitudes can be described in terms of five main characteristics: favorability, attitude accessibility, attitude confidence, persistence, and resistance. **Favorability** refers to how much we like or dislike an attitude object. **Attitude accessibility** refers to how easily and readily an attitude can be retrieved from memory.[3] If you went to a movie last night, you can probably remember with relative ease what your attitude toward it was, just as you are likely to remember your attitude toward an important object, event, or activity with relative ease (such as your attitude toward your first car).

attitude confidence How strongly we hold an attitude.

attitude persistence How long an attitude lasts.

attitude resistance How difficult it is to change an attitude.

Attitudes can also be described in terms of their strength, or **attitude confidence.** In some cases we hold our attitudes very strongly and with a great deal of confidence, whereas in other cases we feel much less certain about them. Attitudes may also vary in their **persistence**, or endurance. The attitudes we hold with confidence may last for an extremely long time, while others may last for only a short time. Finally, attitudes can be described in terms of their **resistance** to subsequent change.[4] Consumers may change their attitudes fairly easily when they are not loyal to a particular brand or know little about a product. However, attitude change is likely to be more difficult when consumers are brand loyal or think they are experts in the product category.

FORMING AND CHANGING ATTITUDES

Marketers can better create or influence consumers' attitudes toward new offerings and novel behaviors when they understand how attitudes are formed. This understanding also helps marketers plan strategies for changing consumer atti-

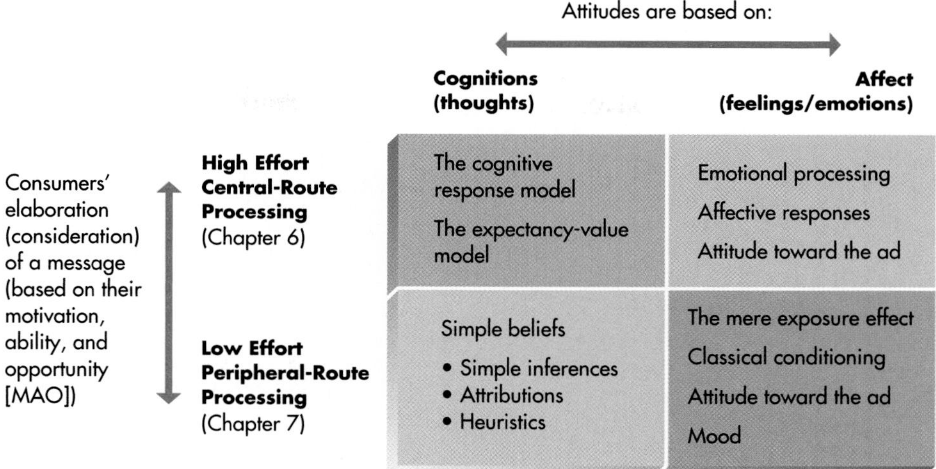

EXHIBIT 6.2
General Approaches to Attitude Formation and Change

As discussed in Chapter 3, consumers' processing differs depending on whether elaboration is high or low. Processing can also be either cognitive or affective. This leads to four basic ways in which consumers can form attitudes. This chapter examines the ways in which attitudes can be formed and changed when consumer effort is high.

tudes about existing offerings and established behaviors. Exhibit 6.2 summarizes general approaches to attitude formation and change processes, providing a useful overview of the topics discussed in this and the next chapter.

The Foundation of Attitudes

As Exhibit 6.2 shows, one approach to attitude formation suggests that attitudes are based on *cognitions (thoughts)* or beliefs.[5] This means that attitudes can be based on thoughts we have about information received from an external source (such as advertising, salesperson, magazines, or a trusted friend) or on information we recall from memory. A second approach suggests that attitudes are based on *emotions.* Sometimes we have a favorable attitude toward an offering (whether it's military service, clothing, or another good or service) simply because it feels good or seems right. Likewise, we can acquire attitudes by observing and vicariously experiencing the emotions of others who use an offering. For example, if you see that people riding a roller coaster are having fun, you may believe that you will too.

A second set of issues affecting attitude formation and change has to do with how much extensive thinking or *elaboration* consumers put forth in forming and changing their attitudes. As Exhibit 6.2 shows, attitude formation and change processes can be described as involving either considerable effort or little effort.

The Role of Effort in Attitude Formation and Change

central-route processing The attitude formation and change process when effort is high.

When do consumers make a conscious effort to form or change an attitude? As discussed in Chapter 3, consumers may sometimes have high motivation, ability, and opportunity (MAO) to process information and make decisions. When MAO is high, consumers are more likely to devote a lot of effort and to experience considerable personal involvement in forming or changing attitudes and making decisions. Some researchers have used the term **central-route processing**

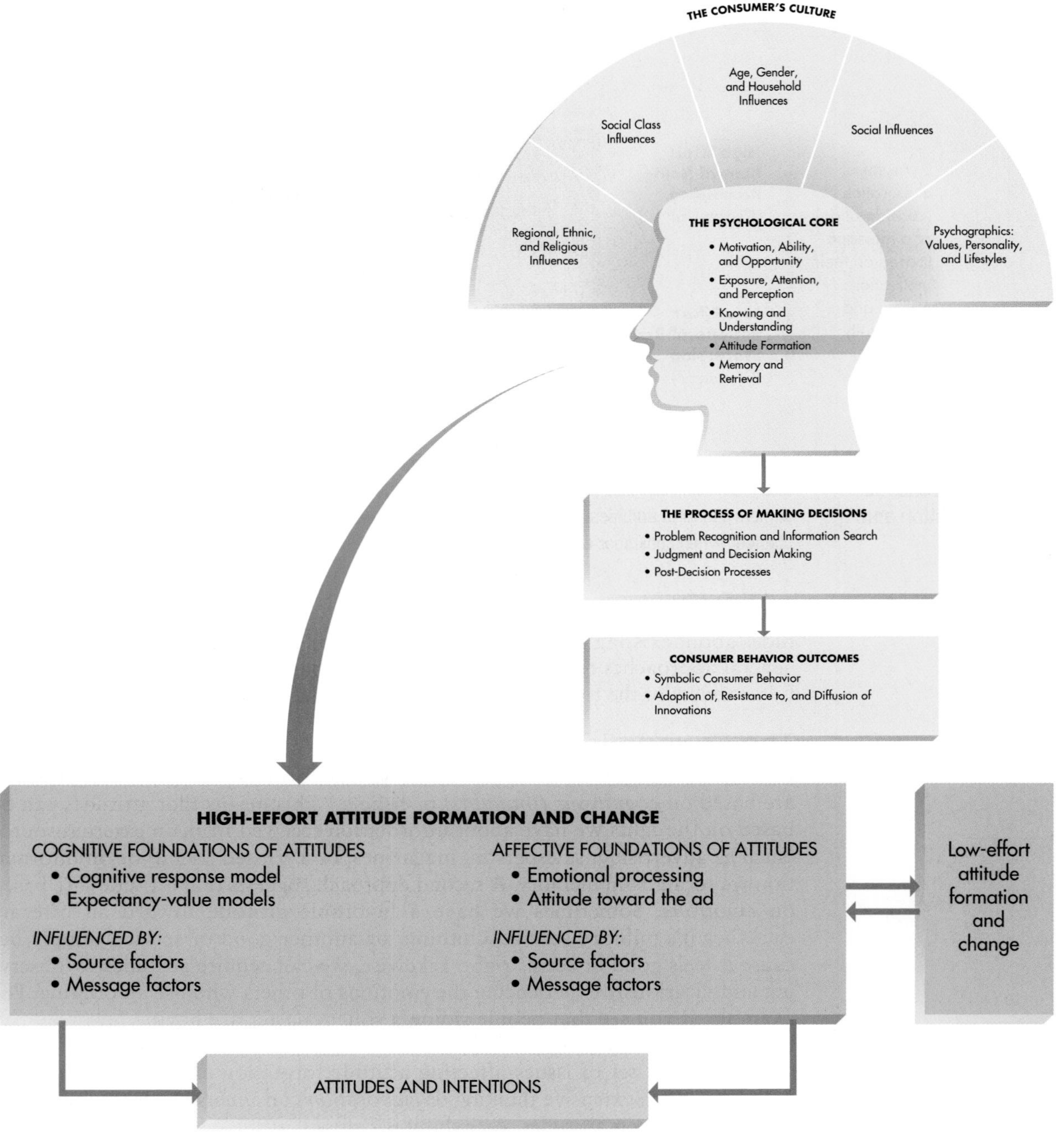

EXHIBIT 6.3
Chapter Overview: Attitude Formation and Change: High Consumer Effort

Following the first two stages (exposure, attention, and perception; and knowledge and understanding), consumers can either form or change their attitudes. This chapter explains how consumers form high-effort attitudes based on both cognition and affect. It also shows how marketers can influence attitudes through source factors (credibility, company reputation, and similarity) and message factors (argument quality, emotional appeals, etc.).

to describe attitude formation and change processes when thinking about a message is likely to involve effort.[6] Processing is central because consumers' attitudes are based on a careful and effortful analysis of the true merits or central issues contained within the message. As a result of this extensive and effortful processing, consumers are likely to form strong, accessible, and confidently held attitudes that are persistent and resistant to change.

When MAO is low, however, consumers' attitudes are based on a more tangential or superficial analysis of the message, not on an effortful analysis of its true merits. Because these attitudes tend to be based on peripheral or superficial cues contained within the message, the term **peripheral-route processing** has been used to describe attitude formation and change that involves limited effort (or low elaboration) on the part of the consumer.

peripheral-route processing The attitude formation and change process when effort is low.

This chapter focuses on several ways in which consumers form and change attitudes when effort (i.e., MAO) is high. The next chapter focuses on how consumers form and change attitudes when effort is low. Because attitudes tend to be more accessible, persistent, resistant to change, and held with confidence when consumers' MAO to process information is high, much of the chapter focuses on what affects the favorability of consumers' attitudes.

Exhibit 6.3 serves as a framework for the ideas discussed in this chapter. It shows that when consumers are likely to devote a lot of effort to processing information, marketers can influence consumer attitudes either (1) *cognitively*—influencing the thoughts or beliefs they have about the offering, or (2) *affectively*—influencing the emotional experiences consumers associate with the offering. Furthermore, marketers can try to influence consumers' attitudes through characteristics of the source used in a persuasive communication, the type of message used, or some combination of both. Finally, after attitudes are formed, they may play a powerful role in influencing consumers' intentions and actual behavior.

THE COGNITIVE FOUNDATIONS OF ATTITUDES

Researchers have proposed various theories to explain how thoughts are related to attitudes when consumers devote a lot of effort to processing information and making decisions. This chapter focuses on the cognitive response model and expectancy-value models.

The Cognitive Response Model

The basic idea behind the cognitive response model is that consumers' thought reactions to a message affect their attitudes. **Cognitive responses** are the thoughts we have when exposed to a communication. These thoughts can take the form of recognitions, evaluations, associations, images, or ideas.[7] Suppose a balding man sees an ad for Rogaine, a product that claims to restore lost hair. In response to this ad, he could think, "I really need a product like this," "This product will never work," or "The guy in the ad was paid to say this." The cognitive response model predicts that these spontaneously generated responses will determine his attitude toward Rogaine.[8]

cognitive responses Thoughts we have in response to a communication.

Consumers' cognitive responses to communications can be classified in three ways:

- **Counterarguments (CAs)** are thoughts that express disagreement with the message (from the preceding example: "This product will never work" or "It will not regrow hair").

counterarguments (CAs) Thoughts that disagree with the message.

support arguments (SAs) Thoughts that agree with the message.

source derogations (SDs) Thoughts that discount or attack the source of the message.

- **Support arguments (SAs)** are thoughts that express agreement with the message ("This sounds great" or "I really need a product like this").
- **Source derogations (SDs)** are thoughts that discount or attack the source of the message ("The guy is lying" or "The guy in the ad was paid to say this").

According to the cognitive response model, these responses affect consumers' attitudes. Specifically, counterarguments and source derogations result in a less favorable initial attitude or resistance to attitude change. In the Rogaine example, thoughts like "It will never work" or "The guy was paid to say this" are likely to lead to a negative attitude toward Rogaine. Thus consumers do not blindly accept and follow suggestions made in persuasive messages; rather, they can use their knowledge about marketers' goals or tactics to effectively cope with or resist these messages.[9] The presence of support arguments, on the other hand, results in positive attitudes. As a result, thoughts like "This sounds great" or "I really need something like this" tend to create a more positive attitude toward the offering. According to the cognitive response model, consumers exert a lot of effort in responding to the message—at least enough effort to generate counterarguments, support arguments, and source derogations.

MARKETING IMPLICATIONS Although marketers want consumers to be exposed to and comprehend their marketing messages, they also want consumers' responses to be positive, not negative. Consumers who generate counterarguments and source derogations will have weak or even negative attitudes toward an offering. Marketers can combat this problem by testing marketing communications for cognitive responses before placing ads in the media. By asking consumers to think aloud while they view the ad or to write down their thoughts immediately after seeing it, marketers can classify the responses, identify problem areas, and strengthen the message.

Consumers tend to generate more counterarguments and fewer support arguments when message content differs from what they already believe. Thus a message supporting handgun control will generate a lot of counterarguments among National Rifle Association members. This **belief discrepancy** creates more counterarguments because consumers want to maintain their existing belief structures and do so by arguing against the message.[10] Consumers also generate more counterarguments and fewer support arguments when the message presents weak arguments. For example, saying that Bic disposable razors come in many colors is not a strong and compelling reason to buy them. In such a situation, consumers may derogate the source (Bic) or generate counterarguments ("Who cares about color?").[11]

belief discrepancy When a message is different from what consumers believe.

In contrast, consumers come up with more support arguments and fewer counterarguments when they are involved with the program in which a commercial appears. In such cases, the program distracts consumers from counterarguing, thereby enhancing the persuasive impact of the message.[12] Finally, consumers react more favorably to communications when they are in a positive mood: they often want to preserve this mood, so they resist counterarguing.[13] •

Expectancy-Value Models

expectancy-value model A widely used model that explains how attitudes form and change.

Expectancy-value models explain how consumers form and change attitudes based on (1) the beliefs or knowledge they have about an object or action and (2) their evaluation of these particular beliefs.[14] According to this model, you might like a Toyota because you believe it is reliable, modestly priced, and stylish—and you think it is good for a car to have these traits.

A variety of expectancy-value models have been proposed in psychology and marketing. These models differ in terms of the components of attitude and how these components should be measured. They also differ in whether they examine consumers' evaluation of a product attribute or its importance.

theory of reasoned action (TORA) A model that provides an explanation of how, when, and why attitudes predict behavior.

The **theory of reasoned action (TORA)** provides an expanded picture of how, when, and why attitudes predict consumer behavior. Exhibit 6.4 and the "Components of the TORA Model" feature explain the basic concepts and show how they are applied. Although research suggests that TORA applies to consumers in different cultures, the power of the model is stronger with U.S. consumers.[15]

attitude specificity How specific the attitude is to the behavior being predicted.

The TORA model improves on previous models in several important ways. First, it incorporates the principle of **attitude specificity**; that is, the more specific the attitude is to the behavior of interest, the more likely the attitude will be related to the behavior. This means that if we are trying to understand consumers' acquisition, usage, and disposition behaviors, we will be more successful if we examine attitudes toward engaging in these behaviors as opposed to attitudes toward offerings in general. Thus, knowing a consumer's attitude toward *buying* a

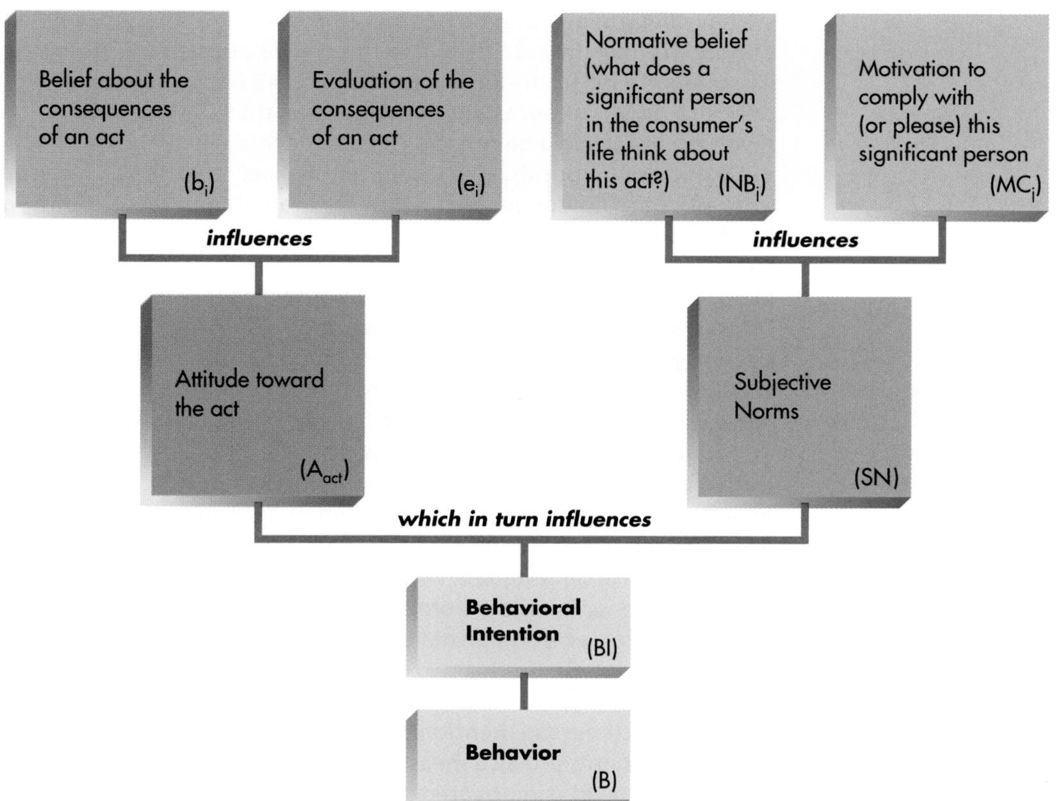

EXHIBIT 6.4
The Theory of Reasoned Action

According to TORA, behavior is a function of our intent to behave (BI), which is determined by our attitude toward performing that behavior (A_{act}) as well as the influence of others' opinions (SN). To form A_{act}, the beliefs we have about the consequences of performing the behavior (b_i) are multiplied by an evaluation of the consequences (e_i) and summed. Similarly, SN is a function of beliefs about what important people think (NB_j) and the motivation to comply with these people (MC_j). The Components of the TORA Model exhibit on pages 136-137 shows these concepts in action.

Components of the TORA Model

behavior (B) What we do.

behavioral intention (BI) What we intend to do.

attitude toward the act (A_{act}) How we feel about doing something.

subjective norms (SN) How others feel about us doing something.

The most basic proposition of the model is that **behavior (B)** is a function of a person's **behavioral intention (BI)**, which in turn is determined by (1) the person's **attitude toward the act (A_{act})** and (2) the **subjective norms (SN)** that operate in the situation. The model then specifies what affects these two components. Consistent with most expectancy-value models, A_{act} is determined by the consumer's *beliefs* (b_i) about the consequences of engaging in the behavior and the consumer's *evaluation* (e_i) of these consequences. Subjective norms are determined by the consumer's *normative beliefs* (NB_j)—or what the consumer thinks someone else wants him or her to do—and the consumer's *motivation to comply* (MC_j) with this person. Although this model might seem complex, it can be illustrated fairly easily with an example.

We begin by identifying the consumer's most important beliefs about the consequences of engaging in the behavior. For example, suppose a consumer named David would like to take skydiving lessons and his beliefs about the consequences are that it will be fun, educational, dangerous, and possibly cost a lot of money. Thus we have determined what beliefs (b_i) David has about skydiving lessons, and we have determined that he has four of them (i = 4). These beliefs can vary in terms of how strongly they are held, and this can be assessed using a subjective probability scale ranging from –3 (very unlikely) to +3 (very likely) (see the exhibit on the opposite page). In our example we can see that David thinks it is very likely that skydiving lessons will be fun (b_1 = +3), somewhat likely they will be educational (b_2 = +2) and dangerous (b_3 = +2), and slightly likely that they will cost a lot of money (b_4 = +1). Each consequence can now be evaluated in terms of how desirable (how bad [–3] to good [+3]) it is. The exhibit on the next page shows that David rates the consequences of potential danger and cost as negative (e_3 = –3 and e_4 = –1) but rates the fun and educational aspects positively (e_1 = +3 and e_2 = +2). To determine David's attitude toward taking skydiving lessons (A_{act}), we multiply each belief strength rating (b_i) by its associated evaluation rating (e_i) and add these multiplied totals (as specified by the model). From these computations, we can see that David has a positive attitude toward taking skydiving lessons (A_{act}= +6).

To predict behavioral intentions, however, we must also examine David's subjective perceptions of the normative influences, also known as subjective norms. There are likely to be people whose opinions and beliefs will affect what David does. We see in the exhibit that there are four people (j = 4) whose opinions matter to David. He can estimate whether each person believes he should or should not take the lessons. This is the normative belief (NB_j) component. We see in the exhibit that David's father is somewhat negative about it (NB_1 = –1) and his mother is very negative (NB_2 = –3), but his two friends think he should take the lessons (NB_3 = +1 and NB_4 = +3). David can also think about how motivated he is to comply with the beliefs of each person mentioned (the MC_j component). As shown in the exhibit, these components are also measured on a seven-point subjective probability scale. In this case David is motivated to comply with each person, particularly his girlfriend (MC_3 = +3). To determine the subjective norm (SN), we multiply each NB by its associated MC and then add these products. In this case, the SN is positive but near zero. Thus David is likely to feel some ambivalence about taking lessons because the opinions of these other people are contradictory.

Finally, the model predicts that behavioral intentions (BI) are determined by the combination of a person's attitudes (A_{act}) and the normative influences that operate in the situation (SN). In this case David is likely to take the lessons because his attitudes are positive and, overall, others have slightly positive feelings about him doing so. Note that A_{act} and SN do not always have an equal impact on BI. In some cases, consumers' behavioral intentions are guided more by what they think (A_{act}); in other cases, they are guided more by the opinions of others (SN).

Applying the Theory of Reasoned Action

Here TORA is used to determine David's intention of taking skydiving lessons. His attitude toward the act (A_{act}) is a function of his beliefs about the consequences (e.g., it will be fun, educational, etc.) as well as his evaluation of these consequences. The strengths of his beliefs are rated on a likelihood scale from –3 to +3 (how likely will skydiving be fun, educational, etc.). His evaluations about these beliefs are rated on a scale of very bad (–3) to very good (+3). For example, it is very good that skydiving is fun; it is very bad that skydiving is dangerous. These numbers are multiplied and added to get a +6 (a positive attitude toward the act of taking skydiving lessons). Another aspect of the model (SN) is based on the opinions of important people in David's life as well as how much he values these opinions. These are also multiplied and summed to get a score of +1. Thus, David is likely to feel some ambivalence about taking lessons because the opinions of significant persons in his life are contradictory.

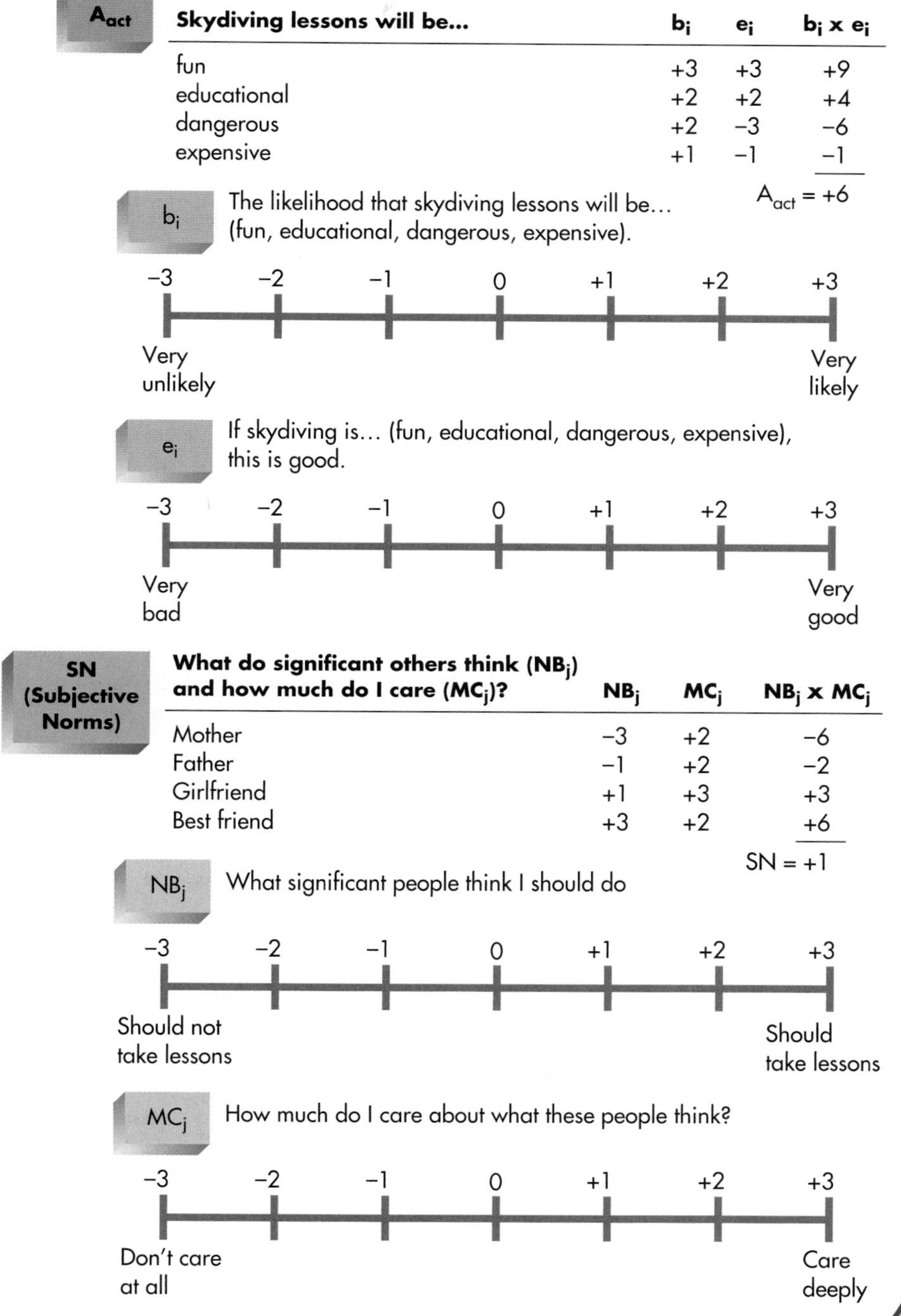

A_{act}

Skydiving lessons will be...	b_i	e_i	$b_i \times e_i$
fun	+3	+3	+9
educational	+2	+2	+4
dangerous	+2	–3	–6
expensive	+1	–1	–1
			A_{act} = +6

b_i
The likelihood that skydiving lessons will be... (fun, educational, dangerous, expensive).
–3 –2 –1 0 +1 +2 +3
Very unlikely
Very likely

e_i
If skydiving is... (fun, educational, dangerous, expensive), this is good.
–3 –2 –1 0 +1 +2 +3
Very bad
Very good

SN (Subjective Norms)

What do significant others think (NB_j) and how much do I care (MC_j)?	NB_j	MC_j	$NB_j \times MC_j$
Mother	–3	+2	–6
Father	–1	+2	–2
Girlfriend	+1	+3	+3
Best friend	+3	+2	+6
			SN = +1

NB_j
What significant people think I should do
–3 –2 –1 0 +1 +2 +3
Should not take lessons
Should take lessons

MC_j
How much do I care about what these people think?
–3 –2 –1 0 +1 +2 +3
Don't care at all
Care deeply

Toyota should predict car purchase behavior better than the attitude toward the *object itself* (the Toyota).

Second, the TORA model looks not only at how consumers' attitudes are formed or changed but also at how other people in the social environment influence consumer behavior. In some situations, **normative influences** from others can play a powerful role in how people behave. For example, if you had a positive attitude toward signing an organ donation card, you might not do so because you thought your parents would be horrified. Normative influences can also make you behave a certain way despite your negative attitude toward doing so. You might have a negative attitude toward eating fast food but do so anyway because of pressure from your friends.

normative influence Social pressure designed to encourage conformity to the expectations of others.

Third, rather than trying to explain behavior per se, the TORA model seeks to predict the intention (tendency) to act. Thus rather than trying to predict whether you will actually buy a Toyota, the TORA model seeks to predict whether you will *intend* to buy one. Trying to predict behavioral intentions from attitudes is much easier than trying to predict actual behaviors because many situational factors could cause a consumer not to engage in an intended behavior.[16] For example, you may intend to buy a Toyota but do not because you are short of money. In addition, an extension of TORA known as the theory of planned behavior seeks to predict behaviors over which consumers have incomplete control by examining perceived behavioral control.[17]

MARKETING IMPLICATIONS

The TORA model helps marketers understand not only what attitudes consumers have but also why consumers have these attitudes and how attitudes can be changed.

Diagnosing existing attitudes. Marketers can use the TORA model to understand why consumers may like or dislike an offering and whether consumers want to engage in or resist a behavior. In particular, this model can help marketers understand a brand's perceived strengths and weaknesses and identify other influential people who might also be targeted (based on their beliefs and their influence over others). Analyzing these factors is a useful way for marketers to diagnose their products' performance in the marketplace.

Devising strategies for attitude change. This model also provides very useful guidance on how marketers can change attitudes, intentions, and (marketers hope) behavior through four major strategies:

1. *Change beliefs.* One possible strategy would be to change the strength of the beliefs that consumers associate with the consequences of acquiring an offering. Specifically, marketers could try to (1) strengthen beliefs that the offering possesses positive, important consequences or (2) lessen the belief that there are negative consequences. To illustrate, Hallmark spent $10 million to convince consumers that its cards aren't expensive.[18] As another example, Mercedes-Benz is using hipper media ads and targeted e-mails to persuade young, affluent car buyers that its entry-level luxury cars are stylish and fun to drive, compared with BMW cars.[19]

   Although marketers commonly use this attitude-change strategy when consumers are more likely to consider the message, it is difficult to induce such a change when consumers already have strong prior beliefs. For example, in trying to market products to post-Soviet Central Asia, some major companies have had to work hard in their marketing efforts to change old consumer myths or beliefs.[20] One such belief involved Barbie: consumers perceived Barbie to be an American brand and thought the product was fake if stamped "Made in Hong

Kong." Likewise, Brazilian coffee producers are challenging the belief that their beans are lower-quality by upgrading their processing methods, winning awards in coffee contests, and pursuing prestigious contracts with Starbucks.[21]

2. *Change evaluations.* Another strategy for changing attitudes is to change consumers' evaluations of the consequences. Consumers' attitudes become more positive when their beliefs are more positive or less negative. A number of American companies, including Levi Strauss, Goodyear, Jim Beam, and Tiffany, have attempted to increase the value of "Made in America" as a sign of quality in selling to European countries.[22] Microsoft sought to change evaluations by adding the *XP* designation to its Windows and Office software as a way of signaling that these products will offer consumers an enhanced usage experience. The supporting ad campaign focused on specific consumer experiences with the software—positive experiences—rather than the technical features of each product.[23]

3. *Add a new belief.* A third strategy is to add a new belief altogether; adding another set of positive beliefs would make the consumer's attitude more positive. This is most effective when the brand has inferior existing features, lower perceived quality, or a higher price compared with its competitors.[24] For example, the electronic Cross Pad introduced the new attribute of "a notepad that uploads right to your computer."[25] In designing the Jeep Liberty, DaimlerChrysler decided on an independent front suspension for a smoother ride while retaining the rugged parts that allow this sport-utility vehicle to go almost anywhere.[26]

4. *Target normative beliefs.* A fourth strategy is to develop communications that specifically target strong normative beliefs as a way of influencing behavior. Northern Illinois University has successfully used a normative campaign to reduce heavy drinking by letting students know that most students have fewer than five drinks when partying.[27] On the other hand, condom ads have been unsuccessful in increasing sales because they have *not* stressed normative beliefs (what others will think of you if you *don't* use them).[28] Note that the importance of normative beliefs varies across cultures. In countries that stress group values over the individual (such as Japan, among other Asian nations), appeals to normative beliefs take on greater significance.[29] ●

HOW COGNITIVELY BASED ATTITUDES ARE INFLUENCED

In the previous sections, you saw how cognitive responses and beliefs can affect consumers' attitudes. In this section, you will see how marketing communications can affect consumers' cognitively based attitudes when the processing effort is extensive. As Exhibit 6.2 shows, the communication source and the message influence how favorable an attitude will be.

Communication Source

Among consumers who process information extensively, those with attitudes based on cognitions are likely to be influenced by believable information. This means marketing messages must be credible to generate support arguments, restrict counterarguments and source derogations, and increase belief strength. Several factors, including source credibility and company reputation, enhance the credibility of a message.

credibility Extent to which the source is trustworthy, expert, or has status.

Source Credibility In many marketing messages, information is presented by a spokesperson, usually a celebrity, an actor, a company representative, or a real consumer. In any sales encounter, the salesperson is a spokesperson for the retailer and the offering. Both the **credibility** of these sources and the credibility of the company influence consumers' attitudes.[30]

In general, sources are credible when they have one or more of three characteristics: trustworthiness, expertise, and status. First, someone who is perceived as trustworthy is more likely to be believed than someone who is not. Because consumers tend to see other consumers' opinions as less biased than persuasive words from official sources, Epinions.com, BizRate.com, and other Web sites invite consumers to post their own reviews of products and services and read reviews that others have posted.[31]

Second, we are more likely to accept a message from someone who is perceived as knowledgeable *or an expert* about the topic than from someone who knows little. For this reason, a salesperson who demonstrates extensive product knowledge will be more credible than an uninformed one.

Third, someone with a high position or status in society can also be perceived as credible. That is why many companies feature their CEOs or founders in ads; company patriarch Robert Mondavi appears in Mondavi wine ads with celebrities like movie director Francis Ford Coppola, while photos of the adventurous founder Jim Thompson are displayed in the stores of Thai Silk Company.[32] In Latin America, having products endorsed by famous and respected people is an effective technique, particularly in Venezuela and Mexico. Pepsi, for example, features the Latin pop star Shakira in some Spanish-language ads.[33]

Research has shown that credible sources have considerable impact on consumers' acceptance of the message when consumers' prior attitudes are negative, when the message deviates greatly from their prior beliefs, when the message is complex or difficult to understand, and when there is a good "match" between the product and endorser.[34] On the other hand, credible sources have less impact when consumers hold their existing attitude with confidence (even a credible source will not convince them otherwise) and when they have a high degree of ability to generate their own conclusions from the message (they have a lot of product-relevant knowledge, particularly if based on direct experience).[35] Also, consumers are less likely to believe that a source is credible when the source (e.g., a celebrity) endorses multiple products.[36]

MARKETING IMPLICATIONS Bill Cosby, Alan Alda, and Candice Bergen have been successful endorsers because consumers perceive these stars as honest and straightforward. Likewise, consumers might perceive a salesperson who has an "honest face" as a credible source of information. Interestingly, a simple two-word ad in the *Wall Street Journal* that stated "Honest Stockbroker" attracted a number of clients.[37] Ordinary people can also be perceived as credible endorsers. Companies such as Home Depot, Wal-Mart, and the U.S. Postal Service have featured employees in their advertising campaigns because the employees add realism and, in many cases, are similar to the target market.[38] In addition, Latin American consumers tend to give positive evaluations to ads featuring real people.[39]

Because of their expertise, sports figures like Tiger Woods and Kobe Bryant have been successful expert sources for athletic apparel and equipment, as well as other products.[40] Expert sources can also be popular, another factor that can contribute to an effective ad. Interestingly, one survey indicated that women endorsers are often seen as more popular and credible than are male endorsers.[41] However, the company or product risks losing some credibility if a celebrity endorser gets into trouble or quits.

A low-credibility source *can* be effective in some circumstances. In particular, if a low-credibility source argues against his or her own self-interest, positive attitude change can result.[42] Political ads, for example, often feature a member of the opposing party who endorses a rival candidate. In addition, the impact of a low-credibility source can actually increase over time (assuming a powerful message). This **sleeper effect** occurs because the memory of the source can decay more rapidly than the memory of the message.[43] Thus consumers may remember the message but not the source. ●

sleeper effect Consumers forget the source of a message more quickly than they forget the message.

Company Reputation When marketing communications do not feature an actual person, consumers judge credibility by the reputation of the company delivering the message.[44] People are more likely to believe—and change their attitudes based on—messages from companies that have a reputation for producing quality products, for dealing fairly with consumers, or for being trustworthy.

strong argument A presentation that features the best or central merits of an offering in a convincing manner.

MARKETING IMPLICATIONS Knowing that reputation influences consumer perceptions and credibility, many companies devote considerable time and money to developing a positive image through corporate advertising. The brokerage firm Charles Schwab, for example, never stops advertising to build its brand, even during market downturns; in any given year, its quarterly ad budget may be $77 million or more. Newcomers entering an industry may spend even more to establish their brands and reputations. E*Trade, an online brokerage firm, spent $521 million on promotions during one recent year.[45] ●

The Message

Just as consumers evaluate whether the source is credible when their processing effort is high, they also evaluate whether the message is credible. Three factors affect the credibility of a message: the quality of its argument, whether it is a one-sided or two-sided message, and whether it is a comparative message.

EXHIBIT 6.5
Argument Quality
When a company announces that its products or services have won awards or endorsements, the company's advertising can become more credible and convincing to consumers.

Source: Courtesy of Phonak.

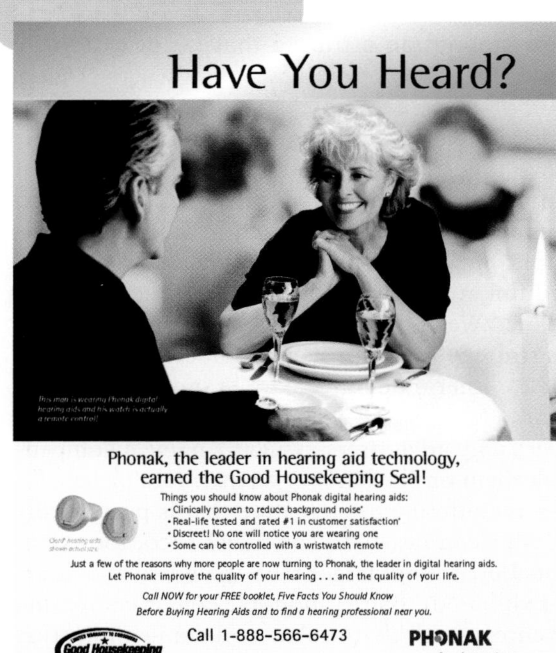

Have You Heard?
Phonak, the leader in hearing aid technology, earned the Good Housekeeping Seal!
Things you should know about Phonak digital hearing aids:
• Clinically proven to reduce background noise*
• Real-life tested and rated #1 in customer satisfaction*
• Discreet! No one will notice you are wearing one
• Some can be controlled with a wristwatch remote
Just a few of the reasons why more people are now turning to Phonak, the leader in digital hearing aids.
Let Phonak improve the quality of your hearing . . . and the quality of your life.
Call NOW for your FREE booklet, Five Facts You Should Know
Before Buying Hearing Aids and to find a hearing professional near you.
Call 1-888-566-6473
Good Housekeeping
Promises
PHONAK
hearing systems
Powered by Innovation

Argument Quality One of the most critical factors affecting whether a message is credible concerns whether it uses strong arguments.[46] **Strong arguments** present the best features or central merits of an offering in a convincing manner. Master Lock has convincingly demonstrated its product's toughness by showing that its lock does not break when you shoot a hole through it. Messages can also present supporting endorsements or research, such as the *Good Housekeeping* Seal or *Consumers Digest's* Best Buy designation (see Exhibit 6.5).

Infomercials—commercial messages that can last 30 or 60 minutes—allow companies enough time to fully explain complicated, technologically advanced, or innovative goods and services. Numerous firms, including Nissan, Nikon, Monster.com, and Humana Healthcare, have successfully used infomercials to present strong arguments and sell offerings.[47] Finally, Internet advertising enables companies to supplement complicated messages with convincing information and to have a positive impact on consumers.[48] Nestlé, for instance, has used online ads embedded with video snippets to promote the European heritage of specialty food brands such as Buitoni and Crosse & Blackwell.[49]

MARKETING IMPLICATIONS If messages are weak and not very compelling, consumers are unlikely to think they offer credible reasons for buying. Saying that you should buy a particular brand of mattress because it comes in decorator fabrics is not very convincing. Nevertheless, messages do not always have to focus on substantive features of the product or service. Less important features can actually play a key role in influencing attitudes when brands are similar and many competitors emphasize the same important attributes.[50] Also, a message should match the amount of effort consumers want to use to process it. A message that is either too simple or too complicated is unlikely to be persuasive.[51] •

one-sided message A marketing message that presents only positive information.

two-sided message A marketing message that presents both positive and negative information.

One- versus Two-Sided Messages Most marketing messages present only positive information. These are called **one-sided messages.** In some instances, however, a **two-sided message**, containing both positive and negative information about an offering, can be effective. For example, Buckley's Mixture has captured 12 percent of the Canadian cough syrup market using blunt two-sided ad messages such as "It tastes awful. And it works" and "Relief is just a yuck away."[52] Like strong message arguments, two-sided messages may affect attitudes by making the message more credible (that is, they increase belief strength) and reducing counterarguments. When consumers see negative information in an ad, they are likely to infer that the company must be honest. By providing reasons for consumers to be interested in the offering despite these problems, the ad encourages consumers to add a new belief.

MARKETING IMPLICATIONS Two-sided messages seem to be particularly effective when (1) consumers are initially opposed to the offering (they already have negative beliefs) or (2) they will be exposed to strong countermessages from competitors.[53] Two-sided messages are also well received by more-intelligent consumers who prefer messages that are more balanced and less biased. However, the use of two-sided advertising is not always in the marketer's best interest. The positive effects of two-sided messages on brand attitudes occur only if the negative message is about an attribute that is not extremely important. •

comparative messages Messages that make direct comparisons with competitors.

Comparative Messages **Comparative messages** show how much better the offering is than a competitor's. Two types of comparative messages have been identified.[54] The most common type is the *indirect comparative message* in which the offering is compared with unnamed competitors (such as "other leading brands" or "Brand X"). For example, Suzuki introduced its midsize XL-7 sport-utility vehicle using ads that poked fun at the impracticalities of larger, competing sport-utility vehicles. The headline "We're big (for a Suzuki), but not too big" reinforced the comparison.[55] This strategy can improve consumers' perceptions of a moderate-share brand relative to other moderate-share brands (but not the market leader).[56]

With *direct comparative advertising,* advertisers explicitly name a competitor or set of competitors and attack them on the basis of an attribute or benefit. This approach is usually used when the offering has a feature that is purportedly better than that of a competitor's. Mexican fast-food chain Del Taco, for example, uses advertising to show that its burritos are larger than the burritos of market leader Taco Bell.[57] In the ad in Exhibit 6.6, Barnesandnoble.com is comparing its title-selection database and inventory with that of Amazon.com—indicating that the former offers more titles than its competitor. Companies such as Pepsi,

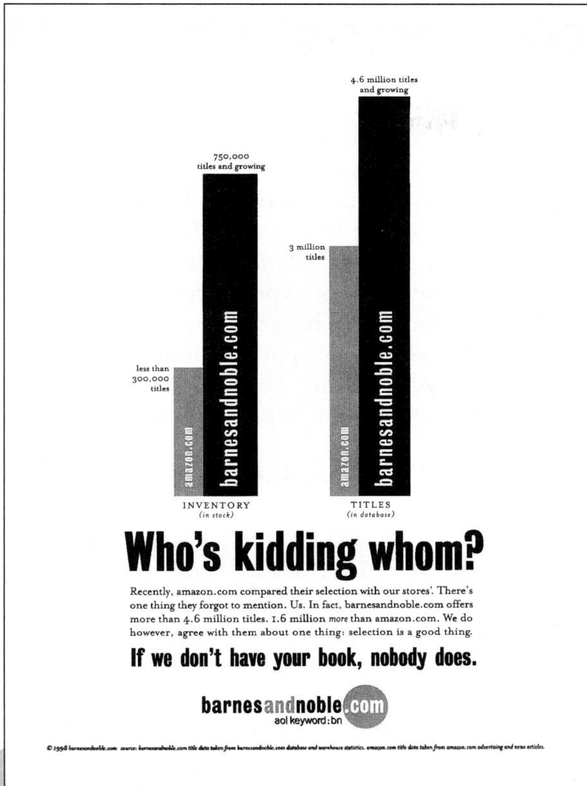

EXHIBIT 6.6
Comparative Advertising
Sometimes ads will mention a competitor by name and point out how a product or service is different from the competitors. In this ad, Barnesandnoble.com is comparing its inventory and title selection with Amazon.com.

Source: barnesandnoble.com.

Levi's, IBM, Dell, AT&T, MCI, Sprint, and Qwest have made heavy use of direct comparative advertising.[58] Salespeople in a personal-selling situation frequently use this technique to convince consumers of the advantages of their brand over the competition.

In general, research shows that direct comparative messages are effective in generating attention and brand awareness and positively increasing message processing, attitudes, intentions, and behavior.[59] They do not, however, have high credibility, as noted earlier. These messages are particularly effective for new brands or for those with a low market share that are attempting to take sales away from more popular brands.[60] Essentially, the new or low-share brand can enhance attitudes by highlighting how it is different from or better than other brands—which gives consumers a credible reason for purchasing the brand. In fact, comparative advertising that stresses differentiation can spur consumers to note the dissimilarities with competing brands.[61] These messages are especially effective when they contain other elements that make them believable, such as a credible source or objective and verifiable claims (a strong argument),[62] and when the featured attribute or benefit is important within the product category.[63]

Furthermore, research shows that consumers who originally receive information in a noncomparative message and are then exposed to a comparative message will revise their evaluations more than when subsequently exposed to another noncomparative message. The reverse is also true: consumers who originally receive information in a comparative message and are then exposed to a noncomparative message will revise their evaluative judgments to a greater degree than when subsequently exposed to another comparative message.[64]

MARKETING IMPLICATIONS Direct comparative messages are best used when consumers' MAO to process the message is high. When MAO is high, consumers exert more effort in processing the message and are less likely to confuse the advertised brand with its competition.[65] Marketers must also be careful that all information contained in the message is factual and verifiable; otherwise, competitors may consider taking legal action. In addition, although it is widely used in the United States and Latin America, comparative advertising is illegal in some countries and closely regulated in the European Union.[66] And some consumers do not like comparative advertising. Japanese consumers, for example, respond better to a softer sell than they do to comparative ads.[67] ●

THE AFFECTIVE (EMOTIONAL) FOUNDATIONS OF ATTITUDES

Most of the consumer research on attitudes when MAO and processing effort are high has focused on the cognitive models of attitude formation. Now, however, researchers are recognizing that consumers might exert a lot of mental energy in processing a message on an emotional basis. Emotional reactions, independent of cognitive structure, may serve as a powerful way of creating attitudes that are favorable, enduring, and resistant to change.[68] This section examines when and how attitudes can be changed through consumers' feelings when MAO and processing effort are high.

affective involvement When a stimulus has strong emotional relevance to a consumer.

affective responses Feelings and images a consumer generates in response to a message.

emotional appeals Messages that elicit an emotional response.

When **affective involvement** with an object or decision is high, consumers can experience fairly strong emotional reactions to a stimulus. These feelings can, in turn, influence attitudes. In this case the consumer's *feelings* act as a source of information, and consumers will rely on these feelings to evaluate the stimulus.[69] Feelings are more likely to play a key role in attitude change when they fit with or are viewed as relevant to the product or service being offered.[70] For example, someone who is in love might have a *more positive attitude* toward an expensive perfume or a nice restaurant than someone who is not experiencing this emotion. Feelings can also be a factor when consumers see others experiencing strong emotion while using an offering or when situational factors hamper the consumer's effort to develop a cognitive attitude.[71] Thus, consumers under severe time pressure could simply recall a previous emotional experience rather than develop a cognitive attitude.

In marketing situations, certain factors can activate experiences or episodes from memory that may be associated with strong emotions.[72] For example, you might experience positive emotions such as joy and excitement if you suddenly see an ad for the car you have just bought. If you are a dog lover, you might experience affective involvement toward a message featuring a cute dog. Maxwell's Hallmark, a store in Phoenix, Arizona, has a secret weapon in battling larger gift stores: it uses two friendly cocker spaniels to attract and retain customers.[73]

Although researchers do not yet have a solid understanding of the emotional bases of attitudes, it is clear that when consumers are emotionally involved in a message, they tend to process it on a general level rather than analytically.[74] This process involves the generation of images or feelings, called **affective responses** (or ARs),[75] rather than cognitive responses. Affective responses are particularly important when the ad builds toward a "peak emotional experience."[76] Consumers can also either recall an emotional experience from memory or vicariously place themselves in the situation and experience the emotions associated with it.[77] These feelings will then influence attitudes. For example, Kodak's "Share Moments, Share Life" ad campaign reminds consumers of the positive feelings generated by pictures of family and friends.[78] For example, in the Sharp ad (Exhibit 6.7), marketers hope that the happy jumping people will create positive affective responses (recalling happy experiences or imagining a similar situation) that might then transfer to the product (Sharp liquid crystal television).

EXHIBIT 6.7
An Emotional Appeal
This ad used feelings and emotions to sell a high technology product. Rather than stressing technical aspects (the cognitive approach), this ad is emphasizing emotions such as happiness, excitement, and "being spirited." Can you think of other products or services that could be sold in a similar manner?

Source: Sharp Electronics Corporation.

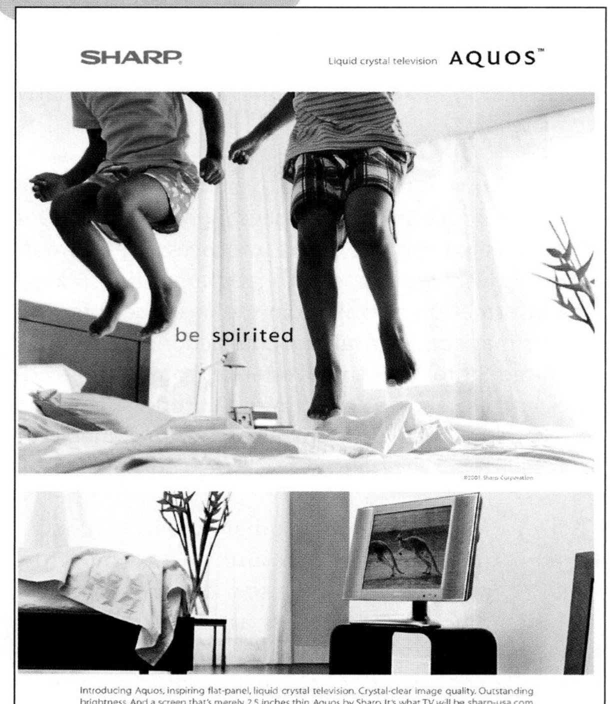

Cross-cultural differences can also influence the effectiveness of **emotional appeals**. One study found that messages evoking ego-focused responses (such as pride or happiness) led to more favorable attitudes in group-oriented cultures, whereas empathetic messages led to more positive attitudes in individualist cultures.[79] The reason for this apparent reversal is that the novelty or uniqueness of these appeals increases the motivation to process and consider the message.

Finally, negative emotions can sometimes have a positive effect on attitude change. In one study the exposure to a public service announcement about child abuse initially created negative emotions (sadness, anger, fear) but then led to a feeling of empathy, and this response led to a decision to help.[80] In addition, consumers can actively try to avoid decisions associated with strong negative emotions by making choices to minimize these emotions.[81]

Note that cognition can still influence whether experienced feelings will affect consumer attitudes. For feelings to have a direct impact on attitudes, consumers must cognitively link them to the offering.[82] To illustrate, if you saw a bank ad showing a tender scene of a father holding his baby, you might experience an immediate emotional response (warmth and joy). However, this feeling will affect your attitude toward the bank only if you consciously make a connection between the feeling and the bank ("This bank makes me feel good" or "I like this bank because it cares about people").

MARKETING IMPLICATIONS Marketers can try to influence emotions as a way of affecting consumer attitudes. In particular, marketers can try to ensure that the emotions experienced in a particular situation will be positive. Car salespeople, for example, often try to do everything possible to make customers happy so that they will develop positive attitudes toward the dealer and the car. The importance of creating positive emotions also explains why airlines, financial institutions, and other service providers place a high value on being friendly. Southwest Airlines, for example, has earned a customer-friendly reputation because, says its president, "we just kill them [passengers] with kindness and caring and attention."[83]

Marketing communications can potentially trigger strong emotions in consumers, although the ability to trigger these emotions is typically quite limited—ads are better at creating low-level moods than they are at creating intense emotions. Nevertheless, in situations where affective involvement in the product or service is often high, marketers may be able to generate the images and feelings necessary to change attitudes. This outcome most often occurs in product and service categories in which a strong pleasure-seeking or symbolic motivation is present—when feelings or symbolic meanings are critical. Mercedes has traded its informational advertising approach for a more emotional appeal. One ad depicts an intimate scene between a father and a son standing in a showroom, communicating that the car is durable enough to hand down from father to son. In Exhibit 6.8, IAMS used an emotional situation (cuddling with puppies) to create positive feelings toward the brand. ●

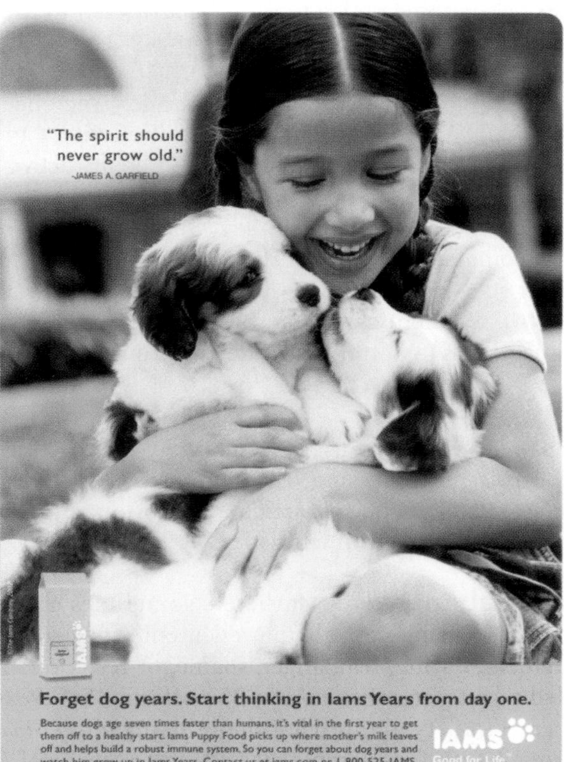

"The spirit should never grow old."
-JAMES A. GARFIELD
Forget dog years. Start thinking in Iams Years from day one.
Because dogs age seven times faster than humans, it's vital in the first year to get them off to a healthy start. Iams Puppy Food picks up where mother's milk leaves off and helps build a robust immune system. So you can forget about dog years and watch him grow up in Iams Years. Contact us at iams.com or 1-800-525-IAMS.
IAMS
Good for Life

EXHIBIT 6.8
Eliciting Positive Emotions
Marketers often use emotional appeals to influence consumer attitudes. In this ad, IAMS employs a situation with high affective involvement—cuddling puppies—to elicit positive emotions in the consumer. It is hoped that consumers will transfer the positive emotions to the brand.

Source: Permission granted by Iams Co.

HOW AFFECTIVELY BASED ATTITUDES ARE INFLUENCED

When MAO and effort are high and attitudes are affectively (emotionally) based, several strategies shown in Exhibit 6.2 can be employed to change attitudes. As with cognitively based attitudes, marketers can use characteristics of the source and the message to change consumers' attitudes by affecting their emotions.

The Source

attractiveness A source characteristic that evokes favorable attitudes if the source is physically attractive, likable, familiar, or similar to ourselves.

match-up hypothesis The idea that the source must be appropriate for the product/service.

Perceived **attractiveness** is an important source characteristic affecting high-effort emotionally based attitudes. Research on source attractiveness suggests that when consumers' MAO and effort are high, attractive sources tend to evoke favorable attitudes if the sources are appropriate for the offering category (e.g., a luxury automobile, fashion, cosmetics, and beauty treatments).[84] This effect has been called the **match-up hypothesis** (the source should match the offering). The relevant attractive source probably enhances attitudes, either by making the ad informative and likable or by affecting consumers' beliefs that the product must be good. A source that is attractive but not relevant can distract the consumer from the message's ideas.[85] When golfer Tiger Woods agreed to endorse American Express, some observers wondered whether he could sell financial services.[86] Others believed that his image of success, hard work, and integrity fit well with the company. Still, research suggests that the match-up hypothesis may be even more powerful for expert sources than for attractive sources, which is why Tiger Woods' endorsement may be particularly effective for golf-related products.[87]

The relationship between attractiveness and attitude change applies to selling encounters as well. Consumers perceive physically attractive salespeople as having more favorable selling skills and are more likely to yield to their requests.[88] Customers also tend to be attracted to and buy from salespeople that the customers perceive as similar to themselves.[89]

MARKETING IMPLICATIONS Marketers need to remember that although attractiveness is most often thought of in terms of physical features, sources can also be attractive if they are perceived as similar, likable, or familiar (in terms of physical appearance or opinions).[90] For example, many sports fans cheered as heavyweight fighter George Foreman staged a successful comeback after a decade in retirement. This made Foreman a likeable and familiar spokesperson for grills and other kitchen appliances.[91] In marketing to China, Nike abandoned its popular Western athletes in favor of popular Chinese athletic heroes (a better match for the Chinese consumer).[92]

The Message

Just as marketers can use characteristics of the source to understand and influence affective processing, they can also use characteristics of the message to influence consumers. In particular, emotional appeals and fear appeals are two important message characteristics.

Emotional Appeals Marketers sometimes attempt to influence consumers' attitudes by using appeals that elicit emotions such as love, wanting, joy, hope, excitement, daring, fear, anger, shame, or rejection. The positive emotions are intended to attract consumers to the offering, whereas the negatives are intended to create anxiety about what might happen to consumers if they do not use the offering. Crest, for example, has advertised its Dual Action Whitening toothpaste using a fear appeal to stir anxiety about not having white teeth. In one ad, three girls are standing under an ultraviolet party light. Their white teeth sparkle, while the teeth of a fourth girl (labeled "Doesn't Use Crest") are barely visible.

Messages can also present situations that express positive emotions with the hope that consumers will vicariously experience these emotions. In these situations marketers can induce consumers to imagine how good the product will make them feel or look. For example, an ad for the impotency drug Viagra shows a happy, dancing couple.[93] Similarly, McDonald's Happy Meals ads concentrate on the emotions surrounding this offering. "For parents, Happy Meal means happy memories; for kids, it means fun, favorite toys, and [entertainment] properties, and favorite food," explains a McDonald's executive. "The area between those is 'special moments,' which gave us the line 'Happy Meals for happy times.'"[94]

Yet emotional appeals may limit the amount of product-related information consumers can process.[95] For example, the ad in Exhibit 6.7 might inhibit cognition about the Sharp products because consumers may be thinking more about feeling good than about the product's features. Thus emotional appeals are more likely to be effective when the arousal of emotions is related to the consumption or use of the product, which is common when hedonic or symbolic motivations are important. For example, some manufacturers of expensive sunglasses have directed their advertising appeals away from functional features, such as sun filters and protection, and toward fashion appeal and sexiness.[96] Also, Volvo switched the focus of some campaigns away from safety and toward "driving pleasure and excitement"—also adding the "enjoy life" slogan—because the brand had developed such a strong image of being safe and stodgy.[97]

MARKETING IMPLICATIONS Typically, marketers attempt to arouse emotions using techniques such as music, emotional scenes, visuals, sex, and attractive sources. To illustrate, Mercedes presented images of a rubber duckie and child, and Goodyear put children from around the world into its advertising in an effort to generate positive feelings.[98] Saturn is trying to create a distinctive image in Japan by departing from the traditional information ads to cast itself as the "cozy" company with friendly employees.[99] Note, however, that arousing emotions is a challenge unless the message has personal relevance.[100] ●

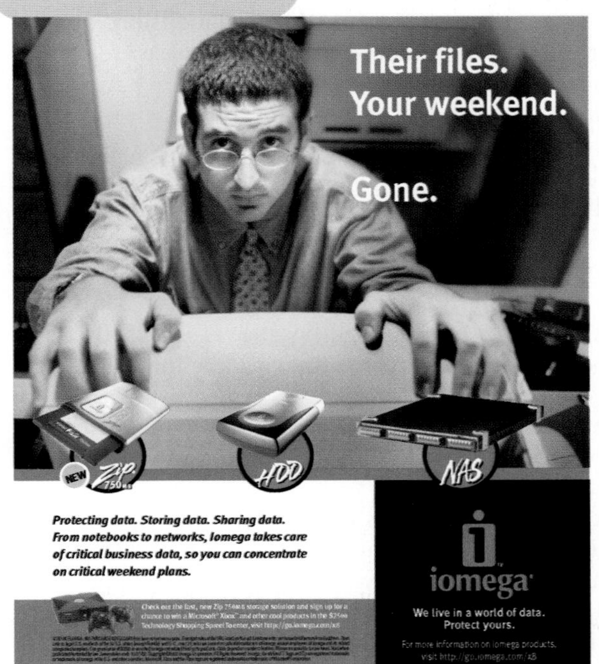

EXHIBIT 6.9
Fear Appeal
This ad stresses the unfortunate consequences of not backing up your files.

Source: Photo courtesy of Iomega Corporation.

Fear Appeals

Fear appeals attempt to elicit fear or anxiety by stressing the negative consequences of either engaging or not engaging in a particular behavior. By arousing this fear, marketers hope consumers will be motivated to think about the message and behave in the desired manner.[101] The ad in Exhibit 6.9, for example, stresses the consequences of not backing up your computer files. Days after a computer virus attacked systems around the world, Symantec debuted an ad campaign emphasizing the risk of not using its antivirus software.[102] Similarly, Wachovia, a financial services firm, used consumers' fears about outliving their retirement money as the basis of a recent ad campaign.[103]

Research examining the effectiveness of fear appeals in changing attitudes and behavior has been mixed. Early studies found that fear appeals were ineffective

fear appeals Messages that stress negative consequences.

because consumers' perceptual defense helped them block out and ignore the message (due to its threatening nature).[104] This research provides one explanation for why the surgeon general's warning on cigarette packages and ads has been largely ineffective. Yet more recent research indicates that fear appeals can work under certain conditions.[105]

MARKETING IMPLICATIONS When can fear appeals be effective? First, the appeal must suggest an immediate action that will reduce the fear. In the ad in Exhibit 6.9, the fear can be easily reduced by backing up computer files. Second, the level of fear must be generally moderate.[106] If the fear induced is too intense (as it was in early studies), the consumers' perceptual defense will take over and the message will not have an impact. Third, at higher levels of involvement, lower levels of fear can be generated because the consumer has a higher motivation to process the information.[107] Factors such as personality, product usage, and socioeconomic status also have an impact on the effectiveness of fear appeals.[108] Finally, the source providing the information must be credible; otherwise, the consumer can easily discount the message by generating counterarguments and source derogations. •

ATTITUDE TOWARD THE AD

attitude toward the ad (A_{ad}) Whether a consumer likes or dislikes an ad.

Although most attitude research has focused on consumers' attitude toward the brand, some evidence suggests that the overall **attitude toward the ad (A_{ad})** in which the brand is advertised will influence brand attitudes and behavior.[109] In other words, if we see an advertisement and like it, our liking for the ad may rub off on the brand and thereby make our brand attitude more positive.

Most A_{ad} research has been done in the context of low effort processing. However, researchers are finding that A_{ad} can also have an impact when consumers devote considerable effort to processing the message. Three major factors have been found to lead to a positive A_{ad} in this context.[110]

utilitarian (functional) dimension The extent to which an ad is informative.

First, more *informative* ads tend to be better liked and generate positive responses.[111] These reactions to the ad will, in turn, have a positive influence on brand attitudes, a factor called the **utilitarian (or functional) dimension**. For example, consumers often like promotions on the Internet because these are seen as more informative than promotions in other media. On the other hand, consumers may have negative attitudes toward ads that are not informative. A good example is the rising negativity toward political ads that are viewed as "mudslinging" and that provide little useful information about the candidates.[112]

hedonic dimension The extent to which an ad creates positive or negative feelings.

Second, consumers can like an ad if it creates positive feelings or emotions (the **hedonic dimension**).[113] We tend to like ads that either make us feel good or elicit positive experiences from memory. This positive attitude can transfer to the brand and make beliefs about the brand (b_i) more positive as well.[114] Thus people might like the ad for Iams pet food (Exhibit 6.8) because it shows affection and cheerful humor, and the positive feelings created might make the consumer's attitudes toward the company more positive. Marketers are also using a variety of techniques to make online advertising seem hip and fun. VF, maker of Lee jeans, incorporates contests, video, and music into its e-mail ad messages and Web sites.[115]

Third, consumers can like an ad because it is interesting—that is, it arouses curiosity and attracts attention. When consumers exert a lot of effort and thoughtfully elaborate on a message, it can be viewed as interesting and generate a positive A_{ad}. This factor helps explain the success of VF's online campaign to promote Lee jeans. VF e-mailed video clips of eccentric characters—such as

Super Greg, an aspiring DJ—to 20,000 consumers who had joined the company's mailing list. Because the ads did not mention the connection with Lee jeans, recipients were intrigued by the videos and forwarded them to friends. Soon consumers were paying close attention to the videos and discussing them with others, raising brand awareness and generating a positive attitude.[116]

WHEN DO ATTITUDES PREDICT BEHAVIOR?

Marketers are interested not only in how attitudes are formed and can be changed but also in knowing whether, when, and why attitudes will predict behavior. The TORA model comes closest to providing this information by predicting which factors affect consumers' behavioral intentions. However, as previously noted, what we intend to do does not always predict what we actually will do. Therefore, marketers also need to consider which factors affect the attitude-behavior relationship. Among the factors that affect whether a consumer's attitudes will influence his or her behavior are:

- *Level of involvement/elaboration.* Attitudes are more likely to predict behavior when cognitive involvement is high and consumers elaborate or think extensively about the information that gives rise to their attitudes.[117] Attitudes also tend to be strong and enduring and therefore more predictive of a consumer's behavior when affective involvement is high. Thus attitudes toward emotionally charged issues such as owning a handgun or getting an abortion tend to be strongly held and related to behavior.
- *Knowledge and experience.* Attitudes are more likely to be strongly held and predictive of behavior when the consumer is knowledgeable about or experienced with the object of the attitude.[118] When making a computer decision, for example, an expert is more likely to form an attitude that is based on more detailed and integrated information than is a novice. This attitude would then be more strongly held and more strongly related to behavior.
- *Analysis of reasons.* Research shows that asking consumers to analyze their reasons for brand preference increases the link between attitude and behavior in situations where behavior is measured soon after attitudes are measured. Marketers should take this finding into account when planning consumer research to support a new product introduction.[119]
- *Accessibility of attitudes.* Attitudes are more strongly related to behavior when they are accessible or "top of mind."[120] Conversely, if an attitude cannot be easily remembered, it will have little effect on behavior. Direct experience (product usage) generally increases attitude accessibility for attributes that must be experienced (e.g., tasted, touched), whereas advertising can produce accessible attitudes for search attributes (e.g., price, ingredients), especially when the level of repetition is high.[121]
- *Attitude confidence.* As we noted earlier, sometimes we are more certain about our evaluations than at other times. Thus another factor affecting the attitude-behavior relationship is attitude confidence. Confidence tends to be stronger when the attitude is based on either a greater amount of information or more trustworthy information. And when we are confident, our attitudes are more likely to predict our behaviors.[122]
- *Specificity of attitudes.* Attitudes tend to be good predictors of behavior when we are very specific about the behavior that they are trying to predict.[123] Thus if we wanted to predict whether a person will take skydiving lessons, measuring

his or her attitude toward skydiving in general would be less likely to predict behavior than measuring his or her attitude toward taking skydiving lessons specifically.

- *Attitude-behavior relationship over time.* When consumers are exposed to an advertising message but do not try the product, their attitude confidence declines over time. Marketers should therefore plan their advertising schedules to reactivate consumer attitudes and attitude confidence through message repetition. On the other hand, trial-based brand attitudes are likely to decline over time even though advertising-based attitudes do not. As a result, marketers should use communications to reinforce the effects of the trial experience and thereby reactivate the attitude.[124]
- *Situational factors.* Intervening situational factors can prevent a behavior from being performed and can thus weaken the attitude-behavior relationship.[125] You might have a very positive attitude toward a Porsche, but you might not buy one because you do not have the money. If you had gone to buy the car, your attitude might not have resulted in a purchase if the dealer was out of stock. In other circumstances, the usage situation may alter the attitude. For example, your attitudes toward different wines might depend on whether you are buying wine for yourself or for a friend.
- *Normative factors.* According to the TORA model, normative factors are likely to affect the attitude-behavior relationship. As one example, you may like going to the ballet, but you do not do so because you think your friends will make fun of you. Although your attitude is positive and should lead to the behavior of attending the ballet, you are more motivated to comply with normative beliefs.
- *Personality variables.* Finally, certain personality types are more likely to exhibit stronger attitude-behavior relationships than are others. Individuals who really like to think about things will evidence stronger attitude-behavior relationships because their attitudes will be based on high elaboration thinking.[126] Also, people who are guided more by their own internal dispositions (called low self-monitors) are more likely to exhibit similar behavior patterns across situations and therefore more consistent attitude-behavior relationships.[127] People who are guided by the views and behaviors of others (called high self-monitors), on the other hand, try to change their behavior to adapt to every unique situation. Thus a high self-monitor's choice of beer might depend on the situation; a low self-monitor would choose the same beer regardless of the circumstances.

SUMMARY

This chapter examined how consumers' attitudes are formed and changed when their MAO to engage in a behavior or process a message is high. In these instances, consumers tend to expend a lot of effort in forming their attitudes. An attitude is a relatively global and enduring evaluation about an offering, issue, activity, person, or event. Attitudes can be described in terms of their favorability, accessibility, confidence, persistence, and resistance. When MAO is high, consumers devote considerable effort to processing a message. Their thoughts and feelings in response to this situation can affect their attitudes, either through a cognitive or an affective route to persuasion.

One cognitive theory, the cognitive response model, holds that attitudes can be based on cognitive responses, the thoughts that consumers have in response to a stimulus. Three categories of cognitive responses are counterarguments, support arguments, and source derogations. A second cognitive theory of attitudes is the expectancy-value approach, which explains how attitudes form and change. The theory of reasoned action (TORA), an extension of this model, predicts that intentions are affected by consumers' attitudes toward the act and normative factors. The TORA model also suggests that marketers can influence consumers' attitudes and intentions by (1) changing beliefs, (2) changing evaluations, (3) adding a new belief, and (4) targeting normative beliefs.

Under elaborative processing, messages can be effective if they (1) have a credible source, (2) have a strong argument, (3) present positive and negative information (under certain circumstances), or (4) involve direct comparisons (if not the market leader). Attitudes are also formed from feelings or emotions such as joy and fear.

Consumers can experience emotions by being affectively involved with a communication or when the message involves an emotional appeal. In either case the consumer processes the communication, and the positive or negative feelings that result can determine attitudes.

When attitudes are affectively based, sources that are likable or attractive can have a positive impact on affective attitude change. Emotional appeals can affect communication processing if they are relevant to the offering (the match-up hypothesis). Fear appeals are a specific type of emotion-eliciting message. A consumer's attitude toward the ad (A_{ad}) can play a role in the attitude change process if the ad is informative or associated with positive feelings. The A_{ad} can then rub off on brand beliefs and attitudes.

Finally, attitudes will better predict a consumer's behavior when (1) involvement is high, (2) knowledge is high, (3) reasons are analyzed, (4) attitudes are accessible, (5) attitudes are held with confidence, (6) attitudes are specific, (7) the attitude-behavior relationship does not decline over time, (8) no situational factors are present, (9) normative factors are not in operation, and (10) we are dealing with certain personality types.

QUESTIONS FOR REVIEW AND DISCUSSION

1. What are attitudes, and what three functions do they serve?
2. How does the cognitive response model differ from expectancy-value models of attitude formation?
3. What role does credibility play in affecting consumer attitudes based on cognitions?
4. What are the advantages and disadvantages of offering a two-sided message about a product?
5. Contrast emotional and fear appeals. Why is each effective? Which do you consider most compelling for products in which you are interested?
6. What three factors may lead to a positive attitude toward the ad (A_{ad}) when consumers devote a lot of effort to processing a message? How can marketers apply these factors when designing advertising messages?

EXERCISES

1. Collect three advertisements (from either magazines or TV) that you think would generate elaborative processing. Perform a detailed analysis of these ads in terms of the following:
    a. What type of cognitive responses might consumers have when seeing/reading these ads? (Be sure to identify counterarguments, support arguments, and source derogations.) Based on these responses, how effective do you think each ad will be in changing attitudes?
    b. Applying the TORA model, what types of attitude-change strategies are these ads using?
    c. What kinds of affective responses (feelings or emotions) might occur? How would these responses affect the attitude change process?
2. Find three ads that you think will generate a fair number of cognitive responses from consumers. Show these ads to a sample of 15 consumers and ask them to think out loud about their reactions while reading the ads. Record these responses either on tape or by hand. Then classify the responses into the categories of counterarguments, source derogations, support arguments, and affective responses. Use this information to answer the following questions:
    a. What are the major strengths of each ad?
    b. What are the major weaknesses of each ad?
    c. How could each ad be improved?
3. Find ten magazine ads that you think will elicit elaborative processing. Analyze these ads for the types of source and message factors discussed in the chapter. Based on this analysis, answer the following questions:
    a. Which types of source and message factors are most frequently used?
    b. Which ads do you think are most effective and why?
    c. Which ads do you think are least effective and why?
4. Interview three people who engage in personal selling for a business. Develop a short questionnaire

that will identify the types of strategies they use to persuade consumers to buy particular products. First, ask some open-ended questions about how the salespeople try to influence consumers. Then ask some specific questions regarding the source and message factors discussed in the chapter. Be sure to ask how often the salespeople use each technique and how effective they think the techniques are.

Summarize this information and answer the following questions:

a. Which types of persuasion techniques are most likely to be used in a personal selling situation?

b. Which message factors are most effective and why?

c. Which message factors are least effective and why?

chapter 7

Attitudes Based on Low Consumer Effort

Introduction: Squawking about a Brand Raises Awareness

Thanks to a feisty white duck squawking "Aflaaaaaac," AFLAC has become a household name across America (see Exhibit 7.1). American Family Life Assurance Company of Columbus—known as AFLAC—had a low profile until 2000, when it kicked off a multimedia campaign to build awareness for the company's supplemental health and life insurance products. Research showed that consumers didn't recognize the AFLAC brand, which prompted the company to look beyond conventional methods of getting its message across. "We realized we are competing for the attention of viewers who are watching not only insurance ads, but entertaining commercials for other products," explains an AFLAC executive.

Then the firm's ad agency observed that AFLAC sounds like a duck squawk, which led to the idea of putting a duck in TV and print commercials. Appearing alongside a jet airliner, riding in a roller coaster, and popping up in other unique situations, the duck reminds consumers of AFLAC's insurance offerings. The duck has become so famous that it serves as the punch line for many talk-show jokes. Thousands of consumers buy stuffed ducks from AFLAC's Web site every year (with the proceeds donated to charity). Not only is the duck generating positive consumer feelings that transfer to the brand, it has helped boost AFLAC's U.S. sales by nearly 30 percent.[1]

The AFLAC campaign illustrates how marketers can influence our attitudes even when we devote little effort to processing a message. Because consumers in this situation do not actively process message arguments or become emotionally involved in the message, marketers must employ other techniques to create positive evaluations of the brand and raise awareness of need situations. This chapter discusses how marketers use techniques such as humor, attractive sources, and emotion to influence attitudes when consumers make little effort to process the message.

EXHIBIT 7.1
The AFLAC Duck
Advertising for the American Family Life Assurance Company of Columbus (AFLAC for short) features this duck to attract attention for the firm's supplemental insurance products.

Source: American Family Life Assurance Company of Columbus (AFLAC).

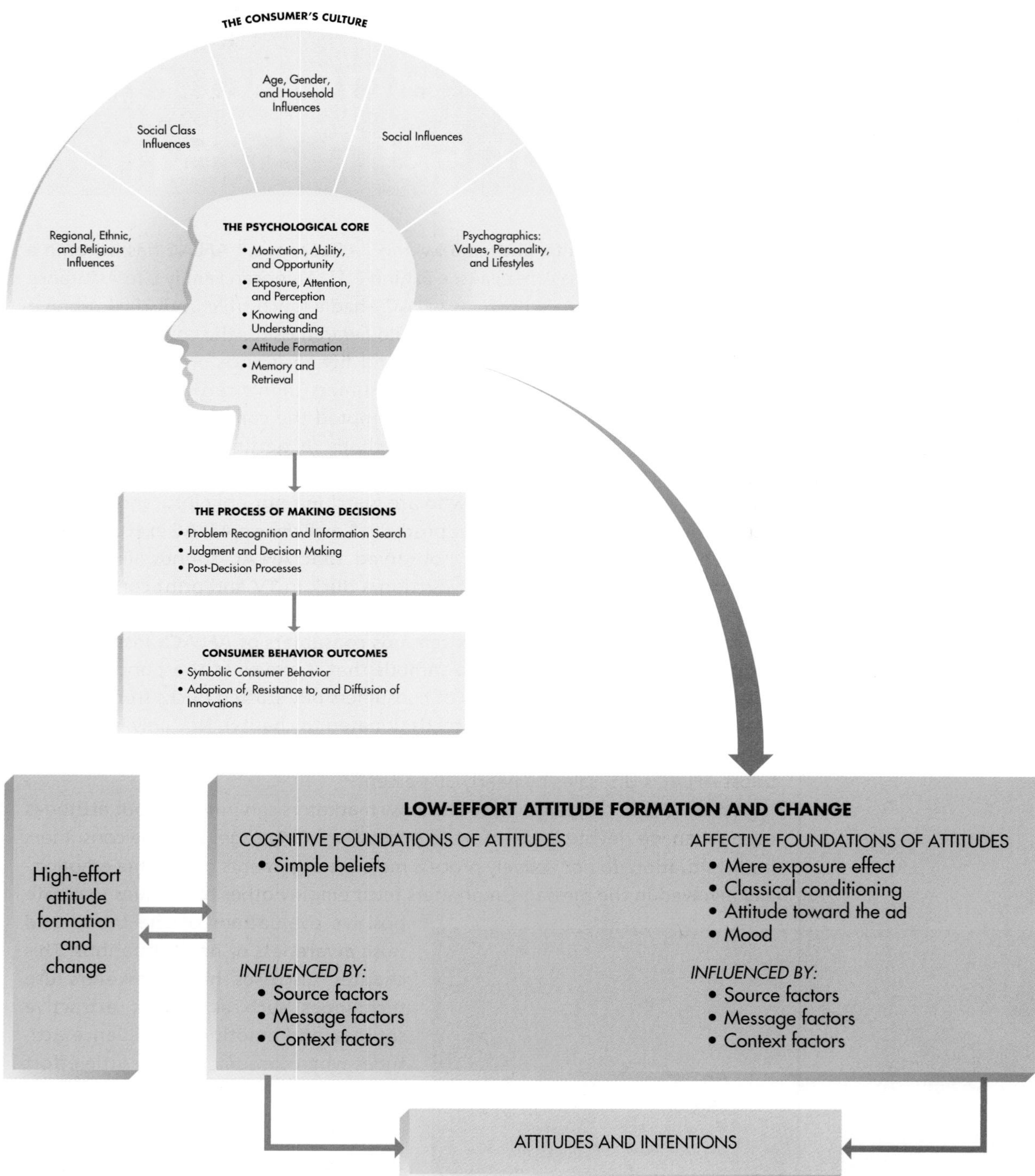

EXHIBIT 7.2
Chapter Overview: Attitude Formation and Change: Low Consumer Effort

Just as in high-effort cases, attitudes can be formed cognitively and affectively in low-effort situations; however, the specific processes are different. Low-effort cognition involves simple beliefs, and affect involves mere exposure, classical conditioning, attitude toward the ad, and mood. Marketers can also influence consumer attitudes cognitively and affectively using source, message, and context factors.

HIGH-EFFORT VERSUS LOW-EFFORT ROUTES TO PERSUASION

When consumers are either unwilling or unable to exert a lot of effort or devote a lot of emotional resources to processing the central idea behind a marketing communication, we characterize it as a low-effort situation. Here, consumers are unlikely to think about what the product means to them, relate empathetically to the characters in the ad, or generate arguments against or in support of the brand message. As a result, when processing effort is low, consumers usually do not form strong beliefs or accessible, persistent, resistant, or confident attitudes.

You saw in Chapter 3 that low-effort situations are those in which consumers do not have the motivation, ability, or opportunity (MAO) to process the information provided. In these situations, consumers tend to be passive recipients of the message. Marketers addressing such situations must therefore use a strategy that takes into account this lower level of processing.

peripheral route to persuasion When MAO is low, marketers try to influence consumer attitudes in ways other than the main message arguments.

peripheral cues Easily processed aspects of a message such as music, an attractive source or picture, or humor.

One way to do this is to create communications that use a different route. Instead of focusing on the key message arguments, the message will be more effective if it takes the **peripheral route to persuasion**.[2] Processing is called *peripheral* when consumers' attitudes are based not on a detailed consideration of the message or their ability to relate to the brand empathetically but on other easily processed aspects of the message, such as the source or visuals, called **peripheral cues**. In particular, consumer attitudes can persist over time if peripheral cues such as visuals are related to the product or service.[3]

Just as there are both cognitive and affective routes to persuasion when processing effort is high, so too can consumers form low-effort attitudes in both a cognitive and an affective manner. Marketers can try to design their ads to enhance the likelihood that consumers' thoughts (the cognitive base), feelings (the affective base), or both will be favorable. Exhibit 7.2 provides a framework for thinking about the peripheral bases of consumer behavior.

Marketers need to understand how consumers form attitudes with low effort because, in most cases, consumers will have limited MAO to process marketing communications. Think about the countless marketing messages you receive every day. How many actually attract your attention and stimulate you to think about the ad and how you feel about the offering? Consider how you normally watch TV. Chances are you have limited exposure to ads because you are channel surfing. You may comprehend very little about the messages because you are watching them in a distracting environment, or you may even tune them out because they feature products you do not care about. These behaviors pose challenges for marketers to overcome.

COGNITIVE BASES OF ATTITUDES WHEN CONSUMER EFFORT IS LOW

Chapter 6 explained how consumers' beliefs form an important cognitive basis for their attitudes. When processing effort is low, attitudes may be based on a few simple and not very strong beliefs, because consumers have not processed the message deeply. Interestingly, because these beliefs are not very strong, marketers may actually be *more* successful in changing them than when processing effort is high. The attitudes of low-effort consumers may be less resistant to attack than those of high-effort consumers because the low-effort people may "let their guard down" and not resist the message or develop counterarguments.

simple inferences When consumers form beliefs based on simple associations.

When processing effort is low, consumers may acquire simple beliefs by forming **simple inferences**. For example, consumers may infer that a brand of champagne is elegant because it is shown with other elegant things, such as a richly decorated room or a woman in an evening dress. Likewise, if an ad is perceived to be similar to the prototypical ad for a product or service category, consumers may believe that the offering is just like the prototypical brand and develop similar attitudes toward both.[4] As noted in Chapter 5, inferred beliefs about the brand may also come from consumers' superficial analysis of its brand name, country of origin, price, or color.

In addition, consumers can form simple beliefs based on attributions or explanations for an endorsement.[5] If consumers attribute an endorsement to the endorser's desire to earn a lot of money, they will not find the message believable. On the other hand, if they perceive that the endorser truly cares about the offering, the ad may be more credible. For example, when Schering-Plough hired New York Mets catcher Mike Piazza to endorse its anti-allergy medication Claritin, Schering's president observed, "Mike Piazza is an ideal spokesperson for this effort, since he is an all-star athlete and a seasonal allergy sufferer who can speak from personal experience."[6]

heuristics Simple rules of thumb used to aid judgments or decisions.

frequency heuristic Beliefs based simply on the number of supporting arguments.

truth effect When consumers believe a statement simply because it has been repeated a number of times.

Finally, consumers can form **heuristics**, or simple rules of thumb, that are easy to invoke and require little thought.[7] For example, consumers could use the heuristic "If it is a well-known brand, it must be good" to infer that brands with more frequent ads are also higher in quality.[8] A special type of heuristic is the **frequency heuristic**, with which consumers form a belief based on the number of supporting arguments.[9] They may think, "It must be good because there are ten reasons why I should like it." Research also indicates that consumers are actually likely to have stronger beliefs when they hear the same message repeatedly this is known as the **truth effect**.[10] Rather than having to think about and evaluate the information, consumers find it easier to use their familiarity with the message as a way of judging its accuracy ("This 'rings a bell' so it must be true").

HOW COGNITIVE ATTITUDES ARE INFLUENCED

Marketers need to consider multiple factors when trying to influence cognitive attitudes. One is the strength and importance of consumers' beliefs. Another is the likelihood that consumers will form favorable beliefs based on the inferences, attributions, and heuristics they use in processing the message. In designing communications that overcome these hurdles, marketers must consider three major characteristics of a communication: (1) the source, (2) the message, and (3) the context in which the message is delivered.

Communication Source

Characteristics of the source play an important role in influencing consumers' beliefs when processing effort is low. Credible sources can serve as peripheral cues for making a simplified judgment, such as "Statements from experts can be trusted" or "Products endorsed by an expert must be good."[11] Note that source expertise is used here as a simple cue in judging the credibility of the message, and, unlike the case in high-effort situations, little cognitive effort is required. Marketers may also increase the chances that consumers will believe the endorsement by ensuring that the endorser does not advertise many other products.

The Message

The message itself can influence attitudes in a number of ways when consumers' processing effort is low.

Category- and Schema-Consistent Information Many elements of a communication affect the inferences that consumers make from a message. For example, consumers may infer that a brand has certain characteristics based on its name ("Healthy Choice cereal must be good for me"). We may make inferences about quality based on price, as discussed earlier, or about attributes based on color, such as when blue suggests coolness. Thus in designing ads for low-effort consumers, marketers pay close attention to the immediate associations consumers have about easily processed visual and verbal information. These associations are likely to be consistent with category and schema information stored in the consumer's memory.

Many Message Arguments The frequency heuristic can also affect consumers' beliefs about the message. As a simplifying rule, consumers do not actually process all the information but simply form a belief based on the number of supporting arguments. For example, White Wave soymilk cartons trumpet multiple benefits, explaining how the product reduces bone loss, inhibits breast cancer, and reduces the risk of heart disease.[12]

Simple Messages In low-processing situations, a simple message is more likely to be effective because consumers will not process a lot of information. Marketers often want to convey basic information and show why a particular brand is superior, especially when it has a point of differentiation that distinguishes it from the competition. However, rather than overloading low-processing consumers with a lot of detailed information about the brand, marketers should provide a simple message that focuses on one or two key points. Pepsi, for instance, promotes the lack of minerals in its Aquafina water with this simple message: "So pure, we promise nothing."[13]

self-referencing Relating a message to one's own experience or self-image.

Involving Messages Marketers will sometimes want to *increase* consumers' involvement with the message to ensure that the information is received. One common strategy is to increase the extent to which consumers engage in **self-referencing**, or relating the message to their own experience or self-image. Studies show that a self-referencing strategy can be effective in developing positive attitudes and intentions, especially if it's used at moderate levels and involvement isn't too low.[14] Similarly, remembering and using the consumer's name in a personal selling context will increase purchase behavior.[15] Finally, consumers will have more favorable attitudes toward brands that are highly descriptive on a specific personality dimension that the consumers consider important or self-descriptive.[16]

MARKETING IMPLICATIONS Marketers can increase self-referencing by (1) directly instructing consumers to use self-reference ("Think of the last time you had a good meal. . ."), (2) using the word *you* in the ad, (3) asking rhetorical questions ("Wouldn't you like your clothes to look this clean?"),[17] or (4) showing visuals of situations to which consumers can easily relate.

mystery ad An ad in which the brand is not identified until the end of the message.

Marketers can employ various other techniques to increase situational involvement and processing effort. One type of involving message is the **mystery ad** (also called the "wait and bait" ad), in which the brand is not identified until the end, thereby arousing the consumer's curiosity and involvement. General Motors took this type of message a step further when it used a "teaser" television commercial challenging consumers to guess the brand of a new sport-utility vehicle and enter a

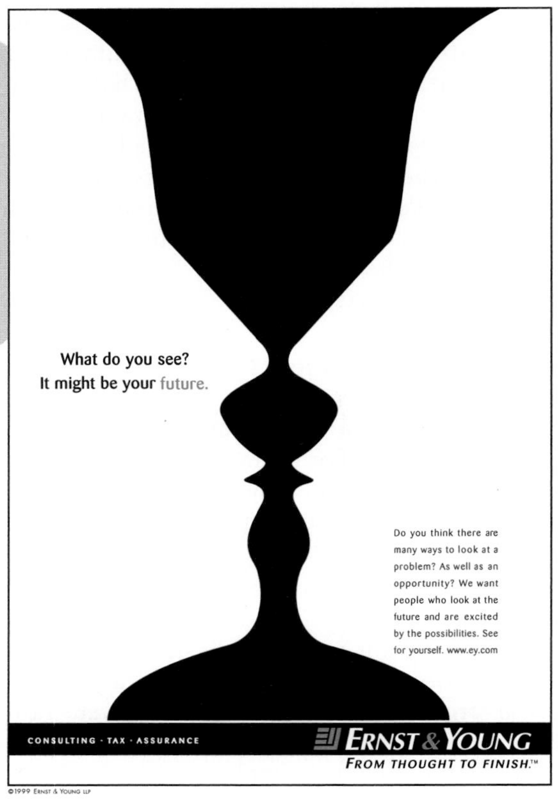

What do you see?
It might be your future.
Do you think there are many ways to look at a problem? As well as an opportunity? We want people who look at the future and are excited by the possibilities. See for yourself. www.ey.com
CONSULTING · TAX · ASSURANCE
ERNST & YOUNG
FROM THOUGHT TO FINISH.™

EXHIBIT 7.3
Increasing Active Processing
This ad tries to draw consumers into the message by challenging them to look at the image in different ways.
Source: Courtesy Ernst & Young LLP.

sweepstakes contest. Consumers most often guessed that the mystery vehicle was a Lexus; weeks later, it was revealed to be a GMC Envoy.[18] Research suggests that this strategy is particularly effective in generating category-based processing and storing brand associations in memory.[19]

Scratch-and-sniff ads have been effective in increasing consumer processing because many consumers cannot resist the excitement of trying something new. Absolut vodka encourages involvement and more active processing on a special Web site (**www.absolutdirector.com**) where consumers can act as movie directors by combining dialogue, plots, and sound effects to create film scenes. Adding to the involvement, consumers can e-mail others with a link to their movie scenes.[20] In Exhibit 7.3, Ernst & Young draws consumers into the message by challenging them to look at the illustration in different ways. ●

Message Context and Repetition

Although source and message factors can influence consumers' attitudes, the context in which the message is delivered can affect the strength of consumer's beliefs and the prominence (or salience) of those beliefs to the consumer. In particular, a company can use message *repetition* to help consumers acquire basic knowledge of important product features or benefits, enhancing the strength and salience of their beliefs. Consumers do not try to process this information actively; rather, the constant repetition increases recall through effortless or **incidental learning.** For example, you may have a prominent belief that GEICO has low insurance rates simply because you have been exposed over and over to that message in its advertising.

incidental learning
Learning that occurs from repetition rather than from conscious processing.

Second, repetition may enhance brand awareness, make a brand name more familiar,[21] make it easier to recognize in the store, increase the likelihood that consumers will remember it when making a decision,[22] and increase confidence in the brand.[23] As you saw early in the chapter, AFLAC's ongoing advertising campaign increased the company's sales by almost 30 percent. Similarly, a series of ads for California avocados increased sales by 16 percent.[24] On the other hand, the Kmart retail chain drew fewer Sunday shoppers and suffered a drop-off in sales after cutting back on Sunday newspaper advertising inserts.[25] Third, as you have seen, repetition can make claims more believable (the truth effect). These repetition effects are even stronger when ads are spaced out over time.[26]

AFFECTIVE BASES OF ATTITUDES WHEN CONSUMER EFFORT IS LOW

The establishment of low-level beliefs based on peripheral cues is not the only way that consumers can form attitudes about brands with little effort. Attitudes can also be based on consumers' affective or emotional reactions to these easily processed peripheral cues. These low-effort affective processes may be due to: (1) the mere exposure effect, (2) classical conditioning, (3) attitude toward the ad, and (4) consumer mood.

The Mere Exposure Effect

mere exposure effect When familiarity leads to liking of an object.

According to the **mere exposure effect**, we tend to prefer familiar objects to unfamiliar ones. Thus our attitudes toward an offering such as a new style of clothing should change as we become more and more familiar with it, regardless of whether we perform any deep cognitive analysis of it. The mere exposure effect may explain why many of the top 30 brands in the 1930s are still in the top 30 today. It is also the reason the music industry likes to have recordings featured on the radio or music videos on TV. Through repeated exposure, consumers become familiar with the music and come to like it.

Because most demonstrations of the mere exposure effect have occurred in tightly controlled laboratory studies, some experts question whether it generalizes to the real world.[27] It is also possible that repeated exposure reduces uncertainty about the stimulus or increases consumers' opportunity to process it[28] and that these factors (rather than mere familiarity) are what affect consumers' attitudes. Yet research shows that mere exposure can help an unknown brand compete against other unknown brands if product performance characteristics are equivalent and consumers invest little processing effort at the time of brand choice.[29] Research also indicates that when consumers can easily process the information from a stimulus to which they have been exposed in the past, they mistakenly believe that the ease in processing is due to liking, truth, or acceptability.[30]

MARKETING IMPLICATIONS If the mere exposure effect is valid, marketers may be able to enhance consumers' liking for a new product or service by repeatedly exposing consumers to the offering or messages about it. Research suggests that when consumers' MAO is low, marketers need to devise creative tactics for increasing exposure to products and messages, perhaps by using the right medium, the right placement within the medium, optimal shelf placement, and sampling.

Consistent with the mere exposure effect, the advertising industry certainly recognizes the importance of developing and maintaining brand-name familiarity. According to advertising authority Leo Bogart, repetition is used to impress "the advertised name upon the consumers' consciousness and make them feel comfortable with the brand."[31] Building brand familiarity is important in many categories; for example, Burger King faced a tough battle when it entered the Japanese market because McDonald's is so well known and strongly preferred there.[32]

wearout Becoming bored with a stimulus.

Note that repeated exposures build familiarity and liking only up to a point.[33] After this, consumers typically experience **wearout**, which means they become bored with the stimulus, and brand attitudes can actually become negative.[34] In fact, research shows that once a persuasive ad has effectively reached the targeted consumer segment, wearout causes a loss of persuasiveness.[35] Marketers can overcome the problem of wearout by developing different executions for the same message or variants on the same offering. Wearout is the reason

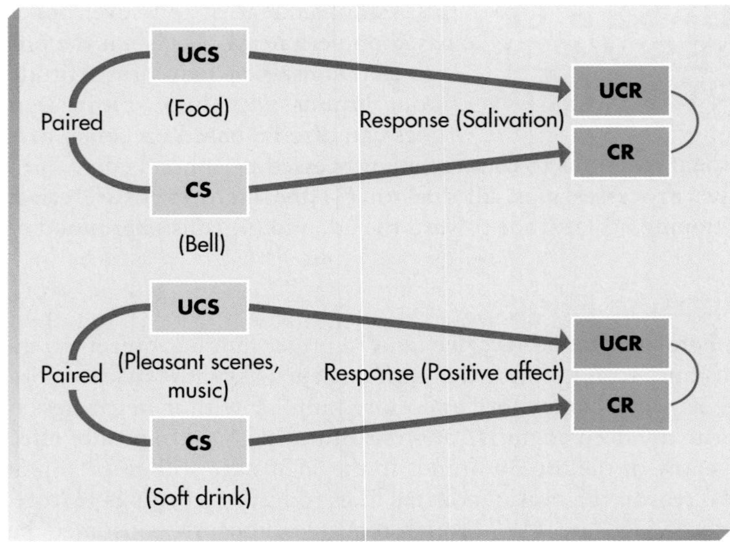

EXHIBIT 7.4
Classical Conditioning
These diagrams illustrate the basic process of classical conditioning. An unconditioned stimulus, or UCS (e.g., food or pleasant scenes), will automatically produce an unconditioned response, or UCR (e.g., salivation or positive affect). By repeatedly pairing the UCS with a conditioned stimulus, or CS (e.g., a bell or soft drink), the CS can be conditioned to produce the same response, a conditioned response, or CR (e.g., salivation or positive affect). Can you think of any other situations in which this process occurs?

classical conditioning Producing a response to a stimulus by repeatedly pairing it with another stimulus that automatically produces this response.

that many advertisers develop an entire campaign of ads rather than a single execution.[36] The goal is to get the same message across in many different ways, the way the familiar but ever-changing "milk mustache" campaign has been used to promote one of the world's most boring products: milk. ●

Classical Conditioning

One way of influencing consumers' attitudes without invoking much processing effort is **classical conditioning.** Classical conditioning became well known from work in the 1900s by the Russian scientist Ivan Pavlov. Normally, hungry dogs will salivate automatically when they see food. Pavlov discovered that he could condition hungry dogs to salivate at the sound of a bell. How did this happen?

According to Pavlov, the food was an *unconditioned stimulus (UCS),* and the salivation response to the food was an *unconditioned response (UCR)* (see Exhibit 7.4). A stimulus is unconditioned when it automatically elicits an involuntary response. In this situation, the dogs automatically salivated when they saw the meat powder. In contrast, a *conditioned stimulus (CS)* is something that does not automatically elicit an involuntary response by itself. Until Pavlov paired the food with the bell, the bell alone was not capable of making the dogs salivate. Repeatedly pairing the conditioned stimulus (the bell) with the unconditioned stimulus (the meat powder) elicited the involuntary unconditioned response (salivation). The dogs came to associate the food and the bell so closely that eventually they salivated upon hearing the bell alone. Because the response could now be evoked in the presence of the conditioned stimulus, the response was said to be a conditioned response (CR). As another illustration of this phenomenon, many cat owners have noticed that their kitties usually come running when they hear the can opener. This behavior occurs because the noise of the can opener has been repeatedly paired with feeding.

MARKETING IMPLICATIONS What possible significance can salivating dogs have for consumer behavior? In fact, classical conditioning theory is sometimes used to explain the effectiveness of marketing communications. Here, however, the unconditioned response is not a physiological one like salivating but rather a psychological one like an emotion. As Exhibit 7.4 shows, certain unconditioned stimuli (such as a happy scene or a catchy jingle) automatically elicit an unconditioned emotional response such as joy or warmth. By repeatedly pairing one of these unconditioned stimuli with a conditioned stimulus, such as the brand name, marketers may be able to evoke the same emotional response (now the conditioned response) to the conditioned stimulus, the brand name itself. Similarly, consumers might be conditioned to have a negative emotional response to an offering such as cigarettes if ads by health advocacy groups repeatedly show the product with stimuli that automatically elicit a negative emotional response (such as pictures of stained teeth).

In one of the first consumer studies to demonstrate classical conditioning, subjects viewed a slide of a blue or beige pen that was matched with a one-minute segment of either pleasant or unpleasant music. Subjects who heard pleasant music selected the pen they viewed with that music 79 percent of the time, whereas only 30 percent of those who heard the unpleasant music selected the pen they had viewed.[37] Although these findings were subject to alternative interpretations (subjects may simply have done what they thought the experimenter wanted them to do or the music may have put the consumers in a more positive mood),[38] more recent and more tightly controlled studies have found support for the classical conditioning phenomenon. For example, by using unconditioned stimuli such as *Star Wars* music and pleasing pictures, experimenters have affected consumers' attitudes toward such conditioned stimuli as geometric figures, colas, and toothpaste.[39] Research has also shown that attitudes created by classical conditioning can be fairly enduring over time.[40]

These studies suggest that conditioning is most likely to occur when:

- the conditioned stimuli–unconditioned stimuli link is relatively novel or unknown. This is why marketers often use unique visuals, such as pictures of beautiful scenery, exciting situations, or pleasing objects, as unconditioned stimuli to create positive feelings.
- the conditioned stimulus precedes the unconditioned stimulus *(forward conditioning)*. Conditioning is weaker when the unconditioned stimulus is presented first *(backward conditioning)* or at the same time as the conditioned stimulus *(concurrent conditioning)*.
- the conditioned stimulus is paired consistently with the unconditioned stimulus.
- the consumer is aware of the link between the conditioned and unconditioned stimuli.
- a logical fit exists between the conditioned and unconditioned stimuli, such as between Michael Jordan and Nike.[41]

Interestingly, the first condition can cause problems for marketers because unconditioned stimuli are often well-known celebrities, music, or visuals for which consumers possess many associations. This situation might suggest that highly visible celebrities are not as effective in creating a classical conditioning effect. However, other research suggests that this problem can be overcome by using highly familiar stimuli such as popular songs and personalities because they elicit very strong feelings in many situations. ●

Attitude Toward the Ad

Another concept that has been useful in understanding the affective bases of attitudes in low-effort situations is the consumer's attitude toward the ad (A_{ad}). Sometimes consumers like an ad so much that they transfer their positive feelings from the ad to the brand.[42] Thus you may decide that you really like Benetton because you find the ads very interesting, or Monster.com because its ads are quite humorous.

One study found that beliefs or knowledge about the brand did not fully account for brand attitudes and that A_{ad} provided a significant additional explanation—brands with liked ads were evaluated more favorably.[43] Furthermore, research in India, Greece, Denmark, New Zealand, and the United States revealed that the A_{ad} principle was globally applicable.[44] In fact, an Advertising Research Foundation project suggests that attitudes toward ads may be the best indicator of advertising effectiveness.[45]

dual-mediation hypothesis Explains how attitudes toward the ad influence brand attitudes.

The **dual-mediation hypothesis** is a somewhat more complex explanation of the relationship between consumers' liking for an ad and brand attitude (see

EXHIBIT 7.5
The Dual-Mediation Hypothesis

This hypothesis explains how attitudes toward the ad (A_{ad}) can influence attitudes toward the brand (A_b) and intentions (I_b). When you read an ad you can have responses (C_{ad}) that are both cognitive (this ad has information about a brand) and affective (positive feelings from finding the ad). These responses may cause you to like the ad (A_{ad}), which can then either (1) make you more accepting of brand beliefs (C_b), leading to a more positive brand attitude (A_b), or (2) give you positive feelings that simply transfer over to the brand (I like the ad so I like the brand). Both processes lead to an increase in intention to purchase.

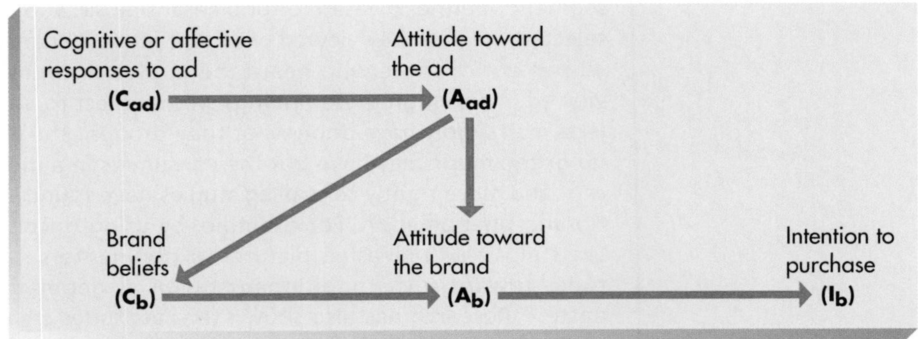

Exhibit 7.5).[46] According to this hypothesis, consumers can have a favorable attitude toward an ad either because they find it believable or because they feel good about it. Thus the dual-mediation hypothesis proposes that A_{ad} can affect brand attitudes (A_b) either through believability or liking. These responses, in turn, may positively affect consumers' intentions to purchase (I_b). Thus consumers who like the ad in Exhibit 7.6 might be more likely to (1) accept the claim that the Nikon F100 is more balanced, agile, and lightweight (C_b) or (2) like Nikon more because they like the ad.

MARKETING IMPLICATIONS The clear implication of the attitude-toward-the-ad theory is that by providing ads that are pleasing, marketers may be able to make consumers' brand attitudes more positive as well. Thus by using techniques such as humor, music, pleasant pictures, and sex (all of which will be discussed in more detail shortly), marketers can develop positive attitudes toward the ad. Procter & Gamble, for example, has abandoned its long tradition of information ads in favor of ads with drama or emotion to "prevent people from hitting the channel changer."[47]

In addition, the effect of ad attitudes on brand attitudes may depend on whether consumers already have a strong attitude toward the brand. When brands are well known and attitudes about them have been formed, consumers may not like the brand more just because they like the ad. However, when brands are new or not well known, consumers' liking for the ad can play a more significant role in their liking for the brand.[48] Studies also suggest that the effect of attitude toward the ad on attitude toward the brand dissipates over time.[49] In other words, as memory of the ad fades, liking for the ad and the brand also becomes weaker. •

Mood

Affective attitudes can also be influenced by the consumer's mood. Here, a stimulus creates a positive or a negative mood; in turn, this mood can affect consumers' reactions to any other stimulus they happen to evaluate. Thus we are more likely to say that we like something if we are in a good mood or say that we dislike something when we are in a bad mood. Mood can therefore bias attitudes in a *mood-congruent direction*. Note that mood is different from classical conditioning because mood (1) does not require a repeated association between two stimuli and (2) can affect consumers' evaluations of any object, not just the stimulus.

According to one study, consumers in a good mood who have a tentative preference for a particular brand tend to ignore negative information about that brand as well as information about a competitor.[50] Still another study found that while consumers tend to like a brand extension less when the product is not very

Nikon
WE TAKE THE WORLD'S GREATEST PICTURES.® YOURS.
The new F100. 785 grams. Eager to please.
Nikon
F100
Introducing the newest addition to Nikon's Total Pro Imaging System, the F100.™ Balanced and agile, it packs heavy duty technology inside its lightweight magnesium alloy frame. You like speed? Try the world's fastest Dynamic Autofocus.
Crisp, sharp exposures? Say hello to 3D Matrix Metering. Even tricky flash situations are a non-issue with its Automatic Balanced Fill-flash system. Now, if it only knew how to fetch. See the F100 at your authorized Nikon dealer.
Photo: Geof Kern ©1999 Nikon Inc.

EXHIBIT 7.6
Affectively Pleasing Ad
This ad is likely to create positive feelings because it is humorous and appealing. Consistent with the dual-mediation hypothesis, a positive A_{ad} may make consumers (1) more likely to accept the claim that the Nikon F100 is more balanced and agile, or (2) like Nikon more because of the ad.

Source: Nikon Inc.

similar to the parent product, consumers in a good mood are more likely to like a brand extension that is moderately similar to the parent product than consumers who are not in a good mood.[51] Moreover, research shows that consumers in a good mood tend to give more weight to positive information when evaluating a product, whereas consumers in a bad mood tend to give more weight to the negative information.[52]

Researchers have examined how lighting influences mood. They found that brighter in-store lighting tends to increase the extent to which shoppers examine and handle merchandise.[53] Brighter lighting does not, however, increase the amount of time consumers spend shopping or the number of purchases they make. Color is also a factor. Warm colors such as red, orange, and yellow tend to be more stimulating and exciting, whereas cool colors such as blue, green, and violet tend to be more soothing.[54]

Consumers may like a brand better when they are put in a good mood by its ads or the programs in which the ads appear. Research has focused on the kinds of emotions or moods that ads invoke and the variety of ways these factors might affect consumers' ad and brand attitudes.[55] One study identified three major categories of affective responses: *SEVA* (surgency, elation, vigor, and activation), which is present when the communication puts the consumer in an upbeat or happy mood; *deactivation feelings,* which include soothing, relaxing, quiet, or pleasant responses; and *social affection,* which are feelings of warmth, tenderness, and caring.[56] For example, Budweiser's "Whassup?" television campaign focuses on friendly relationships among men, in the hope that the ads will generate positive feelings for the beer.[57]

Another study found that ad-induced feelings of warmth and humor could have a direct and positive impact on brand attitudes.[58] Thus the ad for the Nikon camera in Exhibit 7.6 might also generate humor and warm feelings that consumers could transfer to the brand.

MARKETING IMPLICATIONS On the assumption that mood affects consumer behavior, retailers can use physical surroundings and the behavior of store employees to put consumers in a good mood. Warm colors are more likely to draw customers to an outlet but can also create tension. Cool colors, on the other hand, are more relaxing but do not attract customers.[59] Thus when the goal is to stimulate quick purchases or activity, warm colors are more appropriate. Discount stores such as Target and Kmart often use a red-based color scheme. Kmart switched from light blue to red to remove a disadvantage in this area. Warm colors are also appropriate for health clubs, sports stadiums, and fast-food restaurants, where a high level of activity and energy is desirable. The HofferSport store in Nassau, Bahamas, redecorated much of the interior with vivid, warm colors to communicate a lively Caribbean atmosphere and attract young tourists.[60]

On the other hand, cool colors are more appropriate when the goal is to have consumers feel calm or spend time deliberating. Stores that sell expensive consumer goods are a good example. Cole Haan, a high-end shoe company, uses cool green colors in its retail stores to convey a "relaxed but refined" feeling that encourages shoppers to linger.[61] Other businesses that should incorporate cool colors are doctors' offices, hotel rooms, spas, banks, resorts, and upscale restaurants. ●

HOW AFFECTIVE ATTITUDES ARE INFLUENCED

When consumers apply little processing effort and form attitudes based on feelings, the same three factors that influence cognitive reasoning also influence affective attitudes: the communication source, the message, and the context. Again, these factors are based on low-effort processes such as mere exposure, classical conditioning, attitude toward the ad, and mood.

Communication Source

Under conditions of low effort, two factors play a major role in determining whether or not the communication source evokes favorable affective reactions: its physical attractiveness and its likability. These two factors help to explain why marketers like to feature celebrities in ads.

Attractive Sources A huge number of ads feature attractive models, spokespersons, or celebrities, reflecting the long-held belief that beauty sells—especially in the beauty business. Redken, for example, has hired singer Jessica Simpson as a celebrity spokesperson for its professional hair-care products, while actress Elizabeth Hurley smiles out from Estée Lauder cosmetics ads.[62] Supermodel Cindy Crawford, who formerly appeared in Revlon cosmetics ads, is now appearing in ads for Ellen Tracy fashions.[63] Other celebrities featured in beauty ads include Sarah Michelle Gellar (Maybelline) and Uma Thurman (Lancôme).[64]

Research studies generally support the notion that beauty sells. When consumers' motivation to process an advertised message is low, attractive sources will enhance the favorability of consumers' brand attitudes regardless of whether the message arguments are strong or weak.[65] Consumers also rate ads with physically attractive models as more appealing, attractive, eye-catching, impressive, and interesting than ads with unattractive models. These ratings may affect consumers' attitudes toward the products these models sponsor.[66] Moreover, attractiveness can have beneficial effects on advertiser believability and actual purchase.[67] These effects can occur for both male and female models (consumers are most strongly attracted to models of the opposite sex) and have been found to operate for direct-mail responses, point-of-purchase displays, and personal-selling interactions as well.[68]

Likable Sources The likability of the source can influence affective attitudes.[69] For example, Wendy's chairman Dave Thomas was a successful spokesperson because of the homey, warm image he projected. Likable sources may serve as unconditioned stimuli, create a positive mood that affects consumers' evaluations of the ad or brand, and make consumers feel more positive about the endorsed products. Although physically attractive sources can also be likable, sometimes the source can be physically unattractive but have features or a personality that consumers like. Jason Alexander and Jay Leno are well liked, but not generally considered to be extremely attractive.

We also tend to like people of average looks because they are more similar to ourselves and we can better relate to them. Mr. T says he is an effective celebrity spokesperson for Sizzle & Stir dinners because "People know I am a real person. I am just the guy down the street who made it good."[70] Another popular spokesperson is Chris Dollard, a slightly nerdy actor with loose curls who has appeared in ads for Tostitos, J.C. Penney, and MCI.[71] An ad showing a man going overboard to be a doting dad was very popular in Japan (where men are usually depicted as remote corporate warriors).[72] Disabled people are becoming increasingly attractive endorsers for companies such as General Motors, AT&T, IBM, and Sears because marketers want to represent human diversity and because consumers admire courageous individuals.[73]

Celebrity Sources Physical attractiveness and likability explain why celebrities are among the most widely used sources, at times accounting for as much as a third of all television advertising. In particular, celebrity sources can be effective when they are related to the product or service (the match-up hypothesis).[74] Companies may pay huge sums—sometimes as high as $2 to $3 million—to get a celebrity to endorse their products. Basketball star Kobe Bryant earns more than $10 million annually as a spokesperson for McDonald's, Spalding, and other firms.[75] Pepsi hired rapper Busta Rhymes to enhance Mountain Dew's urban image in TV commercials.[76] Even deceased celebrities such as Fred Astaire, James Dean, Marilyn Monroe, Martin Luther King Jr., and Lou Gehrig have strong marketing appeal.[77] Some celebrities place their names on products (e.g., Jimmy Dean's sausage and Paul Newman's salad dressing).[78] Nonprofit organizations also use celebrities to attract attention and influence attitudes. People for the Ethical Treatment of Animals uses Pamela Lee Anderson and Charlize Theron as spokespeople because "we won't get 15 seconds of air time unless we can get a celebrity spokesperson to jump in front of the camera," says its director of policy and communications.[79]

EXHIBIT 7.7
Celebrity Sources
Sometimes popular celebrities can be the source or endorser in a message. Here we see how popular blues guitarist B.B. King is used to present information about the One Touch Ultra System for diabetes testing. This entertainer may generate a positive effect that may transfer to the company.

Source: Courtesy of LifeScan Inc., a Johnson & Johnson Company.

B.B. King
Diabetes for over 10 years
OneTouch® Ultra® System lets you test on your arm too.
Now your fingers have more time to jam.
Less Pain. The freedom to test on your arm which is less painful and gives sensitive fingers a break.*
Less Blood. A tiny blood sample can mean a less painful stick.**
Less Bother. Accurate results in just 5 seconds. Easy sampling with the OneTouch® Ultra® FastDraw™ Design Test Strip.
Test Smart. The more you test, the easier it is to stay in range.
ONETOUCH® Ultra®
OneTouch® changes everything.
KEEP IN TOUCH℠
rewards news information
1.800.227.8862
www.LifeScan.com

Other celebrity sources include cartoon characters. When the Butterfinger candy bar used Bart Simpson as an endorser, sales increased by 26 percent.[80] Joe Camel, now banned in the United States, is alive and well in cigarette advertising in Argentina.[81] Secret agent James Bond has been licensed to sell everything from credit cards to cars to cell phones to watches.[82] Finally, Exhibit 7.7 shows popular blues guitarist B.B. King presenting information about a diabetes testing system.

The Message

Just as the source can influence consumers' feelings and moods, so too can characteristics associated with the message. These message characteristics include pleasant pictures, music, humor, sex, emotional content, and context.

Pleasant Pictures Marketers frequently use pleasant pictures to influence consumers' message processing. Visual stimuli can serve as a conditioned stimulus, affect consumers' mood, or make an ad likable by making it interesting. Research has generally supported the view that pleasant pictures can affect ad and brand attitudes when they are processed peripherally, beyond the effect they have on beliefs about the product.[83] A picture of a sunset, for instance, can influence the choice of a soft drink.[84]

As another example, an ad for 3M's Post-it Notes shows an unusual scene of a 'star' chicken covered with very colorful Post-it Notes, being admired by a group of chickens.[85] Numerous advertisers employ high-powered special effects rivaling those used in the movies. In one ad a Budweiser truck turns into a racing car; in another a speeding car turns into the Exxon tiger (through a process called *morphing*).

Internet advertising often uses pleasing pictures and visuals to catch consumers' attention and generate positive attitudes as well. A key goal of these ads is to look cool, thereby creating positive feelings about the ad.[86] However, advertisers need to find some way of speeding up the processing time for these ads because they often take a long time to download and consumers do not like to wait.[87]

Music Music is frequently used as a communications tool by many companies, including Chevrolet ("Like a Rock") and Nissan (old hits by The Who).[88] Further, the use of music is progressing beyond the traditional use of the "jingle." ITT used crabs, fish, and seals singing the "Hallelujah Chorus" as part of an image campaign.[89] Sometimes the music ads become popular and drive album sales, as was the case with the Crystal Method, Republica, Styx, the Lilys, and Sting, whose "Desert Rose" song played during Jaguar car commercials.[90] Jaguar also used Chris Isaac's "Wicked Game" song to advertise a new luxury sports car in European markets.[91] Molson used upbeat music as the driving force behind its "Anthem" 90-second TV commercial celebrating Canadian heritage and history.[92] McDonald's has even piped music by Bach into its restaurants to scare away troublemakers.[93]

The popularity of music as a marketing device should not be surprising, given that music has been shown to stimulate a variety of positive effects.[94] First, music can be an effective conditioned stimulus for a classical conditioning strategy. Second, music can put the consumer in a positive mood and lead to the development of positive attitudes. Third, music can be effective in generating positive feelings such as happiness, serenity, excitement, and sentimentality. Finally, music can stimulate emotional memories. If a song in an ad reminds you of your high school days or of an old boyfriend or girlfriend, the emotions associated with these memories may transfer to an ad, brand, store, or other attitude object. Several studies have found that music can have a positive effect on purchase intentions.[95]

Whether music evokes a positive affective response depends on the music's structure. Exhibit 7.8 shows several musical characteristics and the emotional responses they may elicit. The style of music used and the product meanings it conveys can vary considerably across different cultures.[96] Marketers must therefore be careful to match their music to the desired affective responses.

Humor Humor is common in TV advertising: 24 to 42 percent of all commercials contain some form of humor.[97] An ad can use humor in many different ways, including puns, understatements, jokes, ludicrous situations, satire, and irony. Although humor is not as widespread in other media as in television, it is nevertheless extensive, particularly in radio.[98] The popularity of humor as a message device is not surprising because it increases liking of both the ad and the brand.[99]

Consumers often rate humorous ad campaigns very positively. Many advertisers of low-involvement products have used humor, including Bud Light, Little Caesar's, Subway, and Snickers. One long-running humorous campaign for Holiday Inn focuses on Mark, a thirtysomething man living at home, and his dysfunctional family. Every time Mark asks his parents for a special amenity, his mother replies, "What does this look like, a Holiday Inn?" Mark finally moves

MUSICAL ELEMENT	EMOTIONAL EXPRESSION: SERIOUS	SAD	SENTIMENTAL	SERENE	HUMOROUS	HAPPY	EXCITING	MAJESTIC	FRIGHTENING
MODE	Major	Minor	Minor	Major	Major	Major	Major	Major	Minor
TEMPO	Slow	Slow	Slow	Slow	Fast	Fast	Fast	Medium	Slow
PITCH	Low	Low	Medium	Medium	High	High	Medium	Medium	Low
RHYTHM	Firm	Firm	Flowing	Flowing	Flowing	Flowing	Uneven	Firm	Uneven
HARMONY	Consonant	Dissonant	Consonant	Consonant	Consonant	Consonant	Dissonant	Dissonant	Dissonant
VOLUME	Medium	Soft	Soft	Soft	Medium	Medium	Loud	Loud	Varied

EXHIBIT 7.8
Musical Characteristics for Producing Various Emotional Expressions

Research has pinpointed the specific effect that various aspects of music can have on feelings. As shown here, the mode, tempo, pitch, rhythm, harmony, and volume of music can influence whether individuals feel serious, sad, sentimental, serene, humorous, happy, excited, majestic, or frightened.

Source: Gordon C. Bruner, "Music, Mood, and Marketing," *Journal of Marketing*, October 1990, p. 100. Reprinted by permission.

into a Holiday Inn hotel and continues his funny antics, such as stealing food from a tray at another guest-room door.[100] Most U.S. products fare very poorly in Japan, but Joy dish detergent was able to capture 20 percent of the market largely by featuring comedian Junji Takada in a series of offbeat ads.[101] And just four days after Isuzu brought back the outrageous liar Joe Isuzu to inject humor into its ads for sport-utility vehicles, company dealerships in Washington, D.C., were already noticing higher consumer traffic.[102]

Humor appears to be more appropriate for low-involvement offerings in which generating positive feelings about the ad is critical.[103] Humor is also most effective when it is tied or related to the offering. Otherwise, consumers will only pay attention to the humor and ignore the brand.[104] For example, the Adobe® Acrobat® ad in Exhibit 7.9 does a good job of tying the humor to the key selling point that sometimes you don't want your document altered.

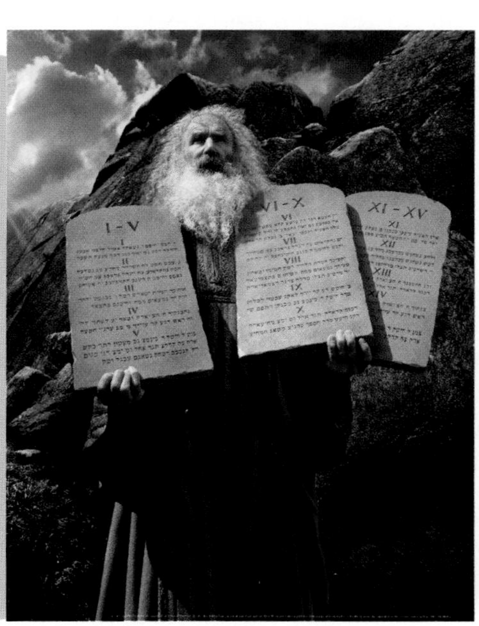

EXHIBIT 7.9
The Use of Humor
This ad uses humor to get across the key point that sometimes you have documents that you don't want altered. Maybe there were fifteen commandments, but we'll never know because Moses didn't have Adobe® Acrobat.®

Source: © 2002 Adobe Systems Incorporated. All rights reserved. Adobe, the Adobe logo, Acrobat, and Tools for the New Work, are either registered trademarks or trademarks of Adobe Systems Incorporated in the United States and/or other countries. Photo

MARKETING IMPLICATIONS Humor tends to work best on TV and radio because they allow for greater expressiveness than other media.[105] Even traditionally hard-sell infomercials are turning to humor. The rock group Barenaked Ladies used a humorous infomercial to launch its "Maroon" album, promoting a fake foot cream that guaranteed to make users into rock stars.[106] Interestingly, the use of humor has also been extended to sales promotions. A company called Communications Diversified creates customized comedy videotapes that can be used as a premium item or sales incentive.[107]

Humor is more effective with certain audiences than with others. In particular, younger, more educated males tend to respond most positively—apparently because aggressive and sexual types of humor appear more frequently than other types of humor and men enjoy this more than women do.[108] Also, humor appears to be more effective for consumers who have either a lower need for cognition or a positive attitude toward the advertised brand.[109]

Finally, humor can be used effectively for consumers throughout the world. One study examined humorous ads from Germany, Thailand, South Korea, and the United States and found that most humorous ads in all four countries contained the same basic structure—contrasts between expected/possible and unexpected/impossible events.[110] However, ads in Korea and Thailand tended to emphasize humor related to group behavior and unequal status relationships, whereas the other two countries focused the humor on individuals with equal status. In all four countries, humor was more likely to be used for pleasure-oriented products. Not all countries appear to employ humor more for low-involvement products than high-involvement ones. German and Thai ads, for example, used humor equally for both types of products. Finally, U.K. marketers tend to use humorous ads more than U.S. marketers.[111] ●

EXHIBIT 7.10
Romantic Message
Sometimes messages have romantic or sexual themes or implications. This ad suggests that romance (and perhaps sex) will be the result of wearing Dark Vanilla perfume.

Source: Courtesy of Coty.

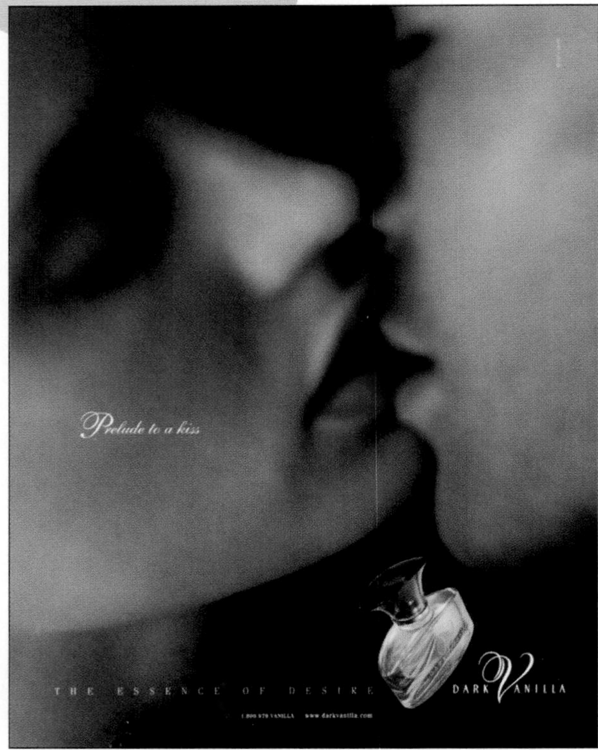

Sex Sex as a communication technique appears in two major forms: sexual suggestiveness and nudity. Sexual suggestiveness involves situations that either portray or imply sexual themes or romance. For example, an ad for Uncle Ben's rice shows a couple flirting with each other in the kitchen.[112] In the United Kingdom, one print ad for Maltesers candy showing a Malteser in a young woman's belly button carried the headline, "The lighter way to get him to do absolutely everything."[113] SSL International, the world's largest condom manufacturer, recently switched from fear appeals to suggestiveness. Now radio ads for its Durex brand of condoms include flirtatious banter between male and female voices.[114] Another good example of sexual suggestiveness is the ad for Dark Vanilla perfume in Exhibit 7.10.

Another use of sex is through nudity or partial nudity, a technique often used by brands in the fragrance industry.[115] Exhibit 7.11 shows an ad from Germany that employs this technique.

You might be surprised to learn that the percentage of ads with sexual overtones has not changed over the years. However, the type of sex appeal has. From 1964 to 1984, the use of sex in the United States became more overt and blatant.[116] As the

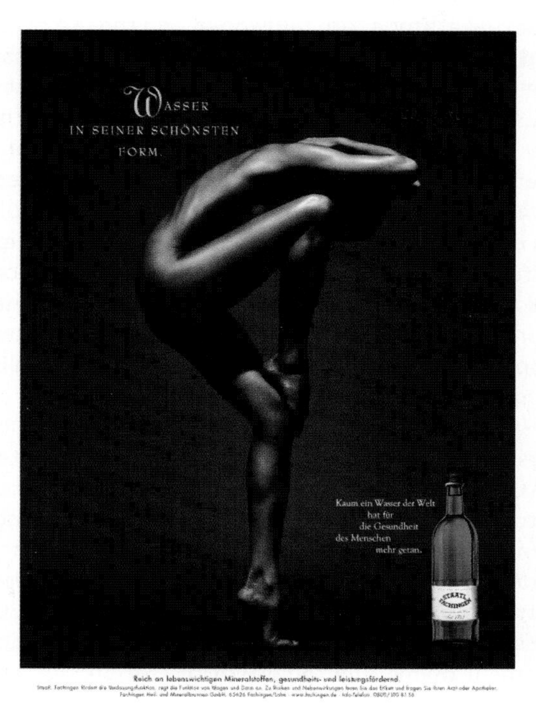

Wasser
in seiner schönsten
Form.
Kaum ein Wasser der Welt
hat für
die Gesundheit
des Menschen
mehr getan.
Staatl. Fachingen
Reich an lebenswichtigen Mineralstoffen, gesundheits- und leistungsfördernd.

EXHIBIT 7.11

Nudity in Advertising

Sometimes ads contain naked or scantily clad models to generate attention or elicit emotions toward a product or service. Here we see an ad from Germany for a mineral water which states "Water in its finest form." The naked model attracts attention and emphasizes the other copy point that this water does a lot to enhance health.

Source: Courtesy of Staatl Fachingen.

country became more conservative in the late 1980s, ads became lighter, more playful, and more subtle, suggestive rather than open.[117] In the 1990s, ads became more blatant again. In addition to the usual product categories in which sex is used (such as jeans and perfume), such diverse categories as cars, gloves, Scotch, and watches are adopting sexual themes.[118] An ad for Timex states, "Make your husband really shine in bed." Women are now being pictured more often as sexual aggressors or equal partners rather than just sex objects. In a Sansabelt campaign women were featured discussing men's pants in a sexually suggestive way.[119]

MARKETING IMPLICATIONS Research on sexual themes in messages suggests that they can be effective in several ways. Sexual messages attract the consumer's attention,[120] and they also have the ability to evoke emotional responses, such as arousal, excitement, or even lust, which can affect consumers' moods and their ad and brand attitudes.[121] However, this effect is not guaranteed. For some consumers, sexual messages can create negative feelings such as embarrassment, disgust, or uneasiness, any of which would have a negative effect. In particular, research has found that women are more likely to react negatively to ads with sexy female models.[122] Women also react more negatively to nudity in general, but more positively to suggestiveness.[123] Men are much more likely than women to buy a product featured in an ad with sexual content. Yet 61 percent of the consumers surveyed in a recent study said they would be less likely to buy products advertised with sexual imagery. In this study, 53 percent of the respondents preferred love imagery over sex imagery in advertising.[124]

An ad for Sony's MiniDisc player was considered offensive because the line "If you play it, they will come" implied that women were objects to be ordered with push-button ease.[125] Similarly, a beer campaign in Hong Kong was called sexist because it featured men describing what they like best about women's legs.[126]

One survey indicated that 84 percent of females and 72 percent of males believe that TV ads place too much emphasis on sex.[127] In another survey, 49 percent said they have been embarrassed in front of friends or family by sexy TV ads, and 47 percent indicated they would not buy a product if they found an ad offensive.[128] Thus the moral is that sexual themes should be used very carefully and should not be demeaning, sexist, or offensive.

Whether consumers will have a positive or negative reaction to a sexual ad often depends on whether the sexual content is appropriate for the product/service. One study found that using a seductive model to sell body oil was very appealing, but having a nude model endorse a ratchet set was not.[129] Thus sexual themes would be relevant for products such as perfume, cologne, suntan lotion, and lingerie but inappropriate for industrial equipment, tools, computers, and household cleaners. Toothpaste brands that sell a "sexier" smile, such as Rembrandt, have been successful in capturing a significant share of the U.S. market.[130]

Finally, consumer reaction to sexual messages varies from culture to culture. In some societies, such as in Europe, sexual attitudes are fairly open and the use of sex in advertising is more widespread than in other countries. Consider the Swissair campaign that featured a carefree nude man flying through the skies, each successive ad showing more of his body.[131] Shown only in Europe and North Africa, the ads increased sales by 30 percent. In other areas (such as Muslim and Asian countries), attitudes are more conservative, and the use of sex is much more restricted. Showing intimacy and kissing, as is done in many ads in the United States, would be totally inappropriate and even offensive in many Asian countries.[132] Consumers in different countries reacted differently to a public-service ad for breast cancer awareness in which men admired an attractive woman wearing a sundress while an announcer stated, "If only women paid as much attention to their breasts as men do." Japanese consumers appreciated the humor, but French consumers disliked the sexual overtones and light treatment of a serious problem.[133] ●

Emotional Content Marketers can plan communications to accommodate or enhance consumers' existing MAO and processing effort in the presence of cognitive attitudes. The same holds true for affective attitudes, which is where emotionally involving messages come into play.

transformational ads Ads that try to increase emotional involvement with the product or service.

One special type of emotional message is called **transformational advertising.**[134] The goal of a transformational ad is to associate the experience of using the product with a unique set of psychological characteristics. These ads try to increase emotional involvement by making the use of the product or service a warmer, more exciting, more pleasing, and richer experience, as opposed to informational ads, which seek only to present factual information. Coca-Cola, for example, is using transformational advertising to convey that "Coke is a part of the pleasure of everyday life, the pleasure of aliveness, relaxation, and being connected," says the company's chief marketing officer. These ads focus on emotional life experiences such as getting married and graduating from high school, as well as on warm feelings for popular figures such as Cal Ripkin Jr.[135]

dramas Ads with characters, a plot, and a story.

Dramas can also increase emotional involvement in a message. A drama message has characters, a plot, and a story about the use of the product or service.[136] This type of message aims to have consumers empathize with the characters and become involved emotionally. For example, over the years Tasters' Choice ran an involving, romantic ad miniseries about a couple who meet over a cup of coffee at a friend's house. Consumers eagerly anticipated each installment of the story.

Message Context The program or editorial context in which an ad appears can affect consumers' evaluation of the message. First, ads embedded in a happy TV program may be evaluated more positively than those in sad programs, especially if the ads are emotional.[137] Similarly, how well we like the program can affect our feelings about the ad and the brand.[138] One explanation is that the programs influence us to process information in a manner consistent with our mood. Or, according to the *excitation transfer hypothesis,* we may mistakenly attribute to the ad our feelings about the TV program.[139]

One note of caution: a TV program can become too arousing and distract viewers from the ads. In an interesting study that compared consumers' reactions to ads during the Super Bowl, ad responses in the winning city were inhibited in contrast to those in the losing and neutral cities.[140] Another study shows that placing ads in violent programs can inhibit processing and ad recall.[141]

SUMMARY

Marketers can use a variety of techniques to change consumers' attitudes when motivation, ability, and opportunity (MAO) are low and the effort consumers use to process information, make decisions, or engage in behavior is also low. When attitudes of low MAO consumers are based on cognitive processing, the message should affect their beliefs, which may be formed by simple inferences, attributions, or heuristics. Marketers can also affect the salience, strength, or favorability of consumers' beliefs on which attitudes are based. Credibility of the source, information consistent with the offering category, a large number of message arguments, simple arguments, and the extent of repetition can influence one or more dimensions of beliefs.

According to the mere exposure effect, when effort (MAO) is low, consumers' attitudes toward an offering become more favorable as they become more familiar with it. Classical conditioning predicts that consumers' attitudes toward an offering (the conditioned stimulus) are enhanced when it is repeatedly paired with a stimulus (the unconditioned stimulus) that evokes a positive emotional response (the unconditioned response). This effect is most likely to occur when the unconditioned stimulus is novel, when the consumer is aware of the link, when the conditioned and unconditioned stimuli fit together, and when the conditioned stimulus precedes the unconditioned one. Furthermore, if consumers like a particular ad (attitudes about the ad are called A_{ad}), these feelings may be transferred to the brand (attitudes about the brand are called A_b). Consumers' moods and their tendency to evaluate an offering in accordance with their moods can also affect attitudes toward an offering.

Finally, marketers can use marketing communications to induce favorable attitudes based on affective processes when consumers' motivation, ability, opportunity, and effort are low. Characteristics of the source (attractiveness, likability); the message (attractive pictures, pleasant music, humor, sex, emotionally involving messages); and the context (repetition, program or editorial context) can influence affective attitudes.

QUESTIONS FOR REVIEW AND DISCUSSION

1. What role do source, message, context, and repetition play in influencing consumers' cognitive attitudes?
2. What is the mere exposure effect, and why is it important to consumers' affective reactions?
3. How does classical conditioning apply to consumers' attitudes when processing effort is low?
4. Explain the dual-mediation hypothesis. What are the implications for affecting consumers' brand attitudes?
5. In low-effort situations, what characteristics of the message influence consumers' affective response?
6. What are the advantages and disadvantages of featuring celebrities in advertising messages?
7. Why must marketers consider local attitudes when planning to use sex in ad messages for different countries?

EXERCISES

1. Watch at least four hours of commercial television. Prepare a chart that lists all the techniques discussed in this chapter across the top as columns (attractive source, likable source, visuals, music, humor, sex, emotion, simple message, repetition, and so on). For each ad, tally which techniques are used. Also briefly assess the effectiveness of each ad in terms of creating positive A_{ad} and A_b, attitudes about the ad and the brand. After collecting this information for all ads viewed during the four hours, answer the following questions:
   a. Which techniques are used most frequently?
   b. In your judgment, which ads tend to be the most effective in influencing attitudes toward the ad and the brand? Why?
   c. In your judgment, which ads tend to be the least effective? Why?
2. Collect five magazines that are directed at different target audiences. Prepare a chart that lists all the techniques discussed in this chapter across the top as columns (attractive source, likable source, visuals, humor, sex, emotion, simple message, repetition, and so on). Down the side of this chart, generate a running list of the different product and service categories that appear in the ads. For each ad in each magazine, make a tally of the type of product advertised and the type(s) of techniques used. Then answer the following questions:
   a. Which techniques are used most frequently?
   b. Do certain techniques tend to be used more often for certain product or service categories?
   c. Do the magazines in general use certain techniques more often for certain target audiences?

chapter 8

Memory and Retrieval

Introduction: Nostalgia Marketing Jogs the Memory

These days, many marketers are trying to create positive attitudes for products by bringing back old brands, ads, symbols, logos, and songs. In fact, marketers have coined a term to describe such marketing efforts—"nostalgia marketing." (See Exhibit 8.1.)

Old brands like Quisp breakfast cereal, the Volkswagen Beetle, and Pokey and Gumby have recently been revitalized. Old television programs have come back, thanks to the success of the Nickelodeon channel. Old brand symbols like StarKist's Charlie the Tuna and KFC's Colonel Sanders are reappearing on packaging and in advertising. Old jingles like Campbell Soup's "Mmm, Mmm Good!" theme and Roto-Rooter's "Call Roto-Rooter, that's the name" refrain are also resurfacing. And popular old songs and rock groups are helping market new products. Consider, for example, Mitsubishi's use of 1970s T-Rex songs in commercials for its Montero sport-utility vehicle.[1] What's driving the popularity of nostalgia marketing? Some of the factors are related to concepts discussed in this chapter.

Consumers in today's fast-paced, information-intensive age are feeling overwhelmed by the new and unfamiliar, which leaves them more receptive to familiar products, songs, and images. Reminders of familiar offerings can also enhance brand awareness and brand knowledge because consumers already have a rich storehouse of personal experiences associated with these offerings in memory. Many of these memories reflect a quieter, more peaceful time. Hearing the name of an old product or seeing an old ad or hearing an old jingle reminds consumers of their positive feelings about this earlier time and makes them feel good. All these concepts are covered in this chapter.

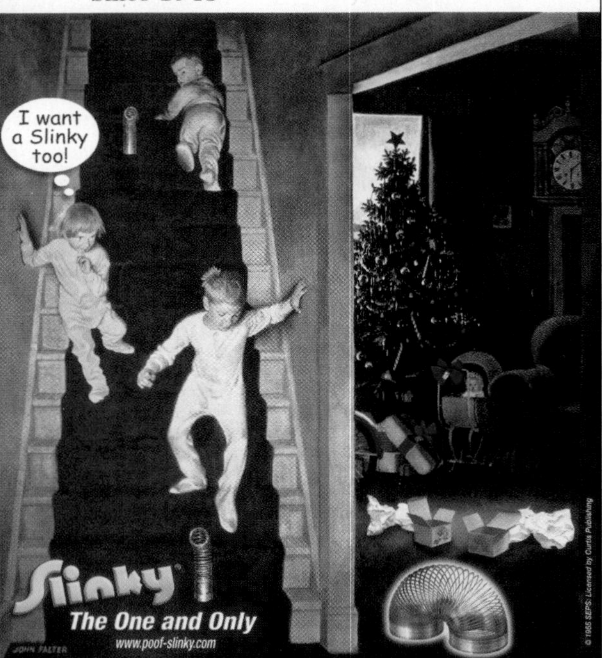

EXHIBIT 8.1

Nostalgia Marketing

Many marketers are using nostalgia marketing to associate their products with pleasant memories consumers may have experienced in their past.

Source: Image courtesy of Poof Products, Inc. © Slinky is a registered trademark of James Industries, Inc. "Christmas Morning" by John Falter © 1955 SEPS: Licensed by Curtis Publishing, Indianapolis IN. All rights reserved. www.curtispublishing.com <http://www.curtispublishing.com>

WHAT IS MEMORY?

consumer memory A personal storehouse of knowledge about products and services, shopping, and consumption experiences.

retrieval The process of remembering.

Consumer memory is a vast personal storehouse of knowledge about products, services, shopping excursions, and consumption experiences. In essence, memory reflects our prior knowledge. **Retrieval** is the process of remembering, or accessing, what we have stored in memory.

We can store and remember information such as what brands or services we have used in the past; features of these products or services; how, where, when, and why we bought them; their price; how, where, when, and why we used them; and whether or not we liked them. We can store and remember information about old products we have disposed of, such as a favorite car we sold. We also have memories of special experiences, for example, a sporting event we attended with friends. The information we store and can retrieve is learned from many sources—marketing communications, the media, word of mouth, and personal experience.

Our memory and ability to retrieve information depend at least in part on our motivation, ability, and opportunity (MAO) to process the information to which we have been exposed. Our ability to carry out day-to-day activities clearly depends on our being able to put new information into our memory and retrieve old information when we need it. Indeed, because we place a high value on the ability to remember, products like gingko biloba and the product depicted in Exhibit 8.2, as well as services like memory improvement seminars, are very popular.

Knowledge, Attitudes, and Memory

We began to discuss certain aspects of memory and retrieval in the preceding three chapters. Chapter 5 noted that information stored in memory affects whether and how we interpret and categorize objects. Chapters 6 and 7 indicated that attitudes are part of our memory—they represent stored summary evaluations of objects. Moreover, we can and often do recall attitudes when we make decisions. Thus, as shown in Exhibit 8.3, memory and retrieval are affected by how we know and understand information through attention, categorization, and comprehension—and by attitude formation processes.

EXHIBIT 8.2
The Value of Memory
We value our memory so highly, we may be willing to take vitamins or supplements that claim to improve our memory.
Source: Courtesy of Natural Balance.

Memory, Retrieval, and Decision Making

How do memory and retrieval influence the way we act and the decisions we make? If you need toothpaste, you might simply remember the brand you bought last time and buy it again the next time you go shopping. You may decide to buy season tickets to a sporting event because you can vividly remember what a

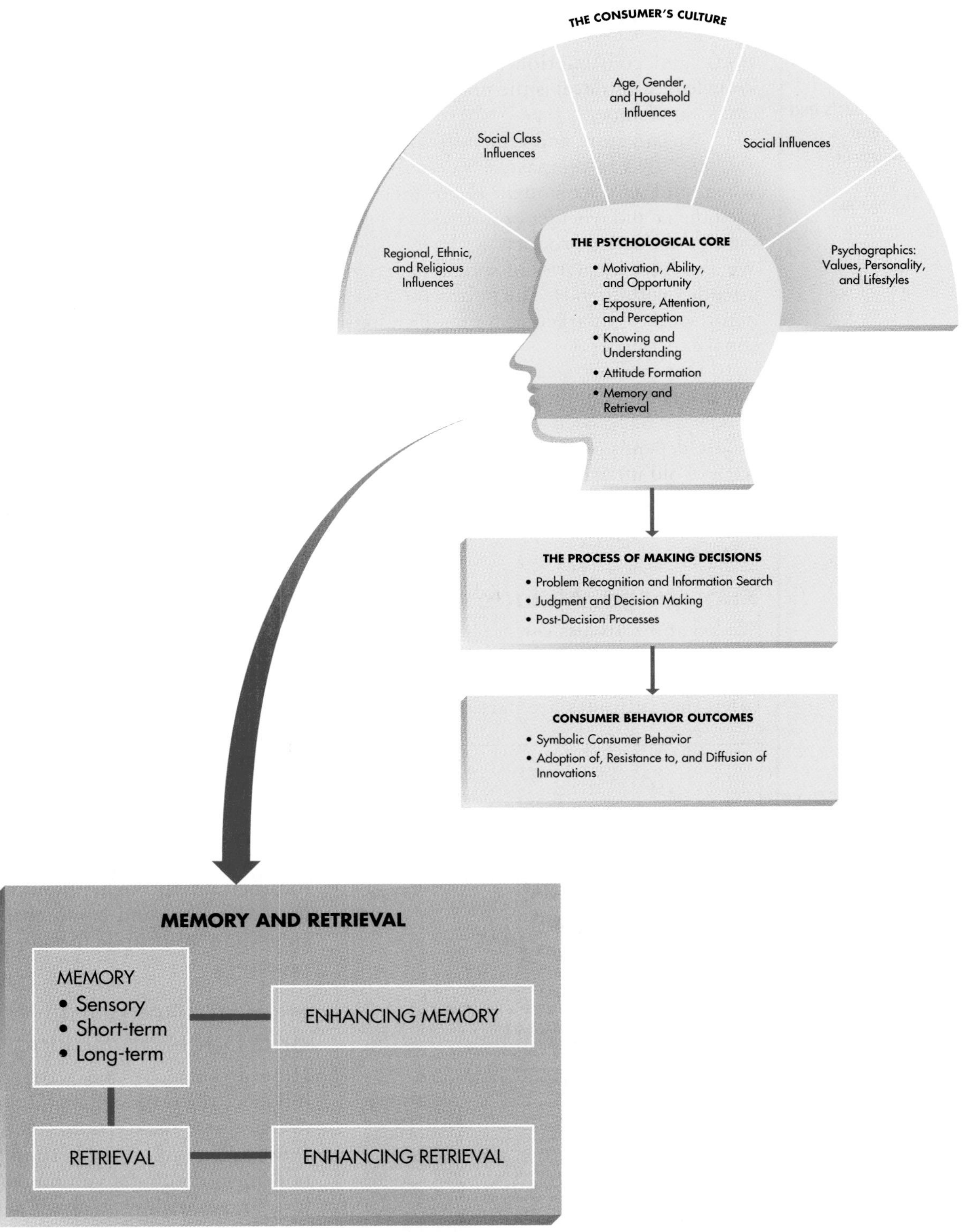

EXHIBIT 8.3
Chapter Overview: Memory and Retrieval

We can identify three types of memory: sensory memory, short-term memory (STM), and long-term memory (LTM). Once information is in memory, it can then be retrieved (recognized or recalled). This chapter shows (1) what influences the transfer of information from STM to LTM and (2) what affects the likelihood that information will be retrieved from memory.

good time you had when you went with your friends. You may decide not to go to a certain restaurant because you remember the bad service from your last visit.

We often receive information about an offering at one time and use that information to make purchase, usage, or disposition decisions at another time. Memory and retrieval make this two-stage process possible.

WHAT ARE THE TYPES OF MEMORY?

Memory represents more than the prior knowledge we discussed in Chapter 5. Exhibit 8.3 indicates three types of memory: sensory memory (iconic and echoic memory), short-term memory (imagery and discursive processing), and long-term memory (autobiographical and semantic memory). Let us look at how we use each of these.

Sensory Memory

Assume for a minute that as you are talking to someone at a party, you happen to overhear other guests talking about a new movie you want to see. You do not want to appear rude, so you try to pay full attention to your dinner partner, but you really want to hear what the others are saying about the movie. Even though you cannot listen to both conversations simultaneously, you can store, for a relatively short period, bits and pieces of the other conversation. So you might be listening to your dinner partner but switch your attention to the other conversation once you hear the word *cool*. As another example, assume that you are doing your homework in front of the TV. Your roommate comes in and says, "That's a great commercial." Although you have not been listening, right after your roommate makes this statement, you realize that you heard the words *Diet Coke*. You realize it is a Diet Coke commercial, and you say, "Yeah, I really like that one."

sensory memory Sensory experiences stored temporarily in memory.

The ability to store sensory experiences temporarily as they are produced is called **sensory memory.** Sensory memory uses a short-term storage area called the sensory store. Sensory memory operates automatically, and if we quickly switch our attention to our sensory store, we may be able to interpret what is in it. If we do not analyze this information right away, however, it disappears from the sensory store, and we cannot determine its meaning.

echoic memory Very brief memory for things we hear.

iconic memory Very brief memory for things we see.

Echoic and Iconic Memory Our sensory store can house information from any of the senses, but **echoic memory**—memory of things we hear—and **iconic memory**—sensory memory of things we see—are the most commonly studied.[2] The Diet Coke example illustrates echoic memory. Here is another example. You may have found that when someone asks you a question and you are not really listening, you can say, "What did you say?" and actually "play back" what the person said. Iconic memory is at work when you drive by a sign and see it quickly, only to realize after you pass that it was a sign for McDonald's.

Characteristics of Sensory Memory Information in sensory memory is stored in its actual sensory form. In other words, we store *"cool"* as it sounds, and we store it exactly, not as a synonym. Information in sensory memory is also short-lived, generally lasting from a quarter of a second to several seconds.[3] If the information is relevant, we will be motivated to process it further, and it may enter what is called short-term memory. However, if we do not analyze that information, it is lost.

Short-Term Memory

short-term memory (STM) The portion of memory where incoming information is encoded or interpreted in light of existing knowledge.

Short-term memory (STM) is the portion of memory where we encode or interpret incoming information in light of existing knowledge.[4] The processes of knowing and understanding discussed in Chapter 5 occur in short-term memory. As you read this book, you are using your short-term memory to comprehend what you read. You also use short-term memory when you watch a TV commercial or make a decision in a store. Thus short-term memory is very important because it is where most of our information processing takes place.

discursive processing The processing of information as words.

imagery processing The processing of information in sensory form.

Imagery and Discursive Processing The information in short-term memory can take one of several forms. When we think about an object, for example, an apple, we might use **discursive processing** and represent it by the word "apple." Alternatively, we could represent it visually, as a picture of an apple, or in terms of its smell, its feel, what it sounds like when we bite into it, or what it tastes like. Representing the visual, auditory, tactile, gustatory, and/or olfactory properties of an apple uses **imagery processing.**[5] Unlike the case of discursive processing, an object in imagery processing bears a close resemblance to the thing being represented.[6] Thus if you were asked to describe an apple and a car, imagery processing would ensure that you preserve their relative sizes.

For both imagery and discursive processing, information in short-term memory varies in how much we elaborate on it.[7] When MAO is low, short-term memory might consist of a simple reproduction of a stimulus, for example, the word *skier* or a picture of a skier. When MAO is high, however, consumers can use elaborated imagery processing to engage in daydreams, fantasies, and visual problem solving, or elaborated discursive processing to think about upcoming events or work out solutions to current problems. For example, if you are thinking about a skiing vacation, you may develop an elaborate fantasy about lounging around the fireplace at a resort hotel; drinking hot cider; and feeling the ache of your tired muscles, the windburn on your face, and the company of your friends. You might also use discursive processing to compare the prices and attributes of various hotels. All this information, whether represented as images or words, can serve as important input for decisions.

Characteristics of Short-Term Memory Short-term memory has two interesting characteristics:

- *Short-term memory is limited.* We can hold only a certain number of things in short-term memory at any one time. For example, if you have to go to the store right now and buy two items, chips and hot dogs, you will have little trouble remembering what to buy. But suppose you have to buy nine items: chips, hot dogs, coffee, cookies, baking soda, plastic wrap, toothpaste, spaghetti sauce, and dog food. Chances are high that you will forget one or more of these items unless you make a shopping list.
- *Short-term memory is short-lived.* The information held in short-term memory is very short-lived unless that information is transferred to long-term memory. Unless we actively try to remember information, it will be lost. This explains why we sometimes learn someone's name only to forget it two minutes later.

MARKETING IMPLICATIONS Short-term memory, particularly imagery processing, has many interesting implications for marketers.

Imagery can create liking for the product. First, imagery processing is used often and affects how we behave. We value some of the products we buy (for example, novels or music) because of the imagery they provide.[8] Thus a product's ability to stimulate multisensory imagery might affect how much we like that product. You may, for example, like novels that are so descriptive that you can actually imagine the sights, sounds, smells, and tastes experienced by the characters in the book.

Imagery can stimulate memories of past experiences. Second, we value some products or promotional tools because they promote imagery that allows us to vicariously experience a past consumption experience. For example, you might keep a sports program or ticket stub because it evokes imagery that allows you to relive the event.

Imagery affects evaluation. Third, the use of imagery can affect the way we evaluate products. Using imagery processing, we may be able to process a lot of information about something simply because more information helps to flesh out the image. Spiegel.com, for example, allows online shoppers to view enlarged photos of different aspects of each product.[9] Adding more information when using discursive processing, however, may lead to information overload.

Imagery affects satisfaction. Finally, imagery may affect how satisfied we are with a product or consumption experience. We may create an elaborate image or fantasy of just what the product or consumption experience will be like (how great we will look in a new car or how relaxing a vacation might be) only to find that it does not materialize as we had imagined. If reality disconfirms our expectations, we may feel dissatisfied. The ad in Exhibit 8.4, for example may stimulate imagery of the fragrant aroma of tropical flowers. If the product does not live up to the outcomes customers imagine, they may be disatified.

Some marketers use imagery to help consumers establish realistic expectations. Lands' End, for example, helps online shoppers envision clothing in use by clicking to see how each item looks on a virtual model set to each consumer's measurements.[10] ●

Long-Term Memory

long-term memory (LTM) The part of memory where information is placed for later use; permanently stored knowledge.

Long-term memory (LTM) is that part of memory where information is permanently stored for later use. Research in cognitive psychology has identified two major types of long-term memory: autobiographical and semantic memory.[11]

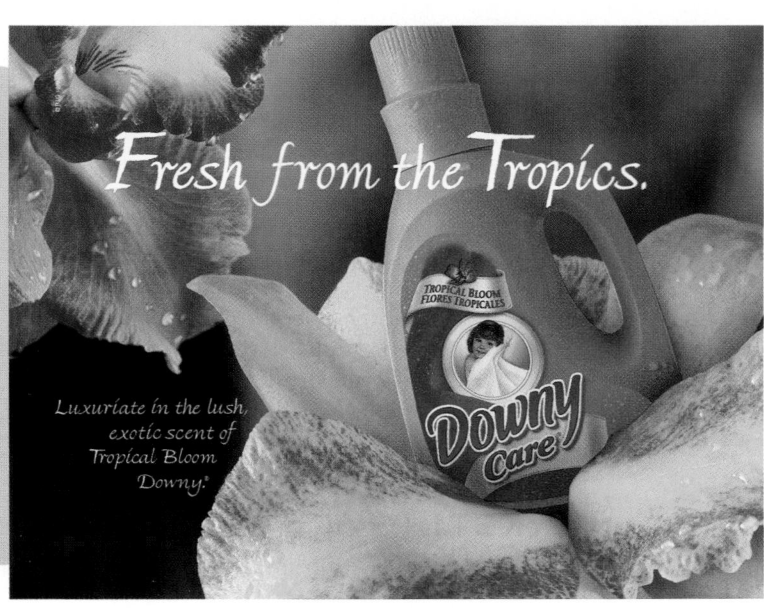

Fresh from the Tropics.
TROPICAL BLOOM
FLORES TROPICALES
Downy Care
Luxuriate in the lush, exotic scent of Tropical Bloom Downy.

EXHIBIT 8.4
Stimulating Imagery Processing
This ad may help consumers imagine the fragrance of tropical flowers. These images may affect consumers' expectations for the product—they will be satisfied with the product if it smells as fragrant as they imagine.

Source: © The Procter & Gamble Company. Used by permission.

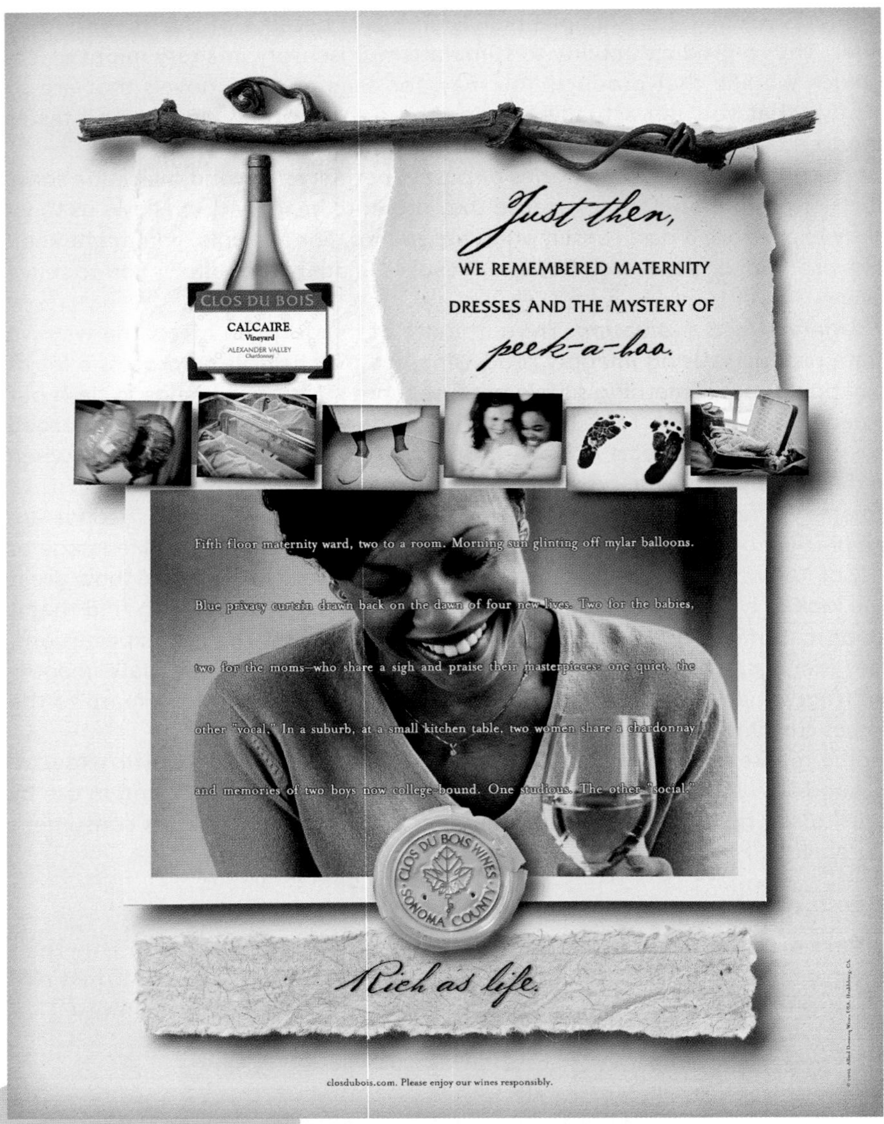

Just then,
WE REMEMBERED MATERNITY
DRESSES AND THE MYSTERY OF
peek-a-boo.
CLOS DU BOIS
CALCAIRE
Vineyard
ALEXANDER VALLEY
Fifth floor maternity ward, two to a room. Morning sun glinting off mylar balloons.
Blue privacy curtain drawn back on the dawn of four new lives. Two for the babies,
two for the moms—who share a sigh and praise their masterpieces: one quiet, the
other "vocal." In a suburb, at a small kitchen table, two women share a chardonnay
and memories of two boys now college-bound. One studious. The other "social."
CLOS DU BOIS WINES
SONOMA COUNTY
Rich as life.
closdubois.com. Please enjoy our wines responsibly.

EXHIBIT 8.5
Autobiographical Memory
This ad for Clos du Bois wines suggests that people can relive pleasant autobiographical memories when they enjoy a relaxing time enjoying Clos du Bois with friends.

Source: Courtesy of Allied Domecq Wines.

Autobiographical Memory **Autobiographical, or episodic, memory** represents knowledge we have about ourselves and our past.[12] It includes past experiences as well as emotions and sensations tied to these experiences. These memories tend to be primarily sensory, mainly involving visual images, although they may also include sounds, smells, tastes, and tactile sensations. In a consumer context, we may have autobiographical memories that relate to acquisition, such as buying a specific product or making a specific shopping trip. And we may have autobiographical memories regarding consumption or disposition, such as attending a particular concert or throwing away a well-worn but loved product. The ad in Exhibit 8.5 shows how autobiographical memory can be used in advertising.

Because each individual has a unique set of experiences, autobiographical memory tends to be very personal and idiosyncratic. If you were asked to remember the road test you took when you got your driver's license, you might have stored in long-term memory the sequence of events that occurred on that day: what car you drove, what your route was, how nervous you were, what your instructor told you to do, and what happened after you passed (or failed!).

Semantic Memory A lot of what we have stored in memory is not related to specific experiences. For example, we have memory for the concept called "dog." We know that dogs have four legs, are furry, wag their tails, and so on. This knowledge is true of all dogs and is not tied to any dog in particular. Knowledge about the world that is detached from specific episodes is called **semantic memory.**

MARKETING IMPLICATIONS

Much of the knowledge we have stored in cognitive categories reflects semantic memory. Thus many of the marketing implications previously presented about knowledge

autobiographical (or episodic) memory Knowledge we have about ourselves and our personal experiences.

semantic memory Knowledge about an entity that is detached from specific episodes.

stored in categories also relate to semantic memory. Autobiographical memory, however, is also important to marketers.

Affecting decision making. Each consumer has a large storehouse of consumer-related experiences whose affective associations can influence the way products and services are evaluated. For example, if you ate at a particular restaurant and found a hair in your food, the memory of this experience might prevent you from eating there again. Positive experiences would have the opposite effect. When selecting a restaurant, you might recall a previous episode in which the food was fabulous or the ambiance romantic—memories that would clearly affect your decision about eating there again.

Promoting empathy and identification. Autobiographical memories can play a role in creating identification with characters in ads. For example, if advertisements for Hefty trash bags can make consumers think about incidents in which their garbage bags split open, consumers may be better able to relate to and empathize with an ad showing inferior bags splitting apart while Hefty bags remain strong.

Cueing and preserving autobiographical memories. As the introduction to this chapter suggested, consumers value some products because they promote autobiographical memories by stimulating feelings of nostalgia—a fondness for the past.[13] Some baby boomers go out of their way to buy older fragrances such as Canoe and Tabu because these products stir up fond memories of teenage years.[14] Consumers often find it important to preserve memories of graduations, weddings, the birth of a child, and so on. Entire industries for products such as film, cameras, video cameras, and diaries focus on consumers' desires to document these autobiographical memories. The scrapbook industry has become a $300 million business.[15] Consumers in many cultures want to preserve autobiographical memories.[16] Consumers who have moved to North America from other countries like India often build shrines in their houses to remind them of the culture they left behind. In the Niger Republic, consumers highly value possessions that remind them of their friends, family, and important events in their lives.

Reinterpreting memories. Research shows that advertising can even affect consumers' autobiographical memories. One study had consumers taste various good- and bad-tasting orange juices and then watch ads that described the products' good taste. Those exposed to the ads remembered the bad-tasting juice as being better tasting than it actually was.[17] ●

HOW MEMORY IS ENHANCED

Because attention and memory are always associated, many of the same factors affect both. Several additional processes, called *chunking, rehearsal, recirculation,* and *elaboration,* also affect memory.[18] These processes are useful for influencing short-term memory or for increasing the likelihood that information will be transferred to long-term memory—with important implications for marketers.

Chunking

chunk A group of items that can be processed as a unit.

Traditionally, researchers have believed that the most individuals can process in short-term memory at any one time is three to seven "chunks" of information. Later studies suggest that the number may be closer to three or four.[19] A **chunk** is a group of items that is processed as a unit. For example, phone numbers are typically grouped into three chunks (621-555-4059).

Because we can process only three to four chunks at any one time, marketers can increase the likelihood that consumers will be able to hold information in short-term memory and transfer it to long-term memory by providing larger bits of information that chunk smaller bits together. For example, acronyms reduce several pieces of information to one chunk. Brand names like IBM and KFC are examples of chunking in a marketing context. Similarly, marketers can facilitate consumers' memory for telephone numbers by providing words rather than individual numbers or digits (1-800-CAL-HOME, 1-800-SEE-2020 or 1-800-GO-U-HAUL). Advertisements might draw conclusions that summarize or chunk disparate pieces of information into a single attribute or benefit. For example, an ad that discusses a food product's calorie, fat, sodium, and sugar content might chunk this information into a conclusion about the product's healthfulness.

Rehearsal

rehearsal The process of actively reviewing material in an attempt to remember it.

Whereas chunking increases the likelihood that information will not be lost from short-term memory, rehearsal affects the transfer of information to long-term memory. **Rehearsal** means that we actively and consciously interact with the material we are trying to remember. We can either silently repeat the material or actively think about the information and its meaning, as we would when studying for an exam.

In marketing contexts, rehearsal is likely to occur only when consumers are motivated to process and remember information. If you are motivated to find the best car on the market, you might study the characteristics of various models so you do not forget them.

When motivation is low, marketers may use tactics to enhance motivation and perpetuate rehearsal. McDonald's revived an old campaign that challenged consumers to remember the contents of a Big Mac: "Two all-beef patties, special sauce, lettuce, cheese, pickles, onions on a sesame seed bun." This challenge was so successful in generating rehearsal that many consumers still remembered the list. Engaging jingles and slogans may be a useful means of inducing rehearsal. Sometimes they work too well, as you may know from going through the day singing a commercial's jingle.

However, one study found that consumers who rehearsed the price paid for a product on the last occasion by physically writing it down (when paying by check or entering the amount into a financial management program, for example) had lower repurchase intentions for that product.[20] The memory of the price presumably enhanced the salience of what consumers had to give up to obtain the product.

Recirculation

recirculation The process by which information is remembered via simple repetition without active rehearsal.

Information can also be transferred to long-term memory through the process of **recirculation.** Water is recirculated when it goes through the same pipe again and again. In the same way, information is recirculated through your short-term memory when you encounter it repeatedly. Unlike rehearsal, with recirculation we make no active attempt to remember the information. Rather, if we do remember, it is because the information has passed through our brain so many times. For example, you can probably recall the names of the streets adjacent to yours or the name of a store near your home—even if you have never gone down these streets, been to the store, or tried to memorize them. Why? Simply because you see them almost every day.

Recirculation is an important principle for marketing because it explains why repetition of marketing communications affects memory, particu-

EXHIBIT 8.6
Recirculation
This ad illustrates the principle of recirculation, as the brand name is repeated multiple times within the single ad.

Source: Courtesy of Bristol-Myers Squibb.

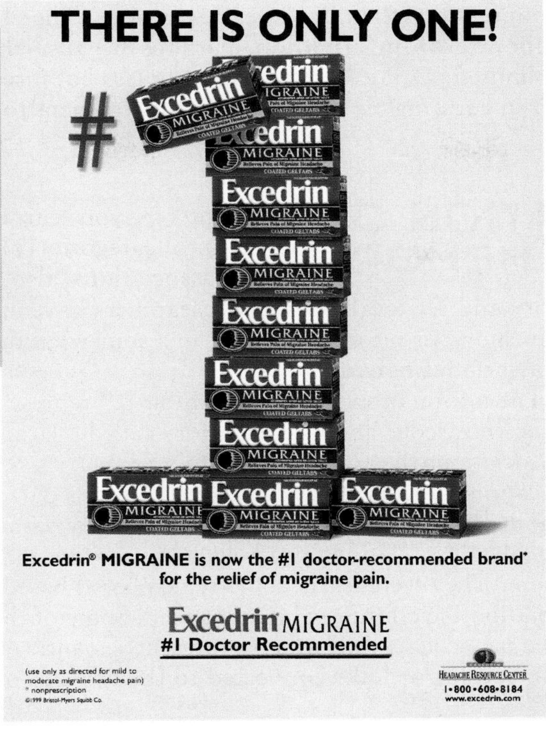

larly in low-involvement situations.[21] Marketers can strengthen the effect of recirculation by creating different ads that repeat the same basic message. To illustrate, a slogan like "Be Young. Have Fun. Drink Pepsi" is likely to be memorable after you have been exposed to it on many occasions, even though the ads may change over time. Recirculation may also explain why communications that repeat the brand name frequently, either within an ad or across communications, tend to produce better memory for the brand name. Knowing that preteens like to play video games over and over, the head of marketing for Burton Snowboard says his firm's snowboards and gear are featured in Sony video games for one reason: "Repetition, repetition, repetition."[22] Recirculation may also be at work if we remember the brand name in Exhibit 8.6.

THERE IS ONLY ONE!
#
Excedrin MIGRAINE
Excedrin® MIGRAINE is now the #1 doctor-recommended brand*
for the relief of migraine pain.
Excedrin MIGRAINE
#1 Doctor Recommended
HEADACHE RESOURCE CENTER
1•800•608•8184
www.excedrin.com

Elaboration

elaboration Transferring information into long-term memory by processing it at deeper levels.

Finally, information can be transferred into long-term memory if it is processed at deeper levels, or **elaborated.**[23] We can try to remember information through rote memorization or rehearsal; however, this type of processing is not always effective. If you have ever memorized material for an exam, you probably noticed that you forgot most of what you learned within two or three days. More enduring memory is established when we try to relate information to prior knowledge and past experiences. If see you an ad for a new product, for instance, you might elaborate on the ad information by trying to think about how to use the product in your day-to-day life. By elaborating on the message in this way, you may have a better memory for the brand and what the ad said about it.

Several strategies familiar from previous chapters enhance the likelihood that consumers will elaborate on information. For example, unexpected or novel stimuli can attract attention and induce elaboration.[24] The makers of Glad trash bags used this principle when they developed an ad featuring actor Robert Mitchum. The 77-year-old actor was an unlikely spokesperson for trash bags—and the incongruity between the product and the actor helped raise consumer memory for Glad bags.[25] Also, an advertising agency study indicates that consumers who pay attention to a particular TV program and think about it are more likely to remember the commercials.[26] Elaboration may explain why children and the elderly tend to remember less from marketing

semantic (or associative) network A set of associations in memory that are linked to a concept.

communications than do other age groups. The elderly may have less ability to elaborate on information, perhaps because their short-term memory is more limited. Children may elaborate less because they have less knowledge, which in turn makes it more difficult for them to think extensively about a message.[27]

ORGANIZATION OF LONG-TERM MEMORY

In Chapter 5, you learned that knowledge is organized into categories and linked to associations. These associations also relate to the concepts of memory and retrieval. Memory researchers have attempted to represent long-term memory, or prior knowledge, in a somewhat different way called a **semantic or associative network.**

The information shown in Exhibit 8.7 represents one consumer's memory or prior knowledge about the category called "vacations." This example depicts the associations the consumer has to a St. Moritz ski vacation, a member of the ski vacation category. That category, in turn, is part of the higher-order "luxury vacation" category. The St. Moritz ski vacation concept is connected to a set of links (called associations and beliefs in previous chapters). How did these links get there? They were learned and remembered based on personal experiences or information the consumer heard or read. Some of these links represent autobiographic memories, while others represent semantic memory. This entire network of associations or links connected to the concept of St. Moritz ski vacation is

EXHIBIT 8.7
A Semantic (or Associative) Network
A semantic network is a set of concepts connected by links. When one concept is activated, others may become activated via the links. Concepts connected by strong links are more likely to activate each other than those connected by weak links.

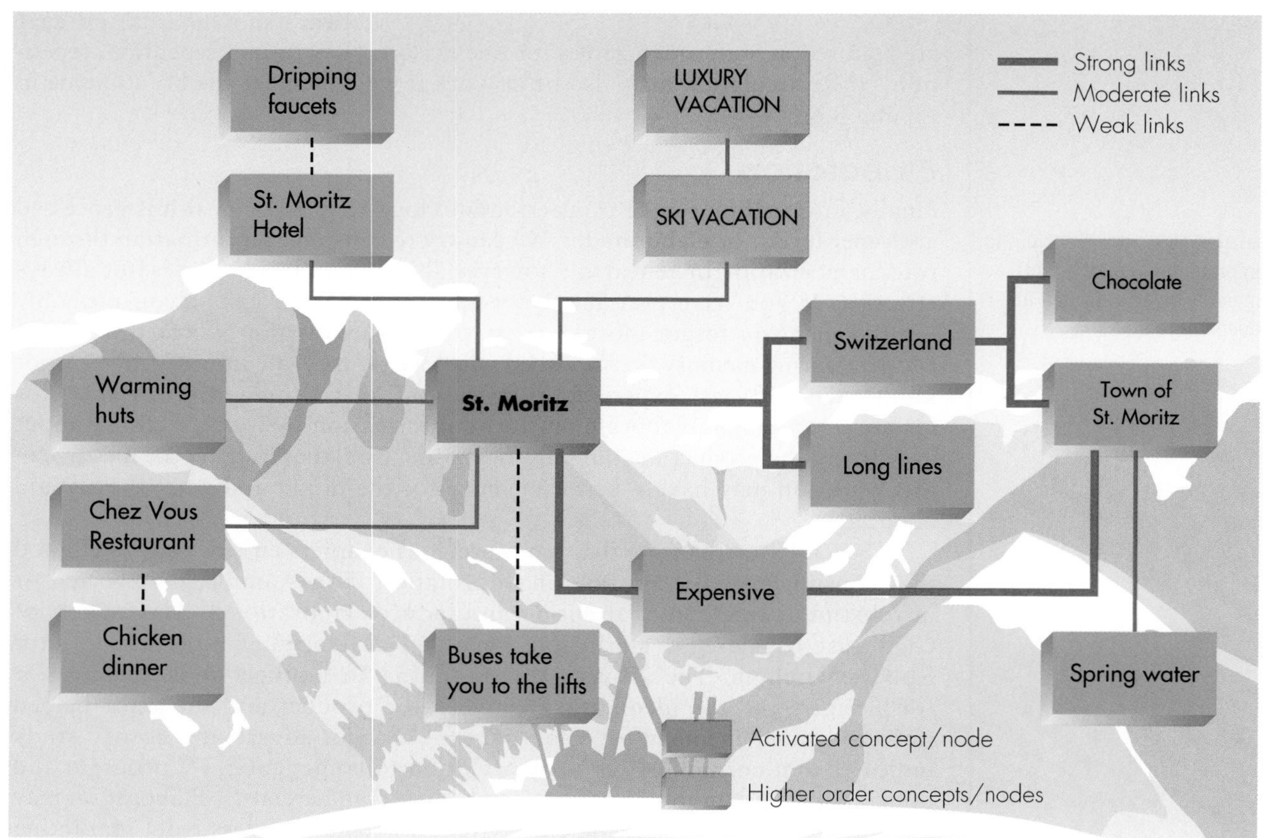

called a semantic (or associative) network. Some researchers think about long-term memory as a series of semantic networks.

Notice in Exhibit 8.7 that the links in the semantic network vary in strength. Strong links, depicted by the thick lines, are firmly established in memory. Others, depicted by the dashed lines, are weakly established in memory. Some links are strong because they have been rehearsed, recirculated, chunked, and elaborated extensively. Others are weak because they have been encountered infrequently, have not been accessed in a long time, or have been processed on a very limited basis.

The entire semantic network represents what is available in this consumer's memory about the concept called "St. Moritz ski vacation." As you will see in the next section, the semantic network and the strength of the links in memory are both important for the process of retrieval.

WHAT IS RETRIEVAL?

Retrieval is the process of remembering. When we retrieve information from memory, we access it from a semantic (or associative) network like the one in Exhibit 8.7.

The Semantic Network

We have a considerable amount of information available in our memory but are able to retrieve or access only some of it at any given time.[28] We have all been in situations in which we try to remember something but cannot. Two factors about the semantic network affect what we remember: trace strength and spreading of activation.[29]

trace strength The extent to which an association (or link) is strongly or weakly linked to a concept in memory.

accessibility The likelihood that an item will be retrieved from long-term memory.

Trace Strength The first factor affecting the semantic network is the strength of the links or associations, known as **trace strength.** The stronger the link that connects information to the product, the more **accessible** the information is. You are more likely to remember that BMW is "the ultimate driving machine" if you have a strong association connecting the car with its slogan. Marketers often try to strengthen our memory links. For example, after research revealed that the majority of U.S. consumers believe family-owned firms make products they can trust, SC Johnson & Son added the tag line "A Family Company" to its advertising and packaging. This helped the maker of Glade, Raid, and Windex strengthen the association with family ownership in the minds of consumers.[30] The more marketers can engage in recirculation, or encourage consumers to rehearse or elaborate on information, the greater the likelihood that the link will be strengthened and consumers will be better able to access that information.

Spreading of Activation A second factor explaining what gets retrieved from memory is called **spreading of activation.** Think of a semantic network as a kind of electric network. Strong links have the potential for generating high-voltage current—weak links the potential for generating low-voltage current. Using the example in Exhibit 8.7, if a concept like St. Moritz is activated in the consumer's semantic network, the strong link between "St. Moritz" and "expensive" will activate or make accessible "expensive." Because the current connecting St. Moritz and expensive is very strong, the electrical potential from this current will spread to adjacent items in the semantic network, particularly along strong links. This spreading of activation will likely lead the consumer to remember the town of St. Moritz. The activation of the concept "St. Moritz" may also activate "Switzerland" and "long lines." Activation from "Switzerland" may, in turn, spread to the concept "chocolate."

Of course, concepts like Switzerland, chocolate, and expensive are linked to many semantic networks, not just to one. Our consumer may think about chocolate when prompted to think about St. Moritz, but chocolate may be linked to other semantic networks that can be cued through spreading of activation. This consumer may start thinking that she recently bought chocolate at a Godiva store, which may lead her to remember that she saw a friend at the store. Spreading of activation explains why we sometimes have seemingly random thoughts as the activation spreads from one semantic network to another.

MAO can influence spreading of activation. If motivation and opportunity to process information are high, the number of activated links can also be quite high. On the other hand, when motivation or opportunity to process are low, only the closest and strongest links might be activated. Individuals with more knowledge about a concept will have a greater ability to process a more detailed semantic network, bringing forth any number of associations.[31]

Because strong links enhance an item's accessibility from memory, they are very important to marketers. The weak links are not unimportant, however. Activation spreads to every link in the semantic network, although the activation may not be sufficient to cause consumers to remember an item. A concept that has been activated but not sufficiently to make it retrievable from memory is said to have been **primed.** It has been given a jump start. Suppose our consumer is trying to remember how she got to the lifts at St. Moritz. The "buses" link is not strongly established in her memory. Activating St. Moritz might prime the bus concept, but the activation is too weak for the consumer to remember the bus. If she later drives by a school, the activation of school might cue buses, and this activation might be sufficient for her to remember that she got to the ski lift in St. Moritz by taking a bus.

priming Activation of a node in memory, often without conscious awareness.

Retrieval Failures

Trace strength and spreading of activation help to explain forgetting—the failure to retrieve information from memory. Forgetting is a fact of life. You might forget to get your car serviced or forget that you are cooking hard-boiled eggs (until they explode). Retrieval failures clearly affect consumers' purchase, consumption, and disposition behaviors.

decay The weakening of nodes or links over time.

Decay In some cases, we forget things because trace strength fades; that is, memory links **decay** over time, often because they are not used. Thus we tend to forget events from childhood because they happened so long ago. The likelihood of decay is reduced when we are repeatedly exposed to information through recirculation or when we retrieve it often from memory.

Sometimes the details or attributes of the information we have learned decay.[32] For example, we might have heard a lot of detailed information about a new movie, such as what the plot was about and who starred in it. Yet later we may remember only something general about it ("I've heard it was good").

That consumers can forget attributes explains some interesting marketing phenomena. For example, consumers may have equally strong memories for brands about which they have heard either very bad or very good things. They forget the information stated about the brands; all they remember is that the brands were in the news. Forgetting also explains the sleeper effect, discussed in Chapter

6, in which consumers show more positive attitudes toward a bad ad as time passes. Researchers believe that over time, consumers forget that an ad lacked credibility and simply remember what the source said about the brand. In essence, memory for the source decays more rapidly than memory for the message.[33]

interference That which causes us not to remember which features go with which brand or concept due to semantic networks being too closely aligned.

Interference Spreading of activation and trace strength explain a second cause of forgetting—interference.[34] **Interference** occurs when semantic networks are so closely aligned that we cannot remember which features go with which brand or concept. Suppose you are watching a car ad that indicates how safe the car is. If you have a lot of information about similar cars stored in memory, you might confuse which attribute is associated with which car. In addition, when consumers are exposed to two or more ads with similar contextual elements, the similarity interferes with brand recall.[35]

Interference also results when one concept is activated so frequently that we cannot activate a different one. Suppose you are trying to recall all 50 states or the items that you have on your grocery list. Chances are you can recall several items very easily and a few more with some difficulty, but the last ones are impossible to remember. The reason is that in trying to remember the missing items, you keep remembering the items you have already recalled, and this interferes with your ability to activate the missing ones.[36] Repeatedly activating the memory trace for the items you have remembered inhibits activation of the other items.

primacy effect The tendency to show greater memory for information that comes first in a sequence.

recency effect The tendency to show greater memory for information that comes last in a sequence.

Primacy and Recency Effects Decay and interference can be used to explain **primacy** and **recency effects**—that is, the fact that things we encountered first or last in a sequence are often most easily remembered. As an example of primacy effects, you are likely to remember the first ad you saw during a commercial break because there was no other advertising information to interfere with it. That information may also be less likely to decay if you rehearse it. The primacy effect explains why, when you study for an exam, you tend to remember best the material you studied first.

As an example of recency effects, you are more likely to remember what you ate for breakfast this morning than what you ate a week ago because (1) this morning's information has not yet decayed, and (2) there is much less information interfering with the retrieval of this information. Based on primacy and recency effects, many advertisers believe that the best placement for an ad is either first or last in a commercial sequence. Some research supports the importance of being first; evidence in support of being last is not as strong.[37]

Retrieval Errors

What we do remember is not always accurate or complete; our memory may be subject to distortion or confusion. You might remember that your friend told you about a great new movie, but it was really your neighbor who told you about it. In addition, memory may be selective, meaning that we retrieve only some information, often either very positive or very negative. In anticipating a vacation, you may remember the good things that happened on your last vacation, but not the bad things. Finally, memory may be distorted. If you had a bad experience with a product, you may later remember experiences that were bad but that did not actually happen. Perhaps you remember that a waitress who treated you badly at a restaurant clunked your coffee down loudly on the table. While this "memory" is consistent with the "bad waitress" experience, it might not have actually happened.[38]

WHAT ARE THE TYPES OF RETRIEVAL?

Consumers can retrieve information through two retrieval systems: explicit and implicit memory.

Explicit Memory

explicit memory Memory of some prior episode achieved by active attempts to remember.

Explicit memory is memory of some prior episode achieved by active attempts to remember it. In this situation, you are consciously trying to remember something that happened in the past. For example, you would use explicit memory to remember what you ordered during a recent trip to In and Out. Consumers try to retrieve information from explicit memory by either recalling it or recognizing it.

recognition The process of determining whether a stimulus has or has not been encountered before.

Recognition **Recognition** occurs when we can identify something we have seen before. Two important types of recognition in marketing are brand recognition (we remember having seen the brand before) and ad recognition (we remember having seen the ad before). Brand recognition is particularly critical for in-store decisions because it helps us identify or locate the brands we want to buy. Logos on brands or packages may be particularly vital for enhancing brand recognition. Johnson & Johnson therefore uses similar package graphics on all its Johnson's baby products to reinforce and build on brand recognition.[39]

recall The ability to retrieve information from memory.

Recall In contrast, **recall** involves a more extensive activation of the links in memory. Thus when we see a Coke display, we use recall to retrieve knowledge about Coke as input for decision making. There are two ways in which we can recall something. *Free recall* exists when we can retrieve something from memory without any help, such as what we had for dinner last night. *Cued recall* exists if we are asked the same question (What did we have for dinner last night?) but need a cue: Was it a vegetarian dish?

Implicit Memory

implicit memory Memory for things without any conscious attempt at remembering them.

Sometimes we remember things without conscious awareness, a phenomenon called **implicit memory.** Suppose as you drive down the highway at high speed, you pass a billboard bearing the word *Caterpillar* (tractors). Later you are asked whether you remember seeing a billboard, and if so, what it was for. You do not remember seeing a billboard, let alone what it was for; you have no explicit memory of it. But if you are asked to say the first word you can think of that begins with *cat-*, you might answer *caterpillar.* You might have encoded something about the billboard without being aware of having even seen it, and hence you might have some information about Caterpillar stored in memory.

How can you have implicit memory of something you cannot explicitly remember? In part, the answer relates to priming. Your brief exposure to the Caterpillar name activated or primed it in your memory. The activation level was not sufficient for the name to be consciously retrieved; however, when you are asked for a word that begins with *cat-*, this activation brings *caterpillar* to mind.

MARKETING IMPLICATIONS Retrieval is clearly an important concept for marketers.

Retrieval as a communication objective. The objective of marketing communications is often to increase retrieval of the brand name, product attribute, or brand benefit.[40] In other cases, the objective of a communication might be to increase consumers' recognition of the brand name, logo or brand symbol, package, advertisement, ad character, brand benefit, and so on. Newer competitors in an established industry work particularly hard to increase consumers' awareness of their brand names. When Priceline.com started selling airline tickets, it spent millions of dollars on multimedia advertising to create brand awareness—which helped the firm attract one million new customers every quarter.[41]

Retrieval affects consumer choices. One study found that Japanese consumers' use of a bank declined as their recognition of the name of the bank declined.[42] Getting consumers to recognize or recall specific claims or slogans is also critical. Furthermore, knowing and remembering this information may serve as useful input to consumers' attitudes, and consumers may invoke this information when making choices among brands. However, the most memorable ads are not necessarily the most effective in generating the desired effect—inducing purchase behavior, for example. Nor are they necessarily effective in achieving objectives such as linking information to the specific brand. In one study, consumers who watched the Super Bowl and its commercials incorrectly attributed the advertising slogan of one telecommunications firm to as many as 13 other companies.[43]

Recall relates to advertising effectiveness. Research shows that it is important for marketers to develop appropriate measures of recognition, recall, and implicit memory when pretesting advertisements.[44] Exhibit 8.8 shows a report from a company that assesses consumers' recall of commercials. Researchers showed consumers a TV commercial and, after 24 hours, asked the consumers what they remembered. This particular page covers cued recall: the percentages indicate how many people remembered the tested ad.

How valuable recognition or recall is to marketers depends, in part, on how consumers typically buy the product. If they typically go through a store aisle and look for the brand they habitually buy, purchase is based on recognition—meaning recognition of the brand name, package, and logo is important. In other cases, product purchase is based on recall. For example, if you are thinking about where you might go for lunch today, the list of places you will consider is likely to depend on which you can recall from memory.

Implicit memory is also important to marketers. Although ad agencies typically measure consumers' explicit memory by what they recall and recognize from an ad, the concept of implicit memory suggests that consumers may have some memory of information in an advertising message even if they do not recognize or recall it. Thus advertisers may try to use measures of implicit memory to gauge whether their ads have affected consumers' memory.

Consumer segments and memory. Unfortunately, although retrieval is an important objective for marketers, not all consumers can remember things equally well. In particular, elderly consumers have difficulty recognizing and remembering brand names and ad claims. Interestingly, research shows that elderly consumers' memory for information from advertising can be improved if they form a mental image of things in the ad, like the claims it makes. Imagery apparently creates a greater number of associations in memory, which, in turn, enhances retrieval.[45] ●

HOW RETRIEVAL IS ENHANCED

Given the importance of retrieval, marketers need to understand how they can enhance the likelihood that consumers will remember something about specific brands. Consumers cannot recognize or recall something unless it is first stored in memory; chunking, rehearsal, and similar factors increase the likelihood that an item will be stored in long-term memory and will be available for retrieval.

Four additional factors—some related to trace strength and spreading of activation—also affect retrieval: (1) the stimulus itself, (2) what it is linked to, (3) the way it is processed, and (4) the characteristics of consumers.

Characteristics of the Stimulus

Retrieval is affected by the salience (prominence) of the stimulus (the message or message medium). It is also affected by the extent to which the item is a prototypical member of a category, whether it uses redundant cues, and the medium that is used to convey information.

Salience Something is salient if it stands out from the larger context in which it is placed because it is bright, big, complex, moving, or prominent in its environment.[46] If you saw a really long commercial or a multipage ad, it might be salient relative to the short commercials or single-page ads that surround it. A visually complex figure in an ad will be salient relative to a simple background, and an animated Internet ad will be salient relative to motionless ones.

EXHIBIT 8.8
Recall Results for a 30-Second Commercial
Some marketing research companies measure the effectiveness of TV commercials by whether consumers can recall them 24 hours after they are aired. This company measures the percentage of program viewers who can recall the commercial if given the name of the product or brand. Recall by various demographic groups is provided.

Source: Jack Haskings and Alice Kendrick, *Successful Advertising Research Methods.* © 1997 by NTC Business Books. Used with permission.

COMMERCIAL	IN-VIEW 30" GTE CORPORATION, "DESERT CC" BASE	PROVED COMMERCIAL REGISTRATION* PCR%
Total Sample, Men	(142)	46
By income (excl. DK/NA/Ref)		
Under $30,000	(71)	44
Over $30,000	(52)	46
By age (excl. DK/NA/Ref)		
18–34	(98)	46
35–49	(44)	46
Total Sample, Women	(165)	50
By income (excl. DK/NA/Ref)		
Under $30,000	(87)	46
Over $30,000	(57)	56
By age (excl. DK/NA/Ref)		
18–34	(84)	50
35–49	(79)	51
30" PCR NORMS	**MEN**	**WOMEN**
All commercials	29	33
All corporate	27	32
18–34	28	33
35–49	26	31

* Proved Commercial Registration (PCR) is defined as the percent of qualified viewers of the program who, given the brand name/product, can recall and accurately describe the commercial on the day following the telecast.

	PITTSBURGH	MINNEAPOLIS	SAN DIEGO
Date	6/18	6/19	6/18
Program	Barnaby Jones	S.W.A.T.	Quincy
Time	8:18 p.m.	7:14 p.m.	8:15 p.m.

EXHIBIT 8.9
Salience
The picture of the huge mound of cheese is salient in this ad for cheese.

Source: Courtesy DDB.

The salience of a stimulus affects retrieval in several ways. For one thing, salient objects tend to attract attention to themselves, drawing attention away from things that are not salient. Because they are prominent, salient stimuli also induce greater elaboration, thereby creating stronger memory traces.[47] This might explain why some research has shown that consumers tend to remember longer commercials better than shorter ones and bigger print ads better than smaller ones. Their length or size makes them salient.[48] The mound of cheese shown in Exhibit 8.9 is likely to be salient because it is so big.

Prototypicality We are better able to recognize and recall prototypical or pioneer brands in a product category (see Chapter 5 for a discussion of prototypicality). Because they have been frequently rehearsed and recirculated, the memory trace for prototypical brands is strong. These brands are also likely to be linked to many other concepts in memory, making their activation highly likely. The fact

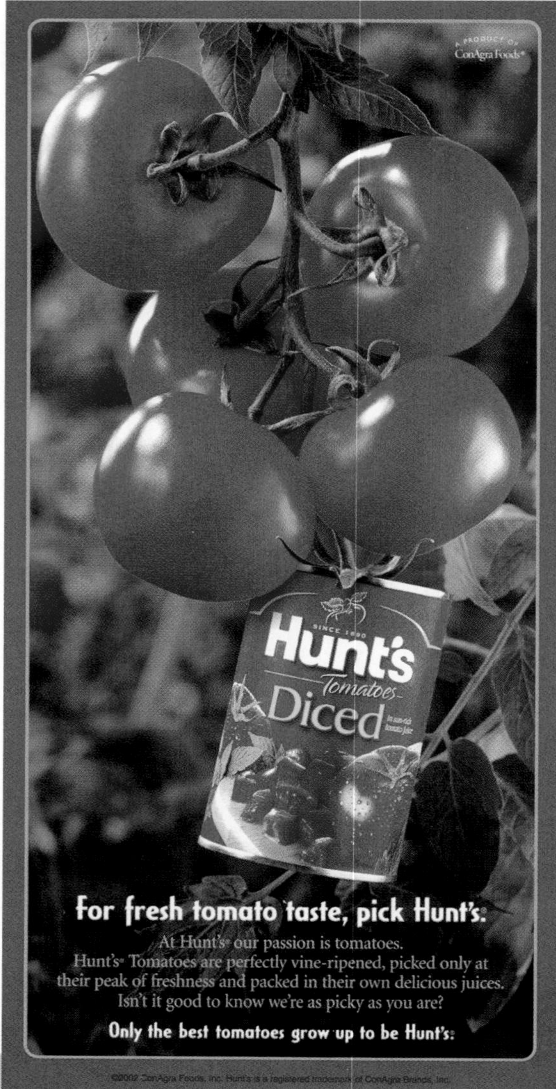

EXHIBIT 8.10
Redundant Cues
The picture of a can of Hunt's Diced Tomatoes hanging from a tomato vine is redundant with the notion that Hunt's uses only the freshest vine-ripened tomatoes.

Source: Courtesy Conagra Foods, Inc.

that we tend to remember these brands may explain why they have been so successful over time and why so many companies fight to establish themselves as category leaders.[49] Coca-Cola, for example, is engaged in intense marketing efforts to establish itself as the market leader in Brazil, Spain, and other countries.[50]

Redundant Cues Memory is enhanced when the information items to be learned seem to go together naturally. Thus our memory of brand name, advertising claims, and pictures presented in ads is better when these elements convey the same information, as in Exhibit 8.10, where the picture and the copy both convey the notion that the tomatoes in Hunt's Diced Tomatoes are fresh. Marketers can also enhance consumers' memory for brands by advertising two complementary products together (such as Special K with Tropicana orange juice) and explaining how they naturally go together.[51] Research indicates that event sponsorship enhances memory when the brand is prototypical—due to prominence in the marketplace—and when the event relates to the brand's core meaning.[52]

The Medium in Which the Stimulus Is Processed Advertisers often wonder whether certain media are more effective than others at enhancing consumer memory. Currently, advertisers are trying to determine whether spending money on Internet ads is a good use of advertising dollars. Some research suggests that consumers tend not to look at or remember Internet ads, whereas other studies suggest that these ads can be as or even more effective in generating brand memory than ads shown in traditional media.[53] A growing number of companies are using Internet advertising to build brand awareness and recognition. The Compaq Computer brand, for example, received more than one million exposures in the first week of its sponsorship of an animated program on the Shockwave.com site.[54] Unfortunately, our understanding of how the choice of medium affects memory is still rudimentary.

What the Stimulus Is Linked To

Retrieval can also be facilitated by what the stimulus is linked to in memory.

Retrieval Cues The associative network concept explains a related way of facilitating retrieval—providing retrieval cues. A **retrieval cue** is a stimulus that facilitates the activation of memory.[55] For example, if you need to remember to go to a sale at Macy's, you might leave a note on your refrigerator that says, "Macy's." When you see the note later, you remember the sale. The note serves as a retrieval cue.

Retrieval cues can be generated internally or externally. Internally, a thought can also cue another thought as in, "Today is December 8. Oh my gosh, it's Mom's birthday!" An external stimulus such as a vending machine, a Web banner, or an in-store display could also serve as a retrieval cue—"Oh, there's the new candy bar I've been hearing about." These same retrieval cues can be used to activate images stored in autobiographical memory. If you see an advertisement for your favorite brand of ice cream, this cue might activate both your positive feelings about ice cream and your memory of past experiences with ice cream. Pictures or videos of ourselves engaging in an activity can serve as powerful retrieval cues to stimulate memories.[56]

The Brand Name as a Retrieval Cue One of the most important types of retrieval cues is the brand name. If we see brand names such as Porsche, Jif, and Nike, we can retrieve information about these and related brands from memory. Research has found, however, that the impact of brand name as a retrieval cue is not the same for recognition as it is for recall.[57]

If marketers want consumers to *recognize* the brand on the store shelf, it is important to have high-frequency words or names to which consumers have been heavily exposed, for example, Coast or Crest. On the other hand, if the goal is to have consumers *recall* the brand and its associations, it is more important to have brand names that (1) evoke rich imagery (Passion, or Old El Paso), (2) are novel or unexpected (Screaming Yellow Zonkers or Toilet Duck), or (3) suggest the product or service and its benefits (Minute Rice or Healthy Request).

retrieval cue A stimulus that facilitates a node's activation in memory.

Other Retrieval Cues In addition to brand names, logos and packages can also act as retrieval cues. The picture of the girl with the umbrella is likely to cue consumers to remember the Morton seasoning products depicted in Exhibit 8.11. Category names are another type of retrieval cue. Thus, encountering the product categories "cars", "peanut butter", or "athletic shoes" might cue the names of specific brands from these categories from memories.

Consumer Implications Retrieval cues have implications for purchasing decisions. Consumers remember very little advertising content when they are actually making a decision in the store.[58] The reason is that advertising is typically seen or heard in a context completely different from the purchase environment. One way to handle this problem is to place a cue from the ad on the brand's package or on an in-store display.[59] This cue will then activate advertising-related links in memory. Thus, packages are sometimes labeled "as seen on TV." Another strategy is to place well-known cues from ads on the package, such as the bear on Snuggle fabric softener, "scrubbing bubbles" on Johnson Wax bathroom cleaner, and "Dig 'em" the Sugar Smacks frog.

MARKETING IMPLICATIONS Retrieval cues also have important implications for marketers. First, these cues can affect what consumers remember from ads.[60] Some research has shown that the most effective retrieval cues match the cues actually used in an ad. Therefore, if an ad uses a picture of an apple, then a picture of an apple, not the word "apple," is the most effective retrieval cue. If the ad uses a particular word, then the actual word, not a picture of what it represents, is the most effective retrieval cue. Other research has shown that music can serve as an effective retrieval cue for ad content, affecting consumers' memories of pictures in an ad.

Interestingly, some marketers have developed features to help consumers generate their own retrieval cues. For example, Amazon.com offers a free service called "Special Occasion Reminders" to help users remember birthdays, anniversaries, and other gift-giving occasions. Users type in each person's name, the month and day of the special occasion, and indicate how far in advance Amazon.com should send an automated reminder. Amazon.com will even e-mail gift suggestions if the user inputs details like the person's age and interests. This service not only acts as a retrieval cue but also facilitates searching and decision making—issues discussed in the next set of chapters. ●

How a Stimulus Is Processed in Short-Term Memory

Another factor affecting retrieval is the way information is processed in short-term memory. One consistent finding is that messages processed through imagery tend to be better remembered than those processed discursively. The reason may be that things processed in imagery form are processed as pictures *and* as words. This **dual coding** provides extra associative links in memory, thereby enhancing the likelihood that the item will be retrieved.

dual coding The representation of a stimulus in two modalities (e.g., pictures and words) in memory.

Information encoded verbally, however, is processed just one way—discursively—so it has only one retrieval path. Nevertheless, imagery processing is not necessarily induced by pictures alone. When you read a novel, you can often generate very vivid images about the story and its characters. In this way, verbal information can also possess imagery-generating properties. Inducing imagery

EXHIBIT 8.11 The Package as Retrieval Cue

Packages sometimes contain information that helps consumers remember what they saw in an ad. The girl with the umbrella (who shows that Morton's salt still pours even when it rains) is used as a retrieval cue on all of Morton's® seasoning products.

Source: Morton®, When It Rains It Pours®, and the Morton Unbrella Girl are registered trademarks of Morton International, Inc.

via pictures, high-imagery words, or imagery instructions may result in dual coding.[61] Dual coding is one reason that marketers often use the audio portion of well-known TV ads as radio commercials. When consumers hear the familiar verbal message, they may provide their own imagery of the visual part, thus promoting dual coding.

Consumer Characteristics Affecting Retrieval

Finally, both consumers' mood and expertise can affect their retrieval of stored memories.

Mood Mood has some very interesting effects on retrieval.[62] First, being in a positive mood can enhance our recall of stimuli in general. Second, we are more likely to recall information that is consistent with our mood. In other words, if we are in a positive mood, we are more likely to recall positive information. Likewise, if we are in a negative mood, we will recall more negative information. From a marketing perspective, if an advertisement can influence a consumer's mood in a positive direction, the recall of relevant information may be enhanced when the consumer is feeling good.

Several explanations account for these mood effects. One is that feelings consumers associate with a concept are linked to the concept in memory. Thus your memory of Disneyland may be associated with the feeling of fun. If you are in a fun mood, the fun concept may be activated, and this activation may spread to Disneyland.[63] Researchers have also suggested that people process information in more detail when mood is intense than when it is weak. More detailed processing, in turn, leads to greater elaboration and higher levels of recall.[64] Another study found that mood influences both elaboration and rehearsal, two processes that enhance memory. In this research, consumers in a positive mood were more likely to readily learn brand names and engage in brand rehearsal.[65]

Expertise Chapter 5 mentioned that compared with novices, experts have more complex category structures in memory with a greater number of higher- and lower-level categories and more detail within each category. Therefore, experts' associative networks are more interconnected than the networks of novices. The complex linkages and the spreading of activation concept explain why experts can recall more brands, brand attributes, and benefits than novices.[66]

SUMMARY

Memory consists of three memory stores, each with different types of memory. Sensory memory (iconic and echoic) involves a very brief analysis of incoming information. Short-term memory represents active working memory and involves imagery and discursive processing. Long-term memory represents the permanent memory store; it includes autobiographical and semantic memory. Consumers will lose information from the sensory store and from short-term memory if they do not further process the information. Long-term memory can be represented as a set of semantic networks with concepts connected by associations or links. Although long-term memory reflects what we have stored, not everything is equally accessible, indicating that memory and retrieval are different phenomena.

To enhance the likelihood that information in long-term memory is stored and to reduce the likelihood that information in memory will be lost, marketers can enhance memory by using principles like chunking, recirculation, rehearsal, and elaboration.

Retrieval is the process of remembering information that is stored in memory. Consumers can retrieve entities when concepts are activated in memory, making the information accessible. Concepts may also be activated by the spreading of activation. Even if the activation potential is not sufficient to retrieve an item, the activation may be sufficient to prime the concept in memory, thereby making that concept more easily retrievable when other cues are present. If a concept or a link to it is not activated often, that concept will "decay" in memory. We may fail to retrieve information, or we may retrieve information that is not accurate.

There are two types of retrieval tasks: those that ask whether we can remember things we have previously encountered—an explicit memory task—and those that *reveal* memory of things for which we have no conscious memory—an implicit memory task. Marketers often use recall and recognition as measures of explicit memory. Because of their importance to retrieval, both recall and recognition serve as objectives for marketing communications, influence consumer choice, and have important strategic implications. Factors that facilitate recognition and recall include characteristics of the information (its salience, prototypicality, redundancy), what it is linked to (retrieval cues), the way it is processed (particularly in imagery mode), and characteristics of consumers (mood and expertise).

QUESTIONS FOR REVIEW AND DISCUSSION

1. How are sensory, short-term, and long-term memory linked?
2. What four techniques can consumers use to enhance their memory?
3. Why are some links in a semantic or associative network weak while others are strong?
4. How can retrieval failures and errors affect consumer memory?
5. How does recognition differ from recall?
6. What is implicit memory, and how can it affect a consumer's ability to retrieve a brand name?
7. How do mood and expertise affect retrieval of memories?

EXERCISES

1. Watch television for two hours (also recording the programs on a VCR), page through two magazines, or spend 20 minutes on the Internet and write down the names of the sites you visit. Without taking any notes about the ads, see how many you can remember afterwards and list them. Why do you think you were able to remember these ads? Now go back to the ads and analyze each in terms of its ability to generate (a) rehearsal, (b) elaboration, (c) recirculation, and (d) interference. Also, analyze them in terms of (e) the information's salience, (f) your mood, and (g) your expertise.
2. Given the results of question 1, suggest how each marketer could make the information in its ad more memorable for consumers.
3. Collect a set of autobiographical memories from members of your class about a common consumer behavior experience (what they did on their last vacation, how they spent a holiday). Compile this information, and analyze it to determine what implications it might have for marketers (vacation marketers, retailers selling holiday items, and so forth).
4. At one time, Cadillac created a TV commercial using actor Dennis Franz, who plays Detective Andy Sipowicz on ABC's *NYPD Blue.* The commercial showed the actor pulling out a notepad and warning a Mercedes driver that he would write him up for driving a luxury car without enough horsepower. The Mercedes driver asked whether Franz was some kind of cop. The actor winked at the camera and said, "Something like that." NBC and CBS refused to run the ad.[67] Using the concepts of spreading of activation, priming, and interference, explain why the networks acted as they did.
5. Collect a set of ads from a magazine. Analyze each ad and determine whether the marketer was trying to establish recall or recognition of information in the ad. Why is recall or recognition an important objective for this marketer? Do you think the marketer was successful in achieving the objective for this ad? Why or why not?
6. Visit a popular Web site such as CNN.com, MSNBC.com, or Travelocity.com. Browse several of the main pages, noting the advertised brands and products. Do any of these ads use trace strength to

make the information more accessible to consumers? Do any use chunking or rehearsal? How does salience operate in this situation? Based on your analysis, is the Internet a particularly good or poor medium for advertising these brands? Explain your answer.

7. After you have completed exercise #1, select one product category that was represented in the advertising you were exposed to. Go to the supermarket and walk through the aisle where those products are stocked and find the advertised brand. How do the brand and packaging act as retrieval cues?

   What redundant cues, if any, are present on the package or at the point of purchase to enhance your memory of this brand? How does the appearance of the supermarket aisle interfere with your memory of this brand or its attributes and benefits? What suggestions can you offer to this marketer for improving its advertising, packaging, or shelf display to enhance memory and retrieval?

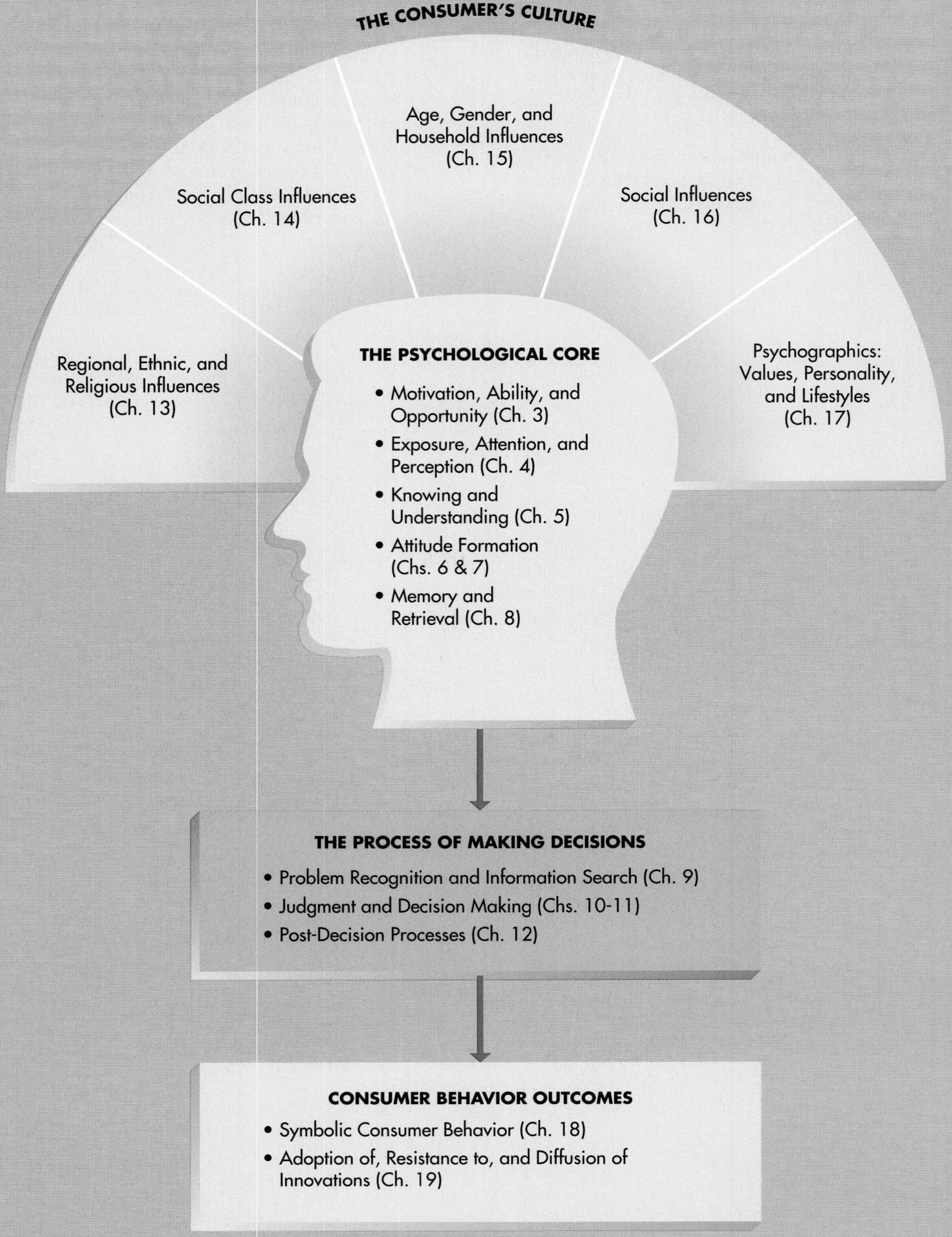

THE CONSUMER'S CULTURE

Regional, Ethnic, and Religious Influences (Ch. 13)

Social Class Influences (Ch. 14)

Age, Gender, and Household Influences (Ch. 15)

Social Influences (Ch. 16)

Psychographics: Values, Personality, and Lifestyles (Ch. 17)

THE PSYCHOLOGICAL CORE

- Motivation, Ability, and Opportunity (Ch. 3)
- Exposure, Attention, and Perception (Ch. 4)
- Knowing and Understanding (Ch. 5)
- Attitude Formation (Chs. 6 & 7)
- Memory and Retrieval (Ch. 8)

THE PROCESS OF MAKING DECISIONS

- Problem Recognition and Information Search (Ch. 9)
- Judgment and Decision Making (Chs. 10-11)
- Post-Decision Processes (Ch. 12)

CONSUMER BEHAVIOR OUTCOMES

- Symbolic Consumer Behavior (Ch. 18)
- Adoption of, Resistance to, and Diffusion of Innovations (Ch. 19)

PART THREE

The Process of Making Decisions

Part Three examines the sequential steps in the consumer decision-making process. Chapter 9 explores the initial steps of this process—problem recognition and information search. Consumers must first realize they have a problem to solve before they can begin the process of making a decision about it. They must then collect information to help make this decision.

As with attitude change, decision making is affected by the amount of effort consumers expend. Chapter 10 examines the decision-making process when consumer effort is high and explores how marketers can influence this extensive decision process. Chapter 11 focuses on decision making when consumer effort is low and discusses how marketers can influence this kind of decision process. Chapter 12 looks at how consumers determine whether they are satisfied or dissatisfied with their decisions and how they learn from choosing and consuming products and services.

chapter 9

Problem Recognition and Information Search

INTRODUCTION: Finding Wheels on the Web

Buying a car? Every month, nearly three million people who are thinking about buying a vehicle visit Edmunds.com, a comprehensive online source of information about new and used cars and trucks. Here, consumers can look up reviews of the latest models, check prices, get tips about buying and selling, learn about used car valuation, and watch video clips of good buying tactics. Consumers can also use the Web site to sign up for wireless access to selected sources of car-related services such as financing, warranties, and insurance.

Originally, Edmunds published books showing market prices for new and used cars. In 1994, the company started putting its information on the Internet for free (see Exhibit 9.1). Now Edmunds.com has become one of the top auto sites on the Web, earning money from advertising and referrals when consumers click to visit a featured partner. All advertising messages are clearly identified so consumers know the source of the information. The company also hosted a traveling auto show that let consumers pay $15 for the chance to test-drive one or more of 50 new models.

"We educate the consumer on what's available, then identify options and avenues," explains Bob Kurilko, Edmunds.com's vice president of product development and marketing, who says that consumers "come in undecided and leave knowing what they want, how much they should pay, and

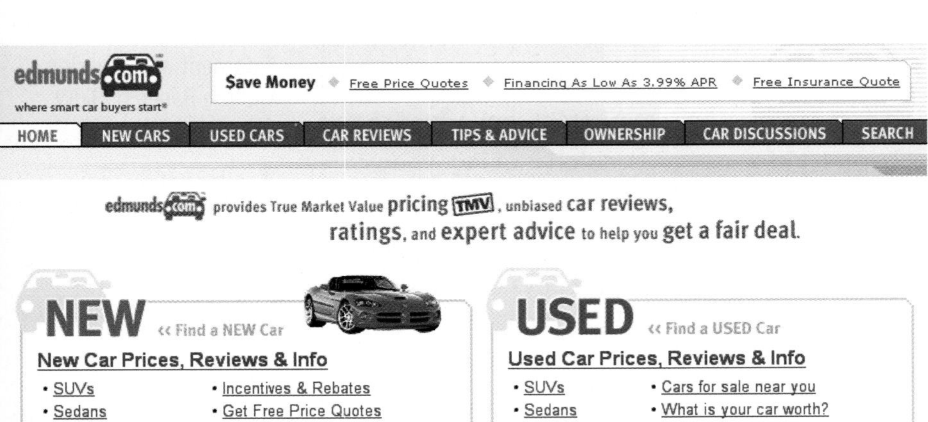

New Vehicle Spotlight
The New Honda Element
Big on function and versatility, the Element gets you (and your stuff) where you need to go. Sponsored by Honda

EXHIBIT 9.1
Getting Information on the Web
Edmunds.com is a very useful Web site from which consumers can collect a lot of information which aids their decision making for an automobile.

Source: © 2003 Edmunds.com Inc.

how to buy it." Car dealers were not initially pleased about consumers using Edmunds.com, observes Kurilko. "But since the Internet's explosion, dealers have had to understand that consumers have the information they need at their fingertips," he says.[1]

Consumers who visit Edmunds.com to research cars illustrate the three central topics of this chapter. Once they realize they need or want a new or used car, consumers enter a state of problem recognition that requires a resolution. They generally start by searching their memory for brands and attributes, a process called internal search. However, most consumers do not have enough information about which car or truck to buy. They therefore conduct an external search for information, in this case on the Internet through Edmunds.com, to support their buying decisions.

As Exhibit 9.2 shows, problem recognition, internal search, and external search represent the early stages of the consumer decision-making process. Although these processes often proceed sequentially, they can also occur simultaneously or in a different order. For example, consumers can be searching for information and suddenly realize that another problem needs to be solved. Also, consumers will not necessarily go through every stage in the exact order every time. However they occur, these three stages are useful in explaining the basic processes that characterize consumer decision making. ●

PROBLEM RECOGNITION

problem recognition The perceived difference between an actual and an ideal state.

ideal state The way we want things to be.

actual state The way things actually are.

The consumer decision process generally begins when the consumer identifies a consumption problem that needs to be solved ("I need a new stereo" or "I'd like some new clothes"). **Problem recognition** is the perceived difference between an ideal and an actual state. This is a critical stage in the decision process because it motivates the consumer to action.

The **ideal state** is the way consumers would like a situation to be (having an excellent stereo or wearing attractive clothing). The **actual state** is the real situation as consumers perceive it now. Problem recognition occurs if consumers become aware of a discrepancy between the actual state and the ideal state ("My stereo is too old" or "My clothing is out of date").

Exhibit 9.3 illustrates the difference between the ideal and actual state. The greater the discrepancy between the actual and ideal state and the higher the level of motivation, ability, and opportunity (MAO), the more likely the consumer is to act. If consumers do not perceive a problem, their motivation to act will be low.

Problem recognition relates not only to acquisition but also to consumption and disposition. Consumers can recognize problems such as needing to decide what to make for dinner, which item of clothing to wear, or whether to replace an old appliance. Procter & Gamble tapped into problem recognition when it discovered that Japanese consumers were squirting out more dish detergent than they needed. This indicated that they needed a more powerful soap, leading to the success of P&G's Joy dishwashing liquid.[2] Because problem recognition stimulates many types of consumer decision making, it is important to understand what contributes to differences between the ideal and the actual state.

The Ideal State: Where We Want to Be

Where do we get our notion of the ideal state? Sometimes we rely on simple expectation, usually based on past experience, about everyday consumption and disposition situations and how products or services fulfill our needs. For example,

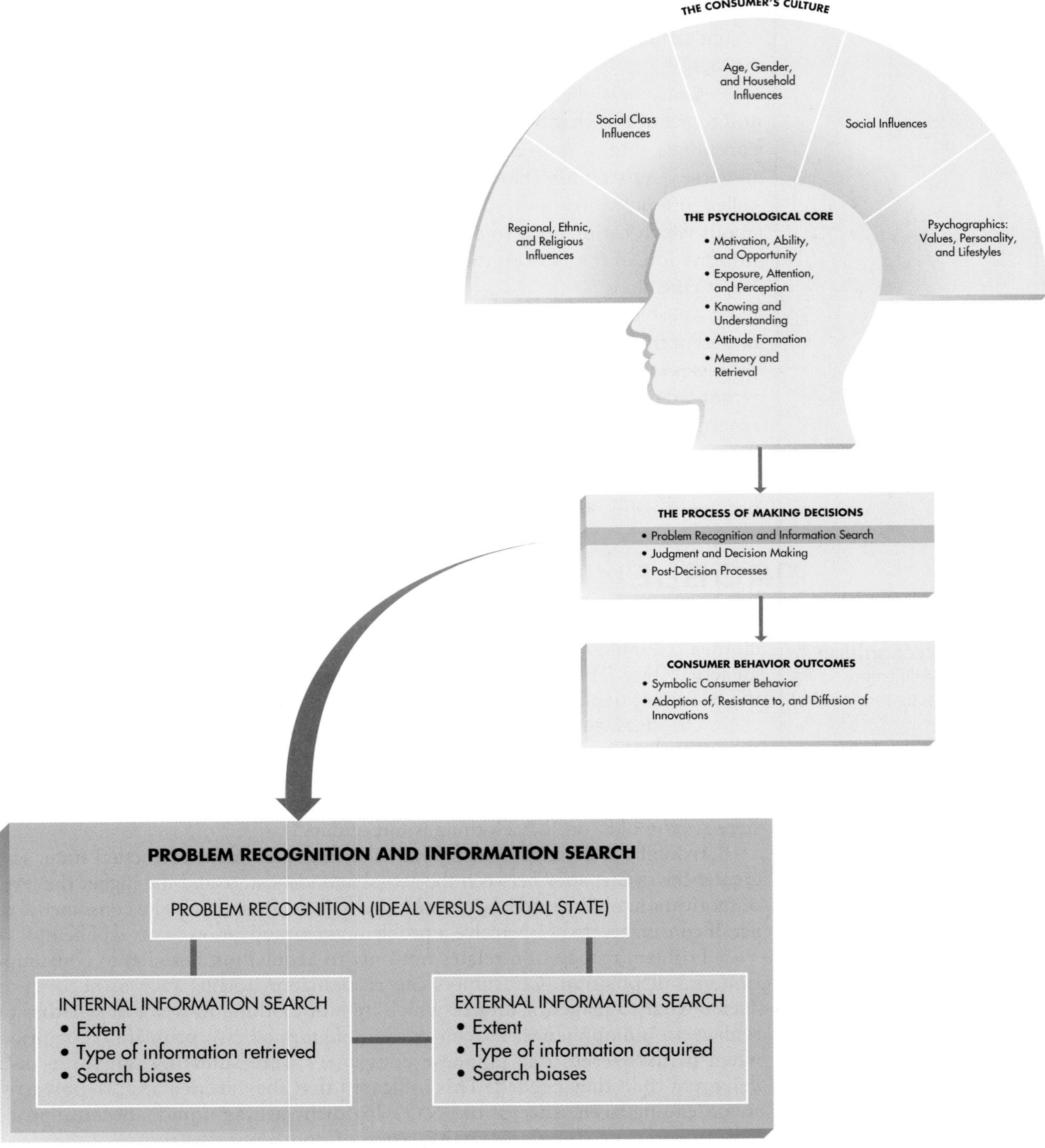

EXHIBIT 9.2
Chapter Overview: Problem Recognition and Information Search

Part Three of the book examines the consumer decision-making process. The first step involves problem recognition (in which the consumer recognizes a problem that needs to be solved). Next the consumer searches for information to solve the problem either internally from memory or externally from outside sources (such as experts, magazines, ads). How much consumers search, what they search for, and the process they go through will be discussed in this chapter.

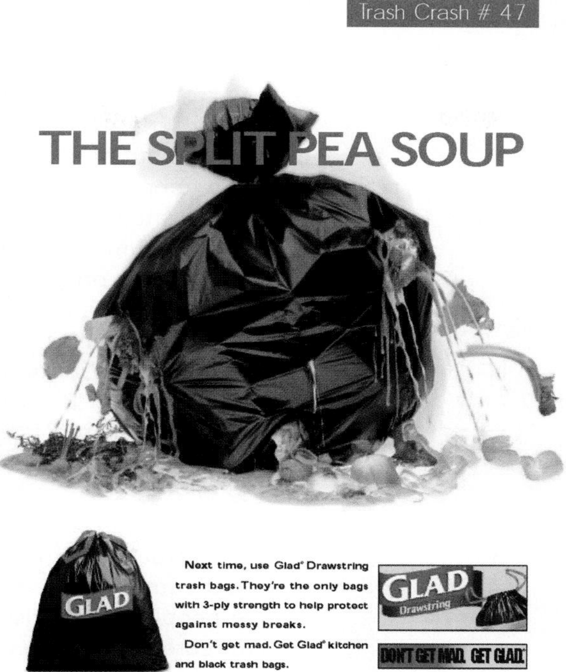

EXHIBIT 9.3
Ideal versus Actual State
This ad is a good illustration of problem recognition and the difference between the actual and ideal state. The ideal state is a strong trash bag that will not break. In this ad, the actual state is a big mess due to a weak bag. GLAD offers the solution to the problem with a strong bag.

Source: ©2002. The GLAD Products Company. Used with permission

we consider how we might look in certain clothes, how clean our house should be, how much fun it would be to vacation in a particular location, which old products we should keep, and so on. The ideal state also can be a function of our future goals or aspirations. For example, many consumers might want to drive a car that will provide them with social status (a Porsche, Mercedes, or Lexus) or to join a club that will bring them the admiration or acceptance of others.

Both expectations and aspirations are often stimulated by our own personal motivations—what we want to be based on our self-image—and by aspects of our own culture. Some societies are more materialistic than others, and therefore the desire for many goods and services may be higher in those cultures. Likewise, social class can exert an influence: many consumers want to be accepted by members of their class or to raise their social standing, leading them to aspire to a higher ideal state. Reference groups also play a critical role, because we strive to be accepted by others and because reference groups serve as a guide to our behavior.

Finally, major changes in personal circumstances, such as getting a promotion or having a baby, can instigate new ideal states. Exhibit 9.4 illustrates another ideal state. When you graduate and start a new job, you are likely to develop new ideal states related to where you live, what you wear, what you drive, and so forth. Since the fall of communism, many Eastern European consumers have been desiring Western goods that were formerly unavailable, thereby creating a new ideal state.

The Actual State: Where We Are Now

Like your perception of the ideal state, your perception of the actual state can be influenced by a variety of factors. Often these are simple physical factors, such as running out of a product, having a product malfunction (the stereo breaks down) or grow obsolete (the computer has insufficient memory), or unexpectedly needing a service (a cavity requires dental work). Needs also play a critical role. If you are hungry or thirsty or if friends make fun of your clothes, your actual state would not be acceptable.

Finally, external stimuli can suddenly change your perceptions of the actual state. If someone tells you that Mother's Day is next Sunday, for example, you might suddenly realize you have not bought a card or present yet. Or opening your closet door may make you realize it is too full.

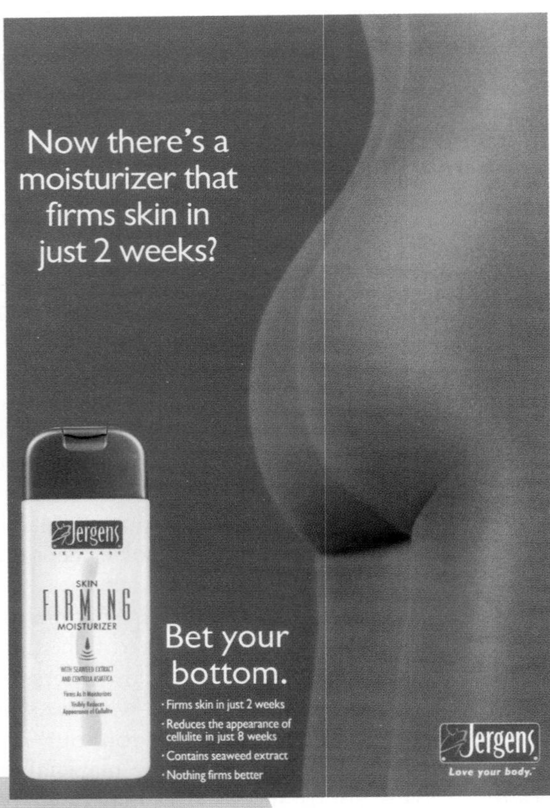

Now there's a moisturizer that firms skin in just 2 weeks?
Jergens
SKIN FIRMING MOISTURIZER
Bet your bottom.
· Firms skin in just 2 weeks
· Reduces the appearance of cellulite in just 8 weeks
· Contains seaweed extract
· Nothing firms better
Jergens
Love your body.

EXHIBIT 9.4
An Ideal State
Many people desire to be attractive and having a firm posterior can be part of this. The Jergen's moisturizer can help consumers achieve this ideal state.

Source: Courtesy of the Andrew Jergens Company.

MARKETING IMPLICATIONS Putting consumers in a state of problem recognition may stimulate the decision process and lead to acquisition, consumption, or disposition of a product or service. Marketing efforts can influence this process. Without problem recognition, marketing efforts are likely to be less effective because the consumer may not be motivated to process information.

In general, marketers use two major techniques to try to stimulate problem recognition. First, they can attempt to create a new ideal state. For example, consumers did not think much about the performance of their athletic shoes in the 1970s. However, today we are continually bombarded with newer and better products that will make us run faster and jump higher—a new ideal state. Some consumers are even willing to pay more than $150 for new higher-tech shoes.

Second, marketers can try to create dissatisfaction with the actual state. The ad in Exhibit 9.5 is directed toward the stressed out worker who has to do "the work of two people." Advertisements for cleaning products such as Febreze, Banish, and Cool Scent are trying to convince smokers to use these products to remove a "smoky smell" from their clothing.[3] A new generation of "polite" cigarettes—with less odor—is now popular with young Japanese consumers.[4] And major tobacco companies are touting the lower toxins or carcinogens in some new cigarette brands.[5] (See Chapter 21 for an in-depth look at the dark side of marketing.)

Whether they create a new ideal state or stimulate dissatisfaction with the actual state, marketers are more likely to have their product or service chosen if they position it as the solution to the consumer's problem. For example, the British food chain Pret A Manger has become successful because, as the French name suggests, its fresh-daily prepackaged sandwiches are "ready to eat"—solving the harried office worker's problem of finding a quick yet healthy and affordable lunch.[6] ●

INTERNAL SEARCH: SEARCHING FOR INFORMATION FROM MEMORY

internal search The process of recalling stored information from memory.

After problem recognition has been stimulated, the consumer will usually begin the decision process to solve the problem. Typically, the next step is **internal search.** As you saw in Chapter 8, almost all decision making involves some form of memory processing. Each consumer has stored in memory a variety of information, feelings, and past experiences that can be recalled when making a decision. For example, at the beginning of the chapter, you saw that consumers who are thinking about buying a car will retrieve their memories of experiences with different car brands.

Because consumers have limited capacity or ability to process information—and because memory traces can decay over time—consumers are likely to recall only a small subset of stored information when they engage in internal search. As a result, researchers are very interested in determining (1) the extent

EXHIBIT 9.5
Creating Dissatisfaction with the Actual State
This ad tries to create dissatisfaction with the actual state. It shows a very busy worker who has a fax machine that cannot keep up with his workload. If consumers can relate to this worker, they will be dissatisfied with their own fax machine (creating problem recognition) and be motivated to look for a new one (hopefully the Panasonic). Can you think of any current product/service situations that you are unhappy with right now?

Source: Courtesy of Panasonic.

of the search; (2) the nature of the search; and (3) the process by which consumers recall information, feelings, and experiences and enter them into the decision process.

How Much Do We Engage in Internal Search?

The degree of internal search can vary widely from the simple recall of only a brand name to more extensive searches through memory for relevant information, feelings, and experiences. On a general level, researchers know that the effort consumers devote to internal search depends on their MAO to process information. Thus consumers will attempt to recall more information when felt involvement, perceived risk, or need for cognition are high. In addition, consumers can engage in active internal search only if information is stored in memory. Consumers with a greater degree of knowledge and experience therefore have a greater ability to search internally. Finally, consumers can recall information from memory only if they have the opportunity to do so. Time pressure or distractions will limit internal search.

What Kind of Information Is Retrieved from Internal Search?

Much of the research on the role of internal search in consumer judgment and decision making has focused on what is recalled. Specifically, researchers have examined the recall of four major types of information: (1) brands, (2) attributes, (3) evaluations, and (4) experiences.[7]

Recall of Brands The set of brands that consumers recall from memory whenever problem recognition has been stimulated is an important aspect of internal search that greatly affects decision making. Rather than remembering all available brands in any given situation, consumers tend to recall a subset of two to eight brands known as a **consideration** or **evoked set.**[8] For example, someone buying bottled water might ordinarily consider Evian and Perrier rather than all possible brands. With product proliferation, however, the number of offerings has increased dramatically. Nestlé alone offers more than 68 water brands (including Perrier), which means more brand competition for inclusion in the consideration set.[9]

consideration (evoked) set The subset of brands evaluated when making a choice.

In general, the consideration set consists of brands that are "top of mind" or easy to remember when making a decision. Some consumers fly rather than take the train—even when the train is faster and cheaper—simply because they do not consider the possibility of train travel.[10] A small consideration set is usually necessary because our ability to recall brand information decreases as the size of the set increases. However, even if we do not recall the entire set from memory, stored information aids the recognition process. For example, stored information can help consumers recognize services in the Yellow Pages or identify brands on the shelf. This is why Nestlé is using television advertising to make its Aero chocolate bar more memorable to U.K. consumers. "With 50 or 60 brands to choose from, our key objective was to get Aero into consumers' consideration set," says an executive at Nestlé's ad agency.[11]

Studies indicate that consideration sets vary in terms of their size, stability, variety, and *preference dispersion* (the equality of preferences toward brands or products in the set). On more familiar occasions and in more familiar locations, such as the occasion of buying snacks at the neighborhood movie theater, consumers have consideration sets that are less stable, are larger in size, and have slightly more variety. In such situations, consumers tend to have stronger preferences for one or two items in the consideration set. This research suggests that a company should enhance its product's linkage with an occasion familiar to consumers—such as movie-going—to increase the chance that the product will be retrieved from memory as part of the consideration set.[12]

According to research, brands that are recalled are more likely to be chosen.[13] However, simply being recalled does not guarantee that a brand will be in the consideration set, because consumers can recall and then reject undesirable alternatives. Also, consumers' choices can be altered by simple manipulation of which brands they recall, even though this may not change their product preferences. Thus if consumers cannot recall brands from memory in order to form a consideration set, the set will tend to be determined by external factors such as availability on the shelf or suggestions of salespeople.[14]

Researchers have looked at the following factors that increase the possibility of consumers recalling a particular brand during internal search and including that brand in the consideration set:

- *Prototypicality.* When consumers engage in internal search, they more easily recall brands that are closest to the prototype or that most resemble other category members, making these more likely to be included in the consideration set than brands that are not typical of the category.[15] For example, Armor All created the category of automotive protectant, and its product is the dominant brand not only in the United States but also in Mexico, Canada, Germany, Japan, and Australia.[16] This brand is more likely than other brands to be in the consideration set when problem recognition for the product exists. As another example, a local food chain in Brazil, Mr. Pizza, has tried to increase inclusion in the consideration set by positioning itself close to the leading foreign chain (Pizza Hut).[17]

- *Brand familiarity.* Well-known brands are more easily recalled during internal search than unfamiliar brands because the memory links associated with these brands tend to be stronger. As a result, companies need to repeat marketing communications continually to keep brand awareness high and associations strong. In Asian cultures, ads with high-meaning pictures and words (e.g., Superman fences with a picture of Superman) are very effective in increasing brand-name recall.[18] Even in low-MAO situations where little processing occurs, incidental ad exposure can increase the likelihood of inclusion in the consideration set.[19] This explains why global brands such as Sony, IBM, McDonald's, Mercedes, and Coca-Cola have high familiarity worldwide and are likely to be in many consumers' consideration sets. Familiarity is also the reason drugs such as Rogaine and Propecia (for men's hair loss) are advertised so heavily.[20] Brand familiarity helps consumers recognize which of the many available brands in the store should be attended to and reduces misidentification of brands.[21] It also operates in the movie business, where Disney and other studios release remakes or sequels that attract audiences because they are based on well-known movies of the past.[22]

- *Goals and usage situations.* As discussed in Chapter 5, consumers have goal-derived and usage-specific categories in memory, such as drinks to bring to the beach, and the activation of these categories will determine which brands they recall during internal search.[23] Thus marketers can attempt to associate products with certain goals and usage situations. For example, Kodak developed the Fun Saver 35 for the category of single-use cameras.[24] Similarly, Domino's Pizza has tried to make a strong impact in Japan by positioning itself as the "food for delivery."[25]
- *Brand preference.* Brands for which the consumer has positive attitudes tend to be recalled more easily and be included in the consideration set more often than brands that evoke negative attitudes.[26] This principle highlights the importance of developing positive brand attitudes. Unilever's Dove brand, for instance, has been associated with moisturizing since the soap debuted in 1955. Unilever has built on positive attitudes toward Dove by extending the brand to body washes, deodorants, and cleansing cloths.[27]
- *Retrieval cues.* By strongly associating the brand with a retrieval cue, marketers can increase the chance that the brand will be included in the consideration set. The Clydesdale horses have helped consumers remember Budweiser for years, and they have been the centerpiece of an aggressive campaign in Japan.[28] Gatorade is currently using a curvy, easy-grip bottle with a green pop-up top as a retrieval cue, much as an hourglass bottle has long served as a retrieval cue for Coca-Cola.[29] The picture of the Michelin man hot air balloon in Thailand is a good example of a retrieval cue.

Recall of Attributes For a variety of reasons, we access only a small portion of the information stored in memory during internal search. Often we cannot remember specific facts about a product or service because our memory of details decreases over time. Thus, the attribute information we recall tends to be in summary or simplified form rather than in its original detail. We would be more likely to remember that a car gets good gas mileage or that it is not expensive than to remember the actual miles per gallon or the exact price.

Nevertheless, consumers can often recall *some* details when they engage in internal search, and the recalled attribute information can strongly influence their brand choices.[30] As a result, researchers have been very interested in determining which factors influence the recall of attribute information in the information search and decision-making processes. Some of the major variables they have identified include:

- *Accessibility or availability.* Information that is more accessible or available—having the strongest associative links—is the most likely to be recalled and entered into the decision process.[31] Information that is perceived as being easy to recall is also more likely to be accessible.[32] Marketers can make information more accessible by repeatedly drawing attention to it in marketing communications or by making the information more relevant.[33] Wal-Mart ads repeatedly stress low prices, hoping that consumers will remember this attribute when they decide where to shop.
- *Diagnosticity.* **Diagnostic information** helps us distinguish objects from one another. If all brands of computers are the same price, then price is not

diagnostic, or useful, in making a decision. On the other hand, if prices vary, consumers can distinguish between them, so the information is diagnostic.[34] If information is both accessible and diagnostic, it has a very strong influence in the decision-making process.[35] If accessible information is not diagnostic, it is less likely to be recalled.

Research shows that negative information tends to be more diagnostic than positive or neutral information, because the former is more distinctive.[36] In other words, because most brands are associated with positive attributes, negative information makes it easier to categorize the brand as different from other brands. Unfortunately, consumers therefore tend to give negative information greater weight in the decision-making process, increasing the chances that the alternative with the negative qualities will be rejected. Obviously, some marketers need to avoid associating their products and services with negative information, to plan a two-sided message campaign, or to divert attention away from the negative feature.

EXHIBIT 9.5A
Retrieval Cues in Advertising
The Michelin Man is a retrieval cue which helps consumers to remember to place this brand in the consideration set.

Source: © AP/Wide World Photos.

In addition, marketers can identify which attributes tend to be most diagnostic for a particular product or service category and try to gain a competitive advantage on one or more of these attributes. In Japan, many consumers like strong drinks, so Budweiser actively markets Buddy beer, which has 6 percent alcohol (versus 5 percent for other brands).[37] Levi Strauss stresses the diagnostic attribute "Made in America" when marketing to European consumers who have an affinity for typically American jeans.[38]

- *Salience*. Research has clearly shown that consumers can recall very salient (prominent) attributes even when their opportunity to process is low.[39] For example, many young women remember Ortho Tri-Cyclen because it has been proven to fight acne, a very salient attribute for this group.[40] For other consumers, price is a highly salient attribute.

Consumers do not always have a strong belief about the salience of an attribute.[41] However, by repeatedly calling attention to an attribute in marketing communications, marketers can increase salience and its impact on the decision.[42] For example, in light of recent research, wine makers are now promoting the positive health benefits of drinking red wine, such as a lower incidence of heart disease.[43] Because of a slow economy in Japan, many Japanese marketers strongly encouraged local consumers to "buy Japanese" and to vacation in their own country, making more salient the attribute of a good or service being Japanese.[44]

diagnostic information Information that helps us discriminate among objects.

Note, however, that an attribute can be highly salient but not necessarily diagnostic. If you are buying a watch, for example, the attribute "tells time" would be highly salient but not very diagnostic. For information to be recalled and entered into the decision, it must have **attribute determinance,** which means being both salient and diagnostic.[45]

attribute determinance Attributes that are both salient and diagnostic.

- *Vividness*. Vivid information is presented as concrete words, pictures, or instructions to imagine (e.g., imagine yourself on a tropical beach), or through word-of-mouth communication. For example, a picture of a hand holding the Canon Elph camera, which is the size of a credit card, is vivid information.[46] Vivid information is easier to recall than less dramatic information but tends to influence judgment and decision making only when consumers have not formed a strong prior evaluation, especially one that is negative.[47] In addition, vividness affects attitudes only when the effort required to process the information matches the amount of effort the consumer is willing to put forth.[48] Otherwise, vivid and nonvivid information affect consumer attitudes in about the same way.

- *Goals.* The consumer's goals will determine which attribute is recalled from memory. For example, if one of your goals in taking a vacation is to economize, you are likely to recall price. Marketers can identify important goals that guide the choice process for consumers and then position their offerings in the context of these goals, such as offering economy vacation packages.

Recall of Evaluations Because our memory for specific details decays rapidly over time, we find overall evaluations or attitudes (that is, our likes and dislikes) easier to remember than specific attribute information. In addition, our evaluations tend to form strong associative links with the brand; this is why it is important for a company to encourage positive consumer attitudes toward its brands. Volkswagen, for instance, changed its advertising for the new Beetle from an emotional appeal to a more informative approach. Using a touch of humor, the company began offering practical information about the interior to counteract negative perceptions that the car was too tiny inside.[49]

Evaluations are also more likely to be recalled by consumers who are actively evaluating the brand when they are exposed to relevant information. For example, if you are ready to buy a new computer and suddenly see an ad for a particular brand, you will probably determine whether you like the brand when you see the ad. This activity is called **online processing.**[50] Afterward, you will more likely recall this evaluation rather than the specific information that led to it. Many times, however, consumers do not have a brand-processing goal when they see or hear an ad. In such cases they do not form an evaluation and are therefore better able to recall specific attribute information, assuming that involvement was high and the information was processed.[51]

online processing The ability of consumers to process an ad as they are viewing it.

Recall of Experiences Internal search can involve the recall of experiences from autobiographical memory, in the form of specific images and the effect associated with them.[52] Like information in semantic memory, experiences that are more vivid, salient, or frequent are the most likely to be recalled. For example, if you have an experience with a product or service that is either unusually positive or unusually negative, you are likely to recall these vivid experiences later. Furthermore, if you repeatedly have a positive experience with a product or service, it will be easier to recall these experiences. For example, some bowling alleys now offer loud music and flashing lights to appeal to younger bowlers and make the experience more fun and exciting.[53]

MARKETING IMPLICATIONS Obviously, marketers want consumers to recall positive experiences related to certain products or services. To illustrate, many Japanese consumers have developed a desire for new products that look old, such as motorcycles, cars, kimonos, and cameras, because these products are reminders of simple, happy times.[54] Marketers often deliberately associate their products or services with common positive experiences or images to increase their recall from memory. Prudential and Sony are just two of many firms that film ads at the Grand Canyon because it is the "quintessential breathtaking experience," and they hope that consumers will tie this positive memory to their brands.[55] •

Is Internal Search Always Accurate?

In addition to being influenced by factors that affect what we recall, we all have processing biases that alter the nature of internal search. These search biases can sometimes lead to the recall of information that results in a less-than-optimal judgment or decision. Three biases have important implications for marketing: confirmation bias, inhibition, and mood.

confirmation bias The greater likelihood of recalling information consistent with our beliefs.

Confirmation Bias **Confirmation bias** refers to our tendency to recall information that reinforces or confirms our overall beliefs rather than contradicting them, thereby making our judgment or decision more positive than it should be. This phenomenon is related to the concept of selective perception—we see what we want to see—and occurs because we strive to maintain consistency in our views. Thus when we engage in internal search, we are more likely to recall information about brands we like or have previously chosen than about brands we dislike or have rejected. Furthermore, when the confirmation bias is operating, we are more likely to recall positive rather than negative information about favored brands. This response can be a problem because, as mentioned earlier, negative information tends to be more diagnostic.

Nevertheless, we sometimes recall contradictory evidence. In fact, we may recall moderately contradictory information because we had consciously thought about it when we first tried to understand it.[56] In most instances, however, consumers tend to recall information that reinforces their overall beliefs.

MARKETING IMPLICATIONS From a marketing perspective, confirmation bias presents a real problem when consumers search internally for only positive information about the competition. One way marketers attack this problem is to draw attention to negative aspects of competitive brands in comparative advertising. Computer companies like Dell and Compaq and telecommunications firms like AT&T and MCI have used this technique. By presenting comparative information in a convincing and credible way, marketers may be able to overcome confirmation bias. •

inhibition The recall of one attribute inhibiting the recall of another.

Inhibition Another internal search bias is associated with limitations in consumers' processing capacity.[57] In this case, all the variables that influence the recall of certain attributes—such as accessibility, vividness, and salience—can actually lead to the **inhibition** of recall for other diagnostic attributes.[58] In buying a house, for example, a consumer might recall information such as the selling price, number of bathrooms, and square footage but not recall other important attributes such as the size of kitchen and the name of the school district. Inhibition can also lead to a biased judgment or decision because consumers may remember but ignore important and useful information.

MARKETING IMPLICATIONS Inhibition is an important aspect of internal search for two reasons. First, consumers may not always consider key aspects of a brand when making a decision, because they recall other, more accessible attributes instead. In particular, if these nonrecalled attributes reflect features that differentiate the brand from others (i.e., if the attributes are diagnostic), the company may want to highlight them in marketing communications. For example, although price advertising is pervasive in the PC market, Dell Computer does not want consumers to forget one of its key differentiating features—service—so it features this attribute (in addition to price) in its advertisements.

Second, marketers can sometimes offset the effect of their brand's disadvantages and/or their competitors' advantages by drawing attention to more vivid or accessible attributes. For example, ads for Cervana deer meat stress that venison is tasty, tender, and low in fat, deflecting attention from the belief that it tastes too gamey.[59] ●

Mood You saw in Chapter 8 that consumers engaged in internal search are most likely to recall information, feelings, and experiences that match their mood.[60] With this in mind, marketing communications that put consumers in a good mood through the use of humor or attractive visuals can enhance the recall of positive attribute information.

EXTERNAL SEARCH: SEARCHING FOR INFORMATION FROM THE ENVIRONMENT

Sometimes a consumer's decision can be based entirely on information recalled from memory. At other times, information is missing or some uncertainty surrounds the recalled information. Then consumers engage in **external search** of outside sources such as dealers, trusted friends or relatives, published sources (magazines, pamphlets, or books), advertisements, the Internet, or the product package. Consumers use external search to collect additional information about which brands are available, as well as the attributes and benefits associated with brands in the consideration set.

external search
The process of collecting information from outside sources (e.g., magazines, dealers, ads).

prepurchase search
A search that occurs to aid a specific decision.

ongoing search
A search that occurs regularly, regardless of whether the consumer is making a choice.

Two types of external search are prepurchase search and ongoing search. **Prepurchase search** occurs in response to the activation of problem recognition. As an example, consumers seeking to buy a new car or truck can get information by visiting dealers, searching Edmunds.com and other Web sites, checking quality rankings, talking to friends, and reading *Consumer Reports*.[61] **Ongoing search** occurs on a regular and continual basis, even when problem recognition is not activated.[62] A consumer might consistently read automotive magazines, visit automotive Web sites, and go to car shows because of a high degree of enduring involvement in cars. Exhibit 9.6 contrasts these two types of searches.

Researchers have examined five key aspects of the external search process: (1) the source of information, (2) the extent of external search, (3) the content of the external search, (4) search typologies, and (5) the process or order of the search.

Where Can We Search for Information?

For either prepurchase or ongoing search, consumers can acquire information from five major categories of external sources:[63]

- *Retailer search.* Visits or calls to stores or dealers, including the examination of package information or pamphlets about brands.
- *Media search.* Information from advertising, online ads, manufacturer-sponsored Web sites, and other types of marketer-produced communications.
- *Interpersonal search.* Advice from friends, relatives, neighbors, and/or other consumers, including those on chat lines.

	Prepurchase Search	Ongoing Search
Determinants	• Involvement in the purchase • Market environment • Situational factors	• Involvement with the product • Market environment • Situational factors
Motives	To make better purchase decisions	• Build a bank of information for future use • Experience fun and pleasure
Outcomes	• Increased product and market knowledge • Better purchase decisions • Increased satisfaction with the purchase outcome	• Increased product and market knowledge leading to – future buying efficiences – personal influence • Increased impulse buying • Increased satisfaction from search, and other outcomes

EXHIBIT 9.6
Types of Information Searches

Consumers can engage in two major types of external search. Prepurchase search occurs in response to problem recognition; the goal is to make better purchase decisions. Ongoing search results from enduring involvement and occurs on a continual basis (independent of problem recognition). Here consumers search for information because they find searching enjoyable (they like to browse).

Source: Peter H. Block, Daniel L. Sherrell, and Nancy M. Ridgeway, "Consumer Search: An Extended Framework," *Journal of Consumer Research*, June 1986, p. 120.

- *Independent search.* Contact with independent sources of information, such as books, non-brand-sponsored Web sites like Edmunds.com, government pamphlets, or magazines.
- *Experiential search.* The use of product samples, product/service trials (such as a test-drive), or experiencing the product online.

Traditionally, retailer and media search, followed by experiential search, have been the most frequently used forms of search. These increase when involvement is higher and knowledge is lower.[64] This finding is significant for marketers because such sources are under their most direct control. Other research indicates that consumers browse two or more sources of information (such as the Internet and catalogs) before making a buying decision. Therefore, marketers and retailers should ensure that brand information is consistent across the various sources.[65]

Consumers increase their use of interpersonal sources as their brand knowledge decreases. Apparently, when consumers' knowledge is limited, they are motivated to seek out the opinions of others. Furthermore, consumers who believe that their purchase and consumption of certain items (usually hedonic or symbolic products and services such as fashion, music, and furniture) will be judged by others tend to seek out interpersonal sources.[66]

Experiential search is also critical for hedonic products and services. Given the importance of sensory stimulation, consumers want to get a "feel" for the offering, so they often try on clothing or listen to a stereo before they buy. Cultural characteristics play a role in external search as well. According to research, consumers who are members of subcultural groups and not culturally assimilated—fully integrated into the surrounding culture—tend to conduct a wider search of external sources. And members of subcultural groups who identify with the surrounding culture are more likely to search for information among media advertisements. Thus, marketers should create informative advertising messages when targeting these consumer segments.[67] Finally, independent search tends to increase as available time increases, but time spent on this type of search is still generally quite low.

Internet Sources The Internet has dramatically altered the way consumers shop and search for information. Now without ever having to leave their homes, consumers have access to almost any type of information they need to make their purchase decisions. As the chapter-opening Edmunds.com vignette shows, consumers find the Internet useful for rapidly searching through mounds of data to find specific information about anything from a long-lost friend to a good used car. Search engines such as Yahoo! and Google allow easy access to information through the use of keywords. In fact, consumers can use the Internet to get information from all five of the sources mentioned above. Sometimes consumers search for specific information; at other times they simply browse.[68]

Marketers should bear in mind, however, that consumers often perceive information from commercial Web sites as biased. Also, consumers see product choice as riskier when they lack access to experiential information until after they have completed an online purchase.[69] This accounts, in part, for the high percentage of online shoppers—as many as 65 percent—who choose to click away before finalizing a purchase.[70] In addition, consumers dislike waiting for graphics-heavy Web advertisements and sites to load, which limits the effectiveness of elaborate display graphics in providing information and encouraging purchases.[71]

Online shopping continues to grow, although it still constitutes only about one percent of all U.S. retail sales. The trend toward Internet shopping has been strongest in the United States. Amazon.com, one of the largest online retail sites, sells nearly 40 million books, videos, and other products in the six weeks preceding Christmas.[72] Now consumers in Europe and Asia are increasing their use of the Internet. Online retailers have realized that U.S. strategies do not work everywhere, and locally tailored sites are becoming popular with European shoppers.[73]

Information Overload Consumers today have access to so much information that they can actually become overloaded. For example, entering a common keyword on an Internet search site can sometimes return more than 100,000 references. In response, some search sites now apply more efficient search techniques that seek to prioritize results by identifying the most popular or frequently accessed sites.[74] Alternatively, search sites such as About.com have subject-matter experts selecting the most important information and narrowing the choice set according to specific criteria. Finally, consumers can use online shopping agents or "bots," like MySimon.com and Dealtime.com, to systematically search the Internet for specific products.[75] Some retailers, however, try to thwart bots because these sites make it too easy for consumers to compare prices.[76]

Simulations Advances in technology and graphics have dramatically improved the online experience. Web site developers can now simulate the retail experience as well as product trials by creating sites that incorporate a variety of special and interactive effects including audio, video, zoom, panoramic views, streaming media, and three-dimensional product representations that can be manipulated.[77] After Lands' End began inviting shoppers to "try on" clothing using a virtual model set to each consumer's body measurements, its online clothing sales rose significantly. Century21.com, a real estate site, offers virtual tours of houses for sale, allowing consumers to simulate a personal visit.[78]

In the "virtual grocery store," marketers have been able to recreate the grocery store environment in impressively accurate detail, complete with visuals and music.[79] Shoppers can "fly down" a 3-D aisle and grab what they want. Research shows that these environments can simulate consumers' search and purchase behavior in grocery stores fairly accurately.[80] They can also aid consumers in their search. For example, if a consumer is looking only for sugarless cereals, the click of a button eliminates all products with sugar, making the consumer's search easier. In addition, these environments aid external information search by allowing consumers to locate exactly what they want anywhere on the site. One downside is that these types of environments have very long downloading times, which has led to limited use.

The Online Community The Internet makes it easy for consumers to share information in an online community. People with a common interest or condition related to a product or service can converse with each other via electronic message boards, chat lines, and other methods.[81] America Online, for example, has hundreds of special-interest communities where consumers can exchange ideas about sports, health, and many other topics.[82] Research indicates that the most common interactions focus on product recommendations and how-to-use-it advice.[83] Often this information is very influential in the decision process because it is not controlled by marketers and it is seen as more credible.

An increasing number of retailers and manufacturers are tracking consumers' online information search and purchase patterns to provide additional assistance. For example, consumers who examine or buy products from Amazon.com can see related or similar items by clicking on a button that says, "Customers who bought this product also bought _____." After tracking customer purchases, the Web site greets customers with, "Welcome back. We've improved our book recommendations." Consumers are then given a list of recommendations that fit their preferences.

MARKETING IMPLICATIONS Not all types of products and services are experiencing success on the Internet. The strongest performance has come from areas such as books, music, videos, travel, toys, high technology, software, consumer electronics, and financial services.[84] On the other hand, marketers are less successful when online shoppers cannot judge the quality of a product such as a sofa (as the defunct furniture retailer Living.com found out) or when they perceive that the delivery cost is high relative to the cost of individual items such as groceries (as the defunct online grocer Webvan.com found out).[85] In some markets consumers will use the Internet to search for information but not to buy, as is the case with homes. The keys to online success are generally super selection, ultraconvenience, and competitive pricing. ●

How Much Do We Engage in External Search?

Much of the research on external search has concentrated on examining how much information consumers acquire prior to making a judgment or decision. One of the key findings is that the degree of search activity is usually quite lim-

EXHIBIT 9.7
Sources of Information Influencing a Technology Purchase

Affluent consumers who are considering the purchase of a consumer electronics product or a computer are influenced by a number of different information sources. Interpersonal sources are more influential than commercial sources.

Source: "How People Buy Technology," *BusinessWeek,* January 21, 2002, p. 10 © BusinessWeek.

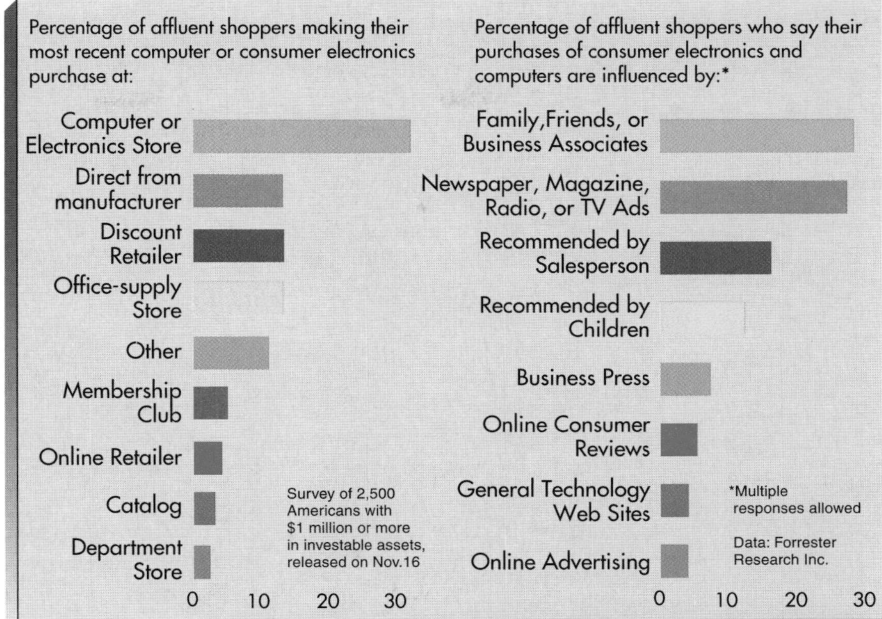

ited, even for purchases that are typically considered important.[86] Researchers have found that more than a third of Australian car buyers made two or fewer trips to the dealer before buying.[87] Exhibit 9.7 shows the sources of information that influence affluent consumers as they purchase computer and electronics products. Note that as more consumers shop on the Internet, search activity may increase because online sources are very convenient. Nevertheless, information search can vary widely from a simple hunt for one or two pieces of information to a very extensive search relying on many sources. In an attempt to explain this variance, researchers have identified a number of causal factors that relate to our motivation, ability, and opportunity to process information.

Motivation to Process Information In general, as the motivation to process information increases, external search will be more extensive. Researchers have identified six factors that increase our motivation to conduct an external search: (1) involvement and perceived risk, (2) the perceived costs and benefits of search, (3) the nature of the consideration set, (4) relative brand uncertainty, (5) attitudes toward the search, and (6) the level of discrepancy of new information.

- *Involvement and perceived risk.* To understand how involvement relates to external search, recall the distinction from Chapter 3 between situational involvement—a response to a particular situation—and enduring involvement, which is an ongoing response. Higher situational involvement will generally lead to greater prepurchase search,[88] whereas enduring involvement relates to ongoing search regardless of whether problem recognition exists.[89] Thus consumers with high enduring involvement with cars or trucks are more likely to read automotive magazines, visit car shows, and engage in other efforts to gain knowledge about cars or trucks on a regular basis.

  Because perceived risk is a major determinant of involvement, it should not be surprising that when consumers face riskier decisions, they engage in more external search activity. One of the key components of perceived risk is uncertainty regarding the consequences of behavior, and consumers use external search as a way to reduce this uncertainty.[90] Consumers are more likely to search when they are uncertain about which brand to choose than when they are uncertain about a specific attribute. Consumers also search more when they are evaluating services rather than products because services are intangible and hence perceived as more uncertain.[91] Finally, consumers will have higher motivation to search if the consequences are more serious, such as those entailing high financial or social risk. This is why consumers often search more extensively for information about higher-priced products or services.

- *Perceived costs and benefits.* External search activity is also greater when its perceived benefits are high relative to its costs.[92] In these situations, consumers who search will benefit by reducing uncertainty, increasing the likelihood of making a better decision, obtaining a better value, and enjoying the shopping process. The costs associated with external search are time, effort, inconvenience, and money (including traveling to stores and dealers). All these factors place psychological or physical strain on the consumer (especially if the distance between stores or dealers is great). In general, consumers tend to continue searching until they perceive that the costs outweigh the benefits. The desire to reduce searching costs explains why many supermarkets now offer a variety of nontraditional items like jewelry, electronics, and furniture. These stores want to become places "where people do all their gift shopping."[93] Note that shopping on the Internet greatly reduces the costs of searching.
- *Consideration set.* If the consideration set contains a number of attractive alternatives, consumers will be motivated to engage in external search to decide which alternative to select. On the other hand, a consideration set that contains only one or two brands reduces the need to search for information.
- *Relative brand uncertainty.* When consumers are uncertain as to which brand is the best, they are more motivated to engage in external search.[94]
- *Attitudes toward search.* Some consumers like to search for information and do so extensively.[95] These consumers generally have positive beliefs about the value and benefits of their search. In particular, extensive search activity appears to be strongly related to the belief that "when important purchases are made quickly, they are regretted."[96] Other consumers simply hate to search and do little.

  Researchers have identified two groups of Internet searchers.[97] Experienced searchers are the most enthusiastic and heaviest users of the Internet, whereas moderate and light users see it as a source of information only, not a source of entertainment or fun. To appeal to the latter group, some companies have created interesting and engaging games to stimulate consumers to search.[98]
- *Discrepancy of information.* Whenever consumers encounter something new in their environment, they will try to categorize it by using their stored knowledge. If a stimulus does not fit into an existing category, consumers will try to resolve this incongruity by engaging in information search, especially when incongruity is at a moderate level and the consumer has limited knowledge about the product category.[99] Consumers are likely to reject highly incongruous information.[100]

  Marketers can capitalize on this tendency by introducing moderate discrepancies between their brand and other brands. For example, an ad for Miele vacuum cleaners made the statement: "Lung Damage Control." This feature is not normally associated with vacuum cleaners (a moderate discrepancy), and the message may motivate consumers to search and find out that the brand has filters to control pollution and allergens.[101]

The same general process applies to the search for information about new products. If a new product is moderately discrepant or incongruent with existing categories of products, the consumer will be motivated to resolve this discrepancy.[102] In particular, consumers explore the most salient attributes in greater depth, rather than search for a lot of additional attributes. From a marketing perspective, this behavior suggests that positioning new products as moderately different from existing brands may induce consumers to search for more information that might, in turn, affect their decision process. A good example is a computer drive that can record DVDs, as compared with traditional drives that play prerecorded DVDs. This moderate discrepancy might stimulate consumers to search for additional product information that could ultimately affect their decision to buy.

Ability to Process Information External search is also strongly influenced by the consumer's ability to process information. Researchers have studied how three variables affect the extent of external information search: (1) consumer knowledge, (2) cognitive abilities, and (3) demographic factors.

- *Consumer knowledge.* Common sense suggests that expert consumers search less because they already have more complex knowledge stored in memory. However, research results on this subject have been mixed.[103] Part of the problem stems from the way in which knowledge is defined. Some studies have measured *subjective knowledge,* the consumer's perception about what he or she knows relative to others. *Objective knowledge* refers to the actual information stored in memory that can be measured with a formal knowledge test. Researchers have linked objective knowledge to information search, although both types of knowledge are somewhat related.

  Specifically, several studies have found an inverted-U relationship between knowledge and search.[104] Consumers with moderate levels of knowledge search the most. They tend to have a higher level of motivation and at least some basic knowledge, which helps them to interpret new information. Experts, on the other hand, search less because they have more knowledge stored in memory, and they also know how to target their search to the most relevant or diagnostic information, ignoring that which is irrelevant—except when the search involves new products. Because experts have more developed memory structures, they have an advantage in learning novel information and can acquire more information about new products.

- *Cognitive abilities.* Consumers with higher basic cognitive abilities, such as IQ and the ability to integrate complex information, are not only more likely to acquire more information than consumers with little or no knowledge, but are also able to process this information in more complex ways.[105]

- *Demographics.* As researchers continue to investigate whether certain types of consumers search more than others, they have discovered a few consistent patterns. For instance, consumers with higher education tend to search more than less educated consumers. This is because more educated consumers have at least moderate levels of knowledge and better access to information sources.[106]

Opportunity to Process Information Consumers who have the motivation and ability to search for information must still have the opportunity to process that information before extensive search can take place. Situational factors that might affect the search process include (1) the amount of information, (2) information format, (3) time available, and (4) the number of items being chosen.

- *Amount of information available.* In any decision situation, the amount of information available to consumers can vary greatly, depending on the number of brands on the market, the attribute information available about each brand, the number of retail outlets or dealers, and the number of other sources of information, such as magazines or knowledgeable friends. In general, consumers do more searching as the amount of available information increases, suggesting that the Internet can generate greater external search. If information is restricted or not available, however, consumers have a hard time engaging in extensive external search.
- *Information format.* The format in which information is presented can also strongly influence the search process. Sometimes information is available from diverse sources or locations, but consumers must expend considerable effort to collect it. In buying insurance, for example, consumers may have to contact different agents or companies to collect information about individual policies.

  In contrast, presenting information in a manner that reduces consumer effort can enhance information search and usage, particularly when the consumer is in the decision mode.[107] For example, in an effort to increase the use of nutritional information, researchers provided a matrix that makes this information easier for consumers to search, thereby improving opportunity.[108] A related study found that consumers increase their use of nutritional information when the rewards of good nutrition are made more explicit.[109] In addition, consumers will engage in more leisurely exploratory searches if information surrounding an object is visually simpler and less cluttered.[110]
- *Time availability.* Consumers who face no time restrictions have more opportunity to search. If consumers are under time pressure, however, they will severely restrict their search activity.[111] Further, consumers will spend less time getting information from different sources as time pressure increases.[112] Note that time pressure is one of the main reasons that consumers search and shop on the Internet.
- *Number of items being chosen.* When consumers are making a decision about multiple items, research suggests that they will conduct a more extensive search with less variability in search patterns than if the decision involves the purchase or use of only one item.[113]

MARKETING IMPLICATIONS The extent to which consumers search for external information has important implications for marketing strategy. First, if many consumers tend to search extensively for a particular product or service, marketers can facilitate the decision process by making information readily available and easily accessible at the lowest cost and with the least consumer effort. To do this, marketers should look at the design of their product packaging, Web sites, ads, and other promotional materials with an eye toward providing information that will alter consumers' attitudes and change their buying behavior. This can be accomplished by providing information about salient and diagnostic attributes, particularly if the brand has a differential advantage. Otherwise, if consumers cannot get the information they need, they may eliminate the brand from their consideration set.

Marketers should also segment the market for any product or service according to search activity. For example, one study found six clusters of searchers in the

EXHIBIT 9.8
In-Store Kiosks Increase Search Opportunity
This in-store kiosk makes it very easy for consumers to collect information on cosmetics while they are shopping.

Source: © Mark Richards/ PhotoEdit.

purchase of a car.[114] Once marketers determine which types of search activities are most likely to occur for their product or service, they can plan to meet the information needs of the consumers in targeted segments. Low-search consumers, for example, will focus on getting a good deal, whereas high searchers will need a lot of attention and information to offset their low levels of confidence and prior satisfaction. Marketers can be very selective in providing low searchers with information, emphasizing only those attributes that are most salient and diagnostic.

Marketers can attempt to stimulate external search by providing information in a highly accessible manner (see Exhibit 9.8). The information kiosk in Exhibit 9.8 makes it very easy for consumers to access company information while they are shopping for cosmetics. For example, the cosmetics retailer Sephora installed in-store interactive kiosks so consumers can quickly and easily access product information, and the Jiffy Lube chain installed Web-enabled kiosks to help customers educate themselves about automotive products.[115] Such opportunities for additional search may lead low searchers to information that will change their attitudes and affect their buying decisions. Marketers can also provide consumers with incentives to search. To illustrate, after Gap.com posted an online coupon good only in Gap stores, the chain was flooded with consumers clutching coupons as they examined merchandise.[116] ●

What Kind of Information Is Acquired in External Search?

Researchers are interested in the types of information that consumers acquire during an external search because this information can potentially play a crucial role in influencing the consumers' judgments and decision making. When searching external sources, consumers usually acquire information about brand name, price, and other attributes.

Brand Name Brand name is the most frequently accessed type of information because it is a central node around which other information can be organized in memory.[117] Thus when we know the brand name, we can immediately activate other relevant nodes. For example, if we know the brand name is Allstate, American Airlines, or IBM, we can draw on a wealth of prior knowledge and associations. Many Internet companies, after seeing the success of Amazon.com, are working hard to build brand name awareness.

Price Consumers search for price information not only because it tends to be diagnostic but also because it can be used to make inferences about other attributes such as quality and value.[118] However, the search for price is less important than we might expect (due to the low overall extent of search), and does not become more important when price variations increase and costs are higher.[119] Furthermore, the importance of price can depend on the culture. As an example, consumers in Japan have not traditionally been fond of discounters. However, they now flock to Fast Retailing and other discount stores to search for the best bargains.[120]

Other Attributes After searching for brand name and price, consumers will search for additional information depending on which attributes are salient and diagnostic in the product or service category. U.S. consumers typically look for reliability, durability, and low price in selecting a car.[121]

Consumers are more likely to access information that is relevant to their goals. For example, if a major goal in choosing a vacation is to maximize excitement, a consumer would probably collect information about a location's available activities, nightlife, and visitors. When consumers switch goals from one purchase occasion to the next, as when looking for an economy car versus one that is fast, the search they perform for the second task is more efficient because they can transfer the knowledge from the first task.[122]

Is External Search Always Accurate?

Consumers can be just as biased in their search for external information as they are during internal search. In particular, consumers tend to search for external information that confirms rather than disconfirms their overall beliefs. In one study, consumers with a strong price-quality belief tended to search more for higher-priced brands.[123] Unfortunately, confirmation bias can lead consumers to avoid important information, resulting in a less-than-optimal decision outcome. Thus if a lower-priced, high-quality brand were available, consumers might never acquire information about it and therefore never select it for purchase.

MARKETING IMPLICATIONS Marketers have to ensure that the specific information consumers seek is easily and readily available. They can do this by emphasizing the information in advertising, on a package, in pamphlets, on Web sites, or through the sales force. In addition, companies must remember that consumers are less likely to choose a brand that performs poorly on attributes that are accessed frequently. Therefore, marketers should be sure that their offerings perform well on attributes that are heavily accessed. Finally, some companies are paying Web search sites such as Yahoo! to return their brand information in a prominent position when consumers perform certain key word searches. To avoid misleading consumers—and to prevent the brands from losing credibility—Yahoo! separates these paid listings in a special "Sponsored Match" section.[124] •

How Do We Engage in External Search?

External search follows a series of sequential steps that can provide further insight into the consumer's decision. These steps include orientation, or getting an overview of the product display; evaluation, or comparing options on key attributes; and verification, or confirming the choice.[125] Researchers have examined the order of information acquisition during evaluation, in particular, because they assume that information acquired earlier in the decision process plays a more significant role than information acquired later.[126] For example, once a brand emerges as the leader early in the search process, subsequent information acquisition and evaluation is distorted in favor of that brand.[127]

Search Stages Consumers tend to access different sources at different stages of the search process. In the early stages, mass media and marketer-related sources tend to be more influential, while interpersonal sources are more critical when the actual decision is made.[128] Consumers are more likely to access information that is especially salient, diagnostic, and goal-related earlier in the search process. However, if they can recall salient, diagnostic information from memory, they will have little need to search for it externally. Thus consumers will search first for information on attributes that provoke greater uncertainty or are less favorable.[129] Consumers also tend to search first for brands that have a higher perceived attractiveness, again pointing to the importance of developing positive attitudes. Finally, research indicates that consumers who are new to a product or service category will start by searching for information about low-risk, well-known brands, progress to a search of lesser-known brands, and then consolidate the information leading to a preference for brands that provide the greatest utility.[130]

searching by brand Collecting information on one brand before moving to another.

searching by attribute Comparing brands on attributes, one at a time.

Searching by Brand or Attribute Two major types of processes are (1) **searching by brand,** in which consumers acquire all the needed information on one brand before moving on to the next, and (2) **searching by attribute,** in which consumers compare brands one attribute at a time.[131] A good example of the latter strategy is price-comparison shopping. Consumers generally prefer to process by attribute because it is simpler and easier.

Also, consumers are very sensitive to the manner in which information is stored in memory and the format in which it is presented in the store.[132] If information is organized by brand, as is the case in most stores where all the information is on packages, consumers will process information by brand. Experts, in particular, tend to process by brand because they have more brand-based knowledge. The fact that consumers are accustomed to processing by brand may bias processing, however, even when information is organized by attribute.[133] In addition, different search strategies affect our decision process differently.[134] Consumers who process by brand remain high in uncertainty until the very end of the search process, whereas those who search by attribute gradually reduce their uncertainty.

Nevertheless, consumers with less knowledge will take advantage of opportunities to process by attribute; for example, by viewing information in a matrix in *Consumer Reports* or in another format that simplifies searching (see Exhibit 9.9). One study found that presenting lists of nutritional information in the grocery store is popular with consumers. The *Consumer Reports'* Rating Charts, which provide information about the top brands and best buys in various product categories in a simple format, is a popular source of information. Another example is *Computer Shopper Magazine,* which presents detailed feature and pricing information to help consumers select a PC. Internet search sites and shopping agents also make it easier for consumers to process by attribute, especially price.

EXHIBIT 9.9
Sources of Consumer Information
Consumer Reports publishes information on the best computer-related products, which makes it easier for consumers to compare brands.

Source:© 2003 by Consumers Union of U.S., Inc. Yonkers, NY 10703-1057, a nonprofit organization. Reprinted with permission from the March 2003 issue of Consumer Reports® for educational purposes only. No commercial use or phtocopying permitted. To learn more about Consumers Union, log onto www.ConsumersReports.org <http://www.ConsumerReports.org>

SUMMARY

This chapter examined the three initial stages of the consumer judgment and decision-making process. Problem recognition, the first stage, is the perceived difference between an ideal state and the actual state. When a discrepancy exists between these two states, the consumer may be motivated to resolve it by engaging in decision making.

Internal search is the recall of information, experiences, and feelings from memory. The extent of internal search generally increases as motivation (involvement, perceived risk), ability (knowledge and experience), and opportunity (lack of time pressure and distractions) increase. Researchers are examining which brands, attributes, evaluations, and experiences consumers recall. In general, aspects that are more salient, diagnostic, vivid, and related to goals are the most likely to be recalled. Several biases exist in internal search: confirmation bias, in which information that reinforces our overall beliefs is remembered; inhibition, in which the recall of some information can inhibit the recall of other attributes; and mood, which refers to our tendency to recall mood-congruent information.

When consumers need more information or are uncertain about recalled information, they engage in external search, acquiring information from outside sources. Two types of external search are prepurchase search (in response to problem recognition) and ongoing search (which continues regardless of problem recognition). During external search, consumers can acquire information from retailers, the media, other people, independent sources, and by experiencing the product. Retailer and media search account for the highest level of search activity, but interpersonal sources increase in importance as consumer knowledge decreases and normative factors increase. Consumers find the Internet a fast and convenient way to search for information.

The extent of external search can vary widely, depending on motivation, ability, and opportunity to search, but it is usually rather limited. Consumers will conduct a more extensive search when they have a higher motivation and opportunity to process information. Situational factors affect the consumer's opportunity to process the information. Brand name and price are the most accessed attributes in an external search. Consumers also tend to exhibit a confirmation bias in their external search. More salient and diagnostic information tends to be accessed earlier. Finally, consumers tend to process either by brand or by attribute. Attribute search is easier and preferred, but often the information is not organized to facilitate such processing.

QUESTIONS FOR REVIEW AND DISCUSSION

1. How does a discrepancy between the ideal state and the actual state affect consumer behavior?
2. What factors affect the inclusion of brands in the consideration set, and why would a company want its brand in the consideration set?
3. How does confirmation bias operate in internal and external searches for information?
4. What six broad groups of sources can consumers consult during external search? Where does the Internet fit in these groups?
5. How do involvement, perceived risk, perceived costs and benefits, and the consideration set affect a consumer's motivation to conduct an external search?
6. When would a consumer be more likely to conduct an external search by brand rather than by attribute? Which search process would a marketer prefer consumers to use—and why?

EXERCISES

1. Find 20 magazine, television, or radio advertisements that you think are trying to instigate problem recognition in consumers. Then group these ads into those you think are (a) trying to influence the ideal state and (b) trying to create dissatisfaction with the actual state. Relate each group of ads to the factors discussed in the chapter on influencing the ideal state and the actual state. Which types of ads do you think are effective and why?
2. Interview five consumers to determine their knowledge about a product or service category for which you think motivation, ability, and opportunity to process are high. Ask consumers to discuss:
   a. all the brands they would consider
   b. what they know about each brand
   c. their evaluations of each brand
   d. any prior experiences they have relative to these brands

After obtaining this information, ask consumers which brand they would choose if they had to pick one right now and whether they would want any additional information before deciding. Finally, analyze this information in terms of the principles discussed in this chapter: recall of brands, attributes, evaluations, and experiences. Do your findings support or contradict these concepts? If so, why? How does internal search relate to the desire for external search?

3. Interview five consumers about their external search activity regarding a product or service category for which you think motivation, ability, and opportunity to search are high. Be sure to ask them questions about
   - **a.** which brands they would search for information on
   - **b.** which types of information they would look for
   - **c.** what sources of information they would use
   - **d.** how much time they would take

Analyze the answers in terms of the external search principles discussed in this chapter: the extent, content, and sources of search. Do your findings support or contradict these concepts?

chapter 10

Judgment and Decision Making Based on High Consumer Effort

INTRODUCTION: Wheels and Deals in Thailand

In Bangkok, Thailand, a DaimlerChrysler salesperson races to complete paperwork on a new Jeep sport-utility vehicle because the customer has been told by her astrologer that she must drive her new vehicle away at exactly 7:49 A.M. With minutes to spare, the deal is closed and the keys are handed over. Another consumer chooses a DaimlerChrysler sport-utility vehicle over a Land Rover because of its durability, powerful engine, and price (half the cost of a Land Rover).

These are two typical occurrences in a country that is one of the world's hottest automotive markets (see Exhibit 10.1). Thais are passionate about their vehicles, listing them as the fifth necessity behind food, lodging, medicine, and clothing. In fact, Thailand is the world's second-largest market for pickup trucks, trailing only the United States. Consequently, many U.S. and Japanese auto companies, including Toyota, Honda, and General Motors, are engaged in a highly competitive battle for market share in Thailand and other Southeast Asian countries.

In addition to selling a large number of dual-cab pickups in Thailand, Toyota launched its Thai-made Altis sedan at the Bangkok auto show. The Altis features details normally found in more expensive cars, which positions the model closer to Toyota's luxury Lexus brand. Honda is also active in the Thai market, where its best-selling models are compact cars and sport-utility vehicles. General Motors produces its Zafira compact minivan in a plant south of Bangkok, and the model's popularity in Europe is attracting considerable interest among Thai consumers.[1]

These manufacturers will succeed in Thailand only if they pay close attention to what consumers want. For example, many consumers have a positive impression of U.S.-made Jeep sport-utility vehicles. Yet only the wealthy in Thailand can afford these models, and many of these peo-

EXHIBIT 10.1
Traffic in Bangkok
Thai consumers are very passionate about their automobiles despite having other means of transportation.

Source: Getty Images.

ple do not do their own driving. And the back seat of such vehicles is not designed for those who spend the day conducting business over the phone while their drivers navigate potholes.

This example points out the importance of understanding the consumer's judgment and decision-making process. Marketers must understand the types of judgments consumers make (vehicles made in the United States must be good) and what types of criteria are important in influencing consumers' decisions (durability, back seat comfort, what others think or say about the purchase, and so on). In addition, marketers must understand the emotions and feelings that influence consumer decisions.

Consumer judgment and decision making when motivation, ability, and opportunity to process are high represent the next stages in the overall model of consumer behavior (see Exhibit 10.2) and are the focus of this chapter. By carefully analyzing the factors that enter into judgment and decision making, marketers can acquire valuable insights that help them develop and market offerings to consumers. ●

HIGH-EFFORT JUDGMENT PROCESSES

judgments Estimating the likelihood of an event or making evaluations.

decision making Making a selection between options or courses of action.

Think about the last time you went to a restaurant. While reviewing the menu, you probably considered some items and thought about how good they would be before making your final choice. In doing so, you were making **judgments,** evaluations or estimates regarding the likelihood of events. Judgments are a critical input into the decision process.

Judgment and **decision making** are often confused with one another. In a consumer context, *judgments* are evaluations or estimates regarding the likelihood that products and services possess certain features or will perform in a certain manner.[2] Judgments do not require the consumer to make a decision. Thus if you see an ad for a new Mexican restaurant, you can form a judgment as to whether you will like it or not, how similar to or different from other Mexican restaurants it is, or how expensive it is. These judgments can serve as input into your decision on whether or not to eat there, but they do not require an actual choice.

In addition, judgment and decision making can involve us in different processes. One study found that consumers searched attributes in a different order during a judgment task as opposed to a decision task.[3] In another study, higher levels of brand familiarity made it easier for consumers to remember information for a judgment but lowered memory in a decision task.[4] Consumers can also act on different preferences depending on whether the task involves choice or a judgment (especially when the product category is unfamiliar).[5] Given the importance of judgment in consumers' information processing, researchers are increasingly examining judgment processes, particularly estimations of likelihood, judgments of goodness or badness, and predictions of the likelihood that two events will occur together.

Judgments of Likelihood and Goodness/Badness

estimation of likelihood Judging how likely it is that something will occur.

An **estimation of likelihood** is our determination of the probability that something will occur. Estimations of likelihood appear in many consumer contexts. For example, when we buy a product or service, we can attempt to estimate its quality and the likelihood that it will satisfy our needs. When we buy clothing, we can estimate the likelihood that others will approve of it. When

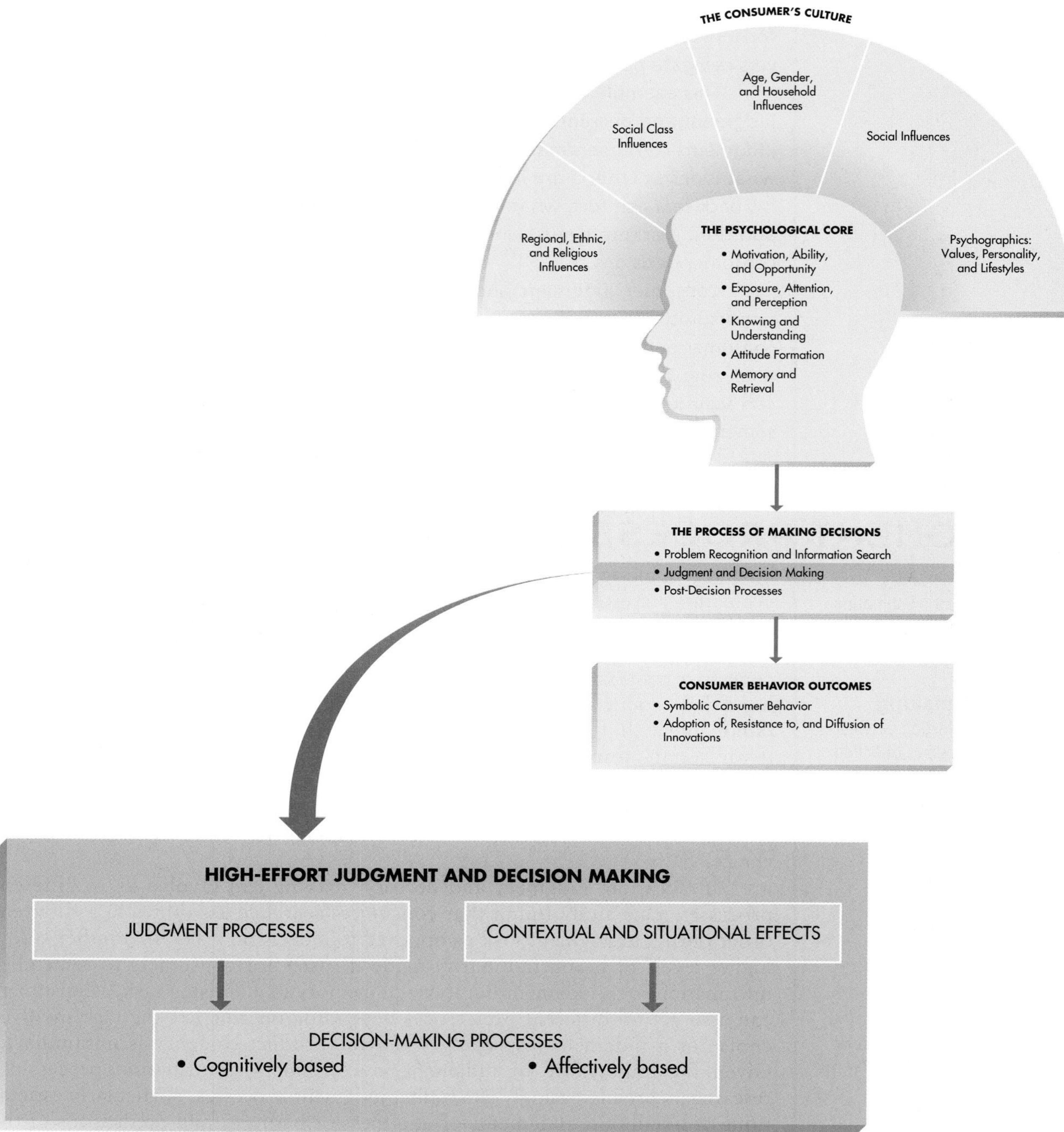

EXHIBIT 10.2
Chapter Overview: Judgment and Decision Making: High Consumer Effort

After problem recognition and search, consumers can engage in some form of judgment or decision making, which can vary in terms of processing effort (from high to low). This chapter looks at high-effort judgment and decision processes. Judgments involve making estimates of how likely something is to occur or how good or bad something is. They serve as inputs into decision making, which can be cognitively or affectively based. The decision-making process can also be influenced by contextual factors such as consumer characteristics, task characteristics, decision framing, and group presence.

we view an ad, we can assess the likelihood that it is truthful. The key point is that estimations of likelihood are at the very core of consumer information processing.

judgment of goodness/badness Evaluating the desirability of something.

Judgments of goodness/badness are the consumer's evaluation of the desirability of product or service features. As an example, in planning a trip we might judge how good or bad it is that Europe is fun and expensive. Most of the research on this kind of judgment has been done in the context of the attitude models covered in Chapter 6. These models suggest that a consumer combines individual judgments into an overall evaluation of goodness or badness in order to form an attitude about the product or service.

anchoring and adjustment process Starting with an initial evaluation and adjusting it with additional information.

Anchoring and Adjustment In making estimations of likelihood and goodness/badness, consumers tend to employ an **anchoring and adjustment process.**[6] They will first anchor the judgment based on some initial value and then make adjustments or "update" the evaluation as they consider additional information. The initial value can be information or an affective response that is readily available from memory or it can be attribute information from the external environment that is encountered first.[7] Consumer values and normative influences can also be strong determinants of the initial value.

To illustrate, Starbucks Coffee has a very positive image in Japan. This factor led a local chain to change its name to Seattle Coffee, hoping to form a positive initial anchor that would encourage consumers to see the shops as similar to Starbucks. Additional information from ads or experience may adjust this initial value upward or downward, but the judgment is more likely to be positive given the Starbucks image. If the prior evaluation of Starbucks had been negative, however, the anchor would most likely have resulted in a negative judgment of quality. Thus the same anchor can lead to two different judgments depending on how it is perceived.

The nature of the initial anchor is extremely important, because it greatly affects the outcome of the judgment. In one study, consumers were asked to make judgments about ground-beef samples. Researchers told one group that the beef was 75 percent lean and told another that it was 25 percent fat. Even though these two statements contain identical information, the "lean" group produced significantly more positive ratings than the "fat" group.[8] We discuss this process, known as *framing,* in more detail later in the chapter.

Anchoring and adjustment can occur in two other ways as well. First, when products are *bundled*—with two or more items offered together—the most important item serves as the anchor, and consumers make adjustments based on evaluations of the remaining items.[9] Second, when low-ability or low-knowledge consumers are evaluating *new* products, they give greater weight to information acquired later in the process, an example of the recency effect.[10]

imagery Imagining an event in order to make a judgment.

Imagery, or visualization, can also play a significant role in the judgment process. Consumers can attempt to construct an image of an event, such as how they will look and feel behind the wheel of a new car, to estimate its likelihood or judge its goodness or badness. Interestingly, visualizing an event can actually make it seem more likely, because consumers may form a positive bias when they imagine themselves using the product.[11] Imagery may also lead consumers to overestimate how satisfied they will be with a product or service.[12] Moreover, when consumers who anticipated satisfaction engaged in imagery, they allocated more mental resources to vivid attributes and weighed those attributes more heavily in forming preferences.[13]

Biases in Judgment Processes If consumers are susceptible to a confirmation bias and they acquire and process only confirming evidence, they become more confident in their judgment than they would be if they acquired negative information. This bias can lead to less-than-optimal choices for future purchases. When consumers are overconfident, they are unlikely to engage in external information search, because they believe that they know almost everything.[14] A study on AIDS found that consumers can have a self-positivity bias ("I am less likely to get AIDS than others") but that this bias can be reduced if important information is made more accessible.[15]

Mood can also have a biasing effect on judgment.[16] Essentially, your mood serves as the initial anchor for your judgment. If you are in a good mood when shopping for a CD, you are more likely to like the new music you hear. One reason for this effect is that consumers want to preserve a good mood and therefore avoid negative information.

In addition, prior brand evaluations can bias judgments. When consumers judge a brand to be good—based on past exposure—they may subsequently fail to learn (and view as important) information about the brand's attributes that are diagnostic of its actual quality.[17] In effect, the favorable brand name "blocks" learning of the product's attributes that really reveal its quality.

MARKETING IMPLICATIONS Marketers can increase the probability that judgments of their products and services are being anchored by a positive initial value by focusing the consumer's attention on certain attributes. For example, even though most consumers will not be able to afford digital TV for a while, a number of electronics firms are heavily advertising this product because it will define the industry leaders—the initial anchor—for years to come.[18] Our judgment of a product can also be affected by our exposure to other products.[19] Thus placing a picture of a low-priced car like the Nissan Altima alongside a Jaguar could make the Jaguar serve as the judgment anchor.

A product's country of origin can serve as an anchor and influence subsequent judgments.[20] For example, the Italian government has spent $25 million on ads to convince consumers that Italian fashions are the finest.[21] In China, domestic brands have had to mount marketing campaigns because consumers now prefer Western versions of the same product.[22] In recent years, U.S.-based Procter & Gamble, Mary Kay Cosmetics, and Avon have successfully captured market share from Chinese brands, as have Japan's Shiseido and Germany's Henkel.[23]

Priming consumers with positive feelings before giving them information will lead them to

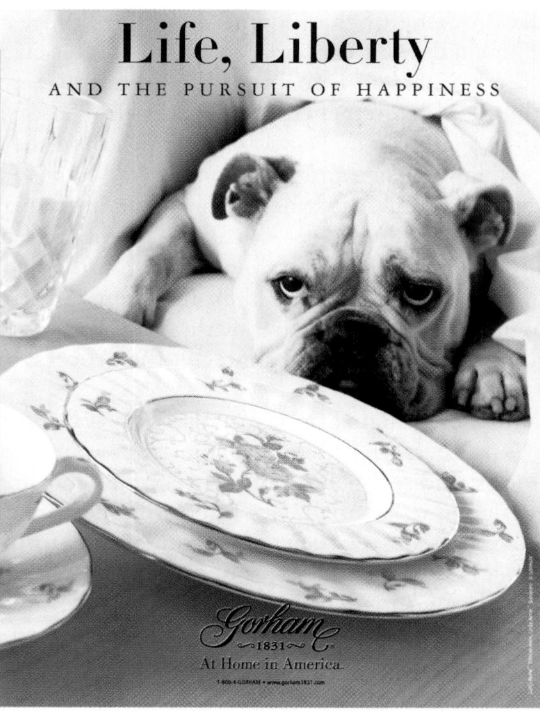

Life, Liberty
AND THE PURSUIT OF HAPPINESS
Gorham
1831
At Home in America.

EXHIBIT 10.3
Anchoring a Judgment
The light humor created by the unhappy dog who doesn't get to lick the plate attempts to prime consumers with positive feelings. Marketers hope consumers will evaluate Gorham china positively as well.

Source: Used by permission of Lenox, Incorporated. © Lenox Incorporated 2002.

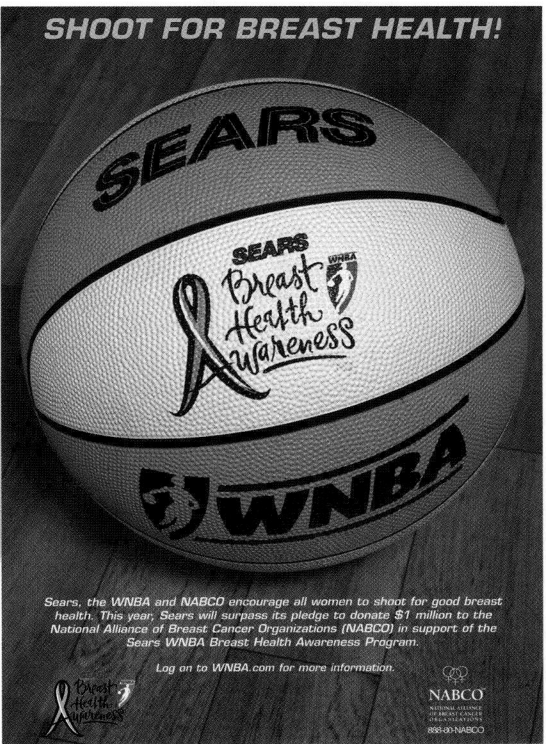
SHOOT FOR BREAST HEALTH!
SEARS
SEARS
Breast Health Awareness
WNBA
Sears, the WNBA and NABCO encourage all women to shoot for good breast health. This year, Sears will surpass its pledge to donate $1 million to the National Alliance of Breast Cancer Organizations (NABCO) in support of the Sears WNBA Breast Health Awareness Program.
Log on to WNBA.com for more information.
Breast Health Awareness
NABCO
NATIONAL ALLIANCE OF BREAST CANCER ORGANIZATIONS
888-80-NABCO

EXHIBIT 10.4
Publicizing Good Works
Companies can contribute to good causes through various activities. When a company publicizes its good works, consumers may develop positive feelings toward the company and, in turn, be more apt to purchase its products and services. In this ad, the WNBA and Sears announce their efforts to support Breast Health Awareness.

Source: Reprinted with permission of WNBA Enterprises, LLC.

evaluate the product or service more positively.[24] The humorous ad in Exhibit 10.3 is a good example of this strategy. Salespeople also prime consumers by recommending (or raving about) a particular product or service. Companies can publicize their good works as is the case of Sears in Exhibit 10.4. Tobacco companies in Hungary are promoting a more positive image by giving money to schools, hospitals, and the Red Cross.[25] Finally, ads suggesting that consumers engage in imagery—like imagining a delicious pizza—can also produce positive judgments.

The judgment process has important implications for the introduction of brand extensions. Consumers reacted so positively to the Martha Stewart brand that the company has expanded it to cover an empire of products and services, including merchandise at Kmart and Zellers, a Martha Stewart by Mail catalog, MarthaStewart.com, *Martha Stewart Living* magazine, and "Ask Martha" newspaper columns.[26] As this example shows, when consumers are exposed to a brand extension, the existing brand name and its positive associations serve as a positive anchor for subsequent judgments of the new product. ●

Conjunctive Probability Assessment

conjunctive probability assessment Estimating the extent to which two events will occur together.

Sometimes consumers estimate the likelihood that two events will occur simultaneously or that a relationship exists between attributes. This estimate is called **conjunctive probability assessment.** Research shows that prior expectations influence its accuracy.[27] For example, consumers might expect that a rich flavor means high calories or that nationally advertised brands are of higher quality than regional ones. When consumers use diagnostic attributes, their judgment improves because they can detect actual relationships between variables. For instance, experts are less guided by country-of-origin stereotypes and more by actual attributes when information is unambiguous.[28]

illusory correlation When consumers think two things occur together when they actually do not.

Sometimes, however, consumers are not adept at making conjunctive probability judgments, and they think a relationship exists when in fact it does not.[29] Such **illusory correlation** is apt to occur when information is ambiguous. To illustrate, just as smokers mistakenly thought "clean," smokeless cigarettes were safer, they may also mistakenly believe that low-toxin and natural cigarettes are safer.[30] This can set up ethical issues, as Chapter 21 discusses. On the other hand, companies need to address inaccuracies that affect their marketing of goods and services. For example, Korean cars and electronic products were originally introduced as budget brands, and now brands such as Hyundai must overcome the perception of low quality as they move into more upscale markets.[31]

HIGH-EFFORT DECISION-MAKING PROCESSES

inept set Options that are unacceptable when making a decision.

inert set Options toward which consumers are indifferent.

In any consumer choice situation, consumers face many available options. Often, they must choose from a set of products, services, brands, or courses of action. At that point, consumers will evaluate the options in the consideration set, find those in the **inept set** unacceptable, and treat those in the **inert set** with indifference.[32] Consumers must also decide how and when to dispose of products and services. Thus to engage in most forms of consumer behavior, consumers must make some type of decision—even if they decide not to choose, which they may do when a great deal of uncertainty exists.[33]

Much of the extensive research on consumer decision making has investigated how we combine the information acquired from internal and external search to make a decision. Researchers have proposed various models of the decision-making process. A basic assumption underlying many of these models is that consumers behave in a cognitive and rational manner, choosing the brand or service with the best combination of features to satisfy their needs. Thus when buying a new stereo, consumers might investigate a set of brands in terms of reliability, power, warranty, and any other salient attributes before selecting the one that maximizes their utility.

Many times, however, consumers do not operate in such a rational manner. In high-elaboration situations, strong feelings might compel a consumer to buy a new CD or a new pair of shoes, even though he or she already has many. Therefore, consumer researchers have recently become interested in how choices are made when the decision is more hedonic or emotional in nature.

Another key finding is that the decision process can vary according to the situation because consumers are highly adaptive to the task.[34] Each choice situation can vary greatly, not only in terms of the types of brands and information evaluated but also in the consumers' motivation, ability, and opportunity (MAO) to process information. Thus the process consumers use to select a car is likely to be very different from the process they use to choose a house, a computer, or any other type of product or service. Furthermore, the type of decision context can change over time as new brands are introduced and information becomes outdated.

Finally, decision-making styles can vary across cultures.[35] Some North Americans, for example, tend to be analytical, to rely on factual information, and to search for solutions to problems. In contrast, in Asian cultures, and particularly in Japan, the *kimochi,* or feeling, generally has to be right; logic is sometimes less important. Similarly, many Saudi Arabians are more intuitive in their decision making and avoid persuasion based on empirical reasoning. Russians are said to place more emphasis on values than on facts, and Germans tend to be theoretical and deductive. In North American and European cultures, decisions are usually made by individuals who control their own fate. In Asian cultures the group is of primary importance, and actions arise at random or from other events, rather than being controlled by individuals.

A key point is that consumers do not follow a uniform process every time they make a decision.[36] Instead, they construct a strategy depending on the nature of the task, and they may employ various decision rules, either alone or in combination. As a result, even though a number of decision-making models have been proposed—including the cognitive and affective models described in the following sections—each may accurately describe decision making under certain circumstances.

HIGH-EFFORT THOUGHT-BASED DECISIONS

cognitive model The process by which consumers combine items of information about attributes to reach a decision.

Cognitive models describe the processes by which consumers combine items of information about attributes to reach a decision in a rational, systematic manner. The various models discussed here are not intended to describe the same process. Rather, they identify *different* processes that may occur when consumers make a decision. Which model a consumer follows depends on both the consumer and the nature of the situation. Furthermore, the situations that different models fit may lead to entirely different selections by the consumer. Finally, consumers may employ a combination of models rather than just one and may not necessarily be aware of the exact process they are following.

Types of Decision Processes

Cognitive models can be classified along two major dimensions: compensatory versus noncompensatory nature, and brand versus attribute processing.

compensatory model A mental cost-benefit analysis model used to make a decision.

Compensatory versus Noncompensatory Models With **compensatory models,** consumers choose the brand that has the greatest number of positive features relative to negative. These models are essentially a type of mental cost-benefit analysis. A key feature is that a negative evaluation on one attribute can be compensated for (hence the name *compensatory*) by positive features on others. To illustrate, for some U.S. consumers, a negative feature of Japanese products is that they are made in another country. However, this shortcoming can be overcome if the products rate highly on other aspects, such as reliability and price.

noncompensatory model Simple decision model in which negative information leads to rejection of the option.

In contrast, with a **noncompensatory model,** negative information leads the consumer to immediately reject the brand or service from the consideration set. In the preceding example, knowing that a product is foreign-made might prevent some consumers from considering it further. Noncompensatory models are easier to implement and require less cognitive effort and strain than compensatory models do.

Brand versus Attribute Models In making a decision, consumers may evaluate *one brand at a time.* Thus, a consumer making a computer purchase might collect information about an IBM computer and make a judgment about it before moving on to the next brand. This type of **brand processing** occurs frequently because the environment—including advertising, dealerships, and so on—is often organized by brands.

brand processing Evaluating one brand at a time.

attribute processing Comparing brands, one attribute at a time.

Attribute processing, on the other hand, occurs when consumers compare across brands, *one attribute at a time.* A good example is price-comparison shopping in which consumers compare each brand on price and select the one with the desired price. Most consumers prefer attribute processing because it is easier than brand processing; however they are not always able to find information available in a manner that facilitates it.

Exhibit 10.5 classifies various cognitive models of decision making according to these two major dimensions.

Compensatory Brand-Processing Models

multiattribute (expectancy-value) model A type of brand-based compensatory model.

Much research has focused on brand-based compensatory models, also called **multiattribute models.** One multiattribute model, the theory of reasoned action (TORA), was discussed in Chapter 6. Under TORA, consumers' attitudes toward an intended act, coupled with their belief about what significant people

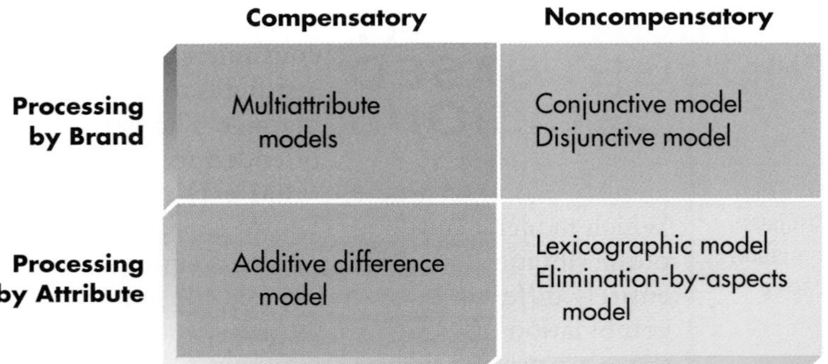

Compensatory
Noncompensatory
Processing by Brand
Multiattribute models
Conjunctive model
Disjunctive model
Processing by Attribute
Additive difference model
Lexicographic model
Elimination-by-aspects model

EXHIBIT 10.5
Types of Cognitive Choice Models
Cognitive decision-making models can be classified along two major dimensions: (a) whether processing occurs one brand at a time or one attribute at a time, and (b) whether they are compensatory (bad attributes can be compensated for by good ones) or noncompensatory (a bad attribute eliminates the brand).

in their lives think is appropriate behavior, predict their intentions of buying, using, or disposing of a product/service.

Various other multiattribute models have been proposed.[37] These models differ in the components they include, usually one or more of these three: (1) belief strength, (2) evaluation, and (3) the importance consumers attach to the attribute or outcome. The boxed insert on page 234 discusses a multiattribute model based mainly on belief strength and importance.

MARKETING IMPLICATIONS Because they identify the beliefs consumers have about the outcomes or attributes associated with buying, using, or disposing of a product or about the attributes that characterize the product, brand-based compensatory models are very useful in identifying which alternatives consumers may choose or reject. These models also help marketers understand which outcomes or attributes associated with the product need to be reinforced or changed.

If consumers do not strongly believe that positive outcomes or attributes are associated with a decision, marketers should stress these outcomes or attributes in their marketing activities so as to strengthen consumers' beliefs. For example, DaimlerChrysler markets its ultracompact smart car in Europe and Japan by stressing fuel efficiency and ease of parking and maneuvering. This helps consumers recognize the positive benefits that compensate for the car's small size.[38]

If marketers analyzing consumer decisions find product weaknesses, they should address these shortcomings by altering the product and communicating the improvements to consumers. For instance, because Ford is a highly trusted brand in Europe, it is attempting to improve Jaguar's quality image by acknowledging that Ford makes Jaguar cars.[39] However, while companies that make changes to remove competitive disadvantages are often able to draw consumers from competitive offerings, they are also reducing differentiation. Therefore, marketers should consider the long-term effects of improvements.[40]

Decision models also help marketers identify weaknesses of competitors which can then be targeted in marketing communications, especially comparative ads. This is important because research shows that consumers with little commitment to a brand will put more weight on negative information because they perceive it as more diagnostic.[41] To illustrate, Ford wanted to induce doubt on the part of Japanese consumers not committed to Volkswagen when it asked in an ad campaign, "Why is the Golf so expensive in Japan?"[42] Facing fierce competition from Lowe's and other rivals that advertise good customer service and product selection, the retail chain Home Depot is countering negative perceptions of clutter and inconsistent customer service by removing wooden pallets from store aisles and restocking shelves during late night or early morning hours so salespeople can focus on customers.[43] ●

Compensatory Attribute-Processing Models

additive difference model Compensatory model in which brands are compared by attribute, two brands at a time.

According to the **additive difference model,** brands are compared by attribute, *two brands at a time.*[44] Consumers evaluate differences between brands on each attribute and then combine them into an overall preference. This process allows trade-offs between attributes—that is, a positive difference on one attribute can offset a negative difference on another.

MARKETING IMPLICATIONS The additive difference model helps marketers determine which attributes or outcomes exhibit the greatest differences among brands—information they can use to improve and properly position their brand. If a brand is performing below a major competitor on a particular attribute, the company needs to enhance consumers' beliefs about its product's superiority. For example, after being vigorously attacked by Dell on the basis of price, Compaq improved its competitive position significantly on this attribute.

On the other hand, if a brand is performing significantly better than competitors on a key attribute, marketers should enhance consumer beliefs by positioning the product or service around this advantage. DaimlerChrysler's smart car, for instance, costs less than $10,000 in Europe and gets high fuel efficiency because of its small size.[45] In South Africa, the fast-food restaurant Africa Hut has become extremely popular because it differs from all other competitors on one key attribute: it serves traditional local dishes such as pap (corn porridge), malamagodu (tripe), morogo (a leafy green vegetable), and skop (sheep's head).[46] ●

Noncompensatory Brand-Processing Models

The compensatory models we have discussed require consumers to exert a significant amount of effort to evaluate each brand on many attributes. Often consumers are not willing to put forth this much effort and instead opt for a simpler noncompensatory process. With noncompensatory brand-processing models, consumers use key attributes to evaluate brands and then eliminate those that are not adequate on any one attribute.[47] These models are called noncompensatory because a negative rating on a key attribute means that the brand is eliminated.

cutoff level For each attribute, the point at which a brand is rejected with a noncompensatory model.

A common feature of noncompensatory models is that the decision process proceeds in a simple, sequential manner. Consumers set up **cutoff levels** for each attribute and reject a brand if it is below the cutoff. For example, gamblers love to pull the lever on "one-armed bandits" and therefore have rejected electronic slot machines.[48] Consumers tend to choose cutoffs that set up the largest difference between accepted and rejected alternatives. Noncompensatory models can be differentiated in terms of cutoff levels and whether the comparison proceeds by brand or by attribute.

conjunctive model A noncompensatory model that sets minimum cutoffs to reject "bad" options.

Conjunctive Model Using a **conjunctive model,** consumers set up minimum cutoffs for each attribute that represent the absolute lowest value they are willing to accept.[49] For example, a consumer might seek to pay less than $20 per month to charge a brief vacation and reject an alternative that costs more than that monthly payment level. The Carnival cruise line has therefore arranged financing to allow consumers to charge a $299 three-day cruise and pay $14 per month for two years. "Some people still perceive cruising as too expensive," explains a Carnival executive. "This just helps us get over that hurdle."[50] Because the cutoffs represent the bare minimum belief strength levels, the psychology of a conjunctive model is to rule out unsuitable alternatives as soon as possible. Consumers will weigh negative information to accomplish this.

disjunctive model A noncompensatory model that sets acceptable cutoffs to find options that are "good."

Disjunctive Model The **disjunctive model** is similar to the conjunctive model with two important exceptions. First, the consumer sets up acceptable levels for the cutoffs—levels that are more desirable. Thus, although $20 per month may be the highest monthly payment a consumer will accept for a vacation, $14 per month may represent a more acceptable level. Second, the consumer bases evaluations on several of the most important attributes, rather than on all, putting the weight on positive information.

MARKETING IMPLICATIONS Identifying consumers' cutoff levels can be very useful for marketers. If a product or service is beyond any of the cutoffs many consumers set, it will be rejected frequently. Therefore, marketers must change consumers' beliefs about these attributes. Until recently many consumers could not afford a cell phone because it was expensive enough to fall beyond the cutoff on price. But now companies offer no-monthly-fee, prepaid packages, allowing many consumers to get phones.[51] As another example, General Motors is trying to move its $80,000 Hummer sport-utility vehicle below the affordability cutoff level by incorporating many Chevy parts to create a smaller version that sells for about $50,000.[52]

In addition, research suggests that marketers can hurt themselves by adding unwanted or unneeded features to products or services because these give the consumer a reason for rejecting the brand.[53] One study found that when two brands offered collector's plate and golf umbrella premiums, the brands were less desirable than when the offer was not made.[54] ●

Noncompensatory Attribute-Processing Models

Two noncompensatory models in which consumers process by attribute are the lexicographic and elimination-by-aspects models.

lexicographic model A noncompensatory model that compares brands by attributes, one at a time.

Lexicographic Model With the **lexicographic model,** consumers order attributes in terms of importance and compare the options one attribute at a time, starting with the most important. If one option dominates, the consumer selects it. If a tie develops, the consumer proceeds to the second most important attribute and continues in this way until only one option remains. Note that a tie occurs if the difference between two options on any attribute is below the just noticeable difference. Thus two brands that cost $2.77 and $2.79 would likely be seen as tied on price. Another common example of a lexicographic strategy is price-comparison shopping, where the most important attribute is, of course, price.

elimination-by-aspects model Similar to the lexicographic model but adds the notion of acceptable cutoffs.

Elimination-by-Aspects Model The **elimination-by-aspects model** is similar to the lexicographic model but incorporates the notion of an *acceptable cutoff*.[55] This model is not as strict as the lexicographic model and more attributes are likely to be considered. Consumers first order attributes in terms of importance and then compare options on the most important attribute. Those options below the cutoff are eliminated, and the consumer continues the process until one option remains.

MARKETING IMPLICATIONS Attribute-processing models not only aid in identifying determinant attributes but also provide additional information on the order in which attributes are evaluated. Thus if many consumers are employing a lexicographic model and a brand is weak on the most important attribute, the company needs to improve on this feature in order to be selected. For example, performance and reliability tend to be the two most critical attributes in the car market, which is why U.S. car manufacturers have had to emphasize these features so heavily to regain consumer confidence.

Marketers can try to change the order of importance so that a major brand advantage is the most critical attribute. Expensive sports cars work hard to do this by touting their performance on different attributes. DaimlerChrysler is promoting its Dodge Viper, for instance, on the basis of the extra-large 500-cubic-inch engine size, while Aston Martin trumpets the powerful V-12 engine of its Vanquish model and Lamborghini stresses the 200 mile-per-hour speed of its Diablo model (see Exhibit 10.6).[56] ●

Multiple Models That Characterize Decision Making

Consumers often use a combination of decision-making strategies.[57] In particular, when many options are available, consumers can use a noncompensatory strategy (conjunctive model) to reduce the size of the consideration set and eliminate poor options, and then use a more thorough model (a compensatory strategy) to evaluate the remaining ones. Or they might use bits and pieces of various strategies in constructing a decision process.[58] Consumers also tend to consolidate or stabilize their brand preferences as they make initial trade-offs in the decision process—preferences that remain stable as consumers continue using attributes to make subsequent choices among available options.[59] Moreover, as consumers learn more about the alternatives or about the decision task, they may change their strategy to adjust to their new knowledge by reordering the importance of attributes or employing a different strategy.[60] Thus consumers tend to be opportunistic and adaptive processors.

MARKETING IMPLICATIONS Given that different models can lead to different choices, marketers may sometimes want to change the process by which consumers make a decision. For example, if most consumers are using a compensatory strategy, switching them to a noncompensatory strategy may be advantageous, particularly if competitors have a major weakness. By convincing consumers not to accept a lower level on an important attribute—that is, not to compensate for the attribute—marketers can sometimes cause consumers to reject competitors from consideration. For example, Adidas

EXHIBIT 10.6
Stressing Performance
Manufacturers of expensive sports cars like to tout the high-performance features of their automobiles. Here is the expensive, high-performance Lamborghini Diablo.

Source: AP/Wide World Photos.

Illustration of Two Compensatory Models

Here's an example of one multiattribute model that uses belief strength and importance weights as its two components. Belief strength represents how strongly consumers hold each belief (some beliefs are held more strongly than others); importance weights represent how important each belief is to a decision (some beliefs are more important than others). The model can be outlined as follows:

$$A_b = \sum_{i=1} (b_i \times I_i)$$

where A_b represents an attitude toward the brand; b_i is the belief strength associated with attribute i, a judgment of likelihood; and I_i is the importance of the attribute. The model can easily be applied to a decision context if we assess A_b for each option in the consideration set. The consumer would choose the option for which he or she has the strongest attitude.

Consider the following example. Suppose Elena wants to go to graduate school at school A, school B, or school C and that the most salient attributes of each school she is considering are qualifications of the faculty, prestige, cost, and distance from home. As shown in the following exhibit, Elena rates b_i and I_i for each option, one at a time. The model then predicts that Elena will select school A because it is rated the most prestigious with the best faculty.

Using the *additive difference model,* Elena first compares school A and school B on the attribute of superior faculty. Using the b_i rating, for example, she finds a difference of +1. She moves on to the prestige attribute, where the difference is +2. Elena continues this process for the other attributes to get a total additive difference of +3, establishing a preference for school A. She repeats the process by comparing school A and school C, again finding that school A is seen as a better choice. (Note that because school A is seen as better than the other two choices, there is no need to compare school B and school C).

Remember that consumers do not formally make these ratings when they make a decision. The numbers are a way of quantifying the mental cost-benefit analysis that consumers might engage in. Nevertheless, compensatory models are useful in helping us identify which factors are most influential in making a decision.

	DESCRIPTION	OUTCOME OR CONSEQUENCES OF THE DECISION	HOW IMPORTANT IS EACH OUTCOME *(1 = not at all; 7 = very important)*	HOW STRONG IS ELENA'S BELIEF THAT THE OUTCOME CHARACTERIZES THE ALTERNATIVE *(−3 = very weak; +3 = very strong)*			ALTERNATIVE CHOSEN AND WHY
				SCHOOL A	***SCHOOL B***	***SCHOOL C***	
THE MULTI-ATTRIBUTE MODEL	Decisions are made by brand-based processing. Each alternative's outcome importance weight is multiplied by its belief strength. These totals are then summed across outcomes. The brand with the highest weighted score is chosen.	Has superior faculty	6	+3	+2	+3	School A is chosen because the sum of its importance weights times their outcome ratings [6x(+3)]+[4x(+3)]+[3x(−1)]+[2x(+1)]= 29. This value is higher than the summed products of the other alternatives (School B= [6x(+2)]+[4x(+1)]+[3x(+1)]+[2x(−1)]= 17, and School C= [6x(+3)]+[4x(−2)]+[3x(+2)]+[2x(0)]= 16).
		Is a more prestigious institution	4	+3	+1	−2	
		Has more expensive tuition	3	−1	+1	+2	
		Is far from home	2	+1	−1	0	
		Weighted Total (sum of each belief strength × its importance)		**29**	**17**	**16**	

			HOW DO THE BELIEF STRENGTH RATINGS COMPARE ACROSS ALTERNATIVES?			
	DESCRIPTION	**OUTCOME**	***SCHOOL A VS. SCHOOL B***	***SCHOOL A VS. SCHOOL C***	***SCHOOL B VS. SCHOOL C***	
THE ADDITIVE DIFFERENCE MODEL	Belief strengths about attributes are compared across brands. The brand with the highest total additive difference across the outcomes is chosen.	Has superior faculty	(+3)−(+2)=+1	(+3)−(+3)=0	(+2)−(+3)= −1	School A is chosen because the additive difference of its belief strength ratings compares more favorably with both School B (+3) and School C (+3). School B isn't seen as any better than School C (additive difference = 0).
		Is a more prestigious institution	(+3)−(+1)=+2	(+3)−(−2)=5	(+1)−(−2)=+3	
		Has more expensive tuition	(−1)−(+1)= −2	(−1)−(+2)= −3	(+1)−(+2)= −1	
		Is far from home	(+1)−(−1)=+2	(+1)−(0)=+1	(−1)−(0)= −1	
		Additive Difference	**+3**	**+3**	**0**	

EXHIBIT

How Elena Might Choose a Graduate School: Compensatory Models*

*Models are compensatory because, for any given alternative, a high rating on one outcome can compensate for a low rating on another outcome.

and Converse have attacked Nike with low-priced shoes, trying to get consumers to reject Nike on the basis of high price.[61]

When consumers are rejecting a brand with a noncompensatory strategy, marketers can try to switch them to a compensatory strategy by arguing that other attributes compensate for a negative. For instance, Precept MC Lady brand golf balls attracted considerable attention after a man used them to win a statewide tournament. Initially, men were put off by the feminine name. However, those who tried the balls liked their performance, and stores began referring to this brand as the "Laddie." The performance and the informal name change helped the MC Lady become America's top-selling golf ball.[62] ●

HIGH-EFFORT FEELING-BASED DECISIONS

The common feature of cognitive models is that decision making proceeds in a sequential and rational manner. Researchers are now increasingly realizing, however, that consumers also possess another processing mode in which they make decisions in a more holistic manner, on the basis of feelings or emotions.[63] In other words, consumers sometimes make decisions simply because they feel right, rather than as the result of a detailed and systematic evaluation. In fact, emotional processing can sometimes overwhelm rational thought and lead consumers to select something that is inconsistent with their rational preferences, making a decision they can sometimes regret later.[64] For instance, even in a poor economy, Japanese consumers bought more jewelry because it felt good.[65] Although our current knowledge of the role of **affective decision making** is still at a preliminary level, some general findings have emerged.

affective decision making Making decisions based on feelings and emotions.

As you saw in Chapter 6, brands can be associated with positive emotions such as love, joy, pride, and elation as well as with negative emotions such as guilt, hate, fear, anxiety, anger, sadness, shame, and greed. These emotions can be recalled to play a central role in the decision process, particularly when consumers perceive them to be relevant to the product or service.[66] This affective processing is frequently experience based.[67] In other words, consumers select an option based on their recall of past experiences and the feelings associated with them.

Consumer feelings are particularly critical for products and services that have hedonic, symbolic, or aesthetic aspects.[68] In choosing a restaurant, clothing, music, entertainment, furniture, or art, for example, consumers will often base their choice on positive associated feelings. A study of rock music found that emotional, sensory, and imagery responses were the most critical in determining liking and intent to purchase recorded music.[69] The marketers of Universal Studios Japan know that visitors want an American experience without giving up local tastes and customs. Therefore, the Osaka theme park has recognizably American architecture, Japanese and English language presentations, and American dishes modified for Japanese preferences.[70]

Emotions also play a key role in deciding what we consume and for how long.[71] We consume products and services that make us feel good more often and for longer periods than ones that do not.

In addition, products and services can serve as a means of removing or reducing negative emotions. Sometimes consumers buy a product, such as new clothing or a new CD, simply to make themselves feel better. In other situations, they may make a choice because of a negative feeling. Many consumers purchase diet foods and drinks, for example, out of guilt or shame.

Negative emotions can also be associated with difficult choices that involve conflict, such as trading off greater safety versus lower price in a car, and consumers will often choose the option that avoids the negative emotion.[72] Moreover, consumers facing emotionally difficult trade-offs between price and quality cope with potentially negative emotions related to quality by choosing the offering with the best quality.[73] Also, brands that require a lot of effort to evaluate may create negative emotions and be selected less frequently than those that require less effort.[74] Finally, when consumers evaluate the outcome of a purchase, they compare what they actually received with what they would have received if they had chosen differently. If a different product or brand would have led to a better outcome, they will regret their actual choice and may switch to the brand they didn't buy on the next purchase occasion.[75]

Imagery plays a key role in emotional decision making.[76] Consumers can attempt to imagine themselves actually consuming the product or service and use any emotions they experience as input for the decision. In choosing a vacation, for example, you can imagine the excitement you might experience from each destination. If these images are pleasant (or negative), they will exert a positive (or negative) influence on your decision process. As shown in Exhibit 10.7, ads can also try to get consumers to imagine themselves in a certain situation. Note that adding information actually makes imagery processing easier (unlike the case in cognitive processing, in which information overload is a threat) because more information makes it easier to form an accurate image. In addition, imagery tends to encourage brand-based processing because images are organized by brand rather than by attribute. Note that when companies designing new products include the customer in imagining visual imagery—creating a new image rather than recalling one from memory—they can produce more original designs.[77]

Consumers can use *both* cognitive and affective processing in making a decision. In fact, they can employ yet another combined strategy in which they first use a compensatory or noncompensatory cognitive model to narrow down a choice set and then use imagery and emotions to make the final decision.[78] In buying a house, for example, consumers often use price, square footage, and number of rooms to narrow down the set and then select the home that "feels right."

EXHIBIT 10.7
Stimulating Imagery through Advertising
Ads sometimes try to induce consumers to imagine themselves in certain situations. When they do, consumers may experience the feelings and emotions that are associated with this situation. This ad for Yankee Candle may stimulate the positive feelings of being in a beautiful forest in autumn.

Source: The Yankee Candle Company, Inc.

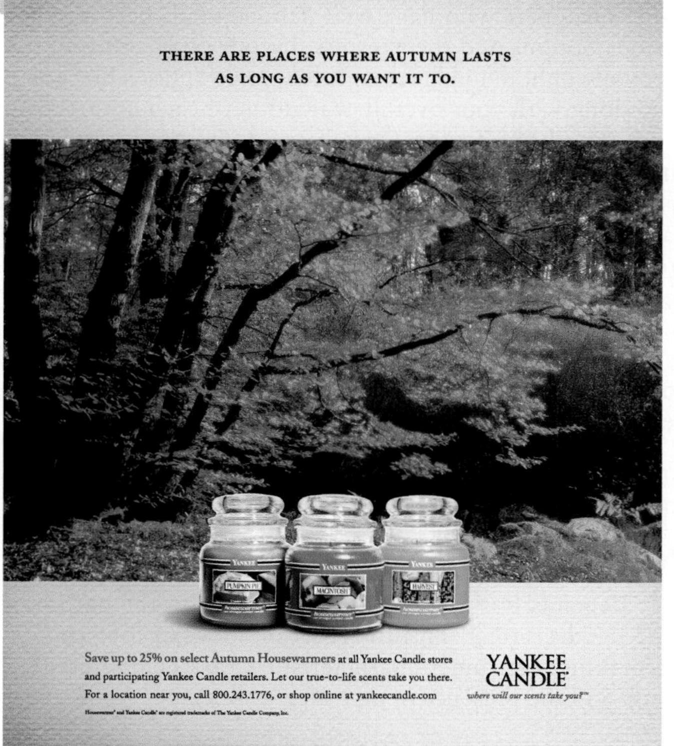

THERE ARE PLACES WHERE AUTUMN LASTS
AS LONG AS YOU WANT IT TO.
YANKEE
PUMPKIN PIE
YANKEE
MACINTOSH
YANKEE
HARVEST
Save up to 25% on select Autumn Housewarmers at all Yankee Candle stores
and participating Yankee Candle retailers. Let our true-to-life scents take you there.
For a location near you, call 800.243.1776, or shop online at yankeecandle.com
YANKEE CANDLE
where will our scents take you?

MARKETING IMPLICATIONS

Marketers can employ a variety of advertising, sales, and promotion techniques to add to the emotional experience surrounding the product or service. Good service or pleasant ambiance in a restaurant or store, for example, can produce positive feelings and experiences that may influence future choices. To provide this kind of ambiance, the main New York City Toys 'R' Us store in Times Square installed a 60-foot Ferris wheel and a giant Tyrannosaurus Rex to entertain shoppers.[79] Many minor league baseball teams generate positive emotions by involving fans in between-innings contests, having animal mascots interact with the audience, and giving away premiums.[80] An ad for American General Insurance shows children strolling through a field while dreamy music plays, all to create a positive feeling.[81] ●

DECISION MAKING WHEN ALTERNATIVES CANNOT BE COMPARED

In the decision-making models discussed thus far, consumers compare alternatives from the same product or service category on the basis of similar attributes or emotions. However, consumers often need to choose from a set of options that may not be directly comparable on the same specific attributes. For example, you might be trying to select entertainment for next weekend and have a choice of going to the movies, eating at a nice restaurant, renting a video, or attending a party. Each alternative has different attributes, making comparisons more difficult.

noncomparable decisions Decisions that involve choosing among products or services from different categories.

alternative-based strategy Developing an overall liking or disliking for each option in order to make a noncomparable decision.

attribute-based strategy Making noncomparable choices by making abstract representations of comparable attributes.

In making these **noncomparable decisions,** consumers adopt either an alternative-based strategy or an attribute-based strategy.[82] Using the **alternative-based strategy** (also called top-down processing), they develop an overall evaluation of each option—perhaps using a compensatory or affective strategy—and base their decision on it. For example, in deciding on weekend entertainment, you could evaluate the pros and cons of each option independently and then select the one you like the best.

Using the **attribute-based strategy,** consumers make comparisons easier for themselves by forming abstract representations of comparable attributes. In this type of bottom-up processing, the choice is constructed or built up. To make a more direct comparison for an entertainment decision, for example, you could construct abstract attributes such as fun, likelihood of impressing a date, and convenience. Because abstractions simplify the decision process, consumers tend to make them even when the options are easy to compare.[83]

Note that both strategies can be employed in different circumstances. When the alternatives are less comparable, consumers tend to use an alternative-based strategy because it is harder to make attribute abstractions.[84] Alternative-based strategies also suit consumers who have well-defined goals because they can easily recall the various options and their results. If your goal is to find fun things to do with a date, you could immediately recall a set of options like going to a movie or eating out, along with your overall evaluation of each option. You would then pick the option with the strongest evaluation. On the other hand, when consumers do not have well-defined goals, they are more likely to use attribute-based processing.

One final point about noncomparable choice is that price is often the one attribute on which alternatives can be compared directly. Consumers typically use price to screen alternatives for the consideration set rather than as the main basis of comparison among noncomparable alternatives. Thus in your decision among entertainment alternatives, you might use cost to generate a set of options that are reasonably affordable, then use an alternative- or attribute-based strategy to make the final decision.

DOES CONTEXT AFFECT HOW DECISIONS ARE MADE?

Consumers use different strategies in different decision contexts, or even for the same decision in different time periods. The best strategy for a specific decision depends both on the consumer and on the nature of the decision.[85] This final section looks at four **contextual effects** on decision making: consumer characteristics, task characteristics, task definition or framing, and the presence of a group.

contextual effects The influence of the decision situation on the decision-making process.

How Consumer Characteristics Can Affect Decision Making

A variety of factors related to consumers affect the nature of the decision process. Consistent with the overall processing model, these factors can be grouped according to consumers' motivation, ability, and opportunity to elaborate on information when making a decision.

Motivation to Process Although we are more likely to use any of the decision processes described in this chapter when our motivation to process is high, the models still differ in the amount of effort they require. As our incentive to make a correct decision increases, we consider the alternatives more carefully,[86] and the likelihood that we will employ a more active compensatory (versus noncompensatory) model increases. We also use a greater number of attributes to make a decision as our involvement increases.[87] On the other hand, if we perceive the decision to be too risky or if it entails an unpleasant task, we may delay making a decision.[88]

Consumers who are in a good mood are more willing to process information and take more time in making a decision than those who are not in a good mood.[89] Mood can also influence the nature of the evaluation. One study found that consumers in a good mood rated a set of audio speakers more positively than did consumers in a bad mood, when their mood was subconsciously influenced by music (awareness caused the consumers to adjust for mood).[90]

Ability to Process Consumers are more likely to understand their preferences and decisions when they can relate the evaluation of a product to its features.[91] When consumers have this "consumption vocabulary," they can use more attributes and information in making a decision. Further, expert consumers have more brand-based prior experience and knowledge and, as a result, tend to select brand-based decision strategies.[92] These consumers also know how to identify diagnostic information and ignore irrelevant attributes in their decision making. In addition, the Internet enables consumers to consider a wider variety of information in their decision process than they could without the ready availability of online research tools. Finally, research indicates that consumers in different cultures tend to use different decision strategies when confronted with information incongruity: North American consumers form evaluations based on attribute information, while East Asian consumers rely on both source and attribute information to form evaluations.[93]

Opportunity to Process As time pressure increases, consumers initially try to process faster.[94] If this technique does not work, they base their decision on fewer attributes and place heavier weight on negative information, eliminating bad alternatives with a noncompensatory strategy such as a conjunctive model.

Time pressure is one of the major reasons that consumers fail to make intended purchases. It can reduce the number of impulsive purchases and shopping time.[95] Consumers may also delay making a decision if they feel uncertain about how to get product information.[96] However, consumers feeling time pressure will defer decisions less when the choice entails high conflict and when the offerings under consideration display common bad features but unique good features.[97]

Finally, whether a consumer is present- or future-oriented can lead to different motivations and choices for different products.[98] *Present-oriented consumers* want to improve their current well-being and prefer products that help them do so, such as relaxing vacations and entertaining books. *Future-oriented consumers* want to develop themselves and select life-enriching vacations and books.

How Task Characteristics Can Affect Decision Making

In addition to consumer characteristics, task characteristics can influence decision making. Researchers have studied two task characteristics: the consideration set and information availability.

The Consideration Set The number and types of alternatives in the consumer's consideration set are key determinants of the decision-making process. With more than 31,000 new products introduced in the United States each year, consumers face more options than ever before, choosing among as many as 16 flavors of Kellogg Eggo waffles and 72 varieties of Pantene hair care products.[99] As the size of our consideration set increases, we must devote additional cognitive effort to making a decision. As consumers, we typically handle this increased load by adopting a combined strategy—narrowing down the set with a noncompensatory model, followed by a compensatory or affectively based strategy.[100]

When the consumer's primary objective is to make a decision, he or she may use trivial attributes to help finalize the decision. For example, if a consumer perceives three brands in the consideration set as equivalent with the exception that one contains a trivial attribute, the consumer is likely to choose the brand with the trivial attribute (arguing that its presence may be useful). If, however, two of the three brands in the consideration set have a particular trivial attribute, the consumer is likely to choose the one without that attribute (arguing that the attribute is unnecessary). In both cases, the consumer used the trivial attribute to complete and justify the final decision.[101]

Merely changing the alternatives in the consideration set can have a major impact on the consumer's decision, even without a change in preferences.[102] Adding inferior brands to the set increases decision accuracy and decreases effort. This phenomenon, called the **attraction effect,** occurs because the inferior brands increase the attractiveness of the dominant brand, making the decision easier.[103] Interestingly, when product information is presented numerically, such as in the form of graphs or charts, the attraction effect is weakened. However, if we receive the information in words, our greater knowledge increases the attraction effect.[104] The attraction effect may not occur at all if consumers are more conscious of price and less conscious of quality.[105]

attraction effect The adding of an inferior brand to a consideration set, which increases the attractiveness of the dominant brand.

The composition of the consideration set is also extremely important because our evaluation of a brand depends on the other brands to which it is compared. In particular, if one brand is clearly more attractive or dominant than others, making a choice does not require much effort.[106] We are more selective in our use of information and process by brand under these conditions. On the other hand, if the brands in the consideration set are similar in attractiveness, we must put forth more effort to make a decision—perhaps using a compensatory or detailed noncompensatory process.[107]

Consumers also tend to possess an **extremeness aversion,** meaning that options perceived as extreme on some particular attribute will seem less attractive than those that are intermediate. Thus people tend to find moderately priced options more attractive than those that are *either* very expensive or very inexpensive. For example, retailer Williams-Sonoma offered two home bread makers; the first one introduced cost $275, and the second cost 50 percent

extremeness aversion The phenomenon that options that are extreme on some attributes are less attractive than those that are moderate on those attributes.

more. Introducing the second, more expensive unit doubled the sales of the first unit.[108] This phenomenon also occurred with Cross pens and microwave ovens.[109]

MARKETING IMPLICATIONS By examining the nature of consumers' consideration sets, marketers can sometimes develop interesting strategies. One way a company can try to gain an advantage is by promoting comparisons with inferior rather than with equal or superior competitors. This approach maximizes the attraction effect and results in a more positive evaluation of the brand. Also, marketers can increase sales of a high-margin item simply by offering a higher-priced option.[110] Thus Panasonic could increase the sales of a $179 microwave oven by offering a slightly larger model at $199. The higher-priced model might not sell well, but it would make the lower-priced model look like a good deal. Another technique is to sell a new improved model alongside the old model at the same price, which makes the new one look better. ●

Availability of Information The amount, quality, and format of the information also affect the decision strategy employed. As you might expect, when a consumer has more information, the decision becomes more complex and the consumer must use a more detailed decision strategy. An increase in the amount of information will lead to a better choice only up to a point; after that the consumer experiences **information overload.**[111]

information overload The negative effect on decision making caused by having too much information.

Good examples of the potential for information overload are ads for pharmaceutical products. The law requires companies to provide detailed prescription information and disclosure of side effects. The sheer amount of information in these ads—usually an entire page of small print—is likely to be overwhelming to most consumers. As another example, one study reports that consumers in both Romania and Turkey have experienced great confusion in judging quality and making choices because "there are so many alternatives now."[112] Information overload can be a problem for U.S. consumers because of the large number of new brands and extensions introduced in many categories.[113] Also, the huge amount of information on the Internet can create overload. Marketers therefore need to be careful not to flood the consumer with too much information; instead they should present only key points.

A lack of available information can also hamper decision making, resulting in poorer-quality decisions and a lower level of satisfaction. Such a lack of both products and information has been a major problem in the former communist countries.[114]

If the quality of information we acquire from either internal or external search is useful or diagnostic, our processing effort is reduced and we make better decisions.[115] Essentially, we can narrow the consideration set relatively quickly because we need fewer attributes. Research shows that consumers tend to give good unique brand features more weight than they give to common features.[116] Another study shows that when consumers lack information about a particular feature, they will use their interpretation of this missing information to support their choice of the option that is superior on the common feature.[117] A focus on quality information further suggests that marketers can benefit from being selective about the information they provide rather than by always focusing on quantity.

On the other hand, if available information is ambiguous, consumers are more likely to stay with their current brand than to risk a new competitive brand, even a superior one.[118] Consumers also can compare numerical attribute information faster and more easily than they can compare verbal information.[119] For example, to help parents select video games, a group of video game manufacturers developed a numerical rating system to indicate the amount of sex and violence in their games.

Finally, the format of the information—that is, the way it is organized in memory or in the external environment—has a major impact on the type of decision strategy employed. For example, a study of VCR purchasers found that consumers are less likely to choose the cheapest brand when products are organized by model (similar offerings by different companies are grouped together) rather than by brand.[120] Thus companies with high-price brands would want the display to be organized by model, and companies offering low-price brands would prefer a brand-based display.

If information is organized by brand, consumers will likely employ a brand-based strategy such as a compensatory, conjunctive, or disjunctive model. On the other hand, if information is organized by attribute or in a matrix, consumers can adopt an attribute-processing strategy, such as the additive difference, lexicographic, or elimination-by-aspects model. Providing information to consumers in a format that requires less effort increases decision effectiveness and accuracy.[121] In one study, consumers presented with a narrative message about vacations used holistic processing to sequence and evaluate the information. The narrative structure is similar to the way consumers acquire information in daily life, so processing was easier; moreover, in processing the narrative, consumers did not consider individual features, which meant negatives had less impact.[122] The ad promoting Flonase in Exhibit 10.8 provides a matrix of information that makes comparison easy. One study found that organizing yogurt by flavor instead of by brand encouraged more comparison shopping on the basis of attribute processing.[123] Sometimes consumers will even restructure information into a more useful format, especially a matrix.[124]

Some researchers expected that the greater availability of information online would allow consumers to readily apply compensatory models. However, consumers do not appear to be using the Internet in this way because such models are still seen as complex and demanding.[125] (Paradoxically, many consumers do want their decision agents, such as their physician or financial or career advisor, to use these rules in making choices.) The Internet also allows consumers to get information by brand, by attribute, or in a matrix, thereby enabling them to structure the decision the way they want to. For Web-based marketers, analyzing consumer reactions to online menu-based choices can help companies estimate each option's utility and develop offerings that satisfy individual consumer needs.[126]

How Decision Framing Can Affect Decision Making

decision framing The initial reference point or anchor in the decision process.

A third contextual influence on the decision process is the manner in which the task is defined or represented, called **decision framing.** This is an important influence because the frame serves as the initial reference point or anchor in the decision process. All subsequent information is processed in light of it. For example, a frame for a car purchase might be: (1) buy an economical car I can afford or (2) buy a car that will impress my friends. Clearly, consumers will use different models and process information differently under these two frames.

Most of the early work on framing studied people's willingness to take risks in a gamble. Results showed that people are more willing to take risks when a choice is framed as a loss rather than as a gain.[127] One study examined consumer preferences for two different coupons.[128] In one condition con-

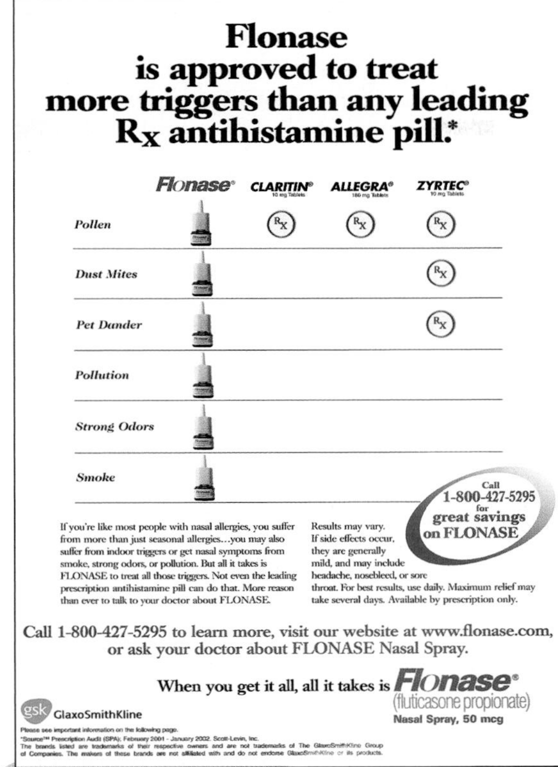

Flonase
is approved to treat
more triggers than any leading
Rx antihistamine pill.*
Flonase®
CLARITIN®
ALLEGRA®
ZYRTEC®
Pollen
Dust Mites
Pet Dander
Pollution
Strong Odors
Smoke
Call 1-800-427-5295 for great savings on FLONASE
If you're like most people with nasal allergies, you suffer from more than just seasonal allergies…you may also suffer from indoor triggers or get nasal symptoms from smoke, strong odors, or pollution. But all it takes is FLONASE to treat all those triggers. Not even the leading prescription antihistamine pill can do that. More reason than ever to talk to your doctor about FLONASE.
Results may vary. If side effects occur, they are generally mild, and may include headache, nosebleed, or sore throat. For best results, use daily. Maximum relief may take several days. Available by prescription only.
Call 1-800-427-5295 to learn more, visit our website at www.flonase.com, or ask your doctor about FLONASE Nasal Spray.
When you get it all, all it takes is Flonase® (fluticasone propionate) Nasal Spray, 50 mcg
gsk GlaxoSmithKline
Please see important information on the following page.
*Source™ Prescription Audit (SPA); February 2001 - January 2002. Scott-Levin, Inc.
The brands listed are trademarks of their respective owners and are not trademarks of The GlaxoSmithKline Group of Companies. The makers of these brands are not affiliated with and do not endorse GlaxoSmithKline or its products.

EXHIBIT 10.8
Providing a Matrix of Information
To facilitate comparisons between a particular brand and its competitors, marketers can provide a matrix of information on the most critical attributes for each brand (reducing decision effort and increasing accuracy).

Source: Copyright GlaxoSmithKline. Used with permission.

sumers were asked to choose between two coupons they could use when buying a jar of Prego spaghetti sauce: With one they would get a free can of Campbell's Tomato and Rice Soup (a 49-cent value), and with another they would buy a can of Campbell's Tomato and Rice Soup and get 49 cents off the total. The first condition was framed as a gain (get something free), and the second was a reduced loss (49 cents off). Even though the coupons had the same value, more consumers opted for the first choice.

Framing relates to other consumer decision contexts as well. Specifically, consumers can either frame their decisions or their decisions can be framed by exposure to external stimuli.

Framing by the Consumer The decision-framing process begins with the consumer's knowledge of the purchase situation.[129] Consumers then activate that portion of memory related to their goals and the situation. For example, the goals to "get food that is on my diet" and "get food that makes me feel good" would probably activate different brands and information from memory and result in different decision processes.

The context in which the product will be used can influence the decision process. Thus you are likely to use different consideration sets, decision criteria, and levels of decision effort when buying beer for yourself and when buying beer for a party. You might buy lower-priced beer for a party because you need a large quantity, but you might be more concerned about image, as well.

One study of mouth-related products (mouthwash, mints, gums and candies, breath sprays, and so on) found that where the product would be used (at home or away from home) and who would use the product (the purchaser or someone else) determined which products were purchased.[130] Another study asked consumers to rate the importance of different attributes for four situations: (1) lunch on a weekday, (2) snack during a shopping trip, (3) evening meal when rushed for time, and (4) evening meal with the family when not rushed for time.[131] Results indicated that attribute importance depended on the situation. Speed and convenience were the most important attributes for situations 1 and 3, whereas variety of menu and popularity with children were most critical for situation 4.

MARKETING IMPLICATIONS The decision-framing process has important implications for both the positioning and segmentation of markets. First, marketers can position the product or service in consumers' goal-related or usage categories. That way, when consumers frame the decision, they will be more likely to consider the brand and important related information. For example, a television ad for Compaq computers showed a businesswoman saving the day by firing off a fax from a cab during a traffic jam.[132] Another ad showed a restaurant owner answering the phone, watching a review of her restaurant on TV, and changing the prices on the menu, all on her computer. In both cases the frame is a computer that solves business problems.

Second, marketers can identify large segments of consumers who have similar goal-related or usage-context categories and market directly to these groups. Thus Reebok introduced a shoe with moving air in the sole to appeal to high-performance consumers.[133] Handspring offered the Treo as a combination mobile phone, handheld computer, and electronic communication device to replace the three separate devices carried by busy people on the move.[134] A company in China labels its products as tea for drivers and tea for watching TV so that consumers will link the brand with a specific use.[135] ●

External Framing Decisions can also be framed by the way in which the problem is structured in the external environment. In the study mentioned earlier in the chapter, consumers who were presented with beef that was 75 percent lean rated it significantly higher than those who were told the beef was 25 percent fat.[136] In another study, industrial buyers who used low price as an initial reference point were less willing to take risks than those with a medium or high price point.[137] Likewise, consumers react more positively when marketers frame the cost of a product as a series of small payments (pennies a day or a few dollars a month) instead of as a large one-time expense.[138] Thus a $299 Carnival cruise seems more attractive when framed as $14 per month.[139]

Whether a decision is framed positively (How good is this product?) or negatively (How bad is this product?) influences the evaluation differently.[140] Consumers are more likely to choose a brand with negatively framed claims about a competitor when elaboration is low, but higher elaboration may lead them to conclude that unfair tactics are being used.[141] Research also shows that consumers with a low need for cognition are more susceptible to the influence of a negatively framed marketing message.[142] In addition, when a decision about options is framed in terms of subtracting unwanted items from a fully loaded product, consumers will choose more options with a higher total option price than if the decision is framed in terms of adding wanted items to a base model.[143]

Priming certain attributes, such as reliability and creativity, can significantly alter judgments of both comparable alternatives like brands of cameras and noncomparable alternatives like computers or cameras.[144] In particular, this priming causes consumers to focus their processing on specific attributes rather than on abstract criteria. Research on charitable contributions found that providing consumers with a high anchor point by asking for $20 increased contributions relative to a low anchor point like a penny.[145] Finally, priming hedonic or symbolic attributes—such as associations—with political concerns (e.g., reduce toxic waste) rather than with functional ones (e.g., no more hassles) can produce a higher willingness to pay for items or social programs.[146]

How Group Context Can Affect Decision Making

A fourth contextual influence on the decision-making process occurs when a consumer makes a decision in the presence of a group, such as deciding what to order when dining out with other people. As each member of the group makes a decision in turn, he or she attempts to balance two sets of goals: (1) goals that are attained by the individual's action alone *(individual-alone)* and (2) goals that are achieved depending on both the individual and the group *(individual-group)*.[147] Because consumers may have to choose a different alternative to achieve each set of goals, they are not always able to achieve both sets of goals simultaneously in group settings.

EXHIBIT 10.9
Goal Classes That Affect Consumer Decision Making

Consumers are not always able to achieve both individual-alone and individual-group goals when making decisions in the context of a group. Trying to achieve individual-group goals can result in either group-variety or group-uniformity, while trying to achieve individual-alone goals allows the consumer to satisfy his or her own taste through the decision.

Source: Dan Ariely and Jonathan Levav, "Sequential Choice in Group Settings: Taking the Road Less Traveled and Less Enjoyed," *Journal of Consumer Research*, vol. 27, December 2000, p. 281. Reprinted with permission of the University of Chicago Press.

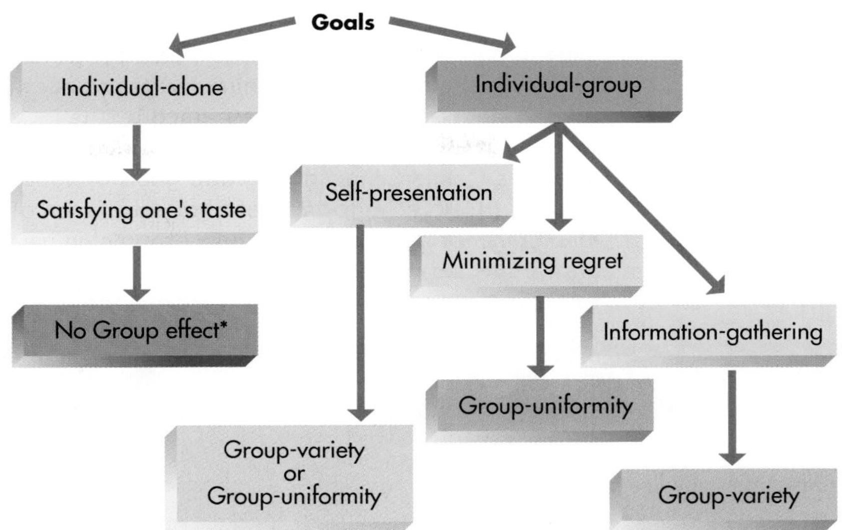

Note. — In cases where informational social influence is present during the decision process, an outcome of group uniformity or variety seeking can result.

In a group, consumers face these three types of individual-group goals, as shown in Exhibit 10.9:

- *Self-presentation.* Consumers seek to convey a certain image by the decisions they make in a group context. When consumers want to use unique choices as positive self-presentation cues or to express their individuality, the result will be variety seeking at the group level. On the other hand, consumers are often more concerned about social norms and therefore make similar choices to blend in, resulting in uniformity at the group level.
- *Minimizing regret.* Consumers who are risk averse and want to minimize regret will tend to make choices that are similar to those made by the rest of the group, leading to uniformity at the group level. This allows group members to avoid any disappointment they might feel if someone else's choice seemed better than their own.
- *Information gathering.* Consumers can learn more about the different choices each has made through interaction with other group members. Whether members actually share choices or simply share their reactions, the result is variety in the totality of choices within the group when consumers see information gathering as a priority. However, when group members are more concerned with self-presentation or loss aversion than with information gathering, they will make similar choices, resulting in group uniformity.

When making a decision in a group context, we try to balance these three individual-group goals with our individual-alone goals. In most group situations, the result is group uniformity, even though individual members may ultimately feel less satisfied by the outcome.

MARKETING IMPLICATIONS The findings about contextual influences on decision making have important implications because marketers can use communications to influence reference points and the way in which decisions are framed. For example, anti-smoking ads now frame the message in terms of a new health problem: impotence.[148] Sales promotions generally are more successful when framed as gains rather than as a reduced loss—consumers prefer to get something for free rather than getting a discount.

Consumer decisions can be framed by the location of products in the store, thereby influencing comparisons. Finally, marketers can use ads and other communications to make individual-group goals a higher priority in group situations, leading to more uniformity of choice in favor of the advertised brand. Beer marketers, for instance, often show group members enjoying only the advertised brand. Such ads reinforce strong social norms and encourage consumers to order the advertised brand when they drink in a social setting. ●

SUMMARY

Judgments simply involve forming evaluations or estimates regarding the likelihood of events, whereas decisions entail the consumer making a choice between options or courses of action. Two major types of judgments are estimations of likelihood and judgments of goodness or badness, both of which can be made by recalling past judgments from memory using either imagery or an anchoring and adjustment process. Consumers may have difficulty making conjunctive probability assessments, which involve determining how two attributes vary together.

Consumers may use one or a combination of various decision-making models: (1) compensatory brand-processing models, which include the multiattribute or expectancy-value model; (2) compensatory attribute-processing models, which include the additive difference model; (3) noncompensatory brand-processing models, which include the conjunctive and disjunctive models; and (4) noncompensatory attribute-processing models, which include the lexicographic and elimination-by-aspects models.

Decisions can also be based on emotions or feelings, using a type of holistic processing in which emotions or images play a key role. In many cases, consumers must make decisions when they cannot directly compare alternatives. To do this, they can use either an alternative-based strategy, in which overall evaluations are made for each option, or an attribute-based strategy, in which abstract representations of attributes are used to make comparisons.

Finally, contextual or situational factors can exert a strong influence on the decision process. These contextual factors can be grouped according to (1) consumer characteristics, such as their motivation, ability, and opportunity to process; (2) task characteristics, such as the nature of the consideration set and the information available; (3) decision framing, either by the environment or by the consumer; and (4) the presence of a group, which causes consumers to try to balance individual-alone goals with individual-group goals.

QUESTIONS FOR REVIEW AND DISCUSSION

1. How does consumer judgment differ from consumer decision making?
2. What is the anchoring and adjustment process, and how does it affect consumer judgment?
3. How do consumers use compensatory and noncompensatory decision-making models?
4. Why do marketers need to know that attribute processing is easier for consumers than brand processing?
5. In what ways do emotions and feelings influence consumer decision making?
6. What four contextual elements affect consumer decision making?

EXERCISES

1. This chapter discussed several types of estimations of likelihood that consumers can make (such as estimating quality or likelihood of satisfaction, goodness/badness). What other types of judgments do consumers make? List as many as possible, and indicate what these judgments have in common.
2. Select a product or service category for which you expect the consumers' motivation, ability, and opportunity to process information to be high. Ask five consumers to describe in detail how they would go about making a decision for this product or service category. First ask them which brands they would consider (the consideration set), and then ask them to describe the specific steps they would go through

in making a decision. Which brand would they choose? After collecting this information, answer the following questions:

a. How do the descriptions provided by the consumers compare with the decision models discussed in this chapter?

b. How do these processes vary for different consumers?

c. Why did one brand tend to be chosen over another?

d. If these processes were representative of many consumers, how might this information be used to develop a marketing strategy?

3. Pick a product or service category that is likely to generate high-elaboration decision making. Identify the most salient attributes for the decision, and collect information about these attributes. Ask ten consumers to rate each attribute in terms of the b_i and I_i ratings from the compensatory model (see the box on page 234) for three major brands in this category. Based on this information, answer the following:

a. What are the strengths and weaknesses of each brand?

b. How would each model described in this chapter provide insights into consumers' decision processes in this situation?

c. How would the information you have collected aid in designing marketing strategy?

chapter 11

Judgment and Decision Making Based on Low Consumer Effort

INTRODUCTION: Are Foreign Brands Better Than Local Brands?

In Vietnam today, brands sold by companies such as Procter & Gamble and Unilever, including locally produced Close-Up toothpaste and Lux soap, are experiencing strong sales. The only problem is that rather than buying these products legally in stores, consumers often purchase them smuggled in from Thailand at higher prices. Pirated videotape versions of movies such as *Lara Croft: Tomb Raider* are also being smuggled into the country. Vietnamese consumers assume that anything *not* made locally is of superior quality even if it has the exact same brand name as an item made in that country. Ironically, this attitude is putting some Vietnamese out of work because local factories are standing idle.[1]

This interesting situation is the result of several factors discussed in this chapter. First, consumers are making an error in judgment by assuming that the products made in Vietnam are inferior in quality. Second, the brands represent common, repeat-purchase products for which consumers will typically not exert much effort in making a choice. Instead, they employ very simple *heuristics*, or rules of thumb, to make these judgments and decisions.[2] The following heuristics may have been factors in this example:

Sometimes consumers simply buy the brand that is most familiar. In Vietnam, consumers desire the smuggled products because they represent well-known brand names, many of which are aggressively advertised within the country.[3] In addition, some consumers use price as a heuristic for making decisions. These smuggled products are highly priced and consumers perceive a price-quality relationship, so they are willing to pay more for these items.

EXHIBIT 11.1

Brands in Vietnam

Well-known international brands are more popular in Vietnam than locally produced products.

Source: © L. Dematteis/The Image Works.

Moreover, when consumers are offered a high-quality product, they may form a positive attitude while consuming it, leading to repeat purchases and perhaps brand loyalty. Some Vietnamese consumers have clearly formed positive attitudes toward the foreign-made brands. Habit is also a factor. Consumers may not buy some products from stores because they are in the habit of buying those items on the black market. Finally, consumers may buy brands simply because they feel good about them. The Vietnamese consumers in this example have positive feelings toward foreign-made brands (see Exhibit 11.1).

When consumers have low motivation, ability, and opportunity (MAO) to process information, their judgment and decision processes are different and involve less effort than when MAO is high. This chapter examines the nature of low-effort judgment and decision making—the next stage in the overall model, as shown in Exhibit 11.2. The focus here is on the cognitive and affective shortcuts or heuristics that consumers use to make judgments and decisions and the marketing implications of this behavior. ●

LOW-EFFORT JUDGMENT PROCESSES

Chapter 10 showed that when effort is high, consumers' judgments—such as estimations of likelihood and goodness/badness—can be cognitively complex. In contrast, when MAO is low, individuals are motivated to simplify the cognitive process by using heuristics to reduce the effort involved in making judgments.[4] Two major types of heuristics are representativeness and availability.

Shortcuts in Making Judgments: The Representativeness Heuristic

representativeness heuristic Making a judgment by simply comparing a stimulus to the category prototype or exemplar.

One way that consumers can make simple estimations or judgments is to make comparisons to the category prototype or exemplar. This categorization process is called the **representativeness heuristic.**[5] For example, if you want to estimate the likelihood that a new toothpaste is of high quality, you might compare it with your prototype for toothpaste, such as Crest.[6] If you see the new brand as similar to the prototype, you will assume that it is also of high quality. This explains why the packaging of many store brands is similar to that of the leading brands in various product categories, seeking outward similarity to suggest that the products themselves share many characteristics of quality.

Like any shortcut, the representativeness heuristic can also lead to biased judgments. The Vietnamese consumers in the chapter-opening example automatically assume anything not made locally is superior in quality (even if the brands are identical); locally produced brands must work to overcome this bias and convince consumers that local products can be good quality.[7]

MARKETING IMPLICATIONS The representativeness heuristic is an important marketing factor because it suggests that companies position products or services close to a prototype that has positive associations in consumers' minds. However, when the shortcut leads to biased judgment, marketers must take steps to overcome it. In the 1960s, radios and electronics made in Japan were considered the prototype for poor-quality merchandise. Japanese firms spent many years producing and heavily marketing high-quality products to overcome this bias. Now Korean electronics firms and car makers are working to overcome the same bias.[8] ●

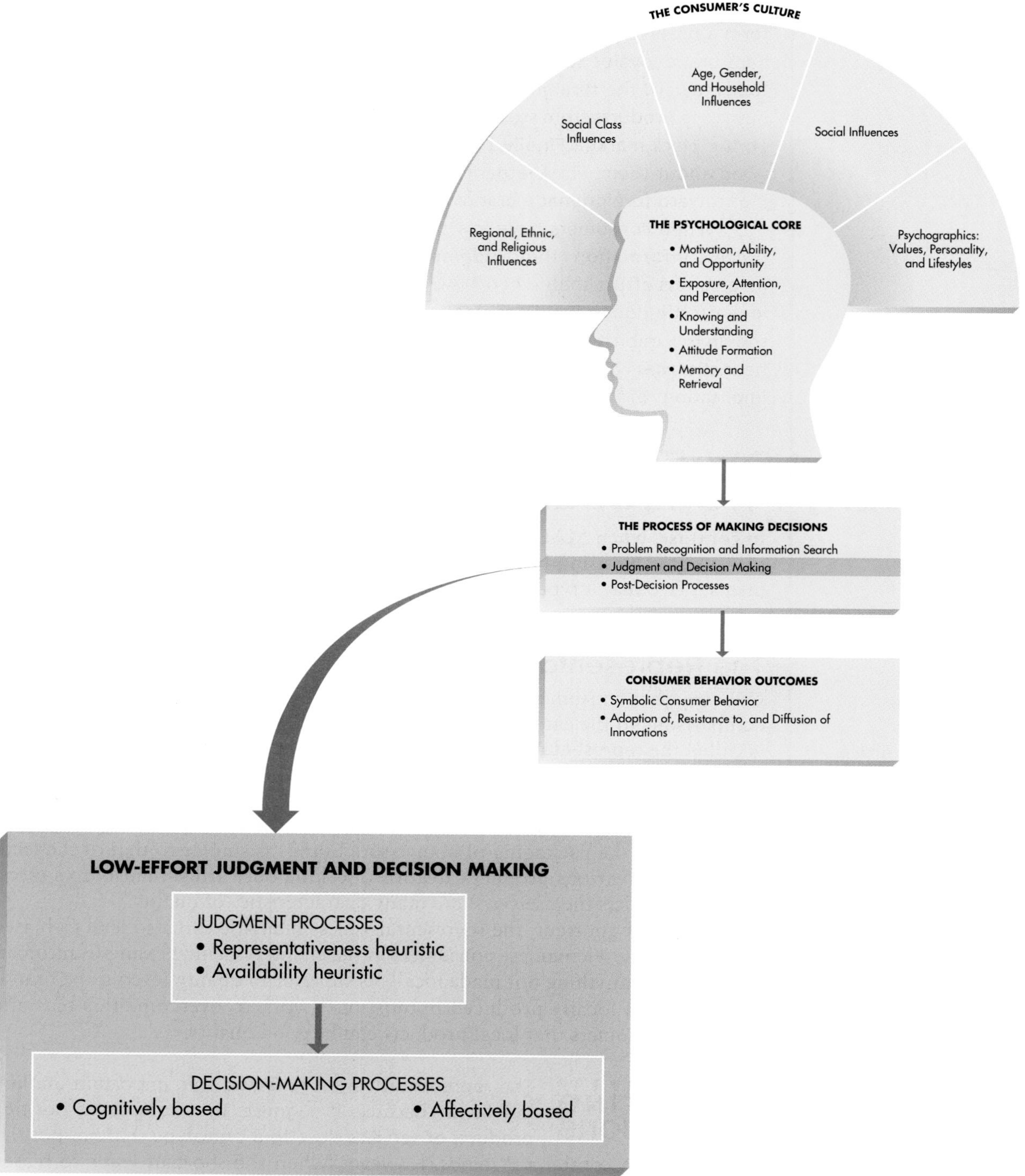

EXHIBIT 11.2

Chapter Overview: Judgment and Decision Making: Low Consumer Effort

In low-effort processing situations, consumers tend to use heuristics or ways of simplifying the judgment or decision. Both cognitively based heuristics (performance-based tactics, habit, price-related tactics, brand loyalty, and normative influences) and affectively based heuristics (affect-related tactics, variety seeking, and impulse) are used to make decisions.

Shortcuts in Making Judgments: The Availability Heuristic

availability heuristic Basing judgments on events that are easy to recall rather than base rate information.

Judgments can also be influenced by the ease with which instances of an event can be brought to mind, a shortcut called the **availability heuristic.**[9] Consumers are more likely to recall more accessible or more vivid events, which influences their judgments. To illustrate, suppose that years ago you purchased a CD player that needed constant repair. Today you may still recall your anger and disappointment when you see this brand. Your experiences greatly color your estimations of quality for this brand, even though the brand might actually have few breakdowns today.

Word-of-mouth communication is another example of accessible information that leads to the use of the availability heuristic. If a friend tells you about all the problems she had with her CD player, this information is likely to affect your estimates of quality, even though her experience might have been an isolated event.

base-rate information How often an event really occurs for all consumers.

These judgments are biased because we tend to ignore **base-rate information**—that is, how often the event really occurs—in favor of information that is more vivid or accessible. One study demonstrated this effect in the context of estimating the probability of refrigerators breaking down.[10] One group was given a set of case histories told by consumers, and another was given actual statistics about the incidence of breakdown. As you might expect, people who read the case histories provided breakdown estimates that were 30 percent higher than those of the statistics group. Another study found that consumers can use both base-rate and case information, but their judgment depends on how the information is structured.[11] As case history information becomes more specific, consumers rely less on base rates. Another reason we do not use more base-rate information is that it is often not available.

law of small numbers The expectation that information obtained from a small number of people represents the larger population.

A related bias is the **law of small numbers**, whereby people expect information obtained from a small sample to be typical of the larger population.[12] If friends inform us that a new CD by a particular artist is really good or that the food at a particular restaurant is terrible, we tend to believe that information, even if most people may not feel the same way. In fact, reliance on small numbers is another reason that word-of-mouth communication can be so powerful. We tend to have confidence that the opinions of friends or relatives are more reflective of the majority than they may actually be.

MARKETING IMPLICATIONS Marketers can attempt to either capitalize on the availability bias or overcome it. To capitalize, they can provide consumers with positive and vivid product-related experiences through the use of marketing communications, or they can ask consumers to imagine such situations. Both strategies will increase consumers' estimates that these events will occur. Or marketers can attempt to stimulate positive word-of-mouth communication. This is what New Line Cinema did when it leaked sketches and trailers for the *Lord of the Rings* movies to fan-maintained Web sites months ahead of each film's opening and provided downloadable screen savers and images that could be passed from fan to fan.[13]

Marketers can attempt to overcome the availability bias by providing consumers with base-rate information about the general population. If this information is vivid and specific, it can help consumers make a less biased judgment. For instance, Bumble Bee ads claim that this brand of tuna is "chosen 2 to 1 over competitors" thanks to a new packing technique.[14] The Internet is an excellent vehicle for providing base-rate information. For example, consumers interested in buying books or music at Amazon.com can see a summary rating and read reviews submitted by other consumers. The availability bias is also a common problem in the context of sweepstakes and lotteries. Consumers often overestimate the likelihood of winning, even though their chances are exceedingly small, because they are exposed to highly vivid and available images of winners in the media. Regulators have attempted to overcome this bias by requiring marketers to clearly post the odds of winning.

The availability bias is quite common in marketing research that uses focus groups to evaluate marketing programs. As discussed in Chapter 2, focus groups consist of as many as 12 consumers who give their opinions on topics ranging from product design to advertising messages. Even though these groups contain a very small number of consumers, marketing managers sometimes mistakenly view the group's responses as mirroring those of the general consumer population.[15] Companies can overcome this problem by checking the findings with a quantitative study using a larger and more representative consumer sample. ●

LOW-EFFORT DECISION-MAKING PROCESSES

Most low-effort judgment and decision situations are not very important in consumers' lives. Clearly, career and family decisions are far more important than deciding which toothpaste or peanut butter to buy. Thus the consumer usually does not want to devote a lot of time and effort to these mundane decisions.[16] In a typical shopping trip, a consumer might purchase 30 to 40 items. Spending even five minutes on each decision would stretch the shopping trip to several hours. Researchers are therefore interested in examining just how consumers make decisions in these low-elaboration situations.

How Does Low-Effort Decision Making Differ from High-Effort Decision Making?

In the discussion of high-effort decision making in Chapter 10, you saw that consumers have certain beliefs about each alternative that are combined to form an attitude that leads to a behavior or a choice. In other words, the consumer engages in *thinking*, which leads to *feelings*, which results in *behaving*. This progression, known as the **hierarchy of effects**, is outlined in Exhibit 11.3.

Herbert Krugman was one of the first researchers to recognize that this traditional hierarchy of effects might not describe all consumer decision-making situations.[17] In studying how television advertising affects consumers, Krugman noticed that, even though viewers could recall ads, the ads appeared to have little impact on viewers' attitudes toward the brand—a finding that is inconsistent with the belief-attitude link. To account for this discrepancy, Krugman hypothesized that advertising influences consumers through a process called *passive* (or *incidental*) *learning*. He viewed television as a primarily low-involvement medium to which viewers do not pay close attention. Viewers also do not link the advertised product or ad to their previous experiences or beliefs. However, through the constant repetition of ad messages, viewers can pick up and retain messages passively. They can therefore pos-

EXHIBIT 11.3
Hierarchy of Effects
When effort is high, consumers actively evaluate brands before making a decision and purchasing. In low-effort situations, consumers think very little before deciding, and beliefs (often based on basic familiarity) lead directly to choice. Consumers make evaluations after the choice, once they have used the product.

High-Effort Hierarchy

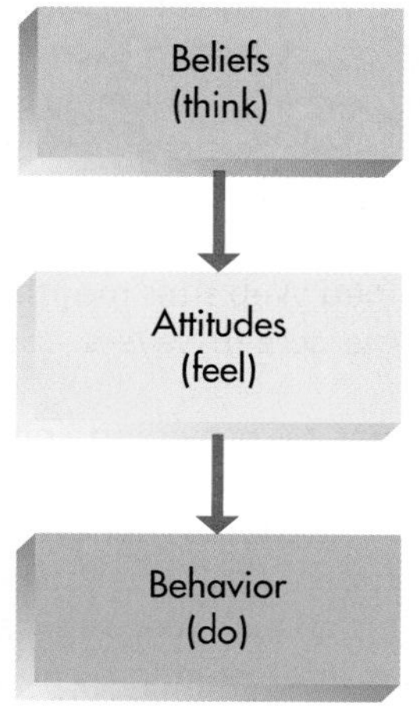

Low-Effort Hierarchy

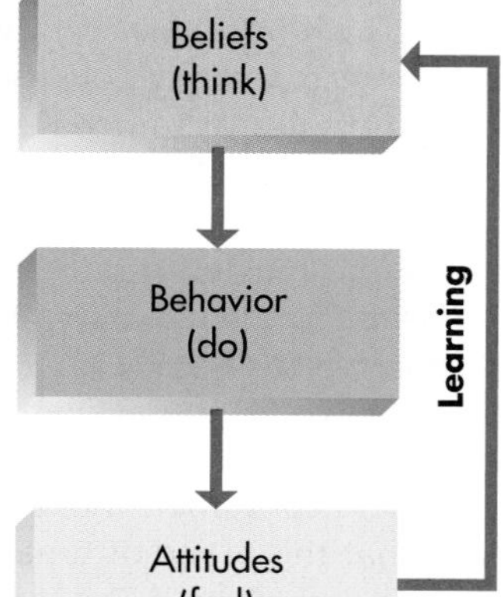

hierarchy of effects The sequence of steps used in decision making.

sess low-level beliefs about the product, a kind of basic familiarity, but not form a strong attitude. As a result, consumers can make purchase decisions without a strong attitude. If a consumer does develop a strong attitude, this tends to occur *after* purchase when the product is being used.

Thus if a consumer sees an ad for Excedrin, she would probably not pay very close attention to it. However, if she sees the ad repeatedly, she would acquire a basic awareness of the brand and the key claims that it is stronger than aspirin and relieves headache pain fast. If she goes to the store to purchase Excedrin, this low-level knowledge may be enough to influence her choice. But only after trying the product will she decide whether she likes or dislikes this brand.

Consistent with Krugman's theory, researchers have proposed an alternative hierarchy of effects for low-effort situations that follows a *thinking-behaving-feeling* sequence.[18] The consumer enters the decision process with a set of low-level beliefs based on brand familiarity and knowledge obtained from repeated exposures to advertising, in-store exposure, or prior usage. These beliefs serve as the foundation for the decision or behavior, in the absence of any attitude. After making the decision and while using the product, the consumer evaluates the brand and may or may not form an attitude, depending on how strongly the brand is liked or satisfies needs. Exhibit 11.3 compares this model with the traditional hierarchy of effects.

Some researchers have challenged the belief-behavior link in the low-involvement hierarchy by noting that consumers sometimes engage in "pure affective choice," making a decision based solely on how they feel rather than on what they think.[19] For example, you might select a flavor of ice cream or a new CD based on positive feelings rather than on any beliefs or knowledge. In these cases the sequence would be feeling, behaving, and then thinking. This type of decision making, which clearly does occur, suggests that consumers can process in both a cognitive and affective manner—a factor in many low-elaboration situations.

Using Simplifying Strategies When Consumer Effort Is Low

Low-effort purchases represent the most frequent type of decisions that consumers make in everyday life. One study of in-store examination of laundry detergent purchases found that the median amount of time taken to make a choice was only 8.5 seconds.[20] Another study of coffee and tissues found very low levels of decision activity, particularly among consumers who purchased the product frequently and possessed a strong brand preference.[21] Findings were similar for analgesics.[22] Some research has examined consumer decision processes across a number of product categories and has even questioned whether there is any decision process at all.[23]

A decision process probably does occur in low-effort situations, but it is simpler, involves less effort, and is qualitatively different from the processes that occur when MAO is high. Two other factors influence the low-MAO decision process. First, the goal is not necessarily to find the best possible brand, called *optimizing*, as is the case with high-elaboration decisions. To optimize here would require more effort than consumers are typically willing to expend. Instead, consumers are more willing to **satisfice**—that is, to find a brand that simply satisfies their needs. It may not be the best, but it is "good enough." The effort required to find the best may simply not be worth it.[24]

satisfice To find a brand that simply satisfies a need even though the brand may not be the best brand.

Second, most low-elaboration decisions are made frequently and repeatedly. In these decisions, consumers may rely on previous information and judgments of satisfaction or dissatisfaction from past consumption. Think of all the times you have purchased toothpaste, breakfast cereal, shampoo, and deodorant. You have acquired information by using these products and from seeing ads, talking to friends, and so forth. Thus you do not need to search for information every time you are in the store. You can simply remember previous decisions and use that information to make your next choice.

choice tactics Simple rules of thumb used to make low-effort decisions.

In these common, repeat-purchase situations, consumers can develop decision heuristics called **choice tactics** that enable them to make quick and effortless decisions.[25] Rather than making a detailed comparison of the various brands, consumers apply these rules to simplify the decision process.

The study of laundry detergents mentioned earlier supports this view.[26] When consumers were asked how they made their choice, several major categories of tactics emerged, among them *price tactics* (it's the cheapest or it's on sale), *affect tactics* (I like it), *performance tactics* (it cleans clothes better), and *normative tactics* (my mother bought it). Other studies have identified additional choice tactics: *habit tactics* (I buy the same brand I bought last time), *brand-loyalty tactics* (I buy the same brand for which I have a strong preference), and *variety seeking tactics* (I need to try something different). Similar results were produced in a study of shampoo and laundry detergent in Singapore.[27] Related patterns of choice-tactic usage were found in a comparison of consumers in Germany, Thailand, and the United States.[28]

Consumers can develop a choice tactic for each repeat-purchase, low-elaboration decision in the product or service category. If the consumer's decision is observed only once, it will appear very limited. Because all prior purchases serve as input to the current decision, it is important to look at a whole series of choices and consumption situations to fully understand consumer decision making.

LEARNING CHOICE TACTICS

The key to understanding low-elaboration decision making is knowing the manner in which consumers learn to use their choice tactics. Certain concepts from the behaviorist tradition in psychology are relevant to understanding the way consumers learn. **Operant conditioning** views behavior as a function of previous actions and of the reinforcements or punishments obtained from these actions.[29] For example, while you were growing up, your parents may have given you a present for making good grades or an allowance for mowing the lawn. You learned that these are good behaviors and you were more likely to do these things again in the future because you were rewarded for them.

operant conditioning The view that behavior is a function of the reinforcements and punishments received in the past.

Reinforcement

Reinforcement usually comes from a feeling of satisfaction that occurs when we as consumers perceive that our needs have been adequately met. This reinforcement increases the probability that we will purchase the same brand again. For example, if you buy Liquid Tide and are impressed by its ability to clean clothes, your purchase will be reinforced and you will be more likely to buy this brand again. One study found that past experience with a brand was by far the most critical factor in brand choice—over quality, price, and familiarity.[30] Other research has shown that information consumers receive from product trials tends to be more powerful and influential than that received from advertising.[31] In particular, the thoughts and emotions consumers experience during a trial can have a powerful influence on evaluations.[32]

Note that consumers often perceive few differences among brands of many products and services.[33] They are unlikely to develop a positive brand attitude when no brand is seen as clearly better than another. However, as long as the consumer is not dissatisfied, the choice tactic he or she used will be reinforced. Suppose you buy the cheapest brand of paper towels. If this brand at least minimally satisfies your needs, you are likely to buy the cheapest brand again—and it may be a different brand next time. Thus reinforcement can occur for either the brand or the choice tactic.

Punishment

Alternatively, consumers can have a bad experience with a product or service, form a negative evaluation of it, and not purchase it again. In operant conditioning terms, this experience is called *punishment.* If you did something bad when you were growing up, your parents may have punished you to make sure you would not behave that way again. In a consumer context, punishment occurs when our needs are not met and we are dissatisfied. Thus we learn not to buy the same brand again.

Punishment may also lead the consumer to reevaluate the choice tactic and choose a different tactic for the next purchase. If you buy the cheapest brand of trash bags and the bags burst when you take out the trash, you could either employ a new tactic (buying the most expensive or the most familiar brand) or upgrade your tactic (buying the cheapest *national* brand).

Repeat Purchase

Consumers learn when the same act is repeatedly reinforced or punished over time, as summarized in Exhibit 11.4. This process occurs whenever we buy a common, repeat-purchase product. Thus we learn and gradually acquire a set of choice tactics that will result in a satisfactory choice in each decision situation. Decision-making models have traditionally ignored the key role of consumption in the decision process, focusing more attention on the processing that occurs immediately prior to the decision. But clearly what takes place

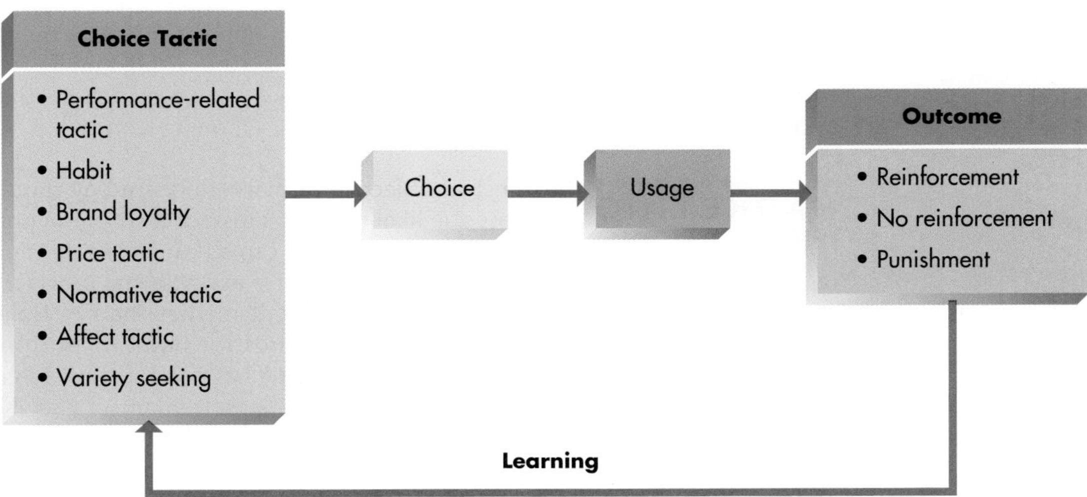

EXHIBIT 11.4 The Learning Process This diagram shows how the outcome of a decision can help consumers learn which choice tactic to apply in a given situation. After consumers apply one of the seven basic types of tactics to make a choice, they take the brand home and use it. During consumption, they can evaluate the brand, which results in one of three basic outcomes: reinforcement (satisfaction leading to positive attitude and repurchase), no reinforcement (leading to tactic reinforcement, but no attitude toward the brand), or punishment (leading to a negative attitude, no repurchase, and tactic reevaluation).

while the product is being consumed has important implications for future acquisition, usage, and disposition decisions. In other words, whether the consumer forms a positive or negative evaluation of the brand or tactic can be an important input into future decisions.

Choice Tactics Depend on the Product

The choice tactics we use often depend on the product category we are considering.[34] For example, we might be brand loyal to Heinz ketchup but always buy the cheapest trash bags. The tactic we learn for a product category depends on which brands are available and our experiences with them. The amount of advertising, price variations, and the number and similarity of brands also influence the type of tactic we employ.[35] Interestingly, the study from Singapore mentioned earlier found a greater similarity in the tactics consumers use for the same product in different cultures (the United States and Singapore) than for products in the same culture.[36] In general, our experiences help us learn what works for each product, and we use these tactics to minimize our decision-making effort for future purchases.

LOW-EFFORT THOUGHT-BASED DECISION MAKING

Each tactic consumers learn for making low-elaboration decisions can have important implications for marketers. As in high-elaboration decisions, these strategies can be divided into two broad categories: thought-based and feeling-based decision making. This section examines cognitive-based decision making, which includes performance-related tactics, habit, brand loyalty, price-related tactics, and normative influences.

Performance as a Simplifying Strategy

performance-related tactics Tactics based on benefits, features, or evaluations of the brand.

When the outcome of the consumption process is positive reinforcement, consumers are likely to use **performance-related tactics** to make their choices. These tactics can represent an overall evaluation (works the best) or focus on a specific attribute or benefit (gets clothes cleaner, tastes better, or has quicker service). Satisfaction is the key: satisfied consumers are likely to develop a positive evaluation of the brand or service and repurchase it based on its features.

MARKETING IMPLICATIONS A principal objective of marketing strategy should be to increase the likelihood of satisfaction through product or service quality. Only then can a brand consistently achieve repeat purchases and loyal users. Campbell's soup, for example, has provided quality products for years, as evidenced by its 75 percent market share.[37] Holiday Inn operators must comply with a variety of standards for hotel room furnishings, amenities, even breakfast offerings so customers will have a consistent, high-quality experience whether they stay in a Holiday Inn in Paris, Rotterdam, or elsewhere.[38]

Advertising can play a central role in influencing performance evaluations by increasing the consumer's expectation of positive reinforcement and satisfaction and lessening the negative effects of an unfavorable consumption experience.[39] Because we see what we want to see and form our expectations accordingly, marketers should select product features or benefits that are important to consumers, help to differentiate the brand from competitors, and convince consumers they will be satisfied if they buy the product. For instance, Coca-Cola gave its Powerade sports drinks differentiating features such as added vitamins and herbs.[40] Chicken of the Sea introduced a Tuna Salad Kit in a pouch, complete with pre-measured amounts of tuna, flavored dressing, and seasoning, for differentiation on the basis of convenience.[41] Another example is the ad for Citrucel in Exhibit 11.5.

Sales promotions such as free samples, price deals, coupons, or premiums (gifts or free merchandise) are often used as an incentive to get the consumer to try the product or service. Marketers hope that if consumers find the product satisfactory, they will continue to buy it when the incentives are withdrawn. These strategies can be successful, however, only if product performance satisfies and reinforces the consumer. They will not overcome dissatisfaction resulting from poor quality or other factors. For example, Snapple failed in Japan, despite heavy promotion, because its beverages had features that Japanese consumers loathe: a cloudy appearance and stuff floating in the bottle.[42] Another caution is that consumers may perceive a price promotion as a signal of lower quality when they are not category experts, when the promotion is not typical of the industry, and when the brand's past behavior is inconsistent.[43] ●

EXHIBIT 11.5
Emphasizing Product Quality
Sometimes ads emphasize features that place the product above the competition. Here Citrucel clearly shows why the brand is better than the main competitor.

Source: Reprinted with permission from GlaxoSmithKline.

Habit as a Simplifying Strategy

Humans are creatures of **habit**. Once we find a convenient way of doing things, we tend to repeat it without really thinking. You probably follow the same routine every morning, drive the same way to work or school, and shop at the same stores. You may even have noticed that students habitually sit in the same general area of the classroom. We do these things because they make life simpler and more manageable.

Sometimes consumers' acquisition, usage, and disposition decisions are based on habit, too. Habit represents one of the simplest and most effortless types of consumer decision making, characterized by: (1) little or no information seeking and (2) little or no evaluation of alternatives. However, habit does not require a strong preference for an offering; rather, it simply involves repetitive behavior and regular purchase.[44] Decision making based on habit also reduces risk.[45] Consumers know the brand will satisfy their needs because they have bought it a number of times in the past. Research supports the effect of habit on low-priced, frequently purchased products. Yet the longer consumers wait to make their next purchase in a product category, the less likely they are to buy the brand they habitually purchase.[46]

habit Doing something the same way every time with little thought.

MARKETING IMPLICATIONS Habit-based decision making has several important implications for marketers who want to develop repeat-purchase behavior and to sell their offerings to habitual purchasers of both that brand and competing products.

Developing repeat-purchase behavior. Getting consumers to acquire or use an offering repeatedly is an important marketing objective because repeat purchases lead to profitability. Marketers can use an operant conditioning technique called **shaping** that leads consumers through a series of steps to a desired response: purchase.[47] Companies often use sales promotion techniques to shape repeat purchase. First, they might offer a free sample to generate brand trial (see Exhibit 11.6 for examples from Thailand). Including a high-value coupon with the sample may induce

shaping Leading consumers through a series of steps to create a desired response.

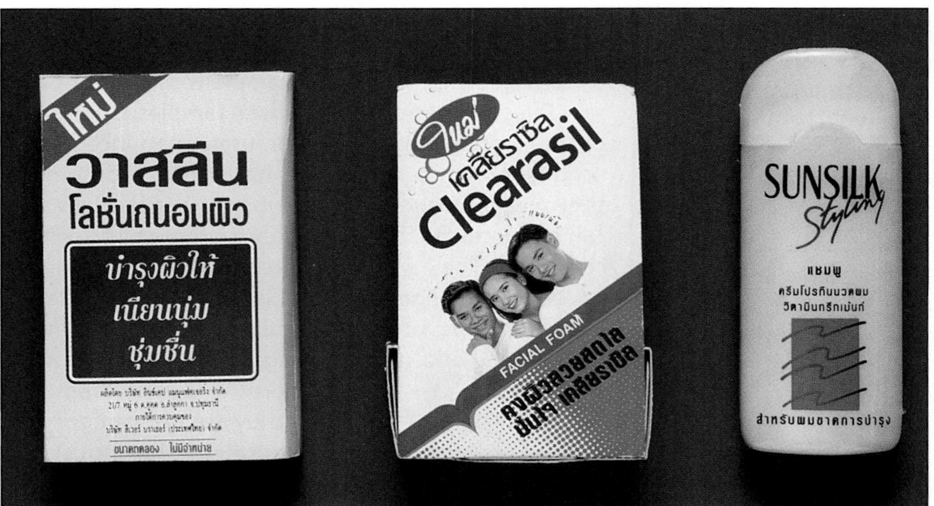

EXHIBIT 11.6
Free Samples
Here are three samples of skin products from Thailand, where sampling is a frequently used marketing tool. Many samples are given out in shopping centers. What types of product samples do you receive?

the consumer to purchase the product. The next step might be to provide a series of lower-value coupons to promote subsequent repurchase. Companies hope that when they withdraw the incentives, the consumer will continue to purchase by habit.

Marketing to habitual purchasers of other brands. A variety of marketing opportunities are available for marketers targeting habitual purchasers of a competing brand. The major goal is to break consumers' habits and induce them to switch to another brand. Because the habitual consumer does not have a strong brand preference, this goal is easier to achieve than it is for brand-loyal consumers. For example, Kellogg's and General Mills are increasing sales of breakfast cereal in Europe by breaking old eating habits in favor of the U.S. tradition of a "quick bite."[48] By observing consumers' habits in taking over-the-counter medications, Procter & Gamble was able to develop more effective packaging for several of its brands, which led consumers to switch.[49]

Sales promotion techniques to induce brand switching include pricing deals, coupons, free samples, and premiums. These special deals may be enough to capture consumers' attention and get them to try the new brand. Procter & Gamble has used coupons generated at the supermarket checkout to target users of a competing dishwashing product. Shoppers who bought Electrasol Tabs received a coupon for a free box of P&G's Cascade Power Tabs.[50] Once the old habit is broken, consumers may continue to purchase the new brand—in this case, Cascade—either because they like it or because they have developed a new habit.

Marketers can also break habits by introducing a new and unique benefit that satisfies consumers' needs better than existing brands. This differential advantage then needs to be heavily advertised to get the word out to consumers. Two examples are Clorox Disinfecting Wipes—promoted as antibacterial and convenient for cleaning household spills—and Hot Pockets wraps, promoted as quick to heat and convenient to eat.[51] Exhibit 11.7 is an example of a product that might induce consumers to switch to French's mustard because it has a unique, no mess cap. In the United Kingdom, Brooke Bond introduced a revolutionary pyramid-shaped tea bag that makes better-tasting tea.[52] Shikishima Baking has tried to break the habits of Japanese consumers by introducing self-buttering bread.[53]

Finally, distribution policies are very important for habitual purchasing. In general, the greater the amount of shelf space a brand has in the store, the more likely the brand is to get consumers' attention. A product's location may be enough to

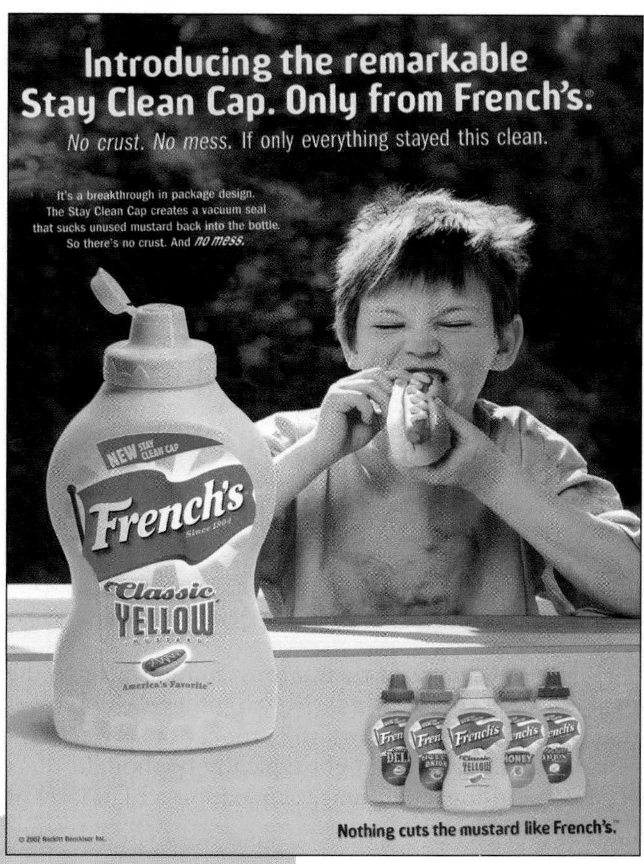

Introducing the remarkable Stay Clean Cap. Only from French's.
No crust. No mess. If only everything stayed this clean.
It's a breakthrough in package design. The Stay Clean Cap creates a vacuum seal that sucks unused mustard back into the bottle. So there's no crust. And no mess.
NEW STAY CLEAN CAP
French's
Classic YELLOW
MUSTARD
America's Favorite
Nothing cuts the mustard like French's.

EXHIBIT 11.7
A New and Unique Benefit
In this ad, French's is advertising a new and unique benefit of a stay clean cap. Thus there is no mess in using this mustard.

Source: © 2002 Reckitt Benckiser Inc. Used by permission.

capture the habitual consumer's attention and plant the idea to buy something else. An end-of-aisle display can sometimes increase a brand's sales by 100 to 400 percent.[54] In one study, eye-catching displays increased sales of frozen dinners by 245 percent, laundry detergent by 207 percent, and salty snacks by 172 percent.[55] In another study, sales of cough and cold syrups rose by 35 percent when in-store promotions were linked to a point-of-purchase brand display.[56] Thus marketers often try to develop interesting displays, such as the award-winning units shown in Exhibit 11.8.

Marketing to habitual purchasers of one's own brand. Marketers need to make sure that the habits of its own repeat-purchase customers are not broken. Because habitual consumers are susceptible to competitors' deals, marketers need to offer comparable deals to build resistance to switching. This is why a fare cut by any one airline is usually matched immediately by all major competitors.

Distribution is also important to prevent habitual consumers from switching to another brand. One major factor that might force a consumer to break a habit is an out-of-stock condition. Without a strong preference, the consumer is more likely to break the habit and buy another brand than to go to another store. In one study, 63 percent of consumers said they would be willing to buy another brand of groceries and canned foods if their preferred brand was not available.[57] Widespread distribution can ensure that the consumer is not forced to buy something else. For Coke, other soft drinks, and teas to be successful in Japan, they must be widely available in that country's vast network of vending machines.[58]

Finally, advertising can induce resistance to switching. By occasionally reminding the consumer of a reason for buying the brand and keeping the brand name "top of mind," marketers may be able to keep consumers from switching. •

Brand Loyalty as a Simplifying Strategy

brand loyalty Buying the same brand repeatedly because of a strong preference.

Brand loyalty occurs when consumers make a conscious evaluation that a brand or service satisfies their needs to a greater extent than others do and decide to buy the same brand repeatedly for that reason.[59] Essentially, brand loyalty results from *very* positive reinforcement of a performance-related choice tactic. Note that the level of commitment to the brand distinguishes brand loyalty from habit. The stronger this evaluation becomes over time, the higher the degree of brand loyalty. To illustrate, if you purchase Heinz ketchup and decide that it is thicker and tastes better than other brands, you will purchase it again. If this evaluation is reinforced repeatedly, you will develop strong brand loyalty. Consumers can also be **multibrand loyal**,[60] or committed to two or more brands they purchase repeatedly. As an example, if you prefer and purchase only Coke and Sprite, you exhibit multibrand loyalty for soft drinks.

multibrand loyal Buying two or more brands repeatedly because of a strong preference.

Brand loyalty results in low-effort decision making because the consumer does not need to process information when making a decision and simply buys

EXHIBIT 11.8A AND B
Award-Winning Displays
By designing eye-popping displays, marketers hope to capture consumers' attention at retail and change their buying habits. This can occur because habitual consumers typically do not have a strong preference for their usual brand. Can you think of any displays that have caught your attention recently?

Source: Designed and produced by Henschel-Steinau, Inc., Englewood, N.J. 07631, U.S.A.

the same brand each time. However, because of their strong commitment to the brand or service, brand-loyal consumers have a relatively high level of involvement with the *brand* whether their involvement with the product or service category is high or low. Thus even though ketchup might typically be thought of as a low-involvement product, the brand-loyal consumer can exhibit a high level of involvement toward the brand Heinz.

MARKETING IMPLICATIONS Brand-loyal consumers form a solid base on which companies can build brand profitability. By identifying the characteristics of these consumers, marketers might discover ways to strengthen brand loyalty. Unfortunately, this task is difficult because marketers cannot obtain a general profile of the brand-loyal consumer that applies to all product categories.[61] In fact, the extent to which a consumer is brand loyal depends on the product category; the consumer who is loyal for ketchup may not be loyal for peanut butter. This means marketers must assess brand loyalty for each specific category.

Identifying brand-loyal customers. One way marketers can identify brand-loyal consumers is to focus on consumer purchase patterns. Consumers who exhibit a particular sequence of purchases (three to four purchases of the same brand in a row) or proportion of purchases (seven or eight out of ten purchases for the same brand) are considered brand loyal.[62] The problem is that because brand loyalty involves both repeat purchases *and* a commitment to the brand, purchase-only measures do not accurately distinguish between habitual and brand-loyal consumers. To truly identify the brand-loyal consumer, marketers must assess both repeat-purchase behavior and a preference for the brand. In one study a measure that looked only at repeat-purchase behavior identified more than 70 percent of the sample of consumers as brand loyal. Adding preference for the brand as a qualifier reduced this percentage to less than 50 percent.[63]

Despite these problems, purchase-only measures of brand loyalty are still widely used in marketing. With the availability of scanner data and online buying information, marketers now have a wealth of information about consumer purchase patterns they can analyze to understand how coupons or pricing changes affect buying. Nevertheless, if the goal is to study brand loyalty, an approach that measures both purchase patterns and preference is preferable.

Developing brand loyalty. Because brand-loyal consumers have a strong brand commitment, they are more resistant to competitive efforts and switching than other consumers. Thus a major goal of marketing is to develop brand loyalty. Knowing that preteen children can be very brand loyal to a particular breakfast cereal, for example, Quaker Oats promotes its Dinosaur Eggs oatmeal as fun and flavorful for children, while advertising the nutritional value and offering discount coupons to build commitment among parents who actually make the purchase.[64] However, the widespread use of pricing deals in the United States has gradually eroded consumer loyalty toward many brands, leading more consumers to buy on the basis of price. Therefore, marketers are now striving to develop consumer loyalty through product quality or sales promotions. Note that this problem has not developed in Europe, where firms use fewer price promotions and loyalty has remained stable.[65]

Developing brand loyalty through product quality. One obvious and critical way to develop brand loyalty is to provide the consumer with a high-quality product that leads to satisfaction. Smithfield Foods has done this with higher-quality pork and beef products, leading to a 20 percent ownership of the U.S. market for pork products despite competition from both branded and unbranded meat products.[66] As another example, Bissinger French Confections creates top-quality candy one piece at a time, building "a tremendous following of people who've been ordering from us for years," says the CEO.[67] In Japan, "low smoke" cigarettes have been successful because of concern about the effects of secondhand smoke.[68]

Recent evidence suggests that consumers will become brand loyal to high-quality brands if these products are offered at a fair price. Consequently, many companies have lowered prices on their major brands.[69] Procter & Gamble, for instance, has cut the price of Luv's, its lowest priced disposable diapers, as part of a plan to increase market share.[70]

Developing brand loyalty through sales promotions. Many companies cultivate brand loyalty through sales promotions. One approach is to use a coupon premium, whereby the consumer saves special coupons, proof-of-purchase seals, or UPC codes to acquire gifts or prizes free or for a small cost. To illustrate, buyers of Betty Crocker baking products can collect box tops to either earn prizes from a gift catalog or earn money for a local school. Buying ten pizzas or CDs to get one free is another type of promotion.

Frequent-flyer programs have been successful in building brand loyalty for airlines such as American and Southwest. Consumers repeatedly fly on the same airline to build up mileage points that can be exchanged for free trips or other goods and services. These programs have even been expanded so that consumers can earn points by using certain phone companies, staying at certain hotels (see Exhibit 11.9), or charging their purchases on certain credit cards. In the Harrah's Entertainment program, for example, consumers earn credits when they gamble or make related purchases at Harrah's properties. Participants then receive credit certificates good for their next visit to Harrah's, which encourages them to return.[71] In France, Quick Burger awards points to consumers every time they eat at the restaurant, and the points can be redeemed for valuable prizes and discounts.[72] In addition, the technique of shaping (discussed earlier) can also be employed to develop brand loyalty.

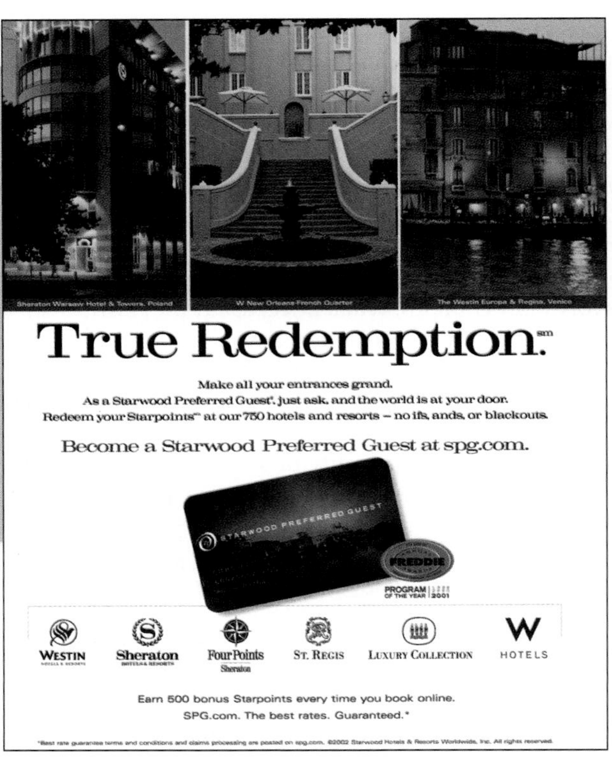

EXHIBIT 11.9
Building Brand Loyalty
Some hotel chains offer programs where consumers can earn 'points' which can then be redeemed for rewards. The Starwood Preferred Guest program offers special treatments and free nights at selected hotels to stimulate repeat stays at Starwood Hotels.

Source: Courtesy of Starwood Hotels and Resorts.

Marketing to brand-loyal consumers of other brands. Marketers want to induce brand-loyal users of competitive brands to switch to their brands. However, because these consumers are strongly committed to other brands, getting them to switch is extremely difficult. As a result, it is usually better to avoid these consumers and try to market toward nonloyal or habitual consumers. The one exception is a brand with a strong point of superiority or differentiation over the competitive brands. In this case the superior attribute might be enough to persuade brand-loyal consumers to switch. For example, Red Bull, an energy drink, has captured market share from other sports drinks with its proprietary formula of vitamins, amino acids, caffeine, and other ingredients.[73] ●

Price as a Simplifying Strategy

price-related tactics Tactics based on price or cost.

Consumers are most likely to use **price-related tactics** such as buying the cheapest, buying the brand on sale, or using a coupon when they perceive few differences among brands and when they have low involvement with the brands in the consideration set. One study found that nine out of ten shoppers entered the store with some strategy for saving money.[74] These strategies are listed in Exhibit 11.10.

Even though price can be a critical factor in many decisions, consumers generally do not remember price information, even for a brand they have just selected.[75] This is because price information is always available in the store, so consumers have little motivation to remember it.

MARKETING IMPLICATIONS Sometimes marketers mistakenly assume that consumers always look for the lowest possible price. Although this assumption is certainly true in some instances, a more accurate statement is that consumers have a zone of acceptance regarding what constitutes an appropriate range of prices for a particular product or service category.[76] As long as the brand falls within this price range, consumers will consider it but reject brands falling either above or below the range. For instance, consumers initially shunned wipe products because they cost more than paper towels and cleaning fluids. Then, after marketers revamped their wipes to promote their germ-killing benefits, consumers began to buy—although some still use price as a primary criterion for choice.[77]

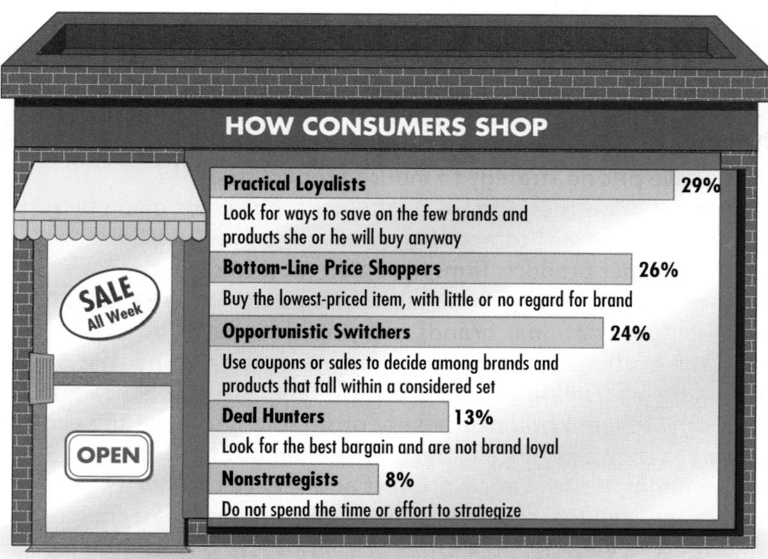

HOW CONSUMERS SHOP
Practical Loyalists 29%
Look for ways to save on the few brands and products she or he will buy anyway
Bottom-Line Price Shoppers 26%
Buy the lowest-priced item, with little or no regard for brand
Opportunistic Switchers 24%
Use coupons or sales to decide among brands and products that fall within a considered set
Deal Hunters 13%
Look for the best bargain and are not brand loyal
Nonstrategists 8%
Do not spend the time or effort to strategize
SALE All Week
OPEN

EXHIBIT 11.10
Money-Saving Strategies
Consumers can use different types of money-saving strategies in their shopping. Which type of shopper are you?

Source: Data from Warwick Baker & Fiore in Laurie Petersen, "The Strategic Shopper," *Adweek's Marketing Week*, March 30, 1992, p. 18.

Consumers may also reject products that are priced too low because they infer that something is wrong with the product. Buyers would be suspicious if a pair of expensive designer jeans were on sale for $9.99. And, as noted earlier, consumers sometimes use price as a heuristic to judge product or service quality (higher price means higher quality). •

Price Perceptions Consumer perceptions play an important role in the use of price-related tactics. Remember that for consumers to perceive two prices as different, the variation must be at or above the just noticeable difference. Thus consumers might not care if one brand of toothpaste is priced at $1.95 and another at $1.99. Consumers also compare a product's price with an internal reference price for such products.

In addition, perceptual processes figure in the consumer's reaction to different price points. Research has consistently indicated that consumers perceive odd prices (those ending with an odd number) as significantly lower than even prices (those ending with an even number); a CD priced at $11.99 will be perceived as less expensive than one priced at $12.00.[78] Consumers tend to be more responsive to price decreases than they are to price increases.[79] Thus lowering the price of a brand or service will increase sales to a greater degree than increasing price by the same amount will decrease sales. Moreover, when a company heavily discounts a product on an infrequent basis, consumers will perceive the average price as lower than if the product goes on sale frequently but with less of a price reduction.[80]

An interesting study found that when companies put restrictions on the deal, such as a purchase or time limit, consumers perceive the deal as more valuable—but only when motivation to process is low.[81] The words companies use to describe the deal can be a factor. One study found that comparing the sale price to the "regular price" worked better in the store, whereas comparison to competitors' prices was more effective at home.[82] Sometimes deals can be confusing, as was McDonald's "Campaign 55." Consumers did not understand that they needed to purchase fries and a drink to get 55-cent burgers.[83]

deal-prone consumers Consumers who are more likely to be influenced by price.

The Deal-Prone Consumer Marketers are interested in identifying **deal-prone consumers** because this segment is suitable for more directly targeted price-related strategies. Unfortunately, research findings on this issue have been mixed. One study found that deal-prone consumers are more likely to be lower-income, older, and less educated than non-deal-prone consumers; other studies have found that higher-income consumers have better access to price information and are therefore more able to act on it.[84] Part of the problem is that consumers react differently to different types of deals: some will be more responsive to coupons, while some will be more responsive to price cuts and to rebates.[85]

MARKETING IMPLICATIONS Pricing strategy is clearly important to marketers, and they can use a variety of pricing techniques, including coupons, price-offs, rebates, and two-for-ones as long as the savings are at or above the just noticeable difference and within the zone of acceptance. P&G's checkout coupon for a free box of Cascade Power Tabs is a good example of an effective pricing strategy to induce product trial.

The importance of deals is evidenced by the deep price cuts made by supermarket chains spurred by the stiff competition from warehouse clubs and discount drugstores. Major consumer products firms have also cut prices in response to competition from store brands. Private-label store brands, which are promoted as being equal in quality to national brands but priced lower, have experienced strong growth in the United States and in Europe. One study found that 66 percent of U.S. shoppers are willing to buy a private-label store product.[86] In the United Kingdom private-label brands are very profitable and have the choicest spots on supermarket shelves.[87] Price wars have broken out in the United States and the United Kingdom in such varied product and service categories as disposable diapers, cigarettes, iced tea, breakfast cereals, and airlines.[88] Fast-food restaurants in Japan have been engaged in a bitter pricing battle, which McDonald's is winning.[89] The ability to search for lower prices is also the reason many consumers like to shop on the Internet.

The importance of value. Consumers are looking for good value—that is, a high-quality brand at a good price. Fast-food chains such as Burger King, McDonald's, and Taco Bell therefore seek to satisfy consumers by offering special "value meals." Note that *value* does not always mean lower price. Consumers will pay a higher price if they believe the product or service provides an important benefit.[90] European consumers, for instance, are willing to pay more for the convenience of premeasured laundry detergent tablets offered under such well-known brands as Wisk and Tide.[91]

One way for marketers to deliver value without lowering prices is to provide a differential benefit and convince consumers that the brand is worth the extra cost. For example, Colgate bet—correctly—that consumers would pay more for Total toothpaste, which has a special germ-fighting ingredient.[92] In Mexico, cosmetics are extremely important to a woman's appearance, and many Mexican women will spare no expense in purchasing these products.[93]

Special pricing. Marketers should avoid using pricing deals too often, or consumers will perceive the special price as the regular price. Then consumers will not buy unless the brand is on sale, resulting in lost profits. This situation has happened in the past to food chains such as Arby's and Domino's. Too many deals can also damage brand loyalty as consumers become too deal oriented and switch brands more often. Thus deals tend to work best when they are used intermittently and selectively. Lower brand loyalty has become a major concern in many product and service categories in the United States and is the reason many companies want to move away from deals and toward brand-building strategies such as advertising and sampling.[94]

The use of pricing deals also varies with the country. Coupons are commonly used in the United States, where 4.5 billion are redeemed every year.[95] Many Web-based sellers use online coupons to attract and retain customers; however, excessive discounts can hurt profitability, as the now closed Vitamins.com site learned after offering $25 off a purchase of $25.01 or more.[96] The trend in the United Kingdom and Italy has been toward fewer coupons of higher value.[97] In many countries coupons are not used for a variety of reasons, including: the allowed discount is too small (Germany), retailers will not accept them (Holland

and Switzerland), and the retail infrastructure cannot accommodate them (Russia and Greece).

Price consciousness is not static. As might be expected, consumers tend to be more price conscious in difficult economic times than in times of prosperity. For more than a decade, the sluggish Japanese economy has contributed to the enormous popularity of discount stores in a country that once scorned them, and coupon use also increased there.[98] Even the Japanese cosmetics industry, known for notoriously high prices, has discounted prices as much as 30 percent. ●

Normative Influences as a Simplifying Strategy

normative choice tactics Low-elaboration decision making that is based on others' opinions.

Sometimes other individuals can influence consumers' low-elaboration decision making. A college freshman may buy the brand of laundry detergent his mother uses at home; a sophomore might buy clothing that her friends like. Our use of such **normative choice tactics** can result from (1) *direct influence*, in which others try to manipulate us, (2) *vicarious observation*, in which we observe others to guide our behavior, and (3) *indirect influence*, in which we are concerned about the opinions of others. Normative tactics are particularly common among inexperienced consumers who have little knowledge. Note that chat groups on the Internet can increase the importance of normative influence in decision making because consumers can talk to each other so easily.

MARKETING IMPLICATIONS If normative tactics are particularly evident in a product or service category, companies can emphasize these motivations in advertising. A good example of this strategy is an ad for Ritz crackers that shows how pleased party guests will be when you "serve it on a Ritz." Consumers often buy expensive imported products to impress others. Marketers can also attempt to stimulate word-of-mouth communication in ways that will be described in Chapter 16. ●

LOW-EFFORT FEELING-BASED DECISION MAKING

The final category of low-effort strategies covers decisions based more on feelings than on cognitive processing. These types of strategies include affective tactics, variety seeking, and impulse purchasing.

Feelings as a Simplifying Strategy

affect Low-level feelings.

At times, consumers will select a brand or service because they like it, even though they may not know why. This behavior relies on very basic, low-level feelings or **affect**. Affect differs from cognitive strategies such as performance-related attitudes in that it does not necessarily result from a conscious recognition of need satisfaction and is usually weaker than an attitude.

affect-related tactics Tactics based on feelings.

Affect is most likely to play a role in the decision process when the product or service is hedonic (rather than functional) and when other factors, such as performance evaluations, price, habit, and normative influences, are not in operation. If you buy Heinz ketchup because it best satisfies your needs or if you usually buy only the cheapest brand of paper towels, affect is less likely to be part of your decision. However, when these factors do not operate in low-effort situations, affect can then play a central role.

affect referral A type of affective tactic in which we simply remember our feelings for the product or service.

Affect Referral **Affect-related tactics** use a form of category-based processing.[99] In other words, we associate brands with global affective evaluations we recall from memory when making a choice, a process called **affect referral** or the "how do I feel about it" heuristic.[100] For instance, when we hear the name *Starbucks*, we might associate it with general feelings of happiness and joy and we might decide to get coffee there based on these feelings, rather than on a detailed evaluation of Starbucks. In one study, consumers choosing between a healthy dessert and a less healthy chocolate cake chose the dessert associated with the most positive affect (the cake) when they had little opportunity to think about the choice. When they had more time to think, however, they chose the healthier dessert, suggesting that affect referral is more of a factor when processing effort is low.[101]

Whenever a consumer encounters a new brand, he or she can also compare it to other brands in the same category. To the extent that the new brand is similar to previously encountered brands, the affect associated with that category can be transferred to the new instance and influence choice.[102] On the other hand, if the new brand is perceived as dissimilar, the consumer is more likely to switch to piecemeal processing, evaluating attributes in the manner described in Chapter 10.[103] For example, teens may perceive the original Jell-O product as old-fashioned and therefore dislike it. However, they may have a very different reaction to X-treme Gel Sticks, a recently introduced version of Jell-O in push-up packaging that comes in green apple and watermelon flavors. Because the product name, the flavors, and the packaging are all dissimilar to traditional Jell-O attributes, teens may be able to evaluate the attributes of the newer product on their own terms rather than in light of their affect for Jell-O.[104]

brand familiarity
Easy recognition of a well-known brand.

Brand Familiarity Affect can also be generated from **brand familiarity** (through the mere exposure effect). In one study, beer drinkers with well-established brand preferences could not distinguish their preferred brand from others in a blind taste test.[105] However, when the beers were identified, consumers rated the taste of their preferred brand significantly higher than the others. Another study found that "buying the most familiar brand" was a dominant choice tactic for inexperienced purchasers of peanut butter. Even when the quality of the most familiar brand was manipulated to be lower than unfamiliar brands, consumers still greatly preferred the familiar brand.[106]

These findings were replicated in a study in Singapore, suggesting that the impact of brand familiarity may be a cross-cultural phenomenon.[107] Another study found that brand name was a more important heuristic cue in a low-elaboration situation than in a high-elaboration one.[108] And, according to research, 27 brands that were tops in their category in 1930 (and thus were most familiar) still rank high today, including Campbell's soup, Ivory soap, and Gold Medal flour.[109] Coca-Cola, the world's most valuable brand, is a household name due, in part, to its consistent, highly visible marketing.[110] Yet aggressively promoted local brands such as Crazy Cola that work hard to gain brand familiarity are outselling Coke and other global brands in Siberia and other areas.[111] Very young children can be influenced by brand names if they are accompanied with visual cues like the Froot Loops toucan.[112]

Visual Attributes Affect plays a key role in determining aesthetic responses to marketing stimuli, especially when visual properties are the only basis for judgment. In Yellow Pages advertising, for example, consumers are more likely to consider firms with color ads and more likely to call those with product-enhancing color.[113] One study found that two key aspects of a product's design produce more positive affective responses to the product.[114] These are *unity*, which means that the visual parts of the design connect in a meaningful way, and *prototypicality*, which means that the object is representative of its category.

MARKETING IMPLICATIONS Given that feelings can play an important role in the decision process, marketers can attempt to create and maintain brand familiarity, build category-based associations, and generate affect through advertising that creates positive attitudes toward the ad. By creating positive affect toward their brand, marketers can increase the probability that it will be selected (all other things being equal).

The power of brand name familiarity was demonstrated years ago when Coca-Cola changed its formula. Even though most consumers preferred the taste of New Coke in blind taste tests, a strong preference for the old formula resurfaced when brand names were identified. In fact, the demand for the old brand was so strong that the company reintroduced Coca-Cola Classic under public pressure. As shown in Exhibit 11.11, Crest is a highly familiar and positively evaluated brand of toothpaste. In Romania and Turkey, buying well-known brand names is very important because it increases a consumer's prestige.[115] Most of the status brands, however, are foreign.

Now that U.S. pharmaceutical companies are permitted to engage in direct-to-consumer advertising, they have raised the brand familiarity of prescription drugs and increased sales for the anti-impotence drug Viagra and the antidepressant drug Zoloft, among others.[116] Johnson & Johnson placed the name of a well-known nonprofit group on its Arthritis Foundation Pain Reliever in the hope that the associated familiarity and affect will transfer over to the brand. The company also donated $1 million to the group.[117] Even the Vatican Library is allowing its name to be placed on various products, including watches, jewelry, and greeting cards.[118]

co-branding An arrangement by which two brands form a partnership to benefit from the power of two.

Many companies now engage in **co-branding**, an arrangement by which two brands form a partnership to benefit from the power of two.[119] Examples include ConAgra and Kellogg's, Kraft and Boboli, and Ocean Spray and Pepsi. Hearst Custom Publishing is co-branding *Jordan* magazine with Nike, which markets sports shoes named after basketball star Michael Jordan.[120] Liquor companies are using co-branding to get around advertising restrictions by placing their name on food (Jack Daniel's Grill with TGI Friday's, and Kahluaccino Drink Mix).[121]

Brands that have positive cross-cultural affect can be marketed internationally. In expanding to Europe and Asia, Nathan's hot dogs hoped that the excitement of New York would create positive category associations and make selling easier.[122] Likewise, U.S. tobacco companies have used a positive "Western" association to sell cigarettes in Eastern Europe.[123] The U.S. image has also benefited companies such as Procter & Gamble, Colgate-Palmolive, and Johnson & Johnson in selling toiletries and detergents in China.[124]

Hedonic products or services—those that involve style or taste—rely heavily on affective associations. The marketing philosophy at Frito-Lay is "If you can make people feel better about what they are eating, the propensity to consume more is there."[125] Finally, the familiarity of packaging can play an important role in influencing brand choice, which explains why Coca-Cola introduced plastic versions of its familiar glass bottle. •

Decision Making Based on Variety-Seeking Needs

Another common consumer-choice tactic in low-effort situations is to try something different. A consumer might regularly buy Johnson's baby shampoo but one day have an urge to try Pantene shampoo—then return to the baby shampoo for later purchases. In marketing and consumer behavior, this phenomenon is called **variety seeking.**

variety seeking Trying something different.

Consumers engage in variety seeking for two major reasons: *satiation* and *boredom*.[126] If you had the same thing for dinner every night or listened to only

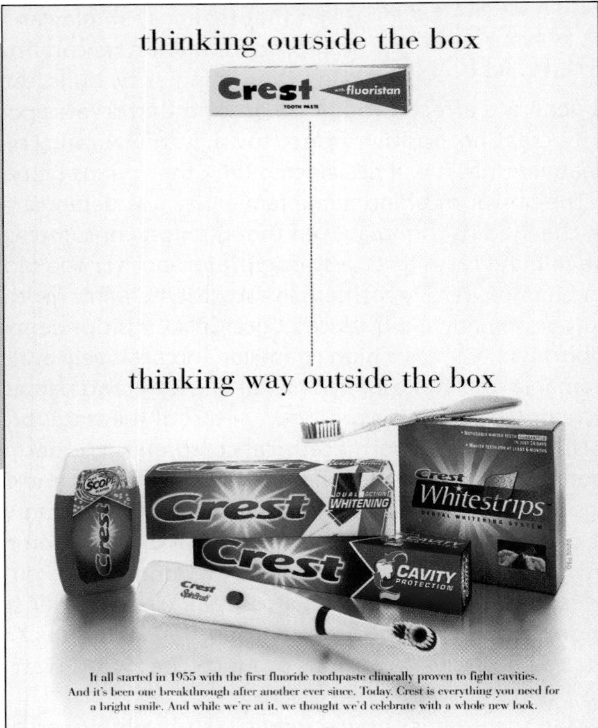

EXHIBIT 11.11
Brand Name Familiarity and Positive Affect
Consumers tend to have more positive feelings toward brands that are more familiar relative to brands that are unfamiliar. The Crest brand is a well-known toothpaste that has been around since 1955.

Source: © The Procter & Gamble Comapny. Used by permission.

one CD over and over, satiation would occur and you would be driven to do something different. Because many consumer decisions occur repeatedly, they can become monotonous. In one study, consumers switched to less-preferred music even though they would have derived more immediate enjoyment from repeating a more-preferred song; later, they had more positive memories of the song sequence that included both favored and less-favored music than of the sequence that included only favored music.[127] Note that variety seeking is not expressed in every product category. It is most likely to occur when involvement is low, there are few differences among brands, and the product is more hedonic than functional.[128] It also tends to occur when consumers become satiated with a particular sensory attribute of a product, such as smell, taste, touch, and visual appearance.[129] Marketers can therefore reduce boredom simply by providing more variety in a product category.[130]

Consumers are motivated to relieve boredom because their level of arousal falls below the **optimal stimulation level (OSL)**—an internal ideal level of stimulation.[131] Repetitive purchasing causes the internal level of stimulation to fall below the OSL, and buying something different is a way of restoring it. In addition, certain consumers need more stimulation and are less tolerant of boredom than others. These **sensation seekers** are more likely to engage in variety seeking and are often the first to try new and trendy products, making them a good market for new offerings.[132]

optimal stimulation level (OSL) The ideal level of stimulation in any situation.

sensation seekers Those who actively look for variety.

Note that purchasing something different is only one way to seek stimulation. Consumers can also express their variety drive by engaging in vicarious exploration and use innovativeness:[133] **Vicarious exploration** occurs when consumers collect information about a product, either from reading or talking with others, or putting themselves in stimulating shopping environments. For example, many people like to go to stores simply to look around or browse—not to buy, just to increase stimulation.

vicarious exploration Seeking information simply for stimulation.

Use innovativeness means using products in a new or different way. For example, a consumer could use an aluminum can that held soup or vegetables to organize nails in a workshop or use baking soda to deodorize a kitty litter box. Consumer use innovativeness actually led to the introduction of a new kitty litter deodorizer product by Arm & Hammer. The woman in Exhibit 11.12 is demonstrating another example of use innovativeness.

use innovativeness The extent to which an old product is put to new uses.

MARY MILKOVISCH MADE A HOUSE WITH RECYCLED BEER CANS.
RUFFIES MADE A TRASH BAG WITH RECYCLED MILK JUGS.
RUFFIES
ECO-CHOICE
Introducing Ruffies* Eco-Choice™ Trash Bags. The first trash bags made with at least 33% recycled plastic bottles (like milk jugs) collected from community recycling centers. Which won't save the planet, of course. But it is something *simple* you can do to help the environment.
ECO-CHOICE™ TRASH BAGS
Made tough. Made with recycled plastic.
RUFFIES

EXHIBIT 11.12
Use Innovativeness
Some consumers think of new and different ways to use products. This consumer made a house with recycled beer cans. Eco-Choice is introducing its plastic bags made with at least 33 percent recycled plastic milk bottles. Have you or anyone you know ever demonstrated use innovativeness?

Source: Carlisle Plastics, Inc.

impulse purchase
An unexpected purchase based on a strong feeling.

MARKETING IMPLICATIONS Marketers sometimes need to recognize consumers' need for variety and take steps to combat it. For example, Colgate has introduced new scented detergents such as Sunshower Fresh Fab, recognizing that consumers may tire of the original scent.[134] The company hopes consumers will express their need for variety by buying Fab in a different scent rather than switching to another brand. As many consumers have tired of the ordinary cola taste, companies have introduced new soft drink flavors such as Pepsi Twist, a lemon-flavored cola.[135] Interestingly, the largest increase in flavored soft drinks occurred in single-serve sizes, which involves less risk than buying a six- or twelve-pack (lending support to the variety-seeking theory).

Marketers can attempt to induce brand switching among variety-seekers by encouraging consumers to "put a little spice into life" and try something different. However, consumers may not like *too* much variety. For example, KFC consumers began to cry "No more" in response to the chain's many menu additions.[136] Consumers also became bored with the many new product introductions in the "new age" beverage category (teas and juices).[137] •

Buying on Impulse

Another common type of decision process that has a strong affective component is the **impulse purchase**, which occurs when consumers suddenly decide to purchase something they had not planned on buying. Impulse purchases are characterized by: (1) an intense or overwhelming feeling of having to buy the product immediately, (2) a disregard for potentially negative purchase consequences, (3) feelings of euphoria and excitement, and (4) a conflict between control and indulgence.[138] They are often instigated by the consumer's exposure to an external stimulus, such as an in-store display, catalog, or TV ad with a phone number. Many consumers decide to travel on impulse (the "spur of the moment").[139]

Researchers estimate that anywhere from 27 to 62 percent of consumer purchases can be considered impulse buys.[140] However, it is important to distinguish between impulse buying and partially planned purchases, or those for which the consumer has an intention to buy the product category but uses the store display to decide which brand to select. When this distinction is made, the proportion of impulse purchases is usually lower.[141] The tendency to engage in impulse purchasing varies; some consumers can be considered highly impulsive buyers, whereas others are not.[142] The tendency to buy on impulse is probably related to other traits such as general acquisitiveness and materialism, sensation seeking, and a liking for recreational shopping.[143] If the costs of impulsiveness are made salient or if normative pressure such as the presence of others with a negative opinion is high, consumers will engage in less impulse purchasing.[144]

MARKETING IMPLICATIONS Many stores organize their merchandise to maximize impulse purchases. Card shops position commonly sought items such as greeting cards near the back so consumers will have to pass a number of displays containing higher-margin, impulse items. As discussed earlier, eye-level and eye-catching displays, including end-of-aisle displays, electronic bulletin boards, and blinking lights, can increase sales dramatically—mostly from impulse purchases.[145] This is why suppliers pay high prices for the best display space in a store.[146] It also explains why the American Greetings and Hallmark Web sites suggest gifts and add-on products when consumers are in the process of sending electronic greeting cards. In addition, package design can increase impulse purchases. In the candy industry, which enjoys a lot of impulse buying, Brach's sold many of its candies in identical pink bags until the company redesigned its packages to have a more dramatic and contemporary look, hoping to increase impulse buying.[147]

Impulse purchasing tends to decline in difficult economic times. In Japan, for example, the lengthy economic recession has led many consumers to buy only what they need, such as clothes and items for children. As a result, marketers have had to reposition many products as necessities rather than as impulse items.[148]

SUMMARY

This chapter examined the nature of consumer judgment and decision making when motivation, ability, and opportunity—and consequently elaboration—are low. In these situations, consumers often make judgments using simplified heuristics or decision rules. When using the representativeness heuristic, consumers base their judgments on comparisons to a category prototype. When using the availability heuristic, they base their judgments on accessibility of information.

Consumers can use choice tactics that are either cognitively based (performance, habit, brand loyalty, price, normative) or based on feelings (affect, variety seeking, impulse). They learn these tactics over repeat purchase occasions through a process similar to operant conditioning.

Performance-related tactics are more likely to be employed when the consumer's needs have been satisfied and the consumer has formed positive attitudes based on consumption, which is why product or service quality is so important. Some consumers purchase by habit or simple repetitive behavior. Marketers want to encourage consumers to continue buying certain brands while attempting to induce users of competing brands to switch. Brand loyalty represents the most desirable situation for marketers because the consumer possesses a strong commitment to the brand and buys it repeatedly. Marketers can build brand loyalty by offering high-quality products as well as by providing special incentives to the consumer for repeat purchases. Price-related tactics can be effective when consumers perceive few differences among brands or when economic motives are extremely important. As long as the price of the brand or service falls within the zone of acceptance, the consumer will consider buying it. When the consumer is inexperienced, has little knowledge, or considers the opinion of others very important, the decision may be guided by normative tactics. In this case, marketers can emphasize normative motivations in their ad messages.

Consumers' use of affect-related tactics implies that marketers should attempt to build and maintain brand familiarity and positive attitudes toward their ads. In addition, marketers need to be aware that some consumers will switch brands because of a need for variety. Finally, many purchases are made on impulse and marketers can organize the purchase environment to induce this type of activity.

QUESTIONS FOR REVIEW AND DISCUSSION

1. How do base-rate information and the law of small numbers bias judgments made on the basis of the availability heuristic?
2. How is the high-effort hierarchy of effects similar to and different from the low-effort hierarchy?
3. What operant conditioning concepts apply to consumer learning?
4. Why is quality an important ingredient in cognitive-based decision making?
5. What is brand loyalty, and what role does it play in low-effort decision making?
6. How do price and value perceptions affect low-effort decision making?

7. When is affect likely to be more of a factor in low-effort decision making?

8. If habit is a simplifying strategy, why do consumers sometimes seek variety?

EXERCISES

1. Interview ten consumers about their decision-making behavior for the following product categories: peanut butter, laundry detergent, canned vegetables, coffee, and ice cream. Ask the consumers to indicate (a) how much time and effort they take in making a decision and (b) how they select the brand they purchase (which choice tactics do they use?). Summarize the responses for each consumer individually and for all consumers; also, answer the following questions:
   - a. On average, how much time and effort do consumers spend on these decisions?
   - b. What are the major types of tactics employed for each category?
   - c. How do the tactics differ for the product categories?
   - d. Do consumers use the same or different tactics across product categories?
   - e. What are the marketing implications of your findings?

2. Pick two common product categories where low-elaboration decision making is likely to occur. Go to your local store and observe 20 consumers making a choice for these two products. Record the amount of time taken and the number of brands examined. If possible, ask consumers why they chose the brand they did immediately after the choice. (Be sure to get the store's permission first.) Summarize this information, and answer the following questions:
   - a. How much time and effort did consumers typically devote to these decisions? Are your findings consistent with those reported in the chapter?
   - b. What were the most common types of choice tactics employed?
   - c. Did the types of choice tactics differ between product categories? If so, why do you think this occurred?

3. Pick ten product or service categories in which low-elaboration decision making is likely to occur. For each category, try to identify the type of choice tactic you would typically use.
   - a. Does this tactic differ across categories?
   - b. If so, why?
   - c. How do you think you learned to use these tactics?

chapter 12

Post-Decision Processes

Introduction: After Consumers Click and Buy

More and more consumers are shopping on the Internet. Most have had positive experiences, but some horror stories have emerged about packages that arrived late, credit cards that were charged for items never purchased or received, sale items that were out of stock, and inadequate customer service to handle questions and inquiries. Online shoppers seeking customer assistance were also frustrated by sluggish or confusing Web sites. Because 28 percent of consumers who experience problems will not buy from that Web site again, companies doing business online need to focus as much on pleasing existing customers as on acquiring new customers.

Retailer Hanover Direct, which operates Domestications, International Male, and other catalogs and Web sites, works hard to prevent customer dissatisfaction. Through research, the company learned that a large percentage of customers who put products into their online shopping carts click away from the site before completing the purchase. In response, Hanover Direct began offering online customer assistance and including a picture of each product in the shopping cart so shoppers could quickly review their purchases before buying. Most important, the company signed up with BizRate.com, an independent site that asks customers to rate their experiences with Hanover Direct. Immediately after a purchase on Hanover Direct, a BizRate screen pops up inviting the customer to rate the shopping experience. One to two weeks later, after the merchandise has been delivered, BizRate sends an e-mail asking the customer to rate the experience one more time. In this way, Hanover Direct can pinpoint problems such as late delivery and make changes that will keep customers coming back in the future. For example, in Exhibit 12.1[1] International Male tries to please and help existing customers with features such as "editor's choice," "find your size," and "free newsletter."

This example illustrates several key topics in this chapter. First, it demonstrates how dissatisfaction can occur when consumers believe that a company has not lived up to their expectations. Second, it highlights

EXHIBIT 12.1
Making Customer Satisfaction a Priority
Source: Courtesy of International Male.

the importance of customer satisfaction as the foundation of a successful business. Third, it shows how customer satisfaction can be a function of good performance, creating positive feelings and perceptions of equity (a fair exchange). Finally, it illustrates how consumers can learn about products and services by experiencing them directly, as Internet shoppers have done.

All these phenomena occur after the consumer has made a decision. This chapter examines the four post-decision processes shown in Exhibit 12.2: dissonance and regret, consumer learning, satisfaction/dissatisfaction, and disposition—all of which have important implications for marketers. ●

POST-DECISION DISSONANCE AND REGRET

Consumers are not always confident in their acquisition, consumption, or disposition decisions. They may feel uncertain as to whether they made the correct choice or even regret the decision they made, as the following sections show.

Dissonance

After you make a decision related to acquisition, consumption, or disposition, you may sometimes feel uncertain about whether you made the correct choice. You might wonder whether you should have bought a shirt or dress other than the one you did, or whether you should have worn something else to a party, or whether you should have kept an old teddy bear instead of throwing it away. **Post-decision dissonance** is most likely to occur when more than one alternative is attractive and the decision is important.[2]

post-decision dissonance A feeling of anxiety over whether the correct decision was made.

Post-decision dissonance can influence consumer behavior because it creates anxiety that the consumer would like to reduce, especially when motivation, ability, and opportunity (MAO) are high. One way of reducing dissonance is to search for additional information from sources such as experts and magazines. This search is very selective and is designed to make the chosen alternative more attractive and the rejected ones less attractive, thereby reducing dissonance.

Regret

post-decision regret A feeling that one has made the wrong purchase decision.

Post-decision regret occurs when consumers perceive an unfavorable comparison between the performance of the chosen option and the performance of the unchosen options. If you consider three cars before making your purchase decision, and then find out that the resale value of the car you bought is much lower than either of the two options, you may regret your purchase and wish you had chosen one of the other cars. In fact, research indicates you may feel regret even if you have no information about the unchosen alternatives—especially if you cannot reverse your decision, have a negative outcome from your chosen alternative, or have made a change from the status quo. Your feelings of regret can also directly influence your intention to buy the same kind of car again.[3] Porsche has used regret in an ad promoting its Carrera 4S model (see Exhibit 12.3 on page 275).

Researchers are also investigating how the consumer's anticipation of post-decision regret can affect a decision about making a purchase and how both pre- and postpurchase price comparisons of alternatives affect regret. One study suggests that if consumers who receive postpurchase information want to avoid feeling regret after a future decision, they should postpone their purchases for a longer period.[4]

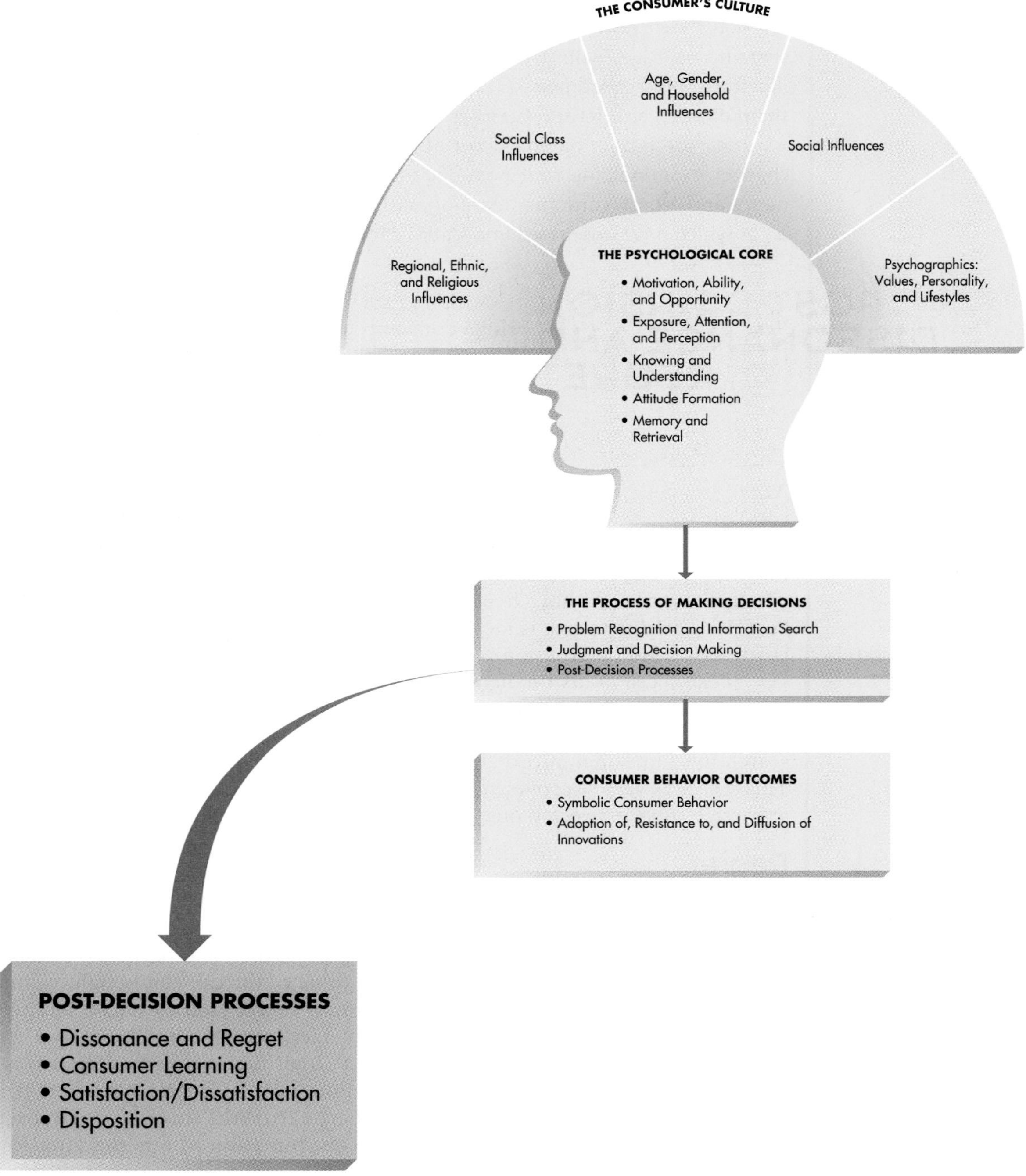

EXHIBIT 12.2

Chapter Overview: Post-Decision Processes

The decision does not end after consumers make a choice or a purchase. Consumers can experience dissonance (anxiety over whether the correct decision was made) or regret after a purchase, learn about the product or service by using it, experience satisfaction or dissatisfaction with the product or service, and eventually dispose of it. This chapter examines the theories and implications underlying each of these important processes.

EXHIBIT 12.3

Advertising Based on Feelings of Regret

In this ad, Porsche uses the theme "buyer's remorse" to encourage consumers to think about how good they will feel after buying the Carrera 4S model.

Source: PORSCHE, CARRERA, 4S, the Porsche Crest and the shape of the PORSCHE 911 CARRERA 4S are registered trademarks of Dr. Ing. h.c.F. Porsche AG. Used with permission of Porsche Cars North America, Inc. Copyrighted by Porsche Cars North America, Inc.

Buyer's remorse.
"Why didn't I do this 10 years ago?"
What better way to make up for lost time than a new 3.6 liter, 320 hp engine? The Carrera 4S. Timeless lines sculpt its wide body. All-wheel drive sticks it to even the most serpentine stretches of road. Post-purchase bliss awaits at your dealer. Contact us at 1-800-PORSCHE or porsche.com.

MARKETING IMPLICATIONS

By helping consumers reduce post-decision dissonance and regret, marketers can diminish any negative feelings related to the product or service. They accomplish this by helping consumers obtain supporting information. For example, consumers who purchase a BMW receive a copy of *BMW Magazine*, which is filled with interesting facts and "feel good" information about the car. This supporting information reduces dissonance and helps consumers develop a positive attitude toward the vehicle. Consumers may also reduce dissonance and regret by reading supporting information in advertisements after a purchase. ●

LEARNING FROM CONSUMER EXPERIENCE*

Earlier chapters explained how consumers acquire knowledge through processes such as information search, exposure to marketing communications, and observation of others. From a practical perspective, when we think about consumer learning, we most often think about this type of learning because it is usually under the direct control of the marketer, who provides information through marketing communications. However, these efforts are often limited because of their low credibility.[5] Consumers assume that these messages are intended to persuade them to buy the product or service and are therefore generally skeptical about the truthfulness of marketing claims.

Experiences that occur during consumption or disposition, however, can be equally—if not more—important sources of consumer knowledge for several reasons. First, the consumer tends to be more motivated to learn under these circumstances. Actually experiencing an event is more involving and interesting than being told about it, and the consumer has more control over what happens. Second, information acquired from experience is more vivid and therefore easier to remember than other types of information.[6] Finally, information about attributes that must be experienced through taste, touch, or smell exerts a stronger influence on consumers' future behavior when it comes from experience or product trial than when it is acquired from advertising or

(*This section draws heavily from an article by Stephen J. Hoch and John Deighton, "Managing What Consumers Learn from Experience," *Journal of Marketing*, April 1989, pp. 1–20.)

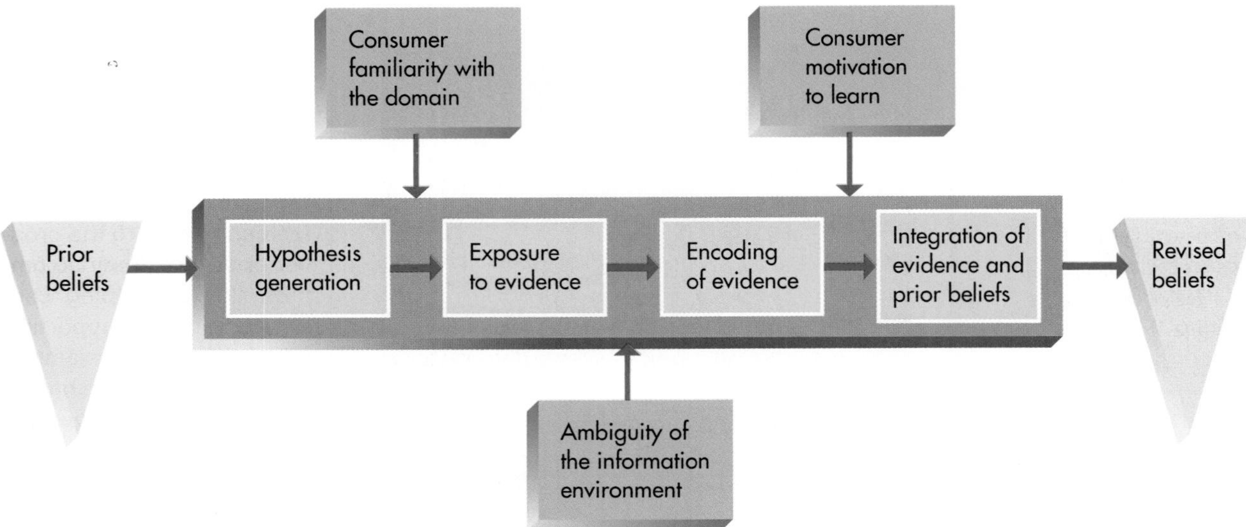

EXHIBIT 12.4
A Model of Learning from Experience

Consumers can acquire a lot of information about products and services by actually experiencing them. This learning process starts with prior beliefs (as one example, "German beers are great"). Upon seeing a new beer from Germany, the consumer can generate hypotheses ("I'll bet this new beer is really good"), get exposure to the evidence (buy the new beer and drink it), encode the evidence (evaluate whether it is good or not), and integrate this evidence with prior beliefs (relate current evaluation with past perceptions). If the beer is not good, the consumer will revise beliefs (not all German beers are good). This entire process is influenced by consumer familiarity, motivation to process, and the ambiguity of the information.

Source: Stephen J. Hoch and John Deighton, "Managing What Consumers Learn from Experience," *Journal of Marketing*, April 1989, pp. 1–20. Reprinted by permission.

word of mouth.[7] For example, an ad can state that a product will taste good, but actually eating it is more likely to result in a strong attitude. On the other hand, repeated exposure to ads can approximate the effect of direct experience when it comes to search or informational attributes such as price or ingredients.[8] If an ad is repeated often enough, it can result in strong beliefs about these characteristics.

A Model of Learning from Consumer Experience

hypothesis testing Testing expectations through experience.

hypothesis generation Forming expectations about the product or service.

exposure to evidence Actually experiencing the product or service.

Consumers can learn from experience by engaging in a process of **hypothesis testing.** On the basis of past experience or another source such as word of mouth or advertising, consumers can form a hypothesis or expectation about a product or service, a consumption experience, or a disposition option and then set out to test it. Such hypotheses are important because without them consumers are less likely to gather the evidence they need to learn. Researchers have proposed that consumers go through four basic stages in testing hypotheses for learning: (1) hypothesis generation, (2) exposure to evidence, (3) encoding of evidence, and (4) integration of evidence and prior beliefs (see Exhibit 12.4). The following example illustrates these four stages.

Suppose a consumer is watching TV and sees an exciting ad for a new Jim Carrey movie. She also remembers some of his previous movies, such as *The Truman Show* or *Ace Ventura*. Based on these sources of information, she **generates a hypothesis** about the quality of the new movie ("It must be great"). Next, she seeks out **exposure to evidence** to either confirm or disprove this hypothesis by going to see the new movie. While watching it, she can assess whether or not it is in fact great; this step is called **encoding the evidence.**

encoding of evidence Processing the information experienced.

Finally, after watching the movie, the consumer can **integrate the evidence** with her existing knowledge or beliefs. If she really likes it, confirming her hypothesis, she may have learned that "you can always count on a Jim Carrey movie to be great." However, if she does not like it, as was the case for some consumers with *The Cable Guy* and *The Majestic,* she may form the new belief that "not all Carrey films are great, and I must be careful in the future."

integration of evidence Combining new information with stored knowledge.

This learning process can occur for any aspect of consumer behavior. In other words, consumers can form hypotheses in relation to acquisition (this product/service will fulfill my needs, buying at a flea market will be fun), consumption (sitting in a hot tub will be soothing, listening to the concert will be fun), or disposition (getting rid of this refrigerator will be easy). Learning from experience is also important when consumers use a purchasing agent—either a person or a computer-aided program that helps consumers make a decision. These agents function by using feedback from repeated hypothesis tests to learn what the consumer likes best.[9]

What Affects Learning from Experience?

Four factors affect learning from experience: (1) motivation, (2) prior familiarity or ability, (3) ambiguity of the information environment or lack of opportunity, and (4) processing biases.

Motivation When consumers are motivated to process information, they will generate a number of hypotheses and seek out information to confirm or disprove them, actively engaging in the process of learning from experience. But when motivation is low, consumers will generate few or no hypotheses and will be less likely to learn unless the learning process involves the simpler processes of classical or operant conditioning (see Chapters 7 and 11). Nevertheless, marketers can still facilitate the learning process when motivation is low, as you will see later in this chapter.

Prior Knowledge or Ability Consumers' prior knowledge or ability affects the extent to which they learn from experience. When knowledge is high, consumers are likely to have well-defined beliefs and expectations and are therefore unlikely to generate new hypotheses. Also, experts are less likely than those with moderate knowledge to search for information.[10] Both these factors inhibit learning. In contrast, low-knowledge consumers lack skills to develop hypotheses to guide the learning process.[11] Without guiding hypotheses, consumers have difficulty collecting evidence and learning. Thus, moderately knowledgeable consumers are the most likely to generate hypotheses and learn from experience. Interestingly, experts do have an advantage in learning information about new products and services, thanks to their more extensive knowledge base.[12]

Ambiguity of the Information Environment or Lack of Opportunity Some situations do not provide the opportunity for consumers to learn from experience, which means consumers may lack sufficient information to confirm or disprove hypotheses.[13] Such **ambiguity of information** occurs because many products and services are similar in quality and consumers can glean little information from the experience.

ambiguity of information A condition whereby decision options are hard to differentiate.

Ambiguous information can strongly affect consumers' ability to learn from experience. When consumers have difficulty determining product quality (for such products as beer and motor oil), they tend to support their hypotheses with information from advertising or word of mouth. The main reason is that consumers cannot disprove the information by experiencing the product, so they see the product as consistent with their prior expectations.[14] Thus for many years consumers believed that Listerine prevented colds and that STP oil treatment improved engine performance because these claims could not be disproved by usage. Obviously, the marketer in situations such as these has an unfair advantage, which is why deception in advertising is such an important topic (see Chapters 4 and 20).

On the other hand, when evidence is unambiguous and the product is clearly good or bad, consumers base their perceptions on actual experience and are able to learn a great deal. Unambiguous information tends to be better remembered and to have a greater impact on future decisions.[15] When evidence is ambiguous, evaluations by both experts and novices are strongly influenced by country-of-origin expectations (e.g., the knowledge that a product was made in Japan), but when evidence is unambiguous, experts ignore this information and make evaluations based on actual quality.[16]

Processing Biases Two biases in information processing—the confirmation bias (Chapter 9) and overconfidence (Chapter 10)—can pose major hurdles to the learning process, particularly when evidence is ambiguous.[17] Specifically, these biases inhibit learning by making consumers avoid both negative and highly diagnostic information. For example, a consumer who believes that all Japanese products are of high quality may ignore contrary evidence and not learn anything new about these products.

Negative information is important to the learning process because it provides a more balanced picture of the situation and allows us to make a more accurate test of hypotheses. Research has also shown that the acquisition of disproving evidence has a strong and rapid impact on consumer learning.[18]

MARKETING IMPLICATIONS Ambiguous information and processing biases often inhibit consumer learning about products and services. From a marketing perspective, these learning principles can have important strategic implications, depending on the market position of the product or service.[19]

Top-dog strategies. A product or service that is the market leader or has a large market share is called a *top dog*. Limitations on learning are advantageous to top dogs because consumers will simply confirm existing beliefs and expectations and display overconfidence, particularly when the motivation to learn is low. Thus consumers are less likely to learn new information that might lead to brand switching.

When motivation to learn is high, however, the consumer will try to acquire information that could be disproving and lead to a switch. Marketers can employ three strategies in this kind of situation. First, the top dog can reinforce the agenda by stating specific claims that justify consumers' evaluation of the brand. For example, in its global advertising, Heinz ketchup tries to give consumers a reason why "Mine's Gotta Have Heinz."[20] Second, marketers can encourage consumers not to acquire new information, which is called *blocking exposure to evidence.* In other words, marketers can try to get across the theme, "Why change if it

EXHIBIT 12.5
Differential Advantage
It is often difficult for consumers to state why one airline is better than another (evidence is ambiguous). Thus the strategy here for AeroMexico is to facilitate comparison with market leaders by pointing out the specific advantages of choosing this airline—the world-class dishes prepared by renowned chefs.

Source: Courtesy of AeroMexico Airlines.

works?" Finally, if evidence about the top dog is unambiguous, the consumer simply needs reinforcement as to why the brand is satisfying—called *explaining the experience*—and needs to be encouraged to try it. For example, KFC, the market leader in Shanghai, touts its quality and value compared to that of small local food vendors. In the United States, the company uses the phrase "There's fast food. Then there's KFC" to differentiate itself from burger competitors.[21]

Underdog strategies. Unlike top dogs, *underdogs* (lower-share brands) have everything to gain by encouraging consumer learning because new information may lead to switching. Thus, the underdog gains an advantage by motivating the consumer to learn. When the consumer is not motivated, underdogs face a more difficult task; they must instigate learning by reducing either the product's costs or its perceived risk.

First, the underdog needs to do everything possible to facilitate comparisons with the market leader, such as using comparative ads, setting up side-by-side displays, or providing information online. Facilitating comparisons is what AeroMexico hopes to accomplish in the ad in Exhibit 12.5. In Japan, Budweiser's Buddy beer touts its alcohol content (6 percent) as higher than that of popular competitors.[22] Nevertheless, overconfidence and confirmation biases may stack the odds against these efforts, and the underdog is unlikely to succeed unless it has a strong and distinct advantage.

Second, marketers can disrupt the agenda by employing advertising to create expectations as well as promotions such as sampling to provide the actual experience. If the evidence is ambiguous, expectations are unlikely to be disconfirmed. For example, Walnut Crest advertised to create expectations for its Chilean Merlot wine by encouraging U.S. consumers to take the "$1,000,000 Taste Challenge." The company provided the experience by arranging for restaurants to offer taste comparisons with higher-priced wines.[23] If the evidence is ambiguous, however, consumer expectations are unlikely to be disproved.

Finally, facilitating product trials is critical when the motivation to learn is low but evidence is unambiguous, because evidence will lead to a positive learning experience. Two common means of encouraging product trial are sampling and coupons. To develop consumers' taste for cranberry sauce in the United Kingdom, Ocean Spray gave away free samples of the product.[24] The coupon offer in Exhibit 12.6 is another example of this strategy. ●

EXHIBIT 12.6

Facilitating Trial

The purpose of this coupon is to lower the financial risk and get consumers to try the advertised product. Would this approach affect your behavior?

Source: © 2002 Reckitt Benckiser Inc. Used by permission.

HOW DO CONSUMERS MAKE SATISFACTION OR DISSATISFACTION JUDGMENTS?

satisfaction The feeling that results when consumers make a positive evaluation or feel happy with a decision.

dissatisfaction The feeling that results when consumers make a negative evaluation or are unhappy with a decision.

After consumers have made acquisition, consumption, or disposition decisions, they can evaluate the outcomes of their decisions. If their evaluations are positive—if they believe their needs or goals have been met—they feel **satisfaction**. Thus you could feel satisfied with the purchase of a new DVD player, the choice of a red wine, or the way you cleaned a cluttered closet. You might also be pleased with a buying experience, a salesperson, or a retail outlet.[25] Satisfaction can be associated with feelings of acceptance, happiness, relief, excitement, and delight.

When consumers have a negative evaluation of an outcome, they feel **dissatisfaction**. Dissatisfaction occurs if you did not enjoy a movie, did not like the taste of a breakfast cereal, were unhappy with a salesperson, or wished you had not thrown something away. Dissatisfaction can be related to feelings of tolerance, distress, sadness, regret, agitation, and outrage.[26]

Most of the research on satisfaction and dissatisfaction has focused on products and services for which the consumer can make an evaluation of both *utilitarian dimensions,* or how well the product or service functions (good or bad), and *hedonic dimensions,* or how it makes someone feel (happy, excited, delighted or sad, regretful, angry).[27] Consumers make a conscious comparison between what they think will happen and actual performance.[28]

Consumers' evaluations and feelings are generally temporary and can change over time. The fact that we are satisfied now does not necessarily mean we will be satisfied the next time. Evaluations also tend to be tied to specific consumption situations—we are satisfied (or not) with the offering as we are using it at the current time. In these ways, satisfaction differs from an attitude, which is relatively enduring and less dependent on the specific situation (see Chapter 5).[29] Note also that a post-decision evaluation can differ from a predecision evaluation in that after using the product, a consumer may judge different attributes and cutoff levels than before.[30] For example, you might like the taste of frozen microwave pizza less after trying it than you thought you would.

Levels of satisfaction vary with our involvement and over time.[31] Specifically, high-involvement consumers tend to express a higher level of satisfaction immediately after purchase, probably due to their more extensive evaluation. However, their satisfaction declines over time. On the other hand, lower-involvement consumers exhibit a lower level of satisfaction initially, but their level of satisfaction tends to increase with greater usage over time.

MARKETING IMPLICATIONS Satisfied customers form the foundation of any successful business. Customer satisfaction leads to repeat purchase, brand loyalty, and positive word of mouth.[32] One study of 100,000 automotive customers found that consumers with different characteristics have different satisfaction thresholds and therefore different repurchase tendencies, even at the same reported satisfaction level.[33] Still, a study of Swedish consumers suggests that satisfaction is especially important for companies that rely on repeat business.[34] High customer satisfaction and repeat purchasing have contributed to Coca-Cola's frequent ranking as the world's most valuable consumer brand.[35] On the Internet, the highly successful retailer Amazon.com attributes 63 percent of its sales to repeat customers.[36]

To further emphasize this point, look at satisfied customers in terms of the profit they bring to the firm. A consumer who shops in an upscale supermarket is estimated to spend more than $50,000 in a decade.[37] Likewise, a satisfied customer is expected to provide $150,000 of business over a lifetime for a car dealer, and an appliance dealer will get $3,000 worth of business over a 20-year period. Even a 5 percent increase in customer retention can raise profits by 25 to 85 percent.[38]

Monitoring customer satisfaction. Not surprisingly, many companies now actively monitor customer satisfaction through the use of market surveys. For example, the American Customer Satisfaction Index (ACSI), which monitors satisfaction in a variety of industries, finds fairly high scores in many cases (see Exhibit 12.7).[39] Pizza Hut regularly conducts telephone surveys of more than 50,000 customers a week to assess performance of both dine-in and carryout service.[40] Procter & Gamble uses the Internet to conduct hundreds of customer surveys every year.[41] In conducting such research, marketers need to measure not only satisfaction but also customer wants and expectations.[42] However, marketers should be aware that when consumers expect to evaluate a product or service, they tend to pay closer attention to negative aspects during consumption and therefore provide less favorable quality and satisfaction evaluations—unless they have low expectations at the outset.[43]

Interestingly, most consumers find enjoyment and satisfaction in their buying experiences. One study found that more than 90 percent of durable-goods purchases were associated with positive feelings.[44] Satisfaction levels also tend to be similar in most European countries.[45] In fact, consumers worldwide are generally satisfied. As a result, some companies are going a step further to focus on building customer loyalty as an indicator of success, in the form of willingness to repurchase and to recommend the product or service to others.[46]

The costs of dissatisfaction. Dissatisfaction can lead to a variety of negative outcomes, including negative word-of-mouth communication, complaints, and reduced purchases with resulting lower profits. If a department store lost 167 customers a month, it would lose $2.4 million in sales (and $280,000 in profit) over the course of just one year.[47] A study of European consumers found that it takes 12 positive experiences to overcome one negative one and that the cost of attracting a new customer is five times the cost of keeping an existing one.[48]

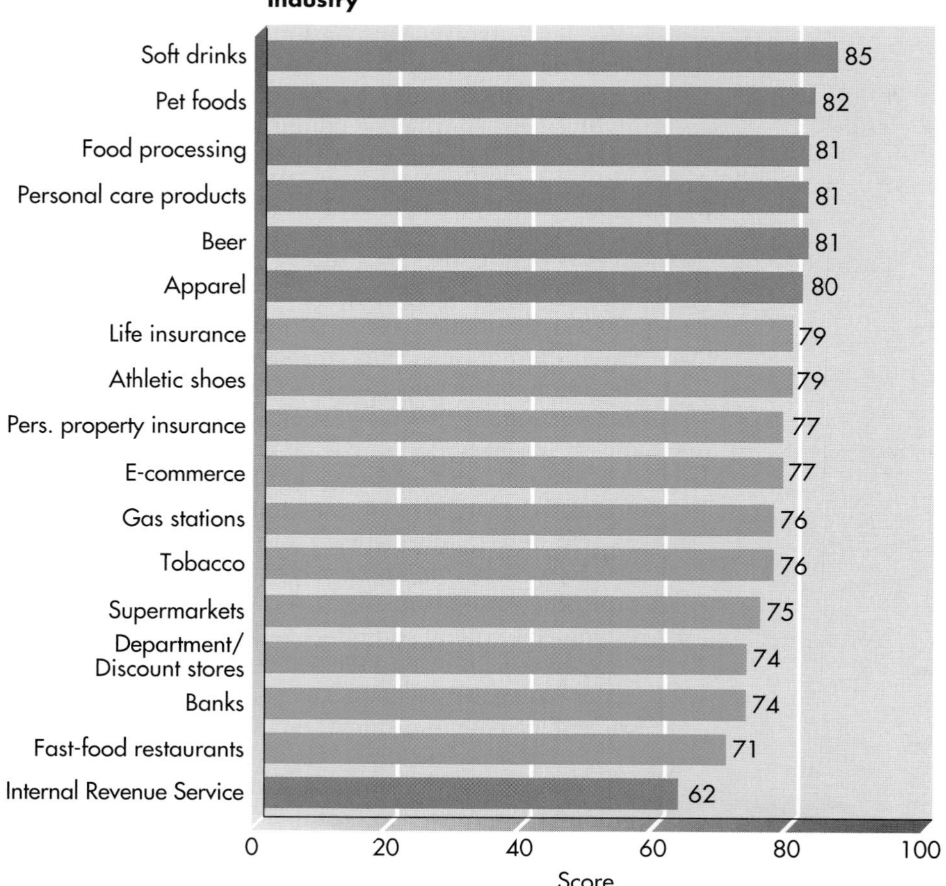

EXHIBIT 12.7

The American Consumer Satisfaction Index

The ACSI measures customer satisfaction performance across a variety of different industries. Here are a few samples.

Source: The University of Michigan Business School, National Quality Research Center.

Addressing dissatisfaction issues can improve customer satisfaction and company performance. After negative publicity and customer complaints tarnished its reputation, Providian Financial, a major credit card firm, retrained its customer service staff and started asking callers whether all their questions had been answered; if not, reps offered to refer questions to higher-level managers. As a result, Providian not only slashed complaints by 40 percent, it also attracted and retained many more customers.[49]

Finally, even though they have more product choices than ever before, consumers in formerly communist countries such as Romania have experienced significant levels of dissatisfaction after the fall of communism.[50] One reason is that these consumers have had difficulty judging quality, and as a result products do not always live up to expectations. Another is that the consumers tend to buy cheaper products in open-air markets where there is no guarantee of quality. ●

The Disconfirmation Paradigm

disconfirmation The existence of a discrepancy between expectations and performance.

The most central concept in the study of satisfaction/dissatisfaction is disconfirmation, diagrammed in Exhibit 12.8. **Disconfirmation** occurs when there is a discrepancy, positive or negative, between our prior expectations and the product's

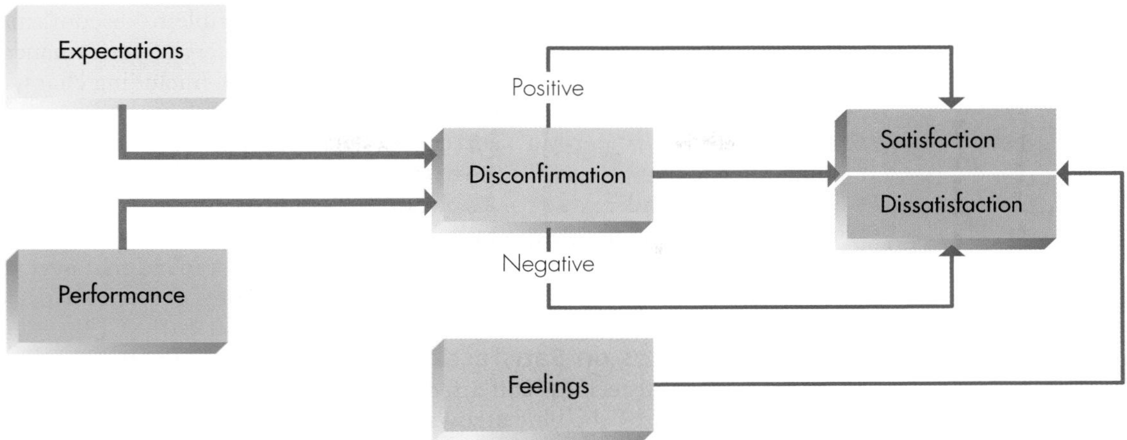

EXHIBIT 12.8
The Disconfirmation Paradigm

Here the disconfirmation paradigm shows how satisfaction or dissatisfaction can occur. Using an example of a new Jim Carrey movie, the consumer enters the situation with expectations (Jim Carrey movies are funny). She can then go see the movie and evaluate it (performance). If she evaluates it as funnier than she expected, positive disconfirmation has occurred and she will be satisfied. If the movie is not funny, a negative disconfirmation and dissatisfaction result. Note that expectations (the likelihood of seeing the movie as funny), performance (whether the movie actually is good), and feelings (positive or negative emotions during viewing) will also affect satisfaction/dissatisfaction (independent of disconfirmation).

expectations Beliefs about how a product/service will perform.

actual performance (see the red arrows in the exhibit).[51] In this case **expectations** are desired product/service outcomes and include "pre-consumption beliefs about overall performance, or . . . the levels or attributes possessed by a product (service)."[52] For example, you might expect a Japanese car to be reliable and fuel efficient, expectations based on advertising, inspection of the product, prior experience with similar products or services, and the experiences of other referent consumers.[53]

performance The measurement of whether the product/service actually fulfills consumers' needs.

Satisfaction Based on Expectations **Performance** measures whether these expected outcomes have been achieved. Performance can either be *objective*—based on the actual performance, which is fairly constant across consumers—or *subjective*—based on individual feelings, which can vary across consumers. The objective performance of a car describes how well it runs, how economical its gas mileage is, or how often it needs repair, whereas subjective performance might include an assessment of how stylish it is or "how good it makes me feel." Research suggests that disconfirmation is based more often on subjective than objective performance.[54] Better-than-expected performance leads to a *positive disconfirmation* and to satisfaction. If performance is as good as expected, a *simple confirmation* has occurred, and this condition will also lead to satisfaction.

In contrast, if performance is lower than expected, the result is *negative disconfirmation* and dissatisfaction. As an illustration, when *Consumer Reports* surveyed customers of national Internet service providers, it found that customers were dissatisfied with Microsoft's MSN service because the performance of its e-mail, technical support, and dial-up connections did not live up to their expectations.[55] A similar problem occurs in formerly communist countries, where consumers often place too much trust in foreign products and then experience dissatisfaction and regret.[56]

Customers' evaluation of services is also susceptible to disconfirmation.[57] Here, customers have expectations related to price and service performance and to intangible characteristics of the facilities and personnel (including characteristics such as reliability, responsiveness, assurance, and empathy).[58] As a service provider, Ukrops' Super Markets stresses "perfectly packed groceries" (even outlining the packing process on the bag) to avoid customer discontent over broken eggs, crushed bread, and soggy ice cream.[59] As another example, Wal-Mart is seeking to exceed customers' expectations by speeding up the check-out process using new technology.[60] Finally, a study of Swedish consumers found that average levels of performance and expectations can predict overall levels of service satisfaction.[61]

Other Influences on Satisfaction Exhibit 12.8 shows that performance, expectations, and feelings can affect satisfaction, *independent* of disconfirmation (as reflected by the blue arrows).[62] To fully understand why satisfaction or dissatisfaction occurs, we must account for all these dimensions together and separately. The simple fact that a product performs well will have a positive influence on satisfaction, independent of expectations.[63] This is particularly true in the case of consumer durables, where risk and involvement are higher. Thus a consumer might not have any expectations about how a new computer may perform and be pleasantly surprised when she sees what it can do. Likewise, the poor performance of a product or service alone can lead to dissatisfaction.[64] If you buy a new DVD player and it does not work well, you could be dissatisfied—even without any prior expectations.

Positive expectations about product or service performance can actually increase the likelihood of satisfaction thanks to the process of *selective perception* by which consumers tend to see what they want to see.[65] In a now classic case, seven of ten consumers participating in a blind taste test preferred the taste of New Coke (which was similar to Pepsi) over the original Coke formula. However, expectations led many consumers to believe that they liked the old Coke better, and they refused to accept the new product.

post-decision feelings Positive or negative emotions experienced while using the products or services.

In addition, positive and negative **post-decision feelings** can help to explain satisfaction or dissatisfaction judgments independent of disconfirmation.[66] If consumers feel good (or bad) while using the product or service, they are more likely to be satisfied (or dissatisfied), independent of their expectations and evaluations of performance. Consumers who are happy or content are most likely to be satisfied, followed by those who experience pleasant surprise. Dissatisfaction is most likely to strike consumers who feel angry or upset, followed by those who experience unpleasant surprise.[67] Finally, the consumer's mood can color post-decision evaluations, particularly when the consumption experience itself is not strongly emotional.[68] For example, you might tend to like a new CD if you are in a good mood when you hear it.

Note that the disconfirmation paradigm is similar to the learning process described earlier. The difference is that satisfaction and dissatisfaction are based on a formal evaluation and feelings, whereas the learning process may not be. For example, you can test the hypothesis that rock music is loud or that Mexican food is spicy without making an assessment of like or dislike. Nevertheless, satisfaction or dissatisfaction can still be an important element of the learning process because it provides us with information.

Finally, research suggests that consumer satisfaction with products need not be transaction-specific and is subject to change. Satisfaction can also be affected by social influences such as family members and may be closely related to consumers' satisfaction with their own lives.[69]

MARKETING IMPLICATIONS Based on the disconfirmation paradigm, marketers need to be very demanding about product or service quality and performance. Better performance leads to fulfilled expectations and satisfaction. For instance, when Pizza Hut entered the market in China, it decided to keep consumers satisfied by using a mild cheese that is overwhelmed by the taste of toppings, because the Chinese have little taste for cheese. The company also substituted pineapple for olives because many Chinese love sweets.[70]

A second important implication is that the expectations created by marketers about product performance can influence the level of consumer satisfaction or dissatisfaction. Raising consumers' expectations of how well the product or service will perform can increase ratings of product performance.[71] When Pizza Hut first opened in China, it knew that pizza was unfamiliar to most Chinese consumers. The firm therefore developed tabletop cards to inform diners that pizza is a healthy food with natural ingredients, creating positive expectations.[72] When Procter & Gamble's Joy dish detergent was introduced in Japan, consumers used too much of the product because more familiar brands were weak. With the marketing pitch "A little bit of Joy cleans better . . . ," P&G created appropriate expectations and was able to satisfy its customers.[73]

Providing consumers with a good warranty or guarantee can create positive expectations that will lead to satisfaction.[74] Unfortunately, this reassurance has been lacking in many developing countries such as Turkey and Romania where many products are of poor quality and do not include warranties. In addition, consumers often do not understand how to use the products (there are few instructions), which leads to further dissatisfaction.[75]

Marketers are setting themselves up for a potential negative disconfirmation and dissatisfaction if customer expectations are too high and companies make promises they cannot keep. To illustrate, many hotels and resorts have met higher customer expectations by improving quality through renovated guest rooms and upgraded facilities. However, the noise and confusion of construction sometimes resulted in guest dissatisfaction—sometimes prompting angry confrontations between annoyed guests and hotel staff.[76]

Marketers should also make sure that customers' feelings about buying and using their offerings are as positive as possible. Making customers feel good allows them to bond with the company and develop loyalty, a form of *relationship marketing* whereby long-term relationships are built with consumers. DaimlerChrysler has sponsored Jeep Jamborees to allow customers to drive their vehicles on rough terrain and "win their hearts."[77] Likewise, cheerful, accommodating salespeople are more likely to generate consumer satisfaction with the encounter, the retailer, and the purchase. Satisfaction was Air Ukraine's major goal when it tried to dissociate itself from the old, unfriendly Russian carrier Aeroflot.[78]

In addition, marketers can use various promotions to increase positive feelings during consumption. The St. Paul Saints, a Minnesota minor league baseball team, gives fans a good feeling about the team using fun promotions such as a Jerry Garcia lookalike contest, in-seat massages, and players reading to young fans in center field.[79] In Hong Kong, a very popular promotion involved trading in old Marlboro boxes for gifts such as lighters, knapsacks, and lanterns.[80] ●

Attribution Theory

Another theory that is useful in determining how and when dissatisfaction occurs is **attribution theory**. This theory was developed by social psychologists to explain how individuals find explanations or causes for effects or behavior.[81] In other words, if someone you do not know suddenly kisses you on the cheek,

attribution theory A theory of how individuals find explanations for events.

you would be motivated to attribute or find an explanation for this event—but how would you do this?

In a marketing context, when a product or service does not fulfill needs, the consumer will attempt to find an explanation. According to attribution theory, three key factors influence the nature of this explanation:

- *Stability*. Is the cause of the event temporary or permanent?
- *Focus*. Is the problem consumer or marketer related?
- *Controllability*. Is the event under the customer's or marketer's control?

Customers are more likely to be dissatisfied if the cause is perceived to be permanent, marketer related, and not under the customer's control. Suppose you find a crack in the windshield of your new car. If you perceive that this is only a chance or temporary occurrence, beyond the control of the marketer (maybe a rock hit the window while you were driving), or your own fault, you will probably not be dissatisfied. On the other hand, if you discover that many other consumers have a similar problem—that is, the cause is more permanent, company related, and under the company's control—you will probably be dissatisfied.

Attribution theory has also found support in research on services, according to a study in which consumers were dissatisfied with a travel agent if a problem was permanent and under the firm's control.[82] Further, in a field study of passengers delayed at an airport, attributions were found to explain the desire either to complain or to fly the same airline again. If consumers saw the delay as permanent and under the airline's control, they were more likely to complain and less likely to fly the airline again.[83]

MARKETING IMPLICATIONS Attribution theory can provide marketers with guidance in how to deal with potential or existing perceptions of consumer dissatisfaction. If the cause of the dissatisfaction actually is permanent, marketer related, and under the marketer's control, something must be done to correct the problem or provide the consumer with restitution. For example, American Airlines added leg room in coach to address customer dissatisfaction with cramped seating, and other airlines are making similar changes.[84] In the banking industry, which counts almost two dissatisfied consumers for every satisfied one, many banks are marketing value-added services such as financial advice, stock quotes, and bill payment in an attempt to satisfy customers.[85]

When a service failure occurs, research indicates that consumers prefer recovery efforts that correspond to the type of failure experienced.[86] In the case of a process failure such as inattentive service, restoring good service and quickly apologizing can reduce dissatisfaction and help restore satisfaction. Restitution is often provided, as well. One of the authors once found a piece of mold at the top of a Coke bottle. The company quickly responded by providing a free case of Coke. Another time he noticed an overcharge for dog food at a grocery store and was immediately given the item free with a sincere apology. Both responses reduced his dissatisfaction.

Alternatively, when consumers perceive that the cause of the dissatisfaction is permanent, marketer related, and under the firm's control when in fact it is not, marketers need to correct these misperceptions. Providing consumers with logical explanations for failure, especially if it was not the company's fault, or providing some form of compensation such as a gift or refund can often reduce feelings of dissatisfaction.[87] For example, Pepsi once faced a serious potential consumer dissatisfaction problem when a syringe was found in a can of Diet Pepsi. Once the company learned that the problem was temporary and not under its control (a consumer had tampered with the can), management quickly launched a media campaign to correct any consumer misperceptions (see Exhibit 12.9). ●

Equity Theory

equity theory A theory that focuses on the fairness of exchanges between individuals, which helps in understanding consumer satisfaction and dissatisfaction.

Equity theory is another approach developed by psychologists that is useful in understanding consumer satisfaction and dissatisfaction. This theory focuses on the nature of exchanges between individuals and their perceptions of these exchanges. In marketing, it has been applied to examining the exchange between a buyer and a seller or a more general institution.[88]

According to equity theory, consumers form perceptions of their own inputs and outputs into a particular exchange. They then compare these perceptions with their perceptions of the salesperson, dealer, or company. For example, when buying a stereo, a consumer's inputs might include information search, decision-making effort, psychological anxiety, and money. The output would be a satisfactory sound system. Seller inputs might include a quality product, selling effort, and a financing plan; a fair profit might constitute the output.

For equity to occur, the buyer must perceive **fairness in the exchange**. Thus the stereo buyer might perceive a fair exchange if he or she purchased a desirable system at a fair price. If the consumer perceives inequity in the exchange—for example, the salesperson did not pay enough attention to the consumer or the deal was not fair—he or she will be dissatisfied. For equity to occur, a perception of fairness must exist on both sides of the exchange, with the consumer perceiving that the seller is also being dealt with fairly. Nevertheless, fairness perceptions tend to be self-centered—that is, biased more toward buyer outcomes and seller inputs than to buyer inputs and seller outcomes.[89]

EXHIBIT 12.9
Addressing Dissatisfaction
In response to a situation in which a syringe was found in a Diet Pepsi can, this ad tells consumers that the company and its employees did not cause the event in any way (thereby correcting any incorrect beliefs that customers might have had).

Source: Courtesy of Pepsi-Cola Company.

Pepsi is pleased to announce...

...nothing.

As America now knows, those stories about Diet Pepsi were a hoax. Plain and simple, not true. Hundreds of investigators have found no evidence to support a single claim.

As for the many, many thousands of people who work at Pepsi-Cola, we feel great that it's over. And we're ready to get on with making and bringing you what we believe is the best-tasting diet cola in America.

There's not much more we can say. Except that most importantly, we won't let this hoax change our exciting plans for this summer.

We've set up special offers so you can enjoy our great quality products at prices that will save you money all summer long. It all starts on July 4th weekend and we hope you'll stock up with a little extra, just to make up for what you might have missed last week.

That's it. Just one last word of thanks to the millions of you who have stood with us.

Drink All The Diet Pepsi You Want.
Uh Huh.

Moreover, research shows that consumers judge the equity of the payment exchanged for service usage by asking themselves, "Am I using this service enough, given what I pay for it?" They will perceive the exchange as more equitable when they have high expectations of service usage levels at first or when the service performance exceeds their normative expectations. And when they perceive the price/usage exchange to be more equitable, they will be more satisfied.[90]

The principles of equity theory complement the disconfirmation paradigm in that equity theory specifies another way dissatisfaction can occur. In other words, both types of processes can be in operation at the same time. However, whereas the disconfirmation paradigm focuses on expectations and performance, equity theory is concerned with more general interpersonal norms governing what is wrong or right and with a consideration of the outcomes for both the seller and buyer, not just the buyer.

MARKETING IMPLICATIONS Equity theory highlights the importance of fairness in marketing exchanges. As long as consumers perceive that their inputs and outputs are equitable in relation to those of the seller, they will be

fairness of exchange The perception that people's inputs are equal to their outputs in an exchange.

satisfied. However, if an inequity exists, consumers will be dissatisfied. In the chapter-opening example, some consumers were dissatisfied with Internet shopping because they perceived an unfair exchange—they were stuck with late delivery or credit card problems. In fact, the Internet is among the top 10 categories of businesses about which consumers complain—especially registering complaints about products ordered online.[91] In Turkey, retail service is generally very poor, leading to dissatisfaction. Consumers often have to wait a long time for service, and after-sale service is frequently bad.[92]

The clear implication is that marketers must work toward providing fair exchanges. This is not always easy because consumers' perceptions of fairness tend to be biased toward themselves. One area in which marketers can most directly affect equity perceptions is the salesperson-customer interaction. In these exchanges, salespeople must make every effort to ensure that their inputs match customer inputs by listening to consumer needs, answering questions, and attempting to provide a good deal. In the automotive industry, Saturn has been successful in offering consumers "a different kind of company"—one that cares about consumers' needs and works hard to fulfill them. The same principles also apply to Internet transactions, where companies like Hanover Direct emphasize customer service to create a fair exchange. Similarly, in the ad in Exhibit 12.10, Coldwell Banker states that its success for 90 years is due to its emphasis on customer service.

Promotions can also increase perceptions of fairness in an exchange. Providing consumers with a lower price or with a free item of merchandise can make consumers feel that they are getting more out of the exchange. This is why many cosmetics companies give consumers free products such as tote bags with a purchase. In addition, companies must ensure that outputs are satisfactory by providing a quality product at a fair price. Wal-Mart, for example, has created strong customer satisfaction by offering "good value every day." •

RESPONSES TO DISSATISFACTION

Marketers must understand the nature of consumers' responses to dissatisfaction because a variety of mostly negative consequences can result. Specifically, dissatisfied consumers can decide to (1) take no action, (2) discontinue purchasing the product or service, (3) complain to the company or to a third party and perhaps return the item, or (4) engage in negative word-of-mouth communication.[93] The last two behaviors in particular have been of great interest to consumer researchers.

Complaints

Surprisingly, the majority of dissatisfied consumers do not complain.[94] Nevertheless, even a few consumer complaints can indicate marketing-related problems that need attention. When consumers complain, they can voice their dissatisfaction to a manufacturer, the retail outlet, regulatory agencies, or the media. Sometimes consumers can take even more drastic action by seeking formal redress through legal means or from governmental regulatory bodies.

Complaints can be related to a variety of matters, such as the product or service, the retail outlet, and the salespeople. Cellular phone service is a growing problem area, with many consumers complaining about confusing and misleading ads, complicated fees, and poor service.[95] Car-rental customers complain about long lines and indecipherable bills.[96] When one newspaper asked readers to indicate their top complaints about area grocery stores, they quickly received over 300 gripes (Exhibit 12.11 lists the top ten). Thus, marketers need to focus on when

EXHIBIT 12.10
Creating Equity in an Exchange
Customer service is one of the main reasons why Coldwell Banker has been successful in the real estate market for over 90 years. In this ad the company discusses its new Internet service for customers, "Coldwell Banker Online," which provides prospective home buyers with housing information.

Source: © Coldwell Banker Corporation.

complaints are likely to occur and what types of people tend to complain.

When Complaints Are Likely to Occur Complaining is more likely to occur when motivation, ability, and opportunity are high. Complaining is also more likely as the level of dissatisfaction or the severity of the problem becomes greater.[97] In equity theory terms, the unfairness of the exchange is higher and the consumer is more motivated to act.[98] Yet the severity of the dissatisfaction alone does not explain complaining behavior. In particular, consumers are less likely to act if they perceive that complaining will take a lot of time and effort, their chances of benefiting from it are low, and the product or service is insignificant.[99]

The more the blame or attribution for dissatisfaction is placed on someone else, particularly on the company or society in general, the greater the motivation and likelihood of complaining.[100] Thus complaining is more likely to occur when consumers feel removed from the problem—that is, when the perceived cause is permanent, marketer related, and volitional.[101]

You might expect that consumers who are aggressive and self-confident would be more likely to complain than those who are not[102] or that consumers with more experience or knowledge ability about how to complain might be more likely to do so than their less savvy counterparts. Neither idea has been strongly supported by evidence, although findings suggest experience may influence the likelihood of complaints. Interestingly, consumers are more likely to complain when they have the time and formal channels of communication. Lack of opportunity and knowledge about how to complain has been a major problem in many developing countries.[103] In Turkey, consumers have lacked the means to complain until recently. However, the opportunity to complain is now influencing the way businesses operate.

Other studies have examined whether demographic and socioeconomic factors are related to complaining behavior. Although the findings have been somewhat mixed, there are several slight tendencies. Complainers tend to be younger, to have a higher income level, and to be less brand loyal than noncomplainers.[104] Researchers have also found that complaining behavior may vary by ethnic group. For example, Mexican American consumers are more likely to complain about certain aspects of goods and services such as delay or nondelivery than are other consumers.[105] Puerto Ricans are less likely to complain than other U.S. consumers because of cultural norms and values.[106]

Complainer Types Finally, research has suggested that there are different types of complainers.[107] *Passives* are the least likely to complain. *Voicers* are likely to complain directly to the retailer or service provider. *Irates* are angry

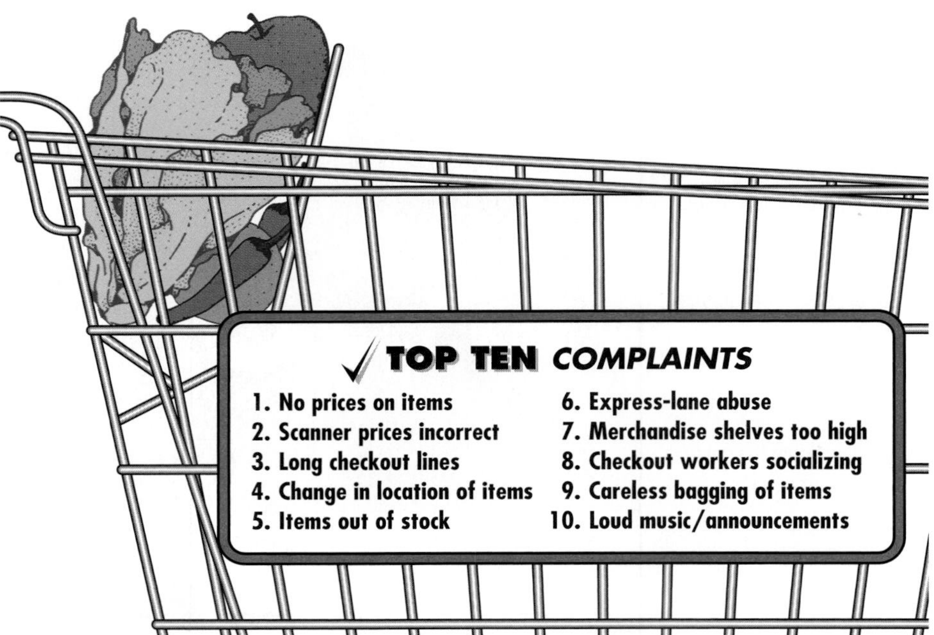

TOP TEN COMPLAINTS
1. No prices on items
2. Scanner prices incorrect
3. Long checkout lines
4. Change in location of items
5. Items out of stock
6. Express-lane abuse
7. Merchandise shelves too high
8. Checkout workers socializing
9. Careless bagging of items
10. Loud music/announcements

EXHIBIT 12.11
Grocery Store Complaints
Consumers have a variety of complaints about products and services. Here are the results of a study of the most common consumer complaints about grocery stores. Do these match with your experience in grocery stores? Marketers can respond to these complaints to increase customer satisfaction.

Source: Data from Kitty Crider, "Grocery Store Gripes," *Austin American Statesman*, October 23, 1991, pp. C1, C2.

consumers who are most likely to engage in negative word of mouth, stop patronage, and complain to the provider but not to a third party such as the media or government. *Activists* engage heavily in all types of complaining, including to a third party. Interestingly, some companies feel that listening to the "customer from hell" actually improves their business because these critics often provide good suggestions.[108] For instance, Holiday Inn learned from surveys that customers were unhappy with the design of the shower, which was too small and tended to collect dirt. In redesigning its hotel bathrooms, the company paid very close attention to everything from the angle of the shower head to elbow room to grout (which captures dirt).[109]

MARKETING IMPLICATIONS Although a large percentage of consumers do not complain, it is still in the marketer's best interests to be responsive when they do. Providing a written response, especially with a coupon or gift, can have a noticeable impact on consumer evaluations.[110] Quick responses, especially ones that involve monetary reimbursement or a fair exchange or refund policy, can lead to greater satisfaction and repeat purchase. Unfortunately, Internet businesses sometimes respond slowly—or not at all—to consumer complaints. In one study, 24 percent of online shoppers never received a response after submitting a complaint, although 38 percent received replies within six hours or sooner.[111] Speedy responses are important because 57 percent of the consumers in a recent survey said that how quickly a Web site responds to their e-mail inquiry influences their decision to make future purchases from that business.[112]

In fact, dissatisfied consumers who have been treated fairly can become even more loyal in the future. For example, a consumer who had set up a complaint Web site to publicize his problems with a Sony electronics product converted the site to an enthusiastic fan site after the company contacted him to resolve the complaint.[113] A study from Singapore found that the length of time taken to respond to a complaint was critical in determining the level of satisfaction—the less time, the higher the satisfaction.[114] In another survey, 90 percent of managers said satisfying the customer was the primary reason for responding to complaints.[115] Thus companies must have an efficient and responsive mechanism for handling these problems.

The online auction site eBay wants to satisfy its 20 million users so they will keep using the site and referring other consumers. This is why eBay established an automated system for recording consumer complaints, forwarding them to eBay representatives, and tracking complaint trends. When customers are not satisfied, their complaints go to higher-level managers for review and resolution. In this way, eBay reduced customer dissatisfaction by 30 percent in one year.[116] At Dell Computer, all employees—from top managers to assembly-line workers—carefully scrutinize customer complaints during a weekly session called "The Hour of Horror" and determine how best to handle these problems. If problems are not resolved within a week, they are reviewed every Friday until they are resolved.[117]

Positive disconfirmation of warranty and service expectations—a response that is better than expected—can result in satisfaction with complaint resolution.[118] For example, a resort hotel in Japan turned a threat of earthquakes on a major holiday weekend to an advantage by offering a free subsequent stay if a large earthquake occurred.[119] Marketers and customers can still experience problems in developing countries, where service is generally poor and warranties are nonexistent.[120]

Sometimes it is in the company's best interest to encourage complaining because dissatisfied consumers who do not complain are more likely to discontinue purchase.[121] But when companies are too responsive to complaints—that is, too eager to please—customers may actually be more likely to complain, even when a complaint is not justified, because they perceive a greater likelihood of success.[122] In particular, consumers are more likely to complain when the cause is ambiguous and the party responsible for the problem is not obvious. Still, by encouraging complaints when justified and actively managing customer problems, the company can retain valued consumers. ●

Responding by Negative Word of Mouth

negative word-of-mouth communication The act of consumers saying negative things about a product or service to other consumers.

When consumers are unhappy with a product or service, they are often motivated to tell others in order to relieve their frustration and to influence others not to purchase the product or do business with the company. **Negative word-of-mouth communication** is more likely to occur when the problem is severe, consumers are not happy with the company's responsiveness, and consumers perceive that the company is at fault.[123] Negative word of mouth can be particularly troublesome because it tends to be highly persuasive and very vivid (and therefore easily remembered), and consumers place great emphasis on it when making decisions.[124] Negative word of mouth is more damaging than complaining because consumers are communicating with other people who might discontinue (or never begin) doing business with the company. Many consumers air gripes on complaint Web sites such as PlanetFeedback.com and consumer-created sites such as "US Worst" (lampooning US West). For companies, these sites present a threat because they are available to consumers worldwide and the information may be unfair, nasty, or a "cheap shot."[125]

MARKETING IMPLICATIONS Marketers need to be responsive to negative word of mouth. Most important, they should make an effort to identify the reason for or source of the difficulty so they can take steps to rectify or eliminate the particular problem with restitution or formal marketing communications. TiVo, which makes a television recording appliance, does this by monitoring complaints on specific Web sites and posting public responses to consumer concerns.[126] ●

IS CUSTOMER SATISFACTION ENOUGH?

Although customer satisfaction should be an extremely important goal for any firm, some companies have questioned whether satisfaction alone is enough to keep customers loyal. As evidence they point out that 65 to 85 percent of customers who defect to competitors' brands say they were either satisfied or very satisfied with the product or service they left.[127] Other studies have found a low correlation between satisfaction and repurchase.[128] Thus customers may need to be "extremely satisfied" or need a stronger reason to stay with a brand or company.[129] Moreover, loyalty depends on whether the product is competitively superior, consumers find its superiority desirable and subject to adoration, the product can be embedded in a social network, and the company works to maintain the network.[130]

customer retention The practice of keeping customers by building long-term relationships.

A key goal for any marketer should therefore be **customer retention**, the practice of working to satisfy customers with the intention of developing long-term relationships with them. A customer-retention strategy attempts to build customer commitment and loyalty by continually paying close attention to all aspects of customer interaction, especially after-sales service. This approach not only strengthens relationships with customers but also increases profits. Specifically, profits can be increased through repeat sales, reduced costs, and referrals.[131]

How can a company retain its customers? Here are some common principles:[132]

- *Care about customers.* Two-thirds of consumers defect because they believe that the company doesn't care about them. Thus, a little caring can go a long way.
- *Remember customers between sales.* Companies can contact consumers to make sure they are not having any problems with the product or service or to acknowledge special occasions such as birthdays and anniversaries.
- *Build trusting relationships.* Provide consumers with expertise and high-quality products and services.
- *Monitor the service-delivery process.* Consumers need the company most when an offering requires service or repairs. Companies should make every effort to respond and show concern in these situations.
- *Provide extra effort.* Companies that go above and beyond the call of duty are more likely to build lasting customer relationships than companies that take the minimalist approach.

DISPOSITION

One more behavior can occur at the post-acquisition stage: disposition.

The Many Ways We Can Dispose of Something

At the most basic level, *disposition* is the throwing away of meaningless or used-up items without any thought. This process occurs on a regular basis for most consumers. Recent studies, however, suggest that disposition is a much richer and more detailed process than researchers once thought.[133]

Disposition is an action we take toward possessions. Although we tend to think of possessions as physical things, they can be defined much more broadly as anything that reflects an extension of the self, including one's body and body parts, other persons, pets, places, services, time periods, and events. For example, you could end a relationship, give a friend an idea, donate an organ, abandon an unhealthy lifestyle, use up all your leisure time, or discontinue a health club membership. Thus the study of disposition relates to all these types of possessions.

Many options are available when a consumer decides that a possession is no longer of immediate use. As outlined in Exhibit 12.12, the item can be (1) given away, which can include passing it along or donating it with or without a tax deduction, (2) traded, (3) recycled, (4) sold, (5) used up, (6) thrown away, (7) abandoned, which means discarding it in a socially unacceptable way, or (8) destroyed.[134] Note that disposition can be *temporary* (loaning or renting the item) or *involuntary* (losing or destroying the item).[135] Here we will focus on permanent, voluntary disposition.

Consumers often have logical and reasonable motives behind their disposition actions.[136] For example, people sell things to earn an economic return and come out ahead. In contrast, they donate something without a tax deduction and pass an item along out of desire to help someone, as well as not wanting the product to go to waste.

Situational and product-related factors can also affect disposition options.[137] For example, when consumers have limited time or storage space, they may be more likely to dispose of a possession by throwing it away, giving it away, or abandoning it. Consumers disposing of a possession of high value are likely to sell it or give it to someone special rather than throw it away. In general, the frequency of different disposition behaviors varies by product category.

Research has examined how consumers dispose of unwanted gifts.[138] They can be laterally recycled (swapped, sold, or passed on to someone else), destroyed, or returned. Destruction is a way of getting revenge against the giver but is usually more of a fantasy than a real action. Retailers need to be aware that returning a gift to a store can be a negative emotional experience for consumers. Disposition can involve more than one individual, as when consumers give old clothes to someone, sell a car, or participate in a neighborhood cleanup, or it can consist of activities of a collective or societal nature such as dumping garbage in the ocean or recycling waste water.[139]

By combining the personal, interpersonal, and societal arenas with the eight types of disposition identified in Exhibit 12.12, we can see that disposition encompasses a wide variety of behaviors. Consumer researchers have only begun to explore these options, focusing mostly on personal disposition. Much work is needed to achieve a more thorough understanding of disposition.

Disposing of Meaningful Objects

Although disposition often means simply getting rid of unwanted, meaningless, or used-up possessions, the process is more involved for certain significant items. Possessions can sometimes be important reflections of the self that are infused with significant symbolic meaning.[140] They define who we are, and they catalog our personal history.[141] In these situations, disposition involves two processes: physical detachment and emotional detachment.

physical detachment Physically disposing of an item.

emotional detachment Emotionally disposing of a possession.

We most often think of disposition in terms of **physical detachment**, the process by which the item is physically transferred to another person or location. However, **emotional detachment** is a more detailed, lengthy, and sometimes painful process. Often, consumers remain emotionally attached to possessions long after they have become physically detached. For example, it may take a person years to come to grips with selling a valued house or car. Giving up a baby or pet for adoption are examples of difficult emotional detachment that sometimes result in grief and mourning. In fact, some pack rats have a difficult time disposing of even minimally valued possessions—as evidenced by overflowing basements, closets, and garages.

The disposition process can be particularly important during periods of role transition, such as puberty, graduation, and marriage.[142] In these instances

EXHIBIT 12.12
Disposition Options
Disposition often means throwing things away; however, there are many additional ways of disposing of an offering (e.g., give away, trade, recycle). In addition, disposition can involve one person (personal focus), two or more people (interpersonal focus), or society in general (societal focus).

Source: Melissa Martin Young and Melanie Wallendorf, "Ashes to Ashes, Dust to Dust: Conceptualizing Consumer Disposition of Possessions," in *Proceedings, Marketing Educators' Conference*, (Chicago: American Marketing Association, 1989), pp. 33–39. Reprinted by permission.

A TAXONOMY OF VOLUNTARY DISPOSITION

METHODS	PERSONAL FOCUS	INTERPERSONAL FOCUS	SOCIETAL FOCUS
Give away: usually to someone who can use it.	Necessarily requires another person as receiver.	Donate body organs; give clothes to the needy; give a baby up for adoption; give an idea to a friend.	Give land to new settlers; give surplus food to the poor; give military advice to an ally.
Trade or exchange it for something else.	Skin grafts; trade sleep time for work time; trade work time for shopping for bargains.	Trade a car; trade stock; barter; exchange ideas with a colleague; switch boyfriends. Swap meets.	Trade tanks for oil; exchange effluent water for a golf course.
Recycle: convert it to something else.	Convert barn beams to paneling; make a quilt of scraps; turkey sandwiches after Thanksgiving.	Recycle newspapers; recycle aluminum cans; manufacturers' recycling of defective parts.	Recycle waste water; convert a slum to a model neighborhood; recycle war ruins as national monuments.
Sell: convert it to money.	Necessarily requires another person as buyer; prostitution; sell one's artwork; sell ideas.	Businesses; sell blood; sell ideals to attain political goals.	Sell wheat; sell weapons; sell land.
Use up: consumption is equivalent to disposal.	Eat food; drive car using up the fuel; shoot ammo; spend one's time; burn wood.	Use employee's time and energy; use someone else's money; use the neighbor's gas.	Use natural fuels or electricity; use a nation's productive capacity; use people as soldiers in wars.
Throw away: discard in a socially acceptable manner.	Put things in the trash; flush the toilet; use a garbage disposal; discard an idea.	Neighborhood cleanup; divorce; end a relationship; resign or retire from a job.	Dump garbage in the oceans; bury nuclear waste.
Abandon: discard in a socially unacceptable manner.	Abandon car on the roadside; abandon morals; abandon an unhealthy, unhappy lifestyle.	Abandon one's child or family; abandon a pet on someone's doorstep; abandon another's trust.	Abandon Vietnam; abandon the Shah of Iran; abandon old satellites in space; abandon the poor.
Destroy: physically damage with intent.	Tear up personal mail; commit suicide; burn house down; shred old pictures.	Raze a building; murder; euthanasia; cremation; abort a child; commit arson.	Conduct war; genocide; execute prisoner; carry out a revolution; burn a flag.

consumers dispose of possessions that are symbols of old roles. Upon getting married, for example, many people dispose of items that signify old relationships, such as pictures, jewelry, and gifts. The disposition of shared possessions is a critical process during divorce. Two types of such disposition have been identified: *disposition to break free*, in which the goal is to free oneself from the former relationship; and *disposition to hold on*, in which the intent is to cling to possessions with the hope that the relationship can be repaired.[143] The more common pattern is breaking free. Sometimes the partners attempt to be fair and distribute possessions evenly; sometimes one of the partners—most likely the initiator of the divorce—is willing to leave most of the possessions to the other partner to relieve guilt. In still other situations, the division of assets can involve a lot of conflict and bitter disagreements as the former partners are motivated by rivalry, punishment, and a desire to cling to power in the relationship.[144]

Consumers also specify how their possessions will be distributed upon death. This process can include giving away valued items to important family members, other individuals, and organizations such as charities and schools, as well as distributing monetary wealth through a will. The subject of intergenerational transfers and inheritance has been of great interest to social scientists.[145]

MARKETING IMPLICATIONS

Marketers need to understand disposition for several reasons. First, disposition decisions often influence later acquisition decisions because a consumer who decides to dispose of a particular item often acquires another. Someone who must buy a new refrigerator because the old one stopped working may decide that the old one did not last long enough and eliminate this brand from future consideration. By understanding why consumers dispose of older brands, particularly when a problem has occurred, marketers may be able to improve their offerings for the future.

Second, marketers have become interested in the way that consumers trade, sell, or give away items for secondhand purchases. Used-merchandise retail outlets and Web sites, flea markets, garage sales, and classified ads are becoming more widespread as consumers increasingly choose to sell or trade old items rather than throw them away. The number of used-merchandise retailers has grown at a rate ten times that of conventional retailers.[146] The market for used CDs, computers, and textbooks is large and continues to grow. Flea markets are quite popular among consumers, not only because they are a different way of disposing of and acquiring products but also because of the hedonistic experience they provide.[147] Consumers enjoy the process of searching and bargaining for items, the festive atmosphere—almost like a medieval fair—and the social opportunities.

Third, product disposition behaviors can sometimes have a major impact on society in general. For example, if product life can be extended by getting consumers to trade or resell items, waste and resource depletion could be reduced. As another example, the state of Texas was having a tremendous problem with litter on its highways and streets. After the state launched a "Don't Mess with Texas" campaign to influence consumers not to litter—featuring members of the Dallas Cowboys and popular local musicians—litter was reduced by 60 percent.

Fourth, by examining broad disposition patterns, we can gain insights that might not otherwise have been possible. To illustrate, one study examined household garbage to identify group differences in food consumption.[148] Researchers found that region of the country accounted most strongly for differences in consumption patterns, followed by cultural status. For instance, people consume more beans in the southwest United States because Mexican food is more popular in that region. The key point is that this type of *trace analysis* may yield more accurate information than self-report questionnaires.

Finally, disposition patterns can sometimes serve as economic indicators.[149] In hard economic times, consumers are more likely to conduct garage sales and decrease the amount and quality of items given to charities such as Goodwill and the Salvation Army. They are also more likely to hold on to major appliances such as stoves, refrigerators, and washing machines for as long as possible. ●

Recycling

We live in an age in which natural resources are rapidly being depleted. Because we can no longer squander resources, the study of disposition behaviors can provide valuable insights for the development of recycling programs. In light of this fact, a number of researchers have been interested in examining factors that relate to recycling.[150] Attitudes toward specific actions such as saving bottles and separating papers have shown promise as predictors of recycling behavior.[151] In addition, research suggests that attitudes toward recycling influence waste recycling and recycling shopping behaviors.[152] Unfortunately, variables such as demographics and psychographics are not strong predictors. What appears to be most useful in understanding consumer recycling is the motivation, ability, and opportunity to recycle.

Motivation to Recycle Consumers are more likely to recycle when they perceive that the benefits outweigh the costs, including money, time, and effort.[153] Immediate benefits or goals include avoiding filling up landfills, reducing waste, reusing materials, and saving the environment. Higher-order goals are to promote health and avoid sickness, achieve life-sustaining ends, and provide for future generations.[154] Note that these benefits are likely to vary across segments. For example, focusing on environmental effects may have little meaning in low-income neighborhoods where family members are being killed in the streets.[155] Also, consumers who perceive that their efforts will have an impact are more motivated to recycle than consumers who do not.[156] Having a clean, convenient place to bring recyclable materials also improves consumer motivation. Tomra Systems, owner of 200 rePlanet recycling kiosks in California, collects recycled beverage containers and gives consumers a receipt exchangeable for cash.[157]

Ability to Recycle Consumers who know how to recycle are more likely to do so than those who do not.[158] One study of German consumers found that a lack of knowledge led to incorrect disposal and therefore less recycling.[159] Consumers must also possess general knowledge about the positive environmental effects of recycling. Finally, consumers must remember to recycle as part of their daily routine.

Opportunity to Recycle If separating, storing, and removing recyclable materials is difficult or inconvenient, consumers will usually avoid doing so. A program in Germany that offered color-coded, large plastic containers on wheels for recyclable materials was quite popular and successful. In addition, to recycle on a regular basis, consumers must break old waste disposal habits and develop new ones. Providing easy-to-use containers also helps consumers in this regard. Also, consumers who buy products such as soft drinks for consumption on the go have less opportunity to recycle the empty bottles and cans.[160] But even one-time-use products can be conveniently recycled. The H. E. Butt Grocery Company in San Antonio has arranged to send thousands of single-use cameras back to Kodak for recycling when consumers bring them in for photo processing.[161]

MARKETING IMPLICATIONS Clearly, marketers can facilitate recycling by increasing consumers' MAO to recycle. Special incentives such as lotteries and contests are effective in increasing motivation. Messages that focus on the negative consequences of not recycling and that are conveyed by personal acquaintances appear to be the most effective means of increasing motivation.[162] For example, sending Boy Scouts to personally deliver messages about the advantages of recycling increased behavior from 11 to 42 percent.[163] Neighborhood block leaders can also be effective. The only drawback is that all these techniques must be reintroduced periodically because their effects are usually temporary.

Marketers can increase consumers' ability to recycle by teaching them how to recycle through personal communications from community or block leaders, flyers, or public service announcements. These messages must be personally relevant and easy to remember. Also, offering tags to place on the refrigerator door can remind consumers to recycle.[164]

Finally, by providing separate containers so recyclable items can be easily put out and collected along with the trash, recycling programs can increase the opportunity to recycle. This type of program has worked well in the United States, Germany, and the Netherlands. Providing easily recyclable products is another way to increase the opportunity to recycle (see Exhibit 12.13). ●

EXHIBIT 12.13
Increasing the Opportunity to Recycle
Companies like Toyota are making it easier for consumers to recycle (increasing opportunity) by offering products that are made of recyclable materials.

Source: Toyota Motors North America, Inc.

TODAY
TOMORROW
TOYOTA
Reduce manufacturing waste going to landfills
Reduce land going to waste
Each year Toyota builds more than one million vehicles in North America. This means that we use a lot of resources—steel, aluminum, and plastics, for instance. But at Toyota, large scale manufacturing doesn't mean large scale waste.
In 1992 we introduced our Global Earth Charter to promote environmental responsibility throughout our operations. And in North America it is already reaping significant benefits. We recycle 376 million pounds of steel annually, and aggressive recycling programs keep 18 million pounds of other scrap materials from landfills.
Of course, no one ever said that looking after the Earth's resources is easy. But as we continue to strive for greener ways to do business, there's one thing we're definitely not wasting. And that's time.
www.toyota.com/tomorrow
©2001

SUMMARY

Consumers sometimes develop post-decision dissonance—a feeling of anxiety or uncertainty regarding a purchasing decision after it has been made. They are motivated to reduce this dissonance by collecting additional information that is used to upgrade the chosen alternative and downgrade the rejected ones. On occasion, they may feel regret when they perceive an unfavorable comparison between the performance of the chosen option and the performance of the unchosen options. In turn, feelings of regret can directly influence the consumer's intention to buy the same product in the future.

Consumers can learn from experience through a process of hypothesis testing in which they attempt to either confirm or disprove expectations by actually engaging in acquisition, consumption, or disposition. This process is influenced by motivation, prior knowledge (familiarity), ambiguity of information, and two types of biases, the confirmation bias and overconfidence. Marketers can use several strategies to influence the learning process, depending on whether the offering is a top dog or an underdog.

Satisfaction is both a subjective feeling and an objective evaluation that a decision has fulfilled a need or goal. Dissatisfaction occurs when consumers have negative feelings and believe that their goals or needs have not been fulfilled. Marketers need to keep consumers satisfied because losing customers can be very costly in the long run.

Three major theories of satisfaction/dissatisfaction are (1) the disconfirmation paradigm, which states that satisfaction occurs when performance disconfirms expectations in a positive way and that dissatisfaction results from negative disconfirmations; (2) attribution theory, which states that dissatisfaction results when the cause of a problem is determined to be permanent, marketer related, and under control; and (3) equity theory, which states that satisfaction results when the buyer perceives fairness in the exchange. Two major ways that consumers can respond to dissatisfaction are by complaining and by engaging in negative word of mouth.

Finally, consumers can dispose of products in a variety of ways. This process has important implications for marketing strategy and an understanding of consumer behavior. Recycling, which is one form of disposition, depends on consumers' motivation, ability, and opportunity to act.

QUESTIONS FOR REVIEW AND DISCUSSION

1. How does post-decision dissonance differ from post-decision regret, and what effect do these have on consumers?
2. Describe how consumers acquire information about goods and services by learning from experience with them.
3. Describe the strategies for dealing with consumer learning that can be used by companies with high market share, and contrast these with strategies used by companies with low market share.
4. How do expectations and performance contribute to disconfirmation?
5. Define attribution theory and equity theory, and explain how they relate to dissatisfaction.
6. In what eight ways can consumers dispose of something?
7. Why is it important for marketers to consider both physical and emotional detachment aspects of consumer disposition?

EXERCISES

1. Pick five durable or nondurable product or service categories. Develop a set of questions to ask consumers to tell (1) how satisfied they are with the offerings in each category, (2) recall any instances when they have been dissatisfied in the past, (3) indicate how they dealt with the situation when they were dissatisfied, and (4) identify how they felt about the company or retailer response (if any). Administer this questionnaire to at least 15 consumers. Based on the data, try to answer the following questions:
   a. With what types of products or services are consumers most satisfied? Why do you think this is the case?
   b. For what products or services are consumers most dissatisfied? Why do you think this is the case?
   c. What are the most common responses to dissatisfaction?
   d. How well have the companies handled dissatisfaction?

2. Interview two marketing professionals (from different companies), either by phone or in person. Ask them to describe in detail (1) how important satisfaction/dissatisfaction is to their business, (2) how they try to generate satisfaction, and (3) what kinds of experiences they have had with dissatisfied consumers and how they handled these problems. Summarize your findings for each topic.

3. Pick five durable and five nondurable products. Develop a set of questions to determine how consumers disposed of each product the last time they needed to do so. Administer the questionnaire to at least ten consumers. Summarize the responses, and answer the following questions:
   - **a.** For each product category, which are the most frequently used methods of disposition?
   - **b.** Which product categories are most alike in terms of disposition patterns? Why?
   - **c.** Which product categories are most dissimilar in terms of disposition patterns? Why?

4. Make an inventory of at least 30 of your possessions. For each, indicate when and how you plan to dispose of it. Also provide detailed reasons for this behavior. Then summarize this information, and answer the following:
   - **a.** Which possessions will be the easiest to dispose of and why?
   - **b.** Which possessions will be the hardest to dispose of and why?
   - **c.** What are your most frequent disposition options and why?

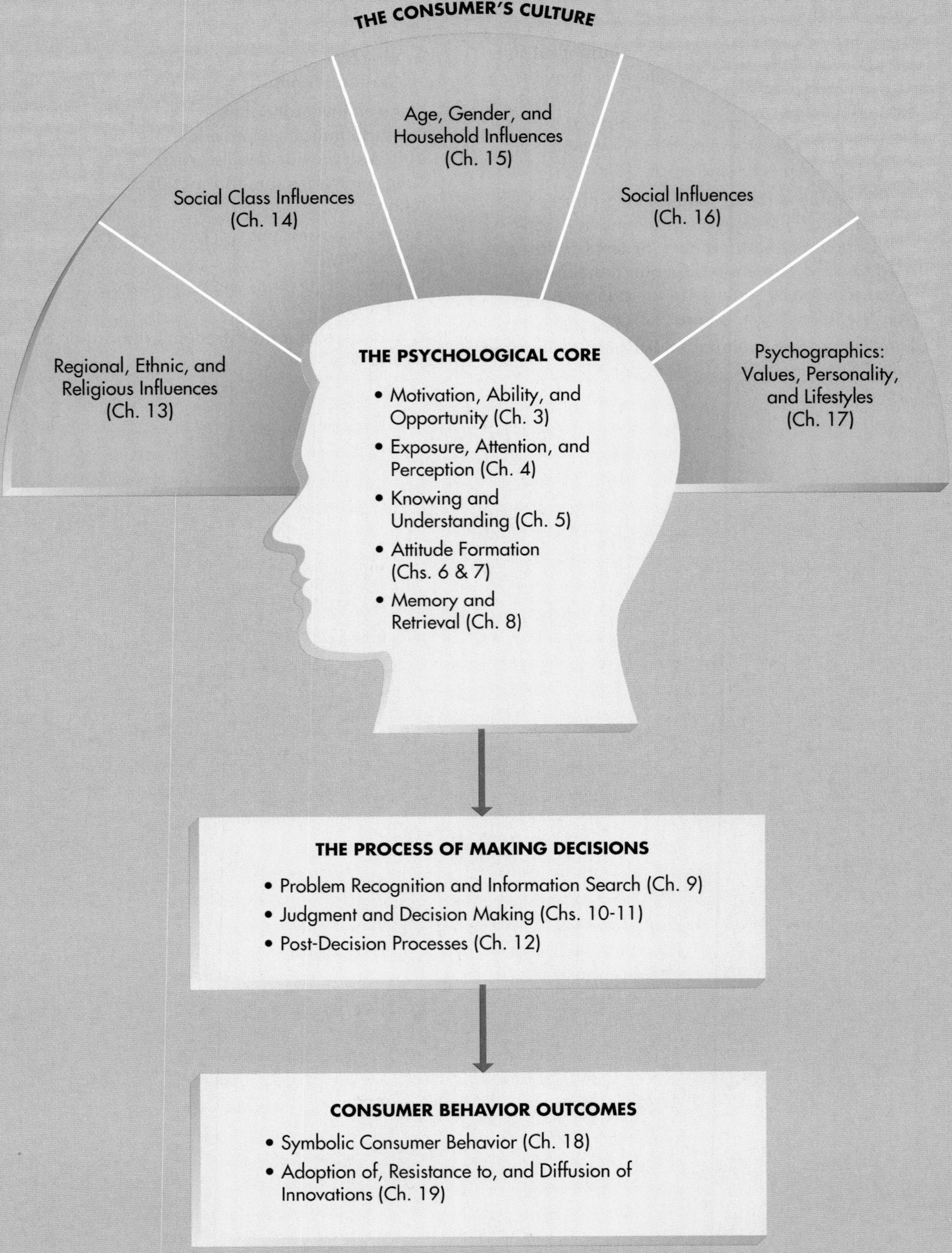

THE CONSUMER'S CULTURE

Regional, Ethnic, and Religious Influences (Ch. 13)

Social Class Influences (Ch. 14)

Age, Gender, and Household Influences (Ch. 15)

Social Influences (Ch. 16)

Psychographics: Values, Personality, and Lifestyles (Ch. 17)

THE PSYCHOLOGICAL CORE

- Motivation, Ability, and Opportunity (Ch. 3)
- Exposure, Attention, and Perception (Ch. 4)
- Knowing and Understanding (Ch. 5)
- Attitude Formation (Chs. 6 & 7)
- Memory and Retrieval (Ch. 8)

THE PROCESS OF MAKING DECISIONS

- Problem Recognition and Information Search (Ch. 9)
- Judgment and Decision Making (Chs. 10-11)
- Post-Decision Processes (Ch. 12)

CONSUMER BEHAVIOR OUTCOMES

- Symbolic Consumer Behavior (Ch. 18)
- Adoption of, Resistance to, and Diffusion of Innovations (Ch. 19)

PART FOUR

The Consumer's Culture

Part Four reflects a "macro" view of consumer behavior, examining how various aspects of the consumer's culture affect behavior. Chapter 13 focuses on how regional, ethnic, and religious groups affect consumer behavior. Chapter 14 examines how social class is determined in various cultures and how it affects consumer decisions and behaviors. Chapter 15 examines how age, gender, and household influences affect consumer behavior and discusses some interesting trends. Chapter 16 considers how, when, and why specific reference groups (such as friends, work groups, clubs) to which we belong can influence consumer decisions and behaviors.

Combined, these external influences can affect our personality, lifestyle, and values, the topics covered in Chapter 17.

Because all of these factors influence consumer behavior, they have many implications for marketing.

chapter 13

Regional, Ethnic, and Religious Influences on Consumer Behavior

INTRODUCTION: Broadcasting Product Placement

Sometimes major TV networks allow advertisers to put *discreet* product placements in programs for a fee. The Hispanic TV network Univision, however, goes further. It invites sponsors to write jingles and skits and prominently display their products on the set of the station's popular show, *Sábado Gigante* (*Gigantic Saturday*).[1] For example, in introducing a segment similar to the *Newlywed Game,* the host announces: "Let's sing to the sponsor who is holding $3,000 for the next contestants," and the audience bursts into the song *"Payless es el amigo de los pies"* ("Payless is the friend of your feet") as the camera pans back and forth from the audience to a display of shoes. The host then states: "Of course you'll feel great at Payless, and a big sale has arrived!" Pointing to a hostess holding a pair of boots, the host announces: "Buy one pair of shoes and take home another at half price. There's great selection for men, women, and children."

Many other products are featured in a similar manner on the four-hour show, and millions of Hispanic consumers in 43 countries love it. In the United States, *Sábado Gigante* reaches more than 20 percent of the Hispanic population (particularly in the South and Southwest) and consistently ranks among the top ten Spanish-language programs. In contrast to the older audience for *Sábado Gigante,* Univision's Telefutura network is targeting younger Hispanics with a music show called *La Cartelera Pepsi* (*Pepsi Hit List*), featuring Spanish rock and pop music. Among the U.S. companies that use advertising

L.A.'s newest Morning News
is in SPANISH
34 KMEX-TV
UNIVISION
Monday-Friday 6-7 a.m
ELLER

EXHIBIT 13.1
Spanish-language Media
Spanish-language stations such as Univision are popular among Hispanic consumers.

Source: A. Ramey/PhotoEdit.

to reach viewers of Univision and Telefutura programs are Pepsi, Sears, J.C. Penney, AT&T, Johnson & Johnson, and Toyota (see Exhibit 13.1).[2]

This example illustrates several important aspects of culture that are central to this chapter. Most important, it demonstrates how consumer behavior can sometimes vary among subgroups of individuals who have unique patterns of ethnicity, customs, and preferences—and how marketers try to reach consumers based on these patterns. It also shows how the region in which consumers reside can influence their behavior. This chapter first discusses how regional influences can affect the consumer. Then it examines subcultures, focusing on three major ethnic groups in the United States (Hispanics, African Americans, and Asian Americans), the use of multicultural marketing, and diversity around the world. Finally, the chapter explores subcultures based on religion (see Exhibit 13.2). ●

REGIONAL INFLUENCES

Because people tend to work and live in the same area, residents in one part of the country can develop patterns of behavior that differ from those in another area. For example, a consumer from New England might enjoy lobster and appreciate colonial architecture, whereas someone from Texas may prefer barbecues and rodeos. This section explores how the region in which we live can affect our consumer behavior. You will learn first about various regions within the United States and then about various regions across the world.

Regions within the United States

Although we can speak of an overall U.S. culture, the United States is a vast country in which various regions have developed unique and distinctive identities. These identities result primarily from differing ethnic and cultural histories. For example, California and the Southwest were originally part of Mexico and therefore reflect a Mexican character. California has also been identified as the "land of opportunity," beginning with the 1849 gold rush and continuing with the lure of Hollywood. The Southwest has integrated its Mexican, Native American, and frontier roots. The eastern seaboard from New England to Georgia has a strong colonial flavor (especially in terms of architecture), reflecting the region's roots as the original 13 British colonies. The wilderness and great expanses of the West and Northwest have greatly determined the more free-spirited personalities of these regions, and the Deep South from Louisiana to Florida owes some of its Dixie, or Southern, character to agriculture, especially the cotton-growing industry, and the rebellion of the Confederacy during the Civil War. Finally, the Midwest is noted for its farms and agriculture.

These statements represent very broad generalizations. Each region also has many unique influences and variations that are too numerous to mention. The key point, however, is that these regional differences may affect consumption patterns. To illustrate, due to strong Mexican influence, consumers in the Southwest prefer spicy food and dishes such as tortillas, salsa, and pinto beans. Interestingly, some types of Mexican (or more accurately Tex-Mex) food such as nachos, chili dogs, and some hot salsas were actually developed in the United States and are only now becoming popular in Mexico.[3] Beef barbecue is particularly popular in Texas due to its large cattle industry, whereas parts of the Deep South lean toward pork barbecue. California has developed a reputation for health consciousness and health foods. Regional differences even show up in the type of stuffing used at Thanksgiving. Cornbread stuffing is

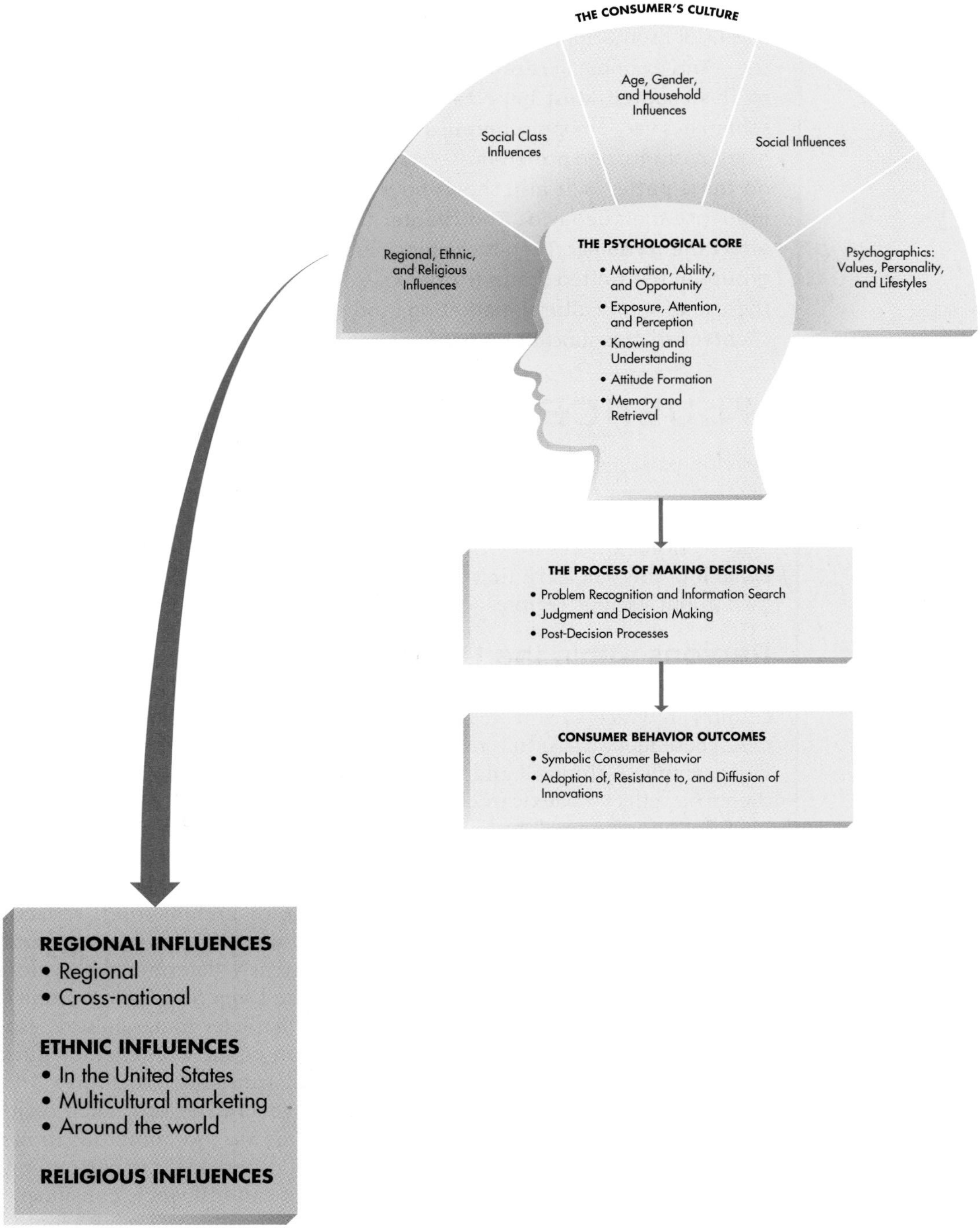

THE CONSUMER'S CULTURE

Regional, Ethnic, and Religious Influences

Social Class Influences

Age, Gender, and Household Influences

Social Influences

Psychographics: Values, Personality, and Lifestyles

THE PSYCHOLOGICAL CORE
- Motivation, Ability, and Opportunity
- Exposure, Attention, and Perception
- Knowing and Understanding
- Attitude Formation
- Memory and Retrieval

THE PROCESS OF MAKING DECISIONS
- Problem Recognition and Information Search
- Judgment and Decision Making
- Post-Decision Processes

CONSUMER BEHAVIOR OUTCOMES
- Symbolic Consumer Behavior
- Adoption of, Resistance to, and Diffusion of Innovations

REGIONAL INFLUENCES
- Regional
- Cross-national

ETHNIC INFLUENCES
- In the United States
- Multicultural marketing
- Around the world

RELIGIOUS INFLUENCES

EXHIBIT 13.2
Chapter Overview: Religion, Ethnicity, and Region
This section of the book examines various aspects of consumer behavior that reflect the consumer as a member of a culture. The region in which one lives, ethnic groups, and religion can affect consumer behavior.

more popular in the South, whereas oyster stuffing is more popular in the North, and Asian families on the West Coast are more likely to substitute rice for stuffing.[4]

Styles of music may also differ in according to region. The Deep South developed a distinct style of southern rock exemplified by the Allman Brothers and Lynyrd Skynyrd. Nashville and Texas have traditionally been strongholds of country music, and Kentucky is known as the home of bluegrass. In the early 1990s, Seattle became recognized as the capital of the "grunge sound," with bands such as Pearl Jam and Soundgarden.

For many years people were moving from rural areas into more heavily populated urban areas. However, tired of high costs, crime, and crowds, more and more U.S. city dwellers have been heading for rural areas. Rural areas are especially attractive for retirement and recreation.[5] In addition, the Internet enables individuals in rural areas to be "connected" and work away from the office.

Nine Nations of North America Nine regions in North America with distinct and identifiable lifestyles and values.

Nine Nations of North America Based on a detailed anthropological study of regional differences, journalist Joel Garreau suggested that the North American continent can be divided into the **Nine Nations of North America**, with consumers in each region emphasizing different values and lifestyles (Exhibit 13.3).[6] Self-respect is valued most in the Empty Quarter, followed by the Islands and MexAmerica. Security is more important in Dixie, New England, and the Breadbasket, and warm relationships with others are most emphasized in the Breadbasket, Ecotopia, and MexAmerica.

These generalizations are admittedly very broad. In fact, a test of the Nine Nations theory found that the regions it identified were no better at predicting consumer values than were the regions used by the U.S. Census Bureau, such as Middle Atlantic and Mountain Pacific.[7] One reason is that considerable variation exists in values and lifestyles among consumers within a region. To compensate, some researchers have tried to go beyond broad regional differences to describe consumers on the basis of more specific characteristics, a technique called *clustering*.

clustering The grouping of consumers according to common characteristics using statistical techniques.

Identifying Regions Based on Clustering Techniques **Clustering** techniques are based on the principle that "birds of a feather flock together."[8] This principle suggests that consumers in the same neighborhood tend to buy the same types of cars, homes, appliances, and other products/services.[9] Systems such as Mosaic (from Experian) and PRIZM (from Claritas) group areas and neighborhoods into more precise clusters based on consumers' similarities on demographic and consumption characteristics. These systems can define a cluster according to similarity of income, education, age, household type, degree of urbanity, attitudes, and product/service preferences, including the type of car owned and preferred radio format. The systems summarize and group all this information using sophisticated statistical techniques such as multivariate regression.

To illustrate, Exhibit 13.4A presents the 62 major types of neighborhoods derived from PRIZM.[10] This system uses data from automobile registrations, consumer product-usage surveys, magazine subscription lists, and other sources to identify clusters or groups of consumers. The 62 clusters can be grouped into the 15 larger clusters in Exhibit 13.4B based on degree of urbanization and socioeconomic status. Note that because clusters are based on

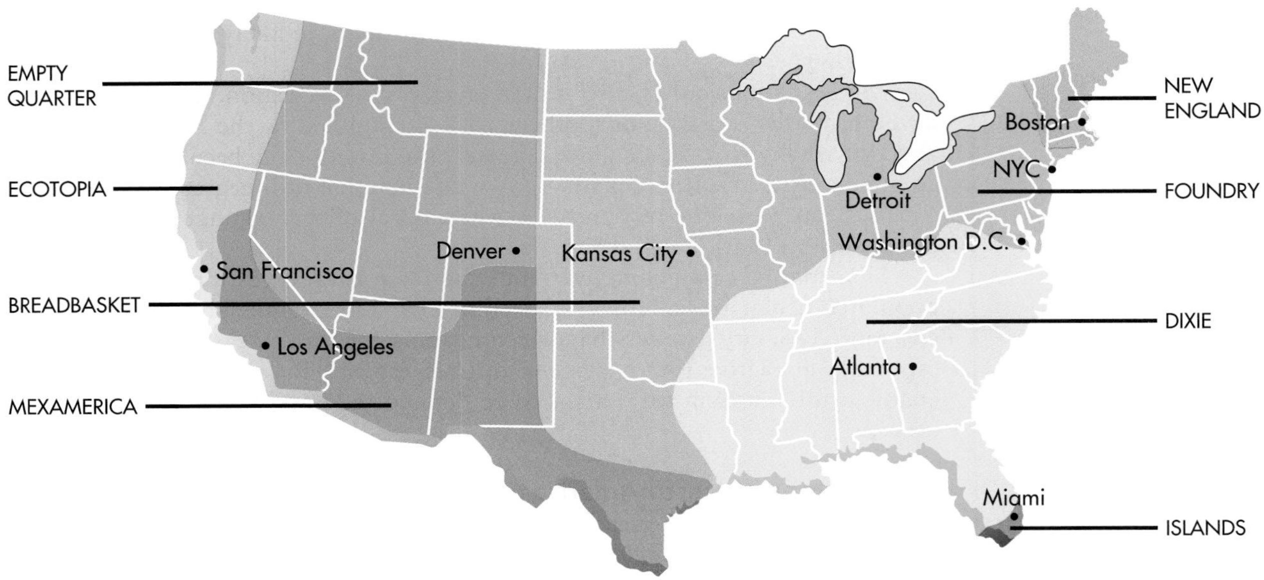

VALUES	NEW ENGLAND	THE FOUNDRY	DIXIE	THE ISLANDS	BREAD-BASKET	MEX-AMERICA	EMPTY QUARTER	ECOTOPIA
Self-respect	22.5%	20.5%	22.5%	25.0%	17.9%	22.7%	35.3%	18.0%
Security	21.7	19.6	23.3	15.6	20.2	17.3	17.6	19.6
Warm relationships with others	14.2	16.7	13.8	9.4	20.5	18.0	5.9	18.5
Sense of accomplishment	14.2	11.7	10.0	9.4	12.4	11.3	8.8	12.2
Self-fulfillment	9.2	9.9	8.4	3.1	7.5	16.0	5.9	12.7
Being well respected	8.3	8.7	11.0	15.6	10.1	2.7	2.9	4.2
Sense of belonging	5.0	8.4	7.5	12.5	7.8	6.7	17.6	7.9
Fun, enjoyment, excitement	5.0	4.5	3.5	9.4	3.6	5.3	5.9	6.9

EXHIBIT 13.3

The "Nine Nations" of North America

Author Joel Garreau divided the United States and Canada into nine major areas, or nations, each of which he believes shares similar values. This map identifies eight "nations" in North America. (The Canadian province of Quebec is not included.) The table shows how values vary according to region. Do you think your region fits these value patterns?

Source: Joel Garreau, *The Nine Nations of North America* (Boston: Houghton Mifflin, 1981), and Lynn R. Kahle, "The Nine Nations of North America and the Value Basis of Geographic Segmentation," *Journal of Marketing*, April 1986, pp. 37–47. Reprinted with permission.

CLUSTER NO.	CLUSTER DESCRIPTION
S1	**ELITE SUBURBS**
01	Blue-Blood Estates (Elite Super-Rich Families)
02	Winner's Circle (Executive Suburban Families)
03	Executive Suites (Upscale White-Collar Couples)
04	Pools & Patios (Established Empty Nesters)
05	Kids & Cul-de-Sacs (Upscale Suburban Families)
U1	**URBAN UPTOWN**
06	Urban Gold Coast (Elite Urban Singles & Couples)
07	Money & Brains (Sophisticated Townhouse Couples)
08	Young Literati (Upscale Singles & Couples)
09	American Dreams (Established Urban Immigrant Families)
10	Bohemian Mix (Bohemian Singles & Couples)
C1	**2ND CITY SOCIETY**
11	Second City Elite (Upscale Executive Families)
12	Upward Bound (Young Upscale White-Collar Families)
13	Gray Power (Affluent Retirees in Sunbelt Cities)
T1	**LANDED GENTRY**
14	Country Squires (Elite Ex-Urban Families)
15	God's Country (Executive Ex-Urban Families)
16	Big Fish, Small Pond (Small Town Executive Families)
17	Greenbelt Families (Young, Middle-Class Town Families)
S2	**THE AFFLUENTIALS**
18	Young Influentials (Upwardly Mobile Singles & Couples)
19	New Empty Nests (Upscale Suburban Fringe Couples)
20	Boomers & Babies (Young White-Collar Suburban Families)
21	Suburban Sprawl (Young Suburban Townhouse Couples)
22	Blue-Chip Blues (Upscale Blue-Collar Families)
S3	**INNER SUBURBS**
23	Upstarts & Seniors (Middle Income Empty Nesters)
24	New Beginnings (Young Mobile City Singles)
25	Mobility Blues (Young Blue-Collar/Service Families)
26	Gray Collars (Aging Couples in Inner Suburbs)
U2	**URBAN MIDSCALE**
27	Urban Achievers (Midlevel, White-Collar, Urban Couples)
28	Big City Blend (Middle-Income Immigrant Families)
29	Old Yankee Rows (Empty-Nest, Middle-Class Families)
30	Mid-City Mix (African-American Singles & Families)
31	Latino America (Hispanic Middle-Class Families)

CLUSTER NO.	CLUSTER DESCRIPTION
C2	**2ND CITY CENTERS**
32	Middleburg Managers (Midlevel White-Collar Couples)
33	Boomtown Singles (Middle Income Young Singles)
34	Starter Families (Young Middle-Class Families)
35	Sunset City Blues (Empty Nests in Aging Industrial Cities)
36	Towns & Gowns (College Town Singles)
T2	**EX-URBAN BLUES**
37	New Homesteaders (Young Middle-Class Families)
38	Middle America (Midscale Families in Midsize Towns)
39	Red, White, & Blue (Small Town Blue-Collar Families)
40	Military Quarters (GIs & Surrounding Off-Base Families)
R1	**COUNTRY FAMILIES**
41	Big Sky Families (Midscale Couples, Kids, & Farmland)
42	New Eco-topia (Rural White/Blue-Collar/Farm Families)
43	River City, USA (Middle-Class, Rural Families)
44	Shotguns & Pickups (Rural Blue-Collar Workers & Families)
U3	**URBAN CORES**
45	Single City Blues (Ethnically Mixed Urban Singles)
46	Hispanic Mix (Urban Hispanic Singles & Families)
47	Inner Cities (Inner-City, Solo-Parent Families)
C3	**2ND CITY BLUES**
48	Smalltown Downtown (Older Renters & Young Families)
49	Hometown Retired (Low-Income, Older Singles, & Couples)
50	Family Scramble (Low-Income Hispanic Families)
51	Southside City (African-American Service Workers)
T3	**WORKING TOWNS**
52	Golden Ponds (Retirement Town Seniors)
53	Rural Industrial (Low-Income, Blue-Collar Families)
54	Norma Rae-ville (Young Families, Bi-Racial Mill Towns)
55	Mines & Mills (Older Families, Mine & Mill Towns)
R2	**HEARTLANDERS**
56	Agri-Business (Rural Farm-Town & Ranch Families)
57	Grain Belt (Farm Owners & Tenants)
R3	**RUSTIC LIVING**
58	Blue Highways (Moderate Blue-Collar/Farm Families)
59	Rustic Elders (Low-Income, Older, Rural Couples)
60	Back Country Folks (Remote Rural/Town Families)
61	Scrub Plant Flats (Older African-American Farm Families)
62	Hard Scrabble (Older Families in Poor, Isolated Areas)

EXHIBIT 13.4A

Sixty-Two Neighborhood Types Derived from PRIZM

Rather than identifying regions in terms of geographical boundaries, marketers can classify consumers according to the type of neighborhood they live in. The logic is that consumers are more likely to share similar characteristics and behaviors with others who live in a comparable neighborhood than with those in a broad region. This exhibit shows 62 types of neighborhoods based on the PRIZM system. Which type of neighborhood do you live in?

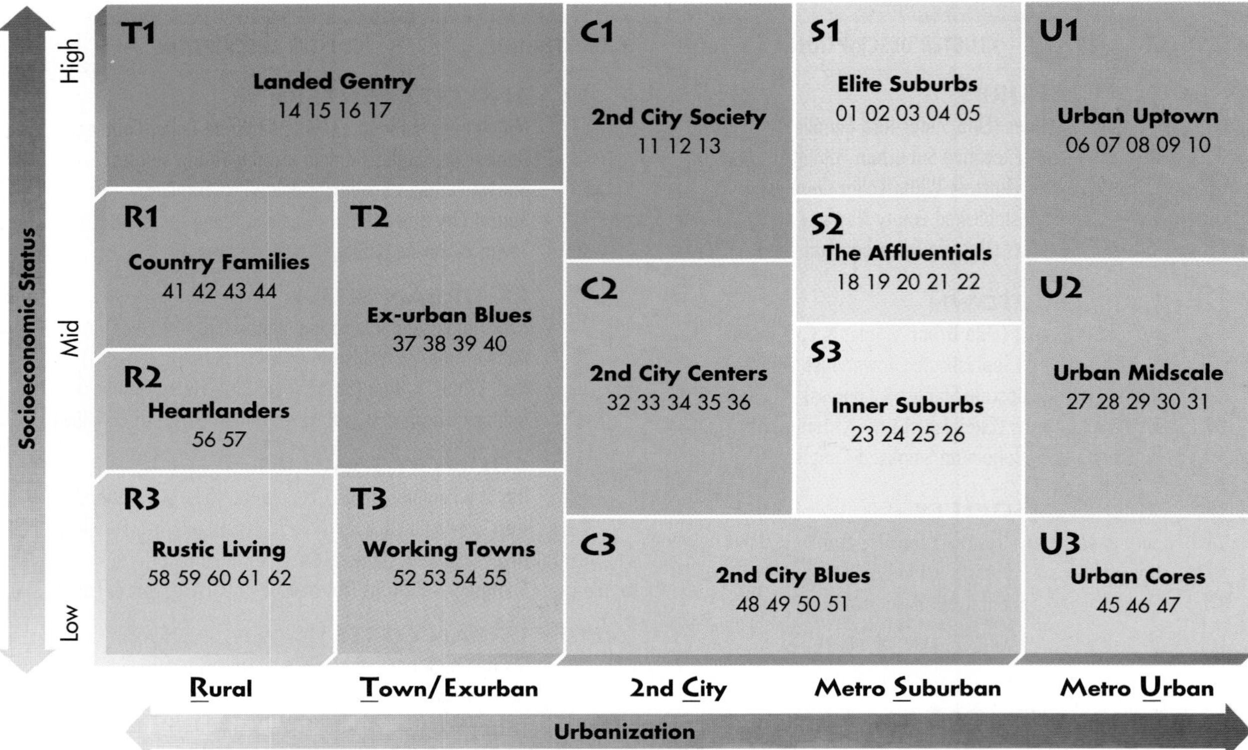

EXHIBIT 13.4B
PRIZM Clusters

Source: PRIZM Cluster reprinted by permission from Claritas, Inc.

common characteristics, not on geography, consumers from different areas of the country may be grouped in the same cluster. The key point is that these more precise clusters allow marketers to segment and target consumers more effectively than broad regional classifications do.

MARKETING IMPLICATIONS Marketers can develop a product, service, or communication to appeal to different regions of the United States. McDonald's sells bratwurst in Minnesota, burritos in California, and lobster sandwiches in Maine.[11] The Southwest is an attractive market for hot cuisines from Mexico, India, Thailand, and Vietnam, as well as for hotter and spicier picante sauces than those sold in northern regions. Likewise, the southern restaurant chain Cracker Barrel changed its menu when it expanded to northern regions, replacing grits with bratwurst.[12]

Based on the Nine Nations theory, an ad stressing self-fulfillment ("Set yourself free with Stouffer's") would seem to be more appropriate for western regions than for the South. Similarly, an appeal to security ("Protect your home from break-ins with Electronic Touch Alarm") might work better in the South than in the West. A number of ads in Texas have a distinct western flavor, reflecting the state's cowboy tradition, and ads directed toward the East Coast may take on a more urban theme. Finally, products can be identified with certain regions such as Florida orange juice, Hawaiian macadamia nuts and suntan lotion, Maine lobsters, and Texas beef.

Marketers can use clustering systems such as PRIZM and Mosaic to help find new customers, develop new products, buy advertising, locate store sites, and target direct mail.[13] In addition, they can use these systems to learn where their customers are, what they like to do, and what media they are exposed to. Hyundai uses PRIZM to target consumers in Kids & Cul-de-Sacs, Bohemian Mix, and other clusters. Within weeks of mailing test-drive offers to consumers in these and other targeted clusters, Hyundai was seeing more test drives and making more sales at a lower cost per vehicle sold.[14] Finally, in deciding where to place a new store, retailers can determine which neighborhoods are most likely to purchase the type of merchandise offered.

Clustering systems are also available for other countries including Germany, Australia, Belgium, South Africa, and Peru. Experian, for example, used its Global Mosaic system to cluster consumers in other countries into 14 common lifestyle categories. This system enables global marketers to target consumers with similar characteristics in different parts of the world.[15] ●

Regions across the World

Clearly, the area of the world in which a consumer resides can influence consumption patterns. As this text has pointed out, cross-cultural variations exist in just about every aspect of consumer behavior. Here are just a few examples of how regions across the world differ in their consumer behavior.

Consumers in different countries vary dramatically in the way they spend their income. Exhibit 13.5 presents a summary of spending patterns from nine different countries around the world.[16] The proportion spent on food is higher in India (52 percent), Kenya (38 percent), Iran (37 percent), Mexico (35 percent), Thailand (30 percent), and Poland (29 percent) than in the United States (10 percent) and Germany (12 percent). The higher percentages reflect lower incomes rather than lavish eating styles.

Consumers in North America, Western Europe, and Asia are more likely to own radios, TVs, and telephones than are consumers in Latin America, Africa, and the Middle East. Note, however, that most urban Latin households (as compared with rural) have a TV and many have a washing machine, VCR, and phone. Other examples include the fact that initially computer ownership was the highest in the United States at 51 percent, but recently other parts of the world have caught up, for example, Japan (57.2 percent), Britain (39 percent), Germany (44 percent), and France (19 percent).[17] Six times as many cars pack the roads in Western Europe as in Eastern Europe. The most Coca-Cola is consumed in North America, followed by Latin America and the European community. The lowest consumption occurs in Asia, the Middle East, and Africa. The top chocolate markets are Switzerland, Britain, and Germany. The need for doctors is highest in Asia, including Indonesia, Thailand, Malaysia, India, and Pakistan. Finally, the fastest growing restaurant cuisines in the United States are Thai, Indian, Vietnamese, and Cajun.[18]

Some nations tend to be strongly associated with certain products, as illustrated in Exhibit 13.6. The consumption of certain types of products is forbidden in certain regions of the world. For example, drinking alcohol and smoking are not allowed in Muslim countries, and religious restrictions forbid the consumption of pork in Israel and beef in India. Food preferences in one part of the world can sometimes appear exotic to people in other areas. The Chinese eat fish stomachs and soup made from bird saliva, natives of Thailand like deep fried chicken heads and claws, and the Iraqis snack on dried, salted locusts.[19] A number of Western habits such as eating snails (particularly in France) and using honey or blue cheese dressing appear equally strange to consumers in other parts of the world.

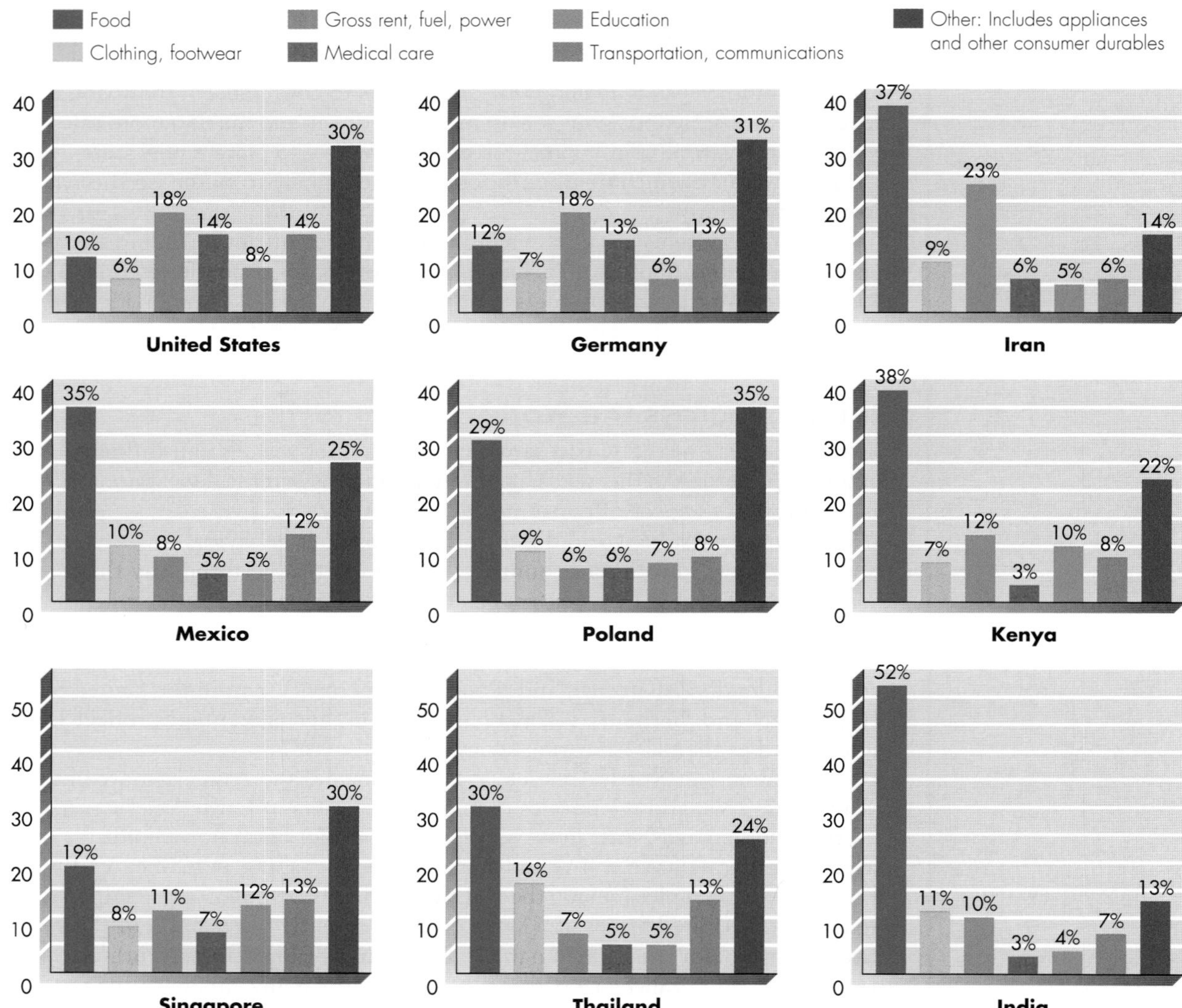

EXHIBIT 13.5

Global Spending Patterns

Consumers in different countries vary widely in how they spend their money. These graphs present the overall spending pattern of nine countries. Western nations (e.g., the United States and Germany) spend proportionately less on food (10 percent and 12 percent, respectively) than India (52 percent), Kenya (38 percent), Iran (37 percent), Mexico (35 percent), Thailand (30 percent), and Poland (29 percent). This statistic reflects the fact that consumers in these six countries typically have less discretionary income.

Source: Ricardo Sookdeo, "The New Global Consumer," *Fortune*, Autumn/Winter 1993, pp. 68–77. Copyright © 1993 by Time Inc. All rights reserved.

Just as in the United States, regional differences in consumer behavior can occur within a specific region of the world. To illustrate, consumers in western India are generally more affluent and more favorably disposed toward premium products, whereas consumers in the north and east are more price conscious. Those in the south tend to be more conservative and utilitarian consumers. Also, in northern India the staple food and drink are wheat and tea; in the south, rice and coffee. Southern Indians tend to be more health conscious and to buy more

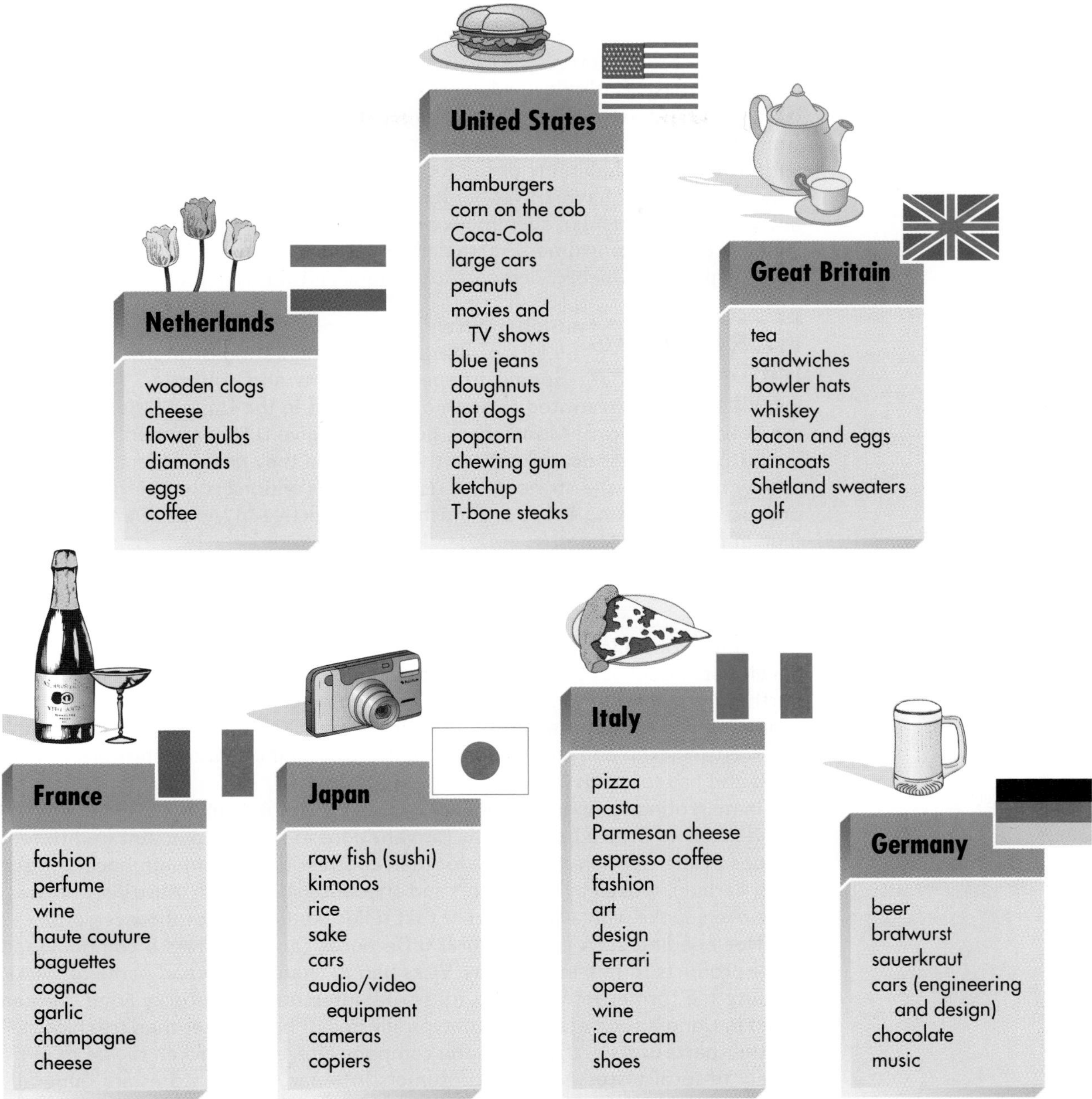

EXHIBIT 13.6
Products and Countries
Many countries tend to be associated with or are known for certain products and services. Here are seven examples. Can you think of any others?

Source: Data from Marieke K. de Mooij and Warren Keegan, *Advertising Worldwide* (Englewood Cliffs, N.J.: Prentice-Hall, 1991).

health and beauty aids and cosmetics because of a desire for fair skin. Finally, southern Indians tend to go to the movies more often and to watch more regional TV due to local language differences, which is why advertising tends to be concentrated in the cinema and on regional TV broadcasts.

In Thailand, the food preferences of northern consumers, particularly near the Cambodian and Burmese borders, differ from the preferences of consumers who live in the central plains (including Bangkok) and in the southern regions on the seacoast. Catholic consumers in the southern part of Germany, particularly Bavaria, have an identity, heritage, and religious orientation that differs from that of the northern and eastern regions which are predominantly Prussian and Protestant. Inhabitants of the former East Germany possess a unique world view as a result of having lived under a police state and command economy for decades.[20] In particular, they focus mainly on home, garden, family, and close friends. Finally, consumers in the different provinces of Canada, especially French-speaking Quebec, demonstrate unique cultural characteristics.

MARKETING IMPLICATIONS Global differences in consumer behavior can sometimes lead to alterations in marketing strategy in order to appeal to specific regions and countries. As shown in Exhibit 13.7, certain strategies are more effective in the United States than they are in Latin America.[21] Money-back guarantees give U.S. consumers confidence, but Latin Americans do not believe them because they never expect to get their money back. Also, the strategies of using famous endorsers or being the official product of a sporting event are much more effective in Venezuela and Mexico than in the United States.

Many companies adjust their marketing to accommodate global consumer differences. McDonald's, for example, offers beer in Germany and wine in France because local consumers typically drink these beverages with their meals. Knowing that Hindu consumers in India do not eat beef for religious reasons, McDonald's developed a beefless Big Mac for that market.[22] In Brazil, the chain has offered northeastern specialties such as *acaraje, bobo de camarao,* and *vatapa.*[23] Other companies also adapt their strategies for different regions. Dunkin' Donuts sells both salty chicken and cheese donuts in Brazil; Domino's Pizza offers pizzas with squid and fish toppings in Japan.[24]

In marketing Pampers disposable diapers, Procter & Gamble developed different versions of a TV ad to account for variations in slang and accent in different regions of the German-speaking world. In contrast to the common hoch Deutsch (high German, spoken by most actors and announcers), Bavarian, Austrian, and Swiss voice-overs spoke with a heavy accent that reflected the styles of those regions.

Not heeding such cross-cultural differences can embarrass a company and cause products to fail. In Germany, Vicks had to change its brand name to Wicks, because the former term is slang for sexual intercourse. Kentucky Fried Chicken failed in Hong Kong because Asians typically boil or broil rather than fry chicken.[25] In other parts of Asia, therefore, the company altered its chicken recipe to more closely fit local tastes. To draw consumers in Japan, where stores are generally small, Office Depot had to downsize its cavernous warehouse stores and reduce the number of office-supply products on the shelves.[26] Adapting strategies to local differences does not ensure success, however. Despite educational programs mounted by Western pharmaceuticals firms, sales of antidepressants remain low in east Asia because mental illness still carries a stigma there and many consumers are treated by alternative healers rather than psychiatrists.[27] ●

ETHNIC INFLUENCES

Ethnicity is another major factor influencing consumer behavior. It is important to emphasize that the many generalizations about ethnic groups discussed here may or may not apply to individual consumers. Rather these generalizations represent only broad group tendencies.

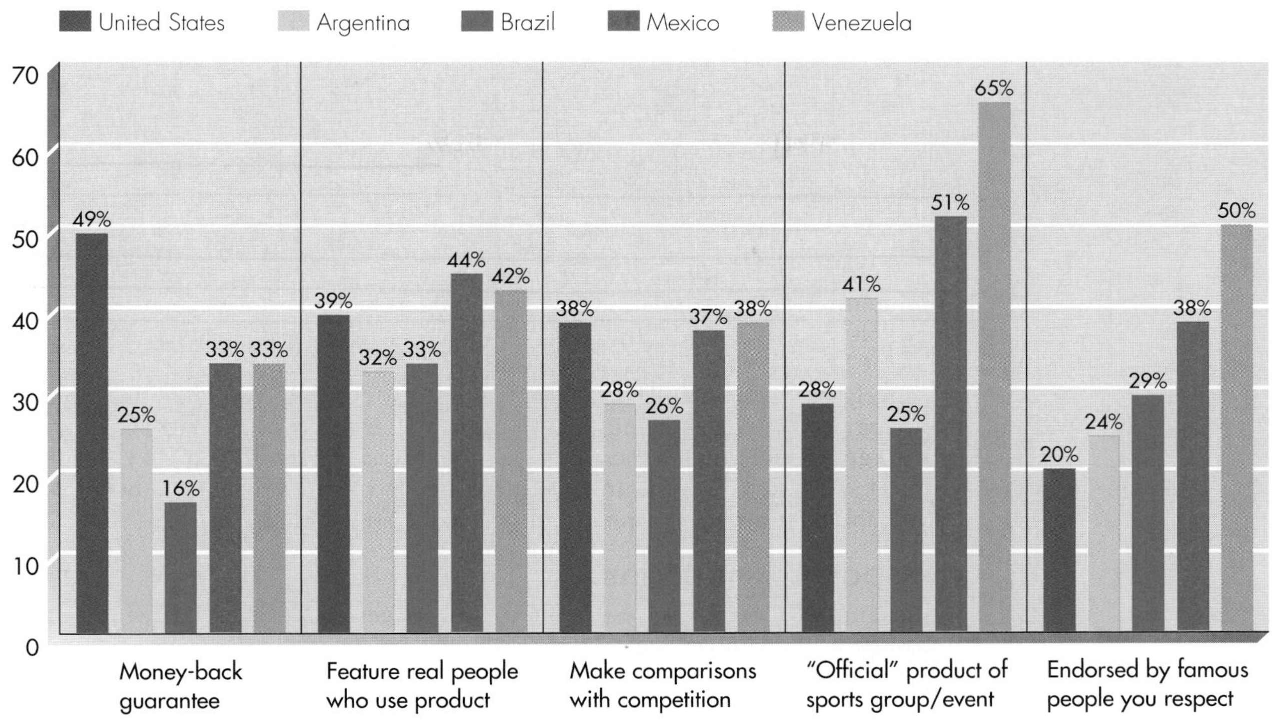

EXHIBIT 13.7
Marketing Strategies in Latin America
Some marketing techniques tend to be more believable or effective in Latin American countries than in the United States. For example, being the official product of a sports group/event or being endorsed by famous and respected people appears to be more effective in several Latin American countries than in the United States.

Source: Adapted from Ignacio Galceran and Jon Berry, "A New World of Consumers," *American Demographics*, March 1995, pp. 27–33. *American Demographics Magazine*, 1995. Reprinted with permission.

ethnic group A subculture with a similar heritage and values.

Throughout the history of the United States, individuals from many different cultures have immigrated to form not only a unique U.S. culture but also a number of subcultures or **ethnic groups** within the larger society. Members of these ethnic groups share a common heritage, set of beliefs, religion, and experiences that set them apart from others in society. Larger groups include the Hispanic, African American, Asian, Jewish, Italian, Irish, Scandinavian, and Polish subcultures. In fact, the Polish population in Chicago is larger than in most cities in Poland.

acculturation Learning how to adapt to a new culture.

These groups tend to be bound together by cultural ties that can, in turn, strongly influence their consumer behavior. In addition, through a process called **acculturation**, members of a subculture must learn to adapt to the host culture. During acculturation, consumers acquire knowledge, skills, and behavior through social interaction, modeling the behavior of others, and reinforcement or receiving rewards for certain behaviors.[28] Thus acculturation is strongly influenced by family, friends, and institutions such as the media, place of worship, and school. Acculturation combines with traditional customs to form a unique consumer culture.

The following sections examine the ethnic composition of the United States and some major population trends.

Ethnic Groups within the United States

The majority of U.S. consumers (commonly referred to as *Anglos*) can trace their ancestry back to one or more European nations, especially England and Germany. However, immigration and population trends are greatly changing the demographic profile of the United States. The non-Anglo population grew 12 times faster than the Anglo population between 1990 and 2000.[29] According to the 2000 Census, the three largest ethnic groups within the U.S. population are African Americans (12.9 percent of the population) Hispanic Americans (12.5 percent), and Asian Americans (4.2 percent).[30] By 2030, nearly half the youth population of the United States will be non-Anglo—primarily Hispanic (see Exhibit 13.8).[31] As a result, the U.S. population is increasingly diverse.

Clearly, U.S. population trends have huge implications for marketers. Collectively, the three main U.S. subcultures already control $900 billion or more in buying power. Their buying power will top $4 trillion within a few decades as these groups continue to increase in size much faster than the general U.S. population.[32] Emerging subcultures represent attractive markets that can be targeted with specific products, communications, and distribution channels.

Hispanic Americans

Hispanic Americans represent one of the largest and fastest growing ethnic groups in the United States today, more than 35 million strong. This section examines the basic characteristics of the Hispanic subculture and then looks at consumption patterns and marketing implications.

Characteristics The Hispanic American market is both huge and diverse. In fact, some have suggested that there is not a single Hispanic market but rather various submarkets with different origins, values, and behaviors.[33] This subcul-

We are the World
Ethnic kids and teens are fueling growth in the youth market.

(UNDER AGE 18)	2001	2010	2020	2030	% CHANGE (2001–2030)
Total Youth	71.0 mil	72.5 mil	77.6 mil	83.4 mil	+18%
Hispanic*	11.3 (16%)	13.7 (16%)	17.2 (22%)	21.0 (25%)	+85%
Non-Hispanic White	45.2 (64%)	42.7 (59%)	42.4 (55%)	42.3 (51%)	–6%
Non-Hispanic Black	10.7 (15%)	11.3 (16%)	12.2 (16%)	13.2 (16%)	+24%
Asian/ Pacific Islander	3.2 (5%)	4.0 (6%)	5.0 (7%)	6.1 (7%)	+94%
Other Non-Hispanic	0.7 (1%)	0.7 (1%)	0.8 (1%)	0.9 (1%)	+27%

(in millions, % of total youth)
*Hispanics can be of any race

Percentages may not equal 100 due to rounding

EXHIBIT 13.8
Ethnic Composition of Under-18 U.S. Consumers

In the coming years, the Hispanic American, African American, Asian American, and other non-Anglo youth population will continue to grow much faster than the Anglo youth population in the United States. By 2030, projections indicate that non-Anglo youngsters under 18 will comprise nearly half of the total U.S. youth population.

Source: Data from U.S. Census Bureau and *American Demographics* calculations, as reported in Rebecca Gardyn, "Habla English?" *American Demographics,* April 2001, p. 55.

ture can be divided into four major groups: Mexican Americans (58.5 percent), living primarily in the Southwest and California; Puerto Ricans (9.6 percent), centered in New York; Central and Southern Americans (8.6 percent); and Cuban Americans (3.5 percent), located primarily in southern Florida.[34]

Levels of Acculturation Hispanics can also be divided into several groups based on their level of acculturation to the host culture: (1) the *acculturated,* who speak mostly English and have a high level of assimilation; (2) the *bicultural,* who can function in either English or Spanish; and (3) the *traditional,* who speak mostly Spanish.[35] In California only 25 percent of Hispanics could be classified as acculturated. This percentage is somewhat higher in Texas. The rate of acculturation tends to be slow, usually taking four generations, because 80 percent of all Hispanics marry other Hispanics. Cuban Americans tend to be the least acculturated and Mexican Americans the most. The proportion of those speaking Spanish at home, more than 70 percent, appears to be on the increase.[36] On the other hand, researchers have found that more than 75 percent of Hispanic youths are bilingual.[37]

Family Orientation and Values Despite this segment's diversity, certain broad generalizations can be made. Foremost, Hispanics have a distinct identity, set of customs and language, as well as a strong family orientation. The Hispanic extended family is usually a large one that includes aunts, uncles, cousins, grandparents, and even godparents. The family is the center of everything, and all family members participate in holidays and festivals. Dinner is often a social event for the entire extended family. Family elders are given the highest respect because of their experience and knowledge.

In addition, Hispanics place a strong emphasis on responsibility, honesty, independence, self-control, inner harmony, and freedom.[38] They can also be characterized by a strong ethnic pride, work ethic, and religious orientation; more than 70 percent are Roman Catholic. Hispanics tend to hold fast to their language, customs, and culture, and they are upwardly mobile. Nevertheless, most Hispanics do not view themselves as materialistic and are not interested in flaunting possessions.[39] Rather, they see themselves as upbeat, colorful, and lively, as reflected by Tejano music, which is very popular among Hispanic consumers.

Demographics The U.S. Hispanic population is also very young. Almost 35 percent of individuals in this ethnic group are under 18 years of age (as compared with 25 percent for the total population).[40] The median age of the Hispanic American population is 26—well below the overall U.S. median age of 35—although the median age of Cuban Americans is 41 and the median age of Mexican Americans is 24.[41] Other important demographics include a lower divorce rate than the general population, reflecting strong family and religious values; larger families with an average of 2.2 children versus fewer than 2 for the general U.S. population; a higher proportion of blue-collar occupations; a median income of $30,700, lower than the general population; and a lower level of education.[42] Note, however, that education and occupational levels have been increasing dramatically in recent years.[43] Politically, Mexicans and Puerto Ricans tend to be Democrats, and Cubans are more likely to be Republican.

Finally, the majority of Hispanic Americans live in urban and suburban areas—particularly Los Angeles, New York, Chicago, Houston, Miami, and San Antonio. However, recent shifts revealed by Census data show a growing Hispanic population in Arkansas, Nevada, and Iowa.[44]

Consumption Patterns Unique Hispanic customs and language have led to identifiable patterns of acquisition and consumption. One of the strongest and most consistent findings is that Hispanic consumers are brand loyal, are likely to buy nationally advertised or prestige brands (particularly those that show an interest in this ethnic group), and are less likely to be lured away by a sale than are other consumers.[45] Thus Hispanics tend to place quality and product reputation ahead of price.

In addition, Hispanics spend more on their children, are more likely to buy fresh produce and meats, and are less likely to eat away from the home than the general population—all due to the focus on family.[46] Because an attractive appearance and good grooming are extremely important, Hispanics spend more on cosmetics and toiletries than the general population. They are therefore 28 percent more likely to buy lipsticks and 44 percent more likely to buy shampoo than the average U.S. consumer, for example.[47] They also tend to spend less on insurance than other Americans.

Food-Consumption Patterns Hispanic American consumers exhibit somewhat unique food-consumption patterns. In particular, they prefer fresh meat and produce, hot spices, canned chilies, and salsas.[48] Delicious meals that please the senses are highly desired, and lowering the fat content would lessen the pleasure. Eight in ten Hispanic Americans cook traditional Hispanic dishes to celebrate Cinco de Mayo (commemorating Mexico's victory over France on May 5, 1862) and other holidays and cultural events.[49] Interestingly, the growth of the Hispanic population is also influencing the rest of the nation's food preferences toward spicier cuisine. As evidence, the sale of salsas has increased dramatically in recent years, whereas ketchup-based cooking is on the decline.[50] The number of Mexican restaurants is rapidly increasing, and fast-food chains such as Taco Bell have become very popular. Hispanic American consumers drink more soft drinks than the general population—and younger members drink more than older members.[51]

intensity of ethnic affiliation How strongly people identify with their ethnic group.

Influence of Acculturation Two important influences on consumption patterns are the consumer's level of acculturation and **intensity of ethnic identification.**[52] Consumers who strongly identify with their ethnic group and are less acculturated into the mainstream culture are more likely to exhibit the consumption patterns of the ethnic group. Strong Hispanic identification leads to a higher level of husband-dominant decisions (discussed in greater detail in Chapter 15).[53] Furthermore, strong identifiers are more likely to be influenced by radio ads, billboards, family members, and coworkers and are less likely than weak identifiers to use coupons.[54] Weak identifiers are more influenced by magazine ads, brochures, the Yellow Pages, *Consumer Reports,* and product labels than are strong identifiers.

The strongest Hispanic identifiers tend to be both recent immigrants and younger Hispanics who were born in the United States but have a powerful desire to rediscover their Hispanic roots.[55] In addition, ethnic identification is more likely to play a role when it is made salient in a particular situation. In other words, a consumer's ethnicity will stand out and influence behavior more when the individual is in the minority than when surrounded by other members of his or her own ethnic group.[56] One study found that minorities adjust to this situation by reducing perceived dissimilarities rather than by increasing similarities between themselves and the majority group.[57]

Finally, a detailed study of Mexican immigration patterns sheds some light on how acculturation occurs.[58] In addition to the social forces mentioned earlier, immigrants adapt to the new consumer environment through trial-and-error learning, by buying and using products and services. After arrival, consumers acquire these items very quickly, particularly buying those that are low-cost, highly visible, not language dependent, and symbolic of both the U.S. and Mexican cultures (including food, clothing, and telephones). Most immigrants strive to buy a car, usually used but still a status symbol generally unattainable in Mexico. Desires for certain products, such as meats, white bread, sugared cereals, and caffeinated drinks, are sometimes stronger among immigrants than among the majority culture.[59]

Note, however, that some Hispanic Americans resist assimilation and desire to maintain their ethnic identity.[60] As an example, a segment of Hispanic Americans strongly dislikes frozen and prepackaged foods. These consumers also tend to buy many items from Mexico, such as foods, soaps, laundry detergents, and recorded music. The editor of *Latina* magazine, which publishes in both English and Spanish, offers another view: "It is now commonly accepted that Hispanics in America are not assimilating but acculturating, that is, taking on the tools necessary to compete and thrive in the dominant society and creating a new hyphenated, hybrid culture."[61]

MARKETING IMPLICATIONS The size, growth rate, characteristics, and spending power of Hispanic Americans lead to a wide variety of marketing implications in areas such as product development, media targeting, advertising messages, promotions, and distribution.

Product development. Marketers are developing specific products and services for the needs and preferences of Hispanic Americans. For example, cosmetics firms, such as Revlon, Maybelline, Cover Girl, Estée Lauder, and L'Oréal, have developed cosmetics designed for consumers with darker skin.[62] One year after Frito-Lay introduced a line of zestier Doritos snacks for the Hispanic American segment, the products were ringing up more than $100 million in annual sales.[63] And McDonald's has introduced a Mexican-style Fiesta Menu in southern California.[64]

Media targeting. Because Hispanic Americans tend to be concentrated in urban areas and share a common language, they can be targeted through the use of Spanish-language media, including TV, radio, print, billboards, and Web sites. Not surprisingly, Hispanic American consumers are heavy users of these media, leading to unprecedented growth in advertising sales.[65] Although radio offers the broadest penetration of Hispanic households, Hispanics spend more time watching television than the general U.S. population. As the chapter-opening example shows, many marketers target adult Hispanic consumers using Spanish-language TV networks. However, targeting younger Hispanic consumers can be more complex. Research suggests that Hispanic teens are more likely to watch English-language TV programs when watching with their siblings, whereas they are more likely to watch Spanish-language programs when watching with their parents.[66] Thus, to maximize its reach, the Chuck E. Cheese pizza chain has begun airing bilingual ads on Nickelodeon and other TV networks.[67]

The number of Spanish-language newspapers is on the rise, and many traditional newspapers publish special editions for Hispanic readers.[68] As a result, many advertising research companies, including Nielsen and Simmons, are closely monitoring Hispanic media patterns.[69]

Advertising messages. Only a small percentage of corporate advertising is directed toward Hispanic Americans, but this percentage is increasing as more firms target the segment. Among the major advertisers targeting Hispanics are Procter & Gamble, AT&T, and Toyota.[70] Advertising is particularly important in this segment because Hispanics tend to buy prestigious or nationally advertised brands.

To illustrate, when Hanes started a print, radio, TV, and Internet advertising campaign targeting Hispanic consumers in Chicago and San Antonio, it increased pantyhose sales by 8 percent.[71] Corona Beer, Mexico's best-selling brand, has boosted U.S. sales by advertising to blue-collar Hispanic workers and linking some promotions to Cinco de Mayo celebrations.[72]

When developing ads, marketers should be guided by the characteristics and consumption patterns of Hispanic Americans (see Exhibit 13.9). Messages that stress family themes repeatedly win the praise of Hispanic American consumers during ad tests.[73] A McDonald's ad showed what looked to most consumers like a birthday party, but the ad had special appeal to Hispanic consumers because they recognized it as a *quinceañera* (a celebration of a girl's coming of age at 15). Ads that portray Hispanics as colorful, upbeat, and lively or that use popular Tejano music also tend to draw a positive response. In addition, advertising can reflect differences between Hispanic segments. In an ad based on the theme, "Coke and your favorite meal," the product was shown with a taco for Mexican Americans, pork loin for Cubans, and chicken and rice for Puerto Ricans.

Hispanics also tend to react positively to ads using ethnic spokespeople, who are perceived as more trustworthy, leading to more positive attitudes toward the brand being advertised.[74] This approach is most effective in environments where ethnicity is more salient (the group is in the minority).[75] Some advertisers try to make ethnic representation in ads proportional to the group's size relative to the general population. This *proportionality criterion* can sometimes be useful in determining how many ethnic members to include in the message.[76]

Hispanics tend to reject image-oriented messages in favor of those that provide clear information about the purpose, benefits, or use of the product or service. When buying a car, for example, Hispanic consumers consult more than four information sources, often checking dealers and print, broadcast, and Internet sources before making a decision; in contrast, the general population consults an average of 1.3 sources.[77] They also tend to interpret visuals and copy literally. All these points suggest that messages directed toward this group need to be straight-

EXHIBIT 13.9
Ad Directed at Hispanic Americans
Hispanics tend to reject image-oriented messages in favor of those that clearly indicate purpose, benefits, or use of the product or service. This ad indicates how an IBM ThinkPad can help a professional woman be successful.

Source: Courtesy of IBM.

forward and clear, especially when communicating with recent immigrants who must be taught how to use products that were unavailable in their native country.

Creating advertising messages for the Hispanic community does not mean simply translating the message into Spanish. Following are several blunders that have been made in translating advertising messages:[78]

- A Coors Light campaign, "Turn It Loose Tonight," was translated literally into Spanish but was interpreted as meaning "Have the Runs Tonight" by Hispanics in the Southwest.
- The slogan for Perdue chickens, "It takes a tough man to make a tender chicken," was translated as, "It takes a sexually excited man to make a chick affectionate."
- The word *bichos* means bugs to Mexicans, but it means a man's private parts to Puerto Ricans. Thus an insecticide ad that claimed to kill all *bichos* left Puerto Ricans wondering.

accommodation theory The more effort one puts forth in trying to communicate with an ethnic group, the more positive the reaction.

Accommodation theory can also apply when marketers develop advertising for Hispanics. This theory predicts that the more effort a source puts into communicating with a group by, for example, using role models and the native language, the greater the reciprocation by this group and the more positive their feelings. As predicted by accommodation theory, advertising in Spanish increases perceptions of the company's sensitivity toward and solidarity with the Hispanic community, thereby creating positive feelings toward the brand and the company.[79] However, using Spanish messages exclusively can lead to negative ad perceptions. Apparently this practice taps into a language insecurity, implying that Hispanics can speak only Spanish. A number of ads directed toward Hispanic Americans are delivered in English because many viewers are either bilingual or highly acculturated. Thus the best strategy may be a combination of English and Spanish messages.

Promotions. The use of sales promotions, such as premiums, sampling, sweepstakes, and pricing deals is also on the rise in this segment. Hispanics are less likely to use coupons, partly because coupons are not available for many ethnic brands, and newer immigrants may not fully understand their purpose (they may be viewed as food stamps and have a negative image).[80] Coupon use tends to increase with acculturation. As evidence, one study found that Hispanics were increasingly buying a brand that used in-store sampling, a cents-off coupon, or a buy-one-get-one-free offer.[81] Another successful promotion featured a Festival Latino that combined coupons with a sweepstakes for cars, trips, and other prizes.[82]

Distribution. More marketers are tailoring the distribution of products and services for Hispanic American consumers. El Guero and Delray Farms in Chicago, Fiesta Market in Texas, Vallarta Foods in Los Angeles, and Varadero supermarkets in southern Florida are full-scale Hispanic markets with a broad selection of Hispanic foods and other products.[83] A mall in Tucson, Arizona, targets Hispanics by advertising in Spanish-language media and providing live mariachi music on holidays such as Cinco de Mayo.[84] In Atlanta, Gainesville Bank and Trust opened Banco Familiar with bilingual staff members and signs, as well as special banking services for the local Hispanic community.[85] ●

African Americans

The African American community represents a large and important segment of the U.S. population. This section examines basic characteristics of this group and its consumption patterns, followed by a discussion of important marketing implications.

Characteristics Nearly 35 million African Americans live in the United States, making up 12.3 percent of the population, and this number is expected to exceed 45 million by 2020.[86] African Americans represent a very diverse group consisting of many subsegments across different levels of income and education, occupations, and regions. The Economic Policy Institute reports that the average African American household income is $31,778, whereas the average Anglo household income is $71,244. At the top income level, U.S. Census data shows that nearly 23 percent of African American married couples have a household income of $75,000 or more, versus nearly 33 percent of Anglo married couples. Also, 15 percent of African Americans have earned a bachelor's or higher degree, compared with 25 percent of Anglos—and the number of African Americans attending college rose 50 percent in the past decade.[87]

Other important characteristics include:[88] (1) a majority of African Americans (54 percent) live in the South; (2) a high proportion live in urban areas, especially the 15 largest U.S. cities; (3) this segment has a younger median age of 28 versus 35 for the population as a whole; (4) this segment has a larger number of single-parent families headed by women; and (5) African Americans watch more TV and have more positive attitudes toward ads than Anglo consumers.[89] African Americans like to join and do things as a group rather than individually. Religious organizations, particularly fundamentalist Protestant groups, are very important to everyday life, leading to a high regard for morality and respect. African Americans are more likely to associate with the Democratic party, although the proportion of black Republican voters is increasing.

Some have argued that the differences between African American and Anglo consumers are not really that great and can be attributed more to income, social class, and urban influences than to race.[90] Furthermore, many aspects of black culture such as music, arts, and athletics have heavily influenced the mainstream culture, thereby reducing differences between African Americans and other ethnic groups.

However, marketers should not assume that African American consumers are similar to the general population in all cases. They can possess differing views on a variety of issues. They are more likely to believe that people should feel free to live, dress, and look the way they want to.[91] Also, African Americans do not necessarily aspire to desert their heritage and assimilate with the majority culture.[92] As incomes rise, a strong desire to preserve a cultural identity develops.

Consumption Patterns A defining element in the consumption patterns of African Americans is the importance of style, self-image, and elegance. "Style—whether captured in an elegant hat, an eloquent phrase, a sophisticated step, or a smooth move—lies at the very heart of the African American culture."[93] Consumption patterns are also related to a strong desire to be recognized and show status. According to research, African Americans often buy premium brands of boys' clothing and alcohol to make a statement about themselves.[94] African Americans tend to be trendsetters in areas such as clothing, music, dance, and language. They have developed their own preferences in fashion and have often been emulated by members of the general population, particularly teenagers.[95]

Traditionally, African American consumers were thought to be more brand loyal than other minority groups, but evidence calls this belief into question.[96] In fact, one study found African American women to be the least brand loyal of all the minority groups studied. Compared with other minorities, African Americans are more likely to pay attention to ads, more willing to pay more for prestigious brands, and less likely to cut back on spending during tough economic times.[97] Furthermore, they respond positively to products and messages targeted toward them and are less likely to trust or buy brands that are not advertised.[98]

African Americans tend to be savvy, investigative, and smart consumers. For example, in the early days of Internet shopping, blacks outspent Anglos nearly two to one; today, 76 percent of African Americans surfing the Web are women.[99] Many blacks enjoy shopping and shop more frequently than other ethnic groups do.[100] In making a purchase, they are more likely to talk to salespeople or to someone knowledgeable about the offering, especially when making investment decisions.[101] They do not exhibit strong store preferences because most retailers have not attempted to appeal to them specifically.

Finally, African American consumers sometimes differ from other groups in terms of the products and services they buy. Among African Americans, the fast-growing categories of products purchased include books, home furnishings, computers, and phone and Internet services. In recent years, as Anglos have cut their purchases of newspapers and magazines, African Americans have increased their spending.[102] Compared with Anglos, blacks are no more likely as a group to consume alcoholic beverages, but blacks who do drink consume more on average each week.

MARKETING IMPLICATIONS African American consumers have a total buying power exceeding $500 billion, and their buying power is multiplying year by year.[103] Not surprisingly, marketers are now devoting more attention to this segment, as evidenced by an increase of advertising dollars from $400 million to more than $800 million in a 10-year period.

Product development. Many marketers focus primarily on products for the unique needs of the African American market. Soft Sheen and African Pride are two leading hair care brands in this market, for example.[104] In addition, marketers that make products for the broader U.S. population are now branching out to design products specifically for black consumers. Companies such as Revlon, Maybelline, and Estée Lauder have developed cosmetics tailored to blacks, and L'eggs sells panty hose shades for darker skin.[105] Clothing manufacturers are designing styles more flattering for the physique of African American women. They are also featuring colorful styles based on African kente cloth.

In the fast-food area, KFC has added menu items such as red beans and rice and greens to appeal to black consumers.[106] Major toy makers such as Mattel (which makes Barbie), Hasbro, and Tyco have designed dolls for the African American market.[107] One Mattel doll called Shani comes in a choice of three complexions—light, medium, and dark—and has a boyfriend named Jamal. Finally, Hallmark introduced the Mahogany line of greeting cards for African Americans, and banks have offered special credit cards that appeal to African American pride.[108]

Media targeting. According to research, strong ethnic identifiers among African American consumers act more positively than weak identifiers to ads placed in racially targeted media.[109] In fact, 82.3 percent of black consumers seek out information from magazines specifically aimed at them.[110] The publications seen as having the highest credibility are *Ebony* and *Essence. BET Weekend* attracts African American readers by distributing its insert inside newspapers.[111] For this segment, Kraft publishes a special magazine, *Food and Family,* featuring recipes and food tips. The company sends the free publication to households in areas with a high African American population.[112] African American TV networks (such as BET) and ethnic programming also represent good vehicles for advertising. Also, African American radio stations have long been a cultural lifeline and represent an efficient advertising vehicle.[113] Mercedes, for example, used radio as its primary medium in a recent campaign targeting affluent African American car buyers in Baltimore, Philadelphia, and Washington, D.C.[114]

Marketers can attempt to reach black consumers through the general media but must be careful to pay close attention to the media habits of blacks. African American consumers represent only 10 to 12 percent of mass-market magazine readership and often prefer different TV programs from other groups.[115]

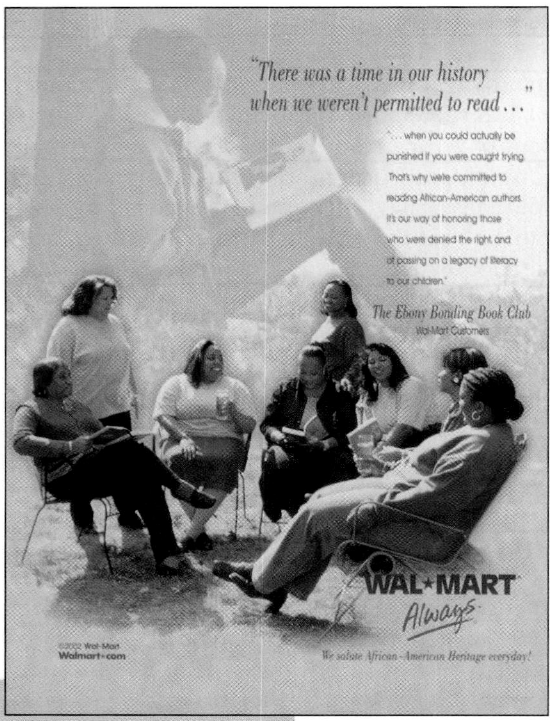

"There was a time in our history when we weren't permitted to read…"
"…when you could actually be punished if you were caught trying. That's why we're committed to reading African-American authors. It's our way of honoring those who were denied the right, and of passing on a legacy of literacy to our children."
The Ebony Bonding Book Club
Wal-Mart Customers
WAL★MART
Always
©2002 Wal-Mart
Walmart.com
We salute African-American Heritage everyday!

EXHIBIT 13.10
Ad Directed at African Americans
Ads directed at African Americans need to express the strong values of this group. This ad for Wal-Mart stresses the value of education and heritage.

Source: Courtesy of Wal-Mart.

Advertising messages. Major advertisers such as General Motors, Procter & Gamble, L'Oreal, and Johnson & Johnson are investing in ad campaigns specifically for this segment.[116] However, African Americans were ignored or given minimal attention in ads for a long time, not only in the United States but in Canada and the United Kingdom as well. In one survey, more than 50 percent of consumers—94 percent of whom were Anglo—said that ads did not include enough blacks.[117] Another survey indicated that more than 60 percent of blacks were alienated by ads because they are "designed for whites."[118] This is in contrast to research showing that distinctive groups such as African Americans will identify more strongly and have more positive evaluations when the advertising source is of the same ethnic group as the target.[119]

Many blacks resent the way they have been portrayed in ads, leading to negative attitudes toward products and services. In the survey mentioned earlier, more than 46 percent of consumers said that blacks were portrayed inaccurately in ads, often appearing in minor and background roles.[120] Although this situation is changing as more ads include African American spokespeople and models, the black models often have lighter skin as opposed to more African features and darker skin.[121] Thus, there is room for improvement in the depiction of African American consumers in ads.

Advertising messages for this segment should take the unique values and expectations of African Americans into account (see Exhibit 13.10) rather than try to use an Anglo strategy.[122] Betty Crocker, for example, developed a targeted campaign around a contest called "Recipes from the Soul," in which black consumers were invited to send in their favorite home-cooking recipes.[123] Ads for banks and financial institutions need to "convey a message of respect."[124] Similarly, McDonald's developed a marketing campaign to convince blacks that they are valued customers.[125] Given that blacks are thorough and smart shoppers, ads should provide specific product and service details and depict real-life situations. Businesses can also "personally invite blacks to purchase their products and services and create advertising that blacks see as relevant, realistic, and positive."[126]

In developing ads, marketers should be careful not to create the impression that blacks are different. Maybelline found that black women wanted to be treated like all other women and be depicted as strong, contemporary, and self-confident.[127] Cadillac also learned not to create an impression of tokenism in creating ads for blacks.[128] Thus successful advertising toward African Americans does not simply mean using black models. The key is the way the message and the themes are portrayed. However, black urban teens have been particularly difficult to target because they are very skeptical of advertising and have few role models they trust.[129]

Marketers must also be cautious of the effect that black models have on consumers outside the targeted segment. One study found that Anglo consumers had less favorable attitudes and were less likely to purchase the product when ads featured black rather than Anglo actors.[130] This problem is pronounced when consumers are prejudiced toward minorities. On an encouraging note, research suggests that younger Anglo consumers are more accepting of minority actors, which may reduce the problem over time.[131] Finally, there are some controversial ethical issues related to marketing toward blacks, such as unfair messages and discrimination.

Promotions. African American consumers respond positively to a variety of sales promotions, including in-store sampling, cents-off coupons, and buy-one-get-one-free offers.[132] Major League Baseball was concerned that blacks account for only 5 percent of ticket sales and have negative perceptions about the league. In response, the teams sponsored special events, including inner-city baseball leagues, and special promotions, such as free tickets, to draw black fans.[133] PepsiCo has successfully wooed younger blacks with promotions featuring hip-hop stars Mary J. Blige and Wyclef Jean. "With the urban youth audience, you really have to gain street credibility first, and you can't do that with a typical mass-marketing campaign," explains Pepsi's director of urban and ethnic marketing.[134]

Distribution. Marketers can also adjust distribution strategies to appeal to African American consumers. KFC outlets in largely black neighborhoods have played upbeat music and dressed employees in traditional African garb with kente ties, vests, and kufu hats.[135] In Atlanta a shopping mall in a predominantly black neighborhood restyled itself as an "Afrocentric retail center."[136] In areas where blacks represent more than 20 percent of the population, J.C. Penney has developed "Authentic African Boutiques" that offer clothing, handbags, hats, and other accessories imported from Africa. Finally, because most black consumers do not have a strong store preference, a number of retailers have hired ethnic specialists to develop special merchandise offerings and advertising.[137] ●

Asian Americans

Asian Americans are the third-largest and fastest growing minority in the United States. The number of Asian Americans has doubled in the last decade to more than 10 million.[138] The largest concentration is in the New York, Los Angeles, and San Francisco metropolitan areas and in Hawaii, where more than 65 percent of the population is of Asian decent. Growth has also been high in other areas, including Dallas—where the Asian American population doubled from 1990 to 2000—and Atlanta, where the population tripled during the same period.[139] Consumers in this subculture have particular characteristics and consumption patterns that affect the way companies target and market to them.

Characteristics The Asian American community is even more diverse than the Hispanic American and African American groups because it consists of people from more than 29 countries, from the Indian subcontinent to the Pacific Ocean, each with its own principles and customs. The six largest groups include immigrants from the Philippines, China, Japan, Korea, Vietnam, and India.[140] In light of this tremendous diversity, it is risky to rely too much on broad statements about Asian Americans as a whole. Nevertheless, we can make a few generalizations.

Many Asian Americans are young, live in multiple-wage-earner households—and thus have greater discretionary income—and are entering their prime earning years. The average annual household income of Asian Americans is about $47,000, and 39 percent have household incomes greater than $75,000, giving them the highest socioeconomic status of any U.S. subculture.[141] They tend to save money, be highly educated, have higher computer literacy, use the Internet more frequently, and hold a higher percentage of professional and managerial jobs than the general population.[142] More than half live in integrated suburbs as opposed to ethnic areas such as a Chinatown, and most tend to be highly assimilated by the second and third generations.

One common denominator of most Asian cultures is the strong emphasis they place on the family, tradition, and cooperation.[143] The group is often more important than the individual. Unmarried children, especially in Chinese American families, are expected to live with their parents. Furthermore, Asian American consumers often stress traditional customs and language, even though their children are generally highly assimilated into the mainstream culture.[144] A very strong work ethic characterizes Confucian subgroups, such as Koreans and Chinese.

Consumption Patterns Although Asian Americans are quite diverse, they exhibit several similar consumption patterns. For example, many Asian Americans shop for fun.[145] They want quality and are willing to pay for it, even though they will still react positively to a good bargain. They are often strongly loyal to high-quality established brands and will frequently recommend products and services to friends and relatives.[146] Thus word-of-mouth communication is very important.

Many consumers, especially the Chinese, have a strong desire to get the "eight bigs:" a color TV, refrigerator, car, camera, VCR, furniture, telephone, and washing machine.[147] Asian Americans are also more likely than other groups to invest in real estate and jewelry. Relationships are extremely important to Asian Americans. Thus companies must show long-term concern and respect for consumers. Furthermore, Asian Americans prefer to deal with family-owned businesses and with companies that have strong reputations for good service.

MARKETING IMPLICATIONS Because Asian Americans are a rapidly growing group with considerable economic power—making more than $254 billion in purchases per year—this subculture has important marketing implications.

Product development. Marketers are increasingly offering products designed with Asian Americans in mind.[148] More companies now offer cosmetic shades that blend better with Asian skin colors and teach consumers appropriate skin care techniques. The Pleasant Company has also developed dolls for the Asian American market. One company mistakenly offered golf balls in a four-pack instead of the usual three-pack. Four is considered an unlucky number because the word *four* sounds similar to the word for death in both Japanese and Chinese.

Media targeting. Although marketers rarely targeted Asian Americans in the past, many are now actively reaching out to this group. For example, TV advertising for the Chinese New Year's parade in both San Francisco and Los Angeles is usually completely sold out by the preceding October, to buyers such as McDonald's, Mazda, Bank of America, and AT&T.[149]

One way of reaching this very diverse group is through native-language newspapers and magazines. Ford has done this, placing newspaper ads in Mandarin, Korean, and Cantonese.[150] The Asian Yellow Pages is also useful, as evidenced by the 5,500-plus Asian businesses in California that advertise in it. In addition, direct mail can be effective. Citibank used direct mail to attract Chinese American depositors with an offer of a gold medallion in exchange for a minimum deposit of $30,000.[151] The Internet is another way to reach Asian Americans. Finally, satellite TV allows Asian American immigrants to watch programs produced in their homelands, interspersed with culturally appropriate programs produced in the United States and accompanied by ads for U.S. products.[152]

Advertising messages. The diversity of languages and customs has inhibited advertising to the Asian market. Nevertheless, Asian Americans have generally responded well to subtle messages that focus on tradition, the family, and cooperation.[153] MCI has been successful by stressing ties to the home. Ads should also present product benefits in a straightforward manner. However, a study found that Asian models tend to be overrepresented in business settings and underrepresented in home and family settings.[154] Emotional messages are generally unacceptable because Asian Americans do not approve of displaying emotions in public.

Asian models may be overrepresented in ads in comparison to their proportion in the population, even though they most typically appear in background roles.[155] At the same time, "ethnically correct" endorsers have been well received. Using Asian models such as Olympic figure skater Michelle Kwan communicates that members of this group are valued customers, which may, in turn, enhance consumers' brand loyalty.[156]

Messages delivered in the native language are often more effective. Despite the diversity of languages within this subculture, marketers may find the effort worthwhile when many consumers from a single subgroup are concentrated in an area. Washington Mutual successfully used a Chinese language campaign in Los Angeles neighborhoods with a large Chinese American population.[157] Northwest Airlines creates formal messages in Japanese to show respectful appreciation to its Japanese American customers.[158] However, simply translating an English message does not always work, which is why Bank of America and many other firms hire ethnic advertising agencies to facilitate the process. In California, Bank of America distributes materials in Chinese, Korean, and Vietnamese, and its ad campaigns feature Asian models and refer to feng shui and other culturally appropriate practices.[159]

Promotions. Evidence suggests that Asian American consumers will respond positively to a variety of promotions, such as pricing deals, coupons, and sponsorship of events. Remy Martin sponsored a Moon Festival Banquet celebrating an important Chinese holiday for influential leaders of the Chinese community in New York.[160] Sampling might also prove to be useful, especially if it demonstrates the quality of the product. Many Japanese American consumers prefer service-oriented promotions, while Chinese and Korean American consumers prefer promotions with tangible rewards.[161]

Distribution. Finally, marketers can design distribution channels for Asian American consumers. The United Savings Bank in San Francisco decorates its branches in popular colors of red and gold.[162] Peterson Bank in Chicago has a special department whose employees speak Korean, and all written materials are available in both English and Korean. A mall near Vancouver (whose customers are 80 percent Chinese Canadians) offers fashions from Hong Kong, a Chinese-language movie theater, a shop with traditional Chinese medicines, and events such as kung fu demonstrations and folk dances.[163] ●

Multicultural Marketing

multicultural marketing Strategies used to appeal to a variety of cultures at the same time.

Ethnic marketing does not necessarily mean complete segmentation. **Multicultural marketing**, in which strategies appeal to a variety of cultures at the same time, is becoming increasingly popular. This strategy requires both a long-term commitment and consideration of ethnic groups from the outset, rather than as an afterthought.[164]

For example, a Schick TV ad showed a variety of different faces, including Asians, Caucasians, African Americans, and Hispanics, dissolving into one another in front of a shaving mirror, thereby recognizing that the "typical" American is multicultural. Another example of multicultural marketing is the

Toyota ad in Exhibit 13.11. Finally, Ford created a multicultural ad in Europe but created a stir when African and Indian models had their faces superimposed or replaced with white models for the Eastern European market, where consumers felt such diversity didn't make sense.[165]

Ethnic Groups around the World

Although few countries are as diverse as the United States, ethnic subcultures do exist in many other nations. It is beyond the scope of this book to discuss each of the numerous ethnic groups around the world, but a few examples should illustrate their importance.

In Canada, the French-speaking subculture has unique motivations and buying habits.[166] French Canadians tend to be lower in income, social class, education, and occupation than the rest of the country; they also have more children and greater family stability. Compared with the rest of the Canadian population, French Canadians use more staples for original or "scratch" cooking; drink more soft drinks, beer, wine, and instant beverages; and consume fewer frozen vegetables, diet drinks, and hard liquor. They also tend to value furniture less than their neighbors. Patriotism and ethnic pride are extremely strong, and this theme has been successfully incorporated into marketing strategies by companies such as Kodak, McDonald's, and KFC.[167]

EXHIBIT 13.11
Multicultural Ad
This ad is a good example of multicultural advertising. Several ethic groups are represented in it.

Source: Photographs copyright Dana Glickstein.

For every expression,
there's a Toyota.
TOYOTA | everyday
©1998 Toyota Motor Sales, U.S.A., Inc. Buckle Up! Do it for those who love you. 1-800-GO-TOYOTA • www.toyota.com

The former Soviet Union was a diverse country, with more than 100 different ethnic groups speaking more than 50 different languages. The breakup of this large nation yielded a number of countries with strong ethnic cores, including Russia, the Baltic countries (Lithuania, Estonia, and Latvia), Belorussia, and Ukraine.

In Thailand more than 80 percent of the population is of Thai origin, but several sizable ethnic subcultures still flourish. The largest, 10 percent of the population, has Chinese roots, and this segment has influenced the Thai culture to a significant degree.[168] Chinese consumers in Thailand exert a powerful economic force because they own many businesses; their influence is also felt in art, religion, and food. This ethnic group has assimilated very well into the main Thai society, and intermarrying is common. As a result, many in this group consider themselves Thai. Other smaller ethnic groups in Thailand include people of Laotian, Indian, and Burmese origin.

India has a diverse ethnic population, with more than 80 languages and 120 dialects spoken in the country. Some villagers need travel only 30 miles from home to reach a destination where they are not able to speak the language. These few examples point up the challenges and opportunities facing marketers who want to reach specific groups within a particular country.

RELIGIOUS INFLUENCES

A final type of subculture is based on religious beliefs. Religion provides individuals with a structured set of beliefs and values that serve as a code of conduct or guide to behavior. It also provides ties that bind people together and make one group different from another. For example, a defining element of Protestantism is the belief that hard work will lead to social mobility. This principle has permeated U.S. culture because most of the original English colonists were Protestant. By stressing strict adherence to its rules and dogmas, the Catholic Church exerts a strong influence on its members and may discourage individualism and innovative thinking. Judaism, on the other hand, stresses individuality and self-education, which can lead to a higher level of innovation, need for achievement, anxiety, and emotionality.[169] Finally, the religious right of born-again Christians who tend to follow televangelists is "anti-elite, anti-intellectual, anti-big government, [and] socially nostalgic and believes in material blessings for those who love the Lord and live right."[170]

Religious influences can sometimes affect consumer behavior. One study found that Jewish consumers were more likely than non-Jews to be exposed in childhood to information from print media, group memberships, and special training; to seek information from TV, magazines, and other media; to adopt new products; to provide information to others; and to remember more information.[171] A study of weekend leisure activities found that price was the most important factor for Protestants, whereas companionship was more critical for Jews. Catholics were more likely to prefer dancing and much less likely to desire sex as an activity than the other groups.[172] Born-again Christians, on the other hand, were less likely to buy on credit, purchase national brands, or attend rock concerts and movies.[173]

Religion can also prevent consuming certain products and services. Mormons are prohibited from using liquor, tobacco, and caffeine, including cola. Orthodox Jews do not eat pork or shellfish, and all meat and poultry must be certified as kosher. Muslims cannot eat pork or drink liquor. Catholic consumers may choose to abstain from eating meat on Fridays during the season of Lent.

Religious subcultures are clearly present in many parts of the world. In India, for example, most of the population is Hindu, but large groups of Muslims, Christians, and Sikhs exhibit different patterns of consumption. Because Hindus are predominantly vegetarian, Indian manufacturers of food and cosmetics must use vegetable-based rather than animal-based oils and shortening in their products. The Sikh religion forbids the consumption of beef and tobacco, and the sale of such products is low in areas where many Sikhs live. Finally, the color green has significance for Muslims, which has led to its frequent use on product packages for this group.

MARKETING IMPLICATIONS

Marketers can segment the market by focusing on religious affiliation, delivering targeted messages and promotions, or using certain media. They can target members of the religious right through the Christian Television Network, religious radio stations, and religious TV programs, which have a total audience of more than 15 million. To reach Christian audiences, marketers can air commercials on Salem Communications' Christian music radio stations in Dallas, Atlanta, Los Angeles, and Chicago.[174] Television is an excellent medium, with more than 20 religious cable networks battling for viewers.[175] In addition, marketers can advertise in one of the many magazines geared to specific religious affiliations.

In planning distribution, marketers can consider stores such as King's House in Scottsdale, Arizona, which specialize in religious products. And more religious institutions are opening gift shops, snack bars, even fitness centers, providing distribution opportunities for suitable goods and services.[176]

For years, local institutions have advertised in newspapers to welcome new members and announce services. Now, faced with flat religious attendance, some religions and congregations are becoming more active in their marketing efforts.[177] The Lutheran Hour Ministries spends $20 million yearly on print, TV, and radio campaigns, stressing family themes rather than specific religious messages. The Catholic Communication Campaign also advertises heavily, using soft-sell themes such as the power of prayer and antiprejudice. Religious ads have moved away from dry, head-and-shoulders shots of preachers to become well-produced messages with slick soundtracks.[178] To attract young people, Protestant and Catholic churches have been offering Taize, a user-friendly type of worship that's "a little bit like disco."[179] Makor, a Jewish religious center in New York City, has partnered with a hip music club to offer jazz along with wine and dinner during religious activities.[180]

Finally, marketers sometimes use religious themes to sell products. A common example is special products or packages produced during times of religious holidays. To appeal to a broad array of consumers and not alienate certain groups, however, marketers generally avoid images with overt religious meaning. This is why Snowmen, Santa Claus, and Christmas trees often replace religious figures at Christmas time.[181] As a public service the Outdoor Advertising Association ran a series of billboards that were all signed by "God." Sample messages included "Love Thy Neighbor," "You think it's hot here?" and "Don't make me come down there." ●

SUMMARY ● ● ● ● ● ● ● ● ● ● ● ● ● ●

Three major aspects of culture have important effects on consumer behavior: regional, ethnic, and religious differences. Consumption patterns may differ in various regions of the United States and the world, leading some marketers to tailor strategies specifically to these regions.

The United States has a number of different ethnic groups, and population trends are dramatically altering the country's demographic profile. The diverse Hispanic population has a distinct identity and language, strong family and religious orientation, a solid work ethic, and youthfulness. These broad characteristics can influence consumption by leading to brand loyalty and the desire for prestigious products, and they have important implications for product development, advertising, media targeting, promotions, and distribution.

The African American population is largely urban, young, social, and religious. Black consumers value prestigious brands and are smart investigative shoppers. The very diverse Asian American subculture is also young, has high socioeconomic status, values the family and the group, and is quite brand loyal. In spite of its language and cultural diversity, this group can be reached with specific marketing strategies.

Many marketers are now taking a multicultural approach by trying to appeal to all subcultures instead of just the majority one. Marketers who want to sell in other countries must also be familiar with important ethnic groups in other areas. Finally, religious values and customs can influence consumer behavior and form the basis of marketing strategies.

QUESTIONS FOR REVIEW AND DISCUSSION

1. Why do the boundaries between the Nine Nations of North America not always coincide with U.S. state boundaries?
2. What is clustering, and why do marketers use it?
3. What are the three main subcultures within the U.S. population?
4. How do acculturation and intensity of ethnic identification affect consumer behavior?
5. Define the accommodation theory, and explain its importance for marketers who target Hispanic Americans.
6. Why would a company adopt multicultural marketing rather than targeting subcultures one by one?
7. Identify some of the ways in which religion can influence consumer behavior.

EXERCISES

1. You have been assigned to develop a marketing strategy for a new fruit drink that provides high energy and is high in nutrients. It is also light and very refreshing, especially on a hot day. How would you market this product in different regions of the world? Develop a detailed marketing plan for two regions that addresses the advertising message, media selection, distribution, and sales promotion.
2. You are developing a marketing strategy for a fashion clothing store chain that wants to specialize in providing products for minorities in your area. The stores plan to sell medium- to high-priced clothing for Hispanic, African American, and Asian American women. Develop a questionnaire to collect information about acquisition and consumption patterns among your potential customers. Be sure to ask questions that will provide insight into your decisions about (a) store design, (b) products offered, (3) pricing, and (4) advertising. Administer this questionnaire to at least ten members of one of the three ethnic groups. Summarize the key findings of your research and make a recommendation in each of the areas mentioned.
3. Pick three product/service categories that you think will show consumption differences across different religious subcultures. Design a questionnaire to assess major consumption patterns for each of these products/services and administer it to at least five consumers in each of the major subcultures. Summarize the responses, and answer the following questions:
   a. How do these cultures vary in terms of consumption?
   b. How would marketing efforts differ for the groups?

chapter 14
Social Class Influences on Consumer Behavior

INTRODUCTION: Class Clash in China

Starting in the early 1990s, some individuals in China—particularly entrepreneurs and managers—began to acquire great wealth as a result of economic reform and more liberal government policies. These "new rich" became big spenders and flaunted their wealth by enrolling their children in private schools and buying expensive items such as cars, TVs and DVDs (see Exhibit 14.1). Initially, many other Chinese people admired these affluent consumers because they had bucked the system.

However, when people learned that their neighbors' newfound prosperity had come at the expense of many others whose standard of living had greatly decreased, making them the "new poor," the status of the new rich changed. Many were looked upon with resentment and were accused of illegally acquiring their wealth. The new rich reacted by becoming very careful not to be conspicuous or learning not to draw attention to themselves. As a result, over 20 percent of China's nightclubs closed as expense accounts dried up, and the rich became more philanthropic. Lavish spending still occurs, but it is now more private. For instance, China is the world's largest market for expensive cognac, at $186 million a year, and pricey Scotch whiskey is almost as popular.

In recent years, the middle class—termed the *middle stratum* in some official Chinese documents—has grown into a sizable segment of the population. In major cities such as Beijing and Shanghai, where foreign firms have invested heavily in production and sales capacity, white-collar workers already outnumber blue-collar workers. Just over 100 million Chinese consumers are considered middle class, and the number could double or triple before the end of this decade, depending on employment trends.[1]

EXHIBIT 14.1
The "New Rich" in China
Some individuals in China have now acquired wealth and can afford items like TVs, DVDs and cars.

Source: Getty Images.

This example illustrates how social class can influence acquisition, consumption, and disposition (see Exhibit 14.2). The concept of social class implies that some people have more power, wealth, and opportunity than others do. Some consumers show off their wealth or possessions by engaging in conspicuous consumption, and certain products and services, such as expensive cognac, can serve as status symbols. Marketers of upscale products often target such consumers. Finally, this example illustrates how some members of society can raise their social standing, a process called *upward mobility,* whereas others may fall to lower levels through *downward mobility*—changes that affect consumer decisions and behavior.

This chapter begins by examining the nature of social class (including its purpose), types of class systems and influences, and ways that social class is measured. Then the chapter discusses some important trends that are influencing and changing social class systems and explains how consumption patterns can vary with social classes. The chapter ends with an analysis of the marketing implications of social class. •

SOCIAL CLASS

social class hierarchy
The grouping of members of society according to status (high to low).

Most societies have a **social class hierarchy** that confers higher status to some classes of people than to others. These social classes consist of identifiable groups of individuals whose behaviors and lifestyles differ from those of members of the other classes. Members of a particular social class tend to share similar values and behavior patterns. Note that social classes are not formal groups with a strong identity, but rather loose collections of individuals with similar life experiences.[2]

Many societies view social class distinctions as important to their existence because they recognize that everyone has a necessary role to play for society to function smoothly. However, some of these roles, such as medical doctor or executive, are more prestigious and more valued than others, such as toll taker or janitor. Nevertheless, the concept of social class is not inherently negative. Even with the inequalities, social class distinctions can help individuals determine what their role in society is or what they would like it to be (their aspirations). Furthermore, all levels of the social class hierarchy make an important contribution to society.

Types of Social Class Systems

Most societies have three major classes: high, middle, and lower. Often, however, finer distinctions are made. The United States, for example, is typically divided into the seven levels presented in Exhibit 14.3.[3] Note that most individuals are concentrated in the middle classes (70 percent of the population). Thailand has five social classes: (1) an aristocracy (descendants of royalty), (2) an elite (composed of top professionals and political leaders), (3) an upper-middle class (merchants, small businesspeople, and white-collar workers), (4) a lower-middle class (craftspeople and skilled laborers), and (5) a lower class (unskilled laborers and peasants).

Although most societies have some kind of hierarchical structure, the size and composition of the classes depend on the relative prosperity of a particular country (see Exhibit 14.4).[4] For example, compared with the United States, Japan and Scandinavia have an even larger and more predominant middle class with much smaller groups above and below. This means there is greater equality among people in the two countries than in other societies. The Japanese structure represents a concerted government effort to abolish the social class system

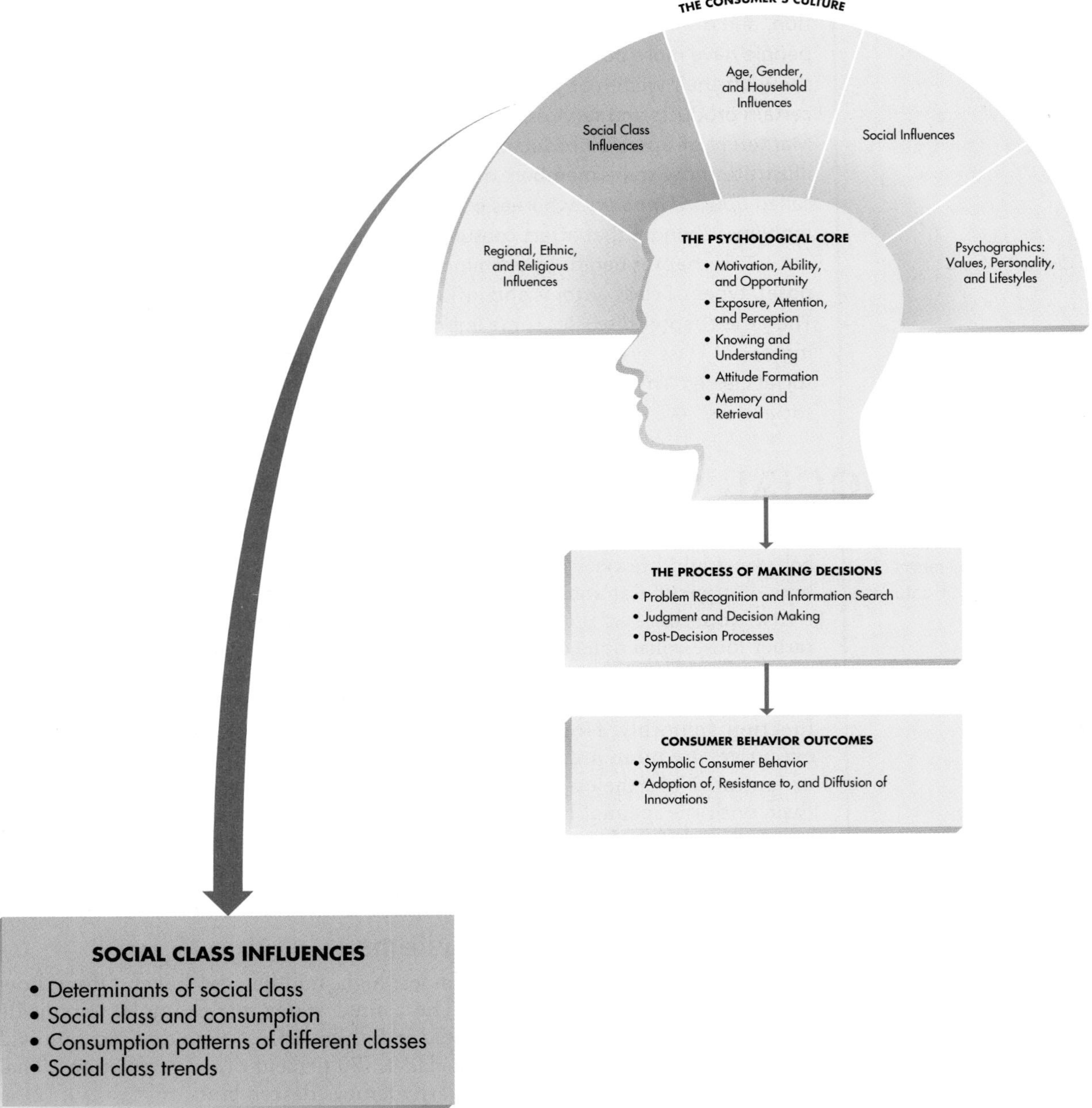

EXHIBIT 14.2
Chapter Overview: Social Class

Social class is another factor that can influence consumer behavior. This chapter examines what determines one's social class (e.g., occupation, education, income), the characteristics of major social classes, and certain social class patterns or trends (upward and downward mobility and fragmentation). Finally, it discusses how social class affects specific outcomes, such as conspicuous consumption, status symbols, compensatory consumption, and the meaning of money.

EXHIBIT 14.3
U.S. Social Classes
Researchers have classified the U.S. social classes in a variety of ways. This exhibit shows a typical classification scheme. Note that the majority of consumers would be considered Middle Americans (70 percent) and that very few are in the top two classes (1.5 percent).

Source: Richard P. Coleman, "The Continuing Significance of Social Class to Marketing," *Journal of Consumer Research*, December 1983, p. 277.

UPPER AMERICANS	*Upper-upper (0.3%):*	The "capital S society" world of inherited wealth, aristocratic names
	Lower-upper (1.2%):	The newer social elite, drawn from current professional, corporate leadership
	Upper-middle (12.5%):	The rest of college graduate managers and professionals; lifestyle centers on private clubs, causes, and the arts
MIDDLE AMERICANS	*Middle class (32%):*	Average pay white-collar workers and their blue-collar friends: live on the "the better side of town," try to "do the proper things"
	Working class (38%):	Average pay blue-collar workers; lead "working class lifestyle" whatever the income, school background, and job
LOWER AMERICANS	*"A lower group of people but not the lowest" (9%):*	Working, not on welfare; living standard is just above poverty; behavior judged "crude," "trashy"
	"Real lower-lower" (7%):	On welfare, visibly poverty stricken, usually out of work (or have the "dirtiest jobs")

and mix together people from all levels of society.[5] Despite this effort, the highly competitive and selective Japanese educational system still restricts entry to higher status positions in the executive and prestigious government ranks. In developing areas such as Latin America and India, on the other hand, the largest concentrations are in the lower classes. Most Latin households are truly poor, whereas India displays a more varied lower-middle class of more than 200 million people. In China, the middle class accounts for about 15 percent of the working population.[6]

In formerly communist countries that stressed equality and sameness, the status hierarchy has changed rapidly. Many citizens now have the opportunity to increase their status, which serves as a strong motivation to "get ahead."[7] At the same time, this sudden social climbing can be quite frightening because it brings with it a feeling of venturing into the unknown.

Interestingly, the upper classes in most societies are more similar to each other than they are to other classes within their own countries because the upper classes tend to be more cosmopolitan and international in orientation.[8] The lower classes, on the other hand, are the most likely to be culture bound—unaware of other cultures and therefore little influenced by them. As a result, they tend to be the most different from the other classes in terms of lifestyles, dress, and eating behaviors. The middle classes are most likely to borrow from other cultures because this practice may represent a means of achieving upward social mobility. Behaving "Western," for example, may serve as a way of achieving status in a Third World country.

Even though the members of a particular class may share similar values, they may maintain these values in different ways. For example, the middle class in the United States can be represented by a lower-level manager with a nonworking spouse, a working couple in which both partners have office jobs, an unmarried

EXHIBIT 14.4
Class Structure by Culture
The relative sizes and structure of social classes vary by culture. Japan and Scandinavia, for example, are characterized by a large middle class with few people above or below. India and Latin America, on the other hand, have a greater proportion of individuals in the lower classes. The United States has a large middle class, but also has significant proportions in the upper and lower classes.

Source: Adapted from Edward W. Cundiff and Marye T. Hilger, *Marketing in the International Environment* (Englewood Cliffs, N.J.: Prentice-Hall, 1988) and Marieke K. de Mooij and Warren Keegan, *Advertising Worldwide* (Englewood Cliffs, N.J.: Prentice-Hall, 1991), p. 96.

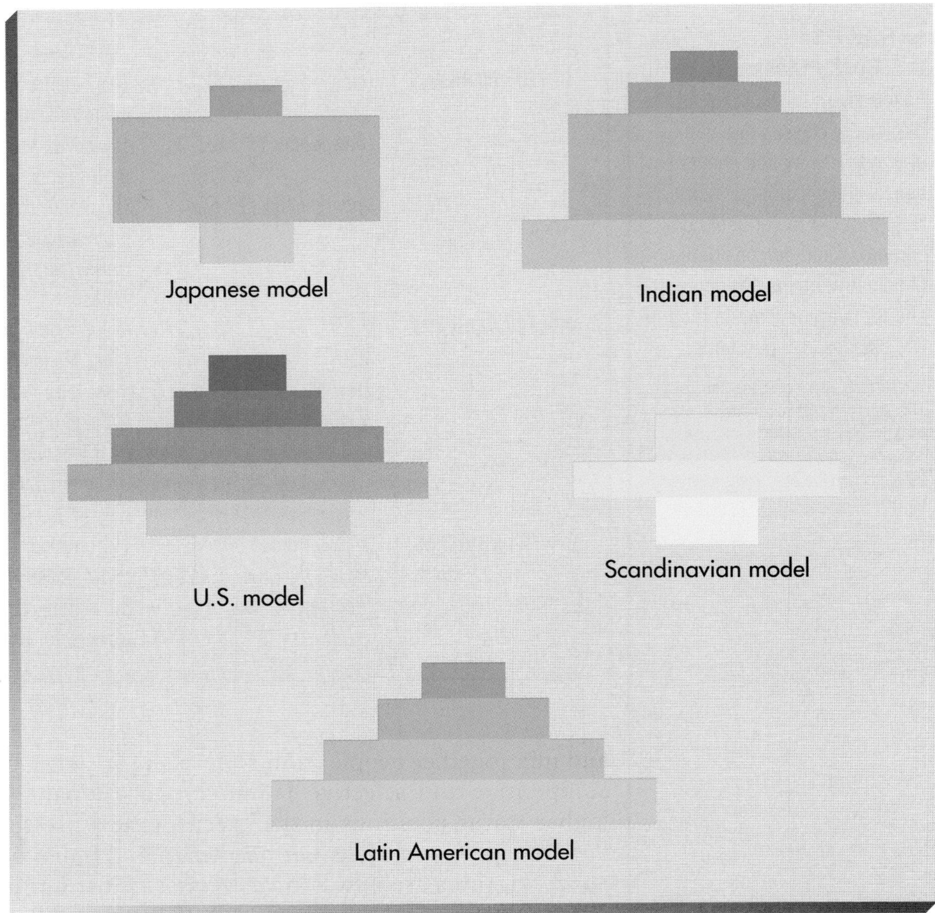

salesperson, a divorced parent with a college degree supporting two children, or the owner of a bowling alley. All these individuals might strive for a better life—an important middle-class value—but might take different paths to get there.

Finally, a particular social class may contain different economic substrata. Specifically, families whose income level is 20 to 30 percent over the median of their class are considered **overprivileged** because they have funds to buy items beyond the basic necessities.[9] **Class average** families are those whose income level is average for their social class. They can therefore afford the type of symbols expected for their status, such as a house, a car, and appropriate clothing. The **underprivileged**, who have incomes below the median, have trouble meeting class expectations.

overprivileged Families with an income higher than the average in their class.

class average Families with an average income in a particular class.

underprivileged Families below the average income in their class.

Social Class Influences

Social class structures are important because they strongly affect norms and values and, therefore, behavior. Given that members of a social class interact regularly with each other (both formally and informally), people are more likely to be influenced by individuals in their own social class than by those in other classes. Note that social class influence is not a cultural straitjacket; it merely reflects the fact that people with similar life experiences are likely to exhibit similar lifestyles and behaviors.[10]

trickle-down effect A theory in which trends that start in the upper classes are then copied by lower classes.

status float Trends that start in the lower and middle classes and move upward.

It is also possible for the norms and behaviors of consumers in one class to influence consumers in other social classes. A traditional and commonly cited theory of class influence is the **trickle-down** effect, whereby lower classes copy trends that begin in the upper classes. As one example, clothing styles that are introduced in the upper class often become popular with other groups. The trickle-down effect occurs because those in lower classes may aspire to raise their social standing by emulating the higher classes. They also accept upper-class influence if they lack the cultural knowledge to make their own judgments of what is and is not acceptable.[11] For example, the middle class often looks to the upper class for guidance on what is "cultural" in music, art, and literature.

More recently, however, the universal validity of the trickle-down theory has been questioned. In some instances, a **status float** can occur, whereby trends start in the lower and middle classes and then spread upward. An excellent example of status float is blue jeans. In the United States this product first gained widespread popularity in the 1950s and 1960s among lower- and middle-class youths, particularly because it symbolized rebellion against the establishment.[12] Eventually this message gained popularity among upper-class youths who wanted to revolt against their parents. In the 1970s and 1980s jeans evolved into a fashion item with the introduction of designer labels. The phenomenon has spread to other countries as well, where even royalty have been seen wearing jeans. Other recent styles, such as tattoos and wearing hats backwards, began in the lower classes and moved into the upper classes. Similarly, some musical styles, particularly blues, rock, and rap music, originated in the lower classes.

How Social Class Is Determined

Examining how social class affects consumer behavior requires a way of classifying consumers into different social classes. Unfortunately, this is not simple, and the exact determinants of social class have been the subject of considerable debate over the years.

Income versus Social Class Many people believe that the more money you have, the higher your social standing is. You may be surprised to learn, however, that income is not strongly related to social class for several reasons.[13] First, income levels often overlap social classes, particularly at the middle and lower levels. For example, many U.S. blue-collar workers have higher incomes than some white-collar workers, yet do not have higher social standing. Second, income increases greatly with age, but older workers do not automatically achieve higher social status. Finally, in many countries an increasing number of dual-career families generate a higher than average income but not necessarily higher status. Thus, although income is one factor related to social class, other factors must be examined to obtain an accurate picture.

Some researchers have argued that income can actually be a better predictor of consumer behavior than social class. However, a more common view is that both factors are important in explaining behavior in different situations.[14] Social class tends to be a better predictor of consumption when it reflects lifestyles and values and does not involve high monetary expenditures, such as for clothes, sports equipment, or furniture. For example, middle-class and lower-class consumers favor different styles of furniture, and middle-class consumers tend to spend more money on furnishing their homes even when income levels are roughly similar. Income, on the other hand, is more useful in explaining the consumption of products and services that are not related to class symbols—such as

OCCUPATION	SCORE	OCCUPATION	SCORE
Physician	88	Mechanic	31
Lawyer	88	Photographer	30
Marketing professor	83	Bank teller	29
Psychologist	82	Hotel receptionist	29
Architect	80	Mail carrier	27
Civil engineer	77	Plumber	27
High school teacher	75	Shoe salesperson	25
Computer scientist	73	Bartender	24
Airplane pilot	68	Farmer	24
Accountant	65	Carpenter	22
Marketing manager	58	Truck driver	21
Actor	52	Hairdresser	19
Athlete	49	Waiter/waitress	19
Sales representative	48	Machine operator	19
Musician	46	Baker	19
Office supervisor	37	Janitor	18
Police detective	38	Crossing guard	17
Secretary	35	Farmworker	17
Firefighter	33	Maid	16

EXHIBIT 14.5
Status Levels of Various Occupations
A variety of indexes have been developed to classify different occupations in terms of their status level. This exhibit presents the status scores of a sample of occupations, using one of these indexes. What major factors do you think cause some occupations to be high in status and others to be low?

Source: Reprinted from Gillian Stevens and Joo Hyun Cho, "Socioeconomic Indexes and the New 1980 Census Occupational Classification Scheme," *Social Science Research*, vol. 14, pp. 142–168. Copyright © 1985 by Academic Press with permission from Elsevier.

boats or recreational vehicles—but that do involve substantial expenditures. Both social class and income are needed to explain behaviors that involve status symbols and significant expenditures such as buying a house or car.

Although income cannot explain social class, social class can often explain how income is used. As one illustration, upper-class consumers are more likely to invest money, whereas the lower classes are more likely to rely on savings accounts in banks. The key point is that social class aids in the understanding of consumer behavior and that social standing is determined by a variety of factors in addition to income.

Occupation and Education The greatest determinant of class standing is occupation, particularly in Western cultures. Specifically, some occupations, especially those that require higher levels of education, skill, or training, are viewed as higher in status than others. Furthermore, individuals with the same occupation tend to share similar income, lifestyles, knowledge, and values.

Researchers can easily measure occupation by asking consumers what they do for a living. They can then code the responses and compare them with published scales of occupational prestige, such as the widely used socioeconomic index (SEI) or the Nam and Powers scale.[15] Exhibit 14.5 shows rankings from the SEI for a sample of occupations.

Note that the perceived status of an occupation may vary from culture to culture. Compared with the United States, for example, professors have higher status in Germany, Japan, China, Thailand, and Nigeria because those countries place more emphasis on education. Engineers typically have higher status in developing countries than they do in developed countries because of the important role engineering plays in integrating industry and technology into society. Finally, the legal profession enjoys much higher prestige in the United States than it does elsewhere in the world.

Education also plays a critical role because it is one of the key determinants of occupation and therefore social class. In fact, educational attainment is considered the most reliable determinant of consumers' income potential and spending patterns.[16] In particular, a college degree is a crucial factor in gaining entry into higher-status occupations. Slightly more than 66 percent of people with bachelor's or advanced degrees are in managerial or professional occupations, compared with 22 percent who have only some college education. This gap will only widen as the need for highly skilled and technical training increases in the information age. In addition, marketers know that highly educated consumers tend to read and travel more and to be less averse to trying new things when compared with rest of the population.

Other Indicators of Social Class Factors such as area of residence, possessions, family background, and social interactions can also indicate class level. The neighborhood in which we live and the amount and types of possessions we

inherited status Status that derives from parents at birth.

earned status Status acquired later in life through achievements.

have are visible signs that often communicate class standing. In terms of family background, researchers distinguish between **inherited status**, which is adopted from parents at birth, and **earned status**, which is acquired later in life from personal achievements.[17] Inherited status serves as the initial anchor point from which values are learned and from which upward or downward mobility can occur. As mentioned previously, members of a social class often interact with each other, so the company we keep also helps to identify our social standing.

The relative importance of these determinants of social class varies from country to country. In formerly communist countries such as Romania, for example, money and possessions are now the strongest determinants of social standing, as opposed to the former criteria of position in the Communist party.[18] In the Arab world, status is determined primarily by social contacts and family position, both of which are considered far more important than money.[19]

Social Class Indexes All the factors mentioned above must be taken into account to determine social class standing, and sociologists have developed a number of indexes to accomplish this task. Over the years the two most widely used tools have been the *Index of Status Characteristics* and the *Index of Social Position*.[20] However, these instruments were developed in the 1940s and 1950s and have recently been criticized as out-of-date. First, the measurement of key variables such as education, occupation, and neighborhood type are based on a society that no longer exists.[21] Second, these indexes fail to account accurately for dual-career households, which generate higher income but not higher status than single-earner households do. Third, the early indexes were based on extensive interviews within a community (called the *reputational method*). These indexes are now difficult to implement because people simply do not know their neighbors as well as they used to.

Computerized Status Index (CSI) A modern index used to determine social class through education, occupation, residence, and income.

status crystallization When consumers are consistent across indicators of social class (income, education, occupation, etc.).

In light of these problems, researchers are using more current indexes such as the **Computerized Status Index (CSI)** (see Exhibit 14.6). This index assesses consumers' education, occupation, area of residence, and income. In contrast to the use of informants for the reputational method, the CSI is easy for interviewers to administer and for consumers to answer.

When consumers are consistent across the various dimensions, social class is easy to determine and **status crystallization** occurs. Sometimes, however, individuals are low on some factors but high on others. Thus a new doctor from an inner-city neighborhood might be inconsistent on factors such as occupation, income, neighborhood, and family background. In situations, consumers can experience stress and anxiety because they do not know exactly where they stand.[22] It is also difficult for marketers to neatly categorize such consumers into one social class or another.

HOW SOCIAL CLASS CHANGES OVER TIME

Social class structures are not necessarily static, unchanging systems. A number of trends and forces are producing an evolution in social class structures in many countries. Three of these key trends are: (1) upward mobility, (2) downward mobility, and (3) social class fragmentation.

Upward Mobility

upward mobility Raising one's status level.

In some cases, individuals can rise to a higher level of status. **Upward mobility** is usually achieved by educational or occupational achievement. In other words, lower- or middle-class individuals can take advantage of educational opportunities, particularly a college education, to facilitate entry into higher

Interviewer circles code numbers (for the computer) which in his/her judgment best fit the respondent and family. Interviewer asks for detail on occupation, then makes rating. Interviewer often asks the respondent to describe neighborhood in own words. Interviewer asks respondent to specify income—a card is presented to the respondent showing the eight brackets—and records R's response. If interviewer feels this is over-statement or under, a "better-judgment" estimate should be given, along with explanation.

EDUCATION:	Respondent	Respondent's spouse
Grammar school (8 yrs or less)	–1	–1
Some high school (9–11 yrs)	–2	–2
Graduated high school (12 yrs)	–3	–3
Some post high school (business, nursing, technical, 1 yr college)	–4	–4
Two, three years of college—possibly Associate of Arts degree	–5	–5
Graduated four-year college (B.A./B.S.)	–7	–7
Master's or five-year professional degree	–8	–8
Ph.D. or six/seven-year professional degree	–9	–9

R's age: ____

Spouse's age: ____

OCCUPATION PRESTIGE LEVEL OF HOUSEHOLD HEAD:
Interviewer's judgment of how head-of-household rates in occupational status.

(Respondent's description—ask for previous occupation if retired, or if R is widow, ask husband's: ______________________)

Chronically unemployed—"day" laborers, unskilled; on welfare	–0
Steadily employed but in marginal semi-skilled jobs; custodians, minimum-pay factory help, service workers (gas attendants, etc.)	–1
Average-skill assembly-line workers, bus and truck drivers, police and firefighters, route deliverymen, carpenters, brick masons	–2
Skilled craftsmen (electricians), small contractors, factory foremen, low-pay salesclerks, office workers, postal employees	–3
Owners of very small firms (2–4 employees), technicians, salespeople, office workers, civil servants with average-level salaries	–4
Middle management, teachers, social workers, lesser professionals	–5
Lesser corporate officials, owners of middle-sized businesses (10–20 employees), moderate-success professionals (dentists, engineers, etc.)	–7
Top corporate executives, "big business" in the professional world (leading doctors and lawyers), "rich" business owners	–9

AREA OF RESIDENCE:
Interviewer's impressions of the immediate neighborhood in terms of its reputation in the eyes of the community.

Slum area: people on relief, common laborers	–1
Strictly working class: not slummy but some very poor housing	–2
Predominantly blue-collar with some office workers	–3
Predominantly white-collar with some well-paid blue-collar	–4
Better white-collar area: not many executives, but hardly any blue-collar either	–5
Excellent area: professionals and well-paid managers	–7
"Wealthy" or "society" type neighborhood	–9

TOTAL FAMILY INCOME PER YEAR:

TOTAL SCORE ________

Under $5,000	–1	$15,000 to $19,999	–4	$35,000 to $49,999	–7
$5,000 to $9,999	–2	$20,000 to $24,999	–5	$50,000 and over	–8
$10,000 to $14,999	–3	$25,000 to $34,999	–6		

Estimated Status ________

(Interviewer's estimate:______________ and explanation:______________________________________)

R's MARITAL STATUS: Married _____ Divorced/Separated _____ Widowed _____ Single _____ (CODE _____)

EXHIBIT 14.6

The Computerized Status Index

The CSI attempts to assess consumers' social class by measuring the various key determinants—education, occupation, area of residence, and income—and combining them to form an overall index. The higher the score, the higher the social standing.

Source: Richard P. Coleman, "The Continuing Significance of Social Class to Marketing," *Journal of Consumer Research*, December 1983, p. 277.

status occupations. "Education is the biggest ticket to the middle class," says one economist, commenting about upward mobility opportunities for lower-class consumers.[23] In the United States, more than one-third of the children of blue-collar workers are college graduates and have about a 30 percent chance of raising their occupational status.[24] The fact that more consumers—of all cultural backgrounds—have access to education has led to a burgeoning middle class and characterizes the United States as the "land of opportunity."

Consumers who excel in a particular occupation can reap rewards and higher status. For example, a mechanic who starts a successful body shop or a talented athlete who signs a lucrative contract may both climb to a higher level of social standing. Statistics indicate that the percentage of business executives from lower-class backgrounds has increased dramatically in the last 40 years.

Nonetheless, upward mobility is not guaranteed. The lower classes, particularly minorities, still face restricted economic and cultural resources as well as educational opportunities. They are therefore statistically less likely than the upper classes to have access to higher-status occupations.[25] As evidence, individuals from higher-status families are twice as likely to maintain their status as members of lower classes are to achieve a higher status. Even after achieving upward mobility, an individual's behavior can still be heavily influenced by his or her former class level because the behaviors associated with the social class in which we grew up were strongly learned. This factor has been called the "Beverly Hillbillies" phenomenon.[26]

Note that the degree of upward mobility may vary across cultures. Typically, Western nations offer the most opportunities for upward advancement, although research shows that opportunities for upward mobility decreased in Canada during the 1980s and 1990s.[27] Even in traditionally rigid class societies such as Great Britain, upward mobility has increased recently, as it has in less developed countries. In formerly communist countries, old party and state bureaucrats have formed the new upper classes because they have the skills and economic knowledge to thrive in the modern environment.[28] The elimination of state-owned companies created many small, privately owned firms and a growing middle class. In Arab countries, the upper and middle class are growing rapidly as a result of oil money and an increase in Western college education, boosting demand for Western goods such as cars, air conditioners, and apparel.[29] Finally, the size of the middle class has been exploding in many developing countries because of increases in international trade which makes affordable goods more available, global communications which show consumers what they have been missing, the number of dual-career families who have greater income, and the need for professionals like managers, accountants, and bankers to support growing economies.[30]

Yet social class mobility can be quite restricted in other countries. In India, a person's educational or occupational opportunities—and therefore social class—are primarily determined by inheritance. In Africa, continuing economic problems have kept upward mobility low.

Downward Mobility

downward mobility The lowering of one's social standing.

Downward mobility, or moving to a lower class, is an increasing trend in many industrialized societies. In the 1970s and 1980s, nearly one-third of the U.S. population suffered a loss in income, and during the 1990s, millions of families slid downward each year.[31] A wide range of individuals, from vice presidents to blue-collar workers, lost their jobs when companies downsized to cut costs during economic slowdowns, and many struggled to find equivalent jobs. When good jobs disappear, so does a comfortable middle-class existence.

Although inflation has slowed in recent years, rising inflation traditionally contributed to downward mobility. When inflation is high, money does not go as far as it once did, so workers feel pressure to work longer and harder. In some cases, both spouses may feel pressure to work. However, when both are employed, the additional expense of child care adds another financial burden. These factors can create stress that threatens the "comfortable life" for many families.[32] In addition, because of increasing material desires, more upper-middle and middle-class families are experiencing significant difficulty in maintaining a lifestyle characteristic of their status level.

status panic The inability of children to reach their parents' level of social status.

Until recently, many parents dreamed of providing their children with a better life and higher status than they had. Some children may now have difficulty reaching their parents' status level, a phenomenon labeled **status panic.**[33] In particular, the children of very successful parents, called *savvy skidders*, often have difficulty achieving the same heights as their parents and must settle for more middle-class careers.

The problem of downward mobility is particularly an issue in formerly communist countries such as East Germany, the Czech Republic, Hungary, and Poland, where the elimination of government-subsidized jobs led to very high unemployment. Many factories closed because their technology was obsolete, and companies found building new plants less expensive than updating old ones. At the same time, prices skyrocketed, resulting in bleak economic conditions. Thus many people now feel worse off than they did before, and workers have faced a loss of class status.

In Japan, there has been both upward and downward mobility.[34] On the one hand, a small group of property owners—the *nyuu ritchi* or *new rich*—has experienced prosperity. However, a greater number—the *nyuu pua* or *new poor*—have suffered and cannot afford to buy a home (costing the equivalent of 18 years of wages).

Regardless of the causes, downward mobility creates disappointment and disillusionment. People in this situation face a constant struggle to provide for the family, fight off depression, and maintain a sense of honor. Sometimes acquisition and consumption can serve the purpose of protecting the person's self-worth. For example, someone might buy a new truck or other item to feel good about himself or herself.[35] Because middle-class consumers in Japan are accustomed to conveying status through the purchase of luxury goods, many have continued to spend lavishly despite the country's prolonged economic problems.[36] Alternatively, downward mobility can lead to a loss of possessions, such as a prized car or home, or to a decrease in consumption if people choose to spend less on items that are less important.

Social Class Fragmentation

social class fragmentation The disappearance of class distinctions.

Interestingly, the old social class distinctions are beginning to disintegrate—a phenomenon called **social class fragmentation.** This fragmentation can be tied to several factors.[37] First, both upward and downward mobility have blurred class divisions. Second, the increased availability of mass media has exposed consumers to the values and norms of other classes and cultures to a greater degree than ever before. In the United States, for example, the TV program *Lifestyles of the Rich and Famous* showed how the richer segments of society spent their time and money. Shows like *The King of Queens* reflect working-class values, and rap and hip-hop music strongly communicate the values and norms of lower-class, inner-city youths to a wide audience in all classes. Music videos and magazines are spreading urban hip-hop fashions to the suburbs and beyond.[38] Thus individuals are now exposed to other classes and can incorporate the idiosyncrasies of these groups into their own behavior.

A third reason for social class fragmentation is that advances in communication technology have increased interaction across social class lines. As one example, the Internet and chat rooms allow strangers to communicate without regard to social class.

These factors have led to the emergence of many social class subsegments with distinct patterns of values and behavior. The United States now has dozens of classes ranging from the suburban elite (superrich families) to the hardscrabble (poor, single-parent families). Examples include upwardly mobile young influentials, God's country (former urban executive families), golden ponders (retirement-town senior citizens), downtown Dixie (African American service-worker families), and young suburbanites.[39] Similar trends are occurring in other countries as well. Exhibit 14.7 identifies some of the traditional and emerging classes in Germany.

HOW DOES SOCIAL CLASS AFFECT CONSUMPTION?

Social class is often viewed as a cause of or motivation for consumer acquisition, consumption, and disposition behaviors. This section examines four major topics: (1) conspicuous consumption, (2) the acquisition of status symbols, (3) compensatory consumption, and (4) the meaning of money.

Conspicuous Consumption

conspicuous consumption The acquisition and display of goods and services to show off one's status.

Conspicuous consumption, also related to social class, is an attempt to offset deficiencies or a lack of esteem by devoting attention to consumption.[40] Conspicuously consumed items are important to their owner because of what they tell others. The visibility of these goods and services is critical because their message can be communicated only if others can see them.

Initially, the concept of conspicuous consumption described the behavior of upper-class consumers who would buy and display very expensive items to communicate their wealth and power. For example, in the 1890s, William H. Vanderbilt's private railway car was designed to be more expensive than that of his rival, Leland Stanford, and his third yacht had to be bigger and better than anyone else's. Today, however, conspicuous consumption can be observed in most social classes.[41] Individuals at all levels can "keep up with the Joneses"—acquiring and displaying the trappings that are characteristic of a respected member of their class. For example, a middle-class family might buy a powerful personal computer to show the neighbors that the family can afford such a purchase. Or a working-class consumer might buy a new motorboat, projection TV, expensive shotgun, or pickup truck to show off to peers.

In the Arab world the newly rich upper classes engage in the conspicuous consumption of items such as cars, planes, and other technologically advanced products. Even in formerly communist countries, consumers now show consumption competitiveness. The idea is that someone who cannot keep up with others might be "the shame of the village."[42]

conspicuous waste Visibly buying products and services that one never uses.

In addition, consumers can engage in **conspicuous waste**. For example, wealthy individuals may buy houses they never use, pianos that no one plays, and cars that no one drives.[43] Note, however, that in today's world some consumers may be moving away from conspicuous consumption toward "experience facilitators" or items that help consumers pursue pastimes that set them apart from

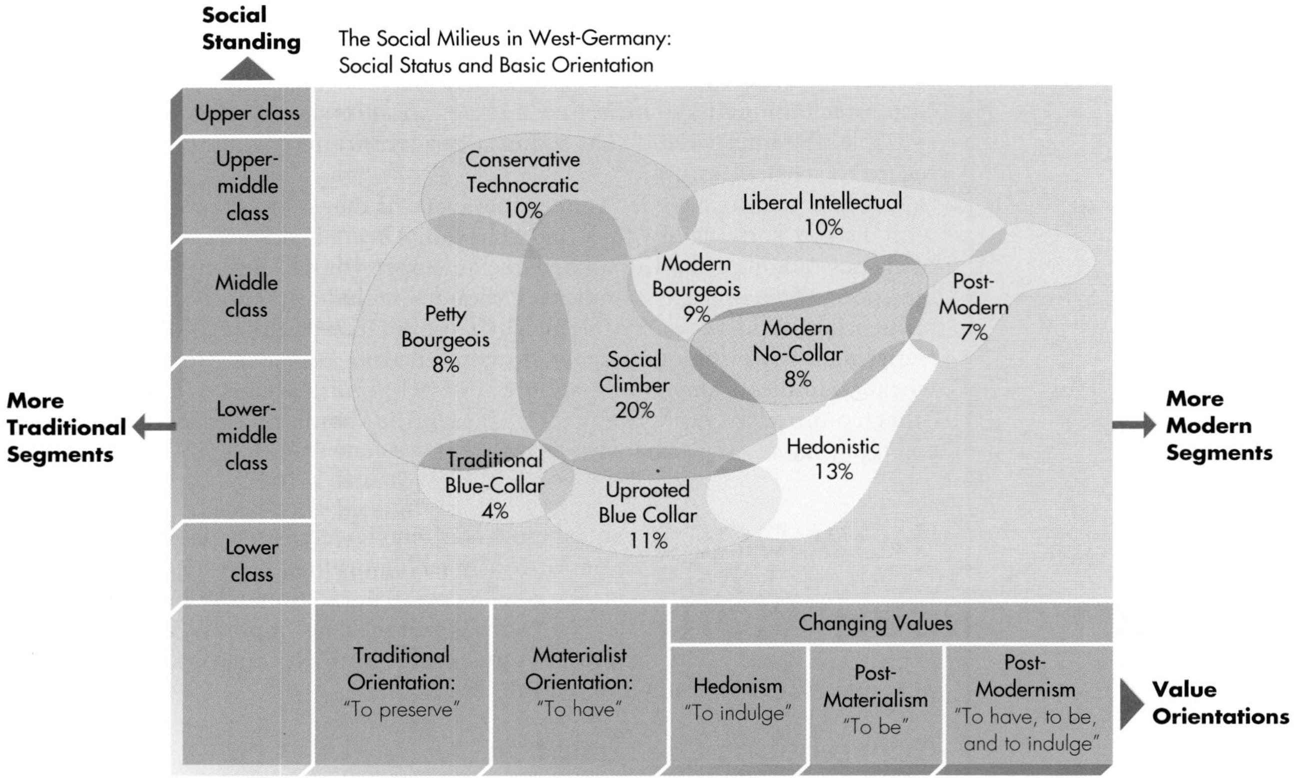

EXHIBIT 14.7
German Social Classes
This exhibit is a detailed depiction of social class structure in German society. The 11 groups are characterized along two dimensions: social standing (low to upper-middle class) and value orientations (traditional to very modern values).

Source: Mariele De Mooij and Warren Keegan, *Advertising Worldwide* (Englewood Cliffs, N.J.: Prentice-Hall, 1991), p. 116. Reprinted by permission of Pearson Education Limited.

the crowd.[44] Evidence of this trend is an increased rate of purchase for electronic gadgets, extreme sports equipment, and adventure travel tours[45] accompanied by a lower rate of purchase for cars, furniture, and restaurant meals.

Status Symbols and Judging Others

status symbols
Products or services that tell others about someone's social class standing.

Highly related to conspicuous consumption is the notion that people often judge others on the basis of what they own or possess. In other words, products or services become **status symbols** to indicate their owners' place in the social hierarchy.[46] Someone who owns an expensive watch or car will likely be viewed as upper class (see Exhibit 14.8) . In the inner city, the latest Nike Jordan sneakers—available only in limited quantities or colors—can be a status symbol.[47] Owning a cellular phone or taking an expensive cruise indicates status in Thailand, and

EXHIBIT 14.8
Conspicuous Consumption
Consumers may judge each other based on the type of watch they wear. This ad implies that wearing a Roger Dubuis watch is a mark of status and prestige.

Source: Courtesy Kevin M. Jenness.

the same is true of having a rock garden or a golf club membership in Japan. In Brazil, eating in fast-food restaurants such as McDonald's and Burger King is a status symbol for lower-middle-class consumers.[48] Similarly, owning a pair of Western jeans, a car, fashion clothing, an apartment, or electronic equipment is a strong indicator of status in formerly communist countries such as Romania.[49]

Thus consumers' quest to acquire items that reflect not only their current social class but also their class aspirations can explain some acquisitions and consumption behavior. Middle-class consumers, for example, characteristically display a strong desire to own a nice house in a respectable neighborhood so that others will judge them in a positive manner. Furthermore, by acquiring items that are considered above their social standing—that is, items that members of their own social class cannot typically afford—consumers can increase their perception of self-worth.

Interestingly, status symbols can sometimes move in a reverse direction, which is called a **parody display**.[50] For example, middle-and-upper class Brazilians now feel hip if they sip caipirinhas (a specialty drink once identified with the lower class) and practice capoeira, a blend of dance and martial arts that was traditionally popular among the lower class.[51] In addition, if certain status symbols become widely possessed, they can lose their status connotations and become **fraudulent symbols**. As an example, designer jeans were an important status symbol in the 1980s but lost popularity when they became too popular. Further, recognizing that luxury brands are often copied by low-price knockoffs for the mass market, Coach and other fashion firms have redesigned their products with more subtle logos (see Exhibit 14.9). The new products are unmistakably upscale but don't "scream 'Coach, Coach, Coach,'" observes a Coach designer.[52]

parody display Status symbols that start in the lower classes and move upward.

fraudulent symbols Symbols that become so widely adopted that they lose their status.

compensatory consumption The consumer behavior of buying products or services to offset frustrations or difficulties in life.

Compensatory Consumption

Compensatory consumption behavior, also related to social class, is an attempt to offset deficiencies or a lack of esteem by devoting attention to consumption.[53] A consumer who is experiencing frustration or difficulties, particularly in terms of career advancement or status level, may attempt to compensate for this lack of success by purchasing desired status symbols, such as a car, house, or nice clothes. These acquisitions help restore lost self-esteem.

Traditionally, compensatory consumption typified the acquisition patterns of the working classes, who would mortgage their future to obtain a house, car, furniture, and other objects that symbolize status and success. More recently, however, middle- and upper-middle-class consumers have exhibited compensatory consumption behavior, particularly members of the baby boom generation in the United States. During the past two decades, many baby boomers have not enjoyed the level of career advancement, gratification, and prosperity that their parents did, due in part to increased job competition, corporate downsizing, and economic uncertainty. To offset their disappointment, baby boomers have increasingly turned toward consumption to achieve gratification.[54] Thus the hippies of the 1960s became very materialistic, as evidenced by their acquisition of the "right" car, fashion clothing, health club memberships, and foreign travel.

In Japan, compensatory consumption has become a major characteristic of middle-class consumers who can no longer afford to buy a home. Not having to spend money on a home gives these consumers more money to buy a variety of status items, such as mink coats, golf memberships, and foreign cars.[55] Even through recent tough economic times, sales of Tiffany diamond jewelry have shown a strong increase.

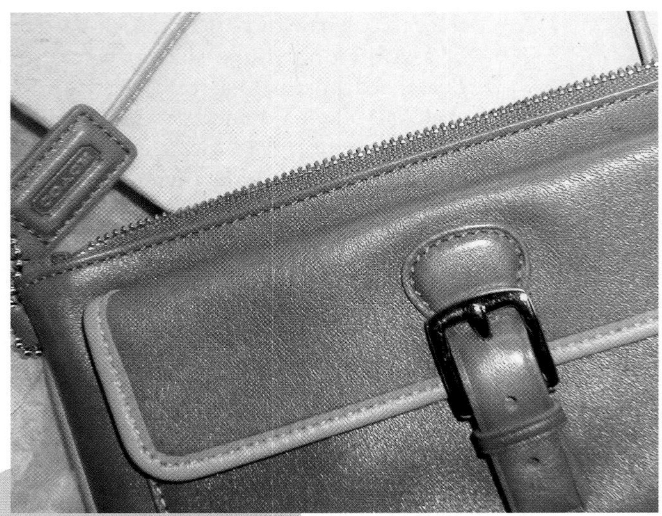

EXHIBIT 14.9
Subtle Logos Grace Status Symbols
To ward off mass market imitations, luxury brands such as Coach have more subtle logos that portray a stronger image of quality.

Source: © Susan Van Etten/PhotoEdit.

The Meaning of Money

An important concept related to social class is money. At the most basic level, economists define *money* as a medium of exchange or standard of payment. Under this view, money fulfills a very functional or utilitarian purpose, enabling people to acquire items needed for everyday living. Often, however, the meaning of money goes beyond the utilitarian and comes to symbolize security, power, love, and freedom.

Consumers learn the meaning of money early in childhood. Parents easily discover that a powerful way of controlling their children is to develop a system of rewards and punishments based on money and buying or not buying things.[56] Children learn that if they behave, get good grades, or do their chores, their parents will buy things for them. This early learning later translates into adult life when money is viewed as a means of acquiring things that will not only bring happiness and life fulfillment but also provide a sense of status and prestige. In some societies this attitude can lead to an almost insatiable desire and quest for making money, which is enhanced by highly visible success stories of those who have "made it" and the belief that "it could happen to anyone, including me." This belief is one reason that state lotteries and get-rich-quick seminars are popular among certain classes.

Marketers must understand money and what it stands for in order to understand consumption patterns. Money allows consumers to acquire status objects that are indicators of social class standing. It is also viewed as a way that consumers can rise to a higher level by acquiring more. Yet the meaning of money does not have to involve physical cash. The ongoing growth in credit and debit card usage shows that transactions need not involve the physical transfer of cash. In Hong Kong, France, and other areas, millions of consumers use "smart cards" like electronic money to pay subway fares, buy snacks from vending machines, and make other purchases.[57] Taking this a step further, shoppers can now set up electronic wallets that allow them to easily make purchases on the Internet.[58]

Of course, consumers vary in terms of how they treat their money. Some people are more likely to spend money to acquire desired items, and others will engage in self-denial in order to save. One study found that spenders tend to be healthier and happier than self-deniers, who tend to have more psychosomatic illnesses and are more unhappy about finances, personal growth, friends, and jobs.[59] However, some individuals who spend more than they have end up in bankruptcy.

Money as Both Good and Evil Money can have both a good and an evil side. On the positive side, money can lead to the acquisition of needed items, a higher quality of life, and the ability to help others and society in general. It also can be perceived as the just reward for hard work. On the downside, the quest for money can lead to obsession, greed, dishonesty, and potentially harmful practices such as gambling, prostitution, and drug dealing, as discussed in Chapter 21. The quest for money can also lead to a variety of negative emotions, such as anxiety, depression, anger, and helplessness.[60] This explains why many religions view money as an evil temptation that should be kept in check. Likewise, even though people generally respect wealthy individuals, they often view the obsessive desire for money with disdain, which means wealthy people may feel alienated from others.[61] Furthermore, people may see individuals who do not share their wealth with others as selfish and greedy.

Money was viewed as an evil in communist countries, where people considered large differences in income to be unfair and immoral. Money played almost no role in acquiring what few goods were available because personal connections and bartering were more important than the exchange of cash. As a result, many consumers in these countries still have trouble understanding the concept of spending and accumulating money.

Money and Happiness The popular belief (especially in Western countries) that money can buy happiness is rarely true. Examples of very wealthy individuals whose lives were generally unhappy and not fulfilling include J. Paul Getty and Howard Hughes.[62] After some people acquire tremendous wealth, money can become meaningless and no longer highly desired. Furthermore, wealthy people can often afford to hire others to do many of the things that they formerly enjoyed, such as gardening and do-it-yourself projects. And, of course, money simply cannot buy love, health, true friendship, and children, among other things. Thus the relentless pursuit of money may not end in the fulfilled dreams that many think it will.

THE CONSUMPTION PATTERNS OF SPECIFIC SOCIAL CLASSES

Earlier sections examined how social class influences acquisition and consumption in general. This section extends the discussion by examining the consumption patterns of specific social classes. Although class distinctions are becoming increasingly blurred, for the sake of simplicity, this discussion will focus on four major groups: (1) the upper class, (2) the middle class, (3) the working class, and (4) the homeless.

The Upper Class

upper class The aristocracy, new social elite, and the upper-middle class.

The **upper class** of most societies is a varied group of individuals who include the aristocracy, the new social elite (or nouveaux riches), and the upper-middle class (professionals). In the United States the aristocracy consists of traditional old-money families who acquired great wealth and power in the late 19th and early 20th centuries and whose current members live on inherited money. Such families include the DuPonts, Vanderbilts, Rockefellers, and Fords. This group represents less than 1 percent of U.S. society. Thus it is really the lower upper and upper middle two groups that are sizable enough to be of major interest to consumer researchers and marketers.

Although small, the upper class is diverse, and its members share a number of common values and lifestyles that relate to consumption behavior. These consumers are more likely to view themselves as intellectual, political, and socially conscious. That self-image leads to an increase in behaviors such as attending the theater, investing in art, purchasing books, traveling (especially to foreign places), donating time and money to good causes, attending prestige schools, and belonging to private clubs. Self-expression is also important, resulting in the purchase of high-quality, prestige brands in good taste. Interestingly, the desire for prestige goods can be traced back to European (especially French) aristocratic classes in earlier centuries, who were the first to engage in the heavy consumption of fine goods, such as art and furniture, and who were later emulated by the upper classes in other societies.[63]

The nouveaux riches represent those in the upper-class segment who have acquired a great deal of status and wealth in their own lifetimes. These people are often workaholics who feel strongly that they have worked hard for their money. In fact, an analysis of literary media and writings about the affluent identified three themes related to their achievement: entrepreneurialism, celebrity status achieved from consumption, and status achieved from artistry/craftsmanship.[64] The affluent are concerned about what others think of them, particularly within their class, and as a result often engage in conspicuous consumption to validate their position in society.[65] They are therefore likely to buy items that are known to be high in price and that can be publicly consumed or displayed, like a Rolls Royce or Mercedes, a Rolex watch, a Mont Blanc pen, designer clothing, or a Wally custom-made yacht.[66] Another nouveau riche characteristic is the tendency to collect items that are symbols of acquired wealth, such as furniture, art objects, cars, and jewelry—items that are known to visibly convey power and wealth. In London, for example, wealthy consumers are paying $5 million or more for luxury penthouses to be designed and placed on the roof of historic apartment buildings.[67]

A study of French consumers found identifiable upper-class preferences for food, sports activities, and items related to health and beauty that differed from those of the lower classes.[68] Being rich enables these consumers to "buy beauty" by belonging to upscale gyms; hiring personal trainers; going to famous health spas; and indulging in herbal body wraps, Swedish and shiatsu massage, facials, manicures, and plastic surgery.[69] Even food becomes a conspicuous consumption item. The more exotic the meal, the more status ascribed to it. Furthermore, the nouveaux riches typically stay in hotels that cost $1,000 or more per night and indulge in expensive hobbies such as car racing. Many vacation in the French Riviera (e.g., San Tropez, Cannes), the Virgin Islands, Hawaii, or Aspen. In addition, America's wealthy individuals tend to live in four types of areas: exclusive suburbs, financial centers (like Manhattan), "big money" retirement areas (e.g., Palm Beach, Florida), and (surprisingly) some sparsely populated counties (with oil wells and huge farms).[70]

The preceding description is not intended to imply that the upper classes are spendthrifts. A more accurate picture is that they save and invest money more than members of other classes.[71] Many are price-conscious. When shopping for holiday gifts, only 49 percent visit upscale stores—the remainder shop at midrange stores such as Macy's and at discount and outlet stores.[72] When they do purchase items for themselves, however, conspicuous consumption is often the goal. Upper-class consumers are also more likely than other classes to engage in careful information search prior to a purchase and are less likely to use price as an indicator of quality; relying instead on actual product characteristics.

Remember that these observations are only broad generalizations and that behaviors can differ within the upper class. Some consumers, for example, may be highly motivated by conspicuous consumption, and others may be more practical and conservative with their money. Thus we can identify subsegments of consumers with specific and unique consumption patterns. As an example, unlike many other upper-class consumers, upper-class white Anglo-Saxon Protestant (WASP) consumers prefer furnishings that are simple and practical but made with high-quality materials and craftsmanship.[73] Two distinct types of apparel preferences among these consumers are practicality (which means simplicity and comfort) and refinement (which conveys social position).

These days, most millionaires do not fit the traditional image of tycoons with stately mansions. In fact, one-third of all U.S. households with assets topping $1 million are headed by consumers aged 39 and younger.[74] The average U.S. millionaire is 54 years old, is married with three children, and has an average household net worth of $9.2 million.[75] More than 72 percent of U.S. millionaires hold college or graduate degrees, and 67.5 percent have annual household incomes of $100,000-plus.[76] At the top end of the spectrum, more than 265,000 U.S. households have a net worth exceeding $10 million.[77] Apart from high-tech ventures, many millionaires make their money in unremarkable businesses such as funeral homes, bowling alleys, and small manufacturing firms.

The Middle Class

middle class Primarily white-collar workers.

The U.S. **middle class** comprises primarily white-collar workers, many of whom have attended college but earned no degree. These consumers want to do the right thing, buy whatever is popular, do whatever is good for the children, and be fashionable.[78] Middle-class consumers also tend to desire a nice home in a nice neighborhood with good schools. As a result, they are likely to spend money on education, shop at somewhat expensive clothing stores with quality brand names, stick with liked brands, be concerned about home furnishings, and buy on credit.

A major feature that distinguishes the middle class is that its members look to the upper class for guidance on certain behaviors such as proper dining etiquette, apparel selections (especially important for those with aspirations of upward mobility), and popular leisure activities such as, golf, tennis, and squash. This tendency also leads to theater attendance, vacations, and adult education classes taken for self-improvement. Furthermore, compared with the lower classes, the middle class spends a greater proportion of its food budget on take-out meals or meals at nice restaurants.

Middle-class values can also determine the types of products and brands middle-class consumers prefer. Exhibit 14.10 presents a sample of product and activity preferences for lower-middle-, middle-, and upper-middle-class U.S. consumers during the past 20 years. Not only are there differences between classes, but changes have occurred in the last decade.

Again, these observations are generalizations and the values and consumption patterns of middle-class consumers vary. Some scholars have suggested, for example, that the United States contains two distinct subsets of middle-class

EXHIBIT 14.10
Middle-Class Preferences
Social class can lead to preferences for different products and services. These preferences have also changed over time. Here are several preferences for lower-middle-, middle-, and upper-middle-class consumers.

Source: Kenneth Labich, "Class in America," *Fortune*, February 7, 1994, p. 116.

CLASS DISTINCTIONS: YOU ARE WHAT YOU CHOOSE

		LOWER-MIDDLE	MIDDLE	UPPER-MIDDLE
Car	1980s	Hyundai	Chevrolet Celebrity	Mercedes
	1990s	Geo	Chrysler minivan	Range Rover
Business shoe (men)	1980s	Sneakers	Wingtips	Cap toes
	1990s	Boots	Rockports	Loafers
Business shoe (women)	1980s	Spike-heel pumps	Mid-heel pump	High-heel pumps
	1990s	High-heel pumps	Dressy flats	One-inch pumps
Alcoholic beverage	1980s	Domestic beer	White wine spritzer	Dom Perignon
	1990s	Domestic lite beer	California Chardonnay	Cristal
Leisure pursuit	1980s	Watching sports	Going to movies	Golf
	1990s	Playing sports	Renting movies	Playing with computers
Hero	1980s	Roseanne Barr	Ronald Reagan	Michael Milken
	1990s	Kathie Lee Gifford	Janet Reno	Rush Limbaugh

consumers.[79] The more traditional middle class moved into the suburbs in the 1950s and 1960s and survived recent difficult economic times. These consumers tend to be politically and culturally liberal and casual about religion. The other group consists of recent arrivals to the middle class, many from ethnic groups (particularly African Americans and Asian Americans) or from rising blue-collar groups. Because tough economic times have threatened their jobs, these consumers tend to be rigidly conservative and like to preserve traditional middle-class values to protect their hard-won gains.

Similar middle-class behavior patterns have been found in other countries. For example, the middle class in Mexico has many similarities to the U.S. middle class, spending much of its disposable income on cars, clothing, vacations, and household goods. However, Mexican middle-class households have a lower average income (around $10,000) compared with their American counterparts.[80] The Mexicans spend more on necessities, rarely use credit, and therefore have little debt repayment. In Russia, 5 million consumers make up the middle class, with an average monthly income of $500. Roughly 85 percent of this group own cars, and most prefer fast-food restaurants from the West.[81]

Finally, rising prosperity has led to an explosion in the size of the middle class in many poorer developing countries around the world.[82] The greatest change has occurred in parts of East Asia (China, India, Indonesia, and South Korea) followed by some Latin American countries (Mexico, Brazil, and Argentina) and Poland and eastern Germany. Personal consumption has risen, as evidenced by greatly increasing sales of typical middle-class items such as washing machines, TVs, DVDs, and stereos. Note that the middle-class incomes can vary dramatically across countries. In China, the average annual middle-class household income is $1,000, compared with about $3,000 in Poland. Furthermore, in Eastern Europe and the Middle East a consumer has to work 40 to 45 days to buy a washing machine, whereas a Western consumer has to work only five. However, the cost of living in these countries is substantially lower than it is in the West, so consumers need less money to buy necessities.

The Working Class

working class Primarily blue-collar workers.

The **working class** is mainly represented by blue-collar workers. The traditional stereotype is of a hard-hatted, middle-aged man, but this image is changing as the working class is becoming younger, more ethnically diverse, more female, somewhat more educated, and more alienated from employers.[83] A key bond among the working class is membership in organized labor unions.

Working-class consumers heavily depend on family members for both economic and social support in many areas, including job opportunities and advice—particularly for key purchases and help during difficult times.[84] As a result, the working class tends to have more of a local orientation socially, psychologically, and geographically than other classes. For example, working-class men exhibit strong preferences for local athletic teams, news segments, and vacations (typically taken less than 2 hours from home). The working class has also demonstrated the strongest resistance to the foreign car invasion in the United States and to abandoning the macho symbol of a large and powerful car or truck.

The working class has in fact remained relatively resistant to change over the years. For example, traditional sex roles have been perpetuated. Women's lives revolve around the home and the children, and their main social contacts are with close relatives, friends, and neighbors—many of whom are lifelong acquaintances. Men's lives focus on their jobs, male camaraderie, and mechanical pursuits like car repair and home improvement.

Like other classes, the working class exhibits identifiable patterns of consumption. For example, the local/home orientation is exemplified in the purchase of products like Schaeffer (versus Heineken) beer, Ford (versus Toyota) pickup trucks, RCA (versus Sony) TVs, Marlboro cigarettes, *Field and Stream* magazine, Black & Decker tools, and McDonald's fast food.[85] Compared with other classes, this group is more likely to eat at home and live in mobile homes.

The working class is also more likely to spend than save, but when they do save, they prefer savings accounts over investments. In addition, working-class consumers are more likely to judge product quality on the basis of price (higher price means higher quality), to shop in mass merchandise or discount stores, and to have less product information when purchasing.[86]

The Homeless*

homeless People at the low end of the status hierarchy.

At the low end of the status hierarchy are the **homeless**. Homeless consumers lack shelter and live on the streets or in makeshift structures, cars, or vacant houses.[87] The homeless represent a very sizable segment of society in some countries. In the United States, the homeless population is estimated to be as high as 7 million.[88] This group, which is growing in size, is made up primarily of drug and alcohol abusers, former mental patients, members of minority female-headed households, and those who have experienced financial setbacks.

(*Much of the discussion in this section is adapted from Ronald Paul Hill and Mark Stamey, "The Homeless in America: An Examination of Possessions and Consumption Behaviors," *Journal of Consumer Research,* December 1990, pp. 303–321.)

Major reasons for homelessness include unemployment, release from mental institutions, drug addiction, and lack of low-cost housing. According to one survey in Austin, Texas, where an estimated 6,000 homeless people live, 51 percent of the respondents were employed but not earning enough to afford a permanent residence.[89]

That the homeless lack basic resources is a sad and troubling problem for many industrialized nations. Along with government relief agencies and volunteers who labor on behalf of these "underclass" citizens, many economists, sociologists, and anthropologists are investigating what persistent homelessness can tell us about our society. The study of consumer behavior can make some contribution to that research.

An overriding characteristic of the homeless is the struggle for survival. In the face of little or no income, homeless consumers have difficulty acquiring necessities such as food, medical care, and other needs for everyday living.[90] These people are not helpless but rather are a "resourceful, determined, and capable group that proactively deals with its lack of resources in the consumer environment."[91] They also maintain their self-esteem by (1) distancing themselves from more dependent individuals on welfare or in shelters and from institutions like the Salvation Army, (2) accepting their street role identity, or (3) telling fictitious stories about past or future accomplishments.[92] In addition, they have lower expectations about acceptable housing than the middle class.

In light of the size and unique behavior patterns of the homeless population, researchers have become interested in its acquisition, consumption, and disposition patterns. In particular, the consumer behavior of the homeless differs from that of the rest of society in two major ways: (1) how they acquire goods and (2) how they use and dispose of them.

Scavenging, a particularly important survival activity, is the finding of used or partially used goods that other individuals and institutions have discarded. Homeless consumers need to scavenge because they are typically denied access to stores and restaurants based on lack of funds and unkempt appearance. They typically find scavenged items in garbage cans and dumpsters. The homeless have become fairly adept at not only locating the best places to scavenge but also finding the most useful and important items in a particular location. For example, they often know which restaurants or grocery stores have the most edible discarded food and sometimes make arrangements with the managers to pick up discards. Many vary their scavenging patterns to avoid detection and move within a wide enough area to provide the needed items. They are therefore a mobile or nomadic society.

Many homeless people also have tools to aid in scavenging and recycling activities. These include items such as shopping carts (to transport materials), tire irons (for protection and for entering abandoned buildings), and ice picks, sledgehammers, and screwdrivers (for removing metal parts). A major problem facing the homeless is how to store and prepare gathered food. Most often they cook over an open fire, but some pirate electricity so they can cook with discarded appliances.

The homeless rarely acquire everything they need by scavenging, which means they need some form of income-producing activity, be it begging, redeeming bottles and cans for the deposit, collecting scrap metal, cleaning windshields at busy intersections, or working as day laborers. When these consumers acquire money, they do not always buy everyday goods. Rather, they prefer to splurge or to buy a special treat such as a hot meal, cigarettes, alcohol, or drugs.

Despite their poverty, most homeless people have some valued possessions. Many try to create some form of home, whether it be an abandoned building or car, a makeshift dwelling built out of scavenged materials, or a spot under a bridge or in a tunnel. Homeless people prefer these habitats to either shelters, which are perceived as dirty and inhospitable, or public places such as bus and train stations and shopping centers, which are patrolled by police and security services. These humble homes can often serve as a source of pride, much like those of other classes. A major challenge for those living in colder climates is keeping warm in the winter. Clothing for the homeless population is often shabby, serving primarily as protection from the environment.

Finally, the consumption and disposition behaviors of the homeless differ from those of the rest of society. In particular, they get the maximum use out of items and discard something only if they have absolutely no further use for it. They often wear clothes and shoes until these items disintegrate or fall apart; they rarely waste food, even if it is spoiled or rotten. Thus the homeless are secondhand consumers because they consume what others have disposed of.

MARKETING IMPLICATIONS Social class can have a variety of marketing implications. In particular, it can serve as a way of segmenting the market, thereby influencing product or service development, the advertising message, media exposure, and outlet selection.

Product or service development. Social class motives and values can determine which products or services consumers desire. Goods and services can be status symbols and motivate acquisition, which is why the upper classes, for example, are willing to pay high prices to satisfy a need for prestige, convenience, and luxury.[93] Therefore, expensive cruises and vacations, luxury automobiles, imported wines, fancy restaurants, and couture clothing can appeal to this group. For example, British restaurateur Sir Terence Conran has been extremely successful in catering to London's chic set with restaurants that feature exotic meals.[94] High-end restaurants such as Park Avenue Café and Wolfgang Puck's Spago are becoming chains to reach the growing affluent market outside the restaurants' original locales.[95] BMW is introducing top-end premium vehicles, including a new Rolls Royce model, for wealthier buyers.[96] Upper-class consumers in the Western hemisphere are a very attractive market for sellers of computers, electronic equipment, and second cars.[97]

The working class, on the other hand, is more concerned with good quality at a fair price, and many products and services are designed to fulfill this desire. Examples include family-rate motels, cafeterias and fast-food restaurants, economy or used cars, and inexpensive multipurpose clothing. In Mexico, the Elektra retail chain caters to working-class customers by making credit available for purchases of televisions and other appliances.[98]

The large size of the middle class makes it a popular target of products and services. In India, for example, marketers are particularly targeting the upper-middle (100 million people) and lower-middle (200 million people) classes. The lower-middle class now accounts for 75 percent of sales of soap and radios; 60 percent of laundry detergents; and up to 50 percent of all soft drinks, shampoo, and color TVs.[99]

Sometimes marketers develop different product lines for different classes. Anheuser-Busch, for example, offers Michelob for the upper-middle class (with a super premium price), Budweiser for the middle class (premium price), and Busch for the working class (low price). Furthermore, Heineken is perceived as an upper-class beer, Coors and Miller as middle class, and Old Style as lower middle.[100] Mercedes is offering smaller and less expensive models to appeal to a broader class of consumers.[101]

Finally, marketers can appeal to the consumers' aspirations for upward mobility by positioning an offering as something that increases one's social standing. To illustrate, a variety of products and services are designed to help consumers become more culturally sophisticated: "best-loved classics" on CD; books on topics such as wine and art appreciation; and television programs that make art, science, and music more accessible.[102] These tools can improve the average person's knowledge of subjects that upper-class people deem culturally important. Also, bankers are increasingly targeting the middle class with services typically reserved for the upper class, such as asset management.[103] Finally, as shown in Exhibit 14.11, products and services can be positioned as evidence that consumers have "made it."

Advertising and personal selling messages. Marketers can design advertising and personal selling messages to appeal to various social classes. Messages directed toward the upper classes, for example, might focus on the themes of "just reward for hard work," "you've made it," or "pamper yourself because you deserve it." Interestingly, in South America marketers for Budweiser abandoned the beer's working-class image to position the brand as the "trendy drink for affluent youth."[104] Certain products and services can be positioned as status symbols (e.g., Godiva chocolates). Johnnie Walker Black Label is by far the most popular whiskey in Thailand because of the status message it conveys. Marketers often appeal to the Japanese upper classes using English words and Western models.[105] Further,

EXHIBIT 14.11
Social Class Aspirations
Sometimes marketers try to appeal to consumers' social class aspirations by positioning a product or service as a symbol of social class standing. Here we see how Bose positions itself as the system for those with a high standard of living.

Source: Courtesy of Bose Corporation.

There are so many reasons to own a Bose® Lifestyle® DVD system.
And we've just added a new one.

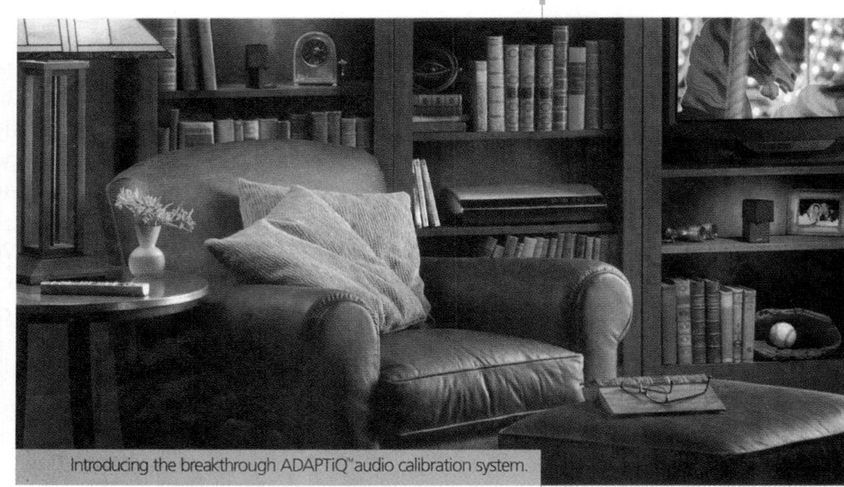
Introducing the breakthrough ADAPTiQ™ audio calibration system.

Customizes sound to your room, so your Lifestyle® DVD system will sound best where it matters most. And it's only from Bose.

No two rooms sound exactly the same. Where you place your speakers, room size and shape, reflective and absorption qualities...even whether a room has rugs or hardwood floors can affect sound. And until now, there wasn't a simple way for home theater systems to account for these variables. Introducing the new ADAPTiQ audio calibration system, now available in Lifestyle® 35 and 28 DVD home entertainment systems. It listens to the sound in your particular room and automatically adjusts your Lifestyle® system to sound its best. So now, no matter what your room's acoustics, you'll enjoy action-packed movies and lifelike music delivered by a system performing to its fullest potential. ▪ The ADAPTiQ system is just one reason you'll enjoy our Lifestyle® systems. Some others: An elegant media center with built-in DVD/CD player. Barely noticeable cube speakers. An Acoustimass® module that produces rich impactful bass. And an advanced universal remote that controls your system – even from another room. Bose Lifestyle® home entertainment systems. Now with the ADAPTiQ system, the height of our technology just got higher.

For a FREE information kit, or names of dealers and Bose stores near you call:
1.800.ASK.BOSE ext.M33 ask.bose.com/wm33

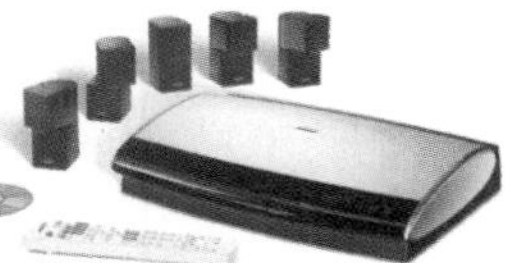

Lifestyle® 35 DVD home entertainment system

BOSE
Better sound through research

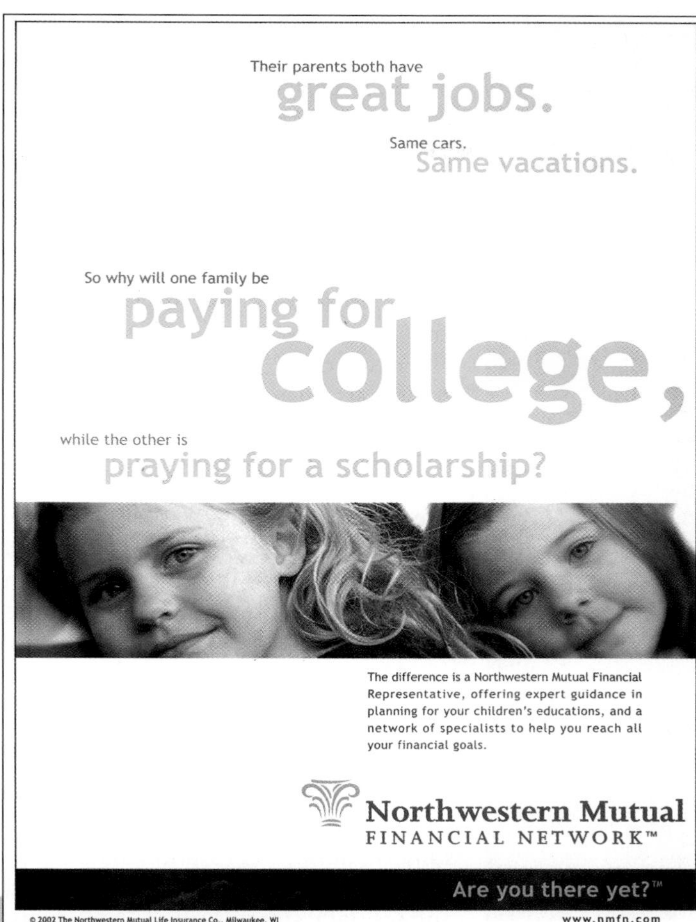

Their parents both have
great jobs.
Same cars.
Same vacations.
So why will one family be
paying for college,
while the other is
praying for a scholarship?
The difference is a Northwestern Mutual Financial Representative, offering expert guidance in planning for your children's educations, and a network of specialists to help you reach all your financial goals.
Northwestern Mutual
FINANCIAL NETWORK™
Are you there yet?™
© 2002 The Northwestern Mutual Life Insurance Co., Milwaukee, WI
www.nmfn.com

EXHIBIT 14.12

An Appeal to Middle-Class Values

College is a very expensive endeavor for many families. However, getting a college education is highly valued by the upper-middle class as a way of getting ahead and improving social standing. This ad for Northwestern Mutual encourages families to plan for their financial future and college.

Source: © 2002 The Northwestern Mutual Life Insurance Co., Milwaukee, WI.

because conspicuous consumption can be an important motivator of consumer behavior, marketing messages can stress the social value or status associated with the product or service. A billboard ad for Rolex, for example, contained the slogan "Get your wrist watched."

Messages successfully directed toward the working class, on the other hand, frequently take on a more localized orientation and focus on home and friends as well as favored activities such as hunting, watching sports events, bowling, and getting together at the local bar. Middle-class messages can focus on themes such as doing the right thing, being fashionable, and doing what's good for the children (see Exhibit 14.12). Advertisers targeting a particular social class within the larger population can be effective by tapping into the group's distinctiveness; when targeting the upper classes, for instance, the advertiser might suggest the group's status as a small, elite group.[106] In addition, messages can use typical members of a social class as role models. The ad in Exhibit 14.13, for example, represents an appeal to the working class.

Media exposure. The classes also differ in their exposure to certain media. Advertisers try to reach the upper classes, especially the nouveaux riches, through targeted magazines and newspapers such as the *Robb Report* (whose readers' average income is $755,000 a year), *Town and Country, Veranda,* and the *New York Times.*[107] Rolex, Giorgio Armani, and other firms also advertise in *Fast Company* and other business magazines to reach moneyed businesspeople.[108] The upper classes tend to restrict their TV viewing to public stations and cultural shows. Members of the upper class are also more likely to fit the profile of the Internet shopper, with higher income and education.[109]

The lower classes, on the other hand, are heavy watchers of TV. Particularly fond of situation comedies, soap operas, and sports programs, this segment is less likely to read magazines and newspapers, compared with other classes. Middle-class consumers, particularly those with only some college, are unique because they tend to be heavy TV watchers and magazine readers.

Outlet selection. Certain outlets are designed to appeal to and pamper upper-class consumers. The merchandise in these stores is generally very expensive, and the service is very personalized.[110] For example, the high-fashion Bijan store on Rodeo Drive in Los Angeles sells by appointment only. With an average of only five customers a day, Bijan sells bulletproof, chinchilla-lined jackets for $27,000; boots for $3,250; and men's perfume in Baccarat crystal bottles for $1,500. Specialty stores such as Prada, Hermes, Louis Vuitton, and Gucci appeal to the upper class by showcasing status products in luxurious settings.[111] Some designers arrange "trunk shows" to preview their latest fashions in selected shops and department stores and take special orders from upscale customers.[112] Conspicuous consumption can also

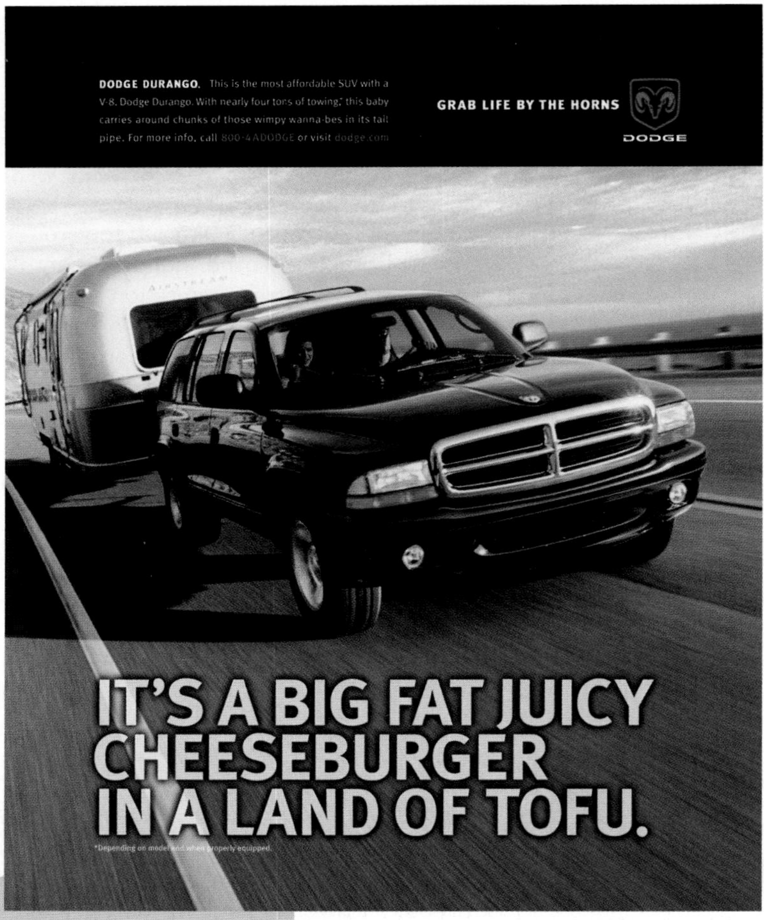

DODGE DURANGO. This is the most affordable SUV with a V-8. Dodge Durango. With nearly four tons of towing,* this baby carries around chunks of those wimpy wanna-bes in its tail pipe. For more info, call 800-4ADODGE or visit dodge.com
GRAB LIFE BY THE HORNS
DODGE
IT'S A BIG FAT JUICY CHEESEBURGER IN A LAND OF TOFU.

EXHIBIT 14.13
Working-Class Role Model
This ad may appeal to working class consumers because it acknowledges the simple value of working with one's hands.

Source: Courtesy of Daimler Chrysler.

be influential because consumers want to acquire items in the "correct" store or outlet, especially if they can be seen doing so (see Exhibit 14.8).[113]

Even mass merchandisers are changing their merchandise mix to offer more snob appeal. Hardware giant Home Depot now offers $7,000 Sub-Zero refrigerators and $39,500 Schonbek chandeliers, and Sears is offering Karastan rugs and Royal Velvet towels in its Great Indoors stores.[114] Even discount merchandisers such as Target sell "cheap chic" apparel and housewares very similar to those offered by pricier retailers.[115] Alternatively, to counter sluggish sales, London's traditionally elitist Savile Row area (famous for clothing) has used aggressive marketing tactics to abandon its stuffy image and appeal more broadly to other classes.[116]

Mass merchandisers and discount stores have successfully targeted working-class consumers by offering quality goods at a good price. Wal-Mart has been extremely adept at understanding the needs and desires of these consumers. Garage sales and resale shops are also popular. Finally, department and specialty stores, such as The Express, Gap, Sears, and Mervyn's, appeal to the middle class by offering fashionable clothing, quality merchandise, and good credit terms.

Note of caution. Although this chapter has discussed social class differences in consumer behavior, marketers have had difficulty in using social class as a segmentation variable for several reasons. First, as noted earlier, a variety of factors such as occupation and income can have opposite effects on social class, which makes social class difficult to measure. Second, variations within a class make social class a better predictor of broad behavior patterns, such as conspicuous product-level choice, than of specific behaviors such as brand choice. Finally, because of social class fragmentation, traditional social class distinctions may be becoming too broad to be truly useful.

As a result, greater segmentation is needed. Marketers are responding by developing their ability to target consumers. For example, "marketers can now pinpoint the class status and buying patterns of just about everyone in the U.S. on a neighborhood-by-neighborhood basis,"[117] thanks in part to the increasing ability to communicate with specific consumers more precisely through direct mail, the Internet, and other interactive media. In the future marketers are likely to use detailed social-class profiles of consumers, rather than traditional broad distinctions. As one example, the American Transportation Television Network (ATTN) directly targets working-class truck drivers at truck stops with reports on traffic conditions, weather reports, and summaries of government regulations.[118] ●

SUMMARY

Individuals in a society can be grouped into different levels of status (upper, middle, and lower), making up a social class hierarchy. Class distinctions are significant because members of a particular class share common life experiences and therefore values and behavior patterns. However, many variations occur within groups.

Although individuals are most likely to be influenced by members of their own class because they regularly interact with them, influence can also cross class lines through the trickle-down effect (when lower classes copy upper-class values and behavior) or the status float effect (when trends start in the lower classes and spread upward).

A variety of factors determine one's level of social class, the most critical of which are occupation and education. Income, area of residence, possessions, family background, and social interactions are also important. Researchers use a battery of items, such as the Computerized Status Index, to measure social class. Three major trends are producing an evolution in social class structures: (1) upward mobility, (2) downward mobility, and (3) social class fragmentation.

Social class causes or motivates acquisition, consumption, and disposition in four major ways. Conspicuous consumption is the acquisition and display of luxury goods and services to demonstrate class status. Also, certain products and services serve as status symbols, and we often judge others on the basis of their possessions. Compensatory consumption occurs when consumers attempt to offset deficiencies in one area by engaging in greater than usual consumption (e.g., buying a new car after losing a job). Finally, the meaning of money can be a key motivator of consumer behavior.

People in each social class generally exhibit specific consumption patterns. The upper class tends to be hardworking, wealthy, socially conscious, and especially concerned with conspicuous consumption. Members of the middle class tend to want to buy the right things and live in a nice neighborhood, and they strongly aspire to higher social standing. The working class is characterized by strong family ties and a local orientation. The homeless struggle for survival by scavenging, recycling, and collecting items that others have discarded. These class distinctions have important marketing implications in areas of product and service development, advertising and personal selling messages, media exposure, and outlet selection.

QUESTIONS FOR REVIEW AND DISCUSSION

1. What is the social class hierarchy?
2. What are the determinants of social class?
3. Why is social class fragmentation taking place?
4. Why would a consumer engage in conspicuous consumption and conspicuous waste?
5. How does parody display differ from status symbols?
6. Under what circumstances does compensatory consumption occur?
7. Why might a company develop different offerings for consumers in different social classes?

EXERCISES

1. Design a battery of questions to measure social class standing. (The CSI in Exhibit 14.6 can be used as a starting point). Make sure to include all the determinants of social class. In addition, pick one product and one service that you think will vary across social class in terms of consumer behavior and develop a series of questions to measure the acquisition and consumption of this product and service (i.e., how much time is spent, what information is collected, where it is purchased, what brands are considered and selected, and so on). Administer this questionnaire to at least 15 consumers who represent the range of social classes, and divide the respondents into three major groups (upper, middle, and lower class). Summarize how the three groups vary in terms of consumption behavior for both the product and service.
2. A travel service has hired you to develop a marketing strategy for a vacation package. The company wants to offer different packages to different social classes. Develop a complete package and marketing strategy for each of the following: the upper class, the middle class, and the working class. Be sure to discuss (1) services offered (including destination, accommodations, and so on), (2) pricing, (3) the advertising message, and (4) media targeting. Summarize the key differences among the three marketing strategies.

chapter 15

Age, Gender, and Household Influences on Consumer Behavior

INTRODUCTION: Generation and Gender Gaps in China

For more than 20 years, the government of mainland China has attempted to curb population growth by limiting urban families to only one child (see Exhibit 15.1). Now the offspring of these one-child families are growing up and exhibiting characteristics very different from those of previous generations. These "little emperors" were raised by doting parents and were given everything from the best clothing to the best education money can buy. As a result, members of this generation are self-confident, ambitious, hardworking, less traditional, and much more materialistic than their parents. This generation is also much more style conscious and freewheeling than other age groups, adopting the same fads and fashions as their counterparts around the world.

Further, young women from this generation are entering professional careers in much greater numbers than their mothers did. As birth rates in the major Chinese cities continue to drop, many in this generation plan to remain single. In one poll, 29 percent of urban Chinese in their twenties said they had little interest in marrying or having children. The age, gender, attitudes, behavior, and buying power of this generation are expected to have a huge impact on the economic future of Asia.[1]

This example illustrates three additional types of influences on consumer behavior, as shown in Exhibit 15.2. First, age can be a factor in acquisition and consumption, and different generations can vary in terms of their behavior. Second, differences in behavior can be based

EXHIBIT 15.1
The Little Emperor
In one-child families in China, children are treated as "little emperors."

Source: Wolfgang Kaehler/CORBIS.

on gender and sex-role factors. Finally, family or household influences can play an important role in influencing consumption activity. This chapter examines all three of these factors and their implications for marketers. ●

HOW AGE AFFECTS CONSUMER BEHAVIOR

Marketers often segment consumers by age. The basic logic is that people of the same age are going through similar life experiences and therefore share many common needs, symbols, and memories, which, in turn, may lead to similar consumption patterns.[2] Regardless of country, age groups are constantly shifting as babies are born, children grow up, adults mature, and people die. This section opens with an overview of age trends in the United States and continues with an examination of four major age groups being targeted by marketers: (1) teens, (2) Generation X, (3) baby boomers, and (4) the 50 and older market.

Age Trends in the United States

The median age of U.S. consumers, which was 32.9 years in 1990, rose to 35.3 years in 2000—the highest it has ever been—reflecting a huge bulge in the 45-to-54-year-old population.[3] However, during the same period, the number of U.S. consumers under 19 years old increased by more than 10 percent, to 80.5 million (see Exhibit 15.3). Youngsters under 5 years old form the smallest part of that group, while teenagers—an important target for many marketers—are a large and growing segment.[4]

American adults (aged 18 and over) now make up more than 74 percent of the overall population. Thanks in part to better medical care and healthier lifestyles, people are living longer, which is why the elderly population continues to expand. Over the past decade, the number of U.S. consumers aged 75 and older grew 26 percent, to nearly 17 million. The overall senior market—starting at age 50—is a growing segment with considerable buying power and is therefore a prime target for marketers, as discussed later in this chapter. However, the segment of younger adults aged 20 to 34 is shrinking, which poses a challenge for marketers seeking to build and sustain brand loyalty during these critical household formation years.[5]

Teens

The transition from childhood to adulthood makes the teen years a time of immense change. During this period, teens strive to develop a distinct identity and self-image, which sometimes results in a rebellion against parents and authority. These years are also marked by a need to gain acceptance from their peers, and teens often do things to be one of the gang. They want to be independent but at the same time dare not deviate too far from the group or face the risk of being rejected.[6] These conflicting forces can create a great deal of pressure and uncertainty. On the other hand, superficially at least, the gap between teens and their parents is smaller than in previous generations. Entire U.S. families dress in jeans and T-shirts, listen to rock and roll, and watch reruns of old TV shows (like *Bewitched* and *Gilligan's Island*), giving parents and kids a common reference point.[7]

A study of 27,000 teens in 44 countries reveals common characteristics and attitudes that cross national boundaries in six distinct segments.[8] The "Thrills and Chills" segment, which includes teens in the United States, Germany, England, and many other European countries, consists of fun-seeking, free-spending consumers

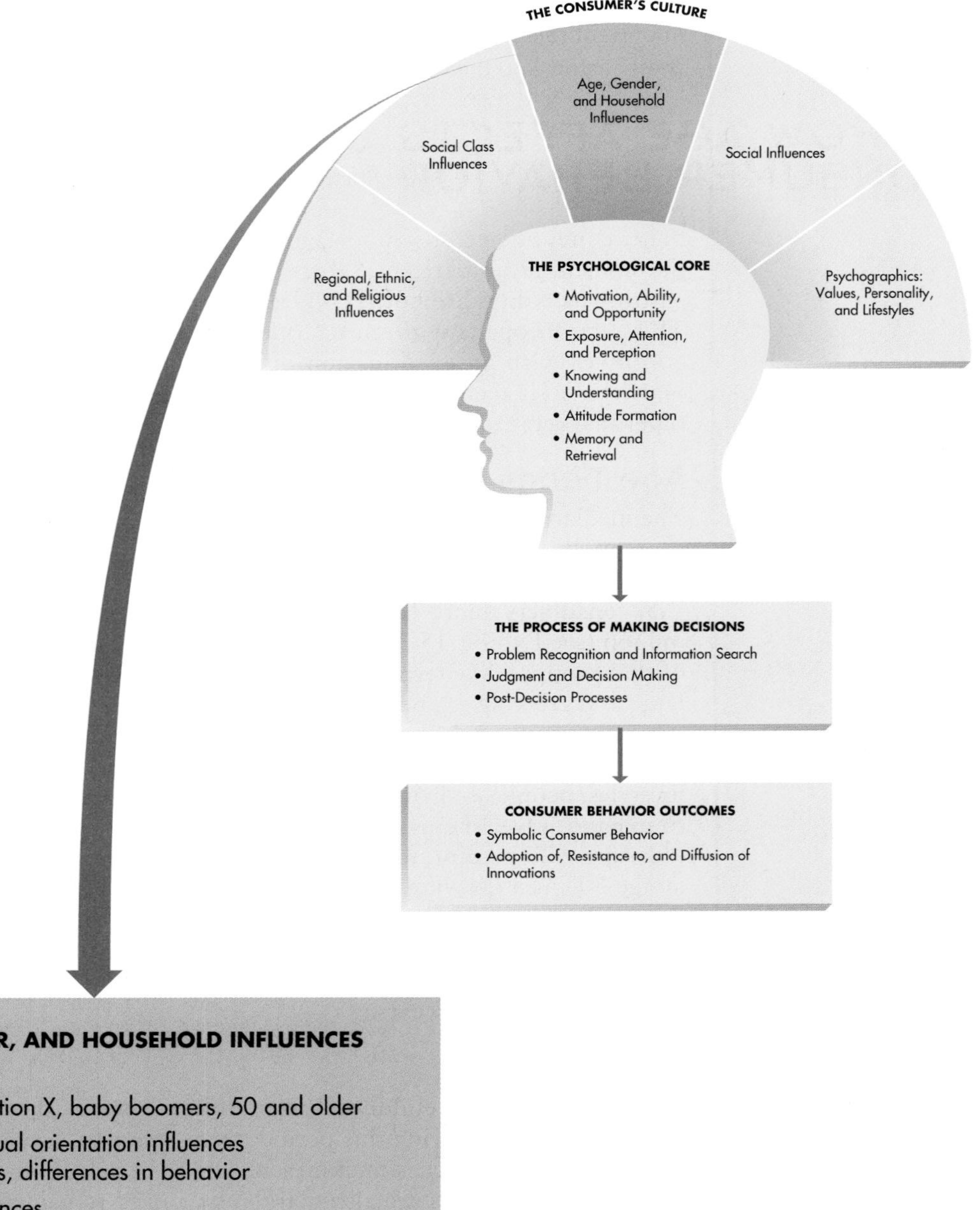

EXHIBIT 15.2
Chapter Overview: Age, Gender, and Household Influences on Consumer Behavior

This chapter shows how factors such as age, gender, and household affect consumer behavior. It examines different age groups (teens, Generation X, baby boomers, and 50 and over), gender and sexual orientation, and types of households. It also discusses changing trends in household structure and how households influence the decision-making process.

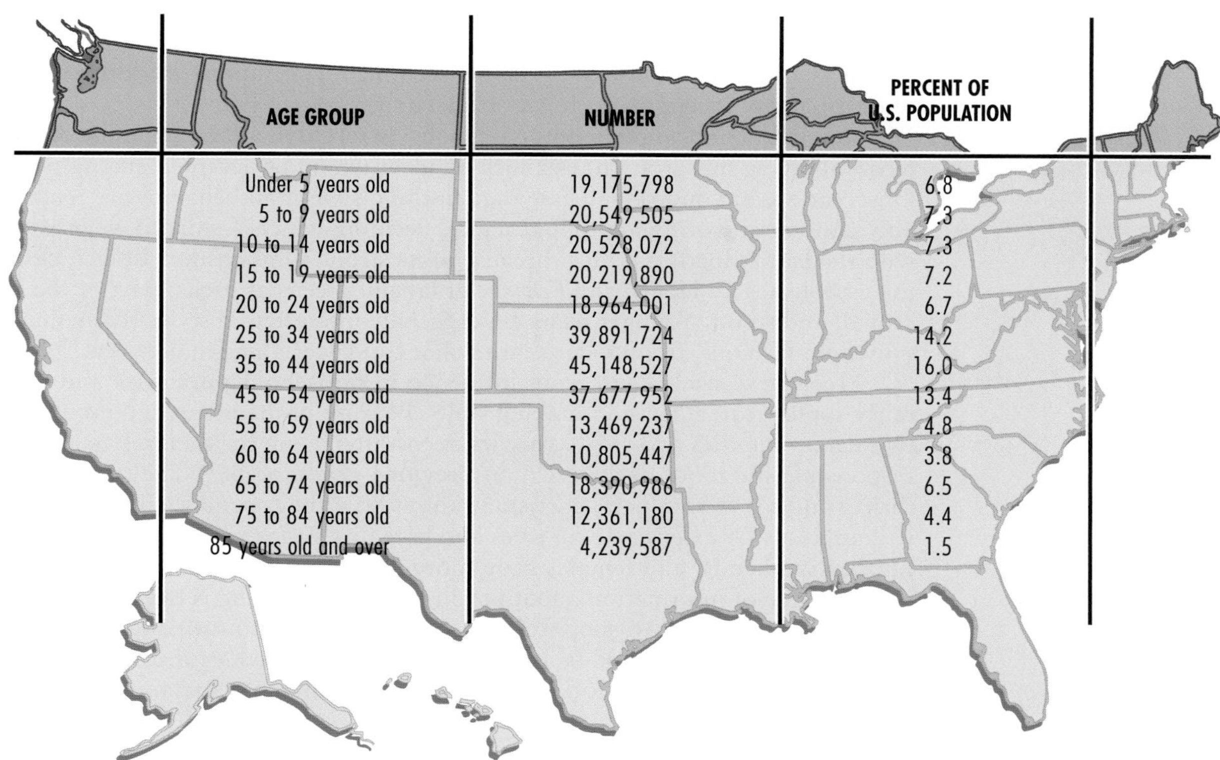

AGE GROUP	NUMBER	PERCENT OF U.S. POPULATION
Under 5 years old	19,175,798	6.8
5 to 9 years old	20,549,505	7.3
10 to 14 years old	20,528,072	7.3
15 to 19 years old	20,219,890	7.2
20 to 24 years old	18,964,001	6.7
25 to 34 years old	39,891,724	14.2
35 to 44 years old	45,148,527	16.0
45 to 54 years old	37,677,952	13.4
55 to 59 years old	13,469,237	4.8
60 to 64 years old	10,805,447	3.8
65 to 74 years old	18,390,986	6.5
75 to 84 years old	12,361,180	4.4
85 years old and over	4,239,587	1.5

EXHIBIT 15.3
The U.S. Population by Age

According to the 2000 Census, consumers up to the age of 19 comprise 28.6 percent of the U.S. population; by comparison, consumers aged 55 and older comprise just 21 percent of the population.

Source: "Profiles of General Demographic Characteristics: 2000 Census of Population and Housing," *U.S. Department of Commerce,* May 2001, p. 3.

from mainly middle-class or upper-class backgrounds. Teens in the "Resigned" segment, covering Denmark, Sweden, Korea, and a number of other countries, have low expectations of the future and of material success, and are alienated from society. The "World Savers" segment, drawn from teens in Hungary, the Philippines, and Venezuela, among other countries, is characterized by altruism, good grades, and high career aspirations. The "Quiet Achievers" in Thailand, China, Hong Kong, Russia, and several other nations conform to societal norms and exhibit an ambitious drive for success. "Bootstrappers" in Nigeria, Mexico, the United States, India, and other countries are family-oriented achievement seekers with hopes and dreams for the future. Finally, "Upholders" in Vietnam, Indonesia, Taiwan, and other nations are dutiful and conforming, seeking a rewarding family life and upholding traditional values.

In general, U.S. teens are very tech-savvy, using the Internet, cell phones, computers, and other digital devices to communicate, play games, do homework, and shop.[9] Knowing this, many parents ask their teenagers to recommend or even make electronics purchases for the household.[10] Far more teenagers earn their own money than ever before, gaining more financial independence than earlier generations did. In Japan, teens with money are sparking a generational battle as they use their income to break free from the strict, traditional world of their parents—spawning new styles and fads that often spread to other parts of the world.[11] At the same time, today's teens are typically more family oriented than previous generations were. Having seen older generations work themselves to death, today's teens prefer to go "back to their roots."[12]

Rock, hip-hop, and rap music symbolizing rebellion are very popular among teens, allowing this group to establish an identity and be accepted among peers. Observations at concerts indicate that clothing styles and behavior are remarkably consistent worldwide. In particular, deciding which T-shirt to wear (often with the band's logo) is critical because of its strong symbolism.[13] In fact, clothing establishes an identity and a way of labeling teens as jocks, part of the in-crowd, and so on. Younger teens are especially interested in styles that emulate grown-up fashions, from underwear to shoes and everything in between.[14]

Teenagers wield increasing influence in household purchases and have fairly sophisticated decision-making skills. Because of the increasing number of two-career families and single parents, teens often shop for themselves and are responsible for more decisions than previous generations.[15] They tend to be thrifty and savvy shoppers, particular about how they spend their money, and willing to search extensively for sales and bargains. Teens tend to do more shopping on weekends, and females shop more than males do.[16] Friends are also a major source of information about products, and socializing is one of the major reasons that teens like to shop. Like adults, teens rely on information from personal sources for high-risk decisions and from mass media for low-risk situations. Because this generation grew up with recycling, many teens will weigh a product's environmental impact before buying.

MARKETING IMPLICATIONS

In the United States teens constitute a very large and growing segment that is expected to reach 35 million by 2010.[17] Their personal purchasing power is a substantial $108 billion, not counting $47 billion more in family purchases.[18] In particular, female teens spend $37 billion a year on beauty and fashion items and influence the spending of another $74 billion. "They shop the broad gamut from cheap to the most expensive," says a drug store executive.[19] Furthermore, as noted above, teens are globally more alike than any other age group.[20] Their universally similar tastes, attitudes, and preferences for music, movies, athletic shoes, clothing, and video games are partly due to popular entertainment and to MTV, which is available in 164 countries. Nonetheless, teens in different regions exhibit some differences, which is why MTV and other marketers are careful to research and address local tastes and behaviors.[21] Compared with U.S. teens, European teens tend to be closer to their parents, watch less TV, and look more to Eastern Europe for cues on fashion and music.

The fact that initial purchases of many products and services are made in the teen years is also important, since brand loyalties established at this time may carry into adulthood. For example, 50 percent of female teens have developed cosmetic brand loyalties by the age of 15[22] (Exhibit 15.4). Teens can also be trendsetters, particularly in areas such as fashion and music. Today's trends often originate from "cool city teens" rather than fashion designers.[23] This is why marketing researchers frequently monitor what's in and what's out among teens for companies such as MTV, Coca-Cola, Pepsi, Levi Strauss, and Microsoft.[24] Companies in Japan have found that the nation's high school girls have an uncanny ability to predict which products will be hits because a fad that catches on with teenagers usually becomes a big trend among consumers in general.[25] However, teen tastes can change very quickly, and popular products may gradually become overexposed and lose their

EXHIBIT 15.4
Teen Loyalties

Teenage consumers are active buyers of a number of products and services and may quickly develop brand loyalty toward their favorite brands. For example, 42 percent of teens buy only one brand of mascara, and 38 percent buy only one brand of eye shadow. Can you think of any brands for which you have been brand loyal since your teen years?

Source: Data from "Those Precocious 13-Year-Olds," *Brandweek*, January 25, 1993, p. 13.

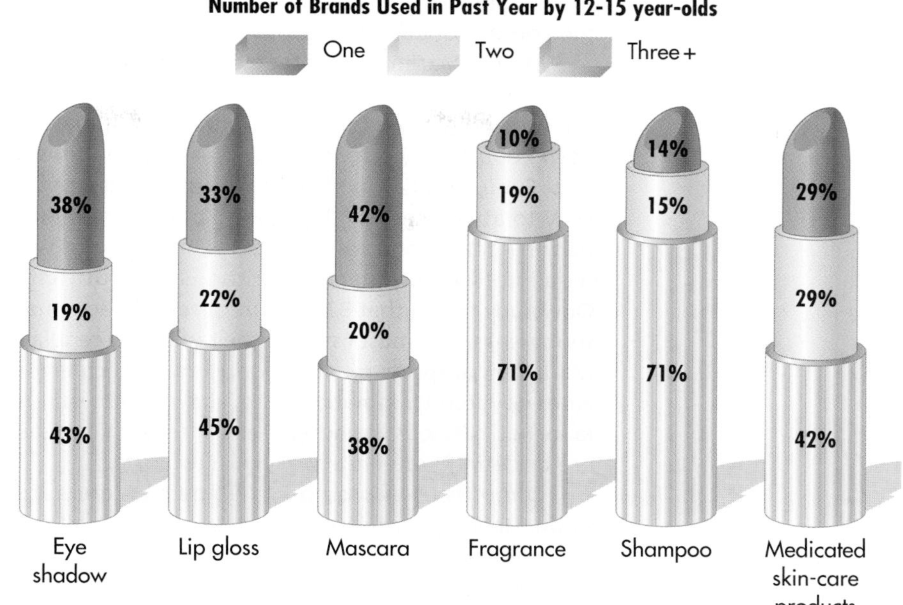

cachet. Knowing this, clothing retailer Abercrombie & Fitch is trying to extend its popularity through edgy advertising and by opening new stores for smaller segments, such as Hollister, geared for teens aged 14 to 18.[26]

The size and purchasing power of the teen market have attracted the attention of marketers offering various goods and services. Many of these are positioned as helping teens deal with the adolescent pressures of establishing an identity, rebelling, and being accepted by peers. For instance, Clairol created XtremeFX hair color for male teens.[27] Gatorade has successfully marketed to teens by offering products that taste lighter and come in funky flavors such as Riptide Rush (a grape and berry blend).[28] In the United Kingdom and in Asia, credit and debit card companies have been targeting teens under age 16 because they are more likely than their parents to embrace the credit culture and use their cards to buy online.[29] Not all is positive, however. Some upscale malls that target affluent women have resisted becoming teen hangouts by offering fewer teen-oriented stores and by playing classical music to drive teens away.[30]

Advertising messages. Advertising messages often incorporate symbols, issues, and language to which teens can relate. Because music and sports tend to be the universal languages of teenagers, popular music and sports figures are frequently featured in ads. The National Football League has been attempting to address declining teen interest in its sport by having pop stars perform at games.[31] Teens are intelligent consumers who are often wary of blatant attempts to influence them.[32] Thus messages need to talk to teenagers, not at them. Furthermore, because they have grown up with videos and computers, today's teens appear to process information faster than earlier generations do.[33] As a result, teens prefer short, snappy phrases to long-winded explanations. For example, an antismoking ad campaign used the tagline "Tobacco: tumor-causing, teeth-staining, smelly puking habit."[34] Note, however, that using slang can sometimes be dangerous because a phrase may already be out-of-date by the time the ad appears, which can make the product or service look "uncool." Finally, many teenagers do not care about the content of advertising and are more concerned with price.

Media. Marketers for teenage consumers can target teens through certain TV networks (especially MTV), TV programs (such as *The Simpsons* and *Seventh Heaven*), magazines (such as *Seventeen* for female teens, *MH-18* for male teens, and *Teen People* for both), and popular-music radio stations.[35] Fashion names such as Gap, Fubu, and Calvin Klein as well as the discount store Target advertise heavily on MTV to attract teens.[36] Target also publishes a magalog—magazine-catalog combination—featuring lifestyle articles interspersed with product information, a technique used by Skechers, American Eagle Outfitters, and others targeting teens.[37] One study found that 83 percent of teens read a major magazine at least once every four weeks, and most listen to the radio on a regular basis, particularly in their cars.[38] Marketers of sports-related products can reach teens through special-interest magazines devoted to snowboarding, surfing, and other sports.[39] More companies have launched catalogs aimed at teens in recent years, and some—such as Limited Too—are targeting preteens with special catalogs.[40]

Other types of promotion. Some marketers are reaching teens through recreation. Heeling Sports, which makes sneakers with built-in wheels, sends teen product ambassadors to perform at amusement parks, malls, skate parks, and college campuses.[41] Some companies communicate with teens in school through electronic communication centers containing calendars of school activities as well as ads.[42] Fast-food chains such as Taco Bell and Pizza Hut now offer menu items in school cafeterias. Channel One, an in-school TV network, intersperses news and features with ads and promotions from sponsors. Over the years, Channel One advertisers have sought to boost brand awareness through promotions such as inviting students to write TV commercials (Snapple) and design art for vending machines (Pepsi). However, critics are concerned about commercialism creeping into the schools; see Chapter 21 for more on the dark side of marketing.[43]

Many companies are going online to reach teens, who are frequent Internet users. For instance, Procter & Gamble promotes its Cover Girl cosmetics by encouraging teens to get a virtual makeover on the company's Web site.[44] Nevertheless teens are fickle users and tend not to be loyal to individual sites. Only if a site appeals to specific interests such as music or movies will it register a lot of visits.[45] ●

Generation X

Generation X (twenty somethings) Individuals born between 1965 and 1976.

Individuals born from 1965 to 1976 are often called **Generation X**. This group is frequently stereotyped as feeling alienated and resentful due to difficulties in career placement and advancement, although many experts dispute this characterization.[46] Within this diverse group, a sizable number of Xers resent being stereotyped and claim their negative image is the invention of those who do not understand their generation.[47] While some underachievers who are pushing 30 hang on to their Generation X "angst," many older members of this group are building careers, having families, and buying homes.[48] Nonetheless, Xers who believe that they may not be able to match or surpass their parents' level of success are apt to feel somewhat disillusioned and be less materialistic than other age groups.

Contrary to the stereotype, Xers are not apathetic slackers. On the contrary, they tend to find success and achievement in being at the very cutting edge of technology. Forty-three percent own their own computers, 70 percent use one every day, and many are hard-core Internet users. Other Xers are finding unique ways to make their fortunes, including a few who have ventured to Vietnam to make investments and start businesses.[49]

A relatively new phenomenon is the so-called boomerang kids. These are Xers who live at home, sometimes well into their 30s or until they marry, to save money.[50] Because parents pay for many essentials (just to keep their homes running), boomerang kids have more discretionary income to spend on entertainment and pleasure and are more likely to buy items like a new car, stereo, or television than their counterparts who must pay utility bills and rent or mortgages. Boomerangers also feel less pressure to settle down than earlier generations and often delay marriage.[51] This trend has led to closer relationships with parents, who are often seen as friends or roommates.

MARKETING IMPLICATIONS The Generation X market represents more than $120 billion in spending power. This group takes the time to research a purchase and appreciates the ability to customize offerings to their personal needs and tastes.[52] It is a key segment for music, movies, budget travel, beer and alcohol, (see Exhibit 15.5) fast food, clothing, jeans, athletic shoes, and cosmetics (although a recent minimalist trend has flattened sales for this category).[53] Xers are also driving the market for PCs, DVDs, and CD-ROMs, online services, and video games, products, and services that are therefore often targeted to them.

EXHIBIT 15.5
Appeal to Generation X
This ad is attempting to appeal to Generation X consumers as they are the key segment for alcohol products.

Source: Jose Cuervo Especial's "Vive Cuervo" ad Campaign.

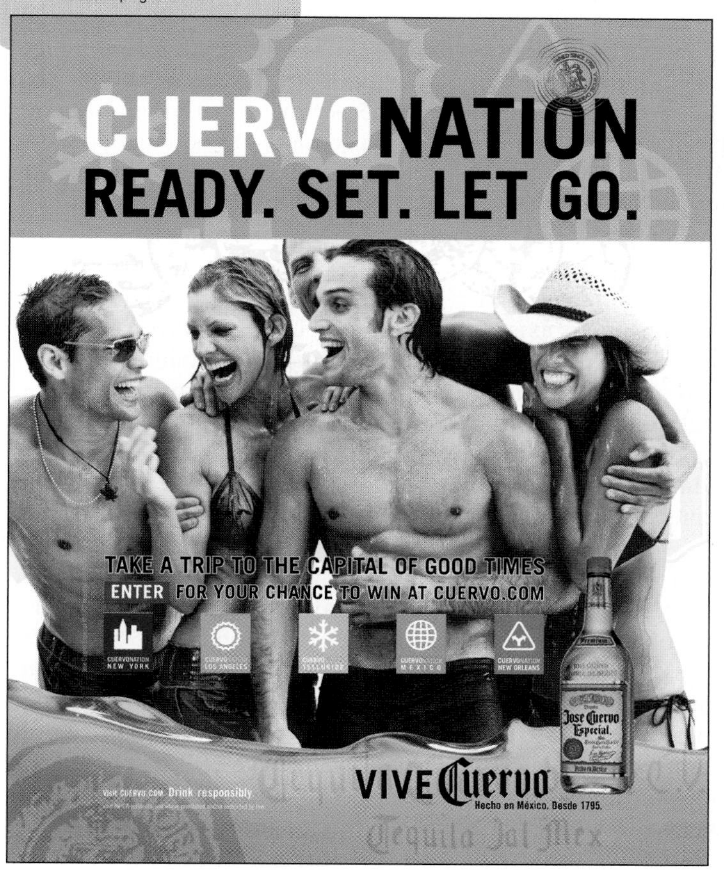

Knowing that Xers spend 24 percent of their discretionary income on eating out, some trendy restaurants have started playing loud techno music to appeal to this group.[54] Eyeing Xers' buying power, Toyota stopped using 1960s music and started using hip-hop and heavy metal songs in car commercials targeting this segment.[55] Because only 5 percent of Xers drink scotch, Dewar's targets young sophisticates and Seagram's positions 7 Crown as a "shooter" (popular among this group).[56] Johnnie Walker is reaching out to Xers with multimedia messages, including a Web site, that subtly link its scotch with entrepreneurial success.[57]

Born and bred on TV, Xers tend to be cynical about obvious marketing techniques.[58] They sometimes find objectionable ads containing: exaggerated claims, stereotypes, unpopular products like cigarettes and alcohol, sexually explicit content, and political, religious, or social messages. However, Xers do react positively to messages they see as clever or in tune with their values and attitudes. In particular, they want to be recognized as their own group and not as mini-baby boomers. Ads should therefore reflect their style, music, fashion, phrases, and interests. For example, Heineken and Mountain Dew have used alternative music and fast-paced videos in ads to change their image and attract this generation.[59] Barq's root beer chose "unglamorous misfits" rather than attractive models for its ad campaign.[60] Ads with the attitude "We know that you know that this is a game" can work well. For example, J & B Scotch ads state: "Drinking J & B cola will make you immortal. Well, OK, it will at least make you fondly remembered by at least some."

Marketers can reach Xers through media vehicles such as popular or alternative music radio stations and TV shows such as *Dawson's Creek*, although Xers watch less TV than other groups do.[61] Magazines such as *Spin* and music-related publications and messages displayed at concerts, sporting events, and popular vacation spots are also attractive vehicles. Mountain Dew, among other companies, sponsors extreme sporting events such as the X Games to reach Xers through special interests.[62]

Increasingly, marketers are using the Internet to reach these Web-savvy consumers.[63] Music and online game sites are especially popular among Xers. Makers of alcohol are using the Internet to communicate with youthful drinkers.[64] To get Xers to donate to charity, ReliefRock offered an online benefit rock music concert rather than send direct-mail letters.[65] To promote its car insurance, State Farm Insurance has run fast-paced online ads that pop up when Xers visit Rollingstone.com and other sites that target this segment.[66]

Targeted sales promotions can also be effective. AT&T offers students a free membership in its Student Advantage discount program.[67] During spring break, many marketers sponsor special events and inundate students with free T-shirts, Frisbees, tank tops, and other items bearing product logos. ●

Baby Boomers

baby boomers
Individuals born between 1946 and 1964.

The 78 million **baby boomers** born between 1946 and 1964 make up the largest demographic group in the United States. Because of their numbers and the fact that many are in their peak earning years, baby boomers have considerable economic power and are a very influential consumer segment. Although boomers are a diverse group, they share many common experiences of the dynamic world of the 1960s and 1970s in which they grew up. In protesting the Vietnam War, this generation created a revolution in social attitudes, music, fashion, and politics, the effects of which are still with us today. This revolution also led to the rise of individualism in which having the freedom to do what you want, when and where you want, is strongly valued.[68]

Subsegments of consumers exist within this very large and diverse group.[69] One group, called middle-aged, overstressed, semiaffluent suburbanites (MOSS), responds positively to marketing efforts that reduce time and effort in shopping and decision making, including product quality, strong packaging, availability, and good service. The 9 million African American boomers form another subsegment. More highly educated than the previous generation and upwardly mobile, these consumers respond to offers targeting their specific values and life experiences.[70]

Some researchers have identified five subgroups of boomers, based on five-year divisions (1946–1951, 1951–1956, and so on). Others suggest three subsegments: leading boomers (born 1946–1950), core boomers (1951–1959), and trailing boomers (1960–1964). Consumers in these subgroups have life experiences in common and may share more attributes with each other than with other segments.[71] If this is true, the oldest and youngest groups would tend to be the most different. Some experts have even suggested the name Gappers for the youngest group (born between 1963 and 1969) because its members fall between boomers and Xers in terms of interests and behavior patterns.[72] Exhibit 15.6 illustrates some of the differences between boomer subgroups and Xers.

EXHIBIT 15.6

The Different Cultures of Boomers and Xers

Author Jonathan Pontell distinguishes between the cultures of the baby boom generation (which he defines as those born between 1942 and 1953), Generation Jones (born between 1954 and 1965, by his definition), and Generation X (born between 1966 and 1978, by his definition).

Source: The Cultural Wasteland, from "Generational Divide," by Allison Stein Wellner, *American Demographics,* Oct. 2000, p. 58. Copyright © 2000, Primedia. All rights reserved.

THE CULTURAL WASTELAND

Generational soundbites, according to author Jonathan Pontell.

	BABY BOOM	GEN JONES	GEN X
Slogan	Make Love, Not War	No Nukes	"Whatever"
Question	Where were you when JFK was shot?	Where's the beef?	Boxers or Briefs?
Demonstration	Chicago Riots	No Nukes March	Battle of Seattle
The 60's	Participants	Witnesses	Oliver Stone Movie
Jewelry	Peace Symbol Necklace	POW Bracelet	Nose Ring
Journalist	Hunter Thompson	John F. Kennedy Jr.	Matt Drudge
News	Walter Cronkite	CNN	CNN.com
Gathering	Woodstock	Live Aid	Lollapalooza
War	Vietnam	"Star Wars"	Persian Gulf War
Hero	JFK	Jerry Brown	Jesse Ventura
Magazine	Ramparts	George	Drudge Report
Scandal	Profumo Affair	Watergate	Monicagate
Gesture	Burn Draft Card	Streaking	Moshing
Hot Spots	San Francisco	Austin	Seattle
Filmakers	Oliver Stone	Spike Lee	Kevin Smith
Feminist	Gloria Steinem	Naomi Wolf	Courtney Love
Poet	Bob Dylan	Bruce Springsteen	Kurt Cobain
Season	Summer of Love	Spring Fever	Winter of Discontent
Anti-	Anti-War	Anti-Nuke	Anti–WTO

MARKETING IMPLICATIONS Because baby boomers have so much buying power, they are the target for many products and services including cars, housing, foreign travel, entertainment, and recreational equipment. Real estate developers are adding whirlpools, bedroom fireplaces, upscale kitchens, and other amenities for baby-boom house buyers.[73] Harley-Davidson has profited by producing heavyweight motorcycles—priced at $17,000 or more—for this segment.[74] Boomers are also heavy consumers of financial services as they look toward retirement and simultaneously pay for their children's college education.[75] They are the heaviest users of frozen dinners and enjoy repackaged "best of" albums as reminders of the music they enjoyed in their teens and young-adult years.[76] Time-pressured baby boomers still like fast food, as they did when they were younger, but many are buying gourmet sandwiches from Cosi, Panera, and other fast-growing restaurant chains as a healthier and more varied alternative to burgers and fries.[77]

baby boomlet (Generation Y) Mini-population explosion from the children of baby boomers.

Many boomers delayed child rearing until their late 20s or 30s and created a mini-population explosion called the **baby boomlet** (now called Generation Y). Thus they are often the target of marketing efforts for children's products and services. To illustrate, much of the growth in minivan sales can be attributed to boomers who want this kind of family vehicle.[78] The ad in Exhibit 15.7 is also directed at baby boomers who are concerned about protecting their children for the future. Marketers have introduced soaps such as Dial for Kids and Baby Dove for this group.[79] Finally, because many baby boomers are in dual-career families, the need for child care services has been increasing rapidly.

An aging population. Because this very large group is getting older, marketers who fail to modify their offerings accordingly will suffer from a shrinking market

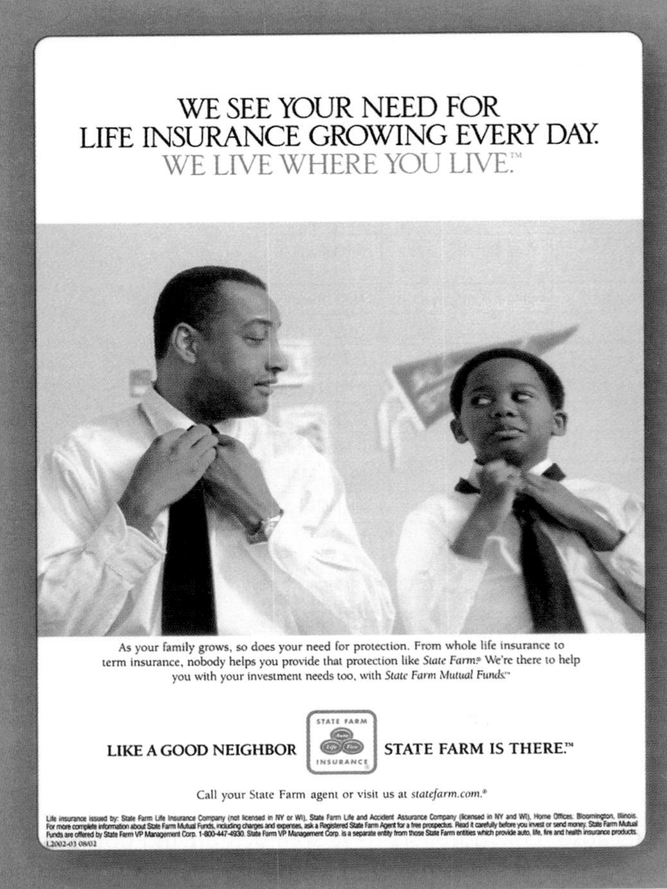

WE SEE YOUR NEED FOR
LIFE INSURANCE GROWING EVERY DAY.
WE LIVE WHERE YOU LIVE.™
As your family grows, so does your need for protection. From whole life insurance to term insurance, nobody helps you provide that protection like State Farm.® We're there to help you with your investment needs too, with State Farm Mutual Funds.℠
LIKE A GOOD NEIGHBOR
STATE FARM
INSURANCE
STATE FARM IS THERE.™
Call your State Farm agent or visit us at statefarm.com.®

EXHIBIT 15.7
Impact of the "Baby Boomlet"
Concern for the future and family protection is now a concern for many baby boomers who now have children.

Source: Copyright, State Farm Mutual Automobile Insurance Company, 1996. Used by permission.

share. Some marketers are developing products and services specifically for the needs of baby boomers. For example, apparel marketers have created jeans in larger sizes and different styles to accommodate the middle-aged physique.[80] The Chico's chain has grown to more than 300 stores by specializing in loose-fitting casual clothing for baby-boom women.[81] To appeal to families that are no longer young, Disney now offers golf, tennis, and adult-education classes.[82]

Many boomers obsessed with aging are a prime market for products and services that help them look and feel young, such as health clubs, body-shaping underwear like the Wonderbra, personal care products, day spas, and plastic surgery.[83] Marketers usually avoid the topic of aging in their communications, however, because boomers are sensitive about the subject.

For a generation that is so concerned with staying youthful, acknowledging adulthood can be a tough admission. This is why some advertisers approach the issue playfully with lines like "Oh no, we've become our parents."[84] An ad for Dewar's shows a bald man with the line: "In an age of miracle hair cures, here's something that will actually grow on you."[85] Vacationing boomers like water parks and water toys at resorts because these activities make them feel young and do not involve strenuous activity.[86] Likewise, in Japan products with a cute cartoon cat, Hello Kitty, have been highly popular among middle-aged consumers who want to show their playful side.[87] As discussed in Chapter 8, marketers like Mitsubishi are using rock music from earlier decades to create a positive and nostalgic feeling.[88] And Cleveland is touting rock connections with the Rock and Roll Hall of Fame to attract boomer tourism.[89] Exhibit 15.8 is a good example of an ad that appeals to baby boomers' sense of nostalgia.

Special marketing communications. Marketers can target boomers through the use of selective media. The VH-1 cable TV network, for example, was created to appeal specifically to boomers' musical interests.[90] Certain cultural TV networks, such as Bravo, the Discovery Channel, and the Arts & Entertainment Network, also tend to attract boomers, as do classic rock radio stations. Some marketers reach boomers through lifestyle-related activities such as home shows, boat shows, and sporting events. Finally, special-interest videos, direct-mail pieces, and targeted Web sites and newsletters can be effective ways of reaching boomers.[91] ●

Fifty and Older

More than 20 percent of the U.S. population is 55 years of age or older, and this percentage is increasing as the baby boomers age.[92] Thanks to pension funds, Social Security, Medicare, retirement savings, and delayed retirement, this generation is relatively well off compared with seniors 20 years ago, although it is also the most varied in terms of wealth, with many poor as well as many rich seniors.[93]

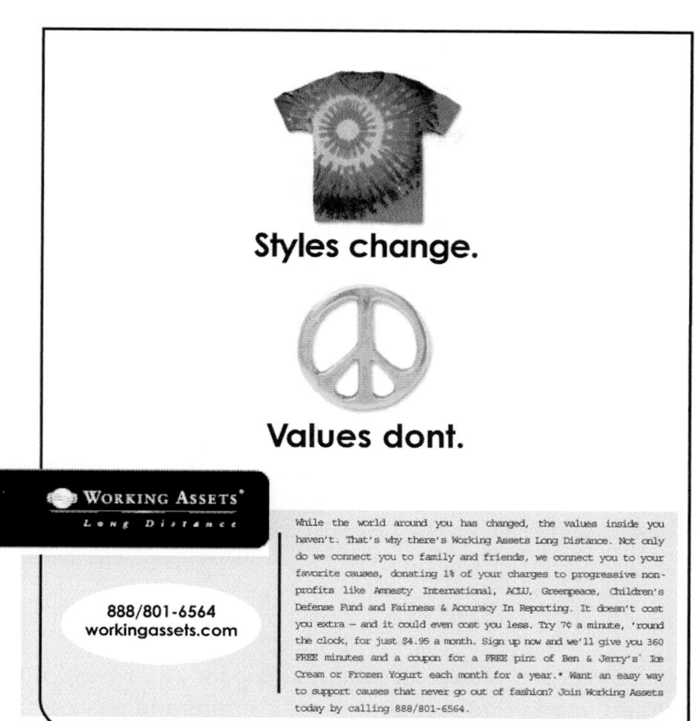

Styles change.
Values dont.
WORKING ASSETS
Long Distance
888/801-6564
workingassets.com
While the world around you has changed, the values inside you haven't. That's why there's Working Assets Long Distance. Not only do we connect you to family and friends, we connect you to your favorite causes, donating 1% of your charges to progressive non-profits like Amnesty International, ACLU, Greenpeace, Children's Defense Fund and Fairness & Accuracy In Reporting. It doesn't cost you extra – and it could even cost you less. Try 7¢ a minute, 'round the clock, for just $4.95 a month. Sign up now and we'll give you 360 FREE minutes and a coupon for a FREE pint of Ben & Jerry's Ice Cream or Frozen Yogurt each month for a year.* Want an easy way to support causes that never go out of fashion? Join Working Assets today by calling 888/801-6564.

EXHIBIT 15.8

An Appeal Directed at Baby Boomers

Tie-died shirts and the peace sign were important symbols when baby boomers were growing up.

Source: Courtesy of Working Assets.

The over-50 market is even more diverse than other age groups.[94] Nevertheless, on a broad level this segment can be divided into two groups that vary significantly in terms of lifestyle and outlook. The **young again** (age 50 to around 65) usually think of themselves as about 15 years younger than they really are in terms of cognitive age.[95] In fact, this group thinks more like older baby boomers (which many are) than like seniors and leads a very active lifestyle. The young again also have considerable discretionary income because they have fewer financial obligations once their children leave home.[96]

The second segment, the **gray market**, consists of consumers over 65.[97] Better medical care and healthier lifestyles have increased the size and economic clout of this group. Because these consumers lived through the Great Depression of the 1930s, their philosophy is to save rather than to spend. Most of these individuals—even those 75 and over—are self-sufficient in most activities, including walking, preparing meals, shopping, housework, and bathing. They do not like being referred to as "old." Finally, women outnumber men in this category because women tend to live longer.

In terms of consumer behavior, information-processing skills tend to deteriorate with age. Therefore, older or mature consumers are less likely to search for information and more likely to have difficulty remembering information and making more complex decisions, especially with large amounts of information.[98] Thus they tend to engage in simpler, more schematic processing.[99] Further, poor recognition memory makes them susceptible to the "truth effect" (believing that often-repeated statements are true—see Chapter 8).[100] As a result, they sometimes need help or consumer education programs when making decisions, as discussed in Chapter 20.[101] Mature consumers also tend to shop more often at discount stores and buy many of the same items that they did when they were younger.[102] Thus they are price sensitive and fairly resistant to the adoption of new products, especially technology products. Exhibit 15.9 shows how the combination of age and income affects companies marketing luxury goods and services.

young again Individuals age 50 to around 65.

gray market Individuals over 65.

MARKETING IMPLICATIONS Mature consumers are an increasingly important target market for many companies. Clearly, this group represents a critical and growing market for health-related and medical products and services and retirement communities (particularly in Florida and the South).[103] Mature consumers already spend more than twice the national average on prescription drugs, accounting for more than 40 percent of all pharmaceutical sales.[104] Marketers of incontinence products for this group are experiencing rapid sales growth.[105] As another example, Allergan has been targeting seniors with information on cataracts and ways to correct the problem.[106]

EXHIBIT 15.9
Marketing Luxury Products by Age

Source: Reprinted with permission from the June 11, 2001 issue of Advertising Age and Donald Ziccardi, Ziccardi Partners Frierson MEE. Copyright © 2001 Crain Communications, Inc.

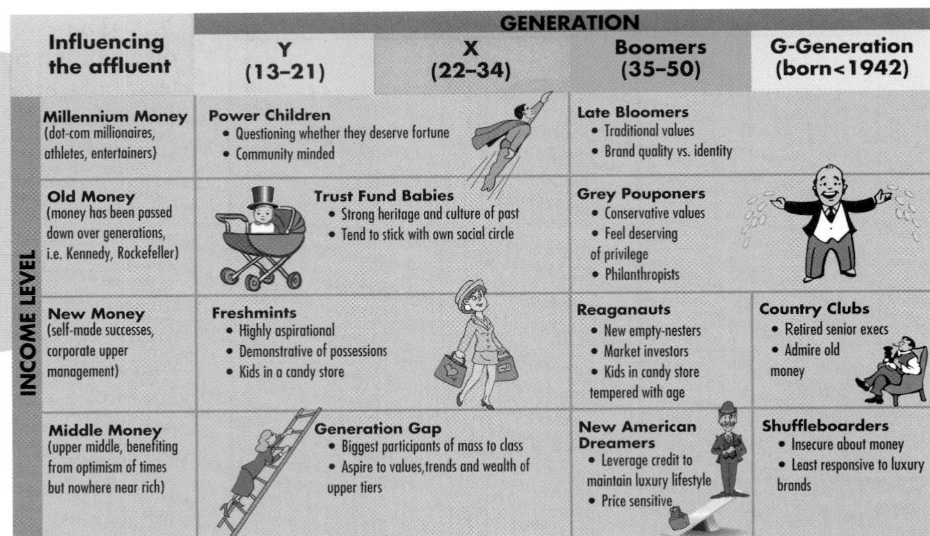

INCOME LEVEL / Influencing the affluent	GENERATION: Y (13–21)	X (22–34)	Boomers (35–50)	G-Generation (born<1942)
Millennium Money (dot-com millionaires, athletes, entertainers)	**Power Children** • Questioning whether they deserve fortune • Community minded		**Late Bloomers** • Traditional values • Brand quality vs. identity	
Old Money (money has been passed down over generations, i.e. Kennedy, Rockefeller)	**Trust Fund Babies** • Strong heritage and culture of past • Tend to stick with own social circle		**Grey Pouponers** • Conservative values • Feel deserving of privilege • Philanthropists	
New Money (self-made successes, corporate upper management)	**Freshmints** • Highly aspirational • Demonstrative of possessions • Kids in a candy store		**Reaganauts** • New empty-nesters • Market investors • Kids in candy store tempered with age	**Country Clubs** • Retired senior execs • Admire old money
Middle Money (upper middle, benefiting from optimism of times but nowhere near rich)	**Generation Gap** • Biggest participants of mass to class • Aspire to values, trends and wealth of upper tiers		**New American Dreamers** • Leverage credit to maintain luxury lifestyle • Price sensitive	**Shuffleboarders** • Insecure about money • Least responsive to luxury brands

In Japan, where consumers 65 and older will soon account for 20 percent of the population, companies are marketing such age-specific goods and services as a health-monitoring talking robot cat and home nursing services.[107]

Other marketers are introducing products and campaigns specifically for the mature market. For instance, chic reading glasses appeal to fashion-conscious seniors, and Johnson & Johnson's Rx Cream fights face wrinkles.[108] Hoping to capitalize on nostalgia, the maker of Burma Shave shaving cream is reviving its well-known roadside advertising signs (originally from the 1930s and 1940s).[109] And firms like Merrill Lynch and T. Rowe Price are offering financial services and products specifically designed to help seniors manage their retirement money.[110]

Many mature consumers have an active lifestyle and buy leisure-based products and services such as educational seminars, travel, and sporting goods. Grandparents spend as much as $30 billion on clothing, toys, and other goods and services for their grandchildren.[111] After years of being criticized for targeting young consumers, makers of beer and wine are taking aim at over-50 drinkers.[112] Offerings whose value lies in a heavy future orientation, however, are not good prospects for the elderly market.[113] Finally, because mature consumers are more likely to resist new products, new offerings should focus on needs rather than on newness.[114]

Specialized marketing communications. Seniors perceive advertisements with positive older role models as more credible than those with younger models.[115] Nevertheless, because American society is considered a youth culture, seniors are more likely to be painted in an unfavorable light than younger consumers and are less likely to appear in ads, a situation that is changing over time.[116] This negative image is probably why mature consumers tend to have a more negative attitude toward ads than younger consumers have. Thus, when advertising to mature consumers, models should be depicted as active, contributing members of society, rather than helpless dependents (see Exhibit 15.10). Mature consumers tend to favor information-oriented messages over imagery. However, marketers should keep messages simple and focus on a few important attributes when targeting this segment.

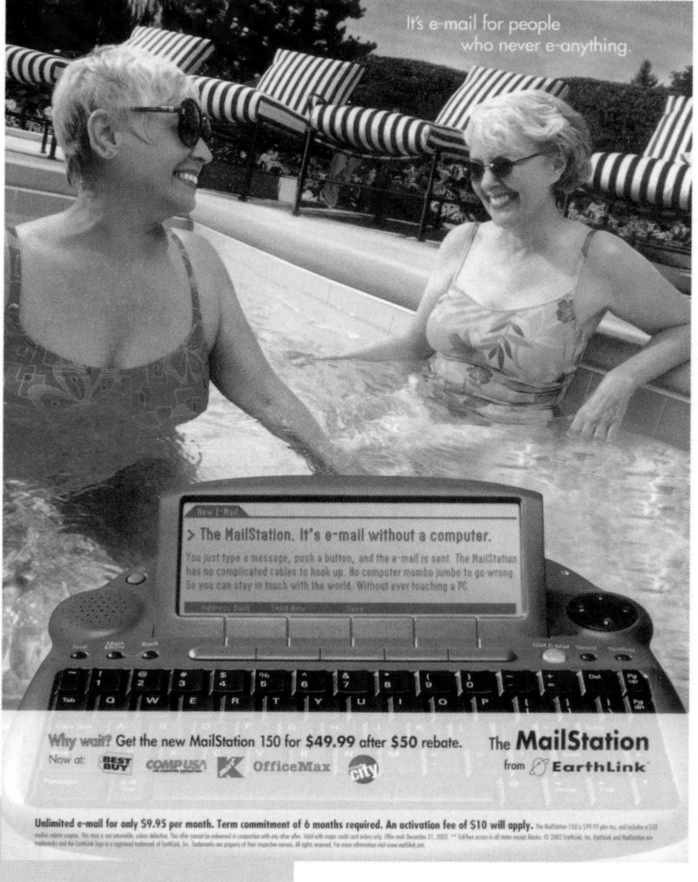

It's e-mail for people
who never e-anything.
New E-Mail
> The MailStation. It's e-mail without a computer.
You just type a message, push a button, and the e-mail is sent. The MailStation has no complicated cables to hook up. No computer mumbo jumbo to go wrong. So you can stay in touch with the world. Without ever touching a PC.
Why wait? Get the new MailStation 150 for $49.99 after $50 rebate.
Now at: BEST BUY COMPUSA OfficeMax city
The MailStation from EarthLink
Unlimited e-mail for only $9.95 per month. Term commitment of 6 months required. An activation fee of $10 will apply.

EXHIBIT 15.10
Image of Older Consumers
Consumers over the age of 50 take offense at being depicted as old. They prefer messages that show them leading active lifestyles, such as this ad for The MailStation.

Source: Courtesy of EarthLink.

Although mature consumers favor programs on public television, CNN, and premium pay cable, they may have more difficulty processing TV messages because of deteriorating processing skills.[117] Marketers can accommodate this condition by making messages bigger, louder, or slower. Mature consumers also tend to be avid readers of both newspapers and magazines, particularly those that focus on news, business, travel, and financial matters. As a result, marketers can reach seniors through this media, including targeted magazines such as *More* (for women), and the Internet (more than 36 percent of consumers between 50 and 64 own a computer and this number is increasing). Further, these consumers spend more time on the Internet than other groups, partly because they have more leisure time.[118]

Specialized sales techniques and promotions. Retailers can design their outlets to provide a more age-friendly shopping environment with features such as easier-to-read labels, comfortable seating, well-lighted parking lots, and shelving arranged so customers do not have to bend.[119] Given the difficulty that seniors have in remembering information, marketers can provide point-of-purchase materials to help this segment make buying decisions. In addition, seniors appreciate convenience, service, feelings of safety, good value, and knowledgeable employees.

Companies are also tailoring their sales techniques to the needs of mature consumers. CSC Insurance Marketing Systems, for example, developed a training program called Selling to Seniors to help its salespeople learn about this market, generate sales leads, perform a needs analysis, and manage customers.[120] Note, however, that because older consumers who seek social interaction from telemarketing calls may not recognize fraudulent offers, consumer education can help this segment avoid being victimized by scams (as discussed in Chapter 20).[121]

Finally, many marketers use special promotions such as senior citizen discounts to attract and retain mature customers. Some seniors are heavy users of these discounts and take advantage of them in many product and service categories.[122] Senior discounts are more effective with the gray market because young again consumers want to avoid showing their age. As an example of a special promotion not involving discounts, Kraft has targeted the senior segment with a joint promotion for Bran Flakes, Maxwell House decaffeinated coffee, and sugar-free Jell-O.[123] ●

HOW GENDER AND SEXUAL ORIENTATION AFFECT CONSUMER BEHAVIOR

Clearly males and females can differ in traits, attitudes, and activities that can affect consumer behavior. Because complete coverage of the many contrasts between men and women is beyond the scope of this text, the following sections will discuss just a few issues that have been the focus of consumer research.

agentic goals Goals that stress mastery, self-efficacy, strength, and assertiveness; characterized as being emotionless.

Sex Roles Have Changed

In most cultures, men and women are expected to behave according to sex-role norms learned very early in childhood. Until recently, males in Western society were expected to be strong, assertive, the primary breadwinner, and emotionless, and were guided by **agentic goals** that stress mastery, self-assertiveness, and self-efficacy.[124] Women, on the other hand, have been guided more by **communal goals** of forming affiliations and fostering harmonious relations with others and have been expected to be relatively submissive, emotional, and home oriented. Remember, however, that these are only general tendencies, subject to considerable individual variation.

On a very general level, men tend to be more competitive, independent, externally motivated, and willing to take risks.[125] In contrast, women tend to be cooperative, interdependent, intrinsically motivated, and risk averse. Men are more apt to derive pleasure from contact sports, hunting, fishing, and working on mechanical tasks, whereas women are more likely to enjoy arts and activities that foster strong social ties.

Over time, however, both female and male roles have been evolving. In particular, many more U.S. women are delaying both marriage and child-bearing in favor of building a career, many times in occupations that were traditionally male dominated, such as management, engineering, and law. Census statistics show that women account for 53 percent of the workforce in the United States.[126] This increase has led to changes in family structure and in women's attitudes in general.

Many women, particularly feminists who are younger and better educated, are placing an increasing value on independence and freedom to do what they want.[127] This factor explains the higher number of women taking vacations by themselves and women's increased rejection of traditional roles related to submissiveness, homemaking, and sexual inhibition. As a result, women have made faster gains in their standard of living in the last two decades than in earlier decades.[128] Further, there are relatively few differences between men and women who engage in the same activities (skateboarding, tennis, and so on), illustrating how roles are changing.[129] The ad in Exhibit 15.11 reflects this trend.

Traditional sex roles are changing in many countries, even those that are very conservative and male dominated. For example, in India, where arranged marriages are still the norm, women's attitudes toward careers, marriage, and the family are undergoing radical changes as more women build careers—especially in high-tech firms—and seek independence.[130] In Japan, where demure kimonos were once the rule, young working women in highly revealing fashions have been

EXHIBIT 15.11
Advertising Appeal Based on Changing Sex Roles
Over time women have been increasingly rejecting traditional roles related to inhibition and submissiveness in favor of those that stress independence and assertiveness. The ad shown here reflects this trend.

Source: Courtesy of Twin Labortories, Inc.

communal goals Goals that stress affiliation and fostering harmonious relations with others; characterized as being submissive, emotional, and home oriented.

flocking to night spots and dance clubs, reflecting a new attitude and challenge to traditional, conservative norms.[131]

Men's sex roles and attitudes have also been changing. In dual-career families, some husbands are assuming greater responsibility for household tasks and child rearing, although a significant number still fail to do their share. Men are now learning that they can express their emotions, be more sensitive, and be more caring and loving fathers. In light of this trend, a Finnish firm developed a "daddy kit" with everything from a tape measure and diaper-changing mat to books on cooking, child care, and songs.[132] An ad for McDonald's in Japan that showed a man doting over his children was surprisingly popular in a country where fathers are most often portrayed as remote corporate warriors.[133]

Note, however, that sex roles and appropriate behavior are dictated by society and may vary from one culture to another. In the United States, for example, some men feel uncomfortable hugging each other, whereas in European and Latin societies such behavior is widely accepted, often as a greeting. In France men kiss each other on the cheek. In certain Muslim countries, the very strict sex roles allow women few rights and require that they be completely covered and kept out of view.

Gender and Sexual Orientation

gender Biological state of being male or female.

sexual orientation A person's preference toward certain masculine or feminine behaviors.

A distinction must be made between gender and sexual orientation. **Gender** refers to a biological state (male or female), whereas **sexual orientation** reflects a person's preference toward certain behaviors. *Masculine* individuals (whether male or female) tend to display male-oriented traits, and *feminine* individuals tend toward female characteristics. In addition, some individuals can be *androgynous,* having both male and female traits. These sexual orientations are important because they can influence an individual's preferences and behavior. For example, women who are more masculine tend to prefer ads that depict nontraditional women.[134]

Traditionally, many marketers used gender for segmenting and targeting consumers in markets such as children's toys. Starting in the 1980s, cultural shifts resulted in a trend toward gender-neutral marketing of toys. In recent years, however, marketers have reverted to gender targeting because research showed preschool children were displaying distinctly male and female play patterns. As a result, Toys 'R' Us redesigned its stores to group toys by gender, and FoxFamily Channels launched separate digital cable channels for boys and girls.[135]

An increasing number of marketers are using sexual orientation to target gay and lesbian consumers for a wide range of products, from cars, beer, and furniture to vacations and greeting cards. In part, this is due to a dramatic rise in the number of same-sex U.S. households. According to Census Bureau statistics, the United States has more than 601,000 same-sex households (304,000 gay male couples and 297,000 lesbian couples), primarily in large metropolitan areas such as San Francisco and New York City.[136] Although gay and lesbian consumers tend to dislike and distrust ad messages more than heterosexual consumers, they are likely to respond to sexual orientation symbols in advertising, such as pink triangles and red AIDS ribbons, and to ads that "reflect their lives and culture."[137] They also respond to marketers and offers they perceive as gay friendly. For example, a Fleet bank ad showing a woman with her pregnant partner carried the copy, "The only aspect of your lifestyle that we're concerned about is improving it."[138]

Differences in Acquisition and Consumption Behaviors

Despite sex-role changes, men and women still exhibit a number of differences in their consumption behaviors. Females are more likely to engage in a detailed, thorough examination of an ad message and then make extended decisions based on product attributes (similar to high MAO decision making), whereas males are selective information processors, driven more by overall themes and simplifying heuristics (similar to low MAO decision making).[139] Males tend to be more sensitive to personally relevant information (consistent with agentic goals), and women pay attention to both personally relevant information and information relevant to others (consistent with communal goals).[140]

Whereas men are more likely to use specific hemispheres of their brain for certain tasks (the right side of the brain for visual and the left side for verbal), women use both hemispheres of their brain for most tasks. Men also appear to be more sensitive to trends in positive emotions experienced during consumption, such as feeling enthusiastic, interested, active, strong, and proud, whereas women display a tendency for negative emotions, such as feeling scared, upset, distressed, and nervous.[141] In addition, men and women differ in the symbolic meaning they attach to products and services.[142] Women are more likely to have shared brand stereotypes for fashion goods, whereas men are more consistent in their images of automobiles.

Men also tend to have more positive attitudes toward and higher involvement with high-tech products than women do.[143] Men are more likely to base decisions on software, prior experience, and reputation, whereas price is more critical for women. During the decision process, men are more likely to consult computer magazines and rely on prior knowledge. In contrast, women use the shopping experience as the primary means of collecting information.

In general, females in the United States enjoy shopping more than males do and see it as a pleasurable, stimulating activity and a way of obtaining social interaction. Men, on the other hand, view shopping in functional terms—as a way of acquiring goods—and regard it as a chore, especially if they hold traditional sex-role stereotypes. These differences extend to holiday gift shopping and garage sales, where men are less likely than women are to get involved and participate.[144] These patterns also hold true in other countries such as Turkey and the Netherlands.

Finally, men and women tend to exhibit different eating patterns. In particular, women are more likely to engage in **compensatory eating**—making up for deficiencies such as lack of social contact or depression by eating.[145]

compensatory eating Making up for lack of social contact or depression by eating.

MARKETING IMPLICATIONS Obviously, many products such as underwear, clothing, and shoes for men, and pantyhose, clothing, shoes, and feminine hygiene products for women, are developed to meet gender-specific needs. In addition, certain products and services appear to be sex-typed or perceived as more appropriate for one gender than the other. A tie, motorcycle, gun, tool kit, and scotch are perceived as more masculine, whereas a food processor, hand lotion, and wine are seen as more feminine.

Note, however, that products may become less sex-typed as sex roles evolve. For example, Charles Schwab and other financial services firms are specifically targeting female investors.[146] More women have started buying Harley-Davidson motorcycles, long a bastion of masculinity.[147] Because 41 percent of the primary decision makers for interior design are female, Glidden introduced Dulux paints with more colorful and stylish packaging to attract this market.[148]

Targeting a specific gender. Marketers often target a particular gender. Here are only a few of many examples: HerInteractive targets girls for its line of Nancy Drew computer games.[149] A Diamond Club campaign encourages women to buy diamonds for themselves—an approach also used by De Beers in China, South Korea, and Taiwan, where women are increasingly buying their own jewelry.[150] In Great Britain, Shell Oil sponsored Women's Workshops to teach women how to perform routine car maintenance. To appeal to men, Halston introduced a cologne, Catalyst, with packages in the shape of test tubes and flasks and the slogan "Boys like to experiment."[151] Interestingly, although the United States is the largest market for men's cologne, men in France, Germany, Britain, Italy, Spain, and Japan all spend more on average for this product.[152] Cosmetics firms have succeeded in getting Japanese males to be more concerned about personal care to the point of tweezing eyebrows and pampering their skin.[153]

In line with changing sex roles, ads are depicting more modern images for both men and women. Men are increasingly shown in emotional and caring roles, whereas women are appearing more frequently in important situations and professional positions. A study of magazine ads found a similar trend in Japan as well.[154]

Some companies have found that "cause marketing" focusing on critical women's and family issues such as domestic violence, rape, breast cancer, AIDS, and children's welfare, is a particularly effective way to reach women.[155] The Lifetime channel was a hit among women with its support for and shows about fighting breast cancer, for example. Also, the Boyds Collection has marketed collectible figurines and stuffed animals to benefit the Starlight Children's Foundation.[156]

Media patterns. Although sex roles are changing, sex differences still exist in media patterns. Marketers can reach men through certain TV programs, especially sports, and magazines such as *Sports Illustrated, GQ, Esquire,* and car and motorcycle publications. Women are more likely than men to watch soap operas and home shopping networks.[157] For example, in selling soap, Lever Brothers advertises to reach women during daytime soap operas, whereas late-night airings are used to reach a more male-oriented audience. Magazines such as *Vogue, Ladies Home Journal, Good Housekeeping, InStyle,* and *Allure* (noted for its hard-nosed reporting about beauty-related issues) target women.[158] The Lifetime channel, has created television shows specifically to attract young females.[159] To appeal to different types of female fitness enthusiasts, Nike placed ads in *Outside* magazine for walking and running shoes and in *Shape* magazine for aerobics shoes. *Sports* and *Jump* magazines were created for women who like sports.[160] *Mode* magazine was created for full-figured professional women with fashion spreads featuring "real" women in clothes they can actually wear, and *More* magazine is aimed at women over 40 and is billed as "smart talk for smart women."[161]

Online retailers are actively designing their sites to attract women Web surfers.[162] For example, *HomeArts* provides a large collection of shopping links aimed at women, and the Victoria's Secret Web site, which sells women's lingerie, attracts a number of men along with the main female audience.[163] In addition, companies like Procter & Gamble and Unilever are launching many brand-specific sites as they target women for soaps, diapers, and other products.[164]

Targeting gay and lesbian consumers. Marketers can reach this market through promotions at events like gay pride parades, ads in targeted magazines such as *Out* and *The Advocate*, specialized Web sites, billboards in select neighborhoods, and—increasingly—television commercials depicting same-sex couples.[165] Bud Light, for example, has sponsored San Francisco's Folsom Street Fair and advertised in *San Francisco Frontiers* magazine.[166] Some Subaru billboards and bus ads show cars bearing the symbol of the gay advocacy group Human Rights Campaign.[167] Saab targets same-sex parents with ads in gay magazines depicting a station wagon with the headline, "A safe car for your children proves to be a fun car for you." In openly targeting gay and lesbian consumers, however, Bud and other marketers have become targets for conservative groups and religious leaders opposed to homosexuality.[168] ●

HOW THE HOUSEHOLD INFLUENCES CONSUMER BEHAVIOR

Some researchers argue that the household is the most important unit of analysis for consumer behavior because many more acquisition, consumption, and disposition decisions are made by households than by individuals. This section defines families and households and examines the different types of households. After exploring some of the major trends that are changing household structure and consumer behavior, the chapter ends with a discussion of how families influence decision making and consumption.

Types of Households

nuclear family Father, mother, and children.

extended family The nuclear family plus relatives such as grandparents, aunts, uncles, and cousins.

A *family* is usually defined as a group of individuals living together who are related by marriage, blood, or adoption. The most typical unit is the **nuclear family**, consisting of a father, mother, and children. The **extended family** consists of the nuclear family plus relatives such as grandparents, aunts, uncles, and cousins. Nearly 4 million U.S. families have three or more generations of parents living with children and grandchildren.[169] In the United States we most often think of *family* in terms of the nuclear family, whereas in many other countries the extended family is the defining unit.

Although the family is important almost everywhere in the world, some countries and cultures exhibit a stronger family orientation than others. In Japan and China, for example, the family is a focal point, and most people feel a very strong sense of obligation to it.[170] The same is true among Latin Americans and U.S. Hispanics.

household A single person living alone or a group of individuals who live together in a common dwelling, regardless of whether they are related.

Household is a broader term that includes a single person living alone or a group of individuals who live together in a common dwelling, regardless of whether they are related. This term includes cohabiting couples (an unmarried male and female living together), gay couples, and singles who are roommates. Because the number of households is on the rise—increasing by 1.35 million each year—marketers and researchers are increasingly thinking in terms of households rather than families.[171]

The traditional stereotype of the American family consisted of a husband as the primary wage earner, a wife who was a non-wage earner at home, and two children under the age of 18. Yet only 6 percent of families fit this profile. Trends such as later marriages, cohabitation, divorce, dual careers, boomerang children, greater longevity, and a lower birth rate have greatly increased the proportion of nontraditional families.[172] The trend of baby boomers settling down has slowed the decrease in married families with children.[173] However, the number of single-parent households headed by women has increased three times faster than the number of two-parent households.[174] Furthermore, 29 percent of all U.S. households consist of married couples without children (because of a conscious choice to have none or because the children have left home).[175] Exhibit 15.12 shows how the types and proportions of households are expected to change over the next few years.

	2000 number	2000 percent	2010 number	2010 percent	2000-2010 percent change
All households	**110,140**	**100.0 %**	**117,696**	**100.0 %**	**6.9 %**
Families	**77,705**	**70.6**	**80,193**	**68.1**	**3.2**
Married couples	60,969	55.4	61,266	52.1	0.5
with children younger than 18*	24,286	22.1	23,433	19.9	–3.5
with children 18+ only	5,318	4.8	6,884	5.8	29.4
with no children	31,365	28.5	30,950	26.3	–1.3
Single fathers	1,523	1.4	1,660	1.4	9.0
Single mothers	7,473	6.8	7,779	6.6	4.1
Other families	7,741	7.0	9,488	8.1	22.6
Nonfamilies	**32,434**	**29.4**	**37,503**	**31.9**	**18.0**
Men living alone	10,898	9.9	12,577	10.7	15.4
Women living alone	16,278	14.8	18,578	15.8	14.1
Other nonfamilies	5,258	4.8	6,347	5.4	20.7

* Includes those with children both younger than age 18 and 18 and older.
Note: Numbers in thousands and percent of all households by type, 2000-2010; and percent change 2000-2010.
Numbers may not add to total due to rounding.

EXHIBIT 15.12
Changes in Household Types

Over the next decade, the profile of the U.S. family will change dramatically. In particular, the proportion of nontraditional families (singles living alone, couples without children, divorced families) is on the rise. As a result, the proportion of families that fit the typical stereotype of husband, wife, and two children is diminishing. Here are some specific projections for each type of household.

Source: Adapted from Joe Schwartz, "Family Traditions: Although Radically Changed, the American Family Is as Strong as Ever," *American Demographics*, March 1987, p. 9. American Demographics, 1987. Reprinted with permission.

family life cycle
Different stages of family life depending on the age of the parents and how many children are living at home.

Households can further differ in terms of the **family life cycle.** As shown in Exhibit 15.13, families can be characterized in terms of the age of the parents and how many children are living at home.[176] Thus families progress from the bachelor stage (young and single) through marriage and having children to being an older couple without children at home. Households may also consist of unmarried singles, couples without children (younger and older), and older couples who delay having children. Various changes such as death or divorce can alter household structure by, for instance, creating single-parent households. The many arrows in the exhibit illustrate how households can change over time.

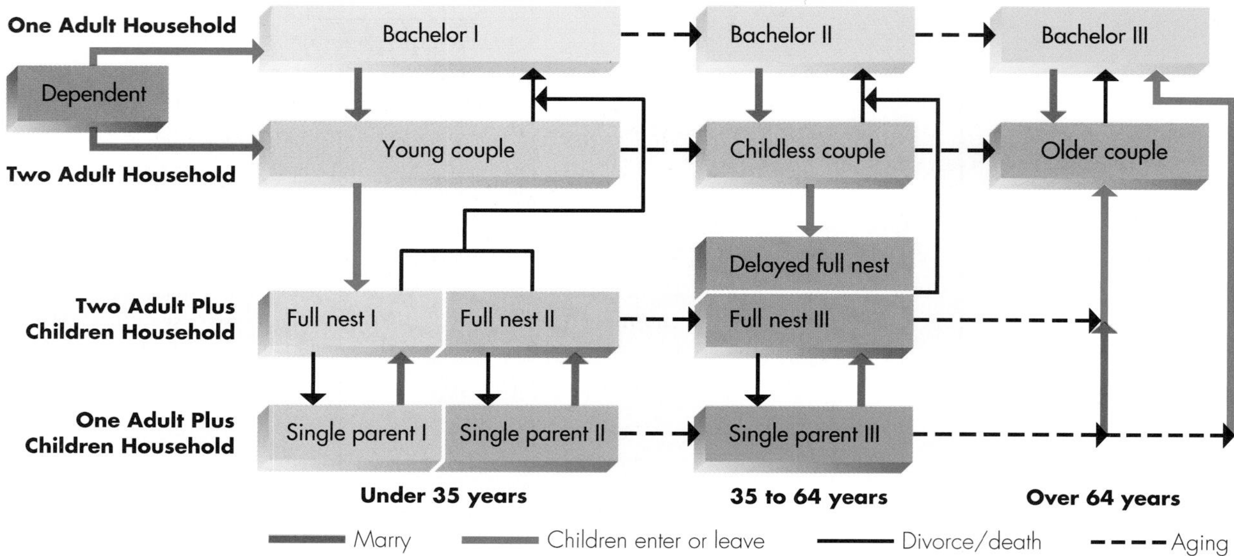

EXHIBIT 15.13
The Family Life Cycle

This chart depicts the varied ways in which families change and mature. Each box represents a stage in the family life cycle, and each line represents a type of change (marriage, divorce, death, children entering or leaving, aging). For example, a typical path might start in bachelorhood and continue through marriage (young couple), having children who then grow up (the three stages of full nest), being an older couple (children living on their own), and being a solitary survivor (one spouse dies). Note that this diagram accounts for other events that can occur (divorce, becoming a single parent, being a childless couple, never marrying). What stage is your family in right now?

Source: Mary C. Gilly and Ben M. Enis, "Recycling the Family Lifecycle," in ed. Andrew A. Michell, *Advances in Consumer Research,* vol. 9 (Ann Arbor, Mich.: Association for Consumer Research, 1982), pp. 271–276. Reprinted by permission.

Households are important to marketers because their needs vary greatly. In general, spending increases as households shift from young singles to young married and then remains high until it falls sharply at the older married or older single stages.[177] However, this pattern depends on what is purchased. New parents tend to spend more on health care, clothing, housing, and food and less on alcohol, transportation, and education. As parents age, they spend more on housing, home maintenance, furnishings, child care, and other household services. Young empty nesters spend more on vehicles, women's clothes, and long-distance telephone services. Older single households and couples increase spending on home-based products, health care, and travel. The affluent gay market is more likely to spend on travel, clothing, and the arts. Finally, households in the midst of a life cycle change are more likely to switch brand preferences and be more receptive to marketing efforts.[178]

These stages do not capture all types of households. Notably missing are same-sex couples and never-married single mothers, both of which are important market segments. Gays and lesbians, for example, represent anywhere from 11 to 23 million consumers in the United States and are relatively affluent and highly educated.[179] In addition, more than 4 million women are never-married mothers between 15 and 44 years old.[180] The largest proportion are teenagers at lower income levels.

Many households consider their pets to be important family members. In the United States more than 60 percent of families own pets, including more than 59 million dogs, 75 million cats, 25 million birds, 250 million fish, and 125 million other animals. Pet owners wield considerable economic power: these households—mostly married couples with no children under 18 years old—spend more than $23 billion a year on pet-related goods and services.[181] Some consumers buy pet mansions, give their pets greeting cards, and dress their pets for holidays.[182]

Animals are an important source of companionship and can even be social facilitators. In Sweden, for example, 83 percent of owners believe that their animals give them the opportunity to talk to other people. In Germany dogs are held in such high regard that they are allowed to accompany their owners into restaurants. Many consumers view animals as surrogate siblings or children (owners can experience what it is like to have children in a limited way). Pets may even be incorporated into family rituals. One study found, for example, that 30 percent of owners celebrated their pet's birthday.

Changing Trends in Household Structure

Five main factors have altered the basic structure and characteristics of households. These include (1) delayed marriage, (2) cohabitation, (3) dual careers, (4) divorce, and (5) smaller families.

Delayed Marriage In many Western societies, an increasing number of individuals are either delaying or avoiding getting married. As evidence, the proportion of never-married U.S. citizens aged 30 to 34 has risen 9.4 percent for men and 6.2 percent for women since 1970, and the proportion of married couples under 25 has decreased in the United States by more then one-third since 1980.[183] For many, careers have become more important than marriage. Because it is now more acceptable for a man and a woman to live together before marriage, many do not see an immediate need to enter into a long-term marital commitment. Nearly 26 percent of all U.S. households, or 27.2 million people, consist of people living alone, and this number is expected to rise during the decade ahead.[184]

The trend toward delayed marriage is important for marketers because single-person households exhibit unique consumption patterns. For example, single men spend more on alcohol, new cars, restaurant meals, clothes, and education than married men do. Essentially, this group consists of college students and "older men (divorced or never married) living like college students." Compared with married women, single women tend to spend more on new cars, shoes, entertainment, candy, and housing (to live in a safe area).[185] Finally, single men are more likely than married ones to give gifts of jewelry, watches, and clothes, whereas single women are more likely than married women to give housewares and small appliances.

By delaying marriage a few years, couples typically find themselves in a better financial position, with greater discretionary income for designer baby clothes, housekeeping services, and high-quality furniture. Parents over 35 with children under 6 spend more than younger parents do on housing, home maintenance, furnishings, child care, transportation, food, and alcohol. In addition, when couples delay marriage, they also delay having children, which has led to an increase in the use of fertility drugs and the incidence of twins and triplets.[186]

Cohabitation As a result of changing social norms, more and more consumers are deciding to live with members of the opposite sex outside marriage. Among the 5 million opposite-sex households, more than half have never been married. Most of the cohabitors (38 percent) are aged 25 to 34, and 20 percent are aged 35 to 44.[187] The highest percentage of unmarried couples living together is in Sweden.

A defining aspect of unmarried couples (compared with married couples) is the tendency of the partners to be more self-oriented. They tend to view possessions as personal rather than joint items and leave open the possibility that the relationship may break down.[188] Identifying possessions as belonging to one or the other protects each person if the relationship ends. In some cases, each partner has his or her own room that contains only that person's items.

Nevertheless, unmarried partners often share expenses, and because both individuals are likely to work, they often have higher discretionary income than married couples of a similar age (with a nonworking spouse). Unmarried couples are therefore more frequent consumers of entertainment, transportation, and vacations than are married couples.

Dual-Career Families The increasing number of dual-career families has had a dramatic impact on household behavior. In general, the two major types of dual-career families are: (1) those in which the woman is concerned about career advancement and personal fulfillment and (2) those in which the woman works out of financial necessity and considers her employment "just a job."[189] The latter group tends to be more like the traditional housewife in terms of outlook and behavior, whereas the former group is more contemporary and progressive.

Dual-career families have several important implications for consumer behavior. First, having two incomes increases discretionary spending.[190] One study found that dual-career families spend more than other families do on child care, eating out, and services in general. Likewise, dual careers mean that the wife is bringing more financial resources to the family, thereby giving her greater clout in influencing family decisions for expensive or important products and services such as vacations, cars, and housing.

Second, the increased burden of having both career and family, or role overload, leaves less time for many activities including cooking, housekeeping, and shopping.[191] This is why dual-career families particularly value products and services that save time, such as microwavable dinners, instant foods, housekeeping services, child care, and fast food, including food delivery services. Interestingly, full-time employment of married women is a major predictor of microwave oven purchases.[192] Because these women have limited shopping time, they are more likely to buy the same brands, be brand loyal, buy impulsively, and use catalogs.

Third, more husbands are taking on household responsibilities, including grocery shopping.[193] This trend is reflected in ads which are targeted to men who are, for example, sharing the responsibility for household cooking. In Asia, however, these ads received a negative response from both men and women because sex roles are viewed more traditionally, even though more men are handling more housework.

Divorce Since 1960, the divorce rate in the United States has more than doubled. Now more than four of every ten U.S. marriages is likely to end in divorce.[194] The trend has recently leveled off, but many divorces still occur each year, and these separations have important implications for consumer behavior. Going through a divorce represents a major transition in which consumers must perform a number of critical tasks—such as disposing of old possessions, forming a new household, and creating new patterns of consumption.[195] Divorce can lead to a major change in lifestyle, and acquiring products and services can be an integral part of forming a new identity and relieving stress during this transition. For example, a recently divorced consumer might buy a new house, car, furniture, or clothing; get a new hairstyle; or go to singles clubs to assume a new image or to feel better.

Divorce also influences household structure. First, if the couple was childless, the newly divorced often adopt many of the singles' acquisition and consumption patterns discussed earlier. However, these new singles are typically older and have greater discretionary income for housing, transportation, and clothing if they are working.

Second, divorce creates single-parent families when children are involved. Estimates are that one in three families in the United States now has only one parent, and most of these families have a female head-of-household, although the proportion of single fathers is growing.[196] These families are time pressured because the single parent must earn an income and raise children, which means convenient products or services—such as packaged or fast foods—are a necessity.[197] Compared with their married counterparts, single parents are likely to have lower than average incomes, spend relatively less on most things, and be renters rather than homeowners.

Finally, divorced individuals with children are remarrying with greater frequency, creating more stepfamilies.[198] Demographers estimate that more than one-third of U.S. families are of this type, and half of all current families will eventually become part of one or more stepfamilies in their lifetime. In nearly two-thirds of stepfamilies, children live with their biological mother, and many such families are lower in income and education and are more youthful than intact families. Due to potential stress and conflicting emotions, about half these families will also end up in divorce. The splintering of families has led some people to predict that members of Generation Y will rely more on friends than on family for emotional stability.[199]

Like other households, stepfamilies can have unique consumption needs. For example, children who travel between families require duplicate supplies of clothes, toothbrushes, and toys.[200] Stepfamilies often plan their vacations around custody considerations.

Smaller Families In many countries the average household size is getting smaller. In particular, boomer and Xer couples are having fewer children because of dual careers, financial burdens, and concern for overpopulation—some couples believe that having more than two children is socially irresponsible. The average family size in the United States is now 3.14 people.[201]

In terms of consumer behavior, smaller family size means consumers have greater discretionary income to spend on recreational items, vacations, education, toys, and entertainment. Smaller families can also spend more on each child. The trend toward smaller families has been key in Japan where parents with fewer children are spending more on education, cultural activities, and colorful clothing.[202] In China one-child families are the rule, as mentioned at the beginning of the chapter, so parents spare no expense in bringing up baby.[203] China is therefore a very attractive market for makers of baby-care products.

Childless married couples are one of the fastest growing types of households. For obvious reasons these households have more discretionary income than other households. Compared with couples who have children, childless couples spend more on food, restaurant meals, entertainment, liquor, clothing, and pets.[204] This trend does not mean that there will be few births in the future. Rather, the baby boomlet will lead to a slight increase in the number of babies born during the next 10 years, which is good news for the makers of children's clothing and toys.

MARKETING IMPLICATIONS Marketers are now recognizing the importance of nontraditional households and are developing offerings that cater to their unique needs. For example, Charles Schwab is targeting single women with ads for its brokerage services that feature the famous divorced mother Sarah Ferguson.[205] Products and services that offer convenience can be marketed specifically to dual-career and divorced households. In Japan, sales of larger American refrigerators are increasing because more women work and can't shop for food daily.[206] In the United States, Procter & Gamble has created ads for Tide that feature adopted children.[207]

Because more husbands from dual-career families and men who are divorced or single are doing more grocery and other types of shopping, retailers are increasingly targeting men.[208] Wives in dual-career households have more clout in expensive decisions, so marketers of costly products and services must appeal to both husband and wife. And in recognition of nontraditional families, Hallmark has developed greeting cards that deal with step-family and cohabitation relationships.[209] •

ROLES THAT HOUSEHOLD MEMBERS PLAY

A key aspect of households is that more than one individual can become involved in acquisition and consumption. This final section discusses various aspects of household consumer behavior, with particular emphasis on **household decision roles** and how household members influence decision processes.

household decision roles Roles that different members play in a household decision.

In a multiperson household, members may perform a variety of tasks or roles in acquiring and consuming a product or service:

- *Gatekeeper.* Household members who collect and control information important to the decision.
- *Influencer.* Household members who try to express their opinions and influence the decision.
- *Decider.* The person or persons who actually determine which product or service will be chosen.
- *Buyer.* The household member who physically acquires the product or service.
- *User.* The household members who consume the product.

Each role can be performed by different household members and by a single individual, subset of individuals, or the entire household. For example, in deciding which DVD to rent, parents might decide on the movie, but the children may play a role, either directly (by stating their preferences) or indirectly (when parents keep their children's likes in mind). One parent may actually go to the store to get the DVD, but the entire family may watch (or consume) it.

In fact, parents are often the deciders and purchasers of items consumed by their children such as clothing, toys, food, and movies. Pull-Ups disposable training pants (Exhibit 15.14) are an example of such a product. Similarly, more than

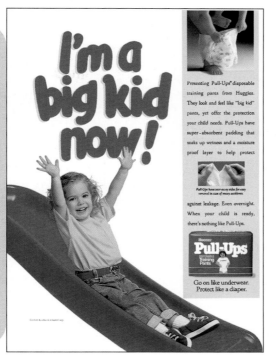

EXHIBIT 15.14
Marketing to Parents and Children
Although young children are the users or consumers of many products and services, parents are usually the deciders of what to purchase. This ad tries to convince parents who have "bigger kids" that Pull-Ups training pants are a beneficial product. Note also, however, that if children this age saw this ad, they might find it appealing because they would think that "I'm a big kid now."

Source: Used with permission of Kimberly-Clark Corporation.

70 percent of men's underwear and fragrance is purchased by wives and girlfriends. On the other hand, children do influence many household decisions, including the choice of radio station when the entire family is listening.[210] Exhibit 15.15 divides household purchases into nine categories, depending on the decision maker and the user.

Household decision roles can be **instrumental**, meaning that they relate to tasks affecting the buying decision, such as when and how much to purchase. Roles can also be **expressive**, which means they indicate family norms such as choice of color or style.[211] Traditionally, the husband fulfilled the instrumental role and the wife the expressive role, but sex-role changes are altering this pattern. Women, for example, are now involved in 65 percent of decisions about buying the household's first computer.[212]

instrumental roles Roles that relate to tasks affecting the buying decision.

expressive roles Roles that involve an indication of family norms.

Conflict can often occur in fulfilling different household roles based on (1) the reasons for buying, (2) who should make the decision, (3) which option to choose, and (4) who gets to use the product or service.[213] For example, because all family members have increased their computer usage, conflict often arises over who gets to use the computer and for how long.[214]

In general, households can resolve conflicts through problem solving, persuasion, bargaining, and politics, although persuasion and problem solving appear to be most frequently used.[215] Note, however, that resolution is often not systematic and rational, but rather a "muddling-through" process in which the household makes a series of small decisions to arrive at a solution.[216] Moreover, many households avoid conflict rather than confront it.

Marketers should recognize that household decisions are more frequent in some circumstances than in others. Specifically, joint decisions are more likely when the perceived risk associated with the decision is high, the decision is very important, there is ample time to make a decision, and the household is young. In addition, household members can influence each other in terms of brand preferences and loyalties, information search patterns, media reliance, and price sensitivities.[217]

The Roles of Spouses

Husbands and wives play different roles in making decisions, and the nature of their influence depends on both the product or service and the couple's relationship. In examining husband-wife influence, a landmark study conducted in Belgium (and replicated in the United States) identified four major categories of decisions:[218]

EXHIBIT 15.15

Buyers and Users

Household purchase decisions can be made by one, some, or all members of the family. Acquired products and services can then be consumed by one, some, or all members. Here is an example of three cells that result from crossing these two factors. Can you think of examples that would fit into the other six cells?

Source: Robert Boutilier, "Pulling the Family's Strings," *American Demographics*, August 1993, pp. 44–48. American Demographics © 1993. Reprinted with permission.

A Consumer \ A Purchase Decision Maker	One member	Some members	All members
One member	1	2 Tennis racket	3
Some members	4 Sugar Pops	5	6
All members	7	8	9 Refrigerator

For Example:

1. Mom and Dad go to buy a new tennis racket for Mom. Dad advises Mom on her purchase. Some members are decision makers and one member is a consumer: cell 2.
2. Mom goes to the grocery store to buy Sugar Pops cereal for her children. She'll never eat the stuff. One member is a decision maker and some members are consumers: cell 4.
3. Mom, Dad, and the kids go to the department store to buy a refrigerator. All members are decision makers and all are consumers: cell 9.

husband-dominant decision Decision made primarily by the male head-of-household.

wife-dominant decision Decision made primarily by the female head-of-household.

autonomic decision Decision equally likely to be made by the husband or wife, but not by both.

syncratic decision Decision made jointly by the husband and wife.

- A **husband-dominant decision** is made primarily by the male head-of-household (e.g., the purchase of lawn mowers and hardware).
- A **wife-dominant decision** is made primarily by the female head-of-household (e.g., children's clothing, women's clothing, groceries, pots and pans, and toiletries).
- An **autonomic decision** is equally likely to be made by the husband or the wife, but not by both (e.g., men's clothing, luggage, toys and games, sporting equipment, stereos, and cameras).
- A **syncratic decision** is made jointly by the husband and wife (e.g., vacations, refrigerators, TVs, living room furniture, carpets, financial planning services, and the family car).

Interestingly, as spouses get nearer to a final decision, the process tends to move toward syncratic decision making and away from the other three types, particularly for more important decisions. These role structures are only general trends, however; the actual influence exerted depends on many factors. First, a spouse will have greater influence when the financial resources he or she brings to the family are higher and he or she has a high level of involvement in the decision.[219] Second, demographic factors, such as total family income, occupation, and education, are also related to the degree of husband-wife influence.[220] Combined, these factors provide a spouse with a perception of power in the decision-making situation. The higher the degree of perceived power, the more likely the spouse will exert influence.

When the family has a strong traditional sex-role orientation, certain tasks are stereotypically considered either masculine or feminine and more decisions tend to be husband-dominated than in less traditional families.[221] For example, Mexican American families tend to have a strong traditional orientation and are characterized by more husband-dominant decisions. Yet sex-role changes, as noted earlier, are influencing husband-wife decisions. In Thailand, for instance, nearly half of the husbands surveyed said they decided what foods their households would eat and they did the family food shopping, traditionally considered the wife's role.[222]

Researchers have found support for the four major patterns of spousal decision roles in a number of countries, although the United States, France, and the Netherlands exhibited a higher level of joint decision making than Venezuela and Gabon, where autonomous decisions were more prevalent.[223] A study of Russian families found that independent decisions occur in less than a quarter of households. The wife makes decisions on toiletries and household cleaning items, and husband dominance occurs only for household durables. Joint decision making is most likely for semidurable goods like small appliances and electronics. Furthermore, in many Latin American countries, husbands dominate most decisions. In the United States, joint decision making is most common among white families, husband dominance is more likely in Japanese American families, and wife dominance is more prevalent in black families.

bargaining A fair exchange of preferences.

concession Giving in on some points to get what one wants in other areas.

Researchers have examined other aspects of spousal decision making as well. For example, through the processes of **bargaining** (which involves a fair exchange) or **concession** (in which a spouse gives in on some points to get what he or she wants in other areas), couples tend to make equitable decisions that result from compromises.[224] Like household decision making, spousal decisions are often not made through a formal, systematic process. Instead, couples use an informal process in which they have limited awareness of each other's knowledge and decision strategy.[225] In fact, husbands and wives are generally not good at estimating their spouse's influence and preferences for products and services. In making these estimations, consumers tend to start with their own preference and adjust for what they think their spouse will like. Unfortunately, this strategy is accurate only when one spouse has actual knowledge of the other's preferences. Sometimes spouses even disagree on whether certain products have been purchased.

The Roles of Children

Children play an important role in household decisions by attempting to influence their parents' acquisition, usage, and disposition behavior. The most common stereotype is that children nag their parents until the adults finally give in. Research finds that although children often make these attempts, their success depends on the type of offering, characteristics of the parents, age of the child, and stage of the decision process.[226] Children are more likely to influence parents for child-related products such as cereals, cookies, candy, snacks, ice cream, and frozen pizza, as well as cars, vacations, and new computer technologies. This is why Hyatt, for example, offers Camp Hyatt with special kid-oriented menus and services.[227] More European families are buying U.S. breakfast cereal, which has never been part of their traditional breakfast, because the kids see TV ads and ask for the advertised cereals.[228] For clothing and toys, children often use the argument that "everyone else has one," and because parents do not want to be identified as "scrimpers," they will often give in.[229]

Interestingly, children consistently overestimate how much influence they have in most decisions.[230] Children tend to have less influence when parents are more involved in the decision process or are more traditional and conservative. Working and single parents, on the other hand, are more likely to give in because they face more time pressures.[231] When parents place more restrictions on TV watching, they tend to yield less, but children's attempts to influence parents increase as parents watch more TV with them.

Another important finding is that the older the child, the more influence he or she will exert.[232] Part of the reason is that younger children tend to have lower involvement in the decision process, and parents are more likely to refuse requests of younger children. As evidence, teens believe they have greater influence when the decision is important to them and the family. Older children also generate their own income, giving them more power.[233]

One study examined the strategies adolescents use in trying to influence parental and family decision making, which include bargaining (making deals), persuasion (trying to influence the decision in their favor), emotional appeals (using emotion to get what they want), and requests (directly asking).[234] Parents, in turn, can use not only the same strategies on their children but also expert (knowledge), legitimate (power), and directive (parental authority) strategies.

The type of household determines the nature of children's influence:

- Authoritarian households stress obedience.
- Neglectful households exert little control.
- Democratic households encourage self-expression.
- Permissive households remove constraints.

Children are more likely to have direct decision control in permissive and neglectful families and to influence decisions in democratic and permissive ones.[235] Also, children's influence varies at different stages of the decision process. It is greatest at the earliest stages of decision making (problem recognition and information search), and declines significantly in the evaluation and choice phases.[236] However, because three out of five parents take their children along when grocery shopping, children may have more influence over grocery purchases than over other purchases.

MARKETING IMPLICATIONS Marketers need to recognize that household decision roles exist and may be performed by different household members. Thus appealing only to deciders or purchasers may be a narrow and relatively ineffective strategy. Marketers who exclusively target children for toys or breakfast cereals, for example, ignore the fact that parents are usually influencers, deciders, and purchasers of these products. Similarly, marketers of men's underwear must take into account that women make the majority of decisions and purchases of these items. Therefore, marketers should determine which family members are involved in each acquisition decision and appeal to all important parties.

For example, many stores offer play areas and baby-sitting centers.[237] The theory is that if kids have fun at a particular store, they will influence their parents to shop there. Fleet Boston Financial Corp. created a FleetKids program, hoping to build early brand loyalty and influence family banking decisions.[238] As another example, Heinz created Funky Purple and Blastin' Green ketchup products to appeal to children.[239] Online marketers know that children use the Internet to send e-mail, play games, do homework, and shop. Older children are heavier Internet users in the United States and United Kingdom, whereas younger children are a major part of the online population in Spain and Italy.[240] Targeting this audience, some Web sites allow kids to shop online without credit cards by setting up special accounts with parental permission.[241] Web sites targeting children under 13 must comply with the Children's Online Privacy Protection Act and obtain parental permission before collecting information from children (see Chapters 20 and 21 for more on regulation and ethical issues).[242]

Marketers sometimes direct their efforts toward the entire family. Marriott offers home-style suites, and Hilton gives parents check-in folders with information about nearby children's attractions and stocks a lending desk with toys, games, and books.[243] Las Vegas has reshaped its image by offering more family-oriented entertainment such as magic acts, jousting tournaments, and horse shows.[244] Direct marketer Lillian Vernon created a special Lilly's Kids catalog of toys and accessories which children and parents can page through together.[245] ●

Household Decision Making versus Household Consumption Behavior

Most of the research mentioned in this chapter focused rather narrowly on decision making. However, more study is needed to better understand the variety of events and processes that can occur when households consume products and services.

To illustrate what consumption patterns can reveal, one study examined how a family used a VCR and its effect on family interactions.[246] Soon after the VCR was purchased, it became the center of family togetherness because it was the basis of a family night for watching movies. The family treated this activity as a major event that dad controlled (as the holder of the remote control). After several months, however, family members became more fragmented in their interests, and individual members began using the VCR for their own needs. Adolescents watched teen movies as a way of identifying with important social or peer groups; the parents watched old movies to bring back memories or teen movies to help them communicate with their children. This example shows how studying consumption patterns can help marketers learn more about the way families communicate and interact.

SUMMARY

Age, gender, and household play important roles in consumer behavior. Age is a key factor because people of the same age have similar life experiences, needs, symbols, and memories that may lead to similar consumption patterns. Teens, who need to establish an identity, are the consumers of tomorrow and have an increasing influence on family decisions. The somewhat disillusioned Generation X consists of smart and cynical young consumers who see through obvious marketing attempts. Baby boomers grew up in a very dynamic and fast-changing world, which affected their values, encouraging individualism and freedom. The 50 and older segment can be divided into two groups—the young again and the gray market. Neither group likes to be thought of as old.

Gender differences also affect consumer behavior. Sex roles are changing. More women are becoming financially independent and working as professionals, and men are learning to become more sensitive and caring. Men and women also differ in terms of consumer traits, information-processing styles, decision-making styles, and consumption patterns. In addition, more marketers are using sexual orientation to target gay and lesbian consumers for various goods and services.

Households include both families and unrelated people living together, as well as singles. The proportion of nontraditional households has increased because of factors such as (1) later marriages, (2) cohabitation, (3) dual-career families, (4) increased divorce, and (5) smaller families. Households exert considerable influence on acquisition and consumption patterns. First, household members can play different roles in the decision process (gatekeeper, influencer, decider, buyer, and user). Second, husbands and wives vary in their influence in the decision process, depending on whether the situation is husband dominant, wife dominant, autonomic, or syncratic. Third, children can influence the decision process by making requests of parents. The nature of this influence partly depends on whether the household is authoritarian, neglectful, democratic, or permissive. However, in general, the older the child, the greater the influence.

QUESTIONS FOR REVIEW AND DISCUSSION

1. What type of U.S. consumers are in the Generation X and baby boomer segments?
2. How have sex roles changed in recent years?
3. What is the difference between gender and sexual orientation, and why is this distinction important for marketers?
4. Define the nuclear family, extended family, and household.
5. What five main factors have altered the basic structure and characteristics of households?
6. What are the five tasks that some household member must perform in acquiring and consuming something?
7. What four major categories of decisions have researchers identified in relation to spouses?

EXERCISES

1. Pick a product or service category that individuals of all age groups consume. Conduct a detailed research analysis of the marketing techniques used to attract the four demographic segments discussed in this chapter in the following areas: (a) brands or services offered, (b) package design, (c) advertising content, (d) media selection, (e) sales promotion, and (f) distribution strategy. Collect this information via a library search, a content analysis of advertising messages and media used, in-store visits, and interviews with marketers. Then answer the following questions:
   a. Which techniques are used to market to multiple age groups?
   b. Which techniques are used to appeal to specific age groups? How do these techniques differ from age group to age group?
2. Conduct a detailed research analysis of the marketing techniques used to appeal to males and females in the following areas: (a) brands or services offered, (b) package design, (c) advertising content, (d) media selection, (e) sales promotion, and (f) distribution strategy. Collect this information in the same manner as described in exercise #1 and then answer the following questions:
   a. Which techniques are used to market to both males and females?
   b. Which specific techniques are used to appeal to males? to females?
3. Pick three products and services that households consume. Conduct an interview of individuals from five families, and ask them to provide a thorough description of the processes used to acquire, consume, and dispose of these products or services. Summarize this information by answering the following questions:
   a. Which specific roles do household members play in the decision process?
   b. What is the nature of husband-wife interaction in the decision?
   c. Which role do children play in the process?
   d. How do household consumption patterns for these products and services differ from individual consumption patterns?
   e. Who disposes of the products and services and why?

chapter 16

Social Influences on Consumer Behavior

INTRODUCTION: Pepsi and Ford Pass the Word on the Web

Pepsi-Cola has taken its long-time battle with Coca-Cola to the Web. Targeting teens in particular, who drink a lot of soft drinks and are heavy Internet users, Pepsi is offering exclusive previews of certain celebrity commercials online. Before the debut of a new Britney Spears television commercial, for example, Pepsi announced an online preview on Yahoo! by sending e-mails to one million teenagers who had registered at one of its Web sites. The company also bought all the advertising space available on Yahoo! during the two days prior to the commercial's debut and built anticipation by rotating 25 different advertising banners promoting the preview. No commercial had ever premiered online, and it drew more than one million consumers in the first four days on Yahoo!

Ford Motor Company of Canada took a different approach when it kicked off a promotion for its Escape sport-utility vehicle by sending e-mails to consumers who had signed up at its Web site. The e-mails invited recipients to win prizes by playing an online game in which they race Escapes on the moon. Forty percent of the recipients clicked to play the game—and each forwarded the game to an average of three friends. In all, nearly 30,000 consumers went to the moon in Ford's game, and 54 percent signed up to receive more e-mails from the company.[1]

Pepsi and Ford are using the Internet to extend their reach among key target markets, build their brands, and improve the likelihood that their promotions will influence consumers to buy, consume, and recommend Pepsi drinks (see Exhibit 16.1) and Ford SUVs. Although both companies started their promotions with e-mails to consumers, they created a buzz by getting recipients to spread the word among other consumers. Very likely many people who viewed the Pepsi ad heard about it from others, just as thousands played the Escape game after receiving forwarded e-mails from friends or relatives.

This chapter explores when and why individuals, groups, and the media (such as the Internet)

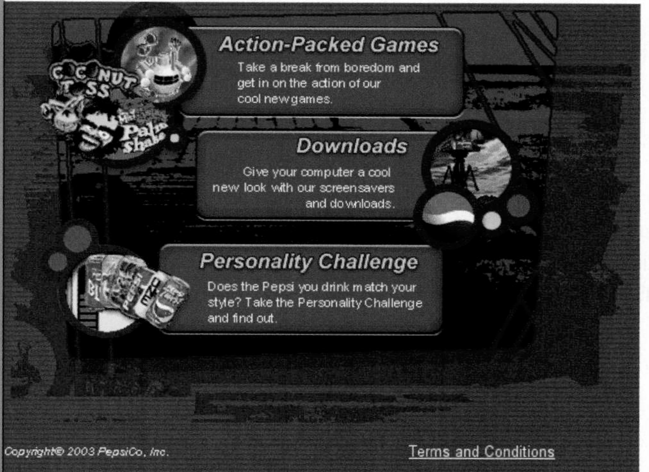

EXHIBIT 16.1
Social Influences Move Online
Web sites are increasingly being used by companies to complement advertising, sales promotions, direct marketing and other elements of the promotion mix and to influence consumers' purchase and usage behaviors.

Source: Copyright © 2003 Pepsico Inc. Used with permission.

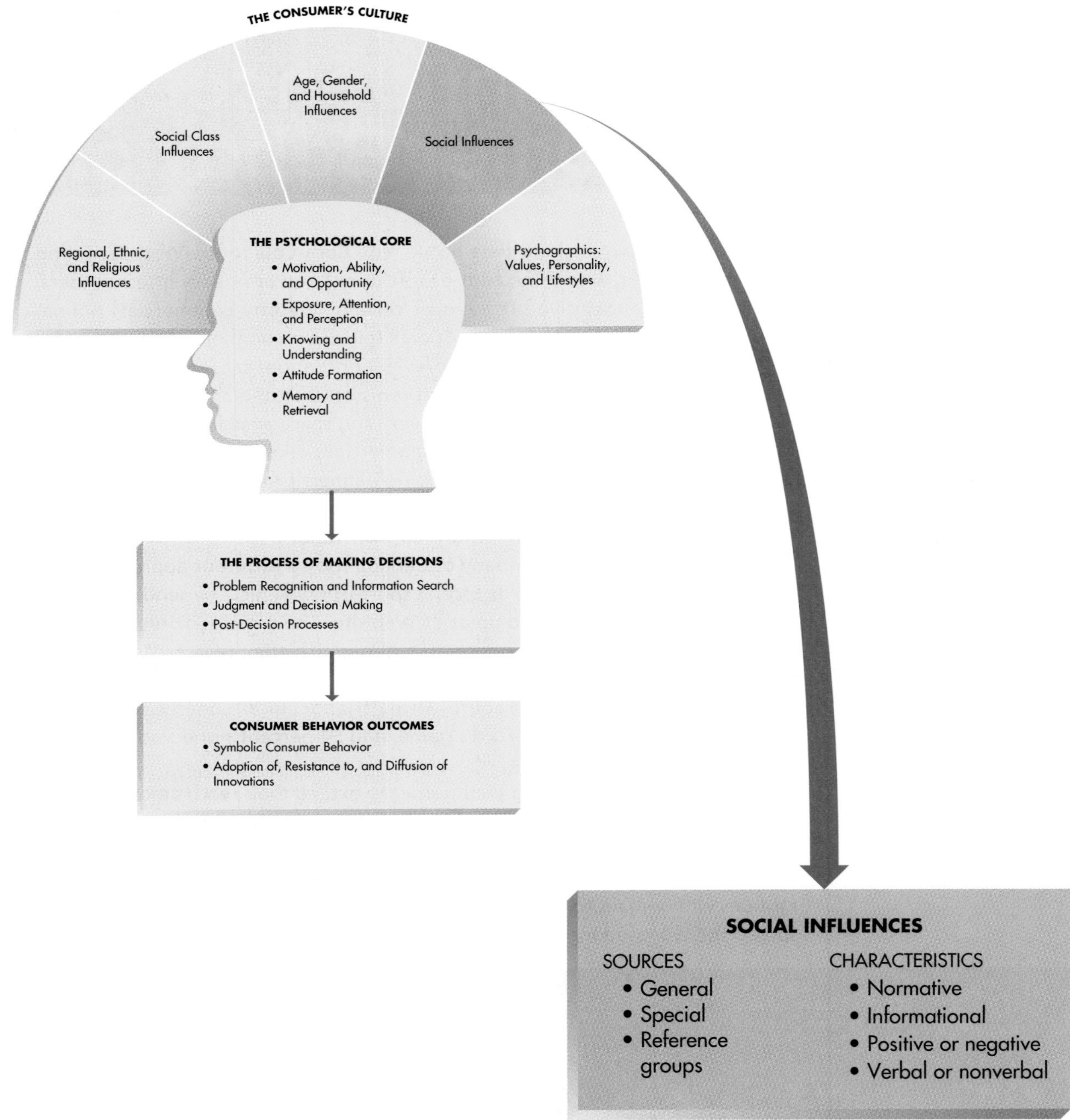

EXHIBIT 16.2
Chapter Overview: Social Influences

This chapter describes various sources of influence (general sources, special sources, and groups) and how they exert influence (by providing normative or informational influence, by providing positive and/or negative information, and by providing information verbally or nonverbally).

social influences Information and pressures from individuals, groups, and the mass media that affect how a person behaves.

affect consumer behavior. Sometimes information and pressures, known as **social influences**, are strong because the information source is very credible; at other times they are strong simply because the source can communicate information widely. Social influence is also powerful when individuals within groups are in frequent contact and have many opportunities to communicate information and perspectives. Certain people in groups are sometimes quite influential because their power or expertise makes others want to follow what they believe or say.

In addition to communicating information, individuals can influence whether, what, when, where, how, how much, and how often consumers think they should acquire, use, and dispose of an offering. Groups can induce not only socially appropriate consumer behaviors but also socially inappropriate and even personally destructive behaviors such as use of illicit drugs. Therefore, marketers need to understand what kinds of social entities create influence, what kinds of influence they create, and what effects their influence attempts can have. Exhibit 16.2 summarizes the social influences that affect consumer behavior. ●

GENERAL SOURCES OF INFLUENCE

Consumers in the opening example learned about the sneak previews from ads, e-mails, and each other. But which sources had the most impact, and why? Exhibit 16.3 offers some answers to this question.

Marketer-Dominated versus Non-Marketer-Dominated Influence

marketer-dominated source Influence delivered from a marketing agent (e.g., advertising, personal selling).

non-marketer-dominated source Influence delivered from an entity outside a marketing organization (e.g., friends, family, the media).

Sources of influence can be described as **marketer dominated** or **non-marketer dominated**, and as delivered via the mass media or personally.

Marketer-Dominated Sources Delivered via Mass Media Marketer-dominated sources that deliver influence through the mass media (cell 1 in Exhibit 16.3) include advertising, sales promotions, publicity, and special events. In the opening example, consumers learned about the Pepsi commercial previews from e-mails and online advertising. Similarly, Macy's and Target influence your purchase behavior by promoting special sales in local newspapers and on television. Companies often announce a new product or service through publicity, and sports teams announce changes in players or managers by holding press conferences.

Marketer-Dominated Sources Delivered Personally Marketer-dominated sources can also deliver information personally (cell 2 in Exhibit 16.3). Salespeople, service representatives, and customer service agents are marketer-dominated personal sources of influence who deliver information in retail outlets, at consumers' homes or offices, over the phone, or at trade shows.

Non-Marketer-Dominated Sources Delivered via Mass Media Influence can also be wielded by non-marketer-dominated sources and delivered via mass media (cell 3 in Exhibit 16.3). Consumer behavior can be affected by news items about new products, movies, and restaurants; product contamination; accidents involving products; and incidences of product abuse or misuse. Consumers shopping for a new car or truck frequently learn about recalls and quality problems from television coverage, Internet sites, *Consumer Reports*, and other media not controlled by the marketer.[2] Certain media sources are particularly

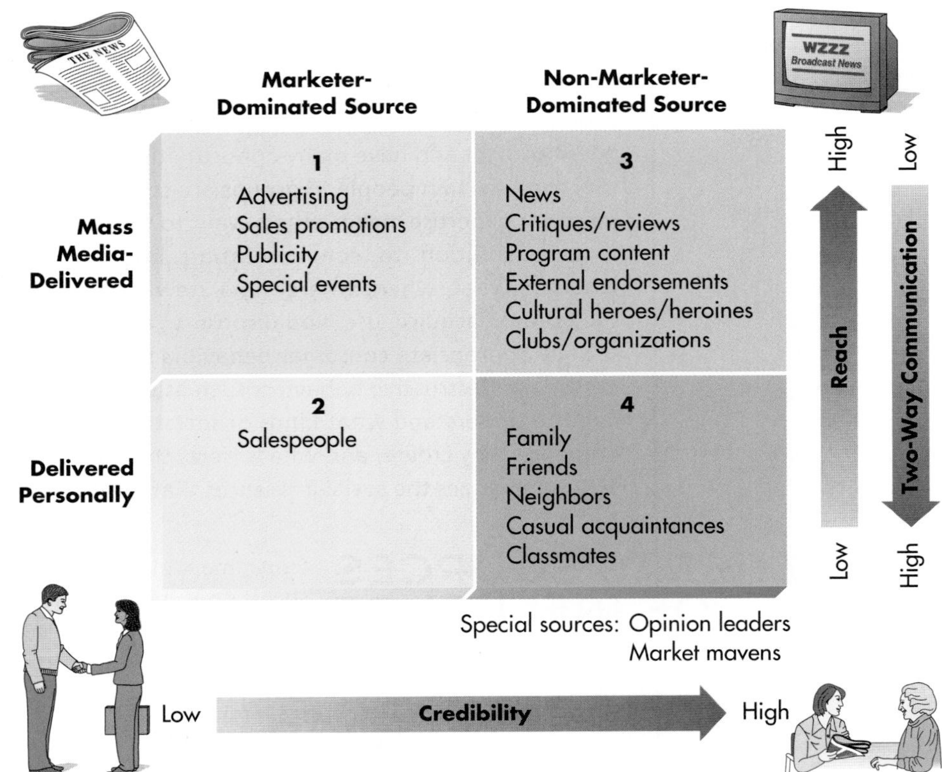

EXHIBIT 16.3
Sources of Influence
Social influence can come from marketer- or non-marketer-dominated sources and can be delivered via the mass media or in person. Non-marketer-dominated sources tend to be more credible. Information delivered via the mass media has the benefit of reaching many people but may not allow for a two-way flow of communication.

powerful sources of influence. Many consumers, for instance, choose movies based on recommendations made by film critics; make dining decisions based on restaurant reviews; make buying decisions based on *Consumer Reports* articles; and book hotel rooms based on the American Automobile Association's ratings. Not long ago, the car manufacturer Skoda, based in the Czech Republic, wanted to change its low-end, low-quality image among U.K. consumers. After Skoda lent test cars to influential journalists from mainstream U.K. publications such as *The Guardian* newspaper, their glowing reports helped boost the car's sales by 23 percent.[3] Celebrities and other well-known figures may also influence consumers' acquisition, usage, and disposition decisions.

Non-Marketer-Dominated Sources Delivered Personally Finally, consumer behavior is influenced by non-marketer-dominated sources that deliver information personally (cell 4 in Exhibit 16.3). Word-of-mouth communication (or "word-of-mouse" online) from friends, family, neighbors, casual acquaintances, and even strangers can affect our consumer behavior, as can the behavior we observe from these people. For example, we might hear from friends that a favorite restaurant is opening a new branch, and we may observe how customers order food in an unfamiliar restaurant (e.g., at the counter, at their table).

How Do These General Sources Differ?

The influence sources shown in Exhibit 16.3 differ in terms of their reach, capacity for two-way communication, and credibility. In turn, these characteristics affect how much influence each source can have with consumers.

Reach Mass media sources are important to marketers because they reach large consumer audiences. Part of the reason the Pepsi commercials achieved such high impressions is that the ads and e-mails reached many people. Now satellite TV, the Internet, and other technologies are spreading marketing messages, product news, the behavior of public figures, and television programs to an increasingly large audience, expanding marketers' reach to other regions and around the world.

Capacity for Two-Way Communication Personally delivered sources of influence are valuable because they provide a two-way flow of information. For example, a car salesperson may have more influence than a car ad because the salesperson can tailor sales information to fit the buyer's information needs, rebut counterarguments, reiterate important and/or complex information, ask questions, and make sure questions are answered.

Personal conversations are often more casual and less purposeful than mass media–delivered information. During a conversation, people are less likely to anticipate what will be said and hence are less likely to take steps to avoid information inconsistent with their own frames of reference. Information from a personal source may also seem more vivid than information from a mass media source because the person speaking somehow makes it more real, which in turn may make it more persuasive.[4]

Credibility Whereas personal and mass media sources differ in their reach and capacity for two-way communication, marketer- and non-marketer-dominated sources differ in their credibility (see Exhibit 16.3). Consumers tend to perceive information delivered through marketer-dominated sources as less credible, more biased, and manipulative. In contrast, non-marketer-dominated sources appear more credible because we do not believe they have a personal stake in our purchase, consumption, or disposition decisions. We are more likely to believe a *Consumer Reports* article on cars than information from a car salesperson. Because non-marketer-dominated sources are credible, they tend to have more influence on consumer decisions than marketer-dominated sources.[5]

Specific personal and mass media sources vary in their credibility. We tend to believe information we hear from people with whom we have strong ties, in part because we are more likely to find them credible.[6] Certain celebrities are also regarded as more credible than others. Tiger Woods is a credible source for golf-related equipment; Denzel Washington is credible as a spokesperson for the Boys and Girls Clubs of America. Likewise, certain magazines have higher credibility. Consumers are more likely to believe articles in *Time* than articles in the *National Enquirer.*

MARKETING IMPLICATIONS Marketers can build on these differences in credibility, reach, and two-way communication capability to influence consumer behavior in various ways.

Use non-marketer-dominated sources to enhance credibility. When possible, marketers should try to have non-marketer-dominated sources promote their offerings (see Exhibit 16.4). Testimonials and word-of-mouth referrals may have considerable impact, particularly if they are delivered through personal communication.[7] Likewise, the media have tremendous power to influence consumption trends and behavior, making or breaking new styles and altering perceptions of what is cool. As an example, *Teen People* and *Teen Magazine* have worked with

EXHIBIT 16.4
Non-marketer-Dominated Sources Enhance Credibility
Ads may be more credible when advertisers use non-marketer-dominated sources in their marketing communications. Here, Eukanuba uses a picture of a dog fed with Eukanuba dog food helping a handicapped person lead a normal life.

Source: Permission granted by Iams Co.

the American Cancer Society to carry stories that deride smoking. As one publisher noted, "We have the power to lead those teens and tell them what brands are hot. . . . We need to leverage that power and make it cool not to smoke."[8]

Sometimes consumers have difficulty determining whether information in the media is from a marketer- or non-marketer-dominated source. Some magazine ads are disguised to look like editorial content, and some magazines feature articles that mention the names of their advertisers. For example, a three-page article in *Home* magazine about the repainting of a cottage mentioned Benjamin Moore paints nine times.[9] On the other hand, consumers who visit the highly popular Allrecipes.com site—which features partner brands such as Betty Crocker and Kraft—can tell it is non-marketer-dominated, serving as an online community for home cooks to swap recipes and offer frank opinions.[10]

Use personal sources to enhance two-way communication. Marketing efforts may be more effective when personal information sources are used. This is why Mary Kay and Avon rely so heavily on personal contacts between representatives and customers. Some businesses like day care centers and tutors survive solely on the basis of word of mouth.

Use a mix of sources to enhance impact. Because marketer- and non-marketer-dominated sources differ in their impact, the effect on consumers may be greatest when marketers use complementary sources of influence. A vitamin marketer, for example, found that although word of mouth had historically sustained the company, competitive pressures forced it to achieve greater reach through advertising. Similarly, given competition from nonbank service providers, banks are finding that word-of-mouth referrals are insufficient to entice consumers to try or stay with a particular bank.[11] Advertisers are finding that mass media ads using superstars are becoming less successful than in the past. Instead, marketing seems to have more impact when these ads are combined with favorable word of mouth.[12] ●

SPECIAL SOURCES OF INFLUENCE

Opinion leaders and market mavens are two special sources that have profound influence. Both are regarded as non-marketer-dominated sources of influence, which adds to their credibility.

Opinion Leaders

opinion leader An individual who acts as an information broker between the mass media and the opinions and behaviors of an individual or group.

An **opinion leader** is someone who acts as an information broker between the mass media and the opinions and behaviors of an individual or group. Opinion leaders are people whose position, expertise, or firsthand knowledge renders them particularly important sources of relevant and credible information, usually in a specific domain. Thus Tyra Banks is an opinion leader for fashion clothing, not for computers. Not all opinion leaders are well known. A coworker may be an opinion leader for computers given her extensive experience with various hardware and software products.

Sometimes opinion leaders are friends or acquaintances who possess these characteristics. In other cases they are professionals like doctors, dentists, or lawyers who advise their patients and clients. Non-marketer-dominated sources like film critics, restaurant reviewers, and *Consumer Reports* also act as information sources. For instance, Hollywood insider Harry Knowles critiques new movies on his Web site Ain't It Cool News (www.aintitcoolnews.com). Celebrities, models, and leaders of various social groups may also serve as opinion leaders for various products or services. Because they are so credible, opinion leaders can play an important role in consumers' acceptance of new products and services. Exhibit 16.5 identifies several celebrity opinion leaders and the categories they influence.

gatekeepers Sources that control the flow of information.

Opinion leaders are part of a general category of **gatekeepers**, people who have special influence or power in deciding whether a product or information will be disseminated to a market. For example, the Beijing Telegraph Administration serves as a gatekeeper because it limits the type of information entering China from the Internet. The Chinese government is also a gatekeeper, prohibiting sexually explicit TV shows and music videos from other countries.[13] Even within the United States, certain people play gatekeeping roles. For example, the search site Yahoo! hires people to keep Web sites that might compromise the integrity of the Yahoo! directory from being included.[14]

Because their influence can be profound even though opinion leaders are not always well-known people, researchers have studied who opinion leaders are and how to target them. They have observed several characteristics.[15] For example, opinion leaders tend to learn a lot about products, are heavy users of mass media, and tend to buy new products when they are first introduced to the marketplace. Opinion leaders are also self-confident, gregarious, and willing to share product information. Interestingly, compared with other consumers, opinion leaders may actually use different criteria to evaluate products and services. One study found that although critics and consumers tend to like the same movies, the critics focus on factors like cinematic excellence, while the public focuses on whether the film is American made, features popular stars, and offers non-objectionable content.[16]

People may become opinion leaders because they have an intrinsic interest in and enjoyment of certain products. In other words, they have enduring involvement in a product category.[17] Opinion leaders might also like the power of having information and sharing it with others. Finally, opinion leaders may communicate information simply because they believe their actions will help others.[18]

Opinion leaders have influence because they generally have no personal stake in whether consumers actually heed their opinions, which is why consumers perceive their opinions as unbiased and credible. In addition, because they have information about and experiences with the product, opinion leaders are often regarded as knowledgeable about acquisition, usage, and disposition options. This is why PC buyers value the comments of opinion leaders such as Walter Mossberg, who writes a technology column for the *Wall Street Journal*—and why

EXHIBIT 16.5
Opinion Leaders
Some—but not all—opinion leaders are well-known people. These well-known opinion leaders have the capacity to influence many people.

Source: Adapted from Rick Martin and Sarah Van Brown, "The Buzz Machine," *Newsweek*, July 27, 1998, pp. 22–26.

WHO ARE THEY?	WHAT ARE THEY KNOWN FOR?	WHO LISTENS TO THEM?
Anna Wintour, editor of *Vogue*	Approving new designers, designs	- Fashion forward consumers
John Doerr, venture capitalist	Funding Silicon Valley start-ups	- Wall Street
George Lundberg, editor of the *Journal of the American Medical Association*	Publishing scientific articles	- Doctors, scientists - Health conscious consumers
Maria Campbell, literary scout	Evaluating how well books will do as movies	- Publishers - Movie producers
Csaba Csere, editor of *Car and Driver* magazine	Providing information to car buffs	- Car dealers - Car manufacturers - Car buffs
Oprah Winfrey, personality, show host, movie star, book club magnate	Popularizing books, people, and ways of dealing with problems	- Book publishers, book buyers - Women
Matt Drudge, Web reporter	Providing news and gossip on the goings on of Washington	- Everyone in Washington
Mark McCarmack, sports agent	Endorsing athletes	- Team owners - Product endorsers - Sports fans
Walter Mossberg, *Wall Street Journal* columnist	Providing straight facts, in easy to digest language, about which software and hardware is worth buying	- Silicon Valley product managers - Consumers contemplating computer hardware or software purchase

PC marketers want Mossberg to review their products. However, simply because they serve as information brokers does not mean that information always flows from opinion leader to consumers. Indeed, opinion leaders often get information by seeking it from others; they are just as likely to be information seekers as providers.[19]

Market Mavens

market maven
A consumer who has and communicates considerable marketplace information to others.

Market mavens are individuals "who have information about *many* products, places to shop, and other facets of the marketplace, and initiate discussions with consumers and respond to requests from consumers for market information."[20] The difference between an opinion leader and a market maven is that a market maven knows a lot about the marketplace in general, such as where and when to shop, what is on sale when, and which products are good and bad. Market mavens are self-confident about their knowledge of the market and their ability to act on that knowledge.[21] Perhaps because of their general interest in the marketplace, market mavens tend to be aware of new products early on, and they are heavy users of a wide range of information sources, both getting and giving

EXHIBIT 16.6

A Scale Measuring Opinion Leadership

Marketers sometimes try to identify opinion leaders because these consumers can be so important to marketing efforts. These scales identify which consumers are opinion leaders and opinion seekers in several product categories.

Source: Leisa Reinecke Flynn, Ronald E. Goldsmith, and Jacqueline K. Eastmen, "Opinion Leaders and Opinion Seekers: Two New Measurements Scales," *Journal of the Academy of Marketing Science*, vol. 24, no. 2, p. 146, copyright © 1996 by Sage Publications, Inc. Reprinted by permission of Sage Publications, Inc.

INITIAL ITEM POOL FOR THE OPINION LEADERSHIP AND OPINION SEEKING SCALES

The questionnaires below ask consumers questions about rock music. A similar version of the questionnaire asks consumers about fashion and environmentally friendly products. Consumers respond to each question using a scale, where 1 means strongly disagree and 7 means strongly agree. People who have a high score on the first scale are classified as opinion leaders in the area of music. Those who score high on the second are opinion seekers in the area of music.

Opinion Leadership

1. Other people rarely ask me about rock CD's before they choose one for themselves. (RS)
2. My opinion on rock [fashion; environmentally friendly products] seems not to count with other people.* (RS)
3. My opinions influence what types of recordings other people buy.
4. Other people think that I am a poor source of information on rock music. (RS)
5. When they choose a rock music recording [fashionable clothing; "green" products], other people do not turn to me for advice.* (RS)
6. Other people rarely come to me for advice about choosing CD's and tapes [fashionable clothing; products that are good for the environment].*
7. People that I know pick rock music [clothing; "green" products] based on what I have told them.*
8. People rarely repeat things I have told them about popular rock music to other people. (RS)
9. What I say about rock music rarely changes other people's minds. (RS)
10. I often persuade other people to buy the rock music [fashions; "green" products] that I like.*
11. I often influence people's opinions about popular rock music [clothing; environmentally correct products.]*

Opinion Seeking

1. When I consider buying a CD or tape [clothes; "green" products], I ask other people for advice.*
2. I don't need to talk to others before I buy CD's or tapes [fashionable clothing; products that are good for the environment].* (RS)
3. Other people influence my choice of rock music.
4. I would not choose a recording without consulting someone else.
5. I rarely ask other people what music [fashions; environmentally friendly products] to buy.* (RS)
6. I like to get others' opinions before I buy a CD or tape [new clothes; "green" products].
7. I feel more comfortable buying a recording [fashion item; product that is good for the environment] when I have gotten other people's opinions on it.*
8. When choosing rock music [fashionable clothing; a "green" product], other people's opinions are not important to me.* (RS)

*Items in the final scales.
(RS): Items reverse scored.

marketplace information. Teenager Ashley Power, founder of Goosehead.com (www.goosehead.com), is a market maven for fashions, music, movies, and other teen interests, which is why MTV and other marketers link to her site.[22]

MARKETING IMPLICATIONS

Marketers use several tactics to influence opinion leaders.

Target opinion leaders. Given their potential impact and the fact that they serve as both seekers and providers of marketplace information, one of the most obvious marketing strategies for reaching opinion leaders and market mavens is to target them directly.[23] For example, doctors may be targeted to help consumers learn about health-related products and services. The Ghana government had more success with its inoculation programs when health workers contacted and gained the approval of an opinion leader—in this case, the local healer—before approaching the public.[24] Marketers must be able to identify opinion leaders if they are to target them. Exhibit 16.6 shows one scale that researchers use to identify opinion leaders.

EXHIBIT 16.7
Using Opinion Leaders in Advertising
Opinion leaders, people whose expertise or knowledge makes them relevant and credible sources of information, can be influential. Jere Marder's position as champion breeder and handler makes her a credible opinion leader for Pro Plan dog food.

Source: © 1999 Ralston Purina Company. Photo by Scott Raffe.

Use opinion leaders in marketing communications. Although opinion leaders' influence may be less effective when delivered through a marketer-dominated source, their expertise and association can still support an offering (see Exhibit 16.7). As an alternative, marketers may use a simulated opinion leader. For example, the major television networks forbid the use of medical professionals or actors playing them to endorse a product. Instead, Mentadent toothpaste has used the wives, husbands, and children of actual dentists. Although these individuals are not experts on toothpaste, their affiliation with real experts presumably gives them some credibility.[25]

Refer consumers to opinion leaders. Finally, marketers can target consumers and ask them to refer to a knowledgeable opinion leader. Ads for Zantac (an ulcer medication) tell ulcer and heartburn sufferers to ask an opinion leader (their doctor) about how the product can help. ●

REFERENCE GROUPS AS SOURCES OF INFLUENCE

Social influence is exerted by specific groups of people as well as by individuals such as opinion leaders and market mavens. A reference group is a set of people with whom individuals compare themselves as a guide to developing their own attitudes, knowledge, and/or behaviors.

Types of Reference Groups

Consumers may relate to three types of reference groups—aspirational, associative, and dissociative.

aspirational reference group A group that we admire and desire to be like.

Aspirational reference groups are groups we admire and wish to be like but are not currently a member of. For example, groupies often aspire to be like members of a rock band. A younger brother may want to be like his older brother and other older children. Some Eastern European youths aspire to be like their U.S. counterparts.[26] Given the high respect accorded to education in Korea, teachers often serve as an aspirational reference group for students in that country.

associative reference group A group to which we currently belong.

Associative reference groups are groups to which we actually belong, such as a clique of friends, an extended family, a particular work group, a club, or a school group. The gender, ethnic, geographic, and age groups to which you belong are also associative reference groups with whom you identify. Exhibit 16.8 shows the associative reference groups in one Illinois high school.

dissociative reference group A group we do not want to emulate.

Dissociative reference groups are groups whose attitudes, values, and behaviors we disapprove of and do not wish to emulate. "Gangsta rap" groups

EXHIBIT 16.8
Associative Reference Groups

The associative reference groups at one high school in Illinois included these "kid-described" groups. Did you have similar groups in your high school? Which one(s) served as associative reference groups for you?

Source: Jerry Adler; With John McCormick and Karen Springen in Chicago, Daniel Pedersen in Atlanta, Nadine Joseph in San Francisco, Ana Figueroa in Los Angeles, and Beth Dickey in Melbourne, Fla., "Beyond Littleton: The Truth about High School," *Newsweek*, May 10, 1999, pp. 56–58.

Jocks rule and nerds still struggle for acceptance just about everywhere. But many schools have their own unique cliques. Take a look at Glenbrook South High in Glenbrook, Illinois: Do any of these groups resemble the groups that existed at your high school? Which ones were associative reference groups for you?

Jocks:	Quintissential athletes.
Nerds:	Superintellectual types.
Trophy case kids:	Named for their hangout under the school awards case. They're punkish in black, hooded sweatshirts.
Wall kids:	Mostly seniors, mostly popular. Lots of preppies and "Abercrombies." Their turf: a wall outside the cafeteria.
Bandies:	Musicians. They stick to themselves outside the rehearsal room. Not especially cool or uncool, just good friends.
Backstage people:	Theatre and arts types (both genders) lounge on couches backstage to talk, do homework, take naps.
Student council kids:	Clean-cut, popular. Lunch time hangout: the council office.

promoting violence are dissociative reference groups for some people. U.S. citizens serve as dissociative reference groups to consumers in some Arab countries, and neo-Nazis serve as dissociative reference groups for many people in Germany and in the United States. Research shows that country music fans are a dissociative reference group for many in the United States—even though these consumers may secretly like the music itself.[27]

MARKETING IMPLICATIONS

The influence of various reference groups has some important implications for marketers.

Associate products with aspirational reference groups. First, by knowing their target consumers' aspirational reference groups, marketers can associate their product with that group and use spokespeople who represent it. Because celebrities' fame and fortune make them an aspirational reference group for some, many companies implicitly or explicitly use celebrities to endorse their products. Reebok is paying Philadelphia 76ers basketball guard Allen Iverson $5 million per year for 10 years to endorse Reebok shoes.[28]

Accurately represent associative reference groups. Second, marketers need to identify and appropriately represent target consumers in ads by accurately reflecting the clothing, hairstyles, accessories, and general demeanor of their associative reference groups.[29] To sell products like skateboards and mountain climbing equipment, for example, many sports marketers develop promotions featuring actual skateboarders and mountain climbers.[30] New Balance features amateur athletes in ads for its sports shoes, which appear in *Outside, Prevention,* and other publications.[31]

Help to develop brand communities. Marketers can help to create a brand community, a specialized group of consumers with a structured set of social relationships centered around a particular brand.[32] These specialized groups demonstrate three characteristics of a community: a shared consciousness, rituals and traditions, and a sense of moral responsibility. Members of a brand community not only buy the product repeatedly, they are extremely committed to it, share information about the brand with other consumers, and influence other community members to remain loyal to the group and the brand. Amazon.com does this online by inviting consumers to post their own reviews of the books, music, and other products it sells.[33] Harley-Davidson does this by organizing events for the 640,000 members of its Harley Owners Group.[34]

Avoid using dissociative reference groups. When appropriate, companies should not use dissociative reference groups in their marketing. McDonald's decided to avoid Ronald McDonald in its promotions in the Middle East because it knew that religious Muslims would not consider a zany, brightly colored clown to be an idol.[35] Similarly, some marketers drop celebrity spokespeople who commit crimes or exhibit other behavior that is offensive to the target market. ●

Characteristics of Reference Groups

Reference groups can be described according to degree of contact, formality, similarity among members, group attractiveness, density, degree of identification, and the strength of the ties connecting members.

Degree of Contact Reference groups vary in their degree of contact. We may have direct and extensive contact with some reference groups like our immediate circle of friends or family but less contact with our former high school classmates. Reference groups with which we have considerable contact tend to exert the greatest influence.[36] A group with which we have face-to-face interaction, such as family, peers, and professors, is a **primary reference group**. In contrast, a **secondary reference group** is one that may influence us even though we have no direct contact with its members. We may be members of groups like the American Marketing Association, an Internet chat group, or a musical fan club. Although we interact with the group only through such impersonal communication channels as newsletters, its behavior and values can still influence our behavior.

primary reference group A group with whom we have physical (face-to-face) interaction.

secondary reference group A group that influences us but with whom we do not have direct contact.

Formality Reference groups also vary in formality. Groups like fraternities, athletic teams, clubs, and classes are formally structured, with rules outlining the criteria for group membership and the expected behavior of members. For example, you must satisfy certain requirements—gaining admission, fulfilling class prerequisites—before you can enroll in particular college courses. Once enrolled, you follow specified rules for appropriate conduct by coming to class on time and taking notes.

Other groups are more ad hoc, less organized, and less structured. For example, your immediate group of friends is not formally structured and likely has no strict set of rules. Likewise, an informal group of local residents may form a neighborhood watch group. People who serve on the same jury, attend the same party, or vacation on the same cruise also may constitute an informal group.

Homophily: The Similarity Among Group Members Groups vary in their **homophily**—or the similarity among the members. When groups are homophilous, reference-group influence tends to be strong because similar people tend to see things in the same way, interact frequently, and develop strong social ties.[37] Group members may have more opportunity to exchange information and are more likely to accept information from one another. Because the sender and receiver are similar, the information they share is also likely to be perceived as credible.

homophily The overall similarity among members in the social system.

Group Attractiveness Research shows that the attractiveness of a particular peer group can affect how members conform through illicit consumption of drugs and other substances.[38] When members perceive a group as very attractive, they have stronger intentions to conform through illicit consumption behavior. Group attractiveness is much less important, however, when a group is capable of socially punishing a member for not conforming by participating in illicit consumption. From a public policy perspective, the implication is that making substance abusers seem less attractive may help U.S. children and teenagers resist illicit activities. Chapters 20 and 21 discuss such issues in more detail.

Density Dense groups are those in which group members all know one another. For example, an extended family that gets together every Sunday operates as a dense social network. In contrast, the network of faculty at a large university is less dense because its members have fewer opportunities to interact, share information, or influence one another. In Korea, network density varies by geographic area. A rural village in Korea may have high density because its families have known each other for generations. By contrast, even though Seoul has a high population density (more than 10 million people), many city dwellers may not know one another, making network density low.

Degree of Identification Some characteristics of the individual within a group contribute to the way groups vary. One is the degree of identification a consumer has with a group. Just because people are members of a group does not mean they use it as a reference group. Even though you may be Hispanic or a senior citizen, you need not necessarily regard similar individuals as part of your reference group.[39] Instead, the influence that a group has on our behavior is affected by the extent to which we identify with it. For example, one study found that consumers who attend sporting events were more likely to buy a sponsor's products when they strongly identified with the team and when they viewed such purchases as a group norm.[40]

tie-strength The extent to which a close, intimate relationship connects people.

Tie-Strength Another characteristic describing individuals within a group is **tie-strength.**[41] A strong tie means that two people are connected by a close, intimate relationship, often characterized by frequent interpersonal contact. A weak tie means that the people have a more distant, nonintimate relationship, with limited interpersonal contact.

Exhibit 16.9 illustrates the concepts of strong and weak ties. In this example, Anne has three very close friends from school: Maria, Kyeung, and Keshia. She also knows Jeff from her health club; Tyrone is Maria's distant cousin. The

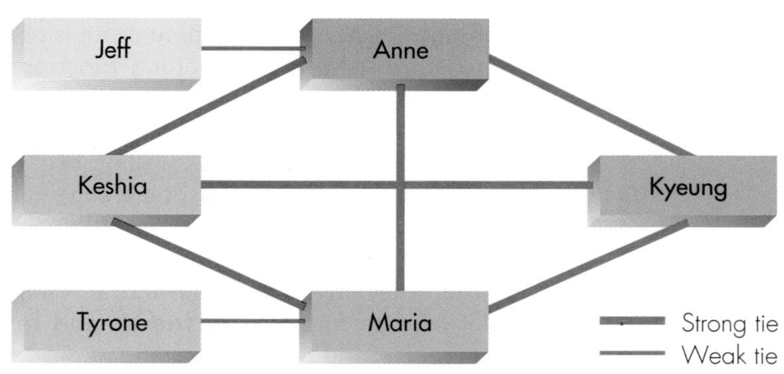

EXHIBIT 16.9
Tie-Strength and Social Influence
Strong ties (denoted by the thick red line) are people with whom we have a close, intimate relationship. As relationships become less close and intimate, tie-strength weakens. If you were a marketer, whom would you target in this network? Why?

solid red lines connect individuals who know one another, with the width of the line indicating how strong the tie is. Thus Anne, Maria, Kyeung, and Keshia are strongly tied to one another. Maria has a weak tie with Tyrone, and Anne has a weak tie with Jeff.

MARKETING IMPLICATIONS

The characteristics that describe reference groups have some important marketing implications.

Understanding information transmission. Homophily, degree of contact, tie-strength, and network density can significantly influence whether, how much, and how quickly information is transmitted between and among consumers within a group. Within dense networks, where consumers are in frequent contact and are connected by strong ties, information about the acquisition, usage, and disposition of an offering—or related offerings—is likely to be transmitted very quickly. The best way for marketers to disseminate information rapidly in a market is to target individuals in dense networks characterized by strong ties and frequent contact.

Formal reference groups as potential targets. Formal reference groups can provide marketers with clear targets for marketing efforts. For example, Mothers Against Drunk Driving can target formal groups like local PTAs, school boards, and so on, and the American Red Cross targets college campuses as part of its blood drives.

Homophilous consumers as targets. Marketers sometimes use the concept of homophily to market their products. If you log on to Amazon.com and find a book you like, the recommendation system points you to more books you might like based on the purchases of others who bought the first book. The principle is that you might share the reading tastes of people that the Web site considers to be similar to you. As another example, Yahoo! distributed branded name cards for students in Singapore to use in exchanging e-mail addresses with peers, thus boosting brand recognition and site usage among this target group.[42]

Targeting the network. Sometimes it makes sense for marketers to target the network itself. Verizon and AT&T Wireless, for example, target families with offers of one large pool of monthly cell phone minutes to be shared among all family members.[43] Health clubs target networks when they offer consumers a discount if a friend joins. Marketers may also encourage referrals by asking consumers to "tell a friend about us."

Understanding the strength of weak ties. Although you might think that weak ties provide little payoff for marketers, the opposite is true. Because weak ties often serve as "bridges" connecting groups, they play a powerful role in propagating information *across* networks. For example, in Exhibit 16.9 Maria serves as a bridge between her four friends and her extended family. Once she gives information to Tyrone, he can communicate it to others with whom he has ties. Weak ties therefore serve a gatekeeping function by transporting information from one group to another.[44]

Marketers can also use weak ties to identify new networks for marketing efforts. For example, direct selling organizations like Avon, Mary Kay cosmetics, and Tupperware and charitable organizations like the American Cancer Society target individual consumers as selling agents and rely on their interpersonal networks for direct selling efforts.[45] Individuals can tap not only consumers with whom they have strong ties but also those with whom ties are weak. Girl Scouts sell cookies not only to friends and relatives but also to neighbors, parents' coworkers, and people shopping at grocery stores. Perhaps because they have recognized the value of this type of selling practice, more marketers are attempting to sell products through home parties. Today, there are home parties for such diverse products as Bible videos, raspberry salsa, and personal computers.[46]

embedded markets
Markets in which the social relationships among buyers and sellers change the way the market operates.

These types of markets are called **embedded markets** because the social relationships among buyers and sellers change the way the market operates.[47] In other words, the fact that you have a social relationship with the seller may influence the way you react to his or her selling efforts. You are more likely to buy Girl Scout cookies from your neighbor's daughter than from a girl you have never met because you want to remain on good terms with your neighbor. Your future interactions with her may depend on whether you buy cookies from her daughter. ●

Reference Groups Affect Consumer Socialization

consumer socialization
The process by which we learn to become consumers.

One way reference groups influence consumer behavior is through socialization, the process by which individuals acquire the skills, knowledge, values, and attitudes that are relevant for functioning in a given domain. **Consumer socialization** is the process by which we learn to become consumers and come to know the value of money; the appropriateness of saving versus spending; and how, when, and where products should be bought and used.[48] Through socialization, consumers learn motives and values as well as the knowledge and skills for consumption, although some observers worry that socialization encourages children to see material goods as a path to happiness, success, and achievement.[49]

Consumer socialization can occur in many ways.[50] Parents may, for example, instill values of thriftiness by (1) directly teaching their children the importance of saving money, (2) letting their children observe them being thrifty, or (3) rewarding children for being thrifty. One study found that direct teaching was the most effective means of instilling consumer skills in younger children. For older children, however, observational learning was most effective.

People as Socializing Agents Clearly, reference groups like family and friends play an important role as socializing agents. Parents affect socialization by influencing what types of products, TV programs, and ads their children are exposed to. Some parents are very concerned about children's exposure to violent and sexually explicit programming and products and actively regulate what their children watch and what games they play.[51] Even grandparents can play a powerful socializing role. In fact, the Office of National Drug Control Policy launched a campaign encouraging grandparents to talk to their grandchildren about drugs. In some cases grandparents' more subdued and less emotionally charged relationship with kids may make them better information sources than parents.[52]

The effect of reference groups as socializing agents can change over time. Parents have substantial influence on young children, but their influence wanes as children grow older and interact more with their peers.[53] Similarly, your high school friends probably had a powerful effect on the values, attitudes, and behaviors you had as a teen, but they likely have much less impact now. Because we associate with many groups throughout our lives, socialization is a lifelong process.

The Media and the Marketplace as Socializing Agents TV programs, movies, music, video games, the Internet, and ads can also serve as socializing agents. Consider the fact that boys are depicted in ads as more knowledgeable, aggressive, active, and instrumental to actions than girls are. Clearly, these sex role stereotypes can affect children's conceptions of what it is like to be a boy versus a girl.[54] In addition, consumer products may be used as socializing agents, which means our childhood toys might have influenced who we are and what was expected of us.[55] One study found that parents were likely to give their boys sporting equipment, machines, military toys, and vehicles and to decorate their rooms with animal motifs. In contrast, girls were more likely to receive dolls, dollhouses, and domestic toys, and their rooms were more likely to be decorated in floral motifs, fringes, ruffles, and lace.[56] Not surprisingly, studies have shown that children of 20 months have already learned to distinguish "boy" toys from "girl" toys. These effects seem to occur at least in part because parents tend to encourage the use of what they consider sex-appropriate toys and discourage cross-sex interests, especially for boys.[57]

As they grow, children can become more suspicious of media and marketplace socializing agents. Some research has found that teens are particularly skeptical of advertising claims.[58]

NORMATIVE INFLUENCE

Thus far you have learned about various sources of influence—general, special, and groups. These sources can exert two types of influence, normative and informational (see Exhibit 16.10).

Assume that you are at a dinner interview with a prospective employer who tells you she is a vegetarian. Although you love beef, you may be reluctant to order it because you want to make a good impression, so you order a vegetarian dish. Your host has just communicated information to you about your expected behavior.

Normative influence, which is what you felt in this example, is social pressure designed to encourage conformity to the expectations of others.[59] Chapter 6 discussed normative influences in the context of how they affect our intentions

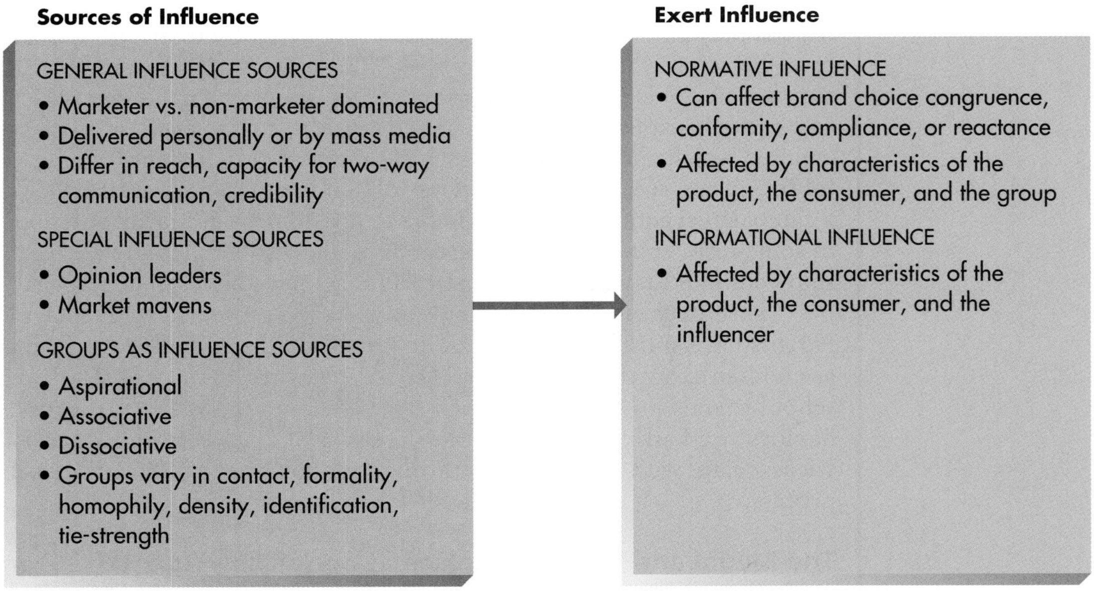

Sources of Influence

GENERAL INFLUENCE SOURCES
- Marketer vs. non-marketer dominated
- Delivered personally or by mass media
- Differ in reach, capacity for two-way communication, credibility

SPECIAL INFLUENCE SOURCES
- Opinion leaders
- Market mavens

GROUPS AS INFLUENCE SOURCES
- Aspirational
- Associative
- Dissociative
- Groups vary in contact, formality, homophily, density, identification, tie-strength

→

Exert Influence

NORMATIVE INFLUENCE
- Can affect brand choice congruence, conformity, compliance, or reactance
- Affected by characteristics of the product, the consumer, and the group

INFORMATIONAL INFLUENCE
- Affected by characteristics of the product, the consumer, and the influencer

EXHIBIT 16.10
Sources of Influence and Types of Influence

General influence sources, special influence sources, and specific groups can affect consumers by exerting normative and/or informational influence.

norms Collective decisions about what constitutes appropriate behavior.

and consumption decisions. The term *normative influence* derives from **norms**, which are society's collective decisions about what behavior should be. For example, we have norms for which brands and stores are cool, norms that discourage stealing and impulsive shopping,[60] and norms about how much food one should eat at a given meal. Morals also exert normative influence about what is right and wrong, and can strongly influence attitudes toward cigarette smoking, for example.[61]

Normative influence implies consumers will be sanctioned or punished if they do not follow the norms and likewise implies consumers will be rewarded for performing the expected behaviors. For example, a prospective boss may deny or reward you with a good job, depending on how you behaved in your interview. Middle school girls may impose sanctions by treating classmates differently when they do not conform to the dress norm.[62] The London department store Harrods bounces consumers who violate its dress code by wearing flip-flop shoes, dirty clothing, or clothing that is too revealing. One woman was even bounced for wearing Lycra leggings.[63]

How Normative Influence Can Affect Consumer Behavior

Normative influence can have several important effects on consumption behaviors.

brand-choice congruence The likelihood that consumers will buy what others in their group buy.

conformity Doing what others in the group do.

Brand-Choice Congruence and Conformity Normative influence affects **brand-choice congruence**—the likelihood that consumers will buy what others in their group buy. Compare, for example, the types of foods, clothes, music, hairstyles, and cars that you buy with the selections of your friends. You and your friends have probably made similar choices.[64]

Normative influence can also affect **conformity**, the tendency for an individual to behave as the group behaves. Conformity and brand-choice congruence may be related. For example, you might conform by buying the same products as others in your group,[65] although brand-choice congruence is not the only way for you to conform. You may also conform by performing activities that the group wants you to perform, such as initiation rites, or by acting the way the group acts. For example, your actions at a party might depend on whether your companions are your parents or your college buddies. In each case you are conforming to a different set of expectations regarding appropriate behavior.

Pressures to conform can be substantial.[66] One study examining group pressure toward underage drinking and drug consumption found that students worried about how others would perceive them if they conformed or refused to conform to the expected behavior of the group. Other studies have shown that conformity increases as more people in the group conform. Interestingly, conformity varies by culture. Compared with consumers in the United States, for example, the Japanese tend to be more group oriented and are more likely to go along with group desires.

compliance Doing what the group or social influencer asks.

Compliance versus Reactance **Compliance**, a somewhat different effect of normative influence, means doing what someone asks us to do. You are complying if, when asked, you donate to a political campaign, fill out a marketing research questionnaire, or purchase Tupperware at a home party. Parents comply with children by purchasing foods, buying toys, or allowing activities (such as parties) that kids request.

reactance Doing the opposite of what the individual or group wants us to do.

However, when we believe our freedom is being threatened, a boomerang effect occurs and we engage in **reactance**—doing the opposite of what the individual or group wants us to do. For example, if a salesperson pressures you too much, you may engage in reactance by saying that you do not want whatever it is he or she is trying to sell.[67] Parents may engage in reactance by staunchly refusing to make a purchase requested by a whining child.

Factors Affecting Normative Influence Strength

The strength of normative influence depends on the characteristics of the product, the consumer, and the group to which the consumer belongs.

Product Characteristics Researchers have hypothesized that reference groups can influence two types of decisions: (1) whether we buy a product within a given product category and (2) what brand we buy. However, whether reference groups affect product and brand decisions also depends on whether the buyer typically consumes the product in private or in public and whether it is a necessity or a luxury. As shown in Exhibit 16.11, mattresses and hot-water heaters are considered privately consumed necessities, whereas camcorders and inline skates can be considered publicly consumed luxuries. Exhibit 16.12 reflects predictions, validated in the United States and Thailand, about when reference groups will affect these decisions.

One prediction is that because we must buy necessity items, reference groups are likely to have little influence on whether we buy such products. However, reference groups might exert some influence on whether we buy a luxury item. For example, your friends will probably not influence whether you buy a hot-water heater or whether you buy shoes, but they might influence whether

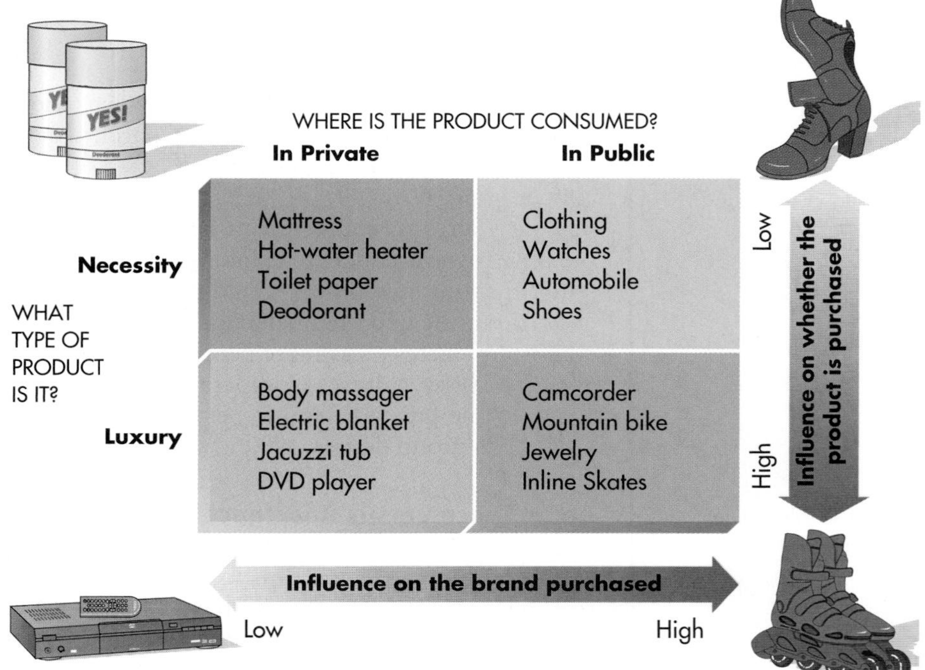

EXHIBIT 16.11
Reference Group Influences on Publicly and Privately Consumed Luxuries and Necessities
Reference groups tend to influence consumption of a product category only when the product is a luxury (not a necessity). Reference groups tend to influence brand only when the product is consumed in public (not when it is consumed in private). Give some examples of your own to illustrate the matrix.

you get inline skates or a body massager. In part, this is because luxury products communicate status—something that may be valued by group members. Also, luxury items may communicate your special interests and values and thus who you are and with whom you associate. As a result, reference groups have more influence on purchases of products that are regarded more as a luxury than a necessity.

A second prediction is that products consumed in public give others the opportunity to observe which brand we have purchased. For example, cars are publicly consumed items, making it very easy for individuals to know whether we are driving a Ferrari or a Ford. In contrast, few people see which brand of mattress we buy because this product is consumed in private. Because different brand images communicate different things to people, reference groups are likely to have considerable influence on the brand we buy when the product is publicly consumed but not when it is privately consumed. Moreover, a publicly consumed product provides opportunities for sanctions. It would be difficult for groups to develop norms and sanctions for violating them when the product is consumed privately. Therefore, reference groups influence product category choice for luxuries but not necessities and influence brand choice for products consumed in public but not those consumed in private.[68]

The significance of the product to the group is yet another characteristic of products that affects normative influence.[69] As discussed in Chapter 18, some products designate membership in a certain group. For example, a varsity sports jacket may signify membership on a sports team and may play a significant role in designating in-group and out-group status. The more central a product is to the group, the greater the normative influence the group exerts over its purchase.

Consumer Characteristics The personalities of some consumers make them readily susceptible to influence by others.[70] Several consumer researchers have developed the scale of "susceptibility to interpersonal influence," which includes the first six items shown in Exhibit 16.12. Consumers who are susceptible to interpersonal influence try to enhance their self-image by acquiring products that they think others will approve of. These consumers are also willing to conform to others' expectations about which products and brands to buy.

In addition, a personality characteristic called "attention to social comparison information" (ATSCI) is related to normative influence. Exhibit 16.12 shows several items from an ATSCI scale. People who are high on this personality trait pay a great deal of attention to what others do and use this information to guide their own behavior. For example, research shows that men feel lower self-esteem when they are exposed to idealized ad images of financial success, just as women and girls feel lower self-perceptions when exposed to idealized ad images of physical attractiveness.[71]

Tie-strength also affects the degree of normative influence. When ties are strong, individuals presumably want to maintain their relationship with others in the group and are therefore motivated to succumb to the group's norms and wishes.[72]

Finally, normative influence is affected by a consumer's identification with the group.[73] A person may be a member of a group such as a family or a subculture with whose attitudes, behaviors, and values he or she does not identify. Normative reference-group influence is weak in such instances.

Group Characteristics The characteristics of the group can influence the degree of normative influence. One characteristic is the extent to which the

ITEMS INDICATING SUSCEPTIBILITY TO INTERPERSONAL INFLUENCE	1. I rarely purchase the latest fashion styles until I am sure my friends approve of them. 2. If other people can see me using a product, I often purchase the brand they expect me to buy. 3. I often identify with other people by purchasing the same products and brands they purchase. 4. To make sure I buy the right product or brand, I often observe what others are buying and using. 5. If I have little experience with a product, I often ask my friends about the product. 6. I frequently gather information from friends or family about a product before I buy.
ITEMS INDICATING ATTENTION TO SOCIAL COMPARISON INFORMATION	1. It is my feeling that if everyone else in a group is behaving in a certain manner, this must be the proper way to behave. 2. I actively avoid wearing clothes that are not in style. 3. At parties, I usually try to behave in a manner that makes me fit in. 4. When I am uncertain how to act in a social situation, I look to the behavior of others for cues. 5. I tend to pay attention to what others are wearing. 6. The slightest look of disapproval in the eyes of a person with whom I am interacting is enough to make me change my approach.

EXHIBIT 16.12 Measuring Susceptibility to Interpersonal Influence and Attention to Social Comparison Information

Individuals differ in whether they are susceptible to influence from others and whether they pay attention to what others do. What conclusions can you draw about yourself based on your answers to these questions? What implications do these questions have for marketers?

Sources: Susceptibility to Interpersonal Influence Scale from William O. Bearden, Richard G. Netemeyer, and Jesse E. Teel, "Measurement of Consumer Susceptibility to Interpersonal Influence," *Journal of Consumer Research,* March 1989, pp. 473–481; ATSCI Scale from William O. Bearden and Randall L. Rose, "Attention to Social Comparison Information: An Individual Difference Factor Affecting Consumer Conformity," *Journal of Consumer Research,* March 1990, pp. 461–471. © 1989 and 1990 University of Chicago Press. Reprinted by permission.

coercive power The extent to which the group has the capacity to deliver rewards and sanctions.

group can deliver rewards and sanctions, also known as the degree of reward power or **coercive power.**[74] For example, your friends are more likely to influence your clothing styles than your neighbors are because your friends have greater opportunity and more motivation—greater coercive power—to deliver sanctions if they consider your clothing inappropriate.

Group cohesiveness and group similarity also affect the degree of normative influence.[75] Cohesive groups and groups with similar members may communicate and interact on a regular basis. Thus they have greater opportunity to convey normative influences and deliver rewards and sanctions.

Finally, normative influence tends to be greater when groups are large and when group members are experts.[76] As an example, you might be more inclined to buy a bottle of wine recommended by a group of wine experts than one recommended by a casual acquaintance.

MARKETING IMPLICATIONS

Marketers can take a variety of specific actions based on normative influences and the factors that affect their strength.

Demonstrate rewards and sanctions for product use/nonuse. Marketers may be able to create normative influence by using advertising to demonstrate rewards or sanctions that can follow from product use or nonuse. For example, Federal Express commercials sometimes show social disapproval arising from nonuse of its delivery services. An ad like the one in Exhibit 16.13 may express or imply that others will evaluate us favorably if we use a certain product.

Create norms for group behavior. Marketing organizations may create groups with norms to guide consumers' behavior. Weight Watchers, for example, is a group with behavior norms. Consumers who adhere to the norms by losing weight are rewarded by group praise. Because influence is greater when consumption is public rather than private, another marketing strategy is to make a private behavior public. Group discussions of eating behavior is one way that Weight Watchers makes private information public.

Create conformity pressures. Marketers may also attempt to create conformity. For example, they may actively associate a product with a certain group so that their product becomes a badge of group membership. They may simulate conformity by showing actors in an ad behaving similarly with respect to a product. Conformity may also be enhanced by publicizing others' conformity, which is what happens at Tupperware parties and at charity fund-raisers like telethons.

Use compliance techniques. The **foot-in-the-door technique** suggests that marketers can enhance compliance by getting a consumer to agree first to a small favor, then to a larger one, and then to an even larger one. For example, a salesperson may first ask a consumer his or her name and then ask what the person thinks of a given product. After complying with these requests, the consumer may be more inclined to comply with the salesperson's ultimate request to purchase the product.[77] Consumers may comply with large marketing research requests such as filling out a long survey if they have first agreed to smaller requests, for example, answering a few research questions over the phone.[78]

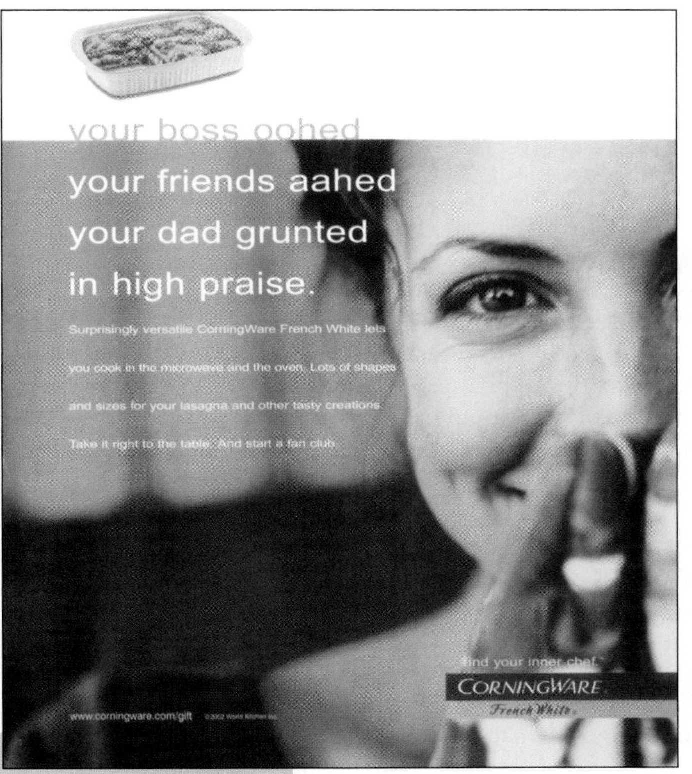

your boss oohed
your friends aahed
your dad grunted
in high praise.
Surprisingly versatile CorningWare French White lets
you cook in the microwave and the oven. Lots of shapes
and sizes for your lasagna and other tasty creations.
Take it right to the table. And start a fan club.
find your inner chef.
CORNINGWARE
French White
www.corningware.com/gift

EXHIBIT 16.13

Ad Using Normative Influence

Normative influence exists when other people can deliver rewards and/or punishments based on whether you conform to their influence attempts. The ad for CorningWare suggests that you will receive great compliments from others if you use CorningWare French White cookware.

Source: Courtesy of World Kitchen, Inc.

foot-in-the-door technique A technique designed to induce compliance by getting an individual to agree first to a small favor, then to a larger one, and then to an even larger one.

With the **door-in-the-face technique**, the marketer first asks the consumer to comply with a very large and possibly outrageous request, then presents a smaller and more reasonable request. For example, a salesperson might ask a consumer whether she wants to buy a $500 piece of jewelry. When the consumer says no, the salesperson might then ask if she wants to buy a set of earrings on sale for only $25.[79] One reason this technique works is that the consumer may perceive that the requestor has given something up by moving from a large to a small request. In turn, the consumer feels obligated to reciprocate by responding to the smaller request.

A third approach is the **even-a-penny-will-help technique**.[80] With this technique, marketers ask the consumer for a very small favor—so small it almost does not qualify as a favor. For example, marketers collecting money for a charity may indicate that even a penny will help those in need. Salespeople making cold calls may tell prospective clients that even one minute of their time will be valuable. Because people would look foolish denying these tiny requests, they usually comply and, in fact, often give an amount appropriate for the situation.

Ask consumers to predict their behavior. Simply asking consumers to predict their own behavior in taking a particular action often increases the likelihood that they will actually behave in that way.[81] For example, a marketer of products containing recycled parts might ask consumers to predict their behavior in supporting the environment by buying or using products made with reclaimed materials. This request may remind consumers that they have previously failed to do enough in living up to their own standards in supporting the environment—in turn, leading to purchases that will fulfill the consumers' self-prophecy.

Provide freedom of choice. Finally, because reactance usually occurs when individuals feel their freedom is being threatened, marketers need to ensure that consumers believe they have freedom of choice. For example, a salesperson might show a variety of styles of a particular dress, discussing the advantages of each. In this way, the consumer feels a greater sense of control over whether to buy at all, and if so, which item to buy. ●

INFORMATIONAL INFLUENCE

In addition to normative influence, reference groups and other influence sources can exert **informational influence** by offering information to help make decisions.[82] For example, chat groups on Internet travel sites exert informational influence by providing travel tips to prospective travelers. Friends exert informational influence by telling you which movie is playing at the local theater, and the media exert informational influence by reporting that certain foods may be health hazards.

door-in-the-face technique A technique designed to induce compliance by first asking an individual to comply with a very large and possibly outrageous request, followed by a smaller and more reasonable request.

even-a-penny-will-help technique A technique designed to induce compliance by asking individuals to do a very small favor—one that is so small it almost does not qualify as a favor.

informational influence The extent to which sources influence consumers simply by providing information.

How Informational Influence Can Affect Consumer Behavior

Informational influence is important because it can affect how much time and effort consumers devote to information search and decision making. Consumers who can get information from others easily may be reluctant to engage in time-intensive information search when making decisions. If, for example, you are looking for a new stereo and a trusted friend tells you that the brand he just bought is the best he has ever had, you might simply buy the same one.

Although information influence can reduce information search, it is sometimes important for marketers to increase the likelihood that consumers will engage in information search. For example, few consumers are likely to know about the benefits of a new, superior offering. The company must therefore launch a campaign to build product awareness and encourage consumers to compare products.

Factors Affecting Informational Influence Strength

The extent to which informational influence is strong or weak depends on the characteristics of the product, of the consumer and the influencer, and of the group.

Product Characteristics Consumers tend to be susceptible to informational influence when considering complex products such as electronic appliances that consumers cannot easily understand how to use.[83] Consumers are also more susceptible to informational influence when they perceive product purchase or usage to be risky.[84] Thus consumers may be affected by information they receive about laser hair removal, given its formidable financial and safety risks. Consumers may also be more open to informational influence when brands are very different from one another. Because consumers have difficulty determining which brand is best for them when the brands are quite distinct, they attach significance to information learned from others.[85]

Consumer and Influencer Characteristics Characteristics of both the consumer and the influencer affect the extent of informational influence. Such influence is likely to be greater when the source or group communicating the information is an expert,[86] especially if the consumer either lacks expertise or has had ambiguous experiences with the product. For example, given their lack of knowledge and confidence about the home-buying process, first-time home buyers are likely to consider carefully the information conveyed by experts such as real estate agents. Personality traits, such as consumers' susceptibility to reference group influence and attention to social comparison information, should also influence the extent to which consumers look to others for cues on product characteristics.[87]

Like normative influence, informational influence is affected by tie-strength. Individuals with strong ties tend to interact frequently, which provides greater opportunities for consumers to learn about products and others' reactions to them. Note that informational influence may actually affect the ties between individuals. When people establish social relationships that involve sharing information, for example, they may become friends in the process.[88]

Finally, culture may influence the impact of informational influence. One study found that U.S. consumers were more likely than Korean consumers to be persuaded by ads with a lot of information. Because the Korean culture often focuses on the group and group compliance, Korean consumers may be more susceptible to normative influence than U.S. consumers are.[89]

Group Characteristics Group cohesiveness also affects informational influence. Specifically, members of cohesive groups have both greater opportunity and perhaps greater motivation to share information.

MARKETING IMPLICATIONS Marketers can incorporate informational influence into their marketing activities in several ways.

Create informational influence by using experts. Because source expertise and credibility affect informational influence, marketers can use sources regarded as expert or credible for a given product category, the way athletic footwear manufacturers use sports stars as spokespeople.

Create a context for informational influence. The likelihood that informational influence will occur depends on the situation. For this reason, marketers should try to create a context for informational influence to occur. One study found that 80 percent of conversations about drinking a new brand of coffee took place in a food-related situation. One way of creating a context for informational influence is to host or sponsor special events related to the product.

Create informational and normative influence. Marketing efforts may be most successful when *both* normative and informational influence attempts are involved. One study found that only 2 percent of consumers donated blood in the absence of any type of influence but between 4 and 8 percent did so when either informational or normative influence was present. However, when both forms of influence were used, 22 percent of the consumers donated blood.[90] Also, because source similarity enhances both normative and informational influence, advertisers might enhance influence by using sources that are similar to their target audience. For example, lottery commercials often show sources similar to the target audience winning the lottery. Web-based recommendation systems are another example.[91] Amazon.com's book recommendations use both normative and informational influence because they indicate what people who have similar book tastes have bought and because they provide information (such as plot summaries and reviews) to help in the decision-making process. ●

DESCRIPTIVE DIMENSIONS OF INFORMATION

In the context of consumer behavior, information can be described by the dimensions of valence and modality.

Valence: Is Information Positive or Negative?

valence Whether information about something is good (positive valence) or bad (negative valence).

Valence describes whether the information is positive or negative. This is very important because researchers have found that negative and positive information affect consumer behavior in different ways.[92] Negative information is more likely than positive information to be communicated. As discussed in Chapter 12, more than half of dissatisfied consumers engage in negative word of mouth. Moreover, dissatisfied consumers complain to three times more people than the number of people satisfied consumers tell about their pleasure.[93] One study found that consumers who were dissatisfied with their home rental situation were likely to tell eight to ten people about their negative experiences.[94]

Researchers also hypothesize that people pay more attention to and give more weight to negative information than they do to positive information. This means negative information is more influential than positive information is.[95] Because most of the information we hear about products and services is positive, negative information may receive more attention—in general, it is surprising, unusual, and different. Negative information may also prompt consumers to attribute problems to the offering itself, not to the consumer who uses it. Thus if you learn that a friend got sick after eating at a new restaurant, you may attribute the outcome to the food (it must be bad) rather than to your friend (he ate too much). Finally, negative information may be diagnostic—that is, we may attach more significance to it because it seems to tell us how offerings differ from one another.

Modality: Does Information Come from Verbal or Nonverbal Channels?

Another dimension describing influence is the modality in which it is delivered—is it communicated verbally or nonverbally? Although norms about group behavior might be explicitly communicated by verbal description, consumers can also infer norms simply by observing how others behave. As an example, you may have a very good idea about what constitutes an appropriate graduation gift because you have observed what others have given in the past. Similarly, informational influence can be delivered verbally or nonverbally. A consumer may learn that a can opener is bad by observing someone struggling with it or by hearing people discuss their experiences with the product.

The Pervasive and Persuasive Influence of Word of Mouth

word of mouth Information about products or services that is communicated verbally.

Marketers are especially interested in a form of influence called **word of mouth**, which refers to information about products or services that is communicated verbally. Word of mouth can affect many consumer behaviors. For example, you may go to see a new movie because your friend said it was great. You may ask a coworker where she gets her hair cut and then go to the same salon. Your neighbor may recommend an electrician, or you may learn from a stranger at the bank that Nordstrom's semiannual sale is next week.[96] More than 40 percent of U.S. consumers seek the advice of family and friends when shopping for doctors, lawyers, or auto mechanics, although men and women differ in how often they seek advice and from whom (see Exhibit 16.14).[97]

Not only is word of mouth pervasive, it is also more persuasive than written information.[98] One study found that word of mouth was the number one source affecting food and household product purchases. It was seven times more

PERCENT OF MEN AND WOMEN WHO CHOOSE SELECTED PEOPLE AS SINGLE MOST-TRUSTED SOURCE FOR SELECTED PRODUCTS AND SERVICES, FOR THREE MOST-TRUSTED SOURCES, 1995

	FIRST-RANKED	PERCENT CHOOSING	SECOND-RANKED	PERCENT CHOOSING	THIRD-RANKED	PERCENT CHOOSING
NEW DOCTOR:						
Men	female relative	26	no one	18	male friend	17
Women	female relative	29	female friend	20	no one	14
WHERE TO GET HAIR CUT:						
Men	no one	38	male friend	25	female relative/friend	12
Women	female friend	45	no one	26	female relative	22
WHAT CAR TO BUY:						
Men	no one	31	male friend	26	male relative	22
Women	male relative	46	male friend	20	no one	19
CAR MECHANIC:						
Men	male friend	40	no one	26	male relative	21
Women	male relative	50	male friend	30	no one	10
WHERE TO GET LEGAL ADVICE:						
Men	male relative	26	male friend	23	no one	17
Women	male relative	31	male friend	16	female relative	14
WHERE TO GET PERSONAL LOAN:						
Men	no one	29	male friend	20	male relative	18
Women	male relative	33	no one	21	professional advisor	12
WHAT MOVIES TO SEE:						
Men	male friend	27	no one	22	female friend	18
Women	female friend	40	no one	19	female relative	15
WHERE TO EAT OUT:						
Men	female friend	26	female relative	21	male friend	21
Women	female friend	42	female relative	18	no one/male relative	11

EXHIBIT 16.14
Gender Differences

Men and women differ in how much they ask others' advice and from whom they seek advice. Women are more likely than men to seek word of mouth from others and to use a broader array of sources.

Source: Martiz Marketing Research Inc. as found in Chip Walker, "Word of Mouth," *American Demographics,* July 1995, pp. 39–45.

effective than print media, twice as effective as broadcast media, and four times more effective than salespeople in affecting brand switching.[99]

Online forums, chat rooms, bulletin boards, and Web sites can potentially magnify the effect of word of mouth. A disgruntled customer can not only tell other people about good and bad consumption experiences in person—he or she can also tell thousands of people with the click of a mouse. Worried about how to respond to online lamentations, some companies regularly monitor the Internet to see whether and how their products are being mentioned in these forums.[100] Ford, for example, uses special software to track online messages and find out what consumers are saying about its vehicles.[101]

viral marketing Online consumer-to-consumer communication that supports a particular offering.

As noted in the opening example, Ford also supports **viral marketing,** online consumer-to-consumer communication that supports a particular offering. Viral marketing is powerful because the source is non-marketer dominated and the message is delivered personally, adding credibility. Hotmail, for example, adds the brief message "Get your free Web based e-mail at Hotmail" to every message sent by a user. As these messages pass from user to user, consumers not only can see that the Hotmail service works, they become aware that their friends are actually using the service. This viral marketing campaign helped Hotmail attract 10 million users in its first year.[102]

MARKETING IMPLICATIONS Word of mouth is important to marketers because it can have a dramatic effect on consumers' product perceptions and an offering's marketplace performance. Many small businesses such as hairstylists, piano instructors, and preschools cannot afford to advertise and rely almost exclusively on word of mouth. Others, such as doctors, dentists, and lawyers, have traditionally been reluctant to advertise, fearing that such promotion will cheapen their professional image. Thus word-of-mouth referrals are a major factor in building and sustaining some businesses. Moreover, product success in some industries is ultimately tied to favorable word of mouth. For example, in preparation for the release of the movie *American Beauty* in the United Kingdom, the distributor arranged for hundreds of screenings to build positive word of mouth and encourage more people to see a film that was not easily described.[103]

Preventing and responding to negative word of mouth. Given its pervasive impact, marketers should be concerned about preventing negative word of mouth and rectifying it once it occurs.[104] Clearly, quality offerings are the best way to prevent negative word of mouth. To rectify negative word of mouth, firms can try to deal with consumers' dissatisfaction before more negative word of mouth spreads. For example, service providers who empathize with consumers' complaints and interact meaningfully with them may reduce the spread of negative word of mouth. In addition, companies are far more successful in reducing negative word of mouth by responding to complaints with an offer of free goods than by ignoring the complaints. In the case of a major crisis, such as Firestone's gigantic tire recall effort, companies must take definite steps to restore consumer confidence (see Exhibit 16.15).[105]

Engineering favorable word of mouth. In addition to creating quality products and services,[106] marketers may also try to engineer favorable word of mouth by targeting opinion leaders and using networking opportunities at trade shows, conferences, and public events. New York–based Kiehl's, for example, has built a $40 million business selling personal care products without advertising or fancy packaging. One way the company generates favorable word of mouth is by giving away up to $1.5 million worth of samples every year so consumers can try the products and tell their friends. Kiehl's also gets good word of mouth from fashion and beauty editors and from celebrity hairdressers who have tried and liked the products.[107] Hebrew National built buzz for its hot dogs by hiring a "Mom Squad" of brand-loyal consumers to drive sport-utility vehicles with brand logos to community events, host home barbecues featuring the hot dogs, and distribute coupons for free packages.[108]

Dealing with rumors. Rumors are a special case of negative word of mouth.[109] Walt Disney, for example, was subjected to false rumors that its movies *Aladdin* and *The Lion King* contained sexually oriented subliminal messages.[110] Companies may use several strategies to deal with false rumors.[111]

- *Do nothing.* Often companies prefer to do nothing because more consumers may actually learn about a rumor from marketers' attempts to correct it. One study found that 35 percent of consumers learned about the rumor that McDonald's used worms in hamburger meat from McDonald's own anti-rumor campaign.[112] However, this strategy can also backfire. Nike has been

EXHIBIT 16.15
Restoring Public Trust
Professional crisis managers recommend these steps when a company is under siege.

Source: Kathryn Kranbold and Erin White, "The Perils and Potential Rewards of Crisis Managing for Firestone," *Wall Street Journal,* September 8, 2000, p. B1. Reprinted with the permission of *The Wall Street Journal* via the Copyright Clearance Center.

DO:	DON'T:
• *Recognize that speed is crucial.* "If you don't have an answer or a solution to the problem, you better be able to tell your audiences that you're working on one," says Rich Blewitt, president of Rowan & Blewitt.	• *Hide what you know.* Being one step behind when evidence of wrongdoing surfaces not only damages your credibility, but also hinders your ability to control the spin, says Victor Kamber, CEO of The Kamber Group.
• *Place customers' interests above your own.* A company must "seem to want to come to the aid of the people in the crisis first, and [put] their own corporate interests last," says Larry Kramer, managing director at GCI Group.	• *Get tied down in the day-to-day details of running the company.* Make this crisis the No. 1 priority. "You've got to have a bunch of people who drop everything and just deal with this," says Mark Braverman, principal, CMG Associates Inc.
• *Take a long-term view.* As the massive Tylenol recall showed, sacrificing a product's image in the short-term can demonstrate responsibility over the long haul.	• *Forget that public perception is more important than reality.* Even if you've done nothing wrong but consumers think you have, their view is what matters, says Steven Fink, president of Lexicon Communications Corp.

accused of condoning low wages and abusive conditions in its Asian factories. Initially, Nike's image suffered in the wake of the very bad publicity it received by not responding vigorously to the attacks. The company has since responded in various ways, including putting links to labor practices and a virtual factory tour on its Web site.[113]

- *Do something locally.* Some companies choose to react locally, putting the rumor to rest on a case-by-case basis. Procter & Gamble sent a packet of information about its man-in-the-moon symbol, long rumored to connote devil worship, only to those consumers who called its hotline. In cases handled locally, companies should brief the personnel who interact with the public about the rumor and how they should respond to it. Management should also try to track down the source of the rumor because it may be tied to a specific source.
- *Do something discreetly.* Companies sometimes do something discreetly about a rumor. For example, when rumors circulated that oil companies were contriving oil shortages out of greed, the firms ran a public relations campaign that highlighted their positive and socially desirable activities. They did not mention the rumor, but the gist of the campaign clearly ran contrary to the rumor's content.
- *Do something big.* At times, companies may do something big with all the media resources at their disposal. They may use advertising to directly confront and refute the rumor, create news refuting the rumor, conduct media interviews about the truth, and hire credible outside opinion leaders to help dispel the rumor. Said Ismail, owner of two Po-Boy Express restaurants in Louisiana, took this approach after receiving phone calls and death threats based on a false rumor—spread via e-mail—that he and his staff had cheered

the terrorist attacks on the World Trade Center. Fighting back, Ismail told his side of the story to newspaper and television reporters. He also enlisted employees and customers to speak to the media on his behalf.[114]

Tracking word of mouth. Whether word of mouth is positive, like referrals, or negative, like product dissatisfaction or rumors, companies may want to try to identify the source. Through a method called *network analysis*, companies can ask consumers where they heard the information and then ask each of those sources where, in turn, they heard the story. By repeating this procedure, marketers can sometimes identify critical information sources.[115] Marketers can also query consumers about the specific information they heard from the source to track the distortion of information and find the key sources responsible for perpetuating it.

If a company can identify critical sources, they may follow up by targeting these sources directly. For example, the company can thank or explicitly reward individuals who are communicating positive word of mouth and acting as referrals. The company can also design referral-incentive programs that reward both the referrer and referee.[116]

Finally, companies should be aware that some institutions can serve as sources of word-of-mouth information. For example, although U.S. consumers may not find the church to be an important clearinghouse for word of mouth, Koreans do. ●

SUMMARY

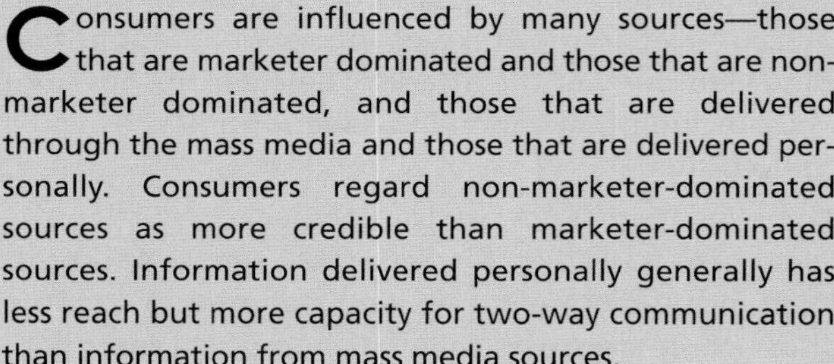

Consumers are influenced by many sources—those that are marketer dominated and those that are non-marketer dominated, and those that are delivered through the mass media and those that are delivered personally. Consumers regard non-marketer-dominated sources as more credible than marketer-dominated sources. Information delivered personally generally has less reach but more capacity for two-way communication than information from mass media sources.

Opinion leaders and market mavens represent special sources of influence. Opinion leaders are experts in a product category; market mavens are individuals involved in the marketplace in general. Marketers may target these individuals explicitly, given their potential to serve as brokers of information, or simulate opinion leaders in marketing communications.

Reference groups are people with whom individuals compare themselves to guide their values, attitudes, and behaviors. Reference groups are associative, aspirational, and dissociative; they can be described according to their degree of contact, formality, homophily, group attractiveness, density, identification, and tie-strength. Reference groups may play a powerful socializing role, influencing consumers' key actions, values, and behaviors.

These influence sources exert normative and informational influence. Normative influence tends to be greater for products that are publicly consumed, considered luxuries, or regarded as a significant aspect of group membership. Normative influence is also strong for individuals who tend to pay attention to social information. Strong ties and identification with the group increase the likelihood that consumers will succumb to normative influences. Finally, normative influence is greater when groups are cohesive, when members are similar, and when the group has the power to deliver rewards and sanctions.

Informational influence operates when individuals affect others by providing information. Consumers are most likely to seek and follow informational influence when products are complex, purchase or use is risky, and brands are distinctive. The more expert the influencer and the more consumers are predisposed to listen to others, the greater the informational influence. Informational influence is also greater when groups are more rather than less cohesive.

Social influence, whether normative or informational, varies in valence and modality. Negative information is communicated to more people and given greater weight in decision making than positive information. Marketers are particularly interested in word-of-mouth information—both positive and negative—which can now be spread even faster and farther through the Internet. Companies may design strategies to identify, target, and reward individuals who serve as positive word-of-mouth referral sources. Sources of negative information, such as rumors, might also be targeted if identified. When dealing with false rumors, companies can do nothing, do something locally, do something discreetly, or do something big.

QUESTIONS FOR REVIEW AND DISCUSSION

1. How do sources of influence differ in terms of marketer domination and delivery?
2. Why do companies sometimes target opinion leaders and market mavens?
3. What are the three types of reference groups, and how can these groups be described?
4. How might consumers respond to normative influence?
5. What three techniques can marketers use to encourage consumer compliance?
6. Differentiate between information valence and modality.
7. Why is word of mouth so important for marketers?

EXERCISES

1. Keep a word-of-mouth log for 24 hours. Document (a) what information you hear, (b) whether it is positive or negative, (c) what effect you think it will have on your behavior, and (d) why. Think about what implications the entries in your log have for marketers.
2. Take an entry in your word-of-mouth log (from exercise #1) and try to track down the source of the information. Did the information flow within a relatively dense social network, or did it flow across social networks via weak ties? Try to diagram the nature of the information flow within and across various groups.
3. Observe a salesperson trying to make a sale. Try to understand which aspects of his or her selling attempts represent informational influence and which represent normative influence. Was the salesperson successful in inducing a sale? Which concepts from this chapter may explain why or why not?
4. As a marketing manager for a new brand of diet hot chocolate, you want to use an opinion leader to stimulate sales of the brand. How might you identify an opinion leader, and what strategies do you have for using an opinion leader in your marketing communications program?
5. You have recently learned that a lot of positive and negative information is being communicated about the new brand of diet hot chocolate. Should your strategy be to try to bolster the positive information or to stop the negative information? Why?

chapter 17

Psychographics: Values, Personality, and Lifestyles

Introduction: Something for Everyone

More than 143 million U.S. consumers—54 percent of the population—have accessed the Internet from home. In addition to researching buying decisions, they are surfing the Web for information, graphics, sounds, and other materials on an extremely wide variety of subjects ranging from cooking and other home-related interests to sports, movies, travel, and fitness. While sex is one of the topics consumers search for most frequently on the Web, listings of the most heavily trafficked Web sites reflect a huge diversity of interests and activities such as search engines, greeting cards, online auctions, and technology. Other popular areas are chat rooms, software and media downloads, games, and the weather. The Internet even attracts so-called cyberchondriacs who regularly visit the hundreds of sites devoted to health and illnesses (see Exhibit 17.1).

Teenagers in particular spend many of their waking hours hunched over computers linked to fellow users or various Web sites. Although more than 70 percent of teens who use the Internet go online to communicate via e-mail and instant messaging, other common uses include researching school assignments and following current events.[1] Some people prefer to communicate online rather than face-to-face, and a growing number of people are choosing to meet and get acquainted online before they date in person.

This brief overview of the Internet's uses illustrates the three topics of this chapter: values, personality, and lifestyles. Values determine which sites people will visit, for example,

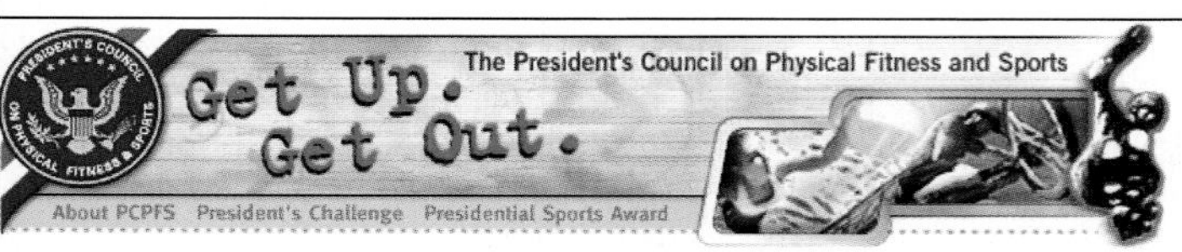

NEWS!

REMARKS OF CHAIRMAN LYNN SWANN AT THE NATIONAL PRESS CLUB

COUNCIL ANNOUNCES NEW FITNESS AWARD TO ENCOURAGE PHYSICAL ACTIVITY

COUNCIL MEMBERS SHARE FITNESS TIPS

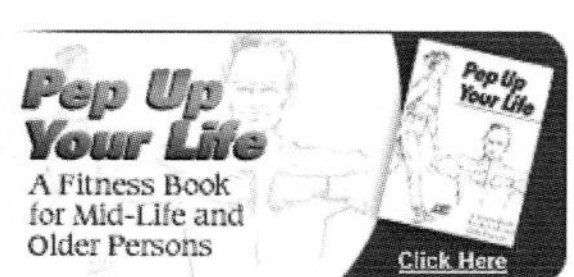

Pep Up Your Life
A Fitness Book for Mid-Life and Older Persons
Click Here

If you're interested in adding life to your years and years to your life, or you need help developing your physical fitness or activity program, we've got you covered.

Our useful information is at your fingertips...ready for you to download and print. Just choose a category to start browsing.

OUR PROGRAMS

The President's Challenge
For teachers, principals, youth and camp, YMCA/YWCA, and club leaders.

FAST FACTS ABOUT THE PRESIDENT'S COUNCIL

Click on the links below for more information:

- New Executive Order for the President's Council.
- Biographies of the new Council members.
- President's Council Fact Sheet.
- Physical Activity Fact Sheet.
- Report *"Physical Activity Fundamental to Preventing Disease"* available online.
- Obesity Still On The Rise, New Data Show

PUBLICATIONS

Reading Room
Index to all PCPFS publications.

PCPFS Research Digests
Quarterly summary of the latest scientific information on specific physical activity topics.

Other Federal Publications

EXHIBIT 17.1
Lifestyle-Related Web Site
This is a Web site that helps consumers stay fit.

Source: The President's Council on Physical Fitness and Sports.

home- or health-related sites or sexually oriented pages. The fact that introverted individuals may feel more comfortable communicating online rather than in person illustrates the influence of personality. Finally, some consumers just enjoy surfing the Web as an activity in and of itself (a lifestyle).

psychographics A description of consumers on the basis of their psychological and behavioral characteristics.

Together, values, personality, and lifestyles constitute the basic components of **psychographics**, the description of consumers based on their psychological and behavioral characteristics. Traditionally, psychographics measured consumer lifestyles, but more modern applications have broadened the approach to include concepts such as the consumers' psychological makeup, their values and personality, and the way they behave with respect to specific products (their usage patterns, attitudes, and emotions).

Marketers use psychographics to gain a more detailed understanding of consumer behavior than they can get from demographic variables like ethnicity, social class, age, gender, and religion. For example, Generation Xers can be divided into several psychographic groups. So-called Yup & Comers (28 percent of Generation Xers) have the highest levels of income and education and are comfortable about themselves and their future. Bystanders (37 percent) are predominantly practical, hardworking women, with a large percentage of Hispanics and African Americans.[2] Playboys (19 percent) are self-absorbed, fun-loving, impulsive types who live on the edge; and Drifters (16 percent) are frustrated, less educated, and seeking status.

Exhibit 17.2 diagrams these psychographic variables and the way they relate to group membership. The following sections examine the major components of psychographic research in greater detail, beginning with values. ●

VALUES

values Enduring beliefs that a given behavior is desirable or good.

Values are enduring beliefs that a given behavior or outcome is desirable or good.[3] For example, you may believe that it is good to be healthy, keep your family safe, have self-respect, and be free. As enduring beliefs, your values serve as standards that guide your behavior across situations and over time. For example, how much you value the environment generally determines the extent to which you litter, recycle, use aerosol cans, or buy recyclable products. Values are so ingrained that most people are not consciously aware of them and have difficulty describing them.

value system Our total set of values and their relative importance.

Our total set of values and their relative importance constitute our **value system**. The way we behave in a given situation is often influenced by how important one value is relative to others.[4] For instance, deciding whether to spend Sunday afternoon relaxing with your family or exercising will be determined by the relative importance you place on family versus health. You feel value conflict when you do something that is consistent with one value but inconsistent with another equally important value. For example, parents who place equal value on convenience and concern for the environment may experience value conflict if they buy disposable diapers for their babies. Similarly, smoking cigarettes may cause conflict for teenagers if they value health and social acceptance equally.

Because values are among the first things children learn, value systems are often in place by age 10. As discussed in Chapter 16, people learn values through the process of socialization, which results from exposure to reference groups and other sources of influence.[5] You may therefore value education because your parents went to college and because they and your teachers encouraged this value. Likewise, the value you place on money, high-tech products, or the environment may come from your exposure to the opinions

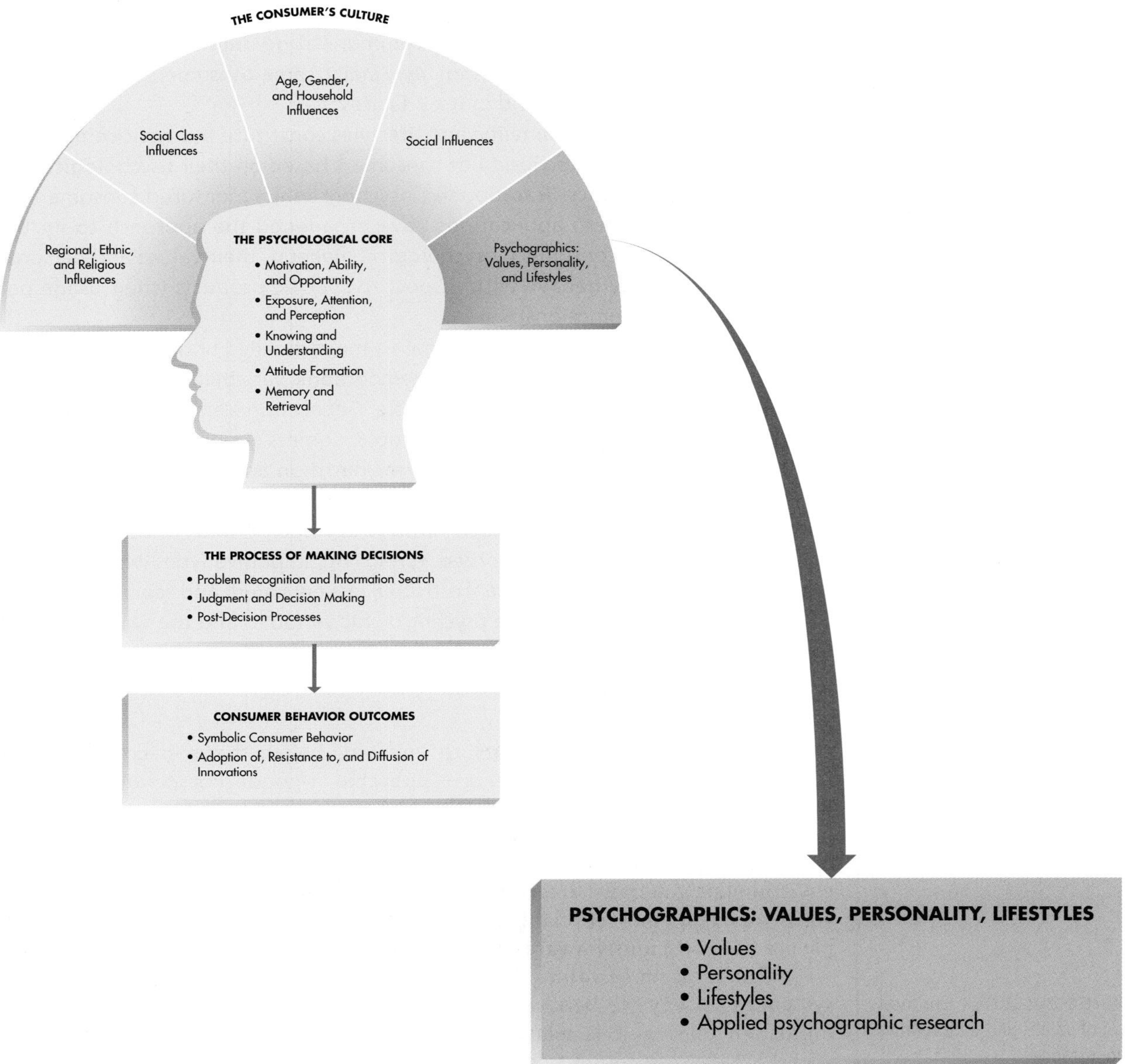

EXHIBIT 17.2 Chapter Overview: Values, Personality, and Lifestyle Previous chapters demonstrated how membership in certain cultural groups (regional, ethnic, social class, etc.) can affect group behaviors. This chapter examines the effect of these cultural influences on an individual level—namely, on values (deeply held beliefs), personality (consumer traits), and lifestyles (behavioral patterns that are manifestations of values and personality). Each of these factors is useful in understanding consumer behavior; in addition, marketers often combine them to obtain an overall psychographic profile of consumers.

of family, friends, or the media. The Cartoon Network, for example, airs anger management spots during children's shows such as *Dragon Ball Z,* which features violent conflicts between characters.[6] Because individuals learn values through exposure to others in institutions and cultures, people within the same group often hold similar values.

Acculturation is the process by which individuals learn the values and behaviors of a new culture (see Chapter 13). For example, immigrants arriving in the United States must learn new values to acculturate to American life. Consumers are more likely to adopt the values of a new culture if they view that culture as attractive and having values similar to their own. Acculturation is also faster when people in the new culture are cohesive, give a lot of verbal and nonverbal signals about what their values are, and express pride in the values they hold.[7]

How Values Can Be Described

global values A person's most enduring, strongly held, and abstract values that hold in many situations.

Values can vary in terms of their specificity. At the broadest level are **global values**, which represent the core of an individual's value system. These values, which are highly enduring, strongly held, and abstract, apply in many situations. For example, because much of U.S. political philosophy is based on the idea of freedom, that value permeates many domains of our lives. We believe that we should have the freedom to speak, go where we want, dress as we please, and live where we want.

One of the many ways of characterizing global values is depicted in Exhibit 17.3. This scheme divides global values into seven categories: maturity, security, prosocial behavior (doing nice things for others), restrictive conformity, enjoyment, achievement, and self-direction. Note that similar categories are placed close together. Thus achievement and self-direction reflect a similar orientation toward the individual as a person, whereas prosocial behavior and restrictive conformity reflect values that relate to how an individual should deal with others.

terminal value A highly desired end state such as social recognition and pleasure.

instrumental value A value needed to achieve a desired end state such as ambition or cheerfulness.

Within the seven domains there are two types of global values: terminal and instrumental. **Terminal values** (shown with an asterisk) are highly desired end states, and **instrumental values** (shown with a plus sign) are those needed to achieve these desired end states. For example, the two terminal values in the prosocial category are equality and salvation. The instrumental values of loving, forgiving, helpfulness, honesty, and belief in God help one achieve these terminal values.[8] Also notice in Exhibit 17.3 that values tend to be polarized. As a result, consumers who place a high value on one set of terminal values place less value on the set on the opposite side of the figure. Thus individuals who value security, maturity, and a prosocial orientation might place less value on enjoyment (on the opposite side). Those who emphasize self-direction and achievement would value prosocial behaviors and restrictive conformity less.

domain-specific values Values that may apply to only a particular area of activities.

Global values are different from **domain-specific values**, which are relevant only to particular areas of activity such as religion, family, or consumption. Materialism is a domain-specific value because it relates to the way we view the acquisition of material goods. Although they differ, global and domain-specific values can be related in that achievement of domain-specific values (such as health) can be instrumental to the achievement of one or more global values (such as inner harmony or self-respect).

The Values That Characterize Western Culture

Given that values are an important influence on behavior, marketers need to understand some of the values that characterize consumption in Western societies. These include materialism, the home, work and play, family and children, health, hedonism, youth, the environment, and technology.

materialism Placing importance on money and material goods.

Materialism One value that has become increasingly prevalent in Western cultures is **materialism**.[9] In a materialistic society, people gauge satisfaction in

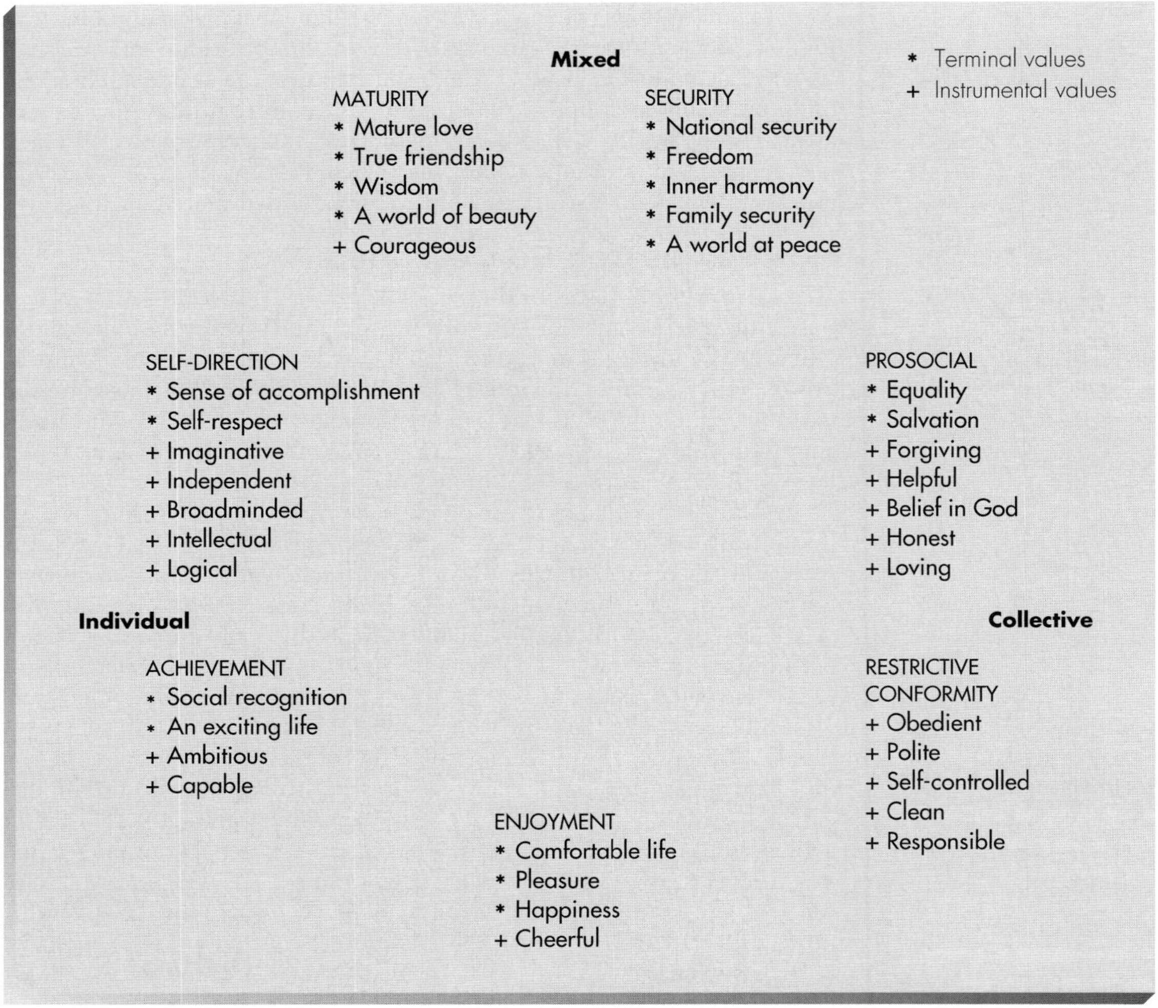

EXHIBIT 17.3
Global Values and Value Categories

One scheme for classifying global values identifies seven major categories. Some values are individual oriented (e.g., self-direction, achievement); others are more collective or group oriented (e.g., prosocial, restrictive conformity). Note that categories close to each other are similar; those farther apart are less so. Terminal values (or highly desired end states) are marked with an asterisk (*); instrumental values have a plus sign (+).

Source: Shalom H. Schwartz and Wolfgang Bilsky, "Toward a Universal Psychological Structure of Human Values," *Journal of Personality and Social Psychology*, vol. 53, no. 3, 1987, pp. 550–562. Copyright © 1987 by the American Psychological Association. Adapted with permission.

terms of what they have or have not acquired in life and in terms of desired possessions. Individuals who are materialistic tend to value items like cars, jewelry, and boats. In contrast, symbolic items such as a mother's wedding gown, family mementos, and photos are more important to those low in materialism.[10] Materialism might lead someone to believe that they will be happy if they have a bigger house, a nicer car, or more expensive clothes.

Materialism may relate to several of the terminal values noted in Exhibit 17.3. For example, possessions may be instrumental in achieving the higher-order value of social recognition. Or materialism may reflect a high value on accomplishment, if people judge self-worth by what they have acquired or their achievement of a comfortable life.

Some people value materialism more highly than others. Not everyone is unhappy with a low-paying job or little discretionary income. Members of communes, nuns, priests, and monks have chosen a lifestyle that rejects material possessions.[11] In addition, growing numbers of people have reassessed their priorities, rejected materialism, and decided to simplify their lives by making and spending less.

Nevertheless, American consumers generally have a materialistic bent, and studies of Japanese and Chinese consumers also reveal an increasing emphasis on a materialistic lifestyle.[12] The desire for material goods is particularly acute in formerly communist countries such as the Czech Republic and Romania, where consumers strive to acquire as many Western goods as possible, especially a car, a TV, and fashionable clothes and shoes.[13]

In a materialistic society, consumers will be receptive to marketing tactics that facilitate the acquisition of goods, such as phone-in or online orders and credit-card payments, and to messages that associate the acquisition of the good with achievement and status, like ads for a Rolex watch. Special sales, coupons, two-for-one deals, bonus packs, and warehouse clubs have done exceptionally well in the United States and Japan, perhaps in part because of consumers' materialistic tendencies. These marketing tactics allow consumers to buy some products cheaply, thus saving money to buy other things.[14] Consumers also want to protect their possessions, creating opportunities for services such as insurance and security companies that protect consumers against loss, theft, or damage.

Home Many consumers place a high value on the home and believe in making it as attractive and as comfortable as possible. Currently, 64 percent of U.S. citizens own their own home, and they spend more time there than in previous eras, a trend called *cocooning*. Because the outside world is becoming more complex, exhausting, and dangerous, consumers often view home as a haven.[15] Also, more and more families view their home as "command central"—a place to coordinate activities and pool resources before members enter the outside world.

Cocooning has resulted in a trend toward more consumption activities taking place inside the home. Take-out and delivery services, video and DVD rentals, pay-per-view movie viewing, and shopping from home are increasingly replacing activities such as eating out, going to the movies, and shopping in stores. This trend is reflected by Blockbuster's appeal to families gathered around the TV at home ("Make It a Blockbuster Night").[16] People are even taking more vacations at home.[17] Furthermore, companies such as House of Fabrics, Home Depot, Michael's, and Expressions, which focus on decorating, crafts, remodeling, and home furnishings, are experiencing growth.

Work and Play Consumers in the United States appear to have a rather schizophrenic approach toward work and play. On the one hand, we are working harder and longer than ever before, partly due to corporate downsizing and an emphasis on productivity. In fact, some companies even arrange for employees' sick children to receive care at special facilities so parents won't have to miss work.[18] However, consumers increasingly value work for its instrumental function in achieving other values such as a comfortable lifestyle, family security, and self-accomplishment (or accomplishing one's life goals). Thus the Protestant work ethic—the value placed on work itself and on the delay of gratification to the exclusion of leisure and pleasure—is less characteristic of consumers today than it was a century ago. A similar work-value trend is evident among the Dutch, who see work as a tool to get money as well as security.[19] In contrast, other cultures attach a different meaning to work. In communist countries such as China and North Korea, consumers value work because of its contribution to the larger social good.

Perhaps because people are working more, they tend to value leisure time as much as they value money. They will pay for services like housecleaning so they can spend more of their nonwork time on leisure activities. One study even found that two-thirds of U.S. consumers were willing to take a salary cut in order to increase their leisure time.[20] Furthermore, the distinction between work and home life is blurring because technological advances such as e-mail and electronic conferencing allow many people to work at home. Many people are also spending more time at work doing household errands (e.g., making doctor appointments) as well as spending part of their weekend time doing job-related work. A study of working mothers found that a strong concern was "juggling, balancing, and fitting it all in" with the "endless array of competing demands" of work and home.[21] In the Netherlands, research identified two main groups among young people: the Yups, who value work as a means to achieve something, and the unambitious, who say, "You can work your whole life, so let's have fun now."[22]

Family and Children Cultures also differ in the values they place on their families and children. Parents in Europe and Asia, for example, tend to value education more than U.S. parents. Among Asian middle-class families, educating children is second in priority only to providing food. This is why children's books have been the largest sellers among Time Life's offerings in the Asian market, representing 55 percent of sales.[23]

Nevertheless, American consumers still place a high value on children. Rather than move their families when they change jobs or get promoted, a small but growing number of parents are commuting to work in another city or state and using e-mail and other technologies to stay in touch with the other parent and their children during the week.[24] U.S. parents are generally quite receptive to child-related products. Consider, for example, the range of cereals, juices, desserts, soft drinks, and other snack products targeting children. Even status luxury goods like Waterford, Mercedes, and Volvo, designers like Liz Claiborne, and high-tech firms like IBM stress family values in their ad campaigns.[25] The ad in Exhibit 17.4 is likely to appeal to consumers who value education.

Health U.S. consumers are placing more value on their health. In part, these concerns are tied to self-esteem because health is defined as having a lean, trim body. However, health is also related to basic concerns about longevity and survival.

Health values are reflected in the increasing number of products that are low in fat, calories, salt, sugar, or cholesterol. Food brands such as Lean Cuisine, Healthy Choice, and Weight Watchers, for example, have been successful because of their low fat content. Just being low fat, however, is not enough. Kellogg's and Unilever have unveiled new lines of functional foods called nutraceuticals that claim to lower cholesterol levels, thereby reducing the risk of heart disease.[26] Coca-Cola, Pepsi, and other marketers are promoting the health benefits of bottled water—the fastest-growing beverage category.[27] Growing concern over pesticides, additives, and contaminants has enhanced demand for organic and vegetarian

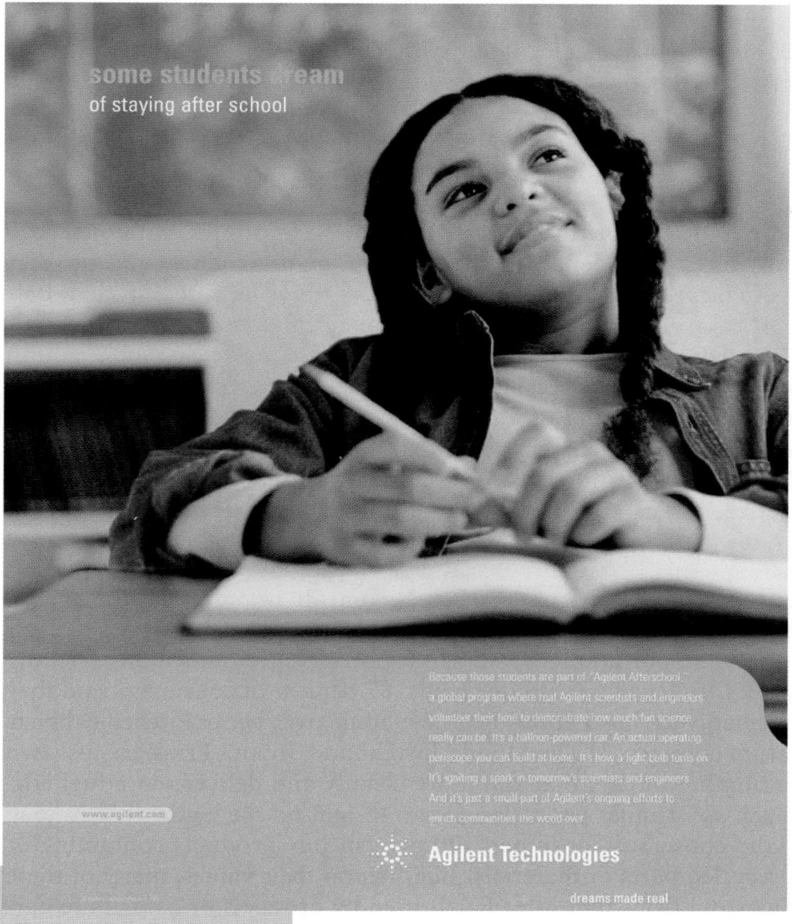

some students dream
of staying after school
Because those students are part of "Agilent Afterschool,"
a global program where real Agilent scientists and engineers
volunteer their time to demonstrate how much fun science
really can be. It's a balloon-powered car. An actual operating
periscope you can build at home. It's how a light bulb turns on.
It's igniting a spark in tomorrow's scientists and engineers.
And it's just a small part of Agilent's ongoing efforts to
enrich communities the world over.
www.agilent.com
Agilent Technologies
dreams made real

EXHIBIT 17.4
Valuing Education
This ad is trying to appeal to individuals who value reading and education.

Source: Reprinted with permission from Agilent Technologies.

foods and boosted sales at specialized chains like Whole Foods.[28] In Europe, health concerns have led to a deep-seated resistance to genetically modified foods.[29]

The emphasis on health has also paved the way for dieting services like Jenny Craig and Weight Watchers, health clubs, and diet aids. Hospitals now offer aerobics, kick-boxing, and aquatics classes to promote wellness. Magazines like *Health, Shape,* and *Runners' World* also exemplify health values. In addition, more consumers are turning to health food stores and alternative medicine for treating and preventing illnesses.[30] Attacks on both adult and youth smoking, bans on smoking in public places, and tobacco and alcohol warning labels in the United States and increasingly in Europe are also consistent with health concerns.[31]

Values and behavior can differ, however. For example, some smokers have become even more determined to maintain their lifestyle, and cigarette stores that provide a smoking "oasis" for these consumers are increasingly popular. Although many consumers say they want to consume less fat, relatively few are buying light or low-fat alternatives.[32] McDonald's McLean burger failed because consumers preferred the traditional, high-fat burgers, and Frito Lay's no fat WOW chips haven't done as well as expected.[33] Even high-fat products like steaks are experiencing strong sales.[34]

In fact, Americans are getting heavier: 61 percent of adults aged 20 to 74, 14 percent of teenagers, and 13 percent of children aged 6 to 11 are overweight.[35] As a result, plus-size clothing outlets, romance novels with overweight heroines, and dating services for overweight people have flourished.[36]

hedonism The principle of pleasure seeking.

Hedonism Consumers are increasingly operating on the principle of **hedonism**, or pleasure seeking, and they desire products and services that simply make them feel good, such as luxury cars, home entertainment centers, and exciting vacations. Airlines appeal to hedonism by offering more leg room and video selections on individual screens, and some truck stops now offer massages, movies, and wedding ceremonies to appeal to their customers' pleasures.[37] And Wendy's, Denny's, and Taco Bell offer late-night hours for consumers who crave fast-food burgers and tacos after midnight.[38]

Hedonism has led to some interesting eating patterns that contradict health values, witnessed by the success of the Chicago Steakhouse chain and Häagen-Dazs ice cream on the one hand, and Healthy Choice fat-free chocolate chip cookies and fat-free frozen yogurt on the other.[39] Furthermore, despite concerns over health, consumers will not switch to low-fat, low-calorie varieties unless they taste good. Consumers are also demanding larger sizes in the foods they consume, which explains the success of products like Pizza Hut's Big Foot Pizza, Healthy Choice's extra portion dinner, Pillsbury's Grand biscuits, and jumbo serving sizes at fast-food restaurants.[40]

Youth Compared with other cultures, the United States has long placed a high value on youth, as evidenced by the wide range of products and services designed to combat or reduce signs of aging (think of wrinkle creams, hair coloring, and hair transplants). Plastic surgery is one of the fastest growing medical specialties for both men and women. Furthermore, more than one million Americans annually receive injections of Botox to reduce and prevent visible wrinkles—at a cost of $300 or more per treatment.[41] Advertising messages also indicate the value we place on youth, as illustrated by Pepsi's "Be Young. Have Fun. Drink Pepsi" campaign. A strong youth orientation is also evident in Latin America, where consumers spend more than $1.6 billion a year on cosmetics.[42]

The Environment The environment has become an important value among U.S. consumers, who are interested in preventing further depletion of environmental resources and pollution as well as supporting environmentally friendly products, services, and activities. In one study, 87 percent of consumers said they would choose energy-saving features in a new home over better kitchen cabinets or other creature comforts.[43] The Honda Insight and Toyota Prius are just two of a growing number of cars that run more cleanly and deliver more fuel efficiency—as much as 71 miles per gallon for an Insight on the highway.[44] Among environmentally conscious consumers, 90 percent buy products containing or packaged in recycled parts or materials. Building on their values, many of these consumers buy from firms that offer Earth-friendly products or contribute part of their profits to environmental causes.[45]

Technology Consumers in Western cultures are fascinated by technological advances. More than ever before they believe that computers, VCRs, ATMs, answering machines, cell phones, and fax machines, not to mention the Internet, improve the quality of their lives. Nevertheless, technological changes are sometimes so rapid that we have trouble keeping up with them, resulting in a renewed emphasis on simplicity or at least on managing complexity. This trend is reflected in the rise of retail concepts like The Body Shop, which sells natural personal care products, as well as a revived interest in classical music and untreated packaging materials like glass, cartons, and paper. Products with features that work automatically are popular because they make it easier for consumers to use the products properly.[46] For example, today's software generally handles more operations and is more user friendly than older software. Thus consumers appear to value technology more for what it can do to make life easier than for the technological advance per se—making technology an instrumental rather than a terminal value.

Why Values Change

Because societies and their institutions are constantly evolving, value systems are also changing. In addition to the key trends already discussed, U.S. values are moving toward casualness in living, more liberal sexual attitudes, greater sophistication in behavior, a change in sex roles, and the wish to be modern.[47] Furthermore, although the United States was different from Western Europe 100 years ago, both cultures, and to a certain extent Japan as well, are becoming more similar in values, even though differences still exist. This increase in value consistency is driven in part by the increase in global communication. For example, Western Europeans regard some of U.S. consumption patterns as attractive. Wealthy Japanese consumers are starting to place greater value on personal preferences, a balanced life, and experiences and less value on traditional expectations, work, and possessions.[48]

Influences on Values

How do values differ across groups of consumers? This section explores the ways that culture, ethnicity, social class, and age can influence our values.

Culture and Values People in different countries are exposed to different cultural experiences, which leads to cross-cultural differences in values. One study found that the three most important values among Brazilians are true friendship, mature love, and happiness, whereas U.S. consumers named family security, world peace, and freedom.[49] Inner harmony ranked 4th in importance among Brazilians but 13th in the United States. These values all differ from the beliefs of consumers in China where the most important values are preserving the best that one has attained, being sympathetic to others, having self-control, and integrating enjoyment, action, and contemplation. A study of women in Germany, France, and the United Kingdom found that the value of "having a familiar routine" is most important for German women, but only 10th in importance for the British and 23rd for the French.[50] "Having beautiful things in the home" and "being with people with up-to-date ideas" are more important to Germans, and "having something to do to keep busy" is more critical to the French and British.

In a classic study, Hofstede identified four main value dimensions along which cultures can vary:[51]

- *Individualism versus collectivism.* The degree to which a culture focuses on the individuals rather than the group.
- *Uncertainty avoidance.* The extent to which a culture prefers structured to unstructured situations.
- *Masculinity versus femininity.* The extent to which a culture stresses masculine values (as defined by Hofstede) such as assertiveness, success, and competition over feminine values such as quality of life, warm personal relationships, and caring.
- *Power distance.* The degree to which a society's members are equal in terms of status.

All cultures can be classified along these four dimensions. Understanding where a given culture falls may provide insight into cross-cultural differences. For example, research showed that tipping in restaurants is less likely to occur in countries where power distance and uncertainty avoidance are low, feminine values are strong, and individualism is high.[52] Another study found that humorous ad themes are more likely to focus on groups in collectivist societies like Thailand and South Korea and on unequal status relationships in countries with high power distance like the United States and Germany.[53]

Ethnic Identification and Values Ethnic groups within a larger culture can have some values that are different from those of other ethnic subcultures. As noted in Chapter 13, Hispanic Americans strongly value the family and home and are therefore less likely to eat away from home than are Anglos.[54] Furthermore, compared with Anglos, Hispanics place more emphasis on equality and inner harmony, and Anglos place more emphasis on having world peace and friendships. African and Asian American subcultures place a high value on the extended family.[55] Because Asian American consumers also value tradition and cooperation, they respond well to subtle messages that focus on these values. In addition to family security, African Americans place a higher value on equality, freedom, a sense of accomplishment, and broadmindedness, whereas their Anglo counterparts value world peace to a greater degree.

Differences in ethnic values are present in many countries around the world. For example, Punjabi consumers in northern India place a high value on entrepreneurialism, since many own family businesses. They hold Western values and place great importance on earning a lot of money, becoming upwardly mobile, and showing off products that indicate wealth or status. They also want to get their children into the right schools where they will have the opportunity to achieve. In contrast, Tamils from the southern part of India place higher value on intellectual pursuits, are idealistic, and spend time in intellectual activities like art, literature, and music. Rather than engaging in conspicuous consumption, these consumers have a simpler lifestyle. Tamils and Punjabis are therefore likely to react very differently to status appeals and services designed to help the individual earn money.

Social Class and Values Different social classes tend to hold specific values, as discussed in Chapter 14. In the United States, working-class consumers have been characterized as valuing family and friendships. Middle-class consumers, in contrast, focus more on individualism, achievement, self-accomplishment, and social recognition. The middle class also values doing the right thing, having a nice home and more possessions, and buying what others buy. Furthermore, as countries in Eastern Europe and other nations embrace market economies, the size of the middle class is increasing dramatically, along with middle-class values that include materialism and a desire for less government control over their lives and greater access to information. Upper-upper-class consumers value giving back to society, and their prosocial orientation spurs them to become active in social, cultural, and civic causes. These consumers also prize self-expression as reflected in their homes, clothing, cars, artwork, and other forms of consumption.[56]

Age and Values Members of a generation often share similar values that differ from those of other generations. For example, your grandparents may value security over hedonism, not because they are older but because they grew up during the Great Depression and suffered economic hardship as children. They therefore view hedonic activities as frivolous and unacceptable. Likewise, baby boomers who grew up in the 1960s—a time of political upheaval, self-indulgence, and rebellion—value hedonism, morality, self-direction, and achievement.[57] Note that it is sometimes very difficult to distinguish values we acquire with age from those we learn from our era. Nevertheless, differences by virtue of age or cohort do exist, and they influence the way we behave as consumers.

MARKETING IMPLICATIONS Marketers need to understand how consumer values affect consumption patterns, market segmentation, new product development, ad development strategy, and ethics.

Consumption patterns. Consumers tend to buy, use, and dispose of products in a manner consistent with their values.[58] Thus marketers can know more about what consumers like if they understand their values. For example, those who value warm relationships with others are more likely to buy gifts, send cards, and make long-distance phone calls than those who place less value on relationships.[59] Consumers buy at The Body Shop not only because of the value the store places on naturalness and health but also because the company emphasizes societal values such as employing orphans in India and buying ingredients from impoverished Brazilian tribes.[60] *Good Housekeeping* was introduced into Japan because many Japanese are questioning their workaholic ways and are anxious to devote more time to home and family.[61] In Taiwan, consumption is guided by Confucian values (in contrast to mainland China), and consumers are therefore frugal and sober and have a finely graded system of status symbols for everything from the home to food.[62]

Interestingly, most international marketing blunders occur because companies do not understand the values of a particular culture.[63] Marketers sometimes adopt an ethnocentric perspective by assuming that the values of consumers in other cultures are similar to their own. Campbell's soup failed in South America because in that region, a mother's behavior is judged by the amount of time and dedication she devotes to domestic duties. Serving canned soup is tantamount to saying you do not care enough about your family.

value segmentation The grouping of consumers by common values.

Market segmentation. Marketers can identify groups of consumers who have a common set of values different from those of other groups, a process called **value segmentation**. For example, Honda segmented the car market based on the value consumers place on environmental issues and then identified some specific demographic variables that described a particular group: primarily married men in their 30s with high incomes and a technical job or an interest in technology or the environment.[64] Then Honda designed the Insight, powered by both gasoline and electricity, to appeal to this group. Like other car manufacturers, Honda offers brands and models for different value segments, such as the Acura brand for materialistic, achievement-oriented consumers. As another example, the People for the Ethical Treatment of Animals (PETA) developed an ad campaign promoting vegetarian values.[65]

Marketers also can use values to understand the attributes that consumers in a particular segment are likely to find important in a product and that may therefore motivate them to choose one brand over another. When buying clothes, individuals who value status might look for attributes like price and luxury, whereas those who value fitting in with the crowd might look for clothing that is trendy.[66] One study found that women's perfume preferences can be grouped according to value segments such as the Fledgling Career Woman, Working-Class Woman, Frustrated Professional, Traditional Housewife, Successful Professional, and Senior Set Woman. In this research, women with higher levels of self-confidence were found to prefer more subtle fragrances.[67]

New product ideas. Values can influence consumers' reactions to new and different products. For example, consumers who highly value change are likely to react very differently to innovations like e-mail, compared with those who value change less.[68] The more a new product is consistent with important consumer values, the greater the likelihood of its success. For example, good-tasting, microwavable, low-fat, and low-calorie frozen entrees succeeded in part because these items are consistent with multiple values like hedonism, time, convenience, health, and technology. Low-fat pet foods are doing well because they are consistent with pet owners' concern for their pets' health.

Ad development strategy. Examining the target segment's value profile can help marketers design more appealing ads.[69] The more compatible the ad copy is with consumers' values, the more likely consumers are to become involved in the message and find it relevant. The ad in Exhibit 17.5 is likely to appeal to females who value independence and broadmindedness. RC Cola appealed to consumers' value of patriotism with images of red, white, and blue, a Fourth of July parade, and a drive-in movie.[70] McDonald's tried to portray itself as a "Thai Patriot," a firm that was contributing positively to the economy, to counter a perception that the company was contributing to Thailand's economic decline.[71] It is important for marketers to connect product attributes and benefits to consumer values because these represent the end state consumers desire to achieve—the driving force behind their consumption of the product.

Marketers must also avoid communications that conflict with cultural values. Benetton created a stir with several ads, including one showing a nun kissing a priest, particularly offensive in predominantly Catholic countries like Italy and France, and one showing pictures of genitalia including those of children.[72] U.S. consumers reacted negatively to a Calvin Klein ad showing underage models in various stages of undress.[73] Consumer groups in Thailand protested an ad that showed Hitler eating an inferior brand of potato chips and being transformed into a good guy by eating the advertised brand.[74]

Ethical considerations. Consumers use values to gauge the appropriateness of others' behavior—including the behavior of marketers. For example, those who value morality might disapprove of products such as X-rated videos and cigarettes, consumption practices like prostitution and gambling, and sexually explicit ads. Consumers also evaluate marketers' behavior for fairness, ethics, and appropriateness.[75] As Chapter 21 explains, marketers should be aware that consumers may boycott, protest, or complain about practices that seem inconsistent with their values of fairness. Johnson & Johnson, for example, has run image ads stressing preventive health care and concern for consumers to counteract the belief that drug manufacturers are "price-gouging medicine men."[76] ●

EXHIBIT 17.5
Reflection of Values
Ads often target consumers' values. This ad is likely to appeal to young women who value independence and broadmindedness.

Source: Photo from Getty Images.

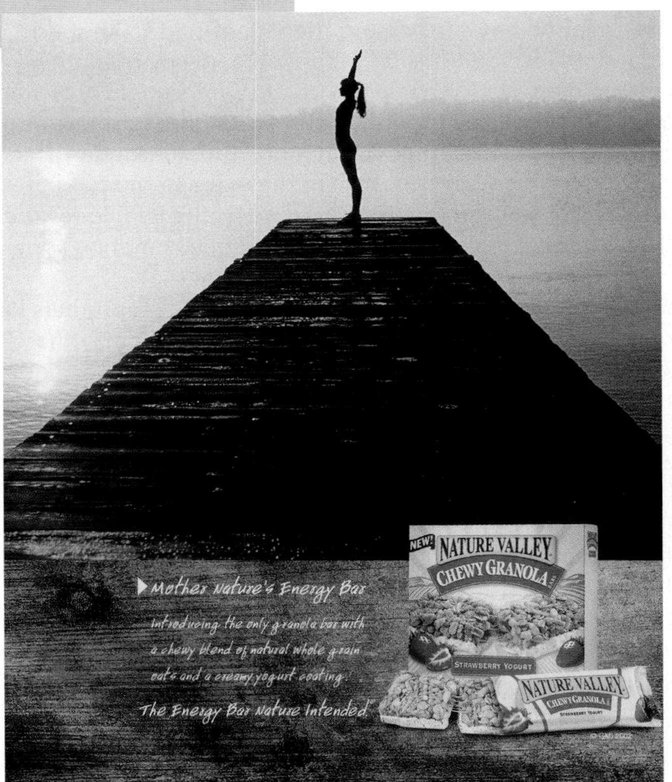

Mother Nature's Energy Bar
Introducing the only granola bar with a chewy blend of natural whole grain oats and a creamy yogurt coating.
The Energy Bar Nature Intended.
NEW!
NATURE VALLEY
CHEWY GRANOLA
STRAWBERRY YOGURT
NATURE VALLEY
CHEWY GRANOLA

How Values Can Be Measured

To segment the market by values, marketers need some means of identifying consumers' values, gauging their importance, and analyzing changes or trends in values. Unfortunately, values are often hard to measure. One reason is that people do not often think about their values and may therefore have a hard time articulating what is really important to them. Another reason is that people may sometimes feel social pressure to respond to a values questionnaire in a given way to make themselves look better in the eyes of the researcher. Therefore, marketers sometimes have to use less obtrusive or more indirect ways of assessing values.

Inferring Values from the Cultural Milieu The least obtrusive way to measure values is to make inferences based on a culture's milieu. For example, advertising has often been used as an indicator of values.[77] Research examining the values portrayed in U.S. print ads between 1900 and 1980 revealed that practicality, the family, modernity, cheapness, wisdom, and uniqueness were among the values that appeared most frequently. Researchers can also use ads to uncover cross-cultural differences in values. One study found that because the People's Republic of China, Taiwan, and Hong Kong are at different levels of economic development and have different political ideologies, different values were reflected in each country's ads.[78] Ads from the People's Republic of China focused on utilitarian themes and promised a better life; Hong Kong ads stressed hedonism and an easier life; and Taiwan ads fell between the other two.

Moreover, researchers have used ads to study trends in values. For example, a historical analysis of Japanese ads found an increasing number of appeals to status, apparently reflecting an increasing value on status.[79] Given the economic changes occurring in China, it is not surprising that local ads are changing from more utilitarian themes to focus on variety in products and product assurances.[80] In addition to studying ads for clues to values, marketers can infer values just by looking at product names. Product names indicative of the values of materialism (More), hedonism (Obsession), time (Minute Rice), technology (Microsoft), and convenience (Reddi-wip) are common in the United States.

Marketers can also identify values reflected in book and magazine titles, TV programs, and the types of people regarded as heroes or heroines. Spoofs like the one in Exhibit 17.6 reflect an attempt to poke fun at the current value of materialism. Even comic books have been used to indicate consumer values. According to research, materialism is portrayed as a valued trait in comic books like *Archie, Uncle Scrooge,* and *Richie Rich*.[81] This study also found that materialism was sometimes viewed as good (bringing happiness and goodwill) and sometimes viewed as bad, abusive, and hurtful. The content of songs is another indicator of values. Many people are concerned that violent song lyrics are an indication of a decline in values, for instance.

One criticism of cultural milieu as an indicator of values is that researchers never know whether culture reflects values or creates them. For example, was Madonna's "Material Girl" successful because consumers value materialism, or did the song promote an attitude that other consumers emulate? In light of this problem, researchers have introduced other methods to measure values.

EXHIBIT 17.6
Spoof of Materialism
Materialistic individuals tend to value their possessions highly and this trait can lead to the desire for many items. The Cutting Edge catalog is poking fun at The Sharper Image catalog and stores, which offer many unusual items for those who have "everything."

Source: © Becker & Mayer! Bellevue, Washington.

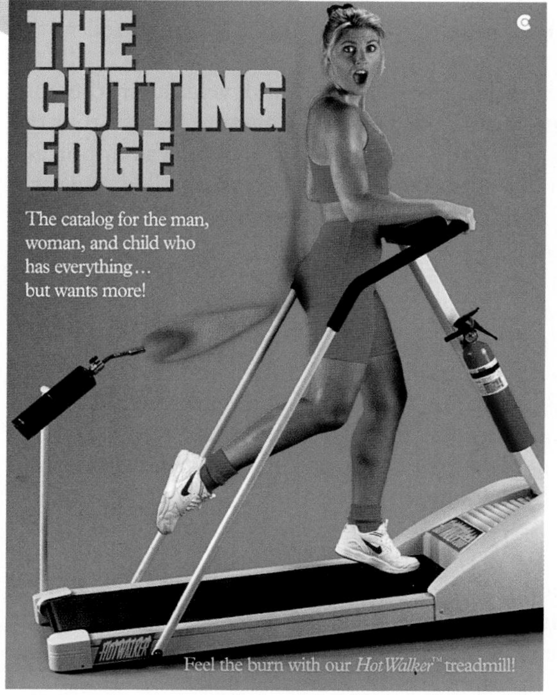

THE CUTTING EDGE
The catalog for the man, woman, and child who has everything… but wants more!
Feel the burn with our HotWalker™ treadmill!

Means-End Chain Analysis Marketers can use the **means-end chain analysis** to gain insight into consumers' values by better understanding which attributes they find important in products. Armed with this information, researchers can work backwards to uncover the values that

PRODUCT	ATTRIBUTE	BENEFIT	INSTRUMENTAL VALUE (driving force)	TERMINAL VALUE
Light beer (I)	Fewer calories	I won't gain weight	Helps make me healthy	I feel good about myself (self-esteem)
Light beer (II)	Fewer calories Great taste Light taste	Less filling Enjoyable/relaxing Refreshing	Good times/fun Friendship Sharing	Belonging
Rice	Comes in boiling bag	Convenient No messy pan to clean up	Saves time	I can enjoy more time with my family (belonging)

EXHIBIT 17.7
An Example of Means-End Chains

According to the means-end chain analysis, product and service *attributes* (e.g., fewer calories) lead to *benefits* (e.g., I won't gain weight) that reflect *instrumental values* (e.g., helps make me healthy) and *terminal values* (e.g., I feel good about myself). This analysis helps marketers identify important values and the attributes associated with them. Can you develop a means-end chain for toothpaste or deodorant?

Sources: Adapted from Jonathan Gutman, "A Means-End Chain Model Based on Consumer Categorization Processes," *Journal of Marketing*, Spring 1982, pp. 60–72; Thomas J. Reynolds and John P. Rochan, "Means-End Based Advertising Research: Copy Testing Is Not Strategy Assessment," *Journal of Business Research*, March 1991, pp. 131–142.

means-end chain analysis A technique that helps us understand how values link to attributes in products and services.

drive consumer decisions.[82] Suppose a consumer likes light beer because it has fewer calories than regular beer. If a researcher asks why it is important to have a beer with fewer calories, the respondent might say, "Because I don't want to gain weight." If the researcher asks why not, the consumer might respond by saying, "I want to be healthy." If asked why again, the consumer might say, "Because I want to feel good about myself." This example is illustrated in the top line of Exhibit 17.7.

Note that this means-end chain has several potential levels. First, the consumer mentioned an important attribute followed by a concrete benefit that the attribute provides. Then the consumer indicated that this benefit was important because it served some instrumental value. This entire process is called a *means-end chain* because the attribute provides the means to a desired end state or terminal value (in this case, self-esteem).

Exhibit 17.7 illustrates other means-end chains that, in combination, reveal several things. First, the same attribute may be associated with very different values. For example, rather than valuing light beer for its health benefits, some consumers may like light beer because they drink it in a social context that leads to a greater sense of belonging. Second, the same value may be associated with very different products and attributes. Thus attributes associated with both light beer and rice may appeal equally to the value of belonging. Third, a given attribute may be linked with multiple benefits and/or values. Thus a consumer might like light beer because it helps her feel healthier and because it facilitates belonging.

Marketers can use means-end chain analysis to identify product attributes that will be consistent with certain values.[83] Not long ago, consumers generally considered sports cars to be expensive and uncomfortable, and ownership took on an aspect of "arrogance and irresponsibility." As a result, manufacturers began offering comfortable cars positioned for "people who have friends" in order to be more in line with current values.[84]

Marketers can also use the means-end chain model to develop advertising strategy. By knowing which attributes consumers find important and which values they associate with those attributes, advertisers can better design ads that appeal to these values and emphasize related attributes. The ad in Exhibit 17.5 suggests the smell of the perfume will help young women be "bad," achieve independence, and perhaps obtain pleasure. Note that the ad need not explicitly link a given attribute with a motive, but allows consumers to implicitly make the linkage.

Finally, marketers can use the means-end chain to segment global markets, cutting across national boundaries to appeal to consumers on the basis of specific benefits and related values.[85] To market yogurt, for instance, a company could identify one segment that values health and reach this segment by focusing on product attributes such as low fat, and identify a second segment that values enjoyment and reach this segment through attributes such as fruit ingredients.

Rokeach Value Survey (RVS) A survey that measures instrumental and terminal values.

Value Questionnaires Marketers can directly assess values by using questionnaires. One of the best-known instruments is the **Rokeach Value Survey (RVS)**. This questionnaire asks consumers about the importance they attach to the 19 instrumental values and 18 terminal values identified in Exhibit 17.3. This questionnaire is standardized and everyone responds to the same set of items, which helps researchers identify the specific values that are most important to a given group of consumers, determine whether values are changing over time, and find out whether values differ for various groups of consumers. One of the drawbacks is that some values measured by the RVS are less relevant to consumer behavior (such as salvation, forgiving, and being obedient). Thus some researchers have recommended the use of a shortened form of the RVS containing only the values most relevant to a consumer context.[86]

List of Values (LOV) A survey that measures nine principle values in consumer behavior.

Others have advocated the use of the **List of Values (LOV)**. This survey technique presents consumers with nine primary values and asks them either to identify the two most important or to rank all nine values by importance. The nine values are (1) self-respect, (2) warm relationships with others, (3) sense of accomplishment, (4) self-fulfillment, (5) fun and enjoyment in life, (6) excitement, (7) sense of belonging, (8) being well respected, and (9) security.[87] The first six are internal values because they derive from the individual; the others are external values. The values can also be described in terms of whether they are fulfilled through interpersonal relationships (warm relationships with others, sense of belonging), personal factors (self-respect, being well respected, self-fulfillment), or nonpersonal things (sense of accomplishment, fun, security, and excitement).

In one study, the LOV predicted consumers' responses to statements that describe their self-reported consumption characteristics ("I am a spender, not a saver," "TV is my main entertainment"), their actual consumption behaviors (the frequency with which they watch movies or the news, read certain magazines, and engage in activities like playing tennis), and their marketplace beliefs ("I believe the number of companies that satisfy consumer complaints is increasing," "I believe the consumer movement has caused prices to increase"). Compared with the RVS, the LOV is a better predictor of consumer behavior, is shorter, and is easier to administer. Finally, the LOV is useful for identifying segments of consumers with similar value systems. Exhibit 17.8 illustrates the relative importance of the nine LOV values in four U.S. segments.[88]

EXHIBIT 17.8
Value Segments
Marketers try to segment consumers in terms of the patterns of values they hold and their relative importance. Here, for example, are four major value segments. Segment A places very high importance on security, and segment D tends to stress warm relationships with others. By identifying value segments, marketers can develop messages that appeal to the specific values of these segments.

Source: Wagner A. Kamakura and Thomas P. Novak, "Value-System Segmentation: Exploring the Meaning of LOV," *Journal of Consumer Research*, June 1992, pp. 112–132. © 1992 University of Chicago Press. All rights reserved.

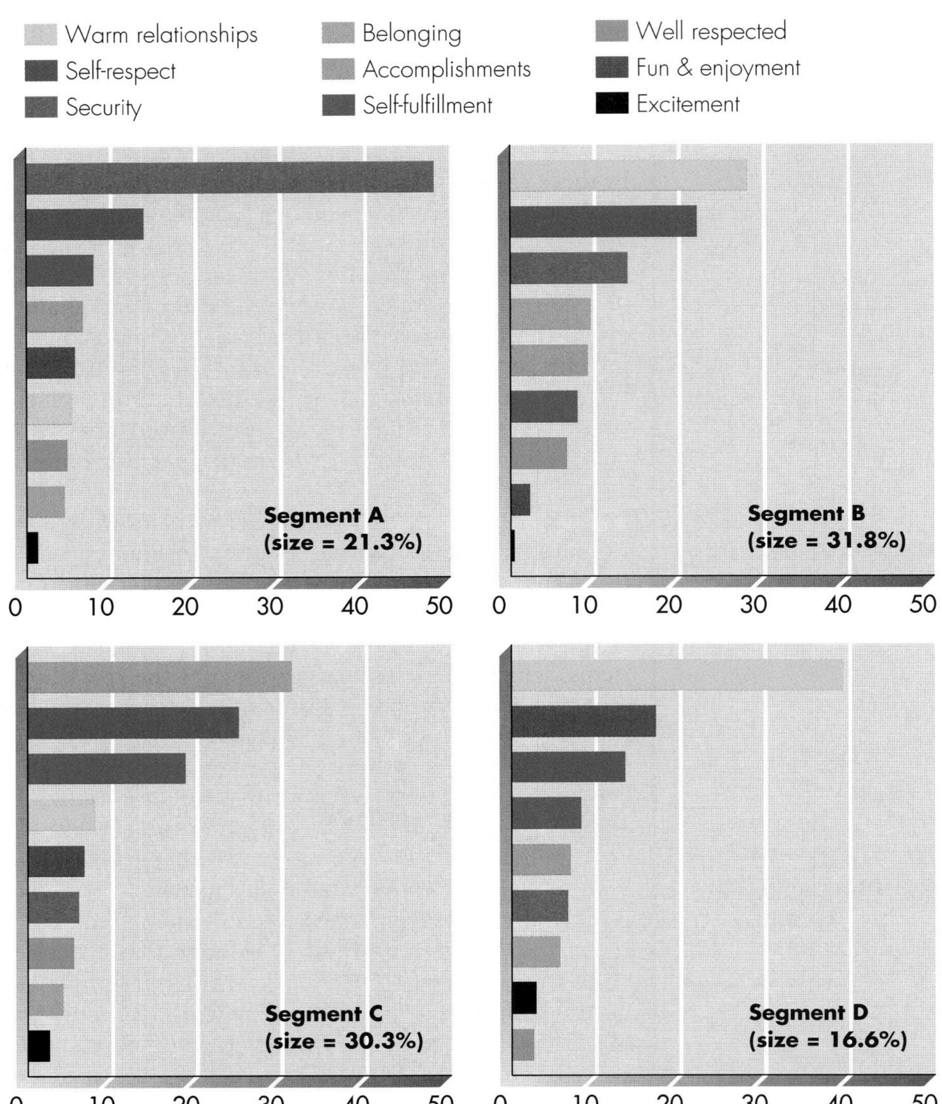

PERSONALITY

Although individuals with comparable backgrounds tend to hold similar values, it is important to remember that people do not always act the same way even when they hold the same values. In listening to a sales pitch, one consumer may state demurely that she finds the product interesting but is not ready to make up her mind right now. Another might act more assertively, interrupting the salesperson midway through his pitch to indicate that she has no interest whatsoever in the product. Thus consumers vary in terms of their personality or the way in which they respond to a particular situation.

personality An internal characteristic that determines how individuals behave in various situations.

Personality consists of the distinctive patterns of behaviors, tendencies, qualities, or personal dispositions that make one individual different from another and lead to a consistent response to environmental stimuli. These patterns are internal characteristics that we are born with or that result from the way we have been raised. The concept of personality helps us understand why people behave differently in different situations.

Research Approaches to Personality

The social sciences provide various approaches to studying personality. This section reviews five that consumer researchers apply: psychoanalytic approaches, trait theories, phenomenological approaches, social-psychological theories, and behavioral approaches.

Psychoanalytic Approaches According to psychoanalytic theories, personality arises from a set of dynamic, unconscious internal struggles within the mind.[89] The well-known psychoanalyst Sigmund Freud proposed that we pass through several developmental stages in forming our personalities. In the first stage, the oral stage, the infant is entirely dependent on others for need satisfaction, and receives oral gratification from sucking, eating, and biting. At the anal stage, the child is confronted with the problem of toilet training. Then in the phallic stage the youth becomes aware of his or her genitals and must deal with desires for the opposite-sex parent (the Oedipal and Electra complexes).

Freud believed that the failure to resolve the conflicts from each stage could influence one's personality. For example, the individual who received insufficient oral stimulation as an infant may reveal this crisis in adulthood through oral-stimulation activities like gum chewing, smoking, and overeating or by distrusting others' motives (including those of marketers). At the anal stage an individual whose toilet training is too restrictive may become obsessed with control and be overly orderly, stubborn, or stingy, resulting in neatly organized closets and records, list making, and excessive saving. These individuals may also engage in extensive information search and deliberation when making decisions. On the other hand, those whose training was overly lenient may become messy, disorganized adults.

Although some of Freud's theories were later questioned by many researchers, the key point is that the subconscious can influence behavior. Consequently, some advertising agencies conduct research to delve deep into consumers' psyches and uncover subconscious reasons why they buy a particular product.[90] This type of research led to the discovery of a deep-seated desire for milk that the dairy industry used in its "Got Milk" campaign.

Trait Theories Trait theorists propose that personality is composed of characteristics that describe and differentiate individuals.[91] For example, people might be described as aggressive, easygoing, quiet, moody, shy, or rigid. Psychologist Carl Jung developed one of the most basic trait theory schemes, suggesting that individuals could be categorized according to their levels of introversion and extroversion.[92] Introverts are shy, prefer to be alone, and are anxious in the presence of others. Introverts tend to avoid social channels and therefore may not find out about new products from others. They are also less motivated by social pressure and more likely to do things that please themselves. In contrast, extroverts are outgoing, sociable, and typically conventional.

More recent work has found that the trait of stability, or consistency in behavior, when combined with the introversion/extroversion dimension, can be used as a basis to represent various personality types (see Exhibit 17.9). For example, a person who is reliable tends to be high on both introversion and stability. In contrast, a passive person is introverted, but neither highly stable nor highly unstable. One interesting feature about this scheme is that the personality

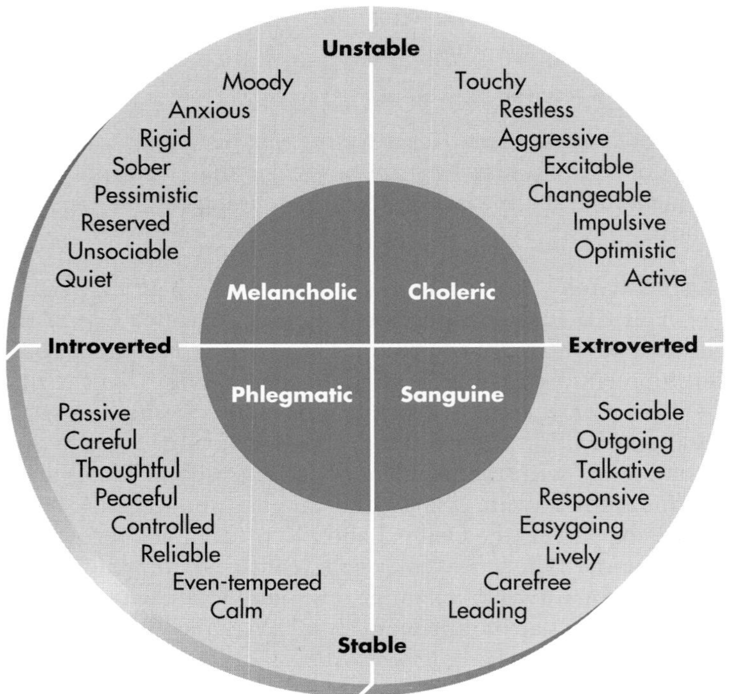

EXHIBIT 17.9
A Trait Conception of Personality Types
Consumers can be classified according to whether they have introverted or extroverted personality traits. These traits can lead to the identification of various personality types (e.g., moody, peaceful, lively, and aggressive). Interestingly, these traits can be grouped into four major groups that correspond to the basic temperaments identified by the ancient Greek physician Hippocrates many centuries ago. How would you classify your personality according to this scheme?

Source: Adapted from Hans Eysenck and S. Rachman, *The Causes and Cures of Neurosis: An Introduction to Modern Behavior Therapy Based on Learning Theory and Principles of Conditioning* (San Diego, Calif.: Knapp, 1965), p. 16.

types identified by these two dimensions match the four temperaments identified by the Greek physician Hippocrates centuries ago—for example, a phlegmatic person is introverted and stable; a melancholic person is introverted and unstable.

Phenomenological Approaches

Phenomenological approaches propose that personality is largely shaped by an individual's interpretations of life events.[93] For example, according to this approach, depression is caused by the way someone interprets key events and the nature of that interpretation, rather than by internal conflicts or traits.

A key concept of the phenomenological approaches is **locus of control,** or people's interpretations of why specific things happen.[94] Individuals with an internal locus of control attribute more responsibility to themselves for good or bad outcomes. These individuals might blame themselves or see themselves as careless when a product fails. Externally controlled individuals, on the other hand, place responsibility on other people, events, or places, rather than on themselves. Thus they might attribute product failure to faulty manufacturing, poor packaging, or the clumsy delivery person.

Locus of control can heavily influence consumers' perceptions of satisfaction in a consumption experience and determine how the consumer feels. To illustrate, consumers who blame themselves for product failure might feel shame, whereas those who blame product failure on an external source might feel anger and irritation. In addition, someone's life theme or goals (concerns that we address in our everyday lives) can greatly influence the meanings he or she derives from ads.[95] Thus a person who is more concerned with family might interpret an ad differently than someone who is more concerned with his or her private self.

Social-Psychological Theories Another group of theories focuses on social rather than biological explanations of personality. These theories propose that individuals act in social situations in order to meet their needs. The researcher Karen Horney, for instance, believed that behavior can be characterized by three major orientations.[96] *Compliant* individuals are dependent on others and are humble, trusting, and tied to a group. *Aggressive* individuals need power, move away from others, and are outgoing, assertive, self-confident, and tough-minded. *Detached* individuals are independent and self-sufficient but suspicious and introverted. These three orientations are measured by the CAD scale.[97] One study found that assertiveness and aggressiveness were significantly related to styles of interaction with marketing institutions.[98] In particular, highly assertive and aggressive people were likely to perceive complaining as acceptable and to enjoy doing it.

locus of control How people interpret why things happen (internal vs. external).

In social-psychological theory, researchers distinguish between state-oriented consumers, who are more likely to rely on subjective norms to guide their behavior, and action-oriented consumers, whose behavior is based more on their own attitudes.[99] Consumers also vary in terms of their attention to information that helps them compare themselves to others (social comparison information). Individuals high on this factor are more sensitive to normative pressure than are those low on this factor.

Behavioral Approaches In contrast to other explanations of personality, behavioral approaches propose that differences in personality are a function of how individuals have been rewarded or punished in the past. According to behavioral approaches, individuals are more likely to have traits or engage in behaviors for which they have received positive reinforcement. They are less likely to maintain characteristics and behaviors for which they have been punished.[100] Thus an individual might be extroverted because parents, caretakers, and other individuals rewarded outgoing behaviors and punished introverted behaviors. Likewise, a consumer might prefer colorful clothing if he or she previously received positive reinforcement for wearing it. Note that these behavioral approaches to personality involve the principles of operant conditioning discussed in Chapter 11.

Determining Whether Personality Characteristics Affect Consumer Behavior

Much of the consumer-related personality research has followed the trait approach and focused on identifying specific personality traits that explain differences in consumers' purchase, use, and disposition behavior. A number of studies have attempted to find a relationship between personality and consumer behavior, but reviews of this research generally conclude that personality is not a good predictor of consumer behavior.[101] One major problem is that researchers developed many of the trait measurement instruments for identifying personality disorders in clinical settings, so these instruments may not be applicable for identifying traits related to consumption behaviors.

In addition, consumer researchers have often attempted to use personality traits inappropriately to explain phenomena. One classic study, which employed the Edwards Personal Preference Schedule (a detailed instrument that measures a variety of personality traits) to examine the difference between Ford and Chevy owners, yielded disappointing results.[102] The only significant difference was that Ford owners were more dominant-aggressive (not a very meaningful or useful finding). Thus personality does not appear to be a good predictor of brand choice.

Although personality has not been shown to be strongly related to consumer behavior, some researchers believe that more reliable measures of traits, developed in a consumer context, would reveal a relationship.[103] For instance, researchers created a consumer self-confidence scale to examine how this trait affects the choice of higher-price alternatives.[104] The association between personality and consumer behavior may be stronger for some types of consumer behavior than for others. For example, although personality may not be very useful in understanding brand choice, it may help marketers understand why some people are more susceptible to persuasion, particularly like a certain ad, or engage in more information processing. The ad in Exhibit 17.10 is also an example of a personality appeal.

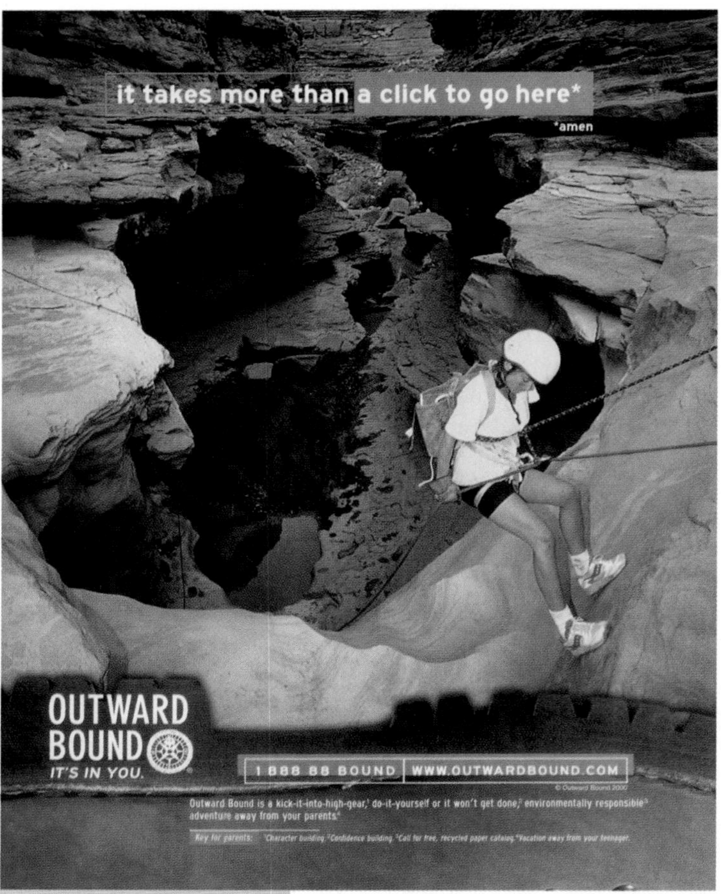

it takes more than a click to go here*
*amen
OUTWARD BOUND
IT'S IN YOU.
1 888 88 BOUND
WWW.OUTWARDBOUND.COM
© Outward Bound 2000
Outward Bound is a kick-it-into-high-gear,[1] do-it-yourself or it won't get done,[2] environmentally responsible[3] adventure away from your parents.[4]
Key for parents: [1]Character building. [2]Confidence building. [3]Call for free, recycled paper catalog. [4]Vacation away from your teenager.

EXHIBIT 17.10
Personality and Ad Appeal
Ad messages are often designed to appeal to certain lifestyles. This ad is directed to those who enjoy a more adventurous or "outdoorsy" lifestyle.

Source: Courtesy of Outward Bound USA.

Marketers may also find personality more useful for targeting some product and service categories than others. In particular, our choice of products and services that involve subjective or hedonic features such as looks, style, and aesthetics may be somewhat related to personality. A good example is the selection of a greeting card, which represents a personal message and therefore is an extension of the sender's personality. Finally, certain types of personality traits may be more related to consumer behavior than others. As described below, these include optimal stimulation level, dogmatism, need for uniqueness, need for cognition, susceptibility to influence, frugality, self-monitoring behavior, and national character.

Optimal Stimulation Level Some activities have the potential to provide some sort of physiological arousal. For example, you might feel more aroused when you drive extremely fast on the highway, ride a roller coaster, see a scary movie, or go to new and different surroundings. Things that are physically stimulating, emotionally energizing, or novel have arousal-inducing potential. However, highly stimulating activities are not always desirable. According to the theory of **optimal stimulation level (OSL)**, people prefer things that are moderately arousing to things that are either too arousing or not arousing at all.[105] For example, you might prefer eating at a restaurant that offers moderately imaginative food to eating at one that offers boring food or one that offers very exotic and unusual food.

optimal stimulation level (OSL) The level of arousal that is most comfortable for an individual.

Even though people generally prefer moderate levels of stimulation, individuals differ in the level of arousal they regard as moderate and optimal. Individuals with a low optimal stimulation level tend to prefer less-arousing activities because they want to avoid going over the edge. In contrast, individuals with a high optimal stimulation level are more likely to seek activities that are very exciting, novel, complex, and different. Consumers with a high need for stimulation might enjoy activities like skydiving, bungee-jumping, gambling, and river rafting.[106] They are also more likely to be innovative and creative.

Individuals with high and low needs for stimulation also differ in the way they approach the marketplace. Those with high stimulation needs tend to be the first to buy new products, to seek information about them, and to engage in variety seeking (buying something different).[107] They are more curious about the ads they watch but may be easily bored by them. These consumers are more likely to buy products associated with greater risk, enjoy shopping in malls with many stores and products, and prefer products and services that deviate from established consumption practices.

dogmatism A tendency to be resistant to change or new ideas.

Dogmatism Consumers can vary in terms of being open- or closed-minded. **Dogmatism** refers to an individual's tendency to be resistant to change and new ideas. Dogmatic or closed-minded consumers are likely to be relatively resistant to new products, new promotions, and new ads. In support, one study found that Nigerian consumers' acceptance of new products depended on how dogmatic the consumers were. The study also found that Muslims were more dogmatic than Christians.[108]

need for uniqueness (NFU) The desire for novelty through the purchase, use, and disposition of products and services.

Need for Uniqueness Consumers who pursue novelty through the purchase, use, and disposition of goods and services are displaying a **need for uniqueness (NFU).**[109] Need for uniqueness covers three behavioral dimensions: creative choice counterconformity (the consumer's choice reflects social distinctiveness yet is one that others will approve), unpopular choice counterconformity (choosing products and brands that do not conform to establish distinctiveness despite possible social disapproval), and avoidance of similarity (losing interest in possessions that become commonplace to avoid the norm and hence reestablish distinctiveness). In one study, consumers with a high need for uniqueness who were asked to explain their decisions made unconventional choices, showing that they were aware that their choices and reasoning were outside the norm.[110] Thus, consumers with a high need for uniqueness may consciously resist conformity by disposing of clothing that has become too popular in favor of emerging fashion trends. They may also express this need by buying hand-crafted or personalized items and by customizing product designs to their particular specifications.

need for cognition (NFC) A trait that describes how much people like to think.

Need for Cognition Consumers who enjoy thinking extensively about things like products, attributes, and benefits are high in the **need for cognition (NFC).**[111] Those with a low need for cognition do not like to think and prefer to take shortcuts or rely on their feelings. Consumers with different needs for cognition differ in terms of their product interests, information search, and reaction to different ad campaigns. Specifically, those with a high need for cognition enjoy products and experiences that carry a serious learning and mastery component such as chess, educational games, and TV shows like *Jeopardy.* They derive satisfaction from searching for and discovering new product features and react positively to long, technically sophisticated ads with details about products or services. They might also scrutinize messages more carefully than other consumers do, considering the credibility or merits of the message.[112] Consumers with low need for cognition, on the other hand, react more positively to short messages using attractive models, humor, or other cues. These individuals tend to make decisions that involve little thinking.

Susceptibility to Influence Consumers also vary in their susceptibility to persuasion attempts, especially those that are interpersonal or face-to-face. Some consumers have a greater desire to enhance their image as observed by others and are therefore willing to be influenced or guided by them.[113] Consumers with lower social and information processing confidence tend to be more influenced by ads than are those with higher self-confidence.

Frugality Frugality is the degree to which consumers take a disciplined approach to short-term acquisitions and are resourceful in using products and services to achieve longer-term goals. Consumers who are high on frugality will, for example, eat leftovers for lunch at work (rather than buy take-out food or

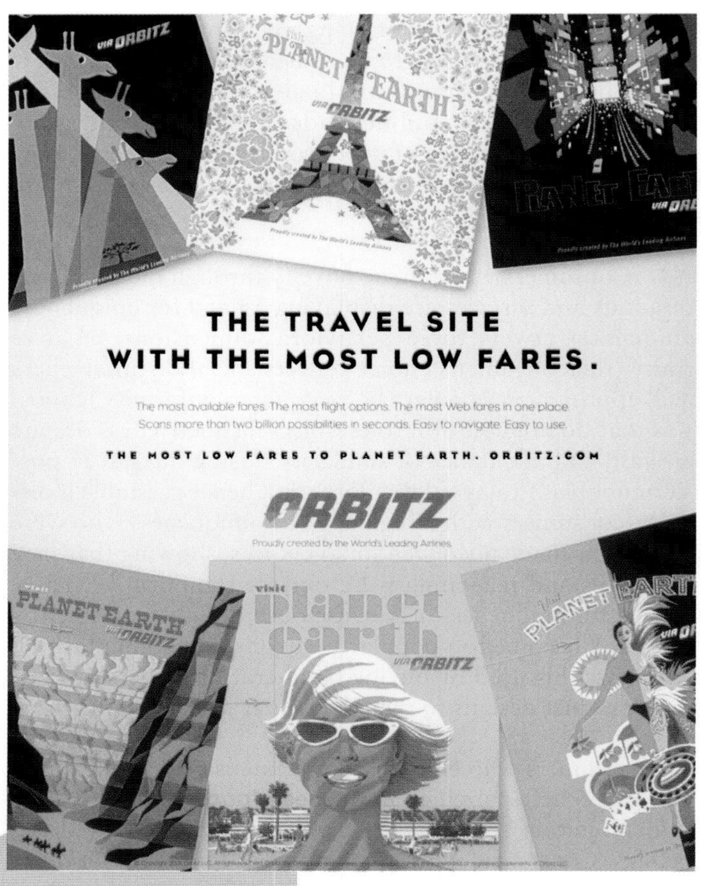

EXHIBIT 17.11
Ad Appealing to Frugality
This ad would appeal to consumers who are frugal and value saving money.

Source: Courtesy of Orbitz.

eat in a restaurant). Research shows that such consumers are less materialistic, less susceptible to the influence of others, and more conscious of price and value than those low in frugality (see Exhibit 17.11).[114]

Self-Monitoring Behavior Individuals differ in the degree to which they look to others for cues on how to behave. High self-monitors are typically sensitive to the desires and influences of others as guides to behavior, and low self-monitors are guided more by their own preferences and desires and are less influenced by normative expectations.[115] High and low self-monitors also differ in their responsiveness to advertising appeals. High self-monitors are more responsive to image-oriented ads and more willing to try and pay more for products advertised with an image consistent with high self-monitoring. In contrast, low self-monitors are generally more responsive to ads that make a quality claim and are more willing to try these products and pay extra for them.

National Character Personality traits can sometimes be used to stereotype people of a particular country as having a **national character**. These characterizations represent only very broad generalizations about a particular country; obviously individuals vary a great deal. To illustrate, the French and Italians are often thought of as emotional and romantic; the British as more reserved. German, French, and U.S. citizens have been characterized as more assertive than their British, Russian, or Italian counterparts. German, British, and Russian consumers can be viewed as "tighter" compared with the "looser" French, Italian, and U.S. consumers.[116] U.S. consumers are also considered more impulsive, risk oriented, and self-confident than Canadians, who are stereotyped as more cautious, restrained, and reserved.

national character
The personality of a country.

Researchers have characterized how countries differ in their needs for achievement, levels of introversion and extroversion, perceptions of human nature as good or evil, and flexibility.[117] Differences in national character are likely to influence individual reactions to marketing. For example, Canadians' aversion to credit cards and borrowing may be tied to their cautious character.[118]

MARKETING IMPLICATIONS Because some personality traits may be related to consumption behavior, marketers can develop products, services, and communications that appeal to various personality types. For example, ads targeting compliant or high self-monitoring consumers should focus on the approval of others, whereas ads and promotions appealing to high optimal stimulation-level consumers or those with a high need for uniqueness might focus on trying something new and different. Coca-Cola, for instance, used word of mouth to attract consumers to its Burn energy drink as a new pub drink distinctly different from Red Bull and other established competitors.[119] Newspapers like the *Village Voice* and *New Times* appeal to individuals who are "hip and irreverent."[120] Finally, Nabisco portrayed its SnackWell's cookies and crackers as a way for women in their 30s with low self-esteem to boost their confidence.[121] ●

LIFESTYLES

lifestyles People's patterns of behavior.

activities, interests, and opinions (AIOs) The three components of lifestyles.

Lifestyles relate closely to consumers' values and personality. Whereas values and personality represent internal states or characteristics, **lifestyles** are manifestations or actual patterns of behavior. In particular, they are represented by a consumer's **activities, interests, and opinions (AIOs)**—see Exhibit 17.12. What people do in their spare time is often a good indicator of their lifestyle. One consumer might like outdoor activities such as skiing or diving, whereas another might prefer to surf the Web or make a scrapbook. Consumers who engage in different activities and have differing opinions and interests may in fact represent distinct lifestyle segments for marketers.

For example, one study identified two lifestyle segments that were most likely to drink and drive: Good Timers, frequent partygoers who are macho and high on sensation seeking, and Problem Kids, who frequently display troublesome behaviors.[122] Another lifestyle segment consists of people with an affinity for nostalgia, or the desire for old things.[123] This segment clearly represents a key market for old movies, books, and antiques. Also, consumers are participating in more extreme sports such as snowmobiling—opening opportunities for marketers of related equipment—whereas group sports are losing popularity.[124]

Lifestyle research can help marketers gain a better understanding of how their product fits into consumers' general patterns of behavior. For example, a study of stomach remedies identified four main lifestyle segments: Severe Sufferers, Active Medicators, Hypochondriacs, and Practicalists.[125] Lifestyles related to cooking include Speed Scratch Cooking, in which people use time-saving techniques and equipment to prepare meals, and Investment Cooking, in which people simultaneously cook many dishes or a large quantity of foods and store some for later consumption.[126]

Finally, consumers in different countries may have characteristic lifestyles. One study found considerable lifestyle differences between Japanese and U.S.

EXHIBIT 17.12
Activities, Interests, and Opinions

Lifestyles are represented by consumers' *activities, interests,* and *opinions.* Here are some major examples of each category. Note that these lifestyles provide a more detailed profile of consumers than their demographics do (the last column).

Source: Joseph T. Plumer, "The Concept and Application of Life Style Segmentation," *Journal of Marketing,* January 1974, pp. 33–37. Reprinted with permission.

ACTIVITIES	INTERESTS	OPINIONS	DEMOGRAPHICS
Work	Family	Themselves	Age
Hobbies	Home	Social issues	Education
Social events	Job	Politics	Income
Vacations	Community	Business	Occupation
Entertainment	Recreation	Education	Family size
Club membership	Fashion	Economics	Dwelling
Community	Food	Products	Geography
Shopping	Media	Culture	City size
Sports	Achievements	Future	Life-cycle stage

women. Japanese women were more home focused, less likely to visit restaurants, less price sensitive, and less likely to drive or go to the movies.[127] Given these preferences, Japanese women would probably spend more time than U.S. women preparing meals at home and would therefore pay more for products that enhance meal quality. Popular lifestyle activities among Russian consumers include going to the movies and theater and participating in sports like soccer, ice hockey, and figure skating.[128] Chinese consumers like to watch sports on TV, go to movies, play cards, read books, and listen to music.[129]

MARKETING IMPLICATIONS Consumer lifestyles can have important implications for market segmentation, communication, and new product ideas.

Market segmentation. Marketers can use lifestyles to identify consumer segments for specific offerings. For example, eyeing the trend toward busier lifestyles, General Mills introduced Chex Morning Mix single-serving pouches for on-the-run breakfasts.[130] Microwavable foods, day care centers, and housecleaning services also appeal to those with busy lifestyles, such as dual-career couples and working women.[131] Consumers with busy work schedules are hiring concierge services such as Circles in Boston to handle errands like passport renewal.[132] This segment is also driving an increase in restaurant take-out orders and Internet shopping.[133] PowerGel was developed as a "fast fuel" for athletes who have no time to chew; the product is simply swallowed.[134] Star Scientific is marketing nicotine-enhanced lozenges for smokers to use in situations where they are unable to smoke.[135] And Ford is targeting hot-rod enthusiasts with its stylish, high-performance Focus model.[136]

Lifestyle segmentation also has important cross-cultural implications. For example, one study of 12 European countries used demographics, activities, behavior toward the media, political inclinations, and mood to identify six Eurotype lifestyle segments: Traditionalists (18 percent of the population), Homebodies (14 percent), Rationalists (23 percent), Pleasurists (17 percent), Strivers (15 percent), and Trendsetters (13 percent).[137] Business travelers to Moscow used to have to settle for a narrow bed in a dingy hotel with little service.[138] Now, Western hotel chains offer services better geared to the typical traveler's lifestyle, such as dry cleaning, room service, and bistros. In Japan, outdoor-oriented consumers are snapping up recreational vehicles—even though many never leave the city.[139] Although alcohol is forbidden in Saudi Arabia, nonalcoholic beers have become very popular among young consumers with an active, hip lifestyle.[140]

Finally, marketers often monitor lifestyle changes to identify new opportunities. For example, many employers have relaxed their business dress codes. In response, many clothiers and retailers are putting more emphasis on casual clothing. As another example, the cocooning trend has enlarged the market for home-related products and services such as home entertainment centers.[141]

Communications. Marketers can design ad messages and promotions to appeal to certain lifestyles, featuring products in the context of desired lifestyles.[142] As golf has become more popular, Nike and other firms are portraying the sport in their ads.[143] Busch beer targets hunters with its "Official Busch Hunting Gear" catalog and store displays of giant inflatable Lab retrievers.[144] Talbots and other service firms have advertised to reach people whose lifestyle does not include watching the Super Bowl.[145]

Lifestyles also influence company media plans. For example, because many fathers have changed their lifestyle to become more involved in child rearing, parenting magazines are adding a focus on male readers and attracting male-oriented

EXHIBIT 17.13
Lifestyle and Media Connections

Source: "Lifestyle and Media Connections," from Michael J. Weiss, Morris B. Holbrook, and John Habich, "Death of the Arts Snob?" *American Demographics*, June 2001, p. 41. Copyright 2001. Media Central, Inc., a PRMEDIA Company. All rights reserved.

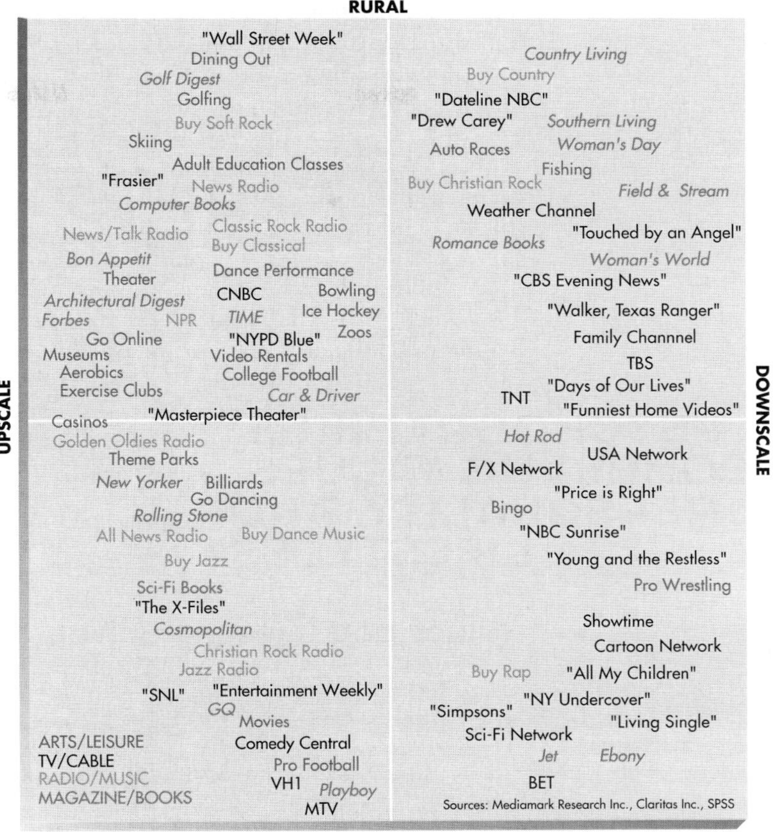

advertising.[146] *Martha Stewart Living,* a magazine for women interested in home and style, now has a competitor in *B. Smith Style,* reflecting the increased size of this segment.[147] Philip Morris even created a lifestyle magazine, *Unlimited,* based on the theme of "Action, Adventure, and Good Times" as a way to appeal to young adults at a time when tobacco marketing is under heavy fire.[148] And companies are using TV commercials to reach couch potatoes in China.[149]

Clearly, the Internet is a very targeted way to communicate with a wide variety of lifestyle segments, particularly those who surf most often (teenagers and young adults). Teenagers are especially fickle surfers, so a site must generate considerable interest to attract and hold these visitors for any length of time.[150] As a result, Pepsi.com and other sites regularly post new games and special features to keep younger visitors returning again and again.[151]

Finally, media usage patterns may be related to lifestyles.[152] For example, consumers who read magazines and newspapers tend to be educated and hold prestige jobs as well as being involved in community and politics. Interestingly, consumers who love to surf the Internet also tend to be heavy TV watchers.[153] One national survey found connections between seemingly unrelated lifestyles and media usage, such as fishing enthusiasts tending to enjoy listening to Christian rock music and reading *Southern Living* (see Exhibit 17.13).[154]

New product ideas. Often marketers can develop new product and service ideas by uncovering unfulfilled needs of certain lifestyle segments. For example, marketers discovered that many workers who bring their lunch to work were tired of sandwiches. In response, companies such as Oscar Mayer, StarKist, and Libby's developed different varieties of easy-to-pack "lunch kits." Trendy coffee houses and brew pubs (also growing in popularity in Japan) provide a place where consumers can separate from work and converse with others.[155] In addition, an increasing number of Japanese consumers like to eat and drink without lifting a finger, and this trend has created a market for products like self-buttering bread, ready-mixed cocktails, and spoonless gelatin.[156] After learning that consumers prefer baby food in easy-to-carry plastic packages, Gerber switched from its traditional single-serving glass jars.[157] And Nike is marketing a wristwatch heart monitor to help athletes monitor their health and performance.[158] ●

PSYCHOGRAPHICS: COMBINING VALUES, PERSONALITY, AND LIFESTYLES

This chapter opened by observing that modern psychographic research tends to combine values, personality, and lifestyle variables. To illustrate this key point, this last section provides a brief description of several psychographic applications in marketing.

Values and Lifestyle Survey

Values and Lifestyle Survey (VALS) A psychographic tool that measures demographic, value, attitude, and lifestyle variables.

One of the most widely known psychographic tools is the **Values and Lifestyle Survey (VALS)**, which is conducted by an organization called SRI. The original VALS study surveyed a broad section of U.S. consumers in the 1970s on several demographic, value, attitude, and lifestyle variables.[159] Although VALS was widely used to identify potential target markets and to understand how to communicate with consumers, by the late 1980s researchers were criticizing it for being outdated and not predicting behavior well. The aging of baby boomers, increased ethnic diversity, more media choices, and changes in values and lifestyles made VALS an invalid tool for describing consumers in the 1990s.

In response to these criticisms, SRI developed VALS2. Because this survey includes only items related to consumer behavior, it is much more closely related to consumption than VALS was. The survey consists of four demographic and 42 attitudinal items. Examples of the latter include "My idea of fun at a national park would be to stay at an expensive lodge and dress up for dinner," "It is the luxuries in life which make life worth living," and "I often crave excitement."[160]

VALS2 incorporates the behavior of U.S. consumers in 170 product categories to create segments based on two factors: (1) consumers' resources, including income, education, self-confidence, health, eagerness to buy, intelligence, and energy level, and (2) their self-orientations, or what motivates them, including their activities and values. VALS2 describes three self-orientations. Principle-oriented consumers are guided by intellectual aspects rather than by feelings or other people's opinions. Status-oriented individuals base their views on the actions and opinions of others and strive to win their approval. Action-oriented consumers desire social or physical action, variety, activity, and risk.

Combining the resource and self-oriented variables, VALS2 identified eight consumer segments (see Exhibit 17.14).[161] At the bottom end of the resource hierarchy are Strugglers (16 percent of the U.S. population), who have the low-

EXHIBIT 17.14
VALS2 American Segments
VALS2 classifies consumers into eight major segments based on two dimensions: resources (education, income, intelligence, etc.) and self-orientation (principle, status, or action orientation), as described in this exhibit. Into which group would you fall?

Source: VALS2, SRI International, Menlo Park, Calif., cited in Judith Waldrop, "Markets with Attitude," *American Demographics,* July 1994, pp. 22–33. American Demographics © 1994. Reprinted with permission.

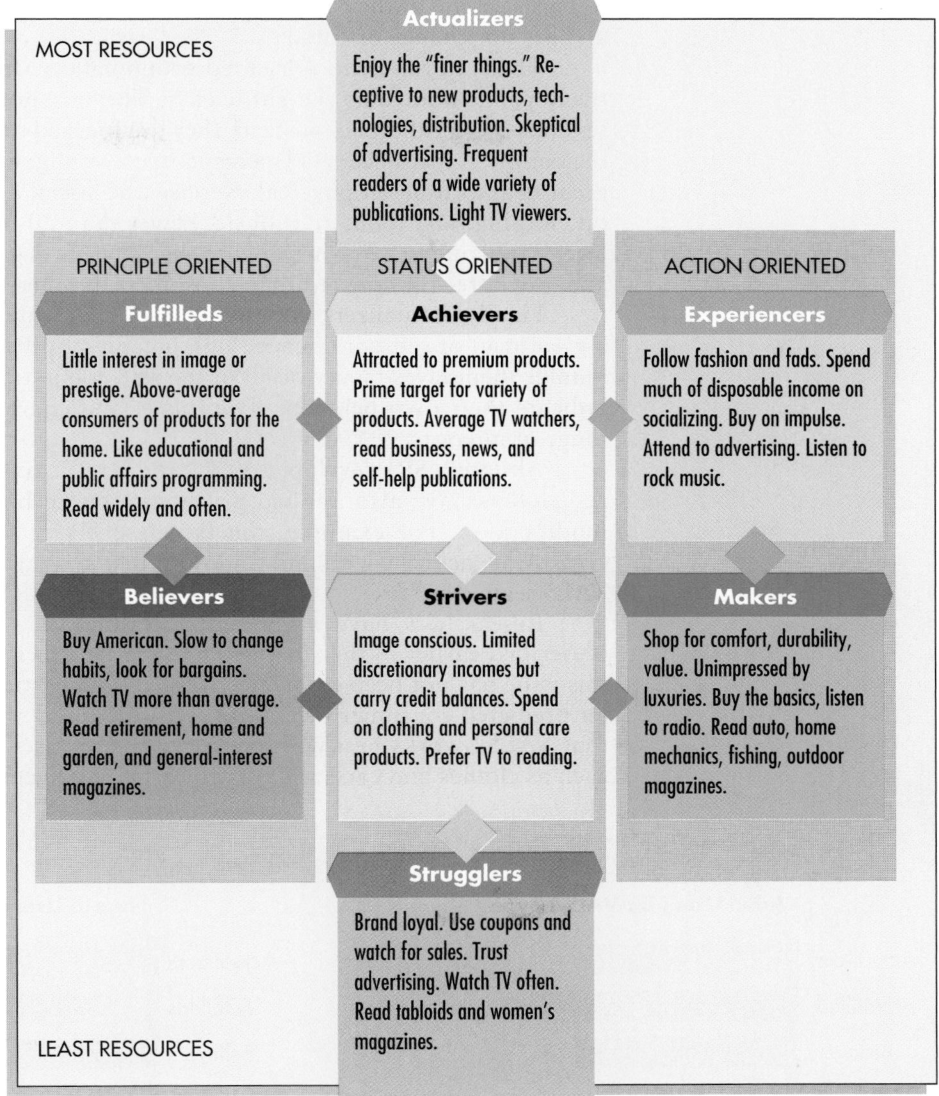

est incomes of the VALS2 segments. Because their focus is on surviving, they are not described by any self-orientation. Believers (17 percent), the largest of the VALS2 segments, are principle-oriented consumers with somewhat modest resources. Believers are poorly educated and have deeply held beliefs about moral codes of conduct and ethics. More than one-third of the consumers in this group are retired. The other principle-oriented group is the Fulfilleds (12 percent), who are mature, responsible, well educated, well informed, and older (more than half are over 50). They are also happy with their families, have high incomes, and are value oriented in their consumption practices.

Status-oriented segments include Strivers (14 percent), who have blue-collar backgrounds and strive to emulate more successful people. Achievers (10 percent) have higher resources, are focused on their work and families, and tend to be successful at their jobs. They are politically conservative, respect authority, and are not change oriented.

Those in the action-oriented group called Makers (12 percent) are relatively young and value self-sufficiency. They are not interested in material possessions or world events; instead, they are focused on family, work, and physical recreation. Experiencers (11 percent) are a young, energetic group who spend a great deal of time on physical exercise and social activities. They spend avidly on clothing, fast food, and music. Fewer than 20 percent have completed college, but many are working toward their college degree. They love new products and are more risk oriented than consumers in other segments.

Finally, Actualizers (8 percent) have the greatest resource base. They have a great deal of self-confidence, high incomes, and education and can therefore indulge themselves in any or all of the self-orientations. They use possessions to indicate their own personal style, taste, and character, and they have a wide range of interests.

Although SRI developed VALS and VALS2 to describe U.S. consumers, its researchers have also applied psychographic techniques in Japan, with some modification. For example, the Japanese VALS has three orientations (self-expression, achievement, and tradition) that serve as the basis for identifying ten VALS segments.[162]

Researchers have argued that techniques such as the List of Values (described earlier in this chapter) may better describe consumer segments, but this issue has not been completely resolved. One study found that the LOV better predicted consumer behavior than VALS, and another did not.[163] Also note that VALS2 works best with products and services that are related to the ego, such as clothes and cars, and for which felt involvement is likely to be high.

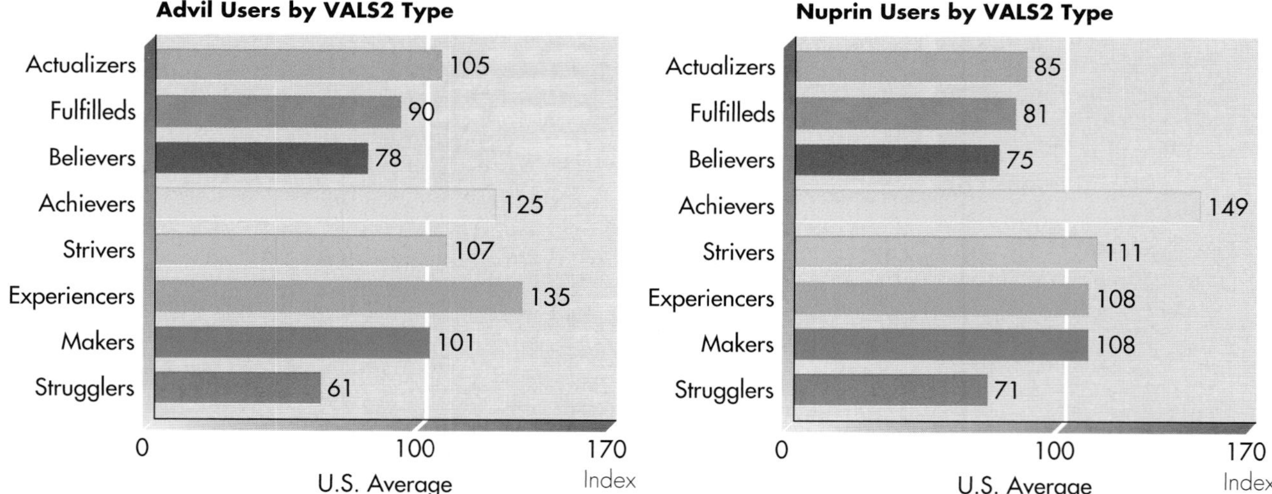

EXHIBIT 17.15
VALS2 Example

This exhibit shows how brand choice varies by VALS2 segment for the ibuprofen analgesic category. Nuprin is preferred by Achievers, and Advil is preferred by Experiencers and Achievers. A clear strategy for Nuprin, then, would be to continue to appeal to Achievers.

Source: Rebecca Pirto, *Beyond Mind Games,* American Demographic Books, pp. 88–89. Copyright 1991 by American Demographics. VALS2, SRI International, Menlo Park, Calif.: cited in Judith Waldrop, "Markets with Attitude," *American Demographics* © 1994. Reprinted with permission.

MARKETING IMPLICATIONS VALS2 can be a useful tool in market segmentation, new product ideas, and especially ad development. To illustrate, marketers can first identify heavy, medium, and light users of a product or service and then examine VALS2 profiles across these segments. Exhibit 17.15 presents possible usage incidences for two major brands in the ibuprofen analgesic category. Achievers are more likely to use Nuprin, whereas Experiencers, followed by Achievers, are more likely to use Advil.[164] Note also that Nuprin fares poorly with Actualizers, who tend to be heavy users of pain relievers. Thus, a strategy for Nuprin would be to continue to appeal to Achievers and try to improve its standing with Actualizers.

Pittsburgh's Iron City beer used VALS2 to improve its image and counteract lagging sales. From research Iron City discovered that it had two main markets: Makers and Believers, who were loyal customers for many years. Strivers and Experiencers, a younger market of consumers, were rejecting the brand. To appeal to these important, yet diverse, segments, Iron City developed an ad campaign juxtaposing images of old Pittsburgh with contemporary, vibrant images of the city as the backdrop for Strivers and Experiencers working hard at having fun. By advertising on television programs and radio stations favored by Strivers and Experiencers, Iron City successfully appealed to these segments and increased its sales by 26 percent.[165] •

Other Applied Psychographic Research

Although VALS2 is probably the best known and most widely used psychographic tool, there are a variety of other ongoing surveys. One well-known annual lifestyle study, the Yankelovich Monitor, assesses key changes in values and lifestyle trends in the United States.[166] The Monitor measures and traces consumers' behavior and feelings toward a wide variety of issues, such as the family, money, institutions, change, stress, and the future. Using these issues, the study follows such major trends as beauty in the home, introspection, anti-bigness, attitudes toward sex, and self-improvement. Yankelovich Partners recently developed another psychographic segmentation system, Monitor Mindbase, with eight major segments and 32 subsegments for more precise targeting.[167]

Many advertising agencies engage in ongoing psychographic research. Common examples include Grey's New Grownups Study, which identifies four types of households based on their ideas about life and use of time; J. Walter Thompson's Life Stages (single, married, married without children, and so on); Ogilvy & Mather's NEW WAVE, which identifies consumer trends; and DDB Needham's Life Style Study.[168] Researchers also study the psychographics of various demographic groups. As one example, the Hispanic Monitor identifies four main segments: Hopeful Loyalists, Recent Seekers (both foreign born), Young Strivers, and Established Adapters.

Some researchers use psychographics to identify global segments of consumers. GlobalScan, conducted by the ad agency Backer Spielvogel Bates Worldwide, surveys consumers in North America, Europe, Australia, Asia, New Zealand, and Venezuela about attitudes, values, media use, product use, and buying patterns. This research has identified five consumer segments: Strivers (26 percent), Achievers (22 percent), Pressured (13 percent), Traditionals (16 percent), and Adapters (18 percent), with 5 percent unclassified.[169] Note, however, that different countries may have different values.

The ad agency DMB&B has used personality traits, values, and products to segment the Russian market. The kuptsi are conservative, narrow-minded people who have roots in prerevolutionary Russia. They do not like foreign products and seek reliability and value in the products they buy. Russian souls are passive and afraid of choice, need reassurance from others that they are buying the right product, and are best persuaded by seeing others buy and successfully use a brand. The students have a broader, more cosmopolitan view of the world and are very open to Western products and ideas. Although they covet Western products, they will often make do with a cheaper version.[170]

Finally, Young & Rubicam has a segmentation scheme called Cross-Cultural Consumer Characterizations, or the 4Cs. Similar to VALS in design, the 4Cs focuses on goals, motivations, and values, as well as lifestyle and purchase patterns. It has identified seven key segments: Resigned Poor, Struggling Poor, Mainstreamers, Aspirers, Succeeders, Transitionals, and Reformers.[171]

Some researchers question whether psychographic techniques fully capture all the variation in consumers' lifestyles. Rather than relying on the traits measured in the research discussed above, one researcher identifies some consumption patterns that do not fit into the VALS framework. These include canonical aesthetics (which relates to traditional Western thought and tastes for art and culture), nurturing mother (in which consumption centers on the home and caring for children), and Jeffersonian America (related to the styles and traditions of a pastoral United States).[172] Another researcher warns that segments can shift with societal changes, economic changes, technological changes, and competitive changes.[173]

SUMMARY

Values are enduring beliefs about things that are important. Consumers learn values through the processes of socialization and acculturation. Our values exist in an organized value system, where some are viewed as more important than others. Terminal values reflect desired end states that guide behavior in many situations. Domain-specific values are relevant within a given sphere of activity. Western cultures tend to highly value materialism, youth, the home, family and children, work and play, health, hedonism, technology, and the environment. Marketers use value-based segmentation to identify groups within the larger market that have a common set of values that differ from those of other groups. Three methods for identifying value-based segments are inferring values based on the cultural milieu of the group, the means-end chain analysis, and questionnaires like the Rokeach Value Survey and the List of Values.

Personality consists of the patterns of behaviors, tendencies, and personal dispositions that make people different from one another. Approaches to the study of personality include (1) the psychoanalytic approach, which sees personality as the result of unconscious struggles within individuals to complete key stages of development; (2) trait theories, which attempt to identify a set of personality characteristics that describe and differentiate individuals, such as introversion, extroversion, and stability; (3) phenomenological approaches, which propose that personality is shaped by an individual's interpretation of life events; (4) social-psychological theories, which focus on the way individuals act in social situations, such as compliant, detached, or aggressive; and (5) behavioral approaches, which view an individual's personality in terms of behavioral responses to past rewards and punishments.

Marketers also measure lifestyles, which are patterns of behavior or activities, interests, and opinions. Lifestyles can provide additional insight into consumers' consumption patterns.

Finally, some marketing researchers use psychographic techniques that involve all these factors—values, personality, and lifestyles—to predict consumer behavior. One of the best-known psychographic tools is the Values and Lifestyle Survey (VALS). VALS2 identifies eight segments of consumers who are similar in their resources and value orientations.

QUESTIONS FOR REVIEW AND DISCUSSION

1. Explain the differences between global values, terminal values, instrumental values, and domain-specific values.
2. What are the four main value dimensions along which national cultures can vary?
3. How do marketers use means-end chain analysis, the Rokeach Value Survey, and the List of Values?
4. How does locus of control affect personality?
5. What are the three components of a consumer's lifestyle?
6. Define psychographics, and discuss its use and potential limitations.

EXERCISES

1. Conduct a content analysis of the advertisements that appear over four issues of a selected magazine. For each ad, record the type of product or service and whether and how each of the following values is reflected in the message: (a) materialism, (b) youthfulness, (c) the home, (d) work and play, (e) the family, (f) health, (g) hedonism, and (h) technology. Summarize this information and answer the following questions:
   a. Which values are most often reflected in the advertisements?
   b. Do certain types of values appear more often for certain types of products?
   c. Which themes appear in relationship to each value?
2. Develop a questionnaire to measure some of the key activities, interests, and opinions of college students. Also develop a series of items to measure the consumption of five product or service categories that may be related to college lifestyles. Administer this questionnaire to 20 fellow students (across different majors if possible). Summarize the results, and answer the following questions:
   a. What are the key lifestyle segments of the college students you surveyed?
   b. For each segment, are there recognizable consumption patterns in terms of products or services?
   c. What general types of marketing strategies would you use to appeal to each group?

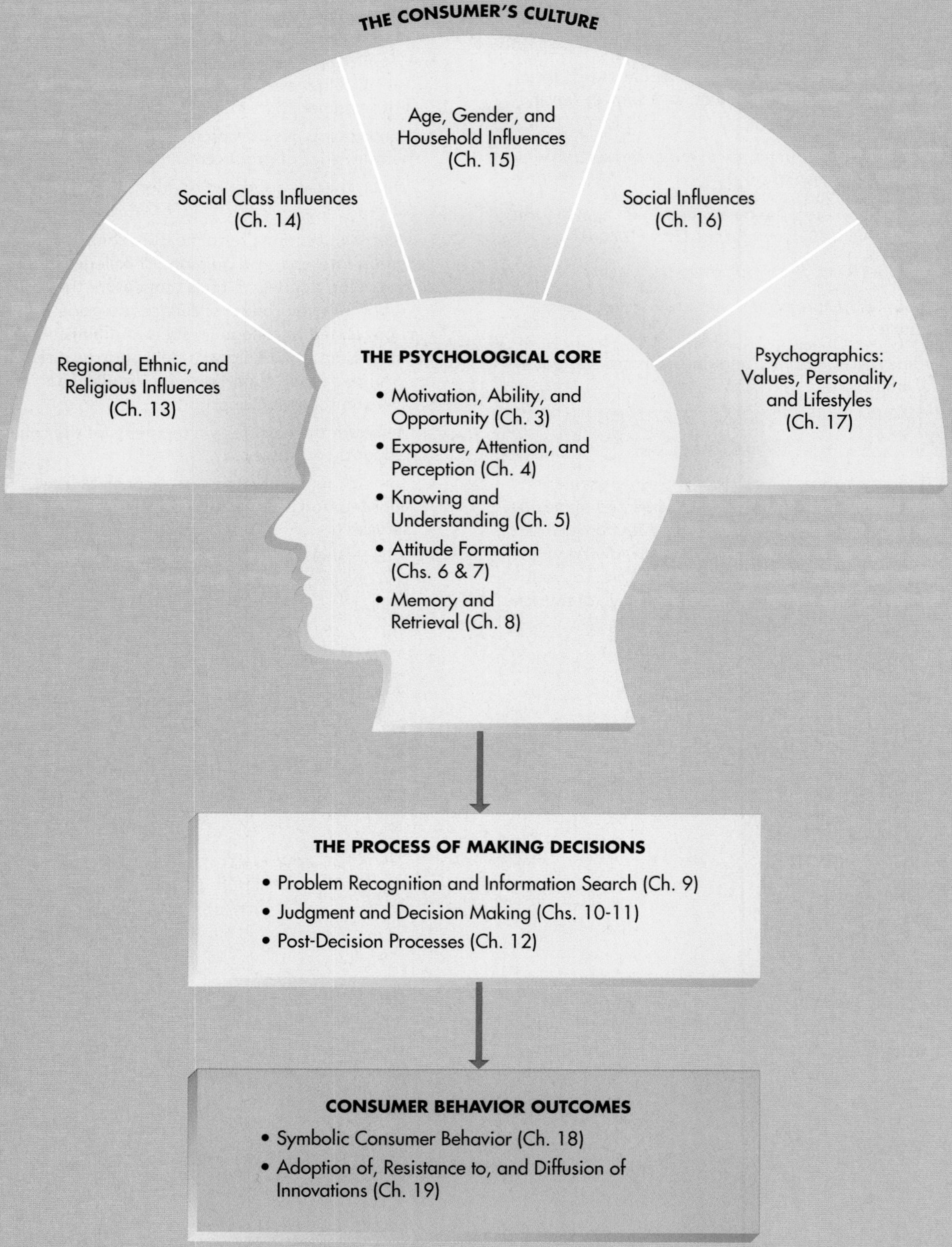

THE CONSUMER'S CULTURE

Regional, Ethnic, and Religious Influences (Ch. 13)

Social Class Influences (Ch. 14)

Age, Gender, and Household Influences (Ch. 15)

Social Influences (Ch. 16)

Psychographics: Values, Personality, and Lifestyles (Ch. 17)

THE PSYCHOLOGICAL CORE

- Motivation, Ability, and Opportunity (Ch. 3)
- Exposure, Attention, and Perception (Ch. 4)
- Knowing and Understanding (Ch. 5)
- Attitude Formation (Chs. 6 & 7)
- Memory and Retrieval (Ch. 8)

THE PROCESS OF MAKING DECISIONS

- Problem Recognition and Information Search (Ch. 9)
- Judgment and Decision Making (Chs. 10-11)
- Post-Decision Processes (Ch. 12)

CONSUMER BEHAVIOR OUTCOMES

- Symbolic Consumer Behavior (Ch. 18)
- Adoption of, Resistance to, and Diffusion of Innovations (Ch. 19)

PART FIVE

Consumer Behavior Outcomes

Part Five examines the outcomes of the numerous influences and decision processes discussed in the preceding chapters. Chapter 18 discusses the fascinating topic of symbolic consumer behavior. Offerings—both products and services—can have deep-felt and significant meanings for consumers. The chapter also highlights some interesting and important consumption rituals.

Chapter 19 builds on the topics of internal decision making and group processes by examining how consumers adopt new offerings and how their adoption decisions affect the spread or diffusion of an offering through a market. This chapter also looks at how social factors influence decision making in a market over time.

chapter 18

Symbolic Consumer Behavior

The Harley-Davidson motorcycle and its accessories, along with its American eagle logo, symbolize personal freedom, patriotism, and machismo to many consumers. Consider that the motorcycles are mainly big, loud, heavy, and very macho. Some devotees paint eagles on their bikes; others tattoo the eagle on their bodies. Bikers sometimes adopt a Western motif, another symbol of freedom, U.S. heritage, and machismo, by dressing in black; wearing leather chaps, boots, and vests; and—for the wildest and most intimidating Harley riders—operating on both sides of the law as "outlaws."

Introduction: The Symbolism of Harley-Davidson

The Harley motorcycle allows some consumers to stand out and break free of their traditional roles—helping them symbolize their uniqueness. Some bikers believe that riding a Harley is like a religious experience. Riding free allows the rider to be close to nature; the throbbing of the machine is like a mantra; and riding is a constant reminder of the risks they take and their vulnerabilities. Some bikers even use Harley paraphernalia as part of religious ceremonies like weddings and funerals.

Many riders view the Harley motorcycle as a very special possession because it symbolizes their connection to others like themselves. Indeed, in addition to the large Harley Owners' Group, a number of specific subgroups have formed: Rich Urban Bikers (RUBS), the Fifth Chapter (a club that also is a support group for recovering alcoholics and addicts), Dykes on Bikes (a lesbian biker club), and Trinity Road Riders (a born-again Christian club). Each group has its own rituals that symbolize group membership. Membership is not auto-

RAINDROPS DODGE IT BASED ON SHEER INTIMIDATION.

EXHIBIT 18.1
Marketers as Creators of Product Meaning
Marketers are one of the several sources that create meaning surrounding a product. This ad by Harley-Davidson clothes reinforces ideas about what it means to be a Harley-Davidson biker.

Source: Courtesy of Harley-Davidson, Inc.

matic, and new group members, who often feel uncomfortable as novices, rely on images of the biker cultivated in magazines like *Biker, Easyriders, American Iron, Supercycle, Independent Biker,* and *HOG Tales.* Harley-Davidson marketing and merchandise also provide ideas about what it means to be a Harley rider (see Exhibit 18.1). Novices use such biker paraphernalia to demonstrate to others that they are true bikers. Once accepted into a biker group, a rider becomes a "brother," forever connected to the group's family. The Bros. Club is, in fact, a cooperative that gives roadside assistance to bikers.

Some owners view their Harleys as sacred, build shrines like special sheds or garages for their bike, and adorn the shrines with Harley posters, calendars, memorabilia, and paraphernalia. They rush to buy limited-edition bikes produced for special occasions such as Harley's 100th birthday. Taboos dictate that one biker is not to touch another's Harley—rather each bike should be revered. Bikers also show respect for their bikes by performing cleaning rituals that enhance and retain their sacred status. Some outlaw bikers are also regarded with sacred status. New bikers feel humbled by their presence, and such outlaw bikers can evoke feelings of admiration and fear even among the most experienced biker enthusiasts.[1]

This chapter describes several key aspects of symbolic consumer behavior, starting with an examination of how offerings acquire symbolic meaning, the functions of symbols, and how they affect our self-concept. Next the chapter explains why some offerings vary in their meaningfulness. Some symbols are special—even sacred—and require consumption practices to keep them so. The chapter ends by showing how meaning is transferred from one individual to another through the process of gift giving (see Exhibit 18.2). ●

SOURCES AND FUNCTIONS OF SYMBOLIC MEANING

To understand why some consumers are so crazy about Harley-Davidson motorcycles, consider where the meaning associated with products and consumption practices like those in the biker subculture comes from and what functions these offerings and activities fulfill. As shown in Exhibit 18.3, the meaning associated with offerings and consumption practices can stem either from our culture or from ourselves as individuals.

Meaning Derived from Culture

cultural categories
The natural grouping of objects that reflect our culture.

cultural principles
Ideas or values that specify how aspects of our culture are organized and/or how they should be perceived or evaluated.

Part of the meaning associated with products derives from our culture (see Exhibit 18.4).[2] Anthropologists suggest that natural categories of objects reflect our culture, including **cultural categories** for time (such as work time and leisure time); space (such as home, office, and safe or unsafe places); and occasions (such as festive versus somber events). We also have cultural categories that reflect our perceptions of various groups of people based on specific characteristics, such as categories of gender, age, social class, and ethnicity.

Implicit in these cultural categories are **cultural principles**—ideas or values that specify how aspects of our culture are organized and how they should be perceived or evaluated. For example, the cultural principles associated with the category known as work time dictate that it is more structured, organized, and precise than leisure time. Cultural principles also give meaning to category-related products. Thus the clothing we associate with work time is also more structured, organized, and precise than the clothing we associate with leisure time. We also have

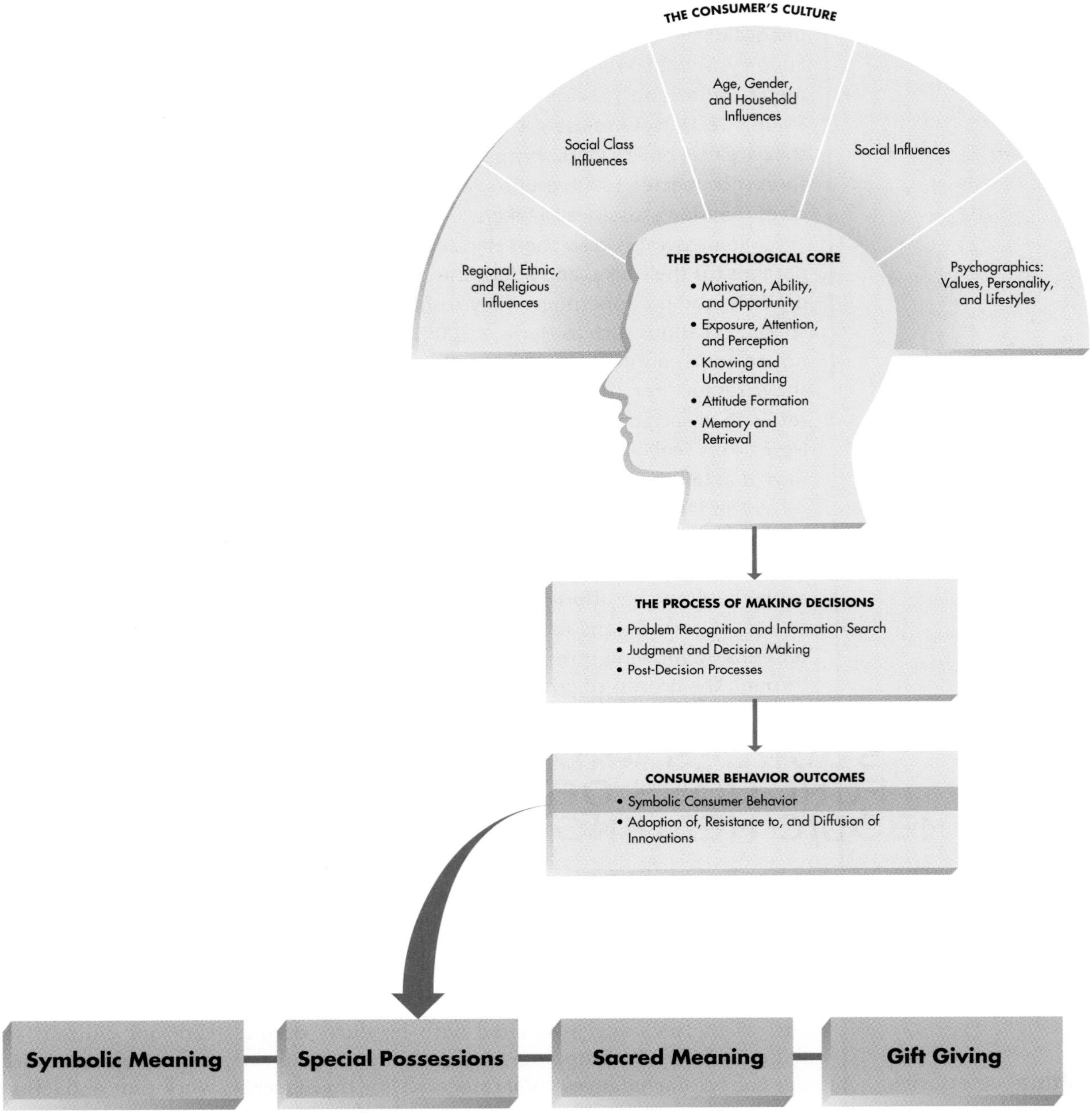

THE CONSUMER'S CULTURE

Regional, Ethnic, and Religious Influences

Social Class Influences

Age, Gender, and Household Influences

Social Influences

Psychographics: Values, Personality, and Lifestyles

THE PSYCHOLOGICAL CORE

- Motivation, Ability, and Opportunity
- Exposure, Attention, and Perception
- Knowing and Understanding
- Attitude Formation
- Memory and Retrieval

THE PROCESS OF MAKING DECISIONS

- Problem Recognition and Information Search
- Judgment and Decision Making
- Post-Decision Processes

CONSUMER BEHAVIOR OUTCOMES

- Symbolic Consumer Behavior
- Adoption of, Resistance to, and Diffusion of Innovations

Symbolic Meaning — Special Possessions — Sacred Meaning — Gift Giving

EXHIBIT 18.2
Chapter Overview

Products and consumption activities can symbolize something about ourselves and our relationships with other people. In this chapter, we consider how products and consumption activities take on and communicate meaning. We also discuss that some possessions and consumption activities take on special or even sacred meaning. Finally, we discuss how gift giving can symbolize how we feel toward a gift recipient.

EXHIBIT 18.3
The Sources and Functions of Consumption Symbols
Consumers use products with various meanings to achieve a set of functions. Combined, these functions help define the consumer's self-concept.

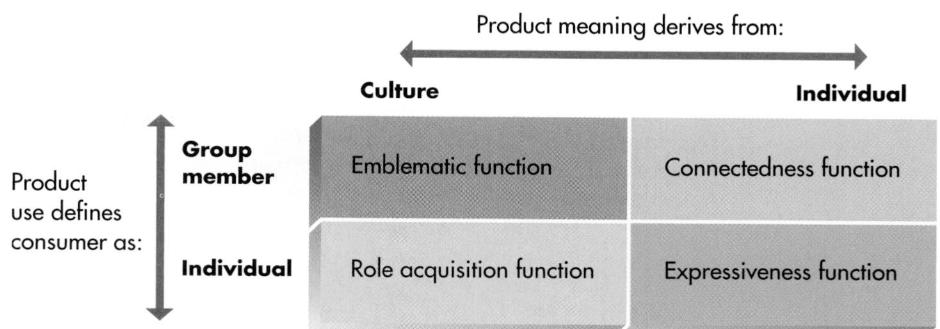

categories for occasions, including festive (vibrant, active, and energetic) and somber (dark, quiet, and inactive). Thus the clothing we associate with celebrations is generally bright, colorful, and comfortable, whereas the clothing we associate with somber activities is often dark, muted, and understated.

Cultural categories of people identified by characteristics such as social status, gender, age, and ethnicity are particularly relevant to the study of symbolic meaning, because we associate various cultural principles with these categories. For example, the category "women" has historically been associated with concepts like delicate, whimsical, expressive, and changeable. In contrast, the category men has historically been associated with concepts like disciplined, stable, and serious. Marketers make products and consumers use them in ways that are consistent with these principles. Thus women's clothing is traditionally more delicate, whimsical, expressive, and changeable than clothing for men. Exhibit 18.4 indicates that by associating and matching product characteristics with cultural principles and categories, we transfer to the product the meaning that exists at the cultural level. For example, we might classify certain clothing as feminine or as suitable for work because we associate it with the corresponding cultural principles and categories.

Exhibit 18.4 also shows that many agents can play a role in this association and matching process. First, product designers and manufacturers introduce new products whose characteristics reflect cultural principles. For example, the Harley-Davidson motorcycle has characteristics that make it "macho." Marketers and advertising agencies may also give products meaning by associating these offerings with certain cultural categories. Thus, Harley-Davidson develops clothing, accessories, and information that communicate what it means to be a biker.[3]

Meaning also comes from nonmarketing sources. Specific people may serve as opinion leaders who shape, refine, or reshape cultural principles and the products and attributes with which they are associated (see Chapter 16). For example, Tiger Woods may define for boys the type of athletic shoe associated with status. Sometimes groups on the margins of society can be agents of change, as when inner-city teens, associated with antiestablishment principles, introduced new styles of clothing that reflected those principles.[4]

Journalists who review new offerings also shape cultural principles and the products associated with them. For example, restaurant reviewers may determine whether a restaurant is associated with principles like status, and style editors may determine whether clothes are associated with young and hip categories or with others. Magazines like *Biker* communicate meaning associated with the

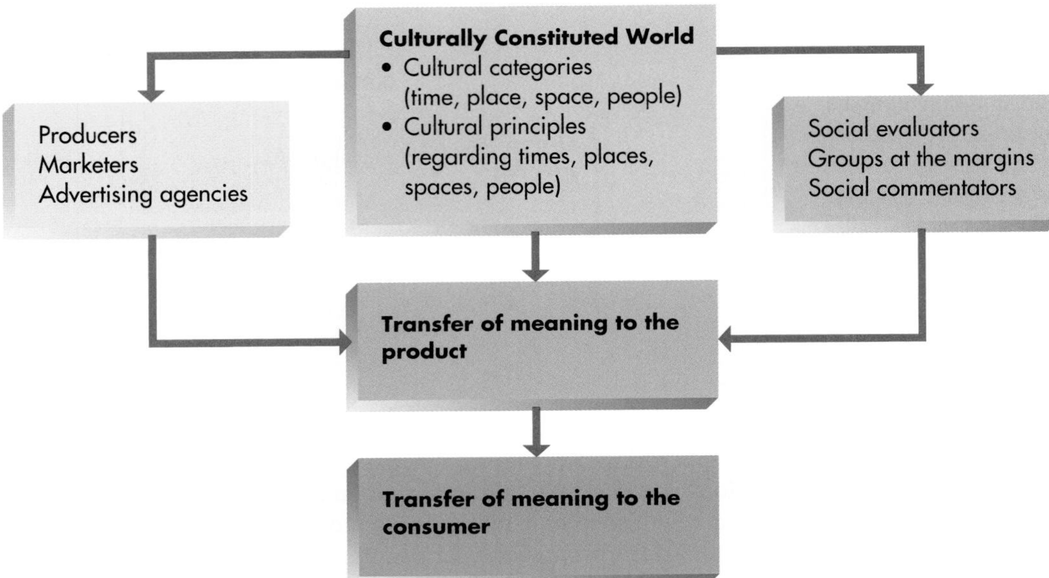

EXHIBIT 18.4
Transfer of Meaning from the Culture to the Product and to the Consumer

Meaning that exists at the level of the culture (e.g., youthful) can become associated with a product (e.g., Pepsi). Marketer-dominated groups (e.g., marketers) and non-marketer-dominated groups (e.g., opinion leaders, the media) can play a powerful role in this association process. The meaning associated with the product can in turn be transferred to the consumer who uses it.

Source: Adapted from Grant McCracken, "Culture and Consumption: A Theoretical Account of the Structure and Movement of the Cultural Meaning of Consumer Goods," *Journal of Consumer Research,* June 1986, pp. 71–84. © 1986 University of Chicago. All rights reserved.

biker category, such as what bikers are like, who they hang around with, and what they like to do. Celebrities like Ricky Martin can also create meaning in products by how they use them. Through all these sources, the meaning inherent in the product gets transferred to the consumer.

Meaning Derived from the Consumer

In addition to the way products derive symbolic meaning from culture, consumers can develop their own individual meanings associated with products. Whether meaning stems from the culture or the consumer, however, consumption symbols can be used to (1) say something about the consumer as a member of a group or (2) say something about the consumer as a unique individual. Combining these two dimensions produces emblematic, role acquisition, connectedness, and expressiveness functions.

The Emblematic Function

emblematic function The use of products to symbolize membership in social groups.

Meaning derived from culture allows us to use products to symbolize our membership in various social groups, an **emblematic function**. Thus dresses are associated with women and clerical collars are associated with priests. The music we listen to may symbolize our age, and the car we drive may symbolize our social status. Consciously or unconsciously, we constantly use products to symbolize the groups to which we belong. At the same time, people who observe us using these products may consciously or unconsciously categorize and make inferences about us and the groups we belong to. Just by looking at someone and his or her possessions, we might be able to tell whether that person is a member of the Mexican American, upper-middle class, or Catholic categories.[5] In particular, offerings may serve as geographic, ethnic, or social class emblems.

Geographic Emblems Products can symbolize geographic identification. For example, brightly colored, loose-fitting clothing symbolizes identification with sunnier regions of the United States, such as California, Arizona, Florida, and Hawaii. The outdoorsy clothing made by Roots symbolizes Canada.[6] Products may also symbolize geographic identification with a region even if used by people who live elsewhere.

EXHIBIT 18.5
Social Class Emblems
Because only relatively wealthy people can afford Wittnauer watches, they symbolize the status and luxury that members of the upper class enjoy.

Source: Courtesy of Wittnauer.

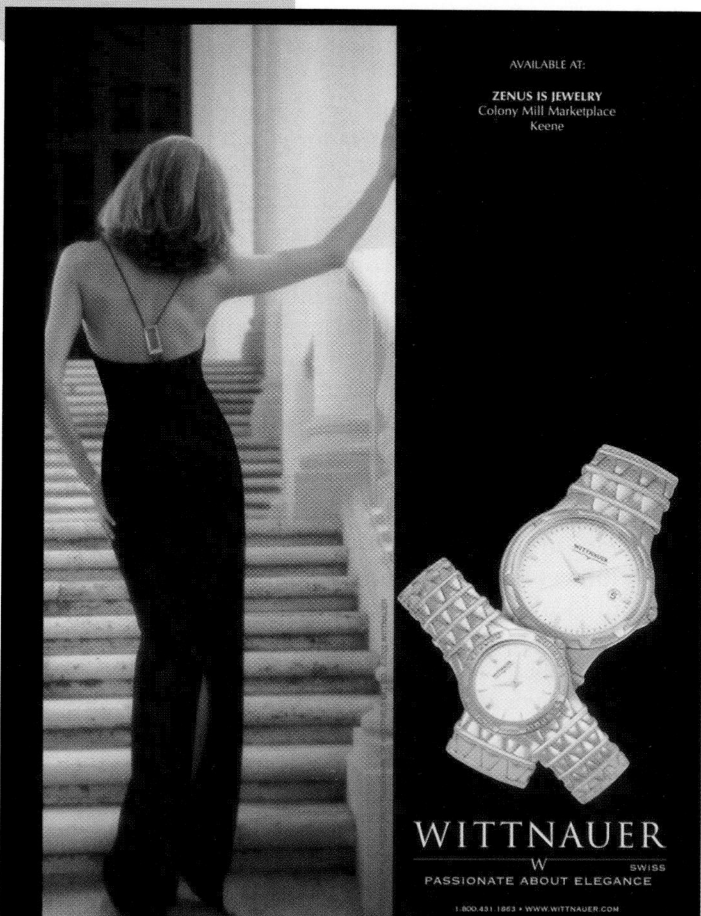

AVAILABLE AT:
ZENUS IS JEWELRY
Colony Mill Marketplace
Keene
WITTNAUER
W
SWISS
PASSIONATE ABOUT ELEGANCE
1.800.431.1863 • WWW.WITTNAUER.COM

Ethnic Emblems Products and consumption activities can symbolize identification with a specific culture or subculture. African Americans sometimes wear African garb to symbolize identification with that culture. In India, Sikh men wear five Ks as symbols of their ethnic and religious affiliation: *kesh* (hair), *kada* (bangle), *kangha* (comb), *kacha* (underpants), and *kirpan* (dagger). Consumers sometimes use ethnic emblems of other cultures or subcultures to differentiate themselves. In Japan, teen rebels have adopted products symbolic of the Latino barrio: low riders; Latino music; and art, fashions, and tattoos with barrio images.[7] Clothing identified with African American urban culture has also become popular among Anglo consumers in the United States.[8]

Consumers commonly use food to express ethnic identity. For example, grilled chicken, chicken mole, and steamed yellowfish reflect U.S., Mexican, and Chinese identities, respectively.[9] Cornmeal serves as an ethnic emblem for Haitians immigrating to the United States.[10] We can also express our ethnic identification by how and when we eat. Cultures differ in whether all elements of the meal are served at once or one item at a time.[11] U.S. families typically eat dinner at about 6:00 p.m., but dinnertime is much later in Spain and Italy.

Social Class Emblems Products can also symbolize social class, such as the watch advertised in Exhibit 18.5. In Mexico the car symbolizes success and luxury because few people can afford to own one.[12] In China, a color TV is an emblem of status and self-worth.[13] Among wealthy American consumers, symbols of social class include helicopters, backyard golf courses, private airplanes, and palatial homes.[14] Consider, also, emblems of membership in the upper-upper class. The cultural principles of upper-upper-class membership include characteristics of refinement, understated restraint, and discipline. So too do the products and consumption activities of this class. One author notes that an upper-class white Anglo-Saxon woman is likely to outfit herself in a loose-fitting wool or cotton cuffed pants in a subdued color, an embroidered wool or cashmere sweater, flats, a small leather handbag, and a small gold bracelet or necklace.[15]

The social classes also use different symbols in consumption rituals. For example, higher and lower social classes in the United States differ greatly in the types of clothing they wear at Thanksgiving, the importance they place on etiquette, the types of serving dishes they use, and even the way they serve a food like butter. The upper-upper-class dinner table will have molded pats of butter (perhaps embossed with the family crest) and individual butter knives and butter plates. In contrast, middle-class families may serve butter on a crystal or china butter plate that is passed from person to person. Lower-class families may pass a tub of butter in its original container, with everyone using the same butter knife.[16]

Countering this type of emblematic function, a growing number of U.S. schools (both public and private) now require students to wear uniforms. Officials and some parents believe that uniforms help curb gang activity, remove social class emblems, and reduce students' anxiety about keeping up with their peers.[17]

Gender Emblems Food, clothing, jewelry, and alcoholic beverages are only some of the product categories associated with membership in the male and female gender categories.[18] One study of consumers in France revealed that meat and certain other foods are viewed as "man" foods, whereas celery and other specific foods are viewed as "woman" foods. In part, associating certain foods with specific gender groups stems from culturally devised notions of fatness and thinness and the appropriateness of these attributes for men and women.

Research also shows that the way a food is eaten reflects its appropriateness for men and women. Fish, for example, must be eaten slowly and delicately, with restraint, and chewed gently to avoid eating bones. According to this researcher, nibbling and picking is more consistent with women's characteristics. In contrast, steak, which may be cut roughly, is chewed intensively, and can be rather messy and bloody, is more consistent with culturally derived characteristics of men.[19] Other researchers have found gender differences in food preferences, with boys preferring chunky peanut butter, for instance, and girls preferring the smooth variety. These preferences may be related to culturally derived associations with boys (rough) and girls (not rough).[20]

Reference Group Emblems The Harley-Davidson example illustrates how products can serve as emblems of membership in a reference group. One reason consumers become outlaw bikers is that they like being members of a reference group with a counterculture ideology. Consumers may also wear private school uniforms, varsity jackets, and special hats, colors, or gang-designated jewelry to symbolize reference group membership. One high school banned rosary beads because students were wearing them as emblems of gang membership.[21]

In addition to products, rituals are sometimes important indicators and affirmations of group membership. For example, rituals like attending the Independence Day parade may reinforce our membership in the "U.S. citizens" group. Other rituals serve as public confirmation that we have become members of a group. Among the upper-upper class, the debutante ball is a ritual that formally introduces 16-year-old girls into the group of women eligible for dating.[22] In Jewish families the ceremony of male circumcision—called a Brith Milah—serves as a ritual inducting a newborn male child into the Jewish faith.

MARKETING IMPLICATIONS Marketers can play three roles in establishing the emblematic function of products.

Symbol development. The first role is symbol development, which identifies cultural principles associated with a category and confers on the product attributes believed to represent those characteristics. For example, Patek Philippe watches have characteristics associated with the upper class: timeless style, understated elegance, precision craftsmanship, precious materials, and price tags that range from $4,700 to $600,000.[23] Sometimes marketers need to ensure that product attributes are appropriately linked with cultural principles. Miller, for example, had to position the *lite* in Lite beer as meaning less filling—an appropriate attribute for men—rather than meaning diet, which would have made the beer seem more feminine. Miller reinforces the masculine image by associating the beer with macho sports figures like former Dallas Cowboys quarterback Troy Aikman.[24]

Symbol communication. The second role is symbol communication. A company can use advertising to charge a product with meaning through the setting for the ad (whether fantasy or naturalistic, interior or exterior, or rural or urban) and through other details such as the time of day and the types of people in the ad—their gender, age, ethnicity, occupation, clothing, body postures, and so on.[25] Each of these ad elements reinforces the meaning associated with the product.

Symbol reinforcement. The third role of marketing in establishing emblematic functions is to design other elements of the marketing mix to reinforce the symbolic image.[26] For instance, a company can use various pricing, distribution, and product strategies to maintain a product's status image. It may give the product a premium price, distribute it through outlets with an upscale image, and incorporate certain features that are appropriate only for the targeted segment. However, marketers may hurt a product's symbolic image if the elements of the marketing mix clash with each other.

Symbol removal. Some marketers have made a business of helping consumers erase symbols associated with groups with whom they no longer identify. For example, the tattoo removal market is growing. Consumers often want tattoos removed because they are emblematic of an earlier time of life or an abandoned reference group and therefore impede the development of new identifications.[27] ●

The Role Acquisition Function

In addition to serving as emblems of group membership, offerings can help us feel more comfortable in new roles. This function is called the **role acquisition function** (see Exhibit 18.3).

role acquisition function The use of products as symbols to help us feel more comfortable in a new role.

Role Acquisition Phases Consumers fill many roles in their lives, and these roles constantly change. You may currently occupy the role of student, son or daughter, brother or sister, and worker. At some point in your life (perhaps even now), you may occupy the role of husband or wife, uncle or aunt, parent, divorcee, grandparent, retiree, widow or widower, and so on.

People typically move from one role to another in three phases.[28] The first phase is separation from the old role. This often means disposing of products associated with the role we are leaving, the way children give up security blankets in their transition from baby to child. Consumers who are divorcing may symbolize the end of the marital relationship by giving away, throwing away, or destroying products that remind them of their former spouses.[29] The second phase is the transition from one role to another, which may be accompanied by experimentation with new identities. During this transition, consumers may be

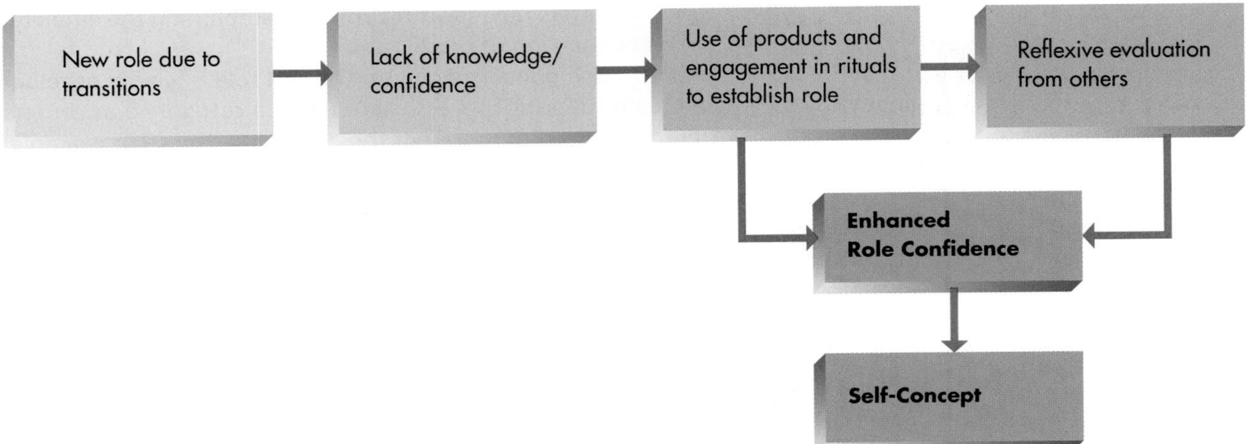

EXHIBIT 18.6
Model of Role Acquisition

When we are entering a new role (e.g., parenthood), we may lack some role confidence. As a result, we engage in activities (e.g., have baby showers) and buy groups of products (e.g., strollers) typically associated with that role. These activities and products, along with the way that others react to our behaviors, enhance our role confidence.

Source: Adapted from Michael Solomon, "The Role of Products as Social Stimuli: A Symbolic Interactionism Perspective," *Journal of Consumer Research*, December 1983, pp. 319–329.

willing to accept new possessions or styles they otherwise would have rejected. Consumers may also construct a new identity through plastic surgery, dieting, new hairstyles, branding, body piercing, and tattooing. The final phase is incorporation, in which the consumer takes on the new role and the identity associated with it.

Use of Symbols and Rituals in Role Transitions Exhibit 18.6 illustrates how and why we use symbols and rituals when we acquire a new role. We often feel uncomfortable with a new role because we are inexperienced in occupying it and have little knowledge about how to fulfill it. A common reaction is to use products stereotypically associated with that role. For example, researchers found that MBAs who were insecure about their job prospects were more likely than other MBAs to use symbols generally associated with the role of businessperson.[30] We often use a group of products to symbolize adoption of a new role. Having the right combination of products is important because without it we may not elicit the appropriate response from others. Imagine the reaction you would get at work if you wore white socks or sneakers with a business suit.

Rituals are also an important part of role transitions. For example, a number of rituals mark the transition from single to married status in the United States—wedding shower, bachelor party, rehearsal dinner, wedding, reception, and honeymoon—each with relevant enabling products.[31] The wedding itself includes clothing for the attendants, flowers, bridal veil, bridal bouquet, pillow for the rings, organ music, wedding clothing for guests, and so on.

reflexive evaluation Feedback from others that tells us whether we are fulfilling a role correctly.

Rituals often involve others whose participation helps validate the role transition. As Exhibit 18.6 shows, we use symbols and engage in rituals to get feedback from participants about whether we are fulfilling the role correctly. This feedback, called **reflexive evaluation**, helps us feel more confident in our role and thus validates our new status. As noted in the opening example, novice

Harley owners require this evaluation from experienced owners before feeling confident in the "biker" role. The next section focuses on marital role transitions and products as symbols of this transition process.

Marital Transitions Products are often an important component in the transition from single to married status. As part of this transition's separation phase, the couple must decide which of their possessions they wish to dispose of and which they will move to their new household. Many times the couple will discard presents from old boyfriends or girlfriends as well as disposing of products symbolizing their former single status. As part of the incorporation phase, the couple acquires new products that are culturally appropriate for the married role and that help them create a mutual history. The ad in Exhibit 18.7 shows some products that may symbolize the move from a single to a newly married state. Clearly, different cultures have different marital rituals. For example, the mother-in-law often gives the keys to the house to a Hindu bride following the wedding, symbolically handing over the charge of running the house.

A similar process operates in the transition from married to single status, as when people divorce. Here, too, people divest possessions in separating from the old role, as each person takes back what was his or hers and they divide their joint possessions. People may deliberately dispose of possessions that remind them of the other person. As one set of researchers notes, "Jettisoning symbols of the ex-spouse . . . may be psychologically necessary in the process of ending the relationship."[32] Some people destroy possessions, which perhaps serves several functions—symbolically representing the destruction of the marriage, punishing the ex-spouse, and eliminating possessions that symbolize the marriage.

People may have difficulty fulfilling other symbolic functions as a result of ending a marriage. For example, one spouse may no longer have the conspicuous consumption items they once used to communicate social status. Thus someone who loses a house and a car (two important symbols of social prestige) may feel a loss of identity. On the other hand, people may acquire products symbolic of their new single status during this role transition, the way some people purchase a sports car.

Cultural Transitions Consumers also change roles when they move to a new culture, often abandoning or disposing of old customs and symbols and adopting new ones in the process. Research suggests that Mexican immigrants faced different and sometimes difficult experiences in moving to the United States.[33] Among these were living in densely grouped housing, shopping in stores with a sometimes overwhelming number of choices, and dealing with unfamiliar

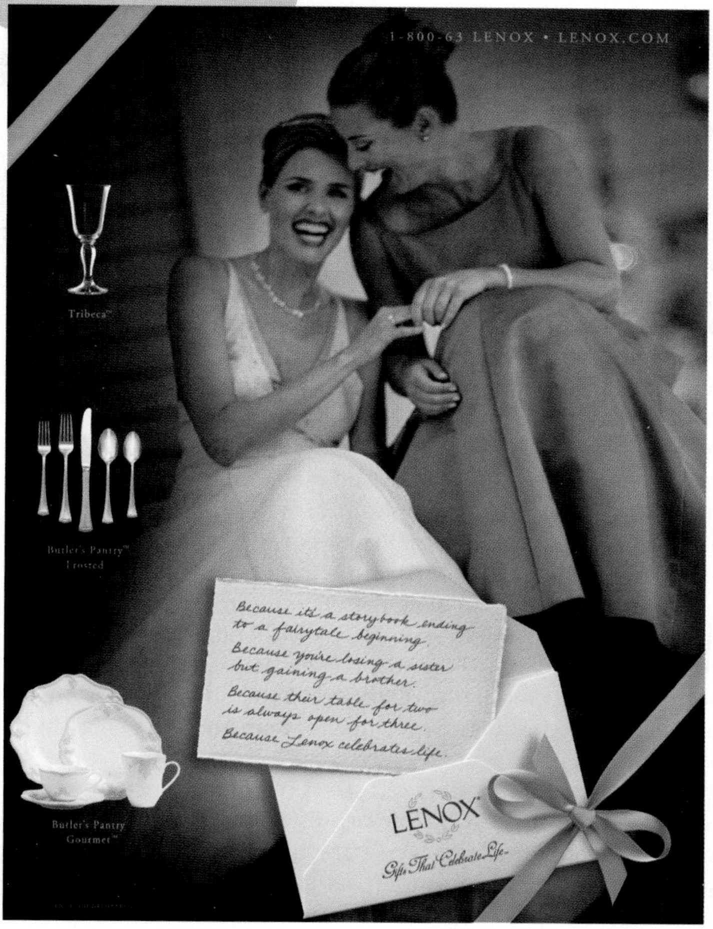

EXHIBIT 18.7
Marital Role Transition Symbols
This ad identifies a set of products that are appropriate as gifts in the transition from single to married status.

Source: Used by permission of Lenox, Incorporated. © Lenox, Incorporated 2002.

currency. As evidence of acculturation, some of the young immigrants in the study were very brand conscious. Yet these immigrants still held on to certain aspects of their culture, including Mexican food and Spanish-language media.

Another study reported on the status symbols acquired by Indians moving to the United States—symbols they did not need in India, where caste and family designate class membership.[34] Research found that Indians sometimes kept transitional items—things that reminded them of their home country and provided a sense of cultural identify—such as music and videos, photographs, heirloom furniture, saris, and jewelry. Whether someone abandons or retains possessions that symbolize the old role may depend on the perceived permanence of the role. The Indians in this study, for example, still considered the possibility of someday returning to India. In fact, expatriates often face frustrating and formidable barriers to inclusion in a new culture, which they seek to overcome by participating in local events and rituals and adapting consumption to local customs while retaining special possessions from home.[35]

Social Status Transitions Newly wealthy individuals, the nouveaux riches, need possessions—usually ostentatious ones—to demonstrate their acquired status and validate their role. This is consistent with the model of symbols and role transitions in Exhibit 18.6, which shows the importance of reflexive evaluation from others to indicate successful role performance. As one author notes, "Consumer satisfaction is derived from audience reactions to the wealth displayed by the purchaser in securing the product or service rather than to the positive attributes of the item in question."[36]

MARKETING IMPLICATIONS

Marketers can apply their knowledge of consumers' role transitions in several ways.

Role transitions and target consumers. Consumers in transition represent an important target market for many firms. Indeed, many of the 3,000-plus pages of ads in *Bride's* magazine explicitly target consumers in their transition to the stage of being married.[37]

Role transitions as means for developing inventory. Because product disposition can be an important aspect of role separation, marketers of secondhand products can acquire inventory by marketing to people engaged in role transitions. For example, secondhand stores might target college students before graduation, knowing that in their role transitions many may wish to dispose of student-related paraphernalia such as furniture and clothing. The online auction firm eBay attracted former Enron employees who put memos and memorabilia up for bid after they lost their jobs following the company's bankruptcy.[38]

Role transitions and product promotions. When consumers are anticipating role changes, marketers may find it useful to promote their products as instrumental in incorporating a new role. For example, marketers tout products from shower fixtures to contraceptives to home computers as acceptable wedding gifts. Furthermore, bridal registries are showing up in places as diverse as Ace Hardware, Tower Records, and the Metropolitan Museum of Art stores.[39] Baby gift registries are on the rise, and marketers position products like wipe warmers and bouncing chairs as important to the new parent role.[40]

Selling product constellations. Marketers can stress the importance of groups of products to consumers in the process of role acquisition.[41] For example, new parents shopping for baby paraphernalia may be attracted to a new crib sold complete with changing table, mattress, waterproof mattress pad, bumpers, quilt, and

They planned their big day
down to the perfect getaway.
Picture the perfect wedding. WeddingChannel.com can help you plan every detail of your dream wedding, just the way you want it. Available 24 hours a day, we offer expert advice, stunning photos and easy-to-use tools to make planning simple. And it's all free of charge.
Combine that with over 20,000 photos of the most beautiful bridal gowns, the finest retailers for gift registry and a directory filled with photos from great reception sites and wedding professionals near you and you've got the perfect wedding resource: WeddingChannel.com.
Planning Made Simple
Guest List Manager | Budget Calculator | Planning Calendar
Personal Wedding Website | Scrapbook | Gift Registry
WeddingChannel.com
Everything you need to plan the perfect wedding. Yours.

EXHIBIT 18.8
Managing Rituals
Some marketers serve customers by providing products and services that help them manage complex transition rituals. WeddingChannel.com does this task for brides-to-be.

Source: Courtesy of WeddingChannel.com.

baby mobile. Businesses featuring product constellations include bridal superstores that offer wedding dresses, attendants' gowns, rented tuxedos, and arrangements with photographers, florists, and limousine companies.[42] Company advertising can suggest that the consumer will earn positive reflexive evaluation from others after using an appropriate constellation of products associated with a given role.

Managing rituals. Marketers can also be instrumental in developing services that facilitate the planning and implementation of the complex rituals surrounding transitions, the way funeral homes perform services in the death ritual. The ad for WeddingChannel.com in Exhibit 18.8 indicates how this firm can be a comprehensive source for helping couples manage the wedding ritual. ●

The Connectedness Function

Although the meaning of offerings that serve emblematic or role acquisition functions derives from the culture, product meaning can also derive from the consumer's role as a member of a group or as an individual (look back at Exhibit 18.3).[43]

connectedness function The use of products as symbols of our personal connections to significant people, events, or experiences.

Products and consumption activities that serve the **connectedness function** express our membership in a group and serve as symbols of our personal connections to significant people, events, or experiences in our lives. For example, you may particularly like a painting or a hat because it was a gift from a close friend. Heirlooms and genealogy studies connect people with their ancestors; family photos connect them to their descendants. People may also value ticket stubs, programs from concerts, and souvenirs as reminders of special people, events, and places.[44] Other products and acts can also symbolize connectedness. Chex Party Mix recipe has been used by families for years and may symbolize connectedness between families and friends (see Exhibit 18.9) when they get together to celebrate holidays and family occasions. As another example, Chinese consumers use large round tables in restaurants to symbolize wholeness and the group's connectedness. During Muslim feasts, everyone shares food from a community plate; those who ask for a separate plate are considered rude.

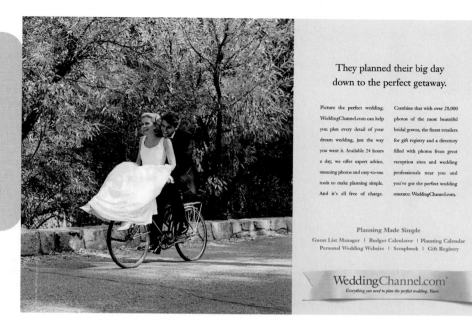

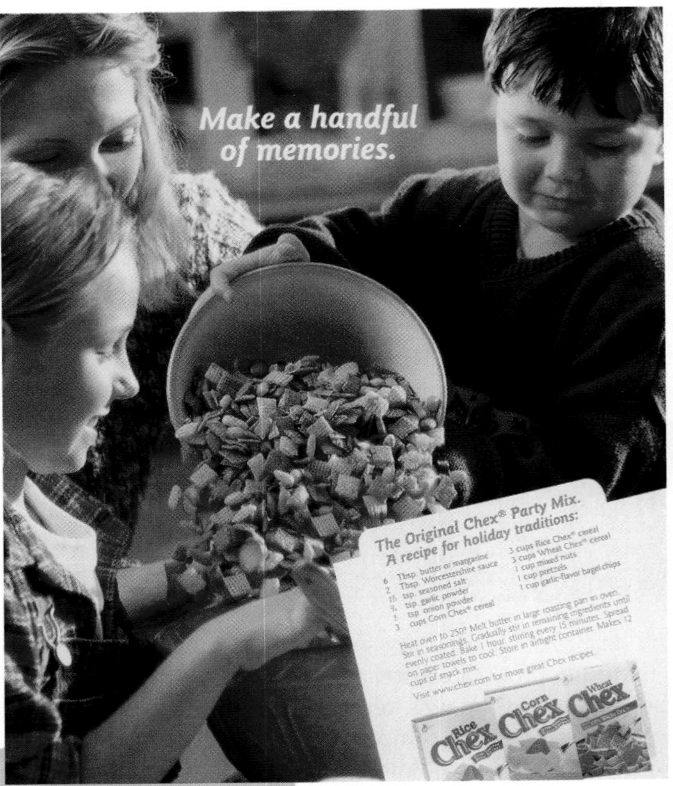

EXHIBIT 18.9
Symbolizing Connectedness
This ad suggests that Chex can symbolize times of family connectedness. Chex Party Mix has been a mainstay snack at social gatherings for many years.

Source: Courtesy of General Mills. Photo by Jeff Johnson.

Rituals may also symbolize connectedness. The U.S. ritual of Thanksgiving is marked by numerous symbols of connectedness.[45] Often family members show their commitment by attending the Thanksgiving gathering—even if they have to travel long distances—and significant others also attend the entire meal or come just for dessert, depending on the seriousness of the relationship. The family may privately denigrate those who live close but do not attend. As part of the Thanksgiving ritual, many families invite people who have nowhere else to go. Cultures like the United States and England also emphasize family connectedness during the Christmas ritual. In other cultures, such as some Eskimo villages in Alaska, the Christmas ritual has more of a community focus.[46]

Each family maintains its own traditions that foster connectedness. Members often strongly resist deviating from these traditions (such as trying a new stuffing recipe). Many families foster connectedness by looking at old family photographs or videos and telling family stories. This sense of connectedness may not only reaffirm social ties but also make us nostalgic about past times.[47]

The Expressiveness Function

As a symbol, a product has the potential to say something about our uniqueness.[48] This **expressiveness function** reflects how unique we are, not how we relate to other people. According to research, Eastern European youths like Western products because these offerings are used to create a distinct appearance that sets them apart.[49] We express our unique personalities through offerings like clothing, home decoration, art, music, leisure activities, and food consumption. Some consumers use body piercing, branding, and tattooing to symbolize their individuality and expressiveness.[50]

expressiveness function The use of products as symbols to demonstrate our uniqueness—how we stand out as different from others.

MARKETING IMPLICATIONS The connectedness and expressive functions lead to several marketing implications. For example, marketers may wish to invoke feelings of nostalgia by connecting their product with people, places, or events. Marketers of toys and games, movies, music, and shoes such as Keds have successfully encouraged consumers to connect these products with special times in their lives.[51] In addition, marketers can suggest that their products enhance uniqueness. For example, one perfume manufacturer advertised that the brand smelled different on every woman and therefore helped to bring out each woman's unique qualities. ●

Multiple Functions

As products and rituals can be used symbolically to serve many functions, a given product may serve several functions simultaneously. Consider, for example, a set of crystal wine goblets received as a wedding present from the bride's grandparents. These goblets could serve an emblematic function because their high price tag may communicate social status. They may also serve a role acquisition function, helping the newlyweds to internalize their new marital roles. Because they were a present from grandparents, the goblets may also serve a connectedness function—symbolizing the newlyweds' special relationship with their grandparents. Finally, if the goblets are personally appealing to the couple, they may symbolize the newlyweds' individual aesthetic tastes, thus serving an expressiveness function.

We sometimes deliberately use products because they fulfill one or more of the four functions noted in Exhibit 18.3. We may choose to dress in a certain way to communicate the group to which we belong or the unique tastes we have, or we might show off photos or artwork to remind ourselves of certain people or occasions. However, we are not always aware of a product's symbolic function, such as the possibility that an item of clothing symbolizes our gender or our age. We may expect certain types of gifts when we go through role transitions like graduation and marriage, but we are probably not conscious that these products help us adjust to our new role. Finally, we may really like an item we got as a gift without realizing that we react this way because it serves as a reminder of the gift giver.

Symbols and Self-Concept

The symbolic functions of products and consumption rituals are important because together they help to define and maintain our self-concept, our mental conception of who we are.[52] Social identity theory proposes that we evaluate brands in terms of their consistency with our individual identities.[53] According to the theory, our self-concept can be decomposed into many separate identities called **actual identity schemas**, including student, worker, daughter, and so on. These identities may be driven, at least in part, by the roles we fulfill. Some identities may be especially salient or central to our self-concept. Our actual identity may be shaped by an **ideal identity schema**—a set of ideas about how the identity we seek would be realized in its ideal form.

actual identity schemas The set of multiple, salient identities that reflect our self-concept.

ideal identity schema A set of ideas about how our identity would be indicated in its ideal form.

Our actual and ideal identity schemas influence which products we use and which consumption practices we engage in. The fact that possessions help shape our identity may explain why people who lose their possessions in natural disasters or wars and people who are in institutions like the military, nursing homes, or prisons often feel a loss of identity.[54] In fact, some consumers who have lost their possessions experience feelings of grief very similar to the feelings that follow the death of a loved one. Some institutions, such as the military and prisons, deliberately strip individuals of their possessions to erase their old identities.[55]

MARKETING IMPLICATIONS

Marketers need to consider several implications stemming from the preceding concepts.

Marketing and the development of consumer self-concepts. Marketers can play a role in both producing and maintaining an individual's self-concept. Although products may help define who we are, we also maintain our self-concept by selecting products with images that are consistent with it. For example, a consumer may purchase Diesel jeans instead of Gap because she views only Diesel as matching her self-image.

Product fit with self-concepts. Marketers should understand how their product fits with the identities of their target consumers and try to create a fit between the image of the brand and the actual or ideal identity of the consumer. Research has found that the more similar a product's image is to a consumer's self-image, the more the consumer likes the product.[56]

Product fit with multiple self-concepts. Because self-images are multifaceted, marketers must also determine whether products consistent with one aspect of the target customers' identity may be inconsistent with another aspect. A new father may react negatively to disposable diapers because though the product is consistent with his new parent identity, it is inconsistent with his environmentally conscious identity.

Advertising fit with self-concepts. Finally, advertising should appeal to the identity concept appropriate for the gender and culture of the targeted segment.[57] Thus, ads targeting women might emphasize mutual reliance, whereas ads targeting men might emphasize autonomy. Similarly, ads targeting consumers in China might stress culturally appropriate themes of group goals and achievement, whereas ads targeting U.S. consumers might stress culturally appropriate themes of personal goals and achievement. ●

SPECIAL POSSESSIONS

Some products come to hold a special, valued position in our minds, though they may or may not be relevant to our self-concepts.[58] For example, one consumer may regard his washing machine as a special possession because it is extremely functional, whereas another may view her skis as special because they give such enjoyment. However, neither consumer may view these products as relevant to their self-concept.[59] Because of the distinction between symbolic products and special possessions, marketers need to understand which products are special and why they become and remain so.

Types of Special Possessions

Researchers have identified the categories of possessions that consumers tend to regard as special.[60] Although almost any possession can be special, many consumers view pets, memory-laden objects, achievement symbols, and collections as having special significance.

Pets As noted in Chapter 15, U.S. consumers tend to regard their pets as very special.[61] Many name their pets, buy them special food and clothes, talk to them, groom them, play with them, photograph them, buy them Christmas presents, take them on vacation, and even buy them health insurance.[62] Often consumers treat pets as family members or as extensions of themselves. Some consumers buy animals whose personality or body type resembles their own and, if someone mistreats their pets, react as if they themselves were being mistreated. In China, the government recently banned consumers from keeping dogs as pets within city limits.[63] But dogs are so special that many Westerners living in China have moved outside the city limits and endure long commutes so they can keep their pets.

Not every culture treats pets as special possessions. Dog owners in Korea typically feed their pets leftovers rather than dog food products. On the other hand, Westerners can be so attached to their pets that they may feel sad or guilty leaving them to go to work or to travel.[64] These feelings have created profitable opportunities for kennel operators, who offer doggie day care and comfortable boarding in temperature-controlled, noise-proof, and hygienic environments.[65]

Memory-Laden Objects Some products acquire special meaning because they evoke memories or emotions of special people, places, or experiences.[66] Examples include heirlooms, antiques, souvenirs, mementos, and gifts from special people. You may value a ticket stub—otherwise just a piece of paper—because it evokes memories of a concert you saw of your favorite band. Similarly, a special song may evoke feelings of sentimentality or nostalgia. Such possessions can be therapeutic for elderly people because they evoke links to other people and happy times. Several researchers report the case of an individual who had to sell a favorite automobile because of a divorce but saved the license plates as a memento of this special possession. Many consumers consider photographs special because they are reminders of special people and create shrines by placing photos on TVs, mantles, and pianos.[67] Possessions that symbolize connectedness clearly have the potential to become special. The ad in Exhibit 18.10 suggests that the advertised Hallmark Christmas ornament may become a special product because it tracks the growth of one's children as they grow.

Achievement Symbols People also regard possessions that symbolize achievement as special. One researcher who studied the Mormon migration to Utah in the 1800s found that people often moved possessions that demonstrated competence. For example, men brought tools, and women brought sewing machines and other objects that had a practical function but also symbolized domestic achievement.[68] Modern-day symbols of achievement might include plaques, college diplomas, trophies, or even conspicuously consumed items like Rolex watches or expensive cars.

EXHIBIT 18.10
Memory-Laden Objects as Special Possessions
Special possessions can be repositories of past experiences, people, or events. This Hallmark ornament is advertised as a potential special possession to parents because it records the growth of their child over a period of years.

Source: Courtesy of Hallmark Cards, Inc.

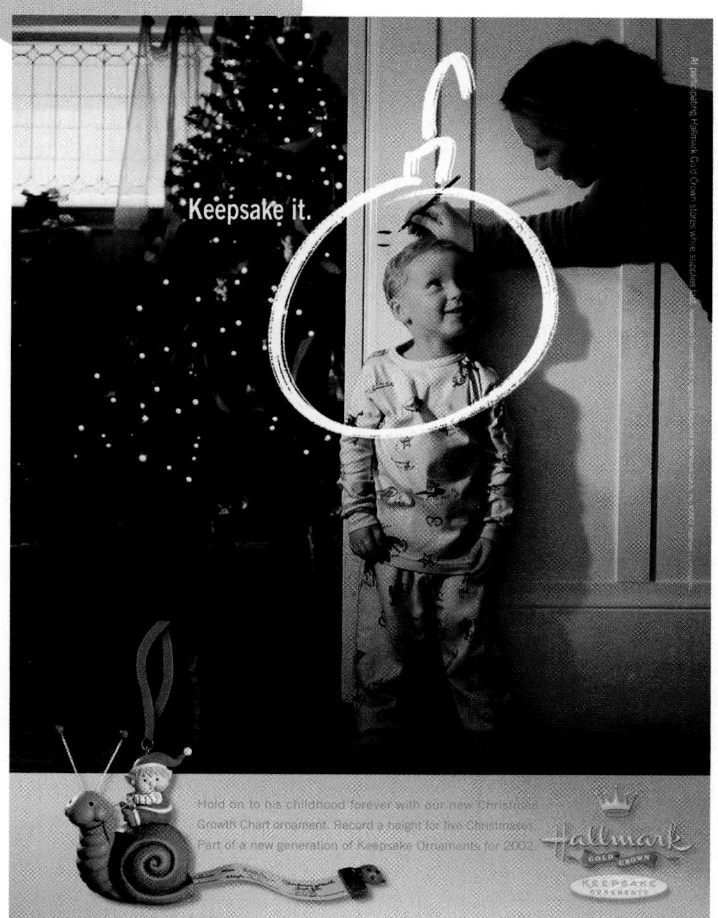

Keepsake it.
Hold on to his childhood forever with our new Christmas
Growth Chart ornament. Record a height for five Christmases.
Part of a new generation of Keepsake Ornaments for 2002.
Hallmark
GOLD CROWN
KEEPSAKE
ORNAMENTS

Collections Collections are special possessions for many. At least one in three U.S. consumers is a collector.[69] Common collectible items include cars; seashells; stones; minerals; CDs; stamps; videos; and childhood objects like GI Joe, baseball cards, Barbie dolls, and cookie jars.[70] Uncommon collectibles include spark plugs, junk mail, drain tiles, and airsickness bags. Firms like the Bradford Exchange, the Franklin Mint, and the Danbury Mint produce collectible items for consumers, but rarity makes items particularly special. For example, a 1910 Honus Wagner baseball card is worth between $400,000 and $600,000 because only 50 still exist.[71] Among the most valuable Olympic collectibles are torches from the 1950s: each of the five or six that remain is worth about $45,000.[72]

Collectors often view their collections as extensions of themselves—sometimes symbolizing an aspect of their occupation, family heritage, or appearance. Researchers have studied a grocery store owner who collected antique product packages, an engineer who collected pocket watches, a woman named Bunny who collected rabbit replicas, and wealthy women who collected monogrammed silver spoons.[73] For some, collections represent a fantasy image of the self.

For example, men who collect baseball cards may be keeping alive the fantasy of themselves as ball players. As is often the case with people who have special possessions, collectors tend to believe that they take better care of their collections than anyone else would.[74]

The Characteristics That Describe Special Possessions

Special possessions have several distinct characteristics.[75] First, consumers will not sell them at market value, if at all. We could never, for example, sell our family pet. We would be unlikely to sell a quilt that was a made by our grandmother, even if someone offered more than its market value. Second, people often buy special possessions with little regard for their price. Collectors, in particular, may pay exorbitant prices to acquire new pieces.

Third, special possessions have few or no substitutes. For example, when our family dog dies, we are unlikely to find or even want to find another like it. Insurance may pay to replace furniture that was damaged in a fire, but new furniture cannot compensate for heirloom pieces that were passed down through generations. In fact, consumers see special possessions as irreplaceable because of the associations with certain events and people in their lives.[76] A fourth characteristic is that people will not discard special possessions, even after they lose their functional value. Children are often reluctant to part with security blankets and stuffed animals and will keep these favorite objects until they are mere threads of fabric. Do your parents still keep your old report cards, bronzed baby shoes, and cards you or others have given to them?

Special possessions might not be used for their original purpose. Some consumers even believe their prized possessions will lose valued properties if used to fulfill their original function. For example, collectibles such as Barbie dolls and Star Wars toys lose their collectible value if they have been removed from their packaging. One study described a woman who collected nutcrackers but would not consider using them to crack nuts.[77] Special possessions can also evoke powerful emotions like achievement, affection, pride, or passion.[78] If these possessions are lost, destroyed, or otherwise disposed of, we may feel depressed, sad, or pained.

Finally, consumers frequently personify special possessions. Some people give names to individual items in a collection, name their houses, or use a feminine or masculine pronoun when referring to their cars or boats. Perhaps even more significant, we often treat these possessions as though they were our partners, feeling such commitment and attachment that we are devastated by their loss.[79]

Why Some Products Are Special

Possessions take on special meaning for several reasons, including their symbolic value, mood-altering properties, and instrumental importance. Exhibit 18.11 shows more specific reasons that underlie these three general categories.

- *Symbolic value.* Possessions may be special, in part, because they fulfill the emblematic, role adoption, connectedness, and expressiveness functions noted earlier in the chapter. For example, we may value art, heirlooms, and jewelry because they are expressions of our style or because they were gifts and tie us to special people.[80] Cars and houses may be valued for their reflection of social class. We value still other possessions, like wedding dresses, because they reflect transitions we have undergone.

- *Mood-altering properties.* Possessions may be special because they have mood-altering properties. For example, trophies, plaques, collections, and

EXHIBIT 18.11
Reasons Why Possessions Are Special

Take a possession you regard as special. Chances are, it is special to you because it has symbolic value, mood-altering properties, and/or utilitarian value.

Source: Adapted from Marsha Richens, "Valuing Things: The Public and Private Meanings of Possessions," *Journal of Consumer Research*, vol. 21, December 1994, pp. 504–521.

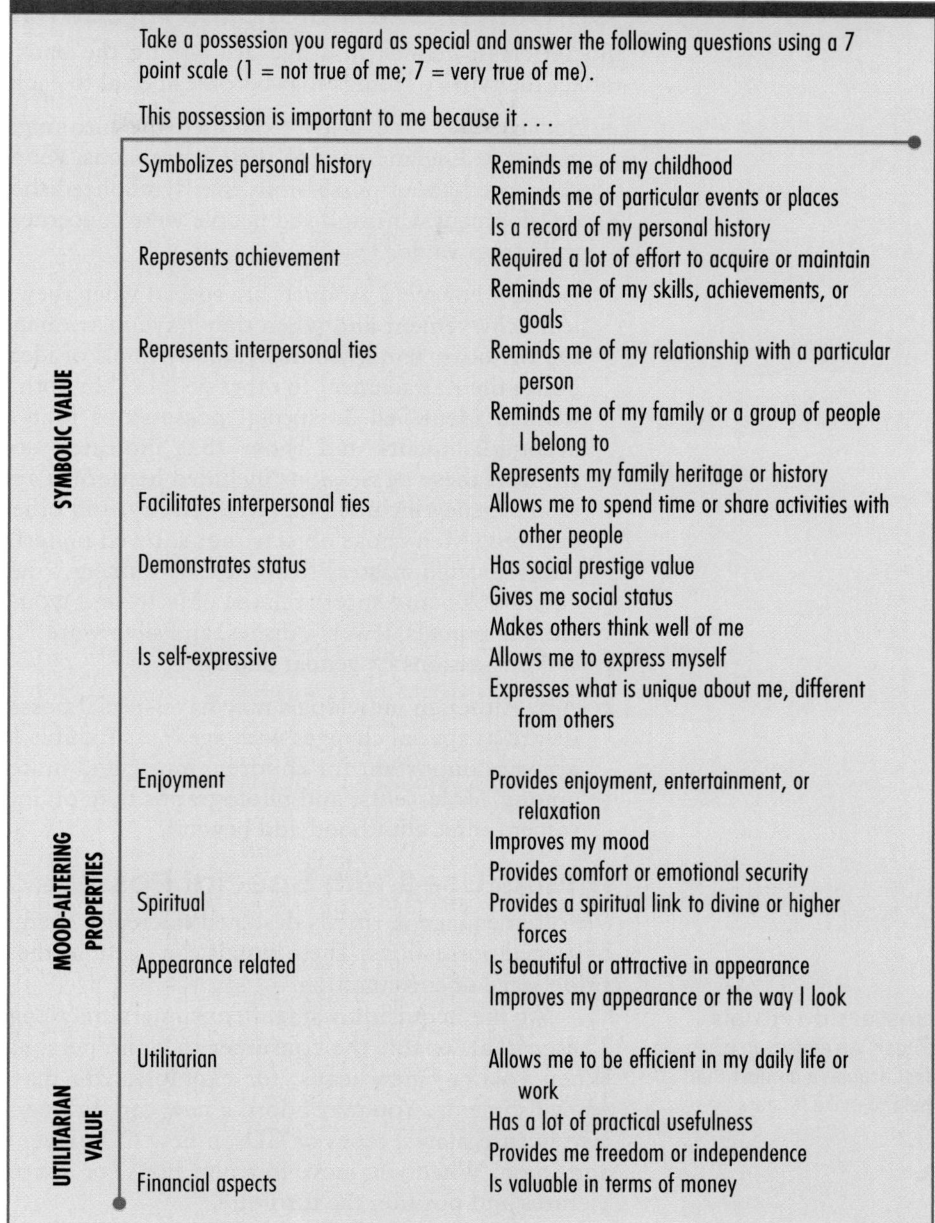

Take a possession you regard as special and answer the following questions using a 7 point scale (1 = not true of me; 7 = very true of me).

This possession is important to me because it . . .

SYMBOLIC VALUE	Symbolizes personal history	Reminds me of my childhood
		Reminds me of particular events or places
		Is a record of my personal history
	Represents achievement	Required a lot of effort to acquire or maintain
		Reminds me of my skills, achievements, or goals
	Represents interpersonal ties	Reminds me of my relationship with a particular person
		Reminds me of my family or a group of people I belong to
		Represents my family heritage or history
	Facilitates interpersonal ties	Allows me to spend time or share activities with other people
	Demonstrates status	Has social prestige value
		Gives me social status
		Makes others think well of me
	Is self-expressive	Allows me to express myself
		Expresses what is unique about me, different from others
MOOD-ALTERING PROPERTIES	Enjoyment	Provides enjoyment, entertainment, or relaxation
		Improves my mood
		Provides comfort or emotional security
	Spiritual	Provides a spiritual link to divine or higher forces
	Appearance related	Is beautiful or attractive in appearance
		Improves my appearance or the way I look
UTILITARIAN VALUE	Utilitarian	Allows me to be efficient in my daily life or work
		Has a lot of practical usefulness
		Provides me freedom or independence
	Financial aspects	Is valuable in terms of money

diplomas can evoke feelings of pride, happiness, and joy.[81] Pets can evoke feelings of comfort. A consumer in one study described her refrigerator as a special possession because making snacks always cheered her up. Others cited stereos and music as favorite possessions because they put these consumers in a good mood.[82]

- *Instrumental importance.* Possessions may be special because they are extremely useful. A consumer who describes her cell phone as special because she uses it constantly to get things done throughout the day is referring to this possession's instrumental value.

Consumer Characteristics Affect What Is Special

Social class, gender, and age are among the background characteristics that affect the types of things that become special to each of us.

- *Social class.* One study examined the meanings people of different social classes in England gave to their possessions. People in the business class were concerned about possessions that symbolized their personal history and self-development. Unemployed people were concerned about possessions that had utilitarian value.[83]
- *Gender.* For men, products are special when they symbolize activity and physical achievement and when they have instrumental and functional features. On the other hand, women value symbols of identity and products that symbolize their attachment to other people.[84] In both Niger and the United States, women identified as special possessions that symbolized their children's accomplishments and those that indicated connectedness. For the U.S. women, these possessions included heirlooms and pictures; for the Nigerian women, they included tapestry, jewelry, and other items passed through generations. Men chose objects that showed material comfort, and possessions that indicated mastery over the environment.[85] Men are more likely to collect cars, books, and sports-related objects, and women are more likely to collect stuffed animals, jewelry, dishes, and silverware.[86] Exhibit 18.12 identifies special possessions by gender and ages.
- *Age.* Although individuals may have special possessions at all ages, what they regard as special changes with age.[87] As Exhibit 18.12 shows, stuffed animals are very important for children; music and motor vehicles are highly prized among adolescents; and photographs take on increasing importance as consumers enter adulthood and beyond.

Rituals Used with Special Possessions

We often engage in rituals designed to create, energize, or enhance the meaning of special possessions. These rituals can occur at the acquisition, usage, or disposition stage of consumption.

possession rituals
Rituals we engage in when we first acquire a product that help to make it "ours."

At the acquisition stage, consumers may engage in **possession rituals.**[88] These rituals enable the consumer to claim personal possession of new goods. When you buy new jeans, for example, you may change the length or add embellishments. You may adorn a new car with personal markers like personalized license plates, tapes or CDs, a new CD player, a special scent, seat covers, and so on. When you move to a new house or apartment, you may rush to hang pictures and position the furniture.

Possession rituals for previously owned goods include wiping away meaning conferred by the former owner.[89] For example, when you buy a new home, you thoroughly clean it, tear down old wallpaper, and take down personal markers like the name on the mailbox. However, it is not always possible to wipe away meaning. In China, for example, consumers often build new houses because of a sense that older structures are "contaminated" by the former occupants.

grooming rituals
Rituals we engage in to bring out or maintain the best in special products.

divestment rituals
Rituals enacted at the disposition stage that are designed to wipe away all traces of our personal meaning in a product.

At the consumption stage, consumers may engage in **grooming rituals** to bring out or maintain the best in special products.[90] Some consumers spend hours washing and waxing their cars or cleaning house before visitors arrive. Sometimes the grooming ritual extends to you personally, as when you spend a lot of time making yourself look good for a special event.

Finally, when the offering loses its symbolic meaning, consumers engage in **divestment rituals**—wiping away all traces of personal meaning. For example,

EXHIBIT 18.12
Frequently Named Special Possessions by Age and Gender

The possessions we regard as special may vary by cultural category (e.g., age and gender). Girls differ from boys and older consumers differ from younger ones in the possessions they regard as special. Can you think of other examples using other cultural categories (e.g., social class)?

Source: Adapted with permission from N. Laura Kamptner, "Personal Possessions and Their Meanings: A Life-Span Perspective," in ed. Floyd W. Rudmin, *To Have Possessions: A Handbook on Ownership and Property*, Special Issue of the *Journal of Social Behavior and Personality*, vol. 6, no. 6, 1991, p. 215.

AGE	MALES	FEMALES
Middle childhood	Sports equipment* Stuffed animals Childhood toys Small appliances Pillows, blankets	Stuffed animals* Dolls Music Jewelry Books
Adolescence	Music Sports equipment Motor vehicles Small appliances Clothing	Jewelry Stuffed animals Music Clothing Motor vehicles Small appliances
Early adulthood	Motor vehicles Music Photographs Jewelry Memorabilia Artwork	Jewelry Photographs Motor vehicles Pillows, blankets Stuffed animals
Middle adulthood	Photographs Jewelry Books Sports equipment Motor vehicles Small appliances	Dishes, silverware Jewelry Artwork Photographs Memorabilia Furniture
Late adulthood	Small appliances Photographs Motor vehicles Artwork Sports equipment	Jewelry Dishes, silverware Photographs Religious Items Furniture

*Items are listed in order from most to least frequently cited.

many people remove the subscription labels before giving away magazines and delete personal files before selling or donating a computer. We might even get rid of a possession in stages—first moving it from the living room to the basement—before we finally decide to sell it or throw it away.

Disposing of Special Possessions

People dispose of special possessions for different reasons and in different ways. Studies show that older consumers make disposition decisions in periods of crisis, when they move to an institution, when approaching death, and to mark rites of passage and progression—although some transfer special possessions only after death, through a will. Sometimes the consumer hopes that giving the object to a relative will invoke memories, express love, or lead to a symbolic immortality; at other times the consumer is seeking control through disposition decisions and timing. An older consumer generally considers which recipient will best appreciate the special object's meaning, continue to use or care for it, or uphold family traditions, or he or she may simply give it to the person who asks first.[91]

SACRED MEANING

sacred entities People, things, and places that are set apart, revered, worshiped, and treated with great respect.

profane things Things that are ordinary and hence have no special power.

Although many possessions are considered special, some are so special they are regarded as sacred. **Sacred entities** are people, things, and places that are set apart, revered, worshiped, and treated with great respect. We may find such entities deeply moving, and we may feel anger and revulsion when they are not accorded their due honor. In contrast, **profane things** are those that are ordinary and hence have no special power. Profane objects are often distinguished from sacred ones by the fact that they are used for more mundane purposes.[92]

Sacred People, Objects, and Places

Movie stars, popular singers, historic figures like John F. Kennedy and Martin Luther King Jr., and religious leaders such as the pope or Gandhi are regarded by many people as sacred. Artifacts from Gandhi's life, including his reading glasses, walking stick, and shawl, are preserved in the town of Ahmedabad as a mark of reverence. The sacred status of famous people is exemplified by the crowds visiting the graves of celebrities like Princess Diana; driving by or visiting homes of living or dead celebrities, for example, Graceland; and visiting Mann's Chinese Theater in Los Angeles to touch the famous handprints and footprints in the sidewalk. Japanese and American baseball fans regard Seattle Mariners slugger Ichiro Suzuki as sacred. Suzuki paraphernalia is popular, Japanese reporters cover all his games, and fans travel from afar to watch him play.[93]

One reason why heirlooms and photographs of ancestors take on sacred status is that we may view our ancestors as heroes. A similar phenomenon explains why we treat as sacred items associated with famous statesmen such as George Washington, Charles de Gaulle, and Winston Churchill. Although not part of our actual past, these heroes were instrumental in formulating national identities. Consumers demonstrate their reverence by visiting the places that mark these historic figures.[94]

Many consumers also regard as sacred such objects as national flags, patriotic songs, art, collections, family recipes, and the Bible and such places as museums, the Vietnam Memorial, the Taj Mahal, and the Great Wall of China. These sacred objects and places evoke powerful emotions, sometimes causing people to weep or feel choked up when viewing them. In addition to sacred people, objects, and places, we may identify certain times and events, religious holidays, weddings, births, deaths, and grace before meals, as sacred.

The Characteristics That Describe Sacred Entities

Sacred entities involve some mystery or myth that raises them above the ordinary.[95] The pope, for example, is viewed as being almost godlike. And legendary figures such as Jim Morrison, Elvis Presley, Marilyn Monroe, and John F. Kennedy are associated with mystery. Second, sacred entities have qualities that transcend time, place, or space. When you enter the Alamo, you may feel as if you were back in the period when the historic fighting took place.

Sacred objects also possess strong approach/avoidance characteristics and create an overwhelming feeling of power and fascination. For example, you may simultaneously desire to be close to but also watch from a distance people you view as heroes and heroines. Encountering sacred entities may evoke certain feelings, such as ecstasy or the sense of being smaller and more humble than the sacred entity. For example, some people may feel that they have accomplished little in comparison to heroes like Abraham Lincoln. Some people feel humbled by the mass of humanity represented by the Vietnam Memorial. Moreover, sacred objects can create strong feelings of attachment, such as the need to take care of and nurture the sacred entity. Often sacred objects involve rituals that dictate how we should behave in the object's presence. For example, Americans know the right and wrong way to treat the national flag.

Sacredness may be maintained by scarcity and exclusivity.[96] For example, the sacred status of special works of art derives from their uniqueness and the fact that their high price maintains their exclusivity. People like Greta Garbo and Jackie Kennedy Onassis became imbued with sacredness by their desire to be out of the public eye, and limiting their public appearances only made them more interesting to their adoring public.

How Sacred Objects Are Profaned

Entities that were once sacred can be made profane if they are not treated with due respect or if they are commercialized and divested of their sacred status. In divorce, for example, some people profane things that were sacred in the marriage by throwing away, giving away, or selling the wedding ring, wedding dress, family furniture, special automobiles, or family jewelry.[97] We can feel considerable revulsion at the profaning of a sacred person or sacred object. In one study, some *Star Trek* fans said they were "barely" able to "stand watching the show" because of the way the series was being commercially exploited.[98]

MARKETING IMPLICATIONS Marketers need to be aware of the sacred meanings of people, objects, places, and events.

Creating and maintaining sacredness. Sometimes marketers create sacredness in objects or people. For example, the promoters of a famous movie star might heighten his sacred status by creating or enhancing his mystery and myth, making him exclusive, and promoting the powerful emotional effect he has on people. Marketers may also help maintain sacredness—for example, by keeping the price of sacred objects like collections, precious works of art, and rare jewelry very high.

Avoiding the profaning of sacred objects. Unsophisticated marketers sometimes profane sacred objects through commercialization. Some consumers believe that Elvis Presley is profaned by commercial Elvis paraphernalia. Selling religious trinkets outside the sacred properties of certain religious sites may profane places such as the Church of Jesus Christ of Latter-Day Saints and the Latter-Day Saint temples. Bruce Springsteen, Paul Simon, and Led Zeppelin are among a group of U.S. artists who have refused to turn their songs into ads. They believe that it is undignified and crass to turn their creative talents and hard work into a tool for selling products.[99]

Product involvement in sacred activities and rituals. In some cases, marketers sell products regarded as instrumental to the continuation or conduct of sacred occasions and rituals. Marketers like Hallmark Cards profitably capitalize on sacred rituals such as Christmas celebrations by selling products (tree ornaments, ribbons, wrapping paper, cards) regarded as important components of these events. ●

THE TRANSFER OF SYMBOLIC MEANING THROUGH GIFT GIVING

This chapter has shown how consumers invest products, times, activities, places, and people with symbolic meaning. Some meanings enhance the special and/or sacred status of the product, and some are instrumental in developing or maintaining the consumer's self-concept. However, another important aspect of symbolic consumption is the transfer of meaning from one individual to another in the context of gift giving.

The Timing of Gifts

Some gift-giving occasions are culturally determined and timed. In the United States, these include Valentine's Day, Mother's Day, Father's Day, and Secretary's Day.[100] Koreans celebrate the 100th day of a baby's life, and families in China celebrate when a baby is 1 month old. Koreans also give gifts to elders and family members on New Year's Day. Consumers in cultures around the world also celebrate various gift-giving holidays such as Christmas, Hanukkah, and Kwanzaa.[101]

Some gift-giving occasions are culturally prescribed but occur at a time that is specific to each individual.[102] These are often the transitions discussed earlier: anniversaries, graduations, birthdays, weddings, bridal and baby showers, retirement parties, and religious transitions such as baptism, first communion, or bar mitzvah. Still other gift-giving occasions are ad hoc, as when we give gifts as part of a reconciliation attempt, to forge an alliance with another person, to cheer someone who is ill, or to thank someone for helping us.

Three Stages of Gift Giving

gestation stage The first stage of gift giving, when we consider what to give someone.

presentation stage The second stage of gift giving, when we actually give the gift.

Gift giving consists of three stages, as shown in Exhibit 18.13. In the **gestation stage** we consider what to give the recipient. The **presentation stage** occurs with the actual giving of the gift. Finally, in the **reformulation stage** we reevaluate the relationship based on the gift-giving experience.

The Gestation Stage The gestation stage before a gift is given involves the motives for and emotions surrounding giving, the nature and meaning of the gift, the value of the gift, and the amount of time spent searching for a gift.

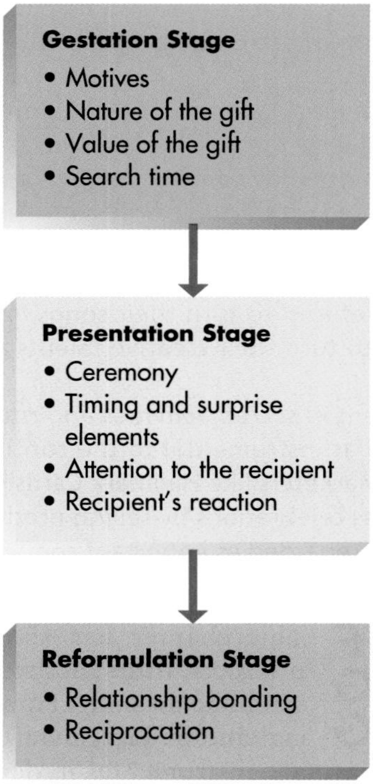

EXHIBIT 18.13
A Model of the Gift-Giving Process
The process of gift giving can be described in terms of three stages: (1) the gestation stage, at which we think about and buy the gift; (2) the presentation stage, at which we actually give the gift; and (3) the reformulation stage, at which we reevaluate our relationship based on the nature of the gift-giving experience. At each stage we can identify several issues that affect the gift-giving process.

Gestation Stage
- Motives
- Nature of the gift
- Value of the gift
- Search time

↓

Presentation Stage
- Ceremony
- Timing and surprise elements
- Attention to the recipient
- Recipient's reaction

↓

Reformulation Stage
- Relationship bonding
- Reciprocation

Motives for and Emotions Surrounding Giving During the gestation stage we develop motives for gift giving.[103] On the one hand, people may give for altruistic reasons—to help the recipient. For example, a relative may give a large cash gift to help a young couple start their married life. We may also give for agnostic reasons because we derive positive emotional pleasure from the act of giving. Or we may give a gift for instrumental reasons, expecting the recipient to give something in return. For example, a secretary may give a boss a nice gift in hopes of getting a raise. Consumers may also give for purely obligatory reasons because they feel the situation or the relationship demands it. Indeed, sometimes we do not react positively to gifts given by others because we now feel the obligation to reciprocate.

Givers sometimes feel anxiety about giving a gift.[104] They may perceive a recipient's demand for perfectionism in an appropriate gift or have limited capacity or confidence as

reformulation stage
The final stage of gift giving, when we reevaluate the relationship based on the gift-giving experience.

resources for choosing the gift. As a result, givers can feel anxious when they are highly motivated to evoke a desired response from recipients but doubt that they will be able to do so. Moreover, gifts may serve to reduce the giver's guilt or alleviate the recipient's hard feelings. In divorce, for example, the spouse who feels responsible for the breakup tends to give the partner more than a fair share, in what is called compensatory giving.[105] Some people may have antagonistic motives for gift giving. For example, if you are invited to the wedding of someone you do not like, you might give the couple something you think is not very beautiful.

The Nature and Meaning of the Gift Several aspects of gift selection signal the giver's feelings toward the recipient. One is the nature of the gift. For example, a worker would not give a boss a gift of lingerie because such items are too personal. Likewise, you would not give good friends a token wedding gift because the relationship dictates something more substantial. Although token gifts may not be appropriate on a clearly defined gift-giving occasion, they can be highly significant when no gift is expected. Spontaneously giving a gift, even something small, can signify love and caring.[106] Thus you may feel quite touched when your significant other buys you "a little something." Similarly, token gifts are quite important for recipients with whom we do not have strong ties. It is appropriate and desirable to send holiday and birthday cards to those whom we do not see very often.[107]

The gift may also symbolize the meaning we wish to transfer to the giver.[108] For example, gifts can symbolize values we regard as appropriate for the recipient, such as domesticity for new brides and grooms, or a new set of expectations. Giving an engagement ring symbolizes expectations regarding commitment and future fidelity, just as giving golf clubs at retirement symbolizes expectations regarding future leisure. Gifts can also be symbolic of the self, as when giving a piece of art or something that the giver has created.

The Value of the Gift The value of the gift is an important element of the gift-selection process. You might splurge on a Mother's Day gift because you want your mother to know how much she means to you. According to one study, men spend more than women on Mother's Day gifts, and non-Anglos spend more than Anglos.[109] The consumer's culture can influence decisions about the value of a gift. In Japan, for example, people lose face if the gift they receive exceeds the value of the gift they have given.[110]

The Amount of Time Spent Searching The amount of time spent searching for a gift symbolizes the nature and intensity of the giver's relationship with the recipient. Men and women differ in how much time and effort they invest in the search for a gift. Women are reportedly more involved in holiday gift shopping than are men.[111] Women also appear to spend more time searching for the perfect gift, whereas men are more likely to settle for something that will do.[112]

The Presentation Stage The presentation stage describes the actual exchange of the gift. Here, the ritual or ceremonial aspects of the giving process become very important.[113]

Ceremony During the presentation stage, the giver decides whether to wrap the gift, and if so, how. Wrapping the present nicely in appropriate paper helps to decommodify, or make more personal, a gift that is otherwise mass-produced.[114] However, how important the gift packaging is depends on the formality and spontaneity of the occasion. For example, unanticipated gifts, such as a boss's surprise gift to an assistant or a wife's surprise gift to her husband, may be less formally wrapped and may even be appropriate if left unwrapped.

Timing and Surprise Both the timing and the possibility of surprise may be important in gift giving. For example, although we know that gift giving is part of the Christmas ritual and that the gifts are even prominently displayed under the tree—sometimes for days before the actual exchange—being surprised by what they contain is often a key element. The excitement of unwrapping an item is heightened by having the recipient guess what the package contains. Although surprise is a valued part of the ritual, it is not always achieved. One study found that right before Christmas, some husbands purchase items that have been chosen in advance by their wives. Here, the gift giving is an orchestrated event with the husband playing the role of "purchasing agent."[115]

Attention to the Recipient Paying attention to the recipient can be a critical dimension in the presentation stage. For example, attendees at wedding showers are expected to watch closely as the bride-to-be opens her gifts.

Recipient's Reaction Another aspect is the reaction the giver hopes to elicit from the recipient, the recipient's actual reaction, and the giver's response to the recipient's reaction. If you spent a lot of time and effort looking for the perfect gift and the recipient opens the package quickly and goes on to the next gift without a word, you will probably feel hurt. As noted earlier, you may also feel anxiety at the presentation stage if you are uncertain about whether the recipient will like your gift.[116]

The Reformulation Stage The reformulation stage marks the third and final stage of the gift-giving process. At this stage, the giver and recipient reevaluate their relationship based on the gift-giving process.

Relationship Bonding A gift may affect the relationship between giver and recipient in different ways, as shown in Exhibit 18.14. An appropriate gift may maintain the strength of the tie between giver and recipient. A gift that is highly valued indicates considerable search costs and may strengthen the relationship between giver and recipient, as might a gift that is a surprise. A gift that is less than expected, one that indicates little prior thought, or no gift at all may weaken the relationship. One study found that gifts could strengthen a relationship by communicating feelings of connection, bonding, and commitment. Gifts can also affirm the relationship, validating existing feelings of commitment. Research suggests that a romantic relationship is likely to last longer when one member gives the other a gift to publicly announce their relationship. On the negative side, inappropriate gifts or those showing limited search effort or interest in the recipient's desires can weaken a relationship, creating the perception that the relationship lacks bonding and connection.[117]

Reciprocation The reformulation stage also has implications for how and whether the recipient will reciprocate on the next gift-giving occasion. If you gave someone a nice gift on one occasion, you would generally expect the recipient to reciprocate on the next occasion. If, on the other hand, you gave a gift that weakened the tie between you and the recipient, the latter may not give you a very nice gift or may give no gift at all on the next gift-giving occasion.

EXHIBIT 18.14
Possible Effect of Gift Giving on the Relationship

Source: Julie A. Ruth, Cele C. Otnes, and Frédéric F. Brunel, "Gift Receipt and the Reformulation of Interpersonal Relationships," *Journal of Consumer Research*, vol. 25, March 1999, p. 389. Reprinted by permission of the University of Chicago Press.

RELATIONAL EFFECT	DESCRIPTION	EXPERIENTIAL THEMES
Strengthening	Gift receipt improves the quality of the relationship between giver and recipient. Feelings of connection, bonding, commitment, and/or shared meaning are intensified.	Ephiphany
Affirmation	Gift receipt validates the positive quality of the relationship between giver and recipient. Existing feelings of connection and/or shared meaning are validated.	Empathy Adherence Affirming farewell Recognition
Negligible effect	The gift-reciept experience has a minimal effect on perceptions of relationship quality.	Superfluity "Error" Charity Overkill
Negative confirmation	Gift receipt validates an existing negative quality of the relationship between giver and recipient. A lack of feelings of connection, bonding, and/or shared meaning is validated.	Absentee Control
Weakening	Gift receipt harms the quality of the relationship between giver and recipient. There is a newly evident or intensified perception that the relationship lacks connection, bonding and/or shared meaning, but the relationship remains.	Burden Insult
Severing	Gift receipt so harms the quality of the relationship between giver and recipient that the relationship is dissolved.	Threat Non affirming farewell

However, some kinds of gift-giving situations or recipients are exempt from reciprocation.[118] For example, if you give someone a gift because she is ill or has experienced some tragedy (say, her house burned down), you will not expect her to reciprocate. Yet if someone unexpectedly gives you a Christmas gift, you will usually feel compelled to rush out and buy him a gift. People of limited financial means (children, students) or of lower status (a secretary as opposed to a boss) may be seen as exempt from giving. Thus it is appropriate for parents to give their children gifts and expect nothing in return. Women have also been reported to feel less obligated to reciprocate in dating-related gift giving, perhaps because of culturally prescribed notions regarding men's generally higher economic power.[119]

MARKETING IMPLICATIONS

Companies can build on several aspects of gift giving to market more effectively to consumers.

Promoting products and services as gifts. Many marketers promote their products for gift-giving occasions, and often gift-giving occasions are the primary focus of their business. Consider, for example that the greeting card industry earns an average of $6 billion a year in revenue in the United States, the majority of which is earned during the Christmas/Hanukkah/Kwanzaa season.[120] In some cases uncommon gifts are promoted as appropriate for various gift-giving occasions. For example, products from blenders and lingerie to stock certificates and power tools are touted as appropriate gifts on Mother's Day. Mortgage companies now offer bridal registries. Rather than buying gifts, gift givers contribute money to the couple's down payment or mortgage. Some retail outlets are known exclusively as gift stores. Here the services the store provides to enhance the presentation of the gift and the salespeople's abilities to point out gifts with special meanings may be important.

Cause-related marketing for frivolous products. Research indicates that consumers who are considering the purchase of a product linked with a gift to charity will prefer a higher-priced brand carrying a larger donation when the product is frivolous rather than practical.[121]

Technology and gift shopping. Technology has created major changes in the gift-giving process. For example, *Bride's* magazine is developing Web pages that will soon allow gift givers to pull up an updated version of the couple's gift registry and buy gifts from retailers.[122] It is interesting to consider whether the reduced search time afforded by these new technologies will alter receivers' feelings about the value of their relationship with the giver.

Ethnicity and holiday shopping. Marketers have also become more sensitive to the ethnic and religious diversity within the United States. For example, because Christmas, Hanukkah, and Kwanzaa are celebrated at about the same time of the year, Archway cookies decided to change its traditional holiday packaging from bells, wreaths, and candles to less culturally specific prints of snowy outdoor scenes.[123]

Alternatives to traditional gifts. Knowing that consumers are becoming weary of the commercialism, hassle, and materialism surrounding gift-giving occasions like Christmas, some charities are adopting the practice of asking consumers to give gifts to people from around the world who are truly in need. For example, the Global Gift Guide, a catalog produced by a nonprofit Christian organization called World Concern, allows consumers to purchase items such as chickens, fish, prenatal care, and business loans for needy families around the world.[124] For similar reasons, travel marketers are touting travel as a holiday gift. More two-income families have less time, more money, and more distance separating them from loved ones, creating a trend toward travel and family reunions at posh resorts around the world and away from holiday shopping.[125] ●

SUMMARY

This chapter discussed the symbolic role that products can play. Consumers use some products as conscious or unconscious badges that designate the various social categories to which they belong. Products and rituals hold symbolic significance when people undergo role transitions; serve as symbols of connection to people, places, and times that have meaning; and are symbols of individuality and uniqueness. The combined symbolic uses of products and rituals affect consumer self-concept.

Consumers regard some possessions as very special. These objects are nonsubstitutable, irreplaceable, will not be sold at market value if at all, and will be purchased with little regard for price. They are rarely discarded, even if their functional value is gone, and they may not even be used for their original functional purpose. We personify these possessions, may feel powerful emotions in their presence, and feel fear or sadness over their potential or actual loss. In part, possessions are special because they serve as emblems, facilitate role transitions, connect us to others, or express our unique styles. They are special because they indicate personal mastery and achievements or are mood enhancing. Background characteristics such as social class, gender, and age all influence the type of object someone regards as special.

Some entities are so special that they are worshiped, set apart, and treated with inordinate respect—that is, they are sacred. In addition to possessions, people, places, objects, times, and events may take on sacred status. Sacred objects transcend time and space and have strong approach/avoidance powers and great fascination. Consumers care for and nurture these entities and often devise special rituals to handle them. Sacred objects can be profaned or made ordinary by commercialization, inappropriate usage, or divestment patterns.

Gift giving is a process of transferring meaning in products from one person to another. Gift-giving occasions are often culturally prescribed but may vary in their timing. The gift-giving process entails three phases: gestation, presentation, and reformulation. The manner in which the first two phases are enacted can affect the long-term viability of the relationship between giver and recipient.

QUESTIONS FOR REVIEW AND DISCUSSION

1. Contrast the emblematic function of a product with the role acquisition function; also contrast the connectedness function of a product with the expressive function.
2. What is reflexive evaluation, and how does it affect role acquisition?
3. How does the ideal identity schema relate to a person's actual identity schemas?
4. What are the three main reasons for possessions taking on special meaning?
5. Why do consumers engage in possession, grooming, and divestment rituals?
6. What are sacred entities, and how are they profaned?
7. Identify the three stages of gift giving, and explain how gift giving can affect relations between the giver and the recipient.

EXERCISES

1. Consider the cultural category of occupational status and the typical clothing of doctors, farmers, waitresses, politicians, businesspeople, truck drivers, and pharmacists. Identify the cultural principles that reflect membership in each of these occupational groups, and explain how the clothing worn by members of each group illustrates these characteristics.
2. Consider two role transitions: graduation and new parenthood. For each, identify the rituals that mark these role transitions and the enabling products that mark their passage. (This task will be easier if you can actually attend a graduation or watch a new parent care for a baby.) Find several advertisements for the products or services that are relevant to these rituals. Identify a set of marketing implications regarding marketing to groups undergoing these transitions.
3. Interview someone you know about one or more possessions that they regard as special/sacred. Try to get them to indicate why these possessions are special and compare their answers with the reasons given in the chapter for why possessions are special. What marketing implications can you derive from their responses?

chapter 19

Adoption of, Resistance to, and Diffusion of Innovations

Introduction: Driving into the Future

The Toyota Prius and the Honda Insight are at the forefront of a new fleet of hybrid cars (see Exhibit 19.1). Driven by stricter federal and state emissions standards in the United States—and a search for better fuel economy—major automotive manufacturers are developing cars, sport-utility vehicles, and trucks equipped with an electric motor to supplement the gasoline engine. Unlike all-electric cars, which have less pep and can go only a limited distance before recharging, the Prius and the Insight rely on their gas motor when drivers need power to pass or in other situations—and recharge the battery while in motion. The compact Prius sedan has a range of about 700 miles on one tank of gas and gets more than 40 miles per gallon. The Insight, a small two-seater, is even more economical, wringing out more than 50 miles per gallon. Moreover, thanks to the electric assist, hybrid vehicle emissions are minimal.

Despite their environmental advantages and the money-saving benefit of lower gas consumption, neither of these cars is racing into sales records. In fact, U.S. consumers buy a total of about 30,000 of these two hybrid cars every year—just a tiny fraction of the 17.2 million vehicles sold annually across the country. One reason may be cost: depending on options, the price tag may be $21,000 or higher, several thousand dollars more than comparable gasoline-only vehicles. Even consumers who are interested in a hybrid vehicle

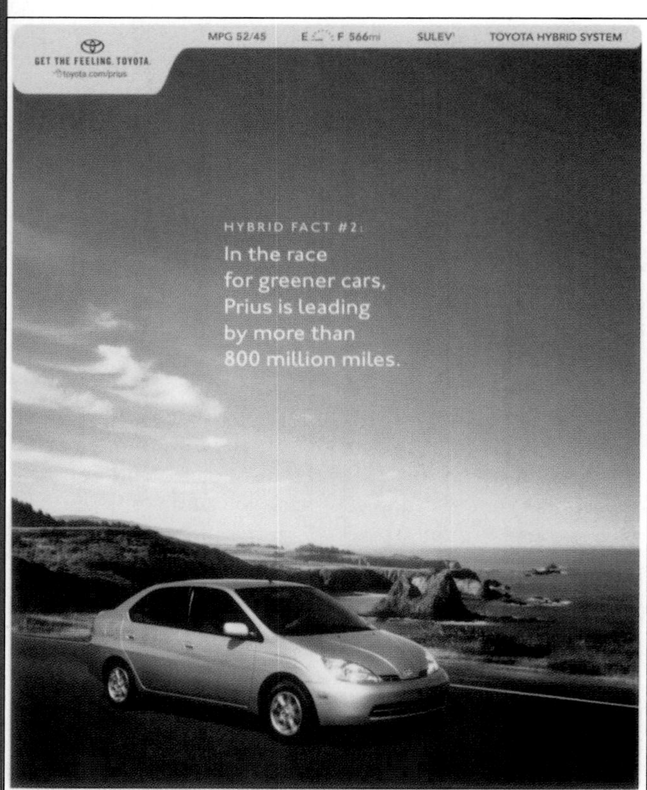

EXHIBIT 19.1
Hybrid Car
Hybrid cars, using a combination of gasoline and electric power, are new entrants in the automotive category. What factors do you think affect how quickly consumers will choose hybrids over traditional automobiles?

Source: Courtesy of Toyota.

because of its fuel efficiency tell researchers they would pay no more than $1,000 over the price of a conventional vehicle. Another reason for the slow start in hybrid vehicle sales is that consumers may still associate such cars with early electric cars—the ones that had to be plugged in for hours to recharge.

Consumers who are interested in new automotive technology and in protecting the environment are among the first purchasers of these hybrid vehicles. Research shows that 57 percent of Prius buyers and 65 percent of Insight buyers are tech-savvy men. Looking ahead to stricter emissions standards and less reliance on fossil fuels, American car manufacturers are also bringing out their own hybrid vehicles. Ford's Escape sport-utility vehicle will soon be available with an optional electric motor-assisted gas engine; General Motors and Chrysler are both getting ready to produce hybrid trucks. Toyota and Honda are also planning to expand their product lines with larger hybrid vehicles. Meanwhile, consumers who want to try before they buy can rent all-electric or hybrid vehicles at specialized rental agencies in California.[1]

Hybrid vehicles reflect some of the basic concepts discussed in this chapter. Innovations in the automotive industry have provided consumers with advantages such as vehicles that are less harmful to the environment while delivering superior fuel economy. Another factor spurring vehicle innovation is government regulation. California, for example, requires that four percent of all vehicles sold in the state have no emissions, and several other states are mulling similar mandates. However, consumers have not rushed to buy all-electric vehicles, because they would have to adjust their behavior to operate the products. Ford's new THINK City electric vehicle, for example, must be plugged in overnight for recharging. It has a plastic body and can accelerate to 65 miles per hour, which would make it legal for use on highways—unlike many earlier electric cars, which moved too slowly for highway use.[2]

Another impediment to hybrid vehicles selling at top speed is their higher price tags. Yet an owner could potentially use much less gasoline and save thousands of dollars over the course of the hybrid vehicle's life. As more people try and then buy hybrids, however, the manufacturers will be able to increase production and lower costs, which in turn will lower prices and make the vehicles more attractive to a wider audience. And more people will see and talk about these innovative cars as a larger number of models become available in the next few years.

This chapter focuses on factors that affect consumers' choice of a new product (see Exhibit 19.2). The chapter opens by describing several types of innovations, which can vary in the kind of novelty they offer and the type of benefit they confer. Next is a discussion of the factors that affect an individual consumer's resistance to or adoption of a new product. Different groups of consumers adopt products at different rates; those who tend to buy new products first are known as innovators, as this section indicates. The final section examines the factors affecting how quickly a new product spreads, or diffuses, through a market. ●

INNOVATIONS

The ability to develop successful new products is critical to a company's sales and future growth. Kraft Foods, for example, regularly rings up $800 million in annual sales just from the new products it launches in a single year.[3] Given the role that new products play in a company's sales and profitability, it is very important for marketers to understand new products and what drives their success.

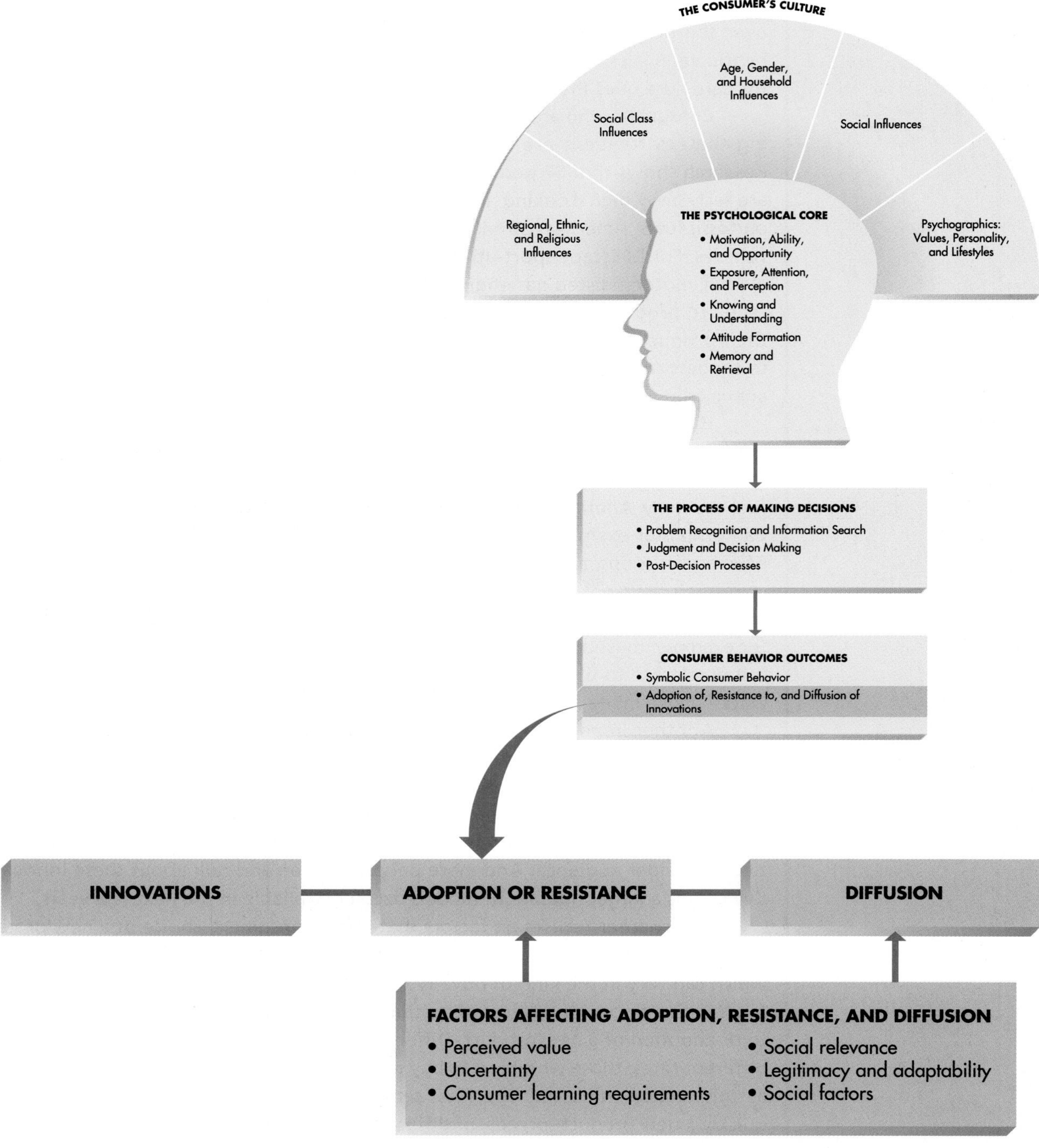

EXHIBIT 19.2
Chapter Overview: Adoption of, Resistance to, and Diffusion of Innovations

Consumers may decide to adopt (e.g., purchase) or resist a new offering (an innovation). Diffusion reflects how fast an innovation spreads through a market. Several things affect adoption, resistance, and diffusion: the type of innovation, its breadth, its characteristics, and the social system in which it is introduced.

Defining an Innovation

innovation An offering that is perceived as new by consumers within a market segment and that has an effect on existing consumption patterns.

A new product, or an **innovation**, is an offering that is new to the marketplace. More formally, an innovation is a product, service, attribute, or idea that consumers within a market segment perceive as new and that has an effect on existing consumption patterns.[4]

Services as well as goods can be innovations. XM Satellite Radio, for example, is a fee-based service that allows drivers to tune in to 100 different 24-hour radio channels on special car stereos wherever they travel in the United States.[5] Ideas can also be described as innovations. For example, social marketers have been active in persuading consumers to adopt such ideas as safe sex, smoke-free workplaces, and abstinence from drugs. In Third World countries social marketers have promoted ideas such as family planning, childhood immunization, and safer and more nutritious food-preparation practices. Often these ideas are supported by related products, such as contraceptives for family planning.[6]

Companies sometimes develop new products to help speed consumers' acceptance of ideas. For example, a product called Baby Think It Over gives teenage girls a realistic glimpse at the responsibilities associated with having a child. The product is a cute, cuddly doll programmed to cry at random intervals throughout the day and night. The only way to stop the baby's crying is to hold and comfort it. Electronic monitors record whether the baby is abused or neglected.[7]

Finally, product attributes can be regarded as innovations. Offering a premade sandwich with the crusts cut off can be innovative for certain segments. J. M. Smucker, well known for jams and jellies, recently introduced frozen Uncrustables, peanut butter and jelly sandwiches made with crustless white bread—a convenient innovation for parents of children who are fussy about their bag lunches.[8] The Discover 2Go℠ ad in Exhibit 19.3 is promoting an innovative product attribute—a mini credit card in a protective case that can be attached to a key chain.

A second aspect of the definition of innovation is that products, services, attributes, packages, and ideas are innovations if they are perceived as new by consumers, whether or not they actually are new. Propecia, a drug introduced to reduce male baldness, is really the same drug that is sold as Proscar and used to treat prostate problems, although consumers are not likely to know this.[9]

Marketers also define "innovation" with respect to a market segment. To illustrate, although disco music has been around since the 1970s, it recently gained popularity in Poland and is perceived as innovative by Polish consumers.[10] Because of small home kitchens and ingrained traditions, the automatic dishwasher is seen as an innovation in Japan, where only 7 percent of households own one.[11] Consumers in Third World countries may regard certain appliances and electronic gadgets as entirely new, even though Americans and consumers in other Western countries regard these items as near necessities.

Innovations bring about changes in consumption patterns, altering how, where, when, whether, or why we

EXHIBIT 19.3
Innovative Attributes
Credit cards, while small, can get lost in a wallet and become less convenient to use. Discover® introduces a credit card with a new attribute—a mini card with a protective case. Attach it to your keychain and it's ready when you need to use it.

Source: Reprinted with permission from Discover® Bank.

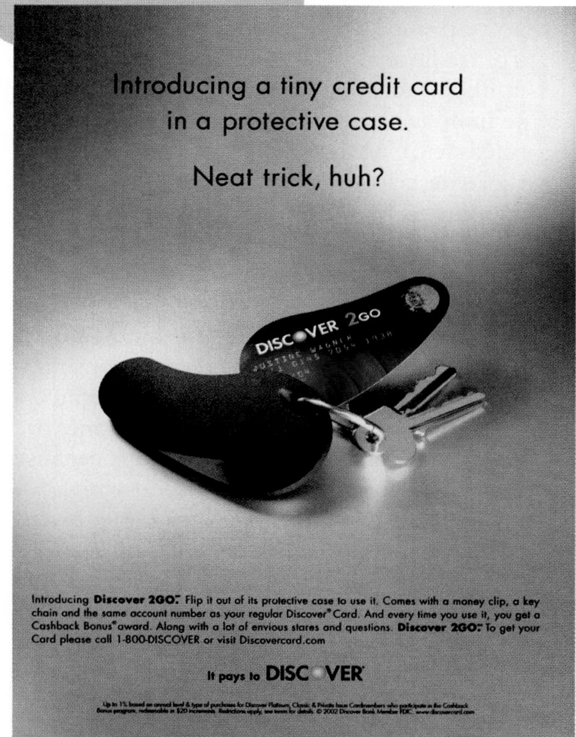

Introducing a tiny credit card
in a protective case.
Neat trick, huh?
DISCOVER 2GO
Introducing Discover 2GO. Flip it out of its protective case to use it. Comes with a money clip, a key chain and the same account number as your regular Discover® Card. And every time you use it, you get a Cashback Bonus® award. Along with a lot of envious stares and questions. Discover 2GO. To get your Card please call 1-800-DISCOVER or visit Discovercard.com
It pays to DISCOVER

acquire products. For example, innovations like Internet shopping have altered the way we buy products. In the Netherlands, consumers can use a handheld scanning device to scan their own groceries while they shop.[12] This innovation changes the acquisition process.

Other innovations may change the way we use products or services. Microwave ovens have changed the way we cook, and e-mail has changed the way we communicate. Innovations like hybrid vehicles change how often drivers must refuel, just as digital cameras change the way people take photographs, alter them, and send them to others.

Finally, some innovations influence disposition behavior. Ideas about recycling have brought about innovations in recyclable packaging materials and reusable containers. Can crushers, composters, and recycling centers were new offerings that affected consumers' disposition behaviors. As another example, consumers who download music onto their computers using MP3 and other technologies will dispose of these files quite differently from albums, CDs, and cassettes.

Marketers classify innovations in three main ways, in terms of: (1) the type of innovation, (2) the type of benefits offered, and (3) the breadth of innovation.

Innovations Characterized by Degree of Novelty

One way to characterize innovations is to describe the degree of change they create in our consumption patterns.[13] A **continuous innovation** has a limited effect on existing consumption patterns. The ad shown in Exhibit 19.4 is an example of a continuous innovation. We would use a continuous innovation in much the same way we used products that came before it. For example, Huggies introduced disposable swimming pants for toddlers who are not yet potty-trained. The product can be worn just like traditional diapers and plastic pants, but unlike traditional disposable diapers, the swimming pants won't "explode" when filled with water. Hybrid vehicles such as those described in the opening example are continuous innovations, because they require little change in the way drivers use and maintain their vehicles. Not surprisingly, most new products are continuous innovations.

EXHIBIT 19.4
Example of Continuous Innovation
The makers of IronKids crustless bread are in touch with the desires of many kids who don't like crust on their bread. Since the idea of crustless bread is not very different from bread with crust, this product would be considered a continuous innovation.

Source: Sara Lee Bakery Group.

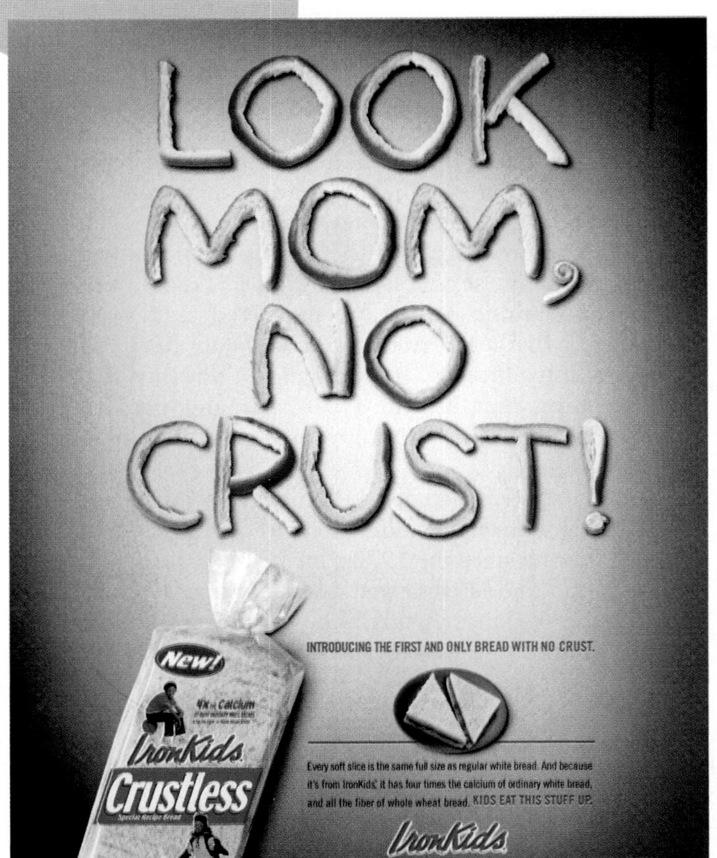

A **dynamically continuous innovation** is one that has a pronounced effect on consumption practices. Often these innovations incorporate a new technology. Cellular phones are dynamically continuous innovations because they change the time and place in which we communicate with other people. Other examples of dynamically continuous innovations include electric cars (which require recharging rather than refueling), handheld computers (which fit in a pocket and are used on the go), and digital cameras (which require no film).

A **discontinuous innovation** is a product so new that we have never known anything

continuous innovation An innovation that has a limited effect on existing consumption patterns.

dynamically continuous innovation An innovation that has a pronounced effect on consumption practices and often involves a new technology.

discontinuous innovation An offering that is so new that we have never known anything like it before.

functional innovation A new product, service, attribute, or idea that provides utilitarian benefits different from or better than existing alternatives.

like it before.[14] For example, a former aeronautics professor has introduced a product called a "skycar"—a machine that flies through the air much like the cars on the TV cartoon *The Jetsons*. The skycar takes off and lands vertically and can fly at speeds up to 300 miles per hour.[15] Products like airplanes, automobiles, computers, televisions, and copy machines were all at one time discontinuous innovations that led to radical changes in consumer behavior.

Discontinuous and dynamically continuous innovations often spawn a host of peripheral products and associated innovations. For example, microwave ovens spawned the introduction of microwavable dishes and pans, as well as new recipes and new food products tailored to microwave cooking. They also fostered the development of products like probes and turntables. And they were responsible for renewed growth in products compatible with microwave cooking practices, such as waxed paper and plastic wrap.

Based on these three broad innovation types—continuous, dynamically continuous, and discontinuous—innovations can be characterized more specifically according to their degree of novelty on a continuum of newness (see Exhibit 19.5). Discontinuous innovations are the most novel and require the most behavioral change, whereas continuous innovations are the least novel and require the least behavioral change.

Innovations Characterized by Benefits Offered

In addition to their degree of novelty, innovations can be characterized by the benefits they offer. Some new products, services, attributes, or ideas are **functional innovations** because they offer functional performance benefits over existing

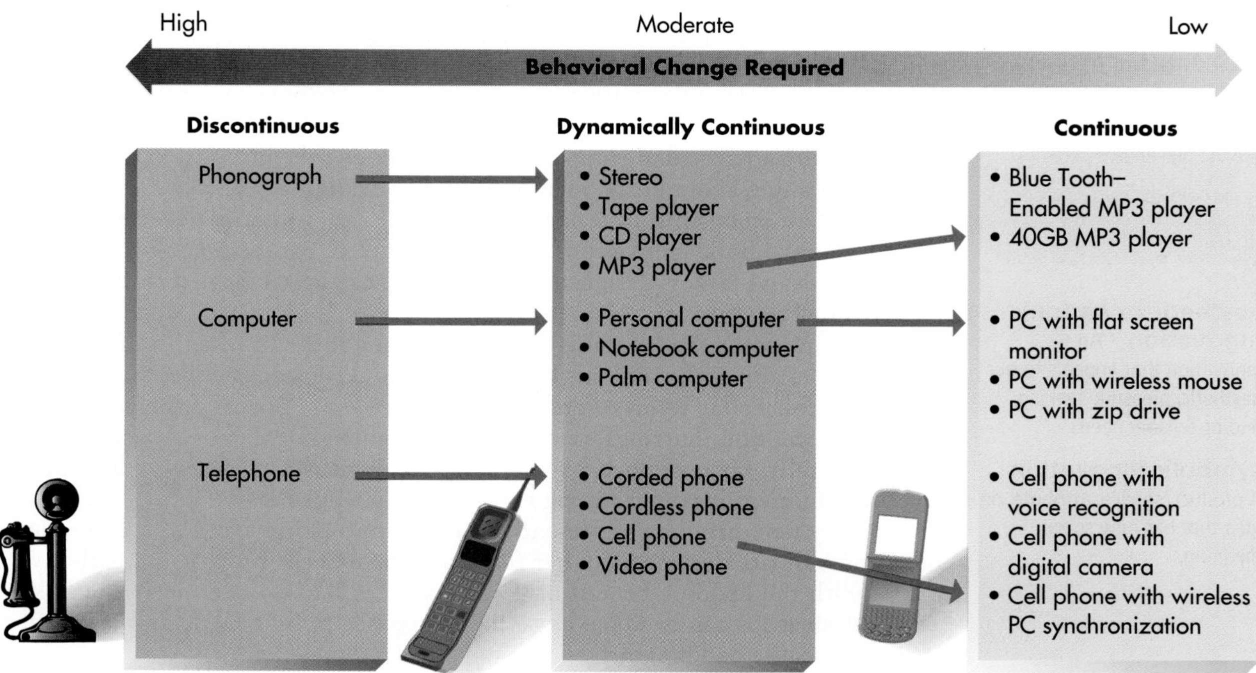

EXHIBIT 19.5 The Innovation Continuum

Innovations vary in how much behavioral change they require on the part of consumers. Discontinuous innovations (products that are radically new when they are first introduced) require considerable change in consumption patterns, whereas continuous innovations (often extensions of existing products) require very little change.

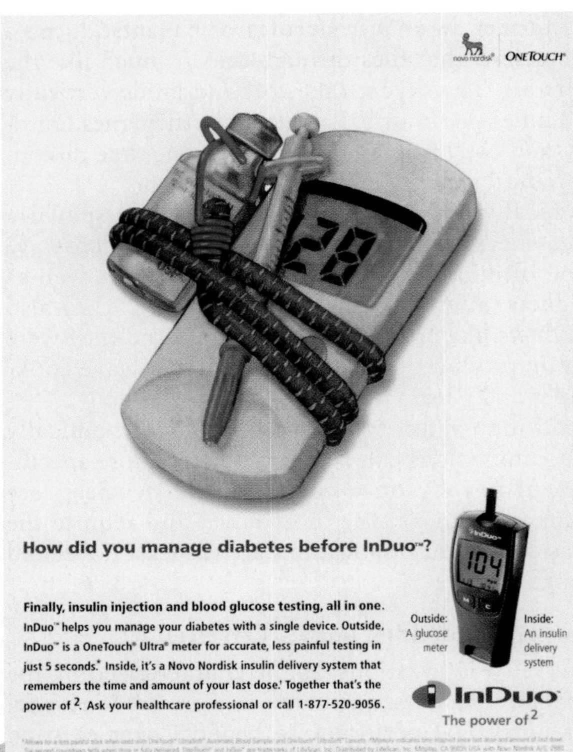

ONETOUCH
How did you manage diabetes before InDuo™?
Finally, insulin injection and blood glucose testing, all in one.
InDuo™ helps you manage your diabetes with a single device. Outside, InDuo™ is a OneTouch® Ultra® meter for accurate, less painful testing in just 5 seconds.* Inside, it's a Novo Nordisk insulin delivery system that remembers the time and amount of your last dose.† Together that's the power of 2. Ask your healthcare professional or call 1-877-520-9056.
Outside: A glucose meter
Inside: An insulin delivery system
InDuo
The power of 2

EXHIBIT 19.6
A Functional Innovation
Drug companies often introduce functional innovations like the one shown here.

Source: Courtesy of LifeScan, Inc., a Johnson & Johnson Company.

alternatives. For example, handheld computers offer consumers functional benefits over desktop and notebook computers, even incorporating options for additional functions such as wireless Web access and cell telephone capabilities.[16]

Often functional innovations rely on new technology that allows better performance than existing alternatives. For example, in Europe consumers can use cell phones to access airline flight arrival and departure schedules, update bank balances, pay for a parking space, buy from vending machines, and receive current stock quotes.[17] In Japan, some cell phones double as digital cameras and digital music players.[18] U.S. consumers can use TiVo personal digital recorders to automatically record hours of television programming, skip commercials, and store recorded programs on a hard drive rather than on tapes.[19] Exhibit 19.6 promotes a new functional innovation called InDuo which tests blood glucose levels in five seconds. The brand also comes with an insulin delivery system that tracks when and how much insulin was last taken.

Aesthetic or hedonic innovations are new products, services, or ideas that appeal to our aesthetic, pleasure-seeking, and/or sensory needs.[20] New forms of dance or exercise, new types of music, new clothing styles, and new types of food all qualify as aesthetic or hedonic innovations. Heinz, for example, has introduced green ketchup, purple ketchup, blue French fries, and chocolate French fries.[21]

aesthetic or hedonic innovation An innovation that appeals to our aesthetic, pleasure-seeking, and/or sensory needs.

symbolic innovation A product, service, attribute, or idea that has new social meaning.

Symbolic innovations are products, services, attributes, or ideas that have new social meaning. In some cases a symbolic innovation is a new offering used exclusively by a particular group of consumers. Using the innovation, therefore, conveys meaning about group membership. For example, new styles of clothing that convey membership in a particular ethnic, age, or gender group may be regarded as symbolic innovations. After the Winter Olympics in Salt Lake City, Roots berets and jackets designed for the Olympics communicated that wearers had attended the event.[22]

In some cases the meaning of the product, not the product itself, is new. For example, although condoms have been around for a long time, their meaning is now couched in terms of preventing the spread of AIDS as opposed to controlling conception. Earrings, once worn by women, are fashionable with men as well. Finally, tattoos, once a symbol of machismo, have gained wide appeal and have different meaning among various consumer groups.

Many new products represent blends of innovation types. For example, nutrition bars are designed to offer functional benefits of protein and carbohydrates with the hedonic benefit of good taste. Similarly, Listerine PocketPaks mouthwash strips can be taken anywhere, have a refreshing taste, and wipe out germs that cause bad breath.[23]

Innovations Characterized by Breadth

Breadth of innovation refers to the range of new and different uses for a particular product. Baking soda, for example, has enjoyed a long life in part because it has been used as a baking ingredient, a tooth polisher, a carpet deodorizer, and a refrigerator deodorizer. Teflon, a product originally designed to keep things from sticking to cookware, is now being used as an ingredient in men's suits. It helps to resist spills, and it retains its resistance through repeated washing and dry cleaning.[24]

ADOPTION OF INNOVATIONS AND RESISTANCE TO ADOPTION

adoption A purchase of an innovation by an individual consumer or household.

Because the success of their new offerings is so important to companies, marketers need to understand how a consumer or household makes an **adoption** decision for an innovation. Adoption decisions represent a continuation of the choice decisions examined in Chapters 10 and 11. Initially, marketers are interested in whether consumers would even consider adopting an innovation, because consumers sometimes resist adoption. Marketers also want to know how consumers adopt products and how they decide whether to buy an innovation. Finally, marketers are interested in when a consumer buys an innovation, in relation to other consumers.

Resistance to Adoption

resistance A desire not to buy an innovation, even in the face of pressure to do so.

Adoption will take place only if consumers do not resist the innovation. **Resistance** is consumers' desire not to buy the innovation, even in the face of pressure to do so.[25] Consumers sometimes resist adopting innovations because it is simpler or seems preferable to continue using a more familiar product or service. For example, many consumers resist switching to new computer operating systems or adopting other high-tech replacement products for their PCs because they fear these new products will be too complicated or will offer few new features that they can actually use.[26]

Resistance may also be high if consumers think that using the product involves some risk. For example, many people initially resisted using ATMs because of the perceived risk.[27] Similar concerns may underlie many consumers' resistance to using credit cards to buy products over the Internet. Exhibit 19.7 shows that consumers often resist new technologies because, although they can create positive effects, they can also create negative effects. When consumers resist a technology, the perceived negative effects of the technology likely outweigh the positive effects.[28]

Note that resistance and adoption are separate concepts. An individual can resist purchasing an innovation without ever progressing to the point of adoption. If an individual does adopt a product, he or she has presumably overcome any resistance that might have existed initially. Marketers have to understand whether, why, and when consumers resist innovations because the product will fail if resistance is too high. Marketers typically use a number of tactics to reduce consumers' resistance to an innovation. As discussed later in this chapter, characteristics of the innovation, the social system in which consumers operate, and marketing tactics all influence consumers' resistance to innovations.

How Consumers Adopt Innovations

In studying consumers' adoption decisions, marketers find it useful to distinguish between high-effort and low-effort decisions. Adoption follows the high-effort hierarchy of effects in a high-effort situation and the low-effort hierarchy of effects in a low-effort situation

High-Effort Hierarchy of Effects In some cases, the consumer becomes aware of an innovation, thinks carefully about it, gathers as much information as possible about it, and forms an attitude based on this information. If his or

EXHIBIT 19.7
Eight Central Paradoxes of Technological Products
Consumers sometimes have mixed reactions to technologies because they create some of the paradoxes noted here. When the negative sides of these paradoxes are salient, consumers will likely resist an innovation.

Source: David Glen Mick and Susan Fournier, "Paradoxes of Technology: Consumer Cognizance, Emotions, and Coping Strategies," *Journal of Consumer Research*, vol. 25, September 1998, p. 126. Used with permission from the University of Chicago Press.

PARADOX	DESCRIPTION
Control/chaos	Technology can facilitate regulation or order, and technology can lead to upheaval or disorder
Freedom/enslavement	Technology can facilitate independence or fewer restrictions, and technology can lead to dependence or more restrictions
New/obsolete	New technologies provide the user with the most recently developed benefits of scientific knowledge, and new technologies are already or soon to be outmoded as they reach the marketplace
Competence/incompetence	Technology can facilitate feelings of intelligence or efficacy, and technology can lead to feelings of ignorance or ineptitude
Efficiency/inefficiency	Technology can facilitate less effort or time spent in certain activities, and technology can lead to more effort or time in certain activities
Fulfills/creates needs	Technology can facilitate the fulfillment of needs or desires, and technology can lead to the development or awareness of needs or desires previously unrealized
Assimilation/isolation	Technology can facilitate human togetherness, and technology can lead to human separation
Engaging/disengaging	Technology can facilitate involvement, flow, or activity, and technology can lead to disconnection, disruption, or passivity

high-effort hierarchy of effects A purchase of an innovation based on considerable decision-making effort.

her attitude is favorable, the consumer may try the product. If the trial experience is favorable, the consumer may decide to adopt the new product. This **high-effort hierarchy of effects** is illustrated in the top half of Exhibit 19.8 and corresponds to the high-effort attitude formation, search, judgment, and choice processes described in earlier chapters.

Consumers' motivation, ability, and opportunity (MAO) determine whether a high-effort adoption process occurs. A high-effort adoption process often takes place when consumers think the innovation incurs psychological, social, economic, financial, or safety risk. For example, the consumer may think that wearing a new style of clothing is socially risky and will wait for others to make the first move. Or the consumer may carefully consider the benefits of buying a DVD player because of the high cost of replacing an entire collection of video tapes with DVDs.

Often a high-effort decision-making process is related to the type of innovation. In particular, consumers are more likely to follow a high-effort decision-making process when the innovation is discontinuous (as opposed to continuous) because they know less about the innovation and must learn about it. A high-effort adoption process may also be used when many people are involved in the decision, as in family or organizational decision-making contexts.[29]

low-effort hierarchy of effects A purchase of an innovation based on limited decision-making effort.

Low-Effort Hierarchy of Effects When the new product involves less risk (as might be the case with a continuous innovation) and when fewer people are involved in the buying process, decision making may follow the **low-effort hierarchy of effects** illustrated in the bottom half of Exhibit 19.8. Here consumers engage in trial after they become aware of the innovation. They devote less decision-making effort to considering and researching the product before they try it,

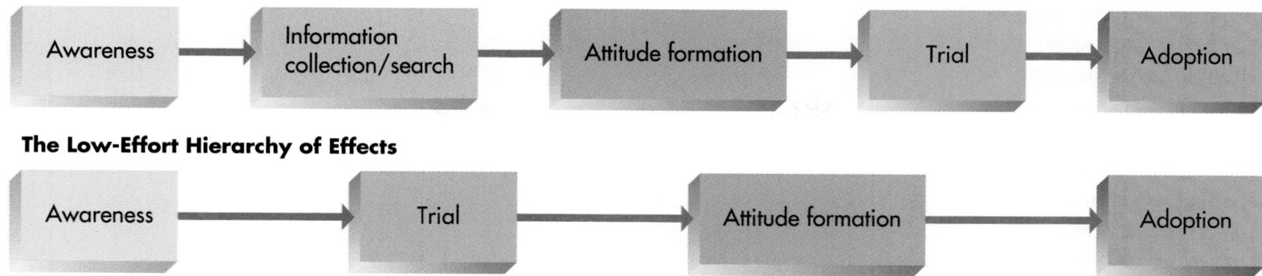

EXHIBIT 19.8 Adoption Decision Process

The amount of effort we engage in before we decide to adopt an innovation varies. In some cases we engage in considerable effort (e.g., extensive information search and evaluation of an offering). In other cases the adoption process involves limited effort. In such cases we first adopt the innovation and then decide whether we like it.

and form attitudes based on the trial. If their attitudes are positive, they may adopt the innovation. With a low-effort hierarchy of effects, the time between awareness of the innovation and its trial or adoption may be brief.

MARKETING IMPLICATIONS Understanding whether consumers' adoption decisions are based on a high- or low-effort adoption process has important implications for marketers. For example, if the adoption involves low effort, marketers need to do all they can to encourage trial because trial affects brand attitudes. To illustrate, when Procter & Gamble introduced Fat-Free Pringles, it distributed free samples of the product to lunchtime crowds in 20 major cities.[30]

If the adoption process is a high-effort one, marketers need to do all they can to reduce the perceived risk associated with the innovation. For example, consumers have largely resisted adopting personal video recorders incorporating the technology from TiVo and its rivals. To reduce resistance, TiVo initially subsidized the cost of manufacturing so Sony and Philips could price the machines at $600 or less, a critical factor in making the financial outlay seem less daunting. TiVo soon developed a new technology that slashed manufacturing costs by almost half, making the device even more affordable for consumers. Celebrities such as Rosie O'Donnell have publicly praised TiVo, as have technology gurus such as the *Wall Street Journal*'s Walter Mossberg. With adopters telling their friends, the positive word of mouth is slowly helping overcome resistance and boost TiVo's sales.[31] ●

Timing of Innovation Adoption Decisions

Consumers differ in the timing of their adoption decisions. One framework identifies five adopter groups based on the timing of their adoption decisions, as shown in Exhibit 19.9.[32] The first 2.5 percent of the market to adopt the innovation are described as innovators. The next 13.5 percent are called early adopters. The next 34 percent are called the early majority. The late majority represent the next 34 percent of adopters. The last 16 percent of the market to purchase the product are called laggards. These adopter groups tend to exhibit different characteristics. For example, innovators have been characterized as venturesome, early adopters as respectable, early majority consumers as deliberate, late majority consumers as skeptical, and laggards as traditional.

Studies of how high-tech products are adopted within organizations reveal additional characteristics of these adopter groups.[33] According to this research,

EXHIBIT 19.9
Profile of Adopter Groups
Some researchers have identified five groups of consumers that differ in when they adopt an innovation relative to others. Innovators are the first in a market to adopt an innovation, and laggards are the last. Certain characteristics (e.g., venturesomeness) are associated with each adopter group.

Source: Adapted with the permission of The Free Press, a Division of Simon & Schuster, Inc., from *Diffusion of Innovations,* 3rd ed., by Everett M. Rogers. Copyright © 1962, 1971, 1983 by The Free Press.

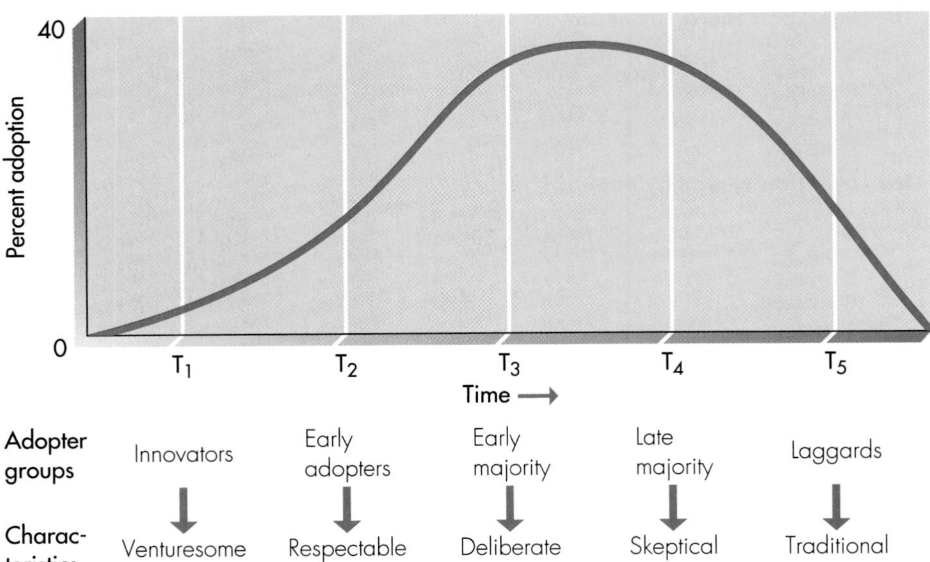

Adopter groups	Innovators	Early adopters	Early majority	Late majority	Laggards
Characteristics	Venturesome	Respectable	Deliberate	Skeptical	Traditional

innovators are technology enthusiasts. They appreciate technologically new products, they want to be the first to get them, and they are willing to live with bugs and deficiencies. Tech-oriented products such as handheld computers and personal digital recorders generally target innovators to gain entry into a market.

Early adopters are visionaries. They admire a technologically new product not so much for its features as for its abilities to create a revolutionary breakthrough in the way things are done. Early adopters who are making buying decisions for their employers want to see a significant return on their investment in new technology. These individuals are less concerned about price, and they willingly serve as opinion leaders for products that provide a revolutionary breakthrough.

As an example of early adopters, one research company has suggested that approximately 16 percent of U.S. households are TAFs—that is, technologically advanced families. These families want faster, newer, and more advanced products that help make home and work life more efficient and fun. Although they realize these new products will be cheaper, faster, and easier to use in the future, they do not want to wait for these market changes. Technologically advanced families tend to be younger and better educated and to have more children than the average U.S. family.[34]

The early majority are pragmatists, seeking innovations that offer incremental, predictable improvements on an existing technology. Because they do not like risk, they care deeply about who is making the innovation and the reputation of the company. They are interested in how well the innovation will fit into established technology systems, and they are concerned about the innovation's reliability. They are price sensitive, and they like to see competitors enter the market, because they can then compare features and be more assured about the product's ultimate feasibility.

Consumers who represent the late majority are conservatives. They are wary of progress and rely on tradition. They often fear high-tech products, and their goal in buying them is to not get stung. They like to buy preassembled products that include everything in a single, easy-to-use package. Consumers who are just now learning to use the Internet are late majority consumers. They are likely to place high value on bundled products that include everything they need (including a connection with an Internet service provider) to access the Internet. However, researchers forecast slow growth in Internet adoption among this group. One reason is lack of credit: 27 percent of U.S. families have no credit card, which most Internet service providers require to cover monthly Internet access fees. Another reason is that late majority adopters see no need to use the Internet at home, in part because many of these consumers can connect to the Internet at work.[35]

Laggards are skeptics. In the PC market, consumers who have yet to buy a PC may be regarded as laggards. Although laggards may resist innovations, marketers can gain insights from understanding why this group is skeptical of an innovation. Why, for example, do some people shun PCs in favor of other methods of storing, analyzing, and communicating information? Do they fear losing or misplacing data not filed in printed form? Do they worry about the security of the information? Or do they believe that PCs are so complex that they will never learn to use one properly?

An important implication of this delineation of adopters into groups is that if an innovation is to spread through the market, it must appeal to every group. Unfortunately, many potentially useful innovations have never gained mass-market appeal because the marketing efforts for them did not acknowledge the characteristics of the adopter groups. For example, Prodigy, a software package for the PC, allowed users to connect to a nationwide computer network via modem. Users could shop, consult online encyclopedias, check the weather and sports, order airline tickets, and perform other functions.

Although Prodigy featured a relatively new technology (appealing to innovators) and promised an innovative way of getting information and ordering products (appealing to early adopters), it did not appeal to the mass market because it did not fit with the early majority's mindset. First, few competitors were producing similar products, so the pragmatic early majority doubted the product would survive and apparently decided that buying it was not a good idea. Moreover, rather than specifying how the software was an incremental improvement on existing products, Prodigy's ads tried to create a vision of a new kind of world.[36] Such a strategy may encourage innovators, but not early adopters.

Some researchers have criticized the five-category scheme of adopter groups because it assumes these categories exist for all types of innovations. The critics say there may be more or fewer categories, depending on the innovation.[37] Also, the assumption that the number of consumers in the adopter categories forms a bell-shaped curve may not be true. For example, unlike the percentages that form the bell-shaped curve in Exhibit 19.9, certain products may attract the first 1 percent of adopters as innovators, the next 60 percent as early adopters, the next 30 percent as the early majority, the following 5 percent as the late majority, and the last 4 percent as laggards.

Some researchers have rejected the definition of innovators as a certain percentage of people who have adopted a product just after it comes on the market. These researchers claim that innovators are instead those who make a decision to buy a new product at any time regardless of the decisions of others.[38] Often such consumers do buy the product soon after it comes to the marketplace, but they do so based on their own feelings, not on the opinions of others.

MARKETING IMPLICATIONS Whether or not marketers accept the five-category adopter scheme, they recognize that consumers who are the first to buy a new product are important for several reasons. First, because innovators adopt new products independently of the opinions of other people, they are more likely to be receptive to information about new products, including information provided by marketers. Second, by virtue of their experience with the innovation, they may also communicate information to others and thus influence the adoption decisions of others. Given these issues, many researchers have attempted to better understand who innovators are and how they can be reached. This knowledge helps marketers design their marketing communications and select appropriate media.

Demographics. Several of the demographic variables described in Chapters 13 through 15 have been linked with the appeal of innovativeness.[39] For example, innovators tend to be younger and to have more income and education than other consumers. In contrast, laggards are older and have less income and education as well as lower occupational status. Religion is sometimes linked with innovation adoption. The Amish, for example, avoid many innovations, including cars, electricity, and telephones.

The fact that these demographic variables are linked with innovativeness makes sense. First, highly educated people tend to be heavier users of media and are therefore likely to learn about new products earlier than less educated people. Second, high-income consumers can afford to buy innovations, and they may perceive less financial risk in adopting something new. Demographic variables such as culture of origin have also been linked with innovativeness. Consumers in Australia and Japan, for example, are regarded as innovators for new technology, which is why these markets have become launching sites for new technologically oriented offerings.[40]

Social influence. Innovators have been linked with the social influence factors discussed in Chapter 16.[41] They tend to have a great deal of social influence beyond their own immediate groups, and they tend to be opinion leaders. Although this finding has not been observed in all research, it makes sense that innovators are able to influence non-adopters because their opinions are shared with and respected by non-adopters.

Personality. Several personality characteristics have also been linked with adoption of innovations.[42] For example, innovators are high in need for stimulation, are inner directed, and are less dogmatic than other consumers. However, the relationships between personality traits and innovativeness are not very strong.[43] Innovators also do less planning and deliberate less than other consumers do when making buying decisions.[44]

Some researchers have proposed that rather than measuring "innate innovativeness" (as a personality trait), a better approach is to examine consumers' willingness to be innovative in a specific consumption domain. For example, an innovator of rock music might respond positively to statements like "In general, I am among the first in my circle of friends to buy a new rock CD when it appears" or "I know the names of new rock acts before other people do." Innovators in the area of fashion, however, might not respond similarly to these statements.[45]

Cultural values. Adoption of innovations has been linked with culture of origin and the values tied to culture. One study of 11 European countries found that innovativeness was associated with cultures that value individualism over collectivism, those that value assertiveness over nurturing, and those that value openness to change over conservatism.[46]

Media involvement. Other research has suggested that innovators are frequent users of the media and rely extensively on external information.[47] They tend to think of themselves as active seekers and disseminators of information.[48] This finding makes sense because to affect others' adoption decisions, innovators must not only get their information somewhere but also be willing to transmit it.

Usage. Finally, innovators may be heavy users within the product category.[49] Consumers who frequently drink soft drinks may be innovators of new beverages because they are in the market often and hence are likely to notice these new products. In addition, innovators are usually experts in the product category, perhaps because of their usage and media involvement. ●

DIFFUSION

diffusion The percentage of the population that has adopted an innovation at a specific point in time.

As increasing numbers of consumers in a market adopt an innovation, the innovation spreads or diffuses through the market. Whereas adoption reflects the behavior of an individual, **diffusion** reflects the behavior of groups of consumers within a market. More specifically, diffusion reflects the percentage of the population that has adopted an innovation at a specific point in time. The diffusion of cell phones in various countries around the world, for example, is quite varied. In the United States and Hong Kong, cell phones are used by more than half of the population; however, in other countries the diffusion of cell phones is just beginning (see Exhibit 19.10).[50]

Because marketers are interested in successfully spreading their offering through a market, they want to know how quickly groups of consumers will adopt innovations. This encompasses two important diffusion issues: how an offering diffuses through the market and how quickly it does so.

EXHIBIT 19.10
Diffusion of Cell Phones
Cell phones have diffused widely through the U.S. market; however, their diffusion is just beginning in Third World countries like Botswana.

Source: © Strauss/Curtis/CORBIS.

How Offerings Diffuse through a Market

One way to examine how offerings spread through a market is to look at the pattern of adoption over time. From the marketers' perspective, life would be easy if everyone adopted the new offering just as soon as it came out on the market. However, this is rarely the case; in fact, several diffusion patterns have been identified.

The S-Shaped Diffusion Curve Some innovations exhibit an **S-shaped diffusion curve**, as illustrated in Exhibit 19.11(a).[51] Following this pattern, products start to spread relatively slowly through the market. As the exhibit shows, a relatively small percentage of the total market has adopted the product between time 1 and time 2. After a certain period, however, the rate of adoption increases dramatically, with many consumers adopting the product within a relatively short period of time. Between times 2 and 3, a dramatic increase occurs in the number of consumers adopting the product. Then adoptions grow at a decreasing rate, and the curve flattens out.

To illustrate, the diffusion of microwave ovens was initially very slow. Then it increased dramatically as consumers became more aware of and knowledgeable about microwave technology and as more products compatible with microwave cooking (snacks, meals, cookware, and so forth) came on the market. Now there is general acceptance of the microwave, and many consumers have one in their house or workplace, which is why the diffusion rate has again slowed.

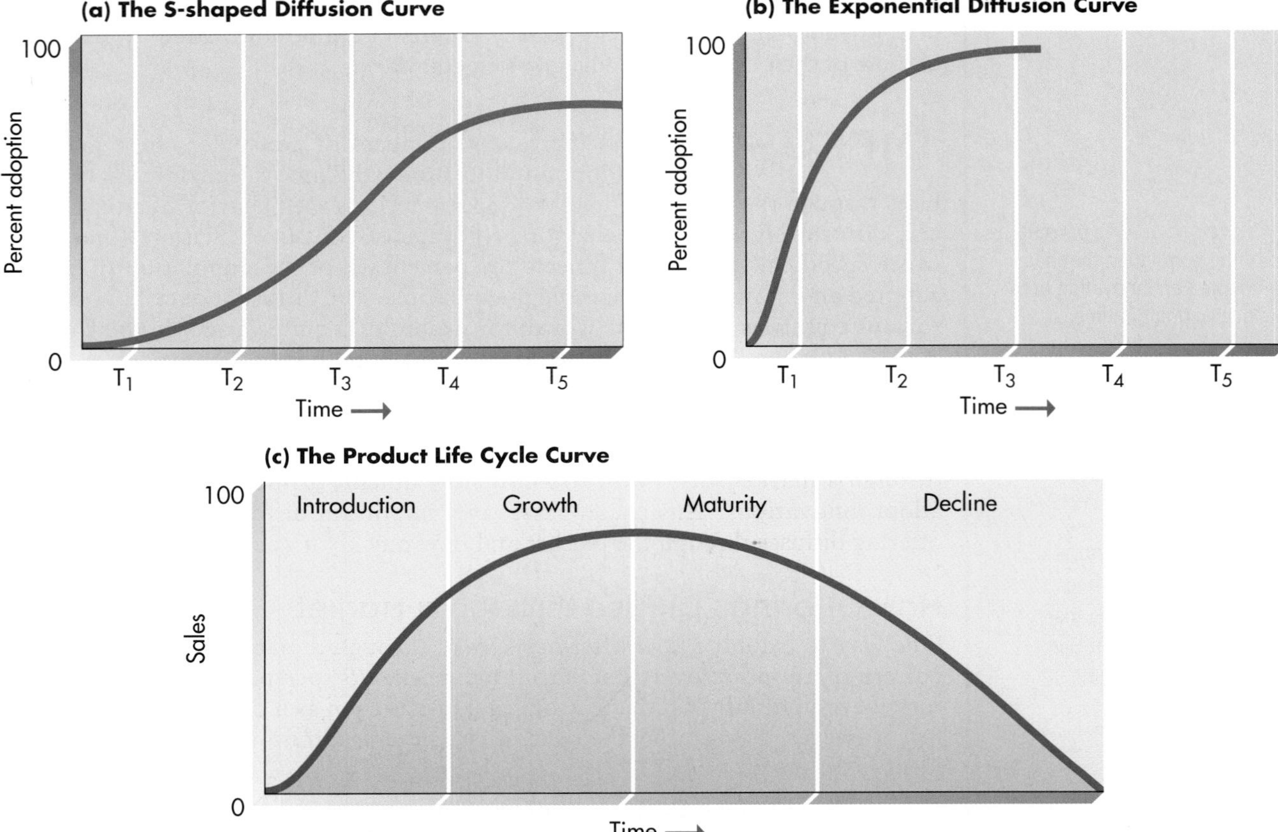

EXHIBIT 19.11
Diffusion and Product Life Cycle Curves

Several diffusion patterns have been identified. (a) With an S-shaped diffusion curve, diffusion starts out slowly, increases rapidly, and then flattens out again. (b) With an exponential diffusion curve, many people adopt the innovation quickly. (c) The product life cycle curve depicts sales (not cumulative diffusion) of an offering over time.

S-shaped diffusion curve A diffusion curve characterized by slow initial growth followed by a rapid increase in diffusion.

exponential diffusion curve A diffusion curve characterized by rapid initial growth.

The Exponential Diffusion Curve Another type of adoption curve is the **exponential diffusion curve**, illustrated in Exhibit 19.11(b).[52] In contrast to the S-shaped curve, the exponential diffusion curve starts out much more quickly, with a large percentage of the market purchasing the product as soon as it is available. However, with each additional time period, the rate of adoption increases at a decreasing rate.

Factors Affecting the Shape of the Diffusion Curve

Many factors influence the ultimate shape of the diffusion curve. In general, marketers might expect an S-shaped diffusion curve when the innovation is associated with some social, psychological, economic, performance, or physical risk. In such situations, consumers might wait to see how other people use and react to the innovation before adopting it. Diffusion may also be slow initially if consumers are not sure whether the product will be on the market for a long period or whether its use carries high switching costs. The diffusion of computers and CD players followed this S-shaped curve. An S-shaped diffusion pattern might also occur when consumers are physically far apart, do not discuss the innovation with others, or do not share the same beliefs.

In contrast, when the innovation involves little risk, switching costs are low, consumers are similar in their beliefs and values, and people talk often about the product and quickly disseminate knowledge throughout the social system, the product may have a rapid takeoff period that follows the exponential curve for diffusion. Note that these curves reflect only the rate at which consumers in the market adopt, not the time period under analysis. In other words, an S-shaped or an exponential curve could reflect diffusion that has occurred over a 1-year or a 30-year period. Furthermore, the curves could reflect the diffusion of either a functional, symbolic, or hedonic innovation.

How Diffusion Relates to the Product Life Cycle

product life cycle A concept that suggests that products go through an initial introductory period followed by periods of sales growth, maturity, and decline.

The **product life cycle** concept (illustrated in Exhibit 19.11(c)) proposes that products initially go through a period of introduction, followed by relatively rapid growth as more competitors enter the market and more consumers adopt the product. As competition increases, weaker competitors drop out and product sales plateau. At some point, however, consumer acceptance wanes, and product sales decline.

Product diffusion and the product life cycle are related but different concepts. Diffusion focuses on the percentage of the market that has adopted the product; diffusion is complete when 100 percent of the market has purchased the product. The product life cycle, on the other hand, deals with sales of the product over time. Second, diffusion curves are generally cumulative—that is, they continue to increase or at least level off over time. However, the product life cycle curve may decline as consumers decide not to purchase the product on future occasions. To illustrate, after an innovation such as the rotary-dial telephone diffused through an entire market, it was replaced by another innovation, the touch-tone phone, and sales of the old product eventually declined as the new innovation took hold.

MARKETING IMPLICATIONS Marketers who understand a product's life cycle can try to prevent that product's decline—perhaps by finding new uses for it. For example, nylon has enjoyed a long life cycle given the myriad uses to which it has been put since its introduction in the 1940s—as an ingredient in clothing, rope, fishing lines, and so on. Rand McNally is extending the life cycle of its detailed maps by packaging them in printed atlases, in software programs, and in other forms.[53] To the extent that marketers develop new uses for a product or encourage use innovativeness, they can lengthen their product's life cycle.

fad A successful innovation that has a very short product life cycle.

Marketers can also try to diagnose the likely life cycle pattern of their offering. Just as diffusion curves differ, so too are there different product life cycle curves. A **fad** is a successful innovation that has a very short product life cycle. Powerpuff Girls, Pokemon cards, scooters, Tae-Bo, and certain diets are examples of fads. As energy drinks such as Red Bull became a fad, Pepsi, Cadbury Schweppes, Coca-Cola and others brought out their own energy drinks to capitalize on consumer interest.[54] Some fads experience a revival years after they first surface. Disco music, a 1970s fad, was revived as a fad just a few years ago.[55] Although the fad for karaoke music peaked some years ago, karaoke dancing has emerged as a more recent fad.[56] Exhibit 19.12 shows another fad.

fashion A successful innovation that has a moderately long and potentially cyclical product life cycle.

A **fashion** or trend is a successful innovation with a lengthier and potentially cyclical life. For example, certain aesthetic styles like art deco run in fashion cycles, as do certain styles of clothing like cargo pants, twin sets, fur, and platform shoes. Some types of foods, like Thai or Mexican, run in fashion cycles, as do certain consumption practices (e.g., breast- versus bottle-feeding infants).

classic A successful innovation that has a lengthy product life cycle.

Finally, a **classic** is a successful innovation that has a lengthy product life cycle. Jeans are a U.S. classic. Others include rock and roll music, Coca-Cola, and hamburgers.

Although the terms *fad, fashion*, and *classic* have most often been applied to aesthetic or hedonic innovations, they can also describe functional and symbolic innovations because the life cycle of these innovations can be similarly variable.

INFLUENCES ON ADOPTION, RESISTANCE, AND DIFFUSION

Knowing that innovations may diffuse quickly or slowly through a market and that the success of a new product depends on how many people within the market adopt it, marketing managers need to understand the factors affecting resistance, adoption, and diffusion. Exhibit 19.2 identifies a number of factors, including characteristics of the innovation itself and of the social system into which it is introduced.

Characteristics of the Innovation

Characteristics of the innovation that can affect resistance, adoption, and diffusion include perceived value, benefits, and costs.

relative advantage Benefits in an innovation superior to those found in existing products.

Perceived Value Consumers perceive that an innovation has value if it offers greater benefits or lower costs than existing alternatives. Products with high perceived value may be more readily adopted than those with low perceived value.

Perceived Benefits An innovation's value to consumers is affected by its perceived **relative advantage**—that is, the extent to which it offers benefits superior to those of existing products. For example, digital phones like those in Europe that allow consumers to charge services to their cellular phone bill offer an advantage of convenience that traditional cellular phones lack.[57] A product or service offers a relative advantage if it can help consumers avoid risks, fulfill their needs, or achieve their goals. Thus the relative advantages of a product should serve as criteria that affect consumers' adoption decisions.

EXHIBIT 19.12
Fads
Examples of fads, including this one, abound. Can you think of other fads?
Source: Getty Images.

Note that a relative advantage is something the product does for the consumer—not something that exists in the product. Thus the relative advantage of hybrid cars such as the Toyota Prius lies not in their features, but in the owners' ability to save money on gasoline and help save the environment. The ad in Exhibit 19.13 emphasizes a product's relative advantage.

Marketers must also bear in mind that many new products have advantages over existing ones, but if consumers do not perceive the advantage or do not think it is important, the innovation will have little impact on adoption. This is what happened to the CueCat, a handheld device that helped consumers locate specific Web pages of participating companies. After consumers connected the CueCat to a PC, they could use it to scan the special barcode embedded in an ad or catalog and immediately find their

EXHIBIT 19.13
Relative Advantage
Innovations are more likely to be adopted when their relative advantages are clear. This ad emphasizes the advantages of Sprint Vision PCS.

Source: Courtesy of Sprint.

Web browsers set for the Web page for that item or information. Although the handheld gadget was fairly easy to use, technology reviewers scoffed at it—and few consumers actually used it, apparently perceiving no relative advantage over simply typing in the Web address.[58]

Perceived Costs Another aspect of the value of a product is its perceived cost. The consumer may perceive two types of costs. One is the actual purchase cost. The higher the purchase cost, the greater the resistance and hence the slower the diffusion. Because hybrid cars offer a number of unique features, these vehicles cost more than other cars. Research shows that consumers perceive the cost to be significantly greater than conventional cars, which is slowing adoption and, in turn, diffusion. In contrast, more efficient manufacturing and higher sales volume have brought prices for DVD players below $100, compared with $600 when this innovation was introduced in the late 1990s. As a result, sales have skyrocketed, leading to faster diffusion.[59]

Another aspect of cost is switching costs—the cost involved in changing from the current product to a new one. This is an issue, for example, for consumers with extensive collections of videotapes who are considering buying a DVD player.

MARKETING IMPLICATIONS If consumers do not perceive that an innovation has a relative advantage, marketers may need to add one by physically redesigning or reengineering the innovation.

Communicate and demonstrate the relative advantage. The company will need to educate consumers who do not understand what a product is or what its relative advantages are. The slow diffusion of WebTV was partly due to the fact that consumers didn't really understand the product, let alone why they should buy it.[60] In contrast, Union Carbide once demonstrated the quality of a new superinsulation product using a dramatic advertisement showing a baby chick in a box lined with the material. After the box containing the chick was placed in a pot of boiling water for more than a minute, the chick emerged completely unharmed. Another way to communicate an innovation's advantage is to use a highly credible and visible opinion leader.

Use price promotions to reduce perceived costs. If consumers perceive that a product is too costly, the company can use special price-oriented sales promotions—price-offs, rebates, or refunds like the one in Exhibit 19.14—to reduce the perceived cost. Marketers can also provide guarantees or warranties that make the product seem less expensive. Alternatively, the marketer may find a cheaper way to manufacture the product and pass on the savings in the form of lower prices for consumers. Marketers of digital watches adopted the latter strategy.

Provide incentives for switching. If innovations are not adopted because consumers think switching costs are high, marketers might provide incentives for switching. For example, companies like America Online offer incentives such as free trial periods for consumers who have never had Internet access or are signed with other Internet service providers. Companies might also use advertising to inform consumers about the costs associated with not switching.

Finally, marketers might be able to force their innovation to become the industry standard, for instance, by having exceptionally high quality, great ease of use, or low price. MPEG-4, a technology standard for condensing huge video files so they can be easily transferred online, is backed by a large number of companies, including Cisco Systems. Although earlier MPEG technologies became widely accepted standards, Windows Media, RealPlayer, and QuickTime are also trying to win wider acceptance within the industry.[61] ●

EXHIBIT 19.14
Enhancing Adoption and Diffusion by Reducing Costs
Coupons are one way of reducing the purchase costs of an innovation.

Source: © The Proctor & Gamble Company. Used by permission.

Uncertainty

In addition to characteristics of the innovation, uncertainty surrounding the innovation can affect adoption, resistance, and diffusion. Two aspects of uncertainty are particularly important. One is doubt about what will become the standard product in the industry. For example, many consumers were reluctant to purchase VCRs because they were not sure whether the VHS or beta format would become the industry standard. MP3's popularity has made it an industry standard for digitally compressing music, although tiny MP3 disks have yet to replace CDs as the industry standard.[62]

A second aspect of uncertainty is the length of the product life cycle. If consumers think the product might be a fad, they are likely to be more resistant than if they think it will become a fashion or a classic. For example, you may forgo spending $80 on platform shoes if you don't believe that they will be in style for very long. Concern over life cycle length is quite legitimate in clothing and high-tech markets, where product improvements often operate on a very short time frame.

MARKETING IMPLICATIONS *Show product adaptability.* When consumers resist innovations because they are worried about a short life cycle, marketers might show how adaptable the product is and hence how likely it is to have a long life cycle. For example, PC marketers can ease the fears of many consumers who do not really know what to do with a computer or why they need one by demonstrating all their fun and convenient applications—using the Internet for shopping, booking airline tickets, doing research, playing games, banking, and so on. ●

Consumer Learning Requirements

A third characteristic affecting resistance, adoption, and diffusion is consumer learning requirements—or what consumers need to do to effectively use the innovation.

compatibility The extent to which the innovation or its usage is consistent with consumer values, norms, and behaviors.

Compatibility Consumers often resist innovations because they see them as incompatible with their needs, values, norms, or behaviors.[63] The more **compatible** the innovation is with consumers' values, norms, and behaviors, the less the resistance and the greater the diffusion (see Exhibit 19.15). Motorola's two-way

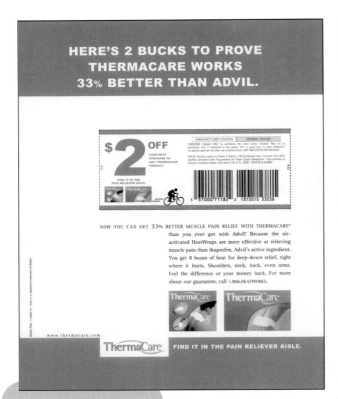

EXHIBIT 19.15
Innovation Incompatibility
Some new products are more compatible with our norms, values, and behaviors than are others. The less compatible an innovation is, the more slowly it will diffuse through a market.

Source: AP/Wide World Photos.

radio is easy to use and compatible with consumers' desires to stay in contact with family members and friends while on outings.[64] Clorox Disinfecting Wipes, a recent new-product hit, is compatible with the way people traditionally clean their kitchens and bathrooms, yet offers the relative advantage of convenience.[65] On the other hand, digital cameras are not as compatible with the way consumers are used to taking and developing photographs, because they operate without film and outside processing.

Some potentially serious consequences can arise when an innovation is not compatible with consumers' values, goals, and behaviors. One case in particular is marketers' attempts to encourage bottle-feeding by mothers in the developing nations of Latin America, Africa, and Asia. Manufacturers' ads showed pictures of mothers with beautiful, fat, healthy babies. The ad copy read, "Give your baby love and Lactogen." (Lactogen is an infant formula.) The ad, which had a modern flavor, was attractive to upper-income, well-educated consumers. It was also attractive to peasant families who aspired to be like the well educated. Unfortunately, most peasant families could not afford the expensive formula, so they diluted it with water, leaving their babies malnourished. Furthermore, they were unused to practices like sterilizing nipples and bottles, so the baby bottles became a haven for bacteria, which made the babies sick. The lack of compatibility between the innovation and the consumers' behavior therefore caused unanticipated problems.[66]

trialability The extent to which an innovation can be tried on a limited basis before it is adopted.

Trialability A second aspect of consumer learning requirements is the **trialability** of the innovation, or the extent to which the product can be tried on a limited basis before it is adopted. Products like the Palm handheld computer are very trialable. The potential user can quickly learn the product's functions to make appointments, keep a phone book, and create to-do lists just by playing with it for a few minutes. However, trialability is virtually impossible with some innovations, such as laser eye surgery. Because trial allows a consumer to see the product's relative advantages and assess the potential risks associated with purchase, products that are easy to try tend to diffuse through the market more quickly than those that do not lend themselves to trial.

Studies suggest that the degree of importance placed on trialability depends on the type of adopter. Trialability may be very important to innovators and early adopters, because they have little else on which to base the value of the innovation. Trialability may be less important for later adopters, who are likely to know many people who have already adopted the innovation and who can therefore speak to its efficacy.[67]

Complexity Complexity is a final learning requirement related to adoption and diffusion. Diffusion is likely to be slow when consumers perceive they will have difficulty understanding or using a new product. Computers, for example, were initially perceived to be very complex, and hence they had a relatively slow diffusion rate. Digital photography is diffusing at a relatively slow rate because consumers perceive complexity in learning to transfer digital images from the camera to the computer, figuring out the software for enhancing images, and printing high-quality photos.[68] Other products, such as cellular phones, have diffused more rapidly, in part because they are easy to use.

MARKETING IMPLICATIONS

Marketers can use several tactics to reduce consumers' resistance to innovations.

Enhance compatibility or reduce complexity. Marketers may be able to reposition an innovation so it appears more consistent with consumers' needs and values. Campbell's soup enjoyed renewed popularity when it was repositioned away from taste and toward nutrition and low calories.[69] Sometimes, however, companies must redesign a product to overcome incompatibility and reduce complexity. For example, because camcorders were initially too complex for the average user, companies like Sharp and Matsushita developed simpler, more user-friendly products.[70]

Educate about compatibility. Companies can use advertising and promotion to show how their innovations are compatible with consumers' needs, values, norms, or behaviors. For example, in Third World countries consumers are not used to modern medicine and the techniques used to avoid many dreaded diseases. One way organizations like the World Health Organization have dealt with this situation is to launch educational programs to demonstrate the value of vaccinations and the procedures that can stop disorders like diarrhea.[71] Advertising can also show how a new offering is easier to use or has more benefits than current alternatives, even if it requires new behaviors.

Use change agents. Another way to enhance perceived compatibility is to use change agents such as opinion leaders (see Chapter 16). Marketers in such diverse fields as farming equipment, medicine, and computers have aimed new products at influential and highly respected people who can be convinced of a new product's merits and who will then spread positive word of mouth to others.[72]

Fit with a system of products. Another way to address incompatibility is to design the innovation to fit with a system of existing products. For example, the Palm handheld computer has done well in part because users can easily transfer data between a Palm handheld and a PC. They can also download programs and games from the Internet for use on the Palm.[73] On the other hand, dishwashers did not fit into home kitchens until builders built spaces and plumbing connections for them.

Force the innovation to be the industry standard. Marketers can sometimes work with regulators to require adoption of the innovation. For example, the use of smoke detectors, seat belts, and lead-free gasoline are all innovations that have been forced into usage by government mandate. As discussed in the chapter-opening example, one reason car manufacturers are introducing more hybrid cars is because of state clean-air requirements mandating zero-emission vehicles.[74]

Use promotions to enhance trialability. Companies can stimulate trial through various promotions. Free samples, for example, encourage trial by people who might otherwise resist using the product. The makers of NutraSweet overcame potential trialability problems by sending millions of consumers free samples of gumballs sweetened with NutraSweet. They chose this approach because NutraSweet is intended as an ingredient in food products, not as a stand-alone product.

Demonstrate compatibility and simplicity. Demonstrations, either live or presented in advertising, can show how compatible the product is with existing needs, values, and behaviors and how simple it is to use. Apple Computer, for example, once held a special promotion called "Take a Mac for a Test Drive," encouraging consumers to take a Macintosh computer home over the weekend to try it out. Companies can also arrange for salespeople to provide demonstrations and discuss the product's benefits with consumers.

Simulate trial. At times, a company may need to simulate trial rather than having consumers actually try the product. For example, some hair salons offer computer systems that allow consumers to see what they would look like with different hair colors and styles. Lands' End invites consumers to personalize the measurements of a "virtual model" on its Web site so they can see how clothing will look on their figure before they buy.[75]

Reduce complexity through product redesign. Sometimes companies can change a product to make it less complex, the way Sharp and others simplified their camcorders. Universal remotes that allow for ready programming of VCRs, for example, are aimed at reducing product complexity. Likewise, 35mm cameras with automatic focusing allow novices to take high-quality pictures without worrying about aperture settings and other complexities. ●

Social Relevance

social relevance The extent to which the innovation can be observed or the extent to which having others observe it has social cachet.

A fourth major factor that affects resistance, adoption, and diffusion is the innovation's **social relevance**, particularly observability and social value. Observability is the extent to which the innovation is observable to others. In general, the more consumers can observe others using the innovation, the more likely they are to adopt it.[76] Consumers are also more likely to learn about new products and their potential benefits when the products are visibly consumed by others. For example, a new shoulder strap designed to distribute the weight of a golf bag gained acceptance among caddies after they saw others using the product.[77] On the other hand, a new scale that announces your body weight is unlikely to be very observable because few people want to weigh themselves in public (or want others to hear their weight!).[78] Thus diffusion is also affected by the public or private nature of the product, as described in Chapter 16.

Social value reflects the extent to which the product has social cachet, which means that it is seen as socially desirable and/or appropriate and therefore generates imitation, speeding diffusion. One study found that farmers adopted certain farming innovations because they were very expensive and thus had social prestige value. These studies also found that the earlier someone adopted the innovation, the more prestige was associated with it.[79] Consumers sometimes adopt aesthetic innovations like new fashions, new hairstyles, and new cars solely on the basis of the social prestige these innovations confer on the user.

Observability and social value both help explain the growing popularity of knee-length socks for basketball players. It began when stars like Seattle Supersonic Moochie Norris and Laker Michael Cooper started wearing them during basketball games. The products are very observable, and their use by sports stars gives them social cachet.[80]

Although social value may enhance diffusion, the diffusion of a product based on a prestige image may actually shorten its life cycle because being adopted by the masses reduces a product's prestige value. For example, designer jeans, once associated with prestige and exclusivity, lost prestige when everyone in the market started to wear them.[81]

MARKETING IMPLICATIONS Marketers can use extensive advertising, promotions, and distribution to overcome problems associated with observability. Observability can also be enhanced by the use of distinctive packaging, styling, and color or unique promotions.[82] Thus many of the techniques discussed in Chapter 4 for enhancing attention and perception may enhance observability. Associating the product with a well-known person or developing ads to suggest that the consumer will be socially rewarded for using the product may also enhance observability. The social relevance of an innovation can be heightened through advertising, particularly advertising that ties product use with potential social approval. Finally, marketers can enhance social value by associating the product with some social entity, cause, or value. Having a new beverage serve as the official drink of the Olympic team might, for example, enhance its social value. ●

Legitimacy and Adaptability

legitimacy The extent to which the innovation follows established guidelines for what seems appropriate in the category.

adaptability The extent to which the innovation can fit with existing products or styles.

Legitimacy and adaptability are two additional factors that influence resistance, adoption, and diffusion, particularly for symbolic and aesthetic innovations.[83] **Legitimacy** refers to the extent to which the innovation follows established guidelines for what seems appropriate in the category. An innovation that is too radical or that does not derive from a legitimate precursor lacks legitimacy. For example, it took the public a long time to accept modern art because it violated the traditions of classical art. Rock and roll and later rap music were initially seen as deviant forms of music. Part of the success of artists like k. d. lang stemmed from their ability to fuse two legitimate music styles (country and rock) into a style that sounded new.

Adaptability, the innovation's potential to fit with existing products or styles, is another factor affecting adoption and diffusion.[84] For example, certain forms of fashion or furniture may be seen as highly adaptable because they can fit with a variety of other fashion or furniture trends. Some functional products, such as PCs, have high adaptability because they can perform a variety of functions. Rock music has proven to be very adaptable as variants from soft rock to punk rock have emerged.

MARKETING IMPLICATIONS Marketers may enhance legitimacy by demonstrating how the innovation came into being. For example, acupuncture may be legitimized by showing the history of the practice in China and its widespread use today. Conversely, if consumers believe the product lacks adaptability, marketers can show that it has uses beyond its original function. For example, the makers of cranberry sauce ask consumers to consider other uses for their product in addition to serving it as a condiment for Thanksgiving dinner.[85] ●

Characteristics of the Social System

Innovations diffuse rapidly or slowly in part because of product characteristics and in part because of the characteristics of the social system into which they are introduced. Both the kinds of people in the target market and the nature of the relationships among the people in the social system will affect the innovation's acceptance.

modernity The extent to which consumers in the social system have positive attitudes toward change.

Modernity Resistance, adoption, and diffusion are affected by the **modernity** of the social system, the extent to which consumers in the system have a positive attitude toward change. Consumers in modern systems value science, technology, and education and are technologically oriented in terms of both the goods produced and the skill of the labor force.[86] The receptivity of consumers toward change, science, and technology is illustrated by the ad in Exhibit 19.16. The more modern the social system, the more receptive its consumers are to new products.

Homophily A second general characteristic of the social system is homophily, or the overall similarity among members of the system. Diffusion is faster when

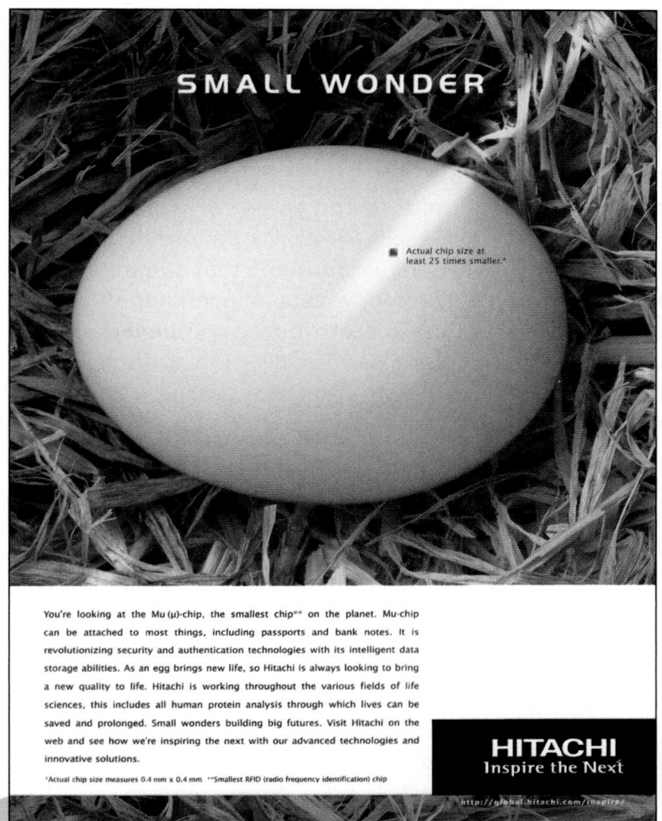

SMALL WONDER
Actual chip size at least 25 times smaller.*
You're looking at the Mu (μ)-chip, the smallest chip** on the planet. Mu-chip can be attached to most things, including passports and bank notes. It is revolutionizing security and authentication technologies with its intelligent data storage abilities. As an egg brings new life, so Hitachi is always looking to bring a new quality to life. Hitachi is working throughout the various fields of life sciences, this includes all human protein analysis through which lives can be saved and prolonged. Small wonders building big futures. Visit Hitachi on the web and see how we're inspiring the next with our advanced technologies and innovative solutions.
*Actual chip size measures 0.4 mm x 0.4 mm **Smallest RFID (radio frequency identification) chip
HITACHI
Inspire the Next
http://global.hitachi.com/inspire/

EXHIBIT 19.16
The Modernity of the Social System and Advertising
The United States is a society that highly values things that are new and technologically sophisticated. As such, this ad should appeal to modernity values of U.S. consumers.

Source: Reprint courtesy of Hitachi AMERICA, Ltd.

consumers in the market are highly similar in terms of education, values, needs, income, and other dimensions.[87] Several factors explain this connection. First, the more similar peoples' backgrounds are, the more likely they are to have similar needs, values, and preferences. Second, similar people are more likely to interact with one another and transmit information. Third, similar people tend to model each other. In addition, normative influence is likely to be higher as homophily grows, increasing the pressure for adopting the innovation and speeding adoption and diffusion.

Physical Distance A third characteristic of the social system is the physical distance between its members. Diffusion tends to be slower when members of the social system are spread apart. Some marketers in Japan have found that high school girls excel at setting trends. No doubt this ability is due to the physical and emotional proximity of girls and their tendency to talk about new products they have seen and used.[88] Likewise, an innovation may experience slower diffusion when consumers are physically separated rather than in physically contiguous cities, states, or countries.[89]

Opinion Leadership A final characteristic of the social system involves the key influencers in the diffusion process. Chapter 16 mentioned that people with credibility, such as experts or opinion leaders, can have considerable influence on adoption and diffusion because they may spread positive or negative product information to others.[90] For example, *US* magazine often features famous celebrity opinion leaders sporting new products juxtaposed with pictures of ordinary readers emulating them. One study analyzing the diffusion of information about family-planning practices among women in a Korean village found that opinion leaders were very important sources of information. Not only was the information communicated by these women important, but the opinion leaders served as bridges connecting spatially related but separate cliques in the village.[91]

MARKETING IMPLICATIONS Marketing efforts can influence resistance, adoption, and diffusion by affecting the social system. For example, if the target market is heterogeneous, companies may need to use targeted communications that show the product's relevance to consumers' unique needs, values, or norms and place the messages in specialized (target-market-specific) media to reach these consumers.

Marketers might also identify consumers who have not adopted the innovation. According to research, nonadopters can be divided into groups with very different characteristics. One group consists of passive consumers who have tried the product but are unlikely to provide much information to others about it. A second is active rejectors who have tried the product but are likely to provide unfavorable word of mouth to others. The third is potential adopters who have not yet tried the product but who may be influenced by active rejectors, active acceptors, or marketers.

Because even a small group can have a big impact on others' adoption decisions, it may be useful to specifically target some of these groups. To illustrate, if potential adopters lack awareness of the innovation, the company can use advertising to build awareness and encourage adoption. Product improvements may, however, be necessary for active rejectors. Thus different marketing strategies may be appropriate for different adopter groups.[92]

Marketing tactics may also affect the nature and extent of word-of-mouth communication. For example, companies can facilitate word of mouth flows about the new product by targeting opinion leaders. Promotions that target the network, rather than the consumer, can be an effective way of speeding diffusion. Newspaper and magazine articles describing the attributes and benefits of an innovation generally have more credibility than communications from the company itself. Special events like trade shows are also ways of showcasing a product, demonstrating its features, and stimulating positive word of mouth. As Chapter 16 indicates, marketers can take a number of steps to track word of mouth, generate positive word of mouth, and counteract negative word of mouth.

Because the elements of the marketing mix can influence diffusion by their effects on both the innovation and the social system, it is not surprising that the more intensive the marketing effort—the advertising, sales promotion, personal selling, and distribution—the faster the innovation spreads through a market.[93] ●

THE CONSEQUENCES OF INNOVATIONS

Although innovations often offer relative advantages that may not have previously existed, they are not always good for society. Several studies have suggested that negative social and economic consequences may arise from the diffusion of an innovation.

One study examined the diffusion of the steel ax among a tribe of aborigines who lived in the Australian bush.[94] Before the innovation was introduced, the stone ax had served as the tribe's principal tool. It was used only by men and was awarded to them as a gift and as payment for work performed. It was generally regarded as a symbol of masculinity and respect. However, missionaries came into the social system with the steel ax and distributed it to men, women, and children. This distribution scheme disrupted the sex and age roles among tribal members and thus affected the social system.

Other innovations can have mixed consequences. For example, some scientists are concerned that strains of genetically engineered corn may threaten monarch butterfly populations. These types of corn have been altered to generate pesticides to counteract caterpillars and other pests that attack corn plants. During the caterpillar stage, monarch butterflies born in milkweed adjacent to cornfields may be exposed to pollen from the altered corn. Although a group of scientists has concluded that these strains of corn do not pose a major risk to monarch caterpillars, more research is being conducted to understand the long-term effects of this innovation.[95]

Innovations can also have negative socioeconomic consequences. For example, a study examining the diffusion of the CAT scanner through the medical community identified two important sociological consequences. First, the innovation tended to diffuse to markets that were generally wealthy, leaving the technology unavailable to families who lived in poorer rural areas. Second, the innovation was expensive and was viewed as driving up health care costs.[96]

Given these types of unanticipated social and economic consequences, we as consumers should be careful to avoid adopting a universally pro-innovation bias.

SUMMARY

Innovations are products, services, ideas, or attributes that consumers in a market segment perceive to be new. Innovations can be characterized as functional, symbolic, or hedonic. They also vary in the degree of behavioral change their adoption requires. Innovativeness in products ranges along a continuum from continuous to discontinuous.

Innovations may represent fads, fashions, or classics and hence may exhibit a short, moderate, or long life cycle. Marketers can extend a product's life cycle by enhancing the breadth of the innovation and by encouraging consumers to find innovative uses for familiar products.

Strategies for marketers of innovations include reducing consumers' resistance to innovations, facilitating consumers' adoption of the innovation, and affecting the diffusion of the innovation through the marketplace. A high-effort as opposed to low-effort hierarchy-of-effects adoption process occurs when the innovation is seen as economically, physically, socially, or psychologically risky. Some individuals, called innovators, are among the first to adopt new products, independently of the decisions of others. Companies may target innovators because their adoption directly or indirectly influences other consumers' adoption decisions through word of mouth or social modeling.

Resistance, adoption, and diffusion are affected by characteristics of the innovation and the social system into which it is introduced. Overcoming resistance is easiest when the innovation is perceived to provide value such as a relative advantage, low price, or low switching costs. In addition, resistance will be lower when the innovation requires minimal learning and when it is highly compatible with existing needs, values, and behaviors; easy to try; easy to use; and low risk. Innovations viewed as high in social relevance, legitimacy, and adaptability encounter less consumer resistance than those regarded as low in social relevance, legitimacy and/or adaptability. Marketers' actions can also affect consumers' perceptions of the innovation's characteristics.

Moreover, the characteristics of the social system in which the innovation operates can affect resistance, adoption, and diffusion. The more dense the social network and the more homophilous the social system, the more likely it is that adopters will transmit information from adopters to nonadopters, which in turn may directly affect the likelihood of adoption. However, the diffusion of an innovation may entail some negative social and economic consequences.

QUESTIONS FOR REVIEW AND DISCUSSION

1. How can innovations be described in terms of degree of novelty and types of benefits? How does the degree of novelty affect consumers' behavioral change?
2. What is the difference between adoption and diffusion? How does the concept of resistance relate to adoption?
3. Under what circumstances might a consumer follow the high-effort hierarchy of effects in adopting an innovation?
4. How can consumers be categorized in terms of their timing of adoption relative to other consumers?
5. What is the product life cycle, and how does it differ from product diffusion?
6. How do consumer learning requirements and social relevance affect resistance, adoption, and diffusion?
7. What characteristics of the social system affect an innovation's acceptance within a market?

EXERCISES

1. Read several publications like *BusinessWeek, Fortune,* or the *Wall Street Journal* and identify two innovative products and/or services.
   a. Why are these offerings innovations? (Relate your answers to the chapter's definition of an innovation.)
   b. What type of innovations are they—continuous, dynamically continuous, discontinuous? Functional, aesthetic, symbolic?
   c. Describe whether you think adoption and diffusion of these offerings will be fast or slow by using concepts associated with the innovations, such as relative advantage, observability, and legitimacy.
   d. Indicate how marketers might overcome resistance and speed adoption and diffusion for those offerings whose diffusion is likely to be slow.
2. Consider a product that you think represents an innovation but that you have not yet purchased. Using the terms discussed in this chapter, indicate why your resistance to this product is high or low.

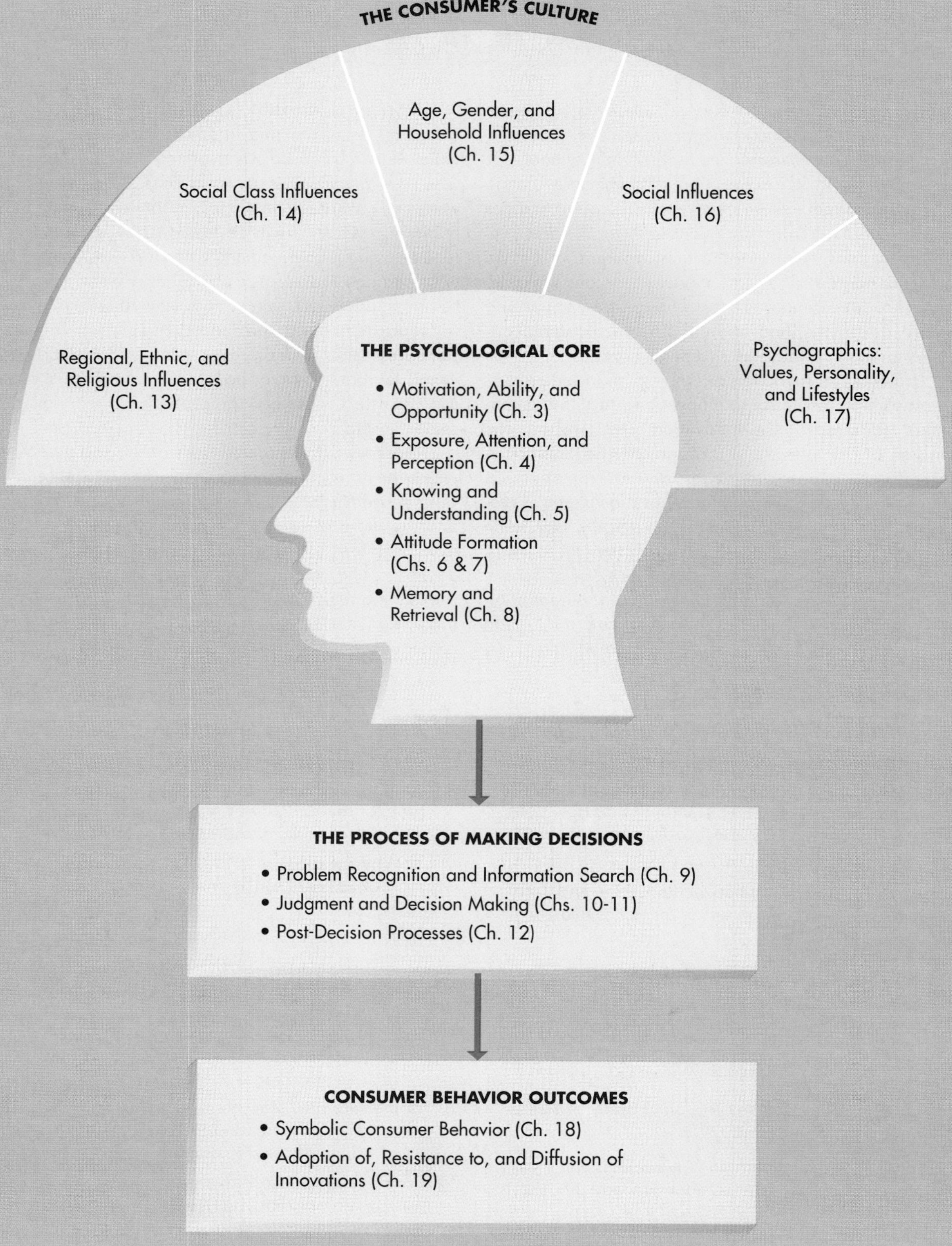

THE CONSUMER'S CULTURE

Regional, Ethnic, and Religious Influences (Ch. 13)

Social Class Influences (Ch. 14)

Age, Gender, and Household Influences (Ch. 15)

Social Influences (Ch. 16)

Psychographics: Values, Personality, and Lifestyles (Ch. 17)

THE PSYCHOLOGICAL CORE

- Motivation, Ability, and Opportunity (Ch. 3)
- Exposure, Attention, and Perception (Ch. 4)
- Knowing and Understanding (Ch. 5)
- Attitude Formation (Chs. 6 & 7)
- Memory and Retrieval (Ch. 8)

THE PROCESS OF MAKING DECISIONS

- Problem Recognition and Information Search (Ch. 9)
- Judgment and Decision Making (Chs. 10-11)
- Post-Decision Processes (Ch. 12)

CONSUMER BEHAVIOR OUTCOMES

- Symbolic Consumer Behavior (Ch. 18)
- Adoption of, Resistance to, and Diffusion of Innovations (Ch. 19)

PART SIX

Consumer Welfare

The final section of the text covers two topics related to consumer welfare that researchers have studied with great interest in recent years. Chapter 20 examines how consumer behavior knowledge and research can be used to protect consumers and design public policy programs to improve our quality of life.

Chapter 21 explores the dark side of consumer behavior and marketing. This chapter focuses on some negative outcomes of consumer-related behaviors as well as on marketers' roles in these issues. The chapter also discusses marketing practices that have been the focus of social commentary in recent years.

chapter 20

Consumerism and Public Policy Issues

INTRODUCTION: Battling over Better Pizza

What exactly does the word *better* mean in an advertisement? That was one of the pivotal issues in a complex legal case involving Papa John's International and Pizza Hut, two of the largest pizza chains in the United States (see Exhibit 20.1). Papa John's had been running an advertising campaign based on the slogan, "Better ingredients, better pizza." After a Pizza Hut commercial decried "skimpy, low-quality" pizza and challenged consumers to find a better pizza than its own products, Papa John's aired a commercial in which Pizza Hut's founder—now a Papa John's franchise owner—stated, "I found a better pizza!" Soon Papa John's was running ads contrasting the quality of its dough with that of "the biggest chain" (presumably Pizza Hut).

At this point, Pizza Hut asked the National Advertising Division (NAD) of the Better Business Bureau to order a halt to its competitor's "Better ingredients, better pizza" campaign. Papa John's backed up its claims by analyzing the two chains' ingredients and presenting consumer research, which prompted the NAD to rule in Papa John's favor. Next, Pizza Hut filed a federal lawsuit charging Papa John's with airing false and misleading advertising. After hearing evidence about how the two chains make their pizzas, the jury found in Pizza Hut's favor. Papa John's appealed the decision on the grounds that its slogan was actually *puffery*—subjective and exaggerated, not meant to be taken literally. The appeals court agreed that the Papa John's slogan was puffery but also said that some of its ads were misleading. Still, the appeals court ruled that Pizza Hut had failed to show that Papa John's ads were misleading consumers into changing their purchasing decisions; Papa John's was allowed to keep its slogan. The U.S. Supreme Court refused to hear the case, leaving the appeals court's decisions intact.[1]

EXHIBIT 20.1
Pizza and Puffery
Who has the *best* pizza?

Source: © Corbis

The fight between Papa John's and Pizza Hut illustrates several important points addressed in this chapter. First, companies sometimes use vague words like "better" in their advertising, assuming that consumers will not believe and act on the literal meaning of these terms. In winning this case, Papa John's successfully argued that its "better" slogan was mere puffery. Second, companies have recourse if they believe consumers are being misled by a competitor's claims. Pizza Hut took its case to the NAD, which is an industry self-regulation agency. Later, it filed suit under federal regulations that protect consumers from false and misleading advertising. Ultimately, the appeals court ruled there was not sufficient evidence proving that consumers had actually been misled by Papa John's ads, illustrating that agencies and groups exist to protect consumers.

This chapter examines these and other issues in public policy and consumerism, starting with a definition of consumerism and an overview of the major consumer rights. A brief description of the government agencies, industry regulations, and consumer groups involved in public policy follows. The remainder of the chapter explores specific issues in consumerism, including advertising and selling practices, product safety, and environmental protection. Examining these issues can help marketers better understand the context and processes surrounding how consumers acquire, consume, and dispose of products and services. ●

WHAT IS CONSUMERISM?

consumerism Activities of government, business, independent organizations, and consumers designed to protect the rights of consumers.

Consumerism is "the set of activities of government, business, independent organizations, and concerned consumers that are designed to protect the rights of consumers."[2] Note that the key focus is on consumer rights. In 1962 President John F. Kennedy proposed the Consumer Bill of Rights to guarantee consumers several basic rights fundamental to the effective functioning of our economic system.[3] These are the rights:

- *Right to safety.* Protection from products or services that might be hazardous to health and safety.
- *Right to be informed.* Protection from fraudulent or misleading advertising and other forms of communications and access to the information needed to make an informed decision.
- *Right to choose.* Access to a variety of products and services at competitive prices wherever possible. If choice is restricted, the government will ensure that consumers receive satisfactory quality and fair prices.
- *Right to be heard.* Full and sympathetic consideration of consumer interests in the formation of government policy.

Since 1962, other presidents have added more consumer rights:

- *Right to consumer education.* Access to knowledge about the products or services acquired and consumed.
- *Right to recourse and redress.* Right to a fair settlement of problems encountered.
- *Right to an environment that enhances the quality of life.* Right to live in an environment that is not threatened by pollution and hazardous waste.

Over the years, these basic consumer rights have formed the foundation for many public policy discussions and decisions as well as much consumer behavior research. Researchers have been especially interested in applying consumer behavior principles, theories, and research methods to better understand consumer issues and offer suggestions to improve consumers' lives. In addition, various government, industry, and advocacy groups and agencies can influence marketing practices and the development of regulations to protect consumer rights.

GROUPS INVOLVED WITH PUBLIC POLICY AND CONSUMERISM

Three types of groups play a major role in the formation of public policy decisions to protect the rights and interests of consumers. These include various government agencies, self-regulating industry groups, and consumer groups.

Government Agencies

Many government agencies look after various consumer interests and regulate fair trade. Although the entire list is too lengthy to present here, Exhibit 20.2 shows the main federal agencies that handle U.S. public policy issues affecting

EXHIBIT 20.2
Federal Agencies Concerned with Consumer Rights

Federal Agency	Responsibility
Federal Trade Commission (FTC)	Originally established to curtail unfair trade practices and limit monopolies, the FTC's role has expanded to include investigating advertising claims, selling practices, and price-fixing and issuing penalties for deceptive advertising and other illegal activities.
Food and Drug Administration (FDA)	The FDA protects consumers from drugs, food, cosmetics, and therapeutic devices that may potentially be harmful, and it is concerned with the amount and nature of information provided about these products on the package or in the advertising.
Federal Communications Commission (FCC)	The FCC regulates interstate television, radio, and wire broadcasts as well as advertisements that appear in these media.
Consumer Product Safety Commission (CPSC)	Originally established to investigate product-related accidents and to recall products that are defective, the CPSC also attempts to identify unsafe products and ban products with an unreasonably high level of risk.
Environmental Protection Agency (EPA)	The EPA is responsible for developing and enforcing standards to protect the environment from threats such as pollution, garbage, and hazardous waste.
National Highway Traffic Safety Administration (NHTSA)	The NHTSA regulates the safety of new and used motor vehicles, investigates dangerous vehicle defects, recalls products when necessary, and sets standards for fuel efficiency in new vehicles.

consumer rights. In addition, other federal, state, and local agencies play an important role, depending on the nature of the problem or situation. Many countries maintain government agencies for consumer protection, as discussed later in this chapter.

Whether consumers should protect themselves from products and services or whether the government should intervene on their behalf is the subject of much debate.[4] Some argue that regulation threatens individual freedom of choice; however, government intervention is sometimes necessary because consumers do not or cannot take adequate measures to protect themselves. Consumers may not accurately assess the risk inherent in the situation, either because they lack the necessary information or because such hazards occur infrequently. As one example, the FDA recently ruled that a Celebrex ad had violated federal regulations by suggesting that the drug was more effective in treating arthritis than the clinical evidence demonstrated.[5] In such a situation, consumers would be unlikely to know the details of the clinical evidence or be able to knowledgeably compare the scientific evidence with the ad's claims.

Industry Self-Regulation

Companies are not always "bad guys" who require constant monitoring to ensure that they deal fairly with consumers. For both ethical and business-related reasons, it is in companies' best interests to be concerned about consumer welfare because it is so closely tied to consumer satisfaction. As a result, numerous industries have set up mechanisms to regulate business activity themselves and to correct problems when necessary. One benefit of self-regulation is that it removes the government from an antagonistic role and reduces its caseload. Concerned about government regulations, for example, which are typically more stringent than voluntary ones, ad agencies have considered setting their own limits on alcohol and tobacco advertising.[6]

NAD/NARB system A system set up by the National Advertising Division to self-regulate advertising messages.

Another excellent example of self-regulation is the **NAD/NARB system**, which the ad industry set up to monitor advertising messages.[7] The National Advertising Division (NAD) monitors ad claims and investigates complaints from consumers, competitors, or local Better Business Bureaus. Within the NAD is the Children's Advertising Review Unit, which monitors ads targeting children.[8] When an ad or infomercial claim is found questionable, the NAD asks advertisers to substantiate it. If the claim cannot be substantiated, the NAD asks the advertiser to alter the message. For example, American Express complained to the NAD that Visa's advertising tag line, "The preferred lodging card," was false and misleading. The NAD said the tagline did not constitute puffery and must be substantiated. Advertisers can appeal NAD decisions to the National Advertising Review Board (NARB), which Visa did. In this case, the NARB backed the NAD's judgment and told Visa to stop using the tag line.[9] In a change from previous procedures, when the NAD/NARB considers a case, the advertisers must now agree that the system's decision is final, ruling out the kind of legal actions described in the opening example about Papa John's and Pizza Hut.[10]

The movie industry and the TV networks often develop their own standards about airing advertising. Under pressure from the FTC and Congress, the film studios are not airing TV commercials for R-rated movies during programs that attract many viewers below 18 years old.[11] For years, the major television networks voluntarily refrained from accepting hard liquor ads. Not long ago, NBC experimented with airing liquor ads but quickly stopped when some federal legislators and consumer advocacy groups raised objections.[12] ABC has content standards covering controversial areas such as ads making medical

EXHIBIT 20.3
Supporting Consumerism

Source: © AP/Wide World Photos.

claims and children's ads.[13] One rule allows doctors to appear in ads, which was previously not permitted, as long as their claims can be substantiated. All four networks also rejected an animal rights campaign promoting vegetarianism because it was considered too controversial.[14]

Finally, companies have the option of taking competitors to court over practices they believe are illegal or unfair, as in the opening example. This can be extremely costly for both sides—Papa John's spent more than $7 million defending its position—but it also allows a company to seek restitution if it has been harmed by a competitor's practices.

Consumer Groups

In addition to government and industry agencies, more than 100 national organizations and 600 local groups look out for various consumer interests. The most well-known groups include Ralph Nader's Public Citizen, National Consumer's League, Consumers Union, Consumer Federation of America, Better Business Bureaus, National Wildlife Federation, and Environmental Defense Fund (see Exhibit 20.3). These groups lobby various government agencies to influence the enactment of legislation and assist consumers in dealing with companies.

Groups like the Politically Correct Squad monitor the media for offensive communications; this organization has attacked Coca-Cola for using reverse sexism in an ad that shows women ogling construction workers.[15] Animal rights groups have put pressure on the National Cattlemen's Beef Association by calling attention to poor treatment of calves and by calling for a veal boycott.[16] EthicAd works with consumer advocates and drug manufacturers to draft voluntary standards for consumer advertising of drugs.[17] And various local consumer groups and media organizations help protect consumer rights through hotlines and investigative reporting.

HOW MARKETING PRACTICES VIOLATE CONSUMER RIGHTS

Regulators have long been interested in the types of information provided in marketing communications and the extent to which they violate consumer rights. This section discusses four areas of concern: (1) deceptive advertising and labeling, (2) deceptive selling practices, (3) advertising to children, and (4) privacy on the Internet.

Deceptive Advertising and Labeling

deception Marketing communications that leave consumers with information or beliefs that are incorrect or cannot be substantiated.

Sometimes marketing communications can leave consumers with information or beliefs that are incorrect or cannot be substantiated, resulting in **deception**. For example, Microsoft had to change its ads for handheld computer software because they were found to focus on features available only on higher-priced wireless models.[18] As defined by the FDA, a *deceptive ad* is one that "either through (1) its verbal content, (2) its design, structure, and/or visual artwork, or (3) the context in which it appears causes at least *n* percent of a representative group of consumers to have a common incorrect impression or belief."[19] (The *n* percent—a percentage of affected consumers, as determined by the federal agency—varies and is determined by the nature of the situation and how severe the consequences of the incorrect belief are.) According to the FTC, deception involves (1) a misrepresentation, omission, or practice that is likely to mislead the consumer, (2) consumers acting as they normally would in relation to a product or service or in a consumption situation, and (3) a material misrepresentation (one that will affect their choice).[20]

Just because consumers hold an incorrect belief, however, does not necessarily mean that deception is present. Remember from Chapter 5 that consumers can simply misunderstand the message.[21] In other words, because mass media is imperfect, every communication is naturally associated with some degree of miscomprehension. However, when a large proportion of consumers hold the same incorrect belief that can be traced to a specific message, then deception is considered to be a problem. According to the FTC, deception occurs when approximately 20 to 25 percent of consumers have an incorrect belief (this percentage may be lower for products or services that affect consumer safety).[22]

The severity of deception is determined by factors such as whether the claim influences behavior, what potentially harmful effects it has on consumers, and the extent to which it creates an unfair advantage in the marketplace.[23] The FTC usually takes action only when the deception causes injury to consumers or unfair losses to competitors. For instance, the agency required iMall and the Home Shopping Network to pay fines of $750,000 and $1.1 million, respectively, for making deceptive claims in Internet ads.[24] However, some consumers, such as children or the elderly, may be more susceptible to deception than other groups and may need more protection.[25]

Types of Deception Deception can occur in a variety of ways.[26] The most obvious type is a company's **false objective claim** about a product or service. For years Listerine claimed to be the mouthwash that "kills germs that cause colds." After research evidence demonstrated that this claim was not valid, the FTC found Listerine guilty of deceptive advertising. Some retailers use "exaggerated reference prices" in ads to make consumers believe that a sale price is a really good deal.[27] The FTC cited Gerber for ads claiming that four out of five pediatricians recommend Gerber baby food when only 12 percent surveyed did so.[28]

false objective claim An invalid claim made by a company.

As discussed in Chapter 5, the name of the product or service or the label can sometimes be misleading.[29] For example, the winemaker Canandaigua Brands was required to alter the labeling of its white zinfandel and chardonnay wines and to use the phrase *with natural flavors* because these brands add fruit flavors that do not conform to zealously guarded pedigrees.[30] Ragu Foods was required to remove the word *fresh* from its spaghetti sauce label because the product is not really "fresh."[31] Various regional marketing groups have been actively monitoring produce labels that misrepresent the origin of a fruit or vegetable.[32]

Puffery As discussed in the opening example, some false or unsubstantiated claims fall outside the realm of regulation. For example, companies may engage in **puffery**, a form of advertising that uses evaluative or subjective terms such as *best, excellent,* or *great* (see Exhibit 20.4). These exaggerated claims cannot be proven, and most consumers do not believe them.[33] However, if "puff" claims are believed and have a significant effect on behavior, then some type of corrective action may be necessary.[34]

puffery Companies' exaggerated claims that are not generally believed by consumers.

Missing Information Consumers can also be deceived by what is *not* said in an ad. Even when everything stated in the ad is true, consumers can be left with a false impression because *information has been left out* or qualifications have

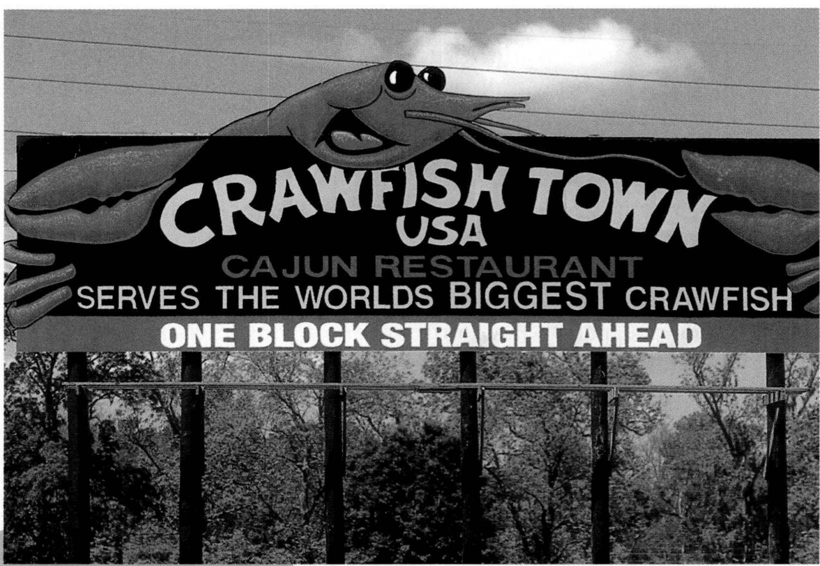

EXHIBIT 20.4
Example of Puffery
Advertisers often use terms like "world's biggest" and "greatest" even though these may be tough to prove.

Source: Eastcott/Momatiuk/The Image Works.

been presented in an inconspicuous place where consumers may not see them.[35] This type of deception is most likely to occur when a consumer's motivation, ability, or opportunity (MAO) to process are low.[36] For example, regulatory agencies have scrutinized weight-loss ads because some lack information about how many consumers lose weight and fail to mention that weight loss may be temporary.[37] As another example, the FTC has said ads from Hewlett-Packard and Microsoft misled consumers into believing that they could access e-mail and the Internet at any time using the Jornada handheld computer. In fact, fine print at the bottom of the ads indicated the need for an optional $350 wireless modem and a phone connection.[38]

Allowing Incorrect Inferences to Be Made Finally, an ad can be deceptive simply because of the way it *interacts with consumers' beliefs*. Even when everything in the ad is accurate, it can still be deceptive because consumers develop an incorrect inference from it. This situation often occurs when consumers infer unrealistically high levels of attribute performance.[39] For example, the FDA required Clorox to change the name of Hidden Valley Ranch Take Heart Dressing to Low Fat Dressing to remove the false impression that the product would contribute to a healthy heart.[40] In the tobacco industry, advertising for low-tar, low-nicotine, and additive-free cigarettes has been attacked because consumers mistakenly believe these cigarettes are healthier for them.[41] In addition, health claims made by a particular food brand can incorrectly cause consumers to believe that all brands in the same category possess the same benefit; however, this can be corrected by printing nutrition information on the package.[42] Research on nutrition information found that consumers tend to draw misleading generalizations or inferences from one claim about an attribute to other, unmentioned attributes. Shoppers might, for instance, think a product advertised as low fat is also low in cholesterol.[43]

The key point is that what the ad actually says does not determine whether or not it is deceptive. What matters is what the consumer *believes* as a result of the ad. Therefore, consumer research studies that assess customers' reactions to advertising messages play a key role in assessing deceptive advertising.[44]

Regulation of Deceptive Advertising The FTC and FDA are the major agencies that regulate deceptive advertising. When companies, consumers, or other organizations complain about an advertising message and the case is severe enough to warrant attention, these agencies will investigate. If the agencies find evidence of potential deception, they will require the offending company to engage in **substantiation** to prove the questionable claims. For example, Wal-Mart and Winn-Dixie were forced to stop claiming that they had the lowest prices and to instead advertise "Everyday Low Prices." Neither chain was able

substantiation Having to prove questionable claims.

to prove that it always had the lowest prices on every product.[45] The Home Shopping Network was asked to substantiate claims about the effectiveness of three vitamin sprays and an aerosol to help quit smoking.[46] The FDA has become more active in seeking substantiation for nutritional claims made by food products, as well as health claims made by certain dietary supplements (that they prevent cancer, thwart hair loss, and so on).[47]

cease-and-desist order An order whereby a company must immediately discontinue all advertising that contains an offending claim.

affirmative disclosure Messages that must be altered to provide correct information.

The FTC and FDA have several options if advertising claims cannot be substantiated. The most common one is to issue a **cease-and-desist order** forcing the company to immediately discontinue all advertising with the offending claim. The makers of heartburn medicines Pepsid AC and Tagamet HB were ordered to withdraw advertising that contained unsubstantiated or misleading claims.[48] Depending on the severity of the problem, the FTC can impose fines or punitive damages. In other cases, it may order **affirmative disclosure**, altering ad claims to provide correct information. For example, the FTC now wants all weight-loss products to provide information about the chances of weight-loss success and to state that this loss may be only temporary.[49] A federal court required *Polo* magazine to publish a disclaimer saying that it has no association with the fashion design house Polo Ralph Lauren.[50] Unfortunately, affirmative disclosure statements can sometimes contribute to uncertainty, be misunderstood, or be misleading.[51] Research shows that these disclosures are likely to effectively correct invalid inferences only when consumers' MAO to process the information are high.[52]

corrective advertising The formal statement a company must make to correct false beliefs.

The agencies may require **corrective advertising** when the infraction is considered very severe and merely ceasing the misleading ad will not dissipate consumer beliefs. (This may occur when an ad has been shown so often that the incorrect belief will persist for a long period.) In these cases, the company must make a formal statement to correct the false consumer belief. For example, Listerine was required to spend more than $10 million over two years on corrective ads to dispel the belief that Listerine prevents colds.[53] One TV ad stated, "While Listerine will not help prevent colds or sore throats or lessen their severity, breath tests prove Listerine fights onion breath better than Scope." Research has generally supported the effectiveness of corrective ads in eradicating false beliefs.[54] However, one study found that *brand* evaluations were likely to be lower after exposure to corrective ads only when prior brand evaluations were negative.[55] Nevertheless, corrective ads did lead to lower evaluations of the *advertiser* when prior attitudes were positive.

Finally, other agencies and groups can also regulate deceptive advertising. As one example, the FCC is quite responsive to consumer complaints about broadcast ads. Various state and local organizations are responsible for monitoring marketing messages that are not national in scope, and the NAD/NARB system provides for industry self-regulation of ad claims.

Deceptive Selling Tactics

Deceptive practices can occur in the context of personal selling. Millions of sales transactions are completed every year through personal selling, telemarketing, and similar sales methods. This volume is bound to lead to instances in which consumers are not treated fairly, which is why regulation has been enacted to protect the interests of consumers. Most companies attempt to prevent abuses because it is in their best interest to please consumers. Nevertheless, some problematic practices have required regulatory attention, including (1) the bait-and-switch technique, (2) misrepresentation of the selling intent, and (3) incorrect statements or promises.

bait-and-switch A technique whereby consumers are attracted by a low price and then enticed to trade up to a more expensive item.

The Bait-and-Switch Technique In the **bait-and-switch** technique, a retailer draws a customer into the store by advertising a product or service at a very attractive low price. The retailer then tries to get the consumer to trade up to a higher priced item by not stocking the advertised item or by making it so unattractive upon close inspection that the consumer will not want it. Encouraging consumers to trade up to another model is not illegal in itself—it can be an honest attempt to better fulfill the consumer's needs. However, it is illegal when the intent is to deceive the consumer.

As an example, the Pennsylvania Bureau of Consumer Protection accused Craftmatic-Contour Industries, Inc., which sells motorized adjustable beds, of using bait-and-switch tactics.[56] Consumers were attracted by beds priced at $400, but salespeople pressured them to buy a bed in the $2,000 to $6,000 range. Although the company vigorously claimed that it was merely "up selling" and not using bait-and-switch tactics, it paid a restitution fine of $300,000. In an investigation of the mail-order camcorder industry, 23 of 32 vendors misrepresented themselves as dealers of a particular brand, and four tried to bait and switch.[57]

When the FTC determines that infractions have occurred, it can impose fines and require corrective advertising. Three carpet retailers in the Washington, D.C. area, for example, were ordered to include the following statement in a conspicuous place in their advertising and to surround the statement with a black border:

> The Federal Trade Commission has found that we engage in bait-and-switch advertising; that is, the salesman makes it difficult to buy the advertised product and he attempts to switch you to a higher priced item.[58]

Misrepresenting the Selling Intent Consumers are often concerned that if they interact with salespeople, they will feel pressured into buying something they may not want. Salespeople realize this and sometimes devise strategies to "trick" consumers into entering a conversation. For example, salespeople might ask consumers to answer a questionnaire or say that consumers have just won a valuable prize. Using these techniques to get a "foot in the door," the salesperson then attempts to sell a product or service. Poor and elderly consumers are often victims of this type of fraud.

postcard scheme A deceptive practice in which a consumer receives a postcard that claims he or she has won a valuable prize but is really a front for intensive selling pressure.

A common example is the **postcard scheme** in which consumers receive a postcard promising cash prizes, free vacations, or expensive cars, usually with the announcement: "Congratulations, you are a guaranteed winner!"[59] When consumers contact the company, they are subjected to an intense selling effort and pressured to buy worthless or unneeded items. In particular, certain land development projects have engaged in this type of activity. Consumers are encouraged to report such misrepresentations through the National Consumer League's toll-free hot line and other avenues. Interestingly, in a study on the ethics of certain sales practices, misrepresentation was one of the most negatively viewed practices.[60]

Incorrect Statements or Promises Another way in which salespeople create legal problems for their company is to make statements, intentionally or not, that cannot be backed up or substantiated. Problem statements can (1) create unintended warranties, (2) dilute the effectiveness of safety warnings, (3) disparage competitive offerings, (4) misrepresent one's own offerings, and (5) interfere with business relationships.[61] Sales managers must therefore carefully educate salespeople about what they can and cannot say and do. In addition, companies that promote "pyramid selling" schemes, such as Amway and Mary Kay, have been under attack because some salespeople are recruited with promises of big money that is unlikely to materialize.[62]

Some selling practices are outright deceptive or fraudulent, and elderly consumers are often victimized by them.[63] For example, unscrupulous telemarketers tell elderly consumers they will win a million dollars if they send a check for a certain amount. In another scheme, salespeople claim to be bank employees and ask for the consumer's account number.[64] One consumer received more than 6,000 calls and pieces of mail for such scams. This situation has led organizations such as the AARP to develop educational programs to help consumers avoid falling victim to fraudulent selling practices.[65]

Despite the potential for abuse and the need for consumer protection, government agencies have often had difficulty regulating personal selling. This is because (1) many sales interactions are verbal and entail little or no written evidence, (2) the abuses usually occur at a local and individual level, making detection more difficult, and (3) it is hard to monitor compliance with the law. Thus protecting consumers from these selling activities is more difficult than protecting them from deceptive advertising.

Advertising to Children

Advertising to children has been the subject of considerable controversy and debate focusing on the effect these ads may have on young, impressionable consumers. The average child spends more than 3 hours a day watching television and is exposed to more than 30,000 ads a year.[66] Networks cluster children's programming in certain time periods, making it easy for marketers to target children and spend heavily to promote toys and other products for this segment.[67] However, advertising to children raises a variety of troubling consumer issues.

Issues Related to Children as Consumers One basic problem is that young children, particularly those under 7 years of age, have not yet developed the cognitive abilities to distinguish between the ad and the program.[68] Even at an age when children can recognize this difference, they still may not understand that the purpose of the ad is to sell them something.[69] Thus young children do not possess the same skepticism as adults and are more likely to believe what they see in ads. Note, however, that children are better at understanding the informational intent ("ads tell you about things") than the persuasive intent.[70]

Another problem is that children can experience difficulties in storing information in long-term memory and retrieving it to use in evaluating ads.[71] Furthermore, ad messages may prey on children's strong needs for sensual satisfaction, play, and affiliation, influencing them to choose material objects over socially oriented options.[72] Critics argue that ads teach children to become materialistic, be impulsive, and seek immediate gratification.

Unfortunately, many parents do not watch television with their children and do not educate or teach them about advertising.[73] As a result, children may be particularly impressionable and subject to having their attitudes and behavior influenced by ads.[74] For example, some younger children believe that little people inside the television set are speaking directly to them. One study found that children who viewed products advertised in school on Channel One liked these products better and had stronger consumption values than those who were not exposed to those ads.[75] Exposure to ads often prompts children to step up requests to parents about buying products, particularly toys, leading to family conflict and disappointed children.[76] Because they do not understand the costs involved, children have been especially vulnerable to ads encouraging them to call 900 numbers for products or services.[77] In fact, mothers say they have more negative perceptions of this practice than of any other activity directed toward children.[78] Children are also exposed to numerous ads for products that shape, often negatively, their impressions of what it means to be an adult.[79]

Over the years, Consumers Union has cited some companies for directing unfair advertising toward children. The consumer group disapproved of Nike and Reebok using emotional appeals and celebrities, and said that some ad messages from Hershey, Colgate-Palmolive, and Procter & Gamble resembled editorial matter.[80]

host selling A technique whereby ads feature a character from a TV show.

When a character in a TV program is also featured in ad messages—a technique called **host selling**—children may easily confuse the program with advertising. For example, PBS came under fire for featuring the popular children's character Barney in pledge drives during children's programming. This led many children to ask their parents to "send money to Barney."[81] The NAD has recommended that no program characters appear in ads within the program or even in adjacent programs, and the FCC now prohibits TV stations from using host selling on children's programs.

Another controversy centers on the types of products advertised. Many ads directed at children promote foods that contain a lot of sugar, such as candy and sugar-coated cereals; critics say these ads encourage bad eating habits. For example, children who watch candy or sugar-coated cereal ads are more likely to ask for these products than to ask for fruit as a snack.[82] Furthermore, children who have been exposed to these ads tend to consume more sugared products and be less well educated about nutrition.

Children's use of the Internet is also a focus for consumer advocates and regulators. Nearly all Web sites targeting children feature some form of advertising.[83] Although parents can use software to block access to some sites, children may not understand the need to avoid giving out personal data and e-mail addresses on the Internet. Internet access thus raises concerns about family privacy as well as about children's ability to differentiate between advertising and nonadvertising material on the Web.

Some Possible Solutions In light of the many issues related to ads targeting children, both the FTC and the FCC have recommended that television stations use a separator between the program and the ad whenever the program is directed toward younger children, particularly on Saturday morning. They recommend including a message in both the video and audio portion of the broadcast prior to and directly after the ads such as "We will return after these messages" before the commercial break, followed by "We now return to [name of the program]" at the end of the break.[84] Such separators have been successful in helping children to distinguish between ads and programming.[85] The FCC has also ruled that TV stations and cable operators must keep records of their commitment to provide three hours of educational children's programming per week and limit children's advertising to a total of 12 minutes per hour on weekdays and 10.5 minutes per hour on weekends.[86]

In response to the problem of advertising sugary foods to children, the FTC has encouraged the use of public service announcements (PSAs) to teach children proper nutritional habits. Unfortunately, this program has had limited success because the PSAs tend to be shown infrequently and simply providing children with basic nutritional information is not sufficient to instill good eating habits. In addition, entertaining or emotional appeals tend to be more effective in reaching the stated goals.[87] Other programs have attempted to educate children about nutrition in schools, hoping that the children will influence their parents to be more conscious of nutrition. Companies such as Red Lobster are providing schools with informational packages about nutrition (in this case, the nutrition of seafood).

The advertising industry has also developed guidelines for children's advertising that are enforced by the Children's Advertising Review Unit (CARU), a wing of the Council of Better Business Bureaus.[88] These guidelines encourage truthful and accurate advertising that recognizes children's cognitive limitations and does not create unrealistic expectations about what products can do. For example, advertisers are expected to accurately portray a product's size, durability, and benefits, and clearly indicate what comes with the product.[89] A recent study found that most advertisers are following these guidelines. However, violations were more likely to occur on cable TV than on network TV, involve the fast-food industry more than other industries, and relate to the amount of time a prize or premium was highlighted.

Educational initiatives by consumer groups and industry organizations are teaching children about the role of advertising.[90] Overall, however, the issue of advertising to children has not been totally resolved; some critics even suggest banning all advertising directed toward children. This position is obviously very controversial and would be strongly opposed by many companies. Supporters of children's advertising maintain that ads deliver useful information to children; teach positive values such as achievement, success, individualism, and fairness; and provide entertainment.[91] Some supporters also believe that very young children are not old enough to buy or significantly influence buying decisions.

Privacy on the Internet

Whereas the issues of deceptive advertising and labeling, deceptive selling practices, and advertising to children relate to protecting consumers from incoming information, privacy on the Internet relates to the flow of personal information from the consumer to outside parties. Privacy is not a new consumer issue, but it has received much more attention recently because the Internet offers the opportunity to collect a lot of detailed information about consumers.[92] Key issues of concern are how much and which information marketers should be allowed to collect, how much of this information should be made public, how it should be used in marketing, whether consumers consent to the collection and use of information, and how consumers can control the flow and use of information.[93] One researcher observes that consumers wind up bearing some of the costs for dealing with unwanted marketing communications—both traditional and online messages—and maintaining control of personal information.[94] The extent of consumer concern and willingness to give personal information varies according to the type of information the online marketer wants to collect.[95] Another study suggests that a company can enhance privacy by providing consumers with more control and information about the benefits they may gain (such as customized offers of products or services) when they allow personal information to be collected.[96]

Online companies are involved in a number of self-regulation strategies to protect consumer privacy. Most Web sites post privacy statements to explain what consumer data they gather, what they do with it, how consumers can review it,

EXHIBIT 20.5
Privacy on the Internet

Source: From Eve M. Caudill and Patrick E. Murphy, "Consumer Online Privacy: Legal and Ethical Issues," Journal of Public Policy and Marketing, Vol. 19, No. 1, Spring 2000, pp. 7–19. Used by permission of The American Marketing Association.

	Goals	Limitations
TRUSTe	Provides guarantee of privacy protection: • Gives a seal of trust to Web sites that submit to application process • Acts as a clearinghouse for privacy violation reports • Provides a children's privacy seal program	• Limited industry compliance • Critics suggest that guidelines go further in protecting privacy
BBBOnline	Provides seal of approval to Web sites that adequately perform through a self-assessment and pay a fee	• Voluntary nature of member company compliance • Enforcement
Alliance for Privacy	Publishes guidelines for member companies to follow in the collection and dissemination of information	• Voluntary nature of member company compliance • Enforcement

and how it is protected. Unfortunately, a survey shows that many of these statements do not provide sufficiently complete explanations.[97] Moreover, a study of privacy- and security-related statements indicates that many commercial Web sites do not post their policies regarding unsolicited consumer contacts, sharing of information with other firms, and allowing consumers to opt out of information sharing.[98] Some organizations grant seals of approval to show consumers that certain Web sites adhere to specific privacy protection guidelines (see Exhibit 20.5).

Government regulators are monitoring privacy issues and taking action to protect certain consumer groups, such as children and seniors. In one case, the FTC found that Liberty Financial Company failed to protect the anonymity of children who participated in its Kids' Website survey.[99] The Children's Online Privacy Protection Act addresses privacy issues related to children's use of the Internet, defining what is acceptable and unacceptable behavior for Internet advertisers.[100] Also, knowing that seniors are more vulnerable to being victimized by Internet-based scams, the FBI's Financial Crimes Squad spends a significant amount of time focusing on this group.[101]

Consumers are increasingly worried about "identity theft," or the stealing of personal information over the Internet.[102] Many consumers fear their credit card numbers will be intercepted by a third party if submitted through the Internet. Thus manufacturers and technology firms are working hard to increase online security.[103] Congress has passed legislation making Internet identity fraud a crime, and the FBI's Internet Fraud Complaint Center invites consumer complaints about this and other online crimes.[104] As the Internet evolves, regulators, marketers, and researchers will closely follow consumer attitudes and behavior to uncover important concerns and provide protection against privacy violations and other problems.

PRODUCT INFORMATION AND SAFETY ISSUES

Government agencies and consumer groups go beyond protecting consumers from unfair practices. They also provide information to help consumers make better decisions and use products and services safely.

Consumer Protection through Information

The purpose of providing consumers with more and better product information is to help them make more informed decisions. For example, the FDA has paid a great deal of attention to the types of nutrition information provided on food labels, in the hope that consumers will purchase and consume these products in a more nutritionally sound manner.[105] As part of this effort, fast-food restaurants are now required to disclose nutrition information about their menu items, with the result that a number of fast-food chains have improved the nutritional content of their offerings. Other types of restaurants may have to provide this type of information in the future, especially to substantiate low-fat or low-salt claims.

Although efforts to inform consumers are instituted with good intentions, a number of problems have arisen, in part because regulators have not based their proposals on a solid understanding of consumer information processing and decision making. Four areas are particularly important for protecting consumers through information: (1) consumer comprehension of information, (2) consumer use of the information, (3) the amount of information provided, and (4) the format of the information.

Can Consumers Comprehend the Information? Unfortunately, the general assumption that consumers can understand and correctly use detailed information when provided is not always valid. A summary of six studies concluded that the vast majority of consumers do not understand basic nutrition information, including common terms such as *calories, fat, carbohydrates,* and *protein.*[106] Also, older consumers (those over 60) are less accurate in their use of nutrition information than younger consumers.[107] Another study found that a large percentage of consumers do not understand the relationship between the contract interest rate and the annual percentage rate when acquiring a loan.[108]

Thus regulators can expect an information program to help consumers make better decisions only when they are certain that consumers can understand the information they are given. One approach is to use educational pamphlets or informal classes to offer instruction on specific topics. However, these programs have generally been difficult to implement because of a lack of consumer interest, suggesting a low MAO level. Some regulators have developed simpler formats that make it easier for consumers to understand the information, as discussed later in the chapter.

Will Consumers Use the Information? A second assumption of consumer information programs is that consumers will actually *use* this information. One study found that fewer than 5 percent of consumers examined nutrition information when selecting breakfast cereals.[109] Other research showed that most consumers look at the front of the package only, especially when health claims are made.[110] Also, after an initial flare-up of public interest, fast-food fare is again becoming fattier because people have a craving for fatty foods and are not motivated to read nutrition information.[111] On the other hand, when the claims made on a food package are inconsistent with the details in the federally required Nutrition Facts panel, consumers are capable of evaluating the panel data and will question the claims rather than the panel data.[112]

These findings have led some to question the validity and usefulness of consumer information programs. Others maintain, however, that even if only 5 percent of consumers use the information, it is still benefiting at least some segment of the population, and one that highly desires it. In support of this view, one study found that consumers who perceive that nutritional information can aid in preventing disease are more likely to read this information on the package.[113] Furthermore, some argue that even though consumers do not pay attention to this information when making a decision, they still might read it while the product is being consumed, such as at the breakfast table.

Can Consumers Be Given Too Much Information? Another subject of controversy is how much information to provide consumers. Chapter 9 mentioned that providing consumers with too much information can result in information overload, consumer confusion, and poorer decisions.[114] Some argue that consumers seldom acquire enough information to become confused—they will stop searching before they reach overload. Regardless, the key point is that more is not always necessarily better. Thus regulators should provide consumers with the most *useful* and *important* information, rather than offering all the details that are available. The value of limited information is a key argument in the fight to shorten the lengthy disclosures required in direct-to-consumer pharmaceutical ads, where a short summary table might be easier to understand.[115]

Can Information Be Made Easier to Use? In light of the three concerns discussed above, regulators have been vitally interested in developing formats that make information easier to understand and use. According to research, formats that make it easier to process information, highlight information so it stands out, or provide a benchmark that allows easy comparisons are more likely to affect consumers' decisions.[116] The Nutrition Facts labeling format was enacted to permit easy comparisons of the nutritional content for different food items and force manufacturers to follow stricter rules in labeling contents, thereby preventing deceptive claims (see Exhibit 20.6).[117] In support, one study found that the new label resulted in slightly more favorable attitudes and perceptions toward nutrition and an increase in the likelihood that consumers would buy a nutritious product.[118] Another study found that the new label improved comprehension of nutrition information but had less impact on the purchase of healthier foods.[119]

Studies indicate that consumers at all education levels can understand nutrition information presented in this format and, as mentioned above, can evaluate the data even in the presence of a conflicting health claim on the package.[120] Further, consumers are more likely to rely on information from the nutrition panel than to rely on claims made on the package, especially when the motivation to process is higher.[121] Some have suggested using verbal (instead of numerical) descriptors to further improve performance. However, when numerical descriptors are used, percentages of nutrient amounts appear to be the most effective.[122] Finally, one study found that using "average brand" values is more effective than using "daily values" as a reference point.[123]

Another example of making information easier for consumers to use is the U.S. government's efforts to standardize the energy-use information provided on various appliances. The goal is to help consumers conserve energy and save money by having the information to compare appliances and choose those that are more energy efficient. The program has had a positive effect on consumer decisions.[124] Changes are also coming in the area of over-the-counter drugs and prescriptions, where the FDA is proposing labeling changes

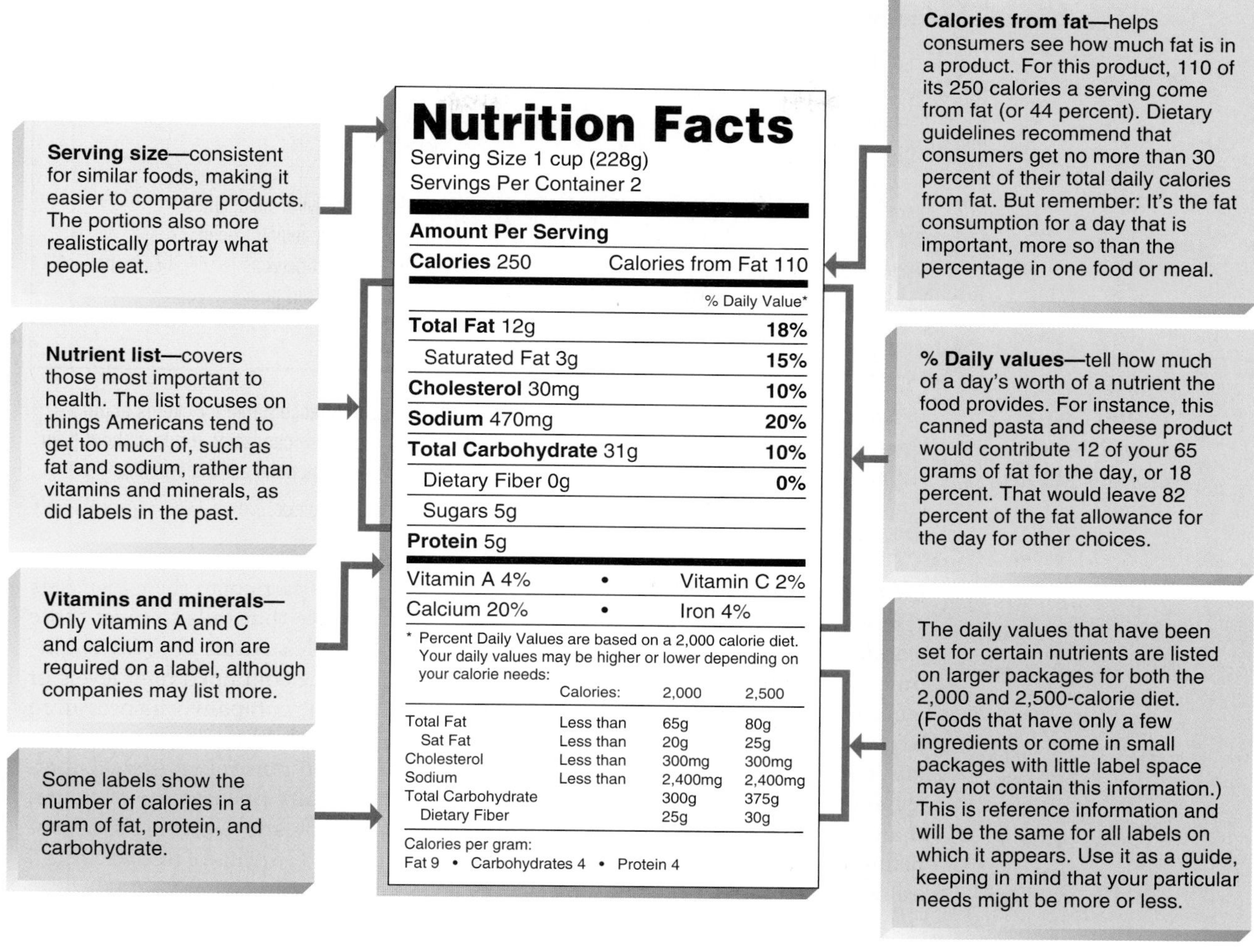

Serving size—consistent for similar foods, making it easier to compare products. The portions also more realistically portray what people eat.
Nutrient list—covers those most important to health. The list focuses on things Americans tend to get too much of, such as fat and sodium, rather than vitamins and minerals, as did labels in the past.
Vitamins and minerals—Only vitamins A and C and calcium and iron are required on a label, although companies may list more.
Some labels show the number of calories in a gram of fat, protein, and carbohydrate.
Nutrition Facts
Serving Size 1 cup (228g)
Servings Per Container 2
Amount Per Serving
Calories 250 Calories from Fat 110
% Daily Value*
Total Fat 12g 18%
Saturated Fat 3g 15%
Cholesterol 30mg 10%
Sodium 470mg 20%
Total Carbohydrate 31g 10%
Dietary Fiber 0g 0%
Sugars 5g
Protein 5g
Vitamin A 4% • Vitamin C 2%
Calcium 20% • Iron 4%
* Percent Daily Values are based on a 2,000 calorie diet. Your daily values may be higher or lower depending on your calorie needs:
Calories: 2,000 2,500
Total Fat Less than 65g 80g
Sat Fat Less than 20g 25g
Cholesterol Less than 300mg 300mg
Sodium Less than 2,400mg 2,400mg
Total Carbohydrate 300g 375g
Dietary Fiber 25g 30g
Calories per gram:
Fat 9 • Carbohydrates 4 • Protein 4
Calories from fat—helps consumers see how much fat is in a product. For this product, 110 of its 250 calories a serving come from fat (or 44 percent). Dietary guidelines recommend that consumers get no more than 30 percent of their total daily calories from fat. But remember: It's the fat consumption for a day that is important, more so than the percentage in one food or meal.
% Daily values—tell how much of a day's worth of a nutrient the food provides. For instance, this canned pasta and cheese product would contribute 12 of your 65 grams of fat for the day, or 18 percent. That would leave 82 percent of the fat allowance for the day for other choices.
The daily values that have been set for certain nutrients are listed on larger packages for both the 2,000 and 2,500-calorie diet. (Foods that have only a few ingredients or come in small packages with little label space may not contain this information.) This is reference information and will be the same for all labels on which it appears. Use it as a guide, keeping in mind that your particular needs might be more or less.

EXHIBIT 20.6 Nutrition Facts Label

The Nutrition Labeling and Education Act of 1990 mandated this format for food labeling. Do you think consumers find this format easy to understand?

Source: Food and Drug Administration, as cited in "New Labels Give Consumers Breakdown in Nutrition," *Austin American Statesman,* May 7, 1994, p. A13.

to better inform consumers and medical personnel about the usage, benefits, and risks of these products.[125] Finally, to prevent companies from exaggerating claims about a dietary supplement's disease-fighting capabilities, the FDA has established specific guidelines for the wording that can be used in making claims (see Exhibit 20.7)

Consumer Protection through Product Safety

Each year consumers suffer a great number of injuries, usually between 15 and 20 million, from product-related accidents. Consumers have the right to be protected from offerings that may be hazardous to their health or safety. A product or service can be potentially harmful to consumers if a problem exists with its quality or features, if it is used by consumers in an unsafe manner, or both.[126]

Acceptable Wording about Structure or Function	Unacceptable Wording about Disease Claims
Maintains healthy lung function	Maintains healthy lungs in smokers
Arouses or increases sexual desire and improves sexual performance	Helps restore sexual vigor, potency, and performance
Helps to maintain cholesterol levels that are already within the normal range	Lowers cholesterol
Supports the immune system	Supports the body's antiviral capabilities
For the relief of occasional sleeplessness	Helps to reduce difficulty falling asleep
'Resolving that irritability that ruins your day'	A reference to helping 'a nervous tension headache'
Helps support cartilage and joint function	A reference to helping 'joint pain'

EXHIBIT 20.7
Acceptable and Unacceptable Claims

This table shows wording that the FDA has deemed acceptable and unacceptable for claims about dietary supplements. In general, claims that a product will cure a disease cannot be made without prior FDA approval, whereas claims about supporting or maintaining body functions are acceptable.

Source: Chris Adams, "Splitting Hairs on Supplement Claims," *Wall Street Journal*, February 22, 2000, p. B1. Reprinted by permission of *The Wall Street Journal* via The Copyright Clearance Center.

Product/Service Problems The government, and in particular, the CPSC, sets safety standards for each industry. A product or service that fails to meet these standards can be recalled or altered. Procter & Gamble's Adult NyQuil Nighttime and Adult Formula 44M brands, for example, once contained high levels of alcohol (25 percent and 24 percent, respectively), and the company was pressured to reduce these levels.[127] The CPSC has also developed child-resistant packaging guidelines for drugs to protect children from accidental poisoning—a real challenge because older adults sometimes have more difficulty opening the packages than children do.[128] Other government agencies actively address consumer problems with products and services. Not long ago, the NHTSA had Firestone recall millions of tires after reports of accidents due to tread separation.[129]

Products for children raise perennial safety issues. Every year World against Toys Causing Harm releases a list of the ten most unsafe toys.[130] Note, however, that some companies have actively disputed the claims made by activists. Even auto airbags, which can save adult lives, have been seriously questioned for their potential to harm children.[131] The NHTSA also discovered that 50 percent of the time that children are in car seats, they are not buckled in safely. This discovery led to new safety rules for car seats.[132]

Seat belts are another focus of government regulation and education efforts. U.S. government efforts to regulate this problem began with requiring seat belts to be installed in all vehicles, followed by public service announcements that educated consumers about the importance of usage. Some of the early campaigns utilized fear appeals, depicting the negative and often grisly consequences of not wearing seat belts. Even though many states also passed seat belt laws, compliance was dramatically lower than desired. A major part of the problem was that consumers simply were not in the habit of wearing the belts and often forgot, even though they would agree that buckling up could save their lives.[133]

Thus, successful driver education programs must not only change consumer attitudes but also give drivers experience to instill the habit of using a seat belt.[134] The NHTSA has sponsored public service announcements featuring a couple dressed for the prom with the slogan "Secure Your Date." (See Exhibit 20.8).[135]

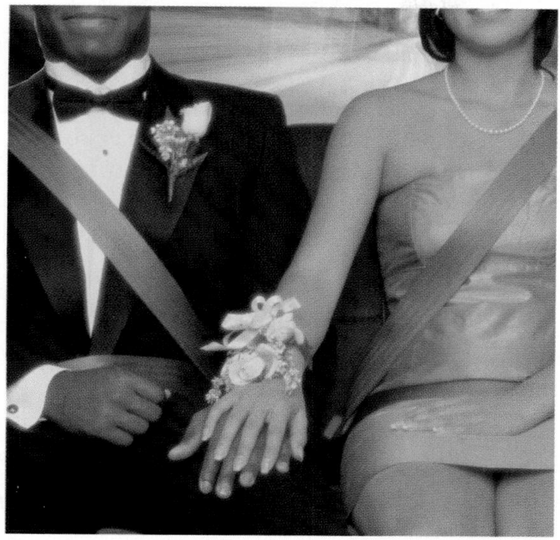

Secure Your Date.
Date of Prom:
Time:
Location:

EXHIBIT 20.8
National Highway Traffic and Safety Administration
This campaign stresses protecting someone you care about. It is hoped that this powerful message will convince consumers to wear their seatbelts.

Source: Produced for the National Highway Traffic Safety Administration by the Academy for Educational Development.

Voluntary self-regulation can help protect consumers. In recent years, for example, car manufacturers such as Ford, General Motors, and Chrysler have recalled various models to fix safety problems.[136] Nevertheless, when a significant infraction occurs, the CPSC, FTC, FDA, EPA, and NHTSA can intercede and propose an appropriate remedial action.[137] To illustrate, the FDA ordered the diet drug Redux off the market because of concerns that it may cause heart valves to leak and had the antihistamine Seldane taken off the market because of dangerous side effects.[138]

Individual consumers can also engage in litigation against companies in situations where the company is liable for a specific problem. In a highly publicized case against McDonald's, a woman was awarded $480,000 in damages because she received severe burns from hot coffee that spilled on her lap.

Incorrect Use of a Product Failure to meet standards accounts for only about 20 percent of product-related injuries.[139] In other cases, injuries occur because consumers use products or services incorrectly. For example, a consumer might combine two combustible chemicals, such as different types of oven cleaners, and cause a fire; spray an insecticide near food preparation areas and poison someone; or use a plunger with a liquid drain opener and accidentally splash the acid on his or her skin.

To reduce these types of dangers, companies are expected to anticipate reasonable risks that may be inherent in the use of a product or service and take steps to avoid them. This expectation is known as the **doctrine of foreseeability**.[140] Under this doctrine, companies can be held responsible if they do not try to prevent or at least minimize misuses that might occur from normal consumption of a product or service. Research on consumer consumption patterns can be particularly useful in identifying common usage problems. For example, it is reasonable for a company to foresee the potential for a consumer to use a plunger with a liquid drain opener. Sometimes, however, consumer misuses are very hard to anticipate, and the company is not usually held responsible. Using a power mower to cut someone's hair would be unexpected, for example, and this abuse would not be the company's fault.

doctrine of foreseeability
The expectation that companies should be able to anticipate normal risky uses of a product/service.

When potential dangers are identified, the company must attempt either to alter the product or to provide clear instructions on how the consumer can avoid potential problems. One of the key tools for protecting consumers from safety hazards is the warning label. Consumers are clearly warned about the danger of using a plunger with liquid drain opener, for instance. Pesticide labels warn consumers to keep the product away from their hands and face and that the product "should not be taken internally." Unfortunately, these warnings are not always as effective as they should be.[141]

New label formats are being developed that should make it easier for consumers to notice and heed the warning when using the product. The label must be easy to locate, perhaps highlighted by different colors or sizes of type, and simple to understand.[142] Companies can also design packaging and labels for poisonous products to make these items especially unattractive to children.[143] Consumer education programs might also be useful in reducing the number of product-related injuries.[144]

Some products or services are inherently risky. Riding a skateboard, bungee jumping, skydiving, driving a car, riding a bicycle, and using a tanning booth involve serious safety risks to the consumer. In these instances, however, consumers are made aware of these potential dangers and use the product at their own risk. Thus companies are not generally held liable for injuries associated with these products or services unless the injury was due to faulty manufacturing or negligence. The gun industry has been fighting lawsuits brought by municipalities that say guns are an unsafe product. Guns are not currently covered by federal consumer-safety regulations, a situation some anti-gun groups are trying to change. Meanwhile, the gun industry has mounted a safety campaign showing the proper use of gun locks and is continuing training and education efforts to teach consumers how to safely use guns.[145]

ENVIRONMENTAL PROTECTION

One final area of consumer rights is the right to an environment that enhances the quality of life—free of hazardous wastes, garbage, and pollutants and with adequate natural resources. Many efforts in this area have focused on developing laws and programs to improve air and water quality and to guard against waste disposal problems, especially hazardous waste.

Environmentally Conscious Behavior

Knowing that motor vehicles are a major cause of air pollution, the U.S. government requires the use of unleaded gasoline and has developed stricter emission control standards to reduce damage to the environment. Authorities in Kathmandu, Nepal, are trying to reduce pollution by replacing diesel-powered vehicles with electric public-transit vehicles.[146] In the past, aerosol spray cans were attacked for pumping volatile organic compounds into the environment, thereby damaging the earth's protective ozone layer. Now manufacturers have developed packaging and manufacturing methods that limit such emissions. Many dry-cleaning businesses use the chemical perc, a possible human carcinogen. In response to public concerns, some "green" dry cleaners have begun operating without the use of this chemical.[147]

Another major concern is the increasing amount of trash or garbage in our environment. Projections say that American consumers will generate 40 percent more trash by the year 2010 and that disposed packaging will account for 30 percent of it.[148] In response, many products (such as Lenor fabric softener in Germany; Jergen's lotion; and Lysol, Windex, and Resolve cleaners) are being sold in refillable containers.[149] Consumers in Romania and other countries reduce waste by using refillable bottles for wine, beer, seltzer, oil, and milk. In addition, companies are being pressured to develop packaging materials that will reduce environmental pollution. For example, the Environmental Defense Fund successfully urged McDonald's to use environmentally friendly packaging such as paper to wrap hamburgers instead of plastic foam containers.[150] Companies that use direct-mail advertising have been pressured to give consumers the option of refusing these materials because of the tremendous waste of ink and

GREEN SEAL
BEFORE YOU BUY A PRODUCT MAKE SURE IT'S PROPERLY SEALED.
Most of the products that sit on the supermarket shelf look harmless. But how can you tell which ones are manufactured with the Earth in mind? It's simple. Just look for the Green Seal. We are a non-profit, environmental labeling organization that certifies products which meet rigorous environmental standards. For more information, write to:
Green Seal, P.O. Box 77438, Washington DC 20013

EXHIBIT 20.9
Labeling Products as Environmentally Friendly
The Green Seal organization awards the Green Seal to products that meet rigorous environmental standards. This seal helps consumers identify products that are environmentally safe.

Source: Green Seal PSA by D.D.B. Needham 1990.

paper associated with junk mail.[151] One study found that stressing societal benefits, self-efficacy, and behavioral control were the most effective ways to induce consumers to reduce household garbage.[152]

The trend toward the use of environmentally friendly products is growing. Nokia is developing cell phones with recyclable and biodegradable parts so discarded phones will not lie forever in landfills.[153] More consumers are abandoning caustic cleaning products in favor of those that are milder and less damaging to the environment.[154] Consumers are also returning to natural cleansers such as baking soda, vinegar, and lemon juice, even if these products are less effective than manufactured cleansers.

One company awards a Green Seal to manufacturers of certain products that meet tough environmental standards (see Exhibit 20.9). This seal makes it easy for environmentally conscious consumers to identify "green," or environmentally friendly, products. Consumers who have a positive attitude toward ecologically conscious living, a negative attitude toward littering, and a perception that pollution is a problem are more likely to buy ecologically packaged products than products without such attributes.[155] Researchers have also found that a *general environmental concern* has an indirect effect on intentions to purchase environmentally sensitive products.[156] Research about recycling shows that specific beliefs about its importance can directly affect whether consumers engage in recycling behaviors and whether they perceive that recycling is inconvenient.[157] Although many consumers express concern for the environment, studies often show that these feelings still do not play a major role in the purchase of many products.[158] On the other hand, environmentally conscious behaviors are most likely to occur when consumers perceive that their actions will make a difference—called *perceived consumer effectiveness.*[159]

Conservation Behavior

conservation Consumer preservation of natural resources.

A second important aspect of environmental protection is **conservation behavior.** The need to conserve has become increasingly important in light of the rapidly escalating problems of garbage disposal and depletion of natural resources. Companies are now realizing that garbage has been a misused resource and are finding creative ways to make products more durable and to reuse materials. For example, Wellman, Inc., has used old soda bottles to make carpeting, Marcal makes paper towels out of undelivered junk mail, and Prestone recycles old antifreeze rather than making it from scratch.[160] Ecofurniture, made of recycled wood, plastic, or paper, is also growing in popularity.[161]

Government and company programs have been developed to encourage consumers to conserve certain resources, especially energy. In particular, consumer researchers have been interested in three major aspects of conservation behavior: *when* are consumers likely to conserve, *who* is most likely to conserve, and *how* can consumers be motivated to conserve?

When Are Consumers Likely to Conserve? In general, consumers are most likely to conserve when they accept personal responsibility for the pollution problem.[162] For example, consumers who perceive that there is an energy shortage because every consumer (including themselves) is using too much are more likely to accept personal blame for this problem and do something about it. However, one of the major obstacles facing conservation programs is actually *getting* consumers to take personal responsibility. Consumers often do not feel accountable for many environmental problems and are therefore not motivated to act.

Thus, for conservation programs to succeed, communications must make the problem personally relevant. For example, in trying to get consumers to conserve energy by turning down the thermostat, communications could focus on how much energy and money the household could save each year and over a long period such as 10 years. Consumers are also most likely to conserve when there are no barriers to doing so, such as the lack of conservation information or salespeople who do not stress conservation.[163]

A study in the Netherlands points out the importance of using social norms to influence consumers' environmental behaviors. This study found that consumers generally perceive that they are more motivated to engage in pro-environmental behavior than other households but are lower in the ability to do so.[164] Further, they believe that ability is the greatest determinant and that their own behavior is influenced by others.

Who Is Most Likely to Conserve? A weak relationship exists between conservation behavior and some demographic characteristics. Younger consumers and individuals with more education are slightly more likely to conserve than other groups.[165] However, researchers have not been able to identify a general profile of "the conserving consumer." Attitudes toward social responsibility and environmental consciousness generally do not relate to conservation behavior.[166] Instead, consumers tend to make environmentally beneficial choices on an activity-by-activity basis.

Physical or structural characteristics of the consumer's residence, such as the type of dwelling and number of appliances, tend to be strongly related to conservation behaviors.[167] Consumers who have fewer appliances and live in apartments and mobile homes are less likely to conserve. A study in the Netherlands found that characteristics of the house, such as the amount of insulation, and behavior of the household members, such as having curtains on the windows and lowering the thermostat when no one is home, were more likely to be related to energy use than factors such as demographics and attitudes.[168]

Researchers have identified three major behaviors of energy conservers: (1) **efficiency behaviors**, which include driving fuel-efficient cars and insulating and weatherizing the home; (2) **curtailment behaviors**, which include lowering the thermostat setting, turning off unneeded lights, and reducing driving by 10 percent; and (3) **demand-shift behaviors**, which include switching to solar heating units and converting from electric appliances to natural gas.[169] Conservation programs are more likely to be effective when they emphasize efficiency behaviors rather than curtailment behaviors.

efficiency behaviors Activities that result in more efficient energy usage.

curtailment behaviors Activities that result in using less energy.

demand-shift behaviors Activities that use more efficient energy sources.

Can Consumers Be Motivated to Conserve? Many organizations and agencies, both government and private, are trying to motivate consumers to conserve. Ads sometimes encourage consumers to use products or packages that conserve resources or to engage in conservation behaviors (see Exhibit 20.10). Another approach is to provide consumers with detailed information about

EXHIBIT 20.10
Emphasizing Conservation
Consumers can sometimes conserve resources by altering their behavior. This ad encourages consumers to conserve water by taking shorter showers.

Source: © David Young-Wolff/PhotoEdit.

conservation through communications, home audits, and appliance labels. Unfortunately, these programs usually have only a limited impact on conservation behavior.[170]

A more promising approach is to provide consumers with incentives to conserve. Providing consumers with a free shower-water flow device, for instance, significantly increased participation in an energy conservation program.[171] Consumers have shown that they prefer incentives such as tax credits to coercive tactics such as higher taxes. In addition, setting goals and providing feedback can be effective in helping consumers curtail energy use.

CONSUMERISM AROUND THE WORLD

Many countries have consumer protection laws, regulatory agencies, and consumer movements, although countries with conservative governments usually impose fewer restrictions on activities.[172] More liberal governments, on the other hand, often seek to protect consumers by creating a more restrictive regulatory environment. Clearly, companies must account for these forces when marketing internationally.

Like the United States, many nations have regulatory agencies to monitor advertising. In France, the Truth in Advertising commission monitors ad messages.[173] In the United Kingdom, advertising is controlled by two organizations: the Advertising Standards Authority (ASA) and the Independent Broadcasting Authority (IBA). The ASA is a self-regulatory agency (including nonindustry members) that monitors nonbroadcast advertising to ensure its honesty and fairness. The IBA is responsible for overseeing radio and television advertising. The British system tends to work more efficiently than similar U.S. organizations because it has better funding and staffing, substantial public participation, stronger remedies for infractions, better organization, and a stronger spirit of cooperation.[174]

Germany has very strict standards for truth in advertising. Deception occurs when research determines that 10 to 15 percent of reasonable consumers, even gullible ones, perceive a message to be misleading.[175] German deception cases are tried in courts (the same is true in France and Belgium). In one highly publicized German case, Philip Morris was ordered to discontinue an ad campaign claiming that passive exposure to cigarette smoke was no more dangerous than eating cookies.[176]

In the Netherlands, the Commercial Code Commission oversees ads. Not long ago, it ruled that a comical mobile phone ad suggesting that phones drive people insane was distasteful and harmful to mental patients.[177] Industry self-regulation is also common in the United Kingdom, Italy, Belgium, Ireland, Switzerland, and the Netherlands; Germany and Austria permit private litigation against companies as well.

Countries also have widely varying laws regarding the legalities of particular marketing practices. In Germany the words *best* or *better* are considered misleading.[178] Finland prohibits newspaper or TV advertising for political groups, religion, alcohol, weight-loss products, or "immoral literature," and the United Kingdom does not allow cigarette or liquor advertising on television. More than 50 European nations have called for bans on tobacco advertising and promotion, even though the European Court of Justice recently overturned a sweeping European Community ban on tobacco ads.[179] After the fall of communism, the Russian government banned cigarette and alcohol ads and then all advertising temporarily until a reasonable set of guidelines could be developed.[180] Regulations regarding advertising to children also vary widely in different countries, which means companies must carefully research local rules when marketing across national boundaries.[181] Other countries often regulate promotion techniques such as premiums, sweepstakes, and free samples more heavily than the United States does.

Advertisers in China have been making widely exaggerated false claims for years.[182] For example, one ad states that a brand of toothpaste cures cancer, and another claims a soap can wash 10 years off a woman's face. Interestingly, local advertisers, and not foreign companies, are the worst offenders. However, the Chinese government is cracking down with comprehensive advertising laws and stiffer enforcement.

Product safety standards are becoming more stringent around the world, particularly in the European Community, which has adopted tougher regulations than the United States.[183] Thus to minimize liability, companies need to maximize product performance and safety. Finally, many consumer activist groups are at work around the world. For example, the environmental movement is strong in many European countries, and the Green Party has been increasing its representation in the German government. International environmental groups such as Greenpeace monitor issues around the globe.

SUMMARY

Consumerism is "the set of activities of government, business, independent organizations, and concerned consumers that are designed to protect the rights of consumers" to (1) be safe, (2) be informed, (3) have choices, (4) be heard, (5) receive consumer education, (6) have recourse and redress, and (7) live in an environment that enhances the quality of life. The various influences on consumerism and public policy issues are government agencies, industry self-regulation, and political consumer groups.

A key public policy issue is deceptive advertising and labeling. Ads can be deceptive when they provide false information, leave out relevant information, or interact with consumers' beliefs to mislead. Deceptive selling techniques include the bait-and-switch technique, misrepresentation of the selling intent, and incorrect statements. Several problems are associated with advertising to children. Young consumers do not have the cognitive capabilities to process ads and must sometimes be protected from certain practices. Regulators, advocacy groups, and consumers are also concerned about privacy on the Internet.

The government is working on ways to help consumers become more informed. To be effective, however, information must be easy to understand, be reasonable in amount, be used by consumers, and appear in an easy-to-use format. The consumer's right to safety is ensured by protection from unsafe products and warnings of dangers or risks when present. Environmental protection and conservation behavior are key public policy issues. Around the world, consumerism issues are being addressed by various rules and regulations enforced by governmental agencies and self-regulation groups.

QUESTIONS FOR REVIEW AND DISCUSSION

1. What are the main government agencies and industry self-regulation groups that address consumer issues?
2. In the context of regulation, how does affirmative disclosure differ from corrective advertising?
3. How have marketers used deceptive selling tactics on consumers?
4. Why is advertising to children so controversial?
5. What are the main consumer privacy issues related to use of the Internet?
6. How does the doctrine of foreseeability relate to product safety?
7. What influences environmentally conscious consumer behavior?

EXERCISES

1. Watch or tape 3 hours of Saturday morning children's television. Code or analyze each ad in terms of the following: (a) type of product advertised, (b) message techniques used (fantasy, humor, music, etc.), (c) emotion evoked, (d) key message delivered, and (e) any aspects you think might confuse young children. Summarize this information and answer the following questions:
   a. What are the most frequently advertised types of products or services? Do you see any ethical problems?
   b. What main techniques are used to influence children? Do you believe that these are reasonable marketing practices?
   c. Did you notice any efforts made to educate children and make them more aware of the advertising? Were these efforts effective?
   d. What types of messages are children being exposed to? Do you see any problems with them?
   e. Did any ads or messages seem to be unfair or unethical? If so, why?
2. Acquire and copy three nutrition labels from packages of food products. Ask ten consumers (as different from one another as possible) to describe what this information means. Alternatively, ask the ten consumers a series of multiple-choice questions about the terms contained on the label. Based on your observations, how well do you think the consumers understood the information? What types of consumers were most likely and least likely to understand the material? What could be done to make it more understandable and useful?
3. This chapter briefly discussed several key public policy issues. Select one of the key issues, and conduct a thorough library search for information about it. Use this information to write a more detailed summary report of the key arguments and possible solutions for this issue.
4. This chapter notes that public policy regulation varies throughout the world. Select a particular country and research the nature of regulation for one of the key issues discussed in this chapter. How do the practices in that country differ from those in the United States? How are they similar?

chapter 21

The Dark Side of Consumer Behavior and Marketing

Introduction: Who Is Collecting Your Personal Data—and Why?

Online companies collect a lot of personal information about you, and you may not even know it. Many Web sites place *cookies*—small data files—on your computer's hard drive to track your movement around each site, determine which pages and items you looked at, and see how long you lingered. Some sites require visitors to provide information such as phone numbers, e-mail addresses, or even Social Security numbers before gaining access to coupons, games, or other online features. Some companies use hidden tracking programs that record your online behavior and analyze it to choose ads for you to see.

When customers become aware that a company is collecting and storing data, they may become concerned about the potential for privacy violation. For example, after Comcast was criticized by consumer groups and legislators for storing data on its customers' online habits, the company agreed to halt the practice. Many sites post privacy policies to explain their data collection practices. However, consumers may not always understand what the company plans to do with the information. Moreover, companies may change their privacy polices or take actions that seem inconsistent with those policies. New Jersey officials investigated Toys 'R' Us, for instance, to learn whether transmitting data gathered online to a technology vendor was inconsistent with the firm's privacy policies. The toy retailer settled by paying a fine,

WORKPLACE SURVEILLANCE | LEGAL DATABASE | RESOURCES & ABOUT US

PRIVACYFOUNDATION

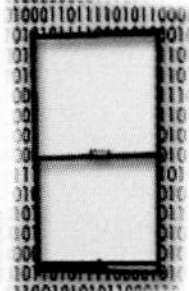

Submit your e-mail for Privacy Watch and Tipsheet updates

Got a News Lead?

Privacy Policy

TOP STORY

Living in the Googleplex

Nation of Voyeurs, Boston Globe   Googlism's Instant Profiles

Five years after its founding by two Stanford grad students, Google dominates the space with tens of millions of Internet searches each day that are rewiring the culture. How so? By every second connecting the nerve-like data points beneath the information glut. Google is fast, free and out-of-control – a technological triumph that makes the notion of Internet privacy look like a gas street lamp in Las Vegas. Google's IPO, needless to say, is anxiously awaited. And where were these story links found? Where else - via Google.

PRIVACY NEWS

Google-opoly: Page-ranking Monopoly Slate, 1/29/03

Predictions About Search Engines Search Engine Guide, 1/28/03

San Diego Ogles Google's Impact Information Week, 1/22/03

Google's Gaggle of Problems Business Week, 1/14/03

Have You Been Googled Lately? Indiana Daily Student, 1/16/03

Total Information Awareness Precursor: Google The American Prospect, 1/28/03

Net Users Try to Elude the Google Grasp N.Y. Times, 7/25/02

Google Tracker Raises Privacy Issues ZDNet, 12/10/00

Search Engine White Paper (pdf) Arnold Information Technology, 1/31/03

Google's Edge ;-) PigeonRank

ADVISORIES & REPORTS

Founding Members of Regulatory DataCorp.

Solicitation: "175 Million E-mail Addresses for $220 U.S."

Interview: David Brin's Naked Truth About Privacy

Comment on Airline Passenger Profiling

A report on the privacy practices of Monster.com

EXHIBIT 21.1

Privacy Advocacy Site

Several organizations, like the one whose Web site is shown here, keep consumers informed about a wide variety of privacy-related issues.

Source: Privacy Foundation.

changing its privacy policy, and posting a prominent link to the policy on its home page. As another example, the pharmaceutical firm Eli Lilly violated its privacy policy by inadvertently revealing the names of people who signed up to receive information from its Prozac.com Web site. The Federal Trade Commission ordered Eli Lilly to set up a system to protect customer data for the next 20 years and to report every year on its security processes.

In some cases, information sharing benefits consumers because they get merchandise or services in exchange for providing personal information. Quicken Loans, for example, offers to personalize communications based on the information customers provide. If a consumer supplies a cell phone or pager number, Quicken Loans will use it to communicate updates on loan status. Quicken's research shows that the majority of its customers find this personalized service valuable. Although adults are capable of weighing the merits of such trade-offs, privacy advocates worry that children will not be able to resist divulging family data online in exchange for gifts.[1] Exhibit 21.1 shows one of a number of advocacy Web sites that keep consumers informed about online privacy issues.

The preceding example illustrates several issues discussed in this chapter. Marketers sometimes engage in practices that could seem distasteful or detrimental to consumers, such as invading their privacy. This chapter also examines whether marketing efforts target children for unsafe products like cigarettes and alcohol, whether activities like advertising make people unhappy with their appearance or what and how much they own, and whether advertising unfairly depicts or represents key segments of our society. In addition, the chapter describes ways that consumers can resist marketing efforts viewed as inappropriate, including individual actions and group actions such as boycotts.

Although these issues represent some of the "dark side" of *marketing*, other issues represent the dark side of *consumer behavior.* This chapter discusses deviant consumer behaviors that stem from uncontrollable sources (compulsive buying, compulsive gambling, and smoking and alcohol addictions) as well as consumer behaviors that are deviant because they are illegal (consumer theft, underage drinking and smoking, and black market transactions). ●

DEVIANT CONSUMER BEHAVIOR

Much of this book has focused on the behavior of the average consumer in an everyday consumption context, but sometimes consumer behavior is regarded as deviant. Behavior is deviant if it is either unexpected or not sanctioned by members of the society. Such behavior may be problematic to the consumer and/or to the society in which the consumer operates. As Exhibit 21.2 indicates, some forms of deviant consumer behavior occur during the purchase or acquisition of the product—before consumers even use it. Three types of deviant *acquisition* behaviors are discussed here: compulsive buying, consumer theft, and black markets. The following section focuses on deviant *consumption* behaviors, including addiction, compulsive consumption, and underage smoking and drinking.

Compulsive Buying

Some individuals buy compulsively, purchasing excessive quantities of items they do not need and sometimes cannot afford. Individuals who buy compulsively gain satisfaction from *buying,* not from *owning* (see part a of Exhibit 21.3).[2]

EXHIBIT 21.2
Framework for Deviant Consumer Behavior
Consumer behavior may be deviant because it involves a physical or psychological abnormality or involves a behavior regarded as illegal. Such deviant behaviors can be associated with the acquisition or usage of offerings.

Stage of the Consumer Behavior Process

Why Deviant?	Deviant acquisition behavior	Deviant usage behavior
Physical/ psychological abnormality	Compulsive buying	Addictive consumption • smoking • drugs • alcohol Compulsive consumption • compulsive gambling • binge eating
Illegal behavior	Consumer theft Black markets	Underage drinking Underage smoking Drug use

Inside the Compulsive Buying Experience Compulsive buying has a strong emotional component, and the emotions run the gamut from the most negative to the most positive.[3] Compulsive buyers feel anxious on days when they do not buy. In fact, compulsive buying may be a response to tension or anxiety. As evidence, some research has found a relationship between compulsive buying and eating disorders like binge eating. While in the store, compulsive buyers may feel great emotional arousal at the stimulation evoked by the store's atmosphere. The act of buying, in turn, brings an immediate emotional high and often a feeling of loss of control (see part b of Exhibit 21.3). However, this emotional high is followed by feelings of remorse, guilt, shame, and depression. Compulsive buyers think that others would be horrified by knowing about these spending habits, and some even hide their purchases in a closet or the trunk of a car.

Buying products in excessive amounts seems antithetical to the buying processes described in earlier chapters. Why then do people buy compulsively? The answer to this question is not simple.

Low Self-Esteem First, compulsive buyers tend to have low self-esteem. In fact, the emotional high consumers experience from compulsive buying comes in part from the attention and social approval they get when they buy. The salesperson can bring considerable satisfaction—being a doting helper, telling consumers how attractive they look in a particular outfit, and saying how thoughtful they are to buy such a nice gift. Consumers can also feel that they are pleasing someone: pleasing the salesperson by buying the product and pleasing the company by making purchases. This attention and the feeling that they are pleasing others may temporarily raise compulsive buyers' self-esteem and act as a reinforcement for buying (see part c of Exhibit 21.3).

Fantasy Orientation Fantasy orientation is a personality trait associated with compulsive buying. Buying makes compulsive buyers feel more important and more grandiose than they actually are. These fantasy feelings may explain how compulsive buyers temporarily avoid or escape thoughts about the financial consequences of their shopping habits.

EXHIBIT 21.3

Quotes from Compulsive Buyers

Compulsive buying can be an emotionally involving experience. Consumers who engage in compulsive buying often enjoy feelings of extra attention or feeling like they are pleasing someone else. But this emotional high may be followed by serious financial and negative emotional consequences.

Source: Thomas O'Guinn and Ronald Faber, "Compulsive Buying: A Phenomenological Perspective," *Journal of Consumer Research*, September 1989, pp. 147–157. © 1989 University of Chicago. All rights reserved.

EMOTIONAL ASPECTS OF COMPULSIVE BUYING

a. "I couldn't tell you what I bought or where I bought it. It was like I was on automatic."

"I really think it's the spending. It's not that I want it, because sometimes I'll just buy it and I'll think, Ugh, another sweatshirt."

b. "But it was like, it was almost like my heart was palpitating, I couldn't wait to get in to see what was there. It was such a sensation. In the store, the lights, the people; they were playing Christmas music. I was hyperventilating and my hands were starting to sweat, and all of a sudden I was touching sweaters and the whole feel of it was just beckoning to me. And if they had a SALE sign up, forget it; I was gone. You never know when you're going to need it. I bought ten shirts one time for $10.00 each."

"It's almost like you're drunk. You're so intoxicated;...I got this great high. It was like you couldn't have given me more of a rush."

FACTORS INFLUENCING COMPULSIVE BUYING

c. "The attention I got there was incredible. She waited on me very nicely, making sure it would fit and if it didn't they would do this and that. And I guess I enjoyed being on the other end of that. I had no idea how I was going to pay for it. I never do."

"I never bought one of anything. I always buy at least two. I still do. I can never even go into the Jewel and buy one quart of milk. I've always got to buy two...It's an act of pleasing. I had been brought up to please everybody and everyone around me because that was the way you got anything was to please. So I thought I was pleasing the store."

FINANCIAL AND EMOTIONAL CONSEQUENCES OF COMPULSIVE BUYING

d. "I would always have to borrow between paychecks. I could not make it between paychecks. Payday comes and I'd pay all my bills, but then I'd piss the rest away, and I'd need to borrow money to eat, and I would cry and cry and cry, and everyone would say, 'Well just make a budget.' Get serious. That's like telling an alcoholic not to go to the liquor store. It's not that simple."

e. "My husband said he couldn't deal with this and he said, 'I'm leaving you. We'll get a divorce. That's it. It's your problem. You did it. You fix it up.'"

"I didn't have one person in the world I could talk to. I don't drink. I don't smoke. I don't do dope. But I can't stop. I can't control it. I said I can't go on like this...My husband hates me. My kids hate me. I've destroyed everything. I was ashamed and just wanted to die."

Alienation Compulsive buyers tend to be somewhat alienated from society; they have fewer friends and social contacts than most people do. Compulsive buying therefore provides an opportunity for social gratification. Consumers may feel as if they are friends with a salesperson who has sold them items on repeated occasions. They may enjoy seeing the UPS driver arrive with a package. By buying, these consumers may feel more integrated and less alienated than they otherwise would.

Family History Finally, compulsive buyers are more likely to come from families whose members show compulsive or addictive behaviors or emotional disorders. For example, one study of Canadian consumers found that compulsive buyers were more likely to come from families showing problems of alcoholism, bulimia, extreme nervousness, or depression. Some evidence suggests that compulsive buying may be hereditary.

1. Please indicate how much you agree or disagree with the statement below. Place an X on the line that best indicates how you feel.

	Strongly agree (1)	Somewhat agree (2)	Neither agree nor disagree (3)	Somewhat disagree (4)	Strongly disagree (5)
a. If I have any money left at the end of the pay period, I just have to spend it.	______	______	______	______	______

2. Please indicate how often you have done each of the following things by placing an X on the appropriate line.

	Very often (1)	Often (2)	Sometimes (3)	Rarely (4)	Never (5)
a. Felt like others would be horrified if they knew of my spending habits	______	______	______	______	______
b. Bought things even though I couldn't afford them	______	______	______	______	______
c. Wrote a check when I knew I didn't have enough money in the bank to cover it	______	______	______	______	______
d. Bought myself something in order to make myself feel better	______	______	______	______	______
e. Felt anxious or nervous on days I didn't go shopping	______	______	______	______	______
f. Made only the minimum payments on my credit cards	______	______	______	______	______

Scoring equation = –9.69 + (*Q*1a x .33) + (*Q*2a x .34) + (*Q*2b x .50) + (*Q*2c x .47) + (*Q*2d x .33) + (*Q*2e x .38) + (*Q*2f x .31).
If scoring is ≤ –1.34, subject is classified as a compulsive buyer.

EXHIBIT 21.4
A Clinical Screening Test for Compulsive Buying

Do you have compulsive buying tendencies? Take this screening test to find out.

Source: Thomas C. O'Guinn and Ronald J. Faber, "A Clinical Screener for Compulsive Buying," *Journal of Consumer Research*, December 1991, pp. 459–469.

Consequences of Compulsive Buying Compulsive buying is more than an annoying habit. Its financial, emotional, and interpersonal consequences can be devastating. Some compulsive buyers spend roughly 50 percent of their income on purchases. To finance their buying habits, they rely extensively on credit cards. They have significantly more credit cards than the general population and are more likely to carry balances within $100 of their credit limit. Because their credit card debt is so great, they tend to pay the minimum monthly balance. They are also more likely to write checks for purchases, even though they know they do not have enough money to pay for them. And compulsive buyers are more likely to borrow money from others to make it from paycheck to paycheck (see part d of Exhibit 21.3).[4] A clinical screening test that incorporates many of these elements is shown in Exhibit 21.4.

Compulsive buying can also wreak devastating emotional and interpersonal consequences. As part e of Exhibit 21.3 indicates, children, spouses, and friends can all be hurt by the spending habits of compulsive buyers.

Compulsive buying raises important ethical questions for marketers; however, research is still needed to clarify these difficult issues.

EXHIBIT 21.5
Consumer Theft
What are the most commonly stolen items? This list breaks them down by type of retailer.

Source: Discount Merchandiser, March 1997, p. 3. Used with permission.

MOST FREQUENTLY STOLEN MERCHANDISE BY TYPE OF RETAILER.

TYPE OF RETAILER	MERCHANDISE
AUTO PARTS	AUTO ACCESSORIES
BOOKS	CASSETTE TAPES
CONSUMER ELECTRONICS	COMPACT DISCS
DEPARTMENT STORES	CLOTHING: SHIRTS
DISCOUNT STORES	CLOTHING, UNDERGARMENTS
DRUGSTORES	CIGARETTES, BATTERIES
FASHION MERCHANDISE	SNEAKERS
GENERAL MERCHANDISE	EARRINGS
GROCERY/SUPERMARKET	OVER-THE-COUNTER MEDICINES
HOME AND HARDWARE	ASSORTED HAND TOOLS
MUSIC	COMPACT DISCS
SHOES	SNEAKERS
SPECIALTY	BED SHEETS
SPECIALTY APPAREL	ASSORTED CLOTHES, SHOES
SPORTING GOODS	ATHLETIC SHOES
THEME PARKS	KEY CHAINS, JEWELRY
TOYS	ACTION FIGURES
VIDEO	VIDEO GAMES
WHOLESALE	PENS, PRERECORDED VIDEO TAPES

Do marketing practices foster compulsive buying? Although research on this issue is scarce, it seems quite likely that enticing sales, attractive displays, doting salespeople, and easy credit foster compulsive buying.

Are marketers ethically bound to help compulsive buyers? Marketers might help compulsive buyers through direct actions such as liberal return policies, sales training in compulsive buying, and denials for credit increases or through indirect actions such as contributions to self-help organizations like Spender Enders. ●

Consumer Theft

Whereas compulsive buying reflects an uncontrollable desire to *purchase* things, consumer theft reflects an uncontrollable desire to *steal* things.

Prevalence of Consumer Theft When we think of consumer theft, we may think first of shoplifting. For retailers, shoplifting is indeed pervasive and significant, with yearly retail losses approximating $30 billion. Furthermore, police reports on shoplifting incidents have been increasing by 5 percent per year for the past decade.[5] Exhibit 21.5 shows the most commonly stolen items from various types of retailers.

Consumer theft is a problem for nonretailers as well.[6] For example, automobile insurance fraud has been estimated to exceed $10 billion per year, and phone service fraud is estimated to exceed $1 billion per year. Hotel theft is also pervasive, with yearly losses exceeding $100 million. Officials at Holiday Inn estimate that a towel is stolen every 11 seconds. Credit card fraud is a problem for Internet businesses in particular. Other common forms of consumer theft include loan fraud; warranty fraud; theft of cable TV services; music, video, and software piracy; coupon fraud; fraudulent returns; and switching or altering price tags. Financial-aid fraud is on the rise as students and parents falsify their income or submit false tax returns to college aid offices. According to the FBI, complaints about online auction fraud, in which consumers steal from other consumers, outnumber all other reports of online crimes.[7]

Factors Affecting Consumer Theft Although you may think that consumer theft is driven by economic need, few demographic variables are associated with theft. Some *forms* of consumer theft are associated with certain demographic groups: shoplifting is most common among teens, and credit card fraud is usually associated with better-educated consumers. However, consumers from all walks of life engage in theft. Moreover, many consumers have engaged in some form of theft at one time. For example, roughly two-thirds of the public admits to having shoplifted.[8]

As shown in Exhibit 21.6, two psychological factors seem to explain theft: (1) the temptation to steal and (2) the ability to rationalize theft behavior. As the exhibit indicates, these factors are, in turn, affected by several other factors: characteristics of the product, the purchase environment, and the consumer.

Temptation to Steal The *temptation* to steal arises when consumers want products that they cannot obtain through legitimate forms of acquisition. Some of these are desires driven by real needs, such as the mother who steals baby formula to feed her child. Others reflect greed, as in the case of upper-class consumers who steal jewelry. Some researchers suggest that marketers are involved by perpetuating materialistic tendencies and creating insatiable desires for new goods and services.[9] Consumers may also be tempted to steal offerings they are too embarrassed to buy through conventional channels (e.g., condoms, pregnancy tests), or offerings they cannot legally buy (e.g., an underage consumer stealing alcohol).[10]

Exhibit 21.6 shows that environmental factors also affect the temptation to steal. Temptation is greater when consumers perceive that they can get away with stealing and that it is worth doing. Thus consumers may assess the perceived risks associated with stealing and getting caught and may consider the benefits of having a product or using a service they did not pay for.[11] Many factors in the environment affect the perceived risks of shoplifting.[12] Stores may be very noisy or crowded, have little or no security, have lax return policies, have few salespeople, contain nooks and crannies, or have price tags that are easily switched, making it easier for consumers to steal without being noticed.

Sometimes people steal for the thrill of doing something they are not supposed to do. This thrill-seeking tendency has been associated with many forms of consumer theft, including price-tag switching and shoplifting.[13]

Rationalizations for Stealing As Exhibit 21.6 shows, consumers also engage in theft because they can somehow *rationalize* their behavior as being either justified or driven by forces outside themselves. For example, consumers may justify stealing a low-ticket item such as grapes from a grocery store or candy from a checkout counter because the item's cost seems so negligible that the word *stealing* hardly seems to apply. Some consumers may believe that stealing is jus-

EXHIBIT 21.6
Motivations for Consumer Theft
Consumers may engage in theft because they (1) feel the temptation to steal and (2) can somehow rationalize their behavior. Various factors associated with the product, the environment, and the consumer can influence temptation and the ability to rationalize.

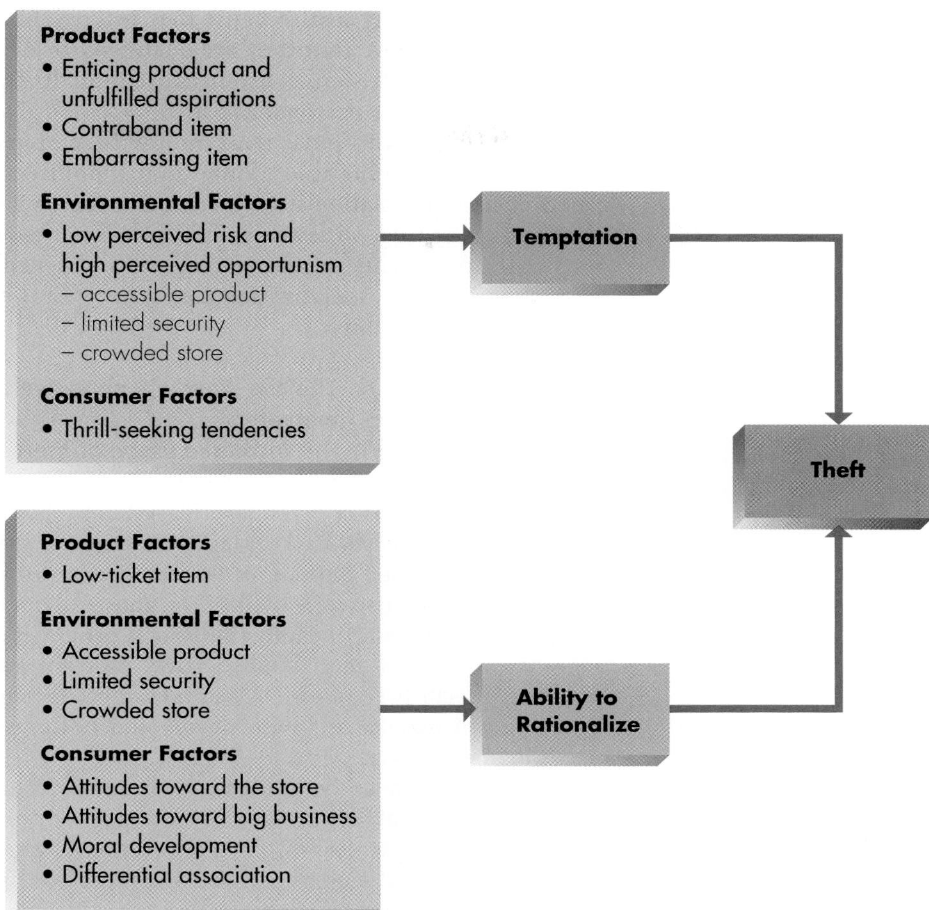

tified because the environment encourages it. Thus the consumer may believe that the marketer "asked for it" by keeping merchandise displays open, having no security guards, or using price tags that can be readily switched. Consumers in crowded stores may become so frustrated by waiting for service that they give up and walk out with their items. They may justify their behavior by thinking that theft is compensation for the unpleasantness they suffered while waiting.[14]

In addition, consumers are likely to rationalize when social influences encourage theft, as in the case of someone who shoplifts on a dare.[15] The consumer rationalizes the behavior through thoughts like "my friend made me do it." Interestingly, researchers have little evidence that dares actually play a large role in the shoplifting behavior of teenagers.[16] "Everybody does it" is another rationalization. In one study, 11 percent of the respondents agreed it was wrong to download online music without paying and copy software without paying—but if they believe that "everybody else does it" they may follow suit.[17]

Consumers are also most likely to rationalize theft when stores have a negative public image. If the store is seen as unfriendly, intimidating, or somehow unfair, consumers may see theft as a way of getting revenge against the retailer. Similarly, consumers may steal because they have negative attitudes toward businesses and because they think that large businesses can readily absorb the losses.

Some consumers may steal because they feel psychologically distanced from the retailer—they believe that they are dealing with a huge faceless conglomerate, not a shop owner. In sum, consumers are more likely to rationalize theft behavior when there is less personalization.[18]

Consumers who have weak moral development may not see the act of stealing as wrong. One study found that shoplifters tend to be rule breakers in general. Some speculation suggests that our society's overall level of moral development is changing, so fewer people view theft as wrong. Some evidence suggests that adolescents' moral restraint is weakened simply by observing their peers shoplift. Thus socialization can affect moral development, which in turn can affect consumer theft.[19]

MARKETING IMPLICATIONS

Theft is clearly a pervasive and expensive problem for marketers.

Increased usage of theft-reducing devices. Businesses spend billions of dollars every year trying to prevent or reduce theft through antitheft devices and improved security systems.[20] Some companies combine closed circuit TVs with sophisticated computer software to track suspicious behavior. Marketers have also used some unusual tactics to reduce theft, including subliminal audio messages that say things like "Do not steal" and "Stealing is a crime."[21]

Covering the costs of theft. Theft hurts consumers because retailers must raise prices to pay for lost merchandise, cover theft insurance, and cover the costs of high-priced security systems.[22] In addition, theft adds to research and development costs as firms experiment with newer and better security systems, which also results in higher prices.

Reducing ability to serve customers. Security systems and procedures may interfere with retailers' abilities to service customers. For example, retailers may have to keep merchandise in glass displays, lock displays, and so on.[23] This added security increases consumers' search costs, making it more difficult and more time consuming for consumers to examine products and for salespeople to service customers. ●

Black Markets

black market An illegal market in which consumers pay (often exorbitant amounts) for items not readily available.

Whereas theft represents situations in which consumers refuse to pay for available items, **black markets** represent situations in which consumers *pay* (often exorbitant amounts) for items *not* readily available. The markets are called black markets because the sellers are unauthorized sellers, which means the buying-selling process is usually illegal. Black markets develop and continue for several reasons. First, some products sold on black markets fulfill basic human needs. Black markets for goods like sugar, salt, blankets, matches, and batteries fulfill functional needs; black markets for drugs, entertainment, and sexual services fulfill experiential needs; and black markets for Swatch watches may fulfill symbolic needs.

Consumers obtain many offerings through black markets.

- *Legal items in short supply.* Some items sold on the black market are legal but in short supply. For example, some consumers buy blocks of tickets to popular sporting events, plays, and concerts and then sell them later at exceptionally high prices. Black markets for car airbags and Cuban cigars have also been prevalent in the United States in recent years.[24] Some black markets deal with the trade of very basic consumer goods. For example, prisoners will trade money and cigarettes for goods like food, books, and clothing.[25]
- *Brands.* In some cases specific brands are sold on the black market, as mentioned in Chapter 11's opening example. The black market for Levi jeans has

been strong in the former Soviet Union. The United States has a black market for frequent-flyer tickets: sellers, who sometimes work through brokers, can get $12 to $15 for each 1,000 miles accrued.[26]

- *Illegal items.* Some goods and services that *cannot legally be sold* to consumers are sold through the black market, such as weapons and products used to build bombs.[27] Black markets for drugs are also common. For example, a large global black market exists for the male potency drug Viagra.[28] Counterfeit products such as fake Gucci shoes are also sold through black markets.[29]

Addictive and Compulsive Consumption

Compulsive buying, consumer theft, and black markets are all forms of deviant *acquisition* behavior; however, in some cases it is not the acquisition process that is deviant but rather how or whether products are *used*. As shown in Exhibit 21.2, consumption behavior can also be deviant either because we lose control over consumption or because it is illegal.

addiction Excessive behavior typically brought on by a chemical dependence.

Addiction

Addiction reflects excessive behaviors typically brought on by a chemical dependence. Addicted consumers feel a great attachment to and dependence on a product or activity and believe that they must use it to function.[30] Individuals can become addicted to many consumer products and services, including cigarettes, drugs, alcohol, exercise, Internet use, TV, video games, collecting, and so on. In many cases, an addiction involves a product that is used repetitively, even if it is dangerous. Although addicted individuals may want to stop consuming the product, they believe that stopping is beyond their control ("I can't help myself"). Often individuals feel shame and guilt over their addiction and try to hide it. Some addicted consumers find strength in groups like Alcoholics Anonymous and Smoke Enders.

Addictive behaviors can be harmful to addicts and to those around them.[31] For example, cigarette smoking has been labeled society's most widespread form of drug dependence. It is the number one preventable cause of death in the United States and is a leading cause of cancer, cardiovascular disease, and chronic obstructive lung disease. The social costs of cigarette smoking are also high. Smokers use more health benefits, take more sick leave, and have more job-related accidents and injuries than nonsmokers do. Although the number of smokers in the United States is declining, smoking is still prevalent, and those who are most vulnerable have the least knowledge about its ill effects. Furthermore, consumers seem to be switching from cigarettes to cigars and chewing tobacco, although these products are just as harmful.

compulsive consumption An irresistible urge to perform an irrational consumption act.

Compulsive Consumption

Compulsive consumption is an irresistible urge to perform an irrational consumption act. For example, betting twice your weekly salary on a race horse is not a rational act, even though compulsive gamblers might engage in this behavior. Similarly, eating two dozen donuts is not rational, but compulsive (binge) eaters might consume food in such quantities.

Compulsive gambling is a special case of compulsive compulsion. An estimated 6 million to 9 million Americans are compulsive gamblers. These individuals suffer from a chronic inability to resist impulses to gamble, and they engage in gambling behavior that is disruptive to both themselves and those around them.[32] Research shows that these consumers are more likely to come from families in which other members exhibited addictive behavior and are more likely to engage in compulsive buying or exhibit alcoholism, be generally impulsive, and view materialism as a measure of success.[33] In fact, scientists have established a strong link between compulsive gambling and consumption of alcohol, tobacco, and illicit drugs.[34]

Typically, compulsive gambling behavior evolves over a series of stages. In the first stage the individual experiences the pleasure of a "big win." During the second stage gambling becomes more reckless, losses pile up, and gambling becomes a central force in the individual's life. Because the consumer cannot obtain a legal loan at this point, he or she turns to loan sharks. The compulsive gambler promises to stop gambling, but cannot. Faced with rising debt and compulsive gambling urges, many gamblers engage in crimes like forgery and embezzlement. The final stage occurs when the gambler realizes that he or she has hit rock bottom. The psychological and financial consequences of compulsive gambling can be disastrous. One study of 54 compulsive gamblers found that each had accumulated debts of nearly $28,000. Ninety-eight percent had turned to crime.[35]

Despite the popular stereotype of the compulsive gambler as a lower-income consumer, compulsive gamblers represent every ethnic and socioeconomic group in society. However, certain groups are particularly susceptible to compulsive gambling. Teens, for example, are four times more likely to engage in compulsive gambling than adults are.[36] The typical compulsive gambler is 39 years old and married; nearly one-third have incomes between $25,000 and $50,000.

Causes of Addictive and Compulsive Consumption Why do some people become addicted to drugs or alcohol or eat or bet compulsively whereas others do not? The answers are neither clear nor simple, and many factors have been implicated in the development of addictive and compulsive tendencies.[37]

Inherited Tendencies Some evidence suggests that addictive tendencies are inherited; for example, genetic markers of alcohol addiction have been the topic of much research. Personality has also been linked to compulsive and addictive behavior. To illustrate, alcohol addiction has been linked with low self-esteem, anxiety, depression, sensation seeking, and antisocial personality disorders. Compared with nonaddicts, addicts are also more likely to exhibit an external locus of control, believing that control or responsibility for events lies in factors outside of themselves. This may explain why addicts find it hard to stop their addictive behavior. Some of these factors (e.g., depression and low self-esteem) may be outcomes of being an addict, however, not factors that predispose one to becoming an addict.

Family-Related Factors Addictive behaviors may also have their roots in dysfunctional families. For example, children of alcoholics are more likely to become alcoholics, perhaps because they model the behavior of their parents. They may also have developed fewer coping mechanisms for dealing with their parents' addiction, thus making them more susceptible to using escapist means like drugs and alcohol. Clearly, addictive and compulsive behaviors are complex and multifaceted problems.

MARKETING IMPLICATIONS *Do marketing activities encourage addictive and compulsive behaviors?* Some might argue that marketing activities encourage addictive and compulsive behaviors. For example, cigarettes are heavily advertised in the United States, and the nicotine in cigarettes is addictive. Public policy makers clearly view marketers as perpetuating this form of addictive consumption. As discussed in Chapter 20, some countries have banned cigarette advertising and require warning labels on ciga-

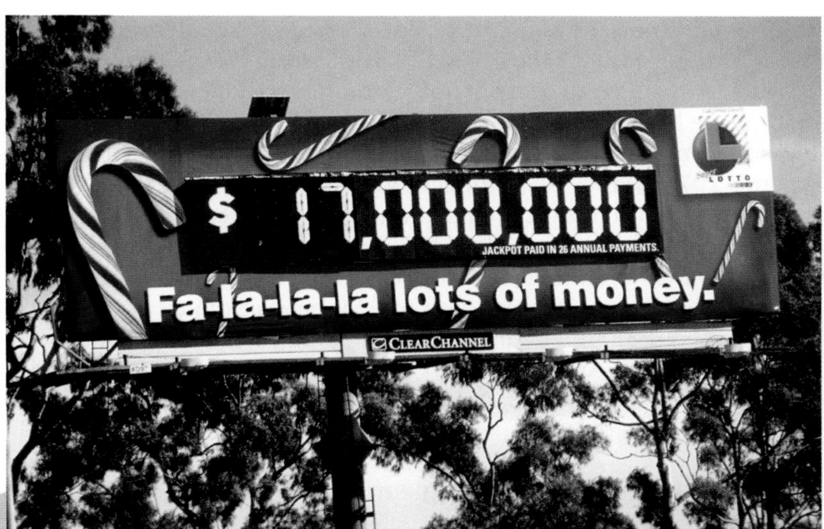

EXHIBIT 21.7
Forms of Gambling
Casinos and lotteries represent common forms of gambling.

Source: © Bill Aron/PhotoEdit.

rette packages, legislative acts that affect marketing practices.

Industry and marketing practices may also perpetuate behaviors like compulsive gambling.[38] Gambling is a fast-growing industry, already legal in places like Las Vegas, New Orleans, and Atlantic City and prevalent on many Indian reservations. Floating riverboat casinos have attracted thousands of Midwest consumers. A number of states have legalized gambling, and others are being pressured by lobbyists to do the same. Moreover, cash-strapped states and governments see casinos and lotteries as important revenue generators. Video Poker machines are available in some states at restaurants, gas stations, convenience stores, and bars. Some 1,400 Internet gambling sites handle $3 billion in bets every year, creating opportunities for 24-hour gambling—even though U.S. citizens cannot legally bet on Web-based casino games.[39]

Other practices encourage gambling as well. Advertising for gambling is increasing. For example, California and New York each spend roughly $30 million a year on state lottery advertising (see Exhibit 21.7). Furthermore, some casinos have installed real-time monitoring systems that show how much a given consumer is winning or losing. When customers sign up for Harrah's Total Rewards program, the company can track their betting and spending activities in any Harrah's casino. The goal is to be able to target customers with appropriate marketing communications.[40] Some people worry that casinos will be targeting people who are big spenders—including those who have gambling problems. Given these trends, it is perhaps not surprising that spending on gambling has increased dramatically over the past 20 years.

Marketing activities that deal with addictive and compulsive consumption. Some marketing activities aim to reduce addictive and compulsive consumption. For example, compulsive gambling hot lines have been established by some states and casinos. These hot lines help suicidal and emotionally distraught compulsive gamblers. Such calls are especially frequent following the Super Bowl—perhaps because the hype surrounding the game makes betting even more enticing to compulsive gamblers.[41] Some people are concerned that gambling industry growth will be followed by increases in the number of consumers who become compulsive gamblers and/or an increase in gambling opportunities for those already hooked. ●

Underage Drinking and Smoking

As mentioned earlier, addictions to alcohol and tobacco represent one form of deviant consumer behavior. However, use of these products is also associated with another deviant consumer behavior: their illegal use by minors.

Prevalence of Underage Drinking and Smoking Although historically states have set different minimum drinking ages, the National Minimum Drinking Age Act now requires states to raise the legal drinking age to 21 in order to receive federal highway funds. Yet even when minors cannot legally consume alcohol and tobacco, many do.[42] High school and junior high school students drink 1.1 billion cans of beer and 35 percent of the wine coolers sold in the United States. Although they cannot legally drink them, teenagers are three times more likely than adults to be aware of lemon-flavored alcoholic beverages and two times more likely than adults to have sampled these products.[43] Half of all junior and senior high school students have consumed alcohol. More than 8 million of the 207 million U.S. students in grades 7 to 12 drink weekly. Nearly one-third of high school students and nearly 45 percent of college students have engaged in "binge drinking" (drinking more than five drinks in one sitting). Four million children are alcoholics or problem drinkers. One million young consumers begin smoking every year, and 90 percent of new smokers are teenagers. An estimated 3,000 children begin smoking each day. These figures are even more dramatic in Asian countries where there are few bans on cigarette adverting. In the Philippines, half of the consumers between the ages of 7 and 17 smoke.

Consequences of Underage Drinking and Smoking The problem of drinking and smoking by underage consumers has consequences for the individual consumer and for society as a whole.[44] Overuse of alcohol has been implicated in 70 percent of campus violence cases, 68 percent of campus property damage cases, and 40 percent of academic failures. Overuse of alcohol is regarded as the primary discipline, emotional, and physical problem on college campuses. Alcohol is also involved in roughly half of teen highway fatalities, half of all youth suicides, and 90 percent of campus hazing deaths. Almost half of all schools polled say that alcohol is the most serious problem they face. Alcohol is even cited as a factor explaining the rising costs of college tuition. Now that colleges are liable for campus drinking incidents, the cost of insurance (and hence tuition) has skyrocketed. Accidents due to drinking also contribute to the high cost of automobile insurance for young consumers. Groups like Mothers Against Drunk Driving (MADD) and Students Against Drunk Driving (SADD) work to enact legislation to punish drinking and driving, use social disapproval to pressure students not to drink and drive, and institute programs that stress the importance of having a designated driver.

Cigarette smoking at an early age is also harmful, causing many health problems like lung cancer and heart disease. Moreover, nonsmokers can be harmed through exposure to secondhand smoke. Use of tobacco products also makes young consumers more vulnerable to the problems of addictive consumption previously noted. Furthermore, in any given year 75 percent of adolescent smokers have tried to quit smoking but cannot do so.[45] As with underage drinking, public interest groups and government organizations publicize the negative health consequences associated with smoking (see Exhibit 21.8).

MARKETING IMPLICATIONS

A number of marketing issues are related to underage drinking and smoking.

Product availability. First, some argue that it is all too easy for underage consumers to buy alcohol and tobacco.[46] They can easily get fake IDs, and store clerks are often lax in checking IDs. Indeed, most underage consumers who smoke buy their own cigarettes, usually at convenience stores and gas stations.

Exposure to advertising. A second issue is whether kids are exposed to too much advertising for alcohol and tobacco and whether such exposure increases the tendency to buy these products. Arguments that disprove and support this notion have been advanced. A recent survey also showed that only 8 percent of consumers identify advertising as a cause of adolescent drinking (the major causes named were peer pressure and having parents who drink). Other studies show that

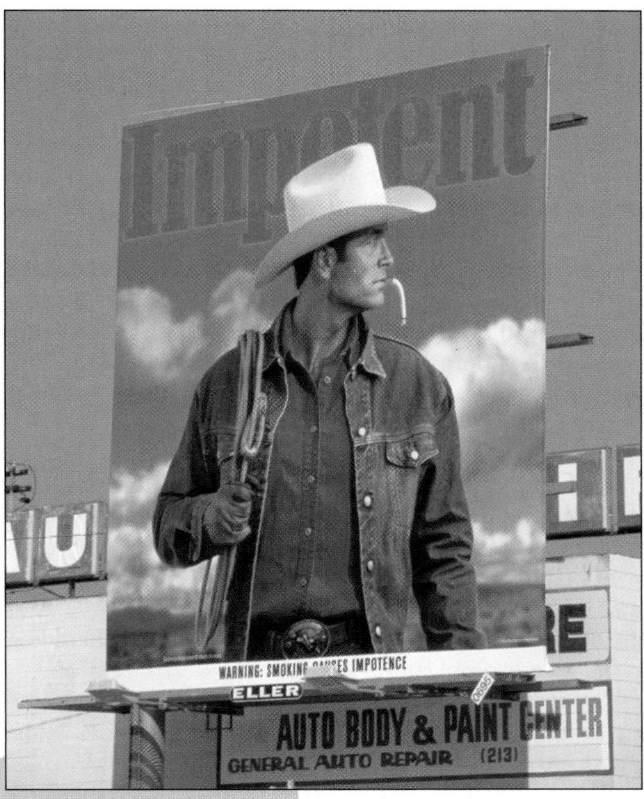

EXHIBIT 21.8
Publicizing the Health Consequences of Smoking
Cigarette smoking at an early age can lead to serious health consequences, including impotence, lung cancer and heart disease. Public interest groups and government organizations sometimes call attention to these negative health consequences.

Source: © David Young-Wolff/PhotoEdit.

peer influence, parental smoking, and self-esteem are the major factors affecting smoking. Some argue that alcohol and cigarette advertising has limited effects on underage consumers.[47]

The United States bans cigarette commercials on TV, and Canada bans almost all cigarette advertising. Nevertheless, children are *exposed* to a lot of alcohol and tobacco advertising.[48] One study found that 15 alcohol commercials are broadcast for every hour of sports programs—and children are heavy viewers of sports. Furthermore, only 3 of 685 alcohol ads televised during 122 sporting events advertised drinking in moderation. Most ads depict alcohol as a positive and appropriate behavior of socially active and beautiful people. Alcohol products are also promoted on the Internet. For example, the Jim Beam site has a "virtual bar." Although the site says consumers must be over 21 to access the bar, checking the actual age of each visitor can be problematic.

Despite the tobacco industry's agreement to avoid marketing to children, many have stepped up advertising in popular adult consumer publications—magazines that many teens also read, which means these underage consumers are being exposed to cigarette ads.[49] Most youthful smokers choose the most heavily advertised brands—further implicating advertising as a cause of smoking behavior. Exposure may be even greater as advertisers look for ways to get around advertising bans.[50] For example, in Canada and some parts of Asia, where tobacco advertising is banned, advertisers use sponsorships and licensed goods to stay in the public eye. These items do not need to carry the Surgeon General's warning label in foreign countries either. Thus consumers may not be warned of the dangers of smoking. California and other states have charged tobacco marketers with reaching children using efforts such as branded matchbooks and billboards at sporting events.[51]

Traditionally, alcohol marketers have voluntarily refrained from advertising hard liquor (anything except beer and wine) on broadcast TV, although some liquor is advertised on cable television and a few companies want to use broadcast TV commercials.[52] Companies are likely to push for hard liquor ads on broadcast TV because beer and other alcoholic beverages are allowed to air commercials; in addition, increases in advertising expenditures have historically been associated with increased alcohol consumption.[53] Moreover, evidence suggests that the more young consumers view alcohol ads, the more they know about these products, and the more likely they are to use them.[54] One study found that almost 90 percent of 11- and 12-year-old children could identify Spuds MacKenzie as a character associated with Budweiser beer—a figure nine times the number who could identify a Coke slogan. Another found that the Budweiser frogs were among the most recognizable TV animals among 9- to 11-year-olds. Still another found that 10-year-old children had no trouble reeling off names of beers and their slogans. Children who were the most aware of these ads were most likely to say that they intended to drink later in life.

A similar effect has been observed with cigarette advertising. Some research shows that teens who smoke are more likely to be aware of and recognize cigarette ads than teens who do not smoke. Furthermore, adolescents who have the greatest exposure to cigarette advertising in general tend to be the heaviest smokers, and the brands that do the most advertising tend to attract a significantly greater proportion of teenagers than adults. Thus teens appear to be particularly sensitive to advertising for cigarettes.

Targeting youth. Third, and perhaps of even more concern, is the suspicion that the cigarette and alcohol manufacturers explicitly target young consumers by portraying advertising images that youths find relevant.[55] The surgeon general, for example, has criticized the alcohol and tobacco industries for using lifestyle appeals that teens find desirable (associating the products with fun, beauty, social acceptance, sports, and sex). Many cigarette ads evoke images such as freedom from authority and independence—themes that clearly appeal to young consumers. Advertising content that shows individuals engaged in risky behavior while consuming alcohol has also been criticized.

Some regulators and critics charge that advertisers target young consumers by using fictional and cartoon characters.[56] The most vehement criticism has been of the use of the cartoon character Joe Camel for Camel cigarettes, a campaign that was withdrawn in 1997.[57] One study found that children were more likely than adults to associate Joe Camel with cigarettes and were more likely than adults to find Joe Camel appealing and to say he was "someone they would like to be friends with." Compared with children who did not like the Joe Camel cartoon character, those who did like him were either ambivalent in their smoking intentions or expressed definite intentions to smoke. Several other studies found that the popularity of the Camel brand increased since the Joe Camel campaign began and almost one-third of adolescents who buy their own cigarettes buy or prefer Camels.[58]

Advertisers claim that such characters have little effect on consumers' desires or purchasing behavior. As one advertiser noted, children are not demanding Metropolitan Life insurance policies that are promoted by Snoopy and Woodstock.[59] Others argue that although children were aware of Joe Camel, their awareness was significantly lower than their awareness of other advertising characters. A study showed that children who were most able to associate Joe Camel with cigarettes had the least favorable image of cigarettes.[60] The alcohol industry also argues that it does not target young consumers and says it has taken great strides to develop ads promoting responsible drinking. Anheuser-Busch alone has spent more than $100 million over the past decade promoting responsible drinking.[61]

Mainstream companies selling smoking and drinking. Fourth, there is concern that mainstream advertisers may be sending inappropriate messages about cigarettes and alcohol even if they don't sell these products. For example, Abercrombie & Fitch recently came under public attack for producing a "back to school" issue of its catalog/magazine targeted to college students. Parents and organizations like MADD were upset over a feature titled "Drinking 101" that offered recipes for 10 hard-core cocktails.[62]

Warning labels and advertisements. Marketers need to be concerned about displaying appropriate warning labels on cigarette and alcohol packages and in ads.[63] Tobacco packages and ads are required to carry the Surgeon General's warning regarding the dangers of smoking (see Exhibit 21.9). Warning labels that reveal the dangers of drinking and driving and the risks of alcohol to pregnant women are also required. Arizona requires businesses that sell alcohol to put up posters warning of the risks of drinking while pregnant. However, these warning labels and posters have not been very effective in changing young consumers' behaviors over long periods.[64] Perhaps one reason is that consumers' perceptual defenses make them tune out these messages. In response, the Surgeon General has called for more

EXHIBIT 21.9
Cigarette Warnings
Cigarette ads and packages must carry one of the Surgeon General's warnings regarding the dangers of smoking. In Canada new warnings with pictures like the one shown here are being used.
Source: Getty Images.

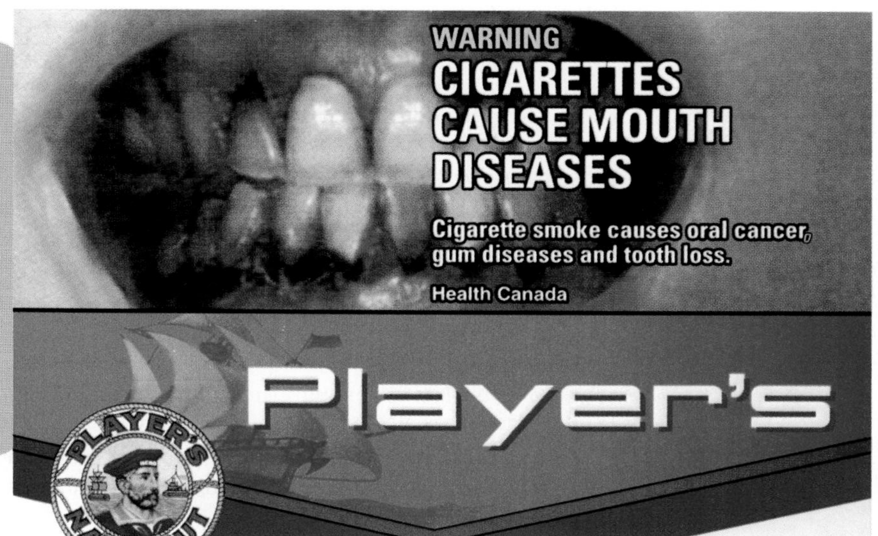

explicit health warnings on labels. Manufacturers now list alcohol levels on their products so consumers clearly understand how strong the beverage is. Some researchers are also experimenting with more attention-getting warning labels and messages. Research found that showing high school students an antismoking advertisement before a movie in which teen characters smoked helped reposition the smoking as a tainted activity.[65] Other researchers have suggested that understanding the rituals involved in underage binge drinking can be the basis of public service announcements to reduce this behavior.[66] ●

NEGATIVE EFFECTS OF MARKETING

Marketing has been implicated as contributing to other negative social outcomes—outcomes that are not necessarily related to deviant acquisition or consumption. Several of these negative effects are examined here, including whether advertising affects self-image, whether it misrepresents or inappropriately depicts certain consumer segments, and whether marketing practices invade consumers' privacy.

Does Advertising Affect Self-Image?

Advertising has long been accused of depicting idealized images of people and their lives. For example, few people have homes like those depicted in ads for household products, and few enjoy holidays in the idealized manner depicted by Hallmark and Royal Caribbean. Advertising may create an idealized image of what one's life *should* be like. If we do not measure up to this idealized image, we may feel dissatisfied. This section considers two aspects of advertising and its impact on self-image:

- Does advertising make consumers dissatisfied with their appearance?
- Does advertising make consumers materialistic and hence dissatisfied with what they own?

Idealized Body Images Male models shown in advertisements are often trim with well-developed muscles and handsome features. The female models who appear in advertisements are mostly young, very thin, and exceedingly beautiful.

Because these ads represent society's conception of the ideal man or woman, they exemplify traits that many men and women will never actually achieve. A particularly salient issue for both men and women is how their body compares to that of thin models.

Obsessions with Thinness American society places great value on thinness as a characteristic of women. As evidence, 70 percent of normal-weight women want to be thinner, and 23 percent of underweight women want to be even thinner than they are.[67] A recent study of 9-year-old girls indicated that roughly 40 percent were dieting. Some children are dieting to such an extent that they are adversely affecting their growth.[68] A New Zealand study found that thinness is popular and dieting is considered normal behavior. The same research found that from the 1950s through the 1980s, women depicted in ads got increasingly thinner.[69] Eating disorders affect up to 3.5 percent of the U.S. population and are increasing dramatically among young women in Japan.[70] In another study, 11 percent of men said they would trade more than five years of their lives to achieve personal weight goals—statistics that closely track women's responses.[71] And men are believed to account for up to 30 percent of the bulimic college population.[72]

This focus on thinness is a relatively recent phenomenon. During the 15th through 18th centuries, being fat was considered fashionable and erotic.[73] Furthermore, being thin is mainly valued in developed countries. In Third World countries, where food is lacking and disease is rampant, weight gain is associated with health and prosperity.[74]

Thinness, Advertising, and Self-Perceptions Certainly, seeing ads with thin models does not make someone become bulimic or anorexic, but do such ads serve as an impetus to consumers with predispositions to eating disorders? Does identification with superthin models create dissatisfaction with one's own body and appearance?[75] Some evidence suggests the answer to these questions is yes.

social comparison theory A theory that proposes that individuals have a drive to compare themselves with other people.

Social comparison theory proposes that individuals have a drive to compare themselves with other people.[76] Consistent with this theory, some research has found that young adult females do compare themselves with models in advertisements and that such self-comparisons can affect self-esteem.[77] Another study suggests that high school girls who are predisposed to unhealthy weight-loss behaviors frequently read fitness and health magazines because they want ideas about losing weight.[78] Seniors are also affected: according to AARP research, 25 percent of older women are currently dieting and 23 percent plan to diet soon.[79]

One outcome of this comparison process is that consumers feel inadequate if they do not live up to the comparison person. Exhibit 21.10 illustrates the statements female consumers in one study made when they looked at magazine ads that featured beautiful models. Interestingly, some research has also found that consumers who view ads with beautiful models reduce their attractiveness ratings of average-looking women. A potentially strong conclusion, based on the research, is that advertising can have an unintended but negative impact on whether men and women are satisfied with their appearance.[80] Clearly, the ad in Exhibit 21.11 is trying to counter this effect.

MARKETING IMPLICATIONS Fortunately, some companies are becoming more sensitive to the effects of such messages. In the fashion industry, demand for plus-size models is up—perhaps in response to

GENERAL COMPARISON	"God! I wish I looked like that." (written comment about a cosmetic ad before discussion began) "There's certain [ads] that I look at and say, 'Wow! I'd sure like to look like that.'" "In high school, you want to think that you could look like that if you try. Then in college, you realize, 'Oh, forget it.'"
ADS GENERATING SPECIFIC BODY COMPARISONS	"When I see ads, I always look at the chest. I like it when she has no chest. Because, you know, I don't either." "I have wide hips. I always look at the hips. I guess I'm just jealous." "When I look at a model I look at the arms, because my arms are awful."
NEGATIVE SELF-FEELINGS FROM VIEWING ADS	"You look at these ads and you feel inadequate, like you can't measure up." "It's frustrating when you start to realize you should look that way—I mean—I can't." "I used to go through these magazines every day and look at [models in the ads] and wish I looked like them. I used to go running every day, and really thought maybe I could look like them. I remember, I even picked one model in particular and cut out ads with her in them. I was pretty obsessed. And I finally realized this wasn't realistic. But I sometimes still look and think, 'Well, maybe.'" "Sometimes [ads with models] can make you feel a little depressed." "They make me feel self-critical." (participant viewing models in swimsuit ads)

EXHIBIT 21.10
Women's Reactions to Idealized Body Images in Ads

One study found that women exposed to ads with beautiful and thin models compared the models with themselves or specific parts of their bodies. In some cases, the ads made consumers feel bad about themselves.

Source: Marsha L. Richins, "Social Comparison and the Idealized Images of Advertising," *Journal of Consumer Research*, June 1991, pp. 71–83.

consumers' demands for different types of women in fashion products and ads.[81] Furthermore, although some women may be unhappy about how they compare with models in ads, women in general are becoming more comfortable with themselves and are more hostile toward advertisers that perpetuate unrealistic images of women.[82] ●

Materialism Advertising has long been criticized for perpetuating materialistic values and making consumers less satisfied with their lives.[83] For example, as advertising content has increasingly depicted materialistic themes, Americans have become more materialistic. Consumers in other countries have also become more materialistic, and the rise in materialism often coincides with the purchase of U.S. products and exposure to U.S. advertisements. Research shows that consumers who watch a lot of television and who find that television commercials are realistic tend to be more materialistic than consumers who do not watch as much television.[84] Television shows may provide a biased or distorted view of reality by showing heroes who seem to have everything at their disposal. Moreover, children are aware of more than 200 brand names by the time they reach first grade, which may influence their future choices.[85]

Social comparison theory would predict that if advertising and the media show individuals with many material possessions, consumers might use advertising as a way of judging their personal accomplishments. Consumers who perceive that they are less well off than the comparison population may be less satisfied with their lives and accomplishments. Some evidence supports this idea. Consumers who watch a lot of advertising tend to overestimate how well off the average consumer is.[86] This misperception sets up a potentially false

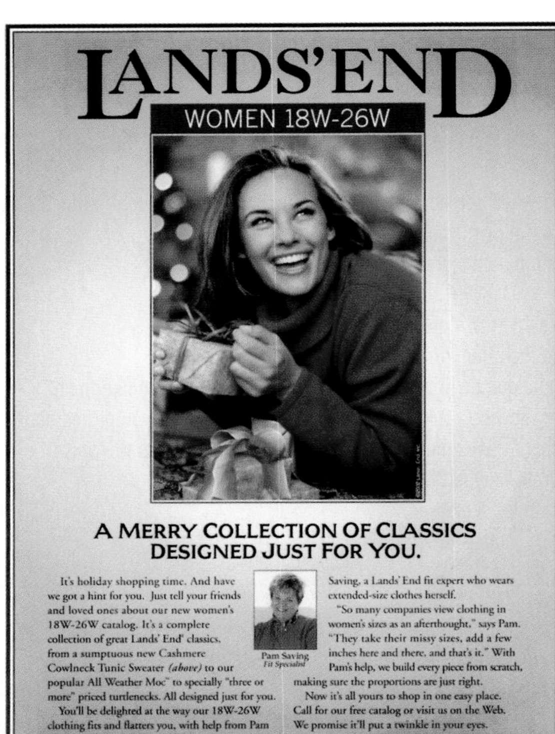

EXHIBIT 21.11
Counteracting the Ideal Image
A number of advertisers are making products to fit normal and larger sized women—and in so doing, promote the message that beautiful women come in all shapes and sizes.

Source: © 2003 Lands' End, Inc. Used with permission.

frame of reference regarding how much the average consumer owns. Moreover, materialistic consumers may pay undue attention to the possessions of others and make inferences about them based on the possessions they own.[87]

Because the material "good life" often depicted in advertising is out of reach for many, consumers are set up for potential dissatisfaction. Governments in some countries have been reluctant to show U.S. ads out of fear that the ads will set off a wave of demand for products the country cannot produce and/or the people cannot afford.[88] In Russia, children who were used to playing with stones and chalk are now encountering ads for toys such as Lego blocks and Barbie dolls and for foods such as Coca-Cola and chocolate bars. As one consumer noted, "Parents are now in the position of disappointing their children in ways that were once impossible."[89] Although little definitive evidence exists to prove that advertising causes materialism and dissatisfaction, the connection is provocative and deserving of more research attention.

Does Advertising Misrepresent Segments of Consumers?

Critics also charge that advertising ignores or inaccurately represents key segments in the marketplace.

Ignoring Key Segments Although women represent 50 percent of the population, they have been conspicuously absent in ads for nondomestic products and large-ticket items like cars.[90] Even when women are represented, the ads often contain male voice-overs. Advertisers have historically believed that male voices are more convincing, more credible, and better at conveying knowledge and expertise than female voices are. When women's voices are used, they are used primarily to speak to dogs, cats, babies, children, and women dieters rather than to the population at large.[91]

Likewise, although African Americans represent roughly 12 percent of the U.S. population and 11 percent of magazine readers, one study found that they appeared in less than 5 percent of all magazine ads and less than 8 percent of television ads. Hispanics and Asians, who are represented in even fewer television commercials, are often shown in primarily background roles when they appear in ads.[92] Others charge that although marketers are more cognizant of the important Hispanic and African American markets, consumers from countries such as Iran, Israel, Poland, Russia, Korea, and Vietnam are often ignored.[93] Sometimes minorities are deliberately excluded from advertising. In Britain, Ford Motor Company was criticized for substituting white faces for black, Indian, and Pakistani workers who appeared in a company brochure.[94] Mature consumers also tend to be underrepresented or, when represented, tend to have minor roles in ads. [95]

Misrepresenting Key Segments Key consumer segments are sometimes represented in advertising in stereotypical or inappropriate ways.[96] For example, women have been represented in gender stereotyped ways (as the mother, wife, homemaker, and sex object), a pattern that holds true whether the products are for men or for women. Women have historically been shown in ads for household cleaning products even though a relatively large number of households are headed by single or divorced men. Women are also more likely than men to be depicted without a paid occupation or shown in lower status occupations than men—a portrayal that does not accurately represent the status of women in the workforce. In contrast, men and boys have been portrayed as knowledgeable, achieving, independent, active, dynamic, masterful, and important.

Both in the United States and in other countries, women and girls have often been depicted as secondary, dependent, nurturing, in need of help, and concerned about appearance. Although many U.S. ads now play up the independence of teenage girls, many ads in Japan depict teenage girls in inappropriately young poses and scenes.[97] Brewing company ads, notorious for portraying scantily clad women, have been criticized for being sexist and discriminating against women.

Stereotypical images of minorities can also be identified.[98] For example, consistent with ethnic stereotypes regarding work ethic, Asian consumers in ads are more likely to appear in work situations than in family or social roles. Some ads stereotype mature consumers in ways that are unflattering.[99] Depictions of the mature consumer as blue-haired, weak, passive, unproductive, ailing, doddering, foolish, and sexless are not uncommon, and advertisers sometimes use stereotypical terms such as *senior citizens, retirees,* and *golden years*. Mature consumers tend to react negatively to ads that show older people leading nonproductive lives. Because many mature consumers view themselves as being 10 to 15 years younger than their actual chronological age, they react more positively to ads whose models are somewhat younger than they are.

MARKETING IMPLICATIONS Alienating consumers by excluding or failing to represent them accurately can negatively affect consumers' images of and attitudes toward brands and companies.[100] Consumers may have more extreme reactions to offensive advertising. Some Canadian women, for example, boycott clothing and cosmetic products that are advertised using inaccurate and unrealistic depictions of women. Given the size of these markets, alienating consumers can be very costly. Therefore, many marketers are taking steps to improve their depiction of key consumer segments.

Represent key segments. Many advertisers have made efforts to represent key segments in their advertising.[101] For example, a recent study found that 26 percent of all commercials shown by ABC, CBS, and NBC during one week of prime-time programming contained African American consumers. Avon, Cover Girl, and other cosmetics firms are using African American celebrities such as Venus and Serena Williams and Brandy in their ads.[102] The representation of mature consumers in print ads has also been on the rise. Some companies have dropped logos and images that represent minorities in stereotypical ways or have modified their logos to present more positive portrayals. For example, Quaker Oats changed Aunt Jemima from a black mammy to a black homemaker—someone akin to Betty Crocker.

Avoid stereotypes. Advertisers are also representing groups in more positive and less stereotypical ways. Several ads have done well by depicting the mature consumer as wise, spunky, romantic, and individualistic. In general, ads that depict mature consumers as active, take-charge doers are more consistent with mature consumers' views of themselves. Similarly, the portrayal of women in advertising is improving.[103] Car companies have begun to depict women as decision makers, and men are now being shown in activities historically associated with women. Some ads, like the one in Exhibit 21.12, show poignant pictures of fathers engaged in fun and nurturing activities with their children.

Tailor communications to key targets. Companies are also recognizing that they must go beyond simply placing a member of a minority group in an ad. Instead, advertisers need to understand more about these consumers.[104] Many companies, including McDonald's, rely on specialty advertising agencies that have in-depth knowledge of these key target groups. ●

Do Marketing Practices Invade Consumers' Privacy?

The opening vignette raised concerns about online companies invading consumers' privacy by collecting information about them, often without their knowledge. Many non-Internet organizations, including retailers, banks, credit reporting agencies, mailing list firms, telephone companies, and insurance and banking companies, also collect and exchange information about consumers through product registration cards, credit applications, sales information, and other techniques.

EXHIBIT 21.12
Changing Images of Men in Advertising
Some advertisers have tried to depict less stereotypical images of men, showing them as prominent figures in sensitive and nurturing roles.

Source: Courtesy of Wear-Dated.

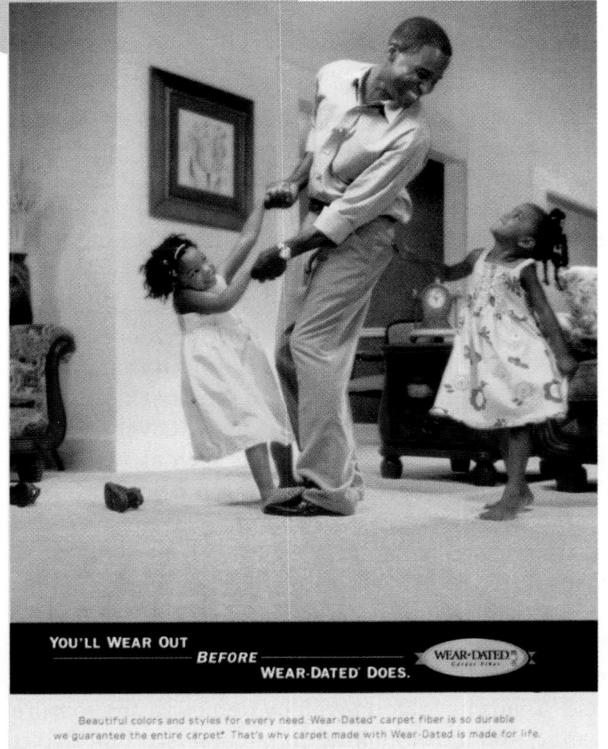

YOU'LL WEAR OUT
BEFORE
WEAR-DATED® DOES.
WEAR-DATED
Beautiful colors and styles for every need. Wear-Dated® carpet fiber is so durable
we guarantee the entire carpet.* That's why carpet made with Wear-Dated is made for life.
www.weardated.com

Sources of Marketing Information Interestingly, much of the information that companies have about consumers is information that consumers themselves provide. For example, marketers can track consumer purchases through scanner data collected at the supermarket checkout. Many catalog companies know a great deal about consumers based on what they buy and which neighborhood they live in. Retailers and banks collect information from the applications that consumers fill out when applying for credit and send many details to the credit reporting agencies, which make data available to other credit companies. And companies are always trying to learn more about consumers through marketing research.

Considerable consumer information also exists in the public domain in the form of zip codes and census data. The government sells this information to marketers who use it to update their mailing lists, target people who have moved, determine consumers' likely income based on the type of neighborhood in which they live, and so on.[105]

Consumers' Responses Consumers are clearly uncomfortable with the amount of information marketers have about them.[106] According to research, 78 percent of consumers believe that businesses collect too much personal information and 88 percent are concerned about threats to their personal privacy. Eighty-two percent perceive a lack of control over how businesses use their personal information, and 41 percent believe that businesses have already invaded their privacy.[107] In a survey about privacy on the Internet, 64 percent of respondents agreed that companies using the Internet should not be allowed to track users for the purposes of sending them marketing messages.[108] In another study, 61 percent of the respondents decided not to use a financial Web site because of concerns about how their personal data would be handled.[109] Consumers also complain that they receive no money when credit card companies, publishers, and catalog companies (among others) sell their names to other companies. Furthermore, consumers must spend time sifting through mailings from companies that have bought their name and wade through unsolicited e-mail from online businesses.[110]

Many consumers do not trust marketers' use of personal information.[111] Consumers worry that companies collect information about them for one purpose but use it for another purpose or sell it to another company without their knowledge. They also worry that personal data is handled by individuals who may not be properly authorized to handle it and who can therefore steal or abuse it. Another worry is that personal data such as credit histories may have errors but that protections against such errors may be inadequate. In addition, consumers and marketers disagree on who should control consumer information. For example, some businesses believe that they own whatever information they legitimately obtain about their customers and they justify their use of consumer information by saying it helps them to provide better products and services to consumers.[112]

MARKETING IMPLICATIONS

Why are consumers so concerned about marketers' use of personal information?

Horror stories hurt all marketers. One of the major reasons for concern is that a small number of unscrupulous marketers use marketing techniques to defraud consumers, such as companies that use telemarketing to defraud elderly consumers of their life savings.[113] These stories get considerable media attention and tarnish the image of all marketers. Consumers are also wary because information disclosures occurring on other fronts make them worry about the lack of privacy in general. For example, more workers are losing jobs or are being denied jobs because information about their current or past health history has been leaked to current or prospective employers.[114]

Communicating how information helps consumers. Marketers believe that consumers worry about privacy because they really do not understand how the information marketers collect is used and how it might benefit consumers. For example, the information collected by catalog companies on such things as consumers' household characteristics, clothing style, and sizes allows marketers to develop customized catalogs. This practice (1) eliminates waste because marketers can more accurately target consumers; (2) better matches products to consumer needs; and (3) keeps costs down so that savings may be passed on to consumers. Tracking personal information online allows firms to help consumers save time by not retyping that information; in addition, the companies can provide customized messages, products, or services tailored to the needs of specific consumers. Excite, for example, lets customers personalize pages to show local weather, news, movie listings, and so on. Customers who develop these personalized pages return to the site 20 times more often than those who do not.[115]

Laws and self-imposed regulation. Consumers are gaining more power against unwanted marketing efforts. In Canada, a privacy code requires direct marketers to give consumers the opportunity to opt out of mailing lists.[116] Although U.S. consumers can write to the Direct Marketing Association and ask that their names not be sold to other companies, many consumers do not know about this option.[117] In Germany, laws prohibit companies from exchanging customer lists. And the European Union (EU) has strict regulations governing the transfer of personal information to companies outside the EU.[118]

The U. S. government is giving businesses a last chance to design self-imposed standards for consumer privacy protection. The Council of Better Business Bureaus and the Alliance for Privacy (a group of 50 top U.S. companies) are developing plans that require members to inform consumers about the personal information being collected online and how that information will be shared.[119] Online businesses can also reassure consumers by paying for an outside firm to conduct a privacy audit showing how they use personal data.[120] ●

How Can Consumers Resist Marketing Practices?

What can consumers do if they are upset about the negative effects of marketing practices? Can consumers change the nature of marketing activities? The answer is yes. Consumers can engage in several forms of consumer resistance.[121]

Individual Resistance Efforts First, consumers who are upset or otherwise dissatisfied with marketing practices can demonstrate dissatisfaction by not patronizing the offending marketer in the future, by complaining to the offending marketer, and/or by spreading negative word of mouth. These individual consumer resistance strategies can be very effective. For example, Calvin Klein withdrew an ad campaign that showed very young girls in provocatively posed positions in response to public outcry and criticisms of child pornography.[122]

Advocacy Groups Group strategies are potentially even more powerful than unorganized consumer efforts. Some formally organized advocacy groups engage in resistance by informing the public about business practices they regard as socially inappropriate (see Exhibit 21.13). The Center for the Study of Commercialism, for example, distributes information via videos, pamphlets, books, and conferences and uses lobbying to stop marketing practices such as Channel One's advertising in schools. *Adbusters,* a magazine published by Canada's Media Foundation, prints articles that make consumers aware of commercial excess, for example, "The McBraining of America" and "The Casino Society."[123] The Center for Food Safety, the Organic Consumers Association, and five other advocacy groups have staged public demonstrations to protest Campbell's Soup's use of ingredients that may be genetically modified, such as soybeans and corn.[124] Teens in Minnesota have formed Target Market as an advocacy group to discourage underage smoking.[125]

EXHIBIT 21.13
Advocacy Advertising
Advocacy groups like the American Anti-Vivisection Society try to bring public attention to business practices regarded as socially, politically, or morally inappropriate.

Source: Courtesy of the American Anti-Vivisection Society.

COMPANION
or research tool?
Experiments on dogs DO NOT save human lives. In 2000, over 70,000 dogs were used in laboratories, most were killed. Many did not receive any relief from pain. Contact AAVS for more information on how to stop cruelty to animals.
801 Old York Road, Jenkintown, PA. 19046
800.SAY.AAVS ¥ www.aavs.org ¥ aavs@aavs.org
aavs
American Anti-Vivisection Society

Boycotts A **boycott** is an organized activity in which consumers avoid purchasing products or services from a company whose policies or practices are seen as unfair or unjust. Organized boycotts are able to gain publicity and are likely to have more impact than the same number of consumers acting on their own.[126] Consumers have

boycott An organized activity in which consumers avoid purchasing products or services from a company whose policies or practices are seen as unfair or unjust.

boycotted products made in foreign sweatshops. Nike, for instance, has come under attack for this practice. In Indonesia, workers might make as little as $.15 per hour, although the shoes sell for $75 and up. People for the Ethical Treatment of Animals has organized boycotts against McDonald's, Burger King, Wendy's, and Safeway to force these firms to insist that their suppliers meet minimal animal welfare standards.[127] Sometimes boycotts are directed against a company's activities rather than against a product itself.[128] Not long ago, the National Hispanic Media Coalition boycotted Capital Cities/ABC because it had not included Latinos and Latin-themed roles in its programs.

Although only 20 national boycotts were recorded by 1981, the number had risen beyond 250 by the early 1990s.[129] This dramatic increase was partly due to government deregulation of businesses and the underfunding of agencies that monitor business practices.[130] Because of perceptions that the government was not regulating business practices, the public took on the action of doing so.

Clearly, boycotts can hurt companies financially. When Pizzeria Uno was besieged by protesters with leaflets decrying its use of coffee from war-torn El Salvador, sales dropped.[131] However, in some cases sales have risen because of boycotts (perhaps because the publicity made the company's name more familiar). For example, StarKist tuna sales rose during a tuna boycott.[132] The primary indicators that a boycott has been successful are not its financial effects, but rather that it (1) changes the offending policies, (2) makes businesses more cautious and responsible in their future activities, and (3) forces changes in the behavior of nontargeted businesses that engage in similarly offensive practices.

SUMMARY

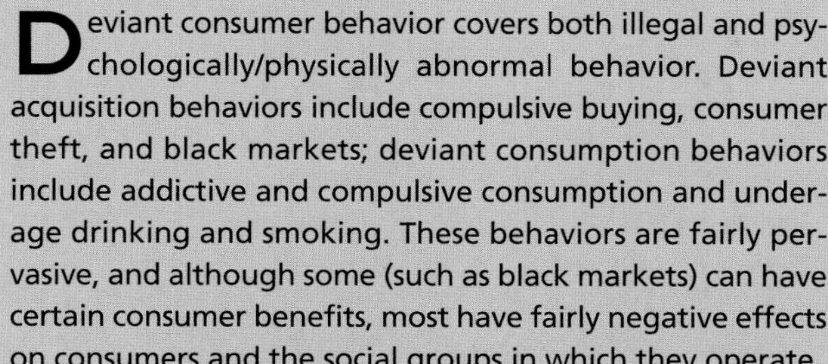

Deviant consumer behavior covers both illegal and psychologically/physically abnormal behavior. Deviant acquisition behaviors include compulsive buying, consumer theft, and black markets; deviant consumption behaviors include addictive and compulsive consumption and underage drinking and smoking. These behaviors are fairly pervasive, and although some (such as black markets) can have certain consumer benefits, most have fairly negative effects on consumers and the social groups in which they operate.

Moreover, critics have questioned whether and/or how much marketing practices influence these behaviors. Advertising has been accused of: perpetuating idealized body images; creating materialistic values; failing to represent key consumer segments; misrepresenting key segments; and invading consumer privacy. In response, many companies are adopting strategies to reduce public criticism and put marketing practices in a more favorable light. At the same time, sophisticated consumers are showing their disapproval of practices regarded as disreputable, objectionable, and/or unethical through individual resistance, support of advocacy groups, and participation in boycotts.

QUESTIONS FOR REVIEW AND DISCUSSION

1. What is compulsive buying, and why is it a problem?
2. How do temptation and rationalization affect consumer theft?
3. How does addictive consumption differ from compulsive consumption?
4. What is social comparison theory, and how does it apply to advertising?
5. Why has advertising been criticized for overlooking or misrepresenting certain consumer segments?
6. What can consumers do to resist marketing practices they perceive as unwanted or unethical?

EXERCISES

1. Visit different types of retail establishments and different service organizations to learn about their yearly losses due to theft, insights about factors affecting theft, whether theft has been increasing or decreasing in recent years, and what they are doing to reduce theft. Report your results to the class. Interview consumers about their theft behavior. Ask consumers whether they have ever engaged in theft and why. Discuss your findings with other members of the class. Do the findings support, enhance, or modify the findings shown in Exhibit 21.6?
2. Collect and share magazine advertisements that deal with cigarettes or alcohol. Do these ads suggest that such advertising (a) is excessive, (b) targets youths, or (c) represents images that are attractive to youths?
3. Collect and share magazine advertisements that use models. Use these advertisements and your own personal experience to argue for or against the idea that advertising perpetuates negative body images.
4. Collect and share magazine advertisements that portray women, minorities, and mature consumers. Based on your observations, evaluate whether advertisers misrepresent these key segments or represent them in stereotypical ways.

ENDNOTES

Chapter 1

1. Natasha Emmons, "Discovery Cove to Expand," *Amusement Business,* July 9, 2001, p. 16; Bruce Orwall, "Would You Spend $179 to Cavort with Dolphins?" *Wall Street Journal,* November 18, 1999, pp. B1, B6.
2. Jacob Jacoby, "Consumer Psychology: An Octennium," in eds. Paul Mussen and Mark Rosenzweig, *Annual Review of Psychology* (Palo Alto, Calif.: Annual Reviews, 1976), pp. 331–358. With permission from the *Annual Review of Psychology,* vol. 27, © 1976, by Annual Reviews.
3. Morris B. Holbrook, "What Is Consumer Research?" *Journal of Consumer Research,* June 1987, pp. 128–132; Russell W. Belk, "Manifesto for a Consumer Behavior of Consumer Behavior," *Scientific Method in Marketing,* 1984, AMA Winter Educators' Conference.
4. Jonathan Arndt, "Role of Product-Related Conversations in the Diffusion of a New Product," *Journal of Marketing Research,* August 1967, pp. 291–295; Vijay Mahajan, Eitan Muller, and Frank M. Bass, "New Product Diffusion Models in Marketing: A Review and Directions," *Journal of Marketing,* January 1990, pp. 1–27.
5. "Dear Data Dog: What's the Most Common Internet Scam?" *American Demographics,* July 1, 2001, p. 26.
6. Jacob Jacoby, Carol K. Berning, and Thomas F. Dietworst, "What about Disposition?" *Journal of Marketing,* April 1977, pp. 22–28.
7. Carolyn Setlow, "A Lesson in Pro-Environmental Retailing," *DSN Retailing Today,* August 20, 2001, p. 16; Tibbet L. Speer, "Growing the Green Market," *American Demographics,* August 1997, pp. 45–49.
8. John L. Mitchell, "Digging for Dollars," *Los Angeles Times,* October 30, 1995, pp. B1, B6.
9. Melanie Trottman, "Antidotes to Airport Rage?" *Wall Street Journal,* August 14, 2000, pp. B1, B6.
10. Andy Dornan, "Killer Apps—Could Mobile Data Be This Century's Tobacco?" *Network Magazine,* February 1, 2001, pp. 14–15; John J. Keller, "Cellular Phones May Affect Use of Pacemakers," *Wall Street Journal,* April 28, 1995, pp. B1, B3; Julia Flynn and John Carey, "More Sound Fury Over Cell Phones: Do They Cause Brain Tumors?" *BusinessWeek,* January 26, 1998, p. 35.
11. Peter K. Francese, "Big Spenders," *American Demographics,* August 1997, pp. 51–58.
12. Dean Takahashi, "Zap! Bop! It's Web Comics," *Wall Street Journal,* April 27, 2000, pp. B1, B12.
13. Mathis Chazanov, "Body Language," *Los Angeles Times: Westside News,* April 30, 1995, pp. 10–15.
14. Pichayaporn Utumporn, "For a Vacation That's a Real Blast, How about Launching a Grenade," *Wall Street Journal,* January 13, 1998, p. B1.
15. Yumiko Ono, "Buttering Up Customers for Margarine," *Wall Street Journal,* June 7, 1994, pp. B1, B6.
16. Barry Newman, "Hungarians Have Cash to Buy Homes If There Were Any," *Wall Street Journal,* July 31, 1995, pp. A1, A4.
17. Craig S. Smith, "U.S. Bank Cards Fight to Win China's Millions," *Wall Street Journal,* July 17, 1995, pp. B1, B5.
18. Adam Cohen, "PayPal's Big Play," *Time,* February 2002, February 11, 2002, p. Y14; "Dreams of a Cashless Society," *The Economist,* May 5, 2001, pp. 65–66.
19. Paula Moore, "Business Bartering Is Bigger Than Ever," *Denver Business Journal,* February 2, 2001, p. 3A; "I'll Trade You a Baby Crib for a Buzz Saw," *BusinessWeek,* May 14, 2001, p. 68.
20. Christina Duff, "At Clothiers, It's Many Unhappy Returns When Buyers Turn Out to Be Borrowers," *Wall Street Journal,* June 2, 1992, pp. B1, B7.
21. Maxine Lans Retsky, "MPAA Sings Different Tune in Copyright Issue," *Marketing News,* March 12, 2001, p. 7; Junda Woo, "Big Copyright Curbs Sought by Industry," *Wall Street Journal,* December 27, 1994, p. B5.
22. See, for example, Valerie S. Folkes, Ingrid M. Martin, and Kamal Gupta, "When to Say When: Effects of Supply on Usage," *Journal of Consumer Research,* December 1993, pp. 467–477.
23. Sara Kehaulani Goo, "Americans Shift Down and Out of Manual Transmissions," *Wall Street Journal,* August 19, 1998, pp. B1, B4.
24. Kevin Goldman, "Company Faces Challenge in Marketing Female Condom," *Wall Street Journal,* July 27, 1994, p. B4.
25. Mark A. Le Turck and Gerald M. Goldhaben, "Effectiveness of Product Warning Labels: Effects of Consumer Information Processing Objectives," *Journal of Public Affairs,* Summer 1989, pp. 111–125.
26. Jacoby, Berning, and Dietworst, "What about Disposition?"
27. Russell W. Belk, "Collecting As Luxury Consumption: Effects on Individuals and Households," *Journal of Economic Psychology,* September 1995, pp. 477–490.
28. Anonymous, "Preferred Plush Targets Tweens' Love of Collecting," *Playthings,* May 2001, p. 67.

29. G. Bruce Knecht and Eleena de Lisser, "Once and for All, Is the Cold Good or Bad for Business?" *Wall Street Journal,* February 6, 1996, pp. B1, B9.

30. Sara McBride, "In Election Whitewash, Dentists Play a Covert but Cleansing Role," *Wall Street Journal,* November 6, 1996, p. B1.

31. Eileen Kinsella, "Eat Grits Sushi, Pitch Ears of Corn and Roll in a Big Bowl of Mush," *Wall Street Journal,* April 19, 1996, p. B1.

32. Khanh T. L. Tran and Erin White, "PlayStation 2: The Chase Is On for First Few," *Wall Street Journal,* October 27, 2000, pp. B1, B4.

33. Erica Mina Okada, "Trade-ins, Mental Accounting, and Product Replacement Decisions," *Journal of Consumer Research,* vol. 27, March 2001, pp. 433–446.

34. Ernest Beck, "In Aisle 10, Soup, Tea—and Bikinis?" *Wall Street Journal,* June 28, 2001, pp. B1, B6.

35. William M. Buckeley, "New Online Casinos May Thwart U.S. Laws," *Wall Street Journal,* May 10, 1995, p. B1.

36. David Whelan, "A Tale of Two Consumers," *American Demographics,* September 1, 2001, pp. 54–57.

37. Mary Beth Grover, "Christmas is Coming: Where's Your Call Center," *Forbes,* December 13, 1999, pp. 86–90; Calmetta Y. Colman and Douglas A. Blackmon, "E-Business: Retailers Strive for Shopping Synergy," *Wall Street Journal,* December 20, 1999, p. B1; Abigail Goldman, "Who'll Be the Internet's Jolliest Holiday Merchants? Customers," *Los Angeles Times,* December 12, 1999, p. 1.

38. Laura Bly, "Orbitz Puts New Spin on Airfares," *USA Today,* June 8, 2001, p. 8D.

39. Nancy Ann Jeffrey, "Attention Shoppers: Get a Loan While Picking Up Groceries," *Wall Street Journal,* December 20, 1995, pp. C1, C18.

40. Lisa Gubernick, "Secondhand Chic," *Forbes,* April 26, 1993, p. 172; Louise Lee, "Secondhand Goods Make First-Rate Gifts, or So More Christmas Shoppers Believe," *Wall Street Journal,* December 19, 1995, p. B1.

41. Leslie Walker, "EBay, Profit Soaring, Raises Sales Estimate for 2001," *Washington Post,* July 20, 2001, p. E02; George Anders, "Yard Sales in Cyberspace," *Wall Street Journal,* April 1, 1999, pp. B1, B12.

42. Shelly Branch, "Campbell's New Soup-to-Go Ads Are Directed at Working Women," *Wall Street Journal,* November 18, 1999, p. B4.

43. Linda L. Price, Eric J. Arnould, and Carolyn Folkman Curasi, "Older Consumers' Disposition of Special Possessions," *Journal of Consumer Research,* vol. 27, September 2000, pp. 179–201.

44. Rob Lenihan, "For Insurance, Shop Online," CNNfn.com, March 20, 2000, **cgi.cnnfn.com/output/pfv/2000/03/20/insurance/q_netinsurance**.

45. Anonymous, "Recycle That PC—For a Fee," *Electronic School,* January 2001, p. 14.

46. Morris B. Holbrook and Meryl P. Gardner, "How Motivation Moderates the Effects of Emotion on the Duration of Consumption," *Journal of Business Research,* July 1998, pp. 241–252.

47. Rasul Bailay, "A Hindu Festival Attracts the Faithful and U.S. Marketers," *Wall Street Journal,* February 12, 2001, p. A18.

48. Emily Nelson, "The Art of the Sale," *Wall Street Journal,* January 11, 2001, pp. B1, B6.

49. Matt Rees, "For Some, Frequent-Flier Miles a Passion," *Los Angeles Times,* April 6, 1995, p. D5.

50. Joseph C. Nunes, "A Cognitive Model of People's Usage Estimations," *Journal of Marketing Research,* vol. 38, November 2000, pp. 397–409.

51. "Overweight Prevalence," *U.S. Department of Health and Human Services,* National Center for Health Statistics, July 10, 2001, **www.cdc.gov/nchs/fastats/overwt.htm**; Shannon Dorcht, "America Weighs In," *American Demographics,* June 1997, pp. 39–45.

52. Elyse Tanouye, "Researchers Report More Patients Ill with Bacterium Resistant to Antibiotics," *Wall Street Journal,* August 24, 1995, p. B9.

53. Philip Kotler and Gary Armstrong, *Principles of Marketing,* 9th ed., p. 6. Copyright 2001 by Prentice-Hall, Inc. Used with permission.

54. Sam Loewenberg, "Western Advertisers Struggle to Conquer the Wild Romanian Frontier," *Los Angeles Times,* June 15, 1995, pp. D4, D9.

55. Margaret McKegney and Normandy Madden, "Tobacco Report Reveals Global Retreat," *Advertising Age,* August 13, 2001, p. 1.

56. Chris Willman, "Unfair Warning: Are the Lyrics of Hip-Hop Artists Being Held to a Different Stickering Standard?" *Entertainment Weekly,* August 17, 2001, p. 70; Corey Moss, "Misunderstood Allen Iverson Skips Hip-Hop for Hoops," *VH1 Daily News,* October 2, 2001, **www.vh1.com/thewire/content/news/1449517.jhtml**; Eben Shapiro, "Ads Denounce Time Warner for Rap Music," *Wall Street Journal,* May 17, 1995, pp. B1, B6.

57. Amy Harmon, "Fun and Games—and Gore," *Los Angeles Times,* May 12, 1995, pp. A1, A28–29.

58. Robert Tomsho, "Costly Funerals Spur a Co-op Movement to Hold Down Bills," *Wall Street Journal,* November 12, 1996, pp. A1, A6.

59. Sarah Lueck, "Contraceptive Sponge May Move Back to Stores After Approval," *Wall Street Journal,* July 13, 2000, p. B16.

60. Stuart Elliott, "A Campaign for AIDS Drug Adds Warning," *New York Times,* May 10, 2001, p. C1.

61. Robert O'Harrow Jr., "3 Web Firms to Pay Fines for Collecting Data on Children," *Washington Post,* April 20, 2001, p. E03.

62. Denise Gellene, "It's Good for You, But Don't Expect Labels to Say That," *Los Angeles Times,* May 8, 1995, pp. D1, D3.

63. James R. Bettman, *An Information Processing Theory of Consumer Choice* (Reading, Mass.: Addison-Wesley, 1979).

Chapter 2

1. Jean Halliday, "Mazda Unveils Protegé," *Advertising Age,* May 7, 2001, p. 51; Rick Kranz, "Mazda Aims at Youth with Powerful Protegé," *Automotive News,* November 6, 2000, p. 57; Michelle Wirth Fellman, "Auto Researchers' Focus on Customers Can Help Drive Sales in Other Industries," *Marketing News*, January 4, 1999, pp. 1, 30–31.

2. Dick McCullough, "Web-Based Market Research Ushers in a New Age," *Marketing News*, September 14, 1998, pp. 27–28.

3. Christopher T. Heun, "Procter & Gamble Readies Market-Research Push," *Information Week,* October 15, 2001, p. 26.

4. Simmons Market Research Bureau, 1994.

5. Tom McGee, "Getting inside Kids' Heads," *American Demographics,* January 1997, pp. 52–55.

6. Hillary Rosner, "Hocus Focus," *Village Voice,* December 15, 1998, p. 43.

7. Chad Rubel, "Two Research Techniques Probe Shoppers' Minds," *Marketing News,* July 29, 1996, p. 16.

8. Kendra Parker, "How Do You Like Your Beef?" *American Demographics,* January 2000, pp. 35–37.

9. Ronald B. Lieber and Joyce E. Davis, "Storytelling: A New Way to Get Close to Your Customer," *Fortune,* February 3, 1997, pp. 102–108.

10. Sandra Yin, "Marketing Tools: The Power of Images," *American Demographics,* November 2001, pp. 32–33.

11. Deborah D. Heisley and Sidney J. Levy, "Autodriving: A Photoelicitation Technique," *Journal of Consumer Research*, December 1991, pp. 257–272.

12. Robin A. Coulter, Gerald Zaltman and Keith S. Coulter, "Interpreting Consumer Perceptions of Advertising: An Application of the Zaltman Metaphor Elicitation Technique," *Journal of Advertising*, 30 Winter 2001, pp. 1–21. January 5, 1999, **www.hbs.edu/units/marketing/zmet**; Morris B. Holbrook, "Collective Stereographic Photo Essays: An Integrated Approach to Probing Consumption Experiences in Depth," *International Journal of Research in Marketing*, July 1998, pp. 201–221.

13. Anonymous, "How Sweet It Is," *American Demographics,* March 2000, p. s18.

14. Lieber and Davis, "Storytelling: A New Way to Get Close to Your Customer."

15. McGee, "Getting inside Kids' Heads."

16. Christine Bittar, "Up in Arms," *Brandweek,* June 18, 2001, pp. 17–18.

17. Faith Keenan, "Dear Diary, I Had Jell-O Today," *BusinessWeek,* April 10, 2001, **www.businessweek.com/technology/content/apr2001/tc20010410_958.htm.**

18. Mike Hofman, "Virtual Shopping," *Inc.,* October 1998, p. 88.

19. David J. Lipke, "Product by Design," *American Demographics,* February 2001, pp. 38–41.

20. Geraldine Brooks, "It's Goo, Goo, Goo, Goo Vibrations at the Gerber Lab," *Wall Street Journal,* December 4, 1996, pp. A1, A6.

21. Emily Nelson, "P&G Checks Out Real Life," *Wall Street Journal*, May 17, 2001, pp. B1, B4.

22. Lieber and Davis, "Storytelling: A New Way to Get Close to Your Customer."

23. Robyn Weisman, "Web Trackers: The Spies in Your Computer," *NewsFactor Network,* November 8, 2001, **www.newsfactor.com/perl/story/14662.html.**

24. Patrick Thibodeau, "Senate Panel Spars over Internet Privacy," *ComputerWorld,* July 13, 2001, **www.cnn.com/2001/TECH/industry/07/13/privacy.legislation.idg.**

25. Jennifer Lach, "Data Mining Digs In," *American Demographics,* July 1999, pp. 38–45.

26. Joe Ashbrook Nickell, "Datamining: Welcome to Harrah's," *Business 2.0,* April 2002, pp. 48–54; Christina Brinkley, "Harrah's Builds Database about Patrons," *Wall Street Journal*, September 2, 1997, pp. B1, B10.

27. Direct Marketing Association, *Profitable Retailing Using Relationship and Database Marketing* (Ithaca, N.Y.: American Demographics Books, 1999).

28. Julia Angwin, "Virgin to Trade Web Use for Personal Data," *Wall Street Journal*, April 10, 2000, p. B16.

29. Janet Logan, "Most E-mail Marketing Never Gets Read," *East Bay Business Times,* October 22, 2001, **eastbay.bcentral.com/eastbay/stories/2001/10/22/smallb4.html.**

30. Jim Rutenberg, "Keeping Up With the Nielsen (Executive) Family," *New York Times,* November 18, 2001, sec. 3, p. 4.

31. **www.arfsite.org,** January 1, 2003.

32. Jacob Jacoby and George J. Szybillo, "Consumer Research in FTC versus Kraft (1991): A Case of Heads We Win, Tails You Lose," *Journal of Public Policy and Marketing*, Spring 1995, pp. 1–14; David W. Stewart, "Deception Materiality, and Survey Research: Some Lessons from Kraft," *Journal of Public Policy and Marketing*, Spring 1995, pp.15–28.

33. Kelly Shermach, "Portrait of the World," *Marketing News*, August 28, 1995, pp. 20–21.

34. Eleena de Lisser, "More Marketers Leaving a (Prepaid) Calling Card," *Wall Street Journal*, July 25, 1994, p. B1.

35. Jennifer Lach, "Summer Overtures," *American Demographics*, June 1999, pp. 38–40.

36. Fara Warner, "Shake-Up in Light Trucks Is Coming Down the Pike—New Marketing, Hybrids and Small, Specialized Runs May Have a Big Impact," *Wall Street Journal,* August 23, 1999, p. B4.

37. Cliff Rothman, "Big Companies Are Openly Courting Gay Consumers," *Los Angeles Times,* May 18, 1999, p. 1; Laura Koss Feder, "Out and About," *Marketing News,* May 25, 1998, p. 1, 20.

38. Allanna Sullivan, "Mobil Bets Drivers Pick Cappuccino over Low Prices," *Wall Street Journal*, January 30, 1995, pp. B1, B4.

39. Marj Carlier, "Chasing Buyers, Shoe Makers Back Races," *Wall Street Journal*, September 13, 1994, pp. B1, B9.

40. Sally D. Goll, "China's (Only) Children Get the Royal Treatment," *Wall Street Journal*, February 8, 1995, pp. B1, B2.

41. Fara Warner, "Condom Seller Lets Users Do the Talking," *Wall Street Journal*, March 22, 1995, pp. B3, B8.

42. Jennifer Lach, "A Sweet Deal," *American Demographics,* January 2000, pp. 10–11; Cyndee Miller, "Study Dispels '80s Stereotypes of Women," *Marketing News*, May 22, 1995, p. 3.

43. Alison Stein Wellner, "Research on a Shoestring," *American Demographics,* April 2001, pp. 38–39.

44. Christina Binkley, "MGM Grand Trumpets Size to Stand Out," *Wall Street Journal*, April 4, 2000, p. B9.

45. Dale Dauten, "Displaying Failures: A Help to Find Success?" *Chicago Tribune*, August 30, 1998, p. 7.

46. McGee, "Getting inside Kids' Heads."

47. Sullivan, "Mobil Bets Drivers Pick Cappuccino over Low Prices."

48. Jennifer Ordonez, "Crunch Time: How Burger King Got Burned in Quest to Make the Perfect Fry," *Wall Street Journal*, January 16, 2001, pp. A1, A8.

49. Elaine Erickson and Elaine Taylor-Gordon, "Finger on the Pulse," *Brandweek*, December 7, 1998, pp. 30–32.

50. Robert McNatt, "Hey, It's Green—It Must Be Healthy," *BusinessWeek*, July 13, 1998, p. 6.

51. Anonymous, "Design For Everyone," *@Issue,* vol. 7, no. 1, pp. 6–13.

52. Benjamin Lipstein, "The Oppenheimer Fund Story: From 14 Million to 27 Billion," in ed. Larry Percy, *Marketing Research That Pays Off* (Birminghampton, N.Y.: Hayworth Press, 1997), pp. 209–248.

53. Mark Robichaux, "Cable Industry Tries Guarantees of Better Service to Polish Image," *Wall Street Journal*, December 1, 1994, p. B1.

54. Carrick Mollenkamp, "Bank of America Seeks Standout Status," *Wall Street Journal*, September 7, 2000, p. B16.

55. Judith Langer, "Focus on Women: Three Decades of Qualitative Research," *Marketing News,* September 14, 1998, pp. 21–22.

56. Charlotte Clarke, "Language Classes," *Marketing Week*, July 24, 1997, pp. 35–39.

57. Emily Nelson, "P&G Peers beyond TV to Reach Targets," *Wall Street Journal*, July 6, 2000, p. B14.

58. Erika Rasmusson, "This Database Is a Heavy Favorite," *Sales and Marketing Management*, June 1998, p. 73.

59. Wanlapa Rerkkriangkrai, "From Bugs to Bahts: 1.6 Million Mosquitoes Turn into One TV," *Wall Street Journal*, November 6, 2000, p. B1.

60. For example, see Sean Dwyer, Orlando Richard, and C. David Shepherd, "An Exploratory Study of Gender and Age Matching in the Salesperson–Prospective Customer Dyad: Testing Similarity-Performance Predictions," *Journal of Personal Selling and Sales Management*, Fall 1998, pp. 55–69.

61. Jennifer M. George, "Salesperson Mood at Work: Implications for Helping Customers," *Journal of Personal Selling and Sales Management*, Summer 1998, pp. 23–30.

62. Robert M. Schindler and Patrick N. Kirby, "Patterns of Rightmost Digits Used in Advertising Prices: Implications for Nine-Ending Effects," *Journal of Consumer Research*, September 1997, pp. 192–201.

63. Jacob Jacoby, Jerry Olson, and Rafael Haddock, "Price, Brand Name, and Product Composition Characteristics as Determinants of Perceived Quality," *Journal of Applied Psychology*, December 1971, pp. 470–479; Kent B. Monroe, "The Influence of Price Differences and Brand Familiarity on Brand Preferences," *Journal of Consumer Research*, June 1976, pp. 42–49.

64. Laura Bird, "Catalogs Cut Shipping, Handling Fees to Inspire Early Christmas Shopping," *Wall Street Journal,* October 24, 1995, pp. B1, B11.

65. Ziv Carmon and Dan Ariely, "Focusing on the Forgone: How Value Can Appear So Different to Buyers and Sellers," *Journal of Consumer Research*, vol. 27, December 2000, pp. 360–370; Tridib Mazumdar and Purushottam Papatla, "An Investigation of Reference Price Segments," *Journal of Marketing Research*, vol. 37, May 2000, pp. 246–258.

66. Dilip Soman and John T. Gourville, "Transaction Decoupling: How Price Bundling Affects the Decision to Consume," *Journal of Marketing Research*, vol. 38, February 2001, pp. 30–44.

67. Martha Brannigan, "Sailing on Sale: Travelers Ride a Wave of Discounts on Cruise Ships," *Wall Street Journal*, July 17, 2000, pp. B1, B4.

68. Gregory L. White, "Car Makers Go Wild for Trucks," *Wall Street Journal*, April 7, 2000, pp. B1, B4.

69. Ronald E. Milliman, "The Influence of Background Music on the Behavior of Restaurant Patrons," *Journal of Consumer Research*, September 1986, pp. 286–289; Richard Yalch and Eric Spannenberg, "Effects of Store Music on Shopping Behavior," *Journal of Services Marketing*, Winter 1990, pp. 31–39; Joseph A. Bellizi, Ayn E. Crowley, and Ronald W. Hasty, "The Effects of Color in Store Design," *Journal of Retailing*, Spring 1983, pp. 21–45.

70. Karen A. Machleit, Sevgin A. Eroglu, and Susan Powell Mantel, "Perceived Retail Crowding and Shopping Satisfaction: What Modifies This Relationship," *Journal of Consumer Psychology*, vol. 9, no. 1, pp. 29–42.

71. Anna Wilde Mathews, "Sagging Frederick's of Hollywood Looks Upmarket," *Wall Street Journal*, July 11, 2000, pp. B1, B4.

72. Kenneth C. Schneider and Cynthia K. Holm, "Deceptive Practices in Marketing Research: The Consumer's Viewpoint," *California Management Review*, Spring 1982, pp. 89–97.

Chapter 3

1. David Whelan, "Investing with Care," *American Demographics*, November 1, 2001, p. 12; Louise Lee, "Brokers Are from Mars, Women Are from Venus," *BusinessWeek*, December 4, 2000, p. 158; Anonymous, "Bridging the Gender Gap," *Chief Executive*, November 2000, p. 10; Joan Raymond, "For Richer and for Poorer," *American Demographics*, July 2000, pp. 58–64.

2. C. Whan Park and Banwari Mittal, "A Theory of Involvement in Consumer Behavior: Problems and Issues," in ed. J. N. Sheth, *Research in Consumer Behavior* (Greenwich, Conn.: JAI Press, 1979), pp. 201–231; Deborah J. MacInnis, Christine Moorman, and Bernard J. Jaworski, "Enhancing and Measuring Consumers' Motivation, Opportunity, and Ability to Process Brand Information from Ads," *Journal of Marketing*, October 1991, pp. 32–53.

3. Deborah J. MacInnis and Bernard J. Jaworski, "Information Processing from Advertisements: Toward an Integrative Framework," *Journal of Marketing*, October 1989, pp. 1–23; Scott B. MacKenzie and Richard A. Spreng, "How Does Motivation Moderate the Impact of Central and Peripheral Processing on Brand Attitudes and Intentions?" *Journal of Consumer Research*, March 1992, pp. 519–529; Richard E. Petty and John T. Cacioppo, *Communication and Persuasion* (New York: Springer-Verlag, 1986). Anthony Greenwald and Clark Leavitt, "Audience Involvement in Advertising: Four Levels," *Journal of Consumer Research*, vol. 11 June 1984, pp. 581–592; Ronald C. Goodstein, "Category-Based Applications and Extensions in Advertising: Motivating More Extensive Ad Processing," *Journal of Consumer Research*, June 1993, pp. 87–99; Ellen Garbarino and Julie A. Edell, "Cognitive Effort, Affect, and Choice," *Journal of Consumer Research*, September 1997, pp. 147–158.

4. Wayne D. Hoyer, "An Examination of Consumer Decision Making for a Common Repeat Purchase Product," *Journal of Consumer Research*, December 1984, pp. 822–829.

5. Richard L. Celsi and Jerry C. Olson, "The Role of Involvement in Attention and Comprehension Processes," *Journal of Consumer Research*, September 1988, pp. 210–224.

6. Marsha L. Richins, Peter H. Bloch, and Edward F. McQuarrie, "How Enduring and Situational Involvement Combine to Create Involvement Responses," *Journal of Consumer Psychology*, September 1992, pp. 143–154; Peter H. Bloch and Marsha L. Richins, "A Theoretical Model for the Study of Product Importance Perceptions," *Journal of Marketing*, Summer 1983, pp. 69–81; Celsi and Olson, "The Role of Involvement in Attention and Comprehension Processes"; Andrew A. Mitchell, "The Dimensions of Advertising Involvement," in ed. Kent Monroe, *Advances in Consumer Research*, vol. 8 (Ann Arbor, Mich.: Association for Consumer Research, 1981), pp. 25–30; Marsha L. Richins and Peter H. Bloch, "After the New Wears Off: The Temporal Context of Product Involvement," *Journal of Consumer Research*, September 1986, pp. 280–285.

7. Michael J. Houston and Michael L. Rothschild, "Conceptual and Methodological Perspectives in Involvement," in ed. S. Jain, *Research Frontiers in Marketing: Dialogues and Directions* (Chicago: American Marketing Association, 1978), pp. 184–187; Richins and Bloch, "After the New Wears Off;" Gilles Laurent and Jean-Noel Kapferer, "Measuring Consumer Involvement Profiles," *Journal of Marketing Research*, February 1985, pp. 41–53.

8. C. Whan Park and S. Mark Young, "Consumer Response to Television Commercials: The Impact of Involvement and Background Music on Brand Attitude Formation," *Journal of Marketing Research*, February 1986, pp. 11–24.

9. Judith Lynne Zaichkowsky, "Measuring the Involvement Construct," *Journal of Consumer Research*, December 1985, pp. 341–352; Laurent and Kapferer, "Measuring Consumer Involvement Profiles."

10. Stefan Fatsis, "Futbol Invades the U.S.—Again," *Wall Street Journal*, April 5, 1996, p. B7.

11. J. Craig Andrews, Syed H. Akhter, Srinivas Durvasula, and Darrel D. Muehling, "The Effect of Advertising Distinctiveness and Message Content Involvement on Cognitive and Affective Responses to Advertising," *Journal of Current Issues and Research in Advertising*, Spring 1992, pp. 45–58; Laura M. Bucholz and Robert E. Smith, "The Role of Consumer Involvement in Determining Cognitive Response to Broadcast Advertising," *Journal of Advertising*, March 1991, pp. 4–17; Darrel D. Muehling, Russell N. Laczniak, and Jeffrey J. Stoltman, "The Moderating Effects of Ad Message Involvement: A Reassessment," *Journal of*

Advertising, June 1991, pp. 29–38; Scott B. MacKenzie and Richard J. Lutz, "An Empirical Examination of the Structural Antecedents of Attitude Toward the Ad in an Advertising Pretesting Context," *Journal of Marketing*, April 1989, pp. 48–65.

12. Barbara Mueller, "Standardization vs. Specialization: An Examination of Westernization in Japanese Advertising," *Journal of Advertising Research*, January–February 1992, pp. 15–24.
13. Tammi S. Feltham and Stephen J. Arnold, "Program Involvement and Ad/Program Consistency as Moderators of Program Context Effects," *Journal of Consumer Psychology*, vol. 3, no. 1, 1994, pp. 51–78; Nader Tavassoli, Clifford Schultz, and Gavan Fitzsimons, "Program Involvement: Are Moderate Levels Best for Ad Memory and Attitude toward the Ad?" *Journal of Advertising Research*, vol. 35, no. 5, 1995, pp. 61–72.
14. Kevin J. Clancy and David W. Lloyd, *Uncover the Hidden Power of Television Programming* (Thousand Oaks, Calif.: Sage Publications, 1999), p. 109.
15. Houston and Rothschild, "Conceptual and Methodological Perspectives in Involvement"; Peter H. Bloch, Daniel Sherrell, and Nancy Ridgway, "Consumer Search: An Extended Framework," *Journal of Consumer Research*, June 1986, pp. 119–126; Peter H. Bloch, Nancy M. Ridgway, and Scott A. Dawson, "The Shopping Mall as Consumer Habitat," *Journal of Retailing*, Spring 1994, pp. 23–42; Richard L. Celsi, Randall L. Rose, and Thomas W. Leigh, "An Exploration of High-Risk Leisure Consumption through Skydiving," *Journal of Consumer Research*, June 1993, pp. 1–23; Eric J. Arnould and Linda L. Price, "River Magic: Extraordinary Experience and the Extended Service Encounter," *Journal of Consumer Research*, June 1993, pp. 24–45; Morris B. Holbrook and Elizabeth C. Hirschman, "The Experiential Aspects of Consumption: Consumer Fantasies, Feelings, and Fun," *Journal of Consumer Research*, September 1982, pp. 132–140; Elizabeth C. Hirschman and Morris B. Holbrook, "Experience Seeking: Emerging Concepts, Methods, and Propositions," *Journal of Marketing*, Summer 1982, pp. 92–101; Morris B. Holbrook, Robert W. Chestnut, Terence A. Oliva, and Eric A. Greenleaf, "Play as a Consumption Experience: The Roles of Emotions, Performance, and Personality in the Enjoyment of Games," *Journal of Consumer Research*, September 1984, pp. 728–739.
16. Celsi and Olson, "The Role of Involvement in Attention and Comprehension Processes"; Greenwald and Leavitt, "Audience Involvement in Advertising"; Laurent and Kapferer, "Measuring Consumer Involvement Profiles"; Zaichkowsky, "Measuring the Involvement Construct"; Michael L. Rothschild, "Perspectives on Involvement: Current Problems and Future Directions," in ed. Tom Kinnear, *Advances in Consumer Research*, vol. 11 (Ann Arbor, Mich.: Association for Consumer Research, 1984), pp. 216–217; Andrew A. Mitchell, "Involvement: A Potentially Important Mediator of Consumer Behavior," in ed. William L. Wilkie, *Advances in Consumer Research*, vol. 6 (Ann Arbor, Mich.: Association for Consumer Research, 1979), pp. 191–196; Petty and Cacioppo, *Communication and Persuasion*.
17. Jennifer L. Aaker and Angela Y. Lee, "'I' Seek Pleasures and 'We' Avoid Pains: The Role of Self-Regulatory Goals in Information Processing and Persuasion," *Journal of Consumer Research*, vol. 28, June 2001, pp. 33–49.
18. Sharon Shavitt, Suzanne Swan, Tina M. Lowrey, and Michaela Wanke, "The Interaction of Endorser Attractiveness and Involvement in Persuasion Depends on the Goal That Guides Message Processing," *Journal of Consumer Psychology*, vol. 3, no. 2, 1994, pp. 137–162; Robert Lawson, "Consumer Decision Making within a Goal-Driven Framework," *Psychology and Marketing*, August 1997, pp. 427–449.
19. Richard P. Bagozzi and Utpal Dholakia, "Goal Setting and Goal Striving in Consumer Behavior," *Journal of Marketing*, vol. 63, 1999, pp. 19–32.
20. Ibid.
21. Abraham H. Maslow, *Motivation and Personality*, 2nd ed. (New York: Harper & Row, 1970).
22. C. Whan Park, Bernard J. Jaworski, and Deborah J. MacInnis, "Strategic Brand Concept-Image Management," *Journal of Marketing*, October 1986, pp. 135–145.
23. Judy Harris and Michael Lynn, "The Manifestations and Measurement of the Desire to Be a Unique Consumer," Proceedings of the 1994 AMA Winter Educators' Conference, Chicago; Kelly Tepper, "Need for Uniqueness: An Individual Difference Factor Affecting Nonconformity in Consumer Responses," Proceedings of the 1994 AMA Winter Educators' Conference, Chicago.
24. Kelly Tepper Tian, William O. Bearden, and Gary L. Hunter, "Consumers' Need For Uniqueness: Scale Development and Validation," *Journal of Consumer Research*, vol. 28, June 2001, pp. 50–66.
25. Laura Petrecca, "Amenities Give Lift to First Class," *Advertising Age*, June 11, 2001, p. S10.
26. John T. Cacioppo and Richard E. Petty, "The Need for Cognition," *Journal of Personality and Social Psychology*, February 1982, pp. 116–131; Douglas M. Stayman and Frank R. Kardes, "Spontaneous Inference Processes in Advertising: Effects of Need for Cognition and Self-Monitoring on Inference Generation and Utilization," *Journal of Consumer Psychology*, vol. 1 no. 2, 1992, pp. 125–142; John T. Cacioppo, Richard Petty, and Katherine Morris, "Effects of Need for Cognition on Message Evaluation, Recall, and Persuasion," *Journal of Personality and Social Psychology*, October 1993, pp. 805–818.
27. P. S. Raju, "Optimum Stimulation Level: Its Relationship to Personality, Demographics, and Exploratory Behavior," *Journal of Consumer*

Research, December 1980, pp. 272–282; Jan-Benedict E. M. Steenkamp, and Hans Baumgartner, "The Role of Optimum Stimulation Level in Exploratory Consumer Behavior," *Journal of Consumer Research*, December 1992, pp. 434–448.

28. Patricia Bellew Gray, "Want to Search Your Soul at a Monastery? Get in Line," *Wall Street Journal*, December 19, 1997, pp. B1, B14.
29. Stuart Elliott, "Study Tries To Help Retailers Understand What Drives the Shopping Habits of Women," *New York Times*, January 17, 2001, p. C6.
30. Robert Roth, *International Marketing Communications* (Chicago: Crain Books, 1982), p. 5.
31. H. Murray, *Thematic Apperception Test Manual* (Cambridge, Mass.: Harvard University Press, 1943); Harold Kassarjian, "Projective Methods," in ed. Robert Ferber, *Handbook of Marketing Research* (New York: McGraw-Hill, 1974), pp. 85–100; Ernest Dichter, *Packaging the Sixth Sense: A Guide to Identifying Consumer Motivation* (Boston: Cahners Books, 1975); Dennis Rook, "Researching Consumer Fantasy," in ed. Elizabeth C. Hirschman, *Research in Consumer Behavior*, vol. 3 (Greenwich, Conn.: JAI Press, 1990), pp. 247–270; David Mick, M. De Moss, and Ronald Faber, "A Projective Study of Motivations and Meanings of Self-Gifts: Implications for Retail Management," *Journal of Retailing*, Summer 1992, pp. 122–144; Mary Ann McGrath, John F. Sherry, and Sidney J. Levy, "Giving Voice to the Gift: The Use of Projective Techniques to Recover Lost Meanings," *Journal of Consumer Psychology*, no. 2, 1993, pp. 171–191.
32. Harold H. Kassarjian and Joel B. Cohen, "Cognitive Dissonance and Consumer Behavior: Reaction to the Surgeon General's Report on Smoking and Health," *California Management Review*, Fall 1965, pp. 55–65; see also Kenneth E. Runyon and David W. Stewart, *Consumer Behavior*, 3rd ed. (Columbus, Ohio: Merrill, 1987).
33. G. H. Smith, *Motivation Research in Advertising and Marketing* (New York: McGraw-Hill, 1954).
34. Dom Del Prete, "Direct Mail Pays Big Dividends for Financial Services Marketers," *Marketing News*, September 29, 1997, pp. 1, 8.
35. Bruce Horovitz, "Marketers Tout Consumer Privacy," *USA Today*, March 1, 2001, p. 3B, **www.usatoday.com/money/media/2001-03-01-privacy.htm.**
36. Jule Kronholz, "It's Summertime and Kids Are Bored. What Else is New?" *Wall Street Journal*, July 23, 1997, pp. A1, A6.
37. Yumiko Ono, "Japan's Fast-Food Companies Cook Up Local Platter to Tempt Local Palates," *Wall Street Journal*, May 29, 1992, pp. B1, B5.
38. Chester Dawson, "Will Tokyo Embrace Another Mouse?" *BusinessWeek*, September 10, 2001, p. 65.
39. Robert Langreth, "Bulletins from the Battle of the Baldness Drug," *Wall Street Journal*, December 19, 1997, pp. B1, B12.
40. Ravi Dhar and Itamar Simonson, "Making Complementary Choices in Consumption Episodes: Highlighting versus Balancing," *Journal of Marketing Research*, vol. 36, February 1999, pp. 29–44.
41. Park, Jaworski, and MacInnis, "Strategic Brand Concept-Image Management."
42. Raymond A. Bauer, "Consumer Behavior as Risk Taking," in ed. Robert S. Hancock, *Dynamic Marketing for a Changing World* (Chicago: American Marketing Association, 1960), pp. 389–398; Grahame R. Dowling, "Perceived Risk: The Concept and Its Measurement," *Psychology and Marketing*, Fall 1986, pp. 193–210; Lawrence X. Tarpey and J. Paul Peter, "A Comparative Analysis of Three Consumer Decision Strategies," *Journal of Consumer Research*, June 1975, pp. 29–37.
43. James R. Bettman, "Perceived Risk and Its Components: A Model and Empirical Test," *Journal of Marketing Research*, May 1973, pp. 184–190.
44. Dana L. Alden, Douglas M. Stayman, and Wayne D. Hoyer, "The Evaluation Strategies of American and Thai Consumers: A Cross Cultural Comparison," *Psychology and Marketing*, March–April 1994, pp. 145–161; Ugur Yavas, Bronislaw J. Verhage, and Robert T. Green, "Global Consumer Segmentation versus Local Market Orientation: Empirical Findings," *Management International Review*, July 1992, pp. 265–272.
45. Vincent W. Mitchell and Michael Greatorex, "Consumer Purchasing in Foreign Countries: A Perceived Risk Analysis," *International Journal of Advertising*, vol. 9 no. 4, 1990, pp. 295–307.
46. Anonymous, "Marketing Briefs," *Marketing News*, March 1995, p. 11.
47. Jacob Jacoby and Leon Kaplan, "The Components of Perceived Risk," in ed. M. Venkatesan, *Advances in Consumer Research*, vol. 3 (Chicago: Association for Consumer Research, 1972), pp. 382–383; Tarpey and Peter, "A Comparative Analysis of Three Consumer Decision Strategies."
48. Jean Halliday, "GM Ads Assure Used Car Buyer," *Advertising Age*, June 11, 2001, p. 10.
49. Joseph N. Boyce, "Landlords Turn to 'Commando' Patrols," *Wall Street Journal*, September 18, 1996, pp. B1, B2.
50. Paula Mergenhagen, "People Behaving Badly," *American Demographics*, August 1997, pp. 37–43.
51. Kathryn Kranhold, "Rogaine Urges the Nonbald to Use Ounces of Prevention," *Wall Street Journal*, September 20, 1999, pp. B1, B4.
52. Abbey Klassen, "Merck Breaks Out Pox Vaccine Spots," *Advertising Age*, June 25, 2001, p. 12.
53. Cyndee Miller, "Condom Sales Cool Off: Carefree Attitudes of Youth, Poor Marketing Are Blamed," *Marketing News*, February 24, 1994, pp. 1, 9.
54. Ibid.

55. Priya Raghubir and Geeta Menon, "AIDS and Me, Never the Twain Shall Meet: The Effects of Information Accessibility on Judgments of Risk and Advertising Effectiveness," *Journal of Consumer Research*, June 1998, pp. 52–63.

56. Shailendra Pratap Jain and Durairaj Maheswaran, "Motivated Reasoning: A Depth-of-Processing Perspective," *Journal of Consumer Research*, vol. 26, March 2000, pp. 358–371; Joan Meyers-Levy and Alice Tybout, "Schema-Congruity as a Basis for Product Evaluation," *Journal of Consumer Research*, June 1989, pp. 39–54.

57. MacInnis and Jaworski, "Information Processing from Advertisements."

58. Joseph W. Alba and J. Wesley Hutchinson, "Dimensions of Consumer Expertise," *Journal of Consumer Research*, March 1987, pp. 411–454; For an excellent overview of measures of consumer knowledge or expertise, see Andrew A. Mitchell and Peter A. Dacin, "The Assessment of Alternative Measures of Consumer Expertise," *Journal of Consumer Research*, December 1996, pp. 219–239.

59. Eric J. Johnson and J. Edward Russo, "Product Familiarity and Learning New Information," *Journal of Consumer Research*, June 1984, pp. 542–550; Merrie Brucks, "The Effects of Product Class Knowledge on Information Search Behavior," *Journal of Consumer Research*, June 1985, pp. 1–16; Alba and Hutchinson, "Dimensions of Consumer Expertise."

60. Oscar Suris, "New Data Help Car Lessees Shop Smarter," *Wall Street Journal*, July 11, 1995, pp. 1, B12.

61. Durairaj Maheswaran and Brian Sternthal, "The Effects of Knowledge, Motivation, and Type of Message on Ad Processing and Product Judgments," *Journal of Consumer Research*, June 1990, pp. 66–73.

62. Jennifer Gregan-Paxton and Deborah Roedder Jonn, "Consumer Learning by Analogy: A Model of Internal Knowledge Transfer," *Journal of Consumer Research*, December 1997, pp. 266–284.

63. Elizabeth C. Hirschman, "Cognitive Complexity, Intelligence, and Creativity: A Conceptual Overview with Implications for Consumer Research," *Research in Marketing*, vol. 3, 1981, pp. 59–99.

64. Jennifer Gregan-Paxton and Deborah Roedder John, "Are Young Children Adaptive Decision Makers? A Study of Age Differences in Information Search Behavior," *Journal of Consumer Research*, March 1995, pp. 567–580.

65. Catherine A. Cole and Gary J. Gaeth, "Cognitive and Age-Related Differences in the Ability to Use Nutrition Information in a Complex Environment," *Journal of Marketing Research*, May 1990, pp. 175–184.

66. Robin Frost, "Women On-Line: Cybergrrl Aims to Show the Way," *Wall Street Journal*, May 30, 1996, p. B8.

67. Cynthia Crossen, "'Merry Christmas to Moi' Shoppers Say," *Wall Street Journal*, December 11, 1997, pp. B1, B14.

68. June Fletcher and Sarah Collins, "The Lazy Gardener," *Wall Street Journal*, June 6, 2001, pp. W1, W16.

69. Peter Wright, "The Time Harassed Consumer: Time Pressures, Distraction, and the Use of Evidence," *Journal of Applied Psychology*, October 1974, pp. 555–561.

70. Danny L. Moore, Douglas Hausknecht, and Kanchana Thamodaran, "Time Compression, Response Opportunity, and Persuasion," *Journal of Consumer Research*, June 1986, pp. 85–99; Priscilla LaBarbera and James MacLaughlin, "Time Compressed Speech in Radio Advertising," *Journal of Marketing*, January 1979, pp. 30–36; Shelly Chaiken and Alice Eagly, "Communication Modality as a Determinant of Message Persuasiveness and Message Comprehensibility," *Journal of Personality and Social Psychology*, March 1976, pp. 605–614; Herbert Krugman, "The Impact of Television Advertising: Learning Without Involvement," *Public Opinion Quarterly*, Fall 1965, pp. 349-356; Patricia A. Stout and Benedicta Burda, "Zipped Commercials: Are They Effective?" *Journal of Advertising*, Fall 1989, pp. 23–32.

71. Park and Young, "Consumer Response to Television Commercials"; Deborah J. MacInnis and C. Whan Park, "The Differential Role of Characteristics of Music on High- and Low-Involvement Consumers' Processing of Ads," *Journal of Consumer Research*, September 1991, pp. 161–173; Shelly Chaiken and Alice Eagly, "Communication Modality as a Determinant of Persuasion: The Role of Communicator Salience," *Journal of Personality and Social Psychology*, August 1983, pp. 605–614.

72. Kenneth Lord and Robert Burnkrant, "Attention Versus Distraction: The Interactive Effect of Program Involvement and Attentional Devices on Commercial Processing," *Journal of Advertising,* March 1993, pp. 47-61; Kenneth R. Lord and Robert E. Burnkrant, "Television Program Effects on Commercial Processing," in ed. Michael J. Houston, *Advances in Consumer Research*, vol. 15 (Provo, Utah: Association for Consumer Research, 1988), pp. 213–218; Gary Soldow and Victor Principe, "Response to Commercials as a Function of Program Context," *Journal of Advertising Research*, February–March 1981, pp. 59–65.

73. Betsy McKay, "PepsiCo Tries to Clarify PepsiOne's Image," *Wall Street Journal*, February 25, 2000, p. B4.

74. Richard Yalch and Rebecca Elmore-Yalch, "The Effect of Numbers on the Route to Persuasion," *Journal of Consumer Research*, June 1984, pp. 522–527.

75. Noel Capon and Roger Davis, "Basic Cognitive Ability Measures as Predictors of Consumer Information Processing Strategies, *Journal of Consumer Research*, June 1984, pp. 551–564.

76. Alison Stein Wellner, "Casting the Health.Net," *American Demographics*, March 2000, pp. 46–49.

77. Rajeev Batra and Michael L. Ray, "Situational Effects of Advertising Repetitions: The Moderating Influence of Motivation, Ability, and Opportunity to Respond," *Journal of Consumer Research*, March 1986, pp. 432–435; Carl Obermiller, "Varieties of Mere Exposure: The Effects of Processing Style and Repetition on Affective Response," *Journal of Consumer Research*, June 1985, pp. 17–30; Arno Rethans, John L. Swazy, and Lawrence J. Marks, "The Effects of Television Commercial Repetition, Receiver Knowledge, and Commercial Length: A Test of the Two-Factor Model," *Journal of Marketing Research*, February 1986, pp. 50–61; Sharmistha Law and Scott A. Hawkins, "Advertising Repetition and Consumer Beliefs: The Role of Source Memory," in ed. William Wells, *Measuring Advertising Effectiveness* (Mahwah, N.J.: Lawrence Erlbaum Associates, 1997), pp. 67–75; Giles D'Sousa and Ram C. Rao, "Can Repeating an Advertisement More Frequently Than the Competition Affect Brand Preference in a Mature Market?" *Journal of Marketing*, 1995, pp. 32–43.

78. Dan Ariely, "Controlling the Information Flow: Effects on Consumers' Decision Making and Preferences," *Journal of Consumer Research*, vol. 27, September 2000, pp. 233–248.

79. Ibid.

80. Fred Vogelstein, "Can Schwab Get Its Mojo Back?" *Fortune*, September 17, 2001, pp. 93–97.

81. Matt Murray, "A Bit of Prosperity and Some Fast Food Fatten Zimbabweans," *Wall Street Journal*, August 8, 1997, pp. A1, A11.

Chapter 4

1. Melanie Wells, "Who Really Needs Madison Avenue?" *Forbes*, October 29, 2001, p. 131; Margaret Mannix, "Search Me, Please," *U.S. News & World Report*, July 30, 2001, p. 37; Becky Ebenkamp, "Return to Peyton Placement," *Brandweek*, June 4, 2001, pp. S10–S17; Tom Daykin, "Miller Sees Gold on Silver Screen," *Milwaukee Journal Sentinel*, May 27, 2001, p. 1D; Allyson Stewart-Allen, "Product Placement Helps Sell Brand," *Marketing News*, February 15, 1999, p. 8; Fara Warner, "Why It's Getting Harder to Tell the Shows from the Ads," *Wall Street Journal*, June 15, 1995, pp. B1, B10.

2. Warner, "Why It's Getting Harder to Tell the Shows from the Ads"; Shelly Branch, "Product Plugs—'M'm M'm Good'?" *Wall Street Journal*, November 14, 2000, pp. B1, B12.

3. Scott Miller, "Formula One Racing Gets Riskier—for Its Sponsors," *Wall Street Journal*, February 25, 2000, pp. B1, B4.

4. Adam Finn, "Print Ad Recognition Readership Scores: An Information Processing Perspective," *Journal of Marketing Research*, May 1988, pp. 168–177.

5. John Battle, "Cashing in at the Register," *Aftermarket Business*, September 1, 1994, pp. 12–13.

6. Robert W. Trott, "Shell Installs TV Sets at Some of Its Gas Stations," *Marketing News*, June 19, 1995, p. 8; Alexei Barrionuevo, "Chevron and BP Amoco Test Web Ads at Pumps," *Wall Street Journal*, June 12, 2000, p. B6.

7. Douglas A. Blackmon, "New Ad Vehicles: Police Cars, School Bus, Garbage Trucks," *Wall Street Journal*, February 20, 1996, pp. B1, B6; Suzanne Vranica, "Think Graffiti Is All That's Hanging in Subway Tunnels? Look Again," *Wall Street Journal*, April 4, 2001, pp. B1, B6; Leslie Chang, "Online Ads in China Go Offline," *Wall Street Journal*, July 30, 2000, pp. B1, B6.

8. Amy Dockser Marcus, "Advertising Breezes Along the Nile River with Signs for Sails," *Wall Street Journal*, July 18, 1997, pp. A1, A11.

9. Kendra L. Darko, "The Power of Opt-In," *American Demographics*, October 1999, pp. 40–44.

10. Lisa Guernsey, "Message to Marketers: RU4 Real?" *New York Times*, June 28, 2001, pp. G1, G8.

11. Paul Surgi Speck and Michael T. Elliott, "Predictors of Advertising Avoidance in Print and Broadcast Media," *Journal of Advertising*, Fall 1997, pp. 61–76.

12. Amy L. Webb, "More Consumers Are Ignoring Ads, Survey Shows," *Wall Street Journal Europe*, June 18, 2001, p. 29.

13. Jeff Howe, "Total Control," *American Demographics*, July 2001, pp. 28–31.

14. Dean M. Krugman, Glen T. Cameron, and Candace McKearney White, "Visual Attention to Programming and Commercials: The Use of In-Home Observations," *Journal of Advertising*, Spring 1995, pp. 1–12; S. Siddarth and Amitava Chattopadhyay, "To Zap or Not to Zap: A Study of the Determinants of Channel Switching during Commercials," *Marketing Science*, vol. 17 no. 2, 1998, pp. 124–138.

15. Sally Beatty, "Fashion Magazines Are Bulging with Ads," *Wall Street Journal*, September 2, 1998, p. B5.

16. Ellen Neuborne, "For Kids on the Web, It's An Ad, Ad, Ad, Ad World," *BusinessWeek*, August 13, 2001, pp. 108–109.

17. Bruce Orwall, "Can Hollywood Shelter Kids from Its Ads?" *Wall Street Journal*, September 29, 2000, pp. B1, B4.

18. Matthew Rose, "Author Learns E-mail Can Sell or Sink a Book," *Wall Street Journal*, August 7, 2000, pp. B1, B6.

19. Andrea Petersen and Jon G. Auerbach, "Online Ad Titans Bet Big in Race to Trace Consumers' Web Tracks," *Wall Street Journal*, November 8, 1999, pp. B1, B4.

20. Wayne Friedman, "Second Down: Super Bowl Spots Are Set to Sell for Below $2 Million, the Second Drop in Prices for the Game in as Many Years," *Advertising Age*, September 3, 2001, p. 3; Joshua Harris Prager, "Hot New Marketing Venue? You're

Sitting on It," *Wall Street Journal*, January 28, 2000, pp. B1, B4.

21. Nadia Mustafa, "Advertisers Wonder: Who's Reading Our Postcards?" *Wall Street Journal*, August 21, 2000, pp. B1, B4.
22. Nick Wingfield, "The Trick Task of Tracking Web Use," *Wall Street Journal*, November 22, 1999, pp. B1, B6; Andrea Petersen, "Plan Is Backed to Count Web-Ad Viewers," *Wall Street Journal*, March 2, 1999, p. B9.
23. Rik Pieters, Edward Rosbergen, and Michel Wedel, "Visual Attention to Repeated Print Advertising: A Test of Scanpath Theory," *Journal of Marketing Research*, vol. 36, November 1999, pp. 424–438.
24. Scott B. MacKenzie, "The Role of Attention in Mediating the Effect of Advertising on Attribute Importance," *Journal of Consumer Research*, September 1986, pp. 174–195; Richard E. Petty and Timothy C. Brock, "Thought Disruption and Persuasion: Assessing the Validity of Attitude Change Experiments," in eds. Richard E. Petty, Thomas Ostrom, and Timothy C. Brock, *Cognitive Responses in Persuasion* (Hillsdale, N. J.: Lawrence Erlbaum, 1981), pp. 55–79.
25. Joe Flint, "Disappearing Act: The Amount of TV Screen Devoted to Show Shrinks," *Wall Street Journal*, March 29, 2001, pp. B1, B6.
26. L. Hasher and R. T. Zacks, "Automatic and Effortful Processes in Memory," *Journal of Experimental Psychology: General*, September 1979, pp. 356–388; W. Schneider and R. M. Shiffrin, "Controlled and Automatic Human Information Processing: I. Detection, Search, and Attention," *Psychological Review*, January 1977, pp. 1–66; R. M. Shiffrin and W. Schneider, "Controlled and Automatic Human Information Processing: II. Perceptual Learning, Automatic Attending, and a General Theory," *Psychological Review*, March 1977, pp. 127–190.
27. Chris Janiszewski, "Preconscious Processing Effects: The Independence of Attitude Formation and Conscious Thought," *Journal of Consumer Research*, September 1988, pp. 199–209; Joan Meyers-Levy, "Priming Effects on Product Judgments: A Hemispheric Interpretation," *Journal of Consumer Research*, June 1989, pp. 76–87.
28. Janiszewski, "Preconscious Processing Effects"; Chris Janiszewski, "The Influence of Print Advertisement Organization on Affect toward a Brand Name," *Journal of Consumer Research*, June 1990, pp. 53–65.
29. Chris Janiszewski, "Preattentive Mere Exposure Effects," *Journal of Consumer Research*, December 1993, pp. 376–392; Janiszewski, "Preconscious Processing Effects"; Janiszewski, "The Influence of Print Advertisement Organization on Affect toward a Brand Name."
30. Janiszewski, "Preattentive Mere Exposure Effects"; Stewart Shapiro and Deborah J. MacInnis, "Mapping the Relationship between Preattentive Processing and Attitudes," in eds. John Sherry and Brian Sternthal, *Advances in Consumer Research*, vol. 19 (Provo, Utah: Association for Consumer Research, 1992), pp. 505–513.
31. Stewart Shapiro, "When an Ad's Influence Is Beyond Our Conscious Control: Perceptual and Conceptual Fluency Effects Caused by Incidental Ad Exposure," *Journal of Consumer Research*, vol. 26, June 1999, pp. 16–36; Stewart Shapiro, Deborah J. MacInnis, and Susan E. Heckler, "The Effects of Incidental Ad Exposure on the Formation of Consideration Sets," *Journal of Consumer Research*, June 1997, pp. 94–104.
32. Celsi and Olson, "The Role of Involvement in Attention and Comprehension Processes."
33. Arch Woodside and J. William Davenport Jr., "The Effect of Salesman Similarity and Expertise on Consumer Purchasing Behavior," *Journal of Marketing Research*, May 1974, pp. 198–202.
34. Robert E. Burnkrant and Daniel J. Howard, "Effects of the Use of Introductory Rhetorical Questions versus Statements on Information Processing," *Journal of Personality and Social Psychology*, December 1984, pp. 1218–1230.
35. Grant McCracken, "Who Is the Celebrity Endorser? Cultural Foundations of the Endorsement Process," *Journal of Consumer Research*, December 1989, pp. 310–321; Jeffrey Burroughs and Richard A. Feinberg, "Using Response Latency to Assess Spokesperson Effectiveness," *Journal of Consumer Research*, September 1987, pp. 295–299.
36. Sue Zeidler, "Victoria's Secret Fashion Show Flaunts Good Ratings," *Yahoo News-Reuters*, November 16, 2001, **dailynews.yahoo.com/htx/nm/20011116/re/retail_victoriassecret_dc_5.html**; "'Victoria's Secret' Comes to Prime Time," *CNN.com*, November 15, 2001, **www.cnn.com/2001/showbiz/tv/11/15/apontv.victorias.secret.ap.**
37. MacInnis and Park, "The Differential Role of Characteristics of Music on High- and Low-Involvement Consumers' Processing of Ads"; David W. Stewart and David H. Furse, *Effective Television Advertising: A Study of 1000 Commercials* (Lexington, Mass.: Lexington Books, 1986); James J. Kellaris and Robert J. Kent, "An Exploratory Investigation of Responses Elicited by Music Varying in Tempo, Tonality, and Texture," *Journal of Consumer Psychology*, March 1993, pp. 381–402; James J. Kellaris, Anthony Cox, and Dena Cox, "The Effects of Background Music on Ad Processing Contingency Explanation," *Journal of Consumer Research*, October 1993, pp. 114–126.
38. Brian Sternthal and Samuel Craig, "Humor in Advertising," *Journal of Marketing*, October 1973, pp. 12–18; Thomas Madden and Marc G. Weinberger, "The Effect of Humor on Attention in Magazine Advertising," *Journal of Advertising*, September 1982, pp. 8–14.
39. Nikhil Deogun, "Pepsi Brings 'Good vs. Evil' to Soda War," *Wall Street Journal*, July 9, 1998, p. B7.

40. Michelle Prather, "What's That Smell?" *Entrepreneur*, July 2001, p. 160; Eleena de Lisser, "Perfume Maker Stirs Up Down-to-Earth Scents," *Wall Street Journal*, April 8, 1998, pp. B1, B2.

41. Alec Klein, "In Photography, Black and White Turns Green Again," *Wall Street Journal*, June 1, 1999, pp. B1, B4.

42. Yih Hwai Lee, "Manipulating Ad Message Involvement through Information Expectancy: Effects on Attitude Evaluation and Confidence," *Journal of Advertising*, vol. 29, no. 2, Summer 2000, pp. 29–42; Joan Meyers-Levy and Alice Tybout, "Schema Congruity as a Basis for Product Evaluation," *Journal of Consumer Research*, June 1989, pp. 39–54. Characteristics of music can also cause surprise; see Kellaris and Kent, "An Exploratory Investigation of Responses Elicited by Music Varying in Tempo, Tonality, and Texture."

43. Laura Q. Hughes and Jack Neff, "Jergens Takes a PSA Tack," *Advertising Age*, June 11, 2001, pp. 4, 47.

44. Dana L. Alden, Ashesh Mukherjee, and Wayne D. Hoyer, "The Effects of Incongruity, Surprise and Positive Moderators on Perceived Humor in Television Advertising," *Journal of Advertising*, vol. 29, no. 2, Summer 2000, pp. 1–15.

45. Edward F. McQuarrie and David Glen Mick, "Visual Rhetoric in Advertising: Text-Interpretive, Experimental, and Reader-Response Analyses," *Journal of Consumer Research*, vol. 26, June 1999, pp. 37–54.

46. Finn, "Print Ad Recognition Readership Scores."

47. W. F. Wagner, *Yellow Pages Report* (Scotts Valley, Calif.: Mark Publishing, 1988); Gerald Lohse, "Consumer Eye Movement Patterns on Yellow Pages Advertising," *Journal of Advertising*, Spring 1997, pp. 61–73.

48. Suzanna Vranica, "Help-Wanted Ads Get Big, Funny, Steamy," *Wall Street Journal*, April 5, 2000, p. B10.

49. Wagner, *Yellow Pages Report*; Lohse, "Consumer Eye Movement Patterns on Yellow Pages Advertising."

50. Yukimo Ono, "'Wobblers' and 'Sidekicks' Clutter Stores, Irk Retailers," *Wall Street Journal*, September 8, 1998, pp. B1, B3.

51. Werner Krober-Riel, "Activation Research: Psychobiological Approaches in Consumer Research," *Journal of Consumer Research*, March 1979, pp. 240–250; Morris B. Holbrook and Donald R. Lehmann, "Form vs. Content in Predicting Starch Scores," *Journal of Advertising Research*, August 1980, pp. 53–62.

52. Ellen Neuborne and Ronnie Weil, "Road Show: The New Face of Billboards," *BusinessWeek*, May 8, 2000, pp. 75–86.

53. Mackenzie, "The Role of Attention in Mediating the Effect of Advertising on Attribute Importance."

54. Elizabeth Jensen, "Blue Bottles, Gimmicky Labels Sell Wine," *Wall Street Journal*, July 7, 1997, pp. B1, B6.

55. Karen V. Fernandez and Dennis L. Rosen, "The Effectiveness of Information and Color in Yellow Pages Advertising," *Journal of Advertising*, vol. 29, no. 2, Summer 2000, pp. 61–73.

56. Chris Janiszewski, "The Influence of Display Characteristics on Visual Exploratory Search Behavior," *Journal of Consumer Research*, December 1998, pp. 290–301.

57. Edward Rosbergen, Rik Pieters, and Michel Wedel, "Visual Attention to Advertising: A Segment-Level Analysis," *Journal of Consumer Research*, December 1997, pp. 305–314.

58. Priya Raghubir and Aradhna Krishna, "Vital Dimensions in Volume Perception: Can the Eye Fool the Stomach?" *Journal of Marketing Research*, vol. 36, August 1999, pp. 313–326.

59. Peter H. Lindsay and Donald A. Norman, *Human Information Processing: An Introduction to Psychology* (New York: Academic Press, 1973).

60. Ibid.

61. Ibid.

62. Gerald J. Gorn, Amitava Chattopadhyay, and Tracey Yi, "Effects of Color as an Executional Cue: They're in the Shade," *Management Science*, October 1997, pp. 1387–1401.

63. Susan Warren, "It's Lustrous, It's Chic, It's Plastic," *Wall Street Journal*, September 1, 1999, pp. B1, B4.

64. Betsy Spethmann, "A New Recipe," *Promo*, May 2001, pp. 39–40.

65. Marnell Jameson, "The Palette Patrol," *Los Angeles Times*, June 13, 1997, pp. E1, E8.

66. Tim Triplett, "Research Probes How Consumers Rely on Color for Their Purchases," *Marketing News*, August 28, 1995, pp. 1, 39.

67. Lindsay and Norman, *Human Information Processing*.

68. Kathryn Kranhold, "Ad Shops Seek 'Demo Love' with Unknown Actors as Strike Wears On," *Wall Street Journal*, August 16, 2000, pp. B1, B4.

69. Ronald E. Millman, "Using Background Music to Affect the Behavior of Supermarket Shoppers," *Journal of Marketing*, Summer 1982, pp. 86–91.

70. Colleen Bazdarich, "In a Buying Mood? Maybe It's the Muzak," *Business 2.0*, March 2002, p. 100.

71. Ronald E. Millman, "The Influence of Background Music on the Behavior of Restaurant Patrons," *Journal of Consumer Research*, September 1986, pp. 286–289; Richard Yalch and Eric Spannenberg, "Effects of Store Music on Shopping Behavior," *Journal of Services Marketing*, Winter 1990, pp. 31–39.

72. Mark I. Alpert and Judy Alpert, "The Effects of Music in Advertising on Mood and Purchase Intentions," Working paper No. 85/86–5–4, Department of Marketing Administration, University of Texas, 1986.

73. Gerald J. Gorn, "The Effects of Music in Advertising on Choice Behavior," *Journal of Marketing*, Winter

1982, pp. 94–101; C. Whan Park and S. Mark Young, "Consumer Response to Television Commercials: The Impact of Involvement and Background Music on Brand Attitude Formation," *Journal of Marketing Research*, February 1986, pp. 11–24; MacInnis and Park, "The Differential Role of Characteristics of Music on High- and Low-Involvement Consumers' Processing of Ads."

74. Lea Goldman, "A Cry in the Wilderness," *Forbes*, May 15, 2000, p. 322.
75. Trygg Engen, *The Perception of Odors* (New York: Academic Press, 1982); Trygg Engen, "Remembering Odors and Their Names," *American Scientist*, September–October 1987, pp. 497–503.
76. T. Schemper, S. Voss, and W. S. Cain, "Odor Identification in Young and Elderly Persons," *Journal of Gerontology*, December 1981, pp. 446–452; J. C. Stevens and W. S. Cain, "Smelling via the Mouth: Effect of Aging," *Perception and Psychophysics*, September 1986, pp. 142–146.
77. W. S. Cain, "Odor Identification by Males and Females: Prediction vs. Performance," *Chemical Senses*, February 1982, pp. 129–142.
78. Beryl Leiff Benderly, "Aroma," *Health*, December 1988, pp. 62–77.
79. M. S. Kirk-Smith, C. Van Toller, and G. H. Dodd, "Unconscious Odour Conditioning in Human Subjects," *Biological Psychology*, vol. 17, 1983, pp. 221–231.
80. Pamela Weentraug, "Sentimental Journeys: Smells Have the Power to Arouse Our Deepest Memories, Our Most Primitive Drives," *Omni*, August 1986, p. 815; Howard Erlichman and Jack N. Halpern, "Affect and Memory: Effects of Pleasant and Unpleasant Odors on Retrieval of Happy and Unhappy Memories," *Journal of Personality and Social Psychology*, May 1988, pp. 769–779; Frank R. Schab, "Odors and the Remembrance of Things Past," *Journal of Experimental Psychology: Learning, Memory and Cognition*, July 1990, pp. 648–655.
81. Theresa Howard, "Who Needs Ads When You've Got Hot Doughnuts Now?" *USA Today*, May 31, 2001, p. B3.
82. Roseanne Harper, "Super Kmart Alters Bakery Presentation," *Supermarket News*, August 15, 1994, pp. 25–26.
83. Susan Reda, "Dollars and Scents," *Stores*, August 1994, p. 38.
84. Thomas K. Grose, "That Odd Smell May Be Your E-mail," *U.S. News & World Report*, August 6, 2001, p. 33.
85. Tara Parker-Pope, "Body Spritzes Promise to Dispel Smokers' Odors," *Wall Street Journal*, March 31, 1998, pp. B1, B14.
86. Andrea Petersen, "Some Dog Owners Now Aspire to Smell as Good as Their Pets," *Wall Street Journal*, February 22, 1996, p. B1.
87. Tony Spleen, "Precut Future Debated: Convenience vs. Taste," *Supermarket News*, February 28, 1994, p. 29.
88. Maxine Wilkie, "Scent of a Market," *American Demographics*, August 1995, pp. 40–49.
89. Jacob Hornik, "Tactile Stimulation and Consumer Response," *Journal of Consumer Research*, December 1992, pp. 449–458.
90. Sak Onkvisit and John J. Shaw, *International Marketing: Analysis and Strategy* (Columbus, Ohio: Merrill, 1989).
91. M. Eastlake Stevens, "REI's X-Treme Sports Retailing," *Colorado Biz*, August 2000, pp. 56–57.
92. Alison Fahey, "Party Hardly," *Brandweek*, October 26, 1992, pp. 24–25.
93. Richard Gibson, "Bigger Burger by McDonald's: A Two Ouncer," *Wall Street Journal*, April 18, 1996, p. B1.
94. Stuart Rogers, "How a Publicity Blitz Created the Myth of Subliminal Advertising," *Public Relations Quarterly*, Winter 1992, pp. 12–18.
95. Martha Rogers and Christine A. Seiler, "The Answer Is No," *Journal of Advertising Research*, March–April 1994, pp. 36–46; W. B. Key, *Subliminal Seduction* (Englewood Cliffs, N. J.: Prentice-Hall, 1973); W. B. Key, *Media Sexploitation* (Englewood Cliffs, N. J.: Prentice-Hall, 1976); W. B. Key, *The Clamplate Orgy* (Englewood Cliffs, N. J.: Prentice-Hall, 1980); Martha Rogers and Kirk H. Smith, "Public Perceptions of Subliminal Advertising: Why Practitioners Shouldn't Ignore This Issue," *Journal of Advertising Research*, March–April 1993, pp. 10–19; Michael Lev, "No Hidden Meaning Here: Survey Sees Subliminal Ads," *New York Times*, June 16, 1991, pp. 22, S12.
96. Sharon Beatty and Del I. Hawkins, "Subliminal Stimulation: Some New Data and Interpretation," *Journal of Advertising*, June 1989, pp. 4–9; Myron Gable, Henry T. Wilkens, Lynn Harris, and Richard Feinberg, "An Evaluation of Subliminally Embedded Sexual Stimuli and Graphics," *Journal of Advertising*, March 1987, pp. 26–32; Dennis L. Rosen and Surendra N. Singh, "An Investigation of Subliminal Embed Effect on Multiple Measures of Advertising Effectiveness," *Psychology and Marketing*, March–April 1992, pp. 157–173; J. Steven Kelly, "Subliminal Embeds in Print Advertising: A Challenge to Advertising Ethics," *Journal of Advertising*, September 1979, pp. 20–24; Anthony R. Pratkanis and Anthony G. Greenwald, "Recent Perspectives on Unconscious Processing: Still No Marketing Applications," *Psychology and Marketing*, Winter 1988, pp. 337–353; Joel Saegert, "Why Marketing Should Quit Giving Subliminal Advertising the Benefit of the Doubt," *Psychology and Marketing*, March–April 1987, pp. 157–173.
97. A. J. Marcel, "Conscious and Unconscious Perception: Experiments on Visual Masking and Word Recognition," *Cognitive Psychology*, June 1983, pp. 197–237; A. J. Marcel, "Conscious and Unconscious

Perception: An Approach to the Relations between Phenomenal Experience and Perceptual Processes," *Cognitive Psychology*, September 1983, pp. 238–300.

98. Ronald C. Goodstein and Ajay Kalra, "Incidental Exposure and Affective Reactions to Advertising," Working paper No. 239, School of Management, University of California at Los Angeles, January 1994.

99. Timothy E. Moore, "Subliminal Advertising: What You See Is What You Get," *Journal of Marketing*, Spring 1982, pp. 38–47.

100. Laura A. Peracchio and Joan Meyers-Levy, "How Ambiguous Cropped Objects in Ad Photos Can Affect Product Evaluations," *Journal of Consumer Research*, June 1994, pp. 190–204.

101. Emily Nelson, "P&G Rides Creative Wave in Target Ads," *Wall Street Journal*, March 3, 2000, p. B5.

Chapter 5

1. Anonymous, "Redox Brands Inc. Introduces New Detergent for Generation X," *Chemical Business Newsbase*, August 13, 2001, p. 35; Matthew Swibel, "Spin Cycle," *Forbes*, April 2, 2001, p. 118, www.forbes.com; Bill Schmitt, "Redox Plans New Spin for Oxydol," *Chemical Week*, July 19, 2000, p. 39.

2. Lawrence W. Barsalou, *Cognitive Psychology: An Overview for Cognitive Scientists* (Hillsdale, N. J.: Lawrence Erlbaum, 1992); James R. Bettman, "Memory Factors in Consumer Choice: A Review," *Journal of Marketing*, Spring 1979, pp. 37–53; Merrie Brucks and Andrew A. Mitchell, "Knowledge Structures, Production Systems and Decision Strategies," in ed. Kent B. Monroe, *Advances in Consumer Research*, vol. 8 (Ann Arbor, Mich.: Association for Consumer Research, 1982), pp. 750–757.

3. Kevin L. Keller, "Conceptualizing, Measuring, and Managing Customer-Based Brand Equity," *Journal of Marketing*, January 1993, pp. 1–22; Deborah J. MacInnis, Kent Nakamoto, and Gayathri Mani, "Cognitive Associations and Product Category Comparisons: The Role of Knowledge Structure and Context," in eds. John F. Sherry and Brian Sternthal, *Advances in Consumer Research*, vol. 19 (Provo, Utah: Association for Consumer Research, 1992), pp. 260–267.

4. Burleigh B. Gardner and Sidney Levy, "The Product and the Brand," *Harvard Business Review*, March–April 1955, pp. 33–39; see also David Ogilvy, *Confessions of an Advertising Man* (New York: Atheneum, 1964).

5. Marianne Wilson, "The Magic of Brand Identity," *Chain Store Age Executive with Shopping Center Age*, February 1994, p. 66.

6. Stewart Owen, "The Landor Image Power Survey: A Global Assessment of Brand Strength," in eds. David A. Aaker and Alexander L. Biel, *Brand Equity and Advertising* (Hillsdale, N. J.: Lawrence Erlbaum, 1993), pp. 11–30.

7. Joseph T. Plummer, "How Personality Makes a Difference," *Journal of Advertising Research*, December 1984–January 1985, pp. 27–31; William D. Wells, Frank J. Andriuli, Fedele J. Goi, and Stuart Seader, "An Adjective Check List for the Study of 'Product Personality,'" *Journal of Applied Psychology*, October 1957, pp. 317–319; Jennifer L. Aaker, "Dimensions of Brand Personality," *Journal of Marketing Research*, August 1997, pp. 347–356.

8. Tim Triplett, "Brand Personality Must Be Managed or It Will Assume a Life of Its Own," *Marketing News*, May 9, 1994, p. 9.

9. Katheryn Kranhold, "Whirlpool Conjures Up Appliance Divas," *Wall Street Journal*, April 27, 2000, p. B14.

10. Anna Wilde Mathews, "Clear Channel Plans to Sell Music Online," *Wall Street Journal*, November 12, 2001, p. B5.

11. Bethany McLean, "Duck and Coverage," *Fortune*, August 13, 2001, pp. 142–143.

12. Gregory L. White, "New Jeep Is Sure to Turn Heads, on the Playground," *Wall Street Journal*, January 9, 2001, pp. B1, B4.

13. Sheri Bridges, Kevin Lane Keller, and Sanjay Sood, "Communication Strategies for Brand Extensions: Enhancing Perceived Fit by Establishing Explanatory Links," *Journal of Advertising*, vol. 29, no. 4, Winter 2000, pp. 1–11; Elyette Roux and Frederic Lorange, "Brand Extension Research: A Review," in eds. Fred von Raiij and Gary Bamoussy, *European Advances in Consumer Research*, vol. 1 (Provo, Utah: Association for Consumer Research, 1993), pp. 492–500; C. Whan Park, Bernard J. Jaworski, and Deborah J. MacInnis, "Strategic Brand Concept-Image Management," *Journal of Marketing*, October 1986, pp. 135–145; David A. Aaker and Kevin L. Keller, "Consumer Evaluations of Brand Extensions," *Journal of Marketing*, January 1990, pp. 27–41; Bernard Simonin and Julie A. Ruth, "Is a Company Known by the Company It Keeps: Assessing the Spillover Effects of Brand Alliances on Consumer Brand Attitudes, *Journal of Marketing Research*, February 1998, pp. 30–42; C. Whan Park, Sung Youl Jun, and Allan D. Shocker, "Composite Branding Alliances: An Investigation of Extension and Feedback Effects, *Journal of Marketing Research*, November 1996, pp. 453–466; MacInnis, Nakamoto, and Mani, "Cognitive Associations and Product Category Comparisons," pp. 260–267; David M. Bousch et al., "Affect Generalization to Similar and Dissimilar Brand Extensions," *Psychology and Marketing*, 1987, pp. 225–237; Susan M. Baroniarczyk and Joseph W. Alba, "The Importance of the Brand in Brand Extension," *Journal of Marketing Research*, May 1994, pp. 214–228.

14. Deborah Roedder John, Barbara Loken, and Christopher Joiner, "The Negative Impact of Extensions: Can Flagship Products Be Diluted?" *Journal of Marketing*, vol. 62, January 1998, pp. 19–32.

15. Rohini Ahluwalia and Zeynep Gürhan-Canli, "The Effects of Extensions on the Family Brand Name: An Accessibility-Diagnosticity Perspective," *Journal of Consumer Research*, December 2000, pp. 371–381; Zeynep Gürhan-Canli and Durairaj Maheswaran, "The Effects of Extensions on Brand Name Dilution and Enhancement," *Journal of Marketing Research*, November 1998, pp. 464–473; Sandra Milberg, C. Whan Park, and Michael S. McCarthy, "Managing Negative Feedback Effects Associated with Brand Extensions: The Impact of Alternative Branding Strategies," *Journal of Consumer Psychology*, vol. 6, no. 2, 1997, pp. 119–140; Barbara Loken and Deborah Roedder-John, "Diluting Brand Beliefs: When Do Brand Extensions Have a Negative Impact," *Journal of Marketing*, July 1993, pp. 71–84; David A. Aaker, *Managing Brand Equity* (New York: The Free Press, 1991).

16. Sarah Ellison, "Body Shop Hopes for New Image with an Omnilife Deal," *Wall Street Journal*, June 8, 2001, p. B4; Emily Nelson and Ann Zimmerman, "Avon Goes Store to Store," *Wall Street Journal*, September 18, 2000, pp. B1, B4.

17. C. Whan Park, Bernard J. Jaworski, and Deborah J. MacInnis, "Strategic Brand Concept-Image Management."

18. Kevin P. Gwinner and John Eaton, "Building Brand Image through Event Sponsorship: The Role of Image Transfer," *Journal of Advertising*, vol. 28, no. 4, Winter 1999, pp. 47–57.

19. Kathryn Kranhold, "Avis to Try Even Harder with Ads Touting High Quality of Service," *Wall Street Journal*, February 18, 2000, p. B9.

20. Gary Strauss, "Squeezing New from Old: More Brands Expand by Tweaking Tried-and-True," *USA Today*, January 4, 2001, p. 1B.

21. Vanessa O'Connell, "Icon Is No Longer Lipton's Cup of Tea," *Wall Street Journal*, May 21, 2001, p. B6.

22. Ogale Idudu, "London's Once-Stuffy Selfridges Now Woos Hipsters," *Wall Street Journal*, September 19, 2000, pp. B1, B4.

23. Sally Beatty, "Recasting the Gun as Sports Equipment, *Wall Street Journal*, April 5, 1999, pp. B1, B4.

24. Evan Ramstad, "Backpacks with Speakers? Electronics Makers Court Jaded Gen Y," *Wall Street Journal*, May 18, 2000, pp. B1, B4.

25. Abbey Klaassen, "St. Joseph: From Babies to Boomers," *Advertising Age*, July 9, 2001, pp. 1, 38.

26. Niraj Dawar and Madan M. Pillutla, "Impact of Product-Harm Crises on Brand Equity: The Moderating Role of Consumer Expectations," *Journal of Marketing Research*, May 2000, pp. 215–226.

27. Thomas W. Leigh and Arno J. Rethans, "Experiences in Script Elicitation within Consumer Decision-Making Contexts," in eds. Richard P. Bagozzi and Alice M. Tybout, *Advances in Consumer Research*, vol. 10 (Ann Arbor, Mich.: Association for Consumer Research, 1983), pp. 667–672; Roger C. Shank and Robert P. Abelson, *Scripts, Plans, Goals, and Understanding: An Inquiry into Human Knowledge Structures* (Hillsdale, N. J.: Lawrence Erlbaum, 1977); Ruth Ann Smith and Michael J. Houston, "A Psychometric Assessment of Measures of Scripts in Consumer Memory," *Journal of Consumer Research*, September 1985, pp. 214–224; R. A. Lakshmi-Ratan and Easwar Iyer, "Similarity Analysis of Cognitive Scripts," *Journal of the Academy of Marketing Science*, Summer 1988, pp. 36–43; C. Whan Park, Easwar Iyer, and Daniel C. Smith, "The Effects of Situational Factors on In-Store Grocery Shopping Behavior: The Role of Store Environment and Time Available for Shopping," *Journal of Consumer Research*, March 1989, pp. 422–432.

28. Eleanor Rosch, "Principles of Categorization," in eds. E. Rosch and B. Lloyd, *Cognition and Categorization* (Hillsdale, N. J.: Lawrence Erlbaum, 1978), pp. 119–160; Barsalou, *Cognitive Psychology.*

29. Rosch "Principles of Categorization"; Barsalou *Cognitive Psychology*; Madhubalan Viswanathan and Terry L. Childers, "Understanding How Product Attributes Influence Product Categorization: Development and Validation of Fuzzy Set-Based Measures of Gradedness in Product Categories," *Journal of Marketing Research*, February 1999, pp. 75–94.

30. Lawrence Barsalou, "Ideals, Central Tendency, and Frequency of Instantiation as Determinants of Graded Structure in Categories," *Journal of Experimental Psychology: Learning, Memory and Cognition*, October 1985, pp. 629–649; Barbara Loken and James Ward, "Alternative Approaches to Understanding the Determinants of Typicality," *Journal of Consumer Research*, September 1990, pp. 111–126; James Ward and Barbara Loken, "The Quintessential Snack Food: Measurement of Product Prototypes," in ed. Richard J. Lutz, *Advances in Consumer Research*, vol. 13 (Provo, Utah: Association for Consumer Research, 1986), pp. 126–131; Gregory S. Carpenter and Kent Nakamoto, "Consumer Preference Formation and Pioneering Advantage," *Journal of Marketing Research*, August 1989, pp. 285–298.

31. Gerald J. Gorn and Charles B. Weinberg, "The Impact of Comparative Advertising on Perception and Attitude: Some Positive Findings," *Journal of Consumer Research*, September 1984, pp. 719–727; Cornelia Pechmann and S. Ratneshwar, "The Use of Comparative Advertising for Brand Positioning: Association versus Differentiation," *Journal of Consumer Research*, September 1991, pp. 145–160; Rita Snyder, "Comparative Advertising and Brand Evaluation: Toward Developing a Categorization Approach," *Journal of Consumer Psychology*, vol. 1, no. 1, 1992, pp. 15–30.

32. Hillary Chura, "Grabbing Bull by Tail," *Advertising Age*, June 11, 2001, pp. 4, 47.

33. John Bissell, "How Do You Market an Image Brand When the Image Falls out of Favor?" *Brandweek*, July 6, 1994, p. 16.

34. Ronald Alsop, "The Best Reputations in High Tech," *Wall Street Journal*, November 18, 1999, pp. B1, B6.

35. "If You Don't Feel Like Fetching the Rental Car, It Fetches You," *Wall Street Journal*, June 10, 1995, pp. B1, B7.

36. Michael D. Johnson, "Consumer Choice Strategies for Comparing Noncomparable Alternatives," *Journal of Consumer Research*, December 1984, pp. 741–753; Michael D. Johnson, "Comparability and Hierarchical Processing in Multialternative Choice," *Journal of Consumer Research*, December 1988, pp. 303–314; James R. Bettman and Mita Sujan, "Effects of Framing of Comparable and Noncomparable Alternatives by Expert and Novice Consumers," *Journal of Consumer Research*, September 1987, pp. 141–154; C. Whan Park and Daniel C. Smith, "Product Level Choice: A Top Down or Bottom Up Process?" *Journal of Consumer Research*, December 1989, pp. 151–162; Janet Whitman, "Nestlé to Give Nescafe Coffees a New Image," *Wall Street Journal*, March 2, 1999, p. B10.

37. Lea Goldman, "A Cry in the Wilderness," *Forbes*, May 15, 2000, p. 322.

38. Barsalou, *Cognitive Psychology.*

39. Alexei Barrionuevo and Ann Zimmerman, "Latest Supermarket Special—Gasoline," *Wall Street Journal*, April 30, 2001, pp. B1, B4.

40. Eleanor Rosch, "Human Categorization," in ed. N. Warren, *Studies in Cross-Cultural Psychology* (New York: Academic Press, 1977), pp. 1–49; A. D. Pick, "Cognition: Psychological Perspectives," in eds. H. C. Triandis and W. Lonner, *Handbook of Cross-Cultural Psychology* (Boston: Allyn & Bacon, 1980), pp. 117–153; Bernd Schmitt and Shi Zhang, "Language Structure and Categorization: A Study of Classifiers in Consumer Cognition, Judgment and Choice," *Journal of Consumer Research*, September 1998, pp. 108–122.

41. Joseph W. Alba and J. Wesley Hutchinson, "Dimensions of Consumer Expertise," *Journal of Consumer Research*, March 1987, pp. 411–454; Deborah Roedder John and John Whitney Jr., "The Development of Consumer Knowledge in Children: A Cognitive Structure Approach," *Journal of Consumer Research*, March 1986, pp. 406–417; Merrie Brucks, "The Effects of Product Class Knowledge on Information Search Behavior," *Journal of Consumer Research*, June 1985, pp. 1–16; Deborah Roedder John and Mita Sujan, "Age Differences in Product Categorization," *Journal of Consumer Research*, March 1990, pp. 452–460. See also Andrew A. Mitchell and Peter A. Dacin, "The Assessment of Alternative Measures of Consumer Expertise," *Journal of Consumer Research*, December 1996, pp. 219–239; C. Whan Park, David L. Mothersbaugh, and Lawrence Feick, "Consumer Knowledge Assessment," *Journal of Consumer Research*, June 1994, pp. 71–82.

42. Joseph W. Alba and J. Wesley Hutchinson, "Knowledge Calibration: What Consumers Know and What They Think They Know," *Journal of Consumer Research*, September 2000, pp. 123–156.

43. Maureen Morrin, "The Impact of Brand Extensions on Parent Brand Memory Structures and Retrieval Processes," *Journal of Marketing Research*, November 1999, pp. 517–525.

44. Yumiko Ono, "Will Good Housekeeping Translate into Japanese?" *Wall Street Journal*, December 30, 1997, pp. B1, B6.

45. "Safety First in Sampling," *Advertising Age*, July 26, 1981.

46. "The Fruit Formerly Known as . . . Prunes to Be Sold as 'Dried Plums' in Bid to Sweeten Image," *Washington Post*, April 15, 2001, p. A4.

47. Ronald C. Goodstein, "Category-Based Applications and Extensions in Advertising: Motivating More Extensive Ad Processing," *Journal of Consumer Research*, June 1993, pp. 87–99; Mita Sujan, "Consumer Knowledge: Effects on Evaluation Strategies Mediating Consumer Judgments," *Journal of Consumer Research*, June 1985, pp. 31–46.

48. Susan T. Fiske, "Schema Triggered Affect: Applications to Social Perception," in eds. Margaret S. Clark and Susan T. Fiske, *Affect and Cognition: The 17th Annual Carnegie Symposium on Cognition* (Hillsdale, N. J.: Lawrence Erlbaum, 1984), pp. 55–78; Susan T. Fiske and Mark A. Pavelchak, "Category-Based vs. Piecemeal-Based Affective Responses: Developments in Schema-Triggered Affect," in eds. Richard M. Sorrentino and E. Tory Higgins, *Handbook of Motivation and Cognition* (New York: Guilford, 1986), pp. 167–203; Joel B. Cohen, "The Role of Affect in Categorization: Toward a Reconsideration of the Concept of Attitude," in ed. Andrew A. Mitchell, *Advances in Consumer Research*, vol. 9 (Ann Arbor, Mich.: Association for Consumer Research, 1982), pp. 94–100.

49. Douglas M. Stayman, Dana L. Alden, and Karen H. Smith, "Some Effects of Schematic Processing on Consumer Expectations and Disconfirmation Judgments," *Journal of Consumer Research*, September 1992, pp. 245–255.

50. David G. Mick, "Levels of Subjective Comprehension in Advertising Processing and Their Relations to Ad Perceptions, Attitudes, and Memory," *Journal of Consumer Research*, March 1992, pp. 411–424.

51. Jacob Jacoby, Wayne D. Hoyer, and David A. Sheluga, *Miscomprehension of Televised Communication* (New York: American Association of Advertising Agencies, 1980); Jacob Jacoby and Wayne D. Hoyer, *The Comprehension and Miscomprehension of Print Communications: An Investigation of Mass Media Magazines* (New York: Advertising Education

Foundation, 1987); see also Jacob Jacoby and Wayne D. Hoyer, "The Miscomprehension of Mass-Media Advertising Claims: A Re-Analysis of Benchmark Data," *Journal of Advertising Research*, June–July 1990, pp. 9–17; Jacob Jacoby and Wayne D. Hoyer, "The Comprehension-Miscomprehension of Print Communication: Selected Findings," *Journal of Consumer Research*, March 1989, pp. 434–444; Fliece R. Gates, "Further Comments on the Miscomprehension of Televised Advertisements," *Journal of Advertising*, Winter 1986, pp. 4–10.

52. Sak Onkvisit and John J. Shaw, *International Marketing: Analysis and Strategy* (Columbus, Ohio: Merrill, 1989), pp. 223–224.

53. Richard L. Celsi and Jerry C. Olson, "The Role of Involvement in Attention and Comprehension Processes," *Journal of Consumer Research*, September 1988, pp. 210–224.

54. Jacob Jacoby, Robert W. Chestnut, and William Silberman, "Consumer Use and Comprehension of Nutrition Information," *Journal of Consumer Research*, September 1977, pp. 119–127.

55. Gary J. Gaeth and Timothy B. Heath, "The Cognitive Processing of Misleading Advertising in Young and Old Adults," *Journal of Consumer Research*, June 1987, pp. 43–54; Deborah Roedder, John and Catherine A. Cole, "Age Differences in Information Processing: Understanding Deficits in Young and Elderly Consumers," *Journal of Consumer Research*, December 1986, pp. 297–315; Catherine A. Cole and Michael J. Houston, "Encoding and Media Effects on Consumer Learning Deficiencies in the Elderly," *Journal of Marketing Research*, February 1987, pp. 55–63.

56. C. Page Moreau, Donald R. Lehmann, and Arthur B. Markman, "Entrenched Knowledge Structures and Consumer Response to New Products," *Journal of Marketing Research*, February 2001, pp. 14–29.

57. Edward T. Hall, *Beyond Culture* (Garden City, N.Y.: Anchor Press/Doubleday, 1976); Onkvisit and Shaw, *International Marketing*, pp. 223–224.

58. Robert Frank, "Big Boy's Adventures in Thailand," *Wall Street Journal*, April 12, 2000, pp. B1, B4.

59. Fara Warner, "Fahrvergnugen Takes a Back Seat," *Adweek's Marketing Week*, June 15, 1992, pp. 1, 6.

60. Onkvisit and Shaw, *International Marketing*.

61. Wayne D. Hoyer, Rajendra K. Srivastava, and Jacob Jacoby, "Examining Sources of Advertising Miscomprehension," *Journal of Advertising*, June 1984, pp. 17–26; Julie A. Edell and Richard Staelin, "The Information Processing of Pictures in Print Advertisements," *Journal of Consumer Research*, June 1983, pp. 45–61; Ann Beattie and Andrew A. Mitchell, "The Relationship between Advertising Recall and Persuasion: An Experimental Investigation," in eds. Linda F. Alwitt and Andrew A. Mitchell, *Psychological Processes and Advertising Effects* (Hillsdale, N. J.: Lawrence Erlbaum, 1985), pp. 129–156.

62. Mick, "Levels of Subjective Comprehension in Advertising Processing and Their Relations to Perceptions, Attitudes, and Memory"; Deborah J. MacInnis and Bernard J. Jaworski, "Information Processing from Advertisements: Toward an Integrative Framework," *Journal of Marketing*, October 1989, pp. 1–23.

63. Katherine Ackley, "R.J. Reynolds to Settle Charges over Ads," *Wall Street Journal*, March 4, 1999, p. B4.

64. Mick, "Levels of Subjective Comprehension in Advertising Processing and Their Relations to Ad Perceptions, Attitudes, and Memory"; David G. Mick and Claus Buhl, "A Meaning-Based Model of Advertising Experiences," *Journal of Consumer Research*, December 1992, pp. 317–338.

65. Jennifer Gregan-Paxton and Deborah Roedder John, "Consumer Learning by Analogy: A Model of Internal Knowledge Transfer," *Journal of Consumer Research*, December 1997, pp. 266–284.

66. Richard D. Johnson and Irwin P. Levin, "More Than Meets the Eye: The Effect of Missing Information on Purchase Evaluations," *Journal of Consumer Research*, September 1985, pp. 169–177; Frank Kardes, "Spontaneous Inference Processes in Advertising: The Effects of Conclusion Omission and Involvement in Persuasion," *Journal of Consumer Research*, September 1988, pp. 225–233; Alba and Hutchinson, "Dimensions of Consumer Expertise."

67. Michaela Wänke, Herbert Bless, and Norbert Schwarz, "Context Effects in Product Line Extensions: Context Is Not Destiny," *Journal of Consumer Psychology*, vol. 7, no. 4, 1998, pp. 299–322.

68. Teresa Pavia and Janeen Arnold Costa, "The Winning Number: Consumer Perceptions of Alpha-Numeric Brand Names," *Journal of Marketing*, July 1993, pp. 85–99; France Leclerc, Bernd H. Schmitt, and Laurette Dube, "Foreign Branding and Its Effects on Product Perceptions and Attitudes," *Journal of Marketing Research*, May 1994, pp. 263–270; Mary Sullivan, "How Brand Names Affect the Demand for Twin Automobiles," *Journal of Marketing Research*, May 1998, pp. 154–165.

69. Emily Nelson, "P&G Tries to Hide Wrinkles in Aging Beauty Fluid," *Wall Street Journal*, May 16, 2000, pp. B1, B4.

70. Akshay R. Rao, Lu Qu, and Robert W. Ruekert, "Signaling Unobservable Product Quality through a Brand Ally," *Journal of Marketing Research*, May 1999, pp. 258–268.

71. Bonnie B. Reece and Robert H. Ducoffe, "Deception in Brand Names," *Journal of Public Policy and Marketing*, 6, 1987, pp. 93–103.

72. Marilyn Chase, "Pretty Soon the Word 'Organic' on Foods Will Mean One Thing" *Wall Street Journal*, August 18, 1997, p. B1.

73. Benjamin A. Holden, "Utilities Pick New, Non-utilitarian Names," *Wall Street Journal*, April 7, 1997, pp. B1, B5.

74. Wendy M. Grossman, "Generic Names Lose Their Luster," *Smart Business*, April 2001, p. 58.

75. Lisa Bronlee, "A Magazine Named Polo Angers a Firm Named Polo Ralph Loren," *Wall Street Journal*, October 21, 1997, p. B10.

76. Susan M. Broniarczyk and Joseph W. Alba, "The Role of Consumers' Intuitions in Inference Making," *Journal of Consumer Research*, December 1994, pp. 393–407.

77. Gary T. Ford and Ruth Ann Smith, "Inferential Beliefs in Consumer Evaluations: An Assessment of Alternative Processing Strategies," *Journal of Consumer Research*, December 1987, pp. 363–371.

78. Irwin P. Levin and Aron M. Levin, "Modeling the Role of Brand Alliances in the Assimilation of Product Evaluations," *Journal of Consumer Psychology*, vol. 9, no. 1, 2000, pp. 43–52.

79. Sung-Tai Hong and Robert S. Wyer Jr., "Determinants of Product Evaluation: Effects of Time Interval between Knowledge of a Product's Country of Origin and Information about Its Specific Attributes," *Journal of Consumer Research*, December 1990, pp. 277–288; Durairaj Maheswaran, "Country of Origin as a Stereotype: Effects of Consumer Expertise and Attribute Strength on Product Evaluations," *Journal of Consumer Research*, September 1994, pp. 354–365; Sung-Tai Hong and Robert S. Wyer Jr., "Effects of Country of Origin and Product-Attribute Information on Product Evaluation: An Information Processing Perspective," *Journal of Consumer Research*, September 1989, pp. 175–187; Johny K. Johansson, Susan P. Douglas, and Ikujiro Nonaka, "Assessing the Impact of Country of Origin on Product Evaluations," *Journal of Marketing Research*, November 1985, pp. 388–396; Maheswaran, "Country of Origin as a Stereotype"; Wai-Kwan Li and Robert S. Wyer Jr., "The Role of Country of Origin in Product Evaluations: Informational and Standard-of-Comparison Effects," *Journal of Consumer Psychology*, 2, 1994, pp. 187–212.

80. Marieke K. De Mooij and Warren Keegan, *Advertising Worldwide* (Hertfordshire, U.K.: Prentice-Hall International, 1991), p. 97.

81. Rajeev Batra, Venkatram Ramaswamy, Dana L. Alden, Jan-Benedict E. M. Steenkamp, and S. Ramachander, "Effects of Brand Local and Nonlocal Origin on Consumer Attitudes in Developing Countries," *Journal of Consumer Psychology*, vol. 9, no. 2, 2000, pp. 83–95.

82. Stephanie N. Mehta, "BellSouth Pushes Harder in Latin America," *Wall Street Journal*, May 24, 1999, p. B10.

83. Zeynep Gürhan-Canli and Durairaj Maheswaran, "Determinants of Country-of-Origin Evaluations," *Journal of Consumer Research*, June 2000, pp. 96–108.

84. Zeynep Gürhan-Canli and Durairaj Maheswaran, "Cultural Variations in Country of Origin Effects," *Journal of Marketing Research*, August 2000, pp. 309–317.

85. Carl McDaniel and R. C. Baker, "Convenience Food Packaging and the Perception of Product Quality," *Journal of Marketing*, October 1977, pp. 57–58.

86. Shelly Branch, "Southern Comfort Is Spirited Into Present," *Wall Street Journal*, June 15, 2001, p. B6.

87. Ralph T. King Jr., "Grapes of Wrath: Kendall-Jackson Sues Gallo Winery in a Battle over a Bottle," *Wall Street Journal*, April 5, 1996, pp. B1, B11.

88. Maxine S. Lans, "Supreme Court to Rule on Colors as Trademarks," *Marketing News*, January 2, 1995, p. 28.

89. Ayn Crowley, "The Two-Dimensional Impact of Color on Shopping," *Marketing Letters*, 1993, pp. 59–69.

90. Donald Lichtenstein and Scott Burton, "The Relationship between Perceived and Objective Price-Quality," *Journal of Marketing Research*, November 1989, pp. 429–443; Etian Gerstner, "Do Higher Prices Signal Higher Quality?" *Journal of Marketing Research*, May 1985, pp. 209–215; Kent Monroe and R. Krishnan, "The Effects of Price on Subjective Product Evaluations," in eds. Jacob Jacoby and Jerry C. Olson, *Perceived Quality: How Consumers View Stores and Merchandise* (Lexington, Mass.: D. C. Heath, 1985), pp. 209–232; Susan M. Petroshius and Kent B. Monroe, "Effect of Product-Line Pricing Characteristics on Product Evaluations," *Journal of Consumer Research*, March 1987, pp. 511–519; Akshay R. Rao and Kent B. Monroe, "The Moderating Effect of Prior Knowledge on Cue Utilization in Product Evaluations," *Journal of Consumer Research*, September 1988, pp. 253–264; Cornelia Pechmann and S. Ratneshwar, "Consumer Covariation Judgments: Theory or Data Driven?" *Journal of Consumer Research*, December 1992, pp. 373–386.

91. Thomas T. Nagle and Reed K. Holden, *The Strategy and Tactics of Pricing*, 2d ed. (Englewood Cliffs, N.J.: Prentice Hall, 1995), pp. 84–85.

92. Ann E. Schlosser, "Applying the Functional Theory of Attitudes to Understanding the Influence of Store Atmosphere on Store Inferences," *Journal of Consumer Psychology*, vol. 7, no. 4, 1998, pp. 345–369.

93. Lauranne Buchanan, Carolyn J. Simmons, and Barbara A. Bickart, "Brand Equity Dilution: Retailer Display and Context Brand Effects," *Journal of Marketing Research*, August 1999, pp. 345–355.

94. Gareth Fenley, "Reinventing Radio Shack," *Display & Design Ideas*, August 2001, pp. 26–27.

95. Tsune Shirai, "What Is an 'International' Mind?" *PHP*, June 1980, p. 25.

96. Barbara Mueller, "Standardization vs. Specialization: An Examination of Westernization in Japanese Advertising," *Journal of Advertising Research*, January–February 1992, pp. 15–22.

97. Margaret C. Campbell and Amna Kirmani, "Consumers' Use of Persuasion Knowledge: The Effects of Accessibility and Cognitive Capacity on Perceptions of an Influence Agent," *Journal of Consumer Research*, June 2000, pp. 69–83.

98. Onkvisit and Shaw, *International Marketing.*

99. Richard J. Harris, Julia C. Pounds, Melissa J. Maiorelle, and Maria Mermis, "The Effect of Type of Claim, Gender, and Buying History on the Drawing of Pragmatic Inferences from Advertising Claims," *Journal of Consumer Psychology*, vol. 2, no. 1, 1993, pp. 83–95; Richard J. Harris, R. E. Sturm, M. L. Kalssen, and J. I. Bechtold, "Language in Advertising: A Psycholinguistic Approach," *Current Issues and Research in Advertising*, The University of Michigan Press. 1986, pp. 1–26; Raymond R. Burke, Wayne S. DeSarbo, Richard L. Oliver, and Thomas S. Robertson, "Deception by Implication: An Experimental Investigation," *Journal of Consumer Research*, March 1988, pp. 483–494.

100. J. Craig Andrews, Scot Burton, and Richard G. Netemeyer, "Are Some Comparative Nutrition Claims Misleading? The Role of Nutrition Knowledge, Ad Claim Type, and Disclosure Conditions," *Journal of Advertising*, vol. 29, no. 3, Fall 2000, pp. 29–42; Terence Shimp, "Do Incomplete Comparisons Mislead?" *Journal of Advertising Research*, December 1978, pp. 21–27; Harris et al., "The Effect of Type of Claim, Gender, and Buying History on the Drawing of Pragmatic Inferences from Advertising Claims;" Gita Johar, "Consumer Involvement and Deception from Implied Advertising Claims," *Journal of Marketing Research*, August 1995, pp. 267–279.

101. Michael Barone and Paul W. Miniard, "How and When Factual Ad Claims Mislead Consumers: Examining the Deceptive Consequences of Copy x Copy Interactions for Partial Comparative Advertisements," *Journal of Marketing Research*, February 1999, pp. 58–74.

Chapter 6

1. Eleftheria Parpis, "New Ammunition," *Adweek*, October 29, 2001, pp. 16+; Ira Teinowitz, "Army Greens: Leo Burnett Gets Bonus Bucks for Recruitment Ads," *Advertising Age*, September 10, 2001, pp. 4+; John Derbyshire, "Is This All We Can Be? The Military Culture and Its Cheapening," *National Review*, April 16, 2001, pp. 30+; "Burnett Puts Boot Camp Online," *Adweek*, February 5, 2001, p. 10; Greg Jaffe, "Uncle Sam Wants Who? New Report Calls Military's Ads Off Target," *Wall Street Journal*, July 6, 2000, pp. B1, B4.

2. Richard E. Petty, H. Rao Unnava, and Alan J. Strathman, "Theories of Attitude Change," in eds. Thomas S. Robertson and Harold H. Kassarjian, *Handbook of Consumer Behavior* (Englewood Cliffs, N. J.: Prentice-Hall, 1991), pp. 241–280.

3. Ida E. Berger and Andrew A. Mitchell, "The Effect of Advertising on Attitude Accessibility, Attitude Confidence, and the Attitude-Behavior Relationship," *Journal of Consumer Research*, December 1989, pp. 269–279.

4. Rohini Ahluwalia, "Examination of Psychological Processes Underlying Resistance to Persuasion," *Journal of Consumer Research*, September 2000, pp. 217–232.

5. Martin Fishbein and Icek Ajzen, *Belief, Attitude, Intention, and Behavior: An Introduction to Theory and Research* (Reading, Mass.: Addison-Wesley, 1975).

6. Petty, Unnava, and Strathman, "Theories of Attitude Change"; Richard Petty and John T. Cacioppo, *Communication and Persuasion* (New York: Springer, 1986).

7. Peter L. Wright, "Message-Evoked Thoughts: Persuasion Research Using Thought Verbalizations," *Journal of Consumer Research*, September 1980, pp. 151–175.

8. Jerry C. Olson, Daniel R. Toy, and Philip A. Dover, "Do Cognitive Responses Mediate the Effects of Advertising Content on Cognitive Structure?" *Journal of Consumer Research*, December 1982, pp. 245–262.

9. Marian Friestad and Peter Wright, "The Persuasion Knowledge Model: How People Cope with Persuasion Attempts," *Journal of Consumer Research*, June 1994, pp. 1–31.

10. Daniel R. Toy, "Monitoring Communication Effects: Cognitive Structure/Cognitive Response Approach," *Journal of Consumer Research*, June 1982, pp. 66–76.

11. Petty, Unnava, and Strathman, "Theories of Attitude Change."

12. Punam Anand and Brian Sternthal, "The Effects of Program Involvement and Ease of Message Counterarguing on Advertising Persuasiveness," *Journal of Consumer Psychology*, vol. 1, no. 3, 1992, pp. 225–238; Kenneth R. Lord and Robert E. Burnkrant, "Attention versus Distraction: The Interactive Effect of Program Involvement and Attentional Devices on Commercial Processing," *Journal of Advertising*, March 1993, pp. 47–60.

13. Deborah J. MacInnis and C. Whan Park, "The Differential Role of Characteristics of Music on High- and Low-Involvement Consumers' Processing of Ads," *Journal of Consumer Research*, September 1991, pp. 161–173; Rajeev Batra and Douglas M. Stayman, "The Role of Mood in Advertising Effectiveness," *Journal of Consumer Research*, September 1990, pp. 203–214.

14. William L. Wilkie and Edgar A. Pessemier, "Issues in Marketing's Use of Multi-Attribute Models," *Journal of Marketing Research*, November 1973, pp. 428–441.

15. Richard P. Bagozzi, Nancy Wong, Shuzo Abe, and Massimo Bergami, "Cultural and Situational Contingencies and the Theory of Reasoned Action: Application to Fast Food Restaurant Consumption," *Journal of Consumer Psychology*, vol. 9, no. 2, 2000, pp. 97–106.

16. Icek Ajzen and Martin Fishbein, "Prediction of Goal-Directed Behavior: Attitudes, Intentions, and Perceived Behavioral Control," *Journal of Experimental Social Psychology*, September 1980, pp. 453–474; Blair H. Sheppard, Jon Hartwick, and Paul R. Warshaw, "The Theory of Reasoned Action: A Meta-Analysis of Past Research with Recommendations for Modifications and Future Research," *Journal of Consumer Research*, December 1988, pp. 325–342.

17. Arti Sahni Notani, "Moderators of Perceived Behavioral Control's Predictiveness in the Theory of Planned Behavior: A Meta-Analysis," *Journal of Consumer Psychology*, vol. 7, no. 3, 1998, pp. 247–271.

18. Calmetta Y. Coleman, "Hallmark to Spend $10 Million to Say Its Cards Aren't Expensive," *Wall Street Journal*, February 12, 1998, p. B6.

19. Jeffrey Ball, "Mercedes Ads Shuck Stodgy Aura for Hipper Tone," *Wall Street Journal*, September 11, 2000, pp. B1, B4.

20. Hugh Pope, "Plying Ex Soviet Asia with Pepsi, Barbie, and Barf," *Wall Street Journal*, June 6, 1998, pp. B1, B6.

21. Miriam Jordan, "Brazil Cultivates a Spot in Gourmet-Coffee Market," *Wall Street Journal*, February 2, 2001, pp. B1, B4.

22. Dana Milbank, "Made in America Becomes a Boast in Europe," *Wall Street Journal*, January 9, 1994, pp. B1, B5.

23. Tobi Elkin, "Microsoft to Focus on Experience: New Attitude Gets New Campaign," *Advertising Age*, February 26, 2001, p. 22.

24. Stephen M. Nowlis and Itamar Simonson, "The Effect of New Product Features on Brand Choice," *Journal of Marketing Research*, February 1996, pp. 36–46.

25. Andrea Petersen, "Cross, IBM Choose Low-Tech Imagery," *Wall Street Journal*, April 30, 1998, p. B5.

26. Jeffrey Ball, "The Softer Side of Jeep," *Wall Street Journal*, April 24, 2001, pp. B1, B4.

27. Mark Frauenfelder, "Social-Norms Marketing," *New York Times Magazine*, December 9, 2001, p. 100.

28. Laura Bird, "Condom Campaign Fails to Increase Sales," *Wall Street Journal*, June 23, 1994, p. B7

29. Barbara Mueller, "Reflections of Culture: An Analysis of Japanese and American Advertising Appeals," *Journal of Advertising Research*, June–July 1987, pp. 51–59.

30. Ronald E. Goldsmith, Barbara A. Lafferty, and Stephen J. Newell, "The Impact of Corporate Credibility and Celebrity Credibility on Consumer Reaction to Advertisements and Brands," *Journal of Advertising*, vol. 29, no. 3, Fall 2000, pp. 43–54; also see Brian Sternthal, Ruby R. Dholakia, and Clark Leavitt, "The Persuasive Effect of Source Credibility: A Situational Analysis," *Public Opinion Quarterly*, Fall 1978, pp. 285–314.

31. Rob Pegoraro, "Logging On: Comparison Shop Till You Just Must Stop," *Washington Post*, November 14, 2000, p. G16.

32. Robert Frank, "Recipe for a Fashion Brand?" *Wall Street Journal*, June 25, 2001, pp. B1, B4; Shelly Branch, "Front and Center: Mondavi Places Patriarch in Ads with Wine Fans," *Wall Street Journal*, August 16, 1999, p. B10.

33. Ignacio Galceran and Jon Berry, "A New World of Consumers," *American Demographics*, March 1995, pp. 26+; "Pepsi Signs Multi-Year Pact with Colombian Pop Star," *Brandweek*, June 11, 2001, p. 10.

34. Amna Kirmani and Baba Shiv, "Effects of Source Congruity on Brand Attitudes and Beliefs: The Moderating Role of Issue-Relevant Elaboration," *Journal of Consumer Psychology*, vol. 7, no. 1, 1998, pp. 25–48.

35. Chenghuan Wu and David R. Schaffer, "Susceptibility to Persuasive Appeals as a Function of Source Credibility and Prior Experience with the Attitude Object," *Journal of Personality and Social Psychology*, April 1987, pp. 677–688.

36. Carolyn Tripp, Thomas D. Jensen, and Les Carlson, "The Effects of Multiple Endorsements by Celebrities on Consumers' Attitudes and Intentions," *Journal of Consumer Research*, March 1994, pp. 535–547.

37. William Power, "Some Brokers Promise That You Will Make Money; Not This One," *Wall Street Journal*, February 23, 1994, p. B1.

38. Joan Voight, "Selling Confidence," *Adweek Southwest*, August 20, 2001, p. 9.

39. Ignacio Galceran and Jon Berry, "A New World of Consumers," *American Demographics*, March 1995, pp. 26–33.

40. "Golfer Tiger Woods Is New Darling of Madison Avenue," *Factiva Advertising & Media Digest*, April 10, 2001, p. 1; Hilary Cassidy, "Spalding Taps Kobe for 'Infusion' Ball, Styled as the Cure for Deflation Blues," *Brandweek*, January 15, 2001, p. 6.

41. Kevin Goldman, "Women Endorsers More Credible Than Men, a Survey Suggests," *Wall Street Journal*, October 22, 1995, p. B1.

42. Sternthal, Dholakia, and Leavitt, "The Persuasive Effect of Source Credibility."

43. Darlene B. Hannah and Brian Sternthal, "Detecting and Explaining the Sleeper Effect," *Journal of Consumer Research*, September 1984, pp. 632–642.

44. Marvin E. Goldberg and Jon Hartwick, "The Effects of Advertiser Reputation and Extremity of Advertising Claim on Advertising Effectiveness," *Journal of Consumer Research*, September, 1990, pp. 172–179.

45. Stacy Forster, "Ads for Online Brokerage Firms Abound Despite Market Slump," *Wall Street Journal*, February 15, 2001, p. B4.

46. Petty, Unnava, and Strathman, "Theories of Attitude Change."; Charles S. Areni and Richard J. Lutz,

"The Role of Argument Quality in the Elaboration Likelihood Model," in ed. Michael J. Houston, *Advances in Consumer Research*, vol. 15 (Provo, Utah: Association for Consumer Research, 1987), pp. 197–203.

47. Jim Edwards, "The Art of the Infomercial," *Brandweek*, September 3, 2001, pp. 14+.

48. Sally Beatty, "Companies Push for Much Bigger, More Complicated On-Line Ads," *Wall Street Journal*, August 20, 1998 p. B1.

49. Kipp Cheng, "Nestlé Takes Web Ad to TV Screen," *Adweek Southwest*, October 22, 2001, p. 7.

50. Timothy B. Heath, Michael S. McCarthy, and David L. Mothersbaugh, "Spokesperson Fame and Vividness Effects in the Context of Issue-Relevant Thinking: The Moderating Role of Competitive Setting," *Journal of Consumer Research*, March 1994, pp. 520–534.

51. Laura A. Peracchio, "Evaluating Persuasion-Enhancing Techniques from a Resource Matching Perspective," *Journal of Consumer Research*, September 1997, pp. 178–191.

52. Joel A. Baglole, "Cough Syrup Touts 'Awful' Taste in U.S.," *Wall Street Journal*, December 15, 1999, p. B10.

53. Michael A. Kamins and Henry Assael, "Two-Sided versus One-Sided Appeals: A Cognitive Perspective on Argumentation, Source Derogation, and the Effect of Disconfirming Trial on Belief Change," *Journal of Marketing Research*, February 1984, pp. 29–39.

54. Cornelia Pechmann and David W. Stewart, "The Effects of Comparative Advertising on Attention, Memory, and Purchase Intentions," *Journal of Consumer Research*, September 1990, pp. 180–191.

55. Theresa Howard, "Suzuki Packs Humor into Ads for SUV Spots That Poke Fun at Huge Vehicles, Appeal to Women and Men," *USA Today*, May 21, 2001, p. B4.

56. Pechmann and Stewart, "The Effects of Comparative Advertising on Attention, Memory, and Purchase Intentions"; Rita Snyder, "Comparative Advertising and Brand Evaluation: Toward Developing a Categorization Approach," *Journal of Consumer Psychology*, vol. 1, no. 1, 1992, pp. 15–30.

57. "Scrappy," *Delaney Report*, February 12, 2001, p. 3.

58. Gene Koprowski, "Theories of Negativity," *Brandweek*, February 20, 1995, pp. 20–22.

59. Dhruv Grewal, Sukumar Kavanoor, Edward F. Fern, Carolyn Costley, and James Barnes, "Comparative versus Noncomparative Advertising: A Meta-Analysis," *Journal of Marketing*, October 1997, pp. 1–15.

60. Pechmann and Stewart, "The Effects of Comparative Advertising on Attention, Memory, and Purchase Intentions."

61. Kenneth C. Manning, Paul W. Miniard, Michael J. Barone, and Randall L. Rose, "Understanding the Mental Representations Created by Comparative Advertising," *Journal of Advertising*, vol. 3, no. 2, Summer 2001, pp. 27+.

62. Jerry B. Gotlieb and Dan Sarel, "Comparative Advertising Effectiveness: The Role of Involvement and Source Credibility," *Journal of Advertising*, vol. 20, no. 1, 1991, pp. 38–45; Koprowski, "Theories of Negativity."

63. Cornelia Pechmann and S. Ratneshwar, "The Use of Comparative Advertising for Brand Positioning: Association versus Differentiation," *Journal of Consumer Research*, September 1991, pp. 145–160.

64. A. V. Muthukrishnan and S. Ramaswami, "Contextual Effects on the Revision of Evaluative Judgments: An Extension of the Omission-Detection Framework," *Journal of Consumer Research*, June 1999, pp. 70–84.

65. Pechmann and Stewart, "The Effects of Comparative Advertising on Attention, Memory, and Purchase Intentions."

66. John Tylee, "New 'Honesty' Laws Could Render Many Campaigns Illegal," *Campaign*, March 17, 2000, p. 16.

67. Barbara Mueller, "Reflections of Culture: An Analysis of Japanese and American Advertising Appeals," *Journal of Advertising Research*, June–July 1987, pp. 51–59.

68. H. Onur Bodur, David Brinberg, and Eloïse Coupey, "Belief, Affect, and Attitude: Alternative Models of the Determinants of Attitude," *Journal of Consumer Psychology*, vol. 9, no. 1, 2000, pp. 17–28.

69. Michel Tuan Pham, "Representativeness, Relevance, and the Use of Feelings in Decision Making," *Journal of Consumer Research*, September 1998, pp. 144–159.

70. MacInnis and Park, "The Differential Role of Characteristics of Music on High- and Low-Involvement Consumers' Processing of Ads."

71. Deborah J. MacInnis and Douglas M. Stayman, "Focal and Emotional Integration: Constructs, Measures and Preliminary Evidence," *Journal of Advertising*, December 1993, pp. 51–66; Chris T. Allen, Karen A. Machleit, and Susan Schultz Kleine, "A Comparison of Attitudes and Emotions as Predictors of Behavior at Diverse Levels of Behavioral Experience," *Journal of Consumer Research*, March 1992, pp. 493–504.

72. Deborah J. MacInnis and Bernard J. Jaworski, "Two Routes to Persuasion in Advertising: Review, Critique, and Research Directions," *Review of Marketing*, vol. 10, 1990, pp. 1–25.

73. Alexia Vargas, "Mom and Pop's Retail Secret: Doggie in the Window," *Wall Street Journal*, December 22, 1999, pp. B1+.

74. C. Whan Park and S. Mark Young, "Consumer Response to Television Commercials: The Impact of Involvement and Background Music on Brand Attitude Formation," *Journal of Marketing Research*, February 1986, pp. 11–24.

75. Rajeev Batra and Michael L. Ray, "Affective Responses Mediating Acceptance of Advertising,"

Journal of Consumer Research, September 1986, pp. 234–249.

76. Hans Baumgartner, Mita Sujan, and Dan Padgett, "Patterns of Affective Reactions to Advertisements: The Integration of Moment-to-Moment Responses into Overall Judgments," *Journal of Marketing Research*, May 1997, pp. 219–232.

77. Deborah J. MacInnis and Bernard J. Jaworski, "Information Processing from Advertisements: Toward an Integrative Framework," *Journal of Marketing*, October 1989, pp. 1–23.

78. "Kodak Debuts New 'Share Moments, Share Life' Advertising Campaign Which Builds on Kodak's Rich Legacy as It Extends Brand Leadership to Digital Imaging," *Business Wire*, March 19, 2001, www.businesswire.com.

79. Jennifer L. Aaker and Patti Williams, "Empathy versus Pride: The Influence of Emotional Appeals across Cultures,' *Journal of Consumer Research*, December 1998, pp. 241–261.

80. Richard P. Bagozzi and David J. Moore, "Public Service Announcements: Emotions and Empathy Guide Prosocial Behavior," *Journal of Marketing*, January 1994, pp. 56–57.

81. May Frances Luce, "Choosing to Avoid: Coping with Negatively Emotion-Laden Consumer Decisions," *Journal of Consumer Research*, March 1998, pp. 409–433.

82. Joel B. Cohen and Charles S. Areni, "Affect and Consumer Behavior," in eds. Thomas S. Robertson and Harold H. Kassarjian, *Handbook of Consumer Behavior* (Englewood Cliffs, N. J.: Prentice-Hall, 1991), pp. 188–240.

83. James Lardner, "Building a Customer-Centric Company," *Business 2.0*, July 10, 2001, pp. 55–59.

84. Petty, Unnava, and Strathman, "Theories of Attitude Change."

85. Harry C. Triandis, *Attitudes and Attitude Change* (New York: Wiley, 1971).

86. Stephen E. Frank, "Can Tiger Woods Sell Financial Services?" *Wall Street Journal*, May 20, 1997, pp. B1, B14.

87. Brian D. Till and Michael Busler, "The Match-Up Hypothesis: Physical Attractiveness, Expertise, and the Role of Fit on Brand Attitude, Purchase Intent, and Brand Beliefs," *Journal of Advertising*, vol. 29, no. 3, Fall 2000, pp. 1–13.

88. Peter H. Reingen and Jerome B. Kernan, "Social Perception and Interpersonal Influence: Some Consequences of the Physical Attractiveness Stereotype in a Personal Selling Situation," *Journal of Consumer Psychology*, vol. 2, no. 1, 1993, pp. 25–38.

89. Scott Ward and Frederick E. Webster Jr., "Organizational Buying Behavior," in eds. Thomas S. Robertson and Harold H. Kassarjian, *Handbook of Consumer Behavior* (Englewood Cliffs, N. J.: Prentice-Hall, 1991), pp. 419–458.

90. Herbert Simon, Nancy Berkowitz, and John Moyer, "Similarity, Credibility, and Attitude Change," *Psychological Bulletin*, January 1970, pp. 1–16.

91. Sam Walker, "George Foreman's Endorsement in Perpetuity Nets $137.5 Million," *Wall Street Journal*, December 10, 1999, p. B9.

92. Sally Goll Beatty, "Bad-Boy Nike Is Playing the Diplomat in China," *Wall Street Journal*, November 10, 1997, pp. B1, B10.

93. Sally Goll Beatty, "Just What Goes in a Viagra Ad? Dancing Couples," *Wall Street Journal*, June 17, 1998, pp. B1, B8.

94. Betsy Spethmann, "Value Ads," *Promo*, March 1, 2001, pp. 74+.

95. Batra and Stayman, "The Role of Mood in Advertising Effectiveness."

96. Kevin Goldman, "The Market for Pricey Sunglasses Heats Up," *Wall Street Journal*, March 22, 1993, pp. B1, B5.

97. "'Enjoy Life'? Hey, We're Trying!" *Automotive News*, September 10, 2001, p. 4; Kevin Goldman, "Volvo Seeks to Soft-Pedal Safety Image," *Wall Street Journal*, March 16, 1993, p. B7.

98. Timothy Aeppel, "Ads for Goodyear Will Take a New Turn," *Wall Street Journal*, August 31, 2001, p. B6; Sally Goll Beatty, "Mercedes Hopes Duckie, Child Broaden Appeal," *Wall Street Journal*, May 21, 1997, pp. B1, B8.

99. Lisa Shuchman, "How Does GM's Saturn Sell Cars in Japan? Very Slowly," *Wall Street Journal*, September 25, 1998, pp. B1, B4.

100. Valerie S. Folkes and Tina Kiesler, "Social Cognition: Consumers' Inferences about the Self and Others," in eds. Thomas S. Robertson and Harold H. Kassarjian, *Handbook of Consumer Behavior* (Englewood Cliffs, N. J.: Prentice-Hall, 1991), pp. 281–315.

101. John F. Tanner, James B. Hunt, and David R. Eppright, "The Protection Motivation Model: A Normative Model of Fear Appeals," *Journal of Marketing*, July 1991, pp. 36–45.

102. Andrea Petersen and Julia Angwin, "High-Tech Marketers Love 'Love Bug,'" *Wall Street Journal*, May 9, 2000, p. B10.

103. Mallorre Dill, "Live Long and Prosper," *Adweek*, February 12, 2001, p. 20.

104. Michael L. Ray and William L. Wilkie, "Fear: The Potential of an Appeal Neglected by Marketing," *Journal of Marketing*, January 1970, pp. 54–62.

105. Ibid.

106. Ibid; Herbert J. Rotfeld, "Fear Appeals and Persuasion: Assumptions and Errors in Advertising Research," in eds. James H. Leigh and Claude R. Martin, *Current Issues and Research in Advertising*

(Ann Arbor, Mich.: Graduate School of Business Administration, University of Michigan, 1990), pp. 155–175.

107. John J. Wheatley, "Marketing and the Use of Fear- or Anxiety-Arousing Appeals," *Journal of Marketing*, April 1971, pp. 62–64; Peter L. Wright, "Concrete Action Plans in TV Messages to Increase Reading of Drug Warnings," *Journal of Consumer Research*, December 1979, pp. 256–269.

108. John J. Burette and Richard L. Oliver, "Fear Appeal Effects in the Field: A Segmentation Approach," *Journal of Marketing Research*, May 1979, pp. 181–190.

109. MacInnis and Jaworski, "Two Routes to Persuasion in Advertising."

110. Thomas J. Olney, Morris B. Holbrook, and Rajeev Batra, "Consumer Responses to Advertising: The Effects of Ad Content, Emotions, and Attitude toward the Ad on Viewing Time," *Journal of Consumer Research*, March 1991, pp. 440–453.

111. Paul W. Miniard, Sunil Bhatla, and Randall L. Rose, "On the Formation and Relationship of Ad and Brand Attitudes: An Experimental and Causal Analysis," *Journal of Marketing Research*, August 1990, pp. 290–303.

112. Sally Goll Beatty, "Executive Fears Effects of Political Ads," *Wall Street Journal*, April 29, 1996, p. B6.

113. Julie A. Edell and Richard E. Staelin, "The Information Processing of Pictures in Print Advertisements," *Journal of Consumer Research*, June 1983, pp. 45–60.

114. Scott B. MacKenzie, Richard J. Lutz, and George E. Belch, "The Role of Attitude toward the Ad as a Mediator of Advertising Effectiveness: A Test of Competing Explanations," *Journal of Marketing Research*, May 1986, pp. 130–143; Pamela M. Homer, "The Mediating Role of Attitude toward the Ad: Some Additional Evidence," *Journal of Marketing Research*, February 1990, pp. 78–86.

115. Kim Cross, "Jean Therapy," *Business 2.0*, January 23, 2001, pp. 70–75; Andrea Petersen, "The Quest to Make URLs Look Cool in Ads," *Wall Street Journal*, February 26, 1997, pp. B1, B3.

116. Cross, "Jean Therapy."

117. Richard E. Petty, John T. Cacioppo, and David W. Schumann, "Central and Peripheral Routes to Advertising Persuasion," *Journal of Consumer Research*, September 1983, pp. 134–148.

118. Smith and Swinyard, "Attitude-Behavior Consistency"; Russell H. Fazio and Mark P. Zanna, "Direct Experience and Attitude-Behavior Consistency," in ed. Leonard Berkowitz, *Advances in Experimental Social Psychology* (New York: Academic Press, 1981), pp. 162–202.

119. Jaideep Sengupta and Gavan J. Fitzsimons, "The Effects of Analyzing Reasons for Brand Preferences: Disruption or Reinforcement?" *Journal of Marketing Research*, vol. 37, August 2000, pp. 318–330.

120. Russell H. Fazio, Martha C. Powell, and Carol J. Williams, "The Role of Attitude Accessibility in the Attitude-to-Behavior Process," *Journal of Consumer Research*, December 1989, pp. 280–288; Berger and Mitchell, "The Effect of Advertising on Attitude Accessibility, Attitude Confidence, and the Attitude-Behavior Relationship."

121. Smith and Swinyard, "Attitude-Behavior Consistency"; Alice A. Wright and John G. Lynch, "Communication Effects of Advertising vs. Direct Experience When Both Search and Experience Attributes Are Present," *Journal of Consumer Research*, March 1995, pp. 708–718.

122. Ida E. Berger, "The Nature of Attitude Accessibility and Attitude Confidence."

123. Fishbein and Ajzen, *Belief, Attitude, Intention, and Behavior*.

124. H. Shanker Krishnan and Robert E. Smith, "The Relative Endurance of Attitudes, Confidence, and Attitude-Behavior Consistency: The Role of Information Source and Delay," *Journal of Consumer Psychology*, vol. 7, no. 3, 1998, pp. 273–298.

125. Ibid.

126. John T. Cacioppo, Richard E. Petty, Chuan Fang Kao, and Regina Rodriguez, "Central and Peripheral Routes to Persuasion: An Individual Difference Perspective," *Journal of Personality and Social Psychology*, 51, 1986, pp. 1032–1043.

127. Mark Snyder and William B. Swan Jr., "When Actions Reflect Attitudes: The Politics of Impression Management," *Journal of Personality and Social Psychology*, vol. 34, 1976, pp. 1034–1042.

Chapter 7

1. Lisa Bertagnoli, "Duck Campaign Is Firm's Extra Insurance," *Marketing News*, August 27, 2001, pp. 5–6; Bethany McLean, "Duck and Coverage," *Fortune*, August 13, 2001, pp. 142–143.

2. Richard E. Petty and John T. Cacioppo, *Attitudes and Persuasion: Classic and Contemporary Approaches* (Dubuque, Iowa: William C. Brown, 1981); Richard E. Petty, John T. Cacioppo, and David Schumann, "Central and Peripheral Routes to Advertising Effectiveness: The Moderating Role of Involvement," *Journal of Consumer Research*, September 1983, pp. 135–146.

3. Jaideep Sengupta, Ronald C. Goodstein, and David S. Boninger, "All Cues Are Not Created Equal: Obtaining Attitude Persistence under Low Involvement Conditions," *Journal of Consumer Research*, March 1997, pp. 315–361.

4. Ronald C. Goodstein, "Category-Based Applications and Extensions in Advertising: Motivating More Extensive Ad Processing," *Journal of Consumer Research*, June 1993, pp. 87–99.

5. Valerie S. Folkes, "Recent Attribution Research in Consumer Behavior: A Review and New Directions,"

Journal of Consumer Research, March 1988, pp. 548–656.

6. "Baseball's Mike Piazza Goes to Bat for Claritin," *Advertising Age,* April 4, 2001, www.adage.com.
7. Shelly Chaiken, "Heuristic versus Systematic Information Processing and the Use of Source versus Message Cues in Persuasion," *Journal of Personality and Social Psychology*, vol. 39, 1980, pp. 752–766; also, "The Heuristic Model of Persuasion," in eds. Mark P. Zanna, J. M. Olson, and C. P. Herman, *Social Influence: The Ontario Symposium*, vol. 5 (Hillsdale, N. J.: Lawrence Erlbaum, 1987), pp. 3–49.
8. Amna Kirmani, "Advertising Repetition as a Signal of Quality: If It's Advertised So Much, Something Must Be Wrong," *Journal of Advertising*, Fall 1997, pp. 77–86.
9. Joseph W. Alba and Howard Marmorstein, "The Effects of Frequency Knowledge on Consumer Decision Making," *Journal of Consumer Research*, June 1987, pp. 14–25.
10. Scott A. Hawkins and Stephen J. Hoch, "Low-Involvement Learning: Memory without Evaluation," *Journal of Consumer Research*, September 1992, pp. 212–225; Lynn Hasher, David Goldstein, and Thomas Toppino, "Frequency and the Conference of Referential Validity," *Journal of Verbal Learning and Verbal Behavior*, February 1977, pp. 107–112.
11. S. Ratneshwar and Shelly Chaiken, "Comprehension's Role in Persuasion: The Case of Its Moderating Effect on the Persuasive Impact of Source Cues," *Journal of Consumer Research*, June 1991, pp. 52–62.
12. Lea Goldman, "A Cry in the Wilderness," *Forbes*, May 15, 2000, p. 322.
13. Betsy McKay, "PepsiCo Bases Water Ads on 'Nothing,'" *Wall Street Journal*, June 25, 2001, p. B10.
14. Robert E. Burnkrant and H. Rao Unnava, Effects of Self-Referencing on Persuasion, *Journal of Consumer Research*, June 1995, pp. 17–26; Sharon Shavitt and Timothy C. Brock," Self-Relevant Responses in Commercial Persuasion," in eds. Jerry C. Olson and Keith Sentis, *Advertising and Consumer Psychology* (New York: Praeger, 1986), pp. 149–171; Kathleen Debevec and Jean B. Romeo, "Self-Referent Processing in Perceptions of Verbal and Visual Commercial Information," *Journal of Consumer Psychology*, vol. 1, no. 1, 1992, pp. 83–102; Joan Myers-Levy and Laura A. Peracchio, "Moderators of the Impact of Self-Reference on Persuasion," *Journal of Consumer Research*, March 1996, pp. 408–423.
15. Daniel J. Howard, Charles Gengler, and Ambuj Jain, "What's in a Name? A Complimentary Means of Persuasion," *Journal of Consumer Research*, September 1995, pp. 200–211.
16. Jennifer L. Aaker, "The Malleable Self: The Role of Self-Expression in Persuasion," *Journal of Marketing Research*, vol. 36, February 1999, pp. 45–57.
17. Robert E. Burnkrant and Daniel J. Howard, "Effects of the Use of Introductory Rhetorical Questions versus Statements on Information Processing," *Journal of Personality and Social Psychology*, December 1984, pp. 1218–1230; James M. Munch, Gregory W. Boller, and John L. Swazy, "The Effects of Argument Structure and Affective Tagging on Product Attitude Formation," *Journal of Consumer Research*, September 1993, pp. 294–302.
18. Jean Halliday, "GMC's New SUV Storms Times Square," *Advertising Age*, March 26, 2001, www.adage.com.
19. Russell H. Fazio, Paul M. Herr, and Martha C. Powell, "On the Development and Strength of Category-Brand Associations in Memory: The Case of Mystery Ads," *Journal of Consumer Psychology*, vol. 1, no. 1, 1992, pp. 1–14.
20. Adrienne Mand, "Absolut Movie-Making Site Continues Branding Trend," *Advertising Age*, September 4, 2001, www.adage.com.
21. Joseph W. Alba, J. Wesley Hutchinson, and John G. Lynch, "Memory and Decision Making," in eds. Thomas S. Robertson and Harold H. Kassarjian, *Handbook of Consumer Behavior* (Englewood Cliffs, N. J.: Prentice-Hall, 1991).
22. H. Rao Unnava and Robert E. Burnkrant, "Effects of Repeating Varied Ad Executions on Brand Name Memory," *Journal of Marketing Research*, November 1991, pp. 406–416.
23. Ida E. Berger and Andrew A. Mitchell, "The Effect of Attitude Accessibility, Attitude Confidence, and the Attitude-Behavior Relationship," *Journal of Consumer Research*, December 1989, pp. 269–279.
24. "Effies," *Adweek's Marketing Week*, June 15, 1992, p. 12.
25. Alice Z. Cuneo, "Kmart CEO Admits Ad Spending Cut a 'Mistake,'" *Advertising Age*, November 27, 2001, www.adage.com.
26. Prashant Malaviya and Brian Sternthal, "The Persuasive Impact of Message Spacing," *Journal of Consumer Psychology*, vol. 6, no. 3, 1997, pp. 233–256.
27. Carl Obermiller, "Varieties of Mere Exposure: The Effects of Processing Style and Repetition in Affective Response," *Journal of Consumer Research*, June 1985, pp. 17–30.
28. Arno Rethans, John L. Swazy, and Lawrence J. Marks, "The Effects of Television Commercial Repetition, Receiver Knowledge, and Commercial Length: A Test of a Two Factor Model," *Journal of Marketing Research*, February 1986, pp. 50–61.
29. William E. Baker, "When Can Affective Conditioning and Mere Exposure Directly Influence Brand Choice?" *Journal of Advertising*, vol. 28, no. 4, Winter 1999, pp. 31–46.
30. Chris Janiszewski and Tom Meyvis, "Effects of Brand Logo Complexity, Repetition, and Spacing on Processing Fluency and Judgment," *Journal of Consumer Research*, vol. 28, June 2001, pp. 18–32.

31. Leo Bogart, *Strategy in Advertising: Matching Media and Messages of Markets and Motivation* (Lincoln, Ill.: NTC Business, 1986), p. 208.
32. Norihiko Shirouzu, "Whoppers Face Entrenched Foes in Japan: Big Macs," *Wall Street Journal*, February 4, 1997, pp. B1, B5.
33. Herbert Krugman, "Why Three Exposures May Be Enough," *Journal of Advertising Research*, December 1972, pp. 11–14.
34. George E. Belch, "The Effects of Television Commercial Repetition on Cognitive Response and Message Acceptance," *Journal of Consumer Research*, June 1982, pp. 56–65.
35. Margaret Henderson Blair, "An Empirical Investigation of Advertising Wearin and Wearout," *Journal of Advertising Research*, vol. 40, November 2000, p. 95.
36. Marian Burke and Julie A. Edell, "Ad Reactions over Time: Capturing Changes in the Real World," *Journal of Consumer Research*, June 1986, pp. 114–118; Curtis P. Haugtvedt, David W. Schumann, Wendy L. Schneier, and Wendy L. Warren, "Advertising Repetition and Variation Strategies: Implications for Understanding Attitude Strength," *Journal of Consumer Research*, June 1994, pp. 176–189.
37. Gerald J. Gorn, "The Effects of Music in Advertising on Choice Behavior: A Classical Conditioning Approach," *Journal of Marketing*, Winter 1982, pp. 94–101.
38. Calvin Bierley, Frances K. McSweeny, and Renee Vannieuwkerk, "Classical Conditioning of Preferences for Stimuli," *Journal of Consumer Research*, December 1985, pp. 316–323; James J. Kellaris and Anthony D. Cox, "The Effects of Background Music in Advertising: A Reassessment," *Journal of Consumer Research*, June 1989, pp. 113–118: Chris T. Allen and Thomas J. Madden, "A Closer Look at Classical Conditioning," *Journal of Consumer Research*, December 1985, pp. 301–315.
39. Bierley, McSweeny, and Vannieuwkerk, "Classical Conditioning of Preferences for Stimuli"; Elnora W. Stuart, Terence A. Shimp, and Randall W. Engle, "Classical Conditioning of Consumer Attitudes: Four Experiments in an Advertising Context," *Journal of Consumer Research*, December 1987, pp. 334–349; Terence A. Shimp, Elnora W. Stuart, and Randall W. Engle, "A Program of Classical Conditioning Experiments Testing Variations in the Conditioned Stimulus and Context," *Journal of Consumer Research*, June 1991, pp. 1–12; Chris T. Allen and Chris A. Janiszewski, "Assessing the Role of Contingency Awareness in Attitudinal Conditioning with Implications for Advertising Research," *Journal of Marketing Research*, February 1989, pp. 30–43.
40. Randi Priluck Grossman and Brian D. Till, "The Persistence of Classically Conditioned Brand Attitudes," *Journal of Advertising*, Spring 1998.
41. Terence A. Shimp, "Neo-Pavlovian Conditioning and Its Implications for Consumer Theory and Research," in eds. Thomas S. Robertson and Harold H. Kassarjian, *Handbook of Consumer Behavior* (Englewood Cliffs, N. J.: Prentice-Hall, 1991), pp. 162–187.
42. Steven P. Brown and Douglas M. Stayman, "Antecedents and Consequences of Attitude toward the Ad: A Meta-analysis," *Journal of Consumer Research*, June 1993, pp. 34–51; Andrew A. Mitchell and Jerry C. Olson, "Are Product Attributes Beliefs the Only Mediator of Advertising Effects on Brand Attitudes?" *Journal of Marketing Research*, August 1981, pp. 318–322; Terence A. Shimp, "Attitude toward the Ad as a Mediator of Consumer Brand Choice," *Journal of Advertising*, vol. 10, no. 2, 1981, pp. 9–15; Christian M. Derbaix, "The Impact of Affective Reactions on Attitudes toward the Advertisement and the Brand: A Step toward Ecological Validity," *Journal of Marketing Research*, November 1995, pp. 470–479.
43. Mitchell and Olson, "Are Product Attributes Beliefs the Only Mediator of Advertising Effects on Brand Attitudes?"
44. Srinivas Durvasula, J. Craig Andrews, Steven Lysonski, and Richard G. Netemeyer, "Assessing the Cross-National Applicability of Consumer Behavior Models: A Model of Attitude toward Advertising in General," *Journal of Consumer Research*, March 1993, pp. 626–636.
45. Russell I. Haley and Allan L. Baldinger, "The ARF Copy Research Validity Project," *Journal of Advertising Research*, April–May 1991, pp. 11–32.
46. Elizabeth S. Moore and Richard J. Lutz, "Children, Advertising, and Product Experiences: A Multimethod Inquiry," *Journal of Consumer Research*, vol. 27, June 2000, pp. 31–48; Scott B. MacKenzie, Richard J. Lutz, and George E. Belch, "The Role of Attitude toward the Ad as a Mediator of Advertising Effectiveness: A Test of Competing Explanations," *Journal of Marketing Research*, May 1986, pp. 130–143; Pamela M. Homer, "The Mediating Role of Attitude toward the Ad: Some Additional Evidence," *Journal of Marketing Research*, February 1990, pp. 78–86; Brown and Stayman, "Antecedents and Consequences of Attitude toward the Ad."
47. Sally Beatty, "P&G Ad Agencies: Please Rewrite Our Old Formulas," *Wall Street Journal*, November 5, 1998, pp. B1, B10.
48. Brown and Stayman, "Antecedents and Consequences of Attitude toward the Ad."
49. Marian Chapman Burke and Julie A. Edell, "Ad Reactions over Time: Capturing Changes in the Real World," *Journal of Consumer Research*, June 1986, pp. 114–118; Amitava Chattopadhyay and Prakash Nedungadi, "Does Attitude toward the Ad Endure? The Moderating Effects of Attention and Delay," *Journal of Consumer Research*, June 1992, pp. 26–33.
50. Margaret G. Meloy, "Mood Driven Distortion of Product Information," *Journal of Consumer Research*, vol. 27, December 2000, pp. 345–359.

51. Michael J. Barone, Paul W. Miniard, and Jean B. Romeo, "The Influence of Positive Mood on Brand Extension Evaluations," *Journal of Consumer Research*, vol. 26, March 2000, pp. 386–400.

52. Rashmi Adaval, "Sometimes It Just Feels Right: The Differential Weighting of Affect-Consistent and Affect-Inconsistent Product Information," *Journal of Consumer Research*, vol. 28, June 2001, pp. 1–17.

53. Charles S. Areni and David Kim, "The Influence of In-Store Lighting on Consumers' Examination of Merchandise in a Wine Store," *International Journal of Research in Marketing*, March 1994, pp. 117–125.

54. Ayn E. Crowley, "The Two-Dimension Impact of Color on Shopping," *Marketing Letters*, vol. 4, no. 1, 1993, pp. 59–69.

55. Julie A. Edell and Marian Chapman Burke, "The Power of Feelings in Understanding Advertising Effects," *Journal of Consumer Research*, December 1987, pp. 421–433; Douglas M. Stayman and David A. Aaker, "Are All Effects of Ad-Induced Feelings Mediated by Aad?" *Journal of Consumer Research*, December 1988, pp. 368–373; Morris B. Holbrook and Rajeev Batra, "Assessing the Role of Emotions as Mediators of Consumer Responses to Advertising," *Journal of Consumer Research*, December 1987, pp. 404–420.

56. Rajeev Batra and Michael L. Ray, "Affective Responses Mediating Acceptance of Advertising," *Journal of Consumer Research*, September 1986, pp. 234–249.

57. Laurel Wentz, "Cannes of Beer: 'Whassup?!' Wins Grand Prix," *Advertising Age*, June 26, 2000, www.adage.com.

58. David A. Aaker, Douglas M. Stayman, and Michael R. Hagerty, "Warmth in Advertising: Measurement, Impact, and Sequence Effects," *Journal of Consumer Research*, March 1986, pp. 365–381.

59. Joseph A. Bellizzi, Ayn E. Crowley, and Ronald W. Hasty, "The Effects of Color in Store Design," *Journal of Retailing*, Spring 1983, pp. 21–45.

60. Alison Embrey, "Sporting Port O'Call," *Display & Design Ideas*, November 2001, pp. 36+.

61. Anna Rachmansky and Kelly Thompson, "Intimate Portrait: Retailers Today Are Favoring Homey Touches over High-Tech Decor," *Footwear News*, July 23, 2001, pp. 58+.

62. "Jessica Simpson Launches 'Irresistible' New Album with Burbank In-Store Appearance," *Business Wire*, June 6, 2001, www.businesswire.com; Dazman Manan, "Chanel Goes for Coco," *New Straits Times*, February 26, 2001, p. 2.

63. Stuart Elliott, "Cindy Crawford, No Longer a Fixture for Revlon, Is Hired to Give Ellen Tracy Apparel Youthful Appeal," *New York Times*, February 13, 2001, p. C7.

64. Ruth La Ferla, "Fevered Pitch: Marketers Hotly Pursue Celebrities," *Dallas Morning News*, April 26, 2001, p. 5C.

65. Curt Haugtvedt, Richard E. Petty, John T. Cacioppo, and T. Steidley, "Personality and Ad Effectiveness: Exploring the Utility of Need for Cognition," in eds. Michael J. Houston, *Advances in Consumer Research*, vol. 15 (Provo, Utah: Association for Consumer Research, 1988), pp. 209–212.

66. Susan M. Petroshius and Kenneth E. Crocker, "An Empirical Analysis of Spokesperson Characteristics on Advertisement and Product Evaluations," *Journal of the Academy of Marketing Science*, Summer 1989, pp. 217–225; Lynn R. Kahle and Pamela M. Homer, "Physical Attractiveness of the Celebrity Endorser: A Social Adaptation Perspective," *Journal of Consumer Research*, March 1985, pp. 954–961.

67. Michael A. Kamins, "An Investigation into the 'Match-Up' Hypothesis in Celebrity Advertising: When Beauty May Be Only Skin Deep," *Journal of Advertising*, vol. 19, no. 1, 1990, pp. 4–13: Marjorie J. Caballero and Paul J. Solomon, "Effects of Model Attractiveness on Sales Response," *Journal of Advertising*, vol. 13, no. 1, 1984, pp. 17–23.

68. Kahle and Homer, "Physical Attractiveness of the Celebrity Endorser"; Kathleen Debevec and Jerome B. Kernan, "More Evidence on the Effects of a Presenter's Physical Attractiveness: Some Cognitive, Affective, and Behavioral Consequences," in ed. Thomas C. Kinnear, *Advances in Consumer Research*, vol. 11 (Provo, Utah: Association for Consumer Research, 1984), pp. 127–132.; Caballero and Solomon, "Effects of Model Attractiveness on Sales Response"; Marjorie J. Caballero and William M. Pride, "Selected Effects of Salesperson Sex and Attractiveness in Direct Mail Advertising," *Journal of Marketing*, January 1984, pp. 94–100; Shelly Chaiken, "Communicator Physical Attractiveness and Persuasion," *Journal of Personality and Social Psychology*, August 1979, pp. 1387–1397; Peter H. Reingen and Jerome B. Kernan, "Social Perception and Interpersonal Influence: Some Consequences of the Physical Attractiveness Stereotype in a Personal Selling Situation," *Journal of Consumer Psychology*, vol. 2, no. 1, 1993, pp. 25–38.

69. Richard E. Petty, H. Rao Unnava, and Alan J. Strathman, "Theories of Attitude Change," in eds. Thomas S. Robertson and Harold H. Kassarjian, *Handbook of Consumer Behavior* (Englewood Cliffs, N. J.: Prentice-Hall, 1991), pp. 241–280; Kahle and Homer, "Physical Attractiveness of the Celebrity Endorser."

70. "Companies Turn to Past to Market Products—Ads Feature TV Stars from Days Gone by in Offbeat Settings," *Wall Street Journal*, April 9, 2001, p. A25.

71. Sally Goll Beatty, "Madison Avenue Picks an Average Joe as '90's Pitchman," *Wall Street Journal*, August 11, 1996, pp. B1, B4.

72. Yumiko Ono, "Japan Warms to Doting Dad Ads," *Wall Street Journal*, May 8, 1997, pp. B1, B12.

73. Joshua Harris Prager, "Disability Can Enable a Modeling Career," *Wall Street Journal*, October 17, 1997, pp. B1, B6.

74. Sengupta, Goodstein, and Boninger, "All Cues Are Not Created Equal."

75. Greg Johnson, "NBA Stars Have Different Appeal in Courting Advertisers," *Los Angeles Times*, June 16, 2001, p. C1.

76. "Dead, Yes—But Still Hot," *BusinessWeek*, June 4, 2001, p. 14.

77. Maureen Tkacik, "The Worlds of Extreme Sport and Hip-Hop Are Hangin' Together," *Wall Street Journal*, August 9, 2001, pp. B1, B4.

78. Kathleen Deveny, "Many Celebrity Foods Enjoy Only 15 Minutes of Fame," *Wall Street Journal*, July 18, 1994, p. B1.

79. Kristin Tillotson, "Kind to Be Cruel? PETA's Intent Might Be Humane, But Using Celebs as Moral Clubs Is Not," *Star-Tribune*, May 27, 2001, p. 3F.

80. "Effies," *Adweek's Marketing Week*, June 15, 1992, p. 14.

81. Jonathan Friedland, "Under Siege in the U.S., Joe Camel Pops up Alive, Well in Argentina," *Wall Street Journal*, September 10, 1996, p. B1.

82. Bruce Orwall, "James Bond Gets a New License to Sell Everything from Credit to Watches," *Wall Street Journal*, June 12, 1997, p. B10.

83. Mitchell and Olson, "Are Product Attributes Beliefs the Only Mediator of Advertising Effects on Brand Attitudes?"; Andrew A. Mitchell, "The Effect of Verbal and Visual Components of Advertisements on Brand Attitudes and Attitude toward the Advertisement," *Journal of Consumer Research*, March 1986, pp. 12–24; Paul W. Miniard, Sunil Bhatla, Kenneth R. Lord, Peter R. Dickson, and H. Rao Unnava, "Picture-Based Persuasion Processes and the Moderating Role of Involvement," *Journal of Consumer Research*, June 1991, pp. 92–107.

84. Paul W. Miniard, Deepak Sirdeshmukh, and Daniel E. Innis, "Peripheral Persuasion and Brand Choice," *Journal of Consumer Research*, September 1992, pp. 226–239.

85. Yumiko Ono, "Making 30 Chickens and Garlands of Post-Its into an Ad, " *Wall Street Journal*, August 20, 1997, pp. B1, B5.

86. Andrea Petersen, "The Quest to Make URL's Look Cool in Ads," *Wall Street Journal*, February 26, 1997, pp. B1, B3.

87. Sally Beatty, "IBM HotMedia Aims to Speed Online Ads," *Wall Street Journal*, October 27, 1998, p. B8; Sally Goll Beatty, "Knock, Knock! Who's There/Noisy New Internet Ads," *Wall Street Journal*, September 3, 1997, pp. B1, B6.

88. Mark Colburn, "Music Sings Volumes about Brands," *Marketing News*, September 10, 2001, p. 16.

89. Gordon Fairclough, "Crabs Sing to Give ITT Industries a 'Name,'" *Wall Street Journal*, September 19, 1998, p. B8.

90. Timothy Finn, "TV Ads Tune In to Pop Music," *Houston Chronicle*, July 1, 2001, p. 3; Sara Scribner, "The Age of Selling Cool," *Hartford Courant*, January 29, 2001, p. D1; Patrick M. Reilly, "TV Commercials Turn Obscure Songs into Radio Hits," *Wall Street Journal*, October 9, 1998, pp. B1, B8.

91. Jean Halliday, "Shifting Gears in Automotive World," *Advertising Age*, July 2, 2001, p. 6.

92. "Molson Canadian Gives Proud Canadians Something to Sing About with Latest Ad," *Canada NewsWire*, June 13, 2001, **www.newswire.ca.**

93. Janine Zuniga, "McDonald's Pipes in Bach to Bug Thugs," *Austin American Statesman*, April 25, 1996, p. C1.

94. Gordon C. Bruner, "Music, Mood, and Marketing," *Journal of Marketing*, October 1990, pp. 94–104; Gorn, "The Effects of Music in Advertising on Choice Behavior"; Judy I. Alpert and Mark I. Alpert, "Background Music as an Influence in Consumer Mood and Advertising Responses," in ed. Thomas K. Srull, *Advances in Consumer Research*, vol. 16 (Provo, Utah: Association for Consumer Research, 1989), pp. 485–491; Meryl Paula Gardner, "Mood States and Consumer Behavior: A Critical Review," *Journal of Consumer Research*, December 1985, pp. 281–300; C. Whan Park and S. Mark Young, "Consumer Response to Television Commercials: The Impact of Involvement and Background Music on Brand Attitude Formation," *Journal of Marketing Research*, February 1986, pp. 11–24.

95. Mark Alpert and Judy Alpert, "Background Music as an Influence in Consumer Mood and Advertising Responses;"Advances in Consumer Research, 16 (Fall 1989) 485–491; Stout and Leckenby, "Let the Music Play."

96. Noel M. Murray and Sandra B. Murray, "Music and Lyrics in Commercials: A Cross-Cultural Comparison between Commercials Run in the Dominican Republic and the United States," *Journal of Advertising*, Summer 1996, pp. 51–64.

97. Marc G. Weinberger and Harlan E. Spotts, "Humor in U.S. vs. U.K. TV Advertising," *Journal of Advertising*, vol. 18, no. 2, 1989, pp. 39–44; Paul Surgi Speck, "The Humorous Message Taxonomy: A Framework for the Study of Humorous Ads," in eds. James H. Leigh and Claude R. Martin, *Current Research and Issues in Advertising* (Ann Arbor, Mich.: University of Michigan, 1991), pp. 1–44.

98. Thomas J. Madden and Marc G. Weinberger, "Humor in Advertising: A Practitioner View," *Journal of Advertising Research*, August–September 1984, pp. 23–29; Stewart and Furse, *Effective Television Advertising*; Thomas J. Madden and Marc C. Weinberger, "The Effects of Humor on Attention in Magazine Advertising," *Journal of Advertising*, vol. 1, no. 3, 1982, pp. 8–14; Marc C. Weinberger and Leland Campbell, "The Use and Impact of Humor in Radio Advertising," *Journal of Advertising Research*, December–January 1991, pp. 44–52.

99. George E. Belch and Michael A. Belch, "An Investigation of the Effects of Repetition on Cognitive and Affective Reactions to Humorous and Serious Television Commercials," in ed. Thomas C. Kinnear, *Advances in Consumer Research*, vol. 11 (Provo, Utah: Association for Consumer Research, 1984), pp. 4–10; Calvin P. Duncan and James E. Nelson, "Effects of Humor in a Radio Advertising Experiment," *Journal of Advertising*, vol. 14, no. 2, 1985, pp. 33–40, 64; Betsy D. Gelb and Charles M. Pickett, "Attitude-toward-the-Ad: Links to Humor and to Advertising Effectiveness," *Journal of Advertising*, vol. 12, no. 2, 1983, pp. 34–42; Betsy D. Gelb and George M. Zinkhan, "The Effect of Repetition on Humor in a Radio Advertising Study," *Journal of Advertising*, vol. 15, no. 2, 1986, pp. 15–20, 34.

100. Lewis Lazare, "Holiday Inn Spots Right on the Mark," *Chicago Sun-Times*, April 9, 2001, p. 53.

101. Nortihiko Shirouzu, "P&G's Joy Makes an Unlikely Splash in Japan," *Wall Street Journal*, December 10, 1997, pp. B1, B8.

102. Mallorre Dill, "Joe Is Back," *Adweek*, February 19, 2001, p. 18.

103. Harlan E. Spotts, Marc. G. Weinberger, and Amy L. Parsons, "Assessing the Use and Impact of Humor on Advertising Effectiveness; A Contingency Approach," *Journal of Advertising*, Fall 1997, pp. 17–32.

104. Brian Sternthal and Samuel Craig, "Humor in Advertising," *Journal of Marketing*, vol. 37, no. 4, 1973, pp. 12–18; Calvin P. Duncan, "Humor in Advertising: A Behavioral Perspective," *Journal of the Academy of Marketing Science*, vol. 7, no. 4, 1979, pp. 285–306; Weinberger and Campbell, "The Use and Impact of Humor in Radio Advertising."

105. Madden and Weinberger, "Humor in Advertising"; Weinberger and Campbell, "The Use and Impact of Humor in Radio Advertising"; Weinberger and Spotts, "Humor in U.S. vs. U.K. TV Advertising."

106. "Barenaked Ladies Break Infomercial on WB," *Advertising Age*, September 5, 2000, **www.adage.com**.

107. Laurie Petersen, "And If You Think This Is Funny," *Adweek's Marketing Week*, September 9, 1991, p. 9.

108. Madden and Weinberger, "Humor in Advertising"; Thomas W. Whipple and Alice E. Courtney, "How Men and Women Judge Humor: Advertising Guidelines for Action and Research," in eds. James H. Leigh and Claude R. Martin, *Current Research and Issues in Advertising* (Ann Arbor, Mich.: University of Michigan, 1981), pp. 43–56.

109. Yong Zhang, "Responses to Humorous Advertising: The Moderating Effect of Need for Cognition," *Journal of Advertising*, Spring 1996: Amitava Chattopadhyay and Kunal Basu, "Prior Brand Evaluation as a Moderator of the Effects of Humor in Advertising," *Journal of Marketing Research*, November 1989, pp. 466–476.

110. Dana L. Alden, Wayne D. Hoyer, and Chol Lee, "Identifying Global and Culture-Specific Dimensions of Humor in Advertising: A Multi-national Analysis," *Journal of Marketing*, April 1993, pp. 64–75; Dana L. Alden, Wayne D. Hoyer, Chol Lee, and Guntalee Wechasara, "The Use of Humor in Asian and Western Advertising: A Four-Country Comparison," *Journal of Asian-Pacific Business*, vol, 1, no. 2, 1995, pp. 3–23.

111. Weinberger and Spotts, "Humor in U.S. vs. U.K. TV Advertising."

112. Christopher Cooper, "Uncle Ben's New Ad Campaign Seeks to Steam up the TV Screen," *Wall Street Journal*, p. B6.

113. Ian Darby, "D'Arcy Injects Sex into Maltesers' 'Lighter Way' Campaign," *Campaign*, June 15, 2001, p. 8.

114. Alessandra Galloni, "In New Global Campaign, Durex Maker Uses Humor to Sell Condoms," *Wall Street Journal*, July 27, 2001, p. B1.

115. Yumiko Ono, "Can Racy Ads Help Revitalize Old Fragrances?" *Wall Street Journal*, November 26, 1996, pp. B1, B10.

116. Lawrence Soley and Gary Kurzbard, "Sex in Advertising: A Comparison of 1964 and 1984 Magazine Advertisements," *Journal of Advertising*, vol. 15, no. 3, 1986, pp. 46–54.

117. Cyndee Miller, "We've Been 'Cosbyized,'" *Marketing News*, April 16, 1990, pp. 1–2; Joshua Levine, "Marketing: Fantasy, Not Flesh," *Forbes*, January 22, 1990, pp. 118–120.

118. Eben Shapiro, "In the Safe-Sex Society, Advertisers Lose Inhibitions about How Much Sex Is Safe," *Wall Street Journal*, December 3, 1993, pp. B1, B6.

119. Lynn G. Coleman, "What Do People Really Lust After in Ads?" *Marketing News*, November 6, 1989, p. 12.

120. Robert S. Baron, "Sexual Content and Advertising Effectiveness: Comments on Belch et al. (1981) and Caccavale et al. (1981)," in ed. Andrew A. Mitchell, *Advances in Consumer Research*, vol. 9 (Ann Arbor, Mich.: Association for Consumer Research, 1982), pp. 428–430.

121. Michael S. LaTour, Robert E. Pitts, and David C. Snook-Luther, "Female Nudity, Arousal, and Ad Response: An Experimental Investigation," *Journal of Advertising*, vol. 19, no. 4, 1990, pp. 51–62.

122. Marilyn Y. Jones, Andrea J. S. Stanaland, and Betsy D. Gelb, "Beefcake and Cheesecake: Insights for Advertisers," *Journal of Advertising*, Summer 1998, pp. 33–52.

123. Rebecca Piirto, "The Romantic Sell," *American Demographics*, August 1989, pp. 38–41.

124. John Fetto, "Where's the Lovin'?" *American Demographics*, February 28, 2001.

125. Kevin Goldman, "Sexy Sony Ad by Leo Burnett Has Electronic Bulletin Board Aflame," *Wall Street Journal*, August 23, 1993, p. B5.

126. Sally D. Goll, "Beer Ads in Hong Kong Criticized as Sexist," *Wall Street Journal*, June 29, 1995, p. B2.

127. Miller, "We've Been 'Cosbyized.'"

128. "Poll on Ads: Too Sexy," *Wall Street Journal*, March 8, 1993, p. B5.

129. Robert A. Peterson and Roger A. Kerin, "The Female Role in Advertisements: Some Experimental Evidence," *Journal of Marketing*, October 1977, pp. 59–63.

130. Kathleen Deveny, "Lure of a Lovelier Smile Prompts a Rush to Buy Do-It-Yourself Teeth Whiteners," *Wall Street Journal*, July 6, 1992, pp. 11, 18.

131. Lisa Bannon and Margaret Studer, "For Two Revealing European Ads, Overexposure Can Have Benefits." *The Wall Street Journal*, June 17, 1993, p. B8.

132. Sak Onkvisit and John J. Shaw, "A View of Marketing and Advertising Practices in Asia and Its Meaning for Marketing Managers," *Journal of Consumer Marketing*, Spring 1985, pp. 5–17.

133. Sarah Ellison, "Sex-Themed Ads Often Don't Travel Well," *Wall Street Journal*, March 31, 2000, p. B7.

134. M. Friestad and Esther Thorson, "Emotion-Eliciting Advertising: Effect on Long Term Memory and Judgment," in ed. R. J. Lutz, *Advances in Consumer Research*, vol. 13 (Provo, Utah: Association for Consumer Research, 1986), pp. 111–116.

135. Betsy McKay, "Coke Taps Ripken for Home-Run Pitch," *Wall Street Journal*, September 7, 2001, p. B6; Betsy McKay, "Coke Aims to Revive 'Feel Good' Factor," *Wall Street Journal*, April 20, 2001, p. B8.

136. Barbara B. Stern, "Classical and Vignette Television Advertising Dramas: Structural Models, Formal Analysis, and Consumer Effects," *Journal of Consumer Research*, March 1994, pp. 601–615; William D. Wells, "Lectures and Dramas," in eds. Pat Cafferata and Alice M. Tybout, *Cognitive and Affective Responses to Advertising* (Lexington, Mass.: D.C. Heath, 1988); John Deighton, Daniel Romer, and Josh McQueen, "Using Dramas to Persuade," *Journal of Consumer Research*, December 1989, pp. 335–343.

137. Marvin E. Goldberg and Gerald J. Gorn, "Happy and Sad TV Programs: How They Affect Reactions to Commercials," *Journal of Consumer Research*, December 1987, pp. 387–403; John P. Murray Jr. and Peter A. Dacin, "Cognitive Moderators of Negative-Emotion Effects: Implications for Understanding Media Context," *Journal of Consumer Research*, March 1996, pp. 439–447.

138. John P. Murray, John L. Lastovicka, and Surendra Singh, "Feeling and Liking Responses to Television Programs: An Examination of Two Explanations for Media-Context Effects," *Journal of Consumer Research*, March 1992, pp. 441–451.

139. S. N. Singh and Gilbert A. Churchill, "Arousal and Advertising Effectiveness," *Journal of Advertising*, vol. 16, no. 1, 1987, pp. 4–10.

140. Mark A. Pavelchak, John H. Antil, and James M. Munch, "The Super Bowl: An Investigation into the Relationship among Program Context, Emotional Experience, and Ad Recall," *Journal of Consumer Research*, December 1988, pp. 360–367.

141. Sally Beatty, "Madison Avenue Should Rethink Television Violence, Study Finds," *Wall Street Journal*, December 1, 1998, p. B8.

Chapter 8

1. Jean Halliday, "Rockin' in the Front Seat," *Advertising Age*, March 16, 2001, **www.adage.com**; Wayne Friedman, "Gumby and Pokey to Tout ABC Summer Reruns," *Advertising Age*, June 11, 2001, pp. 1, 50; Suzanne Barry Osborn, "It's Yesterday Once More," *Chain Store Age Executive*, June 2001, p. 32; Ken Stammen, "Roto-Rooter Jingle Joins Retro Ad Campaigns," *Chicago Sun-Times*, February 9, 2001, p. 53; Jonathan Eig, "How the Web Rescued Quisp from a Cereal Killing," *Wall Street Journal*, April 25, 2000, pp. B1, B10; Keith Naughton and Bill Vlasic, "The Nostalgia Boom," *BusinessWeek*, March 23, 1998, pp. 58–64.

2. G. Sperling, "The Information Available in Brief Visual Presentations," *Psychological Monographs*, vol. 74, 1960, pp. 1–25; U. Neisser, *Cognitive Psychology* (New York: Appleton-Century-Crofts, 1967).

3. R. N. Haber, "The Impending Demise of the Icon: A Critique of the Concept of Iconic Storage in Visual Information Processing," *The Behavioral and Brain Sciences*, March 1983, pp. 1–54.

4. William James (1890) as described in Henry C. Ellis and R. Reed Hunt, *Fundamentals of Human Memory and Cognition* (Dubuque, Iowa: William C. Brown, 1989), pp. 65–66.

5. Deborah J. MacInnis and Linda L. Price, "The Role of Imagery in Information Processing: Review and Extensions," *Journal of Consumer Research*, March 1987, pp. 473–491.

6. Allan Paivio, "Perceptual Comparisons through the Mind's Eye," *Memory and Cognition*, November 1975, pp. 635–647; Stephen M. Kosslyn, "The Medium and the Message in Mental Imagery: A Theory," *Psychological Review*, January 1981, pp. 46–66; MacInnis and Price, "The Role of Imagery in Information Processing."

7. Morris B. Holbrook and Elizabeth C. Hirschman, "The Experiential Aspects of Consumption: Consumer Fantasies, Feelings, and Fun," *Journal of Consumer Research*, September 1982, pp. 132–140; MacInnis and Price, "The Role of Imagery in Information Processing"; Alan Richardson, "Imagery: Definitions and Types," in ed. Aness Sheikh, *Imagery: Current Theory, Research, and Application* (New York: Wiley, 1983), pp. 3–42.

8. Martin S. Lindauer, "Imagery and the Arts," in ed. Aness Sheikh, *Imagery: Current Theory, Research, and Application* (New York: Wiley, 1983), pp. 468–506.

9. Stephanie Miles, "Apparel E-Tailers Spruce Up for Holidays," *Wall Street Journal*, November 6, 2001, p. B6.

10. Ibid.

11. E. Tulving, "Episodic and Semantic Memory," in eds. E. Tulving and W. Donaldson, *Organization and Memory* (New York: Academic Press, 1972), pp. 381–403.

12. Hans Baumgartner, Mita Sujan, and James R. Bettman, "Autobiographical Memories, Affect, and Consumer Information Processing," *Journal of Consumer Psychology*, vol. 1, no. 1, 1992, pp. 53–82.

13. Morris B. Holbrook, "Nostalgia and Consumer Preferences: Some Emerging Patterns of Consumer Tastes," *Journal of Consumer Research*, September 1993, pp. 245–256; Morris B. Holbrook and Robert M. Schindler, "Echoes of the Dear Departed Past: Some Work in Progress on Nostalgia," in eds. Rebecca H. Holman and Michael R. Solomon, *Advances in Consumer Research*, vol. 18 (Provo, Utah: Association for Consumer Research, 1991), pp. 330–333.

14. Robert Johnson, "The Scents of Yesteryear Return," *Wall Street Journal*, November 2, 2000, pp. B1, B4.

15. Sarah Smith, "Trend: Making Memories," *Ladies Home Journal*, November 2000, p14.

16. Annamma Joy and Ruby Roy Dholakia, "Remembrances of Things Past: The Meaning of Home and Possessions of Indian Professionals in Canada," in ed. Floyd W. Rudmin, *To Have Possessions: A Handbook on Ownership and Property, Journal of Social Behavior and Personality* [Special Issue], November 1991, pp. 385–402; Melanie Wallendorf and Eric J. Arnould, "My Favorite Things: A Cross-Cultural Inquiry into Object Attachment, Possessiveness, and Social Linkage," *Journal of Consumer Research*, March 1988, pp. 531–547.

17. Kathryn A. Braun, "Postexperience Advertising Effects on Consumer Memory," *Journal of Consumer Research*, March 1999, pp. 319–334.

18. R. C. Atkinson and R. M. Shiffrin, "Human Memory: A Proposed System and Its Control Processes," in eds. K. W. Spence and J. T. Spence, *The Psychology of Learning and Motivation: Advances in Theory and Research*, vol. 2 (New York: Academic Press, 1968), pp. 89–195.

19. George A. Miller, "The Magical Number Seven, Plus or Minus Two: Some Limits on Our Capacity for Processing Information," *Psychological Review*, March 1956, pp. 81–97; James N. McGregor, "Short-Term Memory Capacity: Limitations or Optimization?" *Psychological Review*, January 1987, pp. 107–108.

20. Dilip Soman, "Effects of Payment Mechanism on Spending Behavior: The Role of Rehearsal and Immediacy of Payments," *Journal of Consumer Research*, vol. 27, March 2001, pp. 460–474.

21. Alan G. Sawyer, "The Effects of Repetition: Conclusions and Suggestions about Experimental Laboratory Research," in eds. G. David Hughes and Michael L. Ray, *Buyer/Consumer Information Processing* (Chapel Hill, N. C.: University of North Carolina Press, 1974), pp. 190–219; George E. Belch, "The Effects of Television Commercial Repetition on Cognitive Response and Message Acceptance," *Journal of Consumer Research*, June 1982, pp. 56–66; H. Rao Unnava and Robert E. Burnkrant, "Effects of Repeating Varied Ad Executions on Brand Name Memory," *Journal of Marketing Research*, November 1991, pp. 406–416; Murphy S. Sewall and Dan Sarel, "Characteristics of Radio Commercials and Their Recall Effectiveness," *Journal of Marketing*, January 1986, pp. 52–60.

22. Eileen Gunn, "Product Placement Prize: Repetition Factor Makes Videogames Valuable Medium," *Advertising Age*, February 12, 2001, p. S10.

23. F. I. M. Craik and R. S. Lockhart, "Levels of Processing: A Framework for Memory Research," *Verbal Learning and Verbal Behavior*, December 1972, pp. 671–684.

24. Susan E. Heckler and Terry L. Childers, "The Role of Expectancy and Relevancy in Memory for Verbal and Visual Information: What Is Incongruency?" *Journal of Consumer Research*, March 1992, pp. 475–492.

25. Kevin Goldman, "Robert Mitchum Adds Class to Trash Bags," *Wall Street Journal*, July 26, 1995, pp. B14.

26. Sally Beatty, "Ogilvy's TV-Ad Study Stresses 'Holding Power' Instead of Ratings," *Wall Street Journal*, June 4, 1999, p. B2.

27. Catherine A. Cole and Michael J. Houston, "Encoding and Media Effects on Consumer Learning Deficiencies in the Elderly," *Journal of Marketing Research*, February 1987, pp. 55–64; Deborah Roedder John and John C. Whitney Jr., "The Development of Consumer Knowledge in Children: A Cognitive Structure Approach," *Journal of Consumer Research*, March 1986, pp. 406–418.

28. Gabriel Biehal and Dipankar Chakravarti, "Consumers' Use of Memory and External Information in Choice: Macro and Micro Perspectives," *Journal of Consumer Research*, March 1986, pp. 382–405; John G. Lynch, Howard Marmorstein, and Michael F. Weigold, "Choices from Sets Including Remembered Brands: Use of Recalled Attributes and Prior Overall Evaluations," *Journal of Consumer Research*, September 1988, pp. 225–233; Valerie S. Folkes, "The Availability Heuristic and Perceived Risk," *Journal of Consumer Research*, June 1988, pp. 13–23.

29. A. M. Collins and E. F. Loftus, "A Spreading Activation Theory of Semantic Processing," *Psychological Review*, November 1975, pp. 407–428; Lawrence W. Barsalou, *Cognitive Psychology: An Overview for Cognitive Scientists* (Hillsdale, N. J.: Lawrence Erlbaum, 1991); John R. Anderson, *Cognitive Psychology and Its Implications* (New York: W. H. Freeman, 1990); Michael Pham and Gita Venkataramani Johar, "Contingent Processes of Source Identification," *Journal of Consumer Research*, December 1997, pp. 249–265.

30. Jack Neff, "S.C. Johnson Ads to Stress 'Family Owned,'" *Advertising Age*, November 13, 2001, **www.adage.com.**

31. Joseph W. Alba and J. Wesley Hutchinson, "Dimensions of Consumer Expertise," *Journal of Consumer Research*, March 1987, pp. 411–454.

32. David C. Riccio, Vita C. Rabinowitz, and Shari Axelrod, "Memory: When Less Is More," *American Psychologist*, November 1994, pp. 917–926.

33. Anthony Pratkanis, Anthony G. Greenwald, M. R. Leipe, and M. Hans Baumgartner, "In Search of Reliable Persuasion Effects: III. The Sleeper Effect Is Dead: Long Live the Sleeper Effect," *Journal of Personality and Social Psychology*, February 1988, pp. 203–218.

34. Raymond Burke and Thomas K. Srull, "Competitive Interference and Consumer Memory for Advertisements," *Journal of Consumer Research*, June 1988, pp. 55–68; Kevin Keller, "Memory and Evaluation Effects in Competitive Advertising Environments," *Journal of Consumer Research*, March 1991, pp. 463–476; Rik G. M. Pieters and Tammo H. A. Bijmolt, "Consumer Memory for Television Advertising: A Field Study of Duration, Serial Position and Competition Effects," *Journal of Consumer Research*, March 1997, pp. 362–372; Tom J. Brown and Michael L. Rothschild, "Reassessing the Impact of Television Advertising Clutter," *Journal of Consumer Research*, June 1993, pp. 138–147; Robert J. Kent and Chris T. Allen, "Competitive Interference Effects in Consumer Memory for Advertising: The Role of Brand Familiarity," *Journal of Marketing*, July 1994, pp. 97–105; H. Rao Unnava and Deepak Sirdeshmukh, "Reducing Competitive Ad Interference," *Journal of Marketing Research*, August 1994, pp. 403–411.

35. Anand Kumar, "Interference Effects of Contextual Cues in Advertisements on Memory for Ad Content," *Journal of Consumer Psychology*, vol. 9, no. 3, 2000, pp. 155–166.

36. Joseph W. Alba and Amitava Chattopadhyay, "Effects of Context and Part-Category Cues on Recall of Competing Brands," *Journal of Marketing Research*, August 1985, pp. 340–349; Joseph W. Alba and Amitava Chattopadhyay, "Salience Effects in Brand Recall," *Journal of Marketing Research*, November 1986, pp. 363–369; Manoj Hastak and Anusre Mitra, "Facilitating and Inhibiting Effects of Brand Cues on Recall, Consideration Set, and Choice," *Journal of Business Research*, October 1996, pp. 121–126.

37. Raymond Burke and Thomas K. Srull, "Competitive Interference and Consumer Memory for Advertising," *Journal of Consumer Research*, June 1988, pp. 55–68; Rik Pieters and Tammo H.A. Bijmolt, "Consumer Memory for Television Advertising: A Field Study of Duration, Serial Position, and Competition Effects," *Journal of Consumer Research*, March 1997, pp. 362–372.

38. Elizabeth F. Loftus, "When a Lie Becomes Memory's Truth: Memory and Distortion after Exposure to Misinformation," *Current Directions in Psychological Science*, August 1992, pp. 121–123.

39. www.johnsonsbaby.com/pro_bath.asp, February 19, 2001.

40. Larry Percy and John R. Rossiter, "A Model of Brand Awareness and Brand Attitude in Advertising Strategies," *Psychology and Marketing*, July–August 1992, pp. 263–274.

41. Ralph King, "The 7 Habits of Highly Persistent Dotcoms," *Business 2.0*, November 2001, pp. 87–94.

42. John Furniss, "Rating American Banks in Japan: Survey Shows Importance of Image," *International Advertiser*, April 1986, pp. 22–23.

43. Bonnie Tsui, "Bowl Poll: Ads Don't Mean Sales," *Advertising Age*, February 5, 2001, p. 33.

44. H. Shanker Krishnan and Dipankar Chakravarti, "Memory Measures for Pretesting Advertisements: An Integrative Conceptual Framework and a Diagnostic Template," *Journal of Consumer Psychology*, vol. 8, no. 1, 1999, pp. 1–37.

45. Cole and Houston, "Encoding and Media Effects on Consumer Learning Deficiencies in the Elderly"; Sharmistha Law, Scott A. Hawkins, and Fergus I. M. Craik, "Repetition-Induced Belief in the Elderly: Rehabilitating Age-Related Memory Deficits," *Journal of Consumer Research*, September 1998, pp. 91–107.

46. Susan T. Fiske and Shelley E. Taylor, *Social Cognition* (New York: McGraw-Hill, 1991).

47. Joseph W. Alba, J. Wesley Hutchinson, and John G. Lynch Jr., "Memory and Decision Making," in eds. Thomas S. Robertson and Harold Kassarjian, *Handbook of Consumer Behavior* (Englewood Cliffs, N. J.: Prentice-Hall, 1991), pp. 1–49.

48. Rik G. M. Pieters and Tammo H. A. Bijmolt, "Consumer Memory for Television Advertising: A Field Study of Duration, Serial Position and Competition Effects," *Journal of Consumer Research*, March 1997, pp. 362–372; David W. Stewart and David H. Furse, *Effective Television Advertising: A Study of 1000 Commercials* (Cambridge, Mass.: Marketing Science Institute, 1986); Pamela Homer, "Ad Size as an Indicator of Perceived Advertising Costs and Effort: The Effects on Memory and Perceptions," *Journal of Advertising*, Winter 1995, pp. 1–12.

49. Frank R. Kardes and Gurumurthy Kalyanaram, "Order of Entry Effects on Consumer Memory and Judgment: An Information Integration Perspective," *Journal of Marketing Research*, August 1992, pp. 343–357; Frank Kardes, Murali Chandrashekaran, and Ronald Dornoff, "Brand Retrieval, Consideration Set Composition, Consumer Choice, and the Pioneering Advantage," *Journal of Consumer Research*, June 1993, pp. 62–75; Frank H. Alpert and Michael A. Kamins, "An Empirical Investigation of Consumer Memory, Attitude, and Perceptions toward Pioneer and Follower Brands," *Journal of Marketing*, October 1995, pp. 34–44.

50. Claudia Penteado, "Coca-Cola Expects to Grow by 7% in Brazil," *Advertising Age*, May 16, 2001, www.adage.com; Hillary Chura and Richard Linnett, "Coca-Cola Readies Massive Global Campaign," *Advertising Age*, April 2, 2001, www.adage.com.

51. Sridar Samu, H. Shankar Krishnan, and Robert E. Smith, "Using Advertising Alliances for New Product Introduction: Interactions between Product Complementarity and Promotional Strategies," *Journal of Marketing*, January 1999, pp. 57–74.

52. Gita Venkatatarmani Johar and Michel Tuan Pham, "Relatedness, Prominence, and Constructive Sponsor Identification," *Journal of Marketing Research*, vol. 36, August 1999, pp. 299–312.

53. Rex Briggs and Nigel Hollis, "Advertising on the Web: Is There Response before Click-Through," *Journal of Advertising Research*, March–April 1997, pp. 33–45.

54. Anonymous, "Click Me," *Smart Business*, March 2001, pp. 111–118.

55. Michael Pham and Gita Venkataramani Johar, "Contingent Processes of Source Identification," *Journal of Consumer Research*, December 1997, pp. 249–265.

56. Deborah D. Heisley and Sidney J. Levy, "Autodriving: A Photoelicitation Technique," *Journal of Consumer Research*, December 1991, pp. 257–272.

57. Joan Meyers-Levy, "The Influence of a Brand Name's Association Set Size and Word Frequency on Brand Memory," *Journal of Consumer Research*, September 1989, pp. 197–207; Alba and Hutchinson, "Dimensions of Consumer Expertise."

58. Cathy J. Cobb and Wayne D. Hoyer, "The Influence of Advertising at Moment of Brand Choice," *Journal of Advertising*, December 1986, pp. 5–27.

59. Keller, "Memory Factors in Advertising," *Journal of Consumer Research*, December 1987, pp. 316-333. J. Wesley Hutchinson and Daniel L. Moore, "Issues Surrounding the Examination of Delay Effects of Advertising," in ed. Thomas C. Kinnear, *Advances in Consumer Research*, vol. 11 (Provo, Utah: Association for Consumer Research, 1984), pp. 650–655.

60. Carolyn Costley, Samar Das, and Merrie Brucks, "Presentation Medium and Spontaneous Imaging Effects on Consumer Memory," *Journal of Consumer Psychology*, vol. 6, no. 3, 1997, pp. 211–231; David W. Sewart and Girish N. Punj, "Effects of Using a Nonverbal (Musical) Cue on Recall and Playback of Television Advertising: Implications for Advertising Tracking," *Journal of Business Research*, May 1998, pp. 39–51.

61. H. Rao Unnava and Robert E. Burnkrant, "An Imagery-Processing View of the Role of Pictures in Print Advertisements," *Journal of Marketing Research*, May 1991, pp. 226–231.

62. Alice M. Isen, "Some Ways in Which Affect Influences Cognitive Processes: Implications for Advertising and Consumer Behavior," in eds. Alice M. Tybout and P. Cafferata, *Advertising and Consumer Psychology* (Lexington, Mass.: Lexington Books, 1989), pp. 91–117; see also Patricia A. Knowles, Stephen J. Grove, and W. Jeffrey Burroughs, "An Experimental Examination of Mood Effects on Retrieval and Evaluation of Advertisement and Brand Information," *Journal of the Academy of Marketing Science*, Spring 1993, pp. 135–143; Gordon H. Bower, "Mood and Memory," *American Psychologist*, February 1981, pp. 129–148; Gordon H. Bower, Stephen Gilligan, and Kenneth Montiero, "Selectivity of Learning Caused by Affective States," *Journal of Experimental Psychology: General*, December 1981, pp. 451–473; Alice M. Isen, Thomas Shalker, Margaret Clark, and Lynn Karp, "Affect, Accessibility of Material in Memory and Behavior: A Cognitive Loop?" *Journal of Personality and Social Psychology*, January 1978, pp. 1–12.

63. Alice M. Isen, "Toward Understanding the Role of Affect in Cognition," in eds. Robert S. Wyer and Thomas K. Srull, *Handbook of Social Cognition* (Hillsdale, N. J.: Lawrence Erlbaum, 1984), pp. 179–236.

64. Alice M. Isen, "Some Ways in Which Affect Influences Cognitive Processes: Implications for Advertising and Consumer Behavior," in eds. Patricia Cafferata and Alice M. Tybout, *Cognitive and Affective Responses to Advertising* (Lexington, Mass.: Lexington Books, 1989), pp. 91–118.

65. Angela Y. Lee and Brian Sternthal, "The Effects of Positive Mood on Memory," *Journal of Consumer Research*, vol. 26, September 1999, pp. 115–127.

66. Alba and Hutchinson, "Dimensions of Consumer Expertise."

67. Sally Goll Beatty, "Networks Nix Ads Featuring Rival TV Stars," *Wall Street Journal*, February 21, 1997, pp. B1, B6.

Chapter 9

1. Karl Greenberg, "Korilko Clicks on Consumers for Edmunds.com," *Brandweek*, May 21, 2001, p. 38; Jean Halliday, "Overhaul Near End for Edmunds.com," *Advertising Age*, April 9, 2001, p. 28; Bob Wallace, "Nothing Simple about Mobile Commerce," *TechWeb*, January 5, 2001, **www.techweb.com**; Karen Lundegaard, "Auto Site Rolls Out a Vintage Campaign," *Wall Street Journal*, July 11, 2000, p. B12.

2. Norihiko Shirouzu, "P&G's Joy Makes an Unlikely Splash in Japan," *Wall Street Journal*, December 10, 1997, pp. B1, B8.

3. Tara Parker-Pope, "Body Spritzes Promise to Dispel Smokers' Odors," *Wall Street Journal*, March 31, 1998, pp. B1, B9.

4. Norihiko Shirouzu, "Low-Smoke Cigarette Catches Fire in Japan," *Wall Street Journal*, September 8, 1997, pp. B1.

5. Bob Garfield, "Softly Lit or Blunt, 'Less Toxic' Cigarette Ads Hint At Health," *Advertising Age*, November 12, 2001, p. 58.

6. Suzanne Kapner, "From a British Chain, Lunch in a New York Minute," *New York Times*, July 29, 2001, sec. 3, p. 4.

7. Joseph W. Alba, J. Wesley Hutchinson, and John G. Lynch, "Memory and Decision Making," in eds.

Thomas C. Roberton and Harold H. Kassarjian, *Handbook of Consumer Behavior* (Englewood Cliffs, N.J.: Prentice Hall, 1991).

8. John R. Hauser and Birger Wernerfelt, "An Evaluation Cost Model of Consideration Sets," *Journal of Consumer Research*, March 1990, pp. 393–408.
9. "Multinationals Tap Into the Bottled Water Market," *Marketing Week*, June 7, 2001, www.mad.co.uk/mw.
10. Susan Carey, "Even When It's Quicker to Travel by Train, Many Fly," *Wall Street Journal*, August 29, 1997, pp. B1, B5.
11. Emma Reynolds, "Nestlé Moves away from Indulgence Angle for Aero Ad," *Marketing*, June 21, 2001, p. 22.
12. Kalpesh Kaushik Desai and Wayne D. Hoyer, "Descriptive Characteristics of Memory-Based Consideration Sets: Influence of Usage Occasion Frequency and Usage Location Familiarity," *Journal of Consumer Research*, vol. 27, December 2000, pp. 309–323.
13. Prakash Nedungadi and J. Wesley Hutchinson, "The Prototypicality of Brands: Relationships with Brand Awareness, Preference, and Usage," in eds. Elizabeth C. Hirschman and Morris B. Holbrook, *Advances in Consumer Research*, vol. 12 (Provo, Utah: Association for Consumer Research, 1985), pp. 498–503; Prakash Nedungadi, "Recall and Consumer Consideration Sets: Influencing Choice without Altering Brand Evaluations," *Journal of Consumer Research*, December 1990, pp. 263–276.
14. Alba, Hutchinson, and Lynch, "Memory and Decision Making."
15. Nedungadi and Hutchinson, "The Prototypicality of Brands"; James Ward and Barbara Loken, "The Quintessential Snack Food: Measurement of Product Prototypes," in ed. Richard J. Lutz, *Advances in Consumer Research*, vol. 13 (Provo, Utah: Association for Consumer Research, 1986), pp. 126–131.
16. "Armor All Wants to Clean Some Son of a Gun's Clock," *Brandweek*, October 18, 1993, pp. 32–33.
17. R. Whitaker Penteado, "Fast-Food Franchises Fight for Brazilian Aficionados," *Brandweek*, June 7, 1993, pp. 20–24.
18. Siew Meng Leong, Swee Hoon Ang, and Lai Leng Tham, "Increasing Brand Name Recall in Print Advertising among Asian Consumers," *Journal of Advertising*, Summer 1996, pp. 65–82.
19. Stewart Shapiro, Deborah J. MacInnis, and Susan E. Heckler, "The Effects of Incidental Ad Exposure on the Formation of Consideration Sets," *Journal of Consumer Research*, June 1997, pp. 94–104.
20. Robert Langreth, "Bulletins for the Battle of the Baldness Drugs," *Wall Street Journal*, December 19, 1997, pp. B1, B6; Yumiko Ono, "Sports Figures Tout Rogaine for Pharmacia," *Wall Street Journal*, December 19, 1997, pp. B1, B6.
21. Alba, Hutchinson, and Lynch, "Memory and Decision Making."
22. Ron Weiskind, "Monkey See, Monkey Redo: If at First You Succeed, Try, Try Again by Remaking the Movie," *Pittsburgh Post-Gazette*, June 17, 2001, p. G-3.
23. S. Ratneshwar and Allan D. Shocker, "Substitution in Use and the Role of Usage Context in Product Category Structures," *Journal of Marketing Research*, August 1991, pp. 281–295.
24. Terry Lefton, "Kodak Teaming with NFL on Single-Use Cameras," *Brandweek*, December 14, 1992, p. 3.
25. Yumiko Ono, "Pizza in Japan Is Adapted to Local Tastes," *Wall Street Journal*, June 4, 1993, p. B1.
26. Nedungadi and Hutchinson, "The Prototypicality of Brands"; Ward and Loken, "The Quintessential Snack Food."
27. Julian E. Barnes, "The Making (Or Possible Breaking) of a Megabrand," *New York Times*, July 22, 2001, sec. 3, pp. 1, 7.
28. Yumiko Ono, "'King of Beers' Wants to Rule More of Japan," *Wall Street Journal*, October 28, 1993, pp. B1, B8.
29. Olga Kharif, "Getting a Grip on Consumer Tastes," *BusinessWeek*, July 16, 2001, p. 12.
30. Gabriel Biehal and Dipankar Chakravarti, "Consumers' Use of Memory and External Information in Choice: Macro and Micro Perspectives," *Journal of Consumer Research*, March 1986, pp. 382–405.
31. Gabriel Biehal and Dipankar Chakravarti, "Information Accessibility as a Moderator of Consumer Choice," *Journal of Consumer Research*, June 1983, pp. 1–14.
32. Michaela Waenke, Gerd Bohner, and Andreas Jurkowitsch, "There Are Many Reasons to Drive a BMW: Does Imagined Ease of Argument Generation Influence Attitudes?" *Journal of Consumer Research*, September 1997, pp. 170–177.
33. Meryl Paula Gardner, "Advertising Effects on Attributes Recalled and Criteria Used for Brand Evaluations," *Journal of Consumer Research*, December 1983, pp. 310–318; Scott B. MacKenzie, "The Role of Attention in Mediating the Effect of Advertising on Attribute Importance," *Journal of Consumer Research*, September 1986, pp. 174–195; Priya Raghubir and Geeta Menon, "AIDS and Me, Never the Twain Shall Meet: The Effects of Information Accessibility on Judgments of Risk and Advertising Effectiveness," *Journal of Consumer Research*, June 1998, pp. 52–63.
34. Fellman and Lynch, "Self-Generated Validity and Other Effects of Measurement;" John G. Lynch, Howard Marmorstein, and Michael F. Weigold, "Choices from Sets Including Remembered Brands: Use of Recalled Attributes and Prior Overall Evaluations," *Journal of Consumer Research*, September 1988, pp. 169–184.

35. Carolyn L. Costley and Merrie Brucks, "Selective Recall and Information Use in Consumer Preferences," *Journal of Consumer Research*, March 1992, pp. 464–474; Geeta Menon, Priya Raghubit, and Norbert Schwarz, "Behavioral Frequency Judgments: An Accessbility-Diagnosticity Framework," *Journal of Consumer Research*, September 1995, pp. 212–228.

36. Paul M. Herr, Frank R. Kardes, and John Kim, "Effects of Word-of-Mouth and Product-Attribute Information on Persuasion: An Accessibility-Diagnosticity Perspective," *Journal of Consumer Research*, March 1991, pp. 454–462.

37. Yumiko Ono, "Anheuser Plays on Tipsiness to Sell Japan Strong Brew," *Wall Street Journal*, November 17, 1998, pp. B1, B4.

38. Milbank, "Made in America Becomes a Boast in Europe."

39. Walter Kintsch and Tuen A. Van Dyk, "Toward a Model of Text Comprehension and Production," *Psychological Review*, September 1978, pp. 363–394; S. Ratneshwar, David G. Mick, and Gail Reitinger, "Selective Attention in Consumer Information Processing: The Role of Chronically Accessible Attributes," in eds. Marvin E. Goldberg, Gerald Gorn, and Richard W. Pollay, *Advances in Consumer Research*, vol. 17 (Provo, Utah: Association for Consumer Research, 1990), pp. 547–553.

40. Anne-Marie Chaker, "Antiacne Campaign Propels Birth-Control Pill," *Wall Street Journal*, September 28, 1998, pp. B1, B4.

41. Jacob Jacoby, Tracy Troutman, Alfred Kuss, and David Mazursky, "Experience and Expertise in Complex Decision Making," in ed. Richard J. Lutz, *Advances in Consumer Research*, vol. 13 (Provo, Utah: Association for Consumer Research, 1986), pp. 469–475.

42. Gardner, "Advertising Effects on Attributes Recalled"; Mackenzie, "The Role of Attention in Mediating the Effect of Advertising."

43. Vanessa O'Connell, "Labels Suggesting the Benefits of Drinking Wine Look Likely," *Wall Street Journal*, October 26, 1998, pp. B1, B3.

44. Jennifer Cody, "Now Marketers in Japan Stress the Local Angle," *Wall Street Journal*, February 23, 1994, p. B1.

45. Mark I. Alpert, "Identification of Determinant Attributes: A Comparison of Methods," *Journal of Marketing Research*, May 1971, pp. 184–191.

46. Emily Nelson, "Camera Makers Focus on Tiny and Cute," *Wall Street Journal*, March 14, 1997, pp. B1, B2.

47. Jolita Kiselius and Brian Sternthal, "Examining the Vividness Controversy: An Availability-Valence Interpretation," *Journal of Consumer Research*, March 1986, pp. 418–431; Herr, Kardes, and Kim, "Effects of Word-of-Mouth and Product-Attribute Information."

48. Punam Anand Keller and Lauren G. Block, "Vividness Effects: A Resource-Matching Perspective," *Journal of Consumer Research*, December 1997, pp. 295–304.

49. Stuart Elliot, "Volkswagen Revamps the Beetle Campaign to Be More Informative," *New York Times*, April 9, 2001, p. C12.

50. Reid Hastie and Bernadette Park, "The Relationship between Memory and Judgment Depends on Whether the Judgment Task Is Memory-Based or On-Line," *Psychological Review*, June 1986, pp. 258–268; Barbara Loken and Ronald Hoverstad, "Relationships between Information Recall and Subsequent Attitudes: Some Exploratory Findings," *Journal of Consumer Research*, September 1985, pp. 155–168.

51. Biehal and Chakravarti, "Consumers' Use of Memory and External Information in Choice"; Jong-Won Park and Manoj Hastak, "Memory-Based Product Judgments: Effects of Involvement at Encoding and Retrieval," *Journal of Consumer Research*, December 1994, pp. 534–547.

52. Hans Baumgartner, Mita Sujan, and James R. Bettman, "Autobiographical Memories, Affect, and Consumer Information Processing," *Journal of Consumer Psychology*, vol. 1, no. 1, 1992, pp. 53–82.

53. Rodney Ho, "Bowling for Dollars, Alleys Try Updating," *Wall Street Journal*, January 24, 1997, pp. B1, B2.

54. Dave Barrager, "Retro Power," *Brandweek*, March 15, 1993, pp. 14–17.

55. Fara Warner, "The Place to Be This Year," *Brandweek*, November 30, 1992, p. 24.

56. Michael J. Houston, Terry L. Childers, and Susan E. Heckler, "Picture-Word Consistency and the Elaborative Processing of Advertisements," *Journal of Marketing Research*, November 1987, pp. 359–369.

57. Joseph W. Alba and Amitava Chattopadhyay, "Salience Effects in Brand Recall," *Journal of Marketing Research*, November 1986, pp. 363–369; Kiselius and Sternthal, "Examining the Vividness Controversy."

58. Alba and Chattopadhyay, "Salience Effects in Brand Recall"; Kiselius and Sternthal, "Examining the Vividness Controversy."

59. "Game Farmers Brand Deer Meat So It's Less Gamey," *Brandweek*, January 11, 1993, p. 7.

60. Gordon H. Bower, "Mood and Memory," *American Psychologist*, February 1981, pp. 129–148; Gordon H. Bower, Stephen Gilligan, and Kenneth Montiero, "Selectivity of Learning Caused by Affective States," *Journal of Experimental Psychology: General*, December 1981, pp. 451–473; Alice M. Isen, Thomas Shalker, Margaret Clark, and Lynn Karp, "Affect, Accessibility of Material in Memory and Behavior: A Cognitive Loop?" *Journal of Personality and Social Psychology*, January 1978, pp. 1–12.

61. Robert L. Simison and Joseph B. White, "Reputation for Poor Quality Still Plagues Detroit," *Wall Street Journal*, May 4, 2000, pp. B1, B4.

62. Peter H. Bloch, Daniel L. Sherrell, and Nancy M. Ridgway, "Consumer Search: An Extended Framework," *Journal of Consumer Research*, June 1986, pp. 119–126.

63. Sharon E. Beatty and Scott M. Smith, "External Search Effort: An Investigation across Several Product Categories," *Journal of Consumer Research*, June 1987, pp. 83–95.

64. Beatty and Smith, "External Search Effort."

65. Lorraine Mirabella, "As Shoppers Change Ways, Retailers Lag," *Baltimore Sun*, January 21, 2001, p. 1D.

66. David F. Midgley, "Patterns of Interpersonal Information Seeking for the Purchase of a Symbolic Product," *Journal of Marketing Research*, February 1983, pp. 74–83.

67. Denver D'Rozario and Susan P. Douglas, "Effect of Assimilation on Prepurchase External Information-Search Tendencies," *Journal of Consumer Psychology*, vol. 8, no. 2, 1999, pp. 187–209.

68. Niranjan J. Raman, "A Qualitative Investigation of Web-Browsing Behavior," in eds. Merrie Brucks and Deborah J. MacInnis, *Advances in Consumer Research*, vol. 24 (Provo, Utah: Association for Consumer Research, 1997), pp. 511–516.

69. Stacy L. Wood, "Remote Purchase Environments: The Influence of Return Policy Leniency on Two-Stage Decision Process," *Journal of Marketing Research*, vol. 38, May 2001, pp. 157–169.

70. Jennifer Rewick, "Clinching the Holiday E-Sale," *Wall Street Journal*, October 9, 2000, pp. B1, B22.

71. Abeer Y. Hoque and Gerald L. Lohse, "An Information Search Cost Perspective for Designing Interfaces for Electronic Commerce," *Journal of Marketing Research*, vol. 36, August 1999, pp. 387–394.

72. Paul A. Greenberg, "Getting Brick and Click Together," *E-Commerce Times*, December 14, 2001, **www.ecommercetimes.com/perl/story/?id=15277**; Jon Swartz, "E-Tailers Ring Up Record Holiday Week," *E-Commerce Times*, December 27, 2001, **www.ecommercetimes.com/perl/story/?id=15520**.

73. Kimberly A. Strassel, "Online Shopping Grows in Europe as Retailers Deal with Problems," *Wall Street Journal*, December 14, 1998, p. B5.

74. Ross Kerber, "Direct Hit Uses Popularity to Narrow Internet Searches," *Wall Street Journal*, July 2, 1998, p. B4.

75. Paul A. Greenberg, "The Bottom Line on Online Shopping Bots," *E-Commerce Times*, July 13, 2001, **www.ecommercetimes.com/perl/story/?id=11999**.

76. Rebecca Quick, "Web's Robot Shoppers Don't Roam Free," *Wall Street Journal*, September 3, 1998, pp. B1, B8.

77. Robyn Weisman, "Technologies That Changed 2001," *Newsfactor.com*, January 3, 2002, **www.newsfactor.com/perl/story/?id=15569**; Sally Beatty, "IBM HotMedia Aims to Speed Online Ads," *Wall Street Journal*, October 27, 1998, p. B8.

78. Mark W. Vigoroso, "The Bottom Line in Web Design: Know Your Customer," *E-Commerce Times*, November 14, 2001, **www.ecommercetimes.com/perl/story/?id=14738**.

79. Dean Takahashi, "Closer to Reality," *Wall Street Journal*, December 7, 1998, p. R8.

80. Burke, Raymond R., "Virtual Shopping: Breakthrough in Marketing Research," *Harvard Business Review*, vol. 74, March–April 1996, pp. 120–131; Feder, Barnaby, "Test Marketers Use Virtual Shopping to Gauge Potential of Real Products," *New York Times*, December 22, 1997, p. C3.

81. Eileen Fischer, Julia Bristor, and Brenda Gainer, "Creating or Escaping Community? An Exploratory Study of Internet Consumers' Behaviors," in eds. Kim P. Corfman and John G. Lynch, eds. *Advances in Consumer Research*, vol. 23 (Provo, Utah: Association for Consumer Research, 1996), pp. 178–182; John Buskin, "Tales from the Front," *Wall Street Journal*, December 7, 1998, p. R6.

82. Larry Weber, *The Provocateur* (New York: Crown Business, 2001), p. 34.

83. Neil A. Granitz and James C. Ward, "Virtual Community: A Sociocognitive Analysis," in eds. Kim P. Corfman and John G. Lynch, *Advances in Consumer Research*, vol. 23 (Provo, Utah: Association for Consumer Research, 1996), pp. 161–166.

84. Jim Sterne, *What Makes People Click: Advertising on the Web*, (Indianapolis, Ind.: Que, 1997).

85. Holly Vanscoy, "Life after Living.com," *Smart Business*, February 2001, pp. 68–10; Clare Saliba, "With Webvan Gone, Where Will Online Shoppers Turn?" *E-Commerce Times*, July 10, 2001, **www.ecommercetimes.com/perl/story/11884.html**.

86. Jacob Jacoby, Robert W. Chestnut, Karl Weigl, and William A. Fisher, "Prepurchase Information Acquisition: Description of a Process Methodology, Research Paradigm, and Pilot Investigation," in ed. Beverlee B. Anderson, *Advances in Consumer Research*, vol. 3 (Cincinnati: Association for Consumer Research, 1976), pp. 306–314; Jacob Jacoby, Robert W. Chestnut, and William Silberman, "Consumer Use and Comprehension of Nutrition Information," *Journal of Consumer Research*, September 1977, pp. 119–128.

87. Geoffrey C. Kiel and Roger A. Layton, "Dimensions of Consumer Information Seeking," *Journal of Marketing Research*, May 1981, pp. 233–239.

88. John O. Claxton, Joseph N. Fry, and Bernard Portis, "A Taxonomy of Prepurchase Information Gathering

Patterns," *Journal of Consumer Research*, December 1974, pp. 35–42.

89. Bloch, Sherrell, and Ridgway, "Consumer Search."

90. R. A. Bauer, "Consumer Behavior as Risk Taking," in ed. Robert S. Hancock, *Dynamic Marketing for a Changing World* (Chicago: American Marketing Association, 1960), pp. 389–398; Rohit Deshpande and Wayne D. Hoyer, "Consumer Decision Making: Strategies, Cognitive Effort, and Perceived Risk," in *1983 Educators' Conference Proceedings* (Chicago: American Marketing Association, 1983), pp. 88–91.

91. Keith B. Murray, "A Test of Services Marketing Theory: Consumer Information Acquisition Activities," *Journal of Marketing*, January 1991, pp. 10–25; Joel E. Urbany, Peter R. Dickson, and William L. Wilkie, "Buyer Uncertainty and Information Search," *Journal of Consumer Research*, September 1989, pp. 208–215.

92. David J. Furse, Girish N. Punj, and David W. Stewart, "A Typology of Individual Search Strategies among Purchasers of New Automobiles," *Journal of Consumer Research*, March 1984, pp. 417–431; Narasimhan Srinivasan and Brian T. Ratchford, "An Empirical Test of a Model of External Search for Automobiles," *Journal of Consumer Research*, September 1991, pp. 233–242; Jacob Jacoby, James J. Jaccard, Imran Currim, Alfred Kuss, Asim Ansari, and Tracy Troutman, "Tracing the Impact of Item-by-Item Information Accessing on Uncertainty Reduction," *Journal of Consumer Research*, September 1994, pp. 291–303.

93. Calmetta Y. Coleman, "Selling Jewelry, Dolls, and TVs Next to Corn Flakes," *Wall Street Journal*, November 19, 1997, pp. B1, B8.

94. Sridhar Moorthy, Brian T. Ratchford, and Debabrata Talukdar, "Consumer Information Search Revisited: Theory and Empirical Analysis," *Journal of Consumer Research*, March 1997, pp. 263–277.

95. Calvin P. Duncan and Richard W. Olshavsky, "External Search: The Role of Consumer Beliefs," *Journal of Marketing Research*, February 1982, pp. 32–43; Girish N. Punj and Richard Staelin, "A Model of Information Search Behavior for New Automobiles," *Journal of Consumer Research*, September 1983, pp. 181–196.

96. Duncan and Olshavsky, "External Search."

97. Kathy Hammond, Gil McWilliam, and Andrea Narholz Diaz, "Fun and Work on the Web: Differences in Attitudes between Novices and Experienced Users," in eds. Joseph W. Alba and J. Wesley Hutchinson, *Advances in Consumer Research*, vol. 25 (Provo, Utah: Association for Consumer Research, 1998), pp. 372–378.

98. Joan E. Rigdon, "Advertisers Give Surfers Games to Play," *Wall Street Journal*, October 28, 1996, pp. B1, B6.

99. Laura A. Peracchio and Alice M. Tybout, "The Moderating Role of Prior Knowledge in Schema-Based Product Evaluation," *Journal of Consumer Research*, December 1996, pp. 177–192.

100. Joan Meyers-Levy and Alice Tybout, "Schema-Congruity as Basis for Product Evaluation," *Journal of Consumer Research*, June 1989, pp. 39–54.

101. Jonathan Welsh, "Vacuums Make Sweeping Health Claims," *Wall Street Journal*, September 9, 1996, pp. B1, B2.

102. Julie L. Ozanne, Merrie Brucks, and Dhruv Grewal, "A Study of Information Search Behavior during Categorization of New Products," *Journal of Consumer Research*, March 1992, pp. 452–463.

103. Punj and Staelin, "A Model of Consumer Information Search Behavior for New Automobiles"; Kiel and Layton, "Dimensions of Consumer Information Seeking."

104. Merrie Brucks, "The Effects of Product Class Knowledge on Information Search Behavior," *Journal of Consumer Research*, June 1985, pp. 1–16; James R. Bettman and C. Whan Park, "Effects of Prior Knowledge and Experience and Phase of the Choice Process on Consumer Decision Processes: A Protocol Analysis," *Journal of Consumer Research*, December 1980, pp. 234–248; Eric J. Johnson and J. Edward Russo, "Product Familiarity and Learning New Information," *Journal of Consumer Research*, June 1984, pp. 542–550; P. S. Raju, Subhas C. Lonial, and W. Glyn Mangold, "Differential Effects of Subjective Knowledge, Objective Knowledge, and Usage Experience on Decision Making; An Exploratory Investigation," *Journal of Consumer Psychology*, vol. 4, no. 2, 1995, pp. 153–180; Joseph W. Alba and J. Wesley Hutchinson, "Dimensions of Consumer Expertise," *Journal of Consumer Research*, March 1987, pp. 411–454.

105. Noel Capon and Roger Davis, "Basic Cognitive Ability Measures as Predictors of Consumer Information Processing Strategies," *Journal of Consumer Research*, June 1984, pp. 551–563.

106. For a summary of a number of studies, see Joseph W. Newman, "Consumer External Search: Amount and Determinants," in eds. Arch Woodside, Jagdish Sheth, and Peter Bennett, *Consumer and Industrial Buying Behavior* (New York: North-Holland, 1977), pp. 79–94; Charles M. Schaninger and Donald Sciglimpaglia, "The Influences of Cognitive Personality Traits and Demographics on Consumer Information Acquisition," *Journal of Consumer Research*, September 1981, pp. 208–216.

107. Scott Painton and James W. Gentry, "Another Look at the Impact of Information Presentation Format," *Journal of Consumer Research*, September 1985, pp. 240–244.

108. J. Edward Russo, Richard Staelin, Catherine A. Nolan, Gary J. Russell, and Barbara L. Metcalf, "Nutrition Information in the Supermarket," *Journal of Consumer Research*, June 1986, pp. 48–70.

109. Christine Moorman, "The Effects of Stimulus and Consumer Utilization of Nutrition Information," *Journal of Consumer Research*, December 1990, pp. 362–374.

110. Chris Janiszewski, "The Influence of Display Characteristics on Visual Exploratory Search Behavior," *Journal of Consumer Research*, December 1998, pp. 290–301.

111. William L. Moore and Donald L. Lehman, "Validity of Information Display Boards: An Assessment Using Longitudinal Data," *Journal of Marketing Research*, November 1980, pp. 296–307; C. Whan Park, Easwar S. Iyer, and Daniel C. Smith, "The Effects of Situational Factors on In-Store Grocery Shopping Behavior: The Role of Store Environment and Time Available for Shopping," *Journal of Consumer Research*, March 1989, pp. 422–433.

112. John R. Hauser, Glen L. Urban, and Bruce D. Weinberg, "How Consumers Allocate Their Time When Searching for Information," *Journal of Marketing Research*, November 1993, pp. 452–466.

113. Alhassan G. Abdul-Muhmin, "Contingent Decision Behavior: Effect of Number of Alternatives to Be Selected on Consumers' Decision Processes," *Journal of Consumer Psychology*, vol. 8, no. 1, 1999, pp. 91–111.

114. Furse, Punj, and Stewart, "A Typology of Individual Search Strategies among Purchasers of New Automobiles."

115. "Radiant Systems Hits Milestone with Sephora," *Business Wire*, January 9, 2001, www.businesswire.com; "Netkey Joins Forces with Autopulse to Roll Out Interactive Kiosks to Educate and Entertain Today's Active Car Owner," *Business Wire*, April 25, 2001, www.businesswire.com.

116. Troy Wolverton and Greg Sandoval, "Net Shoppers Wooed by In-Store Deals," *CNET News.com*, December 12, 2001, http://news.cnet.com/news/0-1007-200-8156745.html.

117. Jacob Jacoby, Robert W. Chestnut, and William A. Fisher, "A Behavioral Process Approach to Information Acquisition in Nondurable Purchasing," *Journal of Marketing Research*, November 1978, pp. 532–544.

118. Kent B. Monroe, "The Influence of Price Differences and Brand Familiarity on Brand Preferences," *Journal of Consumer Research*, June 1976, pp. 42–49.

119. Dhruv Grewal and Howard Marmorstein, "Market Price Variation, Perceived Price Variation, and Consumers' Price Search Decision for Durable Goods," *Journal of Consumer Research*, December 1994, pp. 453–460.

120. "Japanese Retailing: A Yen for Cheap Chic," *The Economist*, June 3, 2000, p. 65; P. H. Ferguson, "Shoppers Leave Ivory Towers for Bargain Basements in Japan," *Austin American Statesman*, December 26, 1993, p. A26.

121. Leonidas C. Leonidou, "Understanding the Russian Consumer," *Marketing and Research Today*, March 1992, pp. 75–83.

122. Cynthia Huffman, "Goal Change, Information Acquisition, and Transfer," *Journal of Consumer Psychology*, vol. 5, no. 1, 1996, pp. 1–26.

123. Deborah Roedder John, Carol A. Scott, and James R. Bettman, "Sampling Data for Covariation Assessment," *Journal of Consumer Research*, March 1986, pp. 406–417.

124. Mark W. Vigoroso, "Search Engine Results That Pay Off," *E-Commerce Times*, December 7, 2001, www.ecommercetimes.com/perl/story/?id=15150.

125. J. Edward Russo and France Leclerc, "An Eye-Fixation Analysis of Choice for Consumer Nondurables," *Journal of Consumer Research*, September 1994, pp. 274–290.

126. Jacoby et al., "Prepurchase Information Acquisition."

127. J. Edward Russo, Margaret G. Meloy, and Husted Medvec, "Predecisional Distortion of Product Information," *Journal of Marketing Research*, November 1998, pp. 438–452.

128. Carol A. Berning and Jacob Jacoby, "Patterns of Information Acquisition in New Product Purchases," *Journal of Consumer Research*, September 1974, pp. 18–22.

129. Itamar Simonson, Joel Huber, and John Payne, "The Relationship between Prior Brand Knowledge and Information Acquisition Order," *Journal of Consumer Research*, March 1988, pp. 566–578.

130. Carrie M. Heilman, Douglas Bowman, and Gordon P. Wright, "The Evolution of Brand Preference and Choice Behaviors of Consumers New to a Market," *Journal of Marketing Research*, vol. 37, May 2000, pp. 139–155.

131. Jacoby et al., "Prepurchase Information Acquisition"; James R. Bettman, *An Information Processing Theory of Consumer Choice* (Reading, Mass.: Addison-Wesley, 1979).

132. Eric J. Johnson and J. Edward Russo, "Product Familiarity and Learning New Information," *Journal of Consumer Research*, June 1984, pp. 542–550; James R. Bettman and P. Kakkar, "Effects of Information Presentation Format on Consumer Information Acquisition Strategies," *Journal of Consumer Research*, March 1977, pp. 233–240.

133. Raj Sethuraman, Catherine Cole, and Dipak Jain, "Analyzing the Effect of Information Format and Task on Cutoff Search Strategies," *Journal of Consumer Psychology*, vol. 3, 1994, pp. 103–136.

134. Jacoby et al., "Tracing the Impact of Item-by-Item Information Accessing on Uncertainty Reduction."

Chapter 10

1. Santan Santivimolnat, "Honda, Toyota Launch Efforts to Boost Sales in Thailand," *Bangkok Post*, November 7, 2001, www.bangkokpost.com; James B. Treece, "Toyota Corolla Altis Debuts for Thai Market," *Bangkok Post*, April 9, 2001, p. 23; Mack Chrysler,

"Manufacturing: Zafira Brings Thai Plant to Life," *Ward's Auto World*, July 2000, www.wardsauto.com; Evelyn Iritani, "Road Warriors," *Los Angeles Times*, July 9, 1995, pp. D1, D6.

2. Michael D. Johnson and Christopher P. Puto, "A Review of Consumer Judgment and Choice," in ed. Michael J. Houston, *Review of Marketing* (Chicago: American Marketing Association, 1987), pp. 236–292.
3. Itamar Simonson, Joel Huber, and John Payne, "The Relationship between Prior Brand Knowledge and Information Acquisition Order," *Journal of Consumer Research*, March 1988, pp. 566–578.
4. Eric J. Johnson and J. Edward Russo, "Product Familiarity and Learning New Information," *Journal of Consumer Research*, June 1984, pp. 528–541.
5. Eloise Coupey, Julie R. Irwin, and John W. Payne, "Product Category Familiarity and Preference Construction, *Journal of Consumer Research*, March 1998, pp. 459–468.
6. Daniel Kahneman and Amos Tversky, "On the Psychology of Prediction," *Psychology Review*, July 1973, pp. 251–275.
7. Joan Meyers-Levy and Alice M. Tybout, "Context Effects at Encoding and Judgment in Consumption Settings: The Role of Cognitive Resources," *Journal of Consumer Research*, June 1997, pp. 1–14.
8. Irwin Levin, "Associative Effects of Information Framing," *Bulletin of the Psychonomic Society*, March 1987, pp. 85–86.
9. Manjit S. Yadav, "How Buyers Evaluate Product Bundles: A Model of Anchoring and Adjustment," *Journal of Consumer Research*, September 1994, pp. 342–353.
10. Gita Venkataramani Johar, Kamel Jedidi, and Jacob Jacoby, "A Varying-Parameter Averaging Model of On-line Brand Evaluations," *Journal of Consumer Research*, September 1997, pp. 232–247.
11. John Carroll, "The Effect of Imagining an Event on Expectations for the Event," *Journal of Experimental Social Psychology*, January 1978, pp. 88–96.
12. Deborah J. MacInnis and Linda L. Price, "The Role of Imagery in Information Processing: Review and Extensions," *Journal of Consumer Research*, March 1987, pp. 473–491.
13. Baba Shiv and Joel Huber, "The Impact of Anticipating Satisfaction on Consumer Choice," *Journal of Consumer Research*, vol. 27, September 2000, pp. 202–216.
14. Calvin P. Duncan and Richard W. Olshavsky, "External Search: The Role of Consumer Beliefs," *Journal of Marketing Research*, February 1982, pp. 32–43.
15. Raghubir and Menon, "AIDS and Me, Never the Twain Shall Meet."
16. Meryl Paula Gardner, "Mood States and Consumer Behavior: A Critical Review," *Journal of Consumer Research*, December 1985, pp. 281–300.
17. Stijn M. J. Van Osselaer and Joseph W. Alba, "Consumer Learning and Brand Equity," *Journal of Consumer Research*, vol. 27, June 2000, pp. 1–16.
18. Evan Ramstad, "Digital-TV Ads Aim to Shuffle Leadership," *Wall Street Journal*, November 3, 1998, p. B16.
19. Paul M. Herr, "Priming Price: Prior Knowledge and Context Effects," *Journal of Consumer Research*, June 1989, pp. 67–75.
20. Sung-Tai Hong and Robert S. Wyer Jr., "Effects of Country-of-Origin and Product-Attribute Information: An Information Processing Perspective," *Journal of Consumer Research*, September 1989, pp. 175–187.
21. Wendy Bounds and Deborah Ball, "Italy Knits Support for Fashion Industry," *Wall Street Journal*, December 15, 1997, p. B8.
22. Craig S. Smith, "Chinese Government Struggles to Rejuvenate National Brands," *Wall Street Journal*, June 24, 1996, pp. B1, B6.
23. Timothy Douek, "China's Cosmetic Fever," February 2001, *Advanstar Communications*, www.findarticles.com/cf_dls/m0HLW/2_168/71016196/p1/article.jhtml.
24. James R. Bettman and Mita Sujan, "Effects of Framing on Evaluation of Comparable and Noncomparable Alternatives by Expert and Novice Consumers," *Journal of Consumer Research*, September 1987, pp. 141–151.
25. Ernest Beck, "Big Tobacco Uses Good Works to Woo Eastern Europe," *Wall Street Journal*, November 10, 1998, pp. B1, B8.
26. Scott Davis and Cathy Halligan, "Extending the Brand," *Target Marketing*, June 1, 2001, pp. 38–45.
27. Hans Baumgartner, "On the Utility of Consumers' Theories in Judgments of Covariation," *Journal of Consumer Research*, March 1995, pp. 634–643; James R. Bettman, Deborah Roedder John, and Carol A. Scott, "Covariation Assessment by Consumers," *Journal of Consumer Research*, December 1986, pp. 316–326; Susan M. Broniarczyk and Joseph W. Alba, "Theory versus Data in Prediction and Correlation Tasks," *Organizational Behavior and Human Decision Processes*, January 1994, pp. 117–139.
28. Durairaj Maheswaran, "Country of Origin as a Stereotype: Effects of Consumer Expertise and Attribute Strength on Product Evaluations," *Journal of Consumer Research*, September 1994, pp. 354–365.
29. Amos Tversky and Daniel Kahneman, "Extensional versus Intuitive Reasoning: The Conjunction Fallacy," *Psychological Review*, October 1983, pp. 293–315.
30. Bob Garfield, "Softly Lit or Blunt, 'Less Toxic' Cigarette Ads Hint at Health," *Advertising Age*, November 12, 2001, p. 58; Gordon Fairclough,

"Tobacco Titans Bid for 'Organic' Cigarette Maker," *Wall Street Journal*, December 10, 2001, pp. B1, B4; Suein Hwang, "Smokers May Mistake 'Clean' Cigarette for Safe," *Wall Street Journal*, September 30, 1995, pp. B1, B2.

31. Moon Ihlwan, "Hyundai Gets Hot," *BusinessWeek*, December 17, 2001, pp. 84–86; David Kiley, "Hyundai's Santa Fe SUV Beats Honda, Toyota," *USA Today*, June 19, 2001, www.usatoday.com/money/autos/2001-05-17-santa-fe.htm; "The Hyundai Syndrome," *Adweek's Marketing Week*, April 20, 1992, pp. 20–21.

32. F. May and R. Homans, "Evoked Set Size and the Level of Information Processing in Product Comprehension and Choice Criteria," in ed. William D. Perrault, *Advances in Consumer Research*, vol. 4 (Chicago: Association for Consumer Research, 1977), pp. 172–175.

33. Ravi Dhar, "Consumer Preference for a No-Choice Option," *Journal of Consumer Research*, September 1997, pp. 215–231.

34. John W. Payne, James R. Bettman, and Eric J. Johnson, "The Adaptive Decision-Maker," in ed. Robin M. Hogarth, *Insights in Decision Making: A Tribute to Hillel Einhorn* (Chicago: University of Chicago Press, 1990).

35. Mariele K. De Mooij and Warren Keegan, *Worldwide Advertising* (London: Prentice-Hall International, 1991).

36. Itamar Simonson, "Get Closer to Your Consumers by Understanding How They Make Choices," *California Management Review*, Summer 1993, pp. 68–84.

37. For a good review of multiattribute models, see William L. Wilkie and Edgar A. Pessemier, "Issues in Marketing's Use of Multiattribute Models," *Journal of Marketing Research*, November 1983, pp. 428–441; Blair H. Sheppard, Jon Hartwick, and Paul R. Warshaw, "The Theory of Reasoned Action: A Meta-analysis of Past Research with Recommendations for Modifications and Future Research," *Journal of Consumer Research*, December 1988, pp. 325–342.

38. Will Pinkston and Scott Miller, "DaimlerChrysler Clears Way for U.S. Debut of 'Smart,'" *Wall Street Journal*, August 20, 2001, pp. B1, B4.

39. Robert L. Simison, "Ford Aims to Resolve Brand Identity Crisis," *Wall Street Journal*, December 15, 1998, p. B6.

40. Timothy B. Heath, Gangseog Ryu, Subimal Chatterjee, Michael S. McCarthy, David L. Mothersbaugh, Sandra Milberg, and Gary J. Gaeth, "Asymmetric Competition in Choice and the Leveraging of Competitive Disadvantages," *Journal of Consumer Research*, vol. 27, December 2000, pp. 291–308.

41. Rohini Ahluwalia, Robert E. Burnkrant, and H. Rao Unnava, "Consumer Response to Negative Publicity: The Moderating Role of Commitment," *Journal of Marketing Research*, vol. 37, May 2000, pp. 203–214.

42. Valerie Reitman, "Strong Sales Rev Up Ad Spending among Car Companies in Japan," *Wall Street Journal*, March 3, 1996, p. B3.

43. Chad Terhune, "Home Depot's Home Improvement," *Wall Street Journal*, March 8, 2001, pp. B1, B4.

44. Amos Tversky, "Intransitivity of Preferences," *Psychological Review*, January 1969, pp. 31–48.

45. Pinkston and Miller, "DaimlerChrysler Clears Way for U.S. Debut of 'Smart.'"

46. Donna Bryson, "Traditional Fare Goes Fast-Food in S. Africa," *Austin American Statesman*, June 4, 1994, p. A16.

47. Peter Wright, "Consumer Choice Strategies: Simplifying vs. Optimizing," *Journal of Marketing Research*, February 1975, pp. 60–67; Noreen Klein and Stewart W. Bither, "An Investigation of Utility-Directed Cutoff Selection," *Journal of Consumer Research*, September 1987, pp. 240–256.

48. Christina Binkley, "Gamblers Prefer One-Armed Bandits That Have Arms," *Wall Street Journal*, February 3, 1997, pp. B1, B8.

49. David Grether and Louis Wilde, "An Analysis of Conjunctive Choice: Theory and Experiments," *Journal of Consumer Research*, March 1984, pp. 373–385.

50. Evan Perez, "Cruising on Credit: Carnival Introduces Vacation Financing to Get More Aboard," *Wall Street Journal*, April 12, 2001, p. B12.

51. Gautam Naik, "Prepaid Plans Open up Cellular-Phone Market," *Wall Street Journal*, September 16, 1998, pp. B1, B4.

52. Gregory L. White, "GM's New Baby Hummer Shares Its Toys with Chevy," *Wall Street Journal*, April 10, 2001, pp. B1, B4.

53. Simonson, "Get Closer to Your Consumers by Understanding How They Make Choices."

54. Itamar Simonson, Ziv Carmon, and Suzanne O'Curry, "Experimental Evidence on the Negative Effect of Product Features and Sales Promotions on Brand Choice," Winter 1994, *Marketing Science*, pp. 23–40.

55. Amos Tversky, "Elimination by Aspects: A Theory of Choice," *Psychological Review*, July 1972, pp. 281–299.

56. Michelle Krebs, "Speed—and Price Tags—Getting Steeper," *Crain's Detroit Business*, October 29, 2001, p. E4.

57. Denis A. Lussier and Richard W. Olshavsky, "Task Complexity and Contingent Processing in Brand Choice," *Journal of Consumer Research*, September 1979, pp. 154–165; Eric J. Johnson and Robert J. Meyer, "Compensatory Choice Models of Noncompensatory Processes: The Effect of Varying Context," *Journal of Consumer Research*, June 1984, pp. 542–551.

58. James R. Bettman, Mary Frances Luce, and John W. Payne, "Constructive Consumer Choice Processes,"

Journal of Consumer Research, December 1998, pp.187–217.

59. Steve Hoeffler and Dan Ariely, "Constructing Stable Preferences: A Look into Dimensions of Experience and Their Impact on Preference Stability," *Journal of Consumer Psychology*, vol. 8, no. 2, 1999, pp. 113–139.

60. Payne, Bettman, and Johnson, "The Adaptive Decision-Maker."

61. Joseph Pereira, "Nike's Rivals Hope Buyers Want Bargains," *Wall Street Journal*, June 2, 1997, pp. B1, B3.

62. Sid Price, "Men Fill Waiting Lists for MC Lady Brand Golf Balls," *St. Louis Business Journal*, September 7, 2001, p. 36.

63. Seymour Epstein, "Integration of the Cognitive and the Psychodynamic Unconscious," *American Psychologist*, August 1994, pp. 709–724.

64. Stephen J. Hoch and George F. Lowenstein, "Time-Inconsistent Preferences and Consumer Self-Control," *Journal of Consumer Research*, March 1991, pp. 492–507.

65. Yumiko Ono, "Tiffany Glitters, Even in Gloomy Japan," *Wall Street Journal*, July 21, 1998, pp. B1, B8.

66. Michel Tuan Pham, "Representativeness, Relevance, and the Use of Feelings in Decision Making," *Journal of Consumer Research*, September 1998, pp. 144–159.

67. Epstein, "Integration of the Cognitive and the Psychodynamic Unconscious."

68. Pham, "Representativeness, Relevance, and the Use of Feelings in Decision Making"; Morris B. Holbrook and Elizabeth C. Hirschman, "The Experiential Aspects of Consumption: Consumer Fantasies, Feelings, and Fun," *Journal of Consumer Research*, September 1982, pp. 132–140.

69. Kathleen T. Lacher and Richard W. Mizerski, "An Exploratory Study of the Responses and Relationships Involved in the Evaluation of, and in the Intention to Purchase New Rock Music," *Journal of Consumer Research*, September 1994, pp. 366–380.

70. Bill Spindle, "Cowboys and Samurai: The Japanizing of Universal," *Wall Street Journal*, March 22, 2001, pp. B1, B6.

71. Morris B. Holbrook and Meryl P. Gardner, "An Approach to Investigating the Emotional Determinants of Consumption Durations: Why Do People Consume What They Consume for as Long as They Consume It?" *Journal of Consumer Psychology*, vol. 2, no. 2, 1993, pp. 123–142.

72. Mary Frances Luce, "Choosing to Avoid: Coping with Negatively Emotion-Laden Consumer Decisions," *Journal of Consumer Research*, March 1998, pp. 409–433.

73. Mary Frances Luce, John W. Payne, and James R. Bettman, "Emotional Trade-off Difficulty and Choice," *Journal of Marketing Research*, vol. 36, May 1999, pp. 143–159.

74. Ellen C. Garbarino and Julie A. Edell, "Cognitive Effort, Affect, and Choice," *Journal of Consumer Research*, September 1997, pp. 147–158.

75. Michael Tsiros and Vikas Mittal, "Regret: A Model of Its Antecedents and Consequences in Consumer Decision Making," *Journal of Consumer Research*, vol. 26, March 2000, pp. 401–417.

76. Ann L. McGill and Punam Anand Keller, "Differences in the Relative Influence of Product Attributes under Alternative Processing Conditions: Attribute Importance versus Ease of Imaginability," *Journal of Consumer Psychology*, vol. 3, no. 1, 1994, pp. 29–50; MacInnis and Price, "The Role of Imagery in Information Processing."

77. Darren W. Dahl, Amitava Chattopadhyay, and Gerald J. Gorn, "The Use of Visual Mental Imagery in New Product Design," *Journal of Marketing Research*, vol. 36, February 1999, pp. 18–28.

78. Joel B. Cohen, "The Role of Affect in Categorization: Toward a Reconceptualization of the Concept of Attitude," in ed. Andrew A. Mitchell, *Advances in Consumer Research*, vol. 9 (Ann Arbor, Mich.: Association for Consumer Research, 1982), pp. 94–100; C. Whan Park and Banwari Mittal, "A Theory of Involvement in Consumer Behavior: Problems and Issues," in ed. Jagdish N. Sheth, *Research in Consumer Behavior* (Greenwich, Conn.: JAI Press, 1985), pp. 201–231.

79. Nanette Byrnes, "A Showstopper on Broadway," *BusinessWeek*, December 24, 2001, p. 54.

80. Christopher Boone, "A League of Our Own," *Navigator*, August–September 2001, pp. 10–15.

81. Deborah Lohse, "Insurers Facing Rivals, Try to Build Brands," *Wall Street Journal*, October 15, 1998, p. B12.

82. Michael D. Johnson, "Consumer Choice Strategies for Comparing Noncomparable Alternatives," *Journal of Consumer Research*, December 1984, pp. 741–753; Michael D. Johnson, "Comparability and Hierarchical Processing in Multialternative Choice," *Journal of Consumer Research*, December 1988, pp. 303–314.

83. Kim P. Corfman, "Comparability and Comparison Levels Used in Choices among Consumer Products," *Journal of Marketing Research*, August 1991, pp. 368–374.

84. C. Whan Park and Daniel Smith, "Product-Level Choice: A Top-Down or Bottom-Up Process?" *Journal of Consumer Research*, December 1989, pp. 289–299.

85. Girish N. Punj and David W. Stewart, "An Interaction Framework of Consumer Decision Making," *Journal of Consumer Research*, September 1983, pp. 181–196.

86. Payne, Bettman, and Johnson, "The Adaptive Decision-Maker."

87. Dennis H. Gensch and Rajshelhar G. Javalgi, "The Influence of Involvement on Disaggregate Attribute Choice Models," *Journal of Consumer Research*, June 1987, pp. 71–82.

88. Eric A. Greenleaf and Donald R. Lehmann, "Reasons for Substantial Delay in Consumer Decision Making," *Journal of Consumer Research*, September 1995, pp. 186–199.

89. Elaine Sherman and Ruth Belk Smith, "Mood States of Shoppers and Store Image: Promising Interactions and Possible Behavioral Effects," in eds. Paul Anderson and Melanie Wallendorf, *Advances in Consumer Research*, vol. 14 (Provo, Utah: Association for Consumer Research, 1987), pp. 251–254.

90. Gerald J. Gorn, Marvin E. Goldberg, and Kunal Basu, "Mood, Awareness, and Product Evaluation," *Journal of Consumer Psychology*, vol. 2, no. 3, 1993, pp. 237–256.

91. Patricia M. West, Christina L. Brown, and Stephen J. Hoch, "Consumption Vocabulary and Preference Formation," *Journal of Consumer Research*, September 1996, pp. 120–135.

92. Johnson and Russo, "Product Familiarity and Learning New Information"; James R. Bettman and C. Whan Park, "Effects of Prior Knowledge and Experience and Phase of the Choice Process on Consumer Decision Processes, A Protocol Analysis," *Journal of Consumer Research*, December 1980, pp. 234–248.

93. Jennifer L. Aaker and Jaideep Sengupta, "Additivity versus Attenuation: The Role of Culture in the Resolution of Information Incongruity," *Journal of Consumer Psychology*, vol. 9, no. 2, 2000, pp. 67–82.

94. Payne, Bettman, and Johnson, "The Adaptive Decision-Maker."

95. C. Whan Park, Easwar S. Iyer, and Daniel C. Smith, "The Effects of Situational Factors on In-Store Grocery Shopping Behavior: The Role of Store Environment and Time Available for Shopping," *Journal of Consumer Research*, March 1989, pp. 422–433.

96. Greenleaf and Lehmann, "Reasons for Substantial Delay in Consumer Decision Making."

97. Ravi Dhar and Stephen M. Nowlis, "The Effect of Time Pressure on Consumer Choice Deferral," *Journal of Consumer Research*, vol. 25, March 1999, pp. 369–384.

98. Michelle M. Bergadaa, "The Role of Time in the Action of the Consumer," *Journal of Consumer Research*, December 1990, pp. 289–302.

99. Emily Nelson, "Too Many Choices Can Cause Frustration among Consumers," *Asian Wall Street Journal*, April 24, 2001, p. N4.

100. Lussier and Olshavsky, "Task Complexity and Contingent Processing in Brand Choice"; Johnson and Meyer, "Compensatory Choice Models of Noncompensatory Processes."

101. Christina L. Brown and Gregory S. Carpenter, "Why Is the Trivial Important? A Reasons-Based Account for the Effects of Trivial Attributes on Choice," *Journal of Consumer Research*, vol. 26, March 2000, pp. 372+.

102. Itamar Simonson and Amos Tversky, "Choice in Context: Tradeoff Contrast and Extremeness Aversion," *Journal of Marketing Research*, August 1992, pp. 281–295.

103. Joel Huber, John W. Payne, and Christopher Puto, "Adding Asymmetrically Dominated Alternatives: Violations of Regularity and the Similarity Hypothesis," *Journal of Consumer Research*, June 1982, pp. 90–98; Srinivasan Ratneshwar, Allan D. Shocker, and David W. Stewart, "Toward Understanding the Attraction Effect: The Implications of Product Stimulus Meaningfulness and Familiarity," *Journal of Consumer Research*, March 1987, pp. 520–533; Sanjay Mishra, U. N. Umesh, and Donald E. Stem, "Antecedents of the Attraction Effect: An Information Processing Approach," *Journal of Marketing Research*, August 1993, pp. 331–349; Yigang Pan, Sue O'Curry, and Robert Pitts, "The Attraction Effect and Political Choice in Two Elections," *Journal of Consumer Psychology*, vol. 4, no. 1, 1995, pp. 85–101.

104. Sankar Sen, "Knowledge, Information Mode, and the Attraction Effect," *Journal of Consumer Research*, June 1998, 64–77.

105. Timothy B. Heath and Subimal Chatterjee, "Asymmetric Decoy Effects on Lower-Quality versus Higher-Quality Brands: Meta-analytic and Experimental Evidence," *Journal of Consumer Research*, December 1995, pp. 268–84.

106. Mukesh Bhargava, John Kim, and Rajendra K. Srivastava, "Explaining Context Effects on Choice Using a Model of Comparative Judgment," *Journal of Consumer Psychology*, vol. 9, no. 3, 2000, pp. 167–177; Noreen M. Klein and Manjit S. Yadav, "Context Effects on Effort and Accuracy: An Enquiry into Adaptive Decision Making," *Journal of Consumer Research*, March 1989, pp. 411–421; Payne, Bettman, and Johnson, "The Adaptive Decision-Maker."

107. Simonson, "Get Closer to Your Consumers by Understanding How They Make Choices."

108. Ibid.

109. Simonson and Tversky, "Choice in Context: Tradeoff Contrast and Extremeness Aversion."

110. Simonson, "Get Closer to Your Consumers by Understanding How They Make Choices."

111. Jacob Jacoby, "Perspectives on Information Overload," *Journal of Consumer Research*, March 1984, pp. 569–573; Kevin Lane Keller and Richard Staelin, "Effects of Quality and Quantity of Information on Decision Effectiveness," *Journal of Consumer Research*, September 1987, pp. 200–213.

112. Ger, "Problems of Marketization in Romania and Turkey."in eds. Clifford Schultz, Russell Belk, and Guliz Ger, *Consumption in Marketizing Economies* (Greenwich, Conn.: JAI Press, 1995).

113. Nelson, "Too Many Choices Can Cause Frustration among Consumers."

114. Sabrina Tavernise, "In Russia, Capitalism of a Certain Size," *New York Times*, July 29, 2001, sec. 3, p. 6; Guliz Ger, Russell Belk, and Dana-Nicoleta Lascu, "The Development of Consumer Desire in Marketing and Developing Economies: The Cases of Romania and Turkey," in eds. Leigh McAlister and Michael L. Rothschild, *Advances in Consumer Research*, vol. 20 (Provo, Utah: Association for Consumer Research, 1993), pp. 102–107.

115. Keller and Staelin, "Effects of Quality and Quantity of Information on Decision Effectiveness."

116. Ravi Dhar and Steven J. Sherman, "The Effect of Common and Unique Features in Consumer Choice," *Journal of Consumer Research*, December 1996, pp. 193–203.

117. Ran Kivetz and Itamar Simonson, "The Effects of Incomplete Information on Consumer Choice," *Journal of Marketing Research*, vol. 37, November 2000, pp. 427–448.

118. A. V. Muthukrishnan, "Decision Ambiguity and Incumbent Brand Advantage," *Journal of Consumer Research*, June 1995, pp. 98–109.

119. Madhubalan Viswanathan and Sunder Narayanan, "Comparative Judgments of Numerical and Verbal Attribute Labels," *Journal of Consumer Psychology*, vol. 3, no. 1, 1994, pp. 79–100.

120. Itamar Simonson, Stephen Nowlis, and Katherine Lemon, "The Effect of Local Consideration Sets on Global Choice between Lower Price and Higher Quality," *Marketing Science*, Fall 1993.

121. Johnson and Russo, "Product Familiarity and Learning New Information"; J. Edward Russo, "The Value of Unit Price Information," *Journal of Marketing Research*, May 1977, pp. 193–201.

122. Rashmi Adaval and Robert S. Wyer Jr., "The Role of Narratives in Consumer Information Processing," *Journal of Consumer Psychology*, vol. 7, no. 3, 1998, pp. 207–245.

123. Itamar Simonson and Russell S. Winer, "The Influence of Purchase Quantity and Display Format on Consumer Preference for Variety," *Journal of Consumer Research*, June 1992, pp. 133–138.

124. Eloise Coupey, "Restructuring: Constructive Processing of Information Displays in Consumer Choice," *Journal of Consumer Research*, June 1994, pp. 83–99.

125. Barbara E. Kahn and Jonathan Baron, "An Exploratory Study of Choice Rules Favored for High-Stakes Decisions," *Journal of Consumer Psychology*, vol. 4, no. 4, 1995, pp. 305–328.

126. John Liechty, Venkatram Ramaswamy, and Steven H. Cohen, "Choice Menus for Mass Customization: An Experimental Approach for Analyzing Customer Demand with an Application to a Web-Based Information Service," *Journal of Marketing Research*, vol. 38, May 2001, pp. 183–196.

127. Daniel Kahneman and Amos Tversky, "Prospect Theory: An Analysis of Decisions under Risk," *Econometrica*, March 1979, pp. 263–291.

128. William B. Diamond and Abhijit Sanyal, "The Effect of Framing on the Choice of Supermarket Coupons," in eds. Marvin E. Goldberg and Gerald Gorn, *Advances in Consumer Research*, vol. 17 (Provo, Utah: Association for Consumer Research, 1990), pp. 488–493.

129. Christopher P. Puto, "The Framing of Buying Decisions," *Journal of Consumer Research*, December 1987, pp. 301–316.

130. Rajendra K. Srivastava, Allan D. Shocker, and George S. Day, "An Exploratory Study of the Influences of Usage Situations on Perceptions of Product Markets," in ed. H. Keith Hunt, *Advances in Consumer Research*, vol. 5 (Ann Arbor, Mich.: Association for Consumer Research, 1978), pp. 32–38.

131. Kenneth E. Miller and James L. Ginter, "An Investigation of Situational Variation in Brand Choice Behavior and Attitude," *Journal of Marketing Research*, February 1979, pp. 111–123.

132. Kevin Goldman, "Computer Companies Try TV Ads' Mass Appeal," *Wall Street Journal*, September 20, 1994, pp. B1, B8.

133. Joseph Pereira, "Can Air Pockets Help Reebok Catch Nike in High Performance Sneaker Marathon?" *Wall Street Journal*, March 27, 1998, pp. B1, B8.

134. Tim Bajarin, "Always the Innovator," *ABCNews.com*, October 18, 2001, **http://more.abcnews.go.com/sections/business/dailynews/silicon_insights_bajarin_011018.html**.

135. Sally D. Goll, "Odds and Ends," *Wall Street Journal*, May 27, 1994, p. B1.

136. Levin, "Associative Effects of Information Framing."

137. Christopher P. Puto, W. E. Patton, and Ronald H. King, "Risk Handling Strategies in Industrial Vendor Selection Decisions," *Journal of Marketing*, January 1987, pp. 89–98.

138. John T. Gourville, "Pennies-a-Day: The Effect of Temporal Reframing on Transaction Evaluation," *Journal of Consumer Research*, March 1998, pp. 395–408.

139. Perez, "Cruising on Credit."

140. Yaacov Schul and Yoav Ganzach, "The Effects of Accessibility of Standards and Decision Framing on Product Evaluations," *Journal of Consumer Psychology*, vol. 4, no. 1, 1995, pp. 61–83.

141. Baba Shiv, Julie A. Edell, and John W. Payne, "Factors Affecting the Impact of Negatively and Positively Framed Ad Messages," *Journal of Consumer Research*, December 1997, pp. 285–294.

142. Yong Zhang and Richard Buda, "Moderating Effects of Need for Cognition on Responses to Positively versus Negatively Framed Advertising Messages," *Journal of Advertising*, vol. 28, no. 2, Summer 1999, pp. 1–15.

143. C. Whan Park, Sung Youl Jun, and Deborah J. MacInnis, "Choosing What I Want versus Rejecting What I Do Not Want: An Application of Decision Framing to Product Option Choice Decisions," *Journal of Marketing Research*, vol. 37, May 2000, pp. 187–202.

144. Bettman and Sujan, "Effects of Framing on Evaluation of Comparable and Noncomparable Alternatives by Expert and Novice Consumers."

145. Cynthia Fraser, Robert E. Hite, and Paul L. Sauer, "Increasing Contributions in Solicitation Campaigns: The Use of Large and Small Anchor-Points," *Journal of Consumer Research*, September 1988, pp. 284–287.

146. Donald P. Green and Irene V. Blair, "Framing and Price Elasticity of Private and Public Goods," *Journal of Consumer Psychology*, vol. 4, no. 1, 1995, pp. 1–32.

147. Dan Ariely and Jonathan Levav, "Sequential Choice in Group Settings: Taking the Road Less Traveled and Less Enjoyed," *Journal of Consumer Research*, vol. 27, December 2000, pp. 279–290.

148. Suein L. Hwang, "How Impotence Became a Weapon Against Smoking," *Wall Street Journal*, November 9, 1998, pp. B1, B4.

Chapter 11

1. Magz Osborne, "'Raider' Leads Charge in Vietnam," *Variety*, August 27, 2001, p. 16; Samantha Marshall, "Soap Smugglers Cleaning Up in Vietnam," *Wall Street Journal*, April 1, 1998, pp. B1, B15.

2. Rohit Deshpande, Wayne D. Hoyer, and Scott Jeffries, "Low Involvement Decision Processes: The Importance of Choice Tactics," in eds. R. F. Bush and S. D. Hunt, *Marketing Theory: Philosophy of Science Perspectives* (Chicago: American Marketing Association, 1982), pp. 155–158; Wayne D. Hoyer, "An Examination of Consumer Decision Making for a Common Repeat Purchase Product," *Journal of Consumer Research*, December 1984, pp. 822–829.

3. "Advertising Surge in Vietnam," *Business Asia*, March 31, 2000, p. 19.

4. Alan Newell and Herbert A. Simon, *Human Problem Solving* (Englewood Cliffs, N. J.: Prentice-Hall, 1972); Daniel Kahneman and Amos Tversky, "On the Psychology of Prediction," *Psychological Review*, July 1973, pp. 237–251.

5. Daniel Kahneman and Amos Tversky, "Subjective Probability: A Judgment of Representativeness," *Cognitive Psychology*, July 1972, pp. 430–454.

6. Sally Beatty, "P&G's Comparisons Defend Toothpaste," *Wall Street Journal*, June 29, 1998, p. B4.

7. Marshall, "Soap Smugglers Cleaning Up in Vietnam."

8. Kiley, "Hyundai's Santa Fe SUV Beats Honda, Toyota"; "The Hyundai Syndrome," *Adweek's Marketing Week*, April 20, 1992, pp. 20–21.

9. Valerie S. Folkes, "The Availability Heuristic and Perceived Risk," *Journal of Consumer Research*, June 1988, pp. 13–23; Johnson and Puto, "A Review of Consumer Judgment and Choice," in ed. Michael J. Houston, *Review of Marketing* (Chicago: American Marketing Association, 1987), pp. 236–292.

10. Peter R. Dickson, "The Impact of Enriching Case and Statistical Information on Consumer Judgments," *Journal of Consumer Research*, March 1982, pp. 398–408.

11. Chezy Ofir and John G. Lynch Jr., "Context Effects on Judgment under Uncertainty," *Journal of Consumer Research*, September 1984, pp. 668–679.

12. Amos Tversky and Daniel Kahneman, "Belief in the Law of Small Numbers," *Psychological Bulletin*, August 1971, pp. 105–110; Amos Tversky and Daniel Kahneman, "Judgment under Uncertainty: Heuristics and Biases," *Science*, September 1974, pp. 1124–1131.

13. Marc Weingarten, "Get Your Buzz to Breed Like Hobbits," *Business 2.0*, January 2002, pp. 96–97.

14. Vanessa O'Connell, "Bumble Bee Tuna Ads Claim a 2-to-1 Edge," *Wall Street Journal*, April 29, 1998, p. B2.

15. Hanjoon Lee, Acito Acito, and Ralph Day, "Evaluation and Use of Marketing Research by Decision Makers: A Behavioral Simulation," *Journal of Marketing Research*, May 1987, pp. 187–196.

16. Hoyer, "An Examination of Consumer Decision Making for a Common Repeat Purchase Product."

17. Herbert E. Krugman, "The Impact of Television Advertising: Learning without Involvement," *Public Opinion Quarterly*, Fall 1965, pp. 349–356.

18. Michael L. Ray, *Marketing Communications and the Hierarchy of Effects* (Cambridge, Mass.: Marketing Science Institute, 1973).

19. Robert B. Zajonc, "Feeling and Thinking: Preferences Need No Inferences," *American Psychologist*, February 1980, pp. 151–175; Robert B. Zajonc and Hazel B. Markus, "Affective and Cognitive Factors in Preferences," *Journal of Consumer Research*, September 1982, pp. 122–131.

20. Hoyer, "An Examination of Consumer Decision Making for a Common Repeat Purchase Product."

21. Cathy J. Cobb and Wayne D. Hoyer, "Direct Observation of Search Behavior in the Purchase of Two Nondurable Products," *Psychology and Marketing*, Fall 1983, pp. 161–179.

22. Alain d'Astous, Idriss Bensouda, and Jean Guindon, "A Reexamination of Consumer Decision Making for a Repeat Purchase Product: Variations in Product Importance and Purchase Frequency," in ed. Thomas K. Srull, *Advances in Consumer Research*, vol. 16 (Provo, Utah: Association for Consumer Research, 1989), pp. 433–438.

23. Richard W. Olshavsky and Donald H. Granbois, "Consumer Decision Making: Fact or Fiction?" *Journal of Consumer Research*, September 1979, pp. 93–100.

24. William E. Baker and Richard J. Lutz, "An Empirical Test of an Updated Relevance-Accessibility Model of Advertising Effectiveness," *Journal of Advertising*, vol. 29, no. 1, Spring 2000, pp. 1–13.

25. Deshpande, Hoyer, and Jeffries, "Low Involvement Decision Processes."

26. Hoyer, "An Examination of Consumer Decision Making for a Common Repeat Purchase Product."

27. Siew Meng Leong, "Consumer Decision Making for Common, Repeat-Purchase Products: A Dual Replication," *Journal of Consumer Psychology*, vol. 2, no. 2, 1993, pp. 193–208.

28. Dana L. Alden, Wayne D. Hoyer, and Guntalee Wechasara, "Choice Strategies and Involvement, A Cross-Cultural Analysis," in ed. Thomas K. Srull, *Advances in Consumer Research*, vol. 16 (Provo, Utah: Association for Consumer Research, 1989), pp. 119–126.

29. Walter A. Nord and J. Paul Peter, "A Behavior Modification Perspective on Marketing," *Journal of Marketing*, Spring 1980, pp. 36–47; Michael Rothschild and William C. Gaidis, "Behavioral Learning Theory: Its Relevance to Marketing and Promotions," *Journal of Marketing*, Spring 1981, pp. 70–78.

30. Holly Heline, "Brand Loyalty Isn't Dead—But You're Not off the Hook," *Brandweek*, June 7, 1994, p. 14.

31. Robert E. Smith and William R. Swinyard, "Information Response Models: An Integrated Approach," *Journal of Marketing*, Winter 1982, pp. 81–93; Robert E. Smith and William R. Swinyard, "Attitude-Behavior Consistency: The Impact of Product Trial vs. Advertising," *Journal of Marketing Research*, August 1983, pp. 257–267.

32. Deanna S. Kempf and Robert E. Smith, "Consumer Processing of Product Trial and the Influence of Prior Advertising: A Structural Modeling Approach," *Journal of Marketing Research*, August 1998, pp. 325–338.

33. Michael L. Rothschild and Michael J. Houston, "The Consumer Involvement Matrix: Some Preliminary Findings," in eds. Barnett A. Greenberg and Danny N. Bellenger, *Proceedings of the American Marketing Association Educators' Conference*, Series no. 41, 1977, pp. 95–98.

34. Wayne D. Hoyer, "Variations in Choice Strategies across Decision Contexts: An Examination of Contingent Factors," in ed. Richard J. Lutz, *Advances in Consumer Research*, vol. 13 (Provo, Utah: Association for Consumer Research, 1986), pp. 32–36.

35. Wayne D. Hoyer and Cathy J. Cobb-Walgren, "Consumer Decision Making across Product Categories: The Influence of Task Environment," *Psychology and Marketing*, Spring 1988, pp. 45–69.

36. Leong, "Consumer Decision Making for Common, Repeat-Purchase Products."

37. Yumiko Ono, "Campbell's New Ads Heat Up Soup Sales," *Wall Street Journal*, March 17, 1994, p. B5.

38. Paulo Prada, "European Inns Take the Hilton Route," *Wall Street Journal*, April 23, 2001, pp. B1, B6.

39. Robert E. Smith, "Integrating Information from Advertising and Trial: Processes and Effects on Consumer Response to Product Information," *Journal of Marketing Research*, May 1993, pp. 204–219.

40. Betsy McKay, "Sports Drinks Refresh Rivalry for Coke, Pepsi," *Wall Street Journal*, May 8, 2001, pp. B1, B4.

41. Alison Paddock, "Craving Convenience. . . But at What Cost?" *Grocery Headquarters*, November 2001, pp. 41+.

42. Norihiko Shirouzu, "Snapple in Japan: How a Splash Dried Up," *Wall Street Journal*, April 15, 1996, pp. B1, B3.

43. Priya Raghubir and Kim Corfman, "When Do Price Promotions Affect Pretrial Brand Evaluations?" *Journal of Marketing Research*, vol. 36, May 1999, pp. 211–222.

44. Jacob Jacoby and David B. Kyner, "Brand Loyalty vs. Repeat Purchasing Behavior," *Journal of Marketing Research*, February 1973, pp. 1–9.

45. Ted Roselius, "Consumer Rankings of Risk Reduction Methods," *Journal of Marketing*, January 1971, pp. 56–61.

46. P. B. Seetharaman, Andrew Ainslie, and Pradeep K. Chintagunta, "Investigating Household State Dependence Effects across Categories," *Journal of Marketing Research*, vol. 36, November 1999, pp. 488–500.

47. Rothschild and Gaidis, "Behavioral Learning Theory."

48. Ernest Beck and Rekha Balu, "Europe is Deaf to Snap! Crackle! Pop!" *Wall Street Journal*, June 22, 1998, pp. B1, B8.

49. Raju Narisetti, "P&G Uses Packaging Savvy on Rx Drug," *Wall Street Journal*, January 30, 1997, pp. B1, B11.

50. Jack Neff, "Coupons Get Clipped," *Advertising Age*, November 5, 2001, pp. 1, 47.

51. Geoffrey A. Fowler, "Towels, Soap, Sponges and Mops, Look Out: Here Come the Wipes," *Wall Street Journal*, August 31, 2001, p. B1; Paddock, "Craving Convenience."

52. Ernest Beck, "New 3-D Tea Bag Rattles Cups in U.K.," *Wall Street Journal*, March 24, 1997, pp. B1, B2.

53. Ronald Curhan, "The Relationship of Shelf Space to Unit Sales: A Review," Working paper, Marketing Science Institute, 1972.

54. Gary F. McKinnon, J. Patrick Kelly, and E. Doyle Robinson, "Sales Effects of Point-of-Purchase In-Store Signing," *Journal of Retailing*, Summer 1981, pp. 49–63.

55. Kathleen Deveny, "Displays Pay Off for Grocery Marketers," *Wall Street Journal*, October 15, 1992, pp. B1, B5.

56. "Study Claims Effectiveness of Point-of-Purchase," *Advertising Age*, July 24, 2001, **www.adage.com**.

57. "Brand Loyalty in the Food Industry," *The Food Institute Report*, November 5, 2001, p. 3.

58. Norihiko Shirouzu, "For Coca-Cola in Japan, Things Go Better with Milk," *Wall Street Journal*, January 20, 1997, pp. B1, B2.

59. George S. Day, "A Two-Dimensional Concept of Brand Loyalty," *Journal of Advertising Research*, August–September 1969, pp. 29–36; Jacoby and Kyner, "Brand Loyalty vs. Repeat Purchasing Behavior"; Jacob Jacoby and Robert W. Chestnut, *Brand Loyalty: Measurement and Management* (New York: Wiley, 1978).

60. Jacob Jacoby, "A Model of Multi-Brand Loyalty," *Journal of Advertising Research*, June–July 1971, p. 26.

61. Ronald E. Frank, William F. Massy, and Thomas L. Lodahl, "Purchasing Behavior and Personal Attributes," *Journal of Advertising Research*, December 1969–January 1970, pp. 15–24.

62. R. M. Cunningham, "Brand Loyalty—What, Where, How Much," *Harvard Business Review*, January–February 1956, pp. 116–128; "Customer Loyalty to Store and Brand," *Harvard Business Review*, November–December 1961, pp. 127–137.

63. Day, "A Two-Dimensional Concept of Brand Loyalty."

64. Janice Rosenberg, "Brand Loyalty Begins Early; Savvy Marketers 'Surround' Kids To Build Connection," *Advertising Age*, February 12, 2001, p. S2.

65. Marnik G. Dekimpe, Martin Mellens, Jan-Benedict E.M. Steenkamp, and Piet Vanden Abeele, "Erosion and Variability in Brand Loyalty," Marketing Science Institute Report No. 96–114, August 1996, pp. 1–25.

66. "Face Value: Bringing Home the Bacon," *The Economist*, December 1, 2001, p. 63.

67. Rifka Rosenwein, "Chocolate 2.0," *Inc. Technology*, September 2001, pp. 190–193.

68. Norihiko Shirouzu, "Low Smoke Cigarette Catches Fire in Japan," *Wall Street Journal*, September 8, 1997, pp. B1.

69. Heline, "Brand Loyalty Isn't Dead."

70. Emily Nelson, "Bottom Line: Diaper Sales Sagging, P&G Thinks Young to Reposition Pampers," *Wall Street Journal*, December 27, 2001, pp. A1, A2.

71. Betsy Spethmann, "Betting on Loyalty Cards," *Promo*, April 1, 2001, p. 90.

72. Bruce Crumley, "Multipoints Adds Up for Quick Burger," *Advertising Age*, November 29, 1993, p. 14.

73. Elizabeth Cohen, "Energy Drinks Pack a Punch, but Is It Too Much?" *CNN.com*, May 29, 2001, **www.cnn.com/2001/HEALTH/diet.fitness/05/29/energy.drinks.02**.

74. Laurie Petersen, "The Strategic Shopper,"*Adweek's Marketing Week*, March 30, 1992, pp. 18–20.

75. Peter D. Dickson and Alan G. Sawyer, "Methods to Research Shoppers' Knowledge of Supermarket Prices," in ed. Richard J. Lutz, *Advances in Consumer Research*, vol. 12 (Provo, Utah: Association for Consumer Research, 1986), pp. 584–587.

76. Chris Janiszewski and Donald R. Lichtenstein, "A Range Theory Account of Price Perception," *Journal of Consumer Research*, vol. 25, March 1999, pp. 353–368; Kent B. Monroe and Susan M. Petroshius, "Buyers' Perception of Price: An Update of the Evidence," in eds. Harold H. Kassarjian and Thomas S. Robertson, *Perspectives in Consumer Behavior*, 3rd ed. (Dallas: Scott-Foresman, 1981), pp. 43–55.

77. Fowler, "Towels, Soap, Sponges and Mops, Look Out: Here Come the Wipes."

78. Mark Stiving and Russell S. Winer, "An Empirical Analysis of Price Endings with Scanner Data," *Journal of Consumer Research*, June 1997, pp. 57–76; Zarrel V. Lambert, "Perceived Prices as Related to Odd and Even Price Endings," *Journal of Retailing*, Fall 1975, pp. 13–22.

79. Kent B. Monroe, "The Influence of Price Differences and Brand Familiarity on Brand Preferences," *Journal of Consumer Research*, June 1976, pp. 42–49.

80. Joseph W. Alba, Carl F. Mela, Terence A. Shimp, and Joel E. Urbany, "The Effect of Discount Frequency and Depth on Consumer Price Judgments," *Journal of Consumer Research*, vol. 26, September 1999, pp. 99–114.

81. J. Jeffrey Inman, Anil C. Peter, and Priya Raghubir, "Framing the Deal: The Role of Restrictions in Accentuating Deal Value," *Journal of Consumer Research*, June 1997, pp. 68–79.

82. Dhruv Grewal, Howard Marmorstein, and Arun Sharma, "Communicating Price Information through Semantic Cues: The Moderating Effects of Situation and Discount Size," *Journal of Consumer Research*, September 1996, pp. 148–155.

83. Richard Gibson, "McDonald's 'Campaign 55' Promotion to Be Clarified and Advertised More," *Wall Street Journal*, May 20, 1997, p. B14.

84. *Supermarket Shoppers in a Period of Economic Uncertainty* (New York: Yankelovich, Skelly, & White, 1982), p. 53; Robert Blattberg, Thomas Buesing, Peter Peacock, and Subrata K. Sen, "Who Is the Deal Prone Consumer?" in ed. H. Keith Hunt, *Advances in Consumer Research*, vol. 5 (Ann Arbor, Mich.: Association for Consumer Research, 1978), pp. 57–62.

85. Donald R. Lichtenstein, Richard G. Netemeyer, and Scot Burton, "Assessing the Domain Specificity of Deal Proneness: A Field Study," *Journal of Consumer Research*, December 1995, pp. 314–326.

86. "Brand Loyalty in the Food Industry."

87. Eleena de Lisser and Kevin Helliker, "Private Labels Reign in British Groceries," *Wall Street Journal*, March 3, 1994, pp. B1, B9.

88. Justin Bateman, "Huggies Closes Gap on Pampers," *Brand Strategy*, July 1, 2001, p. 30; Suein L. Hwang, "Cigarette Makers in Discount War to Lock in Share," *Wall Street Journal*, September 23, 1998, pp. B1, B4;

Elyse Tanouye, "Bayer's Ads Promote Drug for Low Cost," *Wall Street Journal*, May 7, 1996, p. B3; Robert Frank, "Pepsi and Coke Are Expected to Pour Ads for Low-Priced Tea over US," *Wall Street Journal*, June 17, 1996, p. B4

89. Norihiko Shirouzu, "Whoppers Face Entrenched Foes in Japan: Big Macs," *Wall Street Journal*, February 4, 1997, pp. B1, B5.

90. Betsy Spethmann, "Re-Engineering the Price-Value Equation," *Brandweek*, September 20, 1993, pp. 44–47.

91. Christine Bittar, "Tablets, Scents, and Sensibility," *Brandweek*, June 4, 2001, p. S59.

92. Nelson Schwartz, "Colgate Cleans Up," *Fortune*, April 2000, www.fortune.com; Tara Parker-Pope, "Colgate Places a Huge Bet on a Germ-Fighter," *Wall Street Journal*, December 29, 1997, pp. B1, B2.

93. Dianne Solis, "Cost No Object for Mexico's Makeup Junkies," *Wall Street Journal*, June 7, 1994, pp. B1, B6.

94. Kathleen Deveny, "How Country's Biggest Brands Are Faring at the Supermarket," *Wall Street Journal*, March 24, 1994, p. B1.

95. "Redeeming Value," *American Demographics*, October 1, 2001, p. 25.

96. "Penny-Pinchers' Paradise," *BusinessWeek*, January 22, 2001, p. EB12.

97. "International Coupon Trends," *Direct Marketing*, August 1993, pp. 47–49, 83.

98. Bussey, "Japan's Wary Shoppers Worry Two Capitals," *Wall Street Journal*, April 29, 1993, p. A1; Yumiko Ono, "Cosmetics Industry May Get Make-Over," *Wall Street Journal*, August 17, 1993, p. B1.

99. Susan T. Fiske, "Schema Triggered Affect: Applications to Social Perception," in eds. Margaret S. Clark and Susan T. Fiske, *Affect and Cognition: The 17th Annual Carnegie Symposium on Cognition* (Hillsdale, N. J.: Lawrence Erlbaum, 1982), pp. 55–77; Mita Sujan, James R. Bettman, and Harish Sujan, "Effects of Consumer Expectations on Information Processing and Selling Encounters," *Journal of Marketing Research*, November 1986, pp. 346–353.

100. Peter L. Wright, "An Adaptive Consumer's View of Attitudes and Choice Mechanisms as Viewed by an Equally Adaptive Advertiser," in ed. William D. Wells, *Attitude Research at Bay* (Chicago: American Marketing Association, 1976) pp. 113–131.

101. Baba Shiv and Alexander Fedorikhin, "Heart and Mind in Conflict: The Interplay of Affect and Cognition in Consumer Decision Making," *Journal of Consumer Research*, vol. 26, December 1999, pp. 278–292.

102. Susan T. Fiske and Mark A. Pavelchak, "Category-Based versus Piecemeal-Based Affective Responses: Developments in Schema-Triggered Affect," in eds. R. M. Sorrentino and E. T. Higgins, *The Handbook of Motivation and Cognition: Foundations of Social Behavior* (New York: Guilford, 1986) pp. 167–203; David M. Boush and Barbara Loken, "A Process-Tracing Study of Brand Extension Evaluation," *Journal of Marketing Research*, February 1991, pp. 16–28.

103. Fiske, "Schema Triggered Affect"; Mita Sujan, "Consumer Knowledge: Effects on Evaluation Strategies Mediating Consumer Judgments," *Journal of Consumer Research*, June 1985, pp. 31–46.

104. Stephanie Thompson, "Jell-O Sales Jiggle Downward; X-Treme Products Readied," *Advertising Age*, November 19, 2001, www.adage.com/news.cms?newsid=33449.

105. Ralph I. Allison and Kenneth P. Uhl, "Influence of Beer Brand Identification on Taste Perception," *Journal of Marketing Research*, August 1964, pp. 36–39.

106. Wayne D. Hoyer and Stephen P. Brown, "Effects of Brand Awareness on Choice for a Common, Repeat-Purchase Product," *Journal of Consumer Research*, September 1990, pp. 141–148.

107. M. Carole Macklin, "Preschoolers' Learning of Brand Names from Visual Cues," *Journal of Consumer Research*, December 1996, pp. 251–261.

108. Leong, "Consumer Decision Making for Common, Repeat-Purchase Products."

109. Durairaj Maheswaran, Diane M. Mackie, and Shelly Chaiken, "Brand Name as a Heuristic Cue: The Effects of Task Importance and Expectancy Confirmation on Consumer Judgments," *Journal of Consumer Psychology*, vol. 1, no. 4, 1992, pp. 317–336.

110. Richard W. Stevenson, "The Brands with Billion Dollar Names," *New York Times*, October 28, 1988, p. A1.

111. Gerry Khermouch, "The Best Global Brands," *BusinessWeek*, August 6, 2001, pp. 50–57.

112. Betsy McKay, "Siberian Soft-Drink Queen Outmarkets Coke and Pepsi," *Wall Street Journal*, August 23, 1999, pp. B1, B4.

113. Karen V. Fernandez and Dennis L. Rosen, "The Effectiveness of Information and Color in Yellow Pages Advertising," *Journal of Advertising*, vol. 29, no. 2, Summer 2000, pp. 61–73.

114. Robert W. Veryzer and J. Wesley Hutchinson, "The Influence of Unity and Prototypicality on Aesthetic Responses to New Product Designs," *Journal of Consumer Research*, March 1998, pp. 374–394.

115. Guliz Ger, "Problems of Marketization in Romania and Turkey," in eds. Clifford Schultz, Russell Belk, and Guliz Ger, *Consumption in Marketizing Economies* (Greenwich, Conn.: JAI Press, 1995).

116. David Goetzl, "Pfizer Aces Its Advertising Test," *Advertising Age*, December 10, 2001, pp. 51+.

117. Pamela Sebastian, "Nonprofit Group's Name to Go on For-Profit Pills," *Wall Street Journal*, July 13, 1994, p. B1.

118. Rebecca Quick, "Vatican Library Will Allow Companies to Use Its Name," *Wall Street Journal*, October 26, 1996, p. B11.

119. Eric Yang, "Co-brand or Be Damned," *Brandweek*, November 21, 1994, pp. 21–24.

120. Rich Thomaselli and Jon Fine, "Hearst to Launch Michael Jordan Magazine," *Advertising Age*, January 9, 2002, www.adage.com.

121. Laurie Snyder and Elizabeth Jensen, "Liquor Logos Pop up in Some Surprising Places," *Wall Street Journal*, August 26, 1997, pp. B1, B15.

122. Fara Warner, "Nathan's Takes Its Dogs Global," *Adweek's Marketing Week*, June 24, 1991, p. 10.

123. Janet Guyon, "Tobacco Companies Race for Advantage in Eastern Europe While Critics Fume," *Wall Street Journal*, December 28, 1992, pp. B1, B4.

124. Valerie Reitman, "Enticed by Visions of Enormous Numbers, More Western Marketers Move into China," *Wall Street Journal*, July 12, 1993, pp. B1, B6.

125. Karen Benezra, "Brock Party," *Brandweek*, March 27, 1995, pp. 25–30.

126. M. Venkatesan, "Cognitive Consistency and Novelty Seeking," in eds. Scott Ward and Thomas S. Robertson, *Consumer Behavior: Theoretical Sources* (Englewood Cliffs, N. J.: Prentice-Hall, 1973), pp. 354–384; Leigh McAlister, "A Dynamic Attribute Satiation Model of Variety Seeking Behavior," *Journal of Consumer Research*, September 1982, pp. 141–150.

127. Rebecca K. Ratner, Barbara E. Kahn, and Daniel Kahneman, "Choosing Less-Preferred Experiences for the Sake of Variety," *Journal of Consumer Research*, vol. 26, June 1999, pp. 1–15.

128. Hans C.M. Van Trijp, Wayne D. Hoyer, and J. Jeffrey Inman, "Why Switch? Product Category-Level Explanations for True Variety Seeking" *Journal of Marketing Research*, August 1996, pp. 281–292; Wayne D. Hoyer and Nancy M. Ridgway, "Variety Seeking as an Explanation for Exploratory Purchase Behavior: A Theoretical Model," in ed. Thomas C. Kinnear, *Advances in Consumer Research*, vol. 11 (Ann Arbor, Mich.: Association for Consumer Research, 1984), pp. 114–119.

129. J. Jeffrey Inman, "The Role of Sensory-Specific Satiety in Attribute-Level Variety Seeking," *Journal of Consumer Research*, vol. 28, June 2001, pp. 105–120.

130. Saatya Menon and Barbara E. Kahn, "The Impact of Context on Variety Seeking in Product Choices," *Journal of Consumer Research*, December 1995, pp. 285–295.

131. Erich A. Joachimsthaler and John L. Lastovicka, "Optimal Stimulation Level-Exploratory Behavior Models," *Journal of Consumer Research*, December 1984, pp. 830–835.

132. Albert Mehrabian and James Russell, *An Approach to Environmental Psychology* (Cambridge, Mass.: MIT Press, 1974).

133. Linda L. Price and Nancy M. Ridgway, "Use Innovativeness, Vicarious Exploration and Purchase Exploration: Three Facets of Consumer Varied Behavior," in ed. Bruce Walker, *American Marketing Association Educators' Conference Proceedings* (Chicago: American Marketing Association, 1982), pp. 56–60.

134. Bittar, "Tablets, Scents, and Sensibility."

135. Betsy McKay, "Facing Slow Sales, Coke and Pepsi Gear Up for New Battle," *Wall Street Journal*, April 16, 2001, p. B4; Laurie M. Grossman, "Flavored Soda Growth Outpaces Colas as Thirst for Novelty Grows," *Wall Street Journal*, December 14, 1993, p. B8.

136. Michael Selz, "As Fast Food Menus Add Items, Dyspeptic Diners Cry, 'No More,' *Wall Street Journal*, July 25, 1995, pp. B1, B2.

137. Robert Frank, "Fruity Teas and Mystical Sodas Are Boring Consumers," *Wall Street Journal*, October 9, 1996, pp. B1, B2.

138. Dennis W. Rook, "The Buying Impulse," *Journal of Consumer Research*, September 1987, pp. 189–199; Craig J. Thompson, William B. Locander, and Howard R. Pollio, "The Lived Meaning of Free Choice: Existential-Phenomenological Description of Everyday Consumer Experiences of Contemporary Married Women," *Journal of Consumer Research*, December 1990, pp. 346–361.

139. Laura E. Keeton, "Travel Tempts Even the Thrifty to Splurge," *Wall Street Journal*, September 27, 1995, pp. B1, B8.

140. J. Jeffrey Inman and Russell S. Winer, "Where the Rubber Meets the Road: A Model of In-store Consumer Decision Making," *Marketing Science Institute Report Summary*, December 1998, pp. 98–122; "How We Shop . . . From Mass to Market," *Brandweek*, January 9, 1995, p. 17; Danny Bellenger, D. H. Robertson, and Elizabeth C. Hirschman, "Impulse Buying Varies by Product," *Journal of Advertising Research*, December 1978–January 1979, pp. 15–18.

141. Cathy J. Cobb and Wayne D. Hoyer, "Planned vs. Impulse Purchase Behavior," *Journal of Retailing*, Winter 1986, pp. 384–409.

142. Rook, "The Buying Impulse."

143. Russell W. Belk, "Materialism: Trait Aspects of Living in a Material World," *Journal of Consumer Research*, December 1985, pp. 265–280; P. S. Raju, "Optimum Stimulation Level: Its Relationship to Personality, Demographics, and Exploratory Behavior," *Journal of Consumer Research*, December 1980, pp. 272–282; Danny Bellenger and P. K. Korgaonkar, "Profiling the Recreational Shopper," *Journal of Retailing*, Fall 1980, pp. 77–92.

144. Dennis W. Rook and Robert J. Fisher, "Normative Influences on Impulsive Buying Behavior," *Journal of Consumer Research*, December 1995, pp. 305–313; Radhika Puri, "Measuring and Modifying Consumer Impulsiveness: A Cost-Benefit Accessibility Framework," *Journal of Consumer Psychology*, vol. 5, no. 2, 1996, pp. 87–114.

145. Inman and Winer, "Where the Rubber Meets the Road."

146. Nancy Millman, "Horn of Plenty Has Its Price," *Austin American Statesman*, August 8, 1996, pp. D1, D2.

147. Pam Weisz, "Brach's, Tobler Slick Up for Impulse Eyes," *Brandweek*, December 12, 1994, p. 8.

148. Bussey, "Japan's Wary Shoppers Worry Two Capitals."

Chapter 12

1. Alison Stein Wellner, "A New Cure for Shoppus Interruptus," *American Demographics*, August 2000, pp. 44–47.

2. For a review, see William H. Cummings and M. Venkatesan, "Cognitive Dissonance and Consumer Behavior: A Review of the Evidence," *Journal of Marketing Research*, August 1976, pp. 303–308; also see Dieter Frey and Marita Rosch, "Information Seeking after Decisions: The Roles of Novelty of Information and Decision Reversibility," *Personality and Social Psychology Bulletin*, March 1984, pp. 91–98.

3. Michael Tsiros and Vikas Mittal, "Regret: A Model of Its Antecedents and Consequences in Consumer Decision Making," *Journal of Consumer Research*, vol. 26, March 2000, pp. 401–417.

4. Alan D. J. Cooke, Tom Meyvis, and Alan Schwartz, "Avoiding Future Regret in Purchase-Timing Decisions," *Journal of Consumer Research*, vol. 27, March 2001, pp. 447–459.

5. Stephen J. Hoch and John Deighton, "Managing What Consumers Learn from Experience," *Journal of Marketing*, April 1989, pp. 1–20.

6. Allan Pavio, *Imagery and Verbal Processes* (New York: Holt, Rinehart, & Winston, 1981).

7. Robert E. Smith and William R. Swinyard, "Information Response Models: An Integrated Approach," *Journal of Marketing*, Winter 1982, pp. 81–93; Deanna S. Kempf and Robert E. Smith, "Consumer Processing of Product Trial and the Influence of Prior Advertising: A Structural Modeling Approach," *Journal of Marketing Research*, August 1998, pp. 325–338.

8. Ida E. Berger and Andrew A. Mitchell, "The Effect of Advertising on Attitude Accessibility, Attitude Confidence, and the Attitude-Behavior Relationship," *Journal of Consumer Research*, December 1989, pp. 269–279; Alice A. Wright and John G. Lynch Jr., "Communication Effects of Advertising vs. Direct Experience When Both Search and Experience Attributes Are Present," *Journal of Consumer Research*, March 1995, pp. 708–718.

9. Patricia M. West, "Predicting Preferences: An Examination of Agent Learning," *Journal of Consumer Research*, June 1996, pp. 68–80.

10. Merrie Brucks, "The Effects of Product Class Knowledge on Information Search Behavior," *Journal of Consumer Research*, June 1985, pp. 1–16.

11. Joseph W. Alba and J. Wesley Hutchinson, "Dimensions of Consumer Expertise," *Journal of Consumer Research*, March 1987, pp. 411–454.

12. Eric J. Johnson and J. Edward Russo, "Product Familiarity and Learning New Information," *Journal of Consumer Research*, June 1984, pp. 542–551.

13. Stephen J. Hoch and Young-Won Ha, "Consumer Learning: Advertising and the Ambiguity of Product Experience," *Journal of Consumer Research*, October 1986, pp. 221–233.

14. Ibid; Paul Herr, Steven J. Sherman, and Russell H. Fazio, "On the Consequences of Priming: Assimilation and Contrast Effects," *Journal of Experimental Social Psychology*, July 1983, pp. 323–340.

15. Reid Hastie, "Causes and Effects of Causal Attributions," *Journal of Personality and Social Psychology*, July 1984, pp. 44–56; Thomas K. Srull, Meryl Lichtenstein, and Myron Rothbart, "Associative Storage and Retrieval Processes in Person Memory," *Journal of Experimental Psychology: General*, vol. 11, no. 6, 1985, pp. 316–435.

16. Durairaj Maheswaran, "Country of Origin as a Stereotype: Effects of Consumer Expertise and Attribute Strength on Product Evaluations," *Journal of Consumer Research*, September 1994, pp. 354–365.

17. John Deighton, "The Interaction of Advertising and Evidence," *Journal of Consumer Research*, December 1984, pp. 763–770; Hoch and Ha, "Consumer Learning."

18. Bernard Weiner, "Spontaneous Causal Thinking," *Psychological Bulletin*, January 1985, pp. 74–84.

19. Hoch and Deighton, "Managing What Consumers Learn from Experience."

20. Rekha Balu, "Heinz Places Ketchup in Global Account," *Wall Street Journal*, September 9, 1998, pp. B8.

21. Kate MacArthur, "KFC Hopes Seinfeld Star Will Convert Bored Burger Eaters," *Advertising Age*, July 27, 2001, www.adage.com/news.cms?newsID=30246; Kathryn Chen, "KFC Rules Fast-Food Roost in Shanghai," *Wall Street Journal*, December 2, 1997, pp. B1, B12.

22. Yumiko Ono, "Anheuser Plays on Tipsiness to Sell Japan Strong Brew," *Wall Street Journal*, November 17, 1998, pp. B1, B4.

23. Kenneth Hein, "This Fine Wine Is Worth a Cool Million," *Brandweek*, February 5, 2001, p. 40.

24. Joseph Pereira, "Unknown Fruit Takes on Unfamiliar Markets," *Wall Street Journal*, November 9, 1995, pp. B1, B5.

25. Youjae Yi, "A Critical Review of Consumer Satisfaction," *Review of Marketing* (Chicago: American Marketing Association, 1992), pp. 68–123.

26. Richard L. Oliver, "Processing of the Satisfaction Response in Consumption: A Suggested Framework and Research Propositions," *Journal of Consumer Satisfaction, Dissatisfaction, and Complaining Behavior*, vol. 2, 1989, pp. 1–16; Haim Mano and Richard L. Oliver, "Assessing the Dimensionality and Structure of the Consumption Experience: Evaluation, Feeling, and Satisfaction, *Journal of Consumer Research*, December 1993, pp. 451- 466.

27. Haim Mano and Richard L. Oliver, "Assessing the Dimensionality and Structure of the Consumption Experience: Evaluation, Feeling, and Satisfaction," *Journal of Consumer Research*, December 1993, pp. 451–466.

28. Michael D. Johnson, Eugene W. Anderson, and Claes Fornell, "Rational and Adaptive Performance Expectations in a Customer Satisfaction Framework," *Journal of Consumer Research*, March 1995, pp. 695–707.

29. Richard L. Oliver, "Measurement and Evaluation of Satisfaction Processes in Retail Settings," *Journal of Retailing*, Fall 1981, pp. 25–48.

30. Sarah Fisher Gardial, D. Scott Clemons, Robert B. Woodruff, David W. Schumann, and Mary Jane Burns, "Comparing Consumers' Recall of Prepurchase and Postpurchase Evaluation Experiences," *Journal of Consumer Research*, March 1994, pp. 548–560.

31. Marsha L. Richins and Peter H. Bloch, "Post-purchase Satisfaction: Incorporating the Effects of Involvement and Time," *Journal of Business Research*, September 1991, pp. 145–158.

32. Mary C. Gilly and Betsy D. Gelb, "Post-purchase Consumer Processes and the Complaining Consumer," *Journal of Consumer Research*, December 1982, pp. 323–328.

33. Vikas Mattal and Wagner A. Kamakura, "Satisfaction, Repurchase Intent, and Repurchase Behavior: Investigating the Moderating Effect of Customer Characteristics," *Journal of Marketing Research*, vol. 38, February 2001, pp. 131–142.

34. Claes Fornell, "A National Customer Satisfaction Barometer: The Swedish Experience," *Journal of Marketing*, January 1992, pp. 6–21.

35. Gerry Khermouch, "The Best Global Brands," *BusinessWeek*, August 6, 2001, pp. 50–55.

36. Robert D. Hof, "How Amazon Cleared That Hurdle," *BusinessWeek*, February 4, 2002, pp. 60–61; George Anders, "Amazon.com Sales More Than Quadruple," *Wall Street Journal*, July 23, 1998, p. B5.

37. Terry Vavra, "Learning from Your Losses," *Brandweek*, December 7, 1992, pp. 20–22.

38. Tim Triplett, "Product Recall Spurs Company to Improve Customer Satisfaction," *Marketing News*, April 11, 1994, p. 6.

39. "American Customer Satisfaction Index (ACSI) Methodology Report," National Quality Research Center, University of Michigan, December 1995.

40. Chad Rubel, "Pizza Hut Explores Customer Satisfaction," *Marketing News*, March 25, 1996, p. 15.

41. Christopher T. Heun, "Procter & Gamble Readies Market-Research Push," *Information Week*, October 15, 2001, p. 26.

42. Randy Brandt, "Satisfaction Studies Must Measure What the Customer Wants and Expects," *Marketing News*, October 27, 1997, p. 17.

43. Chezy Ofir and Itamar Simonson, "In Search of Negative Customer Feedback: The Effect of Expecting to Evaluate on Satisfaction Evaluations," *Journal of Marketing Research*, vol. 38, May 2001, pp. 170–182.

44. Robert A. Westbrook, "Product/Consumption-Based Affective Responses and Postpurchase Processes," *Journal of Marketing Research*, August 1987, pp. 258–270.

45. Charlotte Klopp and John Sterlickhi, "Customer Satisfaction Just Catching On in Europe," *Marketing News*, May 28, 1990, p. 5.

46. Brad Gale, "Satisfaction Is Not Enough," *Marketing News*, October 27, 1997, p. 18.

47. Vavra, "Learning from Your Losses."

48. Klopp and Sterlickhi, "Customer Satisfaction Just Catching On in Europe."

49. Jon Swartz, "Providian Bounces Back with Revamped Strategy," *USA Today*, December 4, 2001, www.usatoday.com/money/general/2001-05-08-qc2.htm.

50. Guliz Ger, Russell Belk, and Dana-Nicoleta Lascu, "The Development of Consumer Desire in Marketing and Developing Economies: The Cases of Romania and Turkey," in eds. Leigh McAlister and Michael L. Rothschild, *Advances in Consumer Research*, vol. 20 (Provo, Utah: Association for Consumer Research, 1993), pp. 102–107.

51. Richard L. Oliver, "A Cognitive Model of the Antecedents and Consequences of Satisfaction Decisions," *Journal of Marketing Research*, November 1980, pp. 460–469; Yu, "A Critical Review of Consumer Satisfaction," p. 92; see also Douglas M. Stayman, Dana L. Alden, and Karen H. Smith, "Some Effects of Schematic Processing on Consumer Expectations and Disconfirmation Judgments," *Journal of Consumer Research*, September 1992, pp. 240–255.

52. Yi, "A Critical Review of Consumer Satisfaction," p. 92; see also Douglas M. Stayman, Dana L. Alden, and Karen H. Smith, "Some Effects of Schematic Processing on Consumer Expectations and Disconfirmation Judgments," *Journal of Consumer Research*, September 1992, pp. 240–255.

53. Praveen K. Kopalle and Donald R. Lehman, "The Effects of Advertised and Observed Quality on Expectations about New Product Quality," *Journal of Marketing Research*, August 1995, pp. 280–291;

Stephen A. LaTour and Nancy C. Peat, "The Role of Situationally-Produced Expectations, Others' Experiences, and Prior Experiences in Determining Satisfaction," in ed. Jerry C. Olson, *Advances in Consumer Research* (Ann Arbor, Mich.: Association for Consumer Research, 1980), pp. 588–592; Ernest R. Cadotte, Robert B. Woodruff, and Roger L. Jenkins, "Expectations and Norms in Models of Consumer Satisfaction," *Journal of Marketing Research*, August 1987, pp. 305–314.

54. David K. Tse and Peter C. Wilson, "Models of Consumer Satisfaction Formation: An Extension," *Journal of Marketing Research*, May 1988, pp. 204–212.

55. "AOL, MSN at Bottom of Satisfaction Survey," *USA Today*, August 9, 2001, **www.usatoday.com/life/cyber/tech/2001-08-09-isp-survey.htm**.

56. Guliz Ger, "Problems of Marketization in Romania and Turkey," in eds. Clifford Shultz, Russell Belk, and Guliz Ger, *Consumption in Marketizing Economies* (Greenwich, Conn.: JAI Press, 1995).

57. Ruth N. Bolton and James H. Drew, "A Multistage Model of Customers' Assessments of Service Quality and Value," *Journal of Consumer Research*, March 1991, pp. 375–384; Michael D. Johnson, Eugene W. Anderson, and Claes Fornell, "Rational and Adaptive Performance Expectations in a Customer Satisfaction Framework," *Journal of Consumer Research*, March 1995, pp. 695–707.

58. Glenn B. Voss, A. Parasuraman, and Dhruv Grewal, "The Roles of Price, Performance, and Expectations in Determining Satisfaction in Service Exchanges," *Journal of Marketing*, October 1998, pp. 46–61; A. Parasuraman, Valerie A. Zeithaml, and Leonard L. Berry, "SERVQUAL: A Multiple-Item Scale for Measuring Consumer Perceptions of Service Quality," *Journal of Retailing*, Spring 1988, pp. 12–36.

59. Martha Slud, "Properly Packed Sacks Keep Customers Coming Back," *Marketing News*, May 20, 1996, p. 5.

60. Emily Nelson, "Big Retailers Try to Speed Up Checkout Lines," *Wall Street Journal*, March 13, 2000, pp. B1, B6.

61. Johnson, Anderson, and Fornell, "Rational and Adaptive Performance Expectations in a Customer Satisfaction Framework."

62. Tse and Wilson, "Models of Consumer Satisfaction Formation"; Richard L. Oliver, "Cognitive, Affective, and Attribute-Bases of the Satisfaction Response," *Journal of Consumer Research*, December 1993, pp. 418–430; Richard L. Oliver and Wayne S. DeSarbo, "Response Determinants in Satisfaction Judgments," *Journal of Consumer Research*, March 1988, pp. 495–507.

63. Gilbert A. Churchill and Carol Supranant, "An Investigation into the Determinants of Customer Satisfaction," *Journal of Marketing Research*, November 1982, pp. 491–504; Richard L. Oliver and William O. Bearden, "The Role of Involvement in Satisfaction Processes," in eds. Richard P. Bagozzi and Alice M. Tybout, *Advances in Consumer Research*, vol. 10 (Ann Arbor, Mich.: Association for Consumer Research, 1983), pp. 250–255; Paul G. Patterson, "Expectations and Product Performance as Determinants of Satisfaction for a High Involvement Purchase," *Psychology and Marketing*, September–October 1993, pp. 449–465.

64. Robert A. Westbrook and Michael D. Reilly, "Value-Percept Disparity: An Alternative to the Disconfirmation of Expectations Theory of Consumer Satisfaction," in eds. Richard P. Bagozzi and Alice M. Tybout, *Advances in Consumer Research*, vol. 10 (Ann Arbor, Mich.: Association for Consumer Research, 1983), pp. 256–261.

65. William O. Bearden and Jesse E. Teel, "Selected Determinants of Consumer Satisfaction and Complaint Reports," *Journal of Marketing Research*, February 1983, pp. 21–28; John E. Swan and I. Frederick Trawick, "Disconfirmation of Expectations and Satisfaction with a Retail Service," *Journal of Retailing*, Fall 1981, pp. 49–67; Westbrook and Reilly, "Value-Percept Disparity."

66. Westbrook, "Product/Consumption-Based Affective Responses and Postpurchase Processes"; Robert A. Westbrook and Richard L. Oliver, "The Dimensionality of Consumption Emotion Patterns and Consumer Satisfaction," *Journal of Consumer Research*, June 1991, pp. 84–91; Mano and Oliver, "Assessing the Dimensionality and Structure of the Consumption Experience."

67. Westbrook and Oliver, "The Dimensionality of Consumption Emotion Patterns."

68. Paul W. Miniard, Sunil Bhatla, and Deepak Sirdeshmukh, "Mood as a Determinant of Postconsumption Product Evaluations: Mood Effects and Their Dependency on the Affective Intensity of the Consumption Experience," *Journal of Consumer Psychology*, 1992, pp. 173–195.

69. Susan Fournier and David Glen Mick, "Rediscovering Satisfaction," *Journal of Marketing*, vol. 63, October 1999, pp. 5–23.

70. Sally D. Goll, "Pizza Hut Tosses Its Pies into the Ring," *Wall Street Journal*, May 27, 1994, p. B1.

71. Richard W. Olshavsky and John A. Miller, "Consumer Expectations, Product Performance, and Perceived Product Quality," *Journal of Marketing Research*, February 1972, pp. 469–499.

72. Goll, "Pizza Hut Tosses Its Pies into the Ring."

73. Norihiko Shirouzu, "P&G's Joy Makes an Unlikely Splash in Japan," *Wall Street Journal*, December 10, 1997, pp. B1, B8.

74. Diane Halstead, Cornelia Droge, and M. Bixby Cooper, "Product Warranties and Post-purchase Service," *Journal of Services Marketing*, vol. 7, no. 1, 1993, pp. 33–40; Joshua Lyle Wiener, "Are Warranties Accurate Signals of Product Reliability?" *Journal of Consumer Research*, September 1985, pp. 245–250.

75. Ger, "Problems of Marketization in Romania and Turkey."

76. Jesse Drucker, "Hotel Rage: Losing It in the Lobby," *Wall Street Journal*, February 16, 2001, pp. W1, W7.

77. Nichole M. Christain, "One Weekend, 52 Jeeps, a Chance to Bond," *Wall Street Journal*, May 23, 1997, pp. B1, B2.

78. Natalia A. Feduschak and Brian Coleman, "Air Ukraine Promises Friendly Skies, Too," *Wall Street Journal*, October 19, 1992, p. B3.

79. Susan Greco, "Saints Alive!" *Inc.*, August 2001, pp. 44–45.

80. Joanne Lee-Young, "In Hong Kong, Tobacco Promotes Away," *Wall Street Journal*, June 30, 1998, pp. B8.

81. Bernard Weiner, "Reflections and Reviews: Attributional Thoughts about Consumer Behavior," *Journal of Consumer Research*, vol. 27, December 2000, pp. 382–287; Valerie S. Folkes, "Consumer Reactions to Product Failure: An Attributional Approach," *Journal of Consumer Research*, March 1984, pp. 398–409; Valerie S. Folkes, "Recent Attribution Research in Consumer Behavior: A Review and New Directions," *Journal of Consumer Research*, March 1988, pp. 548–565; Richard W. Mizerski, Linda L. Golden, and Jerome B. Kernan, "The Attribution Process in Consumer Decision Making," *Journal of Consumer Research*, September 1979, pp. 123–140.

82. Mary Jo Bitner, "Evaluating Service Encounters: The Effects of Physical Surrounding and Employee Responses," *Journal of Marketing*, April 1990, pp. 69–82.

83. Valerie S. Folkes, Susan Koletsky, and John L. Graham, "A Field Study of Causal Inferences and Consumer Reaction: The View from the Airport," *Journal of Consumer Research*, March 1987, pp. 534–539.

84. Rudy Maxa, "Kinder, Gentler Airlines?" *Marketplace*, February 8, 2000, **www.savvytraveler.com/show/marketplace/2000/02.08.html**.

85. David L. Margulius, "Going to the A.T.M. for More Than a Fistful of Twenties," *New York Times*, January 17, 2002, p. D7; Eleena de Lisser, "Banks Court Disenchanted Customers," *Wall Street Journal*, August 30, 1993, p. B1.

86. Amy K. Smith, Ruth N. Bolton, and Janet Wagner, "A Model of Customer Satisfaction with Service Encounters Involving Failure and Recovery," *Journal of Marketing Research*, vol. 36, August 1999, pp. 356–372.

87. Bitner, "Evaluating Service Encounters."

88. Richard L. Oliver and John E. Swan, "Equity and Disconfirmation Paradigms as Influences on Merchant and Product Satisfaction," *Journal of Consumer Research*, December 1989, pp. 372–383; Elaine G. Walster, G. William Walster, and Ellen Berscheid, *Equity: Theory and Research* (Boston: Allyn & Bacon, 1978).

89. Richard L. Oliver and John L. Swan, "Consumer Perceptions of Interpersonal Equity and Satisfaction in Transactions, A Field Survey Approach," *Journal of Marketing*, April 1989, pp. 21–35.

90. Ruth N. Bolton and Katherine N. Lemon, "A Dynamic Model of Customers' Usage of Services: Usage as an Antecedent and Consequence of Satisfaction," *Journal of Marketing Research*, vol. 36, May 1999, pp. 171–186.

91. Catherine Valenti, "Order with Care: Internet Sees Rapid Growth in Consumer Complaints," *ABC News.com*, November 11, 2001, **http://more.abcnews.go.com/sections/business/dailynews/internet_complaints_011120.html**.

92. Ger, "Problems of Marketization in Romania and Turkey."

93. Day, "Modeling Choices among Alternative Responses to Dissatisfaction"; Marsha L. Richins, "Word-of-Mouth Communication as Negative Information," *Journal of Marketing*, Winter 1983, pp. 68–78.

94. Day, "Modeling Choices among Alternative Responses to Dissatisfaction"; Arthur Best and Alan R. Andreasen, "Consumer Response to Unsatisfactory Purchases," *Law and Society*, Spring 1977, pp. 701–742.

95. Caroline E. Mayer, "Griping about Cellular Bills," *Washington Post*, February 28, 2001, p. G17.

96. Lisa Miller, "Car Rental Industry Promises That Things Will Improve. Really," *Wall Street Journal*, July 17, 1997, pp. A1, A8.

97. Bearden and Teel, "Selected Determinants of Consumer Satisfaction and Complaint Reports."

98. Cathy Goodwin and Ivan Ross, "Consumer Evaluations of Responses to Complaints: What's Fair and Why," *Journal of Services Marketing*, Summer 1990, pp. 53–61.

99. Day, "Modeling Choices among Alternative Responses to Dissatisfaction"; Jagdip Singh and Roy D. Howell, "Consumer Complaining Behavior: A Review," in eds. H. Keith Hunt and Ralph L. Day, *Consumer Satisfaction, Dissatisfaction, and Complaining Behavior* (Bloomington, Ind.: Indiana University Press, 1985).

100. S. Krishnan and S. A. Valle, "Dissatisfaction Attributions and Consumer Complaint Behavior," in ed. William L. Wilkie, *Advances in Consumer Research* (Miami: Association for Consumer Research, 1979), pp. 445–449.

101. Folkes, "Consumer Reactions to Product Failure."

102. Kjell Gronhaug and Gerald R. Zaltman, "Complainers and Noncomplainers Revisited: Another Look at the Data," in ed. Kent B. Monroe, *Advances in Consumer Research* (Ann Arbor, Mich.: Association for Consumer Research, 1981), pp. 159–165.

103. Ger, "Problems of Marketization in Romania and Turkey."

104. Larry M. Robinson and Robert L. Berl, "What about Compliments? A Follow-up Study on Consumer

Complaints and Compliments," in eds. H. Keith Hunt and Ralph L. Day, *Refining Concepts and Measures of Consumer Satisfaction and Complaining Behavior* (Bloomington, Ind.: Indiana University Press, 1980), pp. 144–148.

105. T. Bettina Cornwell, Alan David Bligh, and Emin Babakus, "Complaint Behaviors of Mexican-American Consumers to a Third Party Agency," *Journal of Consumer Affairs*, Summer 1991, pp. 1–18.

106. Sigfredo A. Hernandez, William Strahle, Hector Garcia, and Robert C. Sorenson, "A Cross-Cultural Study of Consumer Complaining Behavior: VCR Owners in the U.S. and Puerto Rico," *Journal of Consumer Policy*, June 1991, pp. 35–62.

107. Jagdip Singh, "A Typology of Consumer Dissatisfaction Response Styles," *Journal of Retailing*, Spring 1990, pp. 57–99.

108. Thomas Petzinger Jr., "Customer from Hell Can Be a Blessing in Disguise for Sales," *Wall Street Journal*, March 1, 1996, p. B1.

109. Emily Nelson, "Shower or Bath? It's a Hotel's Tough Call," *Wall Street Journal*, May 14, 1998, pp. B1, B11.

110. Denise T. Smart and Charles L. Martin, "Manufacturer Responsiveness to Consumer Correspondence: An Empirical Investigation of Consumer Perceptions," *Journal of Consumer Affairs*, Summer 1992, pp. 104–128; Mary Gilly and Betsy Gelb, "Post-purchase Consumer Processes and the Complaining Consumer Behavior," *Journal of Consumer Research*, December 1982, pp. 323–328.

111. Lisa Bertagnoli, "Return to Sender," *Marketing News*, June 18, 2001, p. 3.

112. Tiffany Kary, "Online Retailers Fumble on Customer Care," *CNET News.com*, January 3, 2002, **http://news.com.com/2100-1017-801668.html**.

113. Lou Hirsh, "Consumer Gripe Sites—Hidden Treasure?" *CRM Daily.com*, January 2, 2002, **www.crmdaily.com/perl/story/?id=15555**.

114. Chow-Hou Wee and Celine Chong, "Determinants of Consumer Satisfaction/Dissatisfaction towards Dispute Settlements in Singapore," *European Journal of Marketing*, vol. 25, no. 10, 1991, pp. 6–16.

115. Alan J. Resnick and Robert R. Harmon, "Consumer Complaints and Managerial Response: A Holistic Approach," *Journal of Marketing*, Winter 1983, pp. 86–97.

116. L. Biff Motley, "Speeding Up Handling of Satisfaction Problems," *Bank Marketing*, September 2001, pp. 35+.

117. Stephanie Anderson Forest, "Customers Must Be Pleased, Not Just Satisfied," *BusinessWeek*, August 3, 1992, p. 52.

118. Halstead, Droge, and Cooper, "Product Warranties and Post-purchase Service."

119. Bill Spindle, "Tourists with Quake Discounts Might Ask: Is This Trip Necessary?" *Wall Street Journal*, May 6, 1998, p. B1.

120. Ger, "Problems of Marketization in Romania and Turkey."

121. Claes Fornell and Nicholas M. Didow, "Economic Constraints on Consumer Complaining Behavior," in ed. Jerry C. Olson, *Advances in Consumer Research*, vol. 7 (Ann Arbor, Mich.: Association for Consumer Research, 1980), pp. 318–323; Claes Fornell and Birger Wernerfelt, "Defensive Marketing Strategy by Customer Complaint Management," *Journal of Marketing Research*, November 1987, pp. 337–346.

122. Claes Fornell and Robert A. Westbrook, "The Vicious Cycle of Consumer Complaints," *Journal of Marketing*, Summer 1984, pp. 68–78.

123. Richins, "Word-of-Mouth Communication as Negative Information."

124. Yi, "A Critical Review of Consumer Satisfaction"; Johan Arndt, "Word-of-Mouth Advertising and Perceived Risk," in eds. Harold H. Kassarjian and Thomas R. Robertson, *Perspectives in Consumer Behavior* (Glenview, Ill.: Scott-Foresman, 1968).

125. John Yaukey, "Gotta Gripe? Sites Let You Whine Online," *USA Today*, June 15, 2001, **www.usatoday.com/life/cyber/ccarch/2001-01-17-yaukey.htm**; Hirsch, "Consumer Gripe Sites"; Rebecca Quick, "Cranky Consumers Devise Web Sites to Air Complaints," *Wall Street Journal*, December 26, 1997, pp. B1, B10.

126. Hirsch, "Consumer Gripe Sites"; Quick, "Cranky Consumers Devise Web Sites to Air Complaints."

127. Frederick F. Reichheld, *The Loyalty Effect: The Hidden Force behind Growth* (Boston: Harvard Business School Press, 1996).

128. Priscilla La Barbera and David W. Mazursky, "A Longitudinal Assessment of Consumer Satisfaction/Dissatisfaction: The Dynamic Aspect of Cognitive Processes," *Journal of Marketing Research*, November 1983, pp. 393–404; Ruth Bolton, "A Dynamic Model of the Duration of the Customer's Relationship with a Continuous Service Provider," *Marketing Science*, vol. 17, no. 1, 1998, pp. 45–65.

129. Thomas O. Jones and W. Earl Sasser, "Why Customers Defect," *Harvard Business Review*, November–December 1995, pp. 88–99.

130. Richard L. Oliver, "Whence Consumer Loyalty?" *Journal of Marketing*, vol. 63, 1999, pp. 33–44.

131. Frederick F. Reichheld and W. Earl Sasser, "Zero Defections: Quality Comes to Services," *Harvard Business Review*, September 1990, pp. 105–111; Eugene Anderson, Claes Fornell, and Donald H. Lehman, "Customer Satisfaction, Market Share, and Profitability: Findings from Sweden," *Journal of Marketing*, July 1994, pp. 53–66; Rajendra K. Srivastava, Tassadduq A. Shervani, and Liam Fahey, "Market-Based Assets and Shareholder Value: A Framework for Analysis," *Journal of Marketing*, vol. 62, no. 1, 1998, pp. 2–18.

132. Becky Ebenkamp, "The Complaint Department," *Brandweek*, June 18, 2001, p. 21; Reichheld, *The Loyalty Effect.*

133. Melissa Martin Young and Melanie Wallendorf, "Ashes to Ashes, Dust to Dust: Conceptualizing Consumer Disposition of Possessions," in *Proceedings, Marketing Educators' Conference* (Chicago: American Marketing Association, 1989), pp. 33–39.

134. Ibid; see also Jacob Jacoby, Carol K. Berning, and Thomas F. Dietvorst, "What about Disposition?" *Journal of Marketing*, April 1977, pp. 22–28; Gilbert D. Harrell and Diane M. McConocha, "Personal Factors Related to Consumer Product Disposal," *Journal of Consumer Affairs*, Winter 1992, pp. 397–417.

135. Jacoby, Berning, and Dietvorst, "What about Disposition?"; Young and Wallendorf, "Ashes to Ashes, Dust to Dust."

136. Harrell and McConocha, "Personal Factors Related to Consumer Product Disposal Tendencies."

137. Jacoby, Berning, and Dietvorst, "What about Disposition?"

138. John B. Sherry, Mary Ann McGrath, and Sidney J. Levy, "The Disposition of the Gift and Many Unhappy Returns," *Journal of Retailing*, Spring 1992, pp. 40–65.

139. Young and Wallendorf, "Ashes to Ashes, Dust to Dust."

140. Russell W. Belk, "Possessions and the Extended Self," *Journal of Consumer Research*, September 1988, pp. 139–168.

141. Young and Wallendorf, "Ashes to Ashes, Dust to Dust."

142. Melissa Martin Young, "Disposition of Possessions During Role Transitions," in eds. Rebecca H. Holman and Michael R. Solomon, *Advances in Consumer Research*, vol. 18 (Provo, Utah: Association for Consumer Research, 1991), pp. 33–39.

143. James H. Alexander, "Divorce, the Disposition of the Relationship, and Everything," in eds. Rebecca H. Holman and Michael R. Solomon, *Advances in Consumer Research*, vol. 18 (Provo, Utah: Association for Consumer Research, 1991), pp. 43–48.

144. James H. Alexander, John W. Shouten, and Scott D. Roberts, "Consumer Behavior and Divorce," in eds. Janeen Costa and Russell W. Belk, *Research in Consumer Behavior*, vol. 6 (Greenwich, Conn.: JAI Press, 1993), pp. 153–184.

145. For more information on this topic, see David J. Cheal, "Intergenerational Family Transfers," *Journal of Marriage and the Family*, November 1983, pp. 805–813; Jeffrey P. Rosenfeld, "Bequests from Resident to Resident: Inheritance in a Retirement Community," *The Gerontologist*, vol. 19, no. 6, 1979, pp. 594–600.

146. John F. Sherry Jr., "A Sociocultural Analysis of a Midwestern Flea Market," *Journal of Consumer Research*, June 1990, pp. 13–30.

147. Ibid; Russell W. Belk, John F. Sherry, and Melanie Wallendorf, "A Naturalistic Inquiry into Buyer and Seller Behavior at a Swap Meet," *Journal of Consumer Research*, March 1988, pp. 449–470.

148. Michael D. Reilly and Melanie Wallendorf, "A Comparison of Group Differences in Food Consumption Using Household Refuse," *Journal of Consumer Research*, September 1987, pp. 289–294.

149. Jacoby, Berning, and Dietvorst, "What about Disposition?"

150. For a review, see L. J. Shrum, Tina M. Lowrey, and John A. McCarty, "Recycling as a Marketing Problem: A Framework for Strategy Development," *Psychology and Marketing*, July–August 1994, pp. 393–416.

151. J. M. Hines, H. R. Hungerford, and A. N. Tomera, "Analysis and Synthesis of Research on Responsible Environmental Behavior: A Meta-Analysis," *Journal of Environmental Education*, Winter 1987, pp. 1–8.

152. Abhijit Biswas, Jane W. Licata, Daryl McKee, Chris Pullig, and Christopher Daughtridge, "The Recycling Cycle: Waste Recycling and Recycling Shopping Behaviors," *Journal of Public Policy & Marketing*, vol. 19, Spring 2000, pp. 93–105.

153. Rik G. M. Pieters, "Changing Garbage Disposal Patterns of Consumers: Motivation, Ability, and Performance," *Journal of Public Policy and Marketing*, Fall 1991, pp. 59–76.

154. Richard P. Bagozzi and Pratibha Dabholkar, "Consumer Recycling Goals and Their Effect on Decisions to Recycle," *Psychology and Marketing*, July–August 1994, pp. 313–340.

155. E. Howenstein, "Marketing Segmentation for Recycling," *Environment and Behavior*, March 1993, pp. 86–102.

156. Shrum, Lowrey, and McCarty, "Recycling as a Marketing Problem."

157. Jim Carlton, "Recycling Redefined," *Wall Street Journal*, March 6, 2001, pp. B1, B4.

158. Susan E. Heckler, "The Role of Memory in Understanding and Encouraging Recycling Behavior," *Psychology and Marketing*, July–August 1994, pp. 375–392.

159. Pieters, "Changing Garbage Disposal Patterns of Consumers."

160. Susan Warren, "Recycler's Nightmare: Beer in Plastic," *Wall Street Journal*, November 16, 1999, pp. B1, B4.

161. "Taking Recycling to the Photo Department," *Grocery Headquarters*, May 1, 2001, p. 97.

162. Kenneth R. Lord, "Motivating Recycling Behavior: A Quasi-Experimental Investigation of Message and Source Strategies," *Psychology and Marketing*, July–August 1994, pp. 341–358.

163. S. M. Burn and Stuart Oskamp, "Increasing Community Recycling with Persuasive Communications and Public Commitment," *Journal of Applied Social Psychology*, vol. 16, 1986, pp. 29–41.

164. Heckler, "The Role of Memory in Understanding and Encouraging Recycling Behavior."

Chapter 13

1. This example is from Barbara Martinez, "Dog Food, Toothpaste, and Oreos Star on Popular Hispanic Television Program," *Wall Street Journal*, March 25, 1997, pp. B1, B17.
2. Dianne Solis, "Univision Is Hopeful New Network Will Attract Wider Hispanic Audience," *Dallas Morning News*, January 17, 2002, **www.dallasnews.com**; Steve McClellan, "Hispanic Television," *Broadcasting & Cable*, October 1, 2001, pp. 22+; Ed Leibowitz, "Walk of Fama," *Los Angeles Magazine*, August 2001, p. 24.
3. Ignacio Vazquez, "Mexicans Are Buying 'Made in USA' Food," *Marketing News*, August 31,1998, p. 14.
4. Melanie Wallendorf and Eric Arnould, "We Gather Together: Consumption Rituals of Thanksgiving Day," *Journal of Consumer Research*, June 1991, pp. 13–31.
5. Scott Kilman & Robert L. Rose, "Population of Rural America Is Swelling," *Wall Street Journal*, June 21, 1996, pp. B1, B2.
6. Joel Garreau, *The Nine Nations of North America* (Boston: Houghton-Mifflin, 1981).
7. Lynn R. Kahle, "The Nine Nations of North America and the Value Basis of Geographic Segmentation," *Journal of Marketing*, April 1986, pp. 37–47.
8. Susan Mitchell, "Birds of a Feather," *American Demographics*, February 1995, pp. 40–48.
9. Michael Weiss, "Parallel Universe," *American Demographics*, October 1999, pp. 58–63.
10. Michael J. Weiss, *The Clustering of America* (New York: Harper & Row, 1988); Mitchell, "Birds of a Feather."
11. Greg Johnson, "Beyond Burgers: New McDonald's Menu Makes Run for the Border," *Los Angeles Times*, August 13, 2000, pp. C1+.
12. J. Alex Targuino, "King of Grits Alters Menu to Reflect Northern Tastes," *Wall Street Journal*, August 22, 1997, pp. B1, B5.
13. Mitchell, "Birds of a Feather."
14. Amy Merrick, "New Data Will Let Starbucks Plan Store Openings, Help Blockbuster Stock Its Videos," *Wall Street Journal*, February 14, 2001, pp. B1, B4.
15. Weiss, "Parallel Universe."
16. Ricardo Sookdeo, "The New Global Consumer," *Fortune*, Autumn–Winter 1993, pp. 68–77.
17. Ignacio Galceran and Jon Berry, "A New World of Consumers," *American Demographics*, March 1995, pp. 27–33.
18. Robert Frank, "Thai Food for the World?" *Wall Street Journal*, February 16, 2001, pp. B1, B4.
19. Sak Onkvisit and John J. Shaw, *International Marketing: Analysis and Strategy* (Columbus, Ohio: Merrill, 1989).
20. Ronald A. Fullerton, "Marketing and the Economic Redevelopment in East Germany: Field Observation and Theoretical Analysis," in ed. Luiz V. Dominguez, *Marketing and Economic Reconstruction in the Developing World: Proceedings of the Fourth International Conference on Marketing and Development* (San Jose, Costa Rica: INCAE, 1993), pp. 145–151.
21. Galceran and Berry, "A New World of Consumers."
22. Valerie Reitman, "India Anticipates the Arrival of the Beefless Big Mac," *Wall Street Journal*, October 25, 1993, pp. B1, B5.
23. J. R. Whitaker Penteado, "Fast Food Franchises Fight for the Brazilian Aficionados," *Brandweek*, June 7, 1993, pp. 20–24.
24. Yumiko Ono, "Pizza in Japan Is Adapted to Local Tastes," *Wall Street Journal*, June 4, 1993, p. B1.
25. Onkvisit and Shaw, *International Marketing*.
26. Yumiko Ono, "U.S. Superstores Find Japanese Are a Hard Sell," *Wall Street Journal*, February 14, 2000, pp. B1, B4.
27. Thomas M. Burton, "Makers of Drugs for Mentally Ill Find East Asia Is Resistant Market," *Wall Street Journal*, January 10, 2001, pp. B1, B4.
28. George P. Moschis, *Consumer Socialization* (Lexington, Mass.: D.C. Heath, 1987); Lisa Penaloza, "Atravesando Fronteras/Border Crossings: A Critical Ethnographic Exploration of the Consumer Acculturation of Mexican Immigrants," *Journal of Consumer Research*, June 1994, pp. 32–54.
29. William H. Frey, "Micro Melting Pots," *American Demographics*, June 2001, pp. 20–23.
30. "Profiles of General Demographic Characteristics: 2000 Census of Population and Housing," *U.S. Department of Commerce*, May 2001, p. 3.
31. Rebecca Gardyn, "Habla English?" *American Demographics*, April 2001, pp. 54–57.
32. Joan Raymond, "The Multicultural Report," *American Demographics*, November 2001, pp. S3–S6; Rebecca Gardyn, "True Colors," *American Demographics*, April 2001, pp. 14–17.
33. Cyndee Miller, "Researcher Says U.S. Is More of a Bowl Than a Pot," *Marketing News*, May 10, 1993, p. 6.
34. Pamela Paul, "Hispanic Heterogenity," *Forecast*, June 4, 2001, pp. 1+; Geoffrey Paulin, "A Growing Market: Expenditures by Hispanics," *Monthly Labor Review*, March 1998, pp. 3–21.
35. Carrie Goerne, "Go the Extra Mile to Catch Up with Hispanics," *Marketing News*, December 24, 1990, p. 13; Marlene Rossman, *Multicultural Marketing* (New York: American Management Association, 1994).
36. Patricia Braus, "What Does Hispanic Mean?" *American Demographics*, June 1993, pp. 46–49.
37. Gardyn, "Habla English?"
38. Van R. Wood and Roy Howell, "A Note on Hispanic Values and Subcultural Research: An Alternative View,"

Journal of the Academy of Marketing Science, Winter 1991, pp. 61–67.

39. Diane Crispell, "Materialism among Minorities," *American Demographics*, August 1993, pp. 14–16; Jacqueline Sanchez, "Some Approaches Better Than Others When Targeting Hispanics," *Marketing News*, May 25, 1992, pp. 8, 11.
40. Hillary Chura, "Sweet Spot," *Advertising Age*, November 12, 2001, pp. 1, 16
41. Paul, "Hispanic Heterogeneity."
42. Jerry Dryer, "'Más Queso, Por Favor!'" *Dairy Foods*, November 2001, pp. 16+; Lafayette Jones, "Translating for the Hispanic Market," *Promo*, September 1, 2001, pp. 30+.
43. Joe Schwartz, "Rising Status," *American Demographics*, January 10, 1989, p. 10.
44. Becky Ebenkamp, "Multicultural Marketing Experts Give Their Two Cents on Census Data," *Brandweek*, May 14, 2001, p. 25; Frey, "Micro Melting Pots."
45. Tim Kregor, "Family Affair," *Adweek*, October 8, 2001, pp. 14+; Antonio Guernica, *U.S. Hispanics: A Market Profile* (New York: National Association of Spanish Broadcasters and Strategy Research Corporation, 1980); Christy Fisher, "Poll: Hispanics Stick to Brands—Asian-Americans Shop for Good Price, and African-Americans Look for Quality," *Advertising Age*, February 15, 1993, p. 6.
46. Roberta Bernstein, "Food For Thought," *American Demographics*, May 2000, pp. 39–42; Rodolfo M. Nayga and Oral Capps, "Determinants of Food away from Home Consumption: An Update," *Agribusiness*, November 1992, pp. 549–559.
47. Kregor, "Family Affair."
48. Penaloza, "Atravesando Fronteras/Border Crossings"; Rossman, *Multicultural Marketing*.
49. Dryer, "'Más Queso, Por Favor!'"
50. Kurt Topfer, "U.S. Spice Demand Grows as Ethnic Foods Take Hold," *Chemical Marketing Reporter*, September 14, 1992, p. 26; Molly O'Neil, "New Mainstream: Hot Dogs, Apple Pie, and Salsa," *Supermarket Business*, May 1992, pp. 92, 94.
51. Chura, "Sweet Spot."
52. Humberto Valencia, "Developing an Index to Measure Hispanicness," in eds. Elizabeth C. Hirschman and Morris B. Holbrook, *Advances in Consumer Research*, vol. 12 (Provo, Utah: Association for Consumer Research, 1981), pp. 18–21; Rohit Deshpande, Wayne D. Hoyer, and Naveen Donthu, "The Intensity of Ethnic Affiliation: A Study of the Sociology of Hispanic Consumption," *Journal of Consumer Research*, September 1986, pp. 214–220.
53. Cynthia Webster, "Effects of Hispanic Ethnic Identification on Marital Roles in the Purchase Decision Process," *Journal of Consumer Research*, September 1994, pp. 319–331.
54. Cynthia Webster, "The Effects of Hispanic Subcultural Identification on Information Search Behavior," *Journal of Advertising Research*, September–October 1992, pp. 54–62; Naveen Donthu and Joseph Cherian, "Hispanic Coupon Usage: The Impact of Strong and Weak Ethnic Identification," *Psychology and Marketing*, November–December 1992, pp. 501–510.
55. Gardyn, "Habla English?"; "A Subculture with Very Different Needs," *Adweek*, May 11, 1992, p. 44.
56. Douglas M. Stayman and Rohit Deshpande, "Situational Ethnicity and Consumer Behavior," *Journal of Consumer Research*, December 1989, pp. 361–371.
57. David B. Wooten, "One-of-a-Kind in a Full House: Some Consequences of Ethnic and Gender Distinctiveness," *Journal of Consumer Psychology*, 1995, vol. 4, no. 3, pp. 205–224.
58. Penaloza, "Atravesando Fronteras/Border Crossings."
59. Melanie Wallendorf and Michael D. Reilly, "Ethnic Migration, Assimilation, and Consumption," *Journal of Consumer Research*, December 1983, pp. 292–302.
60. Penaloza, "Atravesando Fronteras/Border Crossings."
61. Dawn Cornitcher, "The Explosive Growth of Ethnic Media in the United States," *Adweek*, May 17, 1999, p. 18.
62. Cyndee Miller, "Cosmetics Firms Finally Discover the Ethnic Market," *Marketing News*, August 30, 1993, p. 2.
63. Chura, "Sweet Spot"; Bernstein, "Food For Thought."
64. Johnson, "Beyond Burgers."
65. McClellan, "Hispanic Television"; Eduardo Porter, "Hispanic TV Takes Off in the U.S.," *Wall Street Journal*, September 7, 2000, p. B1; Thomas C. O'Guinn and Thomas P. Meyer, "Segmenting the Hispanic Market: The Use of Spanish Language Radio," *Journal of Advertising Research*, December 1981, pp. 9–16.
66. Gardyn, "Habla English?"
67. Eduardo Porter, "For Hispanic Marketers, Census Says It All," *Wall Street Journal*, April 24, 2001, p. B8.
68. Anne Marie Kerwin, "NY Times Plans Ad Supplement in Spanish," *Editor and Publisher*, February 27, 1993, pp. 24–25; Hanna Liebman, "Newspapers Hablan Español," *Mediaweek*, August 16, 1993, p. 10.
69. Rick Wartzman and Joe Flint, "Nielsen Ratings Spark a Battle over Just Who Speaks Spanish," *Wall Street Journal*, February 25, 2000, pp. B1, B4.
70. "10 Largest Advertisers to the Hispanic Market, 1999 vs. 2000," *Marketing News*, July 2, 2001, p. 17.
71. Jones, "Translating for the Hispanic Market."
72. Joel Millman, "U.S. Marketers Adopt Cinco de Mayo as National Fiesta," *Wall Street Journal*, May 1, 2001, pp. B1, B4; Suein L. Hwang, "Corona, of the Lime Wedge, Makes Unlikely Comeback," *Wall Street Journal*, November 20, 1997, pp. B1, B13.

73. Jacqueline Sanchez, "Some Approaches Better than Others When Targeting Hispanics," *Marketing News*, May 25, 1992, pp. 8, 11.

74. Rossman, *Multicultural Marketing*.

75. Rohit Deshpande and Douglas M. Stayman, "A Tale of Two Cities: Distinctiveness Theory and Advertising Effectiveness," *Journal of Marketing Research*, February 1994, pp. 57–64.

76. Robert E. Wilkes and Humberto Valencia, "Hispanics and Blacks in Television Commercials," *Journal of Advertising*, March 1989, pp. 19–25.

77. Cristina Merrill, "Where the Cars Are Caliente," *American Demographics*, January 2000, pp. 56–59.

78. Joe Schwartz, "Hispanic Opportunities," *American Demographics*, May 1987, pp. 56–59; Rossman, *Multicultural Marketing*.

79. Scott Koslow, Prem N. Shamdasani, and Ellen E. Touchstone, "Exploring Language Effects in Ethnic Advertising: A Sociolinguistic Perspective," *Journal of Consumer Research*, March 1994, pp. 575–585.

80. Carol J. Kaufman, "Coupon Use in Ethnic Markets: Implications from a Retail Perspective," *Journal of Consumer Marketing*, Winter 1991, pp. 41–51; Christy Fisher, "Marketing to Hispanics: Delivery Systems Foil Couponing," *Advertising Age*, October 15, 1990, p. 47; Christy Fisher, "Marketing to Hispanics: Promotions Trickle Turns into Torrent," *Advertising Age*, October 15, 1990, p. 42.

81. Fisher, "Poll: Hispanics Stick to Brands."

82. Rossman, *Multicultural Marketing*.

83. Lee Zion, "Retail Centers Must Reflect State's Changing Face," *San Diego Business Journal*, July 30, 2001, pp. 6+; Alexia Vargas, "Harvard MBA's Chain Riles Chicago's Hispanic Grocers," *Wall Street Journal*, November 6, 1997, pp. B1, B2.; Mary Ann Linsen, "Store of the Month: Making It in Miami," *Progressive Grocer*, April 1991, pp. 128–136.

84. Laurie M. Grossman, "After Demographic Shift, Atlanta Mall Restyles Itself as Black Shopping Center," *Wall Street Journal*, February 26, 1992, pp. B1, B5.

85. Mike Billips, "Accent Is on Service," *Georgia Trend*, April 2001, pp. 155+.

86. Jim Emerson, "African Americans," *Direct*, September 1, 2001, p. 50; "Profiles of General Demographic Characteristics."

87. "The New Demographics of Black Americans," *BusinessWeek*, December 4, 2000, p. 14; Emerson, "African Americans."

88. "Black Population Surged During '90s: U.S. Census," *Jet*, August 27, 2001, p. 18; Raymond, "The Multicultural Report"; Brigid Schulte, "Blacks Make Gains in Education, Lag in Income, Census Says," *Austin American Statesman*, February 23, 1995, p. A13.

89. Alan J. Bush, Rachel Smith, and Craig Martin, "The Influence of Consumer Socialization Variables on Attitude toward Advertising: A Comparison of African-Americans and Caucasians," *Journal of Advertising*, vol. 28, no. 3, Fall 1999, pp. 13–24.

90. William O'Hare, "Blacks and Whites: One Market or Two?" *American Demographics*, March 1987, pp. 44–48.

91. "Where Blacks, Whites Diverge," *Brandweek*, May 3, 1993, p. 22.

92. Howard Schlossberg, "Many Marketers Still Consider Blacks 'Dark-Skinned Whites,'" *Marketing News*, January 18, 1993, pp. 1, 13.

93. Roland L. Freeman, "Philadelphia's African-Americans: A Celebration of Life," cited in Rossman, *Multicultural Marketing*, p. 140.

94. Bush, Smith, and Martin, "The Influence of Consumer Socialization Variables on Attitude toward Advertising."

95. Debra Goldman, "Black Like Me," *Adweek*, August 24, 1992, p. 25.

96. Cyndee Miller, "Research on Black Consumers: Marketers with Much at Stake Step Up Their Efforts," *Marketing News*, September 13, 1993, pp. 1, 42; Cyndee Miller, "Shopping Patterns Vary Widely Among Minorities," *Marketing News*, January 18, 1993, p. 11.

97. Rhonda Reynolds, "Courting Black Consumers," *Black Enterprise*, September 1993, p. 43.

98. Corliss L. Green, "Ethnic Evaluations of Advertising: Interaction Effects of Strength of Ethnic Identification, Media Placement, and Degree of Racial Composition," *Journal of Advertising*, vol. 28, no. 1, Spring 1999, pp. 49–64; Pepper Miller and Ronald Miller, "Trends Are Opportunities for Targeting African-Americans," *Marketing News*, January 20, 1992, p. 9.

99. "Blacks Get Wired," *Marketing News*, September 15, 1997, p. 1; Gardyn, "True Colors."

100. Martha T. Moore, "Marketers Take Note of Blacks," *USA Today*, August 20, 1993, p. 3B; Reynolds, "Courting Black Consumers"; Christy Fisher, "Retailers Target Ethnic Consumers," *Advertising Age*, September 30, 1991, p. 50.

101. Jennifer Lach, "The Color of Money," *American Demographics*, February 1999, pp. 59–60.

102. Emerson, "African Americans."

103. "Minority Buying Power," *Marketing News*, July 2, 2001, p. 17.

104. "African-Americans Go Natural," *MMR*, December 17, 2001, p. 43.

105. "L'eggs Joins New Approach in Marketing to African American Women," *Supermarket Business*, June 1998, p. 81; Cyndee Miller, "Cosmetics Firms Finally Discover the Ethnic Market," *Marketing News*, August 30, 1993, p. 2.

106. John P. Cortez, "KFC Stores Boast Flavor of Neighborhood," *Advertising Age*, May 31, 1993, pp. 3, 46.

107. Cyndee Miller, "Toy Companies Release Ethnically Correct Dolls," *Marketing News*, September 30, 1991,

pp. 1–2; Maria Mallory and Stephanie Anderson Forest, "Waking Up to a Major Market," *BusinessWeek*, March 23, 1992, pp. 70–73.

108. Janice C. Simpson, "Buying Black," *Time*, August 31, 1992, pp. 52–53; James S. Hirsch, "New Credit Cards Base Appeals on Sexual Orientation and Race," *Wall Street Journal*, November 6, 1995, pp. B1, B9.

109. Green, "Ethnic Evaluations of Advertising."

110. Jake Holden, "The Ring of Truth, *American Demographics*, October 1998, p. 14.

111. Lisa Brownlee, "Magazines Win Black Readers via Newspapers," *Wall Street Journal*, February 6, 1997, pp. B1, B9.

112. Helen Gregory, "Positive Discrimination," *Grocer*, July 21, 2001, pp. 45+.

113. Matthew S. Scott, "Can Black Radio Stations Survive an Industry Shakedown?" *Black Enterprise*, June 1993, pp. 254–260.

114. Frank S. Washington, "Mercedes' New Ad Campaign Targets Affluent Blacks," *Ward's Dealer Business*, October 2001, p. 39.

115. "Black Consumers"; Jeff Jensen, "Blacks Favor Fox, NBC," *Advertising Age*, April 12, 1993, p. 28.

116. "10 Largest Advertisers to the African American Market, 2000," *Marketing News*, July 2, 2001, p. 17.

117. Alan Harman, "Advice to Canadian Papers," *Editor & Publisher*, June 5, 1993, pp. 18–19; Adrienne Ward, "What Roles Do Ads Play in Racial Tension?" *Advertising Age*, August 10, 1992, pp. 1, 35.

118. Reynolds, "Courting Black Consumers"; Russell H. Weigl, James W. Loomis, and Matthew J. Soja, "Race Relations on Prime-Time Television," *Journal of Personality and Social Psychology*, November 1980, pp. 884–893.

119. Jennifer L. Aaker, Anne M. Brumbaugh, and Sonya A. Grier, "Nontarget Markets and Viewer Distinctiveness: The Impact of Target Marketing on Advertising Attitudes," *Journal of Consumer Psychology*, vol. 9, no. 3, 2000, pp. 127–140.

120. Thomas H. Stevenson, "How Are Blacks Portrayed in Business Ads?" *Industrial Marketing Management*, August 1991, pp. 193–199.

121. J. Clinton Brown, "Which Black Is Beautiful?" *Advertising Age*, February 1, 1993, p. 19.

122. Schlossberg, "Many Marketers Still Consider Blacks 'Dark-Skinned Whites'"; William J. Qualls and David J. Moore, "Stereotyping Effects on Consumers' Evaluation of Advertising: Impact of Racial Difference Between Actors and Viewers," *Psychology and Marketing*, Summer 1990, pp. 135–151.

123. "Consumers: It's Not Hip to Be Square," *Promo*, February 2001, www.promo.com.

124. Jamie M. Jamison, "Marketing to the African-American Segment," *Bank Marketing*, December 1993, pp. 21–23.

125. Gregg Cebrynski, "McDonald's Campaign Targets Denver Minorities," *Nation's Restaurant News*, February 9, 1998, pp. 8, 19.

126. Eugene Morris, "The Difference in Black and White," *American Demographics*, January 1993, pp. 44–49.

127. Ann Cooper, "Cosmetics: Changing Looks for Changing Attitudes," *Adweek*, February 22, 1993, pp. 30–36.

128. Eric Hollreiser, "Caddy Tweaks Ad Mix to Woo Blacks," *Brandweek*, November 21, 1994, p. 10.

129. Dan Fost, "Reaching the Hip-Hop Generation," *American Demographics*, May 1993, p. 15.

130. Tommy E. Whittler and Joan DiMeo, "Viewers' Reactions to Racial Cues in Advertising Stimuli," *Journal of Advertising Research*, December 1991, pp. 37–46.

131. Tommy E. Whittler, "Viewers' Processing of Source and Message Cues in Advertising Stimuli," *Psychology & Marketing*, July–August 1989, pp. 287–309.

132. Fisher, "Poll: Hispanics Stick to Brands."

133. William Spain, "Baseball Makes a Pitch for Blacks," *Advertising Age*, August 24, 1992, pp. S1, S4.

134. Maureen Tkacik and Betsy McKay, "Code Red" PepsiCo's Guerrilla Conquest," *Wall Street Journal*, August 17, 2001, p. B5.

135. Cortez, "KFC Stores Boast Flavor of Neighborhood."

136. Grossman, "After Demographic Shift, Atlanta Mall Restyles Itself as Black Shopping Center."

137. Fisher, "Retailers Target Ethnic Consumers"; Carrie Goerne, "Retailers Boost Efforts to Target African-American Consumers," *Marketing News*, June 22, 1992, p. 2.

138. Nicholas Kulish, "U.S. Asian Population Grew and Diversified, Census Shows," *Wall Street Journal*, May 15, 2001, p. B4; "Profiles of General Demographic Characteristics"; Gregory Spencer and Frederick W. Hollman, "U.S. Census Bureau, the Official Statistics," September 21, 1998, pp. 8–9.

139. Frey, " Micro Melting Pots."

140. Raymond, "The Multicultural Report"; James Smart, "Diverse Markets Mean Big Business for Banks," *Bank Marketing*, October 1992, pp. 23–27.

141. Richard H. Levey, "Home Market: With the Right Offer and Approach, Asian Americans Can Be Good Prospects for Loyalty Programs," *Direct*, June 1999, pp. 1+; Raymond, "The Multicultural Report"; Easy Klein, "The Asian-American Market: Climb Aboard the Orient Express," *D & B Reports*, November–December 1990, pp. 38–40; Maria Shao, "Suddenly Asian-Americans Are a Marketer's Dream," *BusinessWeek*, June 17, 1991, pp. 54–55.

142. "Asian Americans Lead the Way Online," *Min's New Media Report*, December 31, 2001.

143. Jonathan Burton, "Advertising Targeting Asians," *Far Eastern Economic Review*, January 21, 1993, pp. 40–41.

144. Alice Z. Cuneo, "Companies Disoriented about Asians," *Advertising Age*, July 9, 1990, pp. S2, S8.

145. Dan Fost, "California's Asian Market," *American Demographics*, October 1990, pp. 34–37; Chui Li, "The Asian Market for Personal Products," *Drug & Cosmetic Industry*, November 1992, pp. 32–36; Klein, "The Asian-American Market."

146. Saul Gitlin, "An Optional Data Base," *Brandweek*, January 5, 1998, p. 16.

147. Rossman, *Multicultural Marketing;* Fost, "California's Asian Market."

148. Li, "The Asian Market for Personal Products"; William Dunn, "The Move Toward Ethnic Marketing," *Nation's Business*, July 1992, pp. 39–41; Rossman, *Multicultural Marketing*.

149. Lisa Marie Petersen, "Advertisers Look to Asian Immigrants," *Mediaweek*, November 30, 1992, p. 2.

150. Julie Cantwell, "Zero Gives New Life to Big 3 in the West; New Plans Include More Dealer Ad Money and Multicultural Marketing," *Automotive News*, November 12, 2001, p. 35.

151. Levey, "Home Market."

152. Cornitcher, "The Explosive Growth of Ethnic Media in the United States."

153. Burton, "Advertising Targeting Asians"; Shao, "Suddenly Asian-Americans Are a Marketer's Dream."

154. Charles R. Taylor and Barbara B. Stern, "Asian-Americans: Television Advertising and the 'Model Minority' Stereotype," *Journal of Advertising*, Summer 1997, pp. 47–62.

155. Ibid.

156. Judy Cohen, "White Consumer Response to Asian Models in Advertising," *Journal of Consumer Marketing*, Spring 1992, pp. 17–27.

157. Christopher Keough, "U.S. Bank Giants Moving to Make Inroads on Asian Turf," *Los Angeles Business Journal*, December 11, 2000, pp. 25+.

158. Levey, "Home Market."

159. Keough, "U.S. Bank Giants Moving to Make Inroads on Asian Turf."

160. Rossman, *Multicultural Marketing*.

161. Levey, "Home Market."

162. "Banking on Asian-Americans," *Sales & Marketing Management*, September 1993, p. 88.

163. Grossman, "After Demographic Shift, Atlanta Mall Restyles Itself as Black Shopping Center."

164. Marlene Rossman, "Inclusive Marketing Shows Sensitivity," *Marketing News*, October 10, 1994, p. 4.

165. Tara Parker Pope, "Ford Puts Blacks in Whiteface, Turns Red," *Wall Street Journal*, February 22, 1996, pp. B8.

166. Onkvisit and Shaw, *International Marketing;* Charles M. Schaninger, Jacques C. Bourgeois, and W. Christian Buss, "French-English Canadian Subcultural Consumption Differences," *Journal of Marketing*, Spring 1985, pp. 82–92.

167. Brian Dunn, "Nationalism in Advertising: Dead or Alive?" *Adweek*, November 22, 1993.

168. Hans Hoefer, *Thailand* (Boston: Houghton Mifflin, 1993).

169. Elizabeth C. Hirschman, "American Jewish Ethnicity: Its Relationship to Some Selected Aspects of Consumer Behavior," *Journal of Marketing*, Summer 1981, pp. 102–110; Elizabeth C. Hirschman, "Religious Affiliation and Consumption Processes: An Initial Paradigm," *Research in Marketing* (Greenwich, Conn.: JAI Press, 1983), pp. 131–170.

170. Thomas C. O'Guinn and Russell W. Belk, "Heaven and Earth: Consumption at Heritage Village, USA," *Journal of Consumer Research*, September 1989, pp. 227–238.

171. Hirschman, "American Jewish Ethnicity."

172. Hirschman, "Religious Affiliation and Consumption Processes."

173. Priscilla L. Barbera, "Consumer Behavior and Born Again Christianity," in eds. Jagdish N. Sheth and Elizabeth C. Hirschman, *Research in Consumer Behavior* (Greenwich, Conn.: JAI Press, 1988), pp. 193–222.

174. Rodney Ho, "Rappin' and Rockin' for the Lord," *Wall Street Journal*, February 28, 2001, pp. B1, B4.

175. Mark Robichaux, "Religious Cable Networks Fight Sin—and One Another," *Wall Street Journal*, August 12, 1996, p. B1.

176. Lisa Miller, "Registers Ring in Sanctuary Stores," *Wall Street Journal*, December 17, 1999, pp. B1, B4; Elizabeth Bernstein, "Holy Frappuccino!" *Wall Street Journal*, August 3, 2001, pp. W1, W8.

177. Fara Warner, "Churches Develop Marketing Campaigns," *Wall Street Journal*, April 17, 1995, p. B4.

178. Lisa Miller, "Religious Ads Go through a Conversion," *Wall Street Journal*, February 24, 1998, p. B7.

179. Lisa Miller, "Trendy Taize Draws Kids with Soft Music and Prayers," *Wall Street Journal*, April 4, 1998, pp. B1, B7.

180. Alison Stein Wellner, "Oh Come All Ye Faithful," *American Demographics*, June 2001, pp. 51–55.

181. Anne Moore, "Silent Night, *Snowy* Night," *Marketing News*, December 8, 1997, pp. 1, 12.

Chapter 14

1. "China's Imported Wine, Spirits Market Gains Momentum," *Xinhua News Agency*, February 6, 2002, www.comtexnews.com; "To Get Rich Is Glorious; China's Middle Class," *The Economist*, January 19, 2002, www.economist.com; Xueguang Zhou, "Economic Transformation and Income Inequality in Urban China: Evidence from Panel Data," *American*

Journal of Sociology, vol. 105, January 2000, pp. 1135+; Ian Johnson, "China's Once-Admired Rich Now Viewed with Disdain," *New Orleans Times-Picayune*, April 9, 1995, p. A29.

2. Pierre Bourdieu, *Language and Symbolic Power* (Cambridge, Mass.: Harvard University Press, 1991).

3. Richard P. Coleman, "The Continuing Significance of Social Class to Marketing," *Journal of Consumer Research*, December 1983, pp. 265–280; Wendell Blanchard, *Thailand, Its People, Its Society, Its Culture* (New Haven, Conn.: HRAF Press, 1990) as cited in Sak Onkvisit and John J. Shaw, *International Marketing: Analysis and Strategy* (Columbus, Ohio: Merrill, 1989), p. 293.

4. Edward W. Cundiff and Marye T. Hilger, *Marketing in the International Environment* (New York: Prentice-Hall, 1988) as cited in Mariele K. DeMooij and Warren Keegan, *Advertising Worldwide* (New York: Prentice-Hall, 1991), p. 96.

5. Onkvisit and Shaw, *International Marketing.*

6. "To Get Rich Is Glorious; China's Middle Class."

7. Russell W. Belk, "Daily Life in Romania," in Consumption in Marketizing Economies, eds. Cliford Shultz II and Güliz (Greenwich, CT: JAI Press, 1994).

8. Ernest Dichter, "The World Consumer," *Harvard Business Review*, July–August 1962, pp. 113–123 as cited in Cundiff and Hilger, *Marketing in the International Environment*, p. 135.

9. Richard P. Coleman, "The Significance of Social Stratification in Selling," in ed. Martin L. Bell, *Marketing: A Maturing Discipline* (Chicago: American Marketing Association, 1960), pp. 171–184.

10. Douglas E. Allen and Paul F. Anderson, "Consumption and Social Stratification: Bourdieu's Distinction," in eds. Chris T. Allan and Deborah Roedder John, *Advances in Consumer Research*, vol. 21 (Provo, Utah: Association for Consumer Research, 1994), pp. 70–73.

11. Pierre Bourdieu, *Distinction: A Social Critique of the Judgment of Taste* (Cambridge, Mass.: Harvard University Press, 1984).

12. Michael R. Solomon, "Deep Seated Materialism: The Case of Levi's 501 Jeans," in ed. Richard J. Lutz, *Advances in Consumer Research*, vol. 13 (Provo, Utah: Association for Consumer Research, 1986), pp. 619–622.

13. Coleman, "The Continuing Significance of Social Class to Marketing."

14. Charles M. Schaninger, "Social Class versus Income Revisited: An Empirical Investigation," *Journal of Marketing Research*, May 1981, pp. 192–208.

15. Gillian Stevens and Joo Hyun Cho, "Socioeconomic Indexes and the New 1980 Census Occupational Classification Scheme," *Social Science Research*, March 1985, pp. 142–168; Charles B. Nam and Mary G. Powers, *The Socioeconomic Approach to Status Measurement* (Houston: Cap and Gown Press, 1983).

16. Diane Crispell, "The Real Middle Americans," *American Demographics*, October 1994, pp. 28–35; Michael Hout, "More Universalism, Less Structural Mobility: The American Occupational Structure in the 1980s," *American Journal of Sociology*, May 1988, pp. 1358–1400.

17. William L. Wilkie, *Consumer Behavior*, 2nd ed. (New York: Wiley, 1990).

18. Güliz Ger, Russell W. Belk, and Dana-Nicoleta Lascu, "The Development of Consumer Desire in Marketizing and Developing Economies: The Cases of Romania and Turkey," in eds. Leigh McAlister and Michael L. Rothschild, *Advances in Consumer Research*, vol. 20 (Provo, Utah: Association for Consumer Research, 1992), pp. 102–107.

19. M. R. Haque, "Marketing Opportunities in the Middle East," in ed. V. H. Manek Kirpalani, *International Business Handbook* (New York: Haworth Press, 1990), pp. 375–416.

20. W. Lloyd Warner, Marchia Meeker, and Kenneth Eells, *Social Class in America* (Chicago: Science Research Associates, 1949); August B. Hollingshead and Fredrick C. Redlich, *Social Class and Mental Illness, A Community Study* (New York: Wiley, 1958).

21. Coleman, "The Continuing Significance of Social Class to Marketing."

22. Gerhard Lenski, "Status Crystallization: A Non-Vertical Dimension of Social Status," *American Sociological Review*, August 1956, pp. 458–464.

23. Alison Stein Wellner, "The Money in the Middle," *American Demographics*, April 2000, pp. 56–64.

24. Benita Eisler, *Class Act: America's Last Dirty Secret* (New York: Franklin Watts, 1983); David L. Featherman and Robert M. Hauser, *Opportunity and Change* (New York: Academic Press, 1978).

25. Allen and Anderson, "Consumption and Social Stratification."

26. Jake Ryan and Charles Sackrey, *Strangers in Paradise: Academics from the Working Class* (Boston: South End Press, 1984).

27. Mary Janigan, Ruth Atherley, Michelle Harries, Brenda Branswell, and John Demont, "The Wealth Gap: New Studies Show Canada's Rich Really Are Getting Richer—and the Poor Poorer—as the Middle Class Erodes," *Maclean's*, August 28, 2000, pp. 42+.

28. Roger Burbach and Steve Painter, "Restoration in Czechoslovakia," *Monthly Review*, November 1990, pp. 36–49; Rahul Jacob, "The Big Rise," *Fortune*, May 30, 1994, pp. 74–80.

29. Haque, "Marketing Opportunities in the Middle East."

30. Jacob, "The Big Rise."

31. Greg J. Duncan, Martha Hill, and Willard Rogers, "The Changing Fortunes of Young and Old," *American Demographics*, August 1986, pp. 26–33; Katherine S. Newman, *Falling from Grace: The Experience of*

Downward Mobility in the American Middle Class (New York: Free Press, 1988); Kenneth Labich, "Class in America," *Fortune*, February 7, 1994, pp. 114–126.

32. Joseph Spiers, "Upper-Middle-Class Woes," *Fortune*, December 27, 1993, pp. 80–86.

33. Newman, *Falling from Grace*; Eisler, *Class Act*.

34. "Japan's Consumer Boom: The Pricey Society," *The Economist*, September 9, 1989, pp. 21–24.

35. Scott D. Roberts, "Consumer Responses to Involuntary Job Loss," in eds. Rebecca H. Holman and Michael R. Solomon, *Advances in Consumer Research*, vol. 18 (Provo, Utah: Association for Consumer Research, 1988), pp. 40–42.

36. Deborah Ball, "Despite Downturn, Japanese Are Still Having Fits for Luxury Goods," *Wall Street Journal*, April 24, 2001, pp. B1, B4.

37. Labich, "Class in America."

38. Lauren Goldstein, "Urban Wear Goes Suburban," *Fortune*, December 21, 1998, pp. 169–172.

39. Labich, "Class in America."

40. John Brooks, *Showing Off in America: From Conspicuous Consumption to Parody Display* (Boston: Little, Brown, 1981); for those interested in reading more about the theory of conspicuous consumption, see Thorstein Veblen, *The Theory of the Leisure Class* (New York: Macmillan, 1899).

41. Christine Page, "A History of Conspicuous Consumption," in eds. Floyd Rudmin and Marsha Richins, *Meaning, Measure, and Morality of Materialism* (Provo, Utah: Association for Consumer Research, 1993), pp. 82–87.

42. Ger, Belk, and Lascu, "The Development of Consumer Desire in Marketizing and Developing Economies."

43. Janeen Arnold Costa and Russell W. Belk, "Nouveaux Riches as Quintessential Americans: Case Studies of Consumption in the Extended Family," in ed. Russell W. Belk, *Advances in Nonprofit Marketing*, vol. 3 (Greenwich, Conn.: JAI Press, 1990), pp. 83–140.

44. Christina Duff, "Indulging in Inconspicuous Consumption," *Wall Street Journal*, April 14, 1997, pp. B1, B4.

45. Chris Koentges, "The Postmodern Age of Adventure," *The Globe and Mail*, February 2, 2002, **www.theglobeandmail.com**.

46. Rebecca H. Holman, "Product Use as Communication: A Fresh Appraisal of a Venerable Topic," in eds. Ben M. Enis and Kenneth J. Roering, *Review of Marketing* (Chicago: American Marketing Association, 1981), pp. 106–119.

47. Gilbert Chan, "Nike Shoe Frenzy Takes 'Status' a Step Beyond," *Sacramento Bee*, March 6, 2001, **www.sacbee.com**.

48. J. R. Whitaker Penteado, "Fast Food Franchises Fight for Brazilian Aficionados," *Brandweek*, June 7, 1993, pp. 20–24.

49. Ger, Belk, and Lascu, "The Development of Consumer Desire in Marketizing and Developing Economies."

50. Brooks, *Showing Off in America.*

51. Stephen Buckley, "Brazil Rediscovers Its Culture; Poor Man's Cocktail, Martial Art Hip Among Middle Class," *Washington Post*, April 15, 2001, p. A16.

52. Teri Agins, "Now, Subliminal Logos," *Wall Street Journal*, July 20, 2001, p. B1.

53. Sigmund Gronmo, "Compensatory Consumer Behavior: Theoretical Perspectives, Empirical Examples and Methodological Challenges," in eds. Paul F. Anderson and Michael J. Ryan, *1984 American Marketing Association Winter Educators' Conference* (Chicago: American Marketing Association, 1984), pp. 184–188.

54. Russell W. Belk, "Yuppies as Arbiters of the Emerging Consumption Style," in ed. Richard J. Lutz, *Advances in Consumer Research*, vol. 13 (Provo, Utah: Association for Consumer Research, 1986), pp. 514–519.

55. Yumiko Ono, "Tiffany Glitters, Even in Gloomy Japan," *Wall Street Journal*, July 21, 1998, pp. B1, B8; "Japan's Consumer Boom: The Pricey Society."

56. Russell W. Belk and Melanie Wallendorf, "The Sacred Meanings of Money," *Journal of Economic Psychology*, March 1990, pp. 35–67.

57. Kristie Lu Stout, "Smart Cards to Wire Hong Kong Schools," *CNN.com*, August 13, 2001, **www.cnn.com/2001/business/asia/08/12/hk.octopuskids**.

58. Thomas E. Weber, "On the Web, the Race for a Better Wallet," *Wall Street Journal*, December 18, 1998, pp. B1, B4.

59. C. Rubenstein, "Your Money or Your Life," *Psychology Today*, vol. 12, 1980, pp. 47–58.

60. Adrian Furnham and Alan Lewis, *The Economic Mind, The Social Psychology of Economic Behavior* (Brighton, Sussex: Harvester Press, 1986); Belk and Wallendorf, "The Sacred Meanings of Money."

61. H. Goldberg and R. Lewis, *Money Madness: The Psychology of Saving, Spending, Loving, and Hating Money* (London: Springwood, 1979).

62. Thomas Wiseman, *The Money Motive* (New York: 1st American, 1974).

63. Rosalind H. Williams, *Dream Worlds: Mass Consumption in Late Nineteenth-Century France* (Berkeley, Calif.: University of California Press, 1982).

64. Elizabeth C. Hirschman, "Secular Immortality and the American Ideology of Affluence," *Journal of Consumer Research*, June 1990, pp. 31–42.

65. Notably not all research has found this to be true. One set of six case studies found that all were comfortable with their status. See Costa and Belk, "Nouveaux Riches as Quintessential Americans."

66. Deborah Ball, "High Style on the High Seas," *Wall Street Journal*, September 14, 2000, pp. B1, B4.

67. Dagmar Aalund, "'Your Penthouse Is *Prefab*-ulous!'" *Wall Street Journal*, May 8, 2000, pp. B1, B6.

68. Bourdieu, *Distinction.*

69. Kevin Helliker, "How Hardy Are Upscale Gyms?" *Wall Street Journal*, February 9, 2001, pp. B1, B6; Priscilla A. LaBarbera, "The Nouveaux Riches, Conspicuous Consumption and the Issue of Self-Fulfillment," in eds. Elizabeth C. Hirschman and Jagdish N. Sheth, *Research in Consumer Behavior* (Greenwich, Conn.: JAI Press, 1988), pp. 179–210; Brooks, *Showing off in America*; Robin Leach and Judith Rich, *Lifestyles of the Rich and Famous.* (Garden City, N.Y.: Doubleday, 1986).

70. Brad Edmondson, "Wealth and Poverty," *American Demographics*, vol. 20, no. 5, 1998, pp. 20–21.

71. C. W. Young, "Bijan Designs a Very Exclusive Image," *Advertising Age*, March 13, 1986, pp. 18, 19, 21, as cited in LaBarbera, "The Nouveaux Riches"; V. Kanti Prasad, "Socioeconomic Product Risk and Patronage Preferences of Retail Shoppers," *Journal of Marketing*, July 1975, pp. 42–47.

72. John Fetto, "Sensible Santas," *American Demographics*, December 2000, pp. 10–11.

73. Elizabeth C. Hirschman, "Upper Class WASPS as Consumers: A Humanist Inquiry," in eds. Elizabeth C. Hirschman and Jagdish Sheth, *Research in Consumer Behavior*, vol. 3 (Greenwich, Conn.: JAI Press, 1988), pp. 115–147.

74. Kathryn Kranhold, "Marketing to the New Millionaire," *Wall Street Journal*, October 11, 2000, pp. B1, B6.

75. Carole Ann King, "The New Wealthy: Younger, Richer, More Proactive," *National Underwriter Life & Health-Financial Services Edition*, February 12, 2001, p. 4.

76. "Who Are the Millionaires?" *Greater Baton Rouge Business Report*, July 31, 2001, p. 9.

77. Trevor Thomas, "'Decamillionaires' Thriving," *National Underwriter Life & Health-Financial Services Edition*, February 12, 2001, p. 10.

78. Coleman, "The Continuing Significance of Social Class to Marketing"; Crispell, "The Real Middle Americans."

79. Labich, "Class in America."

80. "Middle-Class on $10,000 a Year," *American Demographics*, September 1994, pp. 15–17.

81. Dave Montgomery, "Ten Years After Russia's Failed Coup, Middle Class Is Small but Growing," *Knight Ridder*, August 11, 2001.

82. Jacob, "The Big Rise."

83. Rebecca Piirto Heath, "The New Working Class," *American Demographics*, vol. 20, no. 1, January 1998, pp. 51–55.

84. Coleman, "The Continuing Significance of Social Class to Marketing."

85. Michael Solomon and Henry Assael, "The Forest or the Trees: A Gestalt Approach to Symbolic Consumption," in ed. Jean Umiker-Sebek, *Semiotics: New Directions in the Study of Signs for Sale* (Berlin: Mouton de Gruyter, 1987), pp. 189–218; William O'Hare and Barbara O'Hare, "Upward Mobility," *American Demographics*, January 1993, pp. 26–34.

86. Prasad, "Socioeconomic Product Risk and Patronage Preferences of Retail Shoppers"; Stuart Rich and Subhish Jain, "Social Class and Life Cycle as Predictors of Shopping Behavior," *Journal of Marketing Research*, June–July 1987, pp. 51–59.

87. Frank Caro, *Estimating the Numbers of Homeless Families* (New York: Community Service Society of New York, 1981).

88. National Coalition for the Homeless, "How Many People Experience Homelessness?" February 1999, **http://nch.ari.net/numbers.html**.

89. Lakshmi Bhargave, "Homeless Help Themselves With 'Advocate,'" *Daily Texan (Austin)*, February 16, 2000, pp. 1, 8.

90. Richard B. Freeman and Brian Hall, "Permanent Homelessness in America?" *Population Research and Policy Review*, vol. 6, 1987, pp. 3–27.

91. Ronald Paul Hill, "Homeless Women, Special Possessions, and the Meaning of 'Home': An Ethnographic Case Study," *Journal of Consumer Research*, December 1991, pp. 298–310.

92. David A. Snow and Leon Anderson, "Identity Work among the Homeless: The Verbal Construction and Avowal of Personal Identities," *American Journal of Sociology*, May 1987, pp. 1336–1371.

93. LaBarbera, "The Nouveaux Riches."

94. Robert Frank and Lisa Shuchman, "A British Foodie Tries to Tempt Manhattanites," *Wall Street Journal*, August 22, 1997, pp. B1, B2.

95. William M. Bulkeley, "Hold the Ketchup! Chic Restaurants Aim to Sell Haute Cuisine through Chains," *Wall Street Journal*, August 1, 1996, pp. B1, B7.

96. Jeffrey Ball and Scott Miller, "A Battle Fit for the Autobahn," *Wall Street Journal*, February 26, 2001, pp. B1, B6.

97. Ignacio Galceran and Jon Berry, "A New World of Consumers," *American Demographics*, March 1995, pp. 26–31.

98. Peter Katel, "Petro Padillo Longoria: A Retailer Focused on Working-Class Needs," *Time International*, October 15, 2001, p. 49.

99. Rahul Jacob, "India Is Open for Business," *Fortune*, November 16, 1992, pp. 128–130.

100. Kjell Gronhaug and Paul S. Trapp, "Perceived Social Class Appeals of Branded Goods and Services," *Journal of Consumer Marketing*, Winter 1989, pp. 13–18.

101. Ball and Miller, "A Battle Fit for the Autobahn."

102. Allen and Anderson, "Consumption and Social Stratification."

103. Peter Pae, "Private Bankers Court Merely Affluent," *Wall Street Journal*, May 12, 1992, pp. B1, B7.

104. Jonathan Friedland and Michael J. McCarthy, "Pairing Bud with Sushi in South America," *Wall Street Journal*, February 20, 1997, pp. B1, B8.

105. LaBarbera, "The Nouveaux Riches."

106. Sonya A. Grier and Rohit Deshpandé, "Social Dimensions of Consumer Distinctiveness: The Influence of Social Status on Group Identity and Advertising Persuasion," *Journal of Marketing Research*, vol. 38, May 2001, pp. 216–224.

107. Anita Sharpe, "Magazines for the Rich Rake in Readers," *Wall Street Journal*, February 16, 1996, pp. B1, B2.

108. Kranhold, "Marketing to the New Millionaire."

109. Kelly Shermach, "Study Identifies Types of Interactive Shoppers," *Marketing News*, September 25, 1995, p. 22; *eMarketer*, February 3, 2000 (online reference).

110. Rich and Jain, "Social Class and Life Cycle as Predictors of Shopping Behavior."

111. Teri Agins and Deborah Ball, "Designer Stores, in Extra Large," *Wall Street Journal*, June 6, 2001, pp. B1, B12.

112. Teri Agins, "Trunk-Show Chic," *Wall Street Journal*, February 5, 2001, pp. B1, B4.

113. Page, "A History of Conspicuous Consumption."

114. James R. Hagerty, "Gilding the Drill Bit? Hardware Giants Go High End," *Wall Street Journal*, July 28, 1998, pp. B1, B7,

115. Wendy Bounds, "Discounters Dress Up to Lure the Well Heeled Shopper," *Wall Street Journal*, December 3, 1997, pp. B1, B13.

116. Matthew Rose, "Stodgy Savile Row Aims to Suit the Youth," *Wall Street Journal*, March 3, 1996, pp. B1, B5.

117. Labich, "Class in America."

118. Kevin Goldman, "Network Targets Drivers at Truck Stops," *Wall Street Journal*, November 11, 1992, pp. B1, B4.

Chapter 15

1. "UNFPA, China Strengthens Cooperation in Population," *Xinhua News Agency*, January 12, 2002, **www.comtexnews.com**; "China's Baby Bust: A Dwindling Birthrate and an Aging Populace Force China to Rethink Its Family-Planning Policy," *Time International*, July 30, 2001, pp. 18+; "Young and Restless Kids' Tastes Change as Fast in China as Anywhere Else," *Time International*, October 23, 2000, pp. 88+; Joyce Barnathan, "China's Youth," *BusinessWeek*, September 15, 1997, pp. 62E2–62E10.

2. Michael M. Phillips, "Selling by Evoking What Defines a Generation," *Wall Street Journal*, August 13, 1996, pp. B1, B7.

3. "Nation's Median Age Highest Ever, but 65-and-Over Population's Growth Lags, Census 2000 Shows," *U.S. Department of Commerce News*, May 15, 2001, **www.census.gov/press-release/www/2001/cb01cn67.html**.

4. Lisa Vickery, Kelly Greene, Shelly Branch, and Emily Nelson, "Marketers Tweak Strategies as Age Groups Realign," *Wall Street Journal*, May 15, 2001, pp. B1, B4; "Profiles of General Demographic Characteristics: 2000 Census of Population and Housing," U.S. Department of Commerce, May 2001, p. 3.

5. Vickery, Greene, Branch, and Nelson, "Marketers Tweak Strategies as Age Groups Realign."

6. "Teen Clout Grows; Chains React," *MMR*, August 20, 2001, pp. 29+; Howard Schlossberg, "What Teenagers Find Hot Today Will Be Old News Tomorrow," *Marketing News*, December 6, 1993, p. 7.

7. Melinda Beck, "Maybe Rock 'N' Roll Really Is Here to Stay," *Wall Street Journal*, February 5, 1997, pp. B1, B8.

8. "The Six Value Segments of Global Youth," *Brandweek*, May 22, 2000, pp. 38+.

9. David Murphy, "Connecting with Online Teenagers," *Marketing*, September 27, 2001, pp. 31+.

10. Sheree R. Curry, "Wireless Trend Taking Hold," *Advertising Age*, June 25, 2001, p. S2; Wendy Bounds, "Rushing to Cash In on the New Baby Boom," *Wall Street Journal*, August 9, 2000, pp. B1, B4.

11. John C. Jay, "The Valley of the New," *American Demographics*, March 2000, pp. 58–59.

12. Elaine Underwood, "Jean-etics 101," *Brandweek*, August 17, 1992, pp. 14–15.

13. Deena Weinstein, *Heavy Metal, A Cultural Sociology* (New York: Lexington, 1991); Kathryn Joan Fox, "Real Punks and Pretenders," *Journal of Contemporary Ethnography*, October 1987, pp. 344–370; Penelope Eckart, "Clothing and Geography in a Suburban High School," in ed. Conrad Phillip Kottak, *Researching American Culture* (Ann Arbor, Mich.: University of Michigan Press, 1982).

14. Erin White, "Now There's Something New for Back-to-School: Racy Underwear," *Wall Street Journal*, August 3, 2001, p. B1; Megan Scott, "Girls Clamoring for Grown-Up Shoe Styles," *Marketing News*, November 19, 2001, p. 25.

15. Laura Zinn, "Teens: Here Comes the Biggest Wave Yet," *BusinessWeek*, April 11, 1994, pp. 76–86; Lisa Marie Petersen, "I Bought What Was on Sale," *Brandweek*, February 22, 1993, pp. 12–13.

16. Dennis H. Tootelian and Ralph M. Gaedecke, "The Teen Market: An Exploratory Analysis of Income, Spending, and Shopping Patterns," *Journal of Consumer Marketing*, Fall 1994, pp. 35–44; George P. Moschis and Roy L. Moore, "Decision Making among the Young: A Socialization Perspective," *Journal of Consumer Research*, September 1979, pp. 101–112.

17. "To Reach the Unreachable Teen," *BusinessWeek*, September 18, 2000, pp. 78+.

18. "Teen Clout Grows."

19. Ibid.
20. "Those Precocious 13-Year Olds," *Brandweek*, January 25, 1993, p. 13; Shawn Tully, "Teens, the Most Global Market of All," *Fortune*, May 16, 1994, pp. 90–96.
21. Kerry Capell, "MTV's World," *BusinessWeek*, February 18, 2001, pp. 81–84; Sally Beatty and Carol Hymowitz, "How MTV Stays Tuned In to Teens," *Wall Street Journal*, March 21, 2000, pp. B1, B4.
22. Paula Dwyer, "The Euroteens (and How to Sell to Them)," *BusinessWeek*, April 11, 1994, p. 84.
23. Roger Ricklefs, "Marketers Seek Out Today's Coolest Kids to Plug into Tomorrow's Mall Trends," *Wall Street Journal*, July 11, 1996, pp. B1, B2; Michael J. McCarthy, "Stalking the Elusive Teenage Trendsetter," *Wall Street Journal*, November 19, 1998, pp. B1, B10.
24. Beatty and Hymowitz, "How MTV Stays Tuned In to Teens."
25. Norihiko Shirouzu, "Japan's High-School Girls Excel in the Art of Setting Trends," *Wall Street Journal*, April 24, 1998, pp. B1, B7.
26. Erin White, "Abercrombie Seeks to Send Teeny-Boppers Packing," *Wall Street Journal*, August 30, 2001, pp. B1, B4; Rebecca Quick, "Is Ever-So-Hip Abercrombie & Fitch Losing Its Edge with Teens?" *Wall Street Journal*, February 22, 2000, pp. B1, B4.
27. Emily Nelson, "Beauty Makers Now Go Where the Boys Are," *Wall Street Journal*, August 10, 2000, pp. B1, B4.
28. Rekha Balu, "Gatorade Targets Younger Fans in Bid to Best Sports-Drink Rivals," *Wall Street Journal*, January 28, 1998, pp. B7.
29. Murphy, "Connecting with Online Teenagers"; Fara Warner, "Booming Asia Lures Credit-Card Firms," *Wall Street Journal*, November 24, 1995, p. B10.
30. Louise Lee, "To Keep Teens Away, Malls Turn Snooty, "*Wall Street Journal*, October 17, 1996, pp. B1, B9.
31. Patrick M. Reilly and Stefan Fatsis, "NFL Hands the Ball to Pop Stars, Trying to Score with Young Fans," *Wall Street Journal*, August 29, 1997, p. B1.
32. Matthew Grimm, "Irvington, 10533," *Brandweek*, August 17, 1993, pp. 11–13.
33. Helene Cooper, "Once Again, Ads Woo Teens with Slang," *Wall Street Journal*, March 29, 1993, pp. B1, B6; Adrienne Ward Fawcett, "When Using Slang in Advertising: BVC," *Advertising Age*, August 23, 1993, p. S-6.
34. Barbara Martinez, "Antismoking Ads Aim to Gross Out Teens," *Wall Street Journal*, March 21, 1997, pp. B1, B8.
35. Jennie L. Phipps, "Networks Drill Deeper into Teen Market," *Electronic Media*, March 12, 2001, p. 20; Erin White, "Teen Mags for Guys, Not Dolls," *Wall Street Journal*, August 10, 2000, pp. B1, B4; Wendy Bounds, "Teen-Magazine Boom: Beauty, Fashion, Stars, and Sex," *Wall Street Journal*, December 7, 1998, pp. B1, B10.
36. Calmetta Y. Coleman, "Target Aims at Younger Shoppers on MTV," *Wall Street Journal*, April 8, 1999.
37. "To Reach the Unreachable Teen."
38. Jeff Jensen, "A New Read on How to Reach Boys," *Advertising Age*, August 23, 1993, pp. S-10–S-11.
39. Cristina Merrill, "Keeping Up with Teens," *American Demographics*, October 1999, pp. 27–31.
40. Yumiko Ono, "Limited Too Plans a Preteen Catalog Blitz," *Wall Street Journal*, August 25, 1998, p. B8.
41. Leigh Muzslay, "Shoes That Morph from Sneakers to Skates Are Flying out of Stores," *Wall Street Journal*, July 26, 2001, p. B1.
42. Carrie Goerne, "Marketers Try to Get More Creative in Reaching Teens," *Marketing News*, August 5, 1991, pp. 2, 6.
43. Steve Jarvis, "Lesson Plans," *Marketing News*, June 18, 2001, pp. 1, 9–10.
44. Raju Narisetti, "Teenager Rates P&G's Virtual Makeover," *Wall Street Journal*, October 15, 1996, p. B12.
45. Thomas E. Weber, "Where the Boys and Girls Are: Teens Talk about the Web," *Wall Street Journal*, December 24, 1997, pp. B6, B7.
46. Carol Angrisani, "X Marks the Spot," *Brandmarketing*, April 2001, pp. 18+; Jeff Giles, "Generalizations X," *Newsweek*, June 6, 1994, pp. 62–72.
47. Giles, "Generalizations X"; John Flinn, "'Generation X' Plugged in and Purchasing," *Austin American Statesman*, February 4, 1995, pp. A1, A9.
48. Christina Duff, "It's Sad but True: Good Times Are Bad for Real Slackers," *Wall Street Journal*, August 6, 1998, pp. A1, A5; Angrisani, "X Marks the Spot."
49. Bonnie Rochman, "American Twentysomethings Land in Vietnam," *Fortune*, June 24, 1996, pp. 114–126.
50. Pamela Paul, "Echo Boomerang," *American Demographics*, June 2001, pp. 45–49.
51. Kimberly Paterson, "Twentysomething Generation Is Tough to Target," *National Underwriter*, March 21, 1994, pp. 31–32; Randolph E. Schmid, "Young Adults Slow to Leave Home, Quick to Return," *Austin American Statesman*, April 8, 1994, p. A15.
52. Angrisani, "X Marks the Spot."
53. Cyndee Miller, "X Marks the Lucrative Spot, But Some Advertisers Can't Hit Target," *Marketing News*, August 2, 1993, pp. 1, 14; Pat Sloan, "Xers Brush Off Cosmetics Marketers," *Advertising Age*, September 27, 1993, p. 4.
54. Andrea Petersen, "Restaurants Bring in da Noise to Keep Out da Nerds," *Wall Street Journal*, December 30, 1997, pp. B1, B2.
55. Joseph B. White, "Toyota, Seeking Younger Drivers, Uses Hip Hop, Web, Low Prices," *Wall Street Journal*, September 22, 1999, p. B10.

56. Judith Valente, "Scotch Makers Tell Youth It's Hip to Be Old-Fashioned," *Wall Street Journal*, December 29, 1993, pp. B1, B5; Eric Hollreiser, "Seagram Tries '7 & 7' Revisited, with a Slammin' GenX Twist," *Brandweek*, January 30, 1995, p. 14.
57. Shelly Branch, "Johnnie Walker Targets a Younger Market," *Wall Street Journal*, February 7, 2001, p. B14.
58. Alfred Schreiber, "Generation X the Next Big Event Target," *Advertising Age*, June 21, 1993, p. S-3; Robert Gustafson, "Marketing to Generation X? Better Practice Safe Sex," *Advertising Age*, March 7, 1994, p. 26.
59. Gerry Khermouch, "Would You Buy a Heineken from This Dude?" *Brandweek*, February 20, 1995, pp. 1, 6.
60. Sally Goll Beatty, "If Barq's Has Bite, So Do the Spots Wieden Has Made for the Coke Brand," *Wall Street Journal*, June 30, 1997, p. B6.
61. Horst Stipp, "Xers Are Not Created Equal," *Mediaweek*, March 21, 1994, p. 20; Lisa Marie Petersen, "Previews of Coming Attractions," *Brandweek*, March 1993, pp. 22–23.
62. Angrisani, "X Marks the Spot."
63. Laura Koss-Feder, "Want to Catch GenX? Try Looking on the Web," *Marketing News*, June 8, 1998, p. 20.
64. Sally Beatty, Alcohol Firms Boost Online Ads to Youth," *Wall Street Journal*, December 17, 1998, p. B8.
65. Andrea Petersen, "Charities Bet Young Will Come for the Music, Stay for the Pitch," *Wall Street Journal*, September 7, 1996, p. B1.
66. "Insurance Gets Hip," *American Demographics*, January 1, 2002, p. 48.
67. Tibbett L. Speer, "College Come-Ons," *American Demographics*, March 1998, pp. 41–45.
68. Cheryl Russell, "The Power of One," *Brandweek*, October 4, 1993, pp. 27–28, 30, 32.
69. Raymond Kotcher, "Gathering Moss," *Adweek*, November 23, 1992, p. 26; Campbell Gibson, "The Four Baby Booms," *American Demographics*, November 1993, pp. 36–40.
70. Alison Stein Wellner, "The Forgotten Baby Boom," *American Demographics*, February 2001, pp. 46–51.
71. Alison Stein Wellner, "Generational Divide," *American Demographics*, October 2000, pp. 52–58.
72. Heather Graulich, "Do You Fall into the Gap?" *Austin American Statesman*, July 28, 1997, pp. E1, E8.
73. Becca Mader, "Boomer Town," *Business Journal-Milwaukee*, July 20, 2001, p. 21.
74. Ken Brown, "After Roaring through the '90s, Harley's Engine Could Sputter," *Wall Street Journal*, February 12, 2002, www.wsj.com; Joseph Weber, "Harley Investors May Get a Wobbly Ride," *Business Week*, February 11, 2002, p. 65.
75. Peter Francese, "Trend Ticker: Big Spenders," *American Demographics*, September 2001, pp. 30–31; Susan Mitchell, "How Boomers Save," *American Demographics*, September 1994, pp. 22–29; "Baby Boomers Are Top Dinner Consumers," *Frozen Food Age*, February 1994, p. 33.
76. Jeffrey A. Trachtenberg, "Packaging Old Hits to Produce New Hits," *Wall Street Journal*, December 11, 1995, pp. B1, B4.
77. Shirley Leung, "Fast-Food Chains Upgrade Menus, and Profits, with Pricey Sandwiches," *Wall Street Journal*, February 5, 2002, pp. 1+.
78. Fara Warner and Lisa Marie Petersen, "The Magic Bus Updated: Full-Sized Vans Are Back," *Brandweek*, September 30, 1993, pp. 34–35.
79. Penny Warneford and Pam Weisz, "Dial, Lever Eye Baby Boomlet," *Brandweek*, September 19, 1994, pp. 1, 6.
80. Cyndee Miller, "Jeans Marketers Loosen Up, Adjust to Expanding Market," *Marketing News*, August 31, 1992, pp. 6–7.
81. John Finotti, "Back in Fashion: After a Strong Start and Then a Stumble, Specialty Retailer Chico's FAS Is Riding the Baby Boomer Wave," *Florida Trend*, January 2002, pp. 16+.
82. Lisa Bannon, "Disney Decides World Isn't So Small, Creating Education Resort for Boomers," *Wall Street Journal*, March 1, 1996, pp. B1, B2.
83. John Fetto, "Queen for a Day," *American Demographics*, March 2000, pp. 31–32; Francese, "Trend Ticker: Big Spenders"; Patricia Braus, "Boomers against Gravity," *American Demographics*, February 1995, pp. 50–57.
84. Kevin Goldman, "Advertisers Are at Last Treating Baby Boomers Like Grown-Ups," *Wall Street Journal*, December 29, 1993, p. B5.
85. Ernest Beck and Yumiko Ono, "Dewar's Profile Rises as Suitors Swirl Around," *Wall Street Journal*, March 11, 1998, p. B1.
86. Lisa Miller, "Water Toys at Resort Turn Sane Adults into Crazy Kids," *Wall Street Journal*, March 15, 1996, pp. B1, B6.
87. Yumiko Ono, "Kitty-Mania Grips Grown-Ups in Japan," *Wall Street Journal*, December 15, 1998, pp. B1, B4.
88. Jean Halliday, "Rockin' in the Front Seat," *Advertising Age*, March 16, 2001, www.adage.com.
89. Scott McCartney, "Vacations with Ringo, Elvis, and Cobain," *Wall Street Journal*, February 7, 1997, pp. B1, B7.
90. Patrick M. Reilly, "What a Long Strange Trip It's Been," *Wall Street Journal*, April 7, 1999, pp. B1, B4.
91. Vicki Thomas, "Which Media Reach Boomers Best," *Bank Marketing*, July 1993, pp. 68–72.
92. "Profiles of General Demographic Characteristics."
93. Francese, "Trend Ticker: Big Spenders"; Christina Duff, "Profiling the Aged: Fat Cats or Hungry Victims?" *Wall Street Journal*, August 29, 1996, pp. B1, B8.

94. Carol M. Morgan, "The Psychographic Landscape of 50-Plus," *Brandweek*, July 19, 1993, pp. 28–32.

95. Stuart Van Auken and Thomas E. Barry, "An Assessment of the Trait Validity of Cognitive Age Measures," *Journal of Consumer Psychology*, vol. 4, no. 2, 1995, pp. 107–132; Robert E. Wilkes, "A Structural Modeling Approach to the Measurement and Meaning of Cognitive Age," *Journal of Consumer Research*, September 1992, pp. 292–301.

96. Joan Raymond, "The Joy of Empty Nesting," *American Demographics*, May 2000, pp. 49–54.

97. Morgan, "The Psychographic Landscape of 50-Plus"; Phil Goodman, "Marketing to Age Groups Is All in the Mind Set," *Marketing News*, December 6, 1993, p. 4.

98. Catherine A. Cole and Gary J. Gaeth, "Cognitive and Age-Related Differences in the Ability to Use Nutritional Information in a Complex Environment," *Journal of Marketing Research*, May 1990, pp. 175–184; Catherine A. Cole and Siva K. Balasubramanian, "Age Differences in Consumers' Search for Information: Public Policy Implications," *Journal of Consumer Research*, June 1993, pp. 157–169; Deborah Roedder John and Catherine A. Cole, "Age Differences in Information Processing: Understanding Deficits in Young and Elderly Consumers," *Journal of Consumer Research*, December 1986, pp. 297–315.

99. Carolyn Yoon, "Age Differences in Consumers' Processing Strategies: An Investigation of Moderating Differences," *Journal of Consumer Research*, December 1997, pp. 329–342.

100. Sharmistha Law, Scott A Hawkins, and Fergus I.M. Craik, "Repetition-Induced Belief in the Elderly: Rehabilitating Age-Related Memory Deficits," *Journal of Consumer Research*, September 1998, pp. 91–107.

101. Cole and Gaeth, "Cognitive and Age-Related Differences in the Ability to Use Nutritional Information in a Complex Environment," pp. 175–184; Cole and Balasubramanian, "Age Differences in Consumers' Search for Information"; John and Cole, "Age Differences in Information Processing," pp. 297–315.

102. "America's Aging Consumers," *Discount Merchandiser*, September 1993, pp. 16–28; Mary C. Gilly and Valerie A. Zeithaml, "The Elderly Consumer and Adoption of Technologies," *Journal of Consumer Research*, December 1985, pp. 353–357.

103. Michael Moss, "Leon Black Bets Big on the Elderly," *Wall Street Journal*, July 24, 1998, pp. B1, B8.

104. Stephanie Mehta, "Retailer with Vision Aims to Make Fading Eyesight Chic," *Wall Street Journal*, October 23, 1996, pp. B1, B2.

105. Raju Narisetti, "Products to Aid the Incontinent Are Growing Up," *Wall Street Journal*, November 13, 1995, pp. N1, B5.

106. Rhonda L. Rundle, "Allergan's Ads on Cataracts Join Health Debate at Awkward Time," *Wall Street Journal*, March 8, 1999, pp. B14.

107. Yumiko Ono, "An Army of 'Home Helpers' Is Ready to Descend on Japan's Seniors," *Wall Street Journal*, October 7, 1999, pp. B1, B4.

108. Elyse Tanouye, "Pitching Wrinkles as Medical Malady, J&J Launches Rx Cream for Aging Skin," February 13, 1996, pp. B1, B9.

109. Xander Mellish, "Revivers of Burma-Shave Hope to Lure Stubble of a Certain Age," *Wall Street Journal*, December 22, 1995, pp. B12.

110. Kendra Parker, "Reaping What They've Sown," *American Demographics*, December 1999, pp. 34+.

111. Jeff Brazil, "You Talkin' To Me?" *American Demographics*, December 1998, pp. 54–59.

112. Vanessa O'Connell, "Alcohol Makers' New Target: Drinkers over 50," *Wall Street Journal*, August 5, 1998, pp. B1, B4.

113. Bonnie S. Guy, Terri L. Rittenburg, and Douglass K. Hawes, "Dimensions and Characteristics of Time Perceptions among Older Consumers," *Psychology and Marketing*, January–February 1994, pp. 35–56.

114. Dale A. Lunsford and Melissa S. Burnett, "Marketing Product Innovations to the Elderly: Understanding the Barriers to Adoption," *Journal of Consumer Marketing*, Fall 1992, pp. 53–63.

115. Ronald E. Milliman and Robert C. Erffmeyer, "Improving Advertising Aimed at Seniors," *Journal of Advertising Research*, December 1989–January 1990, pp. 31–36.

116. Robin T. Peterson, "The Depiction of Senior Citizens in Magazine Advertisements: A Content Analysis," *Journal of Business Ethics*, September 1992, pp. 701–706; Anthony C. Ursic, Michael L. Ursic, and Virginia L. Ursic, "A Longitudinal Study of the Use of the Elderly in Magazine Advertising," *Journal of Consumer Research*, June 1986, pp. 131–133; John J. Burnett, "Examining the Media Habits of the Affluent Elderly," *Journal of Advertising Research*, October–November 1991, pp. 33–41.

117. John and Cole, "Age Differences in Information Processing"; Burnett, "Examining the Media Habits of the Affluent Elderly."

118. Jim Carlton, "Web Sites, Other PC Wonders Draw Crowds of Retirees," *Wall Street Journal*, January 29, 1998, pp. B1, B11.

119. "America's Aging Consumers"; John and Cole, "Age Differences in Information Processing."

120. David C. Jones, "New Marketing Tool Targets Selling to Seniors," *National Underwriter*, December 20, 1993, p. 5.

121. Jinkook Lee and Loren V. Geistfeld, "Elderly Consumers' Receptiveness to Telemarketing Fraud," *Journal of Public Policy & Marketing*, vol. 18, no. 2, Fall 1999, pp. 208–217; John R. Emshwiller, "Having Lost Thousands to Con Artists, Elderly Widow Tells Cautionary Tale," *Wall Street Journal*, August 9, 1996, pp. B1, B5.

122. Lisa D. Spiller and Richard A. Hamilton, "Senior Citizen Discount Programs: Which Seniors to Target and Why," *Journal of Consumer Marketing*, Summer 1993, pp. 42–51; Kelly Tepper, "The Role of Labeling Processes in Elderly Consumers' Responses to Age Segmentation Cues," *Journal of Consumer Research*, March 1994, pp. 503–519.

123. Yumiko Ono, "Kraft Seeking Joint Marketing Arrangement,' *Wall Street Journal*, March 11, 1996, p. B6.

124. Joan Meyers-Levy, "The Influence of Sex Roles on Judgment," *Journal of Consumer Research*, March 1988, pp. 522–530.

125. Charles S. Areni and Pamela Kiecker, "Gender Differences in Motivation: Some Implications for Manipulating Task-Related Involvement," in ed. Janeen Arnold Costa, *Gender and Consumer Behavior* (Salt Lake City, Utah: University of Utah Printing Service, 1993), pp. 30–43; Brenda Giner and Eileen Fischer, "Women and Arts, Men and Sports: Two Phenomena or One?" in ed. Janeen Arnold Costa, *Gender and Consumer Behavior* (Salt Lake City, Utah: University of Utah Printing Service, 1993), p. 149.

126. "Women in the United States: March 2000 (PPL-121)," *U.S. Department of Commerce*, March 2000, www.census.gov/population/www/socdemo/ppl-121.html.

127. Alladi Venkatesh, "Changing Roles of Women: A Life Style Analysis," *Journal of Consumer Research*, September 1980, pp. 189–197; Eleena de Lisser, "Women Shed Family Baggage on Trips," *Wall Street Journal*, February 9, 1996, pp. B1, B8.

128. Elia Kacapyr, "The Well-Being of American Women," *American Demographics*, August 1998, pp. 30, 32.

129. Beverly A. Browne and Sally K. Francis, "Skateboarders: Gender, Dress, and Social Comparison," in ed. Costa, *Gender and Consumer Behavior*, pp. 46–52.

130. Chen May Yee, "High-Tech Lift for India's Women," *Wall Street Journal*, November 1, 2000, pp. B1, B4; Alladi Venkatesh, "Gender Identity in the Indian Context, a Socio-Cultural Construction of the Female Consumer," in ed. Costa, *Gender and Consumer Behavior*, pp. 119–129.

131. Teresa Watanabe, "Japanese Women Dancing Up a Storm after Work Hours," *Austin American Statesman*, December 19, 1993, p. A24.

132. Matti Huuhtanen, "New Kits Help Dads Cope with Fatherhood," *Austin American Statesman*, December 17, 1994, p. A37.

133. Yumiko Ono, "Japan Warms to McDonald's Doting Dad Ads," *Wall Street Journal*, May 8, 1997, pp. B1, B12.

134. Lynn J. Jaffe and Paul D. Berger, "Impact on Purchase Intent of Sex-Role Identity and Product Positioning," *Psychology and Marketing*, Fall 1988, pp. 259–271.

135. Lisa Bannon, "Why Girls and Boys Get Different Toys," *Wall Street Journal*, February 14, 2000, pp. B1, B4.

136. David Whelan, "Do Ask, Do Tell," *American Demographics*, November 2001, p. 41.

137. John Fetto, "In Broad Daylight," *American Demographics*, February 2001, pp. 16–20; Ronald Alsop, "Cracking the Gay Market Code," *Wall Street Journal*, June 29, 1999, p. B1.

138. Ronald Alsop, "In Marketing to Gays, Lesbians Are Often Left Out," *Wall Street Journal*, October 11, 1999, pp. B1, B4.

139. Joan Meyers-Levy and Durairaj Maheswaran, "Exploring Differences in Males' and Females' Processing Strategies," *Journal of Consumer Research*, June 1991, pp. 63–70; William K. Darley and Robert E. Smith, "Gender Differences in Information Processing Strategies: An Empirical Test of the Selectivity Model in Advertising Response," *Journal of Advertising*, Spring 1995, pp. 41–56; Barbara B. Stern, "Feminist Literary Criticism and the Deconstruction of Ads: A Postmodern View of Advertising and Consumer Responses," *Journal of Consumer Research*, March 1993, pp. 556–566.

140. Meyers-Levy, "The Influence of Sex Roles on Judgment," Joan Meyers-Levy, "Priming Effects on Product Judgments: A Hemispheric Interpretation," *Journal of Consumer Research*, June 1989, pp. 76–86.

141. Laurette Dube and Michael S. Morgan, "Trend Effects and Gender Differences in Retrospective Judgments of Consumption Emotions," *Journal of Consumer Research*, September 1996, pp. 156–162.

142. Richard Elliot, "Gender and the Psychological Meaning of Fashion Brands," in ed. Janeen Arnold Costa, *Gender and Consumer Behavior* (Salt Lake City, Utah: University of Utah Printing Service, 1993), pp. 99–105.

143. Frederica Rudell, "Gender Differences in Consumer Decision Making for Personal Computers: A Test of Hypotheses," and Gary J. Bamossy and Paul Jansen, "Children's Apprehension and Comprehension: Gender Influences on Computer Literacy and Attitude Structures of Personal Computers," in ed. Costa, *Gender and Consumer Behavior*, pp. 1–16 and 17–29.

144. Eileen Fischer and Stephen J. Arnold, "More Than a Labor of Love: Gender Roles and Christmas Gift Shopping," *Journal of Consumer Research*, December 1990, pp. 333–345; Gretchen M. Herrmann, "His and Hers: Gender and Garage Sales," in ed. Costa, *Gender and Consumer Behavior*, pp. 88–98; Mehtap Kokturk and Yonca Karapaza, "A General Profile of Turkish Consumers Based on Gender Differences," in ed. Costa, *Gender and Consumer Behavior*, pp. 107–118.

145. Suzanne C. Grunert, "On Gender Differences in Eating Behavior as Compensatory Consumption," in ed. Costa, *Gender and Consumer Behavior*, pp. 74–86.

146. Margaret Popper, "Why Women Should Surf to Siebert," *BusinessWeek Online*, October 24, 2001, www.businessweek.com; Nancy Ann Jeffrey, "Wall Street's Soft Sell Lures Women Investors," *Wall Street Journal*, July 28, 1995, pp. C1, C6.

147. James H. McAlexander, John H. Shouten, and Harold F. Koenig, "Born to Be Mild? Women in a Male Consumption Domain," in ed. Costa, *Gender and Consumer Behavior*, p. 54.

148. Pam Weisz, "Glidden Makes Fashion Statement to Female Consumers," *Brandweek*, March 27, 1995, p. 14.

149. Khanh T. L. Tran, "Women Assert Computer Games Aren't Male Preserve," *Wall Street Journal*, February 26, 2001, pp. B1, B8.

150. Karen Mazurkewich, "Marketing," *Asian Wall Street Journal*, March 19, 2001, p. 12; Tara Parker-Pope, "All That Glitters Isn't Purchased by Men," *Wall Street Journal*, January 7, 1997, pp. B1, B10.

151. Pam Weisz, "Halston: $10M on Men's Scent," *Brandweek*, September 12, 1994, p. 14.

152. Pat Wechsler, "You're So Vain," *BusinessWeek*, September 8, 1997. p. 6.

153. Yumiko Ono, "Beautifying the Japanese Male," *Wall Street Journal*, March 11, 1999, pp. B1, B8.

154. John B. Ford, Patricia Kramer, Earl D. Honeycutt Jr., and Susan L. Casey, "Gender Role Portrayals in Japanese Advertising: A Magazine Content Analysis," *Journal of Advertising*, Spring 1998, pp. 113–24.

155. Cyndee Miller, "Tapping into Women's Issues Is Potent Way to Reach Market," *Marketing News*, December 6, 1993, pp. 1, 13; Patrick M. Reilly, "Women's Music Tour Handpicks Backers," *Wall Street Journal*, June 9, 1997, pp. B1, B6; Leslie Cauley, "Lifetime's Breast-Cancer Shows Prove to Be Hit with Advertisers," *Wall Street Journal*, October 1, 1998, pp. B12.

156. Stephanie Thompson, "Good Humor's Good Deeds: Unilever Division Plans Ice-Cream Tie-in with World Wildlife Fund," *Advertising Age*, January 8, 2001, p. 6.

157. Patrick M. Reilly, "Hard-Nosed Allure Wins Readers and Ads," *Wall Street Journal*, August 27, 1992, p. B8; Seema Nayyar, "Net TV Soap Ads: Lever Alone Hit Men," *Brandweek*, July 13, 1992, p. 10.

158. Matthew Rose and Suzanne Vranica-Torres, "What Do Women Want—To Read?" *Wall Street Journal*, June 4, 2001, pp. B1, B4.

159. Mark Robichaux, "Lifetime Is Creating New Shows Aimed at Young Female Viewers," *Wall Street Journal*, June 6, 1996, pp. B1, B6.

160. Patrick M. Reilly, "Time Out for Women's Sports Magazines," *Wall Street Journal*, January 19, 1998, p. B8.

161. Teri Agins, "'Real' Women Get a New Magazine Sized for Them," *Wall Street Journal*, December 3, 1996, pp. B8; Wendy Bounds, "Meredith Introduces 'More' for Women," *Wall Street Journal*, June 19, 1998, p. B4.

162. Maricris G. Briones, "On-line Retailers Seek Ways to Close Shopping Gender Gap," *Marketing News*, September 14, 1998, pp. 2, 10.

163. Rebecca Quick, "Victoria's Secret in Cyberspace," *Austin American Statesman*, January 14, 1999, p. E3.

164. Vanessa O'Connell, "Soap and Diaper Makers Pitch to Masses of Web Women," *Wall Street Journal*, July 20, 1998, pp. B1, B4.

165. Ronald Alsop, "Corporate Sponsorships at Gay Pride Parades Alienate Some Activists," *Wall Street Journal*, June 22, 2001, p. B1.

166. Ronald Alsop, "But Brewers Employ In-Your-Mug Approach," *Wall Street Journal*, June 29, 1999, p. B1.

167. Alsop, "Cracking the Gay Market Code."

168. Ronald Alsop, "As Same-Sex Households Grow More Mainstream, Businesses Take Note," *Wall Street Journal*, August 8, 2001, pp. B1, B4.

169. "Multigenerational Households Number 4 Million According to Census 2000," *U.S. Department of Commerce News*, September 7, 2001, **www.census.gov/pressrelease/www/2001/cb01cn182.html**.

170. Sak Onkvisit and John J. Shaw, *International Marketing: Analysis and Strategy* (Columbus, Ohio: Merrill, 1989).

171. Patrick Barta, "Looming Need for Housing a Big Surprise," *Wall Street Journal*, May 15, 2001, pp. B1, B4.

172. "The Future of Households," *American Demographics*, December 1993, pp. 27–40.

173. Christina Diff, "Census Finds Striking Shift in Families," *Wall Street Journal*, May 28, 1998, pp. B1, B13.

174. "Nation's Median Age Highest Ever, But 65-and-Over Population's Growth Lags, Census 2000 Shows." United States Department of Commerce News (soundbite), May 15, 2001. Webpage news release.

175. Pamela Paul, "Childless by Choice," *American Demographics*, November 2001, pp. 45–50.

176. Mary C. Gilly and Ben M. Enis, "Recycling the Family Life Cycle," in ed. Andrew A. Mitchell, *Advances in Consumer Research*, vol. 9 (Ann Arbor, Mich.: Association for Consumer Research, 1982), pp. 271–276; William D. Danko and Charles M. Schaninger, "An Empirical Evaluation of the Gilly-Enis Updated Household Life Cycle Model," *Journal of Business Research*, August 1990, pp. 39–57.

177. Robert E. Wilkes, "Household Life-Cycle Stages, Transitions, and Product Expenditures," *Journal of Consumer Research*, June 1995, pp. 27–42.

178. Alan R. Andreasen, "Life Status Changes and Changes in Consumer Preferences and Satisfaction," *Journal of Consumer Research*, December 1984, pp. 784–794.

179. Rebecca Gardyn, "A Market Kept in the Closet," *American Demographics*, November 2001, pp. 37–43.

180. "The Mommies, in Numbers," *Brandweek*, November 13, 1993, p. 17; Lee Smith, "The New Wave of Illegitimacy," *Fortune*, April 18, 1994, pp. 81–94.

181. John Palmer, "Animal Instincts," *Promo*, May 2001, pp. 25–33; "Pets Can Drive," *American Demographics*,

March 2000, pp. 10–12; Elizabeth C. Hirschman, "Consumers and Their Animal Companions," *Journal of Consumer Research*, March 1994, pp. 616–632; Clinton R. Sanders, "The Animal 'Other': Self-Definition, Social Identity, and Companion Animals," in eds. Marvin E. Goldberg, Gerald Gorn, and Richard W. Pollay, *Advances in Consumer Research*, vol. 17 (Provo, Utah: Association for Consumer Research, 1990), pp. 662–668; Alan Beck and Aaron Katcher, *Between Pets and People: The Importance of Animal Companionship* (New York: Putnam, 1983).

182. Rebecca Gardyn, "VIPs (Very Important Pets)," *American Demographics*, March 2001, pp. 16–18; "Pets Can Drive"; Ellen Graham, "Santa Has Lavish Plans for Cats, Dogs, Birds, Iguanas," *Wall Street Journal*, December 9, 1996, pp. B1, B2; Kathie Jenkins, "It's Dining Cats and Dogs," *Los Angeles Times*, June 22, 1995, pp. H14.

183. U.S. Bureau of the Census, Current Population Reports, Series P-20, No. 410, *Marital Status and Living Arrangements: March 1985* (Washington, D.C.: U.S. Government Printing Office, 1986); Judith Waldrop, "The Fashionable Family," *American Demographics*, March 1988, p. 22.

184. "Multigenerational Households Number 4 Million According to Census 2000." United States Department of Commerce news (soundbite), September 7, 2001. Webpage news release.

185. Patricia Braus, "Sex and the Single Spender," *American Demographics*, November 1993, pp. 28–34.

186. Barbara Carton, "It's a Niche! Twins, Triplets and Beyond," *Wall Street Journal*, February 2, 1999, pp. B1, B4.

187. Rebecca Gardyn, "Unmarried Bliss," *American Demographics,* December 2000, pp. 56–61.

188. Clark D. Olson, "Materialism in the Home: The Impact of Artifacts on Dyadic Communication," in eds. Elizabeth C. Hirschman and Morris B. Holbrook, *Advances in Consumer Research,* vol. 12 (Provo, Utah: Association for Consumer Research, 1985), pp. 388–393.

189. Jeanne L. Hafstrom and Marilyn M. Dunsing, "Socioeconomic and Social-Psychological Influences on Reasons Wives Work," *Journal of Consumer Research,* December 1978, pp. 169–175; Rena Bartos, *The Moving Target: What Every Marketer Should Know about Women* (New York: Free Press, 1982).

190. Rose M. Rubin, Bobye J. Riney, and David J. Molina, "Expenditure Pattern Differentials Between One-Earner and Dual-Earner Households: 1972–1973 and 1984," *Journal of Consumer Research,* June 1990, pp. 43–52; Horacio Soberon-Ferrer and Rachel Dardis, "Determinants of Household Expenditures for Services," *Journal of Consumer Research,* March 1991, pp. 385–397; Don Bellante and Ann C. Foster, "Working Wives and Expenditure on Services," *Journal of Consumer Research,* September 1984, pp. 700–707.

191. Michael D. Reilly, "Working Wives and Convenience Consumption," *Journal of Consumer Research,* March 1982, pp. 407–418; Ralph W. Jackson, Stephen W. McDaniel, and C. P. Rao, "Food Shopping and Preparation: Psychographic Differences of Working Wives and Housewives," *Journal of Consumer Research,* June 1985, pp. 110–113; Janet C. Hunt and B. F. Kiker, "The Effect of Fertility on the Time Use of Working Wives," *Journal of Consumer Research,* March 1981, pp. 380–387; Keith W. Bryant, "Durables and Wives' Employment Yet Again," *Journal of Consumer Research,* June 1988, pp. 37–47.

192. Sharon Y. Nickols and Karen D. Fox, "Buying Time and Saving Time: Strategies for Managing Household Production," *Journal of Consumer Research,* September 1983, pp. 197–208; R. S. Oropesa, "Female Labor Force Participation and Time-Saving Household Technology," *Journal of Consumer Research,* March 1993, pp. 567–579; Eugine H. Fram and Joel Axelrod, "The Distressed Shopper," *American Demographics,* October 1990, pp. 44–45.

193. Linda Thompson and Alexis Walker, "Gender in Families: Women and Men in Marriage, Work, and Parenthood," *Journal of Marriage and the Family,* November 1989, pp. 845–871.

194. Joan Raymond, "The Ex-Files," *American Demographics,* February 2001, pp. 60–64.

195. James H. Alexander, John W. Shouten, and Scott D. Roberts, "Consumer Behavior and Divorce," in eds. Janeen Costa and Russell W. Belk, *Research in Consumer Behavior,* vol. 6 (Greenwich, Conn.: JAI Press, 1993), pp. 153–184.

196. Kalpana Srinivasan, "More Single Fathers Raising Kids, Though Moms Far More Common," *Austin American Statesman,* December 11, 1998, p. A23.

197. Raymond, "The Ex-Files."

198. Barbara Rosewicz, "Here Comes the Bride . . . and for the Umpteenth Time," *Wall Street Journal,* September 10, 1996, pp. B1, B10.

199. Graham, "When Terrible Two's." Ellen Graham, "When the Terrible Twos Become Terrible Teens," *Wall Street Journal*, February 5, 1997, pp.B1, B8.

200. Jan Larson, "Understanding Stepfamilies," *American Demographics,* July 1992, pp. 36–40.

201. "Profiles of General Demographic Characteristics: 2000 Census of Population and Housing," United States Department of Commerce News.

202. Hideo Takayama, "Spending More on Fewer Kids," *Journal of Japanese Trade and Industry,* May 1991, pp. 24–27.

203. Kathy Chen, "Chinese Babies Are Coveted Consumers," *Wall Street Journal,* May 15, 1998, pp. B1, B7.

204. Paul, "Childless by Choice."

205. Vanessa O'Connell and Jon E. Hilsenrath, "Advertisers Are Cautious as Household Makeup Shifts," *Wall Street Journal,* May 15, 2001, pp. B1, B4.

206. Norihiko Shirouzu, "Flouting 'Rules' Sells Fridges in Japan," *Wall Street Journal,* October 31, 1995, pp. B1, B2.

207. Lisa Gubernick, "Adoption in Ads: Trendy, but Touchy," *Wall Street Journal,* July 21, 1998, pp. B1, B8.

208. Lyle V. Harris, "Shopping by Male," *Austin American Statesman,* April 27, 1999, pp. E1, E2.

209. Gardyn, "Unmarried Bliss."

210. Joan Raymond, "Radio-Active," *American Demographics,* October 2000, pp. 28–30.

211. Harry L. Davis, "Dimensions of Marital Roles in Consumer Decision Making," *Journal of Marketing Research,* May 1970, pp. 168–177; Conway Lackman and John M. Lanasa, "Family Decision Making Theory: An Overview and Assessment," *Psychology and Marketing,* March–April 1993, pp. 81–93.

212. "Gender Bender," *American Demographics,* April 2001, p. 25.

213. P. Doyle and P. Hutchinson, "Individual Differences in Family Decision Making," *Journal of the Market Research Society,* October 1973, pp. 193–206; Jagdish N. Sheth, "A Theory of Family Buying Decisions," in ed. J. N. Sheth, *Models of Buyer Behavior* (New York: Harper & Row, 1974), pp. 17–33; Daniel Seymour and Greg Lessne, "Spousal Conflict Arousal: Scale Development," *Journal of Consumer Research,* December 1984, pp. 810–821.

214. Neal Templin, "The PC Wars: Who Gets to Use the Family Computer?" *Wall Street Journal,* October 5, 1996, pp. B1, B2.

215. Sheth, "A Theory of Family Buying Decisions"; Michael A. Belch, George E. Belch, and Donald Sciglimpaglia, "Conflict in Family Decision Making: An Exploratory Investigation," in ed. Jerry C. Olson, *Advances in Consumer Research,* vol. 7 (Chicago: Association for Consumer Research, 1980), pp. 475–479.

216. W. Christian Buss and Charles M. Schaninger, "The Influence of Family Decision Processes and Outcomes," in eds. Richard P. Bagozzi and Alice M. Tybout, *Advances in Consumer Research,* vol. 10 (Ann Arbor, Mich.: Association for Consumer Research, 1983), pp. 439–444.

217. Terry L. Childers and Akshay R. Rao, "The Influence of Familial and Peer-Based Reference Groups on Consumer Decisions," *Journal of Consumer Research,* September 1992, pp. 198–211.

218. Harry L. Davis and Benny P. Rigaux, "Perception of Marital Roles in Decision Processes," *Journal of Consumer Research,* June 1974, pp. 5–14; Mandy Putnam and William R. Davidson, *Family Purchasing Behavior: 11 Family Roles by Product Category* (Columbus, Ohio: Management Horizons, Inc., a Division of Price Waterhouse, 1987).

219. Rosann Spiro, "Persuasion in Family Decision Making," *Journal of Consumer Research,* March 1983, pp. 393–402; Alvin Burns and Donald Granbois, "Factors Moderating the Resolution of Preference Conflict," *Journal of Marketing Research,* February 1977, pp. 68–77.

220. Pierre Filiarault and J. R. Brent Ritchie, "Joint Purchasing Decisions: A Comparison of Influence Structure in Family and Couple Decision Making Units," *Journal of Consumer Research,* September 1980, pp. 131–140; Dennis Rosen and Donald Granbois, "Determinants of Role Structure in Financial Management," *Journal of Consumer Research,* September 1983, pp. 253–258; Spiro, "Persuasion in Family Decision Making"; Kim P. Corfman and Donald R. Lehmann, "Models of Cooperative Group Decision-Making and Relative Influence: An Experimental Investigation of Family Purchase Decisions," *Journal of Consumer Research,* June 1987, pp. 1–13.

221. William J. Qualls, "Household Decision Behavior: The Impact of Husbands' and Wives' Sex Role Orientation," *Journal of Consumer Research,* September 1987, pp. 264–279; Giovanna Imperia, Thomas O'Guinn, and Elizabeth MacAdams, "Family Decision Making Role Perceptions among Mexican-American and Anglo Wives: A Cross-Cultural Comparison," in eds. Elizabeth C. Hirschman and Morris B. Holbrook, *Advances in Consumer Research,* vol. 12 (Provo, Utah: Association for Consumer Research, 1985), pp. 71–74.

222. Michael Flagg, "Asian Marketing," Asian *Wall Street Journal,* March 19, 2001, p. A12.

223. Robert T. Green, Jean-Paul Leonardi, Jean-Louis Chandon, Isabella C. M. Cunningham, Bronis Verhage, and Alain Strazzieri, "Societal Development and Family Purchasing Roles: A Cross-National Study," *Journal of Consumer Research,* March 1983, pp. 436–442; Leonidas C. Leonidou, "Understanding the Russian Consumer," *Marketing and Research Today,* March 1992, pp. 75–83; Sak Onkvisit and John J. Shaw, *International Marketing: Analysis and Strategy* (Columbus, Ohio: Merrill, 1989).

224. Michael B. Menasco and David J. Curry, "Utility and Choice: An Empirical Study of Wife/Husband Decision Making," *Journal of Consumer Research,* June 1989, pp. 87–97; Qualls, "Household Decision Behavior."

225. C. Whan Park, "Joint Decisions in Home Purchasing: A Muddling-Through Process," *Journal of Consumer Research,* September 1982, pp. 151–162; Harry L. Davis, Stephen J. Hoch, and E. K. Easton Ragsdale, "An Anchoring and Adjustment Model of Spousal Predictions," *Journal of Consumer Research,* June 1986, pp. 25–37; Gary M. Munsinger, Jean E. Weber, and Richard W. Hansen, "Joint Home Purchasing by Husbands and Wives," *Journal of Consumer Research,* March 1975, pp. 60–66; Lakshman Krisnamurthi, "The Salience of Relevant Others and Its Effect on Individual and Joint Preferences: An Experimental Investigation," *Journal of Consumer Research,* June 1983, pp. 62–72; Robert F. Krampf, David J. Burns, and Dale M. Rayman, "Consumer Decision Making and the Nature of the Product: A Comparison of Husband and Wife Adoption Process Location," *Psychology and Marketing,* March–April 1993, pp. 95–109.

226. Tamara F. Mangleburg, "Children's Influence in Purchase Decisions: A Review and Critique," in eds.

Marvin E. Goldberg, Gerald Gorn, and Richard W. Pollay, *Advances in Consumer Research,* vol. 17 (Provo, Utah: Association for Consumer Research, 1990), pp. 813–825; Ellen R. Foxman, Patriya S. Tansuhaj, and Karin M. Ekstrom, "Family Members' Perceptions of Adolescents' Influence in Family Decision Making," *Journal of Consumer Research,* March 1989, pp. 481–490; George Belch, Michael A. Belch, and Gayle Ceresino, "Parental and Teenage Influences in Family Decision Making," *Journal of Business Research,* April 1985, pp. 163–176; Lackman and Lanasa, "Family Decision Making Theory."

227. "Parents, Retailers Condition Children to Look for Brand-Name Goods," *Biloxi Sun Herald,* April 22, 2001.

228. Ernest Beck and Rekha Balu, "Europe Is Deaf to Snap! Crackle! Pop!" *Wall Street Journal,* June 22, 1998, pp. B1, B8.

229. Selina S. Guber and Jon Berry, "War Stories from the Sandbox: What Kids Say," *Brandweek,* July 5, 1993, pp. 26–30; Andre Caron and Scott Ward, "Gift Decisions by Kids and Parents," *Journal of Advertising Research,* August–September 1975, pp. 15–20.

230. Mary Lou Roberts, Lawrence H. Wortzel, and Robert L. Berkeley, "Mothers' Attitudes and Perceptions of Children's Influence and Their Effect on Family Consumption," in ed. Jerry C. Olson, *Advances in Consumer Research,* vol. 8 (Ann Arbor, Mich.: Association for Consumer Research, 1981), pp. 730–735; Ellen Foxman and Patriya Tansuhaj, "Adolescents' and Mothers' Perceptions of Relative Influence in Family Purchase Decisions: Patterns of Agreement and Disagreement," in ed. Michael J. Houston, *Advances in Consumer Research,* vol. 15 (Provo, Utah: Association for Consumer Research, 1988), pp. 449–453.

231. Sharon E. Beatty and Salil Talpade, "Adolescent Influence in Family Decision Making: A Replication with Extension," *Journal of Consumer Research,* September 1994, pp. 332–341; Christopher Power, "Getting 'Em While They're Young," *Business Week,* September 9, 1991, pp. 94–95; Scott Ward and Daniel B. Wackman, "Children's Purchase Influence Attempts and Parental Yielding," *Journal of Marketing Research,* November 1972, pp. 316–319.

232. William K. Darley and Jeen-Su Lim, "Family Decision Making in Leisure Time Activities: An Exploratory Analysis of the Impact of Locus of Control, Child Age Influence Factor and Parental Type on Perceived Child Influence," in ed. Richard J. Lutz, *Advances in Consumer Research,* vol. 13 (Ann Arbor, Mich.: Association for Consumer Research, 1986), pp. 370–374; George P. Moschis and Linda G. Mitchell, "Television Advertising and Interpersonal Influences on Teenagers' Participation in Family Consumer Decisions," in ed. Lutz, *Advances in Consumer Research,* vol. 13, pp. 181–186; James E. Nelson, "Children as Information Sources in Family Decisions to Eat Out," in ed. William L. Wilkie, *Advances in Consumer Research,* vol. 6 (Ann Arbor, Mich.: Association for Consumer Research, 1978), pp. 419–423; Beatty and Talpade, "Adolescent Influence in Family Decision Making."

233. Jeff Brazil, "Play Dough," *American Demographics,* December 1999, pp. 57–61.

234. Kay M. Palan and Robert E. Wilkes, "Adolescent-Parent Interaction in Family Decision Making," *Journal of Consumer Research,* September 1997, pp. 159–169.

235. Les Carlson and Sanford Grossbart, "Parental Style and Consumer Socialization of Children," *Journal of Consumer Research,* June 1988, pp. 77–94.

236. Belch, Belch, and Ceresino, "Parental and Teenage Influences in Family Decision Making."

237. Calmetta Y. Coleman, "Supermarkets Build Sales by Beguiling Shoppers' Kids," *Wall Street Journal,* January 19, 1998, pp. B1, B8.

238. Larry Dobrow, "How Old Is Old Enough?" *Advertising Age,* February 4, 2002, p. S4.

239. Shiela Long O'Mara, "Editor's Notes," *Home Accents Today,* October 2001, p. S4.

240. Janae Lepir, "Targeting Online Youth," *Global Cosmetic Industry,* September 2001, p. 56.

241. Rebecca Quick, "New Web Sites Let Kids Shop, Like, without Credit Cards," *Wall Street Journal,* June 14, 1999, pp. B1, B4.

242. Dobrow, "How Old Is Old Enough?"

243. Betsy Spethmann, "Hilton Heads toward Tie-Ins," *Brandweek,* March 8, 1993, p. 4; Christina Binkley, "Marriott Outfits an Old Chain for New Market," *Wall Street Journal,* October 13, 1998, pp. B1, B4.

244. Pauline Yoshihashi, "Stars Fade as Las Vegas Bets on Families," *Wall Street Journal,* February 5, 1993, pp. B1, B2.

245. "Catalogs Look Increasingly at Kids," *Home Textiles Today,* September 24, 2001, p. S36.

246. Thomas C. O'Guinn and Timothy P. Meyer, "The Family VCR: Ordinary Family Life with a Common Textual Product," Working paper, University of Illinois, 1994.

Chapter 16

1. Marc Weingarten, "It's an Ad! It's a Game! It's . . . Both!" *Business 2.0*, March 2002, p. 102; Kenneth Hein, "Pepsi on Yahoo!" *Adweek*, November 12, 2001, p. 7; Charlyn Keathing Chisholm, "Advergaming Enters the I-Marketing Olympics," *E-Commerce Times*, September 11, 2001, **www.ecommercetimes.com/perl/printer/13452**.

2. Robert L. Simison and Joseph B. White, "Reputation for Poor Quality Still Plagues Detroit," *Wall Street Journal*, May 4, 2000, pp. B1, B4.

3. Dana James, "Skoda Is Taken from Trash to Treasure," *Marketing News*, February 18, 2002, pp. 4–5.

4. Frederick Koenig, *Rumor in the Marketplace: The Social Psychology of Commercial Hearsay* (Dover,

Mass.: Auburn House, 1985); Paul M. Herr, Frank R. Kardes, and John Kim, "Effects of Word-of-Mouth and Product-Attribute Information on Persuasion: An Accessibility-Diagnosticity Perspective," *Journal of Consumer Research*, March 1991, pp. 454–462.

5. Paul F. Lazarsfeld, Bernard Berelson, and Hazel Gaudet, *The People's Choice; How the Voter Makes Up His Mind in a Presidential Campaign* (New York: Columbia University Press, 1948); see also Herr, Kardes, and Kim, "Effects of Word-of-Mouth and Product-Attribute Information on Persuasion."

6. Dale Duhan, Scott Johnson, James Wilcox, and Gilbert Harrell, "Influences on Consumer Use of Word-of-Mouth Recommendation Sources," *Journal of the Academy of Marketing Science*, vol. 25, Fall 1997, pp. 283–295.

7. Vicki Clift, "Systematically Solicit Testimonial Letters," *Marketing News*, June 6, 1994, p. 7.

8. Wendy Bounds, "Keeping Teens from Smoking, with Style," *Wall Street Journal*, May 6, 1999, p. B6.

9. Fen Montaigne, "Name That Chintz! How Shelter Magazines Boost Brands," *Wall Street Journal*, March 14, 1997, pp. B1, B8.

10. "How Allrecipes.com Has Avoided Getting Burned," *BusinessWeek Online*, September 29, 2000, **www.businessweek.com/smallbiz/content/sep2000/sb20000929_582.htm**

11. John W. Milligan, "Choosing Mediums for the Message," *US Banker*, February 1995, pp. 42–45.

12. Keiron Culligan, "Word-of-Mouth to Become True Measure of Ads," *Marketing*, February 9, 1995, p. 7.

13. "Wave of Internet Surfers Has Chinese Censors Nervous," *Los Angeles Times*, June 26, 1995, p. D6; Jeffrey A. Trachtenberg, "Time Warner Unit Sets Joint Venture to Market TV Programming in China," *Wall Street Journal*, March 8, 1995, p. B2; Fred D. Reynolds and William R. Darden, "Mutually Adaptive Effects of Interpersonal Communication," *Journal of Marketing Research*, November 1971, pp. 449–454.

14. Kara Swisher, "The Gatekeeper," *Wall Street Journal*, December 8, 1997, pp. R18, R27.

15. Jacob Jacoby and Wayne D. Hoyer, "What If Opinion Leaders Didn't Really Know More: A Question of Nomological Validity," in ed. Kent B. Monroe, *Advances in Consumer Research*, vol. 8 (Chicago: Association for Consumer Research, 1980), pp. 299–302; Robin M. Higie, Lawrence F. Feick, and Linda L. Price, "Types and Amount of Word-of-Mouth Communications about Retailers," *Journal of Retailing*, Fall 1987, pp. 260–277; regarding innovativeness, Terry L. Childers ("Assessment of the Psychometric Properties of an Opinion Leadership Scale," *Journal of Marketing Research*, May 1986, pp. 184–187) found opinion leadership was related to consumer creativity/curiosity and to using products in multiple ways.

16. Morris B. Holbrook, "Popular Appeal versus Expert Judgments of Motion Pictures," *Journal of Consumer Research*, vol. 26, September 1999, pp. 144–155.

17. Marsha L. Richins and Teri Root-Shafer, "The Role of Involvement and Opinion Leadership in Consumer Word of Mouth: An Implicit Model Made Explicit," in ed. Michael J. Houston, *Advances in Consumer Research*, vol. 15 (Provo, Utah: Association for Consumer Research, 1988), pp. 32–36.

18. Audrey Guskey-Federouoch and Robert L. Heckman, "The Good Samaritan in the Marketplace: Motives for Helpful Behavior," Paper presented at the Society for Consumer Psychology Conference, St. Petersburg, Fla., February 1994.

19. Lawrence F. Feick, Linda L. Price, and Robin Higie, "People Who Use People: The Opposite Side of Opinion Leadership," in ed. Richard J. Lutz, *Advances in Consumer Research*, vol. 13 (Provo, Utah: Association for Consumer Research, 1986), pp. 301–305; see also Jagdish N. Sheth, "Word-of-Mouth in Low-Risk Innovations," *Journal of Advertising Research*, June–July 1971, pp. 15–18.

20. Lawrence F. Feick and Linda L. Price, "The Market Maven: A Diffuser of Marketplace Information," *Journal of Marketing*, January 1987, pp. 83–97.

21. William O. Bearden, David M. Hardesty, and Randall L. Rose, "Consumer Self-Confidence: Refinements in Conceptualization and Measurement," *Journal of Consumer Research*, vol. 28, June 2001, pp. 121–134.

22. Heather Holliday, "Instant Power," *Advertising Age*, June 25, 2001, p. s12.

23. See, for example, Dorothy Leonard-Barton, "Experts as Negative Opinion Leaders in the Diffusion of a Technological Innovation," *Journal of Consumer Research*, March 1985, pp. 914–926.

24. Everett M. Rogers, *Diffusion of Innovations* (New York: The Free Press, 1983).

25. Laura Bird, "Consumers Smile on Unilever's Mentadent," *Wall Street Journal*, May 31, 1994, p. B9; Joseph R. Mancuso, "Why Not Create Opinion Leaders for New Product Introduction?" *Journal of Marketing*, July 1969, pp. 20–25.

26. Gabriel Bar-Haim, "The Meaning of Western Commercial Artifacts for Eastern European Youth," *Journal of Contemporary Ethnography*, July 1987, pp. 205–226.

27. Jim Patterson, "Branding Campaign Meant to Take Stigma off Country Music," *Associated Press Newswires*, May 1, 2001.

28. Stefan Fatsis, "Can Iverson Pitch to the Mainstream?" *Wall Street Journal*, June 8, 2001, pp. B1, B4; Stefan Fatsis, "In the NBA, Shoe Money Is No Longer a Slam Dunk," *Wall Street Journal*, May 14, 1998, pp. B1, B5.

29. Basil G. Englis and Michael R. Solomon, "To Be and Not to Be: Lifestyle Imagery, Reference Groups, and the Clustering of America," *Journal of Advertising*, March 1995, pp. 13–28.

30. Stefan Fatsis, "'Rad' Sports Give Sponsors Cheap Thrills," *Wall Street Journal*, May 12, 1995, p. B8.

31. John Gaffney, "Shoe Fetish," *Business 2.0*, March 2002, pp. 98–99.

32. Albert M. Muniz Jr. and Thomas C. O'Guinn, "Brand Community," *Journal of Consumer Research*, vol. 27, March 2001, pp. 412–432.

33. Larry Weber, *The Provocateur* (New York: Crown Business, 2001), p. 116.

34. Jonathan Fahey, "Love Into Money," *Forbes*, January 7, 2002, pp. 60–65.

35. Todd Nissen, "McDonald's Sees Good Results in Middle East," *ClariNet Electronic News Service*, February 20, 1994.

36. A. Benton Cocanougher and Grady D. Bruce, "Socially Distant Referent Groups and Consumer Aspiration," *Journal of Marketing Research*, August 1971, pp. 379–383.

37. Linda L. Price, Lawrence Feick, and Robin Higie, "Preference Heterogeneity and Coorientation as Determinants of Perceived Informational Influence," *Journal of Business Research*, November 1989, pp. 227–242; Jacqueline J. Brown and Peter Reingen, "Social Ties and Word-of-Mouth Referral Behavior," *Journal of Consumer Research*, December 1987, pp. 350–362; Mary C. Gilly, John L. Grahm, Mary Wolfinbarger, and Laura Yale, "A Dyadic Study of Interpersonal Information Search," *Journal of the Academy of Marketing Science*, vol. 26, no. 2, pp. 83–100; George Moschis, "Social Comparison and Informal Group Influence," *Journal of Marketing Research*, August 1976, pp. 237–244.

38. Randall L. Rose, William O. Bearden, and Kenneth C. Manning, "Attributions and Conformity in Illicit Consumption: The Mediating Role of Group Attractiveness," *Journal of Public Policy & Marketing*, vol. 20, no. 1, Spring 2001, pp. 84–92.

39. Rohit Desphande, Wayne D. Hoyer, and Naveen Donthu, "The Intensity of Ethnic Affiliation: A Study of the Sociology of Hispanic Consumption," *Journal of Consumer Research*, September 1986, pp. 214–220; Douglas M. Stayman and Rohit Deshpande, "Situational Ethnicity and Consumer Behavior," *Journal of Consumer Research*, December 1989, pp. 361–371.

40. Robert Madrigal, "The Influence of Social Alliances with Sports Teams on Intentions to Purchase Corporate Sponsors' Products," *Journal of Advertising*, vol. 29, no. 4, Winter 2000, pp. 13–24.

41. Jonathan K. Frenzen and Harry L. Davis, "Purchasing Behavior in Embedded Markets," *Journal of Consumer Research*, June 1990, pp. 1–12; see also Mark S. Granovetter, "The Strength of Weak Ties," *American Journal of Sociology*, May 1973, pp. 1360–1380; Brown and Reingen, "Social Ties and Word-of-Mouth Referral Behavior"; Jonathan K. Frenzen and Kent Nakamoto, "Structure, Cooperation, and the Flow of Market Information," *Journal of Consumer Research*, December 1993, pp. 360–375.

42. Chen May Yee, "Yahoo! Makes Grass-Roots Push in Asia," *Wall Street Journal*, August 1, 2000, p. B9.

43. David Orenstein, "A Family Affair for Mobile Phones," *Business 2.0*, December 26, 2001, **www.business2.com/articles/web/0,1653,36561,FF.html?ref=cnet.**

44. Reingen and Kernan, "Analysis of Referral Networks in Marketing"; Brown and Reingen, "Social Ties and Word-of-Mouth Referral Behavior"; see also Frenzen and Nakamoto, "Structure, Cooperation, and the Flow of Market Information."

45. Nicole Woolsey Biggart, *Charismatic Capitalism* (Chicago: University of Chicago Press, 1989); see also Jonathan K. Frenzen and Harry L. Davis, "Purchasing Behavior in Embedded Markets," *Journal of Consumer Research*, June 1990, pp. 1–12.

46. Barbara Carton, "PCs Replace Lettuce Tubs at Sales Parties," *Wall Street Journal*, March 31, 1997, pp. B1, B10.

47. Frenzen and Davis, "Purchasing Behavior in Embedded Markets."

48. Scott Ward, "Consumer Socialization," *Journal of Consumer Research*, September 1974, pp. 1–16; George P. Moschis, "The Role of Family Communication in Consumer Socialization of Children and Adolescents," *Journal of Consumer Research*, March 1985, pp. 898–913; George P. Moschis, *Consumer Socialization: A Life Cycle Perspective* (Lexington, Mass.: Lexington Books, 1987); Scott Ward, "Consumer Socialization," in eds. Harold H. Kassarjian and Thomas S. Robertson, *Perspectives in Consumer Behavior* (Glenview, Ill.: Scott-Foresman, 1980), pp. 380–396; Les Carlson and Sanford Grossbart, "Parental Style and Consumer Socialization of Children," *Journal of Consumer Research*, June 1988, pp. 77–92.

49. Deborah Roedder John, "Consumer Socialization of Children: A Retrospective Look at Twenty-Five Years of Research," *Journal of Consumer Research*, vol. 26, December 1999, pp. 183–213.

50. Moschis, "The Role of Family Communication in Consumer Socialization of Children and Adolescents"; Harriet L. Rheingold and Kaye V. Cook, "The Contents of Boys' and Girls' Rooms as an Index of Parents' Behavior," *Child Development*, June 1975, pp. 459–463; Scott Ward, Daniel B. Wackman, and Ellen Wartella, *How Children Learn to Buy: The Development of Consumer Information Processing Skills* (Beverly Hills, Calif.: Sage, 1979).

51. Ann Walsh, Russell Laczkiak, and Les Carlson, "Mothers' Preferences for Regulating Children's Television," *Journal of Advertising*, Fall 1998, pp. 23–36.

52. Dave Howland, "Ads Recruit Grandparents to Help Keep Kids from Drugs," *Marketing News*, January 18, 1999, p. 6.

53. Moschis, "The Role of Family Communication in Consumer Socialization of Children and Adolescents"; Conway Lackman and John M. Lanasa, "Family Decision Making Theory: An Overview and Assessment," *Psychology and Marketing*, March–April 1993, pp. 81–93; George P. Moschis, *Acquisition of the*

Consumer Role by Adolescents (Atlanta: Georgia State University, 1978).

54. Beverly A. Browne, "Gender Stereotypes in Advertising on Children's Television in the 1990s: A Cross-National Analysis," *Journal of Advertising*, Spring 1998, pp. 83–96.

55. See, for example, Greta Fein, David Johnson, Nancy Kosson, Linda Stork, and Lisa Wasserman, "Sex Stereotypes and Preferences in the Toy Choices of 20-Month-Old Boys and Girls," *Developmental Psychology*, July 1975, pp. 527–528; Lenore A. DeLucia, "The Toy Preference Test: A Measure of Sex-Role Identification," *Child Development*, March 1963, pp. 107–117; Judith E. O. Blackmore and Asenath A. LaRue, "Sex-Appropriate Toy Preference and the Ability to Conceptualize Toys as Sex-Role Related," *Developmental Psychology*, May 1979, pp. 339–340; Nancy Eisenberg-Berg, Rita Boothby, and Tom Matson, "Correlates of Preschool Girls' Feminine and Masculine Toy Preferences," *Developmental Psychology*, May 1979, pp. 354–355.

56. Donna Rouner, "Rock Music Use as a Socializing Function," *Popular Music and Society*, Spring 1990, pp. 97–108; Thomas L. Eugene, "Clothing and Counterculture: An Empirical Study," *Adolescence*, Spring 1973, pp. 93–112.

57. Fein et al., "Sex Stereotypes and Preferences in the Toy Choices of 20-Month-Old Boys and Girls"; Eisenberg-Berg, Boothby, and Matson, "Correlates of Preschool Girls' Feminine and Masculine Toy Preferences"; Sheila Fling and Main Manosevitz, "Sex Typing in Nursery School Children's Play," *Developmental Psychology*, vol. 7, September 1972, pp. 146–152.

58. Tamara Mangleburg and Terry Bristol, "Socialization and Adolescents' Skepticism toward Advertising," *Journal of Advertising*, Fall 1998, pp. 11–21.

59. Robert E. Burnkrant and Alain Cousineau, "Informational and Normative Social Influence in Buyer Behavior," *Journal of Consumer Research*, December 1975, pp. 206–215; Morton Deutsch and Harold B. Gerard, "A Study of Normative and Informational Influence upon Individual Judgment," *Journal of Abnormal and Social Psychology*, November 1955, pp. 629–636.

60. Dennis Rook and Robert Fisher, "Normative Influences on Impulsive Buying Behavior," *Journal of Consumer Research*," December 1995, pp. 305–313.

61. Paul Rozin and Leher Singh, "The Moralization of Cigarette Smoking in the United States," *Journal of Consumer Psychology*, vol. 8, no. 3, 1999, pp. 321–337.

62. Margaret Talbot, "Girls Just Want to Be Mean," *New York Times Magazine*, February 24, 2002, pp. 24+.

63. Ernest Beck, "Let Labor Lean to Leisurewear: The Harrods Shopper Stays Proper," *Wall Street Journal*, May 27, 1997, p. B1.

64. Peter Reingen, Brian Foster, Jacqueline Brown, and Stephen B. Seidman, "Brand Congruence in Interpersonal Relations: A Social Network Analysis," *Journal of Consumer Research*, December 1984, pp. 771–783.

65. James E. Stafford, "Effects of Group Influence on Consumer Brand Preferences," *Journal of Marketing Research*, February 1966, pp. 68–75.

66. Randall L. Rose, William O. Bearden, and Jesse E. Teel, "An Attributional Analysis of Resistance to Group Pressure Regarding Illicit Drug and Alcohol Consumption," *Journal of Consumer Research*, June 1992, pp. 1–13; see also Bobby J. Calder and Robert E. Burnkrant, "Interpersonal Influences on Consumer Behavior: An Attribution Theory Approach," *Journal of Consumer Research*, June 1977, pp. 29–38, 71; Solomon E. Asch, "Effects of Group Pressure upon the Modification and Distortion of Judgment," in ed. H. Guetzkow, *Groups, Leadership and Men* (Pittsburgh, Pa.: Carnegie Press, 1951); Sak Onkvisit and John J. Shaw, *International Marketing: Analysis and Strategy* (Columbus, Ohio: Merrill, 1989); see also Chin Tiong Tan and John U. Farley, "The Impact of Cultural Patterns on Cognition and Intention in Singapore," *Journal of Consumer Research*, March 1987, pp. 540–544.

67. For a general discussion of reactance behavior, see Mona A. Clee and Robert A. Wicklund, "Consumer Behavior and Psychological Reactance," *Journal of Consumer Research*, March 1980, pp. 389–405.

68. William O. Bearden and Michael J. Etzel, "Reference Group Influence on Product and Brand Purchase Decisions," *Journal of Consumer Research*, 1982, vol. 9, no. 2, pp. 183–194.

69. Robert E. Witt and Grady D. Bruce, "Group Influence and Brand Choice Congruence," *Journal of Marketing Research*, November 1972, pp. 440–443.

70. Bobby J. Calder and Robert E. Burnkrant, "Interpersonal Influences on Consumer Behavior: An Attribution Theory Approach," *Journal of Consumer Research*, June 1977, pp. 29–38; William O. Bearden, Richard G. Netemeyer, and Jesse E. Teel, "Measurement of Consumer Susceptibility to Interpersonal Influence," *Journal of Consumer Research*, March 1989, pp. 473–481; William O. Bearden and Randall L. Rose, "Attention to Social Comparison Information: An Individual Difference Factor Affecting Conformity," *Journal of Consumer Research*, March 1990, pp. 461–471.

71. Charles S. Gulas and Kim McKeage, "Extending Social Comparison: An Examination of the Unintended Consequences of Idealized Advertising Imagery," *Journal of Advertising*, vol. 29, no. 2, Summer 2000, pp. 17–28.

72. C. Whan Park and Parker Lessig, "Students and Housewives: Differences in Susceptibility to Reference Group Influence," *Journal of Consumer Research*, September 1977, pp. 102–110.

73. Robert Fisher and Kirk Wakefield, "Factors Leading to Group Identification: A Field Study of Winners and Losers," *Psychology and Marketing*, January 1998, pp. 23–40.

74. John R. French and Bertram Raven, "The Bases of Social Power," in ed. D. Cartwright, *Studies in Social Power* (Ann Arbor, Mich.: Institute for Social Research, 1969), pp. 150–167.

75. Reingen et al., "Brand Congruence in Interpersonal Relations"; Park and Lessig, "Students and Housewives."

76. Dana-Nicoleta Lascu, William O. Bearden, and Randall L. Rose, "Norm Extremity and Interpersonal Influences on Consumer Conformity," *Journal of Business Research*, March 1995, pp. 200–212.

77. J. L. Freeman and S. Fraser, "Compliance without Pressure: The Foot-in-the-Door Technique," *Journal of Personality and Social Psychology*, August 1966, pp. 195–202.

78. Robert A. Hansen and Larry M. Robinson, "Testing the Effectiveness of Alternative Foot-in-the-Door Manipulations," *Journal of Marketing Research*, August 1980, pp. 359–364; Jacob Hornik, Tamar Zaig, and Diro Shadmon, "Reducing Refusals in Telephone Surveys on Sensitive Topics," *Journal of Advertising Research*, June–July 1991, pp. 48–57; Michael Kamins, "The Enhancement of Response Rates to a Mail Survey through a Labeled Foot-in-the-Door Approach," *Journal of the Market Research Society*, April 1989, pp. 273–284.

79. Robert B. Cialdini, J. E. Vincent, S. K. Lewis, J. Caalan, D. Wheeler, and B. L. Darby, "Reciprocal Concessions Procedure for Inducing Compliance: The Door-in-the-Face Effect," *Journal of Personality and Social Psychology*, February 1975, pp. 200–215; John C. Mowen and Robert Cialdini, "On Implementing the Door-in-the-Face Compliance Strategy in a Marketing Context," *Journal of Marketing Research*, May 1980, pp. 253–258; see also Edward Fern, Kent Monroe, and Ramon Avila, "Effectiveness of Multiple Request Strategies: A Synthesis of Research Results," *Journal of Marketing Research*, May 1986, pp. 144–152.

80. Alice Tybout, Brian Sternthal, and Bobby J. Calder, "Information Availability as a Determinant of Multiple Request Effectiveness," *Journal of Marketing Research*, August 1983, pp. 279–290; John T. Gourville, "Pennies-a-Day: The Effect of Temporal Reframing on Transaction Evaluation," *Journal of Consumer Research*, March 1998, pp. 395–408.

81. Eric R. Spangenberg and Anthony G. Greenwald, "Social Influence by Requesting Self-Prophecy," *Journal of Consumer Psychology*, vol. 8, no. 1, 1999, pp. 61–89.

82. Deutsch and Gerard, "A Study of Normative and Informational Influence upon Individual Judgment"; C. Whan Park and Parker Lessig, "Students and Housewives: Differences in Susceptibility to Reference Group Influences" *Journal of Consumer Research*, 1977, 4 (September), 102–110. Dennis L. Rosen and Richard W. Olshavsky, "The Dual Role of Informational Social Influence: Implications for Marketing Management," *Journal of Business Research*, April 1987, pp. 123–144.

83. Jeffrey D. Ford and Elwood A. Ellis, "A Reexamination of Group Influence on Member Brand Preference," *Journal of Marketing Research*, vol. 17, no. 1, 1980, pp. 125–133; Linda L. Price and Lawrence F. Feick, "The Role of Interpersonal Sources in External Search: An Informational Perspective," in ed. Thomas Kinnear, *Advances in Consumer Research*, vol. 11 (Ann Arbor, Mich.: Association for Consumer Research, 1984), pp. 250–255.

84. Arch G. Woodside and M. Wayne DeLosier, "Effects of Word-of-Mouth Advertising on Consumer Risk Taking," *Journal of Advertising*, September 1976, pp. 17–26.

85. Henry Assael, *Consumer Behavior and Marketing Action*, 4th ed. (Boston: PWS-Kent, 1992).

86. John R. French and Bertram Raven, "The Bases of Social Power," in ed. D. Cartwright, *Studies in Social Power* (Ann Arbor, Mich.: Institute for Social Research, 1959), pp. 150–167; Dana-Nicoleta Lascu, William Bearden, and Randall Rose, "Norm Extremity and Interpersonal Influences on Consumer Conformity," *Journal of Business Research*, March 1995, pp. 200–212; David B, Wooten and Americus Reed II, "Informational Influence and the Ambiguity of Product Experience: Order Effects on the Weighting of Evidence," *Journal of Consumer Psychology*, 1998, vol. 7, no. 1, pp. 79–99.

87. Bearden, Netemeyer, and Teel, "Measurement of Consumer Susceptibility to Interpersonal Influence"; Bearden and Rose, "Attention to Social Comparison Information."

88. Gerald Zaltman and Melanie Wallendorf, *Consumer Behavior: Basic Findings and Management Implications*, 2d ed. (New York: Wiley, 1983); Reingen et al., "Brand Congruence in Interpersonal Relations."

89. Charles R. Taylor, Gordon E. Miracle, and R. Dale Wilson, "The Impact of Information Level on the Effectiveness of U.S. and Korean Television Commercials," *Journal of Advertising*, Spring 1997, pp. 1–18.

90. Stephen A. LaTour and Ajay Manrai, "Interactive Impact of Informational and Normative Influence on Donations," *Journal of Marketing Research*, August 1989, pp. 327–335.

91. Asim Ansari, Skander Essegaier, and Rajeev Kohli, "Internet Recommendation Systems," *Journal of Marketing Research*, vol. 37, August 2000, pp. 363–375.

92. Johan Arndt, "Role of Product-Related Conversations in the Diffusion of a New Product," *Journal of Marketing Research*, August 1967, pp. 291–295.

93. Marsha L. Richins, "Negative Word of Mouth by Dissatisfied Consumers: A Pilot Study," *Journal of Marketing*, January 1983, pp. 68–78.

94. Laurence C. Harmon and Kathleen M. McKenna-Harmon, "The Hidden Costs of Resident Dissatisfaction," *Journal of Property Management*, May–June 1994, pp. 52–55.

95. Herr, Kardes, and Kim, "Effects of Word-of-Mouth and Product-Attribute Information on Persuasion"; Richard W. Mizerski, "An Attribution Explanation of the Disproportionate Influence of Unfavorable Information," *Journal of Consumer Research*, December 1982, pp. 301–310.

96. Brown and Reingen, "Social Ties and Word-of-Mouth Referral Behavior"; Arndt, "Role of Product-Related Conversations in the Diffusion of a New Product"; Laura Yale and Mary C. Gilly, "Dyadic Perceptions in Personal Source Information Search," *Journal of Business Research*, March 1995, pp. 225–238.

97. Chip Walker, "Word of Mouth," *American Demographics*, July 1995, pp. 39–46.

98. Herr, Kardes, and Kim, "Effects of Word-of-Mouth and Product-Attribute Information on Persuasion."

99. Elihu Katz and Paul F. Lazarsfeld, *Personal Influence* (Glencoe, Ill.: Free Press, 1955).

100. Bob Donath, "Shed Some Light: Handling Online Threats to Firm's Image," *Marketing News*, February 16, 1998, p. 12.

101. David Orenstein, "Hidden Treasure," *Business 2.0*, July 10, 2001, pp. 41, 43.

102. Matt Haig, "Spread It by Word of Mouse," *The Guardian*, February 15, 2001, p. 14.

103. Martin Firrell and William Maughan, "Pitching the Movies: Where the Marketing Gets Manic," *Brand Strategy*, March 1, 2001, p. 22.

104. A. Coskun and Cheryl J. Frohlich, "Service: The Competitive Edge in Banking," *Journal of Services Marketing*, Winter 1992, pp. 15–23; Jeffrey G. Blodgett, Donald H. Granbois, and Rockney Waters, "The Effects of Perceived Justice on Complainants' Negative Word-of-Mouth Behavior and Repatronage Intentions," *Journal of Retailing*, Winter 1993, pp. 399–429; Karen Maru File, Ben B. Judd, and Russ A. Prince, "Interactive Marketing: The Influence of Participation on Positive Word-of-Mouth Referrals," *Journal of Services Marketing*, Fall 1992, pp. 5–15; Gary L. Clark, Peter F. Kaminski, and David R. Rink, "Consumer Complaints: Advice on How Companies Should Respond Based on an Empirical Study," *Journal of Services Marketing*, Winter 1992, pp. 41–51.

105. Kathryn Kranhold and Erin White, "The Perils and Potential Rewards of Crisis Managing for Firestone," *Wall Street Journal*, September 8, 2000, pp. B1, B4.

106. Mara Adelman, "Social Support in the Service Sector: The Antecedents, Processes, and Outcomes of Social Support in an Introductory Service," *Journal of Business Research*, March 1995, pp. 273–283; Jerry D. Rogers, Kenneth E. Clow, and Toby J. Kash, "Increasing Job Satisfaction of Service Personnel," *Journal of Services Marketing*, Winter 1994, pp. 14–27.

107. Hilary Stout, "Ad Budget: Zero. Buzz: Deafening," *Wall Street Journal*, December 29, 1999, pp. B1, B4.

108. Sonia Reyes, "Hebrew National Rolls Out 'Mom Squad,'" *Brandweek*, May 28, 2001, p. 6.

109. Michael Kamins, Valerie Folkes, and Lars Perner, "Consumer Responses to Rumors: Good News, Bad News," *Journal of Consumer Psychology*, vol. 6, no. 2, 1997, 165–187.

110. Lisa Bannon, "How a Rumor Spread about Subliminal Sex in Disney's *Aladdin*," *Wall Street Journal*, October 24, 1995, pp. A1, A13.

111. Koenig, *Rumor in the Marketplace*; see also Alice M. Tybout, Bobby J. Calder, and Brian Sternthal, "Using Information Processing Theory to Design Marketing Strategies," *Journal of Marketing Research*, February 1981, pp. 73–79.

112. Susan Goggins as noted in Koenig, *Rumor in the Marketplace*, pp. 163–164.

113. Samantha Marshall, "Labor Problems in Asia Hurt Nike's Image," *Wall Street Journal*, September 26, 1997, p. B18.

114. Patrick Courreges, "Halting Character Assassination: Court of Public Opinion May Provide Only Relief for Ravages of Rumor Mill," *Greater Baton Rouge Business Report*, September 25, 2001, pp. 26+.

115. Reingen and Kernan, "Analysis of Referral Networks in Marketing."

116. Vicki Clift, "Word-of-Mouth Can Be Easily Engineered," *Marketing News*, June 17, 1994, p. 11.

Chapter 17

1. "More Than Half of U.S. Now Wired," *Advertising Age*, February 11, 2002, p. 12; Michael Pastore, "Internet Key to Communication Among Youth," *CyberAtlas*, January 25, 2002, **cyberatlas.com**; Jim Sterne, *Advertising on the Web* (Indianapolis: Que, 1997); Ann Carrns, "www.doctorsmedicines," *Wall Street Journal*, June 10, 1999, pp. B1, B4; Gautam Naik, "In Digital Dorm, Click on Return for Soda," *Wall Street Journal*, January 23, 1997, pp. B1, B8; "Top 25 Web Properties," *Nielsen/NetRatings*, February 17, 2002, **http://209.249.142.16/nnpm/owa/nrpublicreports.toppropertiesweekly**.

2. Karen Benezra, "Don't Mislabel Gen X," *Brandweek*, May 15, 1995, pp. 32–34.

3. Milton Rokeach, *The Nature of Human Values* (New York: Free Press, 1973), p. 5.

4. Wagner A. Kamakura and Jose Alfonso Mazzon, "Value Segmentation: A Model for the Measurement of Values and Value Systems," *Journal of Consumer Research*, September 1991, pp. 208–218; see also Milton Rokeach and Sandra J. Ball-Rokeach, "Stability and Change in American Value Priorities, 1968–1981," *American Psychologist*, May 1989, pp. 775–784; Milton Rokeach, *Understanding Human Values* (New York: Free Press, 1979); Shalom H. Schwartz and Wolfgang Bilsky, "Toward a Universal Psychological Structure of Human Values," *Journal of Personality and Social Psychology*, September 1987, pp. 550–562.

5. Francesco M. Nicosia and Robert N. Mayer, "Toward a Sociology of Consumption," *Journal of Consumer Research*, September 1976, pp. 65–75; Hugh E. Kramer, "The Value of Higher Education and Its Impact on Value Formation," in eds. Robert E. Pitts and Arch G. Woodside, *Personal Values and Consumer Psychology* (Lexington, Mass.: Lexington Books, 1984), pp. 239–251.

6. Sally Beatty, "Kids Are Glued to a Violent Japanese Cartoon Show," *Wall Street Journal*, December 3, 1999, pp. B1, B4.

7. Mary Gilly and Lisa Penaloza, "Barriers and Incentives in Consumer Acculturation," in eds. W. Fred van Raaij and Gary J. Bamossy, *European Advances in Consumer Research*, vol. 1 (Provo, Utah: Association for Consumer Research, 1993), pp. 278–286.

8. Rokeach, *The Nature of Human Values*; Schwartz and Bilsky, "Toward a Universal Psychological Structure of Human Values."

9. Russell W. Belk, "Materialism: Trait Aspects of Living in the Material World," *Journal of Consumer Research*, December 1985, pp. 265–280; Russell W. Belk, "Three Scales to Measure Constructs Related to Materialism: Reliability, Validity, and Relationships to Happiness," in ed. Thomas P. Kinnear, *Advances in Consumer Research*, vol. 11 (Provo, Utah: Association for Consumer Research, 1984), pp. 291–297.

10. Marsha L. Richins, "Special Possessions and the Expression of Material Values," *Journal of Consumer Research*, December 1994, pp. 522–533.

11. Marsha L. Richins and Scott Dawson, "A Consumer Values Orientation for Materialism and Its Measurement: Scale Development and Validation," *Journal of Consumer Research*, December 1992, pp. 303–316.

12. Mary Yoko Brannen, "Cross Cultural Materialism: Commodifying Culture in Japan," in eds. Floyd Rudmin and Marsha Richins, *Meaning, Measure, and Morality of Materialism* (Provo, Utah: The Association for Consumer Research, 1992), pp. 167–180; Dorothy E. Jones, Dorinda Elliott, Edith Terry, Carla A. Robbins, Charles Gaffney, and Bruce Nussbaum, "Capitalism in China," *BusinessWeek*, January 1985, pp. 53–59; see also Tse, Belk, and Zhou, "Becoming a Consumer Society."

13. Ger, "Problems of Marketization in Romania and Turkey," in eds. Schultz, Belk, and Ger, *Consumption in Marketizing Economies*; Güliz Ger, Russell Belk, and Dana–Nicoleta Lascu, "The Development of Consumer Desire in Marketizing and Developing Economies: The Cases of Romania and Turkey," in eds. Leigh McAlister and Michael L. Rothschild, *Advances in Consumer Research*, vol. 20 (Provo, Utah: Association for Consumer Research, 1992), pp. 102–107.

14. P. H. Ferguson, "Shoppers Leave Ivory Towers for Bargain Basements in Japan," *Austin American Statesman*, December 26, 1993, p. A26.

15. Beatriz Terrazas, "In Search of Comfort and Safety, Americans 'Cocooning' in Homes," *Dallas Morning News*, January 10, 2002, **www.dallasnews.com**.

16. Sally Goll Beatty, "Viacom's Blockbuster Rethinks Strategy," *Wall Street Journal*, November 20, 1995, p. B6.

17. Lisa Miller, "The New Dream Vacation Itinerary: Staying at Home," *Wall Street Journal*, October 20, 1996, pp. B1, B6.

18. Molly Cate, "Get Well Centers Lands Birmingham Hospital Job," *Nashville Business Journal*, April 27, 2001, **www.bizjournals.com**.

19. Marleis Welms Floet, "Youth in Holland," *Industry Report*.

20. John P. Robinson, "Your Money or Your Time," *American Demographics*, November 1991, pp. 22–26.

21. Craig J. Thompson, "Caring Consumers: Gendered Consumption Meanings and the Juggling Lifestyle," *Journal of Consumer Research*, March 1996, pp. 388–407.

22. Floet, "Youth in Holland."

23. Christopher T. Linen, "Marketing and the Global Economy," *Direct Marketing*, January 1991, pp. 54–56.

24. Sue Shellenbarger, "Technology Is Helping 'Commuter Families' to Stay in Touch," *Wall Street Journal*, February 14, 2001, p. B1.

25. Joanne Lipman, "Marketers of Luxury Goods Are Turning from Self-Indulgence to Family Values," *Wall Street Journal*, October 22, 1992, pp. B1, B10.

26. Shelly Branch and Ernest Beck, "For Unilever, It's Sweetness and Light," *Wall Street Journal*, April 13, 2000, pp. B1, B4; Vanessa O'Connell, "Food Companies Plan New Pitches for Their Anticholesterol Products," *Wall Street Journal*, December 11, 1998; "Kellogg Unveils Line of Foods Designed to Improve Health," *Wall Street Journal*, November 6, 1998, p. B4.

27. Betsy McKay, "Coke and Pepsi Escalate Their Water Fight," *Wall Street Journal*, May 18, 2001, p. B8.

28. Matthew Grimm, "Veggie Delight," *American Demographics*, August 2000, pp. 66–67.

29. Scott Kilman, "Monsanto Brings 'Genetic' Ads to Europe," *Wall Street Journal*, June 16, 1998, p. B8.

30. John Fetto, "Quackery No More," *American Demographics*, January 2001, pp. 10–11; Matt Murray, "GNC Makes Ginseng, Shark Pills Its Potion for Growth," *Wall Street Journal*, March 15, 1996, pp. B1, B3.

31. Tara Parker-Pope, "Antismoking Sentiment Flares in Europe's Smoke-Filled Cafes," *Wall Street Journal*, August 28, 1996, pp. B1, B8.

32. Kathleen Deveny, "'Light' Foods Are Having Heavy Going," *Wall Street Journal*, March 4, 1993, pp. B1, B8.

33. Nikhil Deogun, "Fat-Free Snacks Aren't Wowing Frito Customers," *Wall Street Journal*, September 14, 1998, pp. B1, B4.

34. Dan Curry, "Skip the Tofu—More Americans Tear Into Steaks," *Wall Street Journal*, March 8, 2001, pp. B1, B4; Kathleen Deveny, "Tempted by Taste, and Tiring of Tofu, Shoppers Are Bringing Home the Bacon," *Wall Street Journal*, March 18, 1993, pp. B1, B7; Laurie Grossman, "Steak Chains Sizzle as Healthier Eaters Splurge on T-Bones When They Dine Out," *Wall Street Journal*, December 14, 1992, pp. B1, B4; Scott Kilman, "Major Companies in the Food Industry Have Little Taste for Organic Products," *Wall Street Journal*, January 10, 1992, pp. B1, B8.

35. John Fetto, "More Is More," *American Demographics*, June 2001, p. 8.

36. Sarah McBride, "Entrepreneurs Cater to a Growing Nation," *Wall Street Journal*, April 10, 1997, pp. B1, B15.

37. Martha Brannigan and Frederic M. Biddle, "Fliers Favor a Jet with Space to Stretch," *Wall Street Journal*, December 12, 1997, pp. B1, B9; Anna Wilde Mathews, "Truck Stops Now Offer Massages, Movies, and Marriages," *Wall Street Journal*, July 22, 1997, pp. B1, B5.

38. Suzanne Vranica, "Wendy's Feeds Off of Nighttime Cravings," *Wall Street Journal*, June 13, 2001, p. B12.

39. Valerie Reitman, "For Frozen Yogurt, a Chill Wind Blows," *Wall Street Journal*, June 3, 1992, p. B1; Curry, "Skip the Tofu."

40. Eben Shapiro, "Portions and Packages Grow Bigger and BIGGER," *Wall Street Journal*, October 12, 1993, pp. B1, B10.

41. "Botox to Be Approved for Cosmetic Purposes," *CNN.com*, February 7, 2002, **www.cnn.com/2002/HEALTH/02/07/botox.cosmetic**.

42. Diane Solis, "Cost No Object for Mexico's Makeup Junkies," *Wall Street Journal*, June 6, 1994, p. B1.

43. David J. Lipke, "Green Homes," *American Demographics*, January 2001, pp. 50–55.

44. Dale Buss, "Green Cars," *American Demographics*, January 2001, pp. 57–61.

45. Rebecca Gardyn, "Saving the Earth, One Click at a Time," *American Demographics*, January 2001, pp. 30–34.

46. Paul Schweitzer, "The Third Millennium: Riding the Waves of Turbulence," *News Tribune*, December 1993, pp. 5–27.

47. Sak Onkvisit and John J. Shaw, *International Marketing: Analysis and Strategy* (Columbus, Ohio: Merrill, 1989), p. 243.

48. Robert Wilk, "INFOPLAN: The New Rich: A Psychographic Approach to Marketing to the Wealthy Japanese Consumer," ESOMAR Conference, Venice, Italy, June 1990, reported in de Mooij and Keegan, *Advertising Worldwide*, pp. 122–129.

49. K. S. Yang, "Expressed Values of Chinese College Students," in eds. K. S. Yang and Y. Y. Li, *Symposium on the Character of the Chinese: An Interdisciplinary Approach* (Taipei, Taiwan: Institute of Ethnology Academic Sinica, 1972), pp. 257–312; see also Oliver H. M. Yau, *Consumer Behavior in China: Customer Satisfaction and Cultural Values* (New York: Rutledge, 1994).

50. Alfred S. Boote, cited in Rebecca Piirto, *Beyond Mind Games* (Ithaca, N.Y.: American Demographic Books, 1991).

51. Geert Hofstede, "National Cultures in Four Dimensions," *International Studies of Management and Organization*, Spring–Summer 1983, pp. 46–74.

52. Michael Lynn, George M. Zinkhan, and Judy Harris, "Consumer Tipping: A Cross-Country Study," *Journal of Consumer Research*, December 1993, pp. 478–488.

53. Dana L. Alden, Wayne D. Hoyer, and Chol Lee, "Identifying Global and Culture-Specific Dimensions of Humor in Advertising: A Multinational Analysis," *Journal of Marketing*, April 1993, pp. 64–75.

54. Van R. Wood and Roy Howell, "A Note on Hispanic Values and Subcultural Research: An Alternative View," *Journal of the Academy of Marketing Science*, Winter 1991, pp. 61–67; see also Humberto Valencia, "Hispanic Values and Subcultural Research," *Journal of the Academy of Marketing Science*, Winter 1989, pp. 23–28.

55. Jonathan Burton, "Advertising Targeting Asians," *Far Eastern Economic Review*, January 21, 1993, pp. 40–41; see also Thomas E. Ness and Melvin T. Smith, "Middle-Class Values in Blacks and Whites," in eds. Pitts and Woodside, *Personal Values and Consumer Psychology*, pp. 231–237.

56. Richard P. Coleman, "The Continuing Significance of Social Class to Marketing," *Journal of Consumer Research*, December 1983, pp. 265–280.

57. William Strauss and Neil Howe, "The Cycle of Generations, *American Demographics*, April 1991, pp. 25–33, 52; see also William Strauss and Neil Howe, *Generations: The History of America's Future, 1584 to 2069* (New York: William Morrow, 1992); Lawrence A. Crosby, James D. Gill, and Robert E. Lee, "Life Status and Age as Predictors of Value Orientation," in eds. Pitts and Woodside, *Personal Values and Consumer Psychology*, pp. 201–218.

58. Sharon Beatty, Lynn R. Kahle, Pamela Homer, and Shekhar Misra, "Alternative Measurement Approaches to Consumer Values: The List of Values and the Rokeach Value Survey," *Psychology and Marketing*, Fall 1985, pp. 181–200.

59. Lynn R. Kahle, *Social Values and Social Change: Adaptation to Life in America* (New York: Praeger, 1983).

60. Judith Valente, "Body Shop Has a Few Aches and Pains," *Wall Street Journal*, August 6, 1993, pp. B1, B12.

61. Yumiko Ono, "Will Good Housekeeping Translate into Japanese?" *Wall Street Journal*, December 30, 1997, pp. B1, B6.

62. Mark Van Roo, "Researching the Taiwan Market: A Very Different Consumer," *Marketing and Research Today*, February 1989, pp. 54–57.

63. Yoram Wind, "The Myth of Globalization," *Journal of Consumer Marketing*, Spring 1986, pp. 23–26.

64. Buss, "Green Cars."

65. Daniel Rosenberg, "Animal-Rights Ad, Toned Down, Still Hits a Wall at the Networks," *Wall Street Journal*, December 29, 1998, p. B5.

66. David K. Tse, John K. Wong, and Chin Tiong Tan, "Towards Some Standardized Cross-Cultural Consumption Values," in ed. Michael J. Houston, *Advances in Consumer Research*, vol. 15 (Provo, Utah: Association for Consumer Research, 1988), pp. 387–393; Ved Prakash, "Segmentation of Women's Market Based on Personal Values and the Means-End Chain Model: A Framework for Advertising Strategy," in ed. Richard J. Lutz, *Advances in Consumer Research*, vol. 13 (Provo, Utah: Association for Consumer Research 1986), pp. 215–220.

67. Rebecca Piirto, *Beyond Mind Games* (Ithaca, N.Y.: American Demographic Books, 1991).

68. Edward F. McQuarrie and Daniel Langmeyer, "Using Values to Measure Attitudes Toward Discontinuous Innovations," *Psychology and Marketing*, Winter 1985, pp. 239–252.

69. Patricia F. Kennedy, Roger J. Best, and Lynn R. Kahle, "An Alternative Method for Measuring Value-Based Segmentation and Advertisement Positioning," in eds. James H. Leigh and Claude R. Martin Jr., *Current Issues and Research in Advertising*, vol. 11 (Ann Arbor, Mich.: Division of Research, School of Business Administration, University of Michigan, 1988), pp. 139–156; Daniel L. Sherrell, Joseph F. Hair Jr., and Robert P. Bush, "The Influence of Personal Values on Measures of Advertising Effectiveness: Interactions with Audience Involvement," in eds. Pitts and Woodside, *Personal Values and Consumer Psychology*, pp. 169–185.

70. Nikhil Deogun, "Seeking Rebound from Obscurity, RC Cola Wraps Itself in the Flag," *Wall Street Journal*, April 1, 1998, p. B8.

71. Pichayaporn Utumporn, "McDonald's Proclaims Itself a Thai Patriot," *Wall Street Journal*, August 10, 1998, p. B6.

72. Lisa Bannon and Margaret Studer, "For 2 Revealing European Ads, Overexposure Can Have Benefits," *Wall Street Journal*, June 17, 1993, p. B8.

73. "Calvin Klein Yanks Ads Showing Teen Skin," *Austin American Statesman*, August 29, 1995, p. C1.

74. Pichayaporn Utumporn, "Ad with Hitler Brings Outcry in Thailand," *Wall Street Journal*, June 5, 1995, p. C1.

75. Robert E. Pitts, John K. Wong, and D. Joel Whalen, "Consumers' Evaluative Structures in Two Ethical Situations: A Means-End Approach," *Journal of Business Research*, March 1991, pp. 119–130.

76. Elyse Tahouye, "Johnson & Johnson Tries to Shape Health-Care Debate with TV Ad," *Wall Street Journal*, May 11, 1993, p. B9.

77. Russell W. Belk and Richard W. Pollay, "Materialism and Status Appeals in Japanese and U.S. Print Advertising," *International Marketing Review*, Winter 1985, pp. 38–47; see also Russell W. Belk, Wendy J. Bryce, and Richard W. Pollay, "Advertising Themes and Cultural Values: A Comparison of U.S. and Japanese Advertising," in eds. K. C. Mun and T. S. Chan, *Proceedings of the Inaugural Meeting of the Southeast Asia Region Academy of International Business* (Hong Kong: The Chinese University of Hong Kong, 1985), pp. 11–20.

78. David K. Tse, Russell W. Belk, and Nan Zhou, "Becoming a Consumer Society: A Longitudinal and Cross-Cultural Content Analysis of Print Ads from Hong Kong, the People's Republic of China, and Taiwan," *Journal of Consumer Research*, March 1989, pp. 457–472.

79. Belk and Pollay, "Materialism and Status Appeals in Japanese and U.S. Print Advertising."

80. Tse, Belk, and Zhou, "Becoming a Consumer Society."

81. Russell W. Belk, "Material Values in the Comics: A Content Analysis of Comic Books Featuring Themes of Wealth," *Journal of Consumer Research*, June 1987, pp. 26–42.

82. For more information on means-end chain analysis, see Beth A. Walker and Jerry C. Olson, "Means-End Chains: Connecting Products with Self," *Journal of Business Research*, March 1991, pp. 111–118; Thomas J. Reynolds and John P. Richon, "Means-End Based Advertising Research: Copy Testing Is Not Strategy Assessment," *Journal of Business Research*, March 1991, pp. 131–142; Jonathan Gutman, "Exploring the Nature of Linkages between Consequences and Values," *Journal of Business Research*, March 1991, pp. 143–148; Thomas J. Reynolds and Jonathan Gutman, "Laddering Theory, Method, Analysis and Interpretation," *Journal of Advertising Research*, February/March 1988, pp. 11–31; Thomas J. Reynolds and Jonathan Gutman, "Laddering: Extending the Repertory Grid Methodology to Construct Attribute-Consequence-Value Hierarchies," in eds. Pitts and Woodside, *Personal Values and Consumer Psychology*, pp. 155–167.

83. Thomas J. Reynolds and J. P. Jolly, "Measuring Personal Values: An Evaluation of Alternative Methods," *Journal of Marketing Research*, November 1980, pp. 531–536; Reynolds and Gutman, "Laddering"; Jonathan Gutman, "A Means-End Model Based on Consumer Categorization Processes," *Journal of Marketing*, Spring 1982, pp. 60–72.

84. T. L. Stanley, "Death of the Sports Car?" *Brandweek*, January 2, 1995, p. 38.

85. Frenkel Ter Hofstede, Jan-Benedict E. M. Steenkamp, and Michel Wedel, "International Market Segmentation Based on Consumer-Product Relations," *Journal of Marketing Research*, vol. 36, February 1999, pp. 1–17.

86. J. Michael Munson and Edward F. McQuarrie, "Shortening the Rokeach Value Survey for Use in Consumer Research," in ed. Michael J. Houston, *Advances in Consumer Research*, vol. 15 (Provo, Utah: Association for Consumer Research, 1988), pp. 381–386.
87. Lynn R. Kahle, Sharon Beatty, and Pamela Homer, "Alternative Measurement Approaches to Consumer Values: The List of Values (LOV) and Values and Life Style (VALS)," *Journal of Consumer Research*, December 1986, pp. 405–409; Kahle, *Social Values and Social Change*.
88. Wagner Kamakura and Thomas P. Novak, "Value-System Segmentation: Exploring the Meaning of LOV," *Journal of Consumer Research*, June 1992, pp. 119–132.
89. Sigmund Freud, *Collected Papers*, vols. I–V (New York: Basic Books, 1959); Erik Erickson, *Childhood and Society* (New York: Norton, 1963); Erik Erickson, *Identity: Youth and Crisis* (New York: Norton, 1968).
90. Yumiko Ono, "Marketers Seek the 'Naked' Truth," *Wall Street Journal*, May 30, 1997, pp. B1, B13.
91. Gordon Allport, *Personality: A Psychological Interpretation* (New York: Holt, Rinehart, & Winston, 1937); Raymond B. Cattell, *The Scientific Analysis of Personality* (Baltimore: Penguin, 1965).
92. Carl G. Jung, *Man and His Symbols* (Garden City, N.Y.: Doubleday, 1964); see also Hans J. Eysenck, "Personality, Stress and Disease: An Interactionistic Perspective," *Psychological Inquiry*, vol. 2, 1991, pp. 221–232.
93. Carl R. Rogers, "Some Observations on the Organization of Personality," *American Psychologist*, September 1947, pp. 358–368; George A. Kelly, *The Psychology of Personal Constructs*, vols. 1 and 2 (New York: Norton, 1955).
94. Bernard Weiner, "Attribution in Personality Psychology," in ed. Lawrence A. Pervin, *Handbook of Personality: Theory and Research* (New York: Guilford, 1990), pp. 465–484; Harold H. Kelly, "The Processes of Causal Attribution," *American Psychologist*, February 1973, pp. 107–128.
95. David Glen Mick and Claus Buhl, "A Meaning-Based Model of Advertising Experiences," *Journal of Consumer Research*, December 1992, pp. 317–338.
96. Karen B. Horney, *Our Inner Conflicts* (New York: Norton, 1945).
97. Joel B. Cohen, "An Interpersonal Orientation to the Study of Consumer Behavior," *Journal of Marketing Research*, August 1967, pp. 270–277; Jon P. Noerager, "An Assessment of CAD—A Personality Instrument Developed Specifically for Marketing Research," *Journal of Marketing Research*, February 1979, pp. 53–59.
98. Marsha L. Richins, "An Analysis of Consumer Interaction Styles in the Marketplace," *Journal of Consumer Research*, June 1983, pp. 73–82.
99. Richard P. Bagozzi, Hans Baumgartner, and Youjae Yi, "State versus Action Orientation and the Theory of Reasoned Action, An Application to Coupon Usage," *Journal of Consumer Research*, March 1992, pp. 505–518; William O. Bearden and Randall L. Rose, "Attention to Social Comparison Information: An Individual Difference Factor Affecting Consumer Conformity," *Journal of Consumer Research*, March 1990, pp. 461–471; Bobby J. Calder and Robert E. Burnkrant, "Interpersonal Influence on Consumer Behavior: An Attribution Theory Approach," *Journal of Consumer Research*, December 1979, pp. 29–38.
100. B. F. Skinner, *About Behaviorism* (New York: Knopf, 1974); B. F. Skinner, *Beyond Freedom and Dignity* (New York: Knopf, 1971).
101. Jacob Jacoby, "Multiple Indicant Approaches for Studying New Product Adopters," *Journal of Applied Psychology*, August 1971, pp. 384–388; Harold H. Kassarjian, "Personality and Consumer Behavior: A Review," *Journal of Marketing Research*, November 1971, pp. 409–418; see also Harold H. Kassarjian, "Personality: The Longest Fad," in ed. William L. Wilkie, *Advances in Consumer Research*, vol. 6 (Ann Arbor, Mich.: Association for Consumer Research, 1979), pp. 122–124.
102. Franklin B. Evans, "Psychological and Objective Factors in the Prediction of Brand Choice," *Journal of Business*, October 1959, pp. 340–369.
103. John L. Lastovicka and Erich A. Joachimsthaler, "Improving the Detection of Personality-Behavior Relationships in Consumer Research," *Journal of Consumer Research*, March 1988, pp. 583–587; Kathryn E. A. Villani and Yoram Wind, "On the Usage of 'Modified' Personality Trait Measures in Consumer Research," *Journal of Consumer Research*, December 1975, pp. 223–228.
104. William O. Bearden, David M. Hardesty, and Randall L. Rose, "Consumer Self-Confidence: Refinements in Conceptualization and Measurement," *Journal of Consumer Research*, vol. 28, June 2001, pp. 121–134.
105. D. E. Berlyne, *Conflict, Arousal and Curiosity*, (New York: McGraw-Hill, 1960); D. E. Berlyne, "Novelty, Complexity, and Hedonic Value," *Perception and Psychophysics*, November 1970, pp. 279–286.
106. Marvin Zuckerman, *Sensation Seeking: Beyond the Optimal Level of Arousal* (Hillsdale, N.J.: Lawrence Erlbaum, 1979); Elizabeth C. Hirschman, "Innovativeness, Novelty Seeking, and Consumer Creativity," *Journal of Consumer Research*, December 1980, pp. 283–295.
107. R. A. Mittelstadt, S. L. Grossbart, W. W. Curtis, and S. P. DeVere, "Optimal Stimulation Level and the Adoption Decision Process," *Journal of Consumer Research*, September 1976, pp. 84–94; P. S. Raju, "Optimum Stimulation Level: Its Relationship to Personality, Demographics, and Exploratory Behavior," *Journal of Consumer Research*, December 1980, pp. 272–282; Jan-Benedict E. M. Steenkamp and Hans Baumgartner, "The Role of Optimum Stimulation Level

in Exploratory Consumer Behavior," *Journal of Consumer Research*, December 1992, pp. 434–448; Erich A. Joachimsthaler and John Lastovicka, "Optimal Stimulation Level—Exploratory Behavior Models," *Journal of Consumer Research*, December 1984, pp. 830–835.

108. Leon G. Schiffman, William R. Dillon, and Festus E. Ngumah, "The Influence of Subcultural and Personality Factors on Consumer Acculturation," *Journal of International Business Studies*, Fall 1981, pp. 137–143.

109. Kelly Tepper Tian, William O. Bearden, and Gary L. Hunter, "Consumers' Need for Uniqueness: Scale Development and Validation," *Journal of Consumer Research*, vol. 28, June 2001, pp. 50–66.

110. Itamar Simonson and Stephen M. Nowlis, "The Role of Explanations and Need for Uniqueness in Consumer Decision Making: Unconventional Choices Based on Reasons," *Journal of Consumer Research*, vol. 27, June 2000, pp. 49–68.

111. John T. Cacioppo, Richard E. Petty, and Chuan F. Kao, "The Efficient Assessment of Need for Cognition," *Journal of Personality Assessment*, June 1984, pp. 306–307; Curtis R. Haugtvedt, Richard E. Petty, and John T. Cacioppo, "Need for Cognition and Advertising: Understanding the Role of Personality Variables in Consumer Behavior," *Journal of Consumer Psychology*, vol. 1, no. 3, 1992, pp. 239–260; Rajeev Batra and Douglas M. Stayman, "The Role of Mood in Advertising Effectiveness," *Journal of Consumer Research*, September 1990, pp. 203–214; John T. Cacioppo, Richard E. Petty, and K. Morris, "Effects of Need for Cognition on Message Evaluation, Recall and Persuasion," *Journal of Personality and Social Psychology*, October 1983, pp. 805–818.

112. Susan Powell Mantel and Frank R. Kardes, "The Role of Direction of Comparison, Attribute-Based Processing, and Attitude-Based Processing in Consumer Preference," *Journal of Consumer Research*, vol. 25, March 1999, pp. 335–352.

113. William O. Bearden, Richard G. Netemeyer, and Jesse H. Teel, "Measurement of Consumer Susceptibility to Interpersonal Influence," *Journal of Consumer Research*, March 1989, pp. 472–480; Peter Wright, "Factors Affecting Cognitive Resistance to Ads," *Journal of Marketing Research*, June 1975, pp. 1–9.

114. John L. Lastovicka, Lance A. Bettencourt, Renée Shaw Hughner, and Ronald J. Kuntze, "Lifestyle of the Tight and Frugal: Theory and Measurement," *Journal of Consumer Research*, vol. 26, June 1999, pp. 85–98.

115. Richard C. Becherer and Lawrence C. Richard, "Self-Monitoring as a Moderating Variable in Consumer Behavior," *Journal of Consumer Research*, December 1978, pp. 159–162; Mark Snyder and Kenneth G. DeBono, "Appeals to Image and Claims about Quality: Understanding the Psychology of Advertising," *Journal of Personality and Social Psychology*, September 1985, pp. 586–597.

116. Dean Peabody, *National Characteristics* (Cambridge, England: Cambridge University Press, 1985); Allan B. Yates, "Americans, Canadians Similar but Vive La Difference," *Direct Marketing*, October 1985, p. 152.

117. Terry Clark, "International Marketing and National Character: A Review and Proposal for an Integrative Theory," *Journal of Marketing*, October 1990, pp. 66–79.

118. Yates, "Americans, Canadians Similar but Vive La Diffèrence."

119. "Getting Burned by Expansion Plans," *Marketing Week*, June 14, 2001, **www.marketingweek.com**.

120. James P. Miller, "Hip and Irreverent, Alternative Papers Grab Readers," *Wall Street Journal*, July 29, 1997, pp. B1, B8.

121. Vanessa O'Connell, "Nabisco Ads Push Cookies for Self-Esteem," *Wall Street Journal*, July 10, 1998, p. B5.

122. John L. Lastovicka, John P. Murray, Erich A. Joachimsthaler, Gaurav Bhalla, and Jim Scheurich, "A Lifestyle Typology to Model Young Male Drinking and Driving," *Journal of Consumer Research*, September 1987, pp. 257–263.

123. Morris B. Holbrook, "Nostalgia and Consumption Preferences: Some Emerging Patterns of Consumer Tastes," *Journal of Consumer Research*, September 1993, pp. 245–256.

124. Sandra Yin, "Going to Extremes," *American Demographics*, June 1, 2001, p. 26.

125. William D. Wells, "Psychographics: A Critical Review," *Journal of Marketing Research*, May 1975, pp. 196–213.

126. Michelle Moran, "Category Analysis: Small Electrics & Consumer Lifestyles Dictate Trends," *Gourmet Retailer*, June 2001, pp. 34+.

127. Onkvisit and Shaw, *International Marketing*, p. 283.

128. Leonidas C. Leonidou, "Understanding the Russian Consumer," *Marketing and Research Today*, March 1992, pp. 75–83.

129. Sam Bradley, "Chinese Consumers Eyeing Hard Goods," *Brandweek*, June 12, 1995, p. 28.

130. Sonia Reyes, "General Mills Finally Chex in With Its First Single-Serve Cereal," *Brandweek*, June 4, 2001, p. 8.

131. Cyndee Miller, "Study Dispels '80s Stereotypes of Women," *Marketing News*, May 22, 1995, p. 3.

132. Alison Stein Wellner, "The End of Leisure?" *American Demographics*, July 2000, pp. 50–56.

133. Kevin Helliker, "Forget Candlelight, Flowers, and Tips: More Restaurants Tout Takeout Service," *Wall Street Journal*, June 15, 1992, pp. B1, B5.

134. Ross Kerber, "Too Busy for Food, Athletes Go for Goo," *Wall Street Journal*, May 1, 1997, pp. B1, B9.

135. Gordon Fairclough, "Will Smokers Swallow a Different Kind of Nicotine?" *Wall Street Journal*, April 27, 2001, pp. B1, B3.

136. Norihiko Shirouzu, "To Project an Aura of Cool, Ford's Focus Model Targets Hot Rodders," *Wall Street Journal*, November 1, 2000, p. B1.

137. ACE Brochure 1989; published by RISC, Paris, France; see also de Mooij and Keegan, *Advertising Worldwide*.

138. Elisabeth Rubinfien, "Travel Alert: Luxury Arrives in Moscow," *Wall Street Journal*, June 29, 1992, p. B7.

139. Yumiko Ono, "Off-Road Vehicles Leave Others in the Dust," *Wall Street Journal*, July 17, 1993, p. B1.

140. Tara Parker-Pope, "Nonalcoholic Beer Hits the Spot in Mideast," *Wall Street Journal*, December 6, 1996, pp. B1, B2.

141. Steve Gelsi, "Pioneer Hits Videophiles with Audio," *Brandweek*, June 19, 1995, p. 16.

142. Basil G. Englis and Michael R. Solomon, "To Be and Not to Be: Life Style Imagery, Reference Groups, and the Clustering of America," *Journal of Advertising*, Spring 1995, pp. 13–28.

143. Kathryn Kranhold, "Golf's High Profile Drives Firms to Take Whack at Big Campaigns," *Wall Street Journal*, July 28, 1997, p. B8.

144. Sally Goll Beatty, "Busch Promotion Takes Aim at Hunters," *Wall Street Journal*, November 19, 1996, p. B1.

145. Erin White, "Talbots to Target Non-Super Bowl Crowd," *Wall Street Journal*, January 27, 2000, p. 18.

146. Chad Rubel, "Parents Magazines Make Room for Daddy," *Marketing News*, February 27, 1995, pp. 1, 5.

147. Wendy Bounds, "What Nerve! Rival Challenges Martha Stewart," *Wall Street Journal*, November 19, 1998, pp. B1, B16.

148. Sally Goll Beatty, "Philip Morris Starts Lifestyle Magazine," *Wall Street Journal*, September 16, 1996, pp. B1, B10.

149. Fara Warner, "TV Study Tips, Lectures Win Chinese Viewers," *Wall Street Journal*, February 18, 1997, pp. B1, B9.

150. Thomas E. Weber, "Where the Boys and Girls Are: Teens Talk about the Web," *Wall Street Journal*, October 24, 1997, pp. B6, B7.

151. Kenneth Hein, "Pepsi on Yahoo!" *Adweek*, November 12, 2001, p. 7.

152. Jacob Hornik and Mary Jane Schlinger, "Allocation of Time to the Mass Media," *Journal of Consumer Research*, March 1981, pp. 343–355.

153. Eben Shapiro, "Web Lovers Love TV, Often Watch Both," *Wall Street Journal*, June 12, 1998, p. B9.

154. Michael J. Weiss, Morris B. Holbrook, and John Habich, "Death of the Arts Snob," *American Demographics*, June 2001, pp. 40–42.

155. Deveny, "For Coffee's Big Three, a Gourmet-Brew Boom Proves Embarrassing Bust"; Gerry Khermouch, "Microbrews Come of Age in the Ways of Marketing," *Brandweek*, October 18, 1993, p. 30; Jennifer Cody, "Deregulation Opens Gate for Flood of Home Brews," *Wall Street Journal*, May 20, 1994, p. B1.

156. Yumiko Ono, "The Bread Can't Yet Put Itself in the Toaster," *Wall Street Journal*, July 21, 1993, p. B1.

157. James Prichard, "Gerber Food to Be Packaged in Plastic Containers Instead of Glass Jars," *Associated Press Newswires*, June 19, 2001.

158. Bernard Wysocki Jr., "Are Profits in Sickness, Or in Health?" *Wall Street Journal*, August 10, 2001, pp. B1, B3.

159. Arnold Mitchell, *Consumer Values: A Typology* (Menlo Park, Calif.: Stanford Research Institute, 1978).

160. Martha Fransworth Riche, "Psychographics for the 1990s," *American Demographics*, July 1989, pp. 24–54.

161. For descriptions of the VALS2 segments, see Riche, "Psychographics for the 1990s"; see also Judith Waldrop, "Markets with Attitude," *American Demographics*, July 1994, pp. 22–33.

162. For a description of these segments, see Piirto, *Beyond Mind Games*.

163. Kahle, Beatty, and Homer, "Alternative Measurement Approaches to Consumer Values"; Thomas P. Novak and Bruce MacEvoy, "On Comparing Alternative Segmentation Schemes: The List of Values (LOV) and Values and Life Styles (VALS)," *Journal of Consumer Research*, June 1990, pp. 105–109.

164. Piirto, *Beyond Mind Games*.

165. Ibid.

166. "The Yankelovich Monitor 1992," *Brandweek*, November 30, 1992, pp. 18–21.

167. David J. Lipke, "Head Trips," *American Demographics*, October 2000, pp. 38–39.

168. Piirto, *Beyond Mind Games*.

169. Jacqueline Silver, "Turning Tables: America and Japan: The Market Opportunities for Companies of the EC," *ESOMAR Conference, America, Japan and the EC '92: The Prospects for Marketing, Advertising and Research* (Venice, Italy, June 18–20, 1990) in Marieke K. de Mooij and Warren Keegan, *Advertising Worldwide* (London: Prentice-Hall International, 1991), p. 122.

170. Cyndee Miller, "From Kuptsi to Cossacks: Ad Agency Divides Russia into Five Segments," *Marketing News*, June 8, 1992, p. 18.

171. Piirto, *Beyond Mind Games*.

172. Douglas B. Holt, "Poststructuralist Lifestyle Analysis: Conceptualizing the Social Patterning of Consumption in Postmodernity," *Journal of Consumer Research*, March 1997, pp. 326–350.

173. Marvin Shoenwald, "Psychographic Segmentation: Used or Abused?" *Brandweek*, January 22, 2001, p. 34.

Chapter 18

1. From John W. Schouten and James H. McAlexander, "Subcultures of Consumption: An Ethnography of the New Bikers," *Journal of Consumer Research*, June 1995, pp. 43–61; Joseph Weber, "Harley Investors May Get a Wobbly Ride," *BusinessWeek*, February 11, 2002, p. 65; Jonathan Fahey, "Love Into Money," *Forbes*, January 7, 2002, pp. 60–65.
2. Grant McCracken, "Culture and Consumption: A Theoretical Account of the Structure and Movement of the Cultural Meaning of Consumer Goods," *Journal of Consumer Research*, June 1986, pp. 71–84; Grant McCracken, *Culture and Consumption* (Indianapolis: Indiana University Press, 1990).
3. McCracken, "Culture and Consumption"; McCracken, *Culture and Consumption*; see also Elizabeth C. Hirschman, Linda Scott, and William B. Wells, "A Model of Product Discourse: Linking Consumer Practice to Cultural Texts," *Journal of Advertising*, Spring 1998, pp. 33–50; Barbara A. Phillips, "Thinking into It: Consumer Interpretation of Complex Advertising Images," *Journal of Advertising*, Summer 1997, pp. 77–86; Cele Otnes and Linda Scott, "Something Old, Something New: Exploring the Interaction between Ritual and Advertising," *Journal of Advertising*, Spring 1996, pp. 33–50; Jonna Holland and James W. Gentry, "The Impact of Cultural Symbols on Advertising Effectiveness: A Theory of Intercultural Accommodation," in eds. Merrie Brucks and Debbie MacInnis, *Advances in Consumer Research*, vol. 24 (Provo, Utah: Association for Consumer Research, 1997), pp. 483–489.
4. Lauren Goldstein, "Urban Wear Goes Suburban," *Fortune*, December 21, 1998, pp. 169–172.
5. For a discussion of how consumers use fashion to both characterize their identity and infer aspects of others' identities, see Craig J. Thompson and Diana L. Haytko, "Speaking of Fashion: Consumers' Use of Fashion Discourses and the Appropriation of Countervailing Cultural Meanings," *Journal of Consumer Research*, June 1997, pp. 15–42.
6. Keith Naughton, "Roots Gets Rad: Trading in Earth Shoes for Hot Berets, the Canadian Firm Plans a U.S. Invasion After Its Olympic Triumph," *Newsweek*, February 25, 2002, p. 36; Larry M. Greenberg, "Marketing the Great White North, Eh?" *Wall Street Journal*, April 21, 2000, p. B1.
7. Julie Laboy, "Clothiers Bring the Barrio to Japanese Teen Rebels," *Wall Street Journal*, April 8, 1998, pp. CA1, CA4.
8. Goldstein, "Urban Wear Goes Suburban."
9. Douglas M. Stayman and Rohit Deshpande, "Situational Ethnicity and Consumer Behavior," *Journal of Consumer Research*, December 1989, pp. 361–371.
10. Laura R. Oswald, "Culture Swapping: Consumption and the Ethnogenesis of Middle-Class Haitian Immigrants," *Journal of Consumer Research*, March 1999, pp. 303–318.
11. Elisabeth Furst, "The Cultural Significance of Food," in ed. Per Otnes, *The Sociology of Consumption: An Anthology* (Oslo, Norway: Solum Forlag, 1988), pp. 89–100.
12. Penaloza, "Atravesando Fronteras/Border Crossings."
13. Kathleen, Brewer Doran, "Symbolic Consumption in China: The Color Television as a Life Statement," in eds. Merrie Brucks and Debbie MacInnis, *Advances in Consumer Research*, vol. 24 (Provo, Utah: Association for Consumer Research, 1997), pp. 128–131.
14. Amy Cortese, "My Jet Is Bigger Than Your Jet," *BusinessWeek*, August 25, 1997, p. 126.
15. Elizabeth C. Hirschman, "Upper Class WASPs as Consumers: A Humanistic Inquiry," in eds. Elizabeth Hirschman and Jagdish N. Sheth, *Research in Consumer Behavior*, vol. 3 (Greenwich, Conn.: JAI Press, 1988), pp. 115–147; see also Elizabeth C. Hirschman, "Primitive Aspects of Consumption in Modern American Society," *Journal of Consumer Research*, September 1985, pp. 142–154; for a study of the symbols of upper-middle class consumers, see Jeffrey F. Durgee, Morris B. Holbrook, and Melanie Wallendorf, "The Wives of Woodville," in ed. Russell W. Belk, *Highways and Buyways: Naturalistic Research from the Consumer Behavior Odyssey* (Provo, Utah: Association for Consumer Research, 1991), pp. 167–177.
16. Melanie Wallendorf and Eric Arnould, "We Gather Together: Consumption Rituals of Thanksgiving Day," *Journal of Consumer Research*, June 1991, pp. 13–31.
17. Stephanie Anderson Forest, "Dressed to Drill," *BusinessWeek*, September 7, 1997, p. 40.
18. For more on the use of clothing as symbols, see Rebecca H. Holman, "Apparel as Communication," in eds. Elizabeth C. Hirschman and Morris B. Holbrook, *Symbolic Consumer Behavior* (Ann Arbor, Mich.: Association for Consumer Research, 1981), pp. 7–15.
19. Pierre Bourdieu, *Distinction: A Social Critique of the Judgment of Taste* (Cambridge, Mass.: Harvard University Press, 1984), for other research on gender associations with food, see Deborah Heisley, "Gender Symbolism in Food," doctoral dissertation, Northwestern University, 1991.
20. Sidney Levy, "Interpreting Consumer Mythology: A Structural Approach to Consumer Behavior," *Journal of Marketing*, vol. 45, no. 3, 1982, pp. 49–62.
21. Nancy Holt, "Glow-in-the-Dark Rosary: Badge of Faith or Forbidden Gang Garb," *Wall Street Journal*, July 22, 1997, p. B1.
22. Jennifer Edison Escalas, "The Consumption of Insignificant Rituals: A Look at Debutante Balls," in eds. Leigh McAlister and Michael L. Rothschild, *Advances in Consumer Research*, vol. 20 (Provo, Utah: Association for Consumer Research, 1993), pp. 709–716.
23. Jean Bond Rafferty, "Surpassing the Test of Time: Patek Philippe," *Town & Country*, January 2002, pp. 98+; Deborah Weisgall, "Buying Time," *Fortune*, September 8, 1997, p. 192.

24. Anonymous, "Miller Lite," *Beverage Dynamics*, January–February 2002, p. 40.

25. Michael R. Solomon, "Building Up and Breaking Down: The Impact of Cultural Sorting on Symbolic Consumption," in eds. Elizabeth C. Hirschman and Jagdish N. Sheth, *Research in Consumer Behavior* (Greenwich, Conn.: JAI Press, 1988), pp. 325–351; McCracken, "Culture and Consumption"; McCracken, *Culture and Consumption.*

26. Solomon, "Building Up and Breaking Down"; C. Whan Park, Bernard J. Jaworski, and Deborah J. MacInnis, "Strategic Brand Concept-Image Management," *Journal of Marketing*, October 1986, pp. 135–145; James H. Leigh and Terrace G. Gabel, "Symbolic Interactionism: Its Effects on Consumer Behavior and Implications for Marketing Strategy," *Journal of Consumer Marketing*, Winter 1992, pp. 27–39.

27. Myrna L. Armstrong and Donata C. Gabriel, "Motivation for Tattoo Removal," *Archives of Dermatology*, April 1996, pp. 412–416.

28. John W. Schouten, "Personal Rites of Passage and the Reconstruction of Self," in eds. Rebecca H. Holman and Michael R. Solomon, *Advances in Consumer Research*, vol. 18 (Provo, Utah: Association for Consumer Research, 1991), pp. 49–51.

29. Melissa Martin Young, "Dispositions of Possessions During Role Transitions," in eds. Rebecca H. Holman and Michael R. Solomon, *Advances in Consumer Research*, vol. 18 (Provo, Utah: Association for Consumer Research, 1991), pp. 33–39.

30. Robert A. Wicklund and Peter M. Gollwitzer, *Symbolic Self-Completion* (Hillsdale, N.J.: Lawrence Erlbaum, 1982).

31. Diane Ackerman, *A Natural History of Love* (New York: Random House, 1994).

32. James H. McAlexander, John W. Schouten, and Scott D. Roberts, "Consumer Behavior and Divorce," in eds. Janeen Arnold Costa and Russell W. Belk, *Research in Consumer Behavior*, vol. 6 (Greenwich, Conn.: JAI Press, 1993), pp. 162; see also Rita Fullerman and Kathleen Debevec, "Till Death Do We Part: Family Dissolution, Transition, and Consumer Behavior," in eds. John F. Sherry and Brian Sternthal, *Advances in Consumer Research*, vol. 19 (Provo, Utah: Association for Consumer Research, 1992), pp. 514–521.

33. Penaloza, "Atravesando Fronteras/Border Crossings"; Melanie Wallendorf and Michael D. Reilly, "Ethnic Migration, Assimilation, and Consumption," *Journal of Consumer Research*, December 1983, pp. 292–302; Rohit Deshpande, Wayne Hoyer, and Naveen Donthu, "The Intensity of Ethnic Affiliation: A Study of the Sociology of Hispanic Consumption," *Journal of Consumer Research*, September 1986, pp. 214–220; for a discussion of acculturation of Chinese Americans, see Wei-Na Lee, "Acculturation and Advertising Communication Strategies: A Cross-Cultural Study of Chinese Americans," *Psychology and Marketing*, September–October 1993, pp. 381–397; for an interesting study on the immigration of Haitian consumers, see Laura R. Oswald, "Culture Swapping: Consumption and the Ethnogenesis of Middle-Class Haitian Immigrants," *Journal of Consumer Research*, March 1999, pp. 303–318; for a discussion of Turkish consumers immigrating to Denmark, see Güliz Gur and Per Østergaard, "Constructing Immigrant Identities in Consumption: Appearance Among the Turko-Danes," in eds. Joseph W. Alba and Wesley Hutchinson, *Advances in Consumer Research*, vol. 25, (Provo, Utah: Association for Consumer Research, 1998), pp. 48–52.

34. Annamma Joy and Ruby Roy Dholakia, "Remembrances of Things Past: The Meaning of Home and Possessions of Indian Professionals in Canada," in ed., Floyd W. Rudmin, *To Have Possessions: A Handbook of Ownership and Property, Journal of Social Behavior and Personality*, Special Issue, vol. 6, no. 6, 1991, 385–402; see also Raj Mehta and Russell W. Belk, "Artifacts, Identity, and Transition: Favorite Possessions of Indians and Indian Immigrants to the United States," *Journal of Consumer Research*, March 1991, pp. 398–411.

35. Craig J. Thompson and Siok Kuan Tambyah, "Trying to Be Cosmopolitan," *Journal of Consumer Research*, vol. 26, December 1999, pp. 214–241.

36. Priscilla A. LaBarbera, "The Nouveaux Riches: Conspicuous Consumption and the Issue of Self-Fulfillment," in eds. Elizabeth C. Hirschman and Jagdish N. Sheth, *Research in Consumer Behavior* (Greenwich, Conn.: JAI Press, 1988), pp. 181–182.

37. Cyndee Miller, "'Til Death Do They Part," *Marketing News*, March 27, 1995, pp. 1–2; for an extensive discussion of consumer life transitions and related products, see Paula Mergenhagen, *Targeting Transitions* (Ithaca, N.Y.: American Demographics Books, 1995).

38. Anonymous, "For Auction Online: Enron's Memos," *New York Times*, January 18, 2002, p. C7.

39. Miller, "'Til Death Do They Part."

40. Rebecca Gardyn, "Rock-a-Buy Baby," *American Demographics*, July 2000, p. 12.

41. Otnes and Scott, "Something Old, Something New."

42. Stephanie Mehta, "Bridal Superstores Woo Couples with Miles of Gowns and Tuxes," *Wall Street Journal*, February 14, 1995, pp. B1, B2.

43. In line with our notion that the meaning of the symbol may derive from the culture as opposed to the individual and that symbols may have public or private meaning, see Marsha L. Richins, "Valuing Things: The Public and Private Meaning of Possessions," *Journal of Consumer Research*, December 1994, pp. 504–521.

44. Mihaly Csikzentmihalyi and Eugene Rochberg-Halton, *The Meaning of Things: Domestic Symbols and the Self* (Cambridge, England: Cambridge University Press, 1981); N. Laura Kamptner, "Personal Possessions and Their Meanings: A Life Span Perspective," *Journal of Social Behavior and Personality*, vol 6, no. 6, 1991, pp. 209–228; see also Richins, "Valuing Things."

45. Wallendorf and Arnould, "We Gather Together."

46. Adam Kuper, "The English Christmas and the Family: Time Out and Alternative Realities," in ed. Daniel

Miller, *Unwrapping Christmas* (Oxford, England: Oxford University Press, 1993), pp. 157–175; Barbara Bodenhorn, "Christmas Present: Christmas Public," in ed. Miller, *Unwrapping Christmas*, pp. 193–216.

47. See, for example, Russell W. Belk, "Possessions and the Sense of Past" in ed. Russell Belk, *Highways* and *Buyways* (Provo, Utah: Association for Consumer Research, 1988).

48. Kelly Tepper Tian, William O. Bearden, and Gary L. Hunter, "Consumers' Need for Uniqueness: Scale Development and Validation," *Journal of Consumer Research*, vol. 28, June 2001, pp. 50–66; Howard L. Fromkin and C. R. Snyder, "The Search for Uniqueness and Valuation of Scarcity," in eds. Kenneth Gergen, Martin S. Greenberg, and Richard H. Willis, *Social Exchanges: Advances in Theory and Research* (New York: Plenum, 1980), pp. 57–75; Csikszenthmihalyi and Rochberg-Halton, *The Meaning of Things*; see also Richins, "Valuing Things."

49. Gabriel Bar-Haim, "The Meaning of Western Commercial Artifacts for Eastern European Youth," *Journal of Contemporary Ethnography*, July 1987, pp. 205–226.

50. Robert P. Libbon, "Datadog," *American Demographics*, September 2000, p. 26.

51. Stacy Baker and Patricia Kennedy, "Death by Nostalgia," in *Advances in Consumer Research* (Provo, Utah: Association for Consumer Research, 1994), vol. 21, pp.169–174; Morris B. Holbrook and Robert Schindler, "Echoes of the Dear Departed Past," in *Advances in Consumer Research*, vol. 18 (Provo, Utah: Association for Consumer Research, 1991), pp. 330–333.

52. Russell W. Belk, "Possessions and the Extended Self," *Journal of Consumer Research*, September 1988, pp. 139–168; A. Dwayne Ball and Lori H. Tasaki, "The Role and Measurement of Attachment in Consumer Behavior," *Journal of Consumer Psychology*, vol. 1, no. 2, 1992, pp. 155–172; M. Joseph Sirgy, "Self-Concept and Consumer Behavior: A Critical Review," *Journal of Consumer Research*, December 1982, pp. 287–300; Robert E. Kleine, Susan Schultz Kleine, and Jerome B. Kernan, "Mundane Consumption and the Self: A Social Identity Perspective," *Journal of Consumer Psychology*, vol. 2, no. 3, 1993, pp. 209–235.

53. Kleine, Kleine, and Kernan, "Mundane Consumption and the Self"; see also Sirgy, "Self-Concept and Consumer Behavior"; M. Joseph Sirgy, *Social Cognition and Consumer Behavior* (New York: Praeger, 1983); George M. Zinkhan and J. W. Hong, "Self-Concept and Advertising Effectiveness: A Conceptual Model of Congruence, Conspicuousness, and Response Mode," in eds. Rebecca Holman and Michael Solomon, *Advances in Consumer Research*, vol. 18 (Provo, Utah: Association for Consumer Research, 1991), pp. 348–354; Morris B. Holbrook, "Patterns, Personalities, and Complex Relationships in the Effects of Self on Mundane Everyday Consumption: These Are 495 of My Most and Least Favorite Things," in eds. John F. Sherry and Brian Sternthal, *Advances in Consumer Research*, vol. 19 (Provo, Utah: Association for Consumer Research, 1992), pp. 417–423.

54. Kleine, Kleine, and Kernan, "Mundane Consumption and the Self."

55. C. R. Snyder and Howard L. Fromkin, *Uniqueness: Human Pursuit of Difference* (New York: Plenum, 1981).

56. Sirgy, "Self-Concept and Consumer Behavior"; Sirgy, *Social Cognition and Consumer Behavior*.

57. Cheng Lu Wang, Terry Bristol, John C. Mowen, and Goutam Chakraborty, "Alternative Modes of Self-Construal: Dimensions of Connectedness-Separateness and Advertising Appeals to the Cultural and Gender-Specific Self," *Journal of Consumer Psychology*, vol. 9, no. 2, 2000, pp. 107–115.

58. Susan E. Schultz, Robert E. Kleine, and Jerome B. Kernan, "These Are a Few of My Favorite Things, Toward an Explication of Attachment as a Consumer Behavior Construct," in ed. Thomas K. Srull, *Advances in Consumer Research*, vol. 16 (Provo, Utah: Association for Consumer Research, 1989), pp. 359–366; Richins, "Valuing Things"; Marsha L. Richins, "Special Possessions and the Expression of Material Values," *Journal of Consumer Research*, December 1994, pp. 522–533.

59. Richins, "Valuing Things."

60. Ibid.

61. Rebecca Gardyn, "VIPs (Very Important Pets)," *American Demographics*, March 2001, pp. 16–18; Belk, "Possessions and the Extended Self"; Elizabeth C. Hirschman, "Consumers and Their Animal Companions," *Journal of Consumer Research*, March 1994, pp. 616–632; see also Clinton R. Sanders, "The Animal 'Other': Self Definition, Social Identity and Companion Animals," in eds. Marvin Goldberg, Jerry Gorn, and Richard Pollay, *Advances in Consumer Research*, vol. 17 (Provo, Utah: Association for Consumer Research, 1990), pp. 662–668.

62. John Fetto, "Pets Can Drive," *American Demographics*, March 2000, pp. 10–12.

63. Kathy Chen, "Tough Rules for Dogs in Beijing Have Some Pet Owners Howling," *Wall Street Journal*, June 20, 1995, p. B1.

64. Libbon, "Datadog."

65. Stephen Mehta, "Executive's Pet Project: A Kennel Chain," *Wall Street Journal*, February 24, 1997, pp. B1, B2.

66. Belk, "Possessions and the Sense of Past"; Susan Schultz Kleine, Robert E. Kleine III, and Chris T. Allen, "How Is a Possession 'Me' or 'Not Me'? Characterizing Types and an Antecedent of Material Possession Attachment," *Journal of Consumer Research*, December 1995, pp. 327–343; McAlexander, Schouten, and Roberts, "Consumer Behavior and Divorce"; Lisa L. Love and Peter S. Sheldon, "Souvenirs: Messengers of Meaning," in eds. Joseph W. Alba and Wesley Hutchinson, *Advances in Consumer Research*, vol. 25

(Provo, Utah: Association for Consumer Research, 1998), pp. 170–175.

67. Belk, "Possessions and the Sense of Past."

68. Russell W. Belk, "Moving Possessions: An Analysis Based on Personal Documents from the 1847–1869 Mormon Migration," *Journal of Consumer Research*, December 1992, pp. 339–361.

69. Temma Ehrenfeld, "Why Executives Collect," *Fortune*, January 11, 1993, pp. 94–97.

70. Russell W. Belk, Melanie Wallendorf, John F. Sherry Jr., and Morris B. Holbrook, "Collecting in a Consumer Culture," in ed. Belk, *Highways and Buyways*.

71. Alexandra Peers, "Baseball's Card of Cards Is Up for Grabs," *Wall Street Journal*, September 20, 1996, pp. B1–B9.

72. Chris Tomasson, "Olympic Collectibles Are an Expensive Passion," *Akron Beacon Journal*, February 10, 2002, www.ohio.com.

73. Russell W. Belk, Melanie Wallendorf, John F. Sherry Jr., Morris Holbrook, and Scott Roberts, "Collectors and Collecting," in ed. Michael J. Houston, *Advances in Consumer Research*, vol. 15 (Provo, Utah: Association for Consumer Research, 1988), pp. 548–553.

74. Belk, Wallendorf, Sherry, Holbrook, and Roberts, "Collectors and Collecting."

75. Russell W. Belk, "The Ineluctable Mysteries of Possessions," in ed. Floyd W. Rudmin, *To Have Possessions: A Handbook on Ownership and Property, Journal of Social Behavior and Personality*, Special Issue, vol. 6, no. 6, 1991, pp. 17–55.

76. Kent Grayson and David Shulman, "Indexicality and the Verification Function of Irreplaceable Possessions: A Semiotic Analysis," *Journal of Consumer Research*, vol. 27, June 2000, pp. 17–30.

77. Belk et al., "Collecting in a Consumer Culture."

78. Susan Fournier, "The Development of Intense Consumer-Product Relationships," Paper presented at the AMA Winter Educator's Conference, St. Petersburg, Fla., February 20, 1994.

79. Fournier, "The Development of Intense Consumer-Product Relationships."

80. Csikszenthmihalyi and Rochberg-Halton, *The Meaning of Things*; Wallendorf and Arnould, "My Favorite Things"; Belk, "Moving Possessions."

81. Csikszenthmihalyi and Rochberg-Halton, *The Meaning of Things*.

82. Ibid.

83. Helga Dittmar, "Meaning of Material Possessions as Reflections of Identity: Gender and Social-Material Position in Society," in ed. Rudmin, *To Have Possessions*, pp. 165–186; see also Helga Dittmar, *The Social Psychology of Material Possessions* (New York: St. Martin's, 1992).

84. Dittmar, "Meaning of Material Possessions as Reflections of Identity"; Kamptner, "Personal Possessions and Their Meanings."

85. Wallendorf and Arnould, "My Favorite Things."

86. Russell W. Belk and Melanie Wallendorf, "Of Mice and Men: Gender Identity in Collecting," in eds. K. Ames and K. Martinez, *The Gender of Material Culture* (Ann Arbor, Mich.: University of Michigan Press), reprinted in ed. Susan M. Pearce, *Objects and Collections* (London: Routledge, 1994), pp. 240–253; Belk et al., "Collectors and Collecting."

87. Elizabeth Myers, "Phenomenological Analysis of the Importance of Special Possessions: An Exploratory Study," in eds. Elizabeth C. Hirschman and Morris B. Holbrook, *Advances in Consumer Research*, vol. 12 (Provo, Utah: Association for Consumer Research, 1985), pp. 560–565.

88. McCracken, "Culture and Consumption"; McCracken, *Culture and Consumption*.

89. Ibid.

90. Ibid.

91. Linda L. Price, Eric J. Arnold, and Carolyn Folkman Curasi, "Older Consumers' Disposition of Special Possessions," *Journal of Consumer Research*, vol. 27, September 2000, pp. 179–201.

92. Russell W. Belk, Melanie Wallendorf, and John F. Sherry Jr., "The Sacred and the Profane in Consumer Behavior: Theodicy on the Odyssey," *Journal of Consumer Research*, June 1989, pp. 1–38.

93. Jack Etkin, "Ichiro Mania: Seattle Outfielder Suzuki Makes It Big in Major Leagues," *Baseball Digest*, December 2001, pp. 40–41.

94. Belk, "Possessions and the Sense of Past."

95. Belk, Wallendorf, and Sherry, "The Sacred and the Profane in Consumer Behavior."

96. Amitai Etzioni, "The Socio-Economics of Property," in ed. Rudmin, *To Have Possessions*, pp. 465–468.

97. McAlexander, Schouten, and Roberts, "Consumer Behavior and Divorce."

98. Robert V. Kozinets, "Utopian Enterprise: Articulating the Meanings of *Star Trek*'s Culture of Consumption," *Journal of Consumer Research*, vol. 28, June 2001, pp. 67–88.

99. Kevin Goldman, "A Few Rockers Give Ad Makers No Satisfaction," *Wall Street Journal*, August 25, 1995, pp. B1, B4.

100. See, for example, Leigh Schmidt, "The Commercialization of the Calendar," *Journal of American History*, December 1991, pp. 887–916.

101. For fascinating historical and sociological accounts of Christmas, see Daniel Miller, "A Theory of Christmas," in ed. Miller, *Unwrapping Christmas*, pp. 3–37; Claude Levi-Strauss, "Father Christmas Executed," in ed. Miller, *Unwrapping Christmas*, pp. 38–54; Belk, "Materialism and the Making of the Modern American Christmas"; Daniel Miller, "Christmas against Materialism in Trinidad," in ed. Miller, *Unwrapping Christmas*, pp. 134–153; Barbara Bodenhorn, "Christmas Present: Christmas Public," in ed. Miller, *Unwrapping Christmas*, pp. 193–216; William B.

Waits, *The Modern Christmas in America* (New York: New York University Press, 1993); and Stephen Nissenbaum, *The Battle for Christmas* (New York: Vantage Books, 1997).

102. John F. Sherry Jr., "Gift Giving in Anthropological Perspective," *Journal of Consumer Research*, September 1983, pp. 157–168.

103. For a discussion of several of these motives, see Sherry, "Gift Giving in Anthropological Perspective"; for research on gender differences in motives, see Mary Ann McGrath, "Gender Differences in Gift Exchanges: New Directions from Projections," *Psychology and Marketing*, August 1995, pp. 229–234; Cele Otnes, Julie A. Ruth, and Constance Milbourne, "The Pleasure and Pain of Being Close: Men's Mixed Feelings about Participation in Valentine's Day Gift Exchange," in eds. Chris Allen and Debbie Roedder-John, *Advances in Consumer Research*, vol. 21 (Provo, Utah: Association for Consumer Research, 1994), pp. 159–164; Cele Otnes, Kyle Zolner, and Tina M. Lowry, "In-Laws and Outlaws: The Impact of Divorce and Remarriage upon Christmas Gift Exchange," in eds. Chris Allen and Debbie Roedder-John, *Advances in Consumer Research*, vol. 21 (Provo, Utah: Association for Consumer Research, 1994), pp. 25–29; for other gift-giving motives, see Russell W. Belk, "Gift Giving Behavior," in ed. Jagdish N. Sheth, *Research in Marketing* (Greenwich, Conn.: JAI Press, 1979), pp. 95–126; Russell W. Belk, "The Perfect Gift," in eds. Cele Otnes and Richard Beltrami, *Gift Giving Behavior: An Interdisciplinary Anthology* (Bowling Green, Ohio: Bowling Green University Popular Press, forthcoming); for a discussion of the roles played by gift givers (the pleaser, the provider, the compensator, the socializer, and the acknowledger), see Cele Otnes, Tina M. Lowrey, and Young Chan Kim, "Gift Selection for Easy and Difficult Recipients," *Journal of Consumer Research*, September 1993, pp. 229–244; Kleine, Kleine, and Allen, "How Is a Possession 'Me' or 'Not Me'?"

104. David B. Wooten, "Qualitative Steps toward an Expanded Model of Anxiety in Gift-Giving," *Journal of Consumer Research*, vol. 27, June 2000, pp. 84–95.

105. McAlexander, Schouten, and Roberts, "Consumer Behavior and Divorce."

106. Russell W. Belk and Gregory S. Coon, "Gift Giving as Agapic Love: An Alternative to the Exchange Paradigm Based on Dating Experiences," *Journal of Consumer Research*, December 1993, pp. 393–417.

107. Sherry, "Gift Giving in Anthropological Perspective"; Mary Searle-Chatterjee, "Christmas Cards and the Construction of Social Relations in Britain Today," in ed. Miller, *Unwrapping Christmas*, pp. 176–192.

108. Belk and Coon, "Gift Giving as Agapic Love"; see also Sherry, "Gift Giving in Anthropological Perspective."

109. Robert P. Libbon, "Datadog," *American Demographics*, May 2000, p. 25.

110. Sak Onkvisit and John J. Shaw, *International Marketing: Analysis and Strategy* (Columbus, Ohio: Merrill, 1989), pp. 241–242.

111. Eileen Fischer and Stephen J. Arnold, "More Than a Labor of Love: Gender Roles and Christmas Shopping," *Journal of Consumer Research*, December 1990, pp. 333–345.

112. John F. Sherry Jr. and Mary Ann McGrath, "Unpacking the Holiday Presence: A Comparative Ethnography of Two Gift Stores," in ed. Elizabeth C. Hirschman, *Interpretive Consumer Research* (Provo, Utah: Association for Consumer Research, 1989), pp. 148–167; see also David Cheal, "Showing Them You Love Them: Gift Giving and the Dialectic of Intimacy," *Sociological Review*, January 1987, pp. 151–169; Lewis Hyde, *The Gift* (New York: Vintage, 1979).

113. See, for example, Theodore Caplow, "Rule Enforcement without Visible Means: Christmas Gift Giving in Middletown," *American Journal of Sociology*, March 1984, pp. 1306–1323.

114. James G. Carrier, "The Rituals of Christmas Giving," in ed. Miller, *Unwrapping Christmas*, pp. 55–74.

115. Mary Ann McGrath, "An Ethnography of a Gift Store: Trappings, Wrappings, and Rapture," *Journal of Retailing*, Winter 1989, p. 434.

116. Wooten, "Qualitative Steps toward an Expanded Model of Anxiety in Gift-Giving."

117. Julie A. Ruth, Cele C. Tones, and Frederic F. Brunel, "Gift Receipt and the Reformulation of Interpersonal Relationships," *Journal of Consumer Research*, March 1999, pp. 385–402; Ming-Hui Huang and Shihti Yu, "Gifts in a Romantic Relationship: A Survival Analysis," *Journal of Consumer Psychology*, vol. 9, no. 3, 2000, pp. 179–188.

118. Belk, "Gift Giving Behavior"; see also Sherry, "Gift Giving in Anthropological Perspective"; for research on this factor and others discussed above, see Rick G. M. Pieters, and Henry S. J. Robben, "Beyond the Horse's Mouth: Exploring Acquisition and Exchange Utility in Gift Evaluation," in eds. Joseph W. Alba and Wesley Hutchinson, *Advances in Consumer Research*, vol. 25, (Provo, Utah: Association for Consumer Research 1998), pp. 160–163.

119. Belk and Coon, "Gift Giving as Agapic Love."

120. Kevin Helliker, "Sweet Sells Year after Year for Hallmark," *Wall Street Journal*, December 20, 1996, pp. B1, B7.

121. Michal Strahilevitz, "The Effects of Product Type and Donation Magnitude on Willingness to Pay More for a Charity-Linked Brand," *Journal of Consumer Psychology*, vol. 8, no. 3, 1999, pp. 215–241.

122. Wendy Bounds, "Here Comes the Bride, Clicking a Mouse," *Wall Street Journal*, January 14, 1999, pp. B1, B3.

123. More Marketers Wish You a Merry Winter," *Wall Street Journal*, December 5, 1996, pp. B1, B12.

124. Joshua Harris Proger, "Out of Ideas? Give a Goat or a Seaweed Body Wrap," *Wall Street Journal*, December 23, 1997, pp. B1, B3.

125. Susan Carey, "Over the River, through the Woods, to a Posh Resort We Go," *Wall Street Journal*, November 21, 1997, pp. B1, B4.

Chapter 19

1. Kristen Gerencher, "Gender Gap: Driving 'Greener' Car Sales," *CBS MarketWatch.com*, March 20, 2002, **www.cbs.marketwatch.com**; Kathryn Kranhold, "Toyota Makes a Bet on New Hybrid Prius," *Wall Street Journal*, July 20, 2000, p. B18.
2. Jeffrey Ball, "How Can Detroit Top the SUV? Think Golf Carts," *Wall Street Journal*, July 20, 2001, pp. B1, B3.
3. Lori Dahm, "Secrets of Success: The Strategies Driving New Product Development at Kraft," *Stagnito's New Products Magazine*, January 2002, pp. 18–19.
4. Hubert Gatignon and Thomas S. Robertson, "Innovative Decision Processes," in eds. Thomas S. Robertson and Harold H. Kassarjian, *Handbook of Consumer Behavior* (New York: Prentice-Hall, 1991), pp. 316–317; see also Everett M. Rogers, *The Diffusion of Innovations* (New York: Free Press, 1983).
5. Larry Armstrong, "Tuning In to Pay Radio," *BusinessWeek*, March 25, 2002, p. 100.
6. Miriam Jordan, "Selling Birth Control to India's Poor," *New York Times*, September 21, 1999, pp. B1, B4.
7. Wilton Woods, "1994 Products of the Year," *Fortune*, December 12, 1994, pp. 198–208.
8. Robert Barker, "No Suckers, Those Smuckers," *BusinessWeek*, March 4, 2002, p. 112.
9. Robert Langreth, "From a Prostate Drug Comes a Pill for Baldness," *Wall Street Journal*, March 20, 1997, pp. B1, B4.
10. Barry Newman, "'Disco Polo' Is Rocking the Pop Foundations of Polish Music Scene," *Wall Street Journal*, February 7, 1996, pp. A1, A8.
11. Yumiko Ono, "Overcoming the Stigma of Dishwashers in Japan," *Wall Street Journal*, May 19, 2000, pp. B1, B4.
12. Tara Parker-Pope, "New Devices Add Up Bill, Measure Shoppers' Honesty," *Wall Street Journal*, June 6, 1995, pp. B1, B13.
13. Thomas S. Robertson, "The Process of Innovation and the Diffusion of Innovation," *Journal of Marketing*, January 1967, pp. 14–19; Thomas S. Robertson, *Innovative Behavior and Communication* (New York: Holt, Reinhart, & Winston, 1971).
14. C. Page Moreau, Arthur B. Markman, and Donald R. Lehmann, "'What Is It?' Categorization Flexibility and Consumers' Responses to Really New Products," *Journal of Consumer Research*, vol. 27, March 2001, pp. 489–498.
15. Peter Waldman, "Great Idea...If It Flies," *Wall Street Journal*, June 24, 1999, pp. B1, B4.
16. Robert Strohmeyer, "Palms Away," *Smart Business*, June 2001, pp. 40–42.
17. Gautam Naik, "You Did *What* on a Cell Phone?" *Wall Street Journal*, June 3, 1999, pp. B1, B6.
18. Peter Landers, "Cellphones Feature Cameras, Video Screens, Keyboards as Japan Plans Upgrade," *Wall Street Journal*, January 18, 2001, pp. B1, B4.
19. Stephen Manes, "Press a Button, Skip the Ads: Digital Tools," *Forbes*, June 11, 2001, p. 146.
20. Alfred R. Petrosky, "Extending Innovation Characteristic Perception to Diffusion Channel Intermediaries and Aesthetic Products," in eds. Rebecca Holman and Michael Solomon, *Advances in Consumer Research*, vol. 18 (Provo, Utah: Association for Consumer Research, 1991), pp. 627–634.
21. Vivan Marino, "When French Fries Go Over the Rainbow," *New York Times*, February 17, 2002, sec. 3, p. 4.
22. Keith Naughton, "Roots Gets Rad: Trading in Earth Shoes for Hot Berets, the Canadian Firm Plans a U.S. Invasion After Its Olympic Triumph," *Newsweek*, February 25, 2002, p. 36.
23. Jack Neff, "Mouthwash Strips Get $40 Mil Push," *Advertising Age*, July 9, 2001, p. 36.
24. Wilton Woods, "Dressed to Spill," *Fortune*, October 17, 1995, p. 209.
25. S. Ram, "A Model of Innovation Resistance," in eds. Melanie Wallendorf and Paul Anderson, *Advances in Consumer Research*, vol. 14 (Provo, Utah: Association for Consumer Research, 1987), pp. 208–212; Jagdish N. Sheth, "Psychology of Innovation Resistance: The Less Developed Concept (LDC) in Diffusion Research," in *Research in Marketing* (Greenwich, Conn.: JAI Press, 1981), pp. 273–282.
26. Don Clark, "Upgrade Fatigue Threatens PC Profits," *Wall Street Journal*, May 14, 1998, pp. B1, B8.
27. Gene Murdock and Lori Franz, "Habit and Perceived Risk as Factors in the Resistance to the Use of ATMs," *Journal of Retail Banking*, February 1983, pp. 20–29.
28. David Glen Mick and Susan Fournier, "Paradoxes of Technology: Consumer Cognizance, Emotions, and Coping Strategies," *Journal of Consumer Research*, September 1998, pp. 123–143.
29. Urban Glen. and Gilbert A. Churchill, "Five Dimensions of the Industrial Adoption Process," *Journal of Marketing Research*, August 1971, pp. 322–327; Charles R. O'Neal, Hans B. Thorelli, and James M. Utterback, "Adoption of Innovation by Industrial Organizations," *Industrial Marketing Management*, March 1973, pp. 235–250; Gerald Zaltman, Robert Duncan, and Jonny Holbek, *Innovations and Organizations (*New York: Wiley, 1973).
30. Tara Parker-Pope, "P&G Puts Lots of Chips on Plan to Give Away Fat-Free Pringles," *Wall Street Journal*, June 23, 1998, p. B8.
31. Monica Hogan, "DirecTV, TiVo Redo DVR Alliance," *Multichannel News*, February 25, 2002, p. 2; "Is TiVo's

Signal Fading?" *BusinessWeek*, September 10, 2001, pp. 72+; Roben Farzad, "Why Shareholders Give TiVo the HeaveHo," *SmartMoney.com*, June 29, 2001, **www.smartmoney.com**.

32. Rogers, *The Diffusion of Innovations.*

33. Geoffrey A. Moore, *Crossing the Chasm* (New York: HarperBusiness, 1991).

34. Cristina Lourosa, "Understanding the User: Who Are the First Ones out There Buying the Latest Gadgets?" *Wall Street Journal*, June 15, 1998, p. R18.

35. Julia Angwin, "Has Growth of the Net Flattened?" *Wall Street Journal*, July 16, 2001, pp. B1, B8.

36. Moore, *Crossing the Chasm.*

37. Robert A. Peterson, "A Note on Optimal Adopter Category Determination," *Journal of Marketing Research*, August 1973, pp. 325–329; see also William R. Darden and Fred D. Reynolds, "Backward Profiling of Male Innovators," *Journal of Marketing Research*, February 1974, pp. 79–85; Steven A. Baumgarten, "The Innovative Communicator in the Diffusion Process," *Journal of Marketing Research*, February 1975, pp. 12–18. Schemes based on consumers' involvement in the new product development process, for example, might be utilized by managers (see Jerry Wind and Vijay Mahajan, "Issues and Opportunities in New Product Development: An Introduction to the Special Issue," *Journal of Marketing Research*, February 1997, pp.1–12).

38. David F. Midgley and Grahame R. Dowling, "Innovativeness: The Concept and Its Measurement," *Journal of Consumer Research*, March 1978, pp. 229–242; Mary Dee Dickerson and James W. Gentry, "Characteristics of Adopters and Non Adopters of Home Computers," *Journal of Consumer Research*, September 1983, pp. 225–235; see also Vijay Mahajan, Eitan Muller, and Rajendra Srivastava, "Determination of Adopter Categories by Using Innovation Diffusion Models," *Journal of Marketing Research*, February 1990, pp. 37–50; Kenneth C. Manning, William O. Bearden, and Thomas J. Madden, "Consumer Innovativeness and the Adoption Process," *Journal of Consumer Psychology*, vol. 4, no. 4, 1995, pp. 329–345.

39. See review in Thomas S. Robertson, Joan Zielinski, and Scott Ward, *Consumer Behavior* (Glenview, Ill.: Scott-Foresman, 1984); see also Dickerson and Gentry, "Characteristics of Adopters and Non Adopters of Home Computers"; Duncan G. Labay and Thomas C. Kinnear, "Exploring the Consumer Decision Process in the Adoption of Solar Energy Systems," *Journal of Consumer Research*, December 1981, pp. 271–277; Kenneth Uhl, Roman Andrus, and Lance Poulsen, "How Are Laggards Different? An Empirical Inquiry," *Journal of Marketing Research*, February 1970, pp. 51–54; Rogers, *The Diffusion of Innovations*, pp. 383–384.

40. Robert A. Guth, "Can Your Cell Phone Shop, Play or Fish?" *Wall Street Journal*, August 3, 2000, p. B1; S. Karene Witcher, "Credit-Card Issuers Find Australia Fertile Ground for Launching Products," *Wall Street Journal*, March 31, 1995, p. B6.

41. Rogers, *The Diffusion of Innovations;* see also Mark S. Granovetter, "The Strength of Weak Ties," *American Journal of Sociology*, May 1973, pp. 1360–1380; John A. Czepiel, "Word-of-Mouth Processes in the Diffusion of a Major Technological Innovation," *Journal of Marketing Research*, May 1974, pp. 172–180.

42. Manning, Bearden, and Madden, "Consumer Innovativeness and the Adoption Process"; Jan-Benedict E.M. Steenkamp and Hans Baumgartner, "The Role of Optimum Stimulation Level in Exploratory Consumer Behavior," *Journal of Consumer Research*, December 1992, pp. 434–448; P. S. Raju, "Optimum Stimulation Level: Its Relationship to Personality, Demographics, and Exploratory Behavior," *Journal of Consumer Research*, December 1980, pp. 272–282.

43. Thomas S. Robertson and James H. Myers, "Personality Correlates of Opinion Leadership and Innovative Buying Behavior," *Journal of Marketing Research*, May 1969, pp. 164–167.

44. Gordon R. Foxall and Christopher G. Haskins, "Cognitive Style and Consumer Innovativeness," *Marketing Intelligence and Planning*, January 1986, pp. 26–46; Gordon R. Foxall, "Consumer Innovativeness: Novelty Seeking, Creativity and Cognitive Style," in eds. Elizabeth C. Hirschman and Jagdish N. Sheth, *Research in Consumer Behavior*, vol. 3 (Greenwich, Conn.: JAI Press, 1988), pp. 79–114.

45. Ronald E. Goldsmith and Charles F. Hofacker, "Measuring Consumer Innovativeness," *Journal of the Academy of Marketing Science*, Summer 1991, pp. 209–221.

46. Jan-Benedict E.M. Steenkamp, Frenkel ter Hofstede, and Michael Wedel, "A Cross-National Investigation into the Individual and National Cultural Antecedents of Consumer Innovativeness," *Journal of Marketing*, April 1999, pp. 55–69.

47. Hubert Gatignon and Thomas S. Robertson, "A Propositional Inventory for New Diffusion Research," *Journal of Consumer Research*, March 1985, pp. 849–867; see also John O. Summers, "Media Exposure Patterns of Consumer Innovators," *Journal of Marketing*, January 1972, pp. 43–49.

48. James J. Engel, Robert J. Kegerreis, and Roger D. Blackwell, "Word-of-Mouth Communication by the Innovator," *Journal of Marketing*, July 1969, pp. 15–19.

49. Dickerson and Gentry, "Characteristics of Adopters and Non Adopters of Home Computers"; Robertson, *Innovative Behavior and Communication;* James W. Taylor, "A Striking Characteristic of Innovators," *Journal of Marketing Research*, February 1977, pp. 104–107; see also Gatignon and Robertson, "A Propositional Inventory for New Diffusion Research"; Elizabeth C. Hirschman, "Innovativeness, Novelty Seeking and Consumer Creativity," *Journal of Consumer Research*, December 1980, pp. 283–295; Engel, Kegerreis, and Blackwell, "Word-of-Mouth Communication by the Innovator."

50. Alex Frew McMillan, "China Cell-Phone Use Hits 140 Million," *CNN.com*, December 21, 2001, **www.cnn.com/2001/BUSINESS/asia/12/21/china.cellphone**;

Miriam Jordan, "It Takes a Cell Phone: A New Nokia Transforms a Village in Bangladesh," *Wall Street Journal*, June 25, 1999, pp. B1, B4.

51. Frank M. Bass, "New Product Growth Models for Consumer Durables," *Management Science*, September 1969, pp. 215–227; Wellesley Dodds, "An Application of the Bass Model in Long-Term New Product Forecasting," *Journal of Marketing Research*, August 1973, pp. 308–311; Roger M. Heeler and Thomas P. Hustad, "Problems in Predicting New Product Growth for Consumer Durables," *Management Science*, October 1980, pp. 1007–1020; Douglas Tigart and Behrooz Farivar, "The Bass New Product Growth Model: A Sensitivity Analysis for a High Technology Product," *Journal of Marketing*, Fall 1981, pp. 81–90.

52. William E. Cox Jr., "Product Life Cycles as Marketing Models," *Journal of Business*, October 1967, pp. 375–384; Rolando Polli and Victor Cook, "Validity of the Product Life Cycle," *Journal of Business*, October 1969, pp. 385–400; D. R. Rink and J. E. Swan, "Product Life Cycle Research: A Literature Review," *Journal of Business Research*, September 1979, pp. 219–242; Robertson, *Innovative Behavior and Communication.*

53. Elizabeth Stanton, "At Rand McNally, Is the Future Drawn to Scale?" *New York Times*, March 17, 2002, sec. 3, p. 4.

54. Hillary Chura, "Grabbing Bull by Tail: Pepsi, Snapple Redouble Efforts to Take on Red Bull Energy Drink," *Advertising Age*, June 11, 2001, p. 4.

55. Joe Queenan, "Back from the Disco Inferno," *American Demographics*, February 1999, pp. 26–28.

56. Khanh T.L. Tran, "'Karaoke for Feet,'" *Wall Street Journal*, August 16, 2000, pp. B1, B4.

57. Naik, "You Did *What* on a Cell Phone?"

58. Elliot Spagat, "A Web Gadget Fizzles, Despite a Salesman's Dazzle," *Wall Street Journal*, June 27, 2001, pp. B1, B4.

59. Elliot Spagat, "At $70 a Pop, Consumers Put Discount DVD Players on Holiday List," *Wall Street Journal*, December 13, 2001, pp. B1, B4.

60. Mark Holmes, "Microsoft 'Out-branded' by TiVo," *Inside Digital TV*, February 6, 2002; Thomas E. Weber, "Why WebTV Isn't Quite Ready for Prime Time," *Wall Street Journal*, January 2, 1997, pp. B1, B11.

61. Gwendolyn Mariano, "Companies Fear Costly MPEG-4 Licenses," *CnetNews.com*, February 8, 2002, www.cnetnews.com.

62. See Lawrence B. Johnson, "The Hottest Designs in Home Entertainment," *USA Today*, January 29, 2002, www.usatoday.com.

63. Gatignon and Robertson, "A Propositional Inventory for New Diffusion Research"; Vijay Mahajan, Eitan Muller, and Frank M. Bass, "New Product Diffusion Models in Marketing: A Review and Directions for Research," *Journal of Marketing*, April 1990, pp. 1–27.

64. Bruce Nussbaum, "Winners: The Best Product Designs of the Year," *BusinessWeek*, May 25, 1998, pp. 78–81.

65. Greg Jacobson, "Proven Brands Rule," *MMR*, January 14, 2002, pp. 29+.

66. Rogers, *The Diffusion of Innovations.*

67. Ibid, p. 231.

68. Al Doyle, "Getting the Perfect Picture," *Technology & Learning*, January 2002, pp. 9–11.

69. Jagdish N. Sheth and S. Ram, *Bringing Innovation to Market,* 1987 (New York: Wiley).

70. David P. Hamilton, "Japanese Firms Focus on Simpler Camcorders," *Wall Street Journal*, May 5, 1993, p. B1.

71. Sheth and Ram, *Bringing Innovation to Market.*

72. Ibid.

73. Strohmeyer, "Palms Away"; Evan Ramstad, "The Pilot Is This Year's Digital Toy, and Those Who Love It Are Passionate," *Wall Street Journal*, April 1, 1997, pp. B1, B5.

74. Kranhold, "Toyota Makes a Bet on New Hybrid Prius."

75. Mark W. Vigoroso, "The Bottom Line in Web Design: Know Your Customer," *E-Commerce Times*, November 14, 2001, www.ecommercetimes.com/perl/story/?id=14738.

76. Robert J. Fisher and Linda L. Price, "An Investigation into the Social Context of Early Adoption Behavior," *Journal of Consumer Research*, December 1992, pp. 477–486.

77. Sandra D. Atchison, "Lifting the Golf Bag Burden," *BusinessWeek*, July 25, 1994, p. 84.

78. June Fletcher, "New Machines Measure That Holiday Flab at Home," *Wall Street Journal*, December 26, 1997, p. B8.

79. Rogers, *The Diffusion of Innovations*, p. 99.

80. Steve McKee, "A Rally with Real Legs: Going Long in the Sock Market," *Wall Street Journal*, June 4, 1999, pp. B1, B3.

81. C. Whan Park, Bernard J. Jaworski, and Deborah J. MacInnis, "Strategic Brand Concept-Image Management," *Journal of Marketing*, October 1986, pp. 135–145.

82. Fisher and Price, "An Investigation into the Social Context of Early Adoption Behavior."

83. Petrosky, "Extending Innovation Characteristic Perception to Diffusion Channel Intermediaries and Aesthetic Products."

84. Alfred Petrosky labels this factor *genrefication* and discusses it in the context of aesthetic innovations. See Petrosky, "Extending Innovation Characteristic Perception to Diffusion Channel Intermediaries and Aesthetic Products."

85. Sheth and Ram, *Bringing Innovation to Market.*

86. Everett M. Rogers and F. Floyd. Shoemaker, *Communication of Innovations* (New York: The Free

Press, 1971); Elizabeth C. Hirschman, "Consumer Modernity, Cognitive Complexity, Creativity and Innovativeness," in ed. Richard P. Bagozzi, *Marketing in the 80s: Changes and Challenges* (Chicago: American Marketing Association, 1980), pp. 152–161.

87. Jaishankar Ganesh, V. Kumar, and Velavan Subramaniam, "Learning Effect in Multinational Diffusion of Consumer Durables: An Exploratory Investigation," *Journal of the Academy of Marketing Science*, vol. 25, Summer 1997, pp. 214–228; Gatignon and Robertson, "A Propositional Inventory for New Diffusion Research."

88. Seth Stevenson, "I'd Like to Buy the World a Shelf-Stable Children's Lactic Drink," *New York Times Magazine*, March 10, 2002, pp. 38+; John C. Jay, "The Valley of the New," *American Demographics*, March 2000, pp. 58–59; Norihiko Shirouzu, "Japan's High-School Girls Excel in Art of Setting Trends, *Wall Street Journal*, April 24, 1998, pp. B1, B7.

89. Gatignon and Robertson, "A Propositional Inventory for New Diffusion Research"; Lawrence A. Brown, Edward J. Malecki, and Aron N. Spector, "Adopter Categories in a Spatial Context: Alternative Explanations for an Empirical Regularity," *Rural Sociology*, Spring 1976, pp. 99–118.

90. Dorothy Leonard-Barton, "Experts as Negative Opinion Leaders in the Diffusion of a Technological Innovation," *Journal of Consumer Research*, March 1985, pp. 914–926.

91. Everett Rogers and D. Lawrence Kincaid, *Communication Networks: Toward a New Paradigm for Research* (New York: Free Press, 1981).

92. Rogers and Kincaid, *Communication Networks*.

93. Frank M. Bass, "The Relationship between Diffusion Curves, Experience Curves, and Demand Elasticities for Consumer Durable Technological Innovations," *Journal of Business*, July 1980, pp. s51–s57; Dan Horskey and Leonard S. Simon, "Advertising and the Diffusion of New Products," *Marketing Science*, Winter 1983, pp. 1–17; Vijay Mahajan and Eitan Muller, "Innovation Diffusion and New Product Growth Models in Marketing," *Journal of Marketing*, Fall 1979, pp. 55–68; Mahajan, Muller, and Bass, "New Product Diffusion Models in Marketing."

94. Lauriston Sharp, "Steel Axes for Stone Age Australians," in ed. Edward H. Spicer, *Human Problems in Technological Change* (New York: Russell Sage Foundation, 1952).

95. S. Milius, "Bt Corn Risk to Monarchs Is 'Negligible,'" *Science News*, September 15, 2001, p. 164; Scott Kilman, "Modified Corn a Threat to Butterfly, Study Says," *Wall Street Journal*, August 22, 2000, p. B8.

96. H. David Banta, "The Diffusion of the Computer Tomography (CT) Scanner in the United States," *International Journal of Health Services*, 10, 1980, pp. 251–269 as reported in Rogers, *The Diffusion of Innovations*, pp. 231–237.

Chapter 20

1. Jim Edwards, "Sour Dough: Pizza Hut v. Papa Johns," *Brandweek*, May 21, 2002, pp. 26+; "'Puffery' Claims No Longer So Easy to Make," *Marketing News*, February 14, 2000, p. 6; Amy Zuber, "Pizza Hut Weights Appeal After Reversal of Papa John's Ad Ban," *Nation's Restaurant News*, October 2, 2000, pp. 6+.

2. Louis Harris and Associates, *Consumerism in the Eighties*, Study No. 822047, 1983, as referenced in John C. Mowen, *Consumer Behavior*, 3rd ed. (New York: Macmillan, 1993), p. 751.

3. Executive Office of the President, *Consumer Advisory Council*, First Report (Washington, D.C.: U.S. Government Printing Office, October 1963).

4. Rachel Dardis, "Risk Regulation and Consumer Welfare," *Journal of Consumer Affairs*, Summer 1988, pp. 303–317.

5. "Celebrex," *Med Ad News*, February 1, 2001, p. 96.

6. Sally Goll Beatty, "Agencies Weigh Regulating Ads for Alcohol, Tobacco Voluntarily," *Wall Street Journal*, December 9, 1996, p. B7.

7. Gary M. Armstrong and Julie L. Ozanne, "An Evaluation of the NAD/NARB Purpose and Performance," *Journal of Advertising*, vol. 12, no. 3, 1983, pp. 15–26; Caleb Solomon, "Gasoline Ads Canceled: Lack of Truth Cited," *Wall Street Journal*, July 21, 1994, pp. B1, B5.

8. Sandra Gurvis, "Nibbling Away at the Truth," *Advertising Age's Creativity*, February 1, 2000, p. 18.

9. "Visa Forced to Change Its Advertisements," *Bank Marketing International*, June 1, 1999, p. 4.

10. Zuber, "Pizza Hut Weighs Appeal."

11. Joanne Jacobs, "Hollywood Gets the Message on Violence," *Denver Post*, January 2, 2001, p. B07.

12. Stuart Elliott, "Facing Outcry, NBC Ends Plan to Run Liquor Ads," *New York Times*, March 21, 2002, **www.nytimes.com.**

13. Rinler Buck, "ABC Amends the Rules for 'The Person in White,'" *Adweek's Marketing Week*, September 9, 1991, p. 11.

14. Daniel Rosenberg, "Animal-Rights Ad, Toned Down, Still Hits a Wall at the Networks," *Wall Street Journal*, December 29, 1998, p. B5.

15. Kevin Goldman, "From Witches to Anorexics, Critical Eyes Scrutinize Ads for Political Correctness," *Wall Street Journal*, May 19, 1994, pp. B1, B10.

16. Daniel Rosenberg, "Veal Industry Focuses on Chefs in Countering Animal-Rights Ads," *Wall Street Journal*, March 18, 1998, p. B3.

17. Kathryn Kranhold, "New Groups Seek Remedy to Drug Ads," *Wall Street Journal*, June 22, 2000, p. B16.

18. "Advertising and Marketing," *Factiva Advertising and Media Digest*, February 26, 2001.

19. Jacob Jacoby and Constance Small, "The FDA Approach to Defining Misleading Advertising," *Journal of Marketing*, October 1975, pp. 65–68.

20. Federal Trade Commission, "Policy Statement on Deception," 45 ATRR 689, October 27, 1983, as cited in Gary T. Ford and John E. Calfee, "Recent Developments in FTC Policy on Deception," *Journal of Marketing*, July 1986, pp. 82–103; also see Jef I. Richards and Ivan L. Preston, "Proving and Disproving Materiality of Deceptive Advertising Claims," *Journal of Public Policy and Marketing*, Fall 1992, pp. 45–56.

21. Jacob Jacoby, Wayne D. Hoyer, and David A. Sheluga, *Miscomprehension of Televised Communication* (New York: American Association of Advertising Agencies, 1980); Jacob Jacoby and Wayne D. Hoyer, *The Comprehension and Miscomprehension of Print Communications: An Investigation of Mass Media Magazines* (New York: The Advertising Education Foundation, 1987).

22. Lee D. Dahringer and Denise R. Johnson, "The Federal Trade Commission Redefinition of Deception and Public Policy Implications: Let the Buyer Beware," *Journal of Consumer Affairs*, vol. 18, 1984, pp. 326–342.

23. Gary Armstrong, Metin Gurol, and Frederick Russ, "Detecting and Correcting Deceptive Advertising," *Journal of Consumer Research*, December 1979, pp. 237–246; Dorothy Cohen, "Unfairness in Advertising Revisited," *Journal of Marketing*, Winter 1982, pp. 73–80; Michael R. Hyman, "Deception in Advertising: A Proposed Complex of Definitions for Researchers, Lawyers, and Regulators," *International Journal of Advertising*, vol. 9, no. 3, 1990, pp. 259–270; Richards and Preston, "Proving and Disproving Materiality of Deceptive Advertising Claims."

24. Bruce Ingersoll, "Home Shopping and iMall to Pay Millions in FTC Ad-Claim Cases," *Wall Street Journal*, April 16, 1999, p. B2.

25. Gary J. Gaeth and Timothy B. Heath, "The Cognitive Processing of Misleading Advertising in Young and Old Adults: Assessment and Training," *Journal of Consumer Research*, June 1987, pp. 43–54.

26. David M. Gardner, "Deception in Advertising: A Conceptual Approach," *Journal of Marketing*, January 1975, pp. 40–46.

27. Joel E. Urbany, William O. Bearden, and Dan C. Weilbaker, "The Effect of Plausible and Exaggerated Reference Prices on Consumer Perceptions and Price Search," *Journal of Consumer Research*, June 1988, pp. 95–110; John Liefield and Louise A. Heslop, "Reference Prices and Deception in Newspaper Advertising," *Journal of Consumer Research*, March 1985, pp. 868–876.

28. Bruce Ingersoll, "Claim by Gerber for Baby Food Was Simply Mush, FTC Alleges," *Wall Street Journal*, March 13, 1997, p. B15.

29. Bonnie B. Reece and Robert H. Ducoffe, "Deception in Brand Names," *Journal of Public Policy and Marketing*, vol. 6, 1987, pp. 93–103.

30. Vanessa O'Connell, "A Wine Label with a Bouquet of Controversy,' *Wall Street Journal*, December 8, 1998, pp. B1, B4.

31. David Kiley, "Ragu Changes Label as 'Fresh' Talk Continues," *Adweek's Marketing Week*, May 6, 1991, p. 4.

32. Aaron Lucchetti, "Produce Sleuths Search for Label Scams," *Wall Street Journal*, June 17, 1997, pp. B1, B6.

33. Ivan L. Preston, "The FTC's Handling of Puffery and Other Selling Claims Made 'By Implication,'" *Journal of Business Research*, June 1977, pp. 155–181.

34. Richard L. Oliver, "An Interpretation of the Attitudinal and Behavioral Effects of Puffery," *Journal of Consumer Affairs*, Summer 1979, pp. 8–27; Terence A. Shimp and Ivan L. Preston, "Deceptive and Nondeceptive Consequences of Evaluative Advertising," *Journal of Marketing*, Winter 1981, pp. 22–32.

35. Gardner, "Deception in Advertising"; Raymond R. Burke, Wayne S. De Sarbo, Richard L. Oliver, and Thomas S. Robertson, "Deception by Implication: An Empirical Investigation," *Journal of Consumer Research*, March 1988, pp. 483–494.

36. Gita Venkataramani Johar, "Consumer Involvement and Deception from Implied Advertising Claims," *Journal of Marketing Research*, August 1995, pp. 267–279.

37. John E. Calfee, "FTC's Hidden Weight Loss Ad Agenda," *Advertising Age*, October 25, 1993, p. 29.

38. Edward Iwata, "Officials Say Deceptive Tech Advertising on Rise; FTC Takes Issue with Claims by Several Well-Known Companies," *USA Today*, May 29, 2001, p. B-1.

39. Burke et al., "Deception by Implication."

40. "Buying the Ranch on Brand Equity," *Brandweek*, October 26, 1992, p. 9.

41. Gordon Fairclough, "Tobacco Titans Bid for 'Organic' Cigarette Maker," *Wall Street Journal*, December 10, 2001, pp. B1, B4; Bob Garfield, "Softly Lit or Blunt, 'Less Toxic' Cigarette Ads Hint at Health," *Advertising Age*, November 12, 2001, p. 58; Carrie Goerne, "Court Ruling Lights Fire under Both Sides in Cigarette Dispute," *Marketing News*, August 17, 1992, p. 6.

42. Sandra J. Burke, Sandra J. Milberg, and Wendy W. Moe, "Displaying Common but Previously Neglected Health Claims on Product Labels: Understanding Competitive Advantages, Deception, and Education," *Journal of Public Policy and Marketing*, Fall 1997, pp. 242–255.

43. J. Craig Andrews, Richard G. Netemeyer, and Scot Burton, "Consumer Generalization of Nutrient Content Claims in Advertising," *Journal of Marketing*, October 1998, pp. 62–75.

44. J. Edward Russo, Barbara L. Metcalf, and Debra Stephens, "Identifying Misleading Advertising," *Journal of Consumer Research*, September 1981, pp. 119–131; Gardner, "Deception in Advertising"; Armstrong, Gurol, and Russ, "Detecting and Correcting Deceptive Advertising."

45. Nikhil Deogun, "Winn-Dixie's Lower Price Tactic Is Referred to FTC by Board," *Wall Street Journal*, December 23, 1996, p. B2.

46. "Feds Charge Shopping Network," *Austin American Statesman*, March 4, 1995, p. A7.

47. Laurie McGinley, "FTC Probes Fat-Content Claims Made by Some Restaurant Chains," *Wall Street Journal*, April 30, 1996, p. B8; Lauran Neergaard, "FDA Requires That Health Claims on Dietary Supplements Be Verifiable," *Austin American Statesman*, December 30, 1993, p. A3.

48. Elyse Tanouye, "Heartburn Drug Makers Feel Judge's Heat," *Wall Street Journal*, October 16, 1995, p. B8.

49. Calfee, "FTC's Hidden Weight Loss Ad Agenda."

50. Wendy Bounds, "Polo Magazine Gets a Whipping from Lauren in Trademark Case," *Wall Street Journal*, July 7, 1997, p. B6.

51. David C. Vladeck, "Truth and Consequences: The Perils of Half-Truths and Unsubstantiated Health Claims for Dietary Supplements," *Journal of Public Policy and Marketing*, vol.19, no. 1, Spring 2000, pp. 132–138; Jacob Jacoby, Margaret C. Nelson, and Wayne D. Hoyer, "Corrective Advertising and Affirmative Disclosure Statements: Their Potential for Confusing and Misleading the Consumer," *Journal of Marketing*, Winter 1982, pp. 61–72; G. Ray Funkhouser, "An Empirical Study of Consumers' Sensitivity to the Wording of Affirmative Disclosure Messages," *Journal of Public Policy and Marketing*, vol. 3, 1984, pp. 26–37; Ellen R. Foxman, Darrel D. Muehling, and Patrick A. Moore, "Disclaimer Footnotes in Ads: Discrepancies between Purpose and Performance," *Journal of Public Policy and Marketing*, vol. 7, 1988, pp. 127–137.

52. Gita Venkataramani Johar and Carolyn J. Simmons, "The Use of Concurrent Disclosures to Correct Invalid Inferences," *Journal of Consumer Research*, vol. 26, March 2000, pp. 307–322.

53. William L. Wilkie, Dennis L. McNeil, and Michael B. Mazis, "Marketing's 'Scarlet Letter': The Theory and Practice of Corrective Advertising," *Journal of Marketing*, Spring 1984, pp. 11–31; Gary M. Armstrong, Metin N. Gurol, and Frederick A. Russ, "A Longitudinal Evaluation of the Listerine Corrective Advertising Campaign," *Journal of Public Policy and Marketing*, vol. 2, 1983, pp. 16–28.

54. Armstrong, Gurol, and Russ, "Detecting and Correcting Deceptive Advertising"; Richard W. Mizerski, Neil K. Allison, and Stephen Calvert, "A Controlled Field Study of Corrective Advertising Using Multiple Exposures and a Commercial Medium," *Journal of Marketing Research*, August 1979, pp. 341–348; Michael B. Mazis and Janice E. Atkinson, "An Experimental Evaluation of a Proposed Corrective Advertising Remedy," *Journal of Marketing Research*, May 1986, pp. 178–183; Tyzoon T. Tyebjee, "The Role of Publicity in FTC Corrective Advertising Remedies," *Journal of Public Policy and Marketing*, 1, 1982, pp. 111–121.

55. Gita Venkataramani Johar, "Intended and Unintended Effects of Corrective Advertising on Beliefs and Evaluations: An Exploratory Analysis," *Journal of Consumer Psychology*, vol. 5, no. 3, 1996, pp. 209–230.

56. Fleming Meeks, "Upselling," *Forbes*, January 8, 1990, pp. 70, 72.

57. Richard W. Easley, James A. Roberts, Mark G. Dunn, and Charles S. Madden, "Diagnosing Consumer Information Problems: An Investigation of Deception on the Mail-Order Video Camcorder Market," *Journal of Public Policy and Marketing*, Fall 1992, pp. 37–44.

58. William L. Wilkie, *Consumer Behavior*, 2nd ed. (New York: Wiley, 1990).

59. Christopher Scanian, "Postcards Offering 'Free Prizes' Can Prove Costly, Experts Warn," *Austin American Statesman*, November 18, 1992, pp. A1, A17.

60. Pratibha A. Dabholkar and James J. Kellaris, "Toward Understanding Marketing Students' Ethical Judgment of Controversial Selling Practices," *Journal of Business Research*, June 1992, pp. 313–329.

61. Karl A. Boedecker, Fred W. Morgan, and Jeffrey J. Stoltman, "Legal Dimensions of Salespersons' Statements: A Review and Managerial Suggestions," *Journal of Marketing*, January 1991, pp. 70–80.

62. Stephanie N. Mehta, "Visions of Wealth and Independence Lead Professionals to Try Multilevel Marketing," *Wall Street Journal*, June 23, 1995, pp. B1, B2.

63. Jinkook Lee and Loren V. Geistfeld, "Elderly Consumers' Receptiveness to Telemarketing Fraud," *Journal of Public Policy and Marketing*, vol. 18, no. 2, Fall 1999, pp. 208–217.

64. "Senior Citizens Warned about Fraud Schemes," *Austin American Statesman*, July 13, 1999, p. B2; John R. Emshwiller, "Having Lost Thousands to Con Artists, Elderly Widow Tells Cautionary Tale," *Wall Street Journal*, August 20, 1995, pp. B1, B5.

65. Samantha Levine, "AARP Educating Elderly on Telemarketing Dangers," *Austin American Statesman*, August 7, 1996, p. A3.

66. A. C. Nielsen Company, *1990 Nielsen Report on Television* (New York: Nielsen Media Research); J. Condry, P. Bence, and C. Scheibe, "Nonprogram Content of Children's Television," *Journal of Broadcasting and Electronic Media*, Summer 1988, pp. 255–270; Carol Lawson, "Guarding the Children's Hour on TV," *New York Times*, January 24, 1991, pp. C1, C13.

67. W. Melody, *Children's Television: The Economics of Exploitation* (New Haven, Conn.: Yale University Press, 1973); Ellen Notar, "Children and TV Commercials: Wave after Wave of Exploitation," *Childhood Education*, Winter 1989, pp. 66–67.

68. Scott Ward, "Consumer Socialization," *Journal of Consumer Research*, September 1974, pp. 1–13; Laurene Krasney Meringoff and Gerald S. Lesser, "Children's Ability to Distinguish Television

Commercials from Program Material," in ed. R. P. Adler, *The Effect of Television Advertising on Children* (Lexington, Mass.: Lexington Books, 1980), pp. 29–42; S. Levin, T. Petros, and F. Petrella, "Preschoolers' Awareness of Television Advertising," *Child Development*, August 1982, pp. 933–937.

69. M. Carole Macklin, "Preschoolers' Understanding of the Informational Function of Advertising," *Journal of Consumer Research*, September 1987, pp. 229–239; Merrie Brucks, Gary M. Armstrong, and Marvin E. Goldberg, "Children's Use of Cognitive Defenses against Television Advertising: A Cognitive Response Approach," *Journal of Consumer Research*, March 1988, pp. 471–482.

70. Mary C. Martin, "Children's Understanding of the Intent of Advertising: A Meta-Analysis," *Journal of Public Policy and Marketing*, Fall 1997, pp. 205–216.

71. Deborah L. Roedder, "Age Differences in Children's Responses to Television Advertising: An Information Processing Approach," *Journal of Consumer Research*, September 1981, pp. 144–153.

72. Jon Berry, "The New Generation of Kids and Ads," *Adweek's Marketing Week*, April 15, 1991, pp. 25–28; Marvin E. Goldberg and Gerald J. Gorn, "Some Unintended Consequences of TV Advertising to Children," *Journal of Consumer Research*, June 1978, pp. 22–29; Gary M. Armstrong and Merrie Brucks, "Dealing with Children's Advertising: Public Policy Issues and Alternatives," *Journal of Public Policy and Marketing*, vol. 7, 1988, pp. 98–113.

73. Bonnie B. Reece, "Children and Shopping: Some Public Policy Questions," *Journal of Public Policy and Marketing*, vol. 5, 1986, pp. 185–194; Armstrong and Brucks, "Dealing with Children's Advertising."

74. Scott Ward and Daniel B. Wackman, "Children's Information Processing of Television Advertising," in ed. Peter Clarke, *New Models for Mass Communication Research* (Beverly Hills, Calif.: Sage, 1973), pp. 119–146; Thomas S. Robertson and John R. Rossiter, "Children and Commercial Persuasion: Testing the Defenses," *Journal of Consumer Research*, June 1974, pp. 13–20; Deborah L. Roedder, Brian B. Sternthal, and Bobby J. Calder, "Attitude-Behavior Consistency in Children's Responses to Television Advertising," *Journal of Marketing Research*, November 1983, pp. 337–349; Scott Ward, Daniel B. Wackman, and Ellen Wartella, *How Children Learn to Buy* (Beverly Hills, Calif.: Sage, 1977).

75. Jeffrey E. Brand and Bradley S. Greenberg, "Commercials in the Classroom: The Impact of Channel One Advertising," *Journal of Advertising Research*, January–February 1994, pp. 18–27.

76. Scott Ward and Daniel Wackman, "Children's Purchase Influence Attempts and Parental Yielding," *Journal of Marketing Research*, August 1972, pp. 316–319; Goldberg and Gorn, "Some Unintended Consequences of TV Advertising to Children"; Tamara F. Mangleburg, "Children's Influence in Purchase Decisions: A Review and Critique," in eds. Marvin E. Goldberg, Gerald Gorn, and Richard W. Pollay, *Advances in Consumer Research*, vol. 17 (Provo, Utah: Association for Consumer Research, 1990), pp. 813–825.

77. Joe Flint, "Proposed 900-Number and Rules Worry Advertisers," *Broadcasting and Cable*, April 5, 1993, p. 44.

78. Russell N. Laczniak, Darrel D. Muehling, and Les Carlson, "Mothers' Attitudes toward 900-Number Advertising Directed at Children," *Journal of Public Policy and Marketing*, Spring 1995, pp. 108–116.

79. Gerald J. Gorn and Renee Florsheim, "The Effects of Commercials for Adult Products on Children," *Journal of Consumer Research*, March 1985, pp. 962–967.

80. Judann Dagnoli, "Consumers Union Hits Kids Advertising," *Advertising Age*, July 23, 1990, p. 4.

81. Mary Lu Carnevale, "Parents Say PBS Stations Exploit Barney in Fund Drives," *Wall Street Journal*, March 19, 1993, pp. B1, B8; Maria Grubbs Hoy, Clifford Young, and John C. Mowen, "Animated Host-Selling Advertisements: Their Impact on Young Children's Recognition, Attitudes, and Behavior," *Journal of Public Policy and Marketing*, vol. 5, 1986, pp. 171–184.

82. Marvin E. Goldberg, Gerald Gorn, and Wendy Gibson, "TV Messages for Snack and Breakfast Foods: Do They Influence Children's Preferences?" *Journal of Consumer Research*, September 1978, pp. 73–81; Debra L. Scammon and Carole L. Christopher, "Nutrition Education with Children via Television," *Journal of Advertising*, vol. 10, 1981, pp. 26–36; Thomas S. Robertson and John R. Rossiter, "Children and Commercial Persuasion: An Attributional Approach," *Journal of Consumer Research*, June 1974, pp. 12–20.

83. "For Kids on the Web, It's an Ad, Ad, Ad, Ad World," *BusinessWeek*, August 13, 2001, pp. 108+.

84. Joan Blatt, Lyle Spencer, and Scott Ward, "A Cognitive-Developmental Study of Children's Reaction to Television Advertising," in eds. E. A. Rubenstein, G. A. Constock, and J. P. Murray, *Television and Social Behavior* (Washington, D.C.: U.S. Government Printing Office, 1972), pp. 452–467.

85. Meringoff and Lesser, "Children's Ability to Distinguish Television Commercials from Program Material."

86. Doug Halonen, "FCC Urged to Monitor Total Hours of Kids TV," *Electronic Media*, September 24, 2002, p. 2; Jon Berry, "Kids' Advocates to TV: 'We've Only Begun to Fight,'" *Adweek's Marketing Week*, April 15, 1991, p. 25.

87. Gerald J. Gorn and Marvin E. Goldberg, "Behavioral Evidence of the Effects of Televised Food Messages on Children," *Journal of Consumer Research*, September 1982, pp. 200–205; Cyndee Miller, "Marketers Find a Seat in the Classroom," *Marketing News*, June 20, 1994, p. 2.

88. Dale Kunkel and Walter Granz, "Assessing Compliance with Industry Self-Regulation of Television Advertising to Children," *Journal of Applied Communication Research*, May 1993, pp. 148–162.

89. "Try to Keep It Simple," *Advertising Age*, February 4, 2002, p. S4.

90. Daniel Golden, "'Media Literacy' Sparks a New Debate Over Commercialism in Schools," *Wall Street Journal*, December 17, 1999, pp. B1, B4.

91. Armstrong and Brucks, "Dealing with Children's Advertising."

92. Eve M. Caudill and Patrick E. Murphy, "Consumer Online Privacy: Legal and Ethical Issues," *Journal of Public Policy and Marketing*, vol. 19, no. 1, Spring 2000, pp. 7–19.

93. Kim Bartel Sheehan and Mariea Grubbs Hoy, "Dimensions of Privacy Concern among Online Consumers," *Journal of Public Policy and Marketing*, vol. 19, no. 1, Spring 2000, pp. 62–73.

94. Ross D. Petty, "Marketing without Consent: Consumer Choice and Costs, Privacy, and Public Policy," *Journal of Public Policy and Marketing*, vol. 19, no. 1, Spring 2000, pp. 42–53.

95. Pamela Paul, "Mixed Signals," *American Demographics*, July 2001, pp.45–49; Joseph Phelps, Glen Nowak, and Elizabeth Ferrell, "Privacy Concerns and Consumer Willingness to Provide Personal Information," *Journal of Public Policy and Marketing*, vol. 19, no. 1, Spring 2000, pp. 27–41.

96. George R. Milne, "Privacy and Ethical Issues in Database/Interactive Marketing and Public Policy: A Research Framework and Overview of the Special Issue," *Journal of Public Policy and Marketing*, vol. 19, no. 1, Spring 2000, pp. 1–6.

97. Mary J. Culnan, "Protecting Privacy Online: Is Self-Regulation Working?" *Journal of Public Policy and Marketing*, vol. 19, no. 1, Spring 2000, pp. 20–26.

98. Anthony D. Miyazaki and Ana Fernandez, "Internet Privacy and Security: An Examination of Online Retailer Disclosures," *Journal of Public Policy and Marketing*, vol. 19, no. 1, Spring 2000, pp. 54–61.

99. Aaron Lucchetti, "FTC Tackles an 'Anonymous' Web Survey," *Wall Street Journal*, May 7, 1999, p. B2.

100. Larry Dobrow, "How Old Is Old Enough?" *Advertising Age*, February 4, 2002, p. S4.

101. Kimberly Bonvissuto, "Net Latest Snare for Senior Scams," *Crain's Cleveland Business*, July 30, 2001, p. 17.

102. Neil Gross and Ira Sager, "Caution Signs along the Road," *Wall Street Journal*, June 22, 1998, pp. B6, B8.

103. Don Clark, "Safety First," *Wall Street Journal*, December 7, 1998, p. R14.

104. Steve Hill, "Safe Hands," *Internet Magazine*, March 2002, pp. 28+.

105. Peter Barton Hutt, "FDA Regulation of Product Claims in Food Labeling," *Journal of Public Policy and Marketing*, Spring 1993, pp. 132–134; Gabriella Stern, "In a Turnabout, Fast-Food Fare Becomes Fattier," *Wall Street Journal*, August 23, 1993, pp. B1, B6; Richard Gibson, "Restaurant Menus' Health Claims May Be Regulated," *Wall Street Journal*, June 2, 1993, p. B1.

106. Jacob Jacoby, Robert W. Chestnut, and William Silberman, "Consumer Use and Comprehension of Nutrition Information," *Journal of Consumer Research*, March 1977, pp. 119–128.

107. Catherine A. Cole and Gary J. Gaeth, "Cognitive and Age-Related Differences in the Ability to Use Nutritional Information in a Complex Environment," *Journal of Marketing Research*, May 1990, pp. 175–184; Catherine A. Cole and Siva K. Balasubramanian, "Age Differences in Consumers' Search for Information: Public Policy Implications," *Journal of Consumer Research*, June 1993, pp. 157–169.

108. Jinkook Lee and Jeanne M. Hogarth, "The Price of Money: Consumers' Understanding of APRs and Contract Interest Rates," *Journal of Public Policy and Marketing*, Spring 1999, pp. 66–76.

109. Jacoby, Chestnut, and Silberman, "Consumer Use and Comprehension of Nutrition Information."

110. Brian Roe, Alan S. Levy, and Brenda M. Derby, "The Impact of Health Claims on Consumer Search and Product Evaluation Outcomes: Results from FDA Experimental Data," *Journal of Public Policy and Marketing*, Spring 1999, pp. 89–105.

111. Stern, "In a Turnabout, Fast-Food Fare Becomes Fattier."

112. Judith A. Garretson and Scot Burton, "Effects of Nutrition Facts Panel Values, Nutrition Claims, and Health Claims on Consumer Attitudes, Perceptions of Disease-Related Risks, and Trust," *Journal of Public Policy and Marketing*, vol. 19, no. 2, Fall 2000, pp. 213–227; Anu Mitra, Manoj Hastak, Gary T. Ford, and Debra Jones Ringold, "Can the Educationally Disadvantaged Interpret the FDA-Mandated Nutrition Facts Panel in the Presence of an Implied Health Claim?" *Journal of Public Policy and Marketing*, vol. 18, no. 1, Spring 1999, pp. 106–117.

113. Lisa R. Szykman, Paul N. Bloom, and Alan S. Levy, "A Proposed Model of the Use of Package Claims and Nutrition Labels," *Journal of Public Policy and Marketing*, Fall 1997, pp. 228–241.

114. For example, see Jacob Jacoby, Donald E. Speller, and Carol A. Kohn, "Brand Choice Behavior as a Function of Information Load," *Journal of Marketing Research*, February 1974, pp. 63–69; Jacob Jacoby, "Perspectives on Information Overload," *Journal of Consumer Research*, March 1984, pp. 432–435; Naresh K. Malhotra, "Reflections on the Information Overload Paradigm in Consumer Decision Making," *Journal of Consumer Research*, March 1984, pp. 436–440; Kevin Lane Keller and Richard Staelin, "Effects of Quality and Quantity of Information on Decision Effectiveness," *Journal of Consumer Research*, September 1987, pp. 200–213.

115. Yumiko Ono, "Fine Print in Drug Ads Sparks a Debate," *Wall Street Journal*, April 1, 1997, pp. B1, B8.

116. J. Edward Russo, Richard Staelin, Catherine A. Nolan, Gary J. Russell, and Barbara L. Metcalf, "Nutrition Information in the Supermarket," *Journal of Consumer Research*, June 1986, pp. 48–70; James R. Bettman and Pradeep Kakkar, "Effects of Information Presentation Format on Consumer Information Acquisition Strategies," *Journal of Consumer Research*, March 1977, pp. 233–240; Cole and Gaeth, "Cognitive and Age–Related Differences in the Ability to Use Nutritional Information"; Christine Moorman, "The Effects of Stimulus and Consumer Characteristics on the Utilization of Nutrition Information," *Journal of Consumer Research*, December 1990, pp. 362–374.

117. Pauline M. Ippolito and Alan D. Mathios, "New Food Labeling Regulations and the Flow of Nutrition Information to Consumers," *Journal of Public Policy and Marketing*, Fall 1993, pp. 118–205; John Sinisi, "New Rules Exact a Heavy Price as Labels Are Recast," *Brandweek*, December 7, 1992, p. 3; Nita Lelyveid, "What's in the Food You Eat," *Austin American Statesman*, May 3, 1994, pp. A7, A13.

118. Scot Burton and Abhijit Biswas, "Preliminary Assessment of Changes in Labels Required by the Nutrition Labeling and Education Act of 1990," *Journal of Consumer Affairs*, Summer 1993, pp. 127–144; Scot Burton, Abhijit Biswas, and Richard Netermeyer, "Effects of Alternative Nutrition Label Formats and Nutrition Reference Information on Consumer Perceptions, Comprehension, and Product Evaluations," *Journal of Public Policy and Marketing*, Spring 1994, pp. 36–47.

119. Christine Moorman, "A Quasi Experiment to Assess the Consumer and Information Determinants of Nutrition Information Processing Activities: The Case of the Nutrition Labeling and Education Act," *Journal of Public Policy and Marketing*, Spring 1996, pp. 28–44.

120. Mitra, Hastak, Ford, and Ringold, "Can the Educationally Disadvantaged Interpret the FDA-Mandated Nutrition Facts Panel"; Gary T. Ford, Manoj Hastak, Anu Mitra, and Debra Jones Ringold, "Can Consumers Interpret Nutrition Information in the Presence of a Health Claim? A Laboratory Investigation," *Journal of Public Policy and Marketing*, Spring 1996, pp. 16–27.

121. Scott B. Keller, Mike Landry, Jeanne Olson, Anne M. Velliquette, Scot Burton, and J. Craig Andrews, "The Effects of Nutrition Package Claims, Nutrition Facts Panels, and Motivation to Process Information on Consumer Product Evaluations," *Journal of Public Policy and Marketing*, Fall 1997, pp. 256–269.

122. Madhubalan Viswanathan, "The Influence of Summary Information on the Usage of Nutrition Information," *Journal of Public Policy and Marketing*, Spring 1994, pp. 48–60: Alan S. Levey, Sara B. Fein, and Raymond E. Schucker, "Performance Characteristics of Seven Nutrition Label Formats," *Journal of Public Policy and Marketing*, Spring 1996, pp. 1–15.

123. Michael J. Barone, Randall L. Rose, Kenneth C. Manning, and Paul W. Miniard, "Another Look at the Impact of Reference Information on Consumer Impressions of Nutrition Information," *Journal of Public Policy and Marketing*, Spring 1996, pp. 55–62.

124. Dennis L. McNeill and William L. Wilkie, "Public Policy and Consumer Information: Impacts of the New Energy Labels," *Journal of Consumer Research*, June 1979, pp. 1–11; R. Bruce Hutton and William L. Wilkie, "Life Cycle Cost: A New Form of Consumer Information," *Journal of Consumer Research*, March 1980, pp. 349–360.

125. "FDA Extends Comment Period for New Labeling," *Medical Marketing and Media*, April 1, 2001, pp. 26–30; Bruce Ingersoll, "FDA Proposes Labels for Drugs Sold at Counter," *Wall Street Journal*, February 27, 1997, p. B8.

126. Fred W. Morgan and Dana I. Avrunin, "Consumer Conduct in Product Liability Litigation," *Journal of Consumer Research*, June 1982, pp. 47–55.

127. Judith S. Riddle, "New Alcohol-Reduced Remedies Put P&G in Re-Marketing Hotseat," *Brandweek*, April 12, 1993, pp. 1, 6.

128. Michael J. McCarthy, "A Design with Twists and Turns," *Wall Street Journal*, February 3, 2000, pp. B1, B4.

129. "Answers Still Elusive in Tire Crisis," *Wall Street Journal*, September 15, 2000, pp. B1, B4.

130. Joseph Pereira, "Toy Story: Industry Strikes Back against Safety Sleuth," *Wall Street Journal*, November 17, 1997, pp. B1, B15.

131. Rob Norton, "Why Airbags Are Killing Kids," *Fortune*, August 19, 1996, p. 40.

132. Asra Q. Nomani, "Regulators Plan Safety Rules for Child Seats," *Wall Street Journal*, February 13, 1997, pp. B1, B12.

133. E. Scott Geller, "Seat Belt Psychology," *Psychology Today*, May 1985, pp. 12–13.

134. Banwari Mittal, "Achieving Higher Seat Belt Usage: The Role of Habit in Bridging the Attitude-Behavior Gap," *Journal of Applied Social Psychology*, September 1988, pp. 993–1016; David L. Ryan and Guy A. Bridgeman, "Judging the Roles of Legislation, Education, and Offsetting Behavior in Seat Belt Use: A Survey and New Evidence from Alberta," *Canadian Public Policy*, March 1992, pp. 27–46.

135. Laura Bird, "U.S. Fears Success May Have Changed Crash Dummies," *Wall Street Journal*, June 8, 1992, pp. B1, B4

136. Oscar Suris, "General Motors Plans to Recall Million Vehicles," *Wall Street Journal*, February 5, 1996; Asra Q. Nomani, "Chrysler Effort to Fix Minivans Has Slow Start," *Wall Street Journal*, February 12, 1996, p. B2; Nichole M. Christain and Asra Q. Nomani, "Ford Recalls 8.7 Million Cars to Fix Ignitions," *Wall Street Journal*, April 26, 1996, pp. B1, B2.

137. George C. Jackson and Fred W. Morgan, "Responding to Recall Requests: A Strategy for Managing Goods Withdrawals," *Journal of Public Policy and Marketing*, vol. 7, 1988, pp. 152–165.

138. Laura Johannes and Steve Stecklow, "Withdrawal of Redux Spotlights Predicament FDA Faces on Obesity," *Wall Street Journal*, September 16, 1997, pp. A1, A10; Bruce Ingersoll, "FDA Proposes to Force Seldane off the Market," *Wall Street Journal*, January 14, 1997, pp. B1, B8.

139. Walter Guzzardi, "The Mindless Pursuit of Safety," *Fortune*, April 9, 1979, pp. 54–64; Mowen, *Consumer Behavior*.

140. James F. Engel, Roger D. Blackwell, and Paul W. Miniard, *Consumer Behavior*, 8th ed. (Fort Worth, Tex.: Dryden Press, 1995).

141. Mark R. Lehto and James M. Miller, "The Effectiveness of Warning Labels," *Journal of Product Liability*, vol. 11, no. 3, 1988, pp. 225–270.

142. James R. Bettman, John W. Payne, and Richard Staelin, "Cognitive Considerations in Designing Labels for Presenting Risk Information," *Journal of Public Policy and Marketing*, vol. 5, 1986, pp. 1–28.

143. Kenneth C. Schneider, "Prevention of Accidental Poisoning through Package and Label Design," *Journal of Consumer Research*, September 1977, pp. 67–75.

144. Richard Staelin, "The Effects of Consumer Education on Consumer Product Safety Behavior," *Journal of Consumer Research*, June 1978, pp. 30–40.

145. Vanessa O'Connell, "Gun Makers to Push Use of Gun Locks," *Wall Street Journal*, May 9, 2001, p. B12.

146. Miriam Jordan, "Electric Buses Put to Test in Nepal," *Wall Street Journal*, May 31, 2000, pp. B1, B4.

147. Stacy Kravetz, "Dry Cleaners' New Wrinkle: Going Green," *Wall Street Journal*, June 3, 1998, pp. B1, B15.

148. Jacquelyn Ottman, "Use Less, Make It More Durable, and Then Take It Back," *Marketing News*, December 7, 1992, p. 13.

149. Seema Nayyar, "Refillable Pouch a Lotions First," *Brandweek*, October 26, 1992, p. 3; Seema Nayyar, "L&F Cleaner Refills Greener," *Brandweek*, September 14, 1992, p. 5; Belk, "Daily Life in Romania."

150. Jaclyn Frierman, "The Big Muddle in Green Marketing," *Fortune*, June 3, 1991, pp. 92–102.

151. Howard Schlossberg, "'Project Clean Mail' Would Fine Tune Direct Marketing," *Marketing News*, September 14, 1992, pp. 18–19.

152. Shirley Taylor and Peter Todd, "Understanding Household Garbage Reduction: A Test of an Integrated Model," *Journal of Public Policy and Marketing*, Fall 1995, pp. 192–204.

153. Anna Peltola, "Finland: Nokia Hopes for Biodegradable Phones in Few Years," *Reuters English News Service*, June 14, 2001, **www.reuters.com**.

154. Kathleen Deveny, "For Growing Band of Shoppers, Clean Means Green," *Wall Street Journal*, April 6, 1993, pp. B1, B7.

155. Charles H. Schwepker and T. Bettina Cornwell, "An Examination of Ecologically Concerned Consumers and Their Intention to Purchase Ecologically Packaged Products," *Journal of Public Policy and Marketing*, Fall 1991, pp. 77–101.

156. Linda F. Alwitt and Robert E. Pitts, "Predicting Purchase Intentions for an Environmentally Sensitive Product," *Journal of Consumer Psychology*, vol. 5, no. 1, 1996, pp. 49–64.

157. John A. McCarty and L. J. Shrum, "The Influence of Individualism, Collectivism, and Locus of Control on Environmental Beliefs and Behavior," *Journal of Public Policy and Marketing*, vol. 20, no. 1, Spring 2001, pp. 93–104.

158. Allan Glass, "Does a Green Message Still Belong on Your Package?" *Brandweek*, October 19, 1992, pp. 26, 28.

159. Pam Scholder Ellen, Joshua Lyle Wiener, and Cathy Cobb-Walgren, "The Role of Perceived Consumer Effectiveness in Motivating Environmentally Conscious Behaviors," *Journal of Public Policy and Marketing*, Fall 1991, pp. 102–117; Thomas C. Kinnear, James R. Taylor, and Sadrudin A. Ahmed, "Ecologically Concerned Consumers: Who Are They?" *Journal of Marketing*, April 1972, pp. 46–57.

160. Jacquelyn Ottman, "Environmentalism Will Be the Trend of the 90s," *Marketing News*, December 7, 1992, p. 13.

161. Cheryl Powell, "The Green Movement Sows Demand for Ecofurniture," *Wall Street Journal*, August 2, 1994, pp. B1, B2.

162. Russell Belk, John Painter, and Richard Semenik, "Preferred Solutions to the Energy Crisis as a Function of Causal Attributions," *Journal of Consumer Research*, December 1981, pp. 306–312.

163. C. Dennis Anderson and John D. Claxton, "Barriers to Consumer Choice of Energy-Efficient Products," *Journal of Consumer Research*, September 1982, pp. 163–170.

164. Rik Peters, Tammo Bijmo, H. Fred van Raaij, and Mark de Kruijk, "Consumers' Attributions of Proenvironmental Behavior, Motivation, and Ability to Self and Others," *Journal of Public Policy and Marketing*, Fall 1998, pp. 215–225.

165. Dorothy Leonard-Barton, "Voluntary Simplicity Lifestyles and Energy Conservation," *Journal of Consumer Research*, December 1981, pp. 243–252.

166. Louise A. Helsop, Lori Moran, and Amy Cousineau, "'Consciousness' in Energy Conservation Behavior: An Exploratory Study," *Journal of Consumer Research*, December 1981, pp. 299–305; Gregory M. Pickett, Norman Kangun, and Stephen J. Grove, "Is There a General Conserving Consumer?" *Journal of Public Policy and Marketing*, Fall 1993, pp. 234–243.

167. Marta Tienda and Osei-Mensah Aborampah, "Energy-Related Adaptations in Low-Income Nonmetropolitan Wisconsin Counties," *Journal of Consumer Research*, December 1981, pp. 265–270.

168. Theo M. M. Verhallen and W. Fred van Raaij, "Household Behavior and the Use of Natural Gas for Heating," *Journal of Consumer Research*, December 1981, pp. 253–257.

169. Gordon H. G. McDougall, John D. Claxton, J. R. Brent Ritchie, and C. Dennis Anderson, "Consumer Energy Research: A Review," *Journal of Consumer Research*, December 1981, pp. 343–354.

170. Ibid; Dennis L. McNeill and William L. Wilkie, "Public Policy and Consumer Information: Impact of the New Energy Labels," *Journal of Consumer Research*, June 1979, pp. 1–11.

171. R. Bruce Hutton and Dennis L. McNeill, "The Value of Incentives in Stimulating Energy Conservation," *Journal of Consumer Research*, December 1981, pp. 291–298; Peter D. Bennett and Noreen Klein Moore, "Consumers' Preferences for Alternative Energy Conservation Policies: A Trade-off Analysis," *Journal of Consumer Research*, December 1981, pp. 313–321; Robert E. Pitts and James L. Wittenbach, "Tax Credits as a Means of Influencing Consumer Behavior," *Journal of Consumer Research*, December 1981, pp. 335–338; Bruce R. Hutton, Gary A. Mauser, Pierre Filiatrault, and Olli T. Ahtola, "Effects of Cost Related Feedback on Consumer Knowledge and Consumption Behavior: A Field Experiment," *Journal of Consumer Research*, December 1986, pp. 327–336; Jeannet H. van Houwelingen and W. Fred van Raaij, "The Effect of Goal-Setting and Daily Electronic Feedback on In-Home Energy Use," *Journal of Consumer Research*, June 1989, pp. 98–105.

172. Edward Cundiff and Marye Hilger Tharpe, *Marketing in the International Environment*, 2nd ed. (Englewood Cliffs, N.J.: Prentice-Hall, 1988).

173. "French Government Announces Crackdown on Racy Ads; DDB Ad Pulled," *Advertising Age*, May 2, 2001, www.adage.com.

174. Gary M. Armstrong and Merrie Brucks, "Dealing with Children's Advertising: Public Policy Issues and Alternatives," *Journal of Public Policy and Marketing*, vol. 7, 1988, pp. 98–113.

175. Ross D. Petty, "Advertising Law in the United States and European Union," *Journal of Public Policy and Marketing*, Spring 1997, pp. 2–13.

176. Matthew Rose, "French Court Blocks Philip Morris Ads That Liken Passive Smoke to Cookies," *Wall Street Journal*, June 27, 1996, B1.

177. "Nielsen in Dutch over Ad," *Austin American Statesman*, April 3, 1999, p. B8.

178. Jean-Pierre Jeannet and Hubert D. Hennessey, *Global Marketing Strategies* (Boston: Houghton Mifflin, 1992); Vern Terpstra and Ravi Sarathy, *International Marketing*, 5th ed. (Chicago: Dryden Press, 1991).

179. Joan Stephenson, "Global Antismoking Measures," *Journal of the American Medical Association*, March 13, 2002, p. 1255; Conor Dignam and Mike Leidig, "Big Tobacco Riding High," *Advertising Age Global*, April 2001, p. 4; Julie Wolf and Ernest Beck, "European Union Seems Set to Ban Most Kinds of Tobacco Advertising," *Wall Street Journal*, December 3, 1997, p. B13.

180. Marcia Kunstel and Joseph Albright, "Russia Mourns Assassination of Famous Television Journalist," *Austin American Statesman*, March 4, 1995, p. A16.

181. Laurel Wentz, "Playing by the Same Rules," *Advertising Age*, December 2, 1991, p. S2.

182. Sally D. Goll, "Chinese Officials Attempt to Ban False Ad Claims," *Wall Street Journal*, February 28, 1995, pp. B1, B9.

183. Terpstra and Sarathy, *International Marketing*.

Chapter 21

1. Jonathan Webdale, "Toysrus.com falls foul of US State ruling on use of cookies," New Media Age, Jan. 10, 2002, p14(1). Reported Reach Deal on Internet Privacy Policies," *The Record*, January 3, 2002, www.bergen.com; Matt Richtel, "Comcast Says It Will Stop Storing Data on Customers," *New York Times*, February 14, 2002, p. C5; Cliff Saran, "Eli Lilly Case Raises Privacy Fears," *Computer Weekly*, January 31, 2002, p. 6; Pamela Paul, "Mixed Signals," *American Demographics*, July 2001, pp. 45–49; Rebecca Gardyn, "Swap Meet," *American Demographics*, July 2001, pp. 51–55; John Fetto, "Candy for Cookies," *American Demographics*, August 2000, p. 10; Rebecca Quick, "On-line Groups Are Offering Up Privacy Plans," *Wall Street Journal*, June 22, 1998, pp. B1, B12.

2. Thomas C. O'Guinn and Ronald J. Faber, "Compulsive Buying: A Phenomenological Exploration," *Journal of Consumer Research*, September 1989, pp. 147–157.

3. Ronald Faber, Gary Christenson, Martina DeZwaan, and James Mitchell, "Two Forms of Compulsive Consumption: Comorbidity of Compulsive Buying and Binge Eating," *Journal of Consumer Research*, December 1995, pp. 296–304; O'Guinn and Faber, "Compulsive Buying"; Ronald J. Faber and Thomas C. O'Guinn, "Compulsive Consumption and Credit Abuse," *Journal of Consumer Policy*, March 1988, pp. 97–109; Gilles Valence, Alain D'Astous, and Louis Fortier, "Compulsive Buying: Concept and Measurement," *Journal of Consumer Policy*, December 1988, pp. 419–433; Rajan Nataraajan and Brent G. Goff, "Compulsive Buying: Toward a Reconceptualization," in ed. Floyd W. Rudman, *To Have Possessions: A Handbook on Ownership and Property* (Corte Madera, Calif.: Select Press, 1991), pp. 307–328; "Compulsive Shopping Could Be Hereditary," *Marketing News*, September 14, 1998, pp. 31; Wayne S. DeSarbo and Elizabeth A. Edwards, "Typologies of Compulsive Buying Behavior: A Constrained Clusterwise Regression Approach," *Journal of Consumer Psychology*, vol. 5, no. 3, 1996, pp. 231–262.

4. Faber and O'Guinn, "Compulsive Consumption and Credit Abuse"; Ronald J. Faber and Thomas C. O'Guinn, "A Clinical Screener for Compulsive Buying," *Journal of Consumer Research*, December

1992, pp. 459–469; O'Guinn and Faber, "Compulsive Buying"; James A. Roberts, "Compulsive Buying among College Students: An Investigation of Its Antecedents, Consequences, and Implications for Public Policy," *Journal of Consumer Affairs*, Winter 1998, pp. 295–319.

5. Janine Latus Musick, "Keeping Would-Be Thieves at Bay," *Nation's Business*, October 1998, pp. 41–43; "Cops and Robbers," *Discount Merchandiser*, March 1997, p. 3.
6. Julia Angwin, "Credit-Card Scams Bedevil E-Stores," *Wall Street Journal*, September 19, 2000, pp. B1, B4; Ronald A. Fullerton and Girish Punj, "Choosing to Misbehave: A Structural Model of Aberrant Consumer Behavior," in eds. Leigh McAlister and Michael Rothschild, *Advances in Consumer Research*, vol. 20 (Provo, Utah: Association for Consumer Research, 1993), pp. 570–574; Ronald A. Fullerton and Girish Punj, "The Unintended Consequences of the Culture of Consumption: A Theory of Consumer Misbehavior," Working paper, University of Hartford, Department of Marketing, 1994; John J. Keller, "Call-Sell Rings Steal Cellular Service," *Wall Street Journal*, March 13, 1992, pp. A5, B3; Jacqueline Simmons, "Hotels Snoop to Stop Guests' Thievery of Everything That Isn't Nailed Down," *Wall Street Journal*, March 17, 1995, pp. B1, B7; "Cops and Robbers"; Steven Stecklow, "Student Applications for Financial Aid Give Lots of False Answers," *Wall Street Journal*, March 11, 1997, pp. A1, A15; Ronald A. Fullerton and Girish Punj, "The Unintended Consequences of the Culture of Consumption: An Historical-Theoretical Analysis of Consumer Misbehavior," *Consumption, Markets and Culture*, vol. 1, no. 4, 1998, pp. 393–423.
7. Robert P. Libbon, "Datadog," *American Demographics*, July 2001, p. 26.
8. Dena Cox, Anthony P. Cox, and George P. Moschis, "When Consumer Behavior Goes Bad: An Investigation of Adolescent Shoplifting," *Journal of Consumer Research*, September 1990, pp. 149–159; Fullerton and Punj, "The Unintended Consequences of the Culture of Consumption"; George P. Moschis, Dena S. Cox, and James J. Kellaris, "An Exploratory Study of Adolescent Shoplifting Behavior," in eds. Melanie Wallendorf and Paul Anderson, *Advances in Consumer Research*, vol. 14 (Provo, Utah: Association for Consumer Research, 1987), pp. 526–530.
9. Fullerton and Punj, "The Unintended Consequences of the Culture of Consumption."
10. Cox, Cox, and Moschis, " When Consumer Behavior Goes Bad."
11. Paul Bernstein, "Cheating—The New National Pastime?" *Business*, October–December 1985, pp. 24–33; Fullerton and Punj, "Some Unintended Consequences of the Culture of Consumption."
12. Fullerton and Punj, "Choosing to Misbehave"; Donald R. Katz, *The Big Store* (New York: Penguin, 1988).
13. Cox, Cox, and Moschis, " When Consumer Behavior Goes Bad"; Moschis, Cox, and Kellaris, "An Exploratory Study of Adolescent Shoplifting Behavior"; Fullerton and Punj, "Some Unintended Consequences of the Culture of Consumption."
14. Katz, *The Big Store*.
15. Cox, Cox, and Moschis, " When Consumer Behavior Goes Bad"; Moschis, Cox, and Kellaris, "An Exploratory Study of Adolescent Shoplifting Behavior."
16. Anthony D. Cox, Dena Cox, Ronald D. Anderson, and George P. Moschis, "Social Influences on Adolescent Shoplifting—Theory, Evidence, and Implications for the Retail Industry," *Journal of Retailing*, Summer 1993, p. 234.
17. John Fetto, "Penny For Your Thoughts," *American Demographics*, September 2000, pp. 8–9.
18. Chok C. Hiew, "Prevention of Shoplifting: A Community Action Approach," *Canadian Journal of Criminology*, January 1981, pp. 57–68.
19. Cox, Cox, and Moschis, " When Consumer Behavior Goes Bad"; Fullerton and Punj, "The Unintended Consequences of the Culture of Consumption"; Fullerton and Punj, "Choosing to Misbehave"; Cox, Cox, Anderson, and Moschis, "Social Influences on Adolescent Shoplifting."
20. Musick, "Keeping Would-Be Thieves at Bay"; Marc Millstein, "Cutting Losses," *Supermarket News*, March 20, 1995, pp. 13–16.
21. Mark McLaughlin, "Subliminal Tapes Urge Shoppers to Heed the Warning Sounds of Silence: 'Don't Steal,'" *New England Business*, February 1987, pp. 36–38.
22. "Retailers to Tighten up Security," *Retail World*, February 22–26, 1999; Charles Goldsmith, "Less Honor, More Case at Europe Minibars," *Wall Street Journal*, March 22, 1996, pp. B6; Simmons, "Hotels Snoop to Stop Guests' Thievery of Everything That Isn't Nailed Down"; Steve Weinstein, "The Enemy Within," *Progressive Grocer*, May 1994, pp. 175–179.
23. Elizabeth Parks, "Let Fragrance Sales Break out of Their Glass Prison," *Drug Store News*, April 3, 1989, p. 28.
24. William Echikson, "Ticket Madness at the World Cup," *BusinessWeek*, July 13, 1998, pp. 126; Joel Engardio, "L.A. Air Bag Thieves May Be Popping up in East County," *Los Angeles Times*, July 1, 1998, p. 1; Ann Marie O'Connon, "Where There's Smoke," *Los Angeles Times*, September 7, 1997, p. A3R.
25. Lisa R. Szykman and Ronald P. Hill, "A Consumer-Behavior Investigation of a Prison Economy," in eds. Janeen Costa Arnold and Russell W. Belk, *Research in Consumer Behavior*, vol. 6 (Greenwich, Conn.: JAI Press, 1993), pp. 231–260; David Bevan, Paul Collier, and Jan Willem Gunning, "Black Markets: Illegality, Information, and Rents," *World Development*, December 1989, pp. 1955–1963.
26. Harvey D. Shapiro, "Buying Miles Is Thrifty—But Iffy," *Los Angeles Times*, March 9, 1995, p. D5.
27. "Hey, Anybody Want a Gun," *The Economist*, May 16, 1998, pp. 47–48; Mark Hosenball and Daniel

Klaidman, "A Deadly Mix of Drugs and Firepower," *Newsweek*, April 19, 1999, p. 27.

28. Jonathan Karp, "Awaiting Knockoffs, Indians Buy Black-Market Viagra," *Wall Street Journal*, July 10, 1998, pp. B1, B2; M. B. Sheridan, "Men Around the Globe Lust after Viagra," *Los Angeles Times*, May 26, 1998, p. 1.
29. Ken Bensinger, "Can You Spot the Fake?" *Wall Street Journal*, February 16, 2001, pp. W1, W14.
30. Elizabeth C. Hirschman, "The Consciousness of Addiction: Toward a General Theory of Compulsive Consumption," *Journal of Consumer Research*, September 1992, pp. 155–179.
31. Christine Gorman, Barbara Dolan, and Glenn Garelik, "Why It's So Hard to Quit Smoking," *Time*, May 30, 1988, p. 131; Gilbert J. Botvin, Catherine J. Goldberg, Elizabeth M. Botvin, and Linda Dusenbury, "Smoking Behavior of Adolescents Exposed to Cigarette Advertising," *Public Health Reports*, March–April 1993, pp. 217–223; James Ryan, Craig Zwerling, and Endel John Orav, "Occupational Risks Associated with Cigarette Smoking: A Prospective Study," *American Journal of Public Health*, January 1992, pp. 29–33; John R. Nelson and Jeanne E. Lukas, "Target: Minorities," *Marketing and Media Decisions*, October 1990, pp. 70–71; Clara Manfreid, Loretta Lacey, Richard Warnecke, and Marianne Buis, "Smoking-Related Behavior, Beliefs, and Social Environment of Young Black Women in Subsidized Public Housing in Chicago," *American Journal of Public Health*, February 1992, pp. 267–272; Tara Parker-Pope, "Health Activists Light into Cigars' Glamorous Image," *Wall Street Journal*, July 8, 1997, pp. B1, B6.
32. Ronald Gaudia, "Effects of Compulsive Gambling on the Family," *Social Work*, May–June 1987, pp. 254–256.
33. Richard G. Netemeyer, Scot Burton, Leslie K. Cole, Donald A. Williamson, Nancy Zucker, Lisa Bertman, and Gretchen Diefenbach, "Characteristics and Beliefs Associated with Probably Pathological Gambling: A Pilot Study with Implications for the National Gambling Impact and Policy Commission," *Journal of Public Policy and Marketing*, vol. 17, no. 2, Fall 1998, pp. 147–160.
34. Laurence Arnold, "Link to Other Addictions Raises New Questions about Gambling," *Associate Press*, June 12, 2001.
35. United Press International, "High Correlation Found between Gambling Addiction and Crime," *ClariNet Electronic News Service*, December 1, 1992.
36. "High Correlation Found between Gambling Addiction and Crime"; Ricardo Chavira, "The Rise of Teenage Gambling," *Time*, February 25, 1991, p. 78.
37. Patricia B. Sutker and Albert N. Allain Jr., "Issues in Personality Conceptualizations of Addictive Behavior," *Journal of Consulting and Clinical Psychology*, April 1988, pp. 172–182; Alex Blaszczynski, Neil McConaghy, and Anna Frankova, "Boredom Proneness in Pathological Gambling," *Psychological Reports*, August 1990, pp. 35–42; John R. Graham and Virginia E. Strenger, "MMPI Characteristics of Alcoholics: A Review," *Journal of Consulting and Clinical Psychology*, April 1988, pp. 197–205; Robert C. McMahon, David Gersh, and Robert S. Davidson, "Personality and Symptom Characteristics of Continuous vs. Episodic Drinkers," *Journal of Clinical Psychology*, January 1989, pp. 161–168; Robert K. Brooner, Chester W. Schmidt, Linda Felch, and George E. Bigelow, "Antisocial Behavior of Intravenous Drug Abusers: Implications for Diagnosis of Antisocial Personality Disorder," *American Journal of Psychiatry*, April 1992, pp. 482–487; Ralph E. Tarter, "Are There Inherited Behavioral Traits That Predispose to Substance Abuse?" *Journal of Consulting and Clinical Psychology*, February 1988, pp. 189–196; Hirschman, "The Consciousness of Addiction."
38. Kevin Heubusch, "Taking Chances on Casinos," *American Demographics*, May 1997, pp. 35–40; Tom Gorman, "Indian Casinos in Middle of Battle over Slots," *Los Angeles Times*, May 9, 1995, pp. A3, A24; Max Vanzi, "Gambling Industry Studies the Odds," *Los Angeles Times*, May 9, 1995, pp. A3, A24; James Popkin, "America's Gambling Craze," *US News and World Report*, March 14, 1994, pp. 42–45; Iris Cohen Selinger, "The Big Lottery Gamble," *Advertising Age*, May 10, 1993, pp. 22–26; Tony Horwitz, "In a Bible Belt State, Video Poker Mutates into an Unholy Mess," *Wall Street Journal*, December 2, 1997, pp. A1, A13; Bruce Orwall, "Place Your Bets," *Wall Street Journal*, March 28, 1996, p. R8; Rebecca Quick, "For Sports Fans, The Internet Is a Whole New Ball Game," *Wall Street Journal*, September 3, 1998, p. B9; Stephen Braun, "Lives Lost in a River of Debt," *Los Angeles Times*, June 22, 1997, pp. A1, A14–A15; Michael McCarthy, "In-Flight Gambling Is Ready to Take Off," *Wall Street Journal*, May 24, 1996, pp. B1, B6; Bruce Orwall, "Like Playing Slots? Casinos Know All about You," *Wall Street Journal*, December 20, 1995, pp. B1, B4.
39. Jeff Harrington, "Booming Online-Gambling Industry Alarms Law-Enforcement, Addiction Experts," *St. Petersburg Times*, April 23, 2001.
40. Joe Ashbrook Nickell, "Datamining: Welcome to Harrah's," *Business 2.0*, April 2002, pp. 48–54.
41. Justin Supon, "Gambling Hotline Braces for Post–Super Bowl Calls," *ClariNet Electronic News Service*, January 27, 1993; Donald Janson, "Two Casinos Post Compulsive Gambler Hot Line," *New York Times*, August 9, 1987, pp. 14, 36.
42. George A. Hacker, "Liquor Advertisements on Television: Just Say No," *Journal of Public Policy and Marketing*, Spring 1998, pp. 139–142; William K. Eaton, "College Binge Drinking Soars, Study Finds," *Los Angeles Times*, June 8, 1994, p. A21; Mike Fuer and Rita Walters, "Mixed Message Hurts Kids: Ban Tobacco, Alcohol Billboards: The Targeting of Children Is Indisputable and Intolerable," *Los Angeles Times*, June 8, 1997, p. M5; Joseph Coleman, "Big Tobacco Still Calls the Shots in Japan," *Marketing News*, August 4, 1997, p. 12.

43. John Machacek, "It's Called Lemonade, But It's Not," *Gannett News Service*, May 10, 2001.

44. Charles S. Clark, "Underage Drinking," *The CQ Researcher*, vol. 2, no. 10, 1992, pp. 219–244; Courtney Leatherman, "College Officials Are Split on Alcohol Policies: Some Seek to End Underage Drinking; Others Try to Encourage 'Responsible Use,'" *Chronicle of Higher Education*, January 31, 1990, pp. A33–A35.

45. Antonia C. Novello, "Alcohol and Tobacco Advertising," *Vital Speeches of the Day*, May 15, 1993, pp. 454–459.

46. Ibid; K. M. Cummings, E. Sciandra, T. F. Pechacek, J. P. Pierce, L. Wallack, S. L. Mills, W. R. Lynn, and S. E. Marcus, "Comparison of the Cigarette Brand Preferences of Adult and Teenaged Smokers—United States, 1989, and 10 U.S. Communities, 1988 and 1990," *Journal of the American Medical Association*, April 8, 1992, p. 1893.

47. Clark, "Underage Drinking;" Erica H. van Roosmalen and Susan A. McDaniel, "Peer Group Influence as a Factor in Smoking Behavior of Adolescents," *Adolescence*, Winter 1989, pp. 801–816; Nancy Twitchell Murphy and Cynthia J. Price, "The Influence of Self-Esteem, Parental Smoking, and Living in a Tobacco Production Region on Adolescent Smoking Behaviors," *Journal of School Health*, December 1988, pp. 401–450; Botvin et al., "Smoking Behavior of Adolescents Exposed to Cigarette Advertising"; Sarah A. McGraw, Kevin W. Smith, Jean J. Schensul, and J. Emilio Carrillo, "Sociocultural Factors Associated with Smoking Behavior by Puerto Rican Adolescents in Boston," *Social Science Medicine*, December 1991, pp. 1355–1364.

48. Associated Press, "Study: Kids Remember Beer Ads," *ClariNet Electronic News Service*, February 11, 1994; Fara Warner, "Cheers! It's Happy Hour in Cyberspace," *Wall Street Journal*, March 15, 1995, pp. B1, B4; Kirk Davidson, "Looking for Abundance of Opposition to TV Liquor Ads," *Marketing News*, January 6, 1997, pp. 4, 30; Rosanna Tamburri, "Dodging Bans on Cigarette Ads in Canada," *Wall Street Journal*, December 27, 1994, p. B5.

49. Dean M. Krugman and Karen Whitehill King, "Teenage Exposure to Cigarette Advertising in Popular Consumer Magazines," *Journal of Public Policy and Marketing*, vol. 19, no. 2, Fall 2000, pp. 183–188; Gordon Fairclough, "Are Cigarette Ads in Magazines Angling for Teens?" *Wall Street Journal*, May 17, 2000, pp. B1, B4.

50. Fara Warner, "Tobacco Brands Outmaneuver Asian Ad Bans," *Wall Street Journal*, August 6, 1996, pp. B1, B3; Eben Shapiro, "Cigarette Makers Outfit Smokers in Icons Eluding Warning and Enraging Activists," *Wall Street Journal*, August 27, 1993, p. B1; Botvin et al., "Smoking Behavior of Adolescents Exposed to Cigarette Advertising"; Novello, "Alcohol and Tobacco Advertising"; Bruce Horovitz, "Most Advertised Cigarettes Are Teens' Choice, Study Says," *Los Angeles Times*, March 13, 1992, p. D4; Cummings et al., "Comparison of the Cigarette Brand Preferences of Adult and Teenaged Smokers."

51. Betsy Spethmann, "Five States Sue RJR," *Promo*, May 2001, p. 22.

52. Vanessa O'Connell, "U.S. Liquor Sellers Want to Run TV Ads," *Wall Street Journal*, May 7, 2001, p. B6; Vanessa O'Connell, "Bacardi Brings Out Bottle in Cable TV Ad for Amaretto," *Wall Street Journal*, April 30, 2001, p. B8.

53. Arch G. Woodside, "Advertising and Consumption of Alcoholic Beverages," *Journal of Consumer Psychology*, vol. 8, no. 2, 1999, pp. 167–186.

54. Elizabeth M. Botvin, Gilbert J. Botvin, John L. Michela, Eli Baker, and Anne D. Filazolla, "Adolescent Smoking Behavior and the Recognition of Cigarette Advertisements," *Journal of Applied Social Psychology*, November 1991, pp. 919–932; Botvin et al., "Smoking Behavior of Adolescents Exposed to Cigarette Advertising"; Richard W. Pollay, S. Siddarth, Michael Siegel, Anne Hadix, Robert K. Merritt, Gary A. Giovino, and Michael P. Eriksen, "The Last Straw? Cigarette Advertising and Realized Market Shares among Youths and Adults, 1979–1993," *Journal of Marketing*, April 1996, pp. 1–16; Joseph DiFranza, John W. Richards, Paul M. Paulman, Nancy Wolf-Gillespie, Christopher Fletcher, Robert D. Jaffe, and David Murray, "RJR Nabisco's Cartoon Camel Promotes Camel Cigarettes to Children," *Journal of the American Medical Association*, December 11, 1991, p. 3149; Cummings et al., "Comparison of the Cigarette Brand Preferences of Adult and Teenaged Smokers."

55. Richard W. Pollay and Ann M. Lavack, "The Targeting of Youths by Cigarette Marketers: Archival Evidence on Trial," in eds. Leigh McAlister and Michael Rothschild, *Advances in Consumer Research*, vol. 20 (Provo, Utah: Association for Consumer Research, 1993), pp. 266–271.

56. See Kathleen J. Kelly, Michael D. Slater, David Karan, and Liza Hunn, "The Use of Human Models and Cartoon Characters in Magazine Advertisements for Cigarettes, Beer, and Nonalcoholic Beverages," *Journal of Public Policy and Marketing*, vol. 19, no. 2, Fall 2000, pp. 189–200.

57. Anonymous, "RJR Denies Link to Teen Smoking, Tobacco: Executive Testifies at Minnesota Trial That Firm Doesn't Use Ads to Attract New Smokers," *Los Angeles Times*, April 21, 1998, p. 13.

58. For more on the Joe Camel controversy, see John E. Calfee, "The Historical Significance of Joe Camel," *Journal of Public Policy and Marketing*, vol. 19, no. 2, Fall 2000, pp. 168–182; Joel B. Cohen, "Playing to Win: Marketing and Public Policy at Odds Over Joe Camel," *Journal of Public Policy and Marketing*, vol. 19, no.2, Fall 2000, pp. 155–167.

59. Richard Morgan, "Is Old Joe Taking Too Much Heat?" *Adweek*, March 16, 1992, p. 44.

60. Reuters, "Joe Camel Doesn't Make Kids Smoke—RJR Funded Survey," *ClariNet Electronic News Service*, February 21, 1994.

61. Clark, "Underage Drinking."

62. Carl Quintanilla, "Du-ude! Clothier's Catalog Sells Students on Drinking," *Wall Street Journal*, July 24, 1998, p. B1.

63. Debra L. Scammon, Robert N. Mayer, and Ken R. Smith, "Alcohol Warnings: How Do You Know When You've Had One Too Many?" *Journal of Public Policy and Marketing*, Spring 1991, pp. 214–228; Michael B. Mazis, Louis A. Morris, and John L. Swasy, "An Evaluation of the Alcohol Warning Label: Initial Survey Results," *Journal of Public Policy and Marketing*, Spring 1991, pp. 229–241; Novello, "Alcohol and Tobacco Advertising"; Richard Gibson and Marj Charlier, "Anheuser Leads the Way in Listing Alcohol Levels," *Wall Street Journal*, March 11, 1993, pp. B1, B2; Richard J. Fox, Dean M. Krugman, James E. Fletcher, and Paul M. Fischer, "Adolescents' Attention to Beer and Cigarette Print Ads and Associated Product Warnings," *Journal of Advertising*, Fall 1998, pp. 57–68.

64. David P. MacKinnon, Rhonda M. Williams-Avery, Kathryn L. Wilcox, and Andrea M. Fenaughty, "Effects of the Arizona Alcohol Warning Poster," *Journal of Public Policy and Marketing*, vol. 18, no. 1, Spring 1999, pp. 77–88.

65. Cornelia Pechmann and Chuan-Fong Shih, "Smoking Scenes in Movies and Antismoking Advertisements Before Movies: Effects on Youth," *Journal of Marketing*, vol. 63, July 1999, pp. 1–13.

66. Debbie Treise, Joyce M. Wolburg, and Cele C. Otnes, "Understanding the 'Social Gifts' of Drinking Rituals: an Alternative Framework for PSA Developers," *Journal of Advertising*, vol. 28, no. 2, Summer 1999, pp. 17–31.

67. U.S. Department of Health and Human Services, as cited in Lague et al., "How Thin Is Too Thin?" *People*, September 20, 1993, pp. 74–80.

68. Hillel Schwartz, "Being Thin Isn't Always Being Happy," *US News and World Report*, February 9, 1987, p. 74.

69. Michael Fay and Christopher Price, "Female Body-Shape in Print Advertisements and the Increase in Anorexia Nervosa," *European Journal of Marketing*, December 1994, pp. 5–19.

70. Isabel Reynolds, "Japan: Feature—Eating Disorders Plague Young Japanese," *Reuters*, June 20, 2001, www.reuters.com.

71. Catherine Fitzpatrick, "How Buff Is Enough? Reality Check Is In the Male," *Milwaukee Journal Sentinel*, June 24, 2001, p. 1-L.

72. Debra Goldman, "Consumer Republic," *Adweek*, May 14, 2001, p. 18.

73. R. Freedman, *Beauty Bound* (Lexington, Mass.: D.C. Heath, 1986).

74. P. S. Powers, *Obesity: The Regulation of Weight* (Baltimore, Md.: Williams and Wilkins, 1980); A. Furnham and N. Alibhai, "Cross-Cultural Differences in the Perception of Female Body Shapes," *Psychological Medicine*, November 1983, pp. 829–837.

75. See also Debra Lynn Stephens, Ronald P. Hill, and Cynthia Hanson, "The Beauty Myth and Female Consumers: The Controversial Role of Advertising," *Journal of Consumer Affairs*, Summer 1994, pp. 137–154.

76. Leon Festinger, "A Theory of Social Comparison Processes," *Human Relations*, May 1954, pp. 117–140.

77. Mary C. Martin and James W. Gentry, "Stuck in the Model Trap: The Effects of Beautiful Models in Ads on Female Pre-Adolescents and Adolescents," *Journal of Advertising*, Summer 1997, pp. 19–33. Marsha L. Richins, "Social Comparison and the Idealized Images of Advertising," *Journal of Consumer Research*, June 1991, pp. 71–83; Richard W. Pollay, "The Distorted Mirror: Reflections on the Unintended Consequences of Advertising," *Journal of Marketing*, April 1986, pp. 18–36; Lague et al., "How Thin Is Too Thin?"

78. Christy Karras, "Study Shows Link Between Fitness Magazines and Eating Disorders," *Associated Press Newswires*, June 20, 2001.

79. Marilyn Gardner, "Slim But Curvy: The Pursuit of Ideal Beauty," *Christian Science Monitor*, January 24, 2001, p. 16.

80. Charles S. Gulas and Kim McKeage, "Extending Social Comparison: An Examination of the Unintended Consequences of Idealized Advertising Imagery," *Journal of Advertising*, vol. 29, no. 2, Summer 2000, pp. 17–28.

81. Calmetta Y. Coleman, "Can't Be Too Thin, but Plus-Size Models Get More Work Now," *Wall Street Journal*, May 3, 1999, pp. A1, A10.

82. Sally Goll Beatty, "Women's Views of Their Lives Aren't Reflected by Advertisers," *Wall Street Journal*, December 19, 1995, p. B2.

83. M. Joseph Sirgy, Dong-Jin Lee, Rustan Kosenko, H. Lee Meadow, Don Rahtz, et al., "Does Television Viewership Play a Role in the Perception of Quality of Life?" *Journal of Advertising*, Spring 1998, pp. 125–143; Pollay, "The Distorted Mirror: Reflections on the Unintended Consequences of Advertising," Russell W. Belk and Richard W. Pollay, "Images of Ourselves: The Good Life in Twentieth Century Advertising," *Journal of Consumer Research*, March 1985, pp. 887–897; Russell W. Belk, "Materialism: Trait Aspects of Living in a Material World," *Journal of Consumer Research*, December 1985, pp. 265–280; Mary Yoko Brannen, "Cross-Cultural Materialism: Commodifying Culture in Japan," in eds. Floyd Rudmin and Marsha L. Richins, *Meaning, Measure, and Morality of Materialism* (Provo, Utah: Association for Consumer Research, 1992), pp. 167–180; Güliz Ger and Russell W. Belk, "Cross-Cultural Differences in Materialism," *Journal of Economic Psychology*, February 1996, pp. 55–77; Marsha L. Richins, "Media, Materialism, and Human Happiness," in eds. Melanie Wallendorf and Paul Anderson, *Advances in Consumer Research*, vol. 14 (Provo, Utah: Association for Consumer Research, 1986), pp. 352–356; Thomas C. O'Guinn and Ronald J. Faber, "Mass Mediated Consumer Socialization: Non-Utilitarian and

Dysfunctional Outcomes," in eds. Melanie Wallendorf and Paul Anderson, *Advances in Consumer Research*, vol. 14 (Provo, Utah; Association for Consumer Research, 1987), pp. 473–477; Ronald J. Faber and Thomas C. O'Guinn, "Expanding the View of Consumer Socialization: A Non-Utilitarian Mass Mediated Perspective," in eds. Elizabeth C. Hirschman and Jagdish N. Sheth, *Research in Consumer Behavior*, vol. 3 (Greenwich, Conn.: JAI Press, 1988), pp. 49–78.

84. Richins, "Media, Materialism and Human Happiness," in eds. Melanie Wallendorf and Paul Anderson, *Advances in Consumer Research*, vol. 14 (Provo, Utah: Association for Consumer Research, 1987), 352–356.

85. Noel C. Paul, "Branded for Life?" *Christian Science Monitor*, April 1, 2002, **www.csmonitor.com/2002/0401/p15s02-wmcn.html.**

86. Richins, "Media, Materialism, and Human Happiness."

87. See for example James M. Hunt, Jerome B. Kernan, and Deborah J. Mitchell, "Materialism as Social Cognition: People, Possessions, and Perception," *Journal of Consumer Psychology*, vol. 5, no. 1, 1996, pp. 65–83.

88. Russell W. Belk, "The Third World Consumer Culture," in ed. Jagdish N. Sheth, *Research in Marketing* (Greenwich, Conn.: JAI Press, 1988), pp. 103–127.

89. Liesl Schillinger, "Barbski," *New Republic*, September 20 and 27, 1993, pp. 10–11.

90. Lynn T. Lovdal, "Sex Role Messages in Television Commercials: An Update," *Sex Roles*, November/December 1989, pp. 715–724; A. E. Courtney and T. Whipple, *Sex Stereotyping in Advertising: An Annotated Bibliography* (Cambridge, Mass.: Marketing Science Institute, 1984).

91. Mary C. Gilly, "Sex Roles in Advertising: A Comparison of Television Advertisements in Australia, Mexico, and the United States," *Journal of Marketing*, April 1988, pp. 75–85.

92. Robert E. Wilkes and Humberto Valencia, "Hispanics and Blacks in Television Commercials," *Journal of Advertising*, December 1989, pp. 19–26; Helena Czepiec and J. Steven Kelly, "Analyzing Hispanic Roles in Advertising: A Portrait of an Emerging Subculture," in eds. James H. Leigh and Claude R. Martin, *Current Issues and Research in Advertising* (Ann Arbor, Mich.: University of Michigan Press, 1983), pp. 219–240.

93. Yuri Radzievsky, "Untapped Markets: Ethnics in the US," *Advertising Age*, June 21, 1993, p. 26.

94. Tara Parker-Pope, "Ford Puts Blacks in Whiteface, Turns Red," *Wall Street Journal*, February 22, 1996, p. B5.

95. Linda E. Swayne and Alan J. Greco, "The Portrayal of Older Americans in Television Commercials," *Journal of Advertising*, Winter 1987, pp. 47–56; Anthony C. Ursic, Michael L. Ursic, and Virginia L. Ursic, "A Longitudinal Study of the Use of the Elderly in Magazine Advertising," *Journal of Consumer Research*, June 1986, pp. 131–134; Walter Gantz, Howard M. Garenberg, and Cindy K. Rainbow, "Approaching Invisibility: The Portrayal of the Elderly in Magazine Advertisements," *Journal of Communication*, January 1980, pp. 56–60.

96. Michael L. Klassen, Cynthia R. Jasper, and Anne M. Schwartz, "Men and Women: Images of Their Relationships in Magazine Advertisements," *Journal of Advertising Research*, March–April 1993, pp. 30–39; Sall Goll Beatty, "Critics Rail at Racy TV Programs but Ads Are Often the Sexiest Fare," *Wall Street Journal*, May 28, 1996, p. A25; Courtney and Whipple, "Sex Stereotyping in Advertising: An Annotated Bibliography"; Beverly A. Browne, "Gender Stereotypes in Advertising on Children's Television in the 1990s: A Cross National Analysis, *Journal of Advertising*, Spring 1998, pp. 83–96; John B. Ford, Patricia Kramer Voli, Earl D. Honeycutt Jr., and Susan L. Casey, "Gender Role Portrayals in Japanese Advertising: A Magazine Content Analysis," *Journal of Advertising*, Spring 1998, pp. 113–124; Gilly, "Sex Roles in Advertising"; F. L. Geis, V. Brown, J. J. Walstedt, and N. Porter, "TV Commercials as Achievement Scripts for Women," *Sex Roles*, April 1984, pp. 513–525; Sally D. Goll, "Beer Ads in Hong Kong Criticized as Sexist," *Wall Street Journal*, June 19, 1995, p. B4; Cyndee Miller, "Babe-Based Beer Ads Likely to Flourish," *Marketing News*, January 6, 1992, p. 1; Jill Hicks Ferguson, Peggy J. Kreshel, and Spencer F. Tinkham, "In the Pages of *Ms:* Sex Role Portrayals of Women in Advertising," *Journal of Advertising*, December 1990, pp. 40–52; see also Michael Klassen, Cynthia R. Jasper, and Anne M. Schwartz, "Men and Women: Images of Their Relationships in Magazine Advertisements," *Journal of Advertising Research*, March–April 1993, pp. 30–40; Kathy Brown, "The Fine Line between Good Taste and Bad Taste Should Be Thicker Than a String Bikini," *Adweek*, April 27, 1992, p. 52.

97. Michael L. Maynard and Charles R. Taylor, "Girlish Images Across Cultures: Analyzing Japanese versus U.S. *Seventeen* Magazine Ads," *Journal of Advertising*, vol. 28, no. 1, Spring 1999, pp. 39–48.

98. Charles R. Taylor and Barbara B. Stern, "Asian-Americans: Television Advertising and the 'Model Minority' Stereotype," *Journal of Advertising*, Summer 1997, pp. 47–61.

99. Alan Greco, "The Elderly as Communicators," *Journal of Advertising Research*, June–July 1988, pp. 39–45; Kevin Goldman, "Seniors Get Little Respect on Madison Avenue," *Wall Street Journal*, September 20, 1993, p. B4; David B. Wolfe, "The Ageless Market," *American Demographics*, July 1987, pp. 26–29, 55–56; Warren A. French and Richard Fox, "Segmenting the Senior Citizen Market," *Journal of Consumer Marketing*, Winter 1985, pp. 61–74.

100. Thomas Stevenson, "How Are Blacks Portrayed in Business Ads?" *Industrial Marketing Management*, August 1991, pp. 193–200; Susan DeYoung, and F. G. Crane, "Females' Attitudes toward the Portrayal of Women in Advertising: A Canadian Study," *International Journal of Advertising*, Summer 1992, pp. 249–256; Leon Wynter, "Global Marketers Learn to Say No to Bad Ads," *Wall Street Journal*, April 1, 1998, p. B1.

101. Wilkes and Valencia, "Hispanics and Blacks in Television Commercials"; Ursic, Ursic, and Ursic, "A Longitudinal Study of the Use of the Elderly in Magazine Advertising"; Phyllis Furman, "The New Wrinkle in Casting," *Madison Avenue*, October 1985, pp. 66–70.

102. Bruce Horovitz, "Color Them Beautiful—and Visible," *USA Today*, May 2, 2001, p. B1.

103. Nancy A. Reese, Thomas W. Whipple, and Alice E. Courtney, "Is Industrial Advertising Sexist?" *Industrial Marketing Management*, November 1987, pp. 231–241; Cyndee Miller, "Liberation for Women in Ads: Nymphettes, June Cleaver Are Out: Middle Ground Is In," *Marketing News*, August 17, 1992, pp. 1, 3; Cyndee Miller, "Michelob Ads Feature Women—And They're Not Wearing Bikinis," *Marketing News*, March 2, 1992, p. 2.

104. Gary Levin, "Shops Make the Most of Ethnic Niches," *Advertising Age*, September 17, 1990, p. 29.

105. Ruth Simon, "Stop Them from Selling Your Financial Secrets," *Money*, March 1992, pp. 99–110.

106. Ellen Foxman and Paula Kilcoyne, "Information Technology, Marketing Practice, and Consumer Privacy: Ethical Issues," *Journal of Public Policy and Marketing*, Spring 1993, p. 106.

107. Carol Krol, "Consumers Reach the Boiling Point Over Privacy Issues," *Advertising Age*, March 29, 1999, p. 22; "Survey Results Show Consumers Want Privacy," *Direct Marketing*, March 1999, p. 10.

108. Kevin Heubusch, "Big Brother and the Internet," *American Demographics*," February 1997, p. 22.

109. Michael Moss, "A Web CEO's Elusive Goal: Privacy," *Wall Street Journal*, February 7, 2000, p. B1, B6.

110. Kim Bartel Sheehan and Mariea Grubbs Hoy, "Flaming, Complaining, Abstaining: How Online Users Respond to Privacy Concerns," *Journal of Advertising*, vol. 28, no. 3, Fall 1999, pp. 37–51; G. Bruce Knecht, "Junk Mail Hater Seeks Profits from Sale of His Name," *Wall Street Journal*, October 13, 1995, pp. B1, B8.

111. Mag Gottleib, "If Trends Continue, Legislative Nightmare Will Become Reality," *Marketing News*, August 16, 1993, pp. A9–A16; H. Jeff Smith, Sandra J. Milberg, and Sandra J. Burke, "Information Privacy: Measuring Individuals' Concerns about Organizational Practices," *MIS Quarterly*, June 1996, pp. 167–196.

112. Foxman and Kilcoyne, " Information Technology, Marketing Practice, and Consumer Privacy."

113. Gottleib, "If Trends Continue, Legislative Nightmare Will Become Reality."

114. Simon, "Stop Them from Selling Your Financial Secrets."

115. Edward Baig, Marcia Stepanek, and Neil Gross, "Privacy," *BusinessWeek*, April 5, 1999, pp. 84–90.

116. Paula Nichols, "Canadian Privacy Code Shows U.S. the Way," *American Demographics*, September 1993, p. 15.

117. Ann Reilly Dowd, "Protect Your Privacy," *Money*, August 1997, pp. 104–115.

118. "Invasion of Privacy: When Is Access to Information Foul—or Fair?" *Harvard Business Review*, September–October 1993, pp. 154–155.

119. Quick, "On-line Groups Are Offering up Privacy Plans."

120. Moss, "A Web CEO's Elusive Goal."

121. N. Craig Smith and Elizabeth Cooper-Martin, "Ethics and Target Marketing: The Role of Product Harm and Consumer Vulnerability," *Journal of Marketing*, July 1997, pp. 1–20; Robert O. Hermann, "The Tactics of Consumer Resistance: Group Action and Marketplace Exit," in eds. Leigh McAlister and Michael Rothschild, *Advances in Consumer Research*, vol. 20 (Provo, Utah: Association for Consumer Research, 1993), pp. 130–134; Lisa Penaloza and Linda L. Price, "Consumer Resistance: A Conceptual Overview," in eds. Leigh McAlister and Michael L. Rothschild, *Advances in Consumer Research*, vol. 20 (Provo, Utah: Association for Consumer Research, 1993), pp. 123–128.

122. Cyndee Miller, "Sexy Sizzle Backfires," *Marketing News*, September 25, 1995, p. 1.

123. Richard W. Pollay, "Media Resistance to Consumer Resistance: On the Stonewalling of 'Adbusters' and Advocates," in eds. Leigh McAlister and Michael Rothschild, *Advances in Consumer Research*, vol. 20 (Provo, Utah: Association for Consumer Research, 1993), p. 129.

124. Scott Kilman, "Campbell Soup Is a Target of Protests Over Biotechnology," *Wall Street Journal*, July 20, 2000, B18.

125. H.J. Cummins, "Judging a Book Cover," *Star-Tribune of the Twin Cities*, January 17, 2001, p. 1E.

126. Jonathan Baron, "Consumer Attitudes about Personal and Political Action," *Journal of Consumer Psychology*, vol. 8, no. 3, 1999, pp. 261–275.

127. Maria Halkias, "PETA Starts Safeway Boycott Over Its Suppliers," *Dallas Morning News*, February 25, 2002, **www.dallasnews.com**.

128. Tony Spleen, "OJ Sales Off 6%, Limbaugh Effect?" *Supermarket News*, May 9, 1994, p. 3; Armando Duron, "Boycott Based on 30 Years of Waiting," *Los Angeles Times*, June 19, 1995, p. F3; Cyndee Miller, "Marketers Weigh Effects of Sweatshop Crackdown," *Marketing News*, May 12, 1997, pp. 1, 19.

129. Dennis Rodkin, "Boycott Power," *Mother Jones*, July–August 1991, pp. 18–19; see also Monroe Friedman, "Consumer Boycotts in the United States, 1970–1980: Contemporary Events in Historical Perspective," *Journal of Consumer Affairs*, Summer 1985, pp. 96–117.

130. Todd Putnam and Timothy Muck, " Wielding the Boycott Weapon for Social Change," *Business and Society Review*, Summer 1991, pp. 5–8.

131. Marcus Mabry and Bruce Sheniz, "Do Boycotts Work?" *Newsweek*, July 6, 1992, pp. 58–59, 61; Dennis E. Garrett, "The Effectiveness of Marketing Boycotts," *Journal of Marketing*, vol. 51, April 1987, pp. 46–57.

132. Rodkin, "Boycott Power."

NAME INDEX

ORGANIZATION/PRODUCT INDEX

SUBJECT INDEX

Supplements to Aid Students

Student Web site

This site provides additional information, guidance, and activities that help enhance concepts presented in the text. Included are

- Chapter previews
- Chapter outlines
- Learning objectives
- Internet exercises with hyperlinks
- Interactive ACE study questions for each chapter

New! *Cases in Consumer Behavior*

A collection of cases that focus on consumer behavior is now available as a shrink-wrap option with this edition. These cases provide a variety of contemporary scenarios to reflect the concepts and topics highlighted in the text.

New! *Wall Street Journal* Subscription

Students whose instructors have adopted the *Wall Street Journal* along with the Hoyer/MacInnis text will receive, shrink-wrapped with their book, a registration card for the 10-week print and online subscription to the *WSJ*. Students must fill out and return the registration card found in the text to initiate these subscription privileges. This text package also includes a copy of the *Wall Street Journal Student Subscriber Handbook*, which explains how to use both print and online versions of the newspaper. The cost of the *WSJ* will be $13.50, in addition to the net cost of the core text. This is sold only as a package with new textbooks; *WSJ* subscriptions cannot be sold as stand-alone items.

FOR THE INSTRUCTOR

- Want an easy way to test your students prior to an exam that ***doesn't*** create more work for you?
- Want to access your supplements ***without*** having to bring them all to class?
- Want to integrate current happenings into your lectures ***without*** all the searching and extra work?
- Want an ***easy*** way to get your course on-line?
- Want to ***free up more time*** in your day to get more done?

Of course you do!

Then check out your
Online Learning Centre!

- Downloadable Supplements
- PageOut
- Online Resources
- Organizational Behaviour Online